HOLT Science Spectrum

A BALANCED APPROACH

Integrating:
- ✓ Chemistry
- ✓ Physics
- ✓ Human Biology
- ✓ Earth Science
- ✓ Space Science
- ✓ Mathematics

KEN DOBSON

JOHN HOLMAN

MICHAEL ROBERTS

HOLT, RINEHART AND WINSTON

A Harcourt Classroom Education Company

Austin • New York • Orlando • Atlanta • San Francisco • Boston • Dallas • Toronto • London

Contributing Writers

Linda K. Butler, Ph.D.
Senior Lecturer
University of Texas at Austin
Austin, TX

Curtis Chubb, Ph.D.
Science Writer
Blanco, TX

Heather Flanagan, Ph.D.
Chemist
Austin, TX

Brook Hall
Science Writer
Loomis, CA

Doug Jenkins
Physics and Physical Science Teacher
Warren Central High School
Bowling Green, KY

Nanette Kalis
Science Writer
Albany, OH

Matt Lee, Ph.D.
Science Editor
Coos Bay, OR

Mitchell Leslie
Science Writer
Stanford University
Stanford, CA

Richard P. Olenick, Ph.D.
Professor of Physics
University of Dallas
Irving, TX

Karen Ross
Science Writer
Georgetown, TX

This adaptation of NELSON BALANCED SCIENCE and NELSON SCIENCE is published by arrangement with Nelson, a division of Stanley Thornes (Publishers) Limited, Walton-on-Thames, UK.

For permission to reprint copyrighted material, grateful acknowledgment is made to the following source: *sci*LINKS is owned and provided by the National Science Teachers Association. All rights reserved.

Printed in the United States of America

ISBN 0-03-054351-7

2 3 4 5 6 7 048 05 04 03 02 01 00

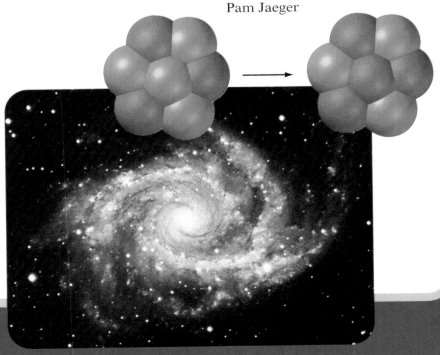

Acknowledgements

Lab Reviewers

Chris Crowell
Brockport High School
Brockport, NY

Bob Iveson
WARD'S Natural Science Est.

James Keefer
Brockport High School
Brockport, NY

Bryan Kommeth
WARD'S Natural Science Est.

Gregory Puskar
Laboratory Manager
Physics Department
West Virginia University
Morgantown, WV

Geof Smith
WARD'S Natural Science Est.

Sharon Wolsky
Rush Henrietta High School
Henrietta, NY

Text Reviewers

Tim Black
Albuquerque, NM

Robert Boyce, Ph.D.
Owner
Robert Boyce Health
Promotion
Charlotte, NC

Larry Brown, Ph.D.
Science Department Chair
Morgan Park Academy
Chicago, IL

Jim Bryn
Physical Science Teacher
Sparks High School
Sparks, NV

Bonnie J. Buratti, Ph.D.
Research Scientist
Jet Propulsion Laboratory
California Institute of
    Technology
Pasadena, CA

G. Lynn Carlson
University of Wisconsin-
Parkside
Racine, WI

David S. Coco, Ph.D.
Research Physicist
University of Texas at Austin
Austin, TX

Bill Conway, Ph.D.
Physics Teacher
Northeastern Illinois
    University
Chicago, IL

Joe Crim, Ph.D.
Professor of Cellular Biology
University of Georgia
Athens, GA

Lillie M. Darke
*Integrated Physics and I.B.
    Chemistry Teacher*
Waltrip High School
Houston, TX

Martha M. Day, Ph.D.
Physical Science Teacher
Whites Creek High School
Whites Creek, TN

William Deutschman, Ph.D.
President
Oregon Laser Consultants
Klamath Falls, OR

Melody Law Ewey
Vice Principal
Holmes Junior High School
Davis, CA

Jean A. Fuller-Stanley, Ph.D.
Chemistry Professor
Wellesley College
Wellesley, MA

Michael Garcia, Ph.D.
Professor of Geology
University of Hawaii
Honolulu, HI

Bruce Gronich
Instructor
University of Texas
    at El Paso
El Paso, TX

David Hamilton, Ed.D.
Physics Teacher
Franklin High School
Portland, OR

John Hubisz, Ph.D.
Physics Professor
North Carolina State
    University
Raleigh, NC

Robert Hudson
Physics Professor Emeritus
Roanoke College
Salem, VA

William Ingham, Ph.D.
Physics Professor
James Madison University
Harrisonburg, VA

Doug Jenkins
Science Teacher
Warren Central High School
Bowling Green, KY

Terry Jimarez
Physical Science Education Specialist
Coronado High School
El Paso, TX

Jennifer Jordan
Integrated Physics and Chemistry Teacher
Fox Technical and Academic High School
San Antonio, TX

John Kudlas, Ph.D.
Science Instructor
Mayo High School
Rochester, MN

Karen Kwitter, Ph.D.
Ebenezer Fitch Professor of Astronomy
Williams College
Williamstown, MA

Joel S. Leventhal, Ph.D.
Research Chemist
USDI Geological Survey
Denver, CO

Timothy Lincoln, Ph.D
Professor of Geology
Albion College
Albion, MI

Jeff Lockwood
Secondary Science Specialist
Tucson Unified School District
Tucson, AZ

Crystal Long
Biology Teacher
Coral Springs High School
Coral Springs, FL

Julie Lutz, Ph.D.
Astronomy Program
Washington State University
Pullman, WA

Edgar McCullough, Jr., Ph.D.
Professor Emeritus Geosciences
University of Arizona
Tempe, AZ

Mickey Musick
Integrated Physics and Chemistry Teacher
Westfield High School
Houston, TX

George T. Ochs
Science Coordinator
Washoe County School District
Reno, NV

Keith Oldham, Ph.D.
Professor of Chemistry
Trent University
Peterborough, Ontario, Canada

Fred Redmore
Professor of Chemistry
Highland Community College
Freeport, IL

Terence M. Phillips, Ph.D., D.Sc.
Professor of Microbiology and Immunology
George Washington University Medical Center
Washington, DC

Walter Robinson, Ph.D.
Department of Atmospheric Sciences
University of Illinois
Urbana, IL

Melanie R. Stewart
Curriculum Consultant
Stow-Munroe Falls City Schools
Stow, OH

William Thwaites, Ph.D.
Professor Emeritus
Biology Department
San Diego State University
San Diego, CA

Richard S. Treptow
Professor of Chemistry
Chicago State University
Chicago, IL

Charles M. Wynn
Professor of Chemistry
Eastern Connecticut State University
Willimantic, CT

Carol Zimmerman, Ph.D.
Exploration Associate
Houston, TX

Table of CONTENTS

Safety in the Laboratory xviii

■ CHAPTER **1**

Introduction to Science 2

   1.1 The Nature of Science 4
   1.2 The Way Science Works 12
   1.3 Organizing Data 20
      Chapter Review 27

Skill-Builder Lab Making Measurements 30

   Math Skills   Conversions 17
                 Writing Scientific Notation 23
                 Using Scientific Notation 24
                 Significant Figures 25

Integrating **Biology**
Connection to **Language Arts**

Unit 1 THE NATURE OF MATTER ━━━━━━━━━━━━━━━ 34

■ CHAPTER **2**

Matter 36

   2.1 What Is Matter? 38
   2.2 Matter and Energy 45
   2.3 Properties of Matter 53
      Chapter Review 61

Inquiry Lab How are the mass and volume of a
   substance related? 57

Design Your Own Lab Testing the Conservation of Mass 64

   Math Skills   Density 56

Science and the Consumer Dry Cleaning:
   How Are Stains Dissolved? 43

Real World Applications Choosing Materials 58

Integrating **Biology • Earth Science • Space Science**

Viewpoints Paper or Plastic at the Grocery Store? 66

H_2O

CHAPTER 3

Atoms and The Periodic Table 68

   3.1 Atomic Structure 70
   3.2 A Guided Tour of the Periodic Table 77
   3.3 Families of Elements 86
   3.4 Using Moles to Count Atoms 95
      Chapter Review 101

Inquiry Lab Why do some metals cost more
   than others? 90

Design Your Own Lab Comparing the Physical
   Properties of Elements 104

   Math Skills   Conversion Factors 98
           Converting Amount to Mass 99
           Converting Mass to Amount 100

Real World Applications Designing Drugs 74

Integrating **Earth Science**
Connection to **Architecture**

3
Li
Lithium
6.941

11
Na
Sodium
22.989 768

19
K
Potassium
39.0983

37
Rb
Rubidium
85.4678

55
Cs
Cesium
132.905 43

87
Fr
Francium
(223.0197)

CHAPTER 4

The Structure of Matter 106

   4.1 Compounds and Molecules 108
   4.2 Ionic and Covalent Bonding 115
   4.3 Compound Names and Formulas 123
   4.4 Organic and
        Biochemical Compounds . **INTEGRATING TECHNOLOGY and Society** 129
      Chapter Review 137

Inquiry Lab Which melts more easily, sugar or salt? 113
Inquiry Lab What properties does a polymer have? 135
Skill-Builder Lab Comparing Two Polymers 140

   Math Skills   Writing Ionic Formulas 125

Integrating **Space Science**
Connections to **Fine Arts • Social Studies**

Career Link Roberta Jordan, Chemist 142

Unit 2 CHANGES IN MATTER ——————————— 144

CHAPTER 5

Chemical Reactions 146
   5.1 The Nature of Chemical Reactions 148
   5.2 Reaction Types 154
   5.3 Balancing Chemical Equations 161
   5.4 Rates of Change 169
      Chapter Review 177

Inquiry Lab Can you write balanced chemical equations ? 167
Inquiry Lab What affects the rates of chemical reactions? 172
Design Your Own Lab Measuring the Rate of a
Chemical Reaction 180

Math Skills Balancing Chemical Equations 165

Real-World Application Self-Heating Meals 151
Science and the Consumer Fire Extinguishers:
Are They All the Same? 164
Integrating **Biology • Earth Science • Environmental Science**
Connections to **Fine Arts • Social Studies**

Viewpoints How Should Life-Saving Inventions
Be Introduced? 182

CHAPTER 6

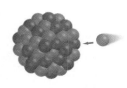

Nuclear Changes 184
   6.1 What Is Radioactivity? 186
   6.2 Nuclear Fission and Fusion 195
   6.3 Dangers and Benefits
      of Nuclear Radiation . . **INTEGRATING TECHNOLOGY and Society** 201
      Chapter Review 207

Skill Builder Lab Simulating Nuclear Decay Reactions 210

Math Skills Nuclear Decay 190
       Half-Life 193

Real-World Application Medical Radiation Exposure 204
Integrating **Earth Science • Space Science**

Career Link Corinna Wu, Science Writer 212

CHAPTER 7

Motion and Forces 216

7.1 Motion. 218
7.2 Acceleration and Force 225
7.3 Newton's Laws of Motion 234
   Chapter Review 241

Inquiry Lab How are action and reaction forces related? 239
Design Your Own Lab Measuring Forces 244

Math Skills Velocity 221
   Momentum 223
   Acceleration. 226
   Newton's Second Law. 236

Real-World Application Hiking. 222
Science and the Consumer Should Air Bags Be Disconnected? 230
Connection to **Social Studies**
Integrating **Mathematics • Space Science**

Viewpoints Should Bicycle Helmets Be Required By Law? . . . 246

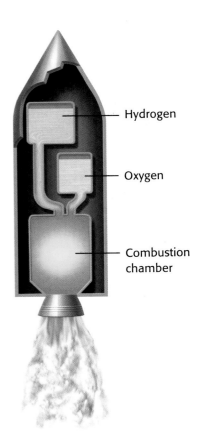

Hydrogen

Oxygen

Combustion
chamber

CHAPTER 8

Work and Energy 248

8.1 Work, Power, and Machines 250
8.2 Simple Machines 257
8.3 What Is Energy? 263
8.4 Conservation of Energy. 272
   Chapter Review 281

Inquiry Lab What is your power output?. 253
Inquiry Lab Is energy conserved in a pendulum? 277
Skill-Builder Lab Determining Energy for a Rolling Ball. 284

Math Skills Work. 251
   Power. 252
   Mechanical Advantage 255
   Gravitational Potential Energy 265
   Kinetic Energy 267
   Efficiency. 279

Real-World Application The Energy in Food 269
Connections to **Social Studies**
Integrating **Biology • Computers and Technology**

Career Link Grace Pierce, Engineer 286

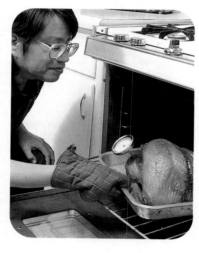

| | CHAPTER **9**

Heat and Temperature 288

9.1 Temperature 290
9.2 Energy Transfer 297
9.3 Using Heat INTEGRATING TECHNOLOGY and *Society* 305
        Chapter Review 313

Inquiry Lab How do temperature and energy relate? 295
Inquiry Lab What color absorbs more radiation? 300
Design Your Own Lab Investigating Conduction by Heat 316

Math Skills Temperature Scale Conversion 294
        Specific Heat 303

Real-World Application Buying Appliances 312

Connection to **Social Studies**
Integrating **Space Science • Health • Earth Science • Biology**

Unit 4 USING ENERGY ————————————————— 318

| | CHAPTER **10**

Waves 320

10.1 Types of Waves 322
10.2 Characteristics of Waves 331
10.3 Wave Interactions 340
        Chapter Review 347

Inquiry Lab How do particles move in a medium? 328
Design Your Own Lab Modeling Transverse Waves 350

Math Skills Wave Speed 336

Science and the Consumer Shock Absorbers:
    Why Are They Important? 326

Connections to **Engineering • Architecture**
Integrating **Earth Science**

Viewpoints Should the Spectrum Be Auctioned?............ 352

CHAPTER 11

Electricity 354

11.1 Electric Charge and Force	356
11.2 Current	363
11.3 Circuits	372
11.4 Magnets and Electromagnetism	379
Chapter Review	387

Inquiry Lab How can materials be classified by resistance?...... 370

Skill-Builder Lab Constructing Electric Circuits 390

Math Skills Resistance 369
Electric Power............................... 376

Science and the Consumer Which Is the Best Type of Battery? 366

Real-World Application The Danger of Electric Shock 368

Connection to **Social Studies**
Integrating **Biology • Earth Science**

Career Link Robert Martinez, Physicist.................... 392

CHAPTER 12

Communication Technology............. 394

12.1 Signals and Telecommunication................	396
12.2 Telephone, Radio, and Television..............	405
12.3 Computers and the Internet .	414
Chapter Review............................	423

Inquiry Lab How do red, blue, and green TV
phosphors produce other colors? 413

Skill-Builder Lab Determining the Speed of Sound ... 426

Science and the Consumer TV by the Numbers:
High-Definition Digital TV..................... 412

Real-World Application Using a Search Engine....... 421

Connections to **Social Studies • Architecture**
Integrating **Biology • Physics**

Unit 5 THE HUMAN BODY ————————— 428

▌CHAPTER 13

Food and Diet 430

13.1 Nutrients and Diet 432
13.2 Energy and Food 441
13.3 Digestion 448
    Chapter Review 455

Inquiry Lab How can you determine which foods contain the
    most vitamin C? 437
Skill-Builder Lab Testing Food for Nutrients 458
Real-World Application Balancing a Diet 439
    Sugar Substitutes 445
    Interpreting Food Labels 447
Connection to Social Studies
Integrating Physics

Viewpoints Should You Buy Genetically Engineered Food? . . . 460

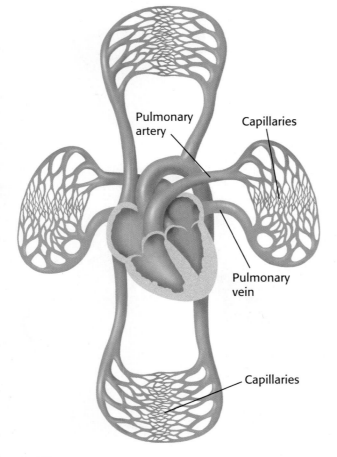

Pulmonary artery

Capillaries

Pulmonary vein

Capillaries

▌CHAPTER 14

Circulation and Respiration 462

14.1 Circulation and the Heart 464
14.2 Breathing and the Lungs 471
14.3 Smoking and Disease 477
    Chapter Review 483

Inquiry Lab How does the structure of
    a heart relate to its function? 468
Inquiry Lab How much air can your
    lungs hold? 475
Design Your Own Lab Studying the Effects
    of Exercise on Circulation and Respiration . 486
Real-World Application Cardiopulmonary
    Resuscitation 472
Connection to Language Arts • Social Studies
Integrating Environmental Science • Chemistry

Career Link Vernon Henderson,
    Trauma Surgeon 488

▌▌CHAPTER 15

Physical Fitness 490

15.1 Bones, Joints, and Muscles 492

15.2 Exercise and Physical Fitness. 501

15.3 Spaceflight **INTEGRATING TECHNOLOGY and Society**
    and Fitness 508

Chapter Review 513

Inquiry Lab How can you estimate the strength
    of a muscle?. 496

Inquiry Lab How can you measure your level
    of aerobic fitness?. 506

Skill-Builder Lab Comparing Skeletal Joints. 516

Real-World Application Anabolic Steroids 502

Connection to **Language Arts**
Integrating **Environmental Science • Physics**

▌▌CHAPTER 16

Disease Prevention and Drug Use 518

16.1 Causes of Disease 520

16.2 Disease Prevention and Treatment 526

16.3 Drugs and Drug Abuse 534

Chapter Review 541

Design Your Own Lab Testing the Effect of Drugs
    on Heart Rate 544

Real-World Application Koch's Postulates 524
    Reading Drug Labels 536

Connection to **Social Studies**
Integrating **Physics • Biology**

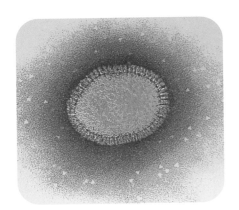

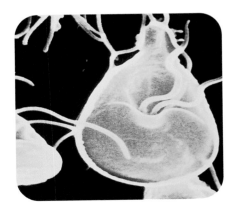

CHAPTER 17

Reproduction and Growth 546

17.1 Human Reproduction 548
17.2 Pregnancy and Birth 555
17.3 Growth and Development 561
     Chapter Review 567

Skill-Builder Lab Investigating the Menstrual Cycle 570

Integrating **Chemistry**
Connections to **Social Studies** • **Language Arts**
    Environmental Science • **Computers and Technology**

Unit 6 EXPLORING EARTH AND SPACE ——————— 572

CHAPTER 18

The Universe 574

18.1 The Universe and Galaxies 576
18.2 Stars and the Sun 585
18.3 The Solar System 592
     Chapter Review 601

Skill-Builder Lab Estimating the Size and
    Power Output of the Sun 604

CHAPTER 19

Planet Earth 606

19.1 Earth's Interior and Plate Tectonics 608
19.2 Earthquakes and Volcanoes 617
19.3 Minerals and Rocks 626
19.4 Weathering and Erosion 633
     Chapter Review 639

Inquiry Lab Can you model tectonic plate boundaries
    with clay? 615

Skill-Builder Lab Analyzing Seismic Waves 642

Integrating **Physics**
Connections to **Social Studies**

Career Link Geerat Vermeij, Paleontologist 644

Crust
Mantle
Outer core
Inner core

▌▌CHAPTER 20

The Atmosphere 646

20.1 Characteristics of the Atmosphere 648
20.2 Water and Wind 656
20.3 Weather and Climate 663
    Chapter Review 671

Design Your Own Lab Measuring Temperature Effects 674
Real-World Application Calculating the Distance
    to a Thunderstorm 665
Integrating **Health • Physics**

Viewpoints Should Laws Require Zero
                Emission Cars? 676

▌▌CHAPTER 21

Using Natural Resources 678

21.1 Organisms and Their Environment 680
21.2 Energy and Resources 688
21.3 Pollution
       and Recycling 697
    Chapter Review 707

Inquiry Lab Why do seasons occur? 685
Inquiry Lab How can oil spills be cleaned up? 703
Skill-Builder Lab Changing the Form of a Fuel 710
Science and the Consumer Sun-Warmed Houses 696
Science and the Consumer Recycling Codes:
    How Are Plastics Sorted? 705
Connection to **Social Studies**
Integrating **Biology**

INTEGRATING TECHNOLOGY and Society

REFERENCE SECTION

Appendix A Study Skills
Reading and Study Skills 714
Math Skills Refresher 722
Graphing Skills 729
Lab Skills 731

Appendix B Useful Data
Table of Densities 734
Morse Code 734
Table of Specific Heats 735
The Electromagnetic Spectrum 735
Periodic Table of the Elements 736
Map of Earth 738
Map of U.S. Natural Resources 740
Weather Map with Symbol Key 740
Star Chart 742

Appendix C Problem Bank 743
Appendix D Selected Answers 751
Glossary 756
Index 767
Credits 777

LABORATORY EXPERIMENTS

Safety in the Laboratory xx
Skill-Builder Lab Making Measurements 30
Design Your Own Lab Testing the
    Conservation of Mass 64
Design Your Own Lab Comparing the
    Physical Properties of Elements 104

Skill-Builder Lab Comparing Polymers 140
Design Your Own Lab Measuring the Rate
    of a Chemical Reaction 180
Skill-Builder Lab Simulating Nuclear
    Decay Reactions 210
Design Your Own Lab Measuring Forces 244
Skill-Builder Lab Determining Energy
    for a Rolling Ball 284
Design Your Own Lab Investigating
    Conduction of Heat 316
Design Your Own Lab Modeling
    Transverse Waves 350
Skill-Builder Lab Constructing
    Electric Circuits 390
Skill-Builder Lab Determining the
    Speed of Sound 426

Skill-Builder Lab Determining the
Speed of Sound 426

Skill-Builder Lab Testing Food
for Nutrients 458

Design Your Own Lab Studying the Effects
of Exercise on Circulation
and Respiration. 486

Skill-Builder Lab Comparing Skeletal Joints . 516

Design Your Own Lab Testing the Effect of
Drugs on Heart Rate 544

Skill-Builder Lab Investigating the
Menstrual Cycle 570

Skill-Builder Lab Estimating the Size
and Power Output of the Sun 604

Skill-Builder Lab Analyzing Seismic
Waves 642

Design Your Own Lab Measuring
Temperature Effects 674

Skill-Builder Lab Changing the Form
of a Fuel 710

Inquiry Labs

How are the mass and volume of a
substance related? 57

Why do some metals cost more
than others? 90

Which melts more easily, sugar or salt? . . . 113

What properties does a polymer have? 135

Can you write balanced chemical
equations? 167

What affects the rates of chemical
reactions? 172

How are action and reaction forces
related? 239

What is your power output when you
climb the stairs? 253

Is energy conserved in a pendulum? 277

How do temperature and energy relate? . . . 295

What color absorbs more radiation? 300

How do particles move in a medium? 328

How can materials be classified by
resistance? 370

How can you make an electromagnet? 384

How do red, blue, and green TV
phosphors produce other colors? 413

How can you determine which foods
contain the most vitamin C? 437

How does the structure of a heart
relate to its function? 468

How much air can your lungs hold? 475

How can you estimate the strength
of a muscle? 496

How can you measure your level
of aerobic fitness? 506

Can you model tectonic plate
boundaries with clay? 615

Why do seasons occur? 685

How can oil spills be cleaned up? 703

Quick ACTIVITIES

Making Observations 14
Kinetic Theory. 48
Convincing John Dalton 73
Constructing a Model 75
Isotopes 84
Elements in Your Food. 88
Building a Close-Packed Structure 118
Polymer Memory 133
Candy Chemistry. 166
Catalysts in Action 173
Modeling Decay and Half-Life 192
Modeling Chain Reactions 199
Newton's First Law 235
A Simple Lever 258
A Simple Inclined Plane 260
Energy Transfer. 275
Sensing Hot and Cold. 291
Convection. 299
Conductors and Insulators. 301
Polarization. 329

Wave Speed 337
Charging Objects. 360
Using a Lemon as a Cell 367
Series and Parallel Circuits 375
Test Your Knowledge of Magnetic Poles . . . 380
Examining Optical Fibers 401
How Fast Are Digital Computers? 416
Testing Foods for Fats 435
Demonstrating the Importance
    of Mechanical Digestion 448
Surface Area 450
Direction of Blood Flow 469
Measuring Breathing Rate 476
Survey of Cigarette Smoking 482
Determining Your Target Heart Rate. 504
Simulating Weightlessness. 511
Thinking Twice 558
Modeling the Universe 582
Using a Star Chart. 588
Measuring Rainfall 659
The Effects of Acid Rain. 700
Observing Air Pollution 701

Math Skills

Conversions. 17
Writing Scientific Notation 23
Using Scientific Notation 24
Significant Figures 25
Density. 56
Conversion Factors 98
Converting Amount to Mass. 99
Converting Mass to Amount. 100
Writing Ionic Formulas 125
Balancing Chemical Equations 165
Nuclear Decay 190
Half-Life. 193
Velocity 221
Momentum 223

Acceleration. 226
Newton's Second Law. 236
Work. 251
Power. 252
Mechanical Advantage 255
Gravitational Potential Energy 265
Kinetic Energy 267
Efficiency. 279
Temperature Scale Conversion 294
Specific Heat 303
Wave Speed 336
Resistance 369
Electric Power 376

REAL WORLD APPLICATIONS

Choosing Materials 58
Designing Drugs 74
Self-Heating Meals 151
Medical Radiation Exposure 204
Hiking 222
The Energy in Food 269

Buying Appliances 312
The Danger of Electric Shock 368
Using a Search Engine 421
Balancing a Diet 439
Sugar Substitutes 445
Interpreting Food Labels 447
Cardiopulmonary Resuscitation 472
Anabolic Steroids 502
Koch's Postulates 524
Reading Drug Labels 536
Calculating the Distance to a
    Thunderstorm 665

Science and the Consumer

Dry Cleaning: How Are Stains
    Dissolved? 43
Fire Extinguishers: Are They
    All the Same? 164
Should a Car's Air Bags Be
    Disconnected? 230
Shock Absorbers: Why Are
    They Important? 326
Which Is the Best Type of Battery? 366
TV by the Numbers: High-Definition
    Digital TV 412
Sun-Warmed Houses 696
Recycling Codes: How Are
    Plastics Sorted? 705

Safety in the Laboratory

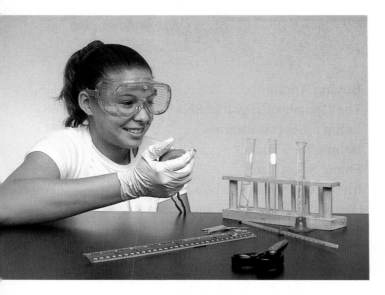

Systematic, careful lab work is an essential part of any science program because lab work is the key to progress in science. In this class, you will practice some of the same fundamental laboratory procedures and techniques that scientists use to pursue new knowledge.

The equipment and apparatus you will use involve various safety hazards, just as they do for working scientists. You must be aware of these hazards. Your teacher will guide you in properly using the equipment and carrying out the experiments, but you must also take responsibility for your part in this process. With the active involvement of you and your teacher, these risks can be minimized so that working in the laboratory can be a safe, enjoyable process of discovery.

Anything can be dangerous if it is misused. Always follow the instructions for the experiment. Pay close attention to the safety notes. Do not do anything differently unless told to do so by your teacher.

If you follow the rules stated on these pages, pay attention to your teacher's directions, and follow the cautions listed on chemical labels, equipment, and in the experiments, then you will stay safe.

These safety rules always apply in the lab

1. **Wear safety goggles, gloves, and a lab apron.**
   Wear these safety devices whenever you are in the lab, not just when you are working on an experiment. Even if you aren't working on an experiment, laboratories contain chemicals that you should protect yourself from. Keep the lab apron strings tied.

   If your safety goggles are uncomfortable or cloud up, ask your teacher for help. Try lengthening the strap, washing the goggles with soap and warm water, or using an anti-fog spray.

2. **No contact lenses in the lab.**
   Contact lenses should not be worn during any investigations using chemicals (even if you are wearing goggles). In the event of an accident, chemicals can get behind contact lenses and cause serious damage before the lenses can be removed. If your doctor requires that you wear contact lenses instead of glasses, you should wear eye-cup safety goggles in the lab. Ask your doctor or your teacher how to use this very important and special eye protection.

3. **NEVER work alone in the lab.**
   Work in the lab only while under the supervision of your teacher. Do not leave equipment unattended while it is in operation.

4. **Wear the right clothing for lab work.**
   Necklaces, neckties, dangling jewelry, long hair, and loose clothing can get caught in moving parts or catch on fire. Tuck in neckties or take them off. Do not wear a necklace or other dangling jewelry, including hanging earrings. It might also be a good idea to remove your wristwatch so that it is not damaged by a chemical splash. Wear shoes that will protect your feet from chemical spills and falling objects—no open-toed shoes or sandals, and no shoes with woven leather straps.

5. **Only books and notebooks needed for the experiment should be in the lab.**
   Only the lab notebook and perhaps the textbook should be used. Keep other books, backpacks, purses, and similar items in your desk or locker.

6. Read the entire experiment before entering the lab.
Memorize the safety precautions. Be familiar with the instructions for the experiment. Only materials and equipment authorized by your teacher should be used. Your teacher will review any applicable safety precautions before the lab. If you are not sure of something, ask your teacher about it.

7. Always heed safety symbols and cautions listed in in the experiments, on handouts, and those posted in the room and given verbally by your teacher.
They are provided for a reason: YOUR SAFETY.

8. Read chemical labels.
Follow the instructions and safety precautions stated on the labels.

9. Be alert and walk with care in the lab.
Sometimes you will have to carry chemicals from the supply station to your lab station. Avoid bumping into other students and spilling the chemicals. Stay at your lab station at other times. Be aware of others near you or your equipment when you are about to do something. If you are not sure of how to proceed, ask.

10. Know the proper fire drill procedures and location of fire exits and emergency equipment.
Make sure you know the procedures to follow in case of a fire or emergency.

11. Know the location and operation of safety showers and eyewash stations.

12. If your clothing catches on fire, do not run; WALK to the safety shower, stand under it, and turn it on.
Call your teacher while you do this.

13. If you get a chemical in your eyes, walk immediately to the eyewash station, turn it on, and lower your head so your eyes are in the running water.
Hold your eyelids open with your thumbs and fingers, and roll your eyeballs around. You have to flush your eyes continuously for at least 15 minutes. Call your teacher while you are doing this.

14. If you spill a chemical on your skin, wash it off with lukewarm water, and call your teacher.
If you spill a solid chemical on your clothing, brush it off carefully without scattering it on somebody else, and call your teacher. If you get liquid on your clothing, wash it off right away using the sink faucet, and call your teacher. If the spill is on your pants or somewhere else that will not fit under the sink faucet, use the safety shower. Remove the pants or other affected clothing while under the shower, and call your teacher. (It may be temporarily embarrassing to remove pants or other clothing in front of your class, but failing to flush that chemical off your skin could cause permanent damage.)

15. Report all accidents to the teacher IMMEDIATELY, no matter how minor.
In addition, if you get a headache, feel sick to your stomach, or feel dizzy, tell your teacher immediately.

16. Report all spills to your teacher immediately.
Call your teacher rather than trying to clean a spill yourself. Your teacher will tell you if it is safe for you to clean up the spill; if not, your teacher will know how the spill should be cleaned up safely.

17. The best way to prevent an accident is to stop it before it happens.
If you have a close call, tell your teacher so that you and your teacher can find a way to prevent it from happening again. Otherwise, the next time, it could be a harmful accident instead of just a close call.

18. Student-designed inquiry investigations, such as the Design Your Own Labs in the textbook must be approved by the teacher before being attempted by the student.

19. DO NOT perform unauthorized experiments or use equipment and apparatus in a manner for which they were not intended.
Use only materials and equipment listed in the activity equipment list or authorized by your teacher. Steps in a procedure should only be performed as described unless your teacher gives you approval to do otherwise.

20. Food, beverages, chewing gum, and tobacco products are NEVER permitted in the lab.

21. For all chemicals, take only what you need. However, if you happen to take too much and have some left over, DO NOT put it back into the container. Ask your teacher what to do with any leftover chemicals.

22. NEVER taste chemicals. Do not touch chemicals or allow them to contact areas of bare skin.

23. Use a sparker to light a Bunsen burner. Do not use matches. Be sure that all gas valves are turned off and that all hot plates are turned off and unplugged when you leave the lab.

24. Use extreme caution when working with hot plates or other heating devices. Keep your head, hands, hair, and clothing away from the flame or heating area, and turn the devices off when they are not in use. Remember that metal surfaces connected to the heated area will become hot by conduction. Remember that many metal, ceramic, and glass items do not always look hot when they are hot. Allow all items to cool before storing.

25. Do not use electrical equipment with frayed or twisted wires.

26. Be sure your hands are dry before using electrical equipment. Before plugging an electrical cord into a socket, be sure the electrical equipment is turned OFF. When you are finished with the device, turn it off. Before you leave the lab, unplug the device, but be sure to turn it off FIRST.

27. Do not let electrical cords dangle from work stations; dangling cords can cause tripping or electrical shocks. The area under and around electrical equipment should be dry; cords should not lie in puddles of spilled liquid.

28. Horseplay and fooling around in the lab are very dangerous. Laboratory equipment and apparatus are not toys; never play in the lab or use lab time or equipment for anything other than their intended purpose.

29. Keep work areas and apparatus clean and neat. Always clean up any clutter made during the course of lab work, put away apparatus in an orderly manner, and report any damaged or missing items.

30. Always thoroughly wash your hands with soap and water at the conclusion of each investigation.

31. Whether or not the lab instructions remind you, all of these rules apply all of the time.

Safety Symbols

The following safety symbols will appear in the laboratory experiments to emphasize important additional areas of caution. Learn what they represent so you can take the appropriate precautions. Remember that the safety symbols represent hazards that apply to a specific activity, but the numbered rules given on the previous pages always apply to all work in the laboratory.

EYE PROTECTION
- Wear safety goggles, and know where the eyewash station is located and how to use it.
- Swinging objects can cause serious injury.
- Avoid directly looking at a light source, as this may cause permanent eye damage.

HAND SAFETY
- Wear latex or nitrile gloves to protect yourself from chemicals in the lab.
- Use a hot mitt to handle resistors, light sources, and other equipment that may be hot. Allow equipment to cool before handling it and storing it.

CLOTHING PROTECTION
- Wear a laboratory apron to protect your clothing.
- Tie back long hair, secure loose clothing, and remove loose jewelry to prevent their getting caught in moving parts or coming in contact with chemicals.

HEATING SAFETY

▷ When using a Bunsen burner or a hot plate, always wear safety goggles and a laboratory apron to protect your eyes and clothing. Tie back long hair, secure loose clothing, and remove loose jewelry.

▷ Never leave a hot plate unattended while it is turned on.

▷ If your clothing catches on fire, walk to the emergency lab shower, and use the shower to put out the fire.

▷ Wire coils may heat up rapidly during experiments. If heating occurs, open the switch immediately, and handle the equipment with a hot mitt.

▷ Allow all equipment to cool before storing it.

CHEMICAL SAFETY

▷ Do not eat or drink anything in the lab. Never taste chemicals.

▷ If a chemical gets on your skin or clothing or in your eyes, rinse it immediately with lukewarm water, and alert your teacher.

▷ If a chemical is spilled, tell your teacher, but do not clean it up yourself unless your teacher says it is OK to do so.

ELECTRICAL SAFETY

▷ Never close a circuit until it has been approved by your teacher. Never rewire or adjust any element of a closed circuit.

▷ Never work with electricity near water; be sure the floor and all work surfaces are dry.

▷ If the pointer of any kind of meter moves off the scale, open the circuit immediately by opening the switch.

▷ Light bulbs or wires that are conducting electricity can become very hot.

▷ Do not work with any batteries, electrical devices, or magnets other than those provided by your teacher.

GLASSWARE SAFETY

▷ If a thermometer breaks, notify your teacher immediately.

▷ Do not heat glassware that is broken, chipped, or cracked. Always use tongs or a hot mitt to handle heated glassware and other equipment because it does not always look hot when it is hot. Allow the equipment to cool before storing it.

▷ If a piece of glassware breaks, do not pick it up with your bare hands. Place broken glass in a specially designated disposal container.

▷ If a light bulb breaks, notify your teacher immediately. Do not remove broken bulbs from sockets.

WASTE DISPOSAL

▷ Use a dustpan, brush, and heavy gloves to carefully pick up broken glass, and dispose of it in a container specifically provided for this purpose.

▷ Dispose of any chemical waste only as instructed by your teacher.

HYGIENIC CARE

▷ Keep your hands away from your face and mouth.

▷ Always wash your hands thoroughly when you are done with an experiment.

CHAPTER 1

Introduction to Science

Chapter Preview

1.1 The Nature of Science
   How Does Science Happen?
   Scientific Theories and Laws

1.2 The Way Science Works
   Science Skills
   Units of Measurement

1.3 Organizing Data
   Presenting Scientific Data
   Writing Numbers in Scientific Notation
   Using Significant Figures

Focus ACTIVITY

Background Imagine that it is 1895 and you are a scientist working in your laboratory. Outside, people move about on foot, on bicycles, or in horse-drawn carriages. A few brave and rich people have purchased the new invention called an automobile. When they can make it run, they ride along the street while the machine sputters, pops, puffs smoke, and frightens both horses and people.

Your laboratory is filled with coils of wire, oddly shaped glass tubes, magnets of all sorts, many heavy glass jars containing liquid and metal plates (batteries), and machines that generate high-voltages. Yellow light comes from a few electric bulbs strung along the ceiling. If more light is needed, it must be daylight coming through windows or light from the old gas lamps along the wall.

It's an exciting time in science because new discoveries about matter and energy are being made almost every day. A few European scientists are even beginning to pay attention to those upstart scientists from America. However, some people believe that humans have learned nearly everything that is worth knowing about the physical world.

Activity 1 Interview someone old enough to have witnessed a lot of technological changes, and ask them what scientific discoveries they think have made the biggest difference in their lifetime. Which changes do you think have been the most important?

Activity 2 A lot has changed since 1895. Research that time period, and find out the cost of a loaf of bread, a dozen eggs, a quart of milk, or a similar common item. How much did the average worker earn in a year? What forms of home entertainment did people have then?

internetconnect

SCI LINKS
NSTA

TOPIC: New discoveries in science
GO TO: www.scilinks.org
KEYWORD: HK1011

Laser-induced fusion is being studied as a way to produce energy for our growing needs. Lasers and fusion reactions would have been outlandish ideas in 1896 when Dr. George Washington Carver started teaching science at the Tuskeegee Institute.

The Nature of Science

science
technology
scientific theory
scientific law

OBJECTIVES

▶ Describe the main branches of natural science and relate them to each other.
▶ Describe the relationship between science and technology.
▶ Distinguish among facts, theories, and laws.
▶ Explain the roles of models and mathematics in scientific theories and laws.

Generally, scientists believe that the universe can be described by basic rules and that these rules can be discovered by careful, methodical study. A scientist may perform experiments to find a new aspect of the natural world, to explain a known phenomenon, to check the results of other experiments, or to test the predictions of current theories.

How Does Science Happen?

Imagine that it is 1895 and you are experimenting with cathode rays. These mysterious rays were discovered almost 40 years before, but in 1895 no one knows what they are. To produce the rays, you create a vacuum by pumping the air out of a sealed glass tube that has two metal rods at a distance from each other, as shown in **Figure 1-1.** When the rods are connected to an electrical source, a current flows through the empty space between the rods, and the rays are produced.

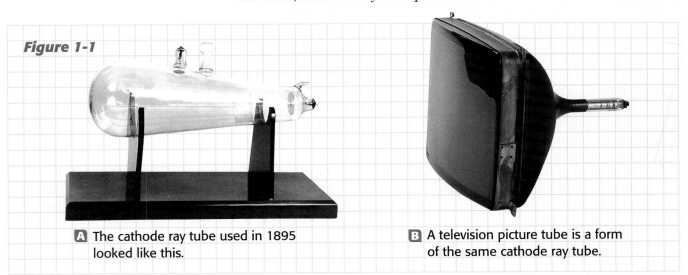

Figure 1-1

A The cathode ray tube used in 1895 looked like this.

B A television picture tube is a form of the same cathode ray tube.

Scientists investigate

You have learned from the work of other scientists and have conducted experiments of your own. From this, you know that when certain minerals are placed inside the tube, the cathode rays make them fluoresce (glow). Pieces of cardboard coated with powder made from these minerals are used to detect the rays. With a very high voltage, even the glass tube itself glows.

Other scientists have found that cathode rays can pass through thin metal foils, but they travel in our atmosphere for only 2 or 3 cm. You wonder if the rays could pass through the glass tube. Others have tried this experiment and have found that cathode rays don't go through glass. But you think that the glow from the glass tube might have outshined any weak glow from the mineral-coated cardboard. So, you decide to cover the glass tube with heavy black paper.

Scientists plan experiments

Before experimenting, you write your plan in your laboratory notebook and sketch the equipment you are using. You make a table in which you can write down the electric power used, the distance from the tube to the fluorescent detector, the air temperature, and anything you observe. You state the idea you are going to test: At a high voltage, cathode rays will be strong enough to be detected outside the tube by causing the mineral-coated cardboard to glow.

Scientists observe

Everything is ready. You want be sure that the black-paper cover doesn't have any gaps, so you darken the room and turn on the tube. The black cover blocks the light from the tube. Just before you switch off the tube, you glimpse a light nearby. When you turn on the tube again, the light reappears.

Then you realize that this light is coming from the mineral-coated cardboard you planned to use to detect cathode rays. The detector is already glowing, and it is on a table almost 1 m away from the tube. You know that 1 m is too far for cathode rays to travel in air. You decide that the tube must be giving off some new rays that no one has seen before. What do you do now?

This is the question Wilhelm Roentgen had to ponder in Würzburg, Germany, on November 8, 1895, when all this happened to him. Should he call the experiment a failure because it didn't give the results he expected? Should he ask reporters to cover this news story? Maybe he should send letters about his discovery to famous scientists and invite them to come and see it.

INTEGRATING

BIOLOGY
In 1928, the Scottish scientist Alexander Fleming was investigating disease-causing bacteria when he saw that one of his cultures contained an area where no bacteria were growing. Instead, an unknown organism was growing in that area. Rather than discarding the culture as a failure, Fleming investigated the unfamiliar organism and found that it was a type of mold. This mold produced a substance that prevented the growth of many disease bacteria. What he found by questioning the results of a "failed" experiment became the first modern antibiotic, penicillin.

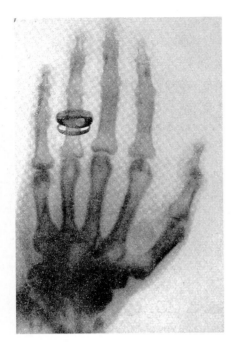

Figure 1-2
Roentgen included this X ray of his wife's hand in one of the first papers he wrote on X rays.

▶ **science** a system of knowledge based on facts or principles

Scientists always test results

Because Roentgen was a scientist, he first repeated his experiment to be sure of his observations. Then he began to think of new questions and to design more experiments to find the answers.

He found that the rays passed through almost everything, although dense materials absorbed them somewhat. If he held his hand in the path of the rays, the bones were visible as shadows on the fluorescent detector, as shown in **Figure 1-2.** When Roentgen published his findings in December, he still did not know what the rays were. He called them *X rays* because *x* represents an unknown in a mathematical equation.

Within 3 months of Roentgen's discovery, a doctor in Massachusetts used X rays to help set the broken bones in a boy's arm properly. After a year, more than a thousand scientific articles about X rays had been published. In 1901, Roentgen received the first Nobel Prize in physics for his discovery.

Science has many branches

Roentgen's work with X rays illustrates how scientists work, but what is **science** about? Science is observing, studying, and experimenting to find the nature of things. You can think of science as having two main branches: social science and natural science. Natural science tries to understand "nature," which really means "the whole universe." Natural science is usually divided into life science, physical science, and Earth science, as shown in **Figure 1-3.**

Life science is *biology*. Biology has many branches, such as *botany*, the science of plants; *zoology*, the science of animals; and *ecology*, the science of balance in nature. Medicine and agriculture are branches of biology too.

Figure 1-3
This chart shows one way to look at science. Modern science has many branches and specialties.

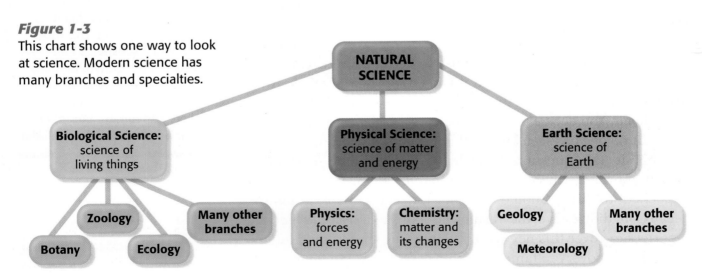

Physical science has two main branches—*chemistry* and *physics*. Chemistry is the science of matter and its changes, and physics is the science of forces and energy.

Some of the branches of Earth science are *geology*, the science of the physical nature and history of the Earth, and *meteorology*, the science of the atmosphere and weather.

This classification of science appears very tidy, like stacks of boxes in a shoe store, but there's a problem with it. As science has progressed, the branches of science have grown out of their little boxes. For example, chemists have begun to explain the workings of chemicals that make up living things, such as DNA, shown in **Figure 1-4.** This science is *biochemistry*, the study of the matter of living things. It is both a life science and a physical science. In the same way, the study of the forces that affect the Earth is *geophysics*, which is both an Earth science and a physical science.

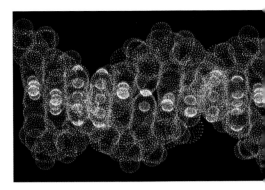

Figure 1-4
Our DNA makes each of us unique.

Science and technology work together

Scientists who do experiments to learn more about the world are practicing *pure science*, also defined as the continuing search for scientific knowledge. Engineers look for ways to use this knowledge for practical applications. This application of science is called technology. For example, scientists who practice pure science want to know how certain kinds of materials, called superconductors, conduct electricity with almost no loss in energy. Engineers focus on how that technology can be used to build high-speed computers.

Technology and science depend on one another, as illustrated by **Figure 1-5.** For instance, scientists did not know that tiny organisms such as bacteria even existed until the technology to make precision magnifying lenses developed in the late 1600s.

▷ **technology** the application of science to meet human needs

A Da Vinci's design for a parachute

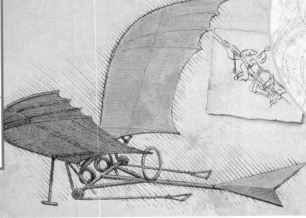

B Da Vinci's design for a helicopter

Figure 1-5
Some of Leonardo da Vinci's ideas could not be built until twentieth-century technology was developed.

Scientific Theories and Laws

People sometimes say things like, "My theory is that we'll see Jaime on the school bus," when they really mean, "I'm guessing that we'll find Jaime on the school bus." People use the word *theory* in everyday speech to refer to a guess about something. In science, a theory is much more than a guess.

Theories and laws are supported by observation

A scientific theory is an explanation that has been tested by repeated observations. Many theories can be tested by observations of experiments in a laboratory or under controlled conditions. Some scientific theories, such as how the continents move, are nearly impossible to test by laboratory experiments because the events occur slowly over long periods of time.

Scientific theories are always being questioned and examined. To be valid, a theory must continue to pass several tests.

▶ A theory must explain observations simply and clearly. The theory that heat is the energy of particles in motion explains how the far end of a metal tube gets hot when you hold the tip over a flame, as shown in **Figure 1-6A.**

▶ Experiments that illustrate the theory must be repeatable. The far end of the tube always gets hot when the tip is held over a flame, whether it is done for the first time or the thirty-first time.

▶ You must be able to predict from the theory. You might predict that anything that makes particles move faster will make the object hotter. Sawing a piece of wood will make the particles move faster. If, as shown in **Figure 1-6B,** you saw rapidly, the saw will get hot.

When you place a hot cooking pot in a cooler place, does the pot become hotter as it stands? No. It will always get cooler. This illustrates a law that states that warm objects always become cooler when they are placed in cooler surroundings. A scientific law states a repeated observation about nature. Notice that the law does not explain why warm objects become cooler.

Mathematics can describe physical events

How would you state the law of gravitation? You could say that something you hold will fall to Earth when you let go. This *qualitative* statement describes with words something you have seen many times. But many scientific laws and theories can be stated as mathematical equations, which are *quantitative* statements.

▶ **scientific theory** a tested, possible explanation of a natural event

▶ **scientific law** a summary of an observed natural event

Figure 1-6
The kinetic theory explains many things that you can observe, such as why both the far end of the tube (A) and the saw blade (B) get hot.

Rectangle Area Equation

$$A = l \times w$$

The rectangle area equation works for all rectangles, whether they are short, tall, wide, or thin.

Universal Gravitation Equation

$$F = G\frac{m_1 m_2}{d^2}$$

In the same way, the universal gravitation equation describes how big the force will be between two galaxies or between Earth and an apple dropped from your hand, as shown in **Figure 1-7**. Quantitative expressions of the laws of science make communicating about science easier. Scientists around the world speak and read many different languages, but mathematics, the language of science, is the same everywhere.

Theories and laws are not absolute

Sometimes theories have to be changed or replaced completely when new discoveries are made. Over 200 years ago, scientists used the *caloric theory* to explain how objects become hotter and cooler. Heat was thought to be an invisible fluid, called caloric, that could flow from a warm object to a cool one. People thought that fires were fountains of caloric that flowed into surrounding objects, making them warmer. The caloric theory could explain everything that people knew about heat.

But the caloric theory couldn't explain why rubbing two rough surfaces together made them warmer. Around 1800, after doing many experiments, some scientists suggested a new theory based on the idea that heat was a result of the motion of particles. The new theory was that heat is really a form of energy that is transferred when fast-moving particles hit others. Because this theory, the *kinetic theory*, explained the old observations as well as the new ones, it was kept and the caloric theory was discarded. You will learn about the kinetic theory in Chapter 2.

Models can represent physical events

When you see the word *model*, you may think of a small copy of an airplane or a person who shows off clothing. Scientists use models too. A scientific model is a representation of an object or event that can be studied to understand the real object or event. Sometimes, like a model airplane, models represent things that are too big, too complex, or too small to study easily.

What does this have to do with the force between two galaxies?

Figure 1-7
For a long time, people believed that gravity was part of the nature of things. Newton described gravitational attraction as a force that varies depending on the mass of the objects and the distance that separates them.

Figure 1-8

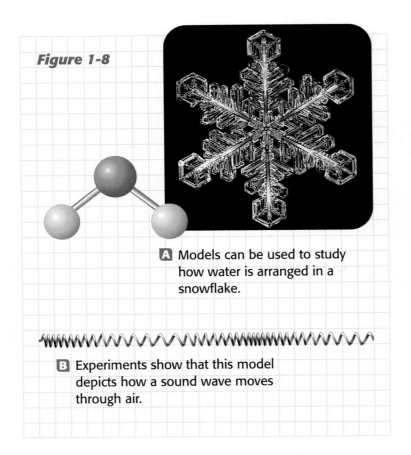

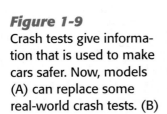

A Models can be used to study how water is arranged in a snowflake.

B Experiments show that this model depicts how a sound wave moves through air.

A model of water is shown in **Figure 1-8A.** Chemists use models to study how water forms an ice crystal, such as a snowflake. Models can be drawings on paper. The drawing in **Figure 1-8B** is a model of a sound wave moving through air. Also, a model can be a mental "picture" or a set of rules that describes what something does. After you have studied atoms in Chapter 3, you will be able to picture atoms in your mind and use models to predict what will happen in chemical reactions.

Scientists and engineers also use computer models. These can be drawings; more often, they are mathematical models of complex systems, such as those shown in **Figure 1-9.** Computer models can save time and money because long and complex calculations are done by a machine.

A

Figure 1-9
Crash tests give information that is used to make cars safer. Now, models (A) can replace some real-world crash tests. (B)

B

46 CO 16 97

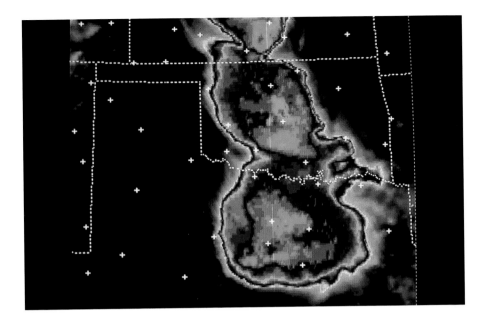

Figure 1-10
Models help forecast the weather and, in cases of dangerous storms, can help save lives.

Computer models have a variety of applications. For example, they can be used instead of expensive crash tests to study the effects of motion and forces in car crashes. Engineers use the predictions from the models to improve the design of cars. *Meteorologists* have computer models such as the one shown in **Figure 1-10,** which uses information about wind speed and direction, air temperature, moisture levels, and ground shape to help forecast the weather.

SECTION 1.1 REVIEW

SUMMARY

▶ A scientist makes objective observations.

▶ A scientist confirms results by repeating experiments and learns more by designing and conducting new experiments.

▶ Scientific laws and theories are supported by repeated observation but may be changed when observations are made that are not consistent with predictions.

▶ Models are used to represent real situations and to make predictions.

CHECK YOUR UNDERSTANDING

1. **Compare and Contrast** the two main branches of physical science.
2. **Explain** how science and technology depend on each other.
3. **Explain** how a scientific theory differs from a guess or an opinion.
4. **Define** *scientific law* and give an example.
5. **Compare and Contrast** a scientific law and a scientific theory.
6. **Compare** quantitative and qualitative descriptions.
7. **Describe** how a scientific model is used, and give an example of a scientific model.
8. **Creative Thinking** How do you think Roentgen's training as a scientist affected the way he responded to his discovery?
9. **Creative Thinking** Pick a common happening, develop a theory about it, and describe an experiment you could perform to test your theory.

The Way Science Works

KEY TERMS
critical thinking
scientific method
variable
length
mass
volume
weight

OBJECTIVES

▶ Understand how to use critical thinking skills to solve problems.
▶ Describe the steps of the scientific method.
▶ Know some of the tools scientists use to investigate nature.
▶ Explain the objective of a consistent system of units, and identify the SI units for length, mass, and time.
▶ Identify what each common SI prefix represents, and convert measurements.

If 16 ounces costs $3.59 and 8 ounces costs $2.19, then . . .

Figure 1-11
Making thoughtful decisions is important in scientific processes as well as in everyday life.

▶ **critical thinking** applying logic and reason to observations and conclusions

Throwing a spear accurately to kill animals for food or to ward off intruders was probably a survival skill people used for thousands of years. In our society, throwing a javelin is an athletic skill, and riding a bicycle or driving a car is considered almost a survival skill. The skills that we place importance on change over time.

Science Skills

Although pouring liquid into a test tube without spilling is a skill that is useful in science, other skills are more important. Planning experiments, recording observations, and reporting data are some of these more important skills. The most important skill is learning to think like a scientist.

Critical thinking

If you are doing your homework and the lights go out, what would you do? Would you call the electric company immediately? A person who thinks like a scientist would first ask questions and make observations. Are lights on anywhere in the house? If so, what would you conclude? Suppose everything electrical in the house is off. Can you see lights in the neighbors' windows? If their lights are on, what does that mean? What if everyone's lights are off?

If you approach the problem this way, you are thinking logically. This kind of thinking is very much like **critical thinking.** You do this kind of thinking when you consider if the giant economy-sized jar of peanut butter is really less expensive than the regular size, as shown in **Figure 1-11,** or consider if a specific brand of soap makes you more attractive.

The Scientific Method

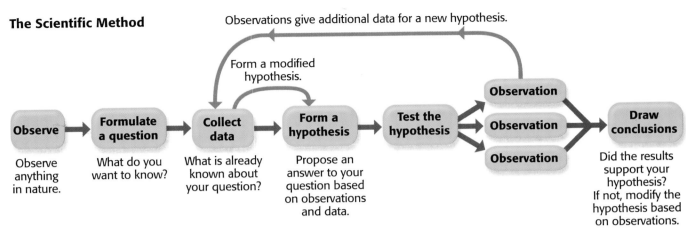

Observations give additional data for a new hypothesis.

Form a modified hypothesis.

Observe — Observe anything in nature.

Formulate a question — What do you want to know?

Collect data — What is already known about your question?

Form a hypothesis — Propose an answer to your question based on observations and data.

Test the hypothesis

Observation
Observation
Observation

Draw conclusions — Did the results support your hypothesis? If not, modify the hypothesis based on observations.

Figure 1-12
The scientific method is a general description of scientific thinking more than an exact path for scientists to follow.

When the lights go out, if you get more facts before you call the power company, you're thinking critically. You're not making a reasonable conclusion if you decide there is a citywide power failure when you observe that your lights are off. You don't have to be a scientist to make observations and use logic.

Using the scientific method

In the scientific method, critical thinking is used to solve scientific problems. The scientific method is a way to organize your thinking about everyday questions as well as about questions that you might think of as scientific. Using the scientific method helps you find and evaluate possible answers. The scientific method is often shown as a series of steps like those in **Figure 1-12.**

Most scientific questions begin with observations—simple things you notice. For example, you might notice that when you open a door, you hear a noise. You ask the question: Why does this door make noise? You may gather data by checking other doors and find that the other doors don't make noise. So you form a *hypothesis*, a possible answer that you can test in some way. If the door makes a noise, then the source of the noise is the doorknob.

Testing hypotheses

Scientists test a hypothesis by doing experiments. How can you design an experiment to test your hypothesis about the door? A good experiment tests only one variable at a time. You might remove the doorknob to see if that stops the squeak.

When you change more than one thing at a time, it's harder to make reasonable conclusions. If you remove the knob, sand the frame, and put oil on the hinges, you may stop the squeak, but you won't know what was causing the squeak. Even if you test one thing at a time, you may not find the answer on the first try. If you take the knob off the door and the door still makes noise, was your experiment a failure?

▶ **scientific method** a series of logical steps to follow in order to solve problems

▶ **variable** anything that can change in an experiment

Quick ACTIVITY

Making Observations

1. Get an ordinary candle of any shape and color.
2. Record all the observations you can make about the candle.
3. Light the candle, and watch it burn for 1 minute.
4. Record as many observations about the burning candle as you can.
5. Share your results with your class, and find out how many different things were observed.

Conducting experiments

In truth, no experiment is a failure. Experiments may not give the results you wanted, but they are all observations of real happenings in the world. A scientist uses the results to revise the hypothesis and to plan a new experiment that tests a different variable. For example, once you know that the doorknob did not cause the squeak, you can revise your hypothesis to see if oiling the door hinges stops the noise.

Scientists often do "what if" experiments to see what happens in a certain situation. These experiments are a form of data collection. Often, as with Roentgen's X rays, experimental results are surprising and lead in new directions.

Scientists always have the question being tested in mind. You can find out if ice is heavier than water without an experiment. Just think about which one floats. The thinking that led to the law of gravitation began in 1666 when Isaac Newton saw an apple fall from a tree. He wondered why objects fall toward the center of Earth rather than in another direction.

Some questions, such as how Earth's continents have moved over millions of years, cannot be answered with experimental data. Instead of getting data from experiments, geologists make observations all over Earth. They also use models based on the laws of physics, such as those shown in **Figure 1-13.**

Using scientific tools

Of course, logical thinking isn't the only skill used in science. Scientists must make careful observations. Sometimes only the senses are needed for observations, as in the case of field botanists using their eyes to identify plants. At other times, special tools are used. Scientists must know how to use these tools, what the limits of the tools are, and how to interpret data from them. Sometimes scientists use light *microscopes*. A light microscope uses lenses to magnify very small objects, such as bacteria, or the details of larger objects, such as the structure of leaves.

Figure 1-13
Computer models of Earth's crust help geologists understand how the continental plates moved in the past and how they may move in the future.

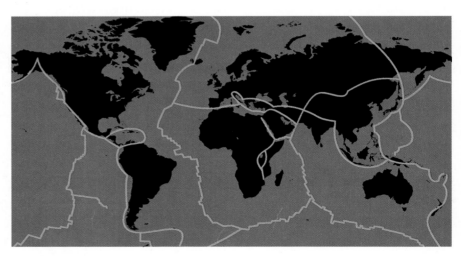

Figure 1-14

A The Gemini North observatory in Hawaii is a new tool for scientists. Its 8.1 m mirror is used to view distant galaxies.

B The Whirlpool galaxy (M51) and its companion NGC5195 are linked by a trail of gas and dust, which NGC5195 has pulled from M51 by gravitational attraction.

Astronomers use *telescopes* with lenses and mirrors to magnify objects that appear small because they are far away, such as the distant stars shown in **Figure 1-14.** Other kinds of telescopes do not form images from visible light. *Radio telescopes* detect the radio signals emitted by distant objects. Some of the oldest, most distant objects in the universe have been found with radio telescopes. Radio waves from those objects were emitted almost 15 billion years ago.

Several different types of *spectrophotometers* break light into a rainbowlike *spectrum*. A chemist can learn a great deal about a substance from the light it absorbs or emits. Physicists use *particle accelerators* to make fragments of atoms move extremely fast and then let them smash into atoms or parts of atoms. Data from these collisions give us information about the structure of atoms.

Units of Measurement

As you learned in Section 1.1, mathematics is the language of science, and mathematical models rely on accurate observations. But if your scientific measurements are in inches and gallons, many scientists will not understand because they do not use these units. For this reason scientists use the International System of Units, abbreviated SI, which stands for the French phrase *le Système Internationale d'Unités*.

Connection to
LANGUAGE ARTS

The word *scope* comes from the Greek word *skopein*, meaning "to see." Science and technology use many different scopes to see things that we can't see with unaided eyes. For example, the telescope gets its name from the Greek prefix *tele-* meaning "distant" or "far." So a telescope is a tool for seeing far.

Making the Connection

Use a dictionary to find out what is seen by a retinoscope, a kaleidoscope, a hygroscope, and a spectroscope.

Table 1-1 SI Base Units

Quantity	Unit	Abbreviation
Length	meter	m
Mass	kilogram	kg
Time	second	s
Temperature	kelvin	K
Electric current	ampere	A
Amount of substance	mole	mol
Luminous intensity	candela	cd

Table 1-2 Prefixes Used for Large Measurements

Prefix	Symbol	Meaning	Multiple of base unit
kilo-	k	thousand	1000
mega-	M	million	1 000 000
giga-	G	billion	1 000 000 000

Table 1-3 Prefixes Used for Small Measurements

Prefix	Symbol	Meaning	Multiple of base unit
deci-	d	tenth	0.1
centi-	c	hundredth	0.01
milli-	m	thousandth	0.001
micro-	μ	millionth	0.000 001
nano-	n	billionth	0.000 000 001

Did You Know ?

SI started with the metric system in France in 1795. The meter was originally defined as 1/10 000 000 of the distance between the North Pole and the Equator.

SI units are used for consistency

When all scientists use the same system of measurement, sharing data and results is easier. SI is based on the metric system and uses the seven SI base units that you see in **Table 1-1.**

Perhaps you noticed that the base units do not include area, volume, pressure, weight, force, speed, and other familiar quantities. Combinations of the base units, called *derived units*, are used for these measurements.

Suppose you want to order carpet for a floor that measures 8.0 m long and 6.0 m wide. You know that the area of a rectangle is its length times its width.

$$A = l \times w$$

The area of the floor can be calculated as shown below.

$$A = 8.0 \text{ m} \times 6.0 \text{ m} = 48 \text{ m}^2$$
(or 48 square meters)

The SI unit of area, m^2, is a derived unit.

SI prefixes are for very large and very small measurements

Look at a meterstick. How would you express the length of a bird's egg in meters? How about the distance you traveled on a vacation trip? The bird's egg might be 1/100 m, or 0.01 m, long. Your trip could have been 800 000 m in distance. To avoid writing a lot of decimal places and zeros, SI uses prefixes to express very small or very large numbers. These prefixes, shown in **Table 1-2** and **Table 1-3,** are all *multiples* of 10.

Using the prefixes, you can now say that the bird's egg is 1 cm (1 *centi*meter is 0.01 m) long and your trip was 800 km (800 *kilo*meters are 800 000 m) long. Note that the base unit of mass is the *kilo*gram, which is already a multiple of the gram.

It is easy to convert SI units to smaller or larger units. Remember that to make a measurement, it takes more of a small unit or less of a large unit. A person's height could be 1.85 m, a fairly small number. In centimeters, the same height would be 185 cm, a larger number.

So, if you are converting to a smaller unit, multiply the measurement to get a bigger number. To write 1.85 m as *centi*meters, you multiply by 100, as shown below.

$$1.85 \; \cancel{m} \times \frac{100 \; cm}{1 \; \cancel{m}} = 185 \; cm$$

If you are converting to a larger unit, divide the measurement to get a smaller number. To change 185 cm to meters, divide by 100, as shown in the following.

$$185 \; \cancel{cm} \times \frac{1 \; m}{100 \; \cancel{cm}} = 1.85 \; m$$

Math Skills

Conversions A roll of copper wire contains 15 m of wire. What is the length of the wire in centimeters?

1 **List the given and unknown values.**
   Given: *length in meters, l* = 15 m
   Unknown: *length in centimeters* = ? cm

2 **Determine the relationship between units.**
   Looking at **Table 1-3,** you can find that 1 cm = 0.01 m. This also means that 1 m = 100 cm.
   You will multiply because you are converting from a larger unit (meters) to a smaller unit (centimeters).

3 **Write the equation for the conversion.**

   $$length \; in \; cm = m \times \frac{100 \; cm}{1 \; m}$$

4 **Insert the known values into the equation, and solve.**

   $$length \; in \; cm = 15 \; \cancel{m} \times \frac{100 \; cm}{1 \; \cancel{m}}$$

   $$length \; in \; cm = 1500 \; cm$$

Practice HINT

If you have done the conversions properly, all the units above and below the fraction will cancel except the units you need.

Practice

Conversions

1. Write 550 *milli*meters as meters.
2. Write 3.5 seconds as *milli*seconds.
3. Convert 1.6 *kilo*grams to grams.
4. Convert 2500 *milli*grams to *kilo*grams.
5. Convert 4.00 *centi*meters to *micro*meters.
6. Change 2800 *milli*moles to moles.
7. Change 6.1 amperes to *milli*amperes.
8. Write 3 *micro*grams as *nano*grams.

internet**connect**

SC*i*LINKS
NSTA

TOPIC: SI units
GO TO: www.scilinks.org
KEYWORD: HK1013

Figure 1-15 Tools for Quantitative Measurements

Quantity	Time	Length
SI Unit	Second, s	Meter, m
Other units	Milliseconds, ms Minutes, min Hours, h	Millimeter, mm Centimeter, cm Kilometer, km
Examples		91m 2 cm 1 mm
Tools		

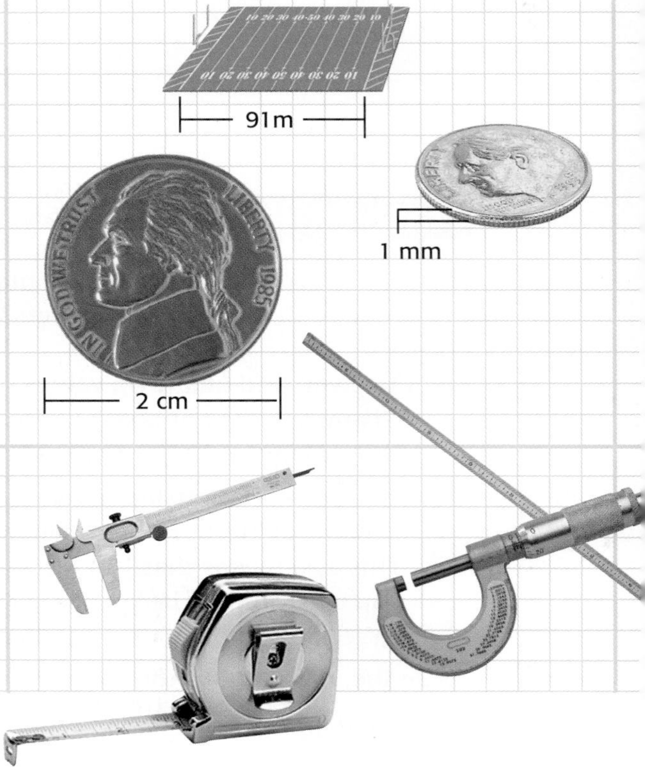

Making measurements

Many observations rely on quantitative measurements. The most basic scientific measurements generally answer questions such as how much time did it take and how big is it?

Often, you will measure time, **length, mass,** and **volume.** The SI units for these quantities and the tools you may use to measure them are shown in **Figure 1-15.**

Although you may hear someone say that he or she is "weighing" an object with a balance, **weight** is not the same as mass. Mass is the quantity of matter and weight is the force with which Earth's gravity pulls on that quantity of matter.

In your lab activities, you will use a graduated cylinder to measure the volume of liquids. The volume of a solid that has a specific geometric shape, such as a rectangular block or a metal cylinder, can be calculated from the length of its surfaces. The volume of small solid objects is usually expressed in cubic centimeters, cm^3. One cubic centimeter is equal to 1 mL.

▶ **length** the straight-line distance between any two points

▶ **mass** a measure of the quantity of matter in an object

▶ **volume** a measure of space, such as the capacity of a container

▶ **weight** the force with which gravity pulls on a quantity of matter

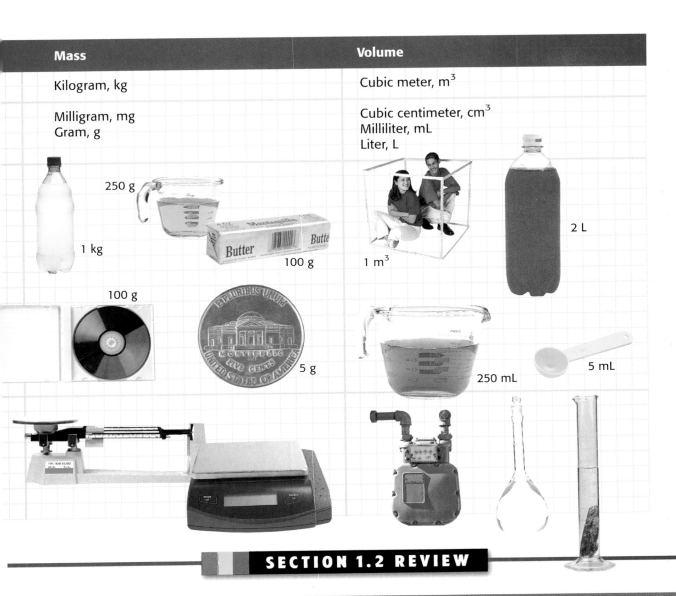

Mass	Volume
Kilogram, kg	Cubic meter, m^3
Milligram, mg Gram, g	Cubic centimeter, cm^3 Milliliter, mL Liter, L

250 g

Butter Butte

1 kg

100 g

100 g

5 g

1 m^3

2 L

250 mL

5 mL

SECTION 1.2 REVIEW

SUMMARY

▶ In the scientific method, a person asks a question, collects data about the question, forms a hypothesis, tests the hypothesis, draws conclusions, and if necessary, modifies the hypothesis based on results.

▶ In an ideal experiment, only one factor, the variable, is tested.

▶ SI has seven base units.

CHECK YOUR UNDERSTANDING

1. **List** three examples each of things that are commonly measured by mass, by volume, and by length.
2. **Explain** why the scientific method is said to be very similar to critical thinking.
3. **Describe** a hypothesis and how it is used. Give an example of a hypothesis.
4. **Explain** why no experiment should be called a failure.
5. **Relate** the discussion of scientists' tools to how science and technology depend on each other.
6. **Explain** the difference between SI base units and derived units. Give an example of each.
7. **Critical Thinking** Why do you think it is wise to limit an experiment to test only one factor at a time?

Organizing Data

scientific notation
precision
significant figures
accuracy

OBJECTIVES

▶ Interpret line graphs, bar graphs, and pie graphs.
▶ Identify the significant figures in calculations.
▶ Use scientific notation and significant figures in problem solving.
▶ Understand the difference between precision and accuracy.

One thing that helped Roentgen discover X rays was that he could read about the experiments other scientists had performed with the cathode ray tube. He was able to learn from their data. Organizing and presenting data are important science skills.

Presenting Scientific Data

Suppose you are trying to determine the speed of a chemical reaction that produces a gas. You can let the gas displace water in a graduated cylinder, as shown in **Figure 1-16.** You read the volume of gas in the cylinder every 10 seconds from the start of the reaction until there is no change in volume for four successive readings. **Table 1-4** shows the data you collect in the experiment.

Because you did the experiment, you saw how the volume changed over time. But how can someone who reads your report see it? To show the results, you can make a graph.

Table 1-4 **Experimental Data**

Time (s)	Volume of gas (mL)	Time (s)	Volume of gas (mL)
0	0	90	116
10	3	100	140
20	6	110	147
30	12	120	152
40	25	130	154
50	43	140	156
60	58	150	156
70	72	160	156
80	100	170	156

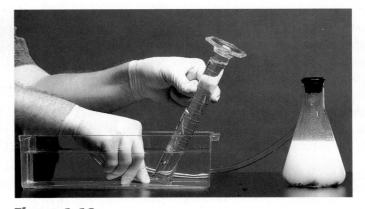

Figure 1-16
The volume of gas produced by a reaction can be determined by measuring the amount of water the gas displaces in a graduated cylinder.

Line graphs are best for continuous changes

Many types of graphs can be drawn, but which one should you use? A *line graph* is best for displaying data that change. Our example experiment has two variables, time and volume. Time is the *independent variable* because you chose the time intervals to take the measurements. The volume of gas is the *dependent variable* because its value depends on what happens in the experiment.

Line graphs are usually made with the *x*-axis showing the independent variable and the *y*-axis showing the dependent variable. **Figure 1-17** is a graph of the data that is in **Table 1-4.**

A person who never saw your experiment can look at this graph and know what took place. The graph shows that gas was produced slowly for the first 20 s and that the rate increased until it became constant from about 50 s to 100 s. The reaction slowed down and stopped after about 140 s.

Bar graphs compare items

A *bar graph* is useful when you want to compare data for several individual items or events. If you measured the melting temperatures of some metals, your data could be presented in a way similar to that in **Table 1-5. Figure 1-18** shows the same values as a bar graph. A bar graph often makes clearer how large or small the differences in individual values are.

Volumes Measured Over Time

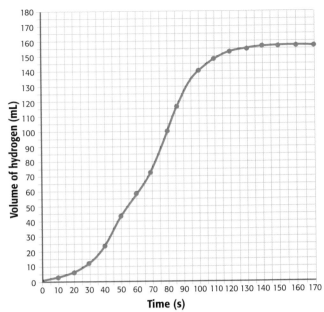

Figure 1-17
Data that change over a range are best represented by a line graph. Notice that many in-between volumes can be read.

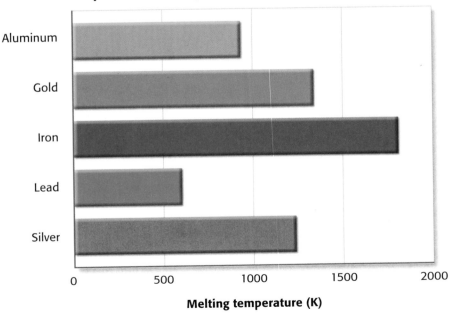

Graph of the Melting Points of Some Common Metals

Table 1-5 **Melting Points of Some Metals**

Element	Melting temp. (K)
Aluminum	933
Gold	1337
Iron	1808
Lead	601
Silver	1235

Figure 1-18
A bar graph is best for data that have specific values for different events or things.

Composition of Calcite

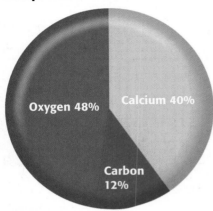

Figure 1-19
A pie chart is best for data that represent parts of a whole, such as the percentage of each element in the mineral calcite.

TOPIC: Presenting scientific data
GO TO: www.scilinks.org
KEYWORD: HK1014

scientific notation a value written as a simple number multiplied by a power of 10

Pie charts show the parts of a whole

A *pie chart* is ideal for displaying data that are parts of a whole. Suppose you have analyzed a compound to find the percentage of each element it contains. Your analysis shows that the compound consists of 40 percent calcium, 12 percent carbon, and 48 percent oxygen. You can draw a pie chart that shows these percentages as a portion of the whole pie, the compound, as shown in **Figure 1-19.**

Writing Numbers in Scientific Notation

Scientists sometimes need to express measurements using numbers that are very large or very small. For example, the speed of light through space is about 300 000 000 m/s. Suppose you want to calculate the time required for light to travel from Neptune to Earth when Earth and Neptune are 4 600 000 000 000 m apart. To find out how long it takes, you would divide the distance between Earth and Neptune by the distance light travels in 1 s.

$$t = \frac{\text{distance from Earth to Neptune (m)}}{\text{distance light travels in 1 s (m/s)}}$$

$$t = \frac{4\ 600\ 000\ 000\ 000\ \text{m}}{300\ 000\ 000\ \text{m/s}}$$

This is a lot of zeros to keep track of when performing a calculation.

To reduce the number of zeros, you can express values as a simple number multiplied by a power of 10. This is called **scientific notation.** Some powers of 10 and their decimal equivalents are shown below.

$$10^4 = 10\ 000$$
$$10^3 = 1000$$
$$10^2 = 100$$
$$10^1 = 10$$
$$10^0 = 1$$
$$10^{-1} = 0.1$$
$$10^{-2} = 0.01$$
$$10^{-3} = 0.001$$

When Earth and Neptune are 4 600 000 000 000 m apart, the distance can be written in scientific notation as 4.6×10^{12} m. The speed of light in space is 3.0×10^8 m/s.

Math Skills

Writing Scientific Notation The adult human heart pumps about 18 000 L of blood each day. Write this value in scientific notation.

1 **List the given and unknown values.**
   Given: *volume,* $V = 18\ 000$ L
   Unknown: *volume,* $V = ? \times 10^?$ L

2 **Write the form for scientific notation.**
   $V = ? \times 10^?$ L

3 **Insert the known values into the form, and solve.**
   First find the largest power of 10 that will divide into the known value and leave one digit before the decimal point. You get 1.8 if you divide 10 000 into 18 000 L. So, 18 000 L can be written as (1.8 × 10 000) L.

   Then write 10 000 as a power of 10. Because $10\ 000 = 10^4$, you can write 18 000 L as 1.8×10^4 L.
   $V = 1.8 \times 10^4$ L

Practice

Writing Scientific Notation

1. Write the following measurements in scientific notation:
   a. 800 000 000 m
   b. 0.0015 kg
   c. 60 200 L
   d. 0.000 95 m
   e. 8 002 000 km
   f. 0.000 000 000 06 kg
2. Write the following measurements in long form:
   a. 4.5×10^3 g
   b. 6.05×10^{-3} m
   c. 3.115×10^6 km
   d. 1.99×10^{-8} cm

Practice HINT

▶ A shortcut for scientific notation involves moving the decimal point and counting the number of places it is moved. To change 18 000 to 1.8, the decimal point is moved four places to the left. The number of places the decimal is moved is the correct power of 10.

$$18\ 000\ \text{L} = 1.8 \times 10^4\ \text{L}$$

▶ When a quantity smaller than 1 is converted to scientific notation, the decimal moves to the right and the power of 10 is *negative*. For example, suppose an *E. coli* bacterium is measured to be 0.000 0021 m long. To express this measurement in scientific notation, move the decimal point to the right.

$$0.000\ 0021\ \text{m} = 2.1 \times 10^{-6}\ \text{m}$$

Using scientific notation

When you use scientific notation in calculations, you follow the rules of algebra for powers of 10. When you multiply two values in scientific notation, you add the powers of 10. When you divide, you subtract the powers of 10.

So the problem about Earth and Neptune can be solved more easily as shown below.

$$t = \frac{4.6 \times 10^{12}\ \text{m}}{3.0 \times 10^8\ \text{m/s}}$$

$$t = \left(\frac{4.6}{3.0} \times \frac{10^{12}}{10^8}\right) \frac{\text{m}}{\text{m/s}}$$

$$t = (1.5 \times 10^{(12-8)})\text{s}$$

$$t = 1.5 \times 10^4\ \text{s}$$

Math Skills

Using Scientific Notation Your state plans to buy a rectangular tract of land measuring 5.36×10^3 m by 1.38×10^4 m to establish a nature preserve. What is the area of this tract in square meters?

1 **List the given and unknown values.**
    Given: *length*, $l = 1.38 \times 10^4$ m
              width, $w = 5.36 \times 10^3$ m
    Unknown: *area*, $A =?$ m^2

2 **Write the equation for area.**
    $A = l \times w$

3 **Insert the known values into the equation, and solve.**
    $A = (1.38 \times 10^4 \text{ m}) (5.36 \times 10^3 \text{ m})$
    Regroup the values and units as follows.
    $A = (1.38 \times 5.36) (10^4 \times 10^3) (\text{m} \times \text{m})$
    When multiplying, add the powers of 10.
    $A = (1.38 \times 5.36) (10^{4+3})(\text{m} \times \text{m})$
    $A = 7.40 \times 10^7 \text{ m}^2$

Practice

Using Scientific Notation

1. Perform the following calculations.
    a. $(5.5 \times 10^4 \text{ cm}) \times (1.4 \times 10^4 \text{ cm})$
    b. $(2.77 \times 10^{-5} \text{ m}) \times (3.29 \times 10^{-4} \text{ m})$
    c. $(4.34 \text{ g/mL}) \times (8.22 \times 10^6 \text{ mL})$
    d. $(3.8 \times 10^{-2} \text{ cm}) \times (4.4 \times 10^{-2} \text{ cm}) \times (7.5 \times 10^{-2} \text{ cm})$

2. Perform the following calculations.

    a. $\dfrac{3.0 \times 10^4 \text{ L}}{62 \text{ s}}$ **c.** $\dfrac{5.2 \times 10^8 \text{ cm}^3}{9.5 \times 10^2 \text{ cm}}$

    b. $\dfrac{6.05 \times 10^7 \text{ g}}{8.8 \times 10^6 \text{ cm}^3}$ **d.** $\dfrac{3.8 \times 10^{-5} \text{ kg}}{4.6 \times 10^{-5} \text{ kg/cm}^3}$

Using Significant Figures

Suppose you need to measure the length of a wire and you have two tape measures. One is marked every 0.001 m, and the other is marked every 0.1 m. Which tape should you use? The tape marked every 0.001 m gives you more **precision.** If you use this tape, you can report a length of 1.638 m. The other tape is only precise to 1.6 m.

Measured quantities are always reported in a way that shows the precision of the measurement. To do this, scientists use **significant figures.** The length of 1.638 m has four significant figures because the digits 1638 are known for sure. The measurement of 1.6 m has two significant figures.

Practice HINT

Because not all devices can display superscript numbers, scientific calculators and some math software for computers display numbers in scientific notation using E values. That is, 3.12×10^4 may be shown as 3.12 E4. Very small numbers are shown with negative values. For example, 2.637×10^{-5} may be shown as 2.637 E–5. The letter *E* signifies exponential notation. The E value is the exponent (power) of 10. The rules for using powers of 10 are the same whether the exponent is displayed as a superscript or as an E value.

▶ **precision** the degree of exactness of a measurement

▶ **significant figures** the digits in a measurement that are known with certainty

24 CHAPTER 1

A Good accuracy and good precision

B Good accuracy and poor precision

C Poor accuracy and good precision

D Poor accuracy and poor precision

If a piece of your tape measure was broken off the tip, you can read 1.638 m precisely, but that number is not accurate. A measured quantity is only as accurate as the tool used to make the measurement. One way to think about the accuracy and precision of measurements is shown in **Figure 1-20.**

Figure 1-20
A ring toss is a game of skill, but it is also a good way to visualize accuracy and precision in measurements.

▷ **accuracy** the extent to which a measurement approaches the true value

Math Skills

Significant Figures Calculate the volume of a room that is 3.125 m high, 4.25 m wide, and 5.75 m long. Write the answer with the correct number of significant figures.

1 List the given and unknown values.
   Given: *length, l* = 5.75 m
      width, w = 4.25 m
      height, h = 3.125 m
   Unknown: *Volume, V* = ? m³

2 Write the equation for volume.
   Volume, V = l × w × h

3 Insert the known values into the equation, and solve.
   $V = 5.75 \text{ m} \times 4.25 \text{ m} \times 3.125 \text{ m}$
   $V = 76.3671875 \text{ m}^3$
   The answer should have three significant figures because the value with the smallest number of significant figures has three significant figures.
   $V = 76.4 \text{ m}^3$

Practice **HINT**

When rounding to get the correct number of significant figures, do you round up or down if the last digit is a 5? Your teacher may have other ways to round, but one very common way is to round to get an even number. For example, 3.25 is rounded to 3.2, and 3.35 is rounded to 3.4. Using this simple rule, half the time you will round up and half the time you will round down.

Practice

Significant Figures
Perform the following calculations, and write the answer with the correct number of significant figures.
1. 12.65 m × 42.1 m
2. 3.02 cm × 6.3 cm × 8.225 cm
3. 3.7 g ÷ 1.083 cm³
4. 3.244 m ÷ 1.4 s

When you use measurements in calculations, the answer is only as precise as the least precise measurement used in the calculation—the measurement with the fewest significant figures. Suppose, for example, that the floor of a rectangular room is measured to the nearest 0.01 m (1 cm). The measured dimensions are reported to be 5.87 m by 8.14 m.

If you use a calculator to multiply 5.87 by 8.14, the display may show 47.7818 as an answer. But you don't really know the area of the room to the nearest 0.0001 m², as the calculator showed. To have the correct number of significant figures, you must round off your results. In this case the correct rounded result is $A = 47.8$ m², which has three significant figures.

Consider one very precise value, 5.8739271 m, and another value that is not as precise, 8.14 m. If you use a calculator to multiply those numbers, you may see 47.813766594 as a result. But the correct rounded result is still 47.8 m² because the least precise value in the calculation had three significant figures.

SECTION 1.3 REVIEW

SUMMARY

▶ Representing scientific data with graphs helps you and others understand experimental results.

▶ Scientific notation is useful for writing very large and very small measurements because it uses powers of 10 instead of strings of zeros.

▶ Accuracy is the extent to which a value approaches the true value.

▶ Precision is the degree of exactness of a measurement.

▶ Expressing data with significant figures tells others how precisely a measurement was made.

CHECK YOUR UNDERSTANDING

1. **Describe** the kind of data that is best displayed as a line graph.
2. **Describe** the kind of data that is best displayed as a pie chart. Give an example of data from everyday experiences that could be placed on a pie chart.
3. **Explain** in your own words the difference between accuracy and precision.
4. **Critical Thinking** An old riddle asks, Which weighs more, a pound of feathers or a pound of lead? Answer the question, and explain why you think people sometimes answer incorrectly.

WRITING SKILL

Math Skills

5. **Convert** the following measurements to scientific notation:
   - **a.** 15 400 mm³
   - **b.** 0.000 33 kg
   - **c.** 2050 mL
   - **d.** 0.000 015 mol
6. **Calculate** the following:
   - **a.** 3.16×10^3 m $\times 2.91 \times 10^4$ m
   - **b.** 1.85×10^{-3} cm $\times 5.22 \times 10^{-2}$ cm
   - **c.** 9.04×10^5 g $\div 1.35 \times 10^5$ cm³
7. **Calculate** the following, and round the answer to the correct number of significant figures.
   - **a.** 54.2 cm² $\times$ 22 cm
   - **b.** 23 500 m $\div$ 89 s

Chapter Highlights

Before you begin, review the summaries of the key ideas of each section, found on pages 11, 19, and 26. The key vocabulary terms are listed on pages 4, 12, and 20.

UNDERSTANDING CONCEPTS

1. Which of the following is not included in physical science?
   a. physics
   b. chemistry
   c. astronomy
   d. zoology
2. What science deals most with energy and forces?
   a. biology
   b. physics
   c. botany
   d. agriculture
3. Using superconductors to build computers is an example of _____.
   a. technology
   b. applied biology
   c. pure science
   d. an experiment
4. A balance is a scientific tool used to measure _____.
   a. temperature
   b. time
   c. volume
   d. mass
5. Which of the following units is an SI base unit?
   a. liter
   b. cubic meter
   c. kilogram
   d. centimeter
6. The quantity 5.85×10^4 m is equivalent to _____.
   a. 5 850 000 m
   b. 58 500 m
   c. 5 840 m
   d. 0.000 585 m
7. Which of the following measurements has two significant figures?
   a. 0.003 55 g
   b. 500 mL
   c. 26.59 km
   d. 2.3 cm
8. The composition of the mixture of gases that makes up our air is best represented on what kind of graph?
   a. pie chart
   b. bar graph
   c. line graph
   d. variable graph
9. Making sure an experiment gives the results you expect is an example of _____.
   a. the scientific method
   b. critical thinking
   c. unscientific thinking
   d. objective observation

Using Vocabulary

WRITING SKILL

10. Physical science was once defined as the science of the nonliving world. Write a paragraph explaining why that definition is no longer accepted.
11. Explain why the observation that the sun sets in the west could be called a scientific law.
12. The volume of a bottle has been measured to be 485 mL. Use the terms *significant figures, accuracy,* and *precision* to explain what this tells you about the way the volume was measured.

BUILDING MATH SKILLS

13. **Graphing**
    The graph at right shows the changes in temperature during a chemical reaction. Study the graph and answer the following questions:

    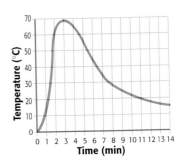

    a. What was the highest temperature reached during the reaction?
    b. How many minutes passed before the highest temperature was reached?
    c. During what period of time was the temperature increasing at a steady rate?
    d. Which occurred more slowly, heating or cooling?

14. Graphing Silver solder is a mixture of 40 percent silver, 40 percent tin, 14 percent copper, and 6 percent zinc. Draw a graph that shows the composition of silver solder.

15. Scientific Notation Write the following measurements in scientific notation:
a. 22 000 mg
c. 65 900 000 m
b. 0.005 km
d. 0.000 003 7 kg

16. Scientific Notation Do the following calculations, and write the answers in scientific notation:
a. 37 000 000 × 7 100 000
b. 0.000 312 ÷ 486
c. 4.6×10^4 cm × 7.5 10^3 cm
d. 8.3×10^6 kg ÷ 2.5×10^9 cm^3

17. Significant Figures Do the following calculations, and write the answers with the correct number of significant figures:
a. 15.75 m × 8.45 m
b. 5650 L ÷ 27 min
c. 0.0058 km × 0.228 km
d. 6271 m ÷ 59.7 s
e. $3.5 \times 10^3 \times 2.11 \times 10^4$

THINKING CRITICALLY

18. Applying Knowledge The picture tube in a television sends a beam of cathode rays to the screen. These are the same invisible rays that Roentgen was experimenting with when he discovered X rays. Use what you know about cathode rays to suggest what produces the light that forms the picture on the screen.

19. Creative Thinking At an air show, you are watching a group of skydivers when a friend says, "We learned in science class that things fall to Earth because of the law of gravitation." Tell what is wrong with your friend's statement, and explain your reasoning.

20. Applying Knowledge You have decided to test the effects of five different garden fertilizers by applying some of each to five separate rows of radishes. What is the independent variable? What factors should you control? How will you measure the results?

21. Interpreting and Communicating A person points to an empty, thick-walled glass bottle and says that the volume is 1200 cm^3. Explain why the person's statement is not as clear as it should be.

DEVELOPING LIFE/WORK SKILLS

22. Interpreting Graphics A consumer magazine has tested several portable stereos and has rated them according to price and sound quality. The data is summarized in the bar graph shown below. Study the graph and answer the following questions:
a. Which brand has the best sound?
b. Which brand has the highest price?
c. Which brand do you think has the best sound for the price?
d. Do you think that sound quality corresponds to price?
e. If you can spend as much as $150, which brand would you buy? Explain your answer.

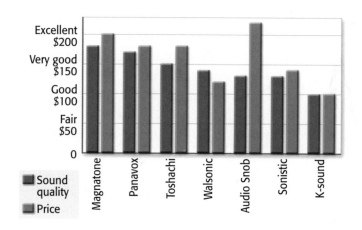

23. Making Decisions You have hired a painter to paint your room with a color that must be specially mixed. This color will be difficult to match if more has to be made. The painter tells you that the total length of your walls is 26 m and all walls are 2.5 m tall. You determine the area $(A = l \times w)$ to be painted is 65 m^2. The painter says that 1 gal of paint will cover about 30 m^2 and that you should order 2 gal of paint. List at least three questions you should ask the painter before you buy the paint.

24. Applying Technology Scientists discovered how to produce laser light in 1960. The substances in lasers emit an intense beam of light when electrical energy is applied. Find out what the word *laser* stands for, and list four examples of technologies that use lasers.

INTEGRATING CONCEPTS

25. Integrating Biology One of the most important discoveries involving X rays came in the early 1950s, when the work of Rosalind Franklin, a British scientist, provided evidence for the structure of a critical substance. Do library research to learn how Franklin used X rays and what her discovery was.

26. Concept Mapping Copy the unfinished concept map given below onto a sheet of paper. Complete the map by writing the correct word or phrase in the lettered box.

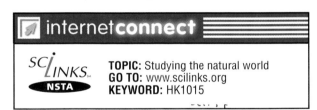

internet**connect**

SCI*LINKS*
NSTA

TOPIC: Studying the natural world
GO TO: www.scilinks.org
KEYWORD: HK1015

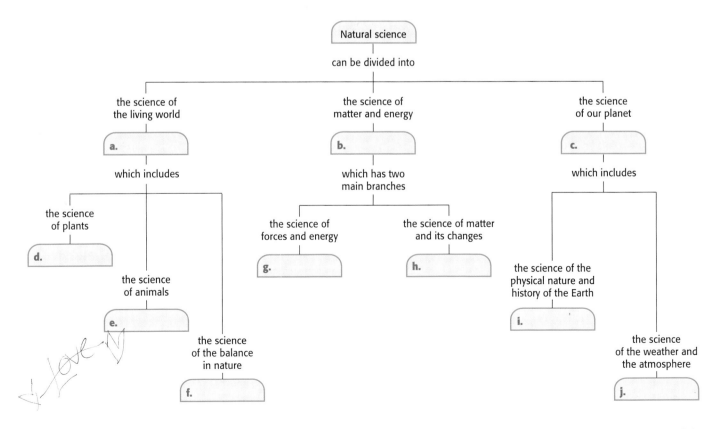

Skill Builder Lab

Introduction

How can you use laboratory tools to measure familiar objects?

Objectives

▸ **Measure** mass, length, volume, and temperature.
▸ **Organize** data into tables and graphs.

Materials

meterstick or metric ruler marked with
    centimeters and millimeters
platform or triple-beam balance
small beaker
wall thermometer
25 mL graduated cylinder
test tubes
small block or box
small rock or irregularly shaped object
basketball, volleyball, or soccer ball
string
sodium chloride (table salt)
sodium hydrogen carbonate
    (baking soda)

Safety Needs

safety goggles

Making Measurements

▶ Preparing for Your Experiment

1. In this laboratory exercise, you will use a meterstick to measure length, a graduated cylinder to measure volume, a balance to measure mass, and a thermometer to measure temperature. You will determine volume by liquid displacement.

▶ Measuring Temperature

2. At a convenient time during the lab, go to the wall thermometer and read the temperature. On the chalkboard, record your reading and the time at which you read the temperature. At the end of your lab measurements, you will make a graph of the temperature readings made by the class.

▶ Measuring Length

3. Measure the length, width, and height of a block or box in centimeters. Record the measurements in a table like **Table 1-6,** shown below. Using the equation below, calculate the volume of the block in cubic centimeters (cm^3), and write the volume in the table.

$$\text{Volume} = \text{length (cm)} \times \text{width (cm)} \times \text{height (cm)}$$
$$V = l \times w \times h$$
$$V = ?\ cm^3$$

4. Repeat the measurements twice more, recording the data in your table. Find the average of your measurements and the average of the volume you calculated.

Table 1-6   **Dimensions of a Rectangular Block**

	Length (cm)	Width (cm)	Height (cm)	Volume (cm³)
Trial 1				
Trial 2				
Trial 3				
Average				

5. To measure the circumference of a ball, wrap a piece of string around the ball and mark the end point. Measure the length of the string using the meterstick or metric ruler. Record your measurements in a table like **Table 1-7,** shown below. Using a different piece of string each time, make two more measurements of the circumference of the ball, and record your data in the table.

6. Find the average of the three values and calculate the difference, if any, of each of your measurements from the average.

Table 1-7   **Circumference of a Ball**

	Circumference (cm)	Difference from average (cm)
Trial 1		
Trial 2		
Trial 3		
Average		—

▶ Measuring Mass

7. Place a small beaker on the balance, and measure the mass. Record the value in a table like **Table 1-8,** shown below. Measure to the nearest 0.01 g if you are using a triple-beam balance and to the nearest 0.1 g if you are using a platform balance.

8. Move the rider to a setting that will give a value 5 g more than the mass of the beaker. Add sodium chloride (table salt) to the beaker a little at a time until the balance just begins to swing. You now have about 5 g of salt in the beaker. Complete the measurement (to the nearest 0.01 or 0.1 g), and record the total mass of the beaker and the sodium chloride in your table. Subtract the mass of the beaker from the total mass to find the mass of the sodium chloride.

9. Repeat steps 7 and 8 two times, and record your data in your table. Find the averages of your measurements, as indicated in **Table 1-8.**

Table 1-8   **Mass of Sodium Chloride**

	Mass of beaker and sodium chloride (g)	Mass of beaker (g)	Mass of sodium chloride (g)
Trial 1			
Trial 2			
Trial 3			
Average			

10. Make a table like **Table 1-8,** substituting sodium hydrogen carbonate for sodium chloride. Repeat steps 7, 8, and 9 using sodium hydrogen carbonate (baking soda), and record your data.

▶ Measuring Volume

11. Fill one of the test tubes with tap water. Pour the water into a 25 mL graduated cylinder.

12. The top of the column of water in the graduated cylinder will have a downward curve. This curve is called a meniscus and is shown in the figure at right. Take your reading at the bottom of the meniscus. Record the capacity of the test tube in a table like **Table 1-9.** Measure the capacity of the other test tubes, and record their capacities. Find the average capacity of the three test tubes.

Table 1-9 **Liquid Volume**

	Volume (mL)
Test tube 1	
Test tube 2	
Test tube 3	
Average	

▶ Measuring Volume by Liquid Displacement

13. Pour about 10 mL of tap water into the 25 mL graduated cylinder. Record the volume as precisely as you can in a table like **Table 1-10,** shown below.

Table 1-10 **Volume of an Irregular Solid**

	Total volume (mL)	Volume of water only (mL)	Volume of object (mL)
Trial 1			
Trial 2			
Trial 3			
Average			

14. Gently drop a small object, such as a stone, into the graduated cylinder; be careful not to splash any water out of the cylinder. You may find it easier to tilt the cylinder slightly and let the object slide down the side. Measure the volume of the water and the object. Record the volume in your table. Determine the volume of the object by subtracting the volume of the water from the total volume.

▶ Analyzing Your Results

1. On a clean sheet of paper make a line graph of the temperatures that were measured with the wall thermometer over time. Did the temperature change during the class period? If it did, find the average temperature, and determine the largest rise and the largest drop.

▶ Defending Your Conclusions

2. On a clean sheet of paper make a bar graph using the data from the three calculations of the mass of sodium chloride. Indicate the average value of the three determinations by drawing a line that represents the average value across the individual bars. Do the same for the sodium hydrogen carbonate masses. Using the information in your graphs, determine whether you measured the sodium chloride or the sodium hydrogen carbonate more precisely.

3. Suppose one of your test tubes has a capacity of 23 mL. You need to use about 5 mL of a liquid. Describe how you could estimate 5 mL.

4. Why is it better to align the meterstick with the edge of the object at the 1 cm mark rather than at the end of the stick?

5. Why is it better to place the meterstick on edge with the scale resting on the surface being measured than on the flat side?

6. Why do you think it is better to measure the circumference of the ball using string than to use a flexible metal measuring tape?

The Nature of Matter

▌ CHAPTER **2**
Matter   **36**

*Viewpoints: Paper or Plastic at
        the Grocery Store?*   **66**

▌ CHAPTER **3**
**Atoms and the
Periodic Table**   **68**

▌ CHAPTER **4**
The Structure of Matter   **106**

*Career Link
        Roberta Jordan, Chemist*   **142**

Matter

Chapter Preview

2.1 What Is Matter?
   Matter
   Pure Substance or Mixture?

2.2 Matter and Energy
   Kinetic Theory
   Energy's Role

2.3 Properties of Matter
   Chemical and Physical Properties
   Chemical and Physical Changes

Atoms are matter

Wood is matter. Because it is fairly rigid and lightweight, wood is a good choice for furniture and buildings. When wood gets hot enough, it chars—its surface turns black. The wood surface breaks down to form another kind of material with different properties, carbon. Nothing you can do to the carbon in the charred residue will cause the carbon to decompose. Carbon is an **element,** and elements are made of **atoms.** An image of some iron atoms is shown in **Figure 2-2.**

Diamonds are made of atoms of the element carbon. The shiny foil wrapped around a baked potato is made of atoms of the element aluminum. The elements that are most abundant on Earth and most abundant in the human body are shown in **Figure 2-3.** Each element also has a one- or two-letter symbol used worldwide to designate it. For example, carbon is C, iron is Fe, copper is Cu, and aluminum is Al. Each of the more than 110 elements that we now know is unique and behaves differently from the rest.

Two or more elements combine chemically to make a compound

Many familiar substances, such as aluminum and iron, are elements. Nylon is another familiar substance, but it is not an element. Nylon is a compound. The basic unit that makes up nylon contains carbon, hydrogen, nitrogen, and oxygen atoms, but each strand actually contains hundreds of these units linked together.

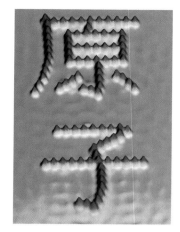

Figure 2-2
This scanning tunneling microscope image shows iron atoms (red) on copper atoms (blue).

▷ **element** a substance that cannot be broken down into simpler substances

▷ **atom** the smallest particle that has the properties of an element

▷ **compound** a substance made of atoms of more than one element bound together

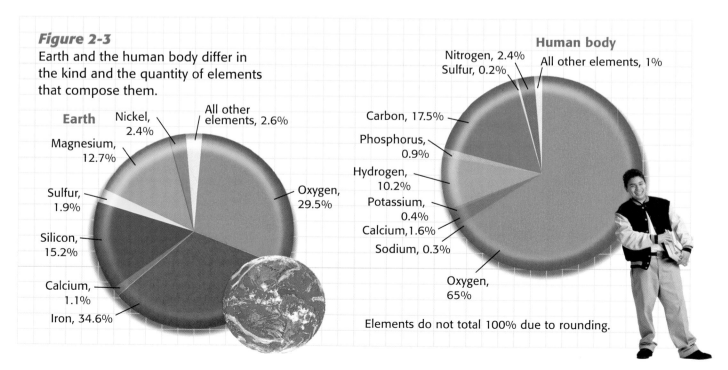

Figure 2-3
Earth and the human body differ in the kind and the quantity of elements that compose them.

Earth

Nickel, 2.4%
All other elements, 2.6%
Magnesium, 12.7%
Sulfur, 1.9%
Oxygen, 29.5%
Silicon, 15.2%
Calcium, 1.1%
Iron, 34.6%

Human body

Nitrogen, 2.4%
Sulfur, 0.2%
All other elements, 1%
Carbon, 17.5%
Phosphorus, 0.9%
Hydrogen, 10.2%
Potassium, 0.4%
Calcium, 1.6%
Sodium, 0.3%
Oxygen, 65%

Elements do not total 100% due to rounding.

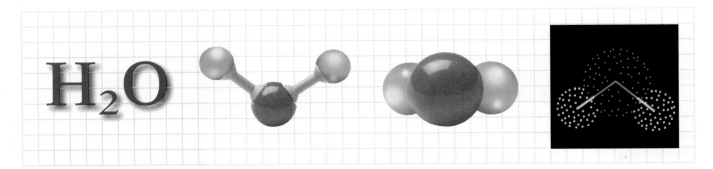

Figure 2-4
A water molecule can be represented as a formula, in physical models, or on a computer.

Every compound is unique and is different from the elements it contains. For example, the elements hydrogen, oxygen, and nitrogen occur in nature as colorless gases. Yet when they combine with carbon to form nylon, the strands of nylon are a flexible solid.

Each unit of iron(III) oxide, which we see often as rust, is made of two atoms of iron and three atoms of oxygen. When elements combine to make a specific compound, the elements always combine in the same proportions. Iron(III) oxide always has two parts of iron for every three parts of oxygen.

▶ **molecule** the smallest unit of a substance that exhibits all of the properties characteristic of that substance

A molecule acts as a unit

Atoms can join together to make millions of different molecules just as letters of the alphabet combine to form different words. A molecular substance you are familiar with is water. A water molecule is made of two hydrogen atoms and one oxygen atom, as shown in **Figure 2-4.**

When oxygen and hydrogen form a molecule of water, the atoms combine and act as a unit. That is what a molecule is—the smallest unit of a substance that behaves like the substance. Most molecules are made of atoms of different elements, just as water is. But a molecule also may be made of atoms of the same element, such as those in **Figure 2-5.** Besides the elements shown in the figure, fluorine, nitrogen, iodine, and bromine form molecules of two atoms. Sulfur forms a molecule of eight atoms, S_8.

Figure 2-5
The atoms of most elements, such as neon, Ne, are found singly in nature. The atoms of some elements form molecules, such as oxygen, O_2, hydrogen, H_2, chlorine, Cl_2, and phosphorus, P_4.

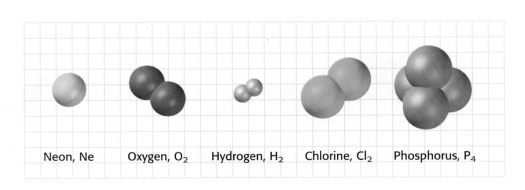

Neon, Ne   Oxygen, O_2 Hydrogen, H_2 Chlorine, Cl_2 Phosphorus, P_4

Chemical formulas represent compounds and molecules

Indigo is the dye originally used to turn jeans blue. The chemical formula for a molecule of indigo, $C_{16}H_{10}N_2O_2$, is shown in **Figure 2-6.** The chemical formula shows how many atoms of each element are in the basic unit of a substance. When the chemical formula is written, the number of atoms of each element in the basic unit is written after the element's symbol as a *subscript.* No subscript number is used if only one atom of an element is present, so the chemical formula for carbon dioxide is CO_2, not C_1O_2.

Numbers placed in front of the chemical formula show the number of molecules. For example, three molecules of table sugar are written as $3C_{12}H_{22}O_{11}$. Each molecule of the sugar contains 12 carbon atoms, 22 hydrogen atoms, and 11 oxygen atoms.

Pure Substance or Mixture?

When people use the word *pure,* they usually mean "not mixed with anything else." "Pure grape juice" contains only the juice of grapes, with nothing added or taken away. In chemistry, the word *pure* means more than this. A pure substance is matter with a fixed composition and definite properties.

Grape juice isn't a pure substance. It is a mixture of many different pure substances, such as water, sugars, acids, and vitamins. The composition of grape juice is not fixed; it can have different amounts of water or sugar or other compounds. Elements and compounds are pure substances, but mixtures are not. Practically all of the things we eat are mixtures. The air we breathe is mainly a mixture of nitrogen and oxygen.

A mixture like grape juice can be separated. The water in grape juice can evaporate, leaving the sugar, acids, and other compounds. Yet the water molecules are not changed by evaporation. A pure substance, like water, cannot be broken down by physical actions such as boiling, melting, or grinding.

Pure substances blended together make mixtures

While a compound is different from the elements that make it, a mixture may have some properties similar to the pure substances that make it. Although you can't see the different substances in grape juice, the mixture has chemical and physical properties in common with its components. For example, grape juice is wet like the water and sweet like the sugar that are in it.

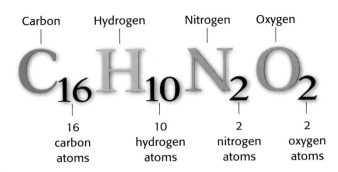

Carbon   Hydrogen   Nitrogen   Oxygen

$C_{16}H_{10}N_2O_2$

16 carbon atoms   10 hydrogen atoms   2 nitrogen atoms   2 oxygen atoms

Figure 2-6
The chemical formula for a molecule of indigo shows that it is made of four elements and 30 atoms.

▶ **chemical formula** the chemical symbols and numbers indicating the atoms contained in the basic unit of a substance

▶ **pure substance** any matter that has a fixed composition and definite properties

▶ **mixture** a combination of more than one pure substance

INTEGRATING

BIOLOGY
Indigo is a natural plant dye made from members of the genus *Indigofera,* which is in the pea family. Before synthetic dyes were developed, indigo was widely grown in the East Indies, in India, and in the Americas. Most indigo species are shrubs 1 to 2 m in height. Leaves and branches of the plants are fermented to yield a paste, which is formed into blocks and then finely ground. The blue color develops as the material is exposed to air.

Figure 2-7

A Flour is suspended in water.

B Salt dissolves in water.

Mixtures are classified by how thoroughly the substances mix

Some mixtures are made by putting solids and liquids together. In **Figure 2-7,** two white powdery solids, flour and salt, are each mixed with water. Despite the physical similarities of these solids, the mixtures they form with water are very different.

The flour doesn't mix well with the water, yielding a cloudy white mixture. You can see that flour does not dissolve in water. A mixture of flour and water is called a *heterogeneous mixture* because the substances aren't uniformly mixed.

The salt-and-water mixture looks very different from the flour-and-water mixture. You cannot see the salt, and the mixture is clear. That's because salt dissolves in water. Even if you leave the mixture for a long time, the salt will not settle out. Salt and water yield a *homogeneous mixture* because the mixing occurs between the individual units and is the same throughout.

Gasoline is a liquid mixture—a homogeneous mixture of at least 100 compounds in various quantities. Because the compounds are **miscible,** gasoline looks like a pure substance even though it isn't.

If you shake a mixture of oil and water, the water will settle out after a while. Oil and water form a heterogeneous mixture. Because oil and water are **immiscible,** you can see two layers in the mixture. **Figure 2-8** shows examples of liquid mixtures.

▶ **miscible** describes two or more liquids that are able to dissolve into each other in various proportions

▶ **immiscible** describes two or more liquids that do not mix into each other

Figure 2-8   Examples of Miscible and Immiscible Liquids

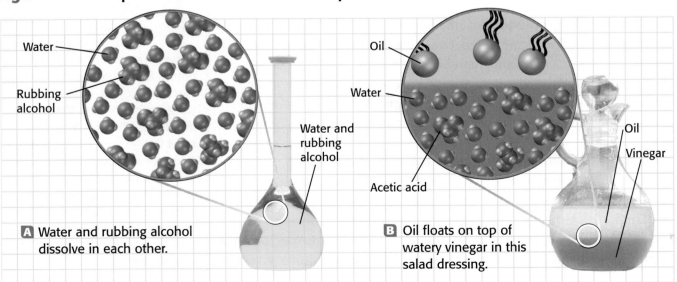

Water

Rubbing alcohol

Water and rubbing alcohol

A Water and rubbing alcohol dissolve in each other.

Oil

Water

Acetic acid

Oil

Vinegar

B Oil floats on top of watery vinegar in this salad dressing.

Dry Cleaning: How Are Stains Dissolved?

Why do some clothes need to be dry cleaned, while others do not? Washing with water and detergents cleans most clothes. But if your clothes have a stubborn stain—such as ink or rust, if you have spilled something greasy on your clothes, or if the label on the clothing recommends dry cleaning, then dry cleaning may be necessary. Dry cleaning is recommended on a clothing label when the fabric does not respond well to water. Certain fabrics, like silk and wool, are usually cleaned without water because water causes them to shrink, take on stubborn wrinkles, or lose their shape.

Stain Removal

Knowing the composition of a stain helps dry cleaners decide how to treat it. Removing a stain that doesn't dissolve in water, such as oil or grease, involves two steps. First, the stain is treated with a substance that loosens the stain. Then the stain is removed when the garment is washed in a mechanical dry cleaner.

If a stain is water-soluble, it will dissolve in water. A water-soluble stain is first treated with a stain remover that is specific to that stain. The stain is then flushed away with a steam gun. After the garment is dry, it is cleaned in a dry-cleaning machine to remove any stains that do not dissolve in water.

Once the fabric has been treated for tough stains, the garment is washed in a dry-cleaning machine.

Dry Cleaning Isn't Really Dry

In spite of its name, dry cleaning does involve liquids. The process uses a liquid solvent instead of water. It is always difficult to remove fats, greases, and oils from fabrics with water-based washing.

A good dry-cleaning solvent must dissolve oil and grease, which trap the water-insoluble particles in the cloth fibers. The most commonly used dry-cleaning solvent is tetrachloroethylene, C_2Cl_4. Tetrachloroethylene is the preferred solvent because oil, grease, and alcohols dissolve in it. Also, tetrachloroethylene is not flammable, and it evaporates easily. This allows it to be recycled by distillation.

In distillation, the components of a mixture are separated based on their rates of evaporation. Upon heating, the component that evaporates most quickly is the first to vaporize and separate from the mixture. When the vapors are cooled, they condense to form a purified sample of that component.

Tetrachloroethylene is suspected of causing some kinds of cancer. To meet the standards of the United States Occupational Safety and Health Administration (OSHA) and other federal guidelines, dry-cleaning machines must be airtight so that no C_2Cl_4 escapes.

Your Choice

1. **Critical Thinking** Explain why it is difficult to remove fats, greases, and oils from fabrics with water-based washing alone.
2. **Critical Thinking** Tetrachloroethylene evaporates more quickly than the fats, grease, and oils it dissolves. Describe how C_2Cl_4 can be recycled by distillation.

internet connect

SCiLINKS
NSTA

TOPIC: Dry cleaning
GO TO: www.scilinks.org
KEYWORD: HK1022

Gases can mix with liquids

Air is a mixture of gases consisting mostly of nitrogen and oxygen. You get oxygen every time you breathe because the gases in air form a homogeneous mixture. Carbonated drinks are also homogeneous mixtures. They contain sugar, flavorings, and carbon dioxide gas, CO_2, dissolved in water. When carbonated drinks are manufactured, the carbon dioxide gas is mixed into the liquid under pressure and forms a solution.

Even a liquid that is not mixed with gas under pressure can contain dissolved gases. If you let a glass of cold water stand overnight, you may be able to see bubbles on the sides of the glass the next morning. The bubbles are some of the air that was dissolved in the cold water.

Carbonated drinks often have a foam on top. A foam is a different kind of gas-liquid mixture. The gas is not dissolved in the liquid but has formed tiny bubbles in it. Eventually, the tiny bubbles join together to form bigger bubbles that can escape from the foam, and the foam collapses.

Other foams are stable and last for a long time. If you whip egg white with enough air, you get a foam. If you heat that foam in an oven, the liquid egg white dries and hardens, and you have a solid foam—meringue.

EARTH SCIENCE
The molten rock in some types of volcanoes contains large quantities of gas. Pumice, a solid foam that occurs naturally on Earth, is a volcanic rock formed by the violent separation of these extremely hot gases from lava. As the exploding lava cools, it traps the gas bubbles. Some pumice is so soft that it is spongy, and some is so light that it floats on water. Often pumice occurs as small pea-size lumps, but it also occurs in deposits large enough to be mined and sold commercially as an abrasive.

SECTION 2.1 REVIEW

SUMMARY

▶ Matter has mass and occupies space.

▶ An element is a substance that cannot be broken down into a simpler substance.

▶ An atom is the smallest particle of matter that has the properties of a particular element.

▶ Atoms can join together to form molecules.

▶ A pure substance that contains two or more elements is a compound.

▶ A pure substance can be represented by a chemical formula.

CHECK YOUR UNDERSTANDING

1. **Define** *chemistry*.
2. **List** the two types of pure substances.
3. **Explain** why light is not matter.
4. **Complete** the following analogy:
   A heterogeneous mixture is to a homogeneous mixture as immiscible liquids are to _____.
5. **Classify** each of the following as an element or a compound:
   a. sulfur, S_8 **c.** carbon monoxide, CO
   b. methane, CH_4 **d.** cobalt, Co
6. **Describe** the makeup of pure water, and write its chemical formula.
7. **Compare and Contrast** mixtures and pure substances. Give an example of each.
8. **Critical Thinking** David and Susan are looking at a jar of honey labeled "Pure Honey." David says, "That means it's natural honey, with nothing else added." Susan says, "It isn't really pure. It's a mixture of lots of different substances." Who is right? Explain your answer.

WRITING SKILL

Matter and Energy

OBJECTIVES

▶ Use the kinetic theory to describe the properties and structures of the different states of matter.

▶ Describe the energy transfers involved in changes of state.

▶ Describe the laws of conservation of mass and conservation of energy, and explain how they apply to changes of state.

▶ **KEY TERMS**
pressure
viscosity
energy
evaporation
condensation
sublimation

If you go to a bakery, such as the one in **Figure 2-9,** you can smell the cookies baking even though you are a long way from the oven. One way to explain this phenomenon is to make some assumptions. First, assume that the particles (molecules and atoms) within substances can move. Second, assume that the molecules and atoms move faster as the temperature rises. A theory based on these assumptions, called the kinetic theory of matter, can be used to explain things like why you can smell cookies baking from far away.

When cookies are baking, energy is transferred from the oven to the cookies. As the temperature in the oven is increased, some molecules within the cookie dough move fast enough to become gases, which in turn spread through the air in the bakery.

Figure 2-9
The substances that make the fresh cookies smell so good may be vanillin, $C_8H_8O_3$, or cinnamaldehyde, C_9H_8O.

Kinetic Theory

Here are the main points of the kinetic theory of matter.

▶ All matter is made of atoms and molecules that act like tiny particles.

▶ These tiny particles are always in motion. The higher the temperature, the faster the particles move.

▶ At the same temperature, more massive (heavier) particles move slower than less massive (lighter) particles.

The kinetic theory is a useful tool for visualizing the differences between the three common states of matter: solids, liquids, and gases.

Common States of Matter

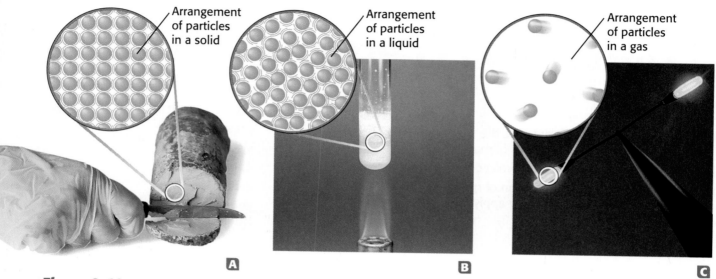

Arrangement of particles in a solid

Arrangement of particles in a liquid

Arrangement of particles in a gas

A **B** **C**

Figure 2-10
Gases, liquids, and solids are the most common states of matter on Earth. Here, the element sodium is shown as (A) the solid metal, (B) melted as a liquid, and (C) as a gas in a sodium-vapor lamp.

The states of matter are physically different

The models for solids, liquids, and gases shown in **Figure 2-10** differ in the distances and angles between molecules or atoms and in how closely these particles are packed together. Gas particles, like those in helium, are in a constant state of motion and rarely stick together. In a liquid, like cooking oil, the particles are closely packed, but they can still slide past each other. Particles in a solid, like iron, are in fixed positions. Most matter found naturally on Earth is either a solid, a liquid, or a gas, but matter also exists in other states.

Gases are free to spread in all directions

Have you noticed that a balloon filled with a "light" gas such as helium goes flat more quickly than a balloon filled with air? You can use the kinetic theory to explain this. The wall of the balloon has tiny holes through which gas particles can escape. The helium particles are smaller and less massive than the nitrogen and oxygen particles found in air. The smaller and less massive particles move faster, so they get through the holes more quickly.

If you leave a jar of perfume open, you will soon smell it from across the room. This is one of the characteristics of a gas—it expands to fill the available space. Kinetic theory can be used to explain this property as well. Under standard conditions of temperature and pressure, particles of a gas move rapidly. Oxygen, O_2, averages almost 500 m/s, and helium, He, travels at more than 1200 m/s. At these speeds, gas particles collide billions of times a second. Like all particles of gas, helium atoms bounce off each other when they collide. As helium atoms bounce around and move freely, they spread to fill the available space.

Figure 2-11

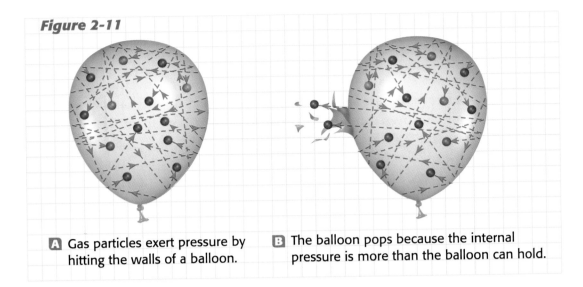

A Gas particles exert pressure by hitting the walls of a balloon.

B The balloon pops because the internal pressure is more than the balloon can hold.

Gases can exert pressure

You may know that a balloon filled with helium is under pressure. The gas in the balloon is pushing out against the balloon walls. The kinetic theory also helps to explain pressure. Helium atoms in the balloon are moving very quickly and are constantly hitting each other and the walls of the balloon, as shown in the model in **Figure 2-11.** Each particle's effect on the balloon wall is tiny, but the battering by millions of particles adds up to a steady force. The pressure inside the balloon is the measure of this steady force per unit area. If too many particles of gas are in the balloon, the battering overcomes the force of the balloon holding the gas in, and the balloon pops.

If you let go of a balloon that you've held pinched at the neck, most of the gas inside rushes out, causing the balloon to shoot through the air. Gases under pressure will escape their container if possible. If there is a lot of pressure in the container, the gas can escape with a lot of force. For this reason, gases in pressurized cylinders and similar containers, like propane tanks for gas grills, can be dangerous and must be handled carefully.

Solids have a rigid structure

If you take an ice cube out of the freezer and put it on a table, the ice will stay there as long as it remains solid. It has the same volume and shape that it had in the ice tray. Unlike gases, a solid does not need a container to have a shape. This is because the structure of a solid is very rigid, and the particles have almost no freedom to change position. The crystals of salt in **Figure 2-12** reflect the ordered arrangement of particles in most solids. The particles are held closely together by strong attractions, yet they can still vibrate around a fixed location.

▶ **pressure** the force exerted per unit area of a surface

Disc One, Module 1:
States of Matter/Classes of Matter
Use the Interactive Tutor to learn more about this topic.

Figure 2-12
The particles in these crystals of salt cannot move freely like the particles in a liquid or a gas can. These crystals of sodium chloride have been magnified 840 times.

▶ **viscosity** the resistance of a fluid to flow

▶ **energy** the ability to change or move matter

Figure 2-13
Your body's heat provides the energy for sweat to evaporate.

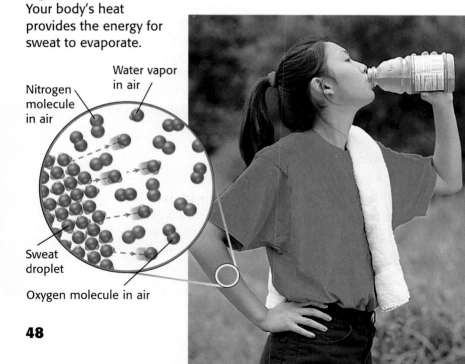

Nitrogen molecule in air

Water vapor in air

Sweat droplet

Oxygen molecule in air

Liquids take the shape of their container

The particles of a liquid are close together, but they are not attracted to each other as strongly as they are in a solid. So the particles in a liquid have more freedom of movement. Because particles in a liquid can move randomly, liquids can spread out on their own. And because liquids and gases can spread, both are classified as *fluids.*

Liquids vary in the rate at which they spread. You know from experience that honey is thicker and flows more slowly than lemonade. This property, **viscosity,** is determined by the attraction between particles in a liquid. The stronger the attraction, the more slowly the liquid will flow, and the higher the viscosity will be.

Energy's Role

What sources of energy would you use if the electricity was off? You might use candles for light and batteries to power a clock. Electricity, candles, and batteries are sources of energy. So is the food you eat. Substances that release heat when they are mixed together are another source of energy. You can think of **energy** as the ability to change or move matter. In Chapter 8, you will learn how energy can be described as the ability to do work.

Energy must be added to cause melting or evaporation

The first major step in the process of recycling aluminum cans is to melt the aluminum. Heating solid aluminum transfers energy to the aluminum atoms. As the atoms gain energy, they vibrate faster. Eventually, they break away from their fixed positions, and the aluminum melts, becoming a liquid. Energy is required to melt aluminum or any solid because the particles must break away from their fixed positions.

You can feel the effects of an energy change when you feel a breeze after you have been perspiring. Energy from your body's molecules is transferred as heat to the water on your skin. When this transfer occurs, your body's molecules cool off and slow down, while the water molecules gain energy and move faster, as shown in **Figure 2-13.**

Figure 2-14
The Changes of State for Water

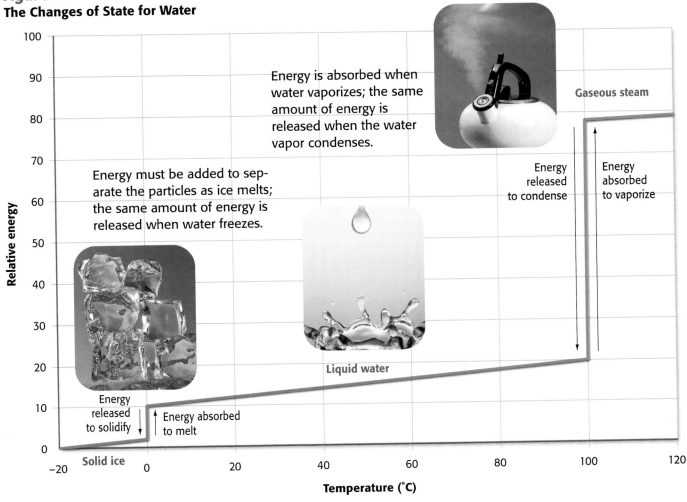

Energy is absorbed when water vaporizes; the same amount of energy is released when the water vapor condenses.

Gaseous steam

Energy must be added to separate the particles as ice melts; the same amount of energy is released when water freezes.

Energy released to condense

Energy absorbed to vaporize

Liquid water

Energy released to solidify

Energy absorbed to melt

Solid ice

Relative energy

Temperature (°C)

Eventually, the fastest moving molecules break away from the liquid surface to form a gas. The water is said to evaporate. It takes energy to separate the particles of a liquid to form a gas.

Evaporation occurs slowly when liquids are cool. But as the temperature of the liquid increases, more of the molecules gain enough energy to break away from the liquid surface and form a gas. If the liquid is heated enough, so many molecules become gas that bubbles form below the surface of the liquid and the liquid boils.

▶ **evaporation** the change of a substance from a liquid to a gas

Energy is transferred in all changes of state

When water vapor condenses to become a liquid or liquid water freezes to form ice, energy is transferred from the water to its surroundings. The water molecules slow down during this energy transfer. The graph in **Figure 2-14** shows the energy transfers that occur as water changes among the three common states of matter.

▶ **condensation** the change of a substance from a gas to a liquid

Figure 2-15
Dry ice (solid carbon dioxide) sublimes to form gaseous carbon dioxide but no liquid.

▶ **sublimation** the change of a substance from a solid to a gas

Some substances do not have a liquid form at normal temperature and pressure. **Figure 2-15** shows solid carbon dioxide, CO_2, undergoing **sublimation,** that is, turning directly into a gas without becoming a liquid. Sometimes, ice made of water molecules sublimes, forming a gas. When left in the freezer for a couple of months, ice cubes get smaller as the ice sublimes.

Changing state does not change composition or mass

Heating or cooling can change the state of a substance. Look at the changes of state that are happening in **Figure 2-16.** Some of the steam is condensing. As this happens, heat is transferred to the surroundings, so the steam cools and turns back into liquid water. Changing the energy of a substance can change the state of the substance, but changing energy does not change the composition of a substance. Ice, water, and steam are all made of H_2O molecules. All that changes is the nature of the attractions between the molecules—strong in a solid and almost nonexistent in a gas.

When an ice cube melts, the mass of the liquid water is the same as the mass of the ice cube. Even though the ice underwent a physical change to produce the water, the mass was not increased or reduced. Similarly, when water boils, the number of water molecules stays the same even as the liquid water loses volume. The mass of the steam is the same as the mass of the liquid water that boiled off.

Figure 2-16
Whether it is ice, water, or steam, water in any form is always made of H_2O molecules.

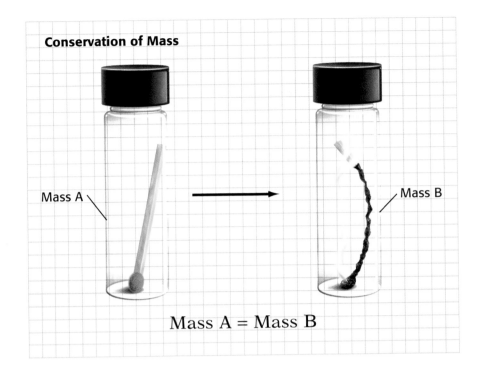

Conservation of Mass

Mass A

Mass B

Mass A = Mass B

Figure 2-17
The match is changed by burning, but the masses of the reactants and the products are equal.

The law of conservation of mass

In chemical changes as well as in physical changes, the total mass of all matter stays the same before and after a change. Matter changes from one form to another, but the total mass stays the same. This is called the law of conservation of mass. The law of conservation of mass is stated as follows.

Mass cannot be created or destroyed.

When you burn a match, it seems to lose mass. The ash has less mass than the original match. But the burning reaction involves gases too, and gases have mass, even though they may be difficult to see or measure. There is also mass in the oxygen that reacts with the match, in the tiny particles that we see as smoke, and in the gases formed in the reaction. The total mass of the reactants (match and oxygen) is the same as the total mass of the products (ash, smoke, and gases), as you can see in **Figure 2-17.**

The law of conservation of energy

Although energy may be converted from one form to another during a physical or chemical change, the total amount of energy before and after the change is always the same. This is the law of conservation of energy, which can be stated as follows.

Energy cannot be created or destroyed.

The law of conservation of energy is described in more detail in Chapter 8.

INTEGRATING

SPACE SCIENCE
Studies of the chemical changes that stars and nebulae undergo are constantly adding to our knowledge. Present estimates are that hydrogen makes up more than 90 percent of the atoms in the universe and constitutes about 75 percent of the mass of the universe. Helium atoms make up most of the remainder. The total of all the other elements contributes very little to the total mass of the universe.

At first glance, starting a car may seem to violate this law. For the tiny amount of energy needed for a person to turn the key in the ignition, a lot of energy results. But the car needs gasoline to run. Gasoline releases energy when it is burned. Because of the arrangement of the atoms in the compounds that make up gasoline, gasoline has stored energy. When this stored energy is considered, the energy before you start the car is equal to the energy afterward.

When you drive a car, gasoline is burned to produce the energy needed to power the car. However, some of the energy from the gasoline is transferred to the surroundings as heat. That is why a car's engine gets hot. The total amount of energy released by the gasoline is equal to the energy used to move the car plus the energy transferred to the surroundings as heat.

When you study nuclear changes and radioactivity in Chapter 6, you will learn that the law of conservation of mass and the law of conservation of energy can be made into one law, which covers all the changes discussed here.

internetconnect

SCILINKS
NSTA

TOPIC: States of matter
GO TO: www.scilinks.org
KEYWORD: HK1023

SECTION 2.2 REVIEW

SUMMARY

▶ The kinetic theory assumes that all matter is made of tiny particles that are always moving.

▶ Solids have a fixed volume and shape.

▶ Gases have a variable volume and shape.

▶ Liquids have a fixed volume but variable shape.

▶ Pressure is the force exerted per unit area of a surface.

▶ The viscosity of a fluid is its resistance to flow.

▶ Energy is the ability to heat, change, or move matter.

▶ Mass and energy are conserved in all changes.

CHECK YOUR UNDERSTANDING

1. **Define** *energy*.
2. **State** the law of conservation of mass and the law of conservation of energy.
3. **List** two examples for each of the three common states of matter.
4. **Rank** the following in order of increasing strength of forces between molecules:
   a. honey   c. water   e. nitrogen gas
   b. marble   d. candle wax
5. **Compare and Contrast** the shape and volume of solids, liquids, and gases.
6. **Predict** which two of the following involve the same energy transfer. Assume that the same substance and the same mass is involved in all four processes.
   a. melting   c. sublimation
   b. evaporation   d. condensation
7. **Describe** the energy transfers that occur when ice melts and water vapor condenses to form liquid water. Portray each state of matter and the change of state using a computer-drawing program.

COMPUTER SKILL

8. **Creative Thinking** Describe a characteristic of gases, and use the kinetic theory to explain how a dog could find you by your scent.

Properties of Matter

OBJECTIVES

▶ Distinguish between chemical and physical properties of matter.

▶ Perform calculations involving density.

▶ Distinguish between chemical and physical changes in matter.

▶ Apply the laws of conservation of mass and conservation of energy to chemical and physical changes.

▶ Evaluate materials and their properties for different uses.

▶ **KEY TERMS**
chemical property
reactivity
physical property
melting point
boiling point
density
buoyancy
chemical change
physical change

The frame and engine of a car are made of steel. Steel is a mixture of iron, small amounts of other metallic elements, and carbon. It is a strong, rigid solid that provides structure and support. The tires are made of a soft, pliable solid that cushions your ride. Liquid gasoline becomes a gas before it burns in the presence of a spark and oxygen. You may not think of the cars you see in **Figure 2-18** as examples of chemistry. However, each of the properties and changes that make these substances useful in cars is described by chemistry.

Chemical and Physical Properties

Some elements, like sodium, react easily with other elements and usually are found as compounds in nature. Other elements, like gold, are much less reactive and often are found uncombined in nature. Magnesium is so reactive it is used to make emergency flares. Light bulbs are filled with argon gas because argon does not react, so the tungsten filament burns longer. All of these are examples of **chemical properties.**

▶ **chemical property** the way a substance reacts with others to form new substances with different properties

Figure 2-18
How substances combine and are used in these cars depends on their physical and chemical properties.

Figure 2-19
Rust is formed when oxygen in moist air reacts with iron to form iron(III) oxide, Fe_2O_3.

Steel

Plastic

Chemical properties describe how a substance reacts

You can see rust on the bumper of a truck in **Figure 2-19.** The steel parts rust, but the rubber and plastic parts, such as those that surround the mirror, do not. The rust results when iron atoms in the steel react to form iron(III) oxide and other compounds. Rubber and plastic do not change in this way; they don't contain iron atoms. Steel, rubber, and plastic have different chemical properties. A chemical property describes how a substance acts when it changes, either by combining with other elements or by breaking apart into new substances. Chemical properties involve the **reactivity** of elements or compounds.

Chemical properties are related to the specific elements that make up substances. The carbon in charcoal will burn and is *flammable.* Flammability is a chemical property that describes whether substances will react in the presence of oxygen and burn when exposed to a flame.

Physical properties remain the same for a pure substance

Unlike chemical properties, **physical properties** can be observed or measured without a change in composition. You can use your senses to observe some of the basic physical properties of a substance: shape, color, odor, and texture. Other physical properties, such as **melting point, boiling point,** strength, hardness, and the ability to conduct electricity, magnetism, or heat, can be measured.

Physical properties remain constant for specific pure substances. At room temperature and atmospheric pressure, all samples of pure water are always colorless and liquid; pure water is never something like a powdery green solid.

▶ **reactivity** the ability of a substance to combine chemically with another substance

▶ **physical property** a characteristic of a substance that can be observed or measured without changing the composition of the substance

▶ **melting point** the temperature at which a solid becomes a liquid

▶ **boiling point** the temperature at which a liquid becomes a gas below the surface

Water boils at 100°C and freezes at 0°C. At atmospheric pressure, pure water always has the same boiling point and melting point. A characteristic of any pure substance is that its boiling point and its melting point are constant. It doesn't matter if you have a lot of water or a little water; the physical properties of the water are constant, regardless of the mass or volume involved. This is true for all pure substances.

Density is a physical property

A substance that has a low density is sometimes referred to as being "light." The balloons in **Figure 2-20** float because they are lighter than the air around them. A substance that has a high density is sometimes referred to as being "heavy." Earth's core is made of iron because it is heavier—more dense—than other substances that are abundant on our planet.

One way to compare the density of two objects of the same size is to hold one in each hand. The lighter one is less dense; the heavier one is more dense. If you held a brick in one hand and an equal-sized piece of sponge in the other hand, you would know instantly that the brick is more dense than the sponge. **Table 2-1** lists the densities of some common substances.

By knowing the density of a substance, you can know if the substance will float or sink. The density of an object is calculated by dividing the object's mass by its volume.

Density Equation

$$D = m/V$$
$$density = mass/volume$$

▶ **density** the mass per unit volume of a substance

Figure 2-20
Helium-filled balloons float upward because helium is lighter—or less dense—than air. Similarly, hot-air balloons rise because hot air is less dense than cool air.

Table 2-1 **Densities of Some Substances**

Substance	Chemical formula	Density in g/cm³
Air, dry	Mixture	0.00129
Brick, common	Mixture	1.9
Gasoline	Mixture	0.7
Helium	He	0.00018
Ice	H_2O	0.92
Iron	Fe	7.86
Lead	Pb	11.3
Nitrogen	N_2	0.00125
Steel	Mixture	7.8
Water	H_2O	1.00

Did You Know ?

The elements osmium and iridium are the two densest substances on Earth. The density of osmium is 22.57 g/cm³. Iridium has a density of 22.42 g/cm³. A piece of either metal the size of a baseball has a mass of approximately 4700 g.

The density of a liquid or a solid usually is reported in units of grams per cubic centimeter (g/cm^3). For example, 10.0 cm^3 of water has a mass of 10.0 g. Its density is 10.0 g for every 10.0 cm^3, or 1.00 g/cm^3. As you learned in Section 1.2, a cubic centimeter contains the same volume as a milliliter. Therefore, in some cases, you may see the density of water expressed as 1 g/mL.

Math Skills

Density If we know that 10.0 cm^3 of ice has a mass of 9.17 g, what is the density of ice?

1 List the given and unknown values.

Given: *mass, m* = 9.17 g

volume, V = 10.0 cm^3

Unknown: *density, D* = ?

2 Write the equation for density.

$$D = \frac{m}{V} \qquad density = \frac{mass}{volume}$$

3 Insert the known values into the equation, and solve.

$$D = \frac{9.17 \text{ g}}{10.0 \text{ cm}^3}$$

$$D = 0.917 \text{ g/cm}^3$$

Practice HINT

▶ When a problem requires you to calculate density, you can use the density equation.

$$D = \frac{m}{V}$$

▶ You can solve for mass by multiplying both sides of the density equation by volume.

$$DV = \frac{m\cancel{V}}{\cancel{V}} \qquad m = DV$$

You will need to use this form of the equation in Practice Problems 6 and 7.

▶ You can solve for volume by dividing both sides of the equation shown above by density.

$$\frac{m}{D} = \frac{\cancel{D}V}{\cancel{D}} \qquad V = \frac{m}{D}$$

You will need to use this form of the equation in Practice Problems 8 and 9.

Practice

Density

1. A piece of tin has a mass of 16.52 g and a volume of 2.26 cm^3. What is the density of tin?

2. A man has a 50.0 cm^3 bottle completely filled with 163 g of a slimy green liquid. What is the density of the liquid?

3. A sealed 2500 cm^3 flask is full to capacity with 0.36 g of a substance. Determine the density of the substance. Guess if the substance is a gas, a liquid, or a solid.

4. A piece of metal has a volume of 6.7 cm^3 and a mass of 75.7 g. Find the metal's density. Using the data in **Table 2-1,** suggest what element the metal could be.

5. The mass of a 125 cm^3 piece of a material is 83.75 g. Determine the density of this material.

6. What is the mass of an object that has a density of 8 g/cm^3 and a volume of 64 cm^3?

7. Different kinds of wood have different densities. The density of pine is generally about 0.5 g/cm^3. What is the mass of a 800 cm^3 piece of pine?

8. What is the volume of 325 g of metal with a density of 9.0 g/cm^3?

9. Diamonds have a density of 3.5 g/cm^3. How big is a diamond that has a mass of 0.10 g ?

The difference in the densities of cream and milk allows us to make skim milk. If whole milk, which has not been homogenized, is allowed to stand, the cream will rise to the top, leaving the more watery milk on the bottom. When the cream is skimmed off, what is left is called skim milk.

In **Figure 2-21,** ice is floating in water because of a difference in the densities of the two substances. Water pushes ice to the surface because ice is less dense than water. The tendency of a less dense substance, like ice, to rise and float in a more dense liquid, like water, is called buoyancy. A cork floats in water because it is less dense than water and the water pushes up against it.

Properties help determine uses

We use physical properties to help us select a substance that may be useful to us. Copper is used in electrical power lines, telephone lines, and electric motors because of its good electrical conductivity. Antifreeze, which contains ethylene glycol (a poisonous liquid), remains a liquid at temperatures that would freeze or boil the water in a car radiator.

Figure 2-21
Ice floats in water because ice is less dense than water.

▶ **buoyancy** the force with which a more dense fluid pushes a less dense substance upward

Inquiry Lab

How are the mass and volume of a substance related?

Materials
✔ 100 mL graduated cylinder
✔ 250 mL beaker with 200 mL water
✔ balance
✔ graph paper

Procedure

1. Make a data table with 3 columns and 12 rows. In the first row, label the columns "Volume of H_2O (mL)," "Mass of cylinder (g) and H_2O (g)," and "Mass of H_2O (g)." In the remaining spaces of the first column, write: 0, 10, 20, 30, 40, 50, 60, 70, 80, 90, and 100. All of your data will be entered on this table.
2. Measure the mass of the empty graduated cylinder, and record it in your data table.
3. Pour the amounts of water listed in the first column of your table from the beaker into the graduated cylinder. Then use the balance to find the mass of the graduated cylinder with the water. Record each value in your data table.
4. On the graph paper, make a graph and label the horizontal x-axis "Mass of water (g)." Mark the x-axis in 10 equal increments for 10, 20, 30, 40, 50, 60, 70, 80, 90 and 100 g. Label the vertical y-axis "Volume of water (mL)." Mark the y-axis in 10 equal increments for 10, 20, 30, 40, 50, 60, 70, 80, 90 and 100 mL.
5. Plot a graph of your data either on paper, on a graphing calculator, or by using a graphing/spreadsheet computer program.

Analysis

1. Use your graph to predict the mass of 55 mL of water and 100 mL of water.
2. Use your graph to predict the volume of 25 g of water and 75 g of water.
3. How could you use your data table to calculate the density of water? How could you use your graph to calculate the density of water? Which method do you think gives better results? Why?

Choosing Materials When you choose materials, you have to make sure their properties are suitable. For example, white acrylic plastic can be used to make false teeth. Sometimes a kind of porcelain is used. Metals are less common, although gold teeth are made sometimes. Fillings usually are made of metal or a special kind of glass.

False teeth have a demanding job to do. They are constantly bathed in saliva, which is corrosive. They must withstand the forces from chewing hard objects, like popcorn or hard candy. The material chosen has to be nontoxic, hard, waterproof, unreactive, tooth-like in appearance, and preferably reasonably priced. Acrylic plastic satisfies these requirements well.

George Washington wore false teeth, but contrary to the legend that they were wood, they were made of hippopotamus bone.

Applying Information

1. Identify some advantages of gold false teeth and Washington's bone teeth.
2. Identify some disadvantages of gold false teeth and Washington's bone teeth.

Chemical and Physical Changes

internetconnect

SCI LINKS
NSTA

TOPIC: Chemical and physical changes
GO TO: www.scilinks.org
KEYWORD: HK1024

▶ **chemical change** a change that occurs when a substance changes composition by forming one or more new substances

Some materials benefit us because they stay in the same state and do not change under normal conditions. Long surgical steel pins are used to reinforce broken bones because surgical steel stays the same even after many years in the human body. Concrete and glass are used as building materials because they change very little under most weather conditions.

Other materials are valued for their ability to change physical states easily. Water is turned into steam to heat homes and factories. Liquid gasoline is changed into a gas so it can burn in car engines.

Still other materials are useful because of their ability to change and combine to form new substances. The compounds in gasoline burn in oxygen to form carbon dioxide and water, releasing energy in the process. This is a **chemical change** because the substances after the change are different from the substances at the beginning.

You see chemical changes happening more often than you may think. When a battery "dies," the chemicals inside the battery have changed so that the battery can no longer supply energy. The oxygen you inhale is used in a series of chemical reactions in your body. You exhale oxygen in carbon dioxide after it has undergone a chemical change. Chemical changes occur when fruits and vegetables ripen and when the food you eat is digested.

Figure 2-22
Electrolysis is a method by which water can be broken down into hydrogen and oxygen gases.

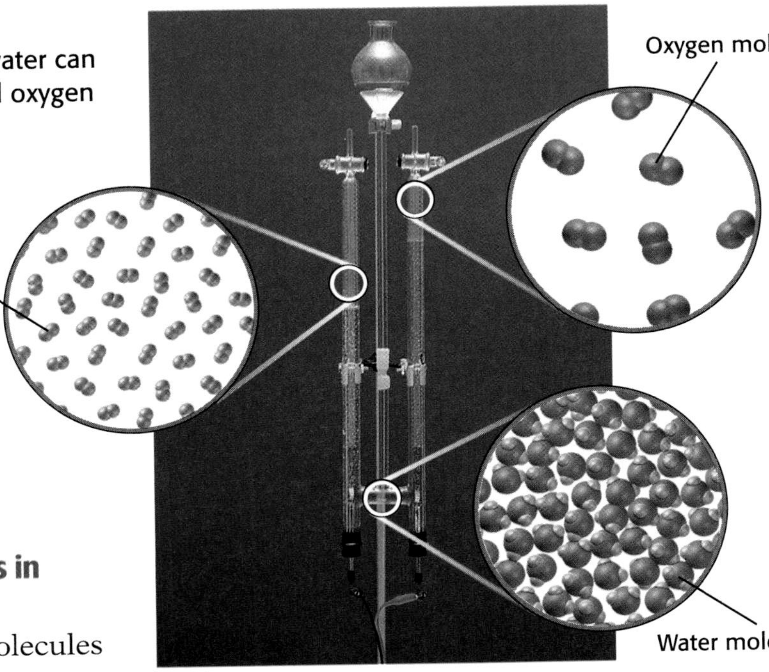

Hydrogen molecule, H₂

Oxygen molecule, O₂

Water molecule, H₂O

Chemical changes are changes in composition

When gasoline burns, the molecules involved combine with the oxygen molecules in air to produce new substances. A chemical change also occurs when a compound breaks apart to form at least two other pure substances. When water is broken down, the atoms of oxygen or hydrogen are not destroyed. Rather, these atoms rearrange to form hydrogen gas, H_2, and oxygen gas, O_2, as shown in **Figure 2-22.** The law of conservation of mass applies to all chemical changes. This is because new atoms are not created, and old atoms are not destroyed.

You can learn about the chemical properties of a substance by observing the chemical changes the substance undergoes. A change in odor or color is a good clue that a substance is changing chemically. When food burns, you can often smell the gases given off by the chemical changes that occur. When paint fades, you can see the effects of chemical changes in the paint.

Physical changes do not change composition

Both quartz crystals and sand are made of SiO_2, but they look very different. When quartz crystals are crushed into sand, a physical change takes place. During physical changes, energy always is absorbed or released. After a physical change, a substance may look different, but the atoms that make up the substance are not changed or rearranged.

Grinding peanuts into peanut butter or pounding a gold nugget into a ring result in physical changes. But physical changes do not change all the properties of a substance. For example, the color of the gold, its melting point, and its density do not change. Melting, freezing, and evaporating are physical changes, too.

▶ **physical change** a change in the physical form or properties of a substance that occurs without a change in composition

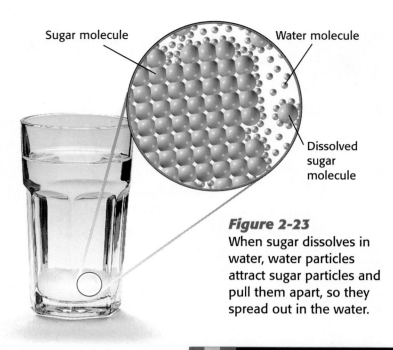

Sugar molecule

Water molecule

Dissolved sugar molecule

Figure 2-23
When sugar dissolves in water, water particles attract sugar particles and pull them apart, so they spread out in the water.

Dissolving is a physical change

When you stir sugar into water, the sugar dissolves and seems to disappear. But the sugar is still there; you can taste the sweetness when you drink the water. **Figure 2-23** shows how the kinetic theory describes this. When sugar dissolves, it seems to disappear because the sugar particles get spread out between the particles of the water. The molecules of the sugar haven't changed because dissolving is a physical change. Dissolving a solid in a liquid, a gas in a liquid, or a liquid in a liquid are all physical changes.

SECTION 2.3 REVIEW

SUMMARY

▶ Chemical properties can be observed when one substance reacts with another.

▶ Physical properties can be observed or measured without changing the composition of matter.

▶ The density of a substance is equal to its mass divided by its volume.

▶ New substances are formed in chemical changes.

▶ Physical changes do not affect all properties because physical changes do not change composition.

▶ Changes of state, including melting, subliming, evaporating, boiling, condensing, and freezing, are physical changes.

CHECK YOUR UNDERSTANDING

1. **Classify** the following as either chemical or physical properties:
   a. is shiny and silvery
   b. melts easily
   c. burns in air
   d. has a density of 2.3 g/cm^3
   e. tarnishes in moist air

2. **Describe** several uses for plastic, and explain why plastic is a good choice for these purposes.

3. **Classify** the following as either a chemical or a physical change:
   a. ice melting in a drink
   b. sugar added to lemonade
   c. mixing vinegar and baking soda to generate bubbles
   d. plants using CO_2 and H_2O to form O_2 and sugar

4. **Explain** why changes of state are physical changes.

5. **Categorize** the following as either absorbing or releasing energy:
   a. solid carbon dioxide going to CO_2 gas
   b. rubbing alcohol evaporating
   c. aluminum solidifying in a mold
   d. chocolate melting

6. **Calculate** the density of a rock that has a mass of 454 g and a volume of exactly 100 cm^3.

7. **Critical Thinking** You need to build a raft. Write a paragraph describing the physical and chemical properties of the raft that would be important to ensure your safety. You are not limited to the properties discussed in this chapter.

WRITING SKILL

Chapter Highlights

Before you begin, review the summaries of the key ideas of each section, found on pages 44, 52, and 60. The key vocabulary terms are listed on pages 38, 45, and 53.

UNDERSTANDING CONCEPTS

1. "Anything that takes up space and has mass" is the definition of _____.
   a. a solid   c. matter
   b. a liquid   d. a gas

2. Which of the following is a compound?
   a. sodium   c. iodine
   b. chlorine   d. water

3. What is the chemical formula for iron(III) oxide?
   a. H_2O c. H_2O_2
   b. NaCl   d. Fe_2O_3

4. Which of the following is a mixture?
   a. air   c. water
   b. salt   d. sulfur

5. Most of the hot flavor in peppers comes from capsaicin, $C_{18}H_{27}NO_3$. Capsaicin is a(n) _____.
   a. element   c. pure substance
   b. mixture   d. atom

6. Which of the following assumptions is not part of the kinetic theory?
   a. All matter is made up of tiny, invisible particles.
   b. The particles are always moving.
   c. Particles move faster at higher temperatures.
   d. Particles are smaller at lower pressure.

7. The cube of metal shown below has a mass of 64 g. The density of the metal is _____.
   a. 2.0 g/cm^3
   b. 4.0 g/cm^3
   c. 8.0 g/cm^3
   d. 21 g/cm^3

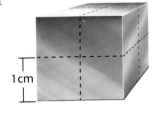

1 cm

8. Three common states of matter are _____.
   a. solid, water, gas
   b. ice, water, gas
   c. solid, liquid, gas
   d. solid, liquid, air

9. Which of the following is a physical change?
   a. melting ice cubes
   b. burning paper
   c. rusting iron
   d. burning gasoline

10. In the figure below, the particles above the cup have _____.
    a. lost enough energy to sublime
    b. gained enough energy to sublime
    c. lost enough energy to evaporate
    d. gained enough energy to evaporate

Using Vocabulary

11. In an alcohol thermometer, the height of a constant amount of liquid alcohol in a thin glass tube increases or decreases as temperature changes. Using what you have learned about the kinetic theory, explain the behavior of the alcohol using the following terms: *lose energy, gain energy, volume (or space), movement, molecules (or particles).*

WRITING SKILL

12. The figure at right shows magnesium burning in the presence of oxygen. Give some evidence that the figure shows signs that a chemical change is occurring.

13. Make a table with two columns. Label one column "Physical properties" and the other "Chemical properties." Put each of the following terms in the proper column: *viscosity, density, reactivity, buoyancy, melting point, corrosion, flammability, dissolving, conducting electricity, tarnishing*.

14. When a candle is burned, the wax seems to disappear, and heat and light are given off. Does this violate the laws of conservation of mass and energy? Explain why or why not.

BUILDING MATH SKILLS

15. **Graphing** The graph below shows some effects of heating on ethylene glycol, the liquid commonly used as antifreeze. Until the temperature is 197°C, is the temperature increasing or decreasing? What physical change is taking place when the ethylene glycol is at 197°C? Describe what is happening to the ethylene glycol molecules at 197°C. How can you tell?

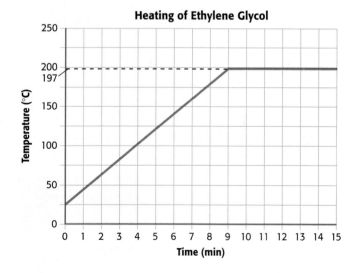

Heating of Ethylene Glycol

16. **Density** A piece of titanium metal has a mass of 67.5 g and a volume of 15 cm³. What is the density of titanium?

17. **Density** If a liquid has a volume of 620 cm³ and a mass of 480 g, what is its density?

18. **Density** A sample of a substance with a mass of 85 g occupies a volume of 110 cm³. What is the density of the substance? Will it float in water?

19. **Density** The density of a piece of brass is 8.4 g/cm³. If its mass is 510 g, find its volume.

20. **Density** What mass of water in grams will fill a tank 100 cm long, 50 cm wide, and 30 cm high?

21. **Density** A graduated cylinder is filled with water to a level of 40.0 mL. When a piece of copper is lowered into the cylinder, the water level rises to 63.4 mL. Find the volume of the copper sample. If the density of the copper is 8.9 g/cm³, what is its mass?

THINKING CRITICALLY

22. **Creative Thinking** Suppose you are planning a journey to the center of the Earth in a self-propelled tunneling machine. List properties of the special materials that would be needed to build the machine.

23. **Applying Knowledge** In the early history of the United States, people would search out sandy stream beds in which small particles of gold were mixed with the sand. The particles were separated by "panning." What properties of the two substances, gold and sand, made panning possible?

24. **Acquiring and Evaluating Data** The air in the Earth's atmosphere is a mixture. Research the atmosphere's contents. What are the main components of the Earth's atmosphere? What is the most abundant substance in the mixture? Is air or nitrogen more dense?

25. Applying Technology Use a computer art program to illustrate a chemical change in which one atom and one molecule interact to form two molecules.

26. Working Cooperatively Suppose you are given a piece of a material that is painted black so you cannot tell its normal appearance. Working in groups of three, plan tests you would do on the material to decide whether it is metal, glass, plastic, or wood.

27. Making Decisions The frame of a tennis racket needs to be strong and stiff, yet light. Tennis racket frames were once made of wood. But to be strong and stiff, the frame had to be thick and heavy. Now rackets can be made from different materials. Make a table of the advantages and disadvantages of each of the materials described in the graphs below.

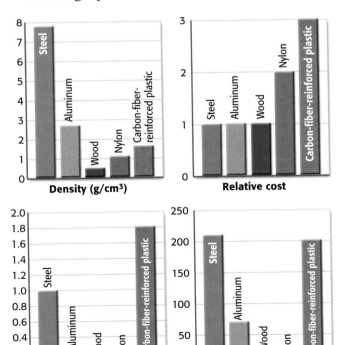

28. Concept Mapping Copy the unfinished concept map below onto a sheet of paper. Complete the map by writing the correct word or phrase in the lettered boxes.

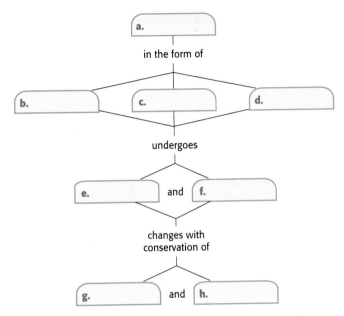

29. Connection to Biology Your body uses the food you eat to do work. However, some of the food energy is lost as heat. How does your body give off this heat?

30. Connection to Language Arts An element is sometimes named for one of its properties, an interesting fact about the element, or for the person who first discovered the element. Research the origin of the name of each of the following elements: promethium, oxygen, iridium, fermium, curium, tantalum, silver, polonium, ytterbium, and hafnium.

internet**connect**

SCLINKS
NSTA

TOPIC: Kinetic theory
GO TO: www.scilinks.org
KEYWORD: HK1025

Design Your Own Lab

Introduction

How can you show that mass is conserved in a chemical reaction between two household substances—vinegar and baking soda?

Objectives

▶ **Measure** the masses of reactants and products in a chemical reaction.

▶ **Design** an experiment to test the law of conservation of mass.

Materials

baking soda (sodium bicarbonate)
vinegar (acetic acid solution)
400 mL beaker (optional)
100 mL graduated cylinder
2 clear plastic cups (capable of holding at least 150 mL each)
balance (with standard masses, if necessary)
2 weighing papers
plastic sandwich bag with zipper-type closure
twist tie

Safety Needs

safety goggles
lab apron
polyethylene gloves
rimmed tray with paper lining

Testing the Conservation of Mass

▶ Observing the Reaction Between Vinegar and Baking Soda

1. On a blank sheet of paper, prepare a table like the one shown below.

	Initial mass (g)	Final mass (g)	Change in mass (g)
Trial 1			
Trial 2			

SAFETY CAUTION Put on a lab apron, safety goggles, and gloves. If you get a chemical on your skin or clothing, wash it off at the sink while calling to your teacher. If you get a chemical in your eyes, immediately flush it out at the eyewash station while calling to your teacher. When mixing chemicals, use a rimmed tray with a paper lining to catch and absorb spills.

2. Place a piece of weighing paper on the balance. Place about 4–5 g of baking soda on the paper. Carefully transfer the baking soda to a plastic cup.

3. Using the graduated cylinder, measure about 50 mL of vinegar. Pour the vinegar into the second plastic cup.

4. Place both cups on the balance, and determine the combined mass of the cups, baking soda, and vinegar to the nearest 0.01 g. Record the combined mass in the first row of your table under "Initial mass."

5. Take the cups off the balance. Carefully and slowly pour the vinegar into the cup that contains the baking soda. To avoid splattering, add only a small amount of vinegar at a time. Gently swirl the cup to make sure the reactants are well mixed.

6. When the reaction has finished, place both cups back on the balance. Determine the combined mass to the nearest 0.01 g. Record the combined mass in the first row of your table under "Final mass."

7. Subtract the final mass from the initial mass, and record the result in the first row of your table under "Change in mass."

▶ Designing Your Experiment

8. Examine the plastic bag and the twist ties. With your lab partners, develop a procedure that will test the law of conservation of mass more accurately than Trial 1 did. Which products' masses were not measured? How can you be sure you measure the masses of all of the reaction products?

9. In your lab report, list each step you will perform in your experiment.

10. Before you carry out your experiment, your teacher must approve your plan.

▶ Performing Your Experiment

11. After your teacher approves your plan, perform your experiment using approximately the same quantities of baking soda and vinegar you used in Trial 1.

12. Record the initial mass, final mass, and change in mass in your table.

▶ Analyzing Your Results

1. Compare the changes in mass you calculated for the first and second trials. What value would you expect to obtain for a change in mass if both trials validated the law of conservation of mass?

2. Was the law of conservation of mass violated in the first trial? Explain your reasoning.

3. If the results of the second trial were different from those of the first trial, explain why.

▶ Defending Your Conclusions

4. Suppose someone performs an experiment like the one you designed and finds that the final mass is much less than the initial mass. Would that prove that the law of conservation of mass is wrong? Explain your reasoning.

viewpoints

Paper or Plastic at the Grocery Store?

As people focus more on the environment, there is a debate raging at the grocery store. It begins with a simple question asked at the checkout counter: "Paper or plastic?"

Some say that paper is a bad choice because making paper bags requires cutting down trees.

Yet these bags are naturally biodegradable, and they recycle easily.

Others say that plastic is not a good choice because plastic bags are made from nonrenewable petroleum products. But recent advances have made plastic bags that can break down when exposed to sunlight. Many stores collect used plastic bags and recycle them to make new ones.

How should people decide which bags to use? What do you think?

> FROM: Jaclyn M., Chicago, IL

I think people should choose paper bags because they can be recycled and reused. There should be a mandatory law that makes sure each community has a weekly recycling service for paper bags.

PAPER!

> FROM: Eric S., Rochester, MN

When it comes down to it, both types of bags can be recycled. However, as we know, not everybody recycles bags. Therefore, paper is a better choice because it is a renewable resource.

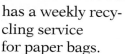

PLASTIC!

> FROM: Christy M., Houston, TX.

I believe we should use more plastic bags in grocery stores. By using paper we are chopping down not only trees but also the homes of animals and plants.

> FROM: Ashley A., Dyer, IN

Plastic is not necessarily better, but is a lot more convenient. You can reuse plastic bags as garbage bags or bags to carry anything you need to take with you. Plastic is also easier to carry when you leave the store. Plastic bags don't get wet in the rain and break, causing you to drop your groceries on the ground.

> FROM: Andrew S., Bowling Green, KY

People should be able to use the bags they want. People that use paper bags should try to recycle them. People that use plastic bags should reuse them. We should be able to choose, as long as we recycle the bags in some way.

> FROM: Alicia K., Coral Springs, FL

Canvas bags would be a better choice than the paper or plastic bags used in stores. Canvas bags are made mostly of cotton, a very renewable resource, whereas paper bags are made from trees, and plastic bags are made from nonrenewable petroleum products.

BOTH or NEITHER!

> Your Turn

1. **Critiquing Viewpoints** Select one of the statements on this page that you *agree* with. Identify and explain at least one weak point in the statement. What would you say to respond to someone who brought up this weak point as a reason you were wrong?

2. **Critiquing Viewpoints** Select one ot the statements on this page that you *disagree* with. Identify and explain at least one strong point in the statement. What would you say to respond to someone who brought up this point as a reason they were right?

3. **Creative Thinking** Make a list of at least 12 additional ways for people to reuse their plastic or paper bags.

4. **Life/Work Skills** Imagine that you are trying to decrease the number of bags being sent to the local landfill. Develop a presentation or a brochure that you could use to convince others to reuse or recycle their bags.

 internet connect

TOPIC: Paper vs. plastic
GO TO: go.hrw.com
KEYWORD: HK1Grocery bag

Which kind of bag do you think is best to use? Why? Share your views on this issue and learn about other viewpoints at the HRW Web site.

CHAPTER 3

Atoms and the Periodic Table

Chapter Preview

3.1 Atomic Structure
What Are Atoms?
What's in an Atom?
Models of the Atom

3.2 A Guided Tour of the Periodic Table
Organization of the Periodic Table
Some Atoms Form Ions
How Do the Structures of Atoms Differ?

3.3 Families of Elements
How Are Elements Classified?
Metals
Nonmetals

3.4 Using Moles to Count Atoms
Counting Things
Calculating with Moles

Focus ACTIVITY

Background Have you ever wondered why coins shine? Coins shine because they are made of metals that reflect light. Another property of metals is that they do not shatter. Metals bend as they are pressed into thin, flat sheets during the coin-making process. All metals share some similarities, but each metal has its own unique chemical and physical properties.

Metals, like everything around us, are made of trillions of tiny units that are too small to see called atoms. Atoms determine the properties of all substances. For example, gold atoms make gold coins softer and shinier than silver coins, which are made of silver atoms. Pennies get their color from the copper atoms they are coated with. In this chapter, you will learn what determines an atom's properties, why atoms are considered the smallest units of elements, and how elements are classified.

Activity 1 What metals do you see during a typical day? Describe their uses and their properties.

Activity 2 Describe several different ways to classify the coins shown on the opposite page.

SC*L*INKS™
NSTA

TOPIC: Metals
GO TO: www.scilinks.org
KEYWORD: HK1031

Atoms determine the properties of objects. For example, metal atoms give these coins their shine and their ability to be pressed flat by this stamping press.

Atomic Structure

Disc One, Module 2:
Models of the Atom
Use the Interactive Tutor to learn more about this topic.

A toms are all around you. They make up the air you are breathing, the chair you are sitting in, and the clothes you are wearing. This book, including this page you are reading, is also made of atoms.

What Are Atoms?

Atoms are tiny units that determine the properties of all matter. The aluminum cans shown in **Figure 3-1** are lightweight and easy to crush because of the properties of the atoms that make up the aluminum.

Our understanding of atoms required many centuries

In the fourth century B.C., the Greek philosopher Democritus suggested that the universe was made of invisible units called atoms. The word *atom* is derived from the Greek word meaning "unable to be divided." He believed movements of atoms caused the changes in matter that he observed.

Although Democritus's theory of atoms explained some observations, Democritus was unable to provide the evidence needed to convince people that atoms really existed. Throughout the centuries that followed, some people supported Democritus's theory. But other theories were also proposed. As the science of chemistry was developing in the 1700s, more emphasis was put on making careful and repeated measurements in scientific experiments. As a result, more-reliable data were collected that were used to favor one theory over another.

Aluminum Atoms

Figure 3-1
The atoms in aluminum, seen here as an image from a scanning tunneling electron microscope, give these aluminum cans their properties.

Atoms are the building blocks of molecules

In 1808, an English schoolteacher named John Dalton proposed his own atomic theory. Dalton's theory was widely accepted because there was much evidence to support it. In his theory, Dalton proposed the following:

- **Every element is made of tiny, unique particles called atoms that cannot be subdivided.**
- **Atoms of the same element are exactly alike.**
- **Atoms of different elements can join to form molecules.**

An atom is the smallest part of an element that still has the element's properties. Imagine dividing a coin made of pure copper until the pieces were too small for you to see. If you were able to continue dividing these pieces, you would be left with the simplest units of the coin—copper atoms. All the copper atoms would be exactly alike. Each copper atom would have chemical properties mostly the same as the coin you started with.

You learned in Chapter 2 that atoms can join. **Figure 3-2** shows how atoms join to form molecules of water. The water we see is actually made of a very large number of water molecules. Whether it gushes downstream in a riverbed or is bottled for us to drink, water is always the same: each molecule is made of two hydrogen atoms and one oxygen atom.

Figure 3-2

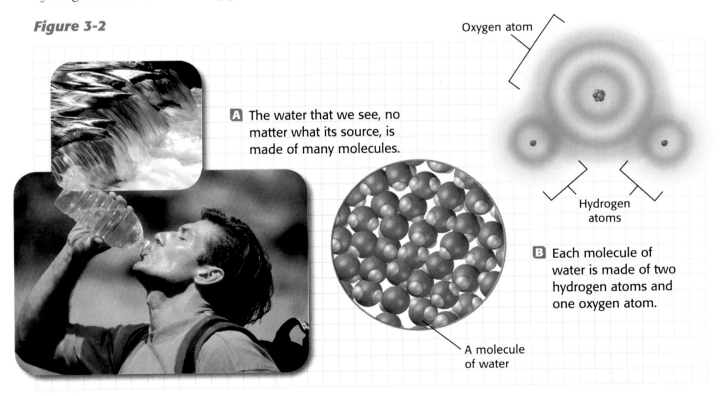

Oxygen atom

A The water that we see, no matter what its source, is made of many molecules.

Hydrogen atoms

B Each molecule of water is made of two hydrogen atoms and one oxygen atom.

A molecule of water

What's in an Atom?

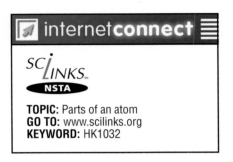

internet**connect**

SC**L**INKS

NSTA

TOPIC: Parts of an atom
GO TO: www.scilinks.org
KEYWORD: HK1032

▶ **nucleus** the center of an atom; made up of protons and neutrons

▶ **proton** a positively charged subatomic particle in the nucleus of an atom

▶ **neutron** a neutral subatomic particle in the nucleus of an atom

▶ **electron** a tiny negatively charged subatomic particle moving around outside the nucleus of an atom

VOCABULARY *Skills Tip*

Remember that **p**rotons *have a* **positive** *charge and* **neutr**ons *are* **neutral.**

Figure 3-3
A helium atom is made of two protons, two neutrons, and two electrons ($2e^-$).

Helium Atom

$2e^-$

Nucleus

Less than 100 years after Dalton published his atomic theory, scientists determined that atoms could be split, or broken down even further. While we now know that there are many different subatomic particles making up atoms, only three of these are involved in the everyday chemistry of most substances.

Atoms are made of protons, neutrons, and electrons

At the center of each atom is a small, dense **nucleus** with a positive electric charge. The nucleus is made of **protons** and **neutrons**. These two subatomic particles are almost identical in size and mass, but protons have a positive charge while neutrons have no charge at all. Moving around outside the nucleus and encircling it is a cloud of very tiny negatively charged subatomic particles with very little mass. These particles are called **electrons.** To get an idea of how far from the nucleus an electron can be, consider this: If the nucleus of a hydrogen atom were the size of a tennis ball, its one electron could be found up to 6.4 km (4 mi) away! A helium atom, shown in **Figure 3-3,** has one more proton and one more electron than a hydrogen atom has. That's because the number of protons and electrons an atom has is unique for each element.

Atoms have no overall charge

You might be surprised to learn that atoms are not charged even though they are made of charged protons and electrons. Atoms do not have a charge because they have an equal number of protons and electrons whose charges exactly cancel. A helium atom has two protons and two electrons. The atom is neutral because the positive charge of the two protons exactly cancels the negative charge of the two electrons.

Charge of two protons:	+2
Charge of two neutrons:	0
Charge of two electrons:	−2
Total charge of a helium atom:	0

Subatomic Particles

Particle	Charge	Mass (kg)	Location in the atom
Proton	+1	1.67×10^{-27}	In the nucleus
Neutron	0	1.67×10^{-27}	In the nucleus
Electron	−1	9.11×10^{-31}	Moving around outside the nucleus

Models of the Atom

Democritus in the fourth century B.C. and later Dalton, in the nineteenth century, thought that the atom could not be split. That theory had to be modified when it was discovered that atoms are made of protons, neutrons, and electrons. Like most scientific models and theories, the model of the atom has been revised many times to explain such new discoveries.

Bohr's model compares electrons to planets

In 1913, the Danish scientist Niels Bohr suggested that electrons in an atom move in set paths around the nucleus much like the planets orbit the sun in our solar system. In Bohr's model, each electron has a certain energy that is determined by its path around the nucleus. This path defines the electron's **energy level.** Electrons can only be in certain energy levels. They must gain energy to move to a higher energy level or lose energy to move to a lower energy level.

One way to imagine Bohr's model is to compare an atom to the stairless building shown in **Figure 3-4.** Imagine that the nucleus is in a very deep basement and that the electronic energy levels begin on the first floor. Electrons can be on any floor of the building but not between floors. Electrons gain energy by riding up in the elevator and lose energy by riding down in the elevator. Higher energy levels are closer together. (Ceiling height decreases toward the top of this modified building.)

According to modern theory, electrons behave more like waves

By 1925, Bohr's model of the atom no longer explained all observations. So a new model was proposed that no longer assumed that electrons orbited the nucleus along definite paths like planets orbiting the sun. In this modern model of the atom, it is believed that electrons behave more like waves on a vibrating string than like particles.

Quick ACTIVITY

Convincing John Dalton
If Dalton were still alive, he might argue: "Atoms are neutral, so they can't be made of charged particles."
Explain why this statement is not true.

internetconnect

SC*LINKS*
NSTA

TOPIC: History of atomic models
GO TO: www.scilinks.org
KEYWORD: HK1033

▶ **energy level** any of the possible energies an electron may have in an atom

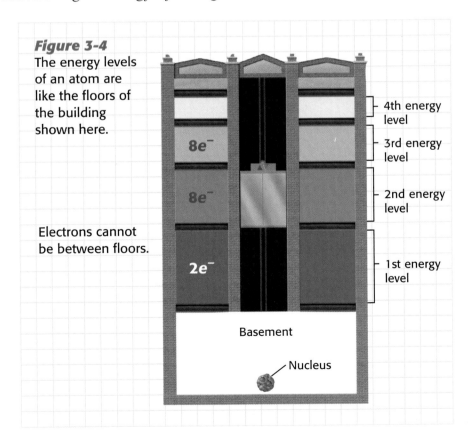

Figure 3-4
The energy levels of an atom are like the floors of the building shown here.

Electrons cannot be between floors.

$8e^-$

$8e^-$

$2e^-$

4th energy level

3rd energy level

2nd energy level

1st energy level

Basement

Nucleus

Designing Drugs In living things, enzymes (compounds that speed up biological reactions) and antibodies (chemical defense agents) use electron arrangements to recognize certain molecules. Because drugs for treating disease and infection are often similar in size and shape to molecules that occur naturally in the body, they can "trick" enzymes and antibodies into behaving in a desired way.

Scientists use computers, along with an equation that represents the wavelike behavior of electrons, to predict the properties of possible new drugs. Computers test how well the drug (shown in yellow in the figure at right) interacts with enzymes and antibodies. Promising compounds are then made. Several prescription medicines on the market today were developed by this process.

Applying Information
Write a paragraph that answers the following questions:

WRITING SKILL

1. How do drugs work?
2. Why are computers used to test a drug before the drug is made?

Imagine the moving blades of a fan, like the one shown in **Figure 3-5.** If you were asked where any one of the blades was located at a certain instant, you would not be able to give an exact answer. In fact, it's nearly impossible to know the exact location of any of the blades because they are moving so quickly. All you know for sure is that each blade could be anywhere within the blurred area you see as the blades turn.

It is also impossible to determine both the exact location of an electron in an atom and its speed and direction. The best scientists can do is calculate the chance of finding an electron in a certain place within an atom. One way to visually show the likelihood of finding an electron in a given location is by shading. The darker the shading, the better the chance of finding an electron at that location. The whole shaded region is called an electron cloud.

Figure 3-5
Just like these blades turning in this fan, the exact positions, speeds, and directions of electrons in an atom cannot be determined.

Constructing a Model

A scientific model is a simplified representation based on limited knowledge that describes how an object looks or functions. In this activity, you will construct your own model.

1. Obtain from your teacher a can that is covered by a sock and sealed with tape. An unknown object is inside the can.
2. Without unsealing the container, try to determine the characteristics of the object inside by examining it through the sock. What is the object's mass?

What is its size, shape, and texture? Record all of your observations in a data table.
3. Remove the taped sock so that you can touch the object without looking at it. Record these observations as well.
4. Use the data you have collected to draw a model of the unknown object.
5. Finally remove the object to see what it is. Compare and contrast the model you made with the object it is meant to represent.

Electrons are found in orbitals within energy levels

The regions in an atom where electrons are found are called **orbitals.** Electrons may occupy four different kinds of orbitals within atoms. The simplest kind of orbital is an *s* orbital. An *s* orbital can have only one possible orientation in space because it is shaped like a sphere, as shown in **Figure 3-6.** An *s* orbital's spherical shape enables it to surround the nucleus of an atom.

A *p* orbital, on the other hand, is dumbbell-shaped and can be oriented three different ways in space, as shown in **Figure 3-7.** The axes on the graphs are drawn to help you picture how these orbitals look in three dimensions. Imagine the *z*-axis being flat on the page. Imagine the dotted lines on the *x*- and *y*-axes going into the page, and the darker lines coming out of the page.

The *d* and *f* orbitals are much more complex. There are five possible *d* orbitals and seven possible *f* orbitals. Although all these orbitals are very different in shape, each can hold a maximum of two electrons.

Electrons usually occupy the lowest energy levels available in an atom. And within each energy level, electrons occupy orbitals with the lowest energy. In any energy level, an *s* orbital has the lowest energy. A *p* orbital has slightly more energy, followed by a *d* orbital. An *f* orbital has the greatest energy.

▶ **orbital** a region in an atom where there is a high probability of finding electrons

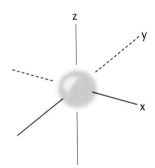

Figure 3-6
An *s* orbital is shaped like a sphere, so it has only one possible orientation in space. An *s* orbital can hold a maximum of two electrons.

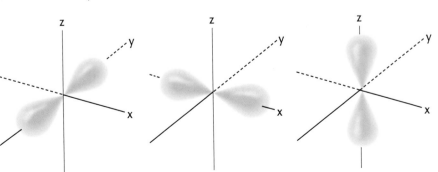

Figure 3-7
Each of these *p* orbitals can hold a maximum of two electrons, so all three together can hold a total of six electrons.

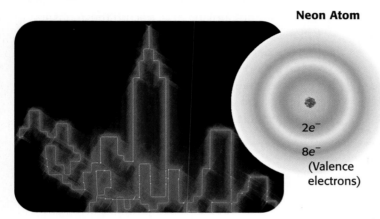

valence electron an electron in the outermost energy level of an atom

Every atom has one or more valence electrons

An electron in the outermost energy level of an atom is called a **valence electron.** The single electron of a hydrogen atom is a valence electron because it is the only electron the atom has. The glowing red sign shown in **Figure 3-8** is made of neon atoms. In a neon atom, two electrons fill the lowest energy level. Its valence electrons, then, are the eight electrons that are farther away from the nucleus in the atom's second (and outermost) energy level.

Neon Atom

$2e^-$

$8e^-$
(Valence electrons)

Figure 3-8
The neon atoms of this sign have eight valence electrons. The sign lights up because atoms first gain energy and then release this energy in the form of light.

SECTION 3.1 REVIEW

SUMMARY

▶ Elements are made of very small units called atoms.

▶ The nucleus of an atom is made of positively charged protons and uncharged neutrons.

▶ Surrounding the nucleus are tiny negatively charged electrons.

▶ Atoms have an equal number of protons and electrons.

▶ In Bohr's model of the atom, electrons orbit the nucleus in set paths much like the planets orbit the sun in our solar system.

▶ In the modern atomic model, electrons are found in orbitals within each energy level.

▶ Electrons in the outermost energy level are called valence electrons.

CHECK YOUR UNDERSTANDING

1. **Summarize** the main ideas of Dalton's atomic theory.
2. **Explain** why Dalton's theory was more successful than Democritus's theory.
3. **List** the charge, mass, and location of each of the three subatomic particles found within atoms.
4. **Predict** how many valence electrons a nitrogen atom has. (Nitrogen has a total of seven electrons, two of which fill the lowest energy level.)
5. **Explain** why oxygen atoms are neutral. (Oxygen has eight positively charged protons.)
6. **Compare** an atom's structure to a ladder. What parts of the ladder correspond to the energy levels of the atom? Identify one way a real ladder is not a good model for the atom.
7. **Explain** how the path of an electron differs in Bohr's model and in the modern model of the atom.
8. **Critical Thinking** In the early 1900s, two associates of New Zealander Ernest Rutherford bombarded thin sheets of gold with positively charged subatomic particles. They found that most of the particles passed right through the sheets but some bounced back as if they had hit something solid. Based on their results, what do you think the majority of an atom is made of? What part of the atom caused the particles to bounce back? (**Hint:** Positive charges repel other positive charges.)

A Guided Tour of the Periodic Table

OBJECTIVES

- ▶ Relate the organization of the periodic table to the arrangement of electrons within an atom.
- ▶ Explain why some atoms gain or lose electrons to form ions.
- ▶ Determine how many protons, neutrons, and electrons an isotope has, given its symbol, atomic number, and mass number.
- ▶ Describe how the abundance of isotopes affects an element's average atomic mass.

▶ **KEY TERMS**
periodic law
period
group
ionization
ion
cation
anion
atomic number
mass number
isotopes
atomic mass unit (amu)
average atomic mass

When you are in a store, chances are you know where to look for your favorite items because they are not placed randomly on the shelves. Similar items are usually grouped together, as shown in **Figure 3-9,** so that you can find what you need quickly. The periodic table organizes all the elements in a similar way.

Organization of the Periodic Table

The periodic table groups similar elements together. This organization makes it easier to predict the properties of an element based on where it is in the periodic table. In the periodic table shown in **Figure 3-10,** on the following pages, elements are represented by their symbols. The elements are also arranged in a certain order. The order is based on the number of protons an atom of that element has in its nucleus.

A hydrogen atom has one proton, so hydrogen is the first element listed in the periodic table. A helium atom has two protons and is the second element listed, and so on. Elements are listed in this order in the periodic table because the periodic law states that when elements are arranged this way, similarities in their properties will occur in a regular pattern.

▶ **periodic law** properties of elements tend to change in a regular pattern when elements are arranged in order of increasing atomic number, or number of protons in their atoms

Figure 3-9
In many stores, similar items are grouped so that they are easier to find.

Figure 3-10

The Periodic Table of the Elements

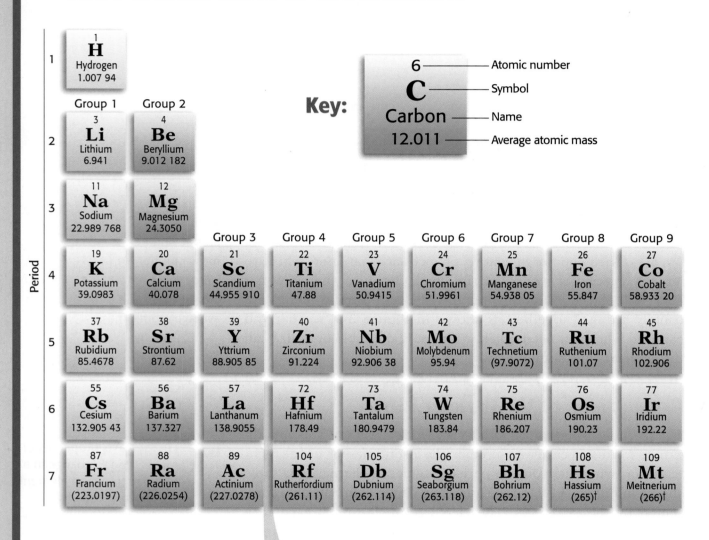

Key:

6	Atomic number
C	Symbol
Carbon	Name
12.011	Average atomic mass

† Estimated from currently available IUPAC data.

* The systematic names and symbols for elements greater than 109 will be used until the approval of trivial names by IUPAC.

go.hrw.com
Visit the HRW Web site to see the most recent version of the periodic table.

Metals
- Alkali metals
- Alkaline-earth metals
- Transition metals
- Other metals

Nonmetals
- Hydrogen
- Semiconductors
- Halogens
- Noble gases
- Other nonmetals

Group 18

2
He
Helium
4.002 602

Group 13	Group 14	Group 15	Group 16	Group 17	
5	6	7	8	9	10
B	**C**	**N**	**O**	**F**	**Ne**
Boron	Carbon	Nitrogen	Oxygen	Fluorine	Neon
10.811	12.011	14.006 74	15.9994	18.998 4032	20.1797
13	14	15	16	17	18
Al	**Si**	**P**	**S**	**Cl**	**Ar**
Aluminum	Silicon	Phosphorus	Sulfur	Chlorine	Argon
26.981 539	28.0855	30.9738	32.066	35.4527	39.948

Group 10	Group 11	Group 12						
28	29	30	31	32	33	34	35	36
Ni	**Cu**	**Zn**	**Ga**	**Ge**	**As**	**Se**	**Br**	**Kr**
Nickel	Copper	Zinc	Gallium	Germanium	Arsenic	Selenium	Bromine	Krypton
58.6934	63.546	65.39	69.723	72.61	74.921 59	78.96	79.904	83.80
46	47	48	49	50	51	52	53	54
Pd	**Ag**	**Cd**	**In**	**Sn**	**Sb**	**Te**	**I**	**Xe**
Palladium	Silver	Cadmium	Indium	Tin	Antimony	Tellurium	Iodine	Xenon
106.42	107.8682	112.411	114.818	118.710	121.757	127.60	126.904	131.29
78	79	80	81	82	83	84	85	86
Pt	**Au**	**Hg**	**Tl**	**Pb**	**Bi**	**Po**	**At**	**Rn**
Platinum	Gold	Mercury	Thallium	Lead	Bismuth	Polonium	Astatine	Radon
195.08	196.966 54	200.59	204.3833	207.2	208.980 37	(208.9824)	(209.9871)	(222.0176)
110	111	112		114		116		118
Uun*	**Uuu***	**Uub***		**Uuq***		**Uuh***		**Uuo***
Ununnilium	Unununium	Ununbium		Ununquadium		Ununhexium		Ununoctium
(269)†	(272)†	(277)†		(285)†		(289)†		(293)†

63	64	65	66	67	68	69	70	71
Eu	**Gd**	**Tb**	**Dy**	**Ho**	**Er**	**Tm**	**Yb**	**Lu**
Europium	Gadolinium	Terbium	Dysprosium	Holmium	Erbium	Thulium	Ytterbium	Lutetium
151.966	157.25	158.925 34	162.50	164.930	167.26	168.934 21	173.04	174.967
95	96	97	98	99	100	101	102	103
Am	**Cm**	**Bk**	**Cf**	**Es**	**Fm**	**Md**	**No**	**Lr**
Americium	Curium	Berkelium	Californium	Einsteinium	Fermium	Mendelevium	Nobelium	Lawrencium
(243.0614)	(247.0703)	(247.0703)	(251.0796)	(252.083)	(257.0951)	(258.10)	(259.1009)	(262.11)

The atomic masses listed in this table reflect the precision of current measurements. (Values listed in parentheses are those of the element's most stable or most common isotope.) In calculations throughout the text, however, atomic masses have been rounded to two places to the right of the decimal.

> **period** a horizontal row of elements in the periodic table

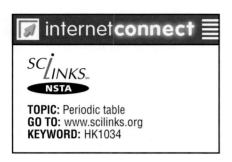

> **group (family)** a vertical column of elements in the periodic table

Figure 3-11
The electronic arrangement of atoms becomes increasingly more complex as you move further right across a period and further down a group of the periodic table.

Using the periodic table to determine electronic arrangement

Horizontal rows in the periodic table are called periods. Just as the number of protons an atom has increases by one as you move from left to right across a period, so does its number of electrons. You can determine how an atom's electrons are arranged if you know where the corresponding element is located in the periodic table.

Hydrogen and helium are both located in Period 1 of the periodic table. **Figure 3-11** shows that a hydrogen atom has one electron in an *s* orbital, while a helium atom has one more electron, for a total of two. Lithium is located in Period 2. A lithium atom is just like a helium atom, except that it has a third electron in an *s* orbital in the second energy level, as follows:

Energy level	Orbital	Number of electrons
1	*s*	2
2	*s*	1

As you continue to move to the right in Period 2, you can see that a carbon atom has electrons in *p* orbitals and *s* orbitals. The locations of the six electrons in a carbon atom are as follows:

Energy level	Orbital	Number of electrons
1	*s*	2
2	*s*	2
2	*p*	2

A nitrogen atom has three electrons in *p* orbitals, an oxygen atom has four, and a fluorine atom has five. **Figure 3-11** shows that a neon atom has six electrons in *p* orbitals. Each orbital can hold two electrons, so all three *p* orbitals are filled.

Elements in the same group have similar properties

Valence electrons determine the chemical properties of atoms. Atoms of elements in the same group, or column, have the same number of valence electrons, so these elements have similar properties. Remember that these elements are not exactly alike, though, because atoms of these elements have different numbers of protons in their nuclei and different numbers of electrons in their filled inner energy levels.

Electron Locations

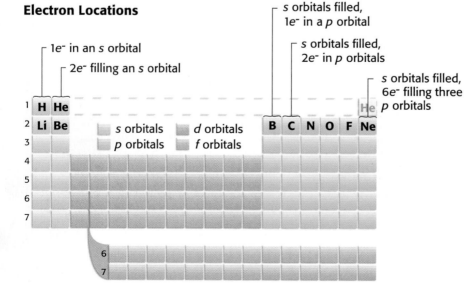

Some Atoms Form Ions

Atoms of Group 1 elements are reactive because their outermost energy levels are only partially filled. Atoms that do not have filled outermost energy levels may undergo a process called ionization. That is, they may gain or lose valence electrons so that they have a full outermost energy level. If an atom gains or loses electrons, it no longer has the same number of electrons as it does protons. Because the charges do not cancel completely as they did before, the ion that forms has a net electric charge, as shown for the lithium ion in **Figure 3-12.**

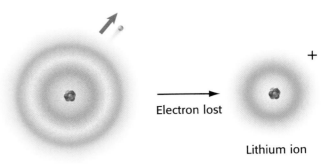

Lithium atom

Electron lost

Lithium ion

Figure 3-12
The valence electron of a reactive lithium atom may be removed to form a lithium ion, Li$^+$, with a 1+ charge.

A lithium atom loses one electron to form a 1+ charged ion

Lithium is located in Group 1 of the periodic table. It is so reactive that it even reacts with air. An electron is easily removed from a lithium atom, as shown in **Figure 3-12.** The model for the atomic structure of lithium explains its reactivity. A lithium atom has three electrons. Two of these electrons occupy the first energy level, but only one electron occupies the second energy level. This single valence electron makes lithium very reactive. Removing this electron forms a positive ion, or cation.

A lithium ion, written as Li$^+$, is much less reactive than a lithium atom because it has a full outermost energy level. Atoms of other Group 1 elements also have one valence electron. They are also reactive and behave similarly to lithium. You will learn more about Group 1 elements in Section 3.3.

▷ **ionization** the process of adding electrons to or removing electrons from an atom or group of atoms

▷ **ion** an atom or group of atoms that has lost or gained one or more electrons and therefore has a net electric charge

▷ **cation** an ion with a positive charge

▷ **anion** an ion with a negative charge

A fluorine atom gains one electron to form a 1– charged ion

Like lithium, fluorine is also very reactive. However, instead of losing an electron to become less reactive, an atom of the element fluorine gains one electron to form an ion with a 1– charge. Fluorine is located in Group 17 of the periodic table, and each atom has nine electrons. Two of these electrons occupy the first energy level, and seven valence electrons occupy the second energy level. A fluorine atom needs only one more electron to have a full outermost energy level. An atom of fluorine easily gains this electron to form a negative ion, or anion, as shown in **Figure 3-13.**

Figure 3-13
A fluorine atom easily gains one valence electron to form a fluoride ion, F$^-$, with a 1– charge.

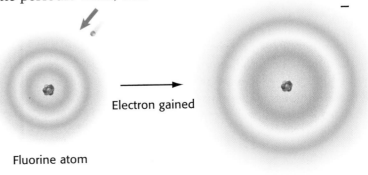

Fluorine atom

Electron gained

Fluoride ion

Ions of fluorine are called fluoride ions and are written as F^-. Because atoms of other Group 17 elements also have seven valence electrons, they are also reactive and behave similarly to fluorine. You will learn more about Group 17 elements in Section 3.3.

How Do the Structures of Atoms Differ?

As you have seen with lithium and fluorine, atoms of different elements have their own unique structures. Because these atoms have different structures, they have different properties. An atom of hydrogen found in a molecule of swimming-pool water has properties very different from an atom of uranium in nuclear fuel.

Atomic number equals the number of protons

▶ **atomic number** the number of protons in the nucleus of an atom

The atomic number, Z, tells you how many protons are in an atom. Remember that atoms are always neutral because they have an equal number of protons and electrons. Therefore, the atomic number also equals the number of electrons the atom has. Each element has a different atomic number. For example, the simplest atom, hydrogen, has just one proton and one electron, so for hydrogen, $Z = 1$. The largest naturally occurring atom, uranium, has 92 protons and 92 electrons, so $Z = 92$ for uranium. The atomic number for a given element never changes.

Mass number equals the total number of subatomic particles in the nucleus

▶ **mass number** the total number of protons and neutrons in the nucleus of an atom

The mass number, A, of an atom equals the number of protons plus the number of neutrons. A fluorine atom has 9 protons and 10 neutrons, so $A = 19$ for fluorine. This mass number includes only the number of protons and neutrons (and not electrons) because protons and neutrons provide most of the atom's mass. Although atoms of an element always have the same atomic number, they can have different mass numbers. **Figure 3-14** shows which subatomic particles in the nucleus of an atom contribute to the atomic number and which contribute to the mass number.

Figure 3-14
Atoms of the same element have the same number of protons and therefore have the same atomic number. But they may have different mass numbers, depending on how many neutrons each atom has.

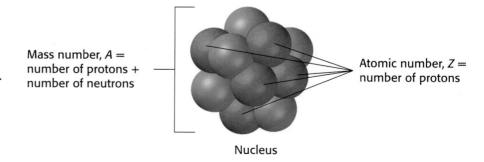

Mass number, A =
number of protons +
number of neutrons

Atomic number, Z =
number of protons

Nucleus

Isotopes of Hydrogen

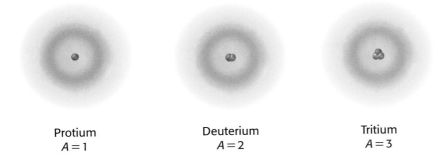

Protium
$A = 1$

Deuterium
$A = 2$

Tritium
$A = 3$

Figure 3-15
Protium has only a proton in its nucleus. Deuterium has both a proton and a neutron in its nucleus, while tritium has a proton and two neutrons.

Isotopes of an element have different numbers of neutrons

Neutrons can be added to an atom without affecting the number of protons and electrons the atom is made of. Many elements have only one stable form, while other elements have different "versions" of their atoms. Each version has the same number of protons and electrons as all other versions but a different number of neutrons. These different versions, or isotopes, vary in mass but are all atoms of the same element because they each have the same number of protons.

The three isotopes of hydrogen, shown in **Figure 3-15,** all share similar chemical properties because each is made of one proton and one electron. The most common hydrogen isotope, protium, has only a proton in its nucleus. A second isotope of hydrogen has a proton and a neutron. The mass number, *A*, of this second isotope is two, and the isotope is twice as massive. In fact, this isotope is sometimes called "heavy hydrogen." It is also known as deuterium, or hydrogen-2. A third isotope has a proton and two neutrons in its nucleus. This third isotope, tritium, has a mass number of three.

▶ **isotopes** any atoms having the same number of protons but different numbers of neutrons

Figure 3-16

🅐 Hydrogen makes up less than 1 percent of Earth's crust. Only 1 out of every 6000 of these hydrogen atoms is a deuterium isotope.

Some isotopes are more common than others

Hydrogen is present on both the sun and on Earth. In both places, protium (the hydrogen isotope without neutrons in its nucleus) is found most often. Only a very small fraction of the less common isotope of hydrogen, deuterium, is found on the sun and on Earth, as shown in **Figure 3-16.** Tritium is an unstable isotope that decays over time, so it is found least often.

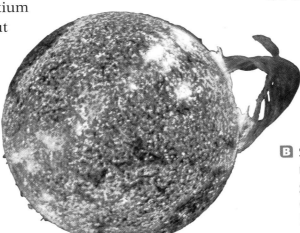

🅑 Seventy-five percent of the mass of the sun is hydrogen, with protium isotopes outnumbering deuterium isotopes 50 000 to 1.

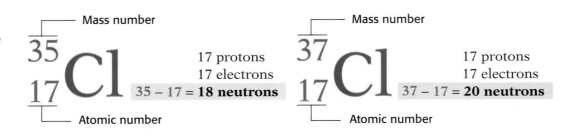

Figure 3-17
One isotope of chlorine has 18 neutrons, while the other isotope has 20 neutrons.

▷ **atomic mass unit (amu)**
a quantity equal to one-twelfth of the mass of a carbon-12 atom

▷ **average atomic mass**
the weighted average of the masses of all naturally occurring isotopes of an element

Calculating the number of neutrons in an atom

Atomic numbers and mass numbers may be included along with the symbol of an element to represent different isotopes. The two isotopes of chlorine are represented this way in **Figure 3-17**. If you know the atomic number and mass number of an atom, you can calculate the number of neutrons it has.

Uranium has several isotopes. The isotope that is used in nuclear reactors is uranium-235, or $^{235}_{92}$U. Like all uranium atoms, it has an atomic number of 92, so it must have 92 protons and 92 electrons. It has a mass number of 235, which means its number of protons and neutrons together is 235. The number of neutrons must be 143.

Mass number (*A*):	235
Atomic number (*Z*):	− 92
Number of neutrons:	143

The mass of an atom

The mass of a single atom is very small. A single fluorine atom has a mass less than one trillionth of a billionth of a gram. Because it is very hard to work with such tiny masses, atomic masses are usually expressed in atomic mass units. An **atomic mass unit (amu)** is equal to one-twelfth of the mass of a carbon-12 atom. This isotope of carbon has six protons and six neutrons, so individual protons and neutrons must each have a mass of about 1.0 amu because electrons contribute very little mass.

Often, the atomic mass listed for an element in the periodic table is an **average atomic mass** for the element as it is found in nature. The average atomic mass for an element is a weighted average, so the more commonly found isotopes have a greater effect on the average than rare isotopes.

Figure 3-18 shows how the natural abundance of chlorine's two isotopes affects chlorine's average atomic mass. The average atomic mass of chlorine is 35.45 amu. This mass is much closer to 35 amu than to 37 amu. That's because the atoms of chlorine with masses of nearly 35 amu are found more often and therefore contribute more to chlorine's average atomic mass than chlorine atoms with masses of nearly 37 amu.

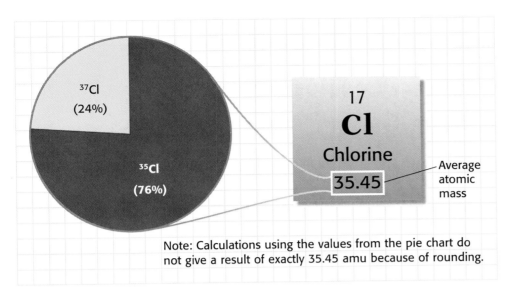

Figure 3-18
The average atomic mass of chlorine is closer to 35 amu than it is to 37 amu because ^{35}Cl isotopes are found more often than ^{37}Cl isotopes.

Note: Calculations using the values from the pie chart do not give a result of exactly 35.45 amu because of rounding.

SECTION 3.2 REVIEW

SUMMARY

▶ Elements are arranged in order of increasing atomic number so that elements with similar properties are in the same column, or group.

▶ Elements in the same group have the same number of valence electrons.

▶ Reactive atoms may gain or lose valence electrons to form ions.

▶ An atom's atomic number is its number of protons.

▶ An atom's mass number is its total number of subatomic particles in the nucleus.

▶ Isotopes of an element have different numbers of neutrons, and therefore have different masses.

▶ An element's average atomic mass is a weighted average of the masses of its naturally occurring isotopes.

CHECK YOUR UNDERSTANDING

1. **Explain** how you can determine the number of neutrons an atom has from an atom's mass number and its atomic number.

2. **Calculate** how many neutrons a phosphorus-32 atom has.

3. **Name** the elements represented by the following symbols:
   - **a.** Li
   - **b.** Mg
   - **c.** Cu
   - **d.** Br
   - **e.** He
   - **f.** S
   - **g.** Na
   - **h.** Fe
   - **i.** K

4. **Compare** the number of valence electrons an oxygen, O, atom has with the number of valence electrons a selenium, Se, atom has. Are oxygen and selenium in the same period or group?

5. **Describe** how a sodium ion differs from a sodium atom. (**Hint:** The behavior of sodium is similar to that of lithium.) Which form of sodium is more likely to be found in nature? Explain your reasoning.

6. **Predict** which isotope of nitrogen is more commonly found, nitrogen-14 or nitrogen-15. (**Hint:** What is the average atomic mass listed for nitrogen in the periodic table?)

7. **Describe** why the elements in the periodic table are arranged in order of increasing atomic number.

8. **Critical Thinking** Before 1937, all naturally occurring elements had been discovered, but no one had found any trace of element 43. Chemists were still able to predict the chemical properties of this element (now called technetium), which is widely used today for diagnosing medical problems. How were these predictions possible? Which elements would you expect to be similar to technetium?

Families of Elements

KEY TERMS

metals

nonmetals

semiconductors

alkali metals

alkaline-earth metals

transition metals

halogens

noble gases

TOPIC: Element families
GO TO: www.scilinks.org
KEYWORD: HK1035

Figure 3-19
(A) Just like the members of this family, (B) elements in the periodic table share certain similarities.

> **OBJECTIVES**
>
> ▶ Locate alkali metals, alkaline-earth metals, and transition metals in the periodic table.
>
> ▶ Locate semiconductors, halogens, and noble gases in the periodic table.
>
> ▶ Relate an element's chemical properties to the electron arrangement of its atoms.

You may have wondered why groups in the periodic table are sometimes called families. Consider your own family. Though each member is unique, you all share certain similarities. All members of the family shown in **Figure 3-19A,** for example, have a similar appearance. Members of a family in the periodic table have many chemical and physical properties in common because they have the same number of valence electrons.

How Are Elements Classified?

Think of each element as a member of a family that is also related to other elements nearby. Elements are classified as metals or nonmetals, as shown in **Figure 3-19B.** This classification groups elements that have similar physical and chemical properties. You will learn more about the chemical properties of elements in Chapter 5.

B

| | Metals |
| Nonmetals |

Note: Sometimes the boxed elements toward the right side of the periodic table are classified as a separate group and called semiconductors or metalloids.

As you can see in **Figure 3-19B,** most elements are metals. Most metals are shiny solids that can be stretched and shaped. They are also good conductors of heat and electricity. All nonmetals, except for hydrogen, are found on the right side of the periodic table. Nonmetals may be solids, liquids, or gases. Solid nonmetals are typically dull and brittle and are poor conductors of heat and electricity. But some elements that are classified as non-metals can conduct under certain conditions. These elements are sometimes considered to be their own group and are called semiconductors or metalloids.

Metals

Many elements are classified as metals. To further classify metals, similar metals are grouped together. There are four different kinds of metals. Two groups of metals are located on the left side of the periodic table. Other metals, like aluminum, tin, and lead, are located toward the right side of the periodic table. Most metals, though, are located in the middle of the periodic table.

The alkali metal sodium is very reactive

Sodium is found in Group 1 of the periodic table, as shown in **Figure 3-20A.** Like other alkali metals, it is soft and shiny and reacts violently with water. For this reason, it must be stored in oil, as shown in **Figure 3-20B,** to prevent it from reacting with moisture in the air.

An atom of an alkali metal is very reactive because it has one valence electron that can easily be removed to form a positive ion. You have already seen in Section 3.2 how lithium, another alkali metal, forms positive ions with a 1+ charge. Similarly, the valence electron of a sodium atom can be removed to form the positive sodium ion Na^+.

Because alkali metals such as sodium are so reactive, they are not found in nature as elements. Instead, they combine with other elements to form compounds. For example, the salt you use to season your food is actually the compound sodium chloride, NaCl. Potassium is another common alkali metal.

Alkali Metals

Group 1

Figure 3-20

Ⓐ The alkali metals are located on the left edge of the periodic table.

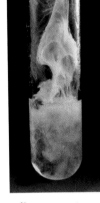

Ⓑ The alkali metal sodium must be stored in oil. Otherwise, it will react violently with moisture and oxygen in the air.

3
Li
Lithium
6.941

11
Na
Sodium
22.989 768

19
K
Potassium
39.0983

37
Rb
Rubidium
85.4678

55
Cs
Cesium
132.905 43

87
Fr
Francium
(223.0197)

▷ **metals** the elements that are good conductors of heat and electricity

▷ **nonmetals** the elements that are usually poor conductors of heat and electricity

▷ **semiconductors** the elements that are intermediate conductors of heat and electricity

▷ **alkali metals** the highly reactive metallic elements located in Group 1 of the periodic table

Alkaline-earth Metals

4 **Be** Beryllium 9.012 182	

Figure 3-21

A The alkaline-earth metals make up the second column of elements from the left edge of the periodic table.

12 **Mg** Magnesium 24.3050
20 **Ca** Calcium 40.078
38 **Sr** Strontium 87.62
56 **Ba** Barium 137.327
88 **Ra** Radium (226.0254)

▶ **alkaline-earth metals**
the reactive metallic elements located in Group 2 of the periodic table

B Fish can escape their predators by hiding among the hard projections of limestone coral reefs that are made of calcium compounds.

Compounds of the alkaline-earth metal calcium are found in limestone and marble

Calcium is in Group 2 of the periodic table, as shown in **Figure 3-21A,** and is an **alkaline-earth metal.** Atoms of alkaline-earth metals, such as calcium, have two valence electrons. Alkaline-earth metals are less reactive than alkali metals, but they may still react to form positive ions with a 2+ charge. When the valence electrons of a calcium atom are removed, a calcium ion, Ca^{2+}, forms. Alkaline-earth metals like calcium also combine with other elements to form compounds.

Calcium compounds make up the hard shells of many sea animals. When the animals die, their shells settle to form large deposits that eventually become limestone or marble, both of which are very strong materials used in construction. Coral is one example of a limestone structure. The "skeletons" of millions of tiny animals combine to form sturdy coral reefs that many fish rely on for protection, as shown in **Figure 3-21B.** Your bones and teeth also get their strength from calcium compounds.

Magnesium is another alkaline-earth metal that has properties similar to calcium. Magnesium is the lightest of all structural materials and is used to build some airplanes. Magnesium, as Mg^{2+}, activates many of the enzymes that speed up processes in the human body. Magnesium also combines with other elements to form many useful compounds. Two magnesium compounds are commonly used medicines—milk of magnesia and Epsom salt.

Quick ACTIVITY

Elements in Your Food

1. For 1 day, make a list of the ingredients in all the foods and drinks you consume.
2. Identify which ingredients on your list are compounds.
3. For each compound on your list, try to figure out what elements it is made of.

Transition Metals

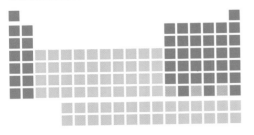

B The transition metals gold, silver, and platinum are often shaped to make jewelry.

Figure 3-22

A The transition metals are located in the middle of the periodic table.

The transition metal gold is mined

Gold is a valuable transition metal. **Figure 3-22A** shows that the transition metals are located in Groups 3–12 of the periodic table. Unlike most other transition metals, gold is not found combined with other elements as an ore but as the free metal.

Transition metals, like gold, are much less reactive than sodium or calcium, but they can lose electrons to form positive ions too. There are two possible cations that a gold atom can form. If an atom of gold loses only one electron, it forms Au^+. If the atom loses three electrons, it forms Au^{3+}. Some transition metals can form as many as four differently charged cations because of their complex arrangement of electrons.

All metals, including transition metals, conduct heat and electricity. They can also be stretched and shaped without breaking. Because gold, silver, and platinum are the shiniest metals, they are often molded into different kinds of jewelry, as shown in **Figure 3-22B.**

There are many other useful transition metals. Copper is often used for electrical wiring or plumbing. Light bulb filaments are made of tungsten. Iron, cobalt, copper, and manganese play vital roles in your body chemistry. Mercury, shown in **Figure 3-23,** is the only metal that is a liquid at room temperature. It is often used in thermometers because it flows quickly and easily without sticking to glass.

▶ **transition metals** the metallic elements located in Groups 3–12 of the periodic table

VOCABULARY *Skills Tip*

The properties of transition metals gradually transition, or shift, from being more similar to Group 2 elements to being more similar to Group 13 elements as you move from left to right across a period.

Figure 3-23
Mercury is an unusual metal because it is a liquid at room temperature. Continued exposure to this volatile metal can harm you because if you breathe in the vapor, it accumulates in your body.

Inquiry Lab

Why do some metals cost more than others?

Procedure

1. The table at right gives the abundance of some metals in Earth's crust. List the metals in order from most to least abundant.
2. List the metals in order of price, from the cheapest to the most expensive.

Analysis

3. If the price of a metal depends on its abundance, you would expect the order to be the same on both lists. How well do the two lists match? Mention any exceptions.
4. The order of reactivity of these metals, from most reactive to least reactive, is aluminum, zinc, chromium, iron, tin, copper, silver, and gold. Use this information to explain any exceptions you noticed in item 3.

5. Create a spreadsheet that can be used to calculate how many grams of each metal you could buy with $100.

Metal	Abundance in Earth's crust (%)	Price ($/kg)
Aluminum (Al)	8.2	1.55
Chromium (Cr)	0.01	0.06
Copper (Cu)	0.0060	2.44
Gold (Au)	0.000 0004	11 666.53
Iron (Fe)	5.6	0.03
Silver (Ag)	0.000 007	154.97
Tin (Sn)	0.0002	6.22
Zinc (Zn)	0.007	1.29

Technetium and promethium are synthetic elements

Technetium and promethium are both man-made elements. They are also both *radioactive*, which means the nuclei of their atoms are continually decaying to produce different elements. There are several different isotopes of technetium. The most stable isotope is technetium-99, which has 56 neutrons. Technetium-99 can be used to diagnose cancer as well as other medical problems in soft tissues of the body, as shown in **Figure 3-24.**

When looking at the periodic table, you might have wondered why part of the last two periods of the transition metals are placed toward the bottom. This keeps the periodic table narrow so that similar elements elsewhere in the table still line up. Promethium is one element located in this bottom-most section. Its most useful isotope is promethium-147, which has 86 neutrons. Promethium-147 is an ingredient in some "glow-in-the-dark" paints.

All elements with atomic numbers greater than 92 are also man-made and are similar to technetium and promethium. For example, americium, another element in the bottom-most section of the periodic table, is also radioactive. Tiny amounts of americium-241 are found in most household smoke detectors. Although it may seem scary to have a radioactive element inside your home, so little of the element is present that it does not affect you.

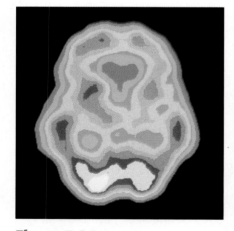

Figure 3-24
With the help of the radioactive isotope technetium-99, doctors are able to confirm that this patient has a healthy brain.

Nonmetals

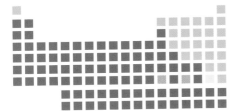

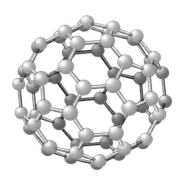

Figure 3-25

Ⓐ Most nonmetals are located on the right side of the periodic table.

Ⓑ The way carbon atoms are connected in the most recently discovered form of carbon resembles the familiar pattern of a soccer ball.

Nonmetals

Except for hydrogen, nonmetals are found on the right side of the periodic table. They include some elements in Groups 13–16 and all the elements in Groups 17 and 18.

Carbon is found in three different forms and can also form many compounds

Carbon and other nonmetals are found on the right side of the periodic table, as shown in **Figure 3-25A.** Although carbon in its pure state is usually found as graphite (pencil "lead") or diamond, the existence of fullerenes, a third form, was confirmed in 1990. The most famous fullerene consists of a cluster of 60 carbon atoms, as shown in **Figure 3-25B.**

Carbon can also combine with other elements to form millions of carbon-containing compounds. Carbon compounds are found in both living and nonliving things. Glucose, $C_6H_{12}O_6$, is a sugar in your blood. A type of chlorophyll, $C_{55}H_{72}O_5N_4Mg$, is found in all green plants. Many gasolines contain isooctane, C_8H_{18}, while rubber tires are made of large molecules with many repeating C_5H_8 units.

Nonmetals and their compounds are plentiful on Earth

Oxygen, nitrogen, and sulfur are other common nonmetals. Each may form compounds or gain electrons to form the negative ions oxide, O^{2-}, sulfide, S^{2-}, and nitride, N^{3-}. The most plentiful gases in the air are the nonmetals nitrogen and oxygen. Although sulfur itself is an odorless yellow solid, many sulfur compounds, like those in rotten eggs and skunk spray, are known for their terrible smell.

Connection to
ARCHITECTURE

The discoverers of the first and most famous fullerene named the molecule *buckminster-fullerene*. Its structure resembles a geodesic dome, a kind of structure designed by American engineer and inventor R. Buckminster Fuller. A geodesic dome encloses the most space using the fewest materials. Any strains caused by the ground shifting or strong winds have little affect on a geodesic dome. That's because the strains are spread evenly throughout the entire structure. These sturdy structures have been used successfully as radar towers in Antarctica in winds as strong as 90 m/s (200 mi/h) for over 25 years. Geodesic domes provide the framework for some sports arenas, theaters, greenhouses, and even some homes.

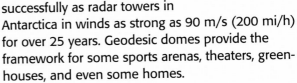

Making the Connection

1. How does the shape of a geodesic dome differ from a more typical building?
2. Explain why energy savings are greater in this kind of structure than in a boxlike building that encloses the same amount of space.

Halogens

Figure 3-26

A The halogens are in the second column from the right of the periodic table.

▶ **halogens** the highly reactive elements located in Group 17 of the periodic table

Group 17

9
F
Fluorine
18.998 4032

17
Cl
Chlorine
35.4527

35
Br
Bromine
79.904

53
I
Iodine
126.904

85
At
Astatine
(209.9871)

B Chlorine keeps pool water bacteria-free for swimmers to enjoy.

Chlorine is a halogen that protects you from harmful bacteria

Chlorine and other halogens are located in Group 17 of the periodic table, as shown in **Figure 3-26A.** You have probably noticed the strong smell of chlorine in swimming pools. Chlorine is widely used to kill bacteria in pools, like the one shown in **Figure 3-26B,** as well as in drinking-water supplies.

Like fluorine atoms, which you learned about in Section 3.2, chlorine atoms are very reactive. As a result, chlorine forms compounds. For example, the chlorine in most swimming pools is added in the form of the compound calcium hypochlorite, $Ca(OCl)_2$. Elemental chlorine is a poisonous yellowish green gas made of pairs of joined chlorine atoms. Chlorine gas has the chemical formula Cl_2. A chlorine atom may also gain an electron to form a negative chloride ion, Cl^-. The attractions between Na^+ ions and Cl^- ions form table salt, NaCl.

Fluorine, bromine, and iodine are other Group 17 elements. Fluorine is a poisonous yellowish gas, bromine is a dark red liquid, and iodine is a dark purple solid. Atoms of each of these elements can also form compounds by gaining an electron to become negative ions. A compound containing the negative ion fluoride, F^-, is used in some toothpastes and added to some water supplies to help prevent tooth decay. Adding a compound containing iodine as the negative ion iodide, I^-, to table salt makes "iodized" salt. You need iodine in your diet for your thyroid gland to function properly.

INTEGRATING

EARTH SCIENCE
No fewer than 81 elements have been detected in sea water. Magnesium (mostly as Mg^{2+} ions) and bromine (mostly as Br^- ions) are two such elements. To recover an element from a sample of sea water, you must evaporate some of the water from the sample. When you do this, sodium chloride crystallizes and the liquid that remains becomes more concentrated in bromide, magnesium, and other ions than the original sea water was, making their recovery easier.

The noble gas neon is inert

Neon is one of the noble gases that make up Group 18 of the periodic table, as shown in **Figure 3-27A.** It is responsible for the bright reddish orange light of "neon" signs. **Figure 3-27B** shows how mixing neon with another substance, such as mercury, can change the color of a sign.

The noble gases are different from most elements that are gases because they exist as single atoms instead of as molecules. Like other members of Group 18, neon is inert, or unreactive, because its outer energy level is full of electrons. For this reason, neon and other noble gases do not gain or lose electrons to form ions. They also don't join with other atoms to form compounds under normal conditions.

Helium and argon are other common noble gases. Helium is less dense than air and is used to give lift to airships and balloons. Argon is used to fill light bulbs because its lack of reactivity prevents filaments from burning.

Semiconductors are intermediate conductors of heat and electricity

Figure 3-28 shows that the elements sometimes referred to as semiconductors or metalloids are clustered toward the right side of the periodic table. Only six elements—boron, silicon, germanium, arsenic, antimony, and tellurium—are semiconductors. Although these elements are classified as nonmetals, each one also has some properties of metals. And as their name implies, semiconductors are able to conduct heat and electricity under certain conditions.

Boron is an extremely hard element. It is often added to steel to increase steel's hardness and strength at high temperatures. Compounds of boron are often used to make heat-resistant glass. Arsenic is a shiny solid that tarnishes when exposed to air. Antimony is a bluish white, brittle solid that also shines like a metal. Some compounds of antimony are used as fire retardants. Tellurium is a silvery white solid whose ability to conduct increases slightly with exposure to light.

Noble Gases

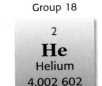

Figure 3-27

A The noble gases are located on the right edge of the periodic table.

B A neon sign is usually reddish orange, but adding a few drops of mercury makes the light a bright blue.

Group 18
2 **He** Helium 4.002 602
10 **Ne** Neon 20.1797
18 **Ar** Argon 39.948
36 **Kr** Krypton 83.80
54 **Xe** Xenon 131.29
86 **Rn** Radon (222.0176)

▶ **noble gases** the unreactive gaseous elements located in Group 18 of the periodic table

Semiconductors

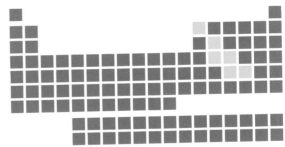

Figure 3-28
Semiconductors are located toward the right side of the periodic table.

Silicon is the most familiar semiconductor

Silicon atoms, usually in the form of compounds, account for 28 percent of the mass of Earth's crust. Sand is made of the most common silicon compound, called silicon dioxide, SiO_2. Silicon is very important for modern technology. Small chips made of silicon, like those shown in **Figure 3-29,** are used in the internal parts of computers.

Silicon and other semiconductors, like germanium, can either conduct electricity, like metals do, or not conduct electricity. The ability of a semiconductor to conduct electricity depends on how charge is manipulated within the semiconductor. This variable nature of semiconductors is what makes computers and other electronic devices work. In some cases, when semiconductors are charged, the charge remains. The memory of a computer is in the form of a gridlike pattern of such charges.

Figure 3-29
Silicon wafers are the basic building blocks of computer chips.

SECTION 3.3 REVIEW

SUMMARY

▶ Metals are shiny solids that conduct heat and electricity.

▶ Alkali metals, located in Group 1 of the periodic table, are very reactive.

▶ Alkaline-earth metals, located in Group 2, are less reactive than alkali metals.

▶ Transition metals, located in Groups 3–12, are not very reactive.

▶ Nonmetals usually do not conduct heat or electricity.

▶ Nonmetals include the inert noble gases in Group 18, the reactive halogens in Group 17, and some elements in Groups 13–16.

▶ Semiconductors are nonmetals that are intermediate conductors of heat and electricity.

CHECK YOUR UNDERSTANDING

1. **Classify** the following elements as alkali, alkaline-earth, or transition metals based on their positions in the periodic table:
   a. iron, Fe   **c.** strontium, Sr
   b. potassium, K   **d.** platinum, Pt
2. **Predict** whether cesium forms Cs^+ or Cs^{2+} ions.
3. **Describe** why chemists might sometimes store reactive chemicals in argon, Ar. To which family does argon belong?
4. **Determine** whether the following substances are likely to be metals or nonmetals:
   a. a shiny substance used to make flexible bed springs
   b. a yellow powder from underground mines
   c. a gas that does not react
   d. a conducting material used within flexible wires
5. **Describe** why atoms of bromine, Br, are so reactive. To which family does bromine belong?
6. **Predict** the charge of a beryllium ion.
7. **Identify** which element is more reactive: lithium, Li, or barium, Ba.
8. **Creative Thinking** Imagine you are a scientist who has just discovered a new element. You have confirmed that the element is a metal but are unsure whether it is an alkali metal, an alkaline-earth metal, or a transition metal. Write a paragraph describing the additional tests you can do to further classify this metal.

WRITING SKILL

3.4

Using Moles to Count Atoms

OBJECTIVES

▶ Explain the relationship between a mole of a substance and Avogadro's constant.

▶ Find the molar mass of an element by using the periodic table.

▶ Solve problems converting the amount of an element in moles to its mass in grams, and vice versa.

▶ KEY TERMS

mole
Avogadro's constant
molar mass
conversion factor

Counting objects is one of the very first things children learn to do. Counting is easy when the objects being counted are not too small and there are not too many of them. But can you imagine counting the grains of sand along a stretch of beach or the stars in the night-time sky? Counting these would be very difficult.

Counting Things

When people count out large numbers of small things, they often simplify the job by using counting units. For example, when you order popcorn at a movie theater, the salesperson does not count out the individual popcorn kernels to give you. Instead, you specify the size of container you want, and that determines how much popcorn you get. So the "counting unit" for popcorn is the size of the container: small, medium, or large.

There are many different counting units

The counting units for popcorn are only an approximation and are not exact. Everyone who orders a large popcorn will not get exactly the same number of popcorn kernels. Many other items, however, require more-exact counting units, as shown in **Figure 3-30.** For example, you usually cannot buy just one egg at the grocery store. Eggs are packaged by the dozen. Items that are needed in large quantities are packaged into groups as well. Grocers buy fruit from farmers in bushels, or 32 qt containers. Copy shops buy paper in reams, or 500-sheet bundles.

Figure 3-30
Eggs are counted by the dozen, peaches are counted by the bushel, and paper is counted by the ream.

An object's mass may sometimes be used to "count" it. For example, if a candy shopkeeper knows that 10 gumballs have a mass of 21.4 g, then the shopkeeper can assume that there are 50 gumballs on the scale when the mass is 107 g (21.4 g × 5).

The mole is useful for counting small particles

Because chemists often deal with large numbers of small particles, they use a large counting unit—the **mole,** abbreviated *mol.* A mole is a collection of a very large number of particles.

602 213 670 000 000 000 000 000 to be exact!

This number is usually written as 6.022×10^{23}/mol and is referred to as **Avogadro's constant.** The constant is named in honor of the Italian scientist Amedeo Avogadro. Avogadro's constant is defined as the number of particles, 6.022×10^{23}, in exactly 1 mol of a pure substance.

One mole of gumballs is 6.022×10^{23} gumballs. One mole of popcorn is 6.022×10^{23} kernels of popcorn. This amount of popcorn would not only cover the United States but form a pile about 500 km (310 mi) high! It is highly unlikely that you will ever come in contact with this much gum or popcorn, so it does not make sense to use moles to count either of these items. The mole is very useful, however, for counting tiny atoms.

Moles and grams are related

The mass in grams of 1 mol of a substance is called its **molar mass.** For example, 1 mol of carbon-12 atoms has a molar mass of 12.00 g. But an entire mole of an element will usually include atoms of several isotopes. So the molar mass of an element in grams is the same as its average atomic mass in amu, which is listed in the periodic table. The average atomic mass listed for carbon in the periodic table is 12.01 amu. One mole of carbon, then, has a mass of 12.01 g. **Figure 3-31** demonstrates this idea for magnesium.

▶ **mole** the SI base unit that describes the amount of a substance

▶ **Avogadro's constant** the number of particles in 1 mol; equals 6.022×10^{23}/mol

▶ **molar mass** the mass in grams of 1 mol of a substance

Did You Know?

Did you know that Avogadro never knew his own constant? Count Amedeo Avogadro (1776–1856) was a lawyer who became interested in mathematics and physics. Avogadro's constant was actually determined by Joseph Loschmidt, a German physicist in 1865, nine years after Avogadro's death.

Figure 3-31
One mole of magnesium (6.022×10^{23} Mg atoms) has a mass of 24.30 g. Note that the balance is only precise to one-tenth of a gram, so it reads 24.3 g.

12
Mg
Magnesium
24.30

You might wonder why 6.022×10^{23} represents the numbers of particles in 1 mol. Experiments have shown that 6.022×10^{23} is the number of carbon-12 atoms in 1 mol of carbon-12. One mole of carbon consists of 6.022×10^{23} carbon atoms, with an average mass of 12.01 amu. So 6.022×10^{23} carbon atoms together have a mass of 12.01 g.

Calculating with Moles

Because the amount of a substance and its mass are related, it is often useful to convert moles to grams, and vice versa. You can use **conversion factors** to relate units.

Using conversion factors

How did the shopkeeper mentioned on page 96 know the mass of 50 gumballs? He multiplied by a conversion factor to determine the number of gumballs on the scale from their combined mass. Multiplying by a conversion factor is like multiplying by 1 because both parts of the conversion factor are always equal.

The shopkeeper knows that exactly 10 gumballs have a combined mass of 21.4 g. This relationship can be written as two equivalent conversion factors, both of which are shown below.

$$\frac{10 \text{ gumballs}}{21.4 \text{ g}} \qquad \frac{21.4 \text{ g}}{10 \text{ gumballs}}$$

The shopkeeper can use one of these conversion factors to determine the mass of 50 gumballs because mass increases in a predictable way as more gumballs are added to the scale, as you can see from **Figure 3-32.**

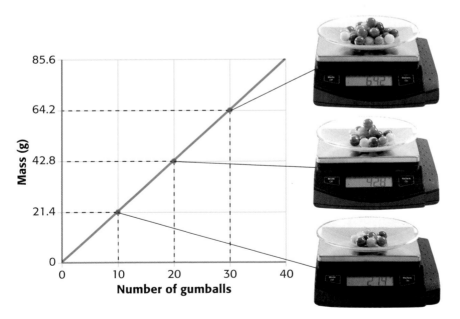

internet connect

SC*LINKS*
NSTA

TOPIC: Avogadro's constant
GO TO: www.scilinks.org
KEYWORD: HK1036

▶ **conversion factor** a ratio equal to one that expresses the same quantity in two different ways

Figure 3-32
There is a direct relationship between the number of gumballs and their mass. Ten gumballs have a mass of 21.4 g, 20 gumballs have a mass of 42.8 g, and 30 gumballs have a mass of 64.2 g.

Math Skills

Conversion Factors What is the mass of exactly 50 gumballs?

1 List the given and unknown values.
Given: mass of 10 gumballs = 21.4 g
Unknown: mass of 50 gumballs = ? g

2 Write down the conversion factor that converts number of gumballs to mass.

The conversion factor you choose should have the unit you are solving for (g) in the numerator and the unit you want to cancel (number of gumballs) in the denominator.

$$\frac{21.4 \text{ g}}{10 \text{ gumballs}}$$

3 Multiply the number of gumballs by this conversion factor, and solve.

$$50 \text{ gumballs} \times \frac{21.4 \text{ g}}{10 \text{ gumballs}} = 107 \text{ g}$$

Practice

Conversion Factors

1. What is the mass of exactly 150 gumballs?
2. If you want 50 eggs, how many dozens must you buy? How many extra eggs do you have to take?
3. If a football player is tackled 1.7 ft short of the end zone, how many more yards does the team need to get a touchdown?

Figure 3-33
There is a direct relationship between the amount of an element and its mass.

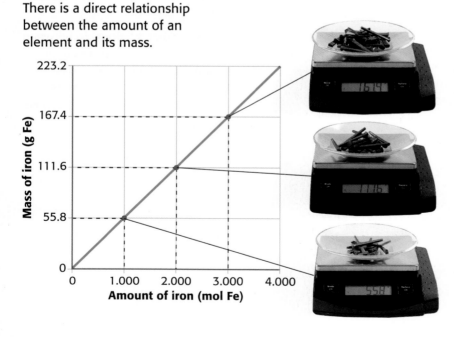

Relating moles to grams

Just as in the gumball example, there is also a relationship between the amount of an element in moles and its mass in grams. This relationship is graphed for iron nails in **Figure 3-33.** Because the amount of iron and the mass of iron are directly related, the graph is a straight line.

An element's molar mass can be used as if it were a conversion factor. Depending on which conversion factor you use, you can solve for either the amount of the element or its mass.

Converting between the amount of an element in moles and its mass in grams is outlined in **Figure 3-34.** For example, you can determine the mass of 5.50 mol of iron by using **Figure 3-34** as a guide. First you must find iron in the periodic table. Its average atomic mass is 55.85 amu. This means iron's molar mass is 55.85 g/mol Fe. Now you can set up the problem using the molar mass as if it were a conversion factor, as shown in the sample problem below.

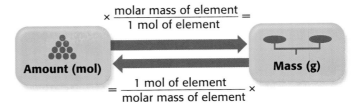

Figure 3-34
The molar mass of an element allows you to convert between the amount of the element and its mass.

Math Skills

Converting Amount to Mass Determine the mass in grams of 5.50 mol of iron.

1 **List the given and unknown values.**
   Given: amount of iron = 5.50 mol Fe
   molar mass of iron = 55.85 g/mol Fe
   Unknown: mass of iron = ? g Fe

2 **Write down the conversion factor that converts moles to grams.**
   The conversion factor you choose should have what you are trying to find (grams of Fe) in the numerator and what you want to cancel (moles of Fe) in the denominator.

$$\frac{55.85 \text{ g Fe}}{1 \text{ mol Fe}}$$

3 **Multiply the amount of iron by this conversion factor, and solve.**

$$5.50 \text{ mol Fe} \times \frac{55.85 \text{ g Fe}}{1 \text{ mol Fe}} = 307 \text{ g Fe}$$

Practice HINT

Notice how iron's molar mass, 55.85 g/mol Fe, includes units (g/mol) and a chemical symbol (Fe). The units specify that this mass applies to 1 mol of substance. The symbol for iron, Fe, clearly indicates the substance. Remember to always include units in your answers and make clear the substance to which these units apply. Otherwise, your answer has no meaning.

Practice

Converting Amount to Mass
What is the mass in grams of each of the following?
1. 2.50 mol of sulfur, S
2. 1.80 mol of calcium, Ca
3. 0.50 mol of carbon, C
4. 3.20 mol of copper, Cu

You can determine the amount of an element from its mass in much the same way, as the next sample problem on the next page shows.

Converting Mass to Amount Determine the amount of iron present in 352 g of iron.

1 **List the given and unknown values.**

Given: mass of iron = 352 g Fe

molar mass of iron = 55.85 g/mol Fe

Unknown: amount of iron = ? mol Fe

2 **Write down the conversion factor that converts grams to moles.**

The conversion factor you choose should have what you are trying to find (moles of Fe) in the numerator and what you want to cancel (grams of Fe) in the denominator.

$$\frac{1 \text{ mol Fe}}{55.85 \text{ g Fe}}$$

3 **Multiply the mass of iron by this conversion factor, and solve.**

$$352 \text{ g Fe} \times \frac{1 \text{ mol Fe}}{55.85 \text{ g Fe}} = 6.30 \text{ mol Fe}$$

SECTION 3.4 REVIEW

SUMMARY

▶ One mole of a substance has as many particles as there are atoms in exactly 12 g of carbon-12.

▶ Avogadro's constant, 6.022×10^{23}/mol, is equal to the number of particles in 1 mol.

▶ Molar mass is the mass in grams of 1 mol of a substance.

▶ An element's molar mass in grams is equal to its average atomic mass in amu.

▶ An element's molar mass can be used to convert from amount to mass, and vice versa.

CHECK YOUR UNDERSTANDING

1. **Define** Avogadro's constant. Describe how Avogadro's constant relates to a mole of a substance.
2. **Determine** the molar mass of the following elements:
   a. manganese, Mn   c. arsenic, As
   b. cadmium, Cd   d. strontium, Sr
3. **List** the two equivalent conversion factors for the molar mass of silver, Ag.
4. **Explain** why a graph showing the relationship between the amount of a particular element and the element's mass is a straight line.
5. **Critical Thinking** Which has more atoms: 3.0 g of iron, Fe, or 2.0 g of sulfur, S?

Math Skills

6. What is the mass in grams of 0.48 mol of platinum, Pt?
7. How many moles are present in 620 g of mercury, Hg?
8. How many moles are present in 11 g of silicon, Si?
9. How many moles are present in 205 g of helium, He?

Chapter Highlights

Before you begin, review the summaries of the key ideas of each section, found on pages 76, 85, 94, and 100. The key vocabulary terms are listed on pages 70, 77, 86, and 95.

UNDERSTANDING CONCEPTS

1. Which of Dalton's statements about the atom was later proven false?
   a. Atoms cannot be subdivided.
   b. Atoms are tiny.
   c. Atoms of different elements are not identical.
   d. Atoms join to form molecules.

2. Which statement is not true of Bohr's model of the atom?
   a. The nucleus can be compared to the sun.
   b. Electrons orbit the nucleus.
   c. An electron's path is not known exactly.
   d. Electrons exist in energy levels.

3. According to the modern model of the atom, _____.
   a. moving electrons form an electron cloud
   b. electrons and protons circle neutrons
   c. neutrons have a positive charge
   d. the number of protons an atom has varies

4. If an atom has a mass of 11 amu and contains five electrons, its atomic number must be _____.
   a. 55   c. 6
   b. 16   d. 5

5. Which statement is true concerning atoms of elements in the same group of the periodic table?
   a. They have the same number of protons.
   b. They have the same mass number.
   c. They have similar chemical properties.
   d. They have the same number of total electrons.

6. The organization of the periodic table is based on _____.
   a. the number of protons in an atom
   b. the mass number of an atom
   c. the number of neutrons in an atom
   d. the average atomic mass of an element

7. Elements with some properties of metals and some properties of nonmetals are known as _____.
   a. alkali metals   c. halogens
   b. semiconductors   d. noble gases

8. An atom of which of the following elements is unlikely to form a positively charged ion?
   a. potassium, K   c. barium, Ba
   b. selenium, Se   d. silver, Ag

9. Atoms of Group 18 elements are inert because _____.
   a. they combine to form molecules
   b. they have no valence electrons
   c. they have filled inner energy levels
   d. they have filled outermost energy levels

10. Which of the following statements about krypton is not true?
    a. Its molar mass is 83.80 g/mol Kr.
    b. Its atomic number is 36.
    c. One mole of krypton atoms has a mass of 41.90 g.
    d. It is a noble gas.

Using Vocabulary

11. How many *protons* and *neutrons* does a silicon, Si, atom have, and where are each of these subatomic particles located? How many *electrons* does a silicon atom have?

TOPIC: Silicon
GO TO: www.scilinks.org
KEYWORD: HK1037

12. Explain why different atoms of the same element always have the same *atomic number* but can have different *mass numbers*. What are these different atoms called?

13. Distinguish between the following:
    a. an *atom* and a *molecule*
    b. an *atom* and an *ion*
    c. a *cation* and an *anion*

14. How is the *periodic law* demonstrated with the *halogens*?

15. What does an element's *molar mass* tell you about the element?

BUILDING MATH SKILLS

16. **Graphing** Use a graphing calculator, a computer spreadsheet, or a graphing program to plot the atomic number on the *x*-axis and the average atomic mass in amu on the *y*-axis for the transition metals in Period 4 of the periodic table (from scandium to zinc). Do you notice a break in the trend near cobalt? Explain why elements with larger atomic numbers do not necessarily have larger atomic masses.

COMPUTER SKILL

17. **Converting Mass to Amount** For an experiment you have been asked to do, you need 1.5 g of iron. How many moles of iron do you need?

18. **Converting Mass to Amount** James is holding a balloon that contains 0.54 g of helium gas. What amount of helium is this?

19. **Converting Amount to Mass** A pure gold bar is made of 19.55 mol of gold. What is the mass of the bar in grams?

20. **Converting Amount to Mass** Robyn recycled 15.1 mol of aluminum last month. What mass of aluminum in grams did she recycle?

THINKING CRITICALLY

21. **Creative Thinking** Some forces push two atoms apart while other forces pull them together. Describe how the subatomic particles in each atom interact to produce these forces.

22. **Applying Knowledge** Explain why magnesium forms ions with the formula Mg^{2+}, not Mg^+ or Mg^-.

23. **Evaluating Data** The figure below shows relative ionic radii for positive and negative ions of elements in Period 2 of the periodic table. Explain the trend in ion size as you move from left to right across the periodic table. Why do the negative ions have larger radii than the positive ions?

0.60	0.31	1.71	1.40	1.36
Li^+	Be^{2+}	N^{3-}	O^{2-}	F^-

24. **Creative Thinking** Although carbon and lead are in the same group, some of their properties are very different. Propose a reason for this. (**Hint:** Look at the periodic table to locate each element and find out how each is classified.)

25. **Problem Solving** How does halving the amount of a sample of an element affect the sample's mass?

DEVELOPING LIFE/WORK SKILLS

26. **Locating Information** Some "neon" signs contain substances other than neon to produce different colors. Design your own lighted sign, and find out which substances you could use to produce the colors you want your sign to be.

27. Making Decisions Suppose you have only 1.9 g of sulfur for an experiment and you must do three trials using 0.030 mol of S each time. Do you have enough sulfur?

28. Communicating Effectively The study of the nucleus produced a new field of medicine called nuclear medicine. Pretend you are writing an article for a hospital newsletter. Describe how radioactive substances called tracers are sometimes used to detect and treat diseases.

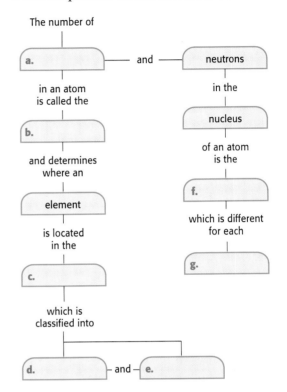

29. Working Cooperatively With a group of your classmates, make a list of 10 elements and their average atomic masses. Calculate the amount in moles for 6.0 g of each element. Rank your elements from the element with the greatest amount to the element with the least amount in a 6.0 g sample. Do you notice a trend in the amounts as atomic number increases? Explain why or why not.

INTEGRATING CONCEPTS

30. Connection to Health You can keep your bones healthy by eating 1200–1500 mg of calcium a day. Use the table below to make a list of the foods you might eat in a day to satisfy your body's need for calcium. How does your typical diet compare with this?

Item, serving size	Calcium (mg)
Plain lowfat yogurt, 1 cup	415
Ricotta cheese, 1/2 cup	337
Skim milk, 1 cup	302
Cheddar cheese, 1 ounce	213
Cooked spinach, 1/2 cup	106
Vanilla ice cream, 1/2 cup	88

31. Concept Mapping Copy the unfinished concept map below onto a sheet of paper. Complete the map by writing the correct word or phrase in the lettered boxes.

The number of

a. ——— and ——— neutrons

in an atom is called the

in the

b.

nucleus

and determines where an

of an atom is the

element

f.

is located in the

which is different for each

c.

g.

which is classified into

d. — and — e.

32. Connection to Physics The big bang theory suggests that the universe began with an enormous explosion. What was formed as a result of the big bang? Describe the matter that was present after the explosion. How much time passed before the elements as we know them were formed?

TOPIC: Origin of elements
GO TO: www.scilinks.org
KEYWORD: HK1038

Design Your Own Lab

Introduction

How can you distinguish metal elements by analyzing their physical properties?

Objectives

▶ **Determine** which physical properties can help you **distinguish** between different metals.

▶ **Identify** unknown metals by **comparing** the data you collect with reference information.

Materials

several unknown metal samples
balance
graduated cylinder
water
several beakers
ice
magnet
stopwatch
metric ruler
wax
hot plate

Safety Needs

safety goggles
gloves
laboratory apron

Comparing the Physical Properties of Elements

▶ Identifying Metal Elements

1. In this lab, you will identify samples of unknown metals by comparing the data you collect with reference information listed in the table at right. Use at least two of the physical properties listed in the table to identify each metal.

▶ Deciding Which Physical Properties You Will Analyze

2. Density is the mass per unit volume of a substance. If the metal is box-shaped, you can measure its length, width, and height, and then use these measurements to calculate the metal's volume. If the shape of the metal is irregular, you can add the metal to a known volume of water and determine what volume of water is displaced.

3. Relative hardness indicates how easy it is to scratch a metal. A metal with a higher value can scratch a metal with a lower value, but not vice versa.

4. Relative heat conductivity indicates how quickly a metal heats or cools. A metal with a value of 100 will heat or cool twice as quickly as a metal with a value of 50.

5. If a magnet placed near a metal attracts the metal, then the metal has been magnetized by the magnet.

▶ Designing Your Experiment

6. With your lab partner(s), decide how you will use the materials provided to identify each metal you are given. There is more than one way to measure some of the physical properties that are listed, so you might not use all of the materials that are provided.

7. In your lab report, list each step you will perform in your experiment.

8. Have your teacher approve your plan before you carry out your experiment.

Physical Properties of Some Metals

Metal	Density (g/mL)	Relative hardness	Relative heat conductivity	Magnetized by magnet?
Aluminum (Al)	2.7	28	100	No
Iron (Fe)	7.9	50	34	Yes
Nickel (Ni)	8.9	67	38	Yes
Tin (Sn)	7.3	19	28	No
Tungsten (W)	19.3	100	73	No
Zinc (Zn)	7.1	28	49	No

▶ Performing Your Experiment

9. After your teacher approves your plan, carry out your experiment. Keep in mind that the more careful your measurements are, the easier it will be for you to identify the unknown metals.

10. Record all the data you collect and any observations you make in your lab report.

▶ Analyzing Your Results

1. Make a table listing the physical properties you compared and the data you collected for each of the unknown metals.

2. Which metals were you given? Explain the reasoning you used to identify each metal.

3. Which physical properties were the easiest for you to measure and compare? Which were the hardest? Explain why.

4. What would happen if you tried to scratch aluminum foil with zinc?

5. Explain why it would be difficult to distinguish between iron and nickel unless you calculate each metal's density.

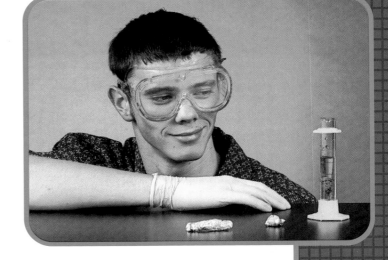

6. Suppose you find a metal fastener and determine that its density is 7 g/mL. What are two ways you could determine whether the unknown metal is tin or zinc?

▶ Defending Your Conclusions

7. Suppose someone gives you an alloy that is made of both zinc and nickel. In general, how do you think the physical properties of the alloy would compare with those of each individual metal?

CHAPTER 4

The Structure of Matter

FLAMMABLE

DANGER! EXTREMELY FLAM-
MABLE LIQUID AND VAPOR.
Causes Eye Irritation. May Be
Harmful If Inhaled or Swallowed.
May Cause Damage To Central
Nervous System. To
neys. Keep container closed. Use with
tion. Do not breathe vapor. Do not get in eyes or
skin. Or on clothing. See Material Safety Data
Sheet (MSDS) for
First Aid: Call A Physician
necessary to breath
flush with plenty of water
If Swallowed:
directed

Chapter Preview

4.1 Compounds and Molecules
What Are Compounds?
Models of Compounds
How Does Structure Affect Properties?

4.2 Ionic and Covalent Bonding
What Holds Bonded Atoms Together?
Ionic Bonds
Metallic Bonds
Covalent Bonds
Polyatomic Ions

4.3 Compound Names and Formulas
Naming Ionic Compounds
Writing Formulas for Ionic Compounds
Naming Covalent Compounds
Chemical Formulas for Covalent Compounds

4.4 Organic and Biochemical Compounds
Organic Compounds
Polymers
Biochemical Compounds

INTEGRATING TECHNOLOGY and Society

Focus ACTIVITY

Background Suddenly, a glass object slips from your hand and crashes to the ground. You watch it break into many tiny pieces as you hear it hit the floor. Glass is a brittle substance. When enough force is applied, it breaks into many sharp, jagged pieces. Glass behaves the way it does because of its composition.

A glass container and a stained glass window have some similar properties because both are made mainly from silicon dioxide. But other compounds are responsible for the window's beautiful colors. Adding a compound of nickel and oxygen to the glass produces a purple tint. Adding a compound of cobalt and oxygen makes the glass deep blue, while adding a compound of copper and oxygen makes the glass dark red.

Activity 1 There are many different kinds of glass, each with its own use. List several kinds of glass that you encounter daily. Describe the ways that each kind of glass differs from other kinds of glass.

Activity 2 Research other compounds that are sometimes added to glass. Describe how each of these compounds changes the properties of glass.

internet connect

SCI**LINKS**
NSTA

TOPIC: Properties of substances
GO TO: www.scilinks.org
KEYWORD: HK1041

Glass is a brittle substance that is made from silicon dioxide, a compound with a very rigid structure. The addition of small amounts of other compounds changes the color of the glass, "staining" it.

Compounds and Molecules

OBJECTIVES

▶ Distinguish between compounds and mixtures.

▶ Relate the chemical formula of a compound to the relative numbers of atoms or ions present in the compound.

▶ Use models to visualize a compound's chemical structure.

▶ Describe how the chemical structure of a compound affects its properties.

I f you step on a sharp rock with your bare foot, you feel pain. That's because rocks are hard substances; they don't bend. Many rocks are made of quartz. Table salt and sugar look similar; both are grainy, white solids. But they taste very different. In addition, salt is hard and brittle and breaks into uniform cube-like granules, while sugar does not. Quartz, salt, and sugar are all compounds. Their similarities and differences result from the way their atoms or ions are joined.

What Are Compounds?

Table salt is a compound made of two elements, sodium and chlorine. When elements combine to form a compound, the compound has properties very different from those of the elements that make it. **Figure 4-1** shows how the metal sodium combines with chlorine gas to form sodium chloride, NaCl, or table salt.

Figure 4-1

(A) The silvery metal sodium combines with (B) poisonous, yellowish green chlorine gas in a violent reaction (C) to form (D) white granules of table salt that you can eat.

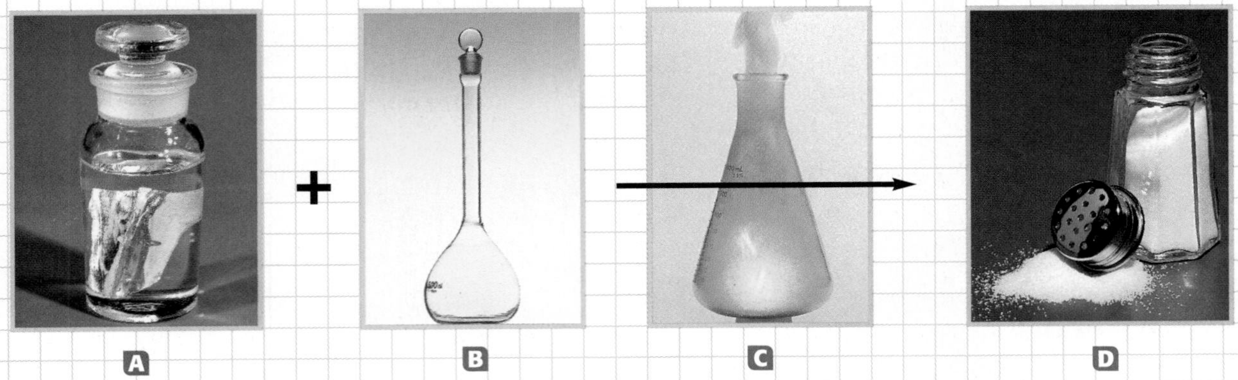

A   +   B   →   C   D

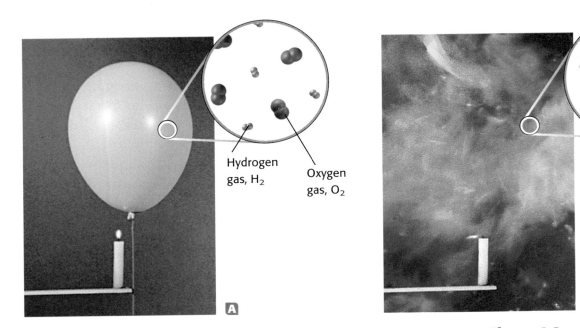

Hydrogen gas, H_2

Oxygen gas, O_2

Water (steam), H_2O

A

B

Chemical bonds distinguish compounds from mixtures

The attractive forces that hold different atoms or ions together in compounds are called **chemical bonds.** Recall from Chapter 2 how compounds and mixtures are different. Mixtures are made of different substances that are just placed together. Each substance in the mixture keeps its own properties.

For example, mixing blue paint and yellow paint makes green paint. Different shades of green can be made by mixing the paints in different proportions, but both original paints remain chemically unchanged.

Figure 4-2 shows that when a mixture of hydrogen gas and oxygen gas is heated, a violent reaction takes place and a compound forms. Chemical bonds are broken, and atoms are rearranged. New bonds form water, a compound with properties very different from those of the original gases.

A compound always has the same chemical formula

The chemical formula for water is H_2O, and that of table sugar is $C_{12}H_{22}O_{11}$. The salt you season your food with has the chemical formula NaCl. A chemical formula shows the types and numbers of atoms or ions making up the simplest unit of the compound.

There is another important way that compounds and mixtures are different. Compounds are always made of the same elements in the same proportion. A molecule of water, for example, is always made of two hydrogen atoms and one oxygen atom. This is true for all water, no matter how much water there is or where it is found. That means water frozen in a comet in outer space and water at 37°C (98.6°F) inside the cells of your body both have the same chemical formula—H_2O.

Figure 4-2
(A) Placing a lit candle under a balloon containing hydrogen gas and oxygen gas causes the balloon to melt, releasing the mixed gases. (B) The mixed gases are ignited by the candle flame, and water is produced.

▶ **chemical bond** the attractive force that holds atoms or ions together

Clay has a layered structure of silicon, oxygen, aluminum, and hydrogen atoms. Artists can mold wet clay into any shape because water molecules let the layers slide over one another. When clay dries, water evaporates and the layers can no longer slide. To keep the dry, crumbly clay from breaking apart, artists change the structure of the clay by heating it. The atoms in one layer bond to atoms in the layers above and below. When this happens, the clay hardens, and the artist's work is permanently set.

Making the Connection

1. Think of other substances that can be shaped when they are wet and that "set" when they are dried or heated.
2. Write a paragraph about one of these substances, and explain why it has these properties. Report your findings to the class.

▶ **chemical structure** the arrangement of bonded atoms or ions within a substance

▶ **bond length** the average distance between the nuclei of two bonded atoms

▶ **bond angle** the angle formed by two bonds to the same atom

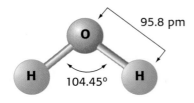

Figure 4-3
The ball-and-stick model in this figure is a giant representation of one molecule of water. A picometer (pm) is equal to 1×10^{-12} m.

Chemical structure shows the bonding within a compound

Although water's chemical formula tells us what atoms it is made of, it doesn't reveal anything about the way these atoms are connected. You can see how a compound's atoms or ions are connected by its **chemical structure.** The structure of a compound can be compared to that of a rope. The kinds of fibers used to make a rope and the way the fibers are intertwined determine how strong the rope is. Similarly, the atoms in a compound and the way the atoms are arranged determine many of the compound's properties.

Two terms are used to specify the positions of atoms relative to one another in a compound. A **bond length** gives the distance between the nuclei of two bonded atoms. And when a compound has three or more atoms, **bond angles** tell how these atoms are oriented. **Figure 4-3** shows the chemical structure of a water molecule. You can see that the way hydrogen and oxygen atoms bond to form water looks more like a boomerang than a straight line.

Models of Compounds

Figure 4-3 is a ball-and-stick model of a water molecule. Ball-and-stick models, as well as other kinds of models, help you "see" a compound's structure by showing you how the atoms or ions are arranged in the compound.

Some models give you an idea of bond lengths and angles

In the ball-and-stick model of water shown in **Figure 4-3,** the atoms are represented by balls. The bonds that hold the atoms together are represented by sticks. Although bonds between atoms aren't really as rigid as sticks, this model makes it easy to see the bonds and the angles they form in a compound.

Structural formulas can also show the structures of compounds. Notice how water's structural formula, which is shown below, is a lot like its ball-and-stick model. The difference is that only chemical symbols are used to represent the atoms.

Space-filling models show the space occupied by atoms

Figure 4-4 shows another way chemists picture a water molecule. It is called a space-filling model because it shows the space that is occupied by the oxygen and hydrogen atoms. The problem with this model is that it is harder to "see" bond lengths and angles.

How Does Structure Affect Properties?

Some compounds, such as the quartz found in many rocks, exist as a large network of bonded atoms. Other compounds, such as table salt, are also large networks, but of bonded positive and negative ions. Still other compounds, such as water and sugar, are made of many separate molecules. Different structures give these compounds different properties.

Compounds with network structures are strong solids

Quartz is sometimes found in the form of beautiful crystals, as shown in **Figure 4-5.** Quartz has the chemical formula SiO_2, and so does the less pure form of quartz, sand. **Figure 4-5** shows that every silicon atom in quartz is bonded to four oxygen atoms. The bonds that hold these atoms together are very strong. All of the Si—O—Si and O—Si—O bond angles are the same. That is, each one is 109.5°. This arrangement continues throughout the substance, holding the silicon and oxygen atoms together in a very strong, rigid structure.

This is why rocks containing quartz are hard and inflexible solids. Silicon and oxygen atoms in sand have a similar arrangement. It takes a lot of energy to break the strong bonds between silicon and oxygen atoms in quartz and sand. That's why the melting point and boiling point of quartz and sand is so high, as shown in **Table 4-1.**

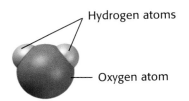

Figure 4-4
This space-filling model of water shows that the two hydrogen atoms take up much less space than the oxygen atom.

internetconnect

SC*LINKS*
NSTA

TOPIC: Structures of substances
GO TO: www.scilinks.org
KEYWORD: HK1042

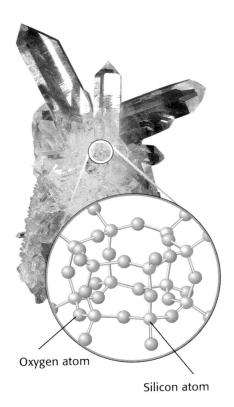

Oxygen atom

Silicon atom

Figure 4-5
Quartz and sand are made of silicon and oxygen atoms bonded in a strong, rigid structure.

Table 4-1 **Some Compounds with Network Structures**

Compound	State (25°C)	Melting point (°C)	Boiling point (°C)
Silicon dioxide, SiO_2 (quartz, sand)	Solid	1700	2230
Magnesium fluoride, MgF_2	Solid	1261	2239
Sodium chloride, NaCl (table salt)	Solid	801	1413

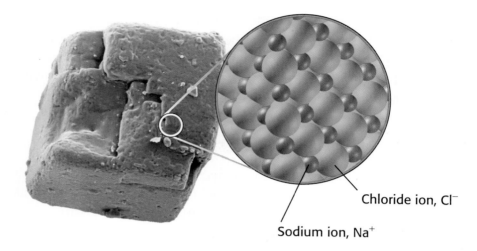

Figure 4-6
Each grain of table salt, or sodium chloride, is composed of a tightly packed network of Na⁺ ions and Cl⁻ ions.

Chloride ion, Cl⁻

Sodium ion, Na⁺

Some networks are made of bonded ions

Like some quartz, table salt—sodium chloride—is found in the form of regularly shaped crystals. Crystals of sodium chloride are cube shaped. Like quartz and sand, sodium chloride is made of a repeating network connected by strong bonds. But the network is not made of atoms. Instead, sodium chloride is made of a network of tightly packed, positively charged sodium ions and negatively charged chloride ions, as shown in **Figure 4-6.** The strong attractions between the oppositely charged ions causes table salt and other similar compounds to have high melting points and boiling points, as shown in **Table 4-1.**

Some compounds are made of molecules

Salt and sugar are both white solids you can eat, but their structures are very different. Unlike salt, sugar is made of molecules. A molecule of sugar, shown in **Figure 4-7,** is made of carbon, hydrogen, and oxygen atoms joined by bonds. Molecules of sugar do attract each other to form crystals. But these attractions are much weaker than those that hold bonded carbon, hydrogen, and oxygen atoms together to make a sugar molecule.

We breathe nitrogen, N_2, oxygen, O_2, and carbon dioxide, CO_2, every day. All three substances are colorless, odorless gases made of molecules. Within each molecule, the atoms are so strongly attracted to one another that they are bonded. But the molecules of each gas have very little attraction for one another. Because the molecules of these gases are not very attracted to one another, they spread out as much as they can. That is why gases can take up a lot of space.

Figure 4-7
Sugar is made of molecules.

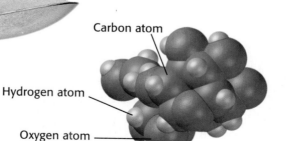

Carbon atom

Hydrogen atom

Oxygen atom

Table 4-2 Comparing Compounds Made of Molecules

Compound	State (25°C)	Melting point (°C)	Boiling point (°C)
Sugar, $C_{12}H_{22}O_{11}$	Solid	185–186	——
Water, H_2O	Liquid	0	100
Dihydrogen sulfide, H_2S	Gas	−85	−60

The strength of attractions between molecules

Compare sugar, water, and dihydrogen sulfide in **Table 4-2.** Although all three compounds are made of molecules, their properties are very different. Sugar is a solid, water is a liquid, and dihydrogen sulfide is a gas. That means that sugar molecules have the strongest attractions for each other, followed by water molecules. Dihydrogen sulfide molecules have the weakest attractions for each other. The fact that sugar and water have such different properties probably doesn't surprise you. Their chemical structures are not at all alike. But what about water and dihydrogen sulfide, which do have similar chemical structures?

Inquiry

Which melts more easily, sugar or salt?

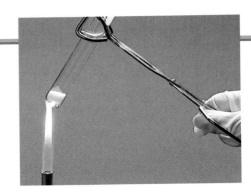

Materials
- ✔ table salt
- ✔ 2 test tubes
- ✔ table sugar
- ✔ stopwatch
- ✔ Bunsen burner
- ✔ tongs

Procedure

SAFETY CAUTION Wear safety goggles and gloves. Tie back long hair, confine loose clothing, and use tongs to handle hot glassware. When heating a substance in a test tube, always point the open end of the test tube away from yourself and others.

1. Use your knowledge of structures to make a hypothesis about whether sugar or salt will melt more easily.
2. To test your hypothesis, place about 1 cm³ of sugar in a test tube.
3. Using tongs, position the test tube with sugar over the flame, as shown in the figure at right. Move the test tube back and forth slowly over the flame. Use a stopwatch to measure the time it takes for the sugar to melt.
4. Repeat steps 2 and 3 with salt. If your sample does not melt within 1 minute, remove it from the flame.

Analysis

1. Which compound is easier to melt? Was your hypothesis right?
2. How can you relate your results to the structure of each compound?

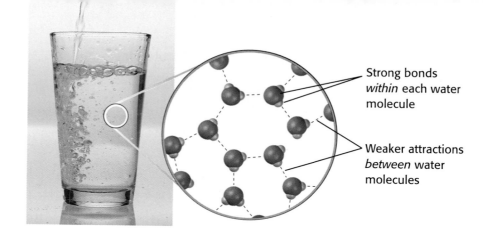

Figure 4-8
Dotted lines indicate the *inter*molecular attractions that occur *between* water molecules, which is often referred to as "hydrogen bonding." Water is a liquid at room temperature because of these attractions.

Strong bonds *within* each water molecule

Weaker attractions *between* water molecules

The higher melting and boiling points of water suggest that water molecules attract each other more than dihydrogen sulfide molecules do. **Figure 4-8** shows how an oxygen atom of one water molecule is attracted to a hydrogen atom of a neighboring water molecule. Water molecules attract each other, but these attractions are not as strong as the bonds holding oxygen and hydrogen atoms together within a molecule.

SECTION 4.1 REVIEW

SUMMARY

- ▶ Atoms or ions in compounds are joined by chemical bonds.

- ▶ A compound's chemical formula shows which atoms or ions it is made of.

- ▶ A model represents a compound's structure visually.

- ▶ Substances with network structures are usually strong solids with high melting and boiling points.

- ▶ Substances made of molecules have lower melting and boiling points.

- ▶ Whether a molecular substance is a solid, a liquid, or a gas depends on the attractions between its molecules at room temperature.

CHECK YOUR UNDERSTANDING

1. **Classify** the following substances as mixtures or compounds:
   a. air
   b. CO
   c. SnF_2
   d. pure water

2. **Explain** why silver iodide, AgI, a compound used in photography, has a much higher melting point than vanillin, $C_8H_8O_3$, a sweet-smelling compound used in flavorings.

3. **Draw** a ball-and-stick model of a boron trifluoride, BF_3, molecule. In this molecule, a boron atom is attached to three fluorine atoms. Each F—B—F bond angle is 120°, and all B—F bonds are the same length.

4. **Predict** which molecules have a greater attraction for each other, C_3H_8O molecules in liquid rubbing alcohol or CH_4 molecules in methane gas.

5. **Explain** why glass, which is made mainly of SiO_2, is often used to make cookware. (**Hint:** What properties does SiO_2 have because of its structure?)

6. **Predict** whether a compound made of molecules that melts at −77.7°C is a solid, a liquid, or a gas at room temperature.

7. **Creative Thinking** A picometer (pm) is equal to 1×10^{-12} m. O—H bond lengths in water are 95.8 pm, while S—H bond lengths in dihydrogen sulfide are 135 pm. Why are S—H bond lengths longer than O—H bond lengths? (**Hint:** Which is larger, a sulfur atom or an oxygen atom?)

Ionic and Covalent Bonding

▶ Explain why atoms sometimes join to form bonds.
▶ Explain why some atoms transfer their valence electrons to form ionic bonds, while other atoms share valence electrons to form covalent bonds.
▶ Differentiate between ionic, covalent, and metallic bonds.
▶ Compare the properties of substances with different types of bonds.

▶ **KEY TERMS**
ionic bond
metallic bond
covalent bond
polyatomic ion

When two atoms join, a bond forms. You have already seen how bonded atoms form many substances. Because there are so many different substances, it makes sense that atoms can bond in different ways.

What Holds Bonded Atoms Together?

Three different kinds of bonds describe the way atoms bond in most substances. In many of the models you have seen so far, the bonds that hold atoms together are represented by sticks. But what bonds atoms in a real molecule?

The outermost energy level of a bonded atom is full of electrons

Atoms bond when their valence electrons interact. You learned in Chapter 3 that atoms with full outermost energy levels are less reactive than atoms with only partly filled outermost energy levels. Generally, atoms join to form bonds so that each atom has a full outermost energy level. When this happens, each atom has an electronic structure similar to that of a noble gas.

When two hydrogen atoms bond, as shown in **Figure 4-9,** the positive nucleus of one hydrogen atom attracts the negative electron of the other hydrogen atom, and vice versa. This pulls

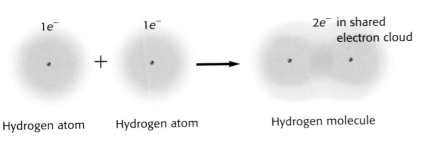

1e⁻   1e⁻   2e⁻ in shared electron cloud

Hydrogen atom   Hydrogen atom   Hydrogen molecule

Figure 4-9
When two hydrogen atoms are very close together, their electron clouds overlap, and a bond forms. The two electrons of the hydrogen molecule that forms are in the shared electron cloud.

Amderican scientist Linus Pauling studied how electrons are arranged within atoms. He also studied the ways that atoms share and exchange electrons. In 1954, he won the Nobel Prize in chemistry for his valuable research.

Later, Pauling fought to ban nuclear weapons testing. Pauling was able to convince more than 11 000 scientists from 49 countries to sign a petition to stop nuclear weapons testing. Pauling won the Nobel Peace Prize in 1962 for his efforts. A year later, a treaty outlawing nuclear weapons testing in the atmosphere, in outer space, and underwater went into effect.

Making the Connection

1. *Electronegativity* is an idea first thought of by Pauling. It tells how easily an atom accepts electrons. Which is more electronegative, a fluorine atom or a calcium atom? Why?

2. Nuclear weapons testing is harmful to humans because of the resulting radiation. Write a paragraph explaining how high levels of radiation can affect your body.

WRITING SKILL

▶ **ionic bond** a bond formed by the attraction between oppositely charged ions

the two atoms closer together. Soon their electron clouds cross each other. The shared electron cloud of the molecule that forms has two electrons (one from each atom). A hydrogen molecule has an electronic structure similar to the noble gas helium. The molecule will not fall apart unless enough energy is added to break the bond.

Bonds can bend and stretch without breaking

Although some bonds are stronger and more rigid than others, all bonds behave more like flexible springs than like sticks, as **Figure 4-10** shows. The atoms move back and forth a little and their nuclei do not always stay the same distance apart. In fact, most reported bond lengths are averages of these distances. Although bonds are not rigid, they still hold atoms together tightly.

Ionic Bonds

Ionic bonds are formed between oppositely charged ions. Atoms of metal elements, such as sodium and calcium, form the positively charged ions. Atoms of nonmetal elements, such as chlorine and oxygen, form the negatively charged ions.

Ionic bonds are formed by the transfer of electrons

Some atoms do not share electrons to fill their outermost energy levels completely. Instead, they transfer electrons. One of the atoms gains the electrons that the other atom loses. Both ions that form usually have filled outermost energy levels. The result is a positive ion and a negative ion, such as the Na^+ ion and the Cl^- ion in sodium chloride.

These oppositely charged ions attract each other and form an ionic bond. Each positive sodium ion attracts several negative chloride ions. These negative chloride ions attract more positive sodium ions, and so on. Soon a network of these bonded ions forms a crystal of table salt.

Figure 4-10
Chemists often use a solid bar to show a bond between two atoms, but real bonds are flexible, like stiff springs.

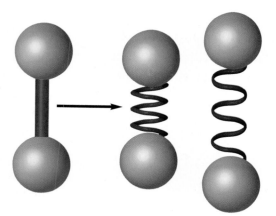

Ionic compounds are in the form of networks, not molecules

Because sodium chloride is a network of ions, it does not make sense to talk about "a molecule of NaCl." In fact, every sodium ion is next to six chloride ions, as shown in **Figure 4-6** on page 112. Instead, chemists talk about the smallest ratio of ions in ionic compounds. Sodium chloride's chemical formula, NaCl, tells us that there is one Na^+ ion for every Cl^- ion, or a 1:1 ratio of ions. This means the compound has a total charge of zero. One Na^+ ion and one Cl^- ion make up a *formula unit* of NaCl.

Not every ionic compound has the same ratio of ions as sodium chloride. An example is calcium fluoride, which is shown in **Figure 4-11.** The ratio of Ca^{2+} ions to F^- ions in calcium fluoride must be 1:2 to make a neutral compound. That is why the chemical formula for calcium fluoride is CaF_2.

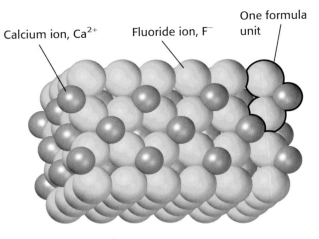

Calcium ion, Ca^{2+} Fluoride ion, F^- One formula unit

Figure 4-11
There are twice as many fluoride ions as calcium ions in a crystal of calcium fluoride, CaF_2. So one Ca^{2+} ion and two F^- ions make up one formula unit of the compound.

When melted or dissolved in water, ionic compounds conduct electricity

Electric current is moving charges. Solid ionic compounds do not conduct electricity because the charged ions are locked into place, causing the melting points of ionic compounds to be very high—often well above 300°C. But if you dissolve an ionic compound in water or melt it, it can conduct electricity. That's because the ions are then free to move, as shown in **Figure 4-12.**

Sodium ion, Na^+

Chloride ion, Cl^-

Water molecule, H_2O

Figure 4-12
Like other ionic compounds, sodium chloride conducts electricity when it is dissolved in water.

Quick ACTIVITY

Building a Close-Packed Structure

Copper and other metals have close-packed structures. This means their atoms are packed very tightly together. In this activity, you will build a close-packed structure using ping pong balls.

1. Place three books flat on a table so that their edges form a triangle.
2. Fill the triangular space between the books with the spherical "atoms." Adjust the books so that the atoms make a one-layer, close-packed pattern, as shown at right.
3. Build additional layers on top of the first layer. How many other atoms does each atom touch? Where have you seen other arrangements that are similar to this one?

internet connect

SCi LINKS
NSTA

TOPIC: Chemical bonding
GO TO: www.scilinks.org
KEYWORD: HK1043

 metallic bond a bond formed by the attraction between positively charged metal ions and the electrons around them

Metallic Bonds

Metals, like copper, shown in **Figure 4-13,** can conduct electricity when they are solid. Metals are also flexible, so they can bend and stretch without breaking. Copper, for example, can be hammered flat into sheets or stretched into very thin wire. What kind of bonds give copper these properties?

Electrons move freely between metal atoms

The atoms in metals like copper form **metallic bonds.** The attraction between one atom's nucleus and a neighboring atom's electrons packs the atoms closely together. This close packing causes the outermost energy levels of the atoms to overlap, as shown in **Figure 4-13.** Therefore, electrons are free to move from atom to atom. This model explains why metals conduct electricity so well. Metals are flexible because the atoms can slide past each other without their bonds breaking.

Figure 4-13
Copper is a flexible metal that melts at 1083°C and boils at 2567°C. Copper conducts electricity because electrons can move freely between atoms.

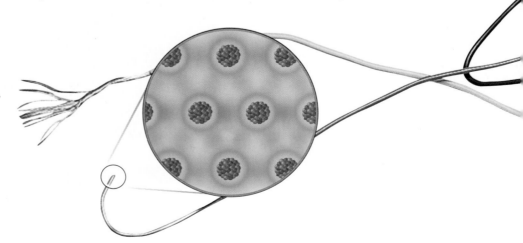

Covalent Bonds

Compounds that are made of molecules, like water and sugar, have **covalent bonds**. Compounds existing as networks of bonded atoms, such as silicon dioxide, are also held together by covalent bonds. Covalent bonds are often formed between nonmetal atoms.

Covalent compounds can be solids, liquids, or gases. Except for silicon dioxide and other compounds with network structures, most covalent compounds have a low melting point— usually below 300°C. In compounds that are made of molecules, the molecules are free to move when the compound is dissolved in water or is melted. But these molecules remain intact and do not conduct electricity because they are not charged.

Atoms joined by covalent bonds share electrons

Some atoms, like the hydrogen atoms in **Figure 4-9,** on page 115, bond to form molecules. **Figure 4-14A** shows how two chlorine atoms bond to form a chlorine molecule, Cl_2. Before bonding, each atom has seven electrons in its outermost energy level. The atoms don't transfer electrons to one another because each needs to gain an electron. If each atom shares one electron with the other atom, then both atoms together have a full outermost energy level. That is, both atoms together have eight valence electrons. The way electrons are shared depends on which atoms are sharing the electrons. Two chlorine atoms are exactly alike. When they bond, electrons are equally attracted to the positive nucleus of each atom. Bonds like this one, in which electrons are shared equally, are called *nonpolar covalent bonds*.

The structural formula in **Figure 4-14B** shows how the chlorine atoms are connected in the molecule that forms. A single line drawn between two atoms indicates that the atoms share two electrons and are joined by one covalent bond.

> ▶ **covalent bond** a bond formed when atoms share one or more pairs of electrons

VOCABULARY *Skills Tip*

Covalent bonds *form when atoms share pairs of* valence *electrons.*

Figure 4-14

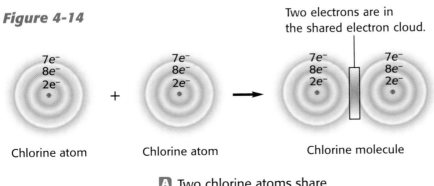

Two electrons are in the shared electron cloud.

Chlorine atom + Chlorine atom → Chlorine molecule

A Two chlorine atoms share electrons equally to form a *nonpolar covalent bond.*

Each chlorine atom has six electrons that are not shared.

One covalent bond (two shared electrons)

B A single line drawn between two chlorine atoms shows that the atoms share two electrons. Dots represent electrons that are not involved in bonding.

Oxygen
Four electrons are in the shared electron cloud.

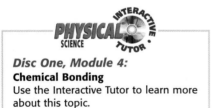

$6e^-$ $6e^-$
$2e^-$ $2e^-$

$:\ddot{O}=\ddot{O}:$

Double covalent bond

Nitrogen
Six electrons are in the shared electron cloud.

$5e^-$ $5e^-$
$2e^-$ $2e^-$

$:N\equiv N:$

Triple covalent bond

Figure 4-15
The elements oxygen and nitrogen have covalent bonds. Electrons not involved in bonding are represented by dots.

▶ **polyatomic ion** an ion made of two or more atoms that are covalently bonded and that act like a single ion

PHYSICAL SCIENCE *INTERACTIVE TUTOR*

Disc One, Module 4:
Chemical Bonding
Use the Interactive Tutor to learn more about this topic.

Atoms may share more than one pair of electrons

Figure 4-15 shows covalent bonding in oxygen gas, O_2 and nitrogen gas, N_2. Notice that the bond joining two oxygen atoms is represented by two lines. This means that two pairs of electrons (a total of four electrons) are shared to form a double covalent bond.

The bond joining two nitrogen atoms is represented by three lines. Two nitrogen atoms form a triple covalent bond by sharing three pairs of electrons (a total of six electrons).

The bond between two nitrogen atoms is stronger than the bond between two oxygen atoms. That's because more energy is needed to break a triple bond than to break a double bond. Triple and double bonds are also shorter than single bonds.

Atoms do not always share electrons equally

When two different atoms share electrons, the electrons are not shared equally. The shared electrons are attracted to the nucleus of one atom more than the other. An unequal sharing of electrons forms a *polar covalent bond*.

Usually, electrons are more attracted to atoms of elements that are located farther to the right and closer to the top of the periodic table. The shading in **Figure 4-16** shows that the shared electrons in the ammonia gas, NH_3, in the headspace of this container, are closer to the nitrogen atom than they are to the hydrogen atoms.

Polyatomic Ions

Until now, we have talked about compounds that have either ionic or covalent bonds. But some compounds have both ionic and covalent bonds. Such compounds are made of **polyatomic ions,** which are groups of covalently bonded atoms that have either lost or gained electrons. A polyatomic ion acts the same as the ions you have already encountered.

Ammonia

80296-01 500 mL

Ammonia Solution
(Household), Science Grade

GENERAL STORAGE

Science Kit & Boreal Laboratories

Figure 4-16
The darker shading around the nitrogen atom as compared to the hydrogen atoms shows that electrons are more attracted to nitrogen atoms than to hydrogen atoms. So the bonds in ammonia are *polar covalent bonds.*

There are many polyatomic ions

Many compounds you use either contain or are made from polyatomic ions. For example, your toothpaste may contain baking soda. Another name for baking soda is sodium hydrogen carbonate, $NaHCO_3$. Hydrogen carbonate, HCO_3^- is a polyatomic ion. Sodium carbonate, Na_2CO_3, is often used to make soaps and other cleaners and contains the carbonate ion, CO_3^{2-}. Sodium hydroxide, $NaOH$, has hydroxide ions, OH^-, and is also used to make soaps. A few of these polyatomic ions are shown in **Figure 4-17.**

Oppositely charged polyatomic ions, like other ions, can bond to form compounds. Ammonium nitrate, NH_4NO_3, and ammonium sulfate, $(NH_4)_2SO_4$, both contain positively charged ammonium ions, NH_4^+. Nitrate, NO_3^-, and sulfate, SO_4^{2-}, are both negatively charged polyatomic ions.

Parentheses group the atoms of a polyatomic ion

You might be wondering why the chemical formula for ammonium sulfate is written as $(NH_4)_2SO_4$ instead of as $N_2H_8SO_4$. The parentheses around the ammonium ion are there to remind you that it acts like a single ion. Parentheses group the atoms of the ammonium ion together to show that the subscript 2 applies to the whole ion. There are two ammonium ions for every sulfate ion. Parentheses are not needed in compounds like ammonium nitrate, NH_4NO_3, because there is a 1:1 ratio of ions.

Always keep in mind that a polyatomic ion's charge applies not only to the last atom in the formula but to the entire ion. The carbonate ion, CO_3^{2-}, has a 2– charge. This means that CO_3, not just the oxygen atom, has the negative charge.

Some polyatomic anion names relate to their oxygen content

You may have noticed that many polyatomic anions are made of oxygen. Most of their names end with *-ite* or *-ate*. These endings do not tell you exactly how many oxygen atoms are in the ion, but they do follow a pattern. Think about sulfate (SO_4^{2-}) and sulfite (SO_3^{2-}), nitrate (NO_3^-) and nitrite (NO_2^-), and chlorate (ClO_3^-) and chlorite (ClO_2^-). The charge of each ion pair is the same. But notice how the ions have different numbers of oxygen atoms. Their names also have different endings.

An *-ate* ending is used to name the ion with one more oxygen atom. The name of the ion with one less oxygen ends in *-ite*. **Table 4-3,** on the next page, lists several common polyatomic anions. As you look at this table, you'll notice that not all of the anions listed have names that end in *-ite* or *-ate*. That's because some polyatomic anions, like hydroxide (OH^-) and cyanide (CN^-), are not named according to any general rules.

Hydroxide ion, OH^-

Carbonate ion, CO_3^{2-}

Ammonium ion, NH_4^+

Figure 4-17
The hydroxide ion (OH^-), carbonate ion (CO_3^{2-}), and ammonium ion (NH_4^+) are all polyatomic ions.

INTEGRATING

SPACE SCIENCE
Most of the ions and molecules in space are not the same as those that are found on Earth or in Earth's atmosphere. C_3H, C_6H_2, and HCO^+ have all been found in space. So far, no one has been able to figure out how these unusual molecules and ions form in space.

Table 4-3 **Some Common Polyatomic Anions**

Ion name	Ion formula	Ion name	Ion formula
Acetate ion	$CH_3CO_2^-$	Hydroxide ion	OH^-
Carbonate ion	CO_3^{2-}	Hypochlorite ion	ClO^-
Chlorate ion	ClO_3^-	Nitrate ion	NO_3^-
Chlorite ion	ClO_2^-	Nitrite ion	NO_2^-
Cyanide ion	CN^-	Phosphate ion	PO_4^{3-}
Hydrogen carbonate ion	HCO_3^-	Phosphite ion	PO_3^{3-}
Hydrogen sulfate ion	HSO_4^-	Sulfate ion	SO_4^{2-}
Hydrogen sulfite ion	HSO_3^-	Sulfite ion	SO_3^{2-}

SECTION 4.2 REVIEW

SUMMARY

▶ Atoms bond when their valence electrons interact.

▶ Cations and anions attract each other to form ionic bonds.

▶ When ionic compounds are melted or dissolved in water, moving ions can conduct electricity.

▶ Atoms in metals are joined by metallic bonds.

▶ Metals conduct electricity because electrons can move from atom to atom.

▶ Covalent bonds form when atoms share electron pairs. Electrons may be shared equally or unequally.

▶ Polyatomic ions are covalently bonded atoms that have either lost or gained electrons. Their behavior resembles that of simple ions.

CHECK YOUR UNDERSTANDING

1. **Determine** if the following compounds are likely to have ionic or covalent bonds.
   a. magnesium oxide, MgO
   b. strontium chloride, $SrCl_2$
   c. ozone, O_3
   d. methanol, CH_4O

2. **Identify** which two of the following substances will conduct electricity, and explain why.
   a. aluminum foil
   b. sugar, $C_{12}H_{22}O_{11}$, dissolved in water
   c. potassium hydroxide, KOH, dissolved in water

3. **Draw** the structural formula for acetylene. Atoms bond in the order HCCH. Carbon and hydrogen atoms share two electrons, and each carbon atom must have a total of four bonds. How many electrons do the carbon atoms share?

4. **Predict** whether a silver coin can conduct electricity. What kind of bonds does silver have?

5. **Describe** how it is possible for calcium hydroxide, $Ca(OH)_2$, to have both ionic and covalent bonds.

6. **Explain** why electrons are shared equally in ozone, O_3, and unequally in carbon dioxide, CO_2.

7. **Analyze** whether dinitrogen tetroxide, N_2O_4, has covalent or ionic bonds. Describe how you reached this conclusion.

8. **Critical Thinking** *Bond energy* measures the energy per mole of a substance needed to break a bond. Which element has the greater bond energy, oxygen or nitrogen? (**Hint:** Which element has more bonds?)

Compound Names and Formulas

▶ Name simple ionic and covalent compounds.

▶ Predict the charge of a transition metal cation in an ionic compound.

▶ Write chemical formulas for simple ionic compounds.

▶ Distinguish a covalent compound's empirical formula from its molecular formula.

KEY TERMS

empirical formula
molecular formula

J ust like elements, compounds have names that distinguish them from other compounds. Although the compounds BaF_2 and BF_3 may have similar chemical formulas, they have very different names. BaF_2 is *barium fluoride*, and BF_3 is *boron trifluoride*. When talking about these compounds, there is little chance for confusion. You can see that the names of these compounds reflect the two elements from which they are formed.

internet connect

SCI*LINKS*

NSTA

TOPIC: Naming compounds
GO TO: www.scilinks.org
KEYWORD: HK1044

Naming Ionic Compounds

Ionic compounds are formed by the strong attractions between cations and anions, as described in Section 4.2. Both ions are important to the compound's structure, so it makes sense that both ions are included in the name.

Names of ionic compounds include the ions of which they are composed

In many cases, the name of the cation is just like the name of the element from which it is made. You have already seen this for many cations. For example, when an atom of the element *sodium* loses an electron, a *sodium ion*, Na^+, forms. Similarly, when a *calcium* atom loses two electrons, a *calcium ion*, Ca^{2+}, forms. And when an *aluminum* atom loses three electrons, an *aluminum ion*, Al^{3+}, forms. These and other common cations are listed in **Table 4-4.** Notice how ions of Group 1 elements have a 1+ charge and ions of Group 2 elements have a 2+ charge.

Table 4-4 **Some Common Cations**

Ion name and symbol	Ion charge
Cesium ion, Cs^+	1+
Lithium ion, Li^+	
Potassium ion, K^+	
Rubidium ion, Rb^+	
Sodium ion, Na^+	
Barium ion, Ba^{2+}	2+
Beryllium ion, Be^{2+}	
Calcium ion, Ca^{2+}	
Magnesium ion, Mg^{2+}	
Strontium ion, Sr^{2+}	
Aluminum ion, Al^{3+}	3+

Table 4-5 Some Common Anions

Element name and symbol	Ion name and symbol	Ion charge
Fluorine, F	Fluoride ion, F^-	1–
Chlorine, Cl	Chloride ion, Cl^-	
Bromine, Br	Bromide ion, Br^-	
Iodine, I	Iodide ion, I^-	
Oxygen, O	Oxide ion, O^{2-}	2–
Sulfur, S	Sulfide ion, S^{2-}	
Nitrogen, N	Nitride ion, N^{3-}	3–

An anion that is made of one element has a name similar to the element. The only difference is the name's ending. **Table 4-5** lists some common anions and shows how they are named. Just like most cations, anions of elements in the same group of the periodic table have the same charge.

NaF is made of sodium ions, Na^+, and fluoride ions, F^-. Therefore, its name is *sodium fluoride*. **Figure 4-18** shows how calcium chloride, another ionic compound, gets its name.

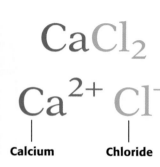

Figure 4-18
Ionic compounds are named for their positive and negative ions.

Some cation names must show their charge

Think about the compounds FeO and Fe_2O_3. According to the rules you have learned so far, both of these compounds would be named *iron oxide*, even though they are not the same compound. Fe_2O_3, the main component of rust, is a reddish brown solid that melts at 1565°C. FeO, on the other hand, is a black powder that melts at 1420°C. These different properties tell us that they are different compounds and should have different names.

Iron is a transition metal. Transition metals may form several cations—each with a different charge. A few of these cations are listed in **Table 4-6.** The charge of the iron cation in Fe_2O_3 is different from the charge of the iron cation in FeO. In cases like this, the cation name must be followed by a Roman numeral in parentheses. The Roman numeral shows the cation's charge. Fe_2O_3 is made of Fe^{3+} ions, so it is named *iron(III) oxide*. FeO is made of Fe^{2+} ions, so it is named *iron(II) oxide*.

Table 4-6 Some Transition Metal Cations

Ion name	Ion symbol	Ion name	Ion symbol
Copper(I) ion	Cu^+	Chromium(II) ion	Cr^{2+}
Copper(II) ion	Cu^{2+}	Chromium(III) ion	Cr^{3+}
Iron(II) ion	Fe^{2+}	Cadmium(II) ion	Cd^{2+}
Iron(III) ion	Fe^{3+}	Titanium(II) ion	Ti^{2+}
Nickel(II) ion	Ni^{2+}	Titanium(III) ion	Ti^{3+}
Nickel(III) ion	Ni^{3+}	Titanium(IV) ion	Ti^{4+}

Determining the charge of a transition metal cation

How can you tell that the iron ion in Fe_2O_3 has a charge of 3+? Like all compounds, ionic compounds have a total charge of zero. This means that the total positive charges must equal the total negative charges. An oxide ion, O^{2-}, has a charge of 2–. Three of them have a total charge of 6–. That means the total positive charge in the formula must be 6+. For two iron ions to have a total charge of 6+, each ion must have a charge of 3+.

Writing Formulas for Ionic Compounds

You have seen how to determine the charge of each ion in a compound if you are given the compound's formula. Following a similar process, you can determine the chemical formula for a compound if you are given its name.

Math Skills

Writing Ionic Formulas What is the chemical formula for aluminum fluoride?

1 **List the symbols for each ion.**
Symbol for an aluminum ion from **Table 4-4**: Al^{3+}
Symbol for a fluoride ion from **Table 4-5**: F^-

2 **Write the symbols for the ions with the cation first.**
$Al^{3+}F^-$

3 **Find the least common multiple of the ions' charges.**
The least common multiple of 3 and 1 is 3. To make a neutral compound, you need a total of three positive charges and three negative charges.
To get three positive charges: you need only one Al^{3+} ion because $1 \times 3+ = 3+$.
To get three negative charges: you need three F^- ions because $3 \times 1- = 3-$.

4 **Write the chemical formula, indicating with subscripts how many of each ion are needed to make a neutral compound.**
AlF_3

Practice HINT

Once you have determined a chemical formula, always check the formula to see if it makes a neutral compound. For this example, the aluminum ion has a charge of 3+. The fluoride ion has a charge of only 1–, but there are three of them for a total of 3–.

$(3-) + (3+) = 0$, so the charges balance, and the formula is neutral.

Practice

Writing Ionic Formulas
Write formulas for the following ionic compounds.
1. lithium oxide
2. beryllium chloride
3. titanium(III) nitride
4. cobalt(III) hydroxide

Naming Covalent Compounds

Covalent compounds, like SiO_2 (silicon dioxide) and CO_2 (carbon dioxide), are named using different rules than those used to name ionic compounds.

Numerical prefixes are used to name covalent compounds of two elements

For two-element covalent compounds, numerical prefixes tell how many atoms of each element are in the molecule. **Table 4-7** lists some of these prefixes. If there is only one atom of the first element, it does not get a prefix. Whichever element is farther to the right in the periodic table is named second and ends in *-ide*.

There are one boron atom and three fluorine atoms in *boron trifluoride*, BF_3. *Dinitrogen tetroxide*, N_2O_4, is made of two nitrogen atoms and four oxygen atoms, as shown in **Figure 4-19.** Notice how the *a* in *tetra* is dropped to make the name easier to say.

Chemical Formulas for Covalent Compounds

Emeralds, shown in **Figure 4-20,** are made of a mineral called beryl. The chemical formula for beryl is $Be_3Al_2Si_6O_{18}$. But how did people determine this formula? It took some experiments. Chemical formulas like this one were determined by first measuring the mass of each element in the compound.

A compound's simplest formula is its empirical formula

Once the mass of each element in a sample of the compound is known, scientists can calculate the compound's **empirical formula,** or simplest formula. An empirical formula tells us the smallest whole-number ratio of atoms that are in a compound. Formulas for most ionic compounds are empirical formulas.

Covalent compounds have empirical formulas, too. The empirical formula for water is H_2O. It tells you that the ratio of hydrogen atoms to oxygen atoms is 2:1. Scientists have to analyze unknown compounds to determine their empirical formulas.

Table 4-7
Prefixes Used to Name Covalent Compounds

Number of atoms	Prefix
1	*Mono-*
2	*Di-*
3	*Tri-*
4	*Tetra-*
5	*Penta-*
6	*Hexa-*
7	*Hepta-*
8	*Octa-*
9	*Nona-*
10	*Deca-*

Figure 4-19
One molecule of *di*nitrogen *tetr*oxide has *two* nitrogen atoms and *four* oxygen atoms.

$$N_2O_4$$
Dinitrogen tetroxide

▶ **empirical formula**
the simplest chemical formula of a compound that tells the smallest whole-number ratio of atoms in the compound

Figure 4-20
Emerald gemstones are cut from the mineral beryl. Very tiny amounts of chromium(III) oxide impurity in the gemstones gives them their beautiful green color.

For example, if a 142 g sample of an unknown compound contains only the elements phosphorus and oxygen and is found to contain 62 g of P and 80 g of O, its empirical formula is easy to calculate. This process is shown in **Figure 4-21.**

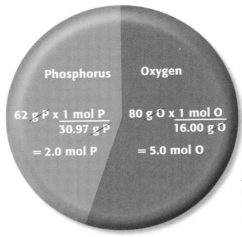

Exactly 142 g of Unknown Compound

Phosphorus

$62 \text{ g P} \times \dfrac{1 \text{ mol P}}{30.97 \text{ g P}}$

$= 2.0 \text{ mol P}$

Oxygen

$80 \text{ g O} \times \dfrac{1 \text{ mol O}}{16.00 \text{ g O}}$

$= 5.0 \text{ mol O}$

$\text{Empirical formula} = P_2O_5$

Figure 4-21
Once you determine the mass of each element in a compound, you can calculate the amount of each element in moles. The empirical formula for the compound is the ratio of these amounts.

Different compounds can have the same empirical formula

It's possible for several compounds to have the same empirical formula because empirical formulas only represent a ratio of atoms. Formaldehyde, acetic acid, and glucose all have the empirical formula CH_2O, as shown in **Table 4-8.** These three compounds are not at all alike, though. Formaldehyde is often used to keep dead organisms from decaying so that they can be studied. Acetic acid gives vinegar its characteristic sour taste and strong smell. And glucose is a sugar that plays a very important role in your body chemistry. Some other formula must be used to distinguish these three very different compounds.

Table 4-8   **Empirical and Molecular Formulas for Some Compounds**

Compound	Empirical formula	Molar mass	Molecular formula	Structure
Formaldehyde	CH_2O	30.03 g/mol	CH_2O	
Acetic acid	CH_2O	60.06 g/mol	$2 \times CH_2O = C_2H_4O_2$	
Glucose	CH_2O	180.18 g/mol	$6 \times CH_2O = C_6H_{12}O_6$	

Molecular formulas are determined from empirical formulas

Formaldehyde, acetic acid, and glucose are all covalent compounds made of molecules. They all have the same empirical formula, but each compound has its own **molecular formula**. A compound's molecular formula tells you how many atoms are in one molecule of the compound.

In some cases, a compound's molecular formula is the same as its empirical formula. The empirical and molecular formulas for water are both H_2O. You can see from **Table 4-8** on the previous page that this is also true for formaldehyde. In other cases, a compound's molecular formula is a small whole-number multiple of its empirical formula. The molecular formula for acetic acid is two times its empirical formula, and that of glucose is six times its empirical formula.

▶ **molecular formula**
a chemical formula that reports the actual numbers of atoms in one molecule of a compound

---

SECTION 4.3 REVIEW

SUMMARY

▶ To name an ionic compound, first name the cation and then the anion.

▶ If an element can form cations with different charges, the cation name must include the ion's charge. The charge is written as a Roman numeral in parentheses.

▶ Prefixes are used to name covalent compounds made of two different elements.

▶ An empirical formula tells the relative numbers of atoms of each element in a compound.

▶ A molecular formula tells the actual numbers of atoms in one molecule of a compound.

▶ Covalent compounds have both empirical and molecular formulas.

CHECK YOUR UNDERSTANDING

1. **Name** the following ionic compounds, specifying the charge of any transition metal cations.
   - **a.** $Ni_3(PO_4)_2$
   - **b.** FeI_2
   - **c.** MnF_3
   - **d.** $CrCl_2$
   - **e.** $NaCN$
   - **f.** CuS

2. **Name** the following covalent compounds:
   - **a.** As_2O_5
   - **b.** SiI_4
   - **c.** P_4S_3
   - **d.** P_4O_{10}
   - **e.** SeO_2
   - **f.** PCl_3

3. **Explain** why Roman numerals must be included in the names of MnO_2 and Mn_2O_7. Name both of these compounds.

4. **Identify** how many fluorine atoms are in one molecule of sulfur hexafluoride.

Math Skills

5. **Creative Thinking** An unknown compound contains 49.47 percent C, 5.20 percent H, 28.85 percent N, and a certain percentage of oxygen. What percentage of the compound must be oxygen? (**Hint:** The sum of the percentages should equal 100 percent.)

6. What is the charge of the cadmium cation in cadmium cyanide, $Cd(CN)_2$, a compound used in electroplating? Explain your reasoning.

7. Determine the chemical formulas for the following ionic compounds:
   - **a.** magnesium sulfate
   - **b.** rubidium bromide
   - **c.** chromium(II) fluoride
   - **d.** nickel(I) carbonate

Organic and Biochemical Compounds

OBJECTIVES

▶ Describe how carbon atoms bond covalently to form organic compounds.

▶ Identify the names and structures of groups of simple organic compounds and polymers.

▶ Identify what the polymers essential for life are made of.

KEY TERMS

organic compound
polymer
biochemical compound
carbohydrate
protein
amino acid

The word *organic* has many different meanings. Most people associate the word *organic* with living organisms. Perhaps you have heard of or eaten organically grown fruits or vegetables. What this means is that they were grown using fertilizers and pesticides that come from plant and animal matter. In chemistry, the word *organic* is used to describe certain compounds.

Organic Compounds

An **organic compound** is a covalently bonded compound made of molecules. Organic compounds contain carbon and, almost always, hydrogen. Other atoms, such as oxygen, nitrogen, sulfur, and phosphorus, are also found in some organic compounds.

Many ingredients of familiar substances are organic compounds. The effective ingredient in aspirin is a form of the organic compound acetylsalicylic acid, $C_9H_8O_4$. Sugarless chewing gum also has organic compounds as ingredients. Two ingredients are the sweeteners sorbitol, $C_6H_{14}O_6$, and aspartame, $C_{14}H_{18}N_2O_5$, both of which are shown in **Figure 4-22.**

▶ **organic compound** any covalently bonded compound that contains carbon

Figure 4-22
The organic compounds sorbitol and aspartame sweeten some sugarless chewing gums.

Sorbitol

Aspartame

Methane

Figure 4-23
Methane is an alkane that has four C–H bonds.

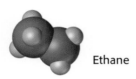

Ethane

Figure 4-24
Ethane, another alkane, has one C–C bond and six C–H bonds.

Figure 4-25
This camper is preparing his dinner on a gas grill fueled by propane. Propane is an alkane that has two C–C bonds and eight C–H bonds.

Propane

Carbon atoms form four covalent bonds in organic compounds

When a compound is made of only carbon and hydrogen atoms, it is called a *hydrocarbon*. Methane, CH_4, is the simplest hydrocarbon. Its structure is shown in **Figure 4-23.** Methane gas is formed when living matter, such as plants, decay, so it is often found in swamps and marshes. The natural gas used in Bunsen burners is also mostly methane. Carbon atoms have four valence electrons to use for bonding. In methane, each of these electrons forms a different C–H single bond.

A carbon atom may also share two of its electrons with two from another atom to form a double bond. Or a carbon atom may share three electrons to form a triple bond. However, a carbon atom can never form more than a total of four bonds.

Alkanes have single covalent bonds

Alkanes are hydrocarbons that have only single covalent bonds. **Figure 4-23** shows that methane, the simplest alkane, has only C–H bonds. But alkanes can also have C–C bonds. You can see from **Figure 4-24** that ethane, C_2H_6, has a C–C bond in addition to six C–H bonds. Notice how each carbon atom in both of these compounds bonds to four other atoms.

Many gas grills are fueled by another alkane, propane, C_3H_8. Propane is made of three bonded carbon atoms. Each carbon atom on the end of the molecule forms three bonds with three hydrogen atoms, as shown in **Figure 4-25.** Each of these end carbon atoms forms its fourth bond with the central carbon atom. The central carbon atom shares its two remaining electrons with two hydrogen atoms. You can see only one hydrogen atom bonded to the central carbon atom in **Figure 4-25** because the second hydrogen atom is on the other side.

Arrangements of carbon atoms in alkanes

The carbon atoms in methane, ethane, and propane all line up in a row because that is their only possible arrangement. When there are more than three bonded carbon atoms, the carbon atoms do not always line up in a row. When they do line up, the alkane is called a *normal alkane,* or *n*-alkane for short. **Table 4-9** shows chemical formulas for the *n*-alkanes that have up to 10 carbon atoms. *Condensed structural formulas* are also included in the table to show how the atoms bond.

The carbon atoms in any alkane with more than three carbon atoms can have more than one possible arrangement. Carbon atom chains may be branched or unbranched, and they can even form rings. **Figure 4-26** shows some of the possible ways six carbon atoms can be arranged when they form hydrocarbons with only single covalent bonds.

Table 4-9 **First 10 *n*-Alkanes**

n-Alkane	Molecular formula	Condensed structural formula
Methane	CH_4	CH_4
Ethane	C_2H_6	CH_3CH_3
Propane	C_3H_8	$CH_3CH_2CH_3$
Butane	C_4H_{10}	$CH_3(CH_2)_2CH_3$
Pentane	C_5H_{12}	$CH_3(CH_2)_3CH_3$
Hexane	C_6H_{14}	$CH_3(CH_2)_4CH_3$
Heptane	C_7H_{16}	$CH_3(CH_2)_5CH_3$
Octane	C_8H_{18}	$CH_3(CH_2)_6CH_3$
Nonane	C_9H_{20}	$CH_3(CH_2)_7CH_3$
Decane	$C_{10}H_{22}$	$CH_3(CH_2)_8CH_3$

Alkane chemical formulas

Except for cyclic alkanes like cyclohexane, the chemical formulas for alkanes follow a special pattern. The number of hydrogen atoms is always two more than twice the number of carbon atoms. This pattern is shown by the chemical formula C_nH_{2n+2}.

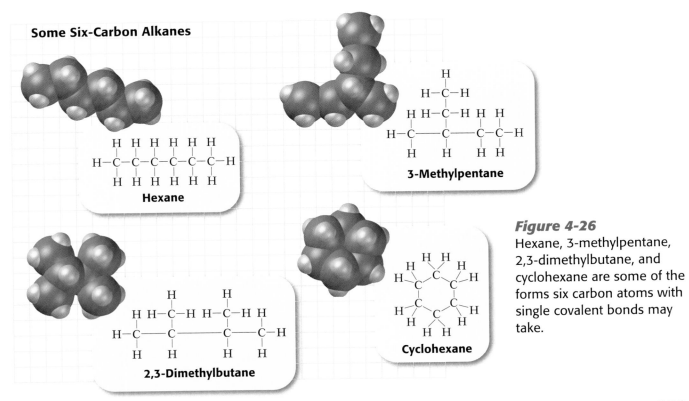

Some Six-Carbon Alkanes

Hexane

3-Methylpentane

2,3-Dimethylbutane

Cyclohexane

Figure 4-26
Hexane, 3-methylpentane, 2,3-dimethylbutane, and cyclohexane are some of the forms six carbon atoms with single covalent bonds may take.

Propene

Ethene

Figure 4-27
The peaches in this plastic container, which is made by joining propene molecules, release ethene gas as they ripen.

Figure 4-28
Many products contain a mixture of the alcohols methanol and ethanol. This mixture is called "denatured alcohol."

Methanol

Ethanol

Alkenes have double carbon-carbon bonds

Alkenes are also hydrocarbons. Alkenes are different from alkanes because they have at least one double covalent bond between carbon atoms. This is shown by C=C. Alkenes are named like alkanes but with the *-ane* ending replaced by *-ene*.

The simplest alkene is ethene (or ethylene), C_2H_4. Ethene is formed when fruit ripens. Propene (or propylene), C_3H_6, is used to make rubbing alcohol and some plastics. The structures of both compounds are shown in **Figure 4-27.**

Alcohols have —OH groups

Alcohols are organic compounds that are made of oxygen as well as carbon and hydrogen. Alcohols have *hydroxyl*, or –OH, groups. The alcohol methanol, CH_3OH, is sometimes added to another alcohol ethanol, CH_3CH_2OH, to make denatured alcohol. Denatured alcohol is found in many familiar products, as shown in **Figure 4-28.** Isopropanol, which is found in rubbing alcohol, has the chemical formula C_3H_8O, or $(CH_3)_2CHOH$. You may have noticed how the names of these three alcohols all end in *-ol*. This is true for most alcohols.

Alcohol molecules behave similarly to water molecules

A methanol molecule is like a water molecule except that one of the hydrogen atoms is replaced by a methyl, or –CH₃, group. Just like water molecules, neighboring alcohol molecules are attracted to one another. That's why many alcohols are liquids at room temperature. Alcohols have much higher boiling points than other organic compounds of similar size.

Polymers

What do the DNA inside the cells of your body, rubber, wood, and plastic soft-drink bottles have in common? They are all made of large molecules called **polymers.**

Many polymers have repeating subunits

Some small organic molecules bond to form long chains called polymers. Polyethene, which is also known as polythene or polyethylene, is the polymer plastic soft-drink bottles are made of. The name *polyethene* tells its structure. *Poly* means "many." *Ethene* is an alkene whose chemical formula is C_2H_4. Therefore, polyethene is "many ethenes," as shown in **Figure 4-29.** The original molecule, in this case C_2H_4, is called a *monomer.*

Some polymers are natural; others are man-made

Rubber, wood, cotton, wool, starch, protein, and DNA are all natural polymers. Man-made polymers are usually either plastics or fibers. Most plastics are flexible and easily molded, whereas fibers form long, thin strands.

Some polymers can be used as both plastics and fibers. For example, polypropene (polypropylene) is molded to make plastic containers, like the one shown in **Figure 4-27,** as well as some parts for cars and appliances. It is also used to make ropes, carpet, and artificial turf for athletic fields.

The elasticity of a polymer is determined by its structure

As with all substances, the properties of a polymer are determined by its structure. Polymer molecules are like long, thin chains. A small piece of plastic or a single fiber is made of billions of these chains. Polymer molecules can be likened to spaghetti. Like a bowl of spaghetti, the chains are tangled but can slide over each other. Soft-drink bottles are made of polyethene, a plastic made of such noodlelike chains. You can crush or dent a soft-drink bottle because the plastic is flexible. Once the bottle has been crushed, though, it does not return to its original shape. That's because polyethene is not elastic.

When the chains are connected to each other, or cross-linked, the polymer becomes elastic. An elastic polymer can be likened to a volleyball net. Like a volleyball net, an elastic polymer can stretch. When the polymer is released, it returns to its original shape. Rubber bands are elastic polymers. As long as a rubber band is not stretched too far, it can shrink back to its original form.

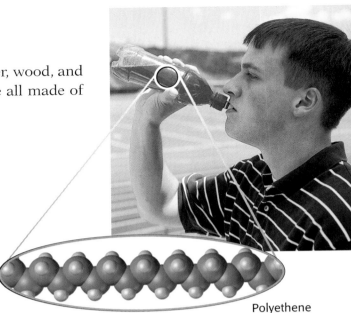

Polyethene

Figure 4-29
Polyethene is a polymer made of many repeating ethene units. As the polymer forms, ethene's double bonds are replaced by single bonds.

▶ **polymer** a large organic molecule made of many smaller bonded units

Quick ACTIVITY

Polymer Memory
Polymers that return to their original shape after stretching can be thought of as having a "memory." In this activity, you will compare the memory of a rubber band with that of the plastic rings that hold a six-pack of cans together.
1. Which polymer stretches better without breaking?
2. Which one has better memory?
3. Warm the stretched six-pack holder over a hot plate, being careful not to melt it. Does it retain its memory?

Biochemical Compounds

biochemical compound any organic compound that has an important role in living things

Biochemical compounds are naturally occurring organic compounds that are very important to living things. Carbohydrates give you energy. Proteins form important parts of your body, like muscles, tendons, fingernails, and hair. The DNA inside your cells gives your body information about what proteins you need. Each of these biochemical compounds is a polymer.

Many carbohydrates are made of glucose

carbohydrate any organic compound that is made of carbon, hydrogen, and oxygen and that provides nutrients to the cells of living things

The sugar glucose is a **carbohydrate.** Glucose provides energy to living things. Starch, also a carbohydrate, is made of many bonded glucose molecules. Plants store their energy as chains of starch.

Starch chains pack closely together in a potato or a pasta noodle. When you eat such foods, enzymes in your body break down the starch, making glucose available as a nutrient for your cells. Glucose that is not needed right away is stored as *glycogen*. When you become active, glycogen breaks apart and glucose molecules give you energy. Athletes often prepare themselves for their event by eating starchy foods. They do this so they will have more energy when they exert themselves later on, as shown in **Figure 4-30.**

Proteins are polymers of amino acids

protein a biological polymer made of bonded amino acids

amino acid any one of 20 different naturally occurring organic molecules that combine to form proteins

Many polymers are made of only one kind of molecule. Starch, for example, is made of only glucose. **Proteins,** on the other hand, are made of many different molecules that are called **amino acids.** Amino acids are made of carbon, hydrogen, oxygen, and nitrogen. Some amino acids also contain sulfur. There are 20 amino acids found in naturally occurring proteins. The way these amino acids combine determines which protein is made.

Figure 4-30
Athletes often eat lots of foods that are high in carbohydrates the day before a big event. This provides them with a ready supply of stored energy.

Inquiry Lab

What properties does a polymer have?

Materials
- ✔ water
- ✔ table sugar
- ✔ 250 mL beakers (2)
- ✔ cornstarch
- ✔ mallet
- ✔ 2 metal pie or cake pans

Procedure

SAFETY CAUTION Wear safety goggles, gloves, and a laboratory apron. Be sure to work in an open space and wear clothes that can be cleaned easily.

1. In one beaker, mix enough sugar with water to make a thick, syrupy liquid.
2. In the second beaker, mix enough cornstarch and water to make a liquid that is like a thick milkshake. The volume of liquid you prepare in this step should be the same as that prepared in step 1.
3. Pour each liquid into a separate pie pan.
4. Hit the liquid in the center of each pie pan with the mallet.

Analysis

1. Do both liquids take the shape of the pans? What does this mean?
2. What happened to the liquid made of sugar and water when it was hit with the mallet? What do you think happened to the molecules of this liquid when you hit the pan?
3. What happened to the liquid made of cornstarch and water when it was hit with the mallet? What happened to the mallet when it hit the liquid? What do you think happened to the molecules of this liquid when you hit it?
4. Which liquid has properties of a polymer? Explain how you reached this conclusion.

Proteins are long chains made of amino acids. A small protein, insulin, is shown in **Figure 4-31.** Many proteins are made of thousands of bonded amino acid molecules. This means that millions of different proteins can be made, each with very different properties. When you eat foods that contain proteins, such as cheese, your digestive system breaks down the proteins into individual amino acids. Later, your cells bond the amino acids in a different order to form whatever protein your body needs.

DNA is a polymer with a complex structure

Your DNA determines your entire genetic makeup. It is made of organic molecules containing carbon, hydrogen, oxygen, nitrogen, and phosphorus.

Figuring out the complex structure of DNA was one of the greatest scientific challenges of the twentieth century. Instead of forming one chain, like many proteins and polymers, DNA is in the form of paired chains, or strands. It has the shape of a twisted ladder known as a *double helix.*

Insulin

Figure 4-31
Insulin controls the use and storage of glucose in your body. Each color in the chain represents a different amino acid.

THE STRUCTURE OF MATTER **135**

Figure 4-32

In DNA, cytosine, C, always pairs with guanine, G. Adenine, A, always pairs with thymine, T.

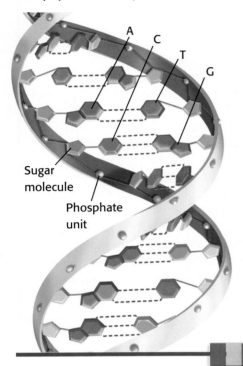

Sugar molecule

Phosphate unit

Your body has many copies of your DNA

Every cell in your body has a copy of your genetic material in the form of chromosomes made of DNA. So your DNA must be able to copy itself. Copying cannot happen unless the two DNA strands are first separated.

Proteins called helicases unwind DNA by separating the paired strands. Proteins called DNA polymerases then pair up new monomers with those already on the strand. At the end of this process, there are two identical strands of DNA.

DNA's structure resembles a twisted ladder

DNA's structure can be likened to a ladder. Alternating sugar molecules and phosphate units correspond to the ladder's sides, as shown in **Figure 4-32.** Attached to each sugar molecule is one of four possible DNA monomers—adenine, thymine, cytosine, or guanine. These DNA monomers pair up with DNA monomers attached to the opposite strand in a predictable way, as shown in **Figure 4-32.** Together, the DNA monomer pairs make up the rungs of the ladder.

SECTION 4.4 REVIEW

SUMMARY

▶ Alkanes have C = H bonds.

▶ Alkenes have C=C and C—H bonds.

▶ Alcohols have one or more —OH groups.

▶ Polymers form when small organic molecules bond to form long chains.

▶ Biochemical compounds are polymers important to living things.

▶ Sugars and starches are carbohydrates that provide energy.

▶ Amino acids bond to form polymers called proteins.

▶ DNA is a polymer shaped like a twisted ladder.

CHECK YOUR UNDERSTANDING

1. **Identify** the following compounds as alkanes, alkenes, or alcohols based on their names:
   a. 2-methylpentane
   b. 3-methyloctane
   c. 1-nonene
   d. butanol
   e. 3-heptene
   f. cyclohexanol

2. **Explain** why the compound CBr_5 does not exist. Give an acceptable chemical formula for a compound made of only carbon and bromine.

3. **Determine** how many hydrogen atoms a compound has if it is a hydrocarbon and its carbon atom skeleton is C=C−C=C.

4. **Compare** the structures and properties of carbohydrates with those of proteins.

5. **Identify** which compound is an alkane: CH_2O, C_6H_{14}, or C_3H_4. Explain your reasoning.

6. **Creative Thinking** *Alkynes*, like alkanes and alkenes, are hydrocarbons. Alkynes have carbon-carbon triple covalent bonds, or C≡C bonds. Draw the structure of the alkyne that has the chemical formula C_3H_4. Can you guess the name of this compound? Explain why there aren't any compounds that have C≡C bonds.

Chapter Highlights

Before you begin, review the summaries of the key ideas of each section, found on pages 114, 122, 128, and 136. The key vocabulary terms are listed on pages 108, 115, 123, and 129.

UNDERSTANDING CONCEPTS

1. Which of the following is not true of compounds made of molecules?
   a. They may exist as liquids.
   b. They may exist as solids.
   c. They may exist as gases.
   d. They have very high melting points.

2. Ionic solids _____.
   a. are formed by networks of ions that have the same charge
   b. melt at very low temperatures
   c. have very regular structures
   d. are sometimes found as gases at room temperature

3. A chemical bond can be defined as _____.
   a. a force that joins atoms together
   b. a force blending nuclei together
   c. a force caused by electric repulsion
   d. All of the above

4. Which substance has ionic bonds?
   a. CO   c. KCl
   b. CO_2 d. O_2

5. Covalent bonds _____.
   a. join atoms in some solids, liquids, and gases
   b. usually join one metal atom to another
   c. are always broken when a substance is dissolved in water
   d. join molecules in substances that have molecular structures

6. A compound has an empirical formula CH_2. Its molecular formula could be ____.
   a. CH_2 c. C_4H_8
   b. C_2H_4 d. either C_2H_4 or C_4H_8

7. The chemical formula for calcium chloride is _____.
   a. CaCl   c. Ca_2Cl
   b. $CaCl_2$ d. Ca_2Cl_2

8. The empirical formula of a molecule _____.
   a. can be used to identify the molecule
   b. is sometimes the same as the molecular formula for the molecule
   c. is used to name the molecule
   d. shows how atoms bond in the molecule

9. All organic compounds _____.
   a. come only from living organisms
   b. contain only carbon and hydrogen
   c. are biochemical compounds
   d. have atoms connected by covalent bonds

10. Which group is not a polymer?
    a. amino acids   c. proteins
    b. carbohydrates   d. plastics

Using Vocabulary

11. Compare the *chemical structure* of oxygen difluoride with that of carbon dioxide. Which compound has the larger *bond angle*? What kind of bonds do both compounds have?

Carbon dioxide   Oxygen difluoride

12. Determine whether the *chemical formula* $C_5H_5N_5$ is the *empirical formula* or *molecular formula* for adenine.

13. Name the following *covalent* compounds:
    a. SF_4 c. PCl_3
    b. N_2O d. P_2O_5

14. Compare the *metallic bonds* of copper with the *ionic bonds* of copper sulfide. Why are metals rather than ionic solids used in electrical wiring?

15. Explain why *proteins* and *carbohydrates* are *polymers*. What is each polymer made of?

BUILDING MATH SKILLS

16. Graphing Which of the graphs below shows how bond length and bond energy are related? Describe the flawed relationships shown by each of the other graphs.

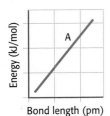
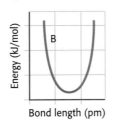
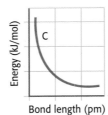

17. Graphing The melting points of elements in the same group of the periodic table follow a pattern. A similar pattern is also seen among the melting points of ionic compounds when the cations are made from elements that are in the same group. To see this, plot the melting point of each of the ionic compounds in the table below on the *y*-axis and the average atomic mass of the element that the cation is made from on the *x*-axis.

a. What trend do you notice in the melting points as you move down Group 2?

b. $BeCl_2$ has a melting point of 405°C. Is this likely to be an ionic compound like the others? Explain. (**Hint:** Locate beryllium in the periodic table.)

c. Predict the melting point of the ionic compound $RaCl_2$. (**Hint:** Check the periodic table, and compare radium's location with the location of magnesium, calcium, strontium, and barium.)

Compound	Melting point (°C)
$MgCl_2$	712
$CaCl_2$	772
$SrCl_2$	868
$BaCl_2$	963

18. Writing Ionic Formulas Determine the chemical formula for each of the following ionic compounds:

a. strontium nitrate, an ingredient in some fireworks, signal flares, and matches

b. sodium cyanide, a compound used in electroplating and treating metals

c. chromium(III) hydroxide, a compound used to tan and dye substances

d. aluminum nitride, a compound used in the computer-chip-making process

e. tin(II) fluoride, the source of fluoride for many toothpastes

f. potassium sulfate, a compound used in the glass-making process

THINKING CRITICALLY

19. Evaluating Data A substance is a solid at room temperature. It is unable to conduct electricity as a solid but can conduct electricity as a liquid. This compound melts at 755°C. Would you expect this compound to have ionic, metallic, or covalent bonds?

20. Creative Thinking Dodecane is a combustible organic compound used in jet fuel research. It is an *n*-alkane made of 12 carbon atoms. How many hydrogen atoms does dodecane have? Draw the structural formula for dodecane.

21. Applying Knowledge The length of a bond depends upon its type. Predict the relative lengths of the carbon-carbon bonds in the following molecules, and explain your reasoning.

$$
\begin{array}{ccc}
\text{H\ \ H} & & \\
| \ \ | & & \\
\text{H}-\text{C}-\text{C}-\text{H} & & \\
| \ \ | & & \\
\text{H\ \ H} & & \\
\textbf{Ethane} & \textbf{Ethene} & \textbf{Ethyne}
\end{array}
$$

H–C≡C–H

22. Influencing Others To get crystals to grow from a mixture of dissolved solid and liquid, a small piece of the solid being grown is sometimes added. The added solid is called a seed crystal. As crystals grow, the mixture must not be disturbed. If it is, the crystals that grow are often small and oddly shaped. Pretend you are starting a small business that sells seed crystals to chemists. Design a brochure to promote your product. In your brochure, discuss why chemists should buy your seed crystals instead of a competitor's.

23. Working Cooperatively For one day, write down all of the ionic compounds listed on the labels of the foods you eat. Also write down the approximate mass you eat of each compound. As a class, make a master list in the form of a computer spreadsheet that includes all of the ionic compounds eaten by the whole class. Identify which compounds were eaten by the most people. Together, create a poster describing the dietary guidelines for the ionic compound that was eaten most often.

COMPUTER SKILL

24. Making Decisions People on low-sodium diets must limit their intake of table salt. Luckily, there are salt substitutes that do not contain sodium. Research different kinds of salt substitutes, and describe how each one affects your body. Determine which salt substitute you would use if you were on a low-sodium diet.

25. Locating Information Numerical recycling codes identify the composition of a plastic so that it can be sorted and recycled. For each of the recycling codes, 1–6, identify the plastic, its physical properties, and at least one product made of this plastic.

26. Concept Mapping Copy the unfinished concept map below onto a sheet of paper. Complete the map by writing the correct word or phrase in the lettered boxes.

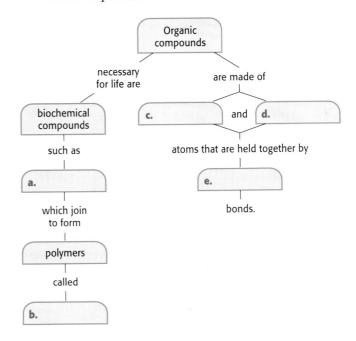

27. Connection to Health The figure below shows how atoms are bonded in a molecule of vitamin C. Which elements is vitamin C made of? What is its molecular formula? Write a paragraph explaining some of the health benefits of taking vitamin C supplements.

WRITING SKILL

internet**connect**

SC*LINKS*
NSTA

TOPIC: Vitamin C
GO TO: www.scilinks.org
KEYWORD: HK1046

Skill Builder Lab

Introduction

Many polymers are able to "bounce back" after they are stretched, bent, or compressed. In this lab, you will compare the bounce heights of two balls made from different polymers.

Objectives

▶ *Synthesize* two different polymers, *shape* each into a ball, and *measure* how high each ball bounces.

▶ *Evaluate* which polymer would make a better toy ball.

Materials

liquid latex
5 percent acetic acid solution (vinegar)
50 percent ethanol solution
sodium silicate solution
deionized water
2 L container
25 mL graduated cylinders (2)
10 mL graduated cylinder
2 medium-sized paper cups
2 wooden craft sticks
paper towels
meterstick

Safety Needs

safety goggles, 3 pairs of gloves
laboratory apron

Comparing Polymers

▶ Preparing for Your Experiment

1. Prepare a data table in your lab report similar to the one shown at right.

▶ Making Latex Rubber

SAFETY CAUTION If you get a chemical on your skin or clothing, wash it off with lukewarm water while calling to your teacher. If you get a chemical in your eyes, flush it out immediately at the eyewash station and alert your teacher.

2. Pour 1 L of deionized water into a 2 L container.

3. Use a 25 mL graduated cylinder to pour 10 mL of liquid latex into one of the paper cups.

4. Clean the graduated cylinder thoroughly with soap and water, then rinse it with deionized water and use it to add 10 mL of deionized water to the liquid latex.

5. Use the same graduated cylinder to add 10 mL of acetic acid solution to the liquid latex-water mixture.

6. Stir the mixture with a wooden craft stick. As you stir, a "lump" of the polymer will form around the stick.

7. Transfer the stick and the attached polymer to the 2 L container. While keeping the polymer underwater, gently pull it off the stick with your gloved hands.

8. Squeeze the polymer underwater to remove any unreacted chemicals, shape it into a ball, and remove the ball from the water.

9. Make the ball smooth by rolling it between your gloved hands. Set the ball on a paper towel to dry while you continue with the next part of the lab.

Bounce Heights of Polymers

| Polymer | Bounce height (cm) | | | | | |
	Trial 1	Trial 2	Trial 3	Trial 4	Trial 5	Average
Latex rubber						
Ethanol-silicate						

10. Wash your gloved hands with soap and water, then remove the gloves and dispose of them. Wash your hands again with soap and water.

▶ Making an Ethanol-silicate Polymer

SAFETY CAUTION Put on a fresh pair of gloves. Ethanol is flammable, so make sure there are no flames or other heat sources anywhere in the laboratory.

11. Use a clean 25 mL graduated cylinder to pour 12 mL of sodium silicate solution into the clean paper cup.

12. Use a 10 mL graduated cylinder to add 3 mL of the ethanol solution to the sodium silicate solution.

13. Stir the mixture with the clean wooden craft stick until a solid polymer forms.

14. Remove the polymer with your gloved hands, and gently press it between your palms until you form a ball that does not crumble. This activity may take some time. Occasionally dripping some tap water on the polymer might be helpful.

15. When the ball no longer crumbles, dry it very gently with a paper towel.

16. Repeat step 10, and put on a fresh pair of gloves.

17. Examine both polymers closely. Record in your lab report how the two polymers are alike and how they are different.

18. Use a meterstick to measure the highest bounce height of each ball when each is dropped from a height of 1 m. Drop each ball five times, and record the highest bounce height each time in your data table.

▶ Analyzing Your Results

1. Calculate the average bounce height for each ball by adding the five bounce heights and dividing by 5. Record the averages in your data table.

2. Based on only their bounce heights, which polymer would make a better toy ball?

▶ Defending Your Conclusions

3. Suppose that making a latex rubber ball costs 22 cents and that making an ethanol-silicate ball costs 25 cents. Does this fact affect your conclusion about which polymer would make a better toy ball? Besides cost, what are other important factors that should be considered?

Analytical Chemist

Have you ever looked at something and wondered what chemicals it contained? That's what analytical chemists do for a living. They use a range of tests to determine the chemical makeup of a sample. To find out more about analytical chemistry as a career, read the interview with analytical chemist Roberta Jordan, who works at the Idaho National Engineering and Environmental Laboratory, in Idaho Falls, Idaho.

In addition to working as an analytical chemist, Roberta Jordan mentors students regularly in the local schools.

"Chemistry is in everything we do. Just to take a breath and eat a meal involves chemistry."

 What is your work as an analytical chemist like?

We deal with radioactive waste generated by old nuclear power plants and old submarines, and we try to find a safe way to store the waste. I'm more like a consultant. A group of engineers that are working on a process will come to me. I tell them what things they need to analyze for and why they need to do that. On the flip side, I'll tell them what techniques they need to use.

 What do you like best about your work?

It forces me to stay current with any new techniques, new areas that are going on in analytical chemistry. And I like the team approach because it allows me to work on different projects.

 What do you find most interesting about your work?

Probably the most interesting thing is to observe how different industries and different labs conduct business. It gives you a broad feel for how chemistry is done.

 What qualities does a good chemist need?

I think you do need to be good at science and math and to like those subjects. You need to be fairly detail-oriented. You have to be precise. You need to be analytical in general, and you need to be meticulous.

What part of your education do you think was most valuable?

I think it was worthwhile spending a lot of energy on my lab work. With any science, the most important part is the laboratory experience, when you are applying those theories that you learn. I'm really a proponent of being involved in science-fair activities.

 What advice do you have for students who are interested in analytical chemistry?

It's worthwhile to go to the career center or library and do a little research. Take the time to find out what kinds of things you could do with your degree. You need to talk to people who have a degree in that field.

 Do you think chemistry has a bright future?

I think that there are a lot of things out there that need to be discovered. My advice is to go for it and don't think that everything we need to know has been discovered. Twenty to thirty years down the road, we will have to think of a new energy source, for example.

internet connect

 SCI LINKS NSTA
TOPIC: Analytical chemistry
GO TO: www.scilinks.org
KEYWORD: HK1499

"One of the things necessary to be a good chemist is you have to be creative. You have to be able to think above and beyond the normal way of doing things to come up with new ideas, new experiments."
—ROBERTA JORDAN

Changes in Matter

▌ CHAPTER **5**

Chemical Reactions   **146**

Viewpoints: How Should Life-Saving
Inventions Be Introduced?   **182**

▌ CHAPTER **6**

Nuclear Changes   **184**

Career Link
Corinna Wu, Science Writer   **212**

Chemical Reactions

Chapter Preview

5.1 **The Nature of Chemical Reactions**
Chemical Reactions Change Substances
Energy and Reactions

5.2 **Reaction Types**
Classifying Reactions
Electrons and Chemical Reactions

5.3 **Balancing Chemical Equations**
Describing Reactions
Determining Mole Ratios

5.4 **Rates of Change**
Factors Affecting Reaction Rates
Equilibrium Systems

Before 1900, oil was refined to make kerosene for lights. Gasoline was a useless byproduct of the refining process.

Focus ACTIVITY

Background Early in the morning in May 1961, everything was quiet. Then a blindingly bright light flashed. The ground shook. A deafening roar filled the air. A Redstone rocket propelled a Project Mercury capsule toward the sky, and the first United States astronaut, Alan B. Shepard, soared 186 km above Earth's surface.

The Redstone rocket was powered by the chemical reaction that occurs between kerosene and oxygen. Kerosene has been used as a fuel to provide heat and light since the 1860s. The same chemical reaction that provided light from lighthouses and kerosene lamps in the days of the sailing ships was launching the United States manned space program.

These days, the space shuttle, which has a mass of about 2 000 000 kg at liftoff, uses a different chemical reaction. But the chemical reaction that sends the shuttle orbiting is neither exotic nor difficult to understand. It is the reaction between hydrogen and oxygen that yields water.

Activity 1 Kerosene and gasoline are just two of the fuels generally produced from crude oil. Visit a fuel distributor in your community and find out what kinds of fuels are available and what makes them different.

Activity 2 Research the octane rating system for gasolines. Find out what the different octane ratings are and what they mean.

The Nature of Chemical Reactions

► **KEY TERMS**
reactant
product
chemical energy
exothermic reaction
endothermic reaction

OBJECTIVES

► Recognize some signs that a chemical reaction is taking place.
► Explain chemical changes in terms of the structure and motion of atoms and molecules.
► Describe the differences between endothermic and exothermic reactions.
► Identify situations involving chemical energy.

If someone talks about chemical reactions, you might think about scientists doing experiments in laboratories. But words like *grow, ripen, decay,* and *burn* describe chemical reactions you see every day. Even your own health is due to chemical reactions taking place inside your body. The food you eat reacts with the oxygen you inhale in processes such as respiration and cell growth. The carbon dioxide formed in these reactions is carried to your lungs, and you exhale it into the environment.

Figure 5-1
Signs of a Chemical Reaction

A When the calcium carbonate in a piece of chalk reacts with an acid, bubbles of carbon dioxide gas are given off.

B When solutions of sodium sulfide and cadmium nitrate are mixed, a solid—yellow cadmium sulfide—settles out of the solution.

C When ammonium dichromate decomposes, energy is released as light and heat.

Chemical Reactions Change Substances

When sugar, water, and yeast are mixed into flour to make bread dough, a chemical reaction takes place. The yeast acts on the sugar to form new substances, including carbon dioxide and lactic acid. You know that a chemical reaction has happened because lactic acid and carbon dioxide are different from sugar. For example, sugar tastes sweet and lactic acid tastes sour. Sourdough bread gets its characteristic taste from lactic acid.

Chemical reactions occur when substances undergo chemical changes to form new substances. Often you can tell that a chemical reaction is happening because you will be able to see changes, such as those in **Figure 5-1.**

Production of gas and change of color are signs of chemical reactions

In bread making, the carbon dioxide gas that is produced expands the dough, causing the bread to rise. This release of gas is a sign that a chemical reaction may be happening.

As the dough bakes, old bonds break and new bonds form. Chemical reactions involving starch and protein make food turn brown when heated. A chemical change happens almost every time there is a change in color.

Chemical reactions rearrange atoms

When gasoline is burned in the engine of a car or boat, a lot of different reactions happen with the compounds that are in the mixture we call gasoline. In a typical reaction, isooctane, C_8H_{18}, and oxygen, O_2, are the reactants. They react and form two products, carbon dioxide, CO_2, and water, H_2O.

The products and reactants contain the same types of atoms: carbon, hydrogen, and oxygen. New product atoms are not created, and old reactant atoms are not destroyed. Atoms are rearranged as bonds are broken and formed. In all chemical reactions, mass is always conserved, as you learned in Chapter 2.

▶ **reactant** a substance that undergoes a chemical change

▶ **product** a substance that is the result of a chemical change

Energy and Reactions

Filling a car's tank with gasoline would be very dangerous if isooctane and oxygen could not be in the same place without reacting. Like most chemical reactions, the isooctane-oxygen reaction needs energy to get started. A small spark provides enough energy to start the reaction. That is why smoking or having any open flame near a gas pump is not allowed.

Energy must be added to break bonds

In each isooctane molecule, like the one shown in **Figure 5-2,** all the bonds to carbon atoms are covalent. In an oxygen molecule, a double covalent bond holds the two oxygen atoms together. For the atoms in isooctane and oxygen to react, all of these bonds have to be broken. This takes energy.

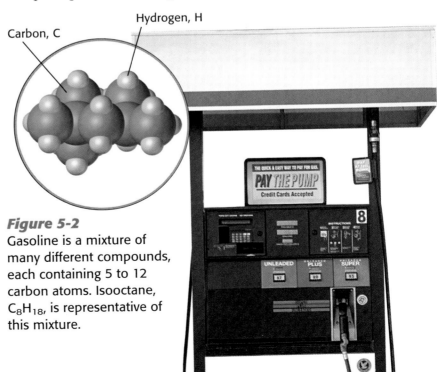

Carbon, C

Hydrogen, H

Figure 5-2
Gasoline is a mixture of many different compounds, each containing 5 to 12 carbon atoms. Isooctane, C_8H_{18}, is representative of this mixture.

Figure 5-3
In photography, light passing through the camera lens causes a chemical reaction on the film. Silver bromide crystals in the gel on the film react to form darker elemental silver, which becomes the negative (A) that is used to make a black and white photograph (B).

A Negative   **B** Photo (positive image)

Many forms of energy can be used to break bonds. Sometimes the energy is transferred as heat, like the spark that starts the isooctane-oxygen reaction. Energy also can be transferred as electricity, sound, or light, as shown in **Figure 5-3.** When molecules collide and enough energy is transferred to separate the atoms, bonds can break.

Forming bonds releases energy

Once enough energy is added to start the isooctane-oxygen reaction, new bonds form to make the products, as shown in **Figure 5-4.** Each carbon dioxide molecule has two oxygen atoms connected to the carbon atom with a double bond. A water molecule is made when two hydrogen atoms each form a single bond with the oxygen atom.

When new bonds form, energy is released. When gasoline burns, energy in the form of heat and light is released as the products of the isooctane-oxygen reaction and other gasoline reactions form. Other chemical reactions can produce electrical energy.

Figure 5-4
The formation of carbon dioxide and water from isooctane and oxygen produces the energy used to power engines.

Reactants		$\longrightarrow$	Products		
Isooctane	**Oxygen**	$\longrightarrow$	**Carbon dioxide**	**Water**	**Energy**
C_8H_{18}	O_2	$\longrightarrow$	CO_2	H_2O	energy
$2C_8H_{18}$ +	$25O_2$	$\longrightarrow$	$16CO_2$ +	$18H_2O$ +	energy

Energy is conserved in chemical reactions

Energy may not appear to be conserved in the isooctane reaction. After all, a tiny spark can set off an explosion. The energy for that explosion comes from the reactants. Often this stored energy is called chemical energy. The total energy of isooctane, oxygen, and their surroundings includes this chemical energy. The total energy before the reaction is equal to the total energy of the products and their surroundings.

Reactions that release energy are exothermic

In the isooctane-oxygen reaction, more energy is released as the products form than is absorbed to break the bonds in the reactants. Like all other combustion reactions, this is an exothermic reaction. After an exothermic reaction, the temperature of the surroundings rises because energy is released. The released energy comes from the chemical energy of the reactants.

Reactions that absorb energy are endothermic

If you put hydrated barium hydroxide and ammonium nitrate together in a flask, the reaction between them takes so much energy from the surroundings that water in the air will condense and then freeze on the surface of the flask. This is an endothermic reaction—more energy is needed to break the bonds in the reactants than is given off by forming bonds in the products.

▶ **chemical energy** the energy stored within atoms and molecules that can be released when a substance reacts

▶ **exothermic reaction** a reaction that transfers energy from the reactants to the surroundings usually as heat

▶ **endothermic reaction** a reaction in which energy is transferred to the reactants usually as heat from the surroundings

internetconnect

SC*LINKS*
NSTA

TOPIC: Corrosion
GO TO: www.scilinks.org
KEYWORD: HK1052

REAL WORLD APPLICATIONS

Self-Heating Meals

Corrosion, the process by which a metal reacts with the oxygen in air or water, is not often wanted. However, corrosion is encouraged in self-heating meals so that the energy from the exothermic reaction can be used. Self-heating meals, as the name implies, have their own heat source.

Each meal contains a package of precooked food, a bag that holds a porous pad containing a magnesium-iron alloy, and some salt water. When the salt water is poured into the bag, the salt water soaks through the holes in the pad of metal alloy and begins to corrode the metals vigorously. Then the sealed food package is placed in the bag. The exothermic reaction raises the temperature of the food by 38°C in 14 minutes.

Applying Information
1. List some people for whom self-heating meals would be useful.
2. What other uses can you think of for this self-heating technology?

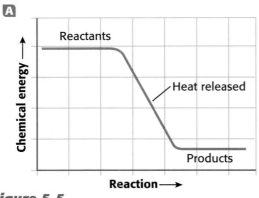

A

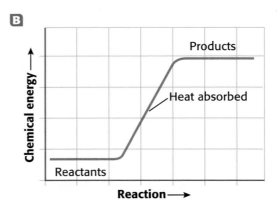

B

Figure 5-5
The general forms for exothermic reactions (A) and endothermic reactions (B) can be described by energy graphs.

When an endothermic reaction occurs, you may be able to notice a drop in temperature. Some endothermic reactions cannot get enough energy as heat from the surroundings to happen; so energy must be added as heat to cause the reaction to take place. The changes in chemical energy for an exothermic reaction and for an endothermic reaction are shown in **Figure 5-5.**

Photosynthesis, like many reactions in living things, is endothermic. In photosynthesis, plants use energy from light to convert carbon dioxide and water to glucose and oxygen, as shown in **Figure 5-6.**

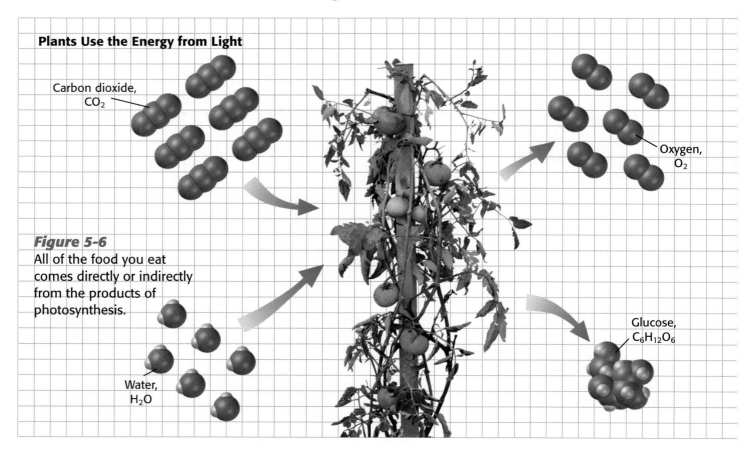

Plants Use the Energy from Light

Carbon dioxide, CO_2

Oxygen, O_2

Figure 5-6
All of the food you eat comes directly or indirectly from the products of photosynthesis.

Water, H_2O

Glucose, $C_6H_{12}O_6$

Figure 5-7

A Some living things, such as this firefly, produce light through a chemical process called bioluminescence.

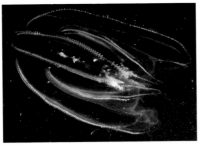

B The comb jelly (*Mnemiopsis leidyi*), shown above, is about 10 cm wide and is native to the Atlantic coast. Comb jellies are not true jellyfish.

INTEGRATING

BIOLOGY

People are charmed by fireflies because these common insects give off light. Scientists have found that fireflies are not alone in this. Some kinds of bacteria, worms, squids, and jellyfish also give off light. This process, called bioluminescence, involves an exothermic reaction made possible by the enzyme luciferase. Scientists can use bacteria that contain luciferase to track the spread of infection in the human body.

Sometimes, reactions are described as exergonic or endergonic. These terms refer to the ease with which the reactions occur. In most cases in this book, exergonic reactions are exothermic and endergonic reactions are endothermic. Bioluminescence, shown in **Figure 5-7,** and respiration are exergonic reactions, and photosynthesis is an endergonic reaction.

SECTION 5.1 REVIEW

SUMMARY

▶ During a chemical reaction, atoms are rearranged.

▶ Signs of a chemical reaction include any of the following: a substance that has different properties than the reactants have; a color change; the formation of a gas or a solid precipitate; or the transfer of energy.

▶ Mass and energy are conserved in chemical reactions.

▶ Chemical energy can be given off or taken in.

▶ Energy must be added to the reactants for bonds between atoms to be broken.

CHECK YOUR UNDERSTANDING

1. **Identify** which of the following is a chemical reaction:
   a. melting ice
   b. burning a candle
   c. rubbing a marker on paper
   d. rusting iron
2. **List** three signs that could make you think a chemical reaction might be taking place.
3. **List** four forms of energy that might be absorbed or released during a chemical reaction.
4. **Classify** the following reactions as exothermic or endothermic:
   a. paper burning with a bright flame
   b. plastics becoming brittle after being left in the sun
   c. a firecracker exploding
5. **Predict** which atoms will be found in the products of the following reactions:
   a. mercury(II) oxide, HgO, is heated and decomposes
   b. limestone, $CaCO_3$, reacts with hydrochloric acid, HCl
   c. table sugar, $C_{12}H_{22}O_{11}$, burns in air to form caramel
6. **Critical Thinking** Calcium oxide, CaO, is used in cement mixes. When water is added, heat is released as CaO forms calcium hydroxide, $Ca(OH)_2$. What signs are there that this is a chemical reaction? Which has more chemical energy, the reactants or the products? Explain your answer.

Reaction Types

▶ **KEY TERMS**

synthesis reaction

decomposition reaction

electrolysis

combustion reaction

single-displacement
   reaction

double-displacement
   reaction

redox reaction

radical

OBJECTIVES

▶ Distinguish among five general types of chemical reactions.

▶ Predict the products of some reactions based on the reaction type.

▶ Describe reactions that transfer or share electrons between molecules, atoms, or ions.

In the last section, you saw how CO_2 is made from sugar by yeast, how isooctane from gasoline burns, and how photosynthesis happens. These are just a few examples of the many millions of possible reactions.

▶ **synthesis reaction** a reaction of at least two substances that forms a new, more complex compound

Classifying Reactions

Even though there are millions of unique substances and many millions of possible reactions, there are only a few general types of reactions. Just as you can follow patterns to name compounds, you also can use patterns to identify the general types of chemical reactions and to predict the products of the chemical reactions.

Synthesis reactions combine substances

Polyethylene, a plastic often used to make trash bags and soda bottles, is produced by a **synthesis reaction** called polymerization. In polymerization reactions, many small molecules join together in chains to make larger structures called polymers. Polyethylene, shown in **Figure 5-8,** is a polymer formed of repeating ethylene molecules.

Hydrogen gas reacts with oxygen gas to form water. In a synthesis reaction, at least two reactants join to form a product. Synthesis reactions have the following general form.

$$A + B \longrightarrow AB$$

The following is a synthesis reaction in which the metal sodium reacts with chlorine gas to form sodium chloride, or table salt.

$$2Na + Cl_2 \longrightarrow 2NaCl$$

Figure 5-8

A molecule of polyethylene is made up of as many as 3500 units of ethylene.

Polyethylene   Ethylene unit

Synthesis reactions always join substances, so the product is a more complex compound than the reactants.

Photosynthesis is another kind of synthesis reaction—the synthesis reaction that goes on in plants. The photosynthesis reaction is shown in **Figure 5-9.**

Decomposition reactions break substances apart

Digestion is a series of reactions that break down complex foods into simple fuels your body can use. Similarly, in what is known as "cracking" crude oil, large molecules made of carbon and hydrogen are broken down to make gasoline and other fuels. Digestion and "cracking" oil are **decomposition reactions,** reactions in which substances are broken apart. The general form for decomposition reactions is as follows.

$$AB \longrightarrow A + B$$

The following shows the decomposition of water.

$$2H_2O \longrightarrow 2H_2 + O_2$$

The **electrolysis** of water is a simple decomposition reaction—water breaks down into hydrogen gas and oxygen gas when an electric current flows through the water.

Combustion reactions use oxygen as a reactant

In Section 5.1 you learned that isooctane forms carbon dioxide and water during combustion. Oxygen is a reactant in every **combustion reaction,** and at least one product of such reactions always contains oxygen.

If the air supply is limited when a carbon-containing fuel burns, there may not be enough oxygen gas for all the carbon to form carbon dioxide. In that case, some carbon monoxide may form. Carbon monoxide, CO, is a poisonous gas that lowers the ability of the blood to carry oxygen. Carbon monoxide has no color or odor, so you can't tell when it is present. When there is not a good air supply during a combustion reaction, not all fuels are converted completely to carbon dioxide. In some combustion reactions, you can tell if the air supply is limited because carbon is given off as small particles that make a dark, sooty smoke.

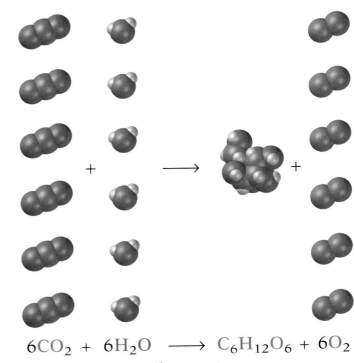

$$6CO_2 + 6H_2O \longrightarrow C_6H_{12}O_6 + 6O_2$$

Figure 5-9
Photosynthesis is the synthesis of glucose and oxygen gas from carbon dioxide and water.

▶ **decomposition reaction** a reaction in which one compound breaks into at least two products

▶ **electrolysis** the decomposition of a compound by an electric current

▶ **combustion reaction** a reaction in which a compound and oxygen burn

internetconnect

SCiLINKS
NSTA

TOPIC: Types of reactions
GO TO: www.scilinks.org
KEYWORD: HK1053

To see how important a good air supply is, look at a series of combustion reactions for methane, CH_4. Because methane has only one carbon atom, it is the simplest carbon-containing fuel. Methane is the primary component in natural gas, the fuel often used in stoves, water heaters, and furnaces.

Methane reacts with oxygen gas to make carbon dioxide and water. Two molecules of oxygen gas are needed for the combustion of each molecule of methane. Therefore, four molecules of oxygen gas are needed for the combustion of two molecules of methane, as shown below.

$$2CH_4 + 4O_2 \longrightarrow 2CO_2 + 4H_2O$$

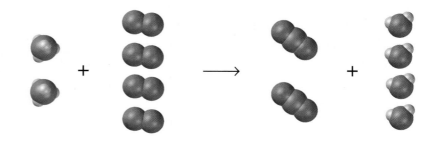

Now look at what happens when less oxygen gas is available. If there are only three molecules of oxygen gas for every two molecules of methane, water and carbon monoxide may form, as shown in the following reaction.

$$2CH_4 + 3O_2 \longrightarrow 2CO + 4H_2O$$

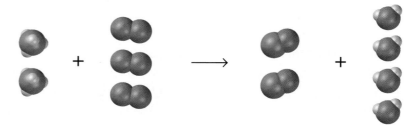

When the air supply is very limited and only two molecules of oxygen gas are available to react with two molecules of methane, water and tiny bits of carbon, or soot, are formed as follows.

$$2CH_4 + 2O_2 \longrightarrow 2C + 4H_2O$$

In single-displacement reactions, elements trade places

Copper(II) chloride dissolves in water to make a bright blue solution. If you add a piece of aluminum foil to the solution, the color fades, and clumps of reddish brown material form. The reddish brown clumps are copper metal. Aluminum replaces copper in the copper(II) chloride, forming aluminum chloride. Aluminum chloride does not make a colored solution, so the blue color fades as the amount of blue copper(II) chloride decreases, as shown in **Figure 5-10.**

The copper atoms are in the form of copper(II) ions, as part of copper(II) chloride, and the aluminum atoms are in the aluminum metal. After the reaction, the aluminum atoms become ions, and the copper atoms become neutral in the copper metal. Because the atoms of one element appear to move into a compound, and atoms of the other element appear to move out, this is called a **single-displacement reaction.** Single-displacement reactions have the following general form.

$$XA + B \longrightarrow BA + X$$

▶ **single-displacement reaction** a reaction in which atoms of one element take the place of atoms of another element in a compound

The single-displacement reaction between copper(II) chloride and aluminum is shown as follows.

$$3CuCl_2 + 2Al \longrightarrow 2AlCl_3 + 3Cu$$

Generally, in a single-displacement reaction, a more reactive element will take the place of a less reactive one.

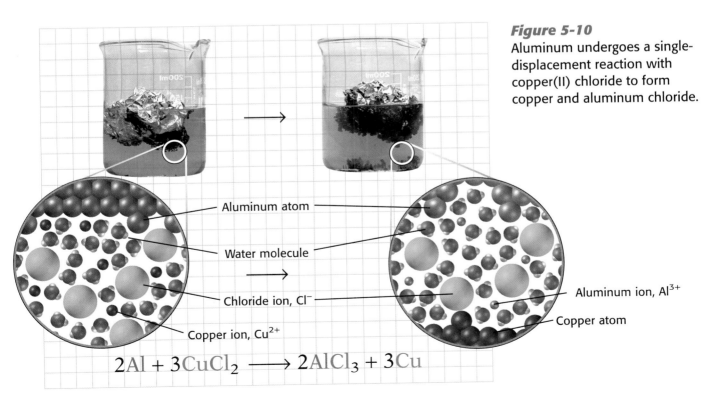

Figure 5-10
Aluminum undergoes a single-displacement reaction with copper(II) chloride to form copper and aluminum chloride.

Aluminum atom

Water molecule

Chloride ion, Cl^-

Copper ion, Cu^{2+}

Aluminum ion, Al^{3+}

Copper atom

$$2Al + 3CuCl_2 \longrightarrow 2AlCl_3 + 3Cu$$

Figure 5-11
Potassium reacts with water in a single-displacement reaction.

Potassium,
K

+

Water,
H₂O

⟶

Potassium hydroxide,
KOH

+

Hydrogen,
H₂

Potassium metal is so reactive that it undergoes a single-displacement reaction with water. A potassium ion appears to take the place of one of the hydrogen atoms in the water molecule. Potassium ions, K^+, and hydroxide ions, OH^-, are formed. The hydrogen atoms displaced from the water join to form hydrogen gas, H_2.

The potassium and water reaction, shown in **Figure 5-11,** is so exothermic that the H_2 may explode and burn instantly. All alkali metals and some other metals undergo single-displacement reactions with water to form hydrogen gas, metal ions, and hydroxide ions.

All of these reactions happen rapidly and give off heat but some alkali metals are more reactive than others. Lithium reacts steadily with water to form lithium ions, hydroxide ions, and hydrogen gas. Sodium and water react vigorously to make sodium ions, hydroxide ions, and hydrogen gas. For potassium, the reaction with water is more violent. Rubidium and cesium are so reactive that the hydrogen gas will explode as soon as they are put into water.

In double-displacement reactions, ions appear to be exchanged between compounds

The yellow lines painted on roads are colored with lead chromate, $PbCrO_4$. This compound can be formed by mixing solutions of lead nitrate, $Pb(NO_3)_2$, and potassium chromate, K_2CrO_4. In solution, these compounds form the ions Pb^{2+}, NO_3^-, K^+, and CrO_4^{2-}. When the solutions are mixed, the yellow lead chromate compound that forms doesn't dissolve in water, so it settles to the bottom. A **double-displacement reaction,** such as this one, occurs when two compounds appear to exchange ions. The general form of a double-displacement reaction is as follows.

$$AX + BY \longrightarrow AY + BX$$

The double-displacement reaction that forms lead chromate is as follows.

$$Pb(NO_3)_2 + K_2CrO_4 \longrightarrow PbCrO_4 + 2KNO_3$$

▶ **double-displacement reaction** a reaction in which a gas, a solid precipitate, or a molecular compound is formed from the apparent exchange of ions between two compounds

Electrons and Chemical Reactions

The general classes of reactions described earlier in this section were used by early chemists, who knew nothing about the parts of the atom. With the discovery of the electron and its role in chemical bonding, another way to classify reactions was developed. We can understand many reactions as transfers of electrons.

Electrons are transferred in redox reactions

The following **reduction/oxidation reaction** is an example of electron transfer. When the metal iron reacts with oxygen to form rust, Fe_2O_3, each iron atom loses three electrons to form Fe^{3+} ions, and each oxygen atom gains two electrons to form the O^{2-} ions.

Substances that accept electrons are said to be *reduced;* substances that give up electrons are said to be *oxidized.* One way to remember this is that the gain of electrons will reduce the positive charge on an ion or will make an uncharged atom a negative ion. Reduction and oxidation are linked. In all redox reactions, one or more reactants is reduced and one or more is oxidized.

Some redox reactions do not involve ions. In these reactions, oxidation is a gain of oxygen or a loss of hydrogen, and reduction is the loss of oxygen or the gain of hydrogen. Respiration and combustion are redox reactions because oxygen gas reacts with carbon compounds to form carbon dioxide. Carbon atoms in CO_2 are oxidized, and oxygen atoms in O_2 are reduced.

Radicals have electrons available for bonding

Many synthetic fibers, as well as plastic bags and wraps, are made by polymerization reactions, as you have already learned. Polymerization reactions can occur when **radicals** are formed.

When a covalent bond is broken such that at least one unpaired electron is left on each fragment of the molecule, these fragments are called radicals. Because an uncharged hydrogen atom has one electron available for bonding, it is a radical. Radicals react quickly to form covalent bonds with other substances, making new compounds. Often, when you see chemical radicals mentioned in the newspaper or hear about them on the radio or television, they are called free radicals.

▶ **reduction/oxidation (redox) reaction** a reaction that occurs when electrons are transferred from one reactant to another

▶ **radicals** the fragments of molecules that have at least one electron available for bonding

Figure 5-12
Radical reactions are used to make polystyrene. Polystyrene foam is often used to insulate or to protect things that can break.

Radicals are part of many everyday reactions besides the making of polymers, such as those shown in **Figure 5-12.** Radicals can also be formed when coal and oil are processed or burned. The explosive combustion of rocket fuel is another reaction involving the formation of radicals.

SECTION 5.2 REVIEW

SUMMARY

▶ Synthesis reactions make larger molecules.

▶ Decomposition breaks compounds apart.

▶ In combustion, substances react with oxygen.

▶ Elements appear to trade places in single-displacement reactions.

▶ In double-displacement reactions, ions appear to move between compounds, resulting in a solid that settles out of solution, a gas that bubbles out of solution, and/or a molecular substance.

▶ In redox reactions, electrons transfer from one substance to another.

CHECK YOUR UNDERSTANDING

1. **Classify** each of the following reactions by type:
   a. $S_8 + 8O_2 \longrightarrow 8SO_2 + heat$
   b. $6CO_2 + 6H_2O \longrightarrow C_6H_{12}O_6 + 6O_2$
   c. $2NaHCO_3 \longrightarrow Na_2CO_3 + H_2O + CO_2$
   d. $Zn + 2HCl \longrightarrow ZnCl_2 + H_2$

2. **Identify** which element is oxidized and which element is reduced in the following reaction.
$$Zn + CuSO_4 \longrightarrow ZnSO_4 + Cu$$

3. **Define** *radical*.

4. **Compare and Contrast** single-displacement and double-displacement reactions based on the number of reactants. Use the terms *compound, atom* or *element,* and *ion*.

5. **Explain** why charcoal grills or charcoal fires should never be used for heating inside a house. (**Hint:** Doors and windows are closed when it is cold, so there is little fresh air.)

6. **Contrast** synthesis and decomposition reactions.

7. **List** three possible results of a double-displacement reaction.

8. **Creative Thinking** Would you expect larger or smaller molecules to be components of a more viscous liquid? Which is likely to be more viscous, crude oil or oil after cracking?

Balancing Chemical Equations

OBJECTIVES

▶ Demonstrate how to balance chemical equations.

▶ Interpret chemical equations to determine the relative number of moles of reactants needed and moles of products formed.

▶ Explain how the law of definite proportions allows for predictions about reaction amounts.

▶ Identify mole ratios in a balanced chemical equation.

▶ Calculate the relative masses of reactants and products from a chemical equation.

▶ **KEY TERMS**

chemical equation
mole ratio

Figure 5-13 shows a combustion reaction you learned about in Section 5.2. You may have seen this reaction in the lab or at home if you have a gas stove. When natural gas burns, methane, the main component, reacts with oxygen gas to form carbon dioxide and water.

Describing Reactions

You can describe this reaction in many ways. You could take a photograph or make a videotape. One way to record the products and reactants of this reaction is to write a word equation.

methane + oxygen ⟶ carbon dioxide + water

▶ **chemical equation** an equation that uses chemical formulas and symbols to show the reactants and products in a chemical reaction

Chemical equations summarize reactions

In Section 5.1, you learned that all chemical reactions are re-arrangements of atoms. This is shown clearly in **Figure 5-13.** A better way to write the methane combustion reaction is as a chemical equation, using the formulas for each substance.

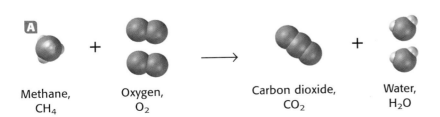

A					
Methane, CH_4	Oxygen, O_2		Carbon dioxide, CO_2	Water, H_2O

Figure 5-13
(A) Methane burns with oxygen gas to make carbon dioxide and water.
(B) A methane flame is used to polish the edges of these glass plates. **B**

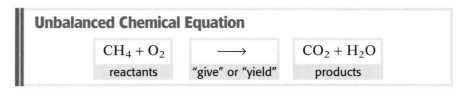

Unbalanced Chemical Equation

$$CH_4 + O_2 \qquad \longrightarrow \qquad CO_2 + H_2O$$

reactants   "give" or "yield"   products

In a chemical equation, such as the one above, the reactants, which are on the left-hand side of the arrow, form the products, which are on the right-hand side. When chemical equations are written, $\longrightarrow$ means "gives" or "yields". People all over the world write chemical equations the same way, as shown in **Figure 5-14.**

Balanced chemical equations account for the conservation of mass

The chemical equation shown above can be made more useful. As written, it does not tell you anything about the amount of the products that will be formed from burning a given amount of methane. When the number of atoms of each element on the right-hand side of the equation matches the number of atoms of each element on the left, then the chemical equation is said to be *balanced*. A balanced chemical equation follows the law of conservation of mass.

How to balance chemical equations

In the previous equation, the number of atoms on each side of the arrow did not match for all of the elements in the equation. Carbon is balanced because one carbon atom is on each side of the equation. However, four hydrogen atoms are on the left, and only two are on the right. Also, two oxygen atoms are on the left, and three are on the right. This can't be correct because atoms can't be created or destroyed in a chemical reaction, as you learned in Chapter 2.

Remember that you cannot balance an equation by changing the chemical formulas. You have to leave the subscripts in the formulas alone. Changing the formulas would mean that different substances were in the reaction. An equation can be balanced only by putting numbers, called coefficients, in front of the chemical formulas.

Because there is a total of four hydrogen atoms in the reactants, a total of four hydrogen atoms must be in the products. Instead of a single water molecule, this reaction makes two water molecules to account for all four hydrogen atoms. To show that two water molecules are formed, a coefficient of 2 is placed in front of the formula for water.

$$CH_4 + O_2 \longrightarrow CO_2 + 2H_2O$$

Figure 5-14
This student is giving a talk on reactions that use copper. You can read the chemical equations even if you can't read Japanese.

Next look at the oxygen. There is a total of four oxygen atoms in the products. Two are in the CO_2, and each water molecule contains one oxygen atom. To get four oxygen atoms on the left side of the equation, two oxygen molecules must react. That would account for all four oxygen atoms.

Balanced Chemical Equation

$$CH_4 + 2O_2 \longrightarrow CO_2 + 2H_2O$$

Now the numbers of atoms for each element are the same on each side, and the equation is balanced, as shown below.

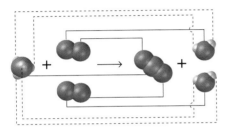

Connection to SOCIAL STUDIES

No one can be sure when fireworks were first used. When the Mongols attacked China in 1232, the defenders used "arrows of flying fire," which some historians think were rockets fired by gunpowder. The Arabs probably used rockets when they invaded the Spanish peninsula in 1249. For hundreds of years, the main use of rockets was to add terror and confusion to battles. In the late 1700s, rockets were used with some success against the British in India. Because of this, Sir William Congreve began to design rockets for England. Congreve's rockets were designed to explode in the air or be fired along the ground.

Making the Connection

British forces used Congreve's rockets during the War of 1812. Research the battle of Fort McHenry. Find out what happened, who won the battle, and what lyrics the rockets inspired.

Information from a balanced equation

You can learn a lot from a balanced equation. In our example, you can tell that each molecule of methane requires two oxygen molecules to react. Each methane molecule that burns forms one molecule of carbon dioxide and two molecules of water. Balanced chemical equations are the standard way chemists write about reactions to describe both the substances in the reaction and the amounts involved.

If you know the formulas of the reactants and products in a reaction, like the one shown in **Figure 5-15,** you can always write a balanced equation, as shown on the following pages.

PHYSICAL SCIENCE INTERACTIVE TUTOR

Disc One, Module 5:
Chemical Equations
Use the Interactive Tutor to learn more about this topic.

Figure 5-15
Magnesium in these fireworks gives off energy as heat and light when it burns to form magnesium oxide.

Fire Extinguishers: Are They All The Same?

A fire is a combustion reaction in progress that is speeded up by high temperatures. Three things are needed for a combustion reaction to occur: a fuel, some oxygen, and an ignition source. If any of these three is absent, combustion cannot occur. So the goal of firefighting is to remove one or more of these parts. Fire extinguishers are effective in firefighting because they separate the fuel from the oxygen supply, which is most commonly air.

Fire extinguishers display codes indicating which types of fires they can put out.

Classes of Fires

A fire is classified by the type of fuel that combusts to produce it. Class A fires involve solid fuels, such as wood and paper. The fuel in a Class B fire is a flammable liquid, like grease, gasoline, or oil. Class C fires involve "live" electric circuits. And Class D fires are fueled by the combustion of flammable metals.

Types of Fire Extinguishers

Different types of fuels require different firefighting methods. Water extinguishers are used on Class A fires, which involve fuels such as most flammable building materials. The steam that is produced helps to displace the air around the fire, preventing the oxygen supply from reaching the fuel.

A Class B fire, in which the fuel is a liquid, is best put out by cold carbon dioxide gas, CO_2. Because carbon dioxide is more dense than air, it forms a layer underneath the air, cutting off the oxygen supply for the combustion reaction.

Class C fires, which involve a "live" electric circuit, can also be extinguished by CO_2. Liquid water cannot be used, or there will be a danger of electric shock. Some Class C fire extinguishers contain a dry chemical that smothers the fire. The dry chemical smothers the fire by reacting with the intermediates that drive the chain reaction that produces the fire. This stops the chain reaction and extinguishes the fire.

Finally, Class D fires, which involve burning metals, cannot be extinguished with CO_2 or water because these compounds may react with some hot metals. For these fires, nonreactive dry powders are used to cover the metal and keep it separate from oxygen. In many cases, the powders used in Class D extinguishers are specific to the type of metal that is burning.

Most fire extinguishers can be used with more than one type of fire. Check the fire extinguishers in your home and school to find out the kinds of fires they are designed to put out.

Your Choice

1. **Making Decisions** Aside from displacing the air supply, how does water or cold CO_2 gas reduce a fire's severity?
2. **Critical Thinking** How is the chain reaction in a Class C fire interrupted by the contents of a dry chemical extinguisher?

internet**connect**

SCI**LINKS** NSTA

TOPIC: Fire extinguishers
GO TO: www.scilinks.org
KEYWORD: HK1057

Math Skills

Balancing Chemical Equations Write the equation that describes the burning of magnesium in air to form magnesium oxide.

1 **Identify the reactants and products.**

Magnesium and oxygen gas are the reactants that form the product, magnesium oxide.

2 **Write a word equation for the reaction.**

$$\text{magnesium} + \text{oxygen} \longrightarrow \text{magnesium oxide}$$

3 **Write the equation using formulas for the elements and compounds in the word equation.**

Remember that some gaseous elements, like oxygen, are molecules, not atoms. Oxygen in air is O_2, not O.

$$Mg + O_2 \longrightarrow MgO$$

4 **Balance the equation one element at a time.**

The same number of each kind of atom must appear on both sides. So far, there is one atom of magnesium on each side of the equation.

Atom	Reactants	Products	Balanced?
Mg	1	1	✔
O	2	1	✘

But there are two oxygen atoms on the left and only one on the right. To balance the number of oxygen atoms, you need to double the amount of magnesium oxide:

$$Mg + O_2 \longrightarrow 2MgO$$

Atom	Reactants	Products	Balanced?
Mg	1	2	✘
O	2	2	✔

This equation gives you two magnesium atoms on the right and only one on the left. So you need to double the amount of magnesium on the left, as follows.

$$2Mg + O_2 \longrightarrow 2MgO$$

Atom	Reactants	Products	Balanced?
Mg	2	2	✔
O	2	2	✔

Now the equation is balanced. It has an equal number of each type of atom on both sides.

Practice **HINT**

▶ Sometimes changing the coefficients to balance one element may cause another element in the equation to become unbalanced. So always check your work.

Balancing Chemical Equations

1. Copper(II) sulfate, $CuSO_4$, and aluminum react to form aluminum sulfate, $Al_2(SO_4)_3$, and copper. Write the balanced equation for this single-displacement reaction.

2. In a double-displacement reaction, sodium sulfide, Na_2S, reacts with silver nitrate, $AgNO_3$, to form sodium nitrate, $NaNO_3$, and silver sulfide, Ag_2S. Balance this equation.

3. Hydrogen peroxide, H_2O_2, is sometimes used as a bleach or as a disinfectant. Hydrogen peroxide decomposes to give water and molecular oxygen. Write a balanced equation for the decomposition reaction.

4. Hydrogen sulfide, H_2S, is a gas that smells like rotten eggs. Write and balance an equation for the oxidation by molecular oxygen of hydrogen sulfide to make sulfuric acid, H_2SO_4.

5. Propane gas, C_3H_8, is commonly used as a fuel for camping stoves and gas barbecue grills. Write and balance the equation for the synthesis of propane from methane in which molecular hydrogen, H_2, is also a product.

Determining Mole Ratios

Look at the reaction of magnesium with oxygen to form magnesium oxide.

$$\text{magnesium} + \text{oxygen} \longrightarrow \text{magnesium oxide}$$

$$2Mg + O_2 \longrightarrow 2MgO$$

The single molecule of oxygen in the equation might be shown as $1O_2$. However, a coefficient of 1 is never written.

Balanced equations indicate particles and moles

One way to read the equation is to say that two atoms of magnesium can react with one molecule of oxygen to give two units of magnesium oxide. This is a good way to understand the reaction. But reactions almost always involve more than one or two atoms.

The equation can also be read as describing mole quantities—2 mol of magnesium can react with 1 mol of oxygen to produce 2 mol of magnesium oxide.

Balanced equations show the conservation of mass

Other ways of looking at the amounts in the reaction are shown in **Figure 5-16.** Notice that there are equal numbers of magnesium and oxygen atoms in the product and in the reactants. The total mass of the reactants is always the same as the total mass of the products.

Quick ACTIVITY

Candy Chemistry
Look at the partial equations below. Using different-colored gumdrops to show atoms of different elements, make models of the reactions by connecting the "atoms" with toothpicks. Use your models to help you balance the following equations. Classify each reaction.

a. $C_3H_8 + O_2 \longrightarrow CO_2 + H_2O$

b. $KI + Br_2 \longrightarrow KBr + I_2$

c. $H_2 + Cl_2 \longrightarrow HCl$

d. $FeS + HCl \longrightarrow FeCl_2 + H_2S$

Figure 5-16 Information from the Balanced Equation: $2Mg + O_2 \longrightarrow 2MgO$

Equation:	2Mg	+	O_2	$\longrightarrow$	2MgO
Amount (mol)	2		1	$\longrightarrow$	2
Molecules	$(6.02 \times 10^{23}) \times 2$		$(6.02 \times 10^{23}) \times 1$	$\longrightarrow$	$(6.02 \times 10^{23}) \times 2$
Mass (g)	24.3 g/mol × 2 mol		32.0 g/mol × 1 mol	$\longrightarrow$	40.3 g/mol × 2 mol
Total mass (g)	48.6		32.0	$\longrightarrow$	80.6
Model				$\longrightarrow$	

The law of definite proportions

What if you want 4 mol of magnesium to react completely? If you have twice as much magnesium as the balanced equation calls for, you will need twice as much oxygen. Twice as much magnesium oxide will be formed. No matter what amounts of magnesium and oxygen are combined or how the magnesium oxide is made, the balanced equation does not change. This follows the law of definite proportions, which states:

A compound always contains the same elements in the same proportions, regardless of how the compound is made or how much of the compound is formed.

Inquiry Lab

Can you write balanced chemical equations?

Materials ✔ 7 test tubes ✔ test-tube rack ✔ labels or wax pencil ✔ 10 mL graduated cylinder
✔ bottles of the following solutions: sodium chloride, NaCl; potassium bromide, KBr; potassium iodide, KI; and silver nitrate, $AgNO_3$

Procedure

SAFETY CAUTION Wear safety goggles and an apron. Silver nitrate will stain your skin and clothes.

1. Label three test tubes, one each for NaCl, KBr, and KI.
2. Using the graduated cylinder, measure 5 mL of each solution into the properly labeled test tube. Rinse the graduated cylinder between each use.
3. Add 1 mL of $AgNO_3$ solution to each of the test tubes. Record your observations.

Analysis

1. What did you observe as a sign that a double-displacement reaction was occurring?
2. Identify the reactants and products for each reaction.
3. Write the balanced equation for each reaction.
4. Which ion(s) produced a solid with silver nitrate?
5. Does this test let you identify all the ions? Why or why not?

Mole ratios can be derived from balanced equations

Whether the magnesium-oxygen reaction starts with 2 mol or 4 mol of magnesium, the proportions remain the same. One way to understand this is to look at the mole ratios from the balanced equation. For 2 mol of magnesium and 1 mol of oxygen, the ratio is 2:1. If 4 mol of magnesium is present, 2 mol of oxygen is needed to react. The ratio is 4:2, which reduces to 2:1.

The mole ratio for any reaction comes from the balanced chemical equation. For example, in the following equation for the synthesis of water, the mole ratio for H_2:O_2:H_2O, using the coefficients, is 2:1:2.

$$2H_2 + O_2 \longrightarrow 2H_2O$$

▶ mole ratio the smallest relative number of moles of the substances involved in a reaction

---

SECTION 5.3 REVIEW

SUMMARY

▶ A chemical equation shows the reactants that combine and the products that result from the reaction.

▶ Balanced chemical equations show the proportions of reactants and products needed for the mass to be conserved.

▶ A compound always contains the same elements in the same proportions, regardless of how the compound is made or how much of the compound is formed.

▶ A mole ratio relates the amounts of any two or more substances involved in a chemical reaction.

CHECK YOUR UNDERSTANDING

1. **Identify** which of the following is a complete and balanced chemical equation:
   a. $H_2O \longrightarrow H_2 + O_2$
   b. $NaCl + H_2O$
   c. $Fe + S \longrightarrow FeS$
   d. $CaCO_3$

2. **Balance** the following equations:
   a. $KOH + HCl \longrightarrow KCl + H_2O$
   b. $Pb(NO_3)_2 + KI \longrightarrow KNO_3 + PbI_2$
   c. $NaHCO_3 \longrightarrow H_2O + CO_2 + Na_2CO_3$
   d. $NaCl + H_2SO_4 \longrightarrow Na_2SO_4 + HCl$

3. **Explain** why the numbers in front of chemical formulas, not the subscripts, must be changed to balance an equation.

4. **Describe** the information needed to calculate the mass of a reactant or product for the following balanced equation:

$$FeS + 2HCl \longrightarrow H_2S + FeCl_2$$

5. **Critical Thinking** Ammonia is manufactured by the Haber process.

$$N_2 + 3H_2 \rightleftharpoons 2NH_3 + heat$$

This involves the reaction of nitrogen with hydrogen to form ammonia. What mass of nitrogen is needed to make 34 g of ammonia?

Rates of Change

OBJECTIVES

▶ Describe the factors affecting reaction rates.

▶ Explain the effect a catalyst has on a chemical reaction.

▶ Explain chemical equilibrium in terms of equal forward and reverse reaction rates.

▶ Apply Le Châtelier's principle to predict the effect of changes in concentration, temperature, and pressure in an equilibrium process.

▶ KEY TERMS

catalyst

enzyme

substrate

equilibrium

Le Châtelier's principle

Chemical reactions can occur at different speeds or rates. Some reactions, such as the explosion of nitroglycerin, shown in **Figure 5-17,** are very fast. Other reactions, such as the burning of carbon in charcoal, are much slower. But what if you wanted to slow down the nitroglycerin reaction to make it safer? What if you wanted to speed up the reaction by which yeast make carbon dioxide, so bread would rise in less time? If you think carefully, you may already know some things about how to change reaction rates.

internetconnect

SciLINKS

NSTA

TOPIC: Factors affecting reaction rate
GO TO: www.scilinks.org
KEYWORD: HK1054

Factors Affecting Reaction Rates

Think about the following observations:

▶ A potato slice takes 5 minutes to fry in oil at 200°C but takes 10 minutes to cook in boiling water at 100°C. Therefore, potatoes cook faster at higher temperatures.

▶ Potato slices take 10 minutes to cook in boiling water, but whole potatoes take about 30 minutes to boil. Therefore, potatoes cook faster if you cut them up into smaller pieces.

These observations relate to the speed of chemical reactions. For any reaction to occur, the particles of the reactants must collide with one another. In each situation where the potatoes cooked faster, the contact between particles was greater, so the cooking reaction went faster.

Figure 5-17
Nitroglycerin can be used as a rocket fuel as well as a medicine for people with heart ailments.

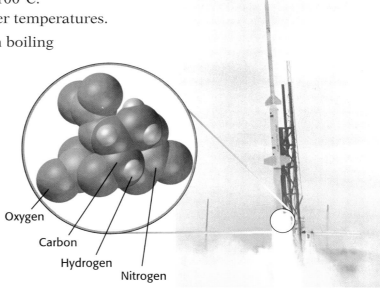

Oxygen

Carbon

Hydrogen

Nitrogen

Figure 5-18

A Mold will grow on bread stored at room temperature.

B Bread stored in the freezer for the same length of time will be free of mold when you take it out.

Figure 5-19
When a solid is divided into pieces, the total surface area becomes larger.

Most reactions go faster at higher temperatures

A potato slice cooks faster in hot oil than in boiling water. Heating food speeds up the chemical reactions that happen in cooking. Cooling food slows down the chemical reactions that result in spoiling, as shown in **Figure 5-18.**

In Chapter 2, you learned that one of the assumptions of the kinetic theory is that particles move faster at higher temperatures. This faster motion increases the energy of the particles and increases the chances that the particles will collide. This means that there are more chances for the particles to react. Because the particles have more chances to react, the reaction will be faster.

A large surface area speeds up reactions

You can save time making mashed potatoes by cutting the potatoes into small pieces before boiling them, because sliced potatoes cook more quickly than whole potatoes. When a whole potato is placed in boiling water, only the outside is in direct contact with the boiling water. As **Figure 5-19** shows, cutting potatoes into pieces allows parts that were inside the potato to be exposed. In other words, the *surface area* of the potato is increased. The surface area of a solid is the amount of the surface that is exposed.

The same holds true for most chemical reactants. If you crush a solid into a powder or dissolve it in a solution, more of the solid surface is exposed. Generally solids that have a large surface area react more rapidly because more particles can come in contact with the other reactants.

Concentrated solutions react faster

Think about a washing machine full of clothes with grass stains on them. If you put a few drops of bleach in the washing machine full of water, little will happen to the dirty clothes. If you pour a bottle of bleach into the washing machine, the stained clothes will be clean. In fact, they may not have any color left. The more concentrated solution has more bleach particles. This means a higher chance for particle collisions with the stains.

Reactions are quicker at higher pressure

Like the concentration of a liquid, the concentration of a gas can be thought of as the number of particles in a given volume. A gas at high pressure is more concentrated than a gas at low pressure because the gas at high pressure has been squeezed into a smaller volume. Gases react faster at higher pressures; the particles have less space, so they have more collisions.

Massive, bulky molecules react slower

The size and shape of the reactant molecules affect the rate of reaction. You know from the kinetic theory of matter, which you studied in Chapter 2, that massive molecules move more slowly than less massive molecules at the same temperature. This means that for equal numbers of massive and "light" molecules of about the same size, the molecules with more mass collide less often with other molecules.

Some molecules, such as large biological compounds, must fit together in a particular way to react. They can collide with other reactants many times, but if the collision occurs on the wrong end of the molecule, they will not react. Generally these compounds react very slowly because many unsuccessful collisions may occur before a successful collision begins the reaction.

Catalysts change the rates of chemical reactions

Why add a substance to a reaction if the substance may not react? This is done all the time in industry when **catalysts** are added to make reactions go faster. Catalysts are not reactants or products. They speed up or slow reactions. Catalysts that slow reactions are called *inhibitors*. Catalysts are used to help make ammonia, to process crude oil, and to accelerate making plastics. Catalysts can be expensive and still be profitable because they can be cleaned or renewed and reused.

Catalysts work in different ways. Most solid catalysts, such as those in car exhaust systems, speed up reactions by providing a surface where the reactants can collect and react. Then the reactants can form new bonds to make the products. Most solid catalysts are more effective if they have a large surface area.

▶ **catalyst** a substance that changes the rate of chemical reactions without being consumed

▶ **enzyme** a protein that speeds up a specific biochemical reaction

internetconnect

SC*LINKS*
NSTA

TOPIC: Catalysts
GO TO: www.scilinks.org
KEYWORD: HK1055

Enzymes are biological catalysts

Enzymes are proteins that are catalysts for chemical reactions in living things. Enzymes are very specific. Each enzyme controls one reaction or set of similar reactions. Some common enzymes and the reactions they control are listed in **Table 5-1.** Most enzymes are fragile. If they are kept too cold or too warm, they tend to decompose. Most enzymes stop working above 45°C.

Table 5-1 **Common Enzymes and Their Uses**

Enzyme	Substrate	What the enzyme does
Amylase	Starch	Breaks down long starch molecules into sugars
Cellulase	Cellulose	Breaks down long cellulose molecules into sugars
DNA polymerase	Nucleic acid	Builds up DNA chains in cell nuclei
Lipase	Fat	Breaks down fat into smaller molecules
Protease	Protein	Breaks down proteins into amino acids.

Figure 5-20

The enzyme hexokinase catalyzes the addition of phosphate to glucose. This model shows the enzyme, in blue, before (A) and after (B) it fits with a glucose molecule, shown in red.

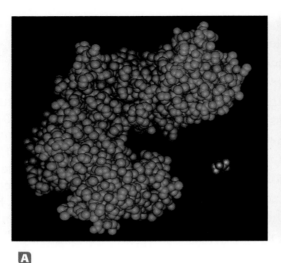

A

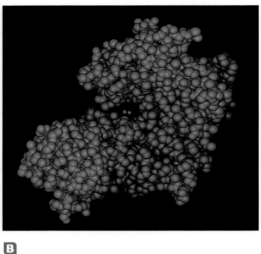

B

▷ **substrate** the specific substance affected by an enzyme

Catalase, an enzyme produced by humans and most other living organisms, breaks down hydrogen peroxide. Hydrogen peroxide is the **substrate** for catalase.

$$2H_2O_2 \xrightarrow{\text{catalase}} 2H_2O + O_2$$

For an enzyme to catalyze a reaction, the substrate and the enzyme must fit exactly—like a key in a lock. This fit is shown in **Figure 5-20.** Enzymes are very efficient. In 1 minute, one molecule of catalase can catalyze the decomposition of 6 million molecules of hydrogen peroxide.

Inquiry Lab

What affects the rates of chemical reactions?

Materials
- ✔ Bunsen burner
- ✔ paper clip
- ✔ 6 test tubes
- ✔ paper ash
- ✔ sandpaper
- ✔ tongs
- ✔ matches
- ✔ 2 sugar cubes
- ✔ steel wool ball, 2 cm diameter
- ✔ graduated cylinder
- ✔ vinegar
- ✔ magnesium ribbon, copper foil strip, zinc strip; each 3 cm long, uniform width

Procedure

SAFETY CAUTION Wear safety goggles and an apron.

1. Label three test tubes 1, 2, and 3. Place 10 mL of vinegar in each test tube. Sandpaper the metals until they are shiny. Then add the magnesium to test tube 1, the zinc to test tube 2, and the copper to test tube 3. Record your observations.
2. Using tongs, hold a paper clip in the hottest part of the burner flame for 30 s. Repeat with a ball of steel wool. Record your observations.
3. Label three more test tubes A, B, and C. To test tube A, add 10 mL of vinegar; to test tube B, add 5 mL of vinegar and 5 mL of water; and to test tube C, add 2.5 mL of vinegar and 7.5 mL of water. Add a piece of magnesium ribbon to each test tube. Record your observations.
4. Using tongs, hold a sugar cube and try to ignite it with a match. Rub paper ash on another cube and try again. Record your observations.

Analysis

1. Describe and interpret your results.
2. For each step, list the factor(s) that influenced the rate of reaction.

Equilibrium Systems

When nitroglycerin explodes, nothing much is left. When an iron nail rusts, given enough time, all the iron is converted to iron(III) oxide and only the rust remains. Even though an explosion occurs rapidly and rusting occurs slowly, both reactions go to completion. Most of the reactants are converted to products, and the amount that is not converted is not noticeable and usually is not important.

Some changes are reversible

You may get the idea that all chemical reactions go to completion if you watch a piece of wood burn or see an explosion. However, reactions don't always go to completion; some reactions are reversible.

For example, carbonated drinks, such as the soda shown in **Figure 5-21,** contain carbon dioxide. These drinks are manufactured by dissolving carbon dioxide in water under pressure. To keep the carbon dioxide dissolved, you need to maintain the pressure by keeping the top on the bottle. Opening the soda allows the pressure to decrease. When this happens, some of the carbon dioxide comes out of solution, and you see a stream of carbon dioxide bubbles. This carbon dioxide change is reversible.

Quick ACTIVITY

Catalysts in Action
1. Pour 2 percent hydrogen peroxide into a test tube to a depth of 2 cm.
2. Pour 2 cm of water into another test tube.
3. Drop a small piece of raw liver into each test tube.
4. Liver contains the enzyme catalase. Watch carefully, and describe what happens. Explain your observations.
5. Repeat steps 1–4 using a piece of liver that has been boiled for 3 minutes. Explain your result.
6. Repeat steps 1–4 again using iron filings instead of liver. What happens?

$$CO_2 \text{ (gas above liquid)} \underset{\substack{\text{decrease} \\ \text{pressure}}}{\overset{\substack{\text{increase} \\ \text{pressure}}}{\rightleftharpoons}} CO_2 \text{ (gas dissolved in liquid)}$$

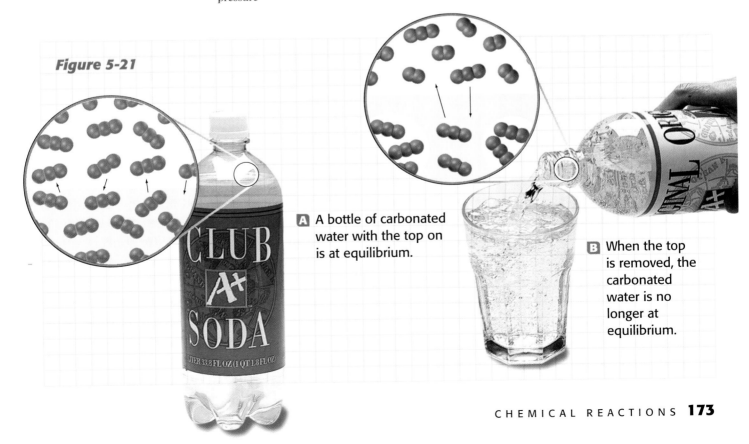

Figure 5-21

A A bottle of carbonated water with the top on is at equilibrium.

B When the top is removed, the carbonated water is no longer at equilibrium.

The reaction can go in either direction. The $\rightleftharpoons$ sign indicates a reversible change. Compare it with the arrow you normally see in chemical reactions, $\longrightarrow$, which indicates a change that goes in one direction—toward completion.

Equilibrium results when rates balance

When a carbonated drink is in a closed bottle, you can't see any changes. The system is in **equilibrium**—a balanced state. This balanced state is dynamic. No changes are apparent, but changes are occurring. If you could see individual molecules in the bottle, you would see continual change. Molecules of CO_2 are coming out of solution constantly. However, CO_2 molecules from the air above the liquid are dissolving at the same time and the same rate.

The result is that the amount of dissolved and undissolved CO_2 doesn't change, even though individual CO_2 molecules are moving in and out of the solution. This is similar to the number of players on the field for a football team. Although different players can be on the field at any time, eleven players are always on the field for each team.

Systems in equilibrium respond to minimize change

When the top is removed from a carbonated drink, the drink is no longer at equilibrium, and CO_2 leaves as bubbles. For equilibrium to be reached, none of the reactants or products can escape.

An example of an equilibrium system is the conversion of limestone, $CaCO_3$, to lime, CaO. Limestone and seashells, which are also made of $CaCO_3$, were used to make lime more than 2000 years ago. By heating limestone in an open pot, lime was produced to make cement. The ancient buildings in Greece and Rome, such as the one shown in **Figure 5-22,** were probably built with cement made by this reaction.

$$CaCO_3 + heat \longrightarrow CaO + CO_2$$

Because the CO_2 gas can escape from an open pot, the reaction proceeds until all of the limestone is converted to lime.

However, if some dry limestone is sealed in a closed container and heated, the result is different. As soon as some CO_2 builds up in the container, the reverse reaction starts. Once the concentrations of the $CaCO_3$, CaO, and CO_2 stabilize, equilibrium is established.

$$CaCO_3 \rightleftharpoons CaO + CO_2$$

If there aren't any changes in the pressure or the temperature, the forward and reverse reactions continue to take place at the same rate. The concentration of CO_2 and the amounts of $CaCO_3$ and CaO in the container remain the same.

▶ **equilibrium** the state in which a chemical reaction and its reverse occur at the same time and at the same rate

VOCABULARY *Skills Tip*

Equilibrium comes from the Latin aequilibris *meaning equally balanced. In Latin,* aequil *means equal, and* libra *means a balance scale. You may have seen the constellation called Libra. The stars in the constellation roughly represent a balance.*

Figure 5-22
Cement for ancient buildings, like this one in Limeni, Greece, probably contained lime made from seashells.

Table 5-2 **The Effects of Change on Equilibrium**

Condition	Effect
Temperature	Increasing temperature favors the reaction that absorbs energy.
Pressure	Increasing pressure favors the reaction that produces less gas.
Concentration	Increasing the concentration of one substance favors the reaction that produces less of that substance.

Figure 5-23
Ammonium sulfate and ammonium phosphate are being dropped from the airplane as fire retardants. The red dye used for identification fades away after a few days.

Le Châtelier's principle predicts changes in equilibrium

Le Châtelier's principle is a general rule that describes the behavior of equilibrium systems.

**If a change is made to a system in chemical equilibrium,
the equilibrium shifts to oppose the change
until a new equilibrium is reached.**

The effects of different changes on an equilibrium system are shown in **Table 5-2.**

Ammonia is a chemical building block used to make fertilizers, dyes, plastics, cosmetics, cleaning products, and fire retardants, such as those you see being applied in **Figure 5-23.** The Haber process, which is used to make ammonia industrially, is exothermic; it releases energy.

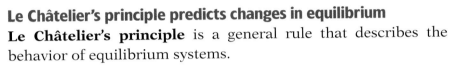

$$\text{nitrogen} + \text{hydrogen} \rightleftharpoons \text{ammonia} + \text{heat}$$

$$N_2 \text{ (gas)} + 3H_2 \text{ (gas)} \rightleftharpoons 2NH_3 \text{ (gas)} + \text{heat}$$

At an ammonia-manufacturing plant, such as the one shown in **Figure 5-24,** production chemists must choose the conditions that favor the highest yield of NH_3. In other words, the equilibrium should favor the production of NH_3.

Figure 5-24
Ammonia, which is manufactured in plants such as this, is used to make ammonium perchlorate—one of the space shuttle's fuels.

INTEGRATING

ENVIRONMENTAL SCIENCE
All living things need nitrogen, which cycles through the environment. Nitrogen gas, N_2, is changed to ammonia by bacteria in soils. Different bacteria in the soil change the ammonia to nitrites and nitrates. Nitrogen in the form of nitrates is needed by plants to grow. Animals eat the plants and deposit nitrogen compounds back in the soil. When plants or animals die, nitrogen compounds are also returned to the soil. Additional bacteria change the nitrogen compounds back to nitrogen gas, and the cycle can start again.

If you raise the temperature, Le Châtelier's principle indicates that the equilibrium will shift to the left, the direction that absorbs energy and makes less ammonia. If you raise the pressure, the equilibrium will move to reduce the pressure according to Le Châtelier's principle. One way to reduce the pressure is to have fewer gas molecules. This means the equilibrium moves to the right—more ammonia—because there are fewer gas molecules on the right side. So to get the most ammonia from this reaction, you need to use a high pressure and a low temperature. The Haber process is a good example of balancing equilibrium conditions to make the most product.

SECTION 5.4 REVIEW

SUMMARY

▶ Increasing the temperature, surface area, concentration, or pressure of reactants may speed up chemical reactions.

▶ Catalysts alter the rate of chemical reactions. Most catalysts speed up chemical reactions. Others, called inhibitors, slow reactions down.

▶ In a chemical reaction, chemical equilibrium is achieved when reactants change to products and products change to reactants at the same time and the same rate.

▶ At chemical equilibrium, no changes are apparent even though individual particles are reacting.

▶ Le Châtelier's principle states that for any change made to a system in equilibrium, the equilibrium will shift to minimize the effects of the change.

CHECK YOUR UNDERSTANDING

1. **Identify** which of the following are examples of chemical equilibrium:
   a. $2NO_2 \rightleftharpoons N_2O_4$
   b. $2H_2O \longrightarrow 2H_2 + O_2$
   c. $N_2 + 3H_2 \rightleftharpoons 2NH_3 + heat$
   d. $H_2 + I_2 \rightleftharpoons 2HI$

2. **List** five factors that may affect the rate of a chemical reaction.

3. **Identify and Explain** an example of Le Châtelier's principle.

4. **Compare and Contrast** a catalyst and an inhibitor.

5. **Analyze** the error in reasoning in the following situation: A person claims that because the overall amounts of reactants and products don't change, a reaction must have stopped.

6. **Describe** what can happen to the reaction rate of a system that is heated and then cooled.

7. **Decide** which way an increase in pressure will shift the following equilibrium system involving ethane, C_2H_6, oxygen, O_2, water, H_2O, and carbon dioxide, CO_2.

   $$2C_2H_6 \text{ (gas)} + 7O_2 \text{ (gas)} \rightleftharpoons 6H_2O \text{ (liquid)} + 4CO_2 \text{ (gas)}$$

8. **Decision Making** Consider the decomposition of solid calcium carbonate to solid calcium oxide and carbon dioxide gas.

   $$heat + CaCO_3 \rightleftharpoons CaO + CO_2 \text{ (gas)}$$

   What conditions of temperature and pressure would you choose to get the most decomposition of $CaCO_3$? Explain your reasoning.

Chapter Highlights

Before you begin, review the summaries of the key ideas of each section, found on pages 153, 160, 168, and 176. The key vocabulary terms are listed on pages 148, 154, 161, and 169.

UNDERSTANDING CONCEPTS

1. When a chemical reaction occurs, atoms are never _____.
   a. ionized
   c. destroyed
   b. rearranged
   d. vaporized

2. In an exothermic reaction, _____.
   a. energy is conserved
   b. the formation of bonds in the product releases more energy than is required to break the bonds in the reactants
   c. energy is released as bonds form
   d. All of the above

3. A + B $\longrightarrow$ AB is an example of a _____.
   a. synthesis reaction
   b. decomposition reaction
   c. single-displacement reaction
   d. double-displacement reaction
   e. redox reaction

4. Which of the following reactions is not an example of a redox reaction?
   a. combustion
   b. rusting
   c. dissolving in salt water
   d. respiration

5. Radicals _____.
   a. form ionic bonds with other ions
   b. result from broken covalent bonds
   c. usually break apart to form smaller components
   d. bind molecules together

6. In any chemical equation, the arrow means _____.
   a. "equals"
   b. "is greater than"
   c. "yields"

7. Hydrogen peroxide, H_2O_2, decomposes to produce water and oxygen gas. The balanced equation for this reaction is _____.
   a. $H_2O_2 \longrightarrow H_2O + O_2$
   b. $2H_2O_2 \longrightarrow 2H_2O + O_2$
   c. $2H_2O_2 \longrightarrow H_2O + 2O_2$
   d. $2H_2O_2 \longrightarrow 2H_2O + 2O_2$

8. Most reactions speed up when _____.
   a. the temperature is lowered
   b. equilibrium is achieved
   c. the concentration of the products is increased
   d. the reactants are in small pieces

9. Enzymes _____.
   a. can be used to speed up almost any chemical reaction
   b. rely on increased surface area to catalyze reactions
   c. catalyze specific biological reactions
   d. always work faster at higher temperatures

10. A system in chemical equilibrium _____.
    a. has particles that don't move
    b. responds to minimize change
    c. is undergoing visible change
    d. is stable only when all of the reactants have been used

Using Vocabulary

11. Explain what it means when a system in equilibrium shifts to favor the products.

12. When wood is burned, energy is released in the forms of heat and light. Describe the reaction, and explain why this change does not violate the law of conservation of energy. Use the terms *combustion, exothermic,* and *chemical energy.*

    WRITING SKILL

13. Translate the following chemical equation into a sentence.
    $$CH_4 + 2O_2 \longrightarrow CO_2 + 2H_2O$$

14. For each of the following changes to the equilibrium system below, predict which reaction will be favored—forward (to the right), reverse (to the left), or neither.

$$H_2 \text{ (gas)} + Cl_2 \text{ (gas)} \rightleftharpoons 2HCl \text{ (gas)} + \text{heat}$$

a. addition of Cl_2
b. removal of HCl
c. increased pressure
d. decreased temperature
e. removal of H_2

BUILDING MATH SKILLS

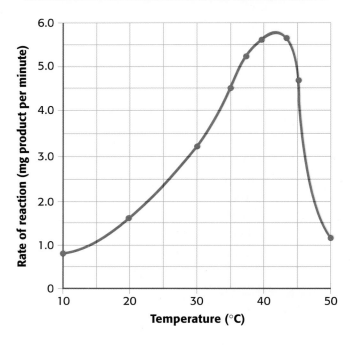

15. Graphing A technician carried out an experiment to study the effect of increasing temperature on a certain reaction. Her results are shown in the graph above.
  a. Between which temperatures does the rate of the reaction rise?
  b. Between which temperatures does the rate of the reaction slow down?
  c. At what temperature is the rate of the reaction fastest?

16. Chemical Equations In 1774, Joseph Priestly discovered oxygen when he heated solid mercury(II) oxide, HgO, and produced the element mercury and oxygen gas. Write and balance this equation.

17. Chemical Equations Aluminum sulfate, $Al_2(SO_4)_3$, is used to fireproof fabrics and to make antiperspirants. It can be formed from a reaction between aluminum oxide, Al_2O_3, and H_2SO_4.

$$Al_2O_3 + 3H_2SO_4 \longrightarrow Al_2(SO_4)_3 + 3H_2O$$

  a. How many moles of $Al_2(SO_4)_3$ would be produced if 6 mol of H_2SO_4 reacted with an unlimited amount of Al_2O_3?
  b. How many moles of Al_2O_3 are required to make 9 mol of H_2O?
  c. If 588 mol of Al_2O_3 reacts with unlimited H_2SO_4, how many moles of each of the products will be produced?

18. Chemical Equations Sucrose, $C_{12}H_{22}O_{11}$, is a sugar used to sweeten many foods. Inside the body, it is broken down to produce H_2O and CO_2.

$$C_{12}H_{22}O_{11} + 12O_2 \longrightarrow 12CO_2 + 11H_2O$$

List all of the mole ratios that can be determined from this equation.

19. Chemical Equations Sulfur burns in air to form sulfur dioxide.

$$S + O_2 \longrightarrow SO_2$$

  a. What mass of SO_2 is formed from 64 g of sulfur?
  b. What mass of sulfur is necessary to form 256 g of SO_2?

20. Chemical Equations Zinc metal will react with hydrochloric acid, HCl, to produce hydrogen gas and zinc chloride, $ZnCl_2$. Write and balance the chemical equation for this reaction.

THINKING CRITICALLY

21. Designing Systems Paper consists mainly of cellulose, a complex compound made up of simple sugars. Suggest a method for turning old newspapers into sugars using an enzyme. What problems would there be? What precautions would need to be taken?

22. Applying Knowledge Molecular models of some chemical reactions are pictured below. Correct the drawings by adding coefficients or drawing molecules with a computer drawing program to reflect balanced equations.

COMPUTER SKILL

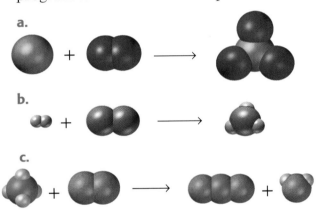

23. Understanding Systems Why is it dangerous to leave a car engine running when the car is in a closed garage?

DEVELOPING LIFE/WORK SKILLS

24. Making Decisions Cigarette smoke contains carbon monoxide. Why do you think carbon monoxide is in the smoke? Why is smoking bad for your health?

25. Interpreting and Communicating Choose several items labeled "biodegradable," and research the decomposition reactions involved. Write balanced chemical equations for the decomposition reactions. Be sure to note any conditions that must occur for the substance to biodegrade. Present your information to the class to inform the students about what products are best for the environment.

INTEGRATING CONCEPTS

26. Concept Mapping Copy the unfinished concept map given below onto a sheet of paper. Complete the map by writing the correct word or phrase in the lettered box.

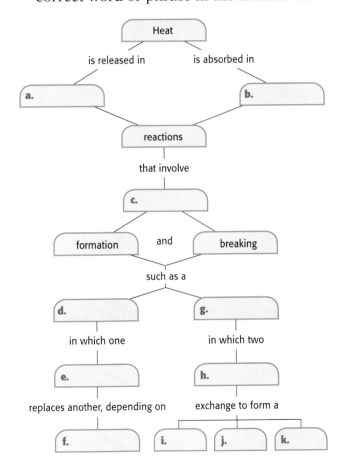

internet**connect**

SCLINKS
NSTA

TOPIC: Biodegradable
GO TO: www.scilinks.org
KEYWORD: HK1056

Design Your Own Lab

Introduction

How can you show that the rate of a chemical reaction depends on the temperature of the reactants?

Objectives

▶ **Measure** the volume of gas evolved to determine the rate of the reaction between zinc and hydrochloric acid.

▶ **Determine** how the rate of this reaction depends on the temperature of the reactants.

Materials

thermometer
metric ruler
stopwatch
heavy scissors
strips of thick zinc foil, 10 mm wide
1.0 M hydrochloric acid
10 mL graduated cylinder
25 mL graduated cylinder
2 sidearm flasks with rubber stoppers
beaker to hold a 10 mL graduated cylinder
rubber tubing
ice
water bath to hold a sidearm flask

Safety Needs

lab apron
safety goggles
polyethylene gloves

Measuring the Rate of a Chemical Reaction

▶ Observing the Reaction Between Zinc and Hydrochloric Acid

1. On a blank sheet of paper, prepare a table like the one shown at right.

   SAFETY CAUTION Hydrochloric acid can cause severe burns. Wear a lab apron, gloves, and safety goggles. If you get acid on your skin or clothing, wash it off at the sink while calling to your teacher. If you get acid in your eyes, immediately flush it out at the eyewash station while calling to your teacher. Continue rinsing for at least 15 minutes or until help arrives.

2. Fill a 10 mL graduated cylinder with water. Turn the cylinder upside down in a beaker of water, taking care to keep the cylinder full. Place one end of the rubber tubing under the spout of the graduated cylinder. Attach the other end of the tubing to the arm of the flask. Place the flask in a water bath at room temperature. Record the initial gas volume of the cylinder and the temperature of the water bath in your data table.

3. Cut a piece of zinc about 50–75 mm long. Measure the length, and record this in your data table. Place the zinc in the sidearm flask.

4. Measure 25 mL of hydrochloric acid in a graduated cylinder.

5. Carefully pour the acid from the graduated cylinder into the flask. Start the stopwatch as you begin to pour. Stopper the flask as soon as the acid is transferred.

6. Record any signs of a chemical reaction you observe.

7. After 15 minutes, determine the amount of gas given off by the reaction. Record the volume of gas in your data table.

	Length of zinc strip (mm)	Initial gas volume (mL)	Final gas volume (mL)	Temperature (°C)	Reaction time (s)
Reaction 1					
Reaction 2					

▶ Designing Your Experiment

8. With your lab partners decide how you will answer the question posed at the beginning of the lab. By completing steps 1–7, you have half the data you need to answer the question. How can you collect the rest of the data?

9. In your lab report, list each step you will perform in your experiment. Because temperature is the variable you want to test, the other variables in your experiment should be the same as they were in steps 1–7.

10. Before you carry out your experiment, your teacher must approve your plan.

▶ Performing Your Experiment

11. After your teacher approves your plan, carry out your experiment. Record your results in your data table.

12. How do the two reactions differ?

▶ Analyzing Your Results

1. Express the rate of each reaction as mL of gas evolved in 1 minute.

2. Which reaction was more rapid?

3. Divide the faster rate by the slower rate, and express the reaction rates as a ratio.

4. According to your results, how does decreasing the temperature affect the rate of a chemical reaction?

▶ Defending Your Conclusions

5. How could you test the effect of temperature on this reaction without using an ice bath?

6. How can you express the rate of each of the two reactions you conducted as a function of the surface area of the zinc?

7. How would you design an experiment to test the effect of surface area on this reaction?

viewpoints

How Should Life-Saving Inventions Be Introduced?

Researchers are developing better fire-proof materials to use inside passenger airplanes. But the new materials are much more expensive than the ones currently used.

Should the Federal Aviation Administration (FAA) require that the new materials be used on all new and old planes, or should it be up to the plane manufacturers and airlines to decide whether to use the new materials?

A similar debate occurs whenever life-saving inventions are introduced, from automobile airbags to better child-safety seats. If the inventions should be used, who should bear the cost? Should it be the federal government, an insurance company, a manufacturer, or the customers?

If the device shouldn't be required at all times, how do you decide when it should be used? When are the risks so small that it doesn't make sense to spend money on another safety device?

What do you think?

> FROM: Stacey F., Rochester, MN.

It should be up to the plane manufacturers because not all companies would be able to afford the cost. The FAA should look into the budgets of all plane companies and companies that can afford it should be required to use the new material.

> FROM: Emily B., Coral Springs, FL

I think it should be up to the plane manufacturers and airlines. The new materials shouldn't be required on planes that are already built or on planes that are being built, because of expenses. However, it would be to an airline's advantage to have the best safety material possible for their customers' sake.

> FROM: Virginia M., Houston, TX

The airlines are responsible for the lives of their passengers, so they should decide. But the FAA should pass a law stating that if the airlines refuse new safety measures, the airlines will accept total responsibility for any accidents that occur.

Leave the Decisions to the Companies Involved

> FROM: April R., Coral Springs, FL

If it can save just one life, it's worth spending money and time on. Eventually the technology will be required on all planes anyway. If an airline chose not to use these materials and there were an accident, there would be liability cases because lives might have been saved. Most people will have no problem spending more for a plane ticket if their safety is ensured.

Require Safety Immediately

> FROM: Carlene de C., Chicago, IL

The FAA should require that all planes— those currently in use and those being built—have fireproof materials. Otherwise, passengers could sue the airline company if they were hurt in a fire and it could have been prevented.

> FROM: Shannon B., Bowling Green, KY

They should put the new fireproof materials on all planes, even the ones that have already been built. The public's health is at risk if a plane malfunctions, and the airlines should want to keep everybody safe. Otherwise they will lose customers.

> Your Turn

1. **Critiquing Viewpoints** Select one of the statements on this page that you *agree* with. Identify and explain at least one weak point in the statement. What would you say to respond to someone who brought up this weak point as a reason you were wrong?

2. **Critiquing Viewpoints** Select one of the statements on this page that you *disagree* with. Identify and explain at least one strong point in the statement. What would you say to respond to someone who brought up this point as a reason they were right?

3. **Life/Work Skills** Imagine that you are preparing to testify in a congressional hearing about this matter. Choose the four most important points you'd make, and draft a statement that explains all of them persuasively.

4. **Working Cooperatively** With your teacher's help, stage a role-playing exercise, with students serving as the panel of congressional representatives preparing to vote on this issue and as witnesses for the airlines, the airplane manufacturers, insurance companies, safety organizations, and a passengers' rights group.

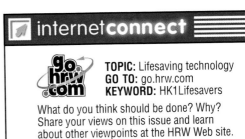

internetconnect

go.hrw.com

TOPIC: Lifesaving technology
GO TO: go.hrw.com
KEYWORD: HK1Lifesavers

What do you think should be done? Why? Share your views on this issue and learn about other viewpoints at the HRW Web site.

CHAPTER 6

Nuclear Changes

Chapter Preview

6.1 What Is Radioactivity?
Nuclear Radiation
Nuclear Decay
Radioactive Decay Rates

6.2 Nuclear Fission and Fusion
Nuclear Forces
Nuclear Fission
Nuclear Fusion

6.3 Dangers and Benefits of Nuclear Radiation
Dangers of Nuclear Radiation
Beneficial Uses of Nuclear Radiation
Nuclear Power

Focus ACTIVITY

Background The painting "Woman Reading Music" was considered one of a series of great finds discovered by Dutch painter and art dealer Han van Meegeren in the 1930s. The previously unknown paintings were believed to be by the great seventeenth century Dutch artist Jan Vermeer. But after World War II, another painting said to be by Vermeer was found in a Nazi art collection, and its sale was traced to van Meegeren. Arrested for collaborating with the Nazis, van Meegeren confessed that both paintings were forgeries. He claimed that he had used one of the fake Vermeers to lure Nazi Germany into returning many genuine paintings to the Dutch.

Was van Meegeren lying to avoid a long prison sentence, or had he really swindled the Nazis? Although X-ray photographs of the painting suggested that it was a forgery, conclusive evidence did not come about until 20 years later. A fraction of the lead in certain pigments used in the painting proved to be radioactive. By measuring the number of radioactive lead nuclei that decayed each minute, experts were able to determine the age of the painting. The fairly rapid decay rate indicated that the paint—and thus the painting—was less than 40 years old.

Activity 1 Radiation exposes photographic film. To test this observation, obtain a small sheet of unexposed photographic film and a new household smoke detector, which contains a radioactive sample. Remove the casing from the detector. In a dark room, place the film next to the smoke detector in a cardboard box and close the box. Be sure that no light can enter the box. After a day, open the box in a dark room and place the film in a thick envelope. Take the film to be processed. Is there an image on the film? How does the image differ from the rest of the film? How can you tell that the image is related to the radioactive source?

Activity 2 Use library resources to research famous art forgeries. How were the forgeries detected? What techniques use radioactive substances to identify the elements in paintings?

Radioactive substances in the paints and canvases used in painting decay over time. These radioactive substances emit nuclear radiation. The amount of radiation emitted can be used to determine how old the painting is and whether the painting is a forgery or not.

internetconnect

SC**LINKS**
NSTA

TOPIC: Radioactive isotopes
GO TO: www.scilinks.org
KEYWORD: HK1071

What Is Radioactivity?

radioactivity
nuclear radiation
alpha particle
beta particle
gamma ray
neutron emission
half-life

> **OBJECTIVES**
>
> ► Identify four types of nuclear radiation and their properties.
> ► Balance equations for nuclear decay.
> ► Calculate the half-life of a radioactive isotope.

In recent years there has been concern about radon gas in buildings and its impact on health. Detectors are used to check the level of radon in a house or a building. Many elements and compounds are dangerous because of the way they react with substances in our bodies. Radon, however, is a gas that, like helium and neon, does not chemically react with substances in the body. Why, then, is it considered a health hazard?

Nuclear Radiation

► **radioactivity** process by which an unstable nucleus emits one or more particles or energy in the form of electromagnetic radiation

Radon is one of many elements that change through **radioactivity.** Radioactive materials, which were mentioned in Chapter 3, have unstable nuclei. These nuclei go through changes by emitting particles or releasing energy, as shown in **Figure 6-1.** After the changes in the nucleus, the element can transform into a different isotope of the same element or change into an entirely different element. This nuclear process is referred to as *nuclear decay.* (Recall from Chapter 3 that isotopes of an element are atoms with the same number of protons but a different number of neutrons in their nuclei.)

► **nuclear radiation** charged particles or energy emitted by an unstable nucleus

The released energy and matter is called **nuclear radiation,** and it can cause damage to living tissue. Nuclear radiation from radon that seeps into houses and buildings is the reason for the health concerns. (Note that the term *radiation* also refers to light or to an energy transfer method between objects at different temperatures. *To avoid confusion, the term* nuclear radiation *will be used to describe radiation associated with nuclear changes.)*

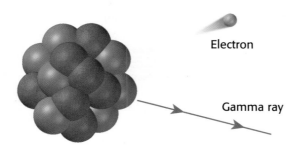

Electron

Gamma ray

Figure 6-1
During radioactivity an unstable nucleus emits one or more particles or high-energy electromagnetic radiation.

Table 6-1 Types of Nuclear Radiation

Radiation type	Symbol	Mass (kg)	Charge	
Alpha particle	$^{4}_{2}He$	6.646×10^{-27}	+2	
Beta particle	$^{0}_{-1}e$	9.109×10^{-31}	−1	
Gamma ray	γ	none	0	
Neutron	$^{1}_{0}n$	1.675×10^{-27}	0	

There are different types of nuclear radiation

Essentially, there are four types of nuclear radiation: alpha particles, beta particles, gamma rays, and neutron emission. Some of their properties are listed in **Table 6-1.** When a radioactive atom decays, the nuclear radiation leaves the nucleus. This nuclear radiation then interacts with nearby matter. The interaction with matter depends in part on the properties of nuclear radiation, like charge, mass, and energy, which are discussed below.

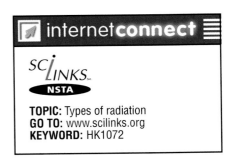

internet connect

SC*LINKS*
NSTA

TOPIC: Types of radiation
GO TO: www.scilinks.org
KEYWORD: HK1072

Alpha particles consist of protons and neutrons

Uranium is a radioactive element that naturally occurs in three isotope forms. One of its isotopes, uranium-238, undergoes nuclear decay by emitting positively charged particles. Ernest Rutherford, noted for discovering the nucleus, named them *alpha (α) rays.* Later, he discovered that alpha rays were actually particles, each made of two protons and two neutrons—the same as helium nuclei. **Alpha particles** are positively charged and more massive than any other type of nuclear radiation.

Alpha particles do not travel far through materials. In fact, they barely pass through a sheet of paper. One factor that limits an alpha particle's ability to pass through matter is the fact that it is massive. Because alpha particles are charged, they remove electrons from—or ionize—matter as they pass through it. This ionization causes the alpha particle to lose energy and slow down further.

▶ **alpha particle** a positively charged particle, emitted by some radioactive nuclei, that consists of two protons and two neutrons

Beta particles are electrons produced from neutron decay

Some nuclei emit another type of nuclear radiation consisting of negatively charged particles. Compared to alpha particles, this type of nuclear radiation travels farther through matter. This nuclear radiation is named the **beta particle,** after the second Greek letter, *beta (β).* Beta particles are fast-moving electrons.

▶ **beta particle** an electron emitted during the radioactive decay of a neutron in an unstable nucleus

Figure 6-2
The element radium, which Marie Curie discovered in 1898, was later found to emit gamma rays.

▶ **gamma ray** high-energy electromagnetic radiation emitted by a nucleus during radioactive decay

Having negative particles come from a positively-charged nucleus puzzled scientists for years. However, in the 1930s, another discovery helped to clear up the mystery: neutrons, which are not charged, decay to form a proton and an electron. The electron, having very little mass, is then ejected from the nucleus at a high speed as a beta particle.

Beta particles easily go through a piece of paper, but most are stopped by 3 mm of aluminum or 10 mm of wood. This greater penetration occurs because beta particles aren't as massive as alpha particles and therefore move faster. But like alpha particles, beta particles can easily ionize other atoms. As they ionize atoms, beta particles lose energy. This property prevents them from penetrating matter very deeply.

Gamma rays are very high energy light

In 1898, Marie Curie, shown in **Figure 6-2,** and her husband, Pierre, isolated the radioactive element radium. In 1900, studies of radium by Paul Villard revealed that the element emitted a new form of nuclear radiation. This radiation was much more penetrating than even beta particles. Following the pattern established by Rutherford, this new kind of nuclear radiation was named the gamma ray, after the third Greek alphabet letter, *gamma* (γ).

Unlike alpha or beta particles, gamma rays are not made of matter and do not have an electric charge. Instead, gamma rays are a form of electromagnetic energy, like visible light or X rays. Gamma rays, however, have more energy than light or X rays.

Because gamma rays have no electrical charge, they do not easily ionize matter. But gamma rays still cause damage because of their high energy. They can go through up to 60 cm of aluminum or 7 cm of lead. Because gamma rays penetrate matter deeply, they are not easily stopped by clothing or most building materials and therefore pose a greater danger to health than either alpha or beta particles.

Neutron radioactivity may occur in a neutron-rich nucleus

Like alpha and beta radiation, neutron emission consists of matter that is emitted from an unstable nucleus. In fact, scientists first discovered the neutron by detecting its emission from a nucleus.

▶ **neutron emission** the release of a high-energy neutron by some neutron-rich nuclei during radioactive decay

Because neutrons have no charge, they do not ionize matter like alpha or beta particles do. Because neutrons do not use their energy ionizing matter, they are able to travel farther through matter than either alpha or beta particles. A block of lead about 15 cm thick is required to stop most fast neutrons emitted during radioactive decay.

Nuclear Decay

When an unstable nucleus emits alpha or beta particles, the number of protons or neutrons changes. For instance, radium-226 (an isotope of radium with the mass number 226) changes to radon-222 by emitting an alpha particle.

A nucleus gives up two protons and two neutrons during alpha decay

Nuclear decay processes can be written as equations similar to those for chemical reactions. The nucleus before decay is like a reactant and is placed on the left side of the equation. The products are placed on the right side. In the case of the alpha decay of radium-226, the decay process is written as follows.

$$^{226}_{88}\text{Ra} \longrightarrow \ ^{222}_{86}\text{Rn} + \ ^{4}_{2}\text{He} \qquad \begin{array}{l} 226 = 222 + 4 \\ 88 = 86 + 2 \end{array}$$

Notice that the mass numbers and the atomic numbers add up. The mass number of the atom before decay is 226 and equals the sum of the mass numbers of the products, 222 and 4. The atomic numbers follow the same principle. The 88 protons in radium before the nuclear decay equals the 86 protons in the radon-222 nucleus and 2 protons in the alpha particle.

A nucleus gains a proton and loses a neutron during beta decay

With beta decay, the form of the equation is the same except the symbol for a beta particle is used. This symbol, with the appropriate mass and atomic numbers, is $^{0}_{-1}e$.

Of course, an electron is not an atom and should not have an atomic number, which is the number of positive charges in a nucleus. But for the sake of convenience, since an electron has a single negative charge, an electron is given an atomic number of –1 when you write a nuclear decay equation. Similarly, the beta particle's mass is so much less than that of a proton or neutron that it can be regarded as having a mass number of 0.

A beta decay process occurs when carbon-14 decays to nitrogen-14 by emitting a beta particle.

$$^{14}_{6}\text{C} \longrightarrow \ ^{14}_{7}\text{N} + \ ^{0}_{-1}e \qquad \begin{array}{l} 14 = 14 + 0 \\ 6 = 7 + (-1) \end{array}$$

In all cases of beta decay, the mass number before and after the decay does not change. Note that the atomic number of the product nucleus increases by 1. This occurs because a neutron

Did You Know?

Ernest Rutherford showed that alpha particles are helium nuclei by trapping alpha particles from radon-222 decay in a glass tube. He then passed a high electric voltage across the gas, causing it to glow. The glow was identical to the glow produced by helium atoms, indicating that the two substances are the same.

Figure 6-3

A nucleus that undergoes beta decay has nearly the same atomic mass afterward, except that it has one more proton and one less neutron.

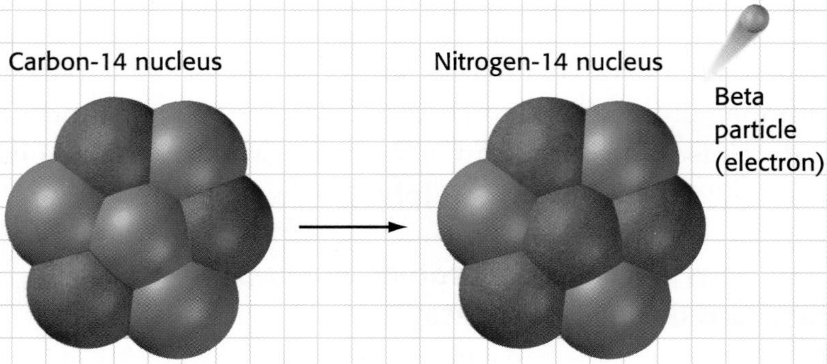

Carbon-14 nucleus

Nitrogen-14 nucleus

Beta particle (electron)

decays into a proton, causing the positive charge of the nucleus to increase by 1, as illustrated in **Figure 6-3.**

When the nucleus undergoes nuclear decay by gamma rays, there is no change in the atomic number of the element. The only change is in the energy content of the nucleus. The results of neutron emission will be discussed in greater detail in the next section.

Math Skills

Nuclear Decay Actinium-217 decays by releasing an alpha particle. Write the equation for this decay process, and determine what element is formed.

1 **Write down the equation with the original element on the left side and the products on the right side.**

Use the letter X to denote the unknown product. Note that the mass and atomic numbers of the unknown isotope are represented by the letters A and Z.

$$^{217}_{89}\text{Ac} \longrightarrow ^{A}_{Z}\text{X} + ^{4}_{2}\text{He}$$

2 **Write math equations for the atomic and mass numbers.**

$$217 = A + 4 \qquad 89 = Z + 2$$

3 **Rearrange the equations.**

$$A = 217 - 4 \qquad Z = 89 - 2$$

4 **Solve for the unknown values, and rewrite the equation with all nuclei represented.**

$$A = 213 \qquad Z = 87$$

The unknown decay product has an atomic number of 87, which is francium, according to the periodic table. The element is therefore $^{213}_{87}\text{Fr}$.

$$^{217}_{89}\text{Ac} \longrightarrow ^{213}_{87}\text{Fr} + ^{4}_{2}\text{He}$$

Practice

Nuclear Decay

Complete the following radioactive-decay equations by identifying the isotope *X*. Indicate whether alpha or beta decay takes place.

1. $^{12}_{5}B \longrightarrow ^{12}_{6}C + ^{A}_{Z}X$

2. $^{225}_{89}Ac \longrightarrow ^{221}_{87}Fr + ^{A}_{Z}X$

3. $^{63}_{28}Ni \longrightarrow ^{A}_{Z}X + ^{0}_{-1}e$

4. $^{212}_{83}Bi \longrightarrow ^{A}_{Z}X + ^{4}_{2}He$

Radioactive Decay Rates

If you were asked to pick up a rock and determine its age, you would probably not be able to do so. After all, old rocks do not look much different from new rocks. How, then, would you go about finding the rock's age? Likewise, how would a scientist find out the age of cloth found at the site of an ancient village?

One way to do it involves radioactive decay. Although it is impossible to predict the moment when any particular nucleus will decay, it is possible to predict the time it takes for half the nuclei in a given radioactive sample to decay. The time in which half a radioactive substance decays is called the substance's **half-life.**

After the first half-life of a radioactive sample has passed, half the sample remains unchanged, as indicated in **Figure 6-4** for carbon-14. After the next half-life, half the remaining half decays, leaving only a quarter of the sample undecayed. Of that quarter, half will decay in the next half-life. Only one-eighth will remain undecayed then. Eventually, the entire sample will decay.

> **half-life** the time required for half a sample of radioactive nuclei to decay

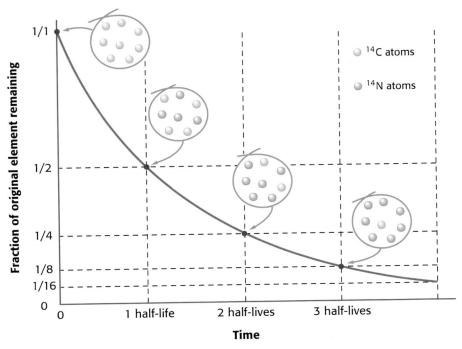

Figure 6-4
With each successive half-life, half the remaining sample decays to form another element.

Table 6-2
Half-lives of Selected Isotopes

Isotope	Half-life	Nuclear radiation emitted
Thorium-219	1.05×10^{-6} s	^4_2He
Hafnium-156	2.5×10^{-2} s	^4_2He
Radon-222	3.82 days	$^4_2\text{He}, \gamma$
Iodine-131	8.1 days	$^0_{-1}e, \gamma$
Radium-226	1599 years	$^4_2\text{He}, \gamma$
Carbon-14	5730 years	$^0_{-1}e$
Plutonium-239	2.412×10^4 years	$^4_2\text{He}, \gamma$
Uranium-235	7.04×10^8 years	$^4_2\text{He}, \gamma$
Potassium-40	1.28×10^9 years	$^0_{-1}e, \gamma$
Uranium-238	4.47×10^9 years	$^4_2\text{He}, \gamma$

Half-life is a measure of how quickly a substance decays

Different radioactive isotopes have different half-lives, as indicated in **Table 6-2.** Half-lives can last from nanoseconds to billions of years, depending on the stability of the nucleus.

If you know how much of a particular radioactive isotope was present in an object at the beginning, you can predict how old the object is. Geologists, people who study the Earth, use the half-lives of long-lasting isotopes, such as potassium-40, to calculate the age of rocks. Potassium-40 decays to argon-40, so the ratio of potassium-40 to argon-40 is smaller for older rocks.

Quick ACTIVITY

Modeling Decay and Half-life

For this exercise, you will need a jar with a lid, 128 pennies, pencil and paper, and a flat work surface.

1. Place the pennies in the jar, and place the lid on the jar. Shake the jar, and then pour the pennies onto the work surface.
2. Separate pennies that are heads up from those that are tails up. Count and record the number of heads-up pennies, and set these pennies aside. Place the tails-up pennies back in the jar.
3. Repeat the process until all pennies have been set aside.

4. For each trial, divide the number of heads-up pennies set aside by the total number of pennies used in the trial. Are these ratios nearly equal to each other? What fraction are they closest to?

Archaeologists use the half-life of radioactive carbon-14 to date more recent materials, such as the remains of an animal or fibers from ancient clothing. All of these materials came from organisms that were once alive. When plants absorb carbon dioxide during photosynthesis, a tiny fraction of the CO_2 molecules contains carbon-14 rather than the more common carbon-12. While the plant is alive, the ratio of the carbon isotopes remains constant. This is also true for animals that eat plants.

When a plant or animal dies, it no longer takes in carbon-14. The amount of carbon-14 decreases through beta decay, while the amount of carbon-12 remains constant. Thus, the ratio of carbon-14 to carbon-12 decreases with time. By measuring this ratio and comparing it with the ratio in a living plant or animal, the age of the once-living organism can be estimated.

Math Skills

Half-life Radium-226 has a half-life of 1599 years. How long would it take seven-eighths of a radium-226 sample to decay?

1 **List the given and unknown values.**
  Given: half-life = 1599 years
    fraction of sample decayed $= \frac{7}{8}$
  Unknown: fraction of sample remaining = ?
    total time of decay = ?

2 **Calculate the fraction of radioactive sample remaining.**
  To find the fraction of sample remaining, subtract the fraction that has decayed from 1.

  fraction of sample remaining = 1 − fraction decayed
  fraction of sample remaining $= 1 - \frac{7}{8} = \frac{1}{8}$

3 **Calculate the number of half-lives needed to equal that fraction.**

  Amount of sample remaining after one half-life $= \frac{1}{2}$

  Amount of sample remaining after two half-lives

  $= \frac{1}{2} \times \frac{1}{2} = \frac{1}{4}$

  Amount of sample remaining after three half-lives

  $= \frac{1}{2} \times \frac{1}{2} \times \frac{1}{2} = \frac{1}{8}$

  Three half-lives are needed for one-eighth of the sample to remain undecayed.

4 **Calculate the total time required for the radioactive decay.**
  Each half-life lasts 1599 years.
  total time of decay $= 3 \text{ half-lives} \times \frac{1599 \text{ y}}{\text{half-life}} = 4797$ years

INTEGRATING

EARTH SCIENCE
The Earth's interior is extremely hot. One reason is because radioactive elements are present in trace amounts beneath the surface of the Earth and their nuclear decay produces energy that raises the temperature of their surroundings

Many radioactive isotopes, like uranium-238, are very dense, which causes them to sink deep into Earth's interior. This is similar to what happens when dense liquids sink below less dense liquids, like syrup does in water.

The long half-lives of these radioactive isotopes can cause some of the surrounding matter to remain hot for billions of years.

Half-life

1. The half-life of iodine-131 is 8.1 days. How long will it take for three-fourths of a sample of iodine-131 to decay?
2. Radon-222 is a radioactive gas with a half-life of 3.82 days. How long would it take for fifteen-sixteenths of a sample of radon-222 to decay?
3. Uranium-238 decays very slowly, with a half-life of 4.47 billion years. What percentage of a sample of uranium-238 would remain after 13.4 billion years?
4. A sample of strontium-90 is found to have decayed to one-eighth of its original amount after 87.3 years. What is the half-life of strontium-90?
5. A sample of francium-212 will decay to one-sixteenth its original amount after 80 minutes. What is the half-life of francium-212?

SECTION 6.1 REVIEW

SUMMARY

▶ Nuclear radiation includes alpha particles, beta particles, gamma rays, and neutron emissions.

▶ Alpha particles are helium-4 nuclei.

▶ Beta particles are electrons emitted by neutrons decaying in the nucleus.

▶ Gamma radiation is an electromagnetic wave like visible light but with much greater energy.

▶ In nuclear decay, the sums of the mass numbers and the atomic numbers of the decay products equal the mass number and atomic number of the decaying nucleus.

▶ The time required for half a sample of radioactive material to decay is called its half-life.

CHECK YOUR UNDERSTANDING

1. **Identify** which of the four common types of nuclear radiation correspond to the following descriptions:
   a. an electron
   b. uncharged particle
   c. can be stopped by a piece of paper
   d. high-energy light
2. **Describe** what happens when beta decay occurs.
3. **Explain** why charged particles do not penetrate matter deeply.

Math Skills

4. **Determine** the product denoted by X in the following alpha decay.

$$^{212}_{86}\text{Rn} \longrightarrow {}^{A}_{Z}\text{X} + {}^{4}_{2}\text{He}$$

5. **Determine** the isotope produced in the beta decay of iodine-131, an isotope used to check thyroid-gland function.

$$^{131}_{53}\text{I} \longrightarrow {}^{A}_{Z}\text{X} + {}^{0}_{-1}e$$

6. **Calculate** the time required for three-fourths of a sample of cesium-138 to decay given that its half-life is 32.2 minutes.
7. **Calculate** the half-life of cesium-135 if seven-eighths of a sample decays in 6×10^6 years.
8. **Critical Thinking** An archaeologist discovers a wooden mask whose carbon-14 to carbon-12 ratio is one-sixteenth the ratio measured in a newly fallen tree. How old does the wooden mask seem to be, given this evidence?

Nuclear Fission and Fusion

OBJECTIVES

▶ Describe how the strong nuclear force affects the composition of a nucleus.

▶ Distinguish between fission and fusion, and provide examples of each.

▶ Recognize the equivalence of mass and energy, and why small losses in mass release large amounts of energy.

▶ Explain what a chain reaction is, how one is initiated, and how it can be controlled.

▶ **KEY TERMS**

strong nuclear force
fission
nuclear chain reaction
critical mass
fusion

In 1939, two German scientists, Otto Hahn and Fritz Strassman, conducted experiments in the hope of forming heavy nuclei. Using the apparatus shown in **Figure 6-5,** they bombarded uranium samples with neutrons, expecting a few nuclei to capture one or more neutrons. They were surprised to discover that the result was less-massive nuclei instead of more-massive nuclei.

It wasn't until their colleague Lise Meitner and her nephew Otto Frisch read the results of Hahn and Strassman's work that an explanation was offered. Meitner and Frisch believed that instead of making heavier elements, the uranium nuclei had split into smaller elements.

Nuclear Forces

Protons and neutrons are tightly packed in the tiny nucleus of an atom. As we saw in the previous section, certain nuclei are unstable and undergo decay by emitting nuclear radiation. Also, an element can have both stable and unstable isotopes. For instance, carbon-12 is a stable isotope, while carbon-14 is unstable and radioactive. The stability of a nucleus depends on the nuclear forces that hold the nucleus together. This force acts between the protons and the neutrons.

Figure 6-5
Using this equipment, Otto Hahn and Fritz Strassman first discovered nuclear fission.

Nuclei are held together by a special force

You may know that like charges repel. But how is it that so many positively charged protons fit into an atomic nucleus without flying apart?

The answer lies in the existence of the **strong nuclear force.** This force causes protons and neutrons in the nucleus to attract each other. The attraction is much stronger than the electric repulsion between protons. However, this attraction due to the strong nuclear force occurs over a very short distance, less than 3×10^{-15} m, or about the width of three protons.

Neutrons contribute to nuclear stability

Due to the strong nuclear force, neutrons and protons in a nucleus attract other protons and neutrons. Because neutrons have no charge, they do not repel each other or the protons. On the other hand, the protons in a nucleus both repel and attract each other, as shown in **Figure 6-6.** In stable nuclei, the attractive forces are stronger than the repulsive forces.

Too many neutrons or protons can cause a nucleus to become unstable and decay

While more neutrons can help hold a nucleus together, there is a limit to how many neutrons a nucleus can have. Nuclei with too many or too few neutrons are unstable and undergo decay.

Nuclei with more than 83 protons are always unstable, no matter how many neutrons they have. These nuclei will always decay, releasing large amounts of energy and nuclear radiation. Some of this released energy is transferred to the various particles ejected from the nucleus, the least massive of which move very fast as a result. The rest of the energy is emitted in the form of gamma rays.

Figure 6-6
The nucleus is held together by the attractions among protons and neutrons. These forces are greater than the electric repulsion among the protons alone.

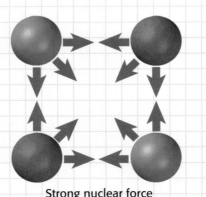

Strong nuclear force
(acts on protons and neutrons alike)

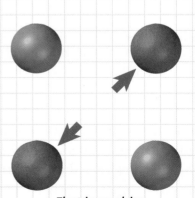

Electric repulsion
(acts on protons)

Nuclear Fission

The process of the production of lighter nuclei from heavier nuclei, which Hahn and Strassman observed, is called fission. In their experiment, uranium-235 was bombarded by neutrons. The products of this fission reaction included two lighter nuclei barium-137 and krypton-84, together with neutrons and energy.

$$^{235}_{92}U + ^1_0n \longrightarrow ^{137}_{56}Ba + ^{84}_{36}Kr + 15^1_0n + energy$$

Notice that the products include 15 neutrons. Uranium-235 can also undergo fission by producing different pairs of lighter nuclei with a different number of neutrons. For example, a different fission of uranium-235 produces strontium-90, xenon-143, and three neutrons. On average, two or three neutrons are released when uranium-235 undergoes fission.

Energy is released during nuclear fission

During fission, as shown in **Figure 6-7,** the nucleus breaks into smaller nuclei. The reaction also releases large amounts of energy. Each dividing nucleus releases about 3.2×10^{-11} J of energy. By comparison, the chemical reaction of one molecule of the explosive trinitrotoluene (TNT) releases only 4.8×10^{-18} J.

In their experiment, Hahn and Strassman determined the masses of all the nuclei and particles before and after the reaction. They found that the overall mass had decreased after the reaction. The missing mass had changed into energy.

The equivalence of mass and energy observed in nature is explained by the special theory of relativity, which Albert Einstein presented in 1905. This equivalence means that matter can be converted into energy and energy into matter. This equivalence is expressed by the following equation.

Mass-Energy Equation

$$Energy = mass \times (speed\ of\ light)^2$$
$$E = mc^2$$

Because c, which is constant, has such a large value, 3.0×10^8 m/s, the energy associated with even a small mass is immense. The mass-equivalent energy of 1 kg of matter is 9×10^{16} J. This is more than the chemical energy of 8 million tons of TNT.

Obviously, it would be devastating if objects around us changed into their equivalent energies. Under ordinary conditions of pressure and temperature, matter is very stable. Objects, such as chairs and tables, never spontaneously change into energy.

▶ **fission** the process by which a nucleus splits into two or more smaller fragments, releasing neutrons and energy

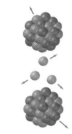

Figure 6-7
When the uranium-235 nucleus is bombarded by a neutron the nucleus breaks apart. It forms smaller nuclei, such as barium-137 and krypton-84, and releases energy through fast neutrons.

Did You Know ❓

Enrico Fermi and his associates achieved the first controlled nuclear reaction in December 1942. The reactor was built on squash courts under the unused football stadium at the University of Chicago. The reactor consisted of blocks of uranium-235 for fuel and graphite to slow the neutrons so that they could be captured by the uranium nuclei and cause fission.

When the total mass of any nucleus is measured, it turns out to be less than the individual masses of the neutrons and protons that make up the nucleus. This missing mass is referred to as the *mass defect*. But what happens to the missing mass? Einstein's equation provides an explanation—it changes into energy. However, the mass defect of a nucleus is very small.

Another way to think about mass defect is to imagine constructing a nucleus by bringing individual protons and neutrons together. During this process a small amount of mass changes into energy, as described by $E = mc^2$.

Neutrons released by fission can start a chain reaction

Have you ever played marbles with lots of marbles in the ring? When one marble is shot into the ring, the resulting collisions cause some of the marbles to scatter. Some nuclear reactions are like this, where one reaction triggers another.

A nucleus that splits when it is struck by a neutron forms smaller product nuclei. These smaller nuclei need fewer neutrons to be held together. Therefore, excess neutrons are emitted. One of these neutrons can collide with another large nucleus, triggering another nuclear reaction. This reaction releases more neutrons, and so it is possible to start a chain reaction.

When Hahn and Strassman continued experimenting, they discovered that each dividing uranium nucleus, on average, produced two or three additional neutrons. Therefore, two or three new fission reactions could be started from the neutrons ejected from one reaction.

If each of these three new reactions produce three additonal neutrons, a total of nine neutrons become available to trigger nine additional fission reactions. From these nine reactions, a total of 27 neutrons are produced, setting off 27 new reactions, and so on. You can probably see from **Figure 6-8** how the reaction of uranium-235 nuclei would quickly result in an uncontrolled **nuclear chain reaction**. Therefore, the ability to create a chain reaction partly depends on the number of neutrons released.

▶ **nuclear chain reaction** a series of fission processes in which the neutrons emitted by a dividing nucleus cause the division of other nuclei

Figure 6-8
A nuclear chain reaction may be triggered by a single neutron.

The chain-reaction principle is used in the nuclear bomb. Two or more masses of uranium-235 are contained in the bomb. These masses are surrounded by a powerful chemical explosive. When the explosive is detonated, all of the uranium is pushed together to create a **critical mass.** The critical mass refers to the minimum amount of a substance that can not only undergo a fission reaction but also sustain a chain reaction. If the amount of fissionable substance is less than the critical mass, a chain reaction will not continue.

▶ **critical mass** the minimum mass of a fissionable isotope in which a nuclear chain reaction can occur

In a nuclear bomb, a chain reaction is started and proceeds very quickly. The result is the release of a large amount of energy in a very short time, causing devastation to the environment and to the life-forms within it for many miles.

The ease with which uranium-235 can make an uncontrolled chain reaction makes it extremely dangerous. Fortunately, the concentration of uranium-235 in nature is too low to start a chain reaction. Almost all of the escaping neutrons are absorbed by the more common and more stable isotope uranium-238.

Chain reactions can be controlled

Not all neutrons released in a fission reaction succeed in triggering a fission reaction. For this reason, the more neutrons that are produced per reaction, the better the chances are of a chain reaction sustaining itself. It is also possible to use materials that will slow a fission chain reaction by absorbing some of the neutrons. In this way, the reaction is controlled, unlike in a nuclear bomb. The energy produced in a controlled reaction can be used to generate electricity.

Quick ACTIVITY

Modeling Chain Reactions

1. To model a fission chain reaction, you will need a small wooden building block and a set of dominoes.
2. Place the building block on a table or counter. Stand one domino upright in front of the block and parallel to one of its sides, as shown at right.
3. Stand two more dominoes vertically, parallel, and symmetrical to the first domino. Continue this process until you have used all the dominoes and a triangular shape is created, as shown at right.
4. Gently push the first domino away from the block so that it falls and hits the second group. Note how more dominoes fall with each step.

Nuclear Fusion

Just as energy is obtained when heavy nuclei break apart, energy can also be obtained when very light nuclei are combined to form heavier nuclei. This type of nuclear process is called **fusion.**

In stars, including the sun, energy is primarily produced when hydrogen nuclei combine, or fuse together, and release tremendous amounts of energy. However, a large amount of energy is needed to start a fusion reaction. This is because all nuclei are positively charged, and they repel each other with an electrical force. Energy is required to bring the hydrogen nuclei close together until the electrical forces are overcome by the attractive nuclear forces between two protons. In stars, the extreme temperatures provide the energy needed to bring hydrogen nuclei together.

Four hydrogen atoms fuse together in the sun to produce a helium atom and enormous energy in the form of gamma rays. This occurs in a multistep process that involves two isotopes of hydrogen: ordinary hydrogen ($_1^1H$), and deuterium ($_1^2H$).

$$_1^1H + _1^1H \longrightarrow _1^2H + \text{two particles}$$
$$_1^2H + _1^1H \longrightarrow _2^3He + _0^0\gamma$$
$$_2^3He + _2^3He \longrightarrow _2^4He + _1^1H + _1^1H$$

SECTION 6.2 REVIEW

SUMMARY

▶ Neutrons and protons in the nucleus are held together by the strong nuclear force.

▶ Nuclear fission takes place when a large nucleus divides into smaller nuclei.

▶ Nuclear fusion occurs when two light nuclei combine.

▶ Mass is converted into energy during both fusion and fission reactions.

CHECK YOUR UNDERSTANDING

1. **Explain** why most isotopes of elements with a high atomic number are radioactive.

2. **Indicate** if the following are fission or fusion reactions.
   a. $_1^1H + _1^2H \longrightarrow _2^3He + \gamma$
   b. $_0^1n + _{92}^{235}U \longrightarrow _{57}^{146}La + _{35}^{87}Br + 3_0^1n$
   c. $_{10}^{21}Ne + _2^4He \longrightarrow _{12}^{24}Mg + _0^1n$
   d. $_{82}^{208}Pb + _{26}^{58}Fe \longrightarrow _{108}^{265}Hs + _0^1n$

3. **Predict** whether the total mass of the 26 protons and 30 neutrons that make up the iron nucleus will be more, less, or equal to 55.847 amu, the mass of an iron atom, $_{26}^{56}Fe$. If it is not equal, explain why.

4. **Critical Thinking** Suppose a nucleus captures two neutrons and decays to produce one neutron, is this process likely to produce a chain reaction? Explain your reasoning.

Dangers and Benefits of Nuclear Radiation

OBJECTIVES

▶ Describe the dangers and possible health effects of exposure to nuclear radiation.

▶ Identify several beneficial uses of nuclear radiation.

▶ Explain the benefits and drawbacks of nuclear power.

KEY TERMS

background radiation
radioactive tracer

When you think about nuclear radiation, do you have a negative reaction? Do you immediately think about danger? The plots of many science-fiction movies and television shows have revolved around the dangers of nuclear radiation, showing it causing mutations or death and destruction.

Dangers of Nuclear Radiation

In many cases, especially when it is used carelessly, nuclear radiation can be extremely dangerous. However, it may surprise you to know that we are exposed to nuclear radiation of some sort every day. This kind of radiation is called **background radiation.** Most of it comes from natural sources, such as the sun, soil, water, and plants, as shown in **Figure 6-9.** The living tissues of most organisms are adapted to survive these low levels of natural nuclear radiation. Only when these background levels are exceeded do problems arise.

▶ **background radiation**
nuclear radiation that arises naturally from cosmic rays and from radioactive isotopes in the soil and air

Figure 6-9
Sources of background radiation are all around us.

Nuclear radiation can ionize atoms in living tissue

When hemoglobin—the molecule in blood that carries oxygen throughout the body—is exposed to excessive amounts of nuclear radiation, its structure is changed. This changed hemoglobin can no longer draw oxygen into the blood, so the body cannot get oxygen as easily.

Most of your body's tissues are made of large molecules. Among these are proteins, carbohydrates, and fats. The chemical properties of these molecules change when the molecules lose or gain electrons through ionization caused by nuclear radiation. If enough molecules in a cell are ionized, the cell no longer functions properly. This can affect the overall health of the body.

Fortunately, the outer skin keeps most radiation outside the body. But if a source of alpha and beta particles is introduced into the body through air, water, or food, the nuclear radiation can severely damage the delicate linings of the body's organs.

Energetic gamma rays and fast neutrons can damage tissues regardless of whether the source of these types of nuclear radiation is inside or outside the body. Nuclear radiation can cause burns in the skin, and it also destroys bone marrow cells, which form red and white blood cells.

High concentrations of radon gas can be dangerous

The potential for internal damage by alpha particles explains the public concern over radon gas. Radon-222 is produced through a series of nuclear reactions of uranium-238 in the Earth's crust. The gas drifts up through the rock and enters the air we breathe.

Outdoors, the radon concentration is low and the gas is less harmful. However, radon can accumulate in the basements of buildings, as shown in **Figure 6-10,** until it reaches dangerous concentrations. The alpha particles emitted by inhaled radon-222 can destroy lung tissue. Prolonged exposure to radon-222 can lead to lung cancer, especially among smokers.

Radiation sickness results from exposure to high levels of nuclear radiation

Not all nuclear radiation causes intense damage to the body's cells. A person exposed for long periods or to high intensities of nuclear radiation will have more damage in his or her cells than a person who is exposed for short periods or to low intensities.

Observable effects from nuclear radiation exposure often do not appear for days or even years. Some common symptoms after serious exposure include a decrease in the number of white blood cells (leucopenia), hair loss, sterility, destruction and death of bones (bone necrosis), and cancer.

Figure 6-10
Radon-222 levels in the air of basements and cellars can become dangerously high. Radon detectors are used to monitor radon-222 levels.

Did You Know ?

Radon-222 problems in homes or offices can be eliminated by sealing cracks in foundations or by installing vents that draw air out of the building.

Nuclear radiation can cause genetic mutations

Long-term effects of nuclear radiation appear when DNA molecules in the body are damaged. As described in Chapter 4, DNA directs the synthesis of proteins by the body, so it contains all the information cells need to function. DNA also carries all the genetic information of an organism. If DNA molecules are extensively damaged by nuclear radiation, the cell may repair them incorrectly, as shown in **Figure 6-11.** When the DNA in reproductive cells is damaged, there is a strong chance of birth defects.

Biologists have observed birth defects in animals that have been exposed to large amounts of nuclear radiation in water or soil. An example of this occurred near the Shiprock Uranium Mine, which operated from 1954 to 1968 in northwestern New Mexico. Radioactive waste from the mine contaminated water that the nearby Navajo used for their sheep and cattle. Although the animals that drank the water remained healthy, the nuclear radiation from the water damaged the DNA in their reproductive cells. This caused their offspring to be born with birth defects.

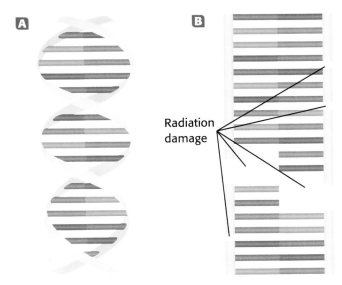

Figure 6-11
After extensive radiation damage, a normal DNA molecule (A) is likely to be rebuilt with its nitrogen bases out of sequence (B).

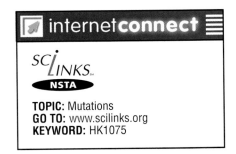

internet**connect**

SCI LINKS
NSTA

TOPIC: Mutations
GO TO: www.scilinks.org
KEYWORD: HK1075

Beneficial Uses of Nuclear Radiation

In spite of their dangers, radioactive substances are highly useful. They have a wide range of applications from medicine to archeological dating.

Small radioactive sources are present in smoke alarms, as shown in **Figure 6-12.** They release alpha particles, which are charged and produce an electric current. If smoke is present in the air, the smoke particles reduce the flow of this current. The drop in current sets off the alarm before dangerous levels of smoke build up.

Nuclear radiation therapy is used to treat cancer

Controlled doses of nuclear radiation are used for treating diseases such as cancer. For example, certain brain tumors can be targeted with small beams of gamma rays. These beams are focused to kill only the tumor cells. The surrounding healthy tissue is harmed only minimally. Different kinds of tumors throughout the body can be treated in a similar way.

Figure 6-12
In a smoke alarm, a small alpha-emitting isotope detects smoke particles in the air.

radioactive tracer a radioactive material added to a substance so that the substance's location can be detected later

Radioactive tracers are used in agriculture, medicine, and scientific research

Radioactive tracers are short-lived isotopes, like magnesium-28, that can be observed with sensitive detectors. On research farms, tracers in flowing water can show how fast water moves through the soil or through the stems and leaves of crops. Geologists use tracers to follow underground water flow.

Tracers are widely used in medicine as well. Tracers that tend to concentrate in affected cells are used to locate tumors. Other tracers can follow the path of drugs in the body to help doctors be sure they are delivered to the desired area.

Nuclear Power

Today, nuclear reactors are used in dozens of countries to generate electricity. Energy produced from fission is used to light the homes of millions of families. There are numerous benefits to this source of energy. Nuclear fission does not produce gaseous pollutants, and there is much more energy in the known uranium reserves than in the known reserves of coal and oil.

Medical Radiation Exposure

Graves's disease is an illness in which the thyroid gland produces excess hormones. This excess causes an increase in metabolism, weight loss (despite a healthy appetite), and an irregular heartbeat.

Graves's disease and similar illnesses can be treated in several ways. Parts of the thyroid gland can be surgically removed, or patients can be treated with radioactive iodine-131. The thyroid cells need iodine to make hormones. When they take in the radioactive iodine-131, the overactive cells are destroyed, and hormone levels drop.

There is some concern that low-level nuclear radiation might cause cancers, such as leukemia. Examine the table below, which shows radiation exposures for different situations and the resulting increased risks in leukemia rates. Note that a *rem* is a unit for measuring doses of nuclear radiation.

Applying Information

1. Given that the typical exposure for radioisotope therapy is about 10 rems, mostly delivered at once, do you think leukemia rates are likely to go up for this group? If so, estimate what risk you would expect.
2. Low-level nuclear radiations and its link to cancers such as leukemia is still in question. Describe what other information would help you evaluate the risks. **WRITING SKILL**

Person tested	Radiation exposure	Measured increased leukemia risk
Hiroshima atomic bomb survivor	27 rem at once	6%
U.S. WW II radiology technician	50 rem over 2 years	0%
Austrian citizen after the nuclear accident at Chernobyl	0.025 rem	0%

Nuclear fission has disadvantages

In nuclear fission reactors, energy is produced by triggering a controlled fission reaction in uranium-235. However, the products of fission reactions are often radioactive isotopes. Therefore, serious safety concerns must be addressed. Radioactive products of fission must be handled carefully so they do not escape in the environment releasing nuclear radiation.

Another safety issue involves the safe operation of the nuclear reactors in which the controlled fission reaction is carried out. A nuclear reactor must be equipped with many safety features in case of a reactor failure. The reactor requires considerable shielding and must meet stricter safety requirements than those required for fossil-fuel-burning power plants. Thus, nuclear power plants are expensive to build.

According to regulations, nuclear power plants can be operated for only about 40 years. After that time, they must be shut down. To avoid accidental contamination, this process is very slow and expensive. Equipment used to take the reactor apart can become contaminated and must also be disposed of as radioactive waste. Because of political opposition, few nuclear power plants have operated for 40 years. This is one of the many factors that limit how effective nuclear power can be.

Nuclear waste must be safely stored

Besides the expenses that occur during the life of a nuclear power plant, there is the expense of storing radioactive materials, such as the fuel rods used in the reactors. After their use they must be placed in safe facilities that are well shielded, as shown in **Figure 6-13.** These precautions are necessary to keep nuclear radiation from leaking out and causing harm to nearby plants and animals. The facilities must also keep nuclear radiation from contacting ground water.

Ideal places for such facilities are sparsely populated areas with little water on the surface or underground. These areas must be free from earthquakes. Even with these considerations, one cannot be sure about long-term safety.

INTEGRATING

SPACE SCIENCE
Unmanned space probes have greatly increased our knowledge of the solar system. Nuclear-powered probes can venture far from the sun without losing power, as solar-powered probes do. *Cassini,* which has been sent to explore Saturn, has been powered by the heat generated by the radioactive decay of plutonium.

Figure 6-13
Storage facilities for nuclear waste must be designed to contain radioactive materials safely for thousands of years.

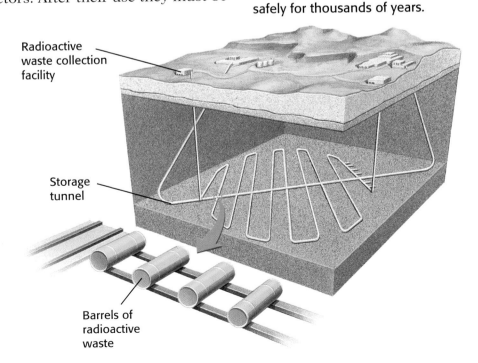

Radioactive waste collection facility

Storage tunnel

Barrels of radioactive waste

The main problem with some radioactive wastes is that they have long half-lives, from hundreds of thousands to millions of years. The oldest human-made structures that are still standing, such as the pyramids of Egypt, are only about 5000 years old. It is hard to imagine whether people could ever build structures that could last 20 to 200 times as long.

Nuclear-fusion reactors are being tested

Another option that holds some promise as an energy source is nuclear fusion. Recall from the last section that fusion takes place when light nuclei, such as hydrogen, are forced together to produce heavier nuclei, such as helium, and energy. Because fusion requires that the electrical repulsion between protons be overcome, these reactions are difficult to produce in the laboratory and have never been produced in a power plant.

The most attractive feature of fusion is that the fuel for it is abundant. Hydrogen is the most common element in the universe and is plentiful in many compounds on Earth, such as water. Earth's oceans could provide enough hydrogen to meet current world energy demands for millions of years.

Unfortunately, practical fusion-based power is far from being a reality. Fusion reactions have some drawbacks. They can produce fast neutrons, a highly energetic and dangerous form of nuclear radiation. Shielding material in the reactor would have to be replaced periodically, increasing the expense of operating a fusion power plant. Lithium can be used to slow down these neutrons, but it is chemically reactive and rare, making its use impractical.

INTEGRATING

SPACE SCIENCE
All heavy elements, from cobalt to uranium, are made when massive stars explode. The pressure produced in the explosion causes nearby nuclei to fuse together, in some cases more than once.

The explosion carries the newly created elements into space. These elements later become parts of new stars and planets. The elements of Earth are believed to have formed in the outer layers of an exploding star.

SECTION 6.3 REVIEW

SUMMARY

▶ Nuclear radiation can damage living cells, causing radiation sickness and birth defects, even death.

▶ Nuclear radiation is used in medicine to diagnose and treat diseases.

▶ Nuclear fission is an alternative to fossil fuels as a source of energy.

CHECK YOUR UNDERSTANDING

1. **Describe** the ways in which nuclear radiation can cause damage to living tissues.
2. **Explain** how gamma rays are used in cancer therapy without harming the patient.
3. **List** several uses for low-level radioactive tracers.
4. **Describe** how sea water could be a source of hydrogen for nuclear fusion.
5. **Critical Thinking** Suppose uranium-238 could undergo fission as easily as uranium-235. Predict how that would change the advantages and drawbacks of fission reactors.

Chapter Highlights

Before you begin, review the summaries of the key ideas of each section, found on pages 194, 200, and 206. The key vocabulary terms are listed on pages 186, 195, and 201.

UNDERSTANDING CONCEPTS

1. When a heavy nucleus decays, it may emit _____.
   a. alpha particles
   b. neutrons
   c. gamma rays
   d. All of the above

2. A neutron decays to form a proton and a(n) _____.
   a. alpha particle
   b. beta particle
   c. gamma ray
   d. emitted neutron

3. After three half-lives, _____ of a radioactive sample remains.
   a. all
   b. one-half
   c. one-third
   d. one-eighth

4. Carbon dating can be used to measure the age of each of the following except _____.
   a. a 7000-year-old human body
   b. a 1200-year-old wooden statue
   c. a 2600-year-old iron sword
   d. a 3500-year-old piece of fabric

5. Of the following elements, only the isotopes of _____ are all radioactive.
   a. nitrogen
   b. gold
   c. sulfur
   d. uranium

6. The strong nuclear force _____.
   a. attracts protons to electrons
   b. holds molecules together
   c. holds the atomic nucleus together
   d. attracts electrons to neutrons

7. The process in which a heavy nucleus splits into two lighter nuclei is called _____.
   a. fission
   b. fusion
   c. alpha decay
   d. a chain reaction

8. Which condition is not necessary for a chain reaction to occur?
   a. The radioactive sample must have a short half-life.
   b. The neutrons from one split nucleus must cause other nuclei to divide.
   c. The radioactive sample must be at critical mass.
   d. Not too many neutrons must be allowed to leave the radioactive sample.

9. Alpha emitters can be dangerous when they are _____.
   a. inhaled into the lungs
   b. consumed in drinking water
   c. eaten in food
   d. All of the above

10. Which of the following is *not* a use for radioactive isotopes?
    a. as tracers for diagnosing disease
    b. as an additive to paints to increase their durability
    c. as a way of treating forms of cancer
    d. as a way to check the thickness of newly made metal sheets

Using Vocabulary

11. How can *radioactivity* affect the atomic number and mass number of a nucleus that changes after undergoing decay?

12. Describe the main differences between the four main types of nuclear *radiation: alpha particles, beta particles, gamma rays,* and *neutron emission.*

13. Would a substance with an extremely short *half-life* be effective as a *radioactive tracer*?

14. For the nuclear *fission* process, how is *critical mass* important in a *chain reaction*?

15. How does nuclear *fusion* account for the energy produced in stars?

16. What is *background radiation,* and what are its sources?

BUILDING MATH SKILLS

17. Graphing Using a graphing calculator or computer graphing program, create a graph for the decay of iodine-131, which has a half life of 8.1 days. Use the graph to answer the following questions:

a. Approximately what percentage of the iodine-131 has decayed after 4 days?

b. Approximately what percentage of the iodine-131 has decayed after 12.1 days?

c. What fraction of iodine-131 has decayed after 2.5 half-lives have elapsed?

d. What percentage of the original iodine-131 remains after 3.5 half-lives?

18. Nuclear Decay Bismuth-212 undergoes a combination of alpha and beta decays to form lead-208. Depending on which decay process occurs first, different isotopes are temporarily formed during the process. Identify these isotopes by completing the equations given below:

a. $^{212}_{83}Bi \longrightarrow ^{\square}_{\square}X + ^{4}_{2}He$

$^{\square}_{\square}X \longrightarrow ^{208}_{82}Pb + ^{0}_{-1}e$

b. $^{212}_{83}Bi \longrightarrow ^{\square}_{\square}Y + ^{0}_{-1}e$

$^{\square}_{\square}Y \longrightarrow ^{208}_{82}Pb + ^{4}_{2}He$

19. Nuclear Decay The longest-lived radioactive isotope yet discovered is the beta-emitter tellurium-130. It has been determined that it would take 2.5×10^{21} years for 99.9% of this isotope to decay. Write the equation for this reaction, and identify the isotope into which tellurium-130 decays.

20. Nuclear Decay It takes about 10^{16} years for just half the samarium-149 in nature to decay by alpha-particle emission. Write the decay equation, and find the isotope that is produced by the reaction.

21. Half-life The ratio of carbon-14 to carbon-12 in a prehistoric wooden artifact is measured to be one-eighth of the ratio measured in a fresh sample of wood from the same region. The half-life of carbon-14 is 5730 years. Determine its age.

22. Half-life Health officials are concerned about radon levels in homes. The half-life of radon-222 is 3.82 days. If a sample of gas taken from a basement contains 4.38 μg of radon-222, how much will remain in the sample after 15.2 days?

THINKING CRITICALLY

23. Applying Knowledge Explain how the equivalence of mass and energy accounts for the small difference between the mass of a uranium-235 nucleus and the masses of the nuclei of its fission fragments.

24. Applying Knowledge Describe the similarities and differences between atomic electrons and beta particles.

25. Creative Thinking Why do people working around radioactive waste in a radioactive storage facility wear badges containing strips of photographic film?

26. Creative Thinking Many radioactive isotopes have half-lives of several billion years. Other radioactive isotopes have half-lives of billionths of a second. Suggest a way in which the half-lives of such isotopes are measured.

27. Problem Solving A radioactive tracer can be used to measure water movement through soil. In order to avoid contamination of ground water, 99.9% of the tracer must decay between the time it is introduced into the soil and the time it reaches the ground-water supply. Estimate this time and calculate the half-life of an ideal tracer that could be used in this application.

28. Allocating Resources An archeologist has collected seven samples from a site: two scraps of fabric, two strips of leather, and three bone fragments. The age of each item must be determined, but the budget for carbon-14 dating is only $4500. Carbon-14 mass spectrometry is an accurate way to find a sample's age, but it costs $820 per sample. Carbon-14 dating by liquid scintillation costs only $400 a sample, but is less reliable. How would you apply either or both of these techniques to the samples to obtain the most reliable information and still stay within your budget?

29. Making Decisions Suppose you are an energy consultant who has been asked to evaluate a proposal to build a power plant in a remote area of the desert. Research the requirements for each of the following types of power plant: nuclear-fission power plant, coal-burning power plant, solar-energy farm. Using information you have learned from this chapter, decide which of these power plants would be best for its surroundings, and write a paragraph supporting your decision.

WRITING SKILL

30. Working Cooperatively Read the following, and discuss with a group of classmates a possible solution to the problem that makes use of radioactivity.

A person believed to be suffering from cancer has been admitted to a hospital. What are some possible methods of diagnosing the patient's conditions? Assuming that cancer is found, how might the disease be treated? Suppose you suspect that another patient is suffering from radiation poisoning. How would you be able to tell?

31. Concept Mapping Copy the unfinished concept map below onto a sheet of paper. Complete the map by writing the correct word or phrase in the lettered boxes.

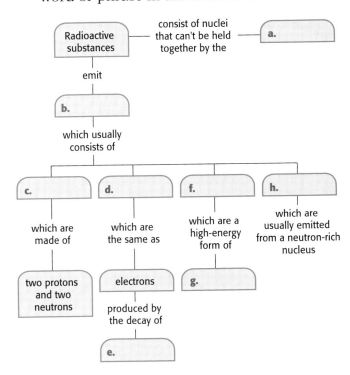

32. Connection to Social Studies Research the philosophical debate surrounding the discovery of radioactive decay. Examine the arguments against the transmutation of elements as presented by scientists such as Lord Kelvin. What ideas were these arguments based on? What experiments convinced most scientists that radioactive elements changed into other elements?

internetconnect

SCiLINKS
NSTA

TOPIC: Radioactive tracers
GO TO: www.scilinks.org
KEYWORD: HK1076

Skill Builder Lab

Introduction

In this lab we will simulate the decay of lead-210 into its isotope lead-206. This decay of lead-210 into its isotope lead-206 occurs in a multistep process. Lead-210, $^{210}_{82}Pb$, first decays into bismuth-210, $^{210}_{83}Bi$, which decays into polonium-210, $^{210}_{84}Po$, which finally decays into the isotope lead-206, $^{206}_{82}Pb$.

Objectives

- **Simulate** the decay of radioactive isotopes by throwing a set of dice.
- **Graph** the results to identify patterns in the amounts of each isotope present.

Materials

10 dice
large paper cup with plastic lid
roll of masking tape
scissors

Simulating Nuclear Decay Reactions

▶ Preparing for Your Experiment

1. On a sheet of paper, prepare a table as shown below. Leave room to add extra rows at the bottom, if necessary.

Throw #	# of dice representing each Isotope			
	$^{210}_{82}Pb$	$^{210}_{83}Bi$	$^{210}_{84}Po$	$^{206}_{82}Pb$
0 (start)	10	0	0	0
1				
2				
3				
4				

2. Place all 10 dice in the cup. Each die represents an atom of $^{210}_{82}Pb$, a radioactive isotope.

3. Put the lid on the cup, and shake it a few times. Then remove the lid, and spill the dice. In this simulation, each throw represents a *half-life*.

4. All the dice that land with *1*, *2*, or *3* up represent atoms of $^{210}_{82}Pb$ that have decayed into $^{210}_{83}Bi$. The remaining dice still represent $^{210}_{82}Pb$ atoms. Separate the two sets of dice. Count the dice, and record the results in your data table.

5. To keep track of the dice representing the decayed atoms, you will make a small mark on them. On a die, the faces with *1*, *2*, and *3* share a corner. With a pencil, draw a small circle around this shared corner, and this die represents the $^{210}_{83}Bi$ atoms.

6. Put all the dice back in the cup, shake them and roll them again. In a decay process, there are two possibilities: some atoms decay and some do not. See the diagram below to track your results.

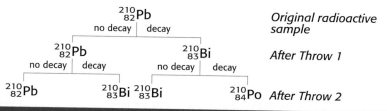

Isotope type	Decays into	Signs of decay	Identifying the atoms in column 2
$^{210}_{82}Pb$	$^{210}_{83}Bi$	Unmarked dice lands on *1, 2,* or *3*	Mark $^{210}_{83}Bi$ by drawing a circle around the corner where faces *1, 2,* and *3* meet.
$^{210}_{83}Bi$	$^{210}_{84}Po$	Dice with one loop lands on *1, 2,* or *3*	Draw a circle around the corner where faces *4, 5,* and *6* meet.
$^{210}_{84}Po$	$^{206}_{82}Pb$	Dice with two loops lands on *1, 2,* or *3*	Put a small piece of masking tape over the two circles
$^{206}_{82}Pb$	Decay ends		

7. After the second throw, we have three types of atoms. Sort the dice into three sets.
   a. The first set consists of dice with a circle drawn on them that landed with *1, 2,* or *3* facing up. These represent $^{210}_{83}Bi$ atoms that have decayed into $^{210}_{84}Po$.
   b. The second set consists of two types of dice: the dice with one circle that did not land on *1, 2,* or *3* (undecayed $^{210}_{83}Bi$) and the unmarked dice that landed with *1, 2,* or *3* facing up (representing the decay of original $^{210}_{82}Pb$ into $^{210}_{83}Bi$).
   c. The third set includes unmarked dice that did not land with *1, 2,* or *3* facing up. These represent the original undecayed $^{210}_{82}Pb$ atoms.
8. After each throw, do the following: separate the different types of atoms in groups, count the atoms in each group, record your data in your table, and mark the dice to identify each isotope. Use the table above as a guide.
9. For your third throw, put all the dice back into the cup. After the third throw, some of the $^{210}_{84}Po$ will decay into the stable isotope $^{206}_{82}Pb$. Use the table above and step 8 to figure out what else happens after the third throw.
10. Continue throwing the dice until all the dice have decayed into $^{206}_{82}Pb$, which is a stable isotope. Hence, these dice will remain unchanged in all future throws.

▶ Analyzing Your Results

1. Write nuclear decay equations for the nuclear reactions modeled in this lab.
2. In your lab report, prepare a graph like the one shown at right. Using a different color or symbol for each atom, plot the data for all four atoms on the same graph.
3. What do your results suggest about how the amounts of $^{210}_{82}Pb$ and $^{206}_{82}Pb$ on Earth are changing over time?

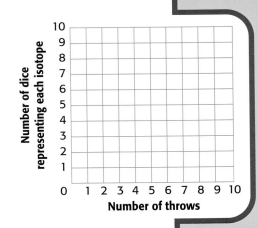

▶ Defending Your Conclusions

4. $^{210}_{82}Pb$ is continually produced through a series of nuclear decays that begin with $^{238}_{92}U$. Does this information cause you to modify your answer to item 3? Explain why.

Science Reporter

Science reporters are usually among the first people to hear about scientific discoveries. News organizations hire science reporters to explain these discoveries to the general public in a clear, understandable, and entertaining way. To learn more about science reporting as a career, read the interview with science reporter Corinna Wu, who writes for Science News *magazine, in Washington, D.C.*

Corinna Wu describes scientific research and discovery in the articles she writes.

"I think writing is something you can learn—it's a craft. Lots of people talk about talents, but I think it's something you can do if you work at it."

 What does a science reporter do?

I write and report news and feature articles for a weekly science news magazine. That entails finding news stories— generally about research. I have to call the researchers and ask them questions about how they did their work and the significance of the work. Then I write a short article explaining the research to ordinary people.

 What is your favorite part of your work?

I like learning about a new subject every week. I get to ask all the stupid questions I was afraid to ask in school.

 How did you become interested in science reporting as a career?

After college, I had a summer internship at NASA, at the Johnson Space Center in Houston, Texas, doing materials research there. I had lots of time to read space news magazines. It was at that time that I realized, "Hey, people write this stuff."

 What kinds of skills are important for a science reporter?

One thing that is really important is to really love writing. If you don't like to write already, it's pretty hard to make yourself do it every day. It helps to have a creative bent, too. It also helps to enjoy explaining things. Science writing by nature is explanatory, more so than other kinds of journalism.

 You have a science background. How does that help you do your job?

I majored in chemistry as an undergraduate and got a master's degree in materials science. I find that I draw on that academic background a lot, in terms of understanding the research.

Do you think a science reporter needs a science background?

Ideally, you should be studying science while writing on the side. But if you have to do one or the other, I'd do science first. It's harder to pick up the science later. Science builds on itself. It takes years to really get a grasp of it.

Why do you think science reporting is important?

Science and technology are becoming part of our everyday lives. It's important for people to keep up on research in these areas. There is an element of education in everything you write.

What advice do you have for students who are interested in science reporting?

Read as much as you can—newspapers, magazines, books. Nothing beats getting real experience writing. If you have a newspaper or magazine at school, get involved in that. You draw on academic experiences—you don't know when they will become useful.

internet connect

SCI**LINKS**
NSTA

TOPIC: Science writer
GO TO: www.scilinks.org
KEYWORD: HK1799

Musical Metal

Science catches up with the shimmering sound of steel drums

By CORINNA WU

More than half a century ago in Trinidad, a teenage Elliot "Ellie" Manette hammered 14 bumps into the steel bottom of an upside-down, 55-gallon oil barrel. Each raised section, when struck, resounded with a clear note.

Manette entered a contest and brought along the new creation. "All the others played small drums," he says, "and I showed up with my big drum. Everyone was surprised."

That humble, street-band instrument would evolve into the modern Caribbean steel drum, or steelpan, loved around the world for its bright, shimmering tones.

Manette, who turns 71 next month, today lives in Morgantown, W.Va., where he has served as an artist-in-residence at West Virginia University for about 5 years. An acknowledged master crafts-man, Manette is also training a group of a dozen apprentices in the art of making and tuning steel drums.

Manette has always worked intuitively. Now, with Manette's help, some scien-tists who are themselves fans of the steel-

A conventional pattern for a tenor drum contains 29 notes arranged in circles of fifths—each note is a musical fifth above or below its neighbors. The notes in the innermost ring are one octave higher than those in the middle ring, which are themselves one octave higher than the notes in the outermost ring.

236

SCIENCE NEWS, VOL. 154

pan have begun to study this intriguing instrument in hopes of divining the techni-cal secrets of its celestial sound. At the University of Texas at El Paso (UTEP), materials scientists and musicians have teamed up to analyze the metallurgy of the drum, connecting what they see under their microscopes with what they hear with their ears.

Lawrence E. Murr, director of UTEP's Materials Research Institute, first encountered steel drums as many people have—on a cruise to the Caribbean. "I'm a metallurgist of sorts, so I got interested in how they work," he says. "I just fell in love with the music. It's a very special sound. I vowed I would get hold of a drum and cut the notes out and look at them."

A step toward doing just that came in 1996 at a cocktail party, where Murr learned that a UTEP music professor, Larry White, had just received a grant to purchase a set of steel drums.

"When we finally got together," Murr says, White "thought I was crazy because I said, 'I really want to take this drums apart to know what makes them tick.'"

Murr recalls White's reaction: "Not my drums!"

Luckily, White agreed to work with Murr—as long as he didn't cut up his new set of steelpans. Searching around for steel drum experts, Murr quickly found Manette, who provided the team with some old drums "they could cut apart and ana-lyze. Manette "was real excit-ed [about the project]," Murr says, "because he was always interested in having somebody do legitimate science on the steel drum."

Manette would like to see materials scientists determine what kind of steel allows him to make the most beautiful sounding drum. Oil barrels made by dif-ferent manufacturers have different steel compositions and, therefore, different properties. Right now, says Manette, "I have no control over the composition. The ideal steel might be very different. We just don't know what it might be."

Soon, White and Murr assembled a

OCTOBER 10, 1998

group of music and engineering students interested in learning more about the instrument. White took Murr's engineering students into his classes to teach them how to read music and play the drums. Meanwhile, the engineers began the task of examining the metal up close.

They studied the microscopic structure of the hammered steel in samples taken from actual drums and tested idealized single-note disks cut from sheets of stain-less steel. What they have found has amazed them, Murr says. "The more research we do, the more we realize that [Manette's] intuition was fortuitous."

The design and processing methods that Manette pioneered, and that steel-pan makers have used ever since the 1940s, turn out to be perfectly suited for producing the drum's complex, rich sound. The researchers will publish their latest results in an upcoming issue of the JOURNAL OF MATERIALS SCIENCE.

When Manette was a youth, dis-carded barrels were abundant in oil-rich Trinidad, so he and his compatriots shaped them to make music. Drums are still made mostly by hand using many of Manette's original techniques.

To form a steelpan, the drum maker first "sinks the head" by hitting the bottom of the barrel with a sledgehammer, making it concave like a bowl. "If you don't do it cor-rectly, it breaks," says Murr. Then, the note-making surfaces are hammered up from underneath, forming raised sections on the bowl's surface. Often, the side of the barrel is cut to make it shorter.

A tenor, or lead, drum can have as many as 32 striking surfaces arranged in a circu-lar pattern. A bass drum might have only three. Other drums in a typical band include what are called guitars and cellos (each with 8 or 9 striking surfaces), which cover the midrange. The drummer strikes the notes with mallets, usually aluminum tubes covered with a piece of rubber.

Grooves or a line of holes bordering the raised surfaces help to isolate them from each other. Nevertheless, hitting one note causes some excitation of neighboring

notes, an effect that contributes to the instrument's intricate sound. "Because the notes are pat-terned onto the same drum head, the vibrational modes of one note will sympa-thetically vibrate with another," Murr explains.

Thomas D. Rossing, a physicist at North-ern Illinois University in DeKalb, has exam-ined the acoustic prop-erties of steel drums with a technique called holographic interfer-ometry. He excites one note electromagnetically at one of its fundamental frequencies, then uses the interferometer to visualize which areas of the playing surface rever-berate. "At amplitudes typical of performance, almost the entire drum vibrates and radiates sound," he reported in the March 1996 PHYSICS TODAY. Such extensive influence of one note on others is unusual in a musical instru-ment.

Through their metallurgical work, the UTEP researchers tried to determine the connections between the structure of the steel and the musical quality of the drum. They learned that drum makers unconsciously take advantage of the phys-

> "Science is a strong tool, a strong way of looking at the world. I feel that trying to introduce people to that way of looking at the world is very important."
> —CORINNA WU

213

Chanposa VII

Motion and Energy

CHAPTER 7
Motion and Forces 216
Viewpoints: Should Bicycle Helmets Be Required By Law? 246

CHAPTER 8
Work and Energy 248
Career Link
Grace Pierce, Engineer 286

CHAPTER 9
Heat and Temperature 288

Motion and Forces

Chapter Preview

7.1 Motion
Speed and Velocity
Momentum

7.2 Acceleration and Force
Acceleration
Force
Friction and Air Resistance
Gravity

7.3 Newton's Laws of Motion
Newton's First Law
Newton's Second Law
Free Fall and Weight
Newton's Third Law

Focus ACTIVITY

Background A car cruises down a track at 48 km/h (30 mi/h). Suddenly, the car smashes into an immovable block of steel and concrete, stopping in only fifteen-hundredths of a second. The occupant is not wearing a seat belt and is thrown against the steering wheel. The occupant's torso experiences the same force of impact it would have received if the occupant had fallen off the roof of a one-story house! The occupant escapes without any injuries because the occupant is a crash-test dummy.

Crash-test dummies come in various sizes and shapes. Each dummy is outfitted with sensors that record how the dummy moves and how hard it presses against different parts of the car during a crash when the dummy is strapped in by a seat belt. Automobile manufacturers use this information to develop and improve seat belts and other safety devices, such as air bags and padded dashboards.

Activity 1 Sit in the driver's seat of a parked car. Without your seat belt fastened, move forward to see what parts of your body would strike the car if you were in a head-on crash. Repeat this test with your seat belt fastened, and then perform the same two tests while sitting in the front passenger seat. Based on your results, where do you think sensors should be placed on a crash-test dummy to provide the most useful information when the dummy is wearing a seat belt? Where should sensors be placed on the dummy when the dummy is not wearing a seat belt?

Activity 2 You can investigate the Earth's pull on objects by using a stopwatch, a board, and two balls of different sizes. Set one end of the board on a chair and the other end on the ground. Time each ball as it rolls down the board. Do this several times with the board at different angles. Does the heavier ball move faster, slower, or take the same amount of time as the lighter one? What factors do you think might have affected the motion of the two balls?

Scientists use crash-test dummies to learn what happens to passengers involved in an automobile accident. During a crash, sensors inside each dummy gather information and feed it to a computer outside the car.

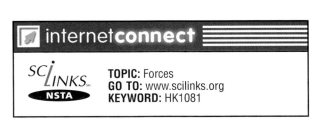

internetconnect

SC*LINKS*
NSTA

TOPIC: Forces
GO TO: www.scilinks.org
KEYWORD: HK1081

Motion

▶ **KEY TERMS**

speed
velocity
momentum

┌─ **OBJECTIVES**

▶ Relate speed to distance and time.
▶ Distinguish between speed and velocity.
▶ Recognize that all moving objects have momentum.
▶ Solve problems involving time, distance, velocity, and momentum.

We are surrounded by moving things. From a car moving in a straight line to a satellite traveling in a circle around the Earth, objects move in a variety of ways. In everyday life motion is so common, it seems to appear very simple. But, in fact, understanding motion requires some new and advanced ideas. How do we know when an object is moving?

Speed and Velocity

An object is moving if its position changes against some background that stays the same. In **Figure 7-1,** a horse is seen galloping against the background of stationary trees. This stationary background is called a *reference frame.* The change in position in a reference frame is measured in terms of the distance traveled by an object from a fixed point.

▶ **speed** distance traveled divided by the time interval during which the motion occurred

Our everyday experience shows that some objects move faster than others. Speed describes how fast an object moves. **Figure 7-1** shows speeds for some familiar things. A flying eagle moves faster than a galloping horse. But how do we determine speed?

Figure 7-1
We encounter a wide range of speeds in our everyday life.

Walking person

1.4 m/s
5.0 km/h
3.1 mi/h

Wheelchair racer

7.3 m/s
26 km/h
16 mi/h

Galloping horse

19 m/s
68 km/h
42 mi/h

3 m/s   5 m/s   10 m/s

Speed measurements involve distance and time

To find speed, you must measure two quantities: distance traveled by an object and the time it takes to travel that distance. Notice that all the speeds shown in **Figure 7-1** are expressed as a distance unit divided by a time unit. The SI unit for speed is meters per second (m/s). Speed is sometimes expressed in other units, such as kilometers per hour (km/h) or miles per hour (mi/h).

Constant speed is the simplest type of motion

When an object covers equal distances in equal amounts of time, it is moving at a constant speed. So what does it mean if a race car has a constant speed of 96 m/s? It means that the race car travels a distance of 96 m every second, as shown in **Table 7-1.**

Speed can be determined from a distance-time graph

We can investigate the relationship between speed, distance, and time by plotting a distance-time graph. The distance covered by an object is noted at regular intervals of time. The time and distance values are plotted along the horizontal and vertical axes respectively. For a race car moving with constant speed, the distance-time graph is a straight line as shown in **Figure 7-2.** The speed of the race car can be found by calculating the slope of the line.

Suppose all objects in **Figure 7-1** are moving at a constant speed. The distance-time graph of each object is drawn in **Figure 7-2.** Notice that the distance-time graph of a faster moving object is steeper than a slower moving object. An object at rest, such as a parked car, has a speed of 0 m/s. Its position does not change as time goes by. So, the distance-time graph of a resting object is a flat line with a slope of zero.

Table 7-1 **Distance-Time Values for a Racing Car**

Time (s)	Distance (m)
0	0
1	96
2	192
3	288
4	384

Figure 7-2
When the motion of an object is graphed by plotting the distance it travels versus time, the slope of the resulting line is the object's speed.

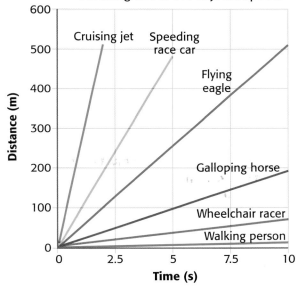

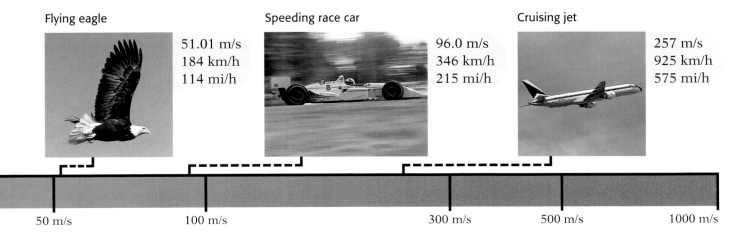

Flying eagle
51.01 m/s
184 km/h
114 mi/h

Speeding race car
96.0 m/s
346 km/h
215 mi/h

Cruising jet
257 m/s
925 km/h
575 mi/h

50 m/s   100 m/s   300 m/s   500 m/s   1000 m/s

Speed is calculated as distance divided by time

Most objects do not move with constant speed. The speed of an object can change from one instant to another. A useful quantity called *average* speed can be defined. Average speed is simply the distance covered by an object divided by the time it takes to travel that distance. From this definition, we can write a simple mathematical formula to calculate average speed.

> **Speed Equation**
>
> $$speed = \frac{distance}{time} \qquad v = \frac{d}{t}$$

Figure 7-3
A wheelchair racer's speed can be determined by timing the racer on a set course.

Suppose a wheelchair racer finishes a 132 m race in 18 s. By inserting the time and distance measurements in the formula, you can calculate the racer's average speed.

$$v = \frac{d}{t} = \frac{132 \text{ m}}{18 \text{ s}} = 7.3 \text{ m/s}$$

The racer's average speed over the entire distance is 7.3 m/s. But the racer probably did not travel at this speed for the whole race. The racer's pace might have been faster at the start of the race and slower near the end as the racer got tired. Suppose we are interested in the average speed during just the first half of the race. To calculate the average speed during the first half, we need to find the time it takes to travel the first 66 m.

► **velocity** quantity describing both speed and direction

Velocity describes both speed and direction

Sometimes, describing the speed of an object is not enough; you may also need to know the direction in which the object is moving. In 1997, a 200 kg (450 lb) lion escaped from a zoo in Florida. The lion was located by searchers in a helicopter. The helicopter crew was able to guide searchers on the ground by reporting the lion's **velocity,** or its speed and direction of motion. The escaped lion's velocity may have been reported as 4.5 m/s *to the north* or 2.0 km/h *toward the highway*.

Without knowing the direction of the lion's motion, it would have been impossible to predict the lion's position. This example shows the importance of knowing the direction of motion, as well as its speed. By specifying both the speed and direction of motion, you get an object's velocity.

Connection to
SOCIAL STUDIES

Many inventions have increased the speed at which people can travel. Cars have greatly changed the relationship between where people live and where they work. This has led to the growth of suburbs surrounding cities.

Making the Connection

1. Use a map to find the shortest straight-line path between your home and school. Calculate how long it would take you to walk to school along this path at a speed of 5.0 km/h.
   (**Hint:** 1 mi = 1.6 km)
2. Now determine the shortest route a school bus could take to go from your house to school. If you were to ride in a school bus that travels an average of 70 km/h (40 mi/h), how long would it take you to get to school?
3. Compare results with your classmates. Explain whether all of you would have gone to the same school 100 years ago.

The direction of motion can be described in various ways. For instance, you can indicate the direction as east, west, south, or north of some fixed point, or you can specify the angle from a fixed line. Also, the direction can be described as positive or negative along the line of motion. So, if a body is moving in one direction, then it has positive velocity, and if it is moving in the opposite direction, then it has negative velocity. *In this book, velocity will always be considered to be positive in the direction of motion.*

Math Skills

Velocity Metal stakes are sometimes placed in glaciers to help measure a glacier's movement. For several days in 1936, Alaska's Black Rapids glacier surged as swiftly as 89 m per day down the valley. Find the glacier's velocity in meters per second. Remember, velocity includes the direction of motion.

1 **List the given and unknown values.**
   Given: *time*, $t = 1$ day
   distance, $d = 89$ m
   Unknown: *velocity*, $v = ?$ (m/s and direction)

2 **Perform any necessary conversions.**
   To find the velocity in meters per second, the value for time must be in seconds.

   $$t = 1 \text{ day} = 24 \text{ h} \times \frac{60 \text{ min}}{1 \text{ h}} \times \frac{60 \text{ s}}{1 \text{ min}}$$

   $$t = 86\,400 \text{ s} = 8.64 \times 10^4 \text{ s}$$

3 **Write the equation for speed.**

   $$speed = \frac{distance}{time} \qquad v = \frac{d}{t}$$

4 **Insert the known values into the equation, and solve.**

   $$v = \frac{d}{t} = \frac{89 \text{ m}}{8.64 \times 10^4 \text{ s}} \quad \text{(For velocity, include direction.)}$$

   $$v = 1.0 \times 10^{-3} \text{ m/s down the valley}$$

Practice HINT

▶ When a problem requires you to calculate velocity, you can use the speed equation on the previous page.
▶ The speed equation can also be rearranged to isolate distance on the left side of the equation in the following way.

$$v = \frac{d}{t}$$

Multiply both sides by t.

$$v \times t = \frac{d}{t} \times t$$

$$d = vt$$

You will need to use this form of the equation in Practice Problem 3.
▶ In Practice Problem 4, you will need to rearrange the equation to isolate time on the left side of the equation.

Practice

Velocity
1. Find the velocity in meters per second of a swimmer who swims exactly 110 m toward the shore in 72 s.
2. Find the velocity in meters per second of a baseball thrown 38 m from third base to first base in 1.7 s.
3. Calculate the distance in meters a cyclist would travel in 5.00 hours at an average velocity of 12.0 km/h to the southwest.
4. Calculate the time in seconds an Olympic skier would take to finish a 2.6 km race at an average velocity of 28 m/s downhill.

Hiking

Hiking Experienced hikers use Naismith's rule to help them calculate the length of a trip. Naismith's rule is as follows:

Allow 1 hour for every 5 km (3 mi) you measure on the map, then add 1 hour for every 600 m (2000 ft) you have to climb.

This rule works for a fit walker who is not carrying a lot of equipment.

Applying Information

1. A group of hikers need to travel from Ambition Lake, at 3293 m (10 805 ft), to Blackcap Mountain, at 3523 m (11 559 ft).

They plan to travel by the route shown on the map at right. Use the map's distance scale to determine how far the hikers have to travel.

2. How many feet must the hikers climb?

3. Use Naismith's rule to calculate how long it will take the hikers to reach their destination.

4. Create a spreadsheet or graphing calculator program that applies Naismith's rule. **COMPUTER SKILL**

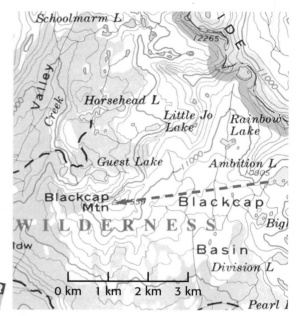

The velocity of an object changes if its speed or direction changes, or both change. If you watch a car's speedometer, you will notice that the speed changes from time to time. This shows a change in the velocity of the car. Even when a car has a constant speed, its velocity can change if the car turns. Why? Because the car's direction has changed.

Momentum

Velocity is not the only important quantity when objects are in motion. For example, a train is more difficult to stop than a car moving along the same path at the same speed. The train is more difficult to stop because it has a greater mass than the car. What if the car is moving very fast and the train is moving very slowly? In that case, is it possible that the car would be more difficult to stop? How do we know which object would be more difficult to stop?

Moving objects have momentum

▶ **momentum** a quantity defined as the product of an object's mass and its velocity

The object with more **momentum** would be more difficult to stop. The momentum of an object depends on both its velocity and its mass. For an object moving in a straight line, momentum is calculated by simply multiplying an object's mass by its velocity.

Like velocity, momentum also has direction. An object's momentum is in the same direction as its velocity. The momentum of the bowling ball shown in **Figure 7-4** is directed toward the pins and is calculated by multiplying its mass and its velocity. The SI unit for momentum is kilograms times meters per second (kg•m/s).

Momentum Equation (for straight-line motion)

$$momentum = mass \times velocity$$
$$p = mv$$

The momentum equation shows that for a given velocity, the more mass an object has, the greater its momentum is. A massive semi truck on the highway, for example, has much more momentum than a sports car traveling at the same velocity. The momentum equation also shows that the faster an object is moving, the greater its momentum is. For instance, a fast-moving train has much more momentum than a slow-moving train with the same mass. If an object is not moving, its momentum is zero.

Figure 7-4
Because of the large mass and high speed of this bowling ball, it has a lot of momentum and is able to knock over the pins easily.

Math Skills

Momentum Calculate the momentum of a 6.00 kg bowling ball moving at 10.0 m/s down the alley.

1 **List the given and unknown values.**
Given: *mass, m* = 6.00 kg
velocity, v = 10.0 m/s down the alley
Unknown: *momentum, p* = ? kg•m/s (and direction)

2 **Write the equation for momentum.**
momentum = mass × velocity
p = mv

3 **Insert the known values into the equation, and solve.**
$p = mv = 6.00 \text{ kg} \times 10.0 \text{ m/s}$
$p = 60.0 \text{ kg•m/s down the alley}$

Practice

Momentum
1. Calculate the momentum of the following objects:
   a. a 75 kg speed skater moving forward at 16 m/s
   b. a 135 kg ostrich running north at 16.2 m/s
   c. a 5.0 kg baby on a train moving eastward at 72 m/s
   d. a 0.8 kg kitten running to the left at 6.5 m/s
   e. a 48.5 kg passenger on a train stopped on the tracks

The law of conservation of momentum

Imagine that two cars of different masses and traveling with different velocities collide head on. Can you predict what will happen after the collision? Momentum can be used to predict the motion of the cars after the collision. This is because in the absence of outside influences, the momentum is conserved.

The total amount of momentum in a system is conserved.

In other words, the total momentum of the two cars before a collision is the same as the total momentum after the collision. This is true if the cars bounce off each other or get tangled together. Cars can bounce off each other to move in opposite directions. If the cars stick together after a head-on collision, the cars will continue in the direction of the car that originally had the greater momentum.

SECTION 7.1 REVIEW

SUMMARY

▶ The average speed of an object is defined as the distance the object travels divided by the time of travel.

▶ The distance-time graph of an object moving at constant speed is a straight line. The slope of the line is the object's speed.

▶ The SI unit for speed is meters per second (m/s).

▶ The velocity of an object consists of both its speed and direction of motion.

▶ The momentum of an object moving in a straight line is calculated by multiplying the object's mass and velocity. An object's momentum is in the same direction as its velocity.

▶ The SI unit for momentum is kilograms times meters per second (kg•m/s).

CHECK YOUR UNDERSTANDING

1. **Identify** the following measurements as speed, velocity, or momentum:
   a. 88 km/h
   b. 10 m/s straight up
   c. 18 kg•m/s down
   d. 19 m/s to the west

2. **Describe** the measurements necessary to find the average speed of a moving train.

3. **Determine** the units of a caterpillar's speed if you measure the distance the caterpillar travels in centimeters and the time it takes to travel this distance in minutes.

4. **Explain** why knowing the velocity of an airplane is more important to a traveler than knowing only the airplane's speed.

5. **Describe** why your velocity changes when you ride a Ferris wheel even if the wheel turns at a constant speed.

6. **Creative Thinking** Describe the motion of a ball in a typical sport. Identify times when the ball moves with a constant velocity and times when its velocity changes.

=== **Math Skills** ===

7. What is the speed in kilometers per hour of a train that travels 3701 km in 87 hours?

8. What is the velocity in meters per second of a sailboat that travels 149 m away from the shore in 16.8 s?

9. What is the momentum of a 1.35 kg baseball moving at 3.75 m/s away from home plate after a hit?

Acceleration and Force

OBJECTIVES

▶ Calculate the acceleration of an object.
▶ Describe how force affects the motion of an object.
▶ Distinguish between balanced and unbalanced forces.
▶ Explain how friction affects the motion of an object.

KEY TERMS
acceleration
force
balanced forces
unbalanced forces
friction
gravity

When you pedal hard to gain speed on your bicycle, your velocity changes. It changes again when you slow down to stop. Your velocity also changes as you round a curve in the road because your direction of motion changes. Any change in velocity is called an acceleration. The cyclist in **Figure 7-5** is accelerating as he turns the corner.

▶ **acceleration** change in velocity divided by the time interval in which the change occurred

Acceleration

To find the acceleration of an object moving in a straight line, we need to measure the object's velocity at different times. For an object moving in a straight line, acceleration can be calculated by dividing the change in the object's velocity by the time in which the change occurs. The change in an object's velocity is symbolized by Δv. The SI unit for acceleration is meters per second per second, or meters per second squared (m/s^2).

Acceleration Equation (for straight-line motion)

$$acceleration = \frac{final\ velocity - initial\ velocity}{time} \qquad a = \frac{\Delta v}{t}$$

Figure 7-5
This cyclist accelerates when he turns a corner even if his speed doesn't change.

What does an acceleration value tell you? If the acceleration is small, that means the speed is increasing very gradually. If the acceleration has a greater value, the object is speeding up more rapidly. For example, a human runner's acceleration is about 2 m/s^2. On the other hand, a sports car that goes from 0 to 96 km/h (60 mi/h) in 3.7 s has an acceleration of 7.2 m/s^2.

Because we use only positive velocity in this book, positive acceleration means the object's velocity will increase—it will speed up. Negative acceleration means the object's velocity will decrease—it will slow down.

Disc Two, Module 9:
Speed and Acceleration
Use the Interactive Tutor to learn more about these topics.

Practice HINT

▶ When a problem asks you to calculate acceleration, you can use the acceleration equation on page 225.

▶ The acceleration equation can also be rearranged to isolate time on the left in the following way.

$$a = \frac{\Delta v}{t}$$

Multiply both sides by t.

$$a \times t = \frac{\Delta v}{\cancel{t}} \times \cancel{t}$$

$$\Delta v = at$$

Divide both sides by a.

$$\frac{\Delta v}{a} = \frac{\cancel{a}t}{\cancel{a}}$$

$$t = \frac{\Delta v}{a}$$

You will need to use this form of the equation in Practice Problem 4.

▶ In Practice Problem 5, you will need to rearrange the equation to isolate final velocity on the left:

$$final\ v = initial\ v + at$$

Math Skills

Acceleration A flowerpot falls off a second-story windowsill. The flowerpot starts from rest and hits the sidewalk 1.5 s later with a velocity of 14.7 m/s. Find the average acceleration of the flowerpot.

1 List the given and unknown values.

Given: *time*, $t = 1.5$ s
initial velocity, initial v = 0 m/s down
final velocity, final v = 14.7 m/s down
Unknown: *acceleration*, $a = ?$ m/s² (and direction)

2 Write the equation for acceleration.

$$acceleration = \frac{final\ v - initial\ v}{time} \qquad a = \frac{\Delta v}{t}$$

3 Insert the known values into the equation, and solve.

$$a = \frac{\Delta v}{t} = \frac{final\ v - initial\ v}{t} = \frac{14.7\ m/s - 0\ m/s}{1.5\ s}$$

$$a = \frac{14.7\ m/s}{1.5\ s} = 9.8\ m/s^2\ down$$

Practice

Acceleration

1. Natalie accelerates her skateboard along a straight path from 0 m/s to 4.0 m/s in 2.5 s. Find her average acceleration.

2. A turtle swimming in a straight line toward shore has a speed of 0.50 m/s. After 4.0 s, its speed is 0.80 m/s. What is the turtle's average acceleration?

3. Find the average acceleration of a northbound subway train that slows down from 12 m/s to 9.6 m/s in 0.8 s.

4. Marisa's car accelerates at an average rate of 2.6 m/s². Calculate how long it takes her car to accelerate from 24.6 m/s to 26.8 m/s.

5. A cyclist travels at a constant velocity of 4.5 m/s westward, then speeds up with a steady acceleration of 2.3 m/s². Calculate the cyclist's speed after accelerating for 5.0 s.

When you press on the gas pedal in a car, you speed up and your acceleration is in the direction of the car's motion. When you press on the brake pedal, your acceleration is opposite to the direction of motion and you slow down. And when you turn the steering wheel, your velocity changes whether or not you speed up or slow down as you make the turn. This is because as you turn a corner the direction of your velocity changes. So acceleration is a common part of many types of motion.

Acceleration can be determined from a velocity-time graph

In the last section you learned that an object's speed can be determined from a distance-time graph of its motion. You can make a velocity-time graph by plotting velocity on the vertical axis and time on the horizontal axis.

A straight line on a velocity-time graph means that the velocity changes by the same amount each time. This is called constant acceleration. The slope of a line on a velocity-time graph gives you the value of the acceleration. A line with a positive slope represents an object that is speeding up. A line with a negative slope represents a slowing object.

The acceleration of an object is zero if its velocity is constant. If you ride your bike in a straight line at a constant speed, you are not accelerating. The bicyclist in **Figure 7-6A** is riding in a straight line with a constant speed of 13.00 m/s, as shown by the data in **Table 7-2.** If you move with a constant speed in a straight line, you are moving with a constant velocity. **Figure 7-6B** and **Figure 7-6C** show two different graphs that tell us about the motion of a cyclist traveling at a constant velocity.

Did You Know ?

The faster a car goes, the longer it takes a given braking force to bring the car to a stop. Braking distance describes how far a car travels between the moment the brakes are applied and the moment the car stops. As a car's speed increases, so does its *braking distance*. For example, when a car's speed is doubled, its braking distance is four times as long.

Figure 7-6

A When you ride your bike straight ahead at a constant speed, you are not accelerating because your velocity does not change.

Table 7-2 Data for a Bicycle with Unchanging Velocity

Time (s)	Velocity (m/s)
0	13.00
1	13.00
2	13.00
3	13.00
4	13.00

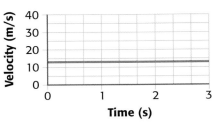

B If you plot the distance traveled against the time it takes, the resulting graph is a straight line with a slope of 13.00 m/s.

C Plotting the velocity against time results in a horizontal line because the velocity does not change. The acceleration is 0 m/s^2.

Figure 7-7

A When you slow down, your velocity changes. Your acceleration is negative because you are decreasing your velocity.

Table 7-3
Data for a Slowing Bicycle

Time (s)	Velocity (m/s)
0	13.00
1	9.75
2	6.50
3	3.25
4	0

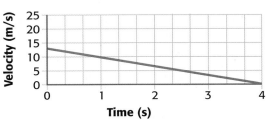

B If you plot the distance you travel against the time it takes you, the distance you travel each second becomes shorter and shorter until you finally stop.

C Plotting the velocity against time results in a line with a negative slope, which means the acceleration is negative.

INTEGRATING

MATHEMATICS

In the seventeenth century, both Sir Isaac Newton and Gottfried Leibniz studied acceleration and other rates of change. Independently, each created calculus, a branch of math that allows for describing rates of change of a quantity like velocity.

▶ **force** the cause of acceleration, or change in an object's velocity

The rider in **Figure 7-7A** is slowing down from 13.00 m/s to 3.25 m/s over a period of 3.00 s, as shown by the data in **Table 7-3.** You can find out the rate at which velocity changes by calculating the acceleration.

$$a = \frac{3.25 \text{ m/s} - 13.00 \text{ m/s}}{3.00 \text{ s}} = \frac{-9.75 \text{ m/s}}{3.00 \text{ s}} = -3.25 \text{ m/s}^2$$

The rider's velocity decreases by 3.25 m/s each second. The acceleration value has a negative sign because the rider is slowing down. **Figure 7-7B** and **Figure 7-7C** show two different graphs describing the motion of an object that is slowing down.

Force

When you throw or catch a ball, you exert a force to change the ball's velocity. What causes an object to change its velocity, or accelerate? Usually, many forces act on an object at any given time. The **net force,** the combination of all of the forces acting on an object, determines whether the velocity of the object will change. An object accelerates in the direction of the net force. It won't accelerate if the net force is zero.

Balanced forces do not change motion

In **Figure 7-8A,** the two teams are engaged in a tug-of-war. Both the teams pull the rope by using their weight and by pushing on the ground. You can imagine that the combined effect of the forces exerted by each team is acting at the center of the rope. If each team exerts an equal force, the rope will not move. **Balanced forces,** such as these, completely cancel each other. The combined force equals zero.

Unbalanced forces do not cancel completely

If opposing forces acting on an object do not have the same strength, they do not cancel each other completely. Such **unbalanced forces** are present in the tug-of-war shown in **Figure 7-8B.** Team 2 moves the rope in its direction because the combined effect from its team members results in a greater force. Although part of the force exerted by Team 2 is canceled by the force exerted by Team 1, the additional, or net, force provided by Team 2 causes the rope to move toward Team 2. Team 1 accelerates to the right because the leftward force is smaller than the rightward force.

What if the forces act in different directions but are not exactly opposite? In this situation, the combination of forces acts like a single force on the object. Like all unbalanced forces, the net force will cause the object to accelerate.

▶ **balanced forces** forces acting on an object that combine to produce a net force equal to zero

▶ **unbalanced forces** forces acting on an object that combine to produce a net nonzero force

VOCABULARY *Skills Tip*

The word force *comes from the Latin word* fortis, *meaning "strength." The word* fortress *comes from the same root.*

**Balanced forces:
no acceleration**

Team 1   Team 2

**Unbalanced forces:
acceleration**

Team 1   Team 2

Figure 7-8

A In a tug-of-war, each side exerts a force on the rope. If the opposing forces are equal, they are *balanced,* and the rope does not move.

B If one force is greater than the other, the forces are *unbalanced,* and the rope moves in the direction of the greater force.

Science and the Consumer

Should a Car's Air Bags Be Disconnected?

Air bags are standard equipment in every new automobile sold in the United States. These safety devices are credited with saving almost 1700 lives between 1986 and 1996. However, air bags have also been blamed for the deaths of 36 children and 20 adults during the same period. In response to public concern about the safety of air bags, the National Highway Traffic Safety Administration has proposed that drivers be allowed to disconnect the air bags on their vehicles.

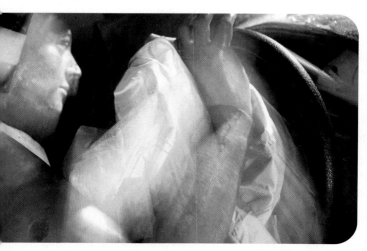

In a collision, air bags explode from a compartment to cushion the passenger's upper body and head.

How Do Air Bags Work?

When a car equipped with air bags crashes into another object, the car comes to an abrupt stop. Sensors in the car detect the sudden change in speed (negative acceleration) and trigger a chemical reaction inside the air bags. This reaction very quickly produces nitrogen gas, causing the bags to inflate and explode out of their storage compartment in a fraction of a second. The inflated air bags cushion the head and upper body of the driver and passengers in the front seat, who keep moving forward at the time of impact because of their inertia. Also, the inflated air bag increases the amount of time over which the stopping force acts. So as the rider moves forward, the air bag absorbs the impact.

What Are the Risks?

Because an air bag inflates suddenly and with great force, it can cause serious head and neck injuries in some circumstances. Seat belts reduce this risk by holding passengers against the seat back, allowing the air bag to inflate before the passenger's head comes into contact with it. In fact, most of the people killed by air bags either were not using seat belts or had not adjusted the seat belts properly.

However, two groups of people are at risk of being injured by air bags even with seat belts on: drivers shorter than about 157 cm (5 ft 2 in.) and infants who ride next to the driver in a rear-facing safety seat.

Alternatives to Disconnecting Air Bags

Always wearing a seat belt and placing child safety seats in the back seat of the car are two easy ways to reduce the risk of injury from air bags. Shorter drivers can buy pedal extenders that allow them to sit farther back and still safely reach the pedals. If the vehicle has a back seat, parents can put their child's safety seat there. Some vehicles without a back seat have a switch that can deactivate the passenger-side air bag. Automobile manufacturers are also working on air bags that inflate less forcefully.

Your Choice

1. **Critical Thinking** Are air bags useful if your car is struck from behind by another vehicle?
2. **Locating Information** Use library resources or the Internet to prepare a report about "smart" air-bag systems.

internet connect

SCILINKS
NSTA

TOPIC: Friction
GO TO: www.scilinks.org
KEYWORD: HK1083

Friction and Air Resistance

Imagine a car that is rolling along a flat, evenly paved street. If no force is acting on the car, the car should keep moving at a constant speed. Experience tells you, however, that the car will keep slowing down until it eventually stops. This steady change in the car's speed gives you a clue that a force must be acting on the car. This unbalanced force that acts against the car's direction of motion is **friction.**

Because of friction, a constant force must be applied to a car on a flat road just to keep it moving. In order for the car to reach a certain speed from rest, the forces on the car must be unbalanced. The force pushing the car forward must be greater than the force of friction opposing the car's motion, as shown in **Figure 7-9A.** Once the car reaches its desired speed, the car will maintain this speed if the forces acting on the car are balanced, as shown in **Figure 7-9B.**

Friction also affects objects that aren't moving. For example, when a truck is parked on a hill with its brakes set, as shown in **Figure 7-9C,** friction provides the force needed to balance the force of gravity and prevent the truck from moving downhill.

Frictional force varies depending on the surfaces in contact

New jogging shoes often have rough rubber soles. Friction between the new shoes and a carpeted floor will be large enough to prevent you from slipping. Frictional forces are relatively great when both surfaces are rough.

▷ **friction** the force between two objects in contact that opposes the motion of either object

Did You Know ?

Another way to think about the effect of force on an object's motion is to use the concept of momentum. The change in momentum for an object is greater when the force is larger or when the force acts over a longer time.

Figure 7-9
Frictional Force and Acceleration

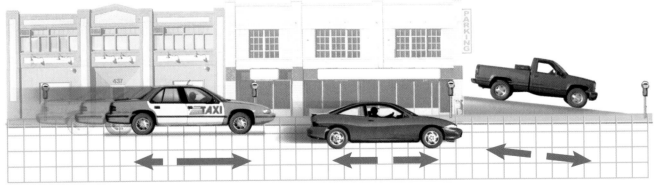

Unbalanced forces: acceleration

A When a car is accelerating, the forces are unbalanced. The force moving the car forward is greater than the opposing force of friction.

Balanced forces: constant speed

B When a car is cruising at constant speed, the force moving the car forward is balanced by the force of friction.

Balanced forces: no motion

C This truck does not roll because the force of friction between the brakes and the wheels balances the force of gravity.

Figure 7-10
With the need for better fuel efficiency and increased speed, car designs have been changed to reduce air resistance. Modern cars are much more aerodynamic.

▶ **gravity** the force of attraction between two particles of matter due to their mass

However, if the soles of your shoes are smooth or if the floor you are walking on has been waxed, you may find it difficult to walk steadily. That's because there is less frictional force if one surface is rough and the other is smooth. Smooth soles and a smooth floor can make it even more difficult to walk because of even less frictional force.

Air resistance is a form of friction

Although friction between a car's tires and the road allows a car to move forward, another type of friction, air resistance, opposes the car's motion. Air resistance is caused by the interaction between the surface of a moving object and the air molecules.

The amount of air resistance on an object depends on its size and shape as well as on the speed with which it moves. Objects with larger surfaces can experience greater air resistance. Air resistance also increases as the object's speed increases. As shown in **Figure 7-10,** car design has changed dramatically over the years. One factor taken into account in designing cars is reducing air resistance. To make cars, trains, and planes move faster without using more fuel, designers have changed the shapes of these vehicles to reduce the resistance between the vehicle and the surrounding air.

Gravity

Gravity is given as the reason why an apple falls down from a tree. But you may not realize that every object exerts a gravitational force on every other object. When an apple breaks from its stem, the apple falls down because the gravitational force between Earth and the apple is much greater than the gravitational force between the apple and the tree. Gravity is different from the forces we have discussed so far, like friction, because the force of gravity acts even when the objects do not touch.

Mass and distance affect gravitational force

The force of gravity between two objects depends on their masses and on the distance between the two objects. The gravitational force between two objects is proportional to the product of their masses. The greater the mass of an object is, the larger the gravitational force it exerts on other objects. For instance, the gravitational force that the person sitting next to you in the classroom exerts on you is so small that you don't even notice it. You can't help but notice Earth's gravitational force because Earth is extremely massive. The gravitational force between most objects around you is very small.

Gravitational force also depends on the distance between two objects, as shown in **Figure 7-11.** The force of gravity changes as the distance between the balls changes. If the distance between the two balls is doubled, the gravitational force between them decreases to one-fourth its original value. If the original distance is tripled, the gravitational force decreases to one-ninth its original value. Gravity is weaker than other types of forces, even though it holds the planets, stars, and galaxies together.

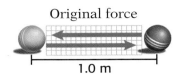

Original force

1.0 m

$$\frac{\text{Original force}}{9}$$

3.0 m

Figure 7-11
Gravitational force rapidly grows weaker as the distance between two objects increases.

SECTION 7.2 REVIEW

SUMMARY

▶ Acceleration is a change in the velocity of an object. An object accelerates when it speeds up, slows down, or changes direction. Acceleration is caused by a force.

▶ For straight-line motion, average acceleration is defined as the change in an object's velocity per unit time.

▶ The SI unit for acceleration is meters per second squared (m/s^2).

▶ The forces that act on an object combine to act effectively as one force.

▶ Friction is the force between two objects in contact; it opposes the motion of either object.

▶ Gravity is the force of attraction that two particles of matter exert on each other. It is proportional to their mass and inversely proportional to the square of the distance between them.

CHECK YOUR UNDERSTANDING

1. **Describe** three ways in which a car's velocity will change.
2. **Identify** a situation involving balanced forces. Describe the net force, and explain how this force affects the motion of an object.
3. **Identify** a situation involving unbalanced forces. Describe the net force, and explain how it affects the motion of an object.
4. **Evaluate** the following situations, and decide if an unbalanced force is present:
   a. A car turns right without slowing down.
   b. A spacecraft moves in one direction at a constant speed.
   c. A cyclist coasts downhill, going faster and faster.
   d. A tennis racket hits a tennis ball.
5. **Arrange** the following pairs of surfaces in order of most friction to least friction:
   a. a shoe sole and a waxed basketball court
   b. a shoe sole and the frozen surface of a lake
   c. a shoe sole and the sidewalk
6. **Creative Thinking** Explain why Venus, which is slightly less massive than Earth, experiences a stronger gravitational pull from the sun than Earth does.

Math Skills

7. What is the average acceleration of a car that starts from rest and then moves straight ahead reaching 18 m/s in 12 s?
8. Which will be moving faster after 3.0 s, a cyclist maintaining a constant velocity of 15 m/s straight ahead or a race car accelerating forward from a stoplight at 4.0 m/s^2?

Newton's Laws of Motion

KEY TERMS

inertia
free fall
terminal velocity

OBJECTIVES

▶ State Newton's three laws of motion, and apply them to physical situations.
▶ Calculate force, mass, and acceleration with Newton's second law.
▶ Recognize that the free-fall acceleration near Earth's surface is independent of the mass of the falling object.
▶ Explain the difference between mass and weight.
▶ Identify paired forces on interacting objects.

Every motion you observe or experience is related to a force. Sir Isaac Newton described the relationship between motion and force in three laws that we now call Newton's laws of motion. Newton's laws apply to a wide range of motion—a caterpillar crawling on a leaf, a person riding a bicycle, or a rocket blasting off into space.

Newton's First Law

If you slide your book across a rough surface, such as carpet, the book will soon come to rest. On a smooth surface, such as ice, the book will slide much farther before stopping. Because there is less frictional force between the ice and the book, the force must act over a longer time before the book comes to a stop. Without friction, the book would keep sliding forever. This is an example of Newton's first law, which is stated as follows.

An object at rest remains at rest and an object in motion maintains its velocity unless it experiences an unbalanced force.

You experience the effect described by Newton's first law when you ride in a car. As the car comes to a stop, you can feel your body continue to move forward. Your seat belt and the friction between your pants and the seat stop your forward motion. They provide the unbalanced rearward force needed to bring you to a stop as the car stops.

Because infants are more fragile than adults, they are placed in special backward-facing car seats, as shown in **Figure 7-12**. The force that is needed to bring the baby to a stop is safely spread out over the baby's entire body.

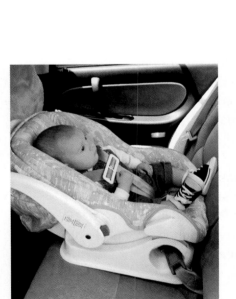

Figure 7-12
During an abrupt stop, this baby would continue to move forward. The backward-facing car seat distributes the force that holds the baby in the car.

Newton's First Law

1. Place an index card over a glass, and set a coin on top of the index card.
2. With your thumb and forefinger, quickly flick the card sideways off the glass. Observe what happens to the coin. Does the coin move with the index card?
3. Try again, but this time slowly pull the card sideways and observe what happens to the coin.
4. Use Newton's first law to explain your results.

Inertia is the tendency of an object at rest to remain at rest or, if moving, to continue moving with a constant velocity. All objects have inertia because they resist changes in motion. An object with very little mass, such as a baseball, can be accelerated with a small force. But it takes a much larger force to accelerate a car, which has a large mass.

▷ **inertia** the tendency of an object to remain at rest or in motion with a constant velocity

Newton's Second Law

Newton's first law describes what happens when the net force acting on an object is zero: the object either remains at rest or continues moving at a constant velocity. What happens when the net force acting on an object is not zero? Newton's second law describes the effect of this unbalanced force on the motion of an object.

Force equals mass times acceleration

Newton's second law, which describes the relationship between mass, force, and acceleration, can be stated as follows.

The unbalanced force acting on an object equals the object's mass times its acceleration.

Mathematically, Newton's second law can be written as follows.

Newton's Second Law
$$force = mass \times acceleration$$
$$F = ma$$

Consider the difference between pushing an empty shopping cart and pushing the same cart filled with groceries, as shown in **Figure 7-13.** If you push the cart with the same amount of force in each situation, the empty cart will have a greater acceleration because it has a smaller mass than the full cart. The same amount of force in each case produces different accelerations because the masses are different.

Figure 7-13
Because the full cart has a larger mass than the empty cart, the same force gives the empty cart a greater acceleration.

What would happen if you and a friend each pushed an empty cart but you used more force? The cart you pushed would have a greater acceleration. When two masses are the same, a greater force provides a greater acceleration.

Although the force in these cases is a push, Newton's second law applies regardless of the type of force involved. The acceleration is always in the direction of the net force.

Force is measured in newtons

Newton's second law can be used to derive the SI unit of force, the newton (N). One newton is the force that can give a mass of 1 kg an acceleration of 1 m/s^2, expressed as follows.

$$1 \text{ N} = 1 \text{ kg} \times 1 \text{ m/s}^2$$

The pound (lb) is sometimes used as a unit of force. One newton is equivalent to 0.225 lb. Conversely, 1 lb is equal to 4.448 N.

Math Skills

Newton's Second Law Zookeepers lift a stretcher that holds a sedated lion. The total mass of the lion and stretcher is 175 kg, and the lion's upward acceleration is 0.657 m/s^2. What is the unbalanced force necessary to produce this acceleration of the lion and the stretcher?

1 List the given and unknown values.
   Given: *mass*, $m = 175$ kg
                acceleration, $a = 0.657$ m/s^2
   Unknown: *force*, $F = ?$ N

2 Write the equation for Newton's second law.
   force = mass × acceleration
   $F = ma$

3 Insert the known values into the equation, and solve.
   $F = 175 \text{ kg} \times 0.657 \text{ m/s}^2$
   $F = 115 \text{ kg·m/s}^2 = 115$ N

Practice HINT

▶ When a problem requires you to calculate the unbalanced force on an object, you can use Newton's second law on the previous page.
▶ The equation for Newton's second law can be rearranged to isolate mass on the left side of he equation in the following way.
   $F = ma$
   Divide both sides by *a*.
   $$\frac{F}{a} = \frac{m\cancel{a}}{\cancel{a}}$$
   $$m = \frac{F}{a}$$
   You will need to use this form of the equation in Practice Problem 2.
▶ In Practice Problem 3 you will need to rearrange the equation to isolate acceleration on the left side.

Practice

Newton's Second Law

1. What is the net force necessary for a 1.6×10^3 kg automobile to accelerate forward at 2.0 m/s^2?

2. A baseball accelerates downward at 9.8 m/s^2. If the gravitational force acting on the baseball is 1.4 N, what is the baseball's mass? (**Hint:** Assume gravity is the only force acting on the ball.)

3. A sailboat and its crew have a combined mass of 655 kg. If the sailboat experiences an unbalanced force of 895 N pushing it forward, what is the sailboat's acceleration?

Free Fall and Weight

When gravity is the only force acting on an object, it is said to be in free fall. The free-fall acceleration of an object is directed toward the center of the Earth. Because free-fall acceleration results from the force due to gravity, it is often abbreviated as the letter g. Near Earth's surface, g is approximately equal to 9.8 m/s^2.

▶ **free fall** the motion of a body when only the force of gravity is acting on it

Free-fall acceleration near Earth's surface is constant

In the absence of air resistance, all objects near Earth's surface accelerate at the same rate, regardless of their mass. This means that if you dropped a 1.5 kg book and a 15 kg rock from the same height, they would hit the ground at about the same moment. For simplicity, we will disregard air resistance for all calculations in this book. We will assume that all objects on Earth accelerate at exactly 9.8 m/s^2.

Why do all objects have the same free-fall acceleration? Newton's second law shows that acceleration depends on both the force on an object and its mass. A heavier object experiences a greater gravitational force than a lighter object. But a heavier object is also harder to accelerate because it has more mass. The extra mass of the heavy object exactly compensates for the additional gravitational force.

Weight equals mass times free-fall acceleration

The force on an object due to gravity is called its weight. On Earth, your weight is simply the amount of gravitational force exerted on you by Earth. If you know the free-fall acceleration, g, acting on a body, you can use $F = ma$ (Newton's second law) to calculate the body's weight. Weight equals mass times free-fall acceleration. Mathematically, this is expressed as follows.

$$weight = mass \times free\text{-}fall\ acceleration$$
$$w = mg$$

Note that because weight is a force, the SI unit of weight is the newton. For example, a small apple weighs about 1 N. A 1.0 kg book has a weight of 1.0 kg $\times$ 9.8 m/s^2 = 9.8 N.

You may have seen pictures of astronauts floating in the air, as shown in **Figure 7-14.** Does this mean that they don't experience gravity? In orbit, astronauts, the space shuttle, and all objects on board experience free fall due to the Earth's gravity. In fact, the astronauts and their surroundings all accelerate at the same rate. Therefore, the floor of the shuttle does not push up against the astronauts and the astronauts appear to be floating. This situation is referred to as *apparent weightlessness.*

Figure 7-14
In the low gravity environment of the orbiting space shuttle, astronauts experience apparent weightlessness.

INTEGRATING

SPACE SCIENCE
Because the planets in our solar system have different masses and sizes, the value of *g* is different on each planet. Find the weight of a 58 kg person on the following planets:

Earth, where *g* = 9.8 m/s²

Mars, where *g* = 3.7 m/s²

Venus, where *g* = 8.8 m/s²

Neptune, where *g* = 11.8 m/s²

terminal velocity the maximum velocity reached by a falling object that occurs when the resistance of the medium is equal to the force due to gravity

Weight is different from mass

Mass and weight are easy to confuse. Although mass and weight are proportional to one another, they are not the same. Mass is a measure of the amount of matter in an object. Weight is the gravitational force an object experiences due to its mass.

The weight of an object depends on gravity, so a change in an object's location will change the object's weight. For example, consider a 66 kg astronaut. On Earth, this astronaut weighs 66 kg × 9.8 m/s²=650 N (about 150 lb), but on the moon's surface, where *g* is only 1.6 m/s², the astronaut would weigh 66 kg × 1.6 m/s²=110 N (about 24 lb). The astronaut's mass remains the same on Earth, the moon, or an orbiting space shuttle, but the gravitational force acting on the astronaut changes in each place.

Weight influences shape

Gravity influences the shapes of living things. On land, large animals must have strong skeletons to support their mass against gravity. The woody trunks of trees serve the same function. For organisms that live in water, however, the downward force of gravity is balanced by the upward forces of the water. For many of these creatures, strong skeletons or other supporting structures are unnecessary. Because a jellyfish has no skeleton, it can drift gracefully through the water but collapses if it washes up on the beach.

Velocity is constant when air resistance balances weight

Both air resistance and gravity act on objects moving through Earth's atmosphere. For a falling object, when the force of air resistance becomes equal to the gravitational force on the object—the weight—it stops accelerating, as shown in **Figure 7-15.** This happens because the air resistance acts in the opposite direction to the weight. When these two forces are equal, the object stops accelerating and reaches its maximum velocity, the **terminal velocity.**

When sky divers begin their jump, their parachutes are closed. Once they leap from the plane, they are accelerated toward Earth by gravity. As their velocity increases, the force they experience due to air resistance increases. When air resistance and the force of gravity are equal, they reach a terminal velocity of about 320 km/h (200 mi/h). But when they open the parachute, their air resistance increases greatly. For a while, this slows them down. Eventually, they reach a new terminal velocity of several kilometers per hour allowing them to land safely.

Figure 7-15

When a sky diver reaches terminal velocity, the force of gravity is balanced by air resistance.

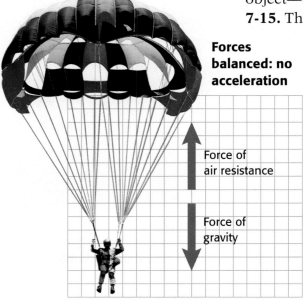

Forces balanced: no acceleration

Force of air resistance

Force of gravity

Newton's Third Law

When you kick a soccer ball with your foot, as shown in **Figure 7-16,** you notice the effect of the force exerted by your foot on the ball. The ball experiences a change in motion. But is this the only force present? Do you feel a force on your foot when kicking the ball? In fact, the soccer ball exerts an equal and opposite force on your foot. The force exerted on the ball by your foot is the action force, and the force exerted on your foot by the ball is the reaction force.

Figure 7-16
According to Newton's third law, the soccer ball and the foot shown in this photo exert equal and opposite forces on one another.

Note that the action and reaction forces are applied to different objects. These forces are equal and opposite, but this is not a case of balanced forces because two different objects are involved. The action force acts on the ball, and the reaction force acts on the foot. This is an example of Newton's third law, also called the law of action and reaction.

For every action force, there is an equal and opposite reaction force.

Newton's third law implies that forces always occur in pairs. But the action and reaction force of a force pair act on different objects. Also, action and reaction forces occur at the same time.

Newton's third law is used in rocketry. Rockets were invented many centuries ago. They have many different sizes and designs, but the basic principle remains the same.

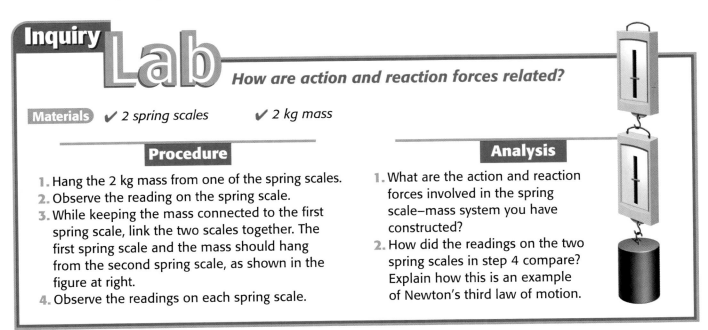

Inquiry Lab

How are action and reaction forces related?

Materials ✔ 2 spring scales   ✔ 2 kg mass

Procedure

1. Hang the 2 kg mass from one of the spring scales.
2. Observe the reading on the spring scale.
3. While keeping the mass connected to the first spring scale, link the two scales together. The first spring scale and the mass should hang from the second spring scale, as shown in the figure at right.
4. Observe the readings on each spring scale.

Analysis

1. What are the action and reaction forces involved in the spring scale–mass system you have constructed?
2. How did the readings on the two spring scales in step 4 compare? Explain how this is an example of Newton's third law of motion.

Figure 7-17

All forces occur in action-reaction pairs. In this case, the upward push on the rocket equals the downward push on the exhaust gases.

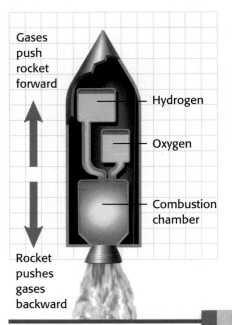

Gases push rocket forward

Hydrogen

Oxygen

Combustion chamber

Rocket pushes gases backward

The push of the hot gases through the nozzle is matched by an equal push in the opposite direction on the combustion (burning) chamber, which accelerates the rocket forward.

Figure 7-17 is a representation of a liquid-fuel rocket. Liquid oxygen and liquid hydrogen are held in separate compartments, as shown. The oxygen and hydrogen react in a combustion chamber to produce a gas with a great deal of energy. This energy causes the gas to press out equally in all directions inside the rocket. The pressure of the gas against one side of the rocket balances the pressure of the gas against the opposite side. However, because the bottom of the combustion chamber is open, gas escapes through the nozzle. Thus, the force of the gas against the front of the rocket is not balanced at the back of the rocket. This unbalanced force pushes the rocket forward.

Rockets burn up most of their fuel during the early stages of flight, mainly because the rocket has more mass to accelerate because of the unused fuel it carries. As the fuel is used, the rocket's mass decreases and the force needed to produce a given acceleration decreases. Because air is more dense in Earth's lower atmosphere, the rocket also experiences greater air resistance initially.

SECTION 7.3 REVIEW

SUMMARY

▶ An object at rest remains at rest and an object in motion maintains a constant velocity unless it experiences an unbalanced force (Newton's first law).

▶ The unbalanced force acting on an object equals the object's mass times its acceleration, or $F = ma$ (Newton's second law).

▶ The SI unit for force is the newton (N). Weight equals mass times free fall acceleration, or $W = mg$.

▶ For every action force, there is an equal and opposite reaction force (Newton's third law).

CHECK YOUR UNDERSTANDING

1. **State** each of Newton's three laws of motion in your own words, and give an example that demonstrates each law.
2. **Explain** the difference between mass and weight. Does the weight of an object ever change? If so, when?
3. **Identify** the action and reaction forces in each of the following cases:
   a. your hand pushing against a wall
   b. a hammer pounding a nail
   c. a stone striking the bottom of a well
   d. a book sliding to a stop on the ground
4. **Critical Thinking** Using Newton's laws, predict what will happen when a car traveling on an icy road
   a. comes to a sharp bend.
   b. has to stop quickly.

Math Skills

5. What is the acceleration of a boy on a skateboard if the unbalanced forward force on the boy is 15 N? The total mass of the boy and skateboard is 58 kg.
6. How much does a 5.0 kg puppy weigh on Earth?

Chapter Highlights

Before you begin, review the summaries of the key ideas of each section, found on pages 224, 233, and 240. The key vocabulary terms are listed on pages 218, 225, and 234.

UNDERSTANDING CONCEPTS

1. If you jog for 1 hour and travel 10 km, 10 km/h describes your _____.
   - a. momentum
   - b. average speed
   - c. displacement
   - d. acceleration

2. _____ is speed in a certain direction.
   - a. Acceleration
   - b. Friction
   - c. Momentum
   - d. Velocity

3. Which of the following objects is not accelerating?
   - a. a ball being juggled
   - b. a woman walking at 2.5 m/s along a straight road
   - c. a satellite circling Earth
   - d. a braking cyclist

4. The newton is a measure of _____.
   - a. mass
   - b. length
   - c. force
   - d. acceleration

5. _____ is a force that opposes the motion between two objects in contact with each other.
   - a. Motion
   - b. Friction
   - c. Acceleration
   - d. Velocity

6. Automobile seat belts are necessary for safety because of a passenger's _____.
   - a. inertia
   - b. weight
   - c. speed
   - d. gravity

7. The winner of the shot-put event in the Olympics is the person who best uses _____.
   - a. Newton's first law
   - b. Newton's second law
   - c. air resistance
   - d. the law of gravity

8. An example involving action-reaction forces is _____.
   - a. air escaping from a toy balloon
   - b. a rocket traveling through the air
   - c. a ball bouncing off a wall
   - d. All of the above

Using Vocabulary

9. State whether 30 m/s to the west represents a *speed*, a *velocity*, or both.

10. Describe the motion of a cyclist at the start of a race. In your answer, use the terms *velocity, acceleration, force,* and *friction.*

11. A wrestler weighs in for the first match on the moon. Will he weigh more or less on the moon? Explain your answer using the terms *weight, mass, force,* and *gravity.*

12. "There is no *gravity* in outer space." Write a paragraph explaining whether this statement is true or false. **WRITING SKILL**

13. Describe a sky diver's jump from the airplane to the ground. In your answer, use the terms *air resistance, gravity,* and *terminal velocity.*

BUILDING MATH SKILLS

14. **Graphing** The following graphs describe the motion of four different balls—*a, b, c,* and *d.* Using the graphs below, state whether each ball is accelerating, sitting still, or moving at a constant velocity.

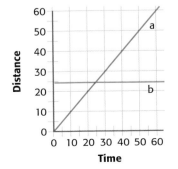
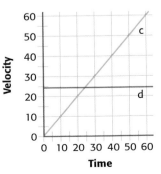

15. Velocity An airplane traveling from San Francisco northeast to Chicago travels 1260 km in 3.5 hours. What is the airplane's velocity?

16. Velocity Heather and Matthew take 45 s to walk eastward along a straight road to a store 72 m away. What is their average velocity?

17. Velocity Simpson drives his car with an average velocity of 85 km/h toward the east. How long will it take him to drive 560 km on a perfectly straight highway?

18. Momentum Calculate the momentum of an 85 kg man jogging north along the highway at 2.65 m/s.

19. Momentum Calculate the momentum of a 9.1 kg toddler who is riding in a car moving east at 89 km/h.

20. Acceleration A driver is traveling east on a dirt road when she spots a pothole ahead. She slows her car from 14.0 m/s to 5.5 m/s in 6.0 s. What is the car's acceleration?

21. Acceleration How long will it take a cyclist with a forward acceleration of -0.50 m/s^2 to bring a bicycle with an initial forward velocity of 13.5 m/s to a complete stop?

22. Force A 5.5 kg watermelon is pushed across a table. If the acceleration of the watermelon is 4.2 m/s^2 to the right, what is the net force exerted on the watermelon?

23. Force A block pushed with a force of 13.5 N accelerates at 6.5 m/s^2 to the left. What is the mass of the block?

24. Force The net force on a 925 kg car is 37 N as it pulls away from a stop sign. Find the car's acceleration.

25. Weight A bag of sugar has a mass of 2.26 kg. What is its weight in newtons on the moon, where the acceleration due to gravity is one-sixth that on Earth? (**Hint:** On Earth, $g = 9.8$ m/s^2.)

THINKING CRITICALLY

26. Interpreting Graphics Two cars are traveling east on a highway, as shown in the figure below. After 5.0 s, they are side by side at the *next* telephone pole. The distance between the poles is 70.0 m. Determine the following quantities:
  a. the distance car A has traveled during the 5.0 s interval
  b. the distance car B has traveled during the 5.0 s interval
  c. the average velocity of car A during this 5.0 s time interval
  d. the average velocity of car B during this 5.0 s time interval

27. Applying Knowledge If the average velocity of a sea gull in a given time interval is 0 m/s, what can you say about the position of the sea gull at the end of the time interval?

28. Applying Knowledge Which object has more momentum in each of the following?
  a. a car and train with the same velocity
  b. a moving ball and a still bat
  c. two identical balls moving at the same speed in the same direction
  d. two identical balls moving at the same speed in opposite directions

29. Problem Solving Why will a boat use more fuel to travel 32 km/h against the wind in a rainstorm than it would to travel at the same velocity for the same time on a sunny day with no wind?

30. Creative Thinking According to Newton's second law, twice the net force results in twice the acceleration. Explain why a stone weighing 20 N doesn't fall twice as fast as a stone weighing 10 N.

31. Applying Knowledge If you doubled the net force acting on a moving object, how would the object's acceleration be affected?

32. Problem Solving How will acceleration change if the mass being accelerated is tripled but the net force is halved?

DEVELOPING LIFE/WORK SKILLS

33. Allocating Resources A pizza-delivery car can travel 11 km for every liter (L) of gasoline it uses (26 mi/gal). If the driver's average speed is 28 km/h (18 mi/h), how many hours can the driver travel before emptying a full 35 L gas tank?

34. Making Decisions If you were an engineer designing an air-bag system, would you want the air bag to release vertically or horizontally from its storage compartment? Explain your reasoning. (**Hint:** Consider the direction of the force of the air bag.)

35. Working Cooperatively Read the following arguments about rocket propulsion. With a small group, determine which is correct. Use a diagram to explain your answer.
a. Rockets cannot travel in outer space because there is nothing for the gas exiting the rocket to push against.
b. Rockets can travel in outer space because gas exerts an unbalanced force on the front of the rocket. This net force causes the acceleration.
c. Argument b can't be true. The action and reaction forces will be equal and opposite. Therefore, the forces will balance, and no movement would be possible.

INTEGRATING CONCEPTS

36. Concept Mapping Copy the unfinished concept map below onto a sheet of paper. Complete the map by writing the correct word or phrase in the lettered boxes.

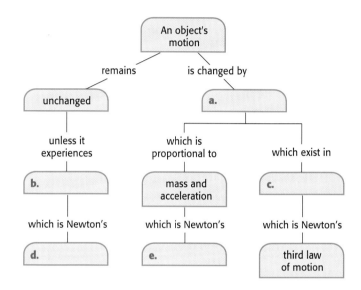

37. Connection to Social Studies Research Galileo's work on falling bodies. What did he want to demonstrate? What theories did he try to refute? What arguments did he use to persuade others that he was right? Did he depend on experiments and observations, logic, or other approaches?

38. Integrating Health When you exercise, you move all or parts of your body to oppose various forces. Identify the forces that oppose your body during the following exercises: push-ups, running, and swimming.

internetconnect

SC*LINKS*
NSTA

TOPIC: Graphing speed, velocity, acceleration
GO TO: www.scilinks.org
KEYWORD: HK1085

Design Your Own Lab

Introduction

How can you use a rubber band to measure the force necessary to break a human hair?

Objectives

▶ **Build** and calibrate an instrument that measures force.

▶ **Use** your instrument to measure how much force it takes to stretch a human hair until it breaks.

Materials

rubber bands of various sizes
large and small metal paper clips
pen or pencil
metric ruler
standard hooked masses ranging
    from 10–200 g
comb or hairbrush

Safety Needs

Safety goggles

Measuring Forces

▶ Testing the Strength of a Human Hair

1. Obtain a rubber band and a paper clip.
2. Carefully straighten the paper clip so that it forms a double hook. Cut the rubber band and tie one end to the ring stand and the other end to one of the paper clip hooks. Let the paper clip dangle.
3. In your lab report, prepare a table as shown below.
4. Measure the length of the rubber band. Record this length in **Table 1**.
5. Hang a hooked mass from the lower paper clip hook. Supporting the mass with your hand, allow the rubber band to stretch downward slowly. Then remove your hand carefully so the rubber band does not move.
6. Measure the stretched rubber band's length. Record the mass that is attached and the rubber band's length in **Table 1**. Calculate the change in length by subtracting your initial reading of the rubber band's length from the new length.
7. Repeat steps 5 and 6 three more times using different masses each time.
8. Convert each mass (in grams) to kilograms using the following equation.
$$\text{mass (in kg)} = \text{mass (in g)} \div 1000$$
Record your answers in **Table 1**.
9. Calculate the force (weight) of each mass in newtons using the following equation.
$$\text{Force (in N)} = \text{mass (in kg)} \times 9.81 \text{ m/s}^2$$
Record your answers in **Table 1**.

Table 1   Calibration

Rubber-band length (cm)	Change in length (cm)	Mass on hook (g)	Mass on hook (kg)	Force (N)
	0	0	0	0

▶ Designing Your Experiment

10. With your lab partner(s), devise a plan to measure the force required to break a human hair using the instrument you just calibrated. How will you attach the hair to your instrument? How will you apply force to the hair?

11. In your lab report, list each step you will perform in your experiment.

12. Have your teacher approve your plan before you carry out your experiment.

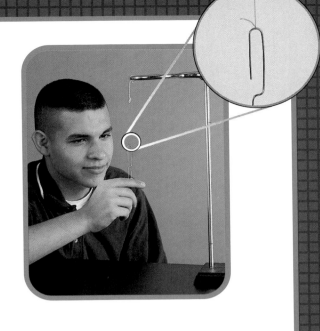

▶ Performing Your Experiment

13. After your teacher approves your plan, gently run a comb or brush through a group member's hair several times until you find a loose hair at least 10 cm long that you can test.

14. In your lab report, prepare a data table similar to the one shown at right to record your experimental data.

15. Perform your experiment on three different hairs from the same person. Record the maximum rubber-band length before the hair snaps for each trial in **Table 2**.

Table 2 **Experimentation**

Trial	Rubber-band length (cm)	Force (N)
Hair 1		
Hair 2		
Hair 3		

▶ Analyzing Your Results

1. Plot your calibration data in your lab report in the form of a graph like the one shown at right. On your graph, draw the line or smooth curve that fits the points best.

2. Use the graph and the length of the rubber band for each trial of your experiment to determine the force that was necessary to break each of the three hairs. Record your answers in **Table 2**.

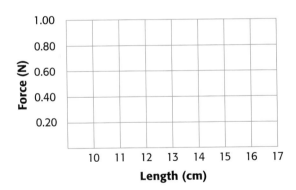

▶ Defending Your Conclusions

3. Suppose someone tells you that your results are flawed because you measured length and not force. How can you show that your results are valid?

viewpoints

Should Bicycle Helmets Be Required by Law?

In some communities, bicyclists are required by law to wear a helmet and can be ticketed if they do not. Few people dispute the fact that bicycle helmets can save lives when used properly.

But others say that it is a matter of private rights and that the government should not interfere. Should it be up to bicyclists to decide whether or not to wear a helmet and to suffer any consequences?

But are the consequences limited to the rider? Who will pay when the rider gets hurt? Should the rider bear the cost of an injury that could have been prevented?

Is this an issue of public health or private rights? What do you think?

> FROM: Chad A., Rochester, MN

More and more people are getting head injuries every year because they do not wear a helmet. Nowadays helmets look so cool— I wouldn't be ashamed to wear one.

Require Bicycle Helmets

> FROM: Laurel R., Coral Springs, FL

I believe that this is a public issue only for people under the age of 12. Children 12 and under still need guidance and direction about safety and they are usually the ones riding their bicycles out in the road or in traffic. Often they don't pay attention to cars or other motor vehicles around them.

> FROM: Jocelyn B., Chicago, IL

They should treat helmets the same way they treat seatbelts. I was in a tragic bike accident when I was 7. I was jerked off my bike, and I slid on the glass-laden concrete. To make a long story short, I think there should be a helmet law because people just don't know the danger.

> FROM: Megan J., Bowling Green, KY.

Although wearing a bicycle helmet can be considered a matter of public health, the rider is the one at risk. It is a personal choice, no matter what the public says.

> FROM: Melissa F., Houston, TX

Bicycle helmets shouldn't be required by law. Helmets are usually a little over $20, and if you have five kids, the helmets alone cost $100. You'd still have to buy the bikes.

Don't Require Bicycle Helmets

> FROM: Heather R., Rochester, MN

It has to do with private rights. The police have more serious issues to deal with, like violent crimes. Bicycle riders should choose whether or not they want to risk their life by riding without a helmet.

Your Turn

1. **Critiquing Viewpoints** Select one of the statements on this page that you *agree* with. Identify and explain at least one weak point in the statement. What would you say to respond to someone who brought up this weak point as a reason you were wrong?

2. **Critiquing Viewpoints** Select one of the statements on this page that you *disagree* with. Identify and explain at least one strong point in the statement. What would you say to respond to someone who brought up this point as a reason they were right?

3. **Creative Thinking** Suppose you live in a community that does not have a bicycle helmet law. Design a campaign to persuade people to wear helmets, even though it isn't required by law. Your campaign could include brochures, posters, and newspaper ads.

4. **Acquiring and Evaluating Data** When a rider falls off a bicycle, the rider continues moving at the speed of the bicycle until the rider strikes the pavement and slows down rapidly. For bicycle speeds ranging from 5.0 m/s to 25.0 m/s, calculate what acceleration would be required to stop the rider in just 0.50 s. How large is the force that must be applied to a 50.0 kg rider to cause this acceleration? Organize your data and results in a series of charts or graphs.

 internet**connect**

TOPIC: Bicycle helmets
GO TO: go.hrw.com
KEYWORD: HK1Helmet

Should helmets be required by law? Why or why not? Share your views on this issue and learn about other viewpoints at the HRW Web site.

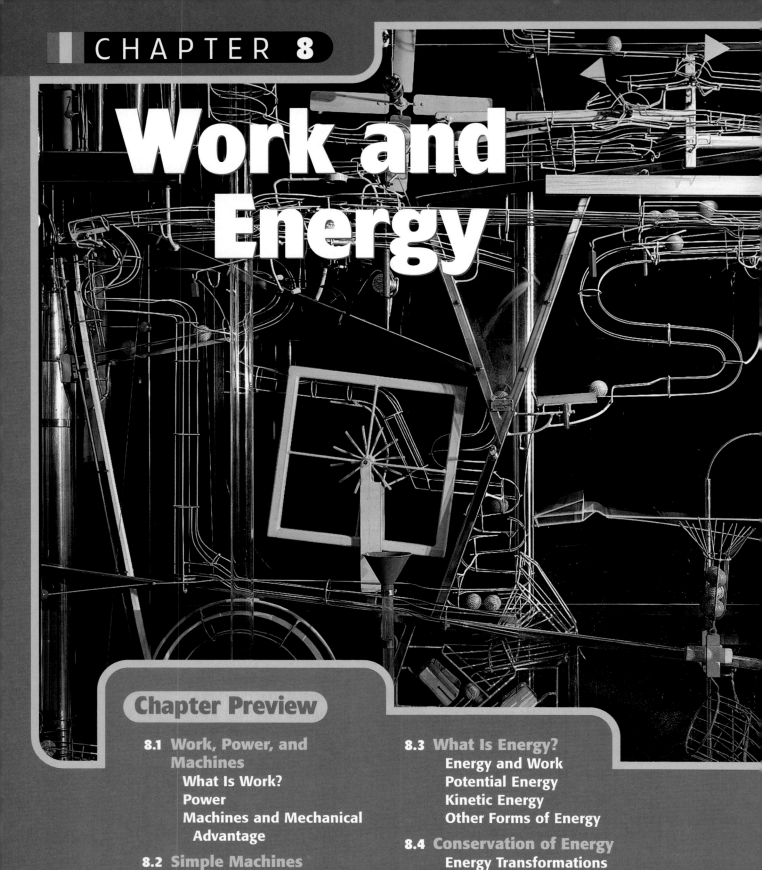

CHAPTER 8

Work and Energy

Chapter Preview

8.1 Work, Power, and Machines
  What Is Work?
  Power
  Machines and Mechanical
    Advantage

8.2 Simple Machines
  The Lever Family
  The Inclined Plane Family
  Compound Machines

8.3 What Is Energy?
  Energy and Work
  Potential Energy
  Kinetic Energy
  Other Forms of Energy

8.4 Conservation of Energy
  Energy Transformations
  The Law of Conservation
    of Energy
  Efficiency of Machines

Kinetic sculptures are sculptures that have moving parts. The changes in the motion of different parts of a kinetic sculpture can be explained in terms of forces or in terms of energy transformations.

Focus ACTIVITY

Background The collection of tubes, tracks, balls, and blocks of wood shown at left is an audio-kinetic sculpture. A conveyor belt lifts the balls to a point high on the track, and the balls wind their way down as they are pulled by the force of gravity and pushed by various other forces. They twist through spirals, drop straight down tubes, and sometimes go up and around loops as if on a roller coaster. Along the way, the balls trip levers and bounce off elastic membranes. The sculpture uses the energy of the falling balls to produce sounds in wood blocks and metal tubes.

This kinetic sculpture can be considered a machine or a collection of many small machines. It uses the motion of the balls to produce a desired musical effect. Other kinetic sculptures may incorporate simple machines such as levers, wheels, and screws. The American artist Alexander Calder, shown at left, is well known for his hanging mobiles that move in response to air currents.

This chapter introduces the basic principles of energy that explain the motions and interactions of machines and of parts within machines—including kinetic sculptures.

Activity 1 Look around your kitchen or garage. What kinds of tools or utensils do you see? How do these tools help with different kinds of projects? For each tool, consider where force is applied to the tool and how the tool may apply force to another object. Is the force transferred to another part of the tool? Is the force that the tool can exert on an object larger or smaller than the force exerted on the tool?

Activity 2 Any piece of artwork that moves is a kinetic sculpture. Design and construct a kinetic sculpture of your own. Some ideas for materials include hangers, rubber bands, string, wood and metal scraps, and old toys.

internet**connect**

SCiLINKS
NSTA

TOPIC: Machines
GO TO: www.scilinks.org
KEYWORD: HK1091

Work, Power, and Machines

OBJECTIVES

▶ Define *work* and *power*.

▶ Calculate the work done on an object and the rate at which work is done.

▶ Use the concept of mechanical advantage to explain how machines make doing work easier.

▶ Calculate the mechanical advantage of various machines.

PHYSICAL SCIENCE INTERACTIVE TUTOR

Disc Two, Module 10: Work
Use the Interactive Tutor to learn more about this topic.

▶ **work** a quantity that measures the effects of a force acting over a distance

Figure 8-1
As this weightlifter holds the barbell over her head, is she doing any work on the barbell?

If you needed to change a flat tire, you would probably use a car jack to lift the car. Machines—from complex ones such as a car to relatively simple ones such as a car jack, a hammer, or a ramp—help people get things done every day.

What Is Work?

Imagine trying to lift the front of a car without using a jack. You could exert a lot of force without moving the car at all. Exerting all that force might seem like hard work. In science, however, the word **work** has a very specific meaning.

Work is done only when force causes a change in the motion of an object. Work is calculated by multiplying an applied force by the distance over which the force is applied. In this book, we will always assume that the force used to calculate work is pushing or pulling along the same line as the direction of motion.

Work Equation

$$work = force \times distance$$
$$W = F \times d$$

In the case of trying to lift the car, you might apply a large force, but if the distance that the car moves is equal to zero, the work done on the car is also equal to zero.

However, once the car moves even a small amount, you have done some work on it. You could calculate how much by multiplying the force you have applied by the distance the car moves.

The weightlifter in **Figure 8-1** is applying a force to the barbell as she holds it overhead, but the barbell is not moving. Is she doing any work on the barbell?

Work is measured in joules

Because work is calculated as force times distance, it is measured in units of newtons times meters, N•m. These units are also called *joules* (J). In terms of SI base units, a joule is equivalent to $1 \text{ kg} \cdot \text{m}^2/\text{s}^2$.

$$1 \text{ N} \cdot \text{m} = 1 \text{ J} = 1 \text{ kg} \cdot \text{m}^2/\text{s}^2$$

Because these units are all equal, you can choose whichever unit is easiest for solving a particular problem. Substituting equivalent units will often help you cancel out other units in a problem.

You do about 1 J of work when you slowly lift an apple, which weighs about 1 N, from your waist to the top of your head, a distance of about 1 m. Three push-ups require about 1000 J of work.

INTEGRATING

BIOLOGY

You may not do any work on a car if you try to lift it without a jack, but your body will still get tired from the effort because you are doing work on the muscles inside your body.

When you try to lift something, your muscles contract over and over in response to a series of electrical impulses from your brain. With each contraction, a tiny bit of work is done on the muscles. In just a few seconds, this can add up to thousands of contractions and a significant amount of work.

Math Skills

Work Imagine a father playing with his daughter by lifting her repeatedly in the air. How much work does he do with each lift, assuming he lifts her 2.0 m and exerts an average force of 190 N?

1 **List the given and unknown values.**
   Given: *force, F* = 190 N
   distance, d = 2.0 m
   Unknown: *work, W* = ? J

2 **Write the equation for work.**
   work = *force* × *distance* $W = F \times d$

3 **Insert the known values into the equation, and solve.**
   $W = 190 \text{ N} \times 2.0 \text{ m} = 380 \text{ N} \cdot \text{m} = 380 \text{ J}$

Practice

Work

1. A crane uses an average force of 5200 N to lift a girder 25 m. How much work does the crane do on the girder?
2. An apple weighing 1 N falls through a distance of 1 m. How much work is done on the apple by the force of gravity?
3. The brakes on a bicycle apply 125 N of frictional force to the wheels as the bicycle travels 14.0 m. How much work have the brakes done on the bicycle?
4. While rowing in a race, John uses his arms to exert a force of 165 N per stroke while pulling the oar 0.800 m. How much work does he do in 30 strokes?
5. A mechanic uses a hydraulic lift to raise a 1200 kg car 0.5 m off the ground. How much work does the lift do on the car?

Practice HINT

▶ In order to use the work equation, you must use units of newtons for force and units of meters for distance. Practice Problem 5 gives a mass in kilograms instead of a weight in newtons. To convert from mass to force (weight), use the definition of weight from Section 7.3:

$$w = mg$$

where *m* is the mass in kilograms and $g = 9.8 \text{ m/s}^2$. Then plug the value for weight into the work equation as the force.

Power

Running up a flight of stairs doesn't require any more work than walking up slowly, but it is definitely more exhausting. The amount of time it takes to get work done is another important factor when considering work and machines. The quantity that measures this is **power.** Power is defined as the rate at which work is done, that is, how much work is done in a certain amount of time.

> **power** a quantity that measures the rate at which work is done

Power Equation

$$power = \frac{work}{time} \qquad P = \frac{W}{t}$$

Running up the stairs takes less time than walking. How does reducing the time in this equation affect the power if the amount of work stays the same?

Power is measured in watts

Power is measured in SI units called *watts* (W). A watt is the amount of power required to do 1 J of work in 1 s, about as much power as you need to lift an apple over your head in 1 s. You must be careful not to confuse the abbreviation for watts, W, with the symbol for work, *W*. You can tell which one is meant by the context in which it appears and by whether it is in italics.

Did You Know ?

Another common unit of power is horsepower (hp). This originally referred to the average power output of a draft horse. One horsepower equals 746 W. With that much power, a horse could raise a load of 746 apples, weighing 1 N each, by 1 m every second.

Math Skills

Power It takes 100 kJ of work to lift an elevator 18 m. If this is done in 20 s, what is the average power of the elevator during the process?

1 List the given and unknown values.
> **Given:** *work*, $W = 100$ kJ $= 1 \times 10^5$ J
> *time*, $t = 20$ s
> The distance of 18 m will not be needed to calculate power.
> **Unknown:** *power*, $P = ?$ W

2 Write the equation for power.
$$power = \frac{work}{time} \qquad P = \frac{W}{t}$$

3 Insert the known values into the equation, and solve.
$$P = \frac{1 \times 10^5 \text{ J}}{20 \text{ s}} = 5 \times 10^3 \text{ J/s} = 5 \times 10^3 \text{ W}$$
$$P = 5 \text{ kW}$$

Practice

Power

1. While rowing in a race, John does 3960 J of work on the oars in 60.0 s. What is his power output in watts?
2. Every second, a coal-fired power plant produces enough electricity to do 9×10^8 J (900 MJ) of work. What is the plant's power output in watts (or in megawatts)?
3. Using a jack, a mechanic does 5350 J of work to lift a car 0.500 m in 50.0 s. What is the mechanic's power output?
4. Suppose you are moving a 300 N box of books. Calculate your power output in the following situations:
   a. You exert a force of 60.0 N to push the box 12.0 m in 20.0 s.
   b. You lift the box 1 m onto a truck in 3 s.
5. Anna walks up the stairs on her way to class. She weighs 565 N and the stairs go up 3.25 m vertically.
   a. Calculate her power output if she climbs the stairs in 12.6 s.
   b. What is her power output if she climbs the stairs in 10.5 s?

Practice HINT

▶ In order to calculate power in Practice Problems 4 and 5, you must first use the work equation to calculate the work done in each case.

Inquiry Lab

What is your power output when you climb the stairs?

Materials ✔ flight of stairs ✔ stopwatch ✔ meterstick

Procedure

1. Determine your weight in newtons. If your school has a scale that weighs in kilograms, multiply your mass in kilograms by 9.8 m/s² to determine your weight in newtons. If your school has a scale that weighs in pounds, you can use the conversion factor of 4.45 N/lb.
2. Divide into pairs. Have your partner use the stopwatch to time how long it takes you to walk quickly up the stairs. Record the time. Then switch roles and repeat.
3. Measure the height of one step in meters. Multiply the number of steps by the height of one step to get the total height of the stairway.
4. Multiply your weight in newtons by the height of the stairs in meters to get the work you did in joules. Recall the work equation: *work = force × distance,* or *W = F × d.*
5. To get your power in watts, divide the work done in joules by the time in seconds that it took you to climb the stairs.

Analysis

1. How would your power output change if you walked up the stairs faster?
2. What would your power output be if you climbed the same stairs in the same amount of time while carrying a stack of books weighing 20 N?
3. Why did you use your weight as the force in the work equation?

Figure 8-2
A jack makes it easier to lift a car by multiplying the input force and spreading the work out over a large distance.

Machines and Mechanical Advantage

Which is easier, lifting a car yourself or using a jack as shown in **Figure 8-2**? Which requires more work? Using a jack is obviously easier. But you may be surprised to learn that using a jack doesn't require less work. You do the same amount of work either way, but the jack makes the work easier by allowing you to apply less force at any given moment.

Machines multiply and redirect forces

Machines help us do work by redistributing the work that we put into them. Machines can change the direction of an input force, or they can increase an output force by changing the distance over which the force is applied. This process is often called multiplying the force.

Work input equals work output

Compare the amount of work required to lift a box straight onto the bed of a truck, as shown in **Figure 8-3A**, with the amount of work required to push the same box up a ramp, as shown in **Figure 8-3B.** When the mover lifts straight up, he must apply 225 N of force for a short distance. Using the ramp, he has to apply only 75.0 N of force, but he must apply the force over a longer distance. The work done is the same in both cases.

Both a car jack and a loading ramp make doing work easier by increasing the distance over which the force is applied. As a result, the force required at any point is reduced. But the amount of work you put into the machine—the work input—is equal to the amount you get out—the work output.

Figure 8-3
(A) When lifting a box straight up, a mover applies a large force over a short distance.
(B) Using a ramp to lift the box, the mover applies a smaller force over a longer distance.

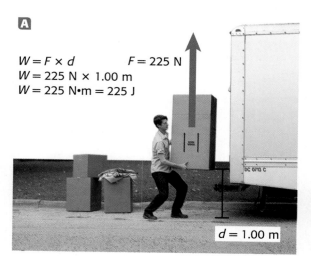

A

$W = F \times d$ $F = 225$ N
$W = 225$ N $\times$ 1.00 m
$W = 225$ N•m $= 225$ J

$d = 1.00$ m

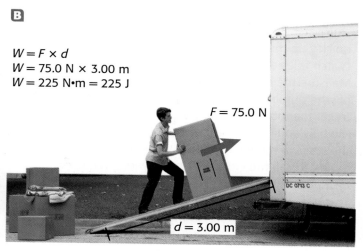

B

$W = F \times d$
$W = 75.0$ N $\times$ 3.00 m
$W = 225$ N•m $= 225$ J

$F = 75.0$ N

$d = 3.00$ m

Mechanical advantage tells how much a machine multiplies force or increases distance

A ramp makes doing work easier by increasing the distance over which force is applied. But how long should the ramp be? An extremely long ramp would allow the mover to use very little force, but he would have to push the box a long distance. A very short ramp, on the other hand, would be too steep and would not help him very much.

To solve problems like this, scientists and engineers use a number that describes how much the force or distance is multiplied by a machine. This number is called the mechanical advantage, and it is defined as the ratio between the output force and the input force. It is also equal to the ratio between the input distance and the output distance.

▶ **mechanical advantage**
a quantity that measures how much a machine multiplies force or distance

Mechanical Advantage Equation

$$mechanical\ advantage = \frac{output\ force}{input\ force} = \frac{input\ distance}{output\ distance}$$

A machine with a mechanical advantage of greater than 1 multiplies the input force. Such a machine can help you move or lift heavy objects, such as a car or a box of books. A machine with a mechanical advantage of less than 1 does not multiply force, but increases distance and speed. When you swing a baseball bat, your arms and the bat together form a machine that increases speed without multiplying force.

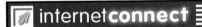
internetconnect

SCiLINKS
NSTA

TOPIC: Mechanical advantage
GO TO: www.scilinks.org
KEYWORD: HK1092

Math Skills

Mechanical Advantage Calculate the mechanical advantage of a ramp that is 5.0 m long and 1.5 m high.

1 List the given and unknown values.
  Given: *input distance* = 5.0 m
    output distance = 1.5 m
  Unknown: *mechanical advantage* = ?

2 Write the equation for mechanical advantage.
  Because the information we are given involves only distance, we only need part of the full equation:
  $$mechanical\ advantage = \frac{input\ distance}{output\ distance}$$

3 Insert the known values into the equation, and solve.
  $$mechanical\ advantage = \frac{5.0\ \cancel{m}}{1.5\ \cancel{m}} = 3.3$$

▶ The mechanical advantage equation can be rearranged to isolate any of the variables on the left.

▶ For practice problem 4, you will need to rearrange the equation to isolate output force on the left.

▶ For practice problem 5, you will need to rearrange to isolate ouput distance. When rearranging, use only the part of the full equation that you need.

Practice

Mechanical Advantage

1. Calculate the mechanical advantage of a ramp that is 6.0 m long and 1.5 m high.
2. Determine the mechanical advantage of an automobile jack that lifts a 9900 N car with an input force of 150 N.
3. A sailor uses a rope and pulley to raise a sail weighing 140 N. The sailor pulls down with a force of 140 N on the rope. What is the mechanical advantage of the pulley?
4. Alex pulls on the handle of a claw hammer with a force of 15 N. If the hammer has a mechanical advantage of 5.2, how much force is exerted on a nail in the claw?
5. While rowing in a race, John pulls the handle of an oar 0.80 m on each stroke. If the oar has a mechanical advantage of 1.5, how far does the blade of the oar move through the water on each stroke?

SECTION 8.1 REVIEW

SUMMARY

▶ Work is done when a force causes an object to move. This meaning is different from the everyday meaning of *work*.

▶ Work is equal to force times distance. The most commonly used SI unit for work is joules.

▶ Power is the rate at which work is done. The SI unit for power is watts.

▶ Machines help people by redistributing the work put into them. They can change either the size or the direction of the input force.

▶ The mechanical advantage of a machine describes how much the machine multiplies force or increases distance.

CHECK YOUR UNDERSTANDING

1. **Explain** how you can exert a large force on an object without doing any work.
2. **Determine** if work is being done on the objects in the following three situations:
   a. lifting a spoonful of soup to your mouth
   b. holding a stack of books motionless over your head
   c. letting a pencil fall to the ground
3. **Describe** how a lever can increase the force without changing the amount of work being done.
4. **Critical Thinking** Which has a greater mechanical advantage—a long, thin wedge or a short, wide wedge?

Math Skills

5. How much work in joules is done by a person who uses a force of 25 N to move a desk 3.0 m?
6. A bus driver applies a force of 55.0 N to the steering wheel, which in turn applies 132 N of force on the steering column. What is the mechanical advantage of the steering wheel?
7. A student who weighs 400 N climbs a 3 m ladder in 4 s.
   a. How much work does the student do?
   b. What is the student's power output?
8. An outboard engine on a boat can do 1.0×10^6 J of work in 50.0 s. Calculate its power in watts. Convert your answer to horsepower (1 hp = 746 W).

Simple Machines

OBJECTIVES

▶ Name and describe the six types of simple machines.

▶ Discuss the mechanical advantage of different types of simple machines.

▶ Recognize simple machines within compound machines.

▶ **KEY TERMS**

simple machines

compound machines

The most basic machines of all are called simple machines. Other machines are either modifications of simple machines or combinations of several simple machines. **Figure 8-4** shows examples of the six types of simple machines. Simple machines are divided into two families, the lever family and the inclined plane family.

▶ **simple machine** one of the six basic types of machines of which all other machines are composed

The Lever Family

To understand how levers do work, imagine using a claw hammer to pull out a nail. As you pull on the handle of the hammer, the head turns around the point where it meets the wood. The force you apply to the handle is transferred to the claw on the other end of the hammer. The claw then does work on the nail.

Figure 8-4 **The Six Simple Machines**

Simple lever

Pulley

Wheel and axle

Simple inclined plane

Wedge

Screw

The lever family

The inclined plane family

The Three Classes of Levers

Figure 8-5

A All first-class levers have a fulcrum in the middle of an arm; the input force acts on one end, and the other end applies an output force.

C Third-class levers multiply distance rather than force. As a result, they have a mechanical advantage of less than 1. The human body contains many third-class levers.

B In a second-class lever, the fulcrum is at one end of the arm and the input force is applied to the other end. The wheel of a wheelbarrow is a fulcrum.

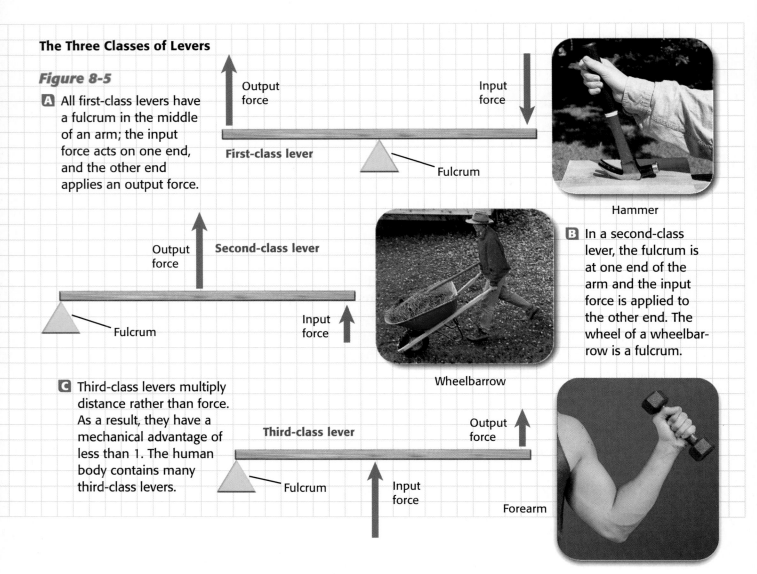

Output force

Input force

First-class lever

Fulcrum

Hammer

Output force

Second-class lever

Fulcrum

Input force

Wheelbarrow

Third-class lever

Output force

Fulcrum

Input force

Forearm

Levers are divided into three classes

All levers have a rigid *arm* that turns around a point called the *fulcrum*. Force is transferred from one part of the arm to another. In that way, the original input force can be multiplied or redirected into an output force. Levers are divided into three classes depending on the location of the fulcrum and of the input and output forces.

Figure 8-5A shows a claw hammer as an example of a first-class lever. First-class levers are the most common type. A pair of pliers is made of two first-class levers joined together.

Figure 8-5B shows a wheelbarrow as an example of a second-class lever. Other examples of second-class levers include nutcrackers and hinged doors.

Figure 8-5C shows the human forearm as an example of a third-class lever. The biceps muscle, which is attached to the bone near the elbow, contracts a short distance to move the hand a large distance.

Pulleys are modified levers

You may have used pulleys to lift things, as when raising a flag to the top of a flagpole or hoisting a sail on a boat. A pulley is another type of simple machine in the lever family.

Figure 8-6A shows how a pulley is like a lever. The point in the middle of a pulley is like the fulcrum of a lever. The rest of the pulley behaves like the rigid arm of a first-class lever. Because the distance from the fulcrum is the same on both sides of a pulley, a single, fixed pulley has a mechanical advantage of 1.

Using moving pulleys or more than one pulley at a time can increase the mechanical advantage, as shown in **Figure 8-6B** and **Figure 8-6C.** Multiple pulleys are sometimes put together in a single unit called a *block and tackle*.

Figure 8-6 **The Mechanical Advantage of Pulleys**

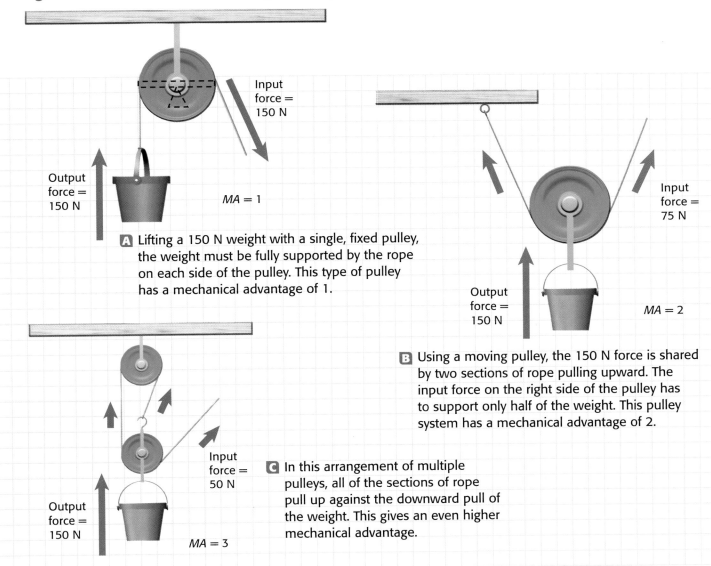

Input force = 150 N

Output force = 150 N

MA = 1

A Lifting a 150 N weight with a single, fixed pulley, the weight must be fully supported by the rope on each side of the pulley. This type of pulley has a mechanical advantage of 1.

Input force = 75 N

Output force = 150 N

MA = 2

B Using a moving pulley, the 150 N force is shared by two sections of rope pulling upward. The input force on the right side of the pulley has to support only half of the weight. This pulley system has a mechanical advantage of 2.

Input force = 50 N

Output force = 150 N

MA = 3

C In this arrangement of multiple pulleys, all of the sections of rope pull up against the downward pull of the weight. This gives an even higher mechanical advantage.

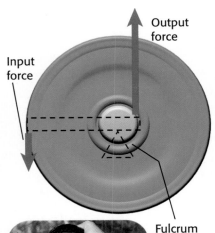

Figure 8-7
How is a wheel and axle like a lever? How is it different from a pulley?

A wheel and axle is a lever or pulley connected to a shaft

The steering wheel of a car is another kind of simple machine: a wheel and axle. A wheel and axle is made of a lever or a pulley (the wheel) connected to a shaft (the axle), as shown in **Figure 8-7.** When the wheel is turned, the axle also turns. When a small input force is applied to the steering wheel, the force is multiplied to become a large output force applied to the steering column, which turns the front wheels of the car. Screwdrivers and cranks are other common wheel-and-axle machines.

The Inclined Plane Family

Earlier we showed how pushing an object up a ramp requires less force than lifting the same object straight up. A loading ramp is another type of simple machine, an inclined plane.

Inclined planes multiply and redirect force

When you push an object up a ramp, you apply a force to the object in a direction parallel to the ramp. The ramp then redirects this force to lift the object upward. For that reason, the output force of the ramp is shown in **Figure 8-8A** as an arrow pointing straight up.

An inclined plane turns a small input force into a large output force by spreading the work out over a large distance. Pushing something up a long ramp that climbs gradually is easier than pushing something up a short, steep ramp.

A Simple Inclined Plane
1. Make an inclined plane out of a board and a stack of books.
2. Tie a string to an object that is heavy but has low friction, such as a metal toy car or a roll of wire. Use the string to pull the object up the plane.
3. Still using the string, try to lift the object straight up through the same distance.
4. Which action required more force? In which case did you do more work?

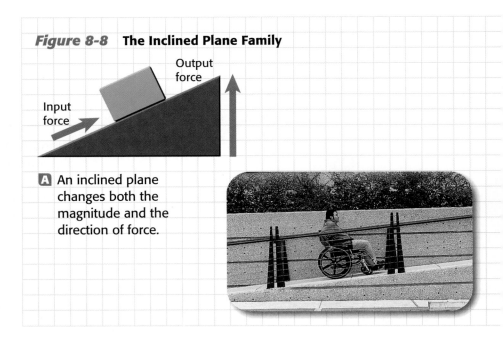

Figure 8-8   The Inclined Plane Family

A An inclined plane changes both the magnitude and the direction of force.

A wedge is a modified inclined plane

When an ax blade or a splitting wedge hits a piece of wood, it pushes through the wood and breaks it apart, as shown in **Figure 8-8B**. An ax blade is an example of a wedge, another kind of simple machine in the inclined plane family. A wedge functions like two inclined planes back to back. Using a wedge is like pushing a ramp instead of pushing an object up the ramp. A wedge turns a single downward force into two forces directed out to the sides. Some types of wedges, such as nails, are used as fasteners.

A screw is an inclined plane wrapped around a cylinder

A type of simple machine that you probably use often is a screw. The threads on a screw look like a spiral inclined plane. In fact, a screw is an inclined plane wrapped around a cylinder, as shown in **Figure 8-8C.** Like pushing an object up a ramp, tightening a screw with gently sloping threads requires a small force acting over a large distance. Tightening a screw with steeper threads requires more force. Jar lids are screws that people use every day. Spiral staircases are also common screws.

The ancient Egyptians built dozens of large stone pyramids as tombs for the bodies of kings and queens. The largest of these is the pyramid of Khufu at Giza, also called the Great Pyramid. It is made of more than 2 million blocks of stone. These blocks have an average weight of 2.5 tons, and the largest blocks weigh 15 tons. How did the Egyptians get these huge stones onto the pyramid?

Making the Connection

1. The Great Pyramid is about 140 m tall. How much work would be required to raise an average-sized pyramid block to this height? (2.5 tons = 2.2×10^4 N)
2. If the Egyptians used ramps with a mechanical advantage of 3, then an average block could be moved with a force of 7.3×10^3 N. If one person can pull with a force of 525 N, how many people would it take to pull an average block up such a ramp?

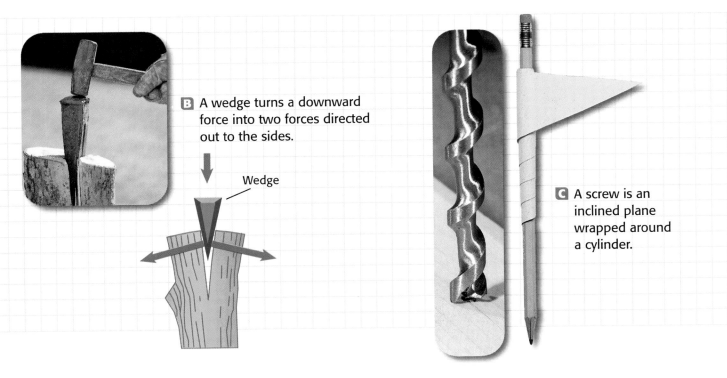

B A wedge turns a downward force into two forces directed out to the sides.

Wedge

C A screw is an inclined plane wrapped around a cylinder.

Figure 8-9
A bicycle is made of many simple machines.

Compound Machines

Many devices that you use every day are made of more than one simple machine. A machine that combines two or more simple machines is called a compound machine. A pair of scissors, for example, uses two first class levers joined at a common fulcrum; each lever arm has a wedge that cuts into the paper. Most car jacks use a lever in combination with a large screw.

Of course, many machines are much more complex than these. How many simple machines can you identify in the bicycle shown in **Figure 8-9**? How many can you identify in a car?

▶ **compound machine**
a machine made of more than one simple machine

SECTION 8.2 REVIEW

SUMMARY

▶ The most basic machines are called simple machines. There are six types of simple machines in two families.

▶ Levers have a rigid arm and a fulcrum. There are three classes of levers.

▶ Pulleys and wheel-and-axle machines are also in the lever family.

▶ The inclined plane family includes inclined planes, wedges, and screws.

▶ Compound machines are made of two or more simple machines.

CHECK YOUR UNDERSTANDING

1. **List** the six types of simple machines.
2. **Identify** the kind of simple machine represented by each of these examples:
   a. a drill bit   **b.** a skateboard ramp   **c.** a boat oar
3. **Describe** how a lever can increase the force without changing the amount of work being done.
4. **Explain** why pulleys are in the lever family.
5. **Compare** the mechanical advantage of a long, thin wedge with that of a short, wide wedge. Which is greater?
6. **Critical Thinking** Can an inclined plane have a mechanical advantage of less than 1?
7. **Critical Thinking** Using the principle of a lever, explain why it is easier to open a door by pushing near the knob than by pushing near the hinges. What class of lever is a door?
8. **Creative Thinking** Choose a compound machine that you use every day, and identify the simple machines that it contains.

What Is Energy?

▶ Explain the relationship between energy and work.
▶ Define *potential energy* and *kinetic energy*.
▶ Calculate kinetic energy and gravitational potential energy.
▶ Distinguish between mechanical and nonmechanical energy.
▶ Identify nonmechanical forms of energy.

▶ **KEY TERMS**
potential energy
kinetic energy
mechanical energy

The world around you is full of energy. When you see a flash of lightning and hear a thunderclap, you are observing light and sound energy. When you ride a bicycle, you have energy just because you are moving. Even things that are sitting still have energy waiting to be released. We use other forms of energy, like nuclear energy and electrical energy, to power things in our world, from submarines to flashlights. Without energy, living organisms could not survive. Our bodies use a great deal of energy every day just to stay alive.

Energy and Work

When you stretch a slingshot, as shown in **Figure 8-10,** you are doing work, and you transfer energy to the elastic band. When the elastic band snaps back, it may in turn transfer that energy again by doing work on a stone in the slingshot. Whenever work is done, energy is transformed or transferred to another system. In fact, one way to define energy is as the ability to do work.

Energy is measured in joules

While work is done only when an object experiences a change in its motion, energy can be present in an object or a system when nothing is happening at all. But energy can be observed only when it is transferred from one object or system to another, as when a slingshot transfers the energy from its elastic band to a stone in the sling.

The amount of energy transferred from the slingshot can be measured by how much work is done on the stone. Because energy is a measure of the ability to do work, energy and work are expressed in the same units—joules.

Figure 8-10
A stretched slingshot has the ability to do work.

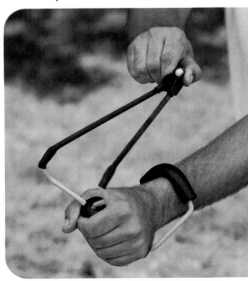

Potential Energy

Stretching a rubber band requires work. If you then release the stretched rubber band, it will fly away from your hand. The energy used to stretch the rubber band is stored so that it can do work at a later time. But where is the energy between the time you do work on the rubber band and the time you release it?

Potential energy is stored energy

A stretched slingshot or a rubber band stores energy in a form called potential energy. Potential energy is sometimes called energy of position because it results from the relative positions of objects in a system. The rubber band has potential energy because the two ends of the band are far away from each other. The energy stored in any type of stretched or compressed elastic material, such as a clock spring or a bungee cord, is called *elastic potential energy*.

The apple in **Figure 8-11** will fall if the stem breaks off the branch. The energy that could potentially do work on the apple results from its position above the ground. This type of stored energy is called *gravitational potential energy*. Any system of two or more objects separated by a distance contains gravitational potential energy resulting from the gravitational attraction between the objects.

Gravitational potential energy depends on both mass and height

An apple at the top of the tree has more gravitational potential energy with respect to the Earth than a similar apple on a lower branch. But if two apples of different mass are at the same height, the heavier apple has more gravitational potential energy than the lighter one.

Because it results from the force of gravity, gravitational potential energy depends both on the mass of the objects in a system and on the distance between them.

Figure 8-11
This apple has gravitational potential energy. The energy results from the gravitational attraction between the apple and Earth.

▶ **potential energy** the stored energy resulting from the relative positions of objects in a system

🖼 internet**connect** ≣

SC*L*INKS
NSTA

TOPIC: Potential energy
GO TO: www.scilinks.org
KEYWORD: HK1094

Gravitational Potential Energy Equation

$$grav.\ PE = mass \times free\text{-}fall\ acceleration \times height$$
$$PE = mgh$$

In this equation, notice that mg is the weight of the object in newtons, which is the same as the force on the object due to gravity. So this equation is really just a calculation of force times distance, like the work equation.

The height used in the equation for gravitational potential energy is usually measured from the ground. However, in some cases, a relative height might be more important. For example, if an apple were in a position to fall into a bird's nest on a lower branch, the apple's height above the nest could be used to calculate the apple's potential energy relative to the nest.

Math Skills

Gravitational Potential Energy A 65 kg rock climber ascends a cliff. What is the climber's gravitational potential energy at a point 35 m above the base of the cliff?

1 List the given and unknown values.
   Given: *mass, m* = 65 kg
   height, h = 35 m
   free-fall acceleration, g = 9.8 m/s^2
   Unknown: *gravitational potential energy, PE* = ? J

2 Write the equation for gravitational potential energy.
   $PE = mgh$

3 Insert the known values into the equation, and solve.
   $PE = (65 \text{ kg})(9.8 \text{ m/s}^2)(35 \text{ m})$
   $PE = 2.2 \times 10^4 \text{ kg} \cdot \text{m}^2/\text{s}^2 = 2.2 \times 10^4 \text{ J}$

▶ The gravitational potential energy equation can be rearranged to isolate height on the left.
   $mgh = PE$
   Divide both sides by *mg*, and cancel.
   $$\frac{\cancel{mg}h}{\cancel{mg}} = \frac{PE}{mg}$$
   $$h = \frac{PE}{mg}$$

You will need this version of the equation for practice problem 3.

▶ For practice problem 4, you will need to rearrange the equation to isolate mass on the left. When solving these problems, use *g* = 9.8 m/s^2.

Practice

Gravitational Potential Energy

1. Calculate the gravitational potential energy in the following systems:
   a. a car with a mass of 1200 kg at the top of a 42 m high hill
   b. a 65 kg climber on top of Mount Everest (8800 m high)
   c. a 0.52 kg bird flying at an altitude of 550 m
2. Lake Mead, the reservoir above Hoover Dam, has a surface area of approximately 640 km^2. The top 1 m of water in the lake weighs about 6.3×10^{12} N. The dam holds that top layer of water 220 m above the river below. Calculate the gravitational potential energy of the top 1 m of water in Lake Mead.
3. A science student holds a 55 g egg out a window. Just before the student releases the egg, the egg has 8.0 J of gravitational potential energy with respect to the ground. How far is the student's arm from the ground in meters? (**Hint:** Convert the mass to kilograms before solving.)
4. A diver has 3400 J of gravitational potential energy after stepping up onto a diving platform that is 6.0 m above the water. What is the diver's mass in kilograms?

Kinetic Energy

Once an apple starts to fall from the branch of a tree, as in **Figure 8-12A,** it has the ability to do work. Because the apple is moving, it can do work when it hits the ground or lands on the head of someone under the tree. The energy that an object has because it is in motion is called kinetic energy.

Kinetic energy depends on mass and speed

A falling apple can do more work than a cherry falling at the same speed. That is because the kinetic energy of an object depends on the object's mass.

As an apple falls, it accelerates. The kinetic energy of the apple—its ability to do work—increases as it speeds up. In fact, the kinetic energy of a moving object depends on the square of the object's speed.

> **Kinetic Energy Equation**
>
> $$kinetic\ energy = \tfrac{1}{2} \times mass \times speed\ squared$$
> $$KE = \tfrac{1}{2}mv^2$$

Figure 8-12B shows a graph of kinetic energy versus speed for a falling apple that weighs 1.0 N. Notice that kinetic energy is expressed in joules. Because kinetic energy is calculated using both mass and speed squared, the base units are kg•m^2/s^2, which are equivalent to joules.

▶ **kinetic energy** the energy of a moving object due to its motion

VOCABULARY *Skills Tip*

Kinetic *comes from the Greek word* kinetikos, *which means "motion."*

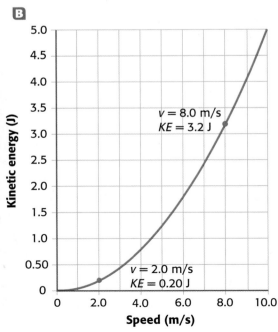

Figure 8-12
(A) A falling apple can do work on the ground underneath—or on someone's head.
(B) A small increase in the speed of an apple results in a large increase in kinetic energy.

Kinetic energy depends on speed more than mass

The line on the graph of kinetic energy versus speed curves sharply upward as speed increases. At one point, the speed is 2.0 m/s and the kinetic energy is 0.20 J. At another point, the speed has increased four times to 8.0 m/s. But the kinetic energy has increased 16 times, to 3.2 J. In the kinetic energy equation, speed is squared, so a small increase in speed produces a large increase in kinetic energy.

You may have heard that car crashes are much more dangerous at speeds above the speed limit. The kinetic energy equation provides a scientific reason for that fact. Because a car has much more kinetic energy at higher speeds, it can do much more work—which means much more damage—in a collision.

internetconnect

SCILINKS
NSTA

TOPIC: Kinetic energy
GO TO: www.scilinks.org
KEYWORD: HK1095

Math Skills

Kinetic Energy What is the kinetic energy of a 44 kg cheetah running at 31 m/s?

1 **List the given and unknown values.**
    Given: *mass, m* = 45 kg
            speed, v = 31 m/s
    Unknown: *kinetic energy, KE* = ?

2 **Write the equation for kinetic energy.**
$$\text{kinetic energy} = \tfrac{1}{2} \times \text{mass} \times \text{speed squared}$$
$$KE = \tfrac{1}{2}mv^2$$

3 **Insert the known values into the equation, and solve.**
$$KE = \tfrac{1}{2}(44 \text{ kg})(31 \text{ m/s})^2$$
$$KE = 2.1 \times 10^4 \text{ kg} \cdot \text{m}^2/\text{s}^2 = 2.1 \times 10^4 \text{ J}$$

Practice

Kinetic Energy

1. Calculate the kinetic energy in joules of a 1500 kg car moving at the following speeds:
   a. 29 m/s
   b. 18 m/s
   c. 42 km/h (**Hint:** Convert the speed to meters per second before substituting into the equation.)
2. A 35 kg child has 190 J of kinetic energy after sledding down a hill. What is the child's speed in meters per second at the bottom of the hill?
3. A bowling ball traveling 2.0 m/s has 16 J of kinetic energy. What is the mass of the bowling ball in kilograms?

Practice HINT

▶ The kinetic energy equation can be rearranged to isolate speed on the left.
$$\tfrac{1}{2}mv^2 = KE$$
Multiply both sides by $\dfrac{2}{m}$.
$$\left(\dfrac{2}{m}\right) \times \tfrac{1}{2}mv^2 = \left(\dfrac{2}{m}\right) \times KE$$
$$v^2 = \dfrac{2KE}{m}$$
Take the square root of each side.
$$\sqrt{v^2} = \sqrt{\dfrac{2KE}{m}}$$
$$v = \sqrt{\dfrac{2KE}{m}}$$
You will need this version of the equation for practice problem 2.

▶ For practice problem 3, you will need to use the equation rearranged with mass isolated on the left:
$$m = \dfrac{2KE}{v^2}$$

Other Forms of Energy

Apples have potential energy when they are hanging on a branch above the ground, and they have kinetic and potential energy when they are falling. The sum of the potential energy and the kinetic energy in a system is called mechanical energy.

Apples can also give you energy when you eat them. What kind of energy is that? In almost every system, there are hidden forms of energy that are related to the motion and arrangement of atoms that make up the objects in the system.

Energy that lies at the level of atoms and that does not affect motion on a large scale is sometimes called *nonmechanical energy*. However, a close look at the different forms of energy in a system usually reveals that they are in most cases just special forms of kinetic or potential energy.

mechanical energy
the sum of the kinetic and potential energy of large-scale objects in a system

Atoms and molecules have kinetic energy

You learned in Chapter 2 that atoms and molecules are constantly in motion. Therefore, these tiny particles have kinetic energy. Like a bowling ball hitting pins, kinetic energy is transferred between particles through collisions. The average kinetic energy of particles in an object increases as the object gets hotter and decreases as it cools down. In Chapter 9, you will learn more about how the kinetic energy of particles relates to heat and temperature.

Figure 8-13 shows the motion of atoms in two parts of a horseshoe at different temperatures. In both parts, the iron atoms inside the horseshoe are vibrating. The atoms in the hotter part of the horseshoe are vibrating more rapidly than the atoms in the cooler part, so they have greater kinetic energy.

Figure 8-13
The atoms in a hot object, such as this horseshoe, have kinetic energy. The kinetic energy is related to the object's temperature.

If a scientist wanted to analyze the motion of a horseshoe in a game of "horseshoes," the motion of particles inside the shoes would not be important. For the sake of that study, the energy due to the motion of the atoms would be considered nonmechanical energy.

However, if the same scientist wanted to study the change in the properties of iron when heated in a black-smith's shop, the motion of the atoms would become significant to the study, and the kinetic energy of the particles within the horseshoe would then be viewed as mechanical energy.

Chemical reactions involve potential energy

In a chemical reaction, bonds between atoms break apart. When the atoms bond together again in a new pattern, a different substance is formed. Both the formation of bonds and the breaking of bonds involve changes in energy. The amount of *chemical energy* associated with a substance depends in part on the relative positions of the atoms it contains.

Because chemical energy depends on position, it is a kind of potential energy. Reactions that release energy involve a decrease in the potential energy within substances. For example, when a match burns, as shown in **Figure 8-14,** the release of stored energy from the match head produces light and an explosion of hot gas. For more on chemical energy, review Chapter 5.

Living things get energy from the sun

Where do you get the energy you need to live? It comes in the form of chemical energy stored in the food you eat. But where did that energy come from? When you eat a meal, you are eating either plants or animals, or both. Animals also eat plants or other animals, or both. At the bottom of the food chain are plants and algae that derive their energy directly from sunlight.

Plants use *photosynthesis* to turn the energy in sunlight into chemical energy. This energy is stored in sugars and other organic molecules that make up cells in living tissue. When your body digests food, these molecules from plants or animals are transferred to your own cells. When your body needs energy, some of the organic molecules are broken down through *respiration.* Respiration releases the energy your body needs to live.

Figure 8-14
When a match burns, the chemical energy stored inside the head of the match is released, producing light and an explosion of hot gas.

The Energy in Food
We get energy from the food we eat. This energy is often measured by another unit, the Calorie. One Calorie is equivalent to 4186 J.

Applying Information
1. Look at the nutrition label on this "energy bar." How many Calories of energy does the bar contain?

2. Calculate how many joules of energy the bar contains by multiplying the number of Calories by the conversion factor of 4186 J/Cal.

3. An average person needs to take in about 10 million joules of energy every day. How many energy bars would you have to eat to get this much energy?

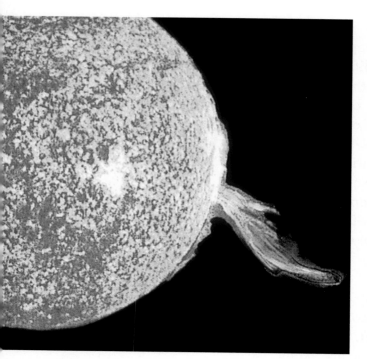

Figure 8-15
The nuclei of atoms contain enormous amounts of energy. The sun is fueled by nuclear fusion reactions in its core.

The sun gets energy from nuclear reactions

The sun, shown in **Figure 8-15,** not only gives energy to living things but also keeps our whole planet warm and bright. And the energy that reaches Earth from the sun is only a small portion of the sun's total energy output. How does the sun produce so much energy?

The sun's energy comes from nuclear fusion, a type of reaction in which light atomic nuclei combine to form a heavier nucleus. Nuclear power plants use a different process, called nuclear fission, to release nuclear energy. In fission, a single heavy nucleus is split into two or more lighter nuclei. In both fusion and fission, small quantities of mass are converted into large quantities of energy.

In Section 6.2, you learned that mass is converted to energy during nuclear reactions. This nuclear energy is a kind of potential energy stored by the forces holding subatomic particles together in the nuclei of atoms.

Electricity is a form of energy

The lights and appliances in your home are powered by another form of energy, electricity. Electricity results from the flow of charged particles through wires or other conducting materials. Moving electrons can increase the temperature of a wire and cause it to glow, as in a light bulb. Moving electrons also create magnetic fields, which can do work to power a motor or other devices. The lightning shown in **Figure 8-16** is caused by electrons traveling through the air between the ground and a thundercloud. You will learn more about electricity in Chapter 11.

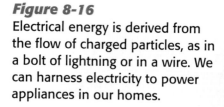

Figure 8-16
Electrical energy is derived from the flow of charged particles, as in a bolt of lightning or in a wire. We can harness electricity to power appliances in our homes.

Light can carry energy across empty space

An asphalt surface on a bright summer day is hotter where light is shining directly on it than it is in the shade. Light energy travels from the sun to Earth across empty space in the form of *electromagnetic waves.*

A beam of white light can be separated into a color spectrum, as shown in **Figure 8-17.** Light toward the blue end of the spectrum carries more energy than light toward the red end. You will learn more about electromagnetic waves and the electromagnetic spectrum in Chapter 10.

Figure 8-17
Light is composed of electromagnetic waves, which can carry energy across empty space.

SECTION 8.3 REVIEW

SUMMARY

▶ Energy is the ability to do work.

▶ Like work, energy is measured in joules.

▶ Potential energy is stored energy.

▶ Elastic potential energy is stored in any stretched or compressed elastic material.

▶ The gravitational potential energy of an object is determined by its mass, its height, and *g,* the free-fall acceleration due to gravity. *PE = mgh.*

▶ An object's kinetic energy, or energy of motion, is determined by its mass and speed. $KE = \frac{1}{2}mv^2$.

▶ Potential energy and kinetic energy are forms of mechanical energy.

▶ In addition to mechanical energy, most systems contain nonmechanical energy.

▶ Nonmechanical energy does not usually affect systems on a large scale.

CHECK YOUR UNDERSTANDING

1. **List** three different forms of energy.
2. **Explain** how energy is different from work.
3. **Explain** the difference between potential energy and kinetic energy.
4. **Determine** what form or forms of energy apply to each of the following situations, and specify whether each form is mechanical or nonmechanical:
   a. a Frisbee flying though the air
   b. a hot cup of soup
   c. a wound clock spring
   d. sunlight
   e. a boulder sitting at the top of a cliff
5. **Critical Thinking** Water storage tanks are usually built on towers or placed on hilltops. Why?
6. **Creative Thinking** Name one situation in which gravitational potential energy might be useful, and name one situation where it might be dangerous.

Math Skills

7. Calculate the gravitational potential energy of a 93.0 kg sky diver who is 550 m above the ground.
8. What is the kinetic energy in joules of a 0.02 kg bullet traveling 300 m/s?
9. Calculate the kinetic or potential energy in joules for each of the following situations:
   a. a 2.5 kg book held 2.0 m above the ground
   b. a 15 g snowball moving through the air at 3.5 m/s
   c. a 35 kg child sitting at the top of a slide that is 3.5 m above the ground
   d. an 8500 kg airplane flying at 220 km/h

Conservation of Energy

▶ KEY TERMS

efficiency

OBJECTIVES

▶ Identify and describe transformations of energy.
▶ Explain the law of conservation of energy.
▶ Discuss where energy goes when it seems to disappear.
▶ Analyze the efficiency of machines.

Imagine you are sitting in the front car of a roller coaster, such as the one shown in **Figure 8-18.** The car is pulled slowly up the first hill by a conveyor belt. When you reach the crest of the hill, you are barely moving. Then you go over the edge and start to race downward, speeding faster and faster until you reach the bottom of the hill. The wheels are roaring along the track. You continue to travel up and down through a series of smaller humps, twists, and turns. Finally, you climb another hill almost as big as the first, drop down again, and then coast to the end of the ride.

Figure 8-18
The tallest roller coaster in the world is the Fujiyama, in Fujikyu Highland Park, Japan. It spans 70 m from its highest to lowest points.

Energy Transformations

In the course of a roller coaster ride, energy changes form many times. You may not have noticed the conveyor belt at the beginning, but in terms of energy it is the most important part of the ride. All of the energy required for the entire ride comes from work done by the conveyor belt as it lifts the cars and the passengers.

The energy from that initial work is stored as gravitational potential energy at the top of the first hill. After that, the energy goes through a series of transformations, or changes, turning into kinetic energy and turning back into potential energy. A small quantity of this energy is transferred as heat to the wheels and as vibrations that produce a roaring sound in the air. But whatever form the energy takes during the ride, it is all there from the very beginning.

Potential energy can become kinetic energy

Almost all of the energy of a car on a roller coaster is potential energy at the top of a tall hill. The potential energy gradually changes to kinetic energy as the car accelerates downward. At the bottom of the lowest hill, the car has a maximum of kinetic energy and a minimum of potential energy.

Figure 8-19A shows the potential energy and kinetic energy of a car at the top and the bottom of the biggest hill on the Fujiyama roller coaster. Notice that the system has the same amount of energy, 354 kJ, whether the car is at the top or the bottom of the hill. That is because all of the gravitational potential energy at the top changes to kinetic energy as the car goes down the hill. When the car reaches the lowest point, the system has no potential energy because the car cannot go any lower.

Kinetic energy can become potential energy

When the car is at the lowest point on the roller coaster, it has no more potential energy, but it has a lot of kinetic energy. This kinetic energy can do the work to carry the car up another hill. As the car climbs the hill, the car slows down, decreasing its kinetic energy. Where does that energy go? Most of it turns back into potential energy as the height of the car increases.

At the top of a smaller hill, the car will still have some kinetic energy, along with some potential energy, as shown in **Figure 8-19B.** The kinetic energy will carry the car forward over the crest of the hill. Of course, the car could not climb a hill taller than the first one without an extra boost. The car does not have enough energy.

Figure 8-19

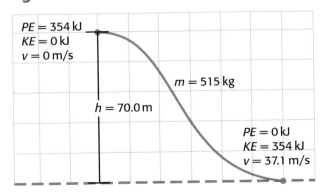

$PE = 354\,kJ$
$KE = 0\,kJ$
$v = 0\,m/s$

$m = 515\,kg$

$h = 70.0\,m$

$PE = 0\,kJ$
$KE = 354\,kJ$
$v = 37.1\,m/s$

A As a car goes down a hill on a roller coaster, potential energy changes to kinetic energy.

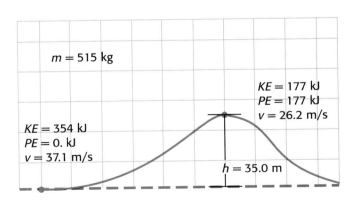

$m = 515\,kg$

$KE = 177\,kJ$
$PE = 177\,kJ$
$v = 26.2\,m/s$

$KE = 354\,kJ$
$PE = 0.\,kJ$
$v = 37.1\,m/s$

$h = 35.0\,m$

B At the top of this small hill, half the kinetic energy has become potential energy. The rest of the kinetic energy carries the car over the crest of the hill at high speed.

Energy transformations explain the flight of a ball

The relationship between potential energy and kinetic energy can explain motion in many different situations. Let's look at some other examples.

A tennis player tosses a 0.05 kg tennis ball into the air to set up for a serve, as shown in **Figure 8-20.** He gives the ball 0.5 J of kinetic energy, and it travels straight up. As the ball rises higher, the kinetic energy is converted to potential energy. The ball will keep rising until all the kinetic energy is gone. At its highest point, the ball has 0.5 J of potential energy. As the ball falls down again, the potential energy changes back to kinetic energy.

Imagine that a tennis trainer wants to know how high the ball will go when it is given 0.5 J of initial kinetic energy by a tennis player. The trainer could make a series of calculations using force and acceleration, but in this case using the concept of energy transformations is easier. The trainer knows that the ball's initial kinetic energy is 0.5 J and that its mass is 0.05 kg. To find out how high the ball will go, the trainer has to find the point where the potential energy equals its initial kinetic energy, 0.5 J. Using the equation for gravitational potential energy, the height turns out to be 1 m above the point that the tennis player releases the ball.

Figure 8-20
The kinetic energy of the ball at the bottom of its path equals the potential energy at the top of the path.

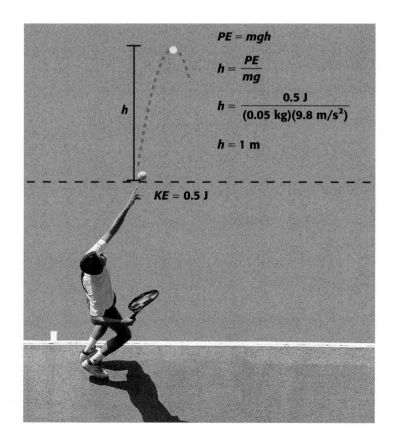

$$PE = mgh$$

$$h = \frac{PE}{mg}$$

$$h = \frac{0.5 \text{ J}}{(0.05 \text{ kg})(9.8 \text{ m/s}^2)}$$

$$h = 1 \text{ m}$$

$$KE = 0.5 \text{ J}$$

Energy transformations explain a bouncing ball

Before a serve, a tennis player usually bounces the ball a few times while building concentration. The motion of a bouncing ball can also be explained using energy principles. As the tennis player throws the ball down, she adds kinetic energy to the potential energy the ball has at the height of her hand. The kinetic energy of the ball then increases steadily as the ball falls because the potential energy is changing to kinetic energy.

When the ball hits the ground, there is a sudden energy transformation as the kinetic energy of the ball changes to elastic potential energy stored in the compressed tennis ball. The elastic potential energy then quickly changes back to kinetic energy as the ball bounces upward.

If all of the kinetic energy in the ball changed to elastic potential energy, and that elastic potential energy all changed back to kinetic energy during the bounce, the ball would bounce up to the tennis player's hand. Its speed on return would be exactly the same as the speed at which it was thrown down. If the ball were dropped instead of thrown down, it would bounce up to the same height from which it was dropped.

Mechanical energy can change to other forms of energy

If changes from kinetic energy to potential energy and back again were always complete, then balls would always bounce back to the same height they were dropped from and cars on roller coasters would keep gliding forever. But that is not the way things really happen.

When a ball bounces on the ground, not all of the kinetic energy changes to elastic potential energy. Some of the kinetic energy compresses the air around the ball, making a sound, and some of the kinetic energy makes the ball, the air, and the ground hotter. Because these other forms of energy are not directly due to the motion or position of the ball, they can be considered nonmechanical energy. With each bounce, the ball loses some mechanical energy, as shown in **Figure 8-21.**

Likewise, a car on a roller coaster cannot keep moving up and down the track forever. The total mechanical energy of a car on a roller coaster constantly decreases due to friction and air resistance. This energy does not just disappear though. Some of it increases the temperature of the track, the car's wheels, and the air. Some of the energy compresses the air, making a roaring sound. Often, when energy seems to disappear, it has really just changed to a nonmechanical form.

Figure 8-21
With each bounce of a tennis ball, some of the mechanical energy changes to nonmechanical energy.

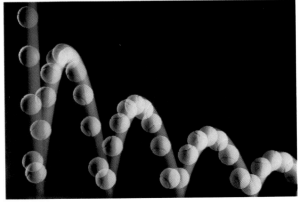

The Law of Conservation of Energy

In our study of machines in Section 8.1, we saw that the work done on a machine is equal to the work that it can do. Similarly, in our study of the roller coaster, we found that the energy present at the beginning of the ride is present throughout the ride and at the end of the ride, although the energy continually changes form. The energy in each system does not appear out of nowhere and never just disappears.

This simple observation is based on one of the most important principles in all of science—the law of conservation of energy. Here is the law in its simplest form.

Energy cannot be created or destroyed.

In a mechanical system such as a roller coaster or a swinging pendulum, the energy in the system at any time can be calculated by adding the kinetic and potential energy to get the total mechanical energy. The law of conservation of energy requires that at any given time, the total energy should be the same.

Energy doesn't appear out of nowhere

Energy cannot be created from nothing. Imagine a girl jumping on a trampoline. After the first bounce, she rises to a height of 0.5 m. After the second bounce, she rises to a height of 1 m. Because she has greater gravitational potential energy after the second bounce, we must conclude that she added energy to her bounce by pushing with her legs. Whenever the total energy in a system increases, it must be due to energy that enters the system from an external source.

Energy doesn't disappear

Because mechanical energy can change to nonmechanical energy due to friction, air resistance, and other factors, tracing the flow of energy in a system can be difficult. Some of the energy may leak out of the system into the surrounding environment, as when the roller coaster produces sound as it compresses the air. But none of the energy disappears; it just changes form.

Systems may be open or closed

Energy has many different forms and can be found almost everywhere. Accounting for all of the energy in a given situation can be complicated. To make studying a situation easier, scientists often limit their view to a small area or a small number of objects. These boundaries define a system.

INTEGRATING

COMPUTERS AND TECHNOLOGY

In order for a flashlight to work, there must be a supply of energy.

A flashlight battery contains different chemicals that can react with each other to release energy. When the flashlight is turned on, chemical potential energy changes to electrical energy, and electrons begin to flow through a wire attached to the battery. Inside the bulb, the wire filament begins to glow, and the energy is transformed into light energy.

After the flashlight has been used for a certain amount of time, the battery will run out of energy. It will have to be replaced or recharged. You will learn more about batteries in Chapter 11.

A system might include a gas burner and a pot of water. A scientist could study the flow of energy from the burner into the pot and ignore the small amount of energy going into the pot from the lights in the room, from a hand touching the pot, and so on.

When the flow of energy into and out of a system is small enough that it can be ignored, the system is called a *closed system*. Most systems are *open systems*, which exchange energy with the outside. Earth is an open system, as shown in **Figure 8-22.** Is your body an open or closed system?

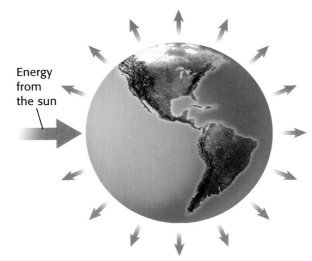

Energy from the sun

Figure 8-22
Earth is an open system because it receives energy from the sun and radiates some of its own energy out into space.

Inquiry Lab

Is energy conserved in a pendulum?

Materials
- ✔ 1–1.5 m length of string
- ✔ pencil with an eraser
- ✔ meterstick
- ✔ nail or hook in the wall above a chalkboard
- ✔ pendulum bob
- ✔ level

Procedure

1. Hang the pendulum bob from the string in front of a chalkboard. On the board, draw the diagram as shown in the photograph at right. Use the meterstick and the level to make sure the horizontal line is parallel to the ground.
2. Pull the pendulum ball back to the "X." Make sure everyone is out of the way; then release the pendulum and observe its motion. How high does the pendulum swing on the other side?
3. Let the pendulum swing back and forth several times. How many swings does the pendulum make before the ball noticeably fails to reach its original height?
4. Stop the pendulum and hold it again at the "X" marked on the board. Have another student place the eraser end of a pencil on the intersection of the horizontal and vertical lines. Make sure everyone is out of the way again, especially the student holding the pencil.
5. Release the pendulum again. This time its motion will be altered halfway through the swing as the string hits the pencil. How high does the pendulum swing now? Why?

6. Try placing the pencil at different heights along the vertical line. How does this affect the motion of the pendulum? If you put the pencil down close enough to the arc of the pendulum, the pendulum will do a loop around it. Why does that happen?

Analysis

1. Use the law of conservation of energy to explain your observations in steps 2–6.
2. If you let the pendulum swing long enough, it will start to slow down, and it won't rise to the line any more. That suggests that the system has lost energy. Has it? Where did the energy go?

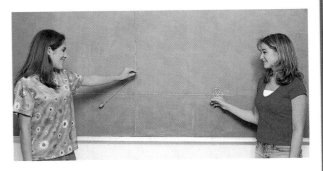

Efficiency of Machines

If you use a pulley to raise a sail on a sailboat like the one in **Figure 8-23,** you have to do work against the forces of friction in the pulley. You also have to lift the added weight of the rope and the hook attached to the sail. As a result, only some of the energy that you transfer to the pulley is available to raise the sail.

Not all of the work done by a machine is useful work

Because of friction and other factors, only some of the work done by a machine is applied to the task at hand; the machine also does some incidental work that does not serve any intended purpose. In other words, there is a difference between the total work done by a machine and the *useful* work done by the machine, that is, work that the machine is designed or intended to do.

Although all of the work done on a machine has some effect on the output work that the machine does, the output work might not be in the form that you expect. In lifting a sail, for example, some of the work available to lift the sail, which would be useful work, is transferred away as heat that warms the pulley, which is not a desired effect. The amount of useful work might decrease slightly more if the pulley squeaks, because some energy is "lost" as it dissipates into forces that vibrate the pulley and the air to produce the squeaking sound.

Efficiency is the ratio of useful work out to work in

The **efficiency** of a machine is a measure of how much useful work it can do. Efficiency is defined as the ratio of useful work output to total work input.

> #### Efficiency Equation
> $$efficiency = \frac{useful\ work\ output}{work\ input}$$

Efficiency is usually expressed as a percentage. To change an answer found using the efficiency equation into a percentage, just multiply by 100 and add the percent sign, "%."

A machine with 100 percent efficiency would produce exactly as much useful work as the work done on the machine. Because every machine has some friction, no machine has 100 percent efficiency. The useful work output of a machine never equals—and certainly cannot exceed—the work input.

Figure 8-23
Like all machines, the pulleys on a sailboat are less than 100 percent efficient.

▷ **efficiency** a quantity, usually expressed as a percentage, that measures the ratio of useful work output to work input

Efficiency A sailor uses a rope and an old, squeaky pulley to raise a sail that weighs 140 N. He finds that he must do 180 J of work on the rope in order to raise the sail by 1 m (doing 140 J of work on the sail). What is the efficiency of the pulley? Express your answer as a percentage.

1 **List the given and unknown values.**

Given: *work input* = 180 J

useful work output = 140 J

Unknown: *efficiency* = ? %

2 **Write the equation for efficiency.**

$$efficiency = \frac{useful\ work\ output}{work\ input}$$

3 **Insert the known values into the equation, and solve.**

$$efficiency = \frac{140\ J}{180\ J} = 0.78$$

To express this as a percentage, multiply by 100 and add the percent sign, "%."

$efficiency = 0.78 \times 100 = 78\%$

Practice HINT

▶ The efficiency equation can be rearranged to isolate any of the variables on the left

▶ For practice problem 2, you will need to rearrange the equation to isolate *work input* on the left side.

▶ For practice problem 3, you will need to rearrange to isolate *useful work output*.

▶ When using these rearranged forms to solve the problems, you will have to plug in values for *efficiency*. When doing so, do not use a percentage, but rather convert the percentage to a decimal by dropping the percent sign and dividing by 100.

Practice

Efficiency

1. Alice and Jim calculate that they must do 1800 J of work to push a piano up a ramp. However, because they must also overcome friction, they actually must do 2400 J of work. What is the efficiency of the ramp?

2. It takes 1200 J of work to lift the car high enough to change a tire. How much work must be done by the person operating the jack if the jack is 25 percent efficient?

3. A windmill has an efficiency of 37.5 percent. If a gust of wind does 125 J of work on the blades of the windmill, how much output work can the windmill do as a result of the gust?

Perpetual motion machines are impossible

Figure 8-24 shows a machine designed to keep on going forever without any input of energy. These theoretical machines are called *perpetual motion machines.* Many clever inventors have devoted a lot of time and effort to designing such machines. If such a perpetual motion machine could exist, it could provide a never-ending supply of energy.

Figure 8-24
Theoretically, a perpetual motion machine could keep going forever without any energy loss or energy input.

Because energy always leaks out of a system, no machine has 100 percent efficiency. In other words, every machine needs at least a small amount of energy input to keep going. Unfortunately, that means that perpetual motion machines are impossible. But new technologies, from magnetic trains to high speed microprocessors, reduce the amount of energy leaking from systems so that energy can be used as efficiently as possible.

SECTION 8.4 REVIEW

SUMMARY

▶ Energy readily changes from one form to another.

▶ In a mechanical system, potential energy can become kinetic energy, and kinetic energy can become potential energy.

▶ Mechanical energy can change to nonmechanical energy as a result of friction, air resistance, or other means.

▶ Energy cannot be created or destroyed, although it may change form. This is called the law of conservation of energy.

▶ A machine cannot do more work than the work required to operate the machine. Because of friction, the work output of a machine is always somewhat less than the work input.

▶ The efficiency of a machine is the ratio of the useful work performed by the machine to the work required to operate the machine.

CHECK YOUR UNDERSTANDING

1. **State** the law of conservation of energy in your own words.
2. **List** three situations in which potential energy becomes kinetic energy and three situations in which kinetic energy becomes potential energy.
3. **Describe** the rise and fall of a basketball using the concepts of kinetic energy and potential energy.
4. **Explain** why machines are not 100 percent efficient.
5. **Applying Knowledge** Use the concepts of kinetic energy and potential energy to describe the motion of a child on a swing. Why does the child need a push from time to time?
6. **Creative Thinking** Using what you have learned about energy transformations, explain why the driver of a car has to continuously apply pressure to the gas pedal in order to keep the car cruising at a steady speed, even on a flat road. Does this situation violate the law of conservation of energy? Why or why not?

Math Skills

7. **Efficiency** When you do 100 J of work on the handle of a bicycle pump, it does 40 J of work pushing the air into the tire. What is the efficiency of the pump?
8. **Efficiency and Power** A river does 6500 J of work on a water wheel every second. The wheel's efficiency is 12 percent.
   a. How much work in joules can the axle of the wheel do in a second?
   b. What is the power output of the wheel?
9. **Efficiency and Work** John is using a pulley to lift the sail on his sailboat. The sail weighs 150 N and he must lift it 4.0 m.
   a. How much work must be done on the sail?
   b. If the pulley is 50 percent efficient, how much work must John do on the rope in order to lift the sail?

Chapter Highlights

Before you begin, review the summaries of the key ideas of each section, found on pages 256, 262, 271, and 280. The key vocabulary terms are listed on pages 250, 257, 263, and 272.

UNDERSTANDING CONCEPTS

1. _____ is defined as force acting over a distance.
   a. Power
   b. Energy
   c. Work
   d. Potential energy

2. The quantity that measures how much a machine multiplies force is called _____.
   a. mechanical advantage
   b. leverage
   c. efficiency
   d. power

3. Scissors are an example of _____.
   a. a lever
   b. a wedge
   c. a wheel and axle
   d. a compound machine

4. The unit that measures 1 J of work done each second is the _____.
   a. power
   b. newton
   c. watt
   d. mechanical advantage

5. Joules could be used to measure _____.
   a. the work done in lifting a bowling ball
   b. the potential energy of a bowling ball held in the air
   c. the kinetic energy of a rolling bowling ball
   d. All of the above

6. Which of the following situations does *not* involve potential energy being changed into kinetic energy?
   a. an apple falling from a tree
   b. shooting a dart from a spring-loaded gun
   c. pulling back on the string of a bow
   d. a creek flowing downstream

7. _____ is determined by both mass and velocity.
   a. Work
   b. Power
   c. Potential energy
   d. Kinetic energy

8. Energy that does not involve the large-scale motion or position of objects in a system is called _____.
   a. potential energy
   b. mechanical energy
   c. nonmechanical energy
   d. conserved energy

9. The law of conservation of energy states that _____.
   a. the energy of a system is always decreasing
   b. no machine is 100 percent efficient
   c. energy is neither lost nor created
   d. Earth has limited energy resources

Using Vocabulary

10. Write one sentence using *work* in the scientific sense, and write another sentence using it in a different, nonscientific sense. Explain the difference in the meaning of *work* in the two sentences.

WRITING SKILL

11. The first page of this chapter shows an example of *kinetic sculpture*. You have now also learned the definition of *kinetic energy*. Given your knowledge of these two terms, what do you think the word *kinetic* means?

12. A can opener is a *compound machine*. Name three *simple machines* that it contains.

13. For each of the following, state whether the system contains primarily *kinetic energy* or *potential energy:*
  a. a stone in a stretched slingshot
  b. a speeding race car
  c. water above a hydroelectric dam
  d. the water molecules in a pot of boiling water

14. An elephant and a mouse race up the stairs. The mouse beats the elephant by a full second, but the elephant claims, "I am more powerful than you are, and this race has proved it." Use the definitions of *work* and *power* to support the elephant's claim.

15. How is *energy* related to *work, force,* and *power?*

BUILDING MATH SKILLS

16. You and two friends apply a force of 425 N to push a piano up a 2.0 m long ramp.
  a. **Work** How much work in joules has been done when you reach the top of the ramp?
  b. **Power** If you make it to the top in 5.0 s, what is your power output in watts?
  c. **Mechanical Advantage** If lifting the piano straight up would require 1700 N of force, what is the mechanical advantage of the ramp?

17. A crane uses a block and tackle to lift a 2200 N flagstone to a height of 25 m.
  a. **Work** How much work is done on the flagstone?
  b. **Efficiency** In the process, the crane's hydraulic motor does 110 kJ of work on the cable in the block and tackle. What is the efficiency of the block and tackle?
  c. **Potential Energy** What is the potential energy of the flagstone when it is 25 m above the ground?

18. A 2.0 kg rock sits on the edge of a cliff 12 m above the beach.
  a. **Potential Energy** Calculate the potential energy in the system.
  b. **Energy Transformations** The rock falls off the cliff. How much kinetic energy will it have just before it hits the beach? (Ignore air resistance.)
  c. **Kinetic Energy** Calculate the speed of the rock just before it hits the beach. (For help, see Practice Hint on page 267.)
  d. **Conservation of Energy** What happens to the energy after the rock hits the beach?

THINKING CRITICALLY

19. Interpreting Graphics The diagram below shows five different points on a roller coaster.

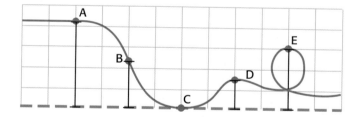

  a. List the points in order from the point where the car would have the greatest potential energy to the point where it would have the least potential energy.
  b. Now list the points in order from the point where the car would have the greatest kinetic energy to the point where it would have the least kinetic energy.
  c. How are your two lists related to each other?

20. Critical Thinking Use the law of conservation of energy to explain why the work output of a machine can never exceed the work input.

21. Applying Knowledge If a bumper car triples its speed, how much more work can it do on a bumper car at rest? (**Hint:** Use the equation for kinetic energy.)

22. Understanding Systems When a hammer hits a nail, there is a transfer of energy as the hammer does work on the nail. However, the kinetic energy and potential energy of the nail do not change very much. What happens to the work done by the hammer? Does this violate the law of conservation of energy?

DEVELOPING LIFE/WORK SKILLS

23. Applying Knowledge You are trying to pry the lid off a paint can with a screwdriver, but the lid will not budge. Should you try using a shorter screwdriver or a longer screwdriver? Explain.

24. Designing Systems Imagine you are trying to move a piano into a second-floor apartment. It will not fit through the stairwell, but it will fit through a large window 3.0 m off the ground. The piano weighs 1800 N and you can exert only 290 N of force. Design a compound machine or system of machines you could use to lift the piano to the height of the window.

INTEGRATING CONCEPTS

25. Connection to Sports A baseball pitcher applies a force to the ball as his arm moves a distance of 1.0 m. Using a radar gun, the coach finds that the ball has a speed of 18 m/s after it is released. A baseball has a mass of 0.15 kg. Calculate the average force that the pitcher applied to the ball. (**Hint:** You will need to use both the kinetic energy equation and the work equation.)

26. Concept Mapping Copy the unfinished concept map below onto a sheet of paper. Complete the map by writing the correct word or phrase in the lettered boxes.

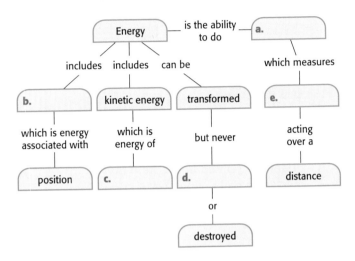

27. Connection to Earth Science Many fuels come from fossilized plant and animal matter. How is the energy stored in these fuels? How do you think that energy got into the fuels in the first place?

28. Connection to Biology When lifting an object using the biceps muscle, the forearm acts as a lever with the fulcrum at the elbow. The input work is provided by the biceps muscle pulling up on the bone. Assume that the muscle is attached 1.0 cm from the elbow and that the total length of the forearm from elbow to palm is 32 cm. How much force must the biceps exert to lift an object weighing 12 N? What class of lever is the forearm in this example?

TOPIC: Energy and sports
GO TO: www.scilinks.org
KEYWORD: HK1097

Skill Builder Lab

Introduction

Raised objects have gravitational potential energy. Moving objects have kinetic energy. How are these two quantities related in a system that involves a ball rolling down a ramp?

Objectives

- ▶ *Measure* the height, distance traveled, and time interval for a ball rolling down a ramp.
- ▶ *Calculate* the ball's potential energy at the top of the ramp and its kinetic energy at the bottom of the ramp.
- ▶ *Analyze* the relationship between potential energy and kinetic energy.

Materials

golf ball, racquet ball, or handball
board, at least 90 cm (3 ft) long
stack of books, at least 60 cm (2 ft) high
box
meterstick
masking tape
stopwatch
balance

Safety Needs

safety goggles

Determining Energy for a Rolling Ball

▶ Preparing for Your Experiment

1. On a blank sheet of paper, prepare a table like the one shown below.

Table I **Potential Energy and Kinetic Energy**

	Height 1	Height 2	Height 3
Mass of ball (kg)			
Length of ramp (m)			
Height of ramp (m)			
Time ball traveled, first trial (s)			
Time ball traveled, second trial (s)			
Time ball traveled, third trial (s)			
Average time ball traveled (s)			
Final speed of ball (m/s)			
Final kinetic energy of ball (J)			
Initial potential energy of ball (J)			

2. Measure the mass of the ball, and record it in your table.

3. Place a strip of masking tape across the board close to one end, and measure the distance from the tape to the opposite end of the board. Record this distance in the row labeled "Length of ramp."

4. Make a catch box by cutting out one side of a box. ◆

5. Make a stack of books approximately 30 cm high. Build a ramp by setting the taped end of the board on top of the books, as shown in the photograph on the next page. Place the other end in the catch box. Measure the vertical height of the ramp at the tape, and record this value in your table as "Height of ramp."

▶ Making Time Measurements

6. Place the ball on the ramp at the tape. Release the ball, and measure how long it takes the ball to travel to the bottom of the ramp. Record the time in your table.

7. Repeat step 6 two more times and record the results in your table. After three trials, calculate the average travel time and record it in your table.

8. Repeat steps 5–7 with a stack of books approximately 45 cm high, and repeat the steps again with a stack approximately 60 cm high.

▶ Analyzing Your Results

1. Calculate the average speed of the ball using the following equation:

$$average\ speed = \frac{length\ of\ ramp}{average\ time\ ball\ traveled}$$

2. Multiply average speed by 2 to obtain the final speed of the ball, and record the final speed.

3. Calculate and record the final kinetic energy of the ball by using the following equation:

$$KE = \frac{1}{2} \times mass\ of\ ball \times (final\ speed)^2$$

$$KE = \frac{1}{2}mv^2$$

4. Calculate and record the initial potential energy of the ball by using the following equation:

$$grav.\ PE = mass\ of\ ball \times (9.8\ m/s^2) \times height\ of\ ramp$$

$$PE = mgh$$

▶ Defending Your Conclusions

5. For each of the three heights, compare the ball's potential energy at the top of the ramp with its kinetic energy at the bottom of the ramp.

6. How did the ball's potential and kinetic energy change as the height of the ramp was increased?

7. Suppose you perform this experiment and find that your kinetic energy values are always just a little less than your potential energy values. Does that mean you did the experiment wrong? Why or why not?

CareerLink

Civil Engineer

In a sense, civil engineering has been around since people started to build structures. Civil engineers plan and design public projects, such as roads, bridges, and dams, and private projects, such as office buildings. To learn more about civil engineering as a career, read the profile of civil engineer Grace Pierce, who works at Traffic Systems, Inc., in Orlando, Florida.

As a civil engineer, Grace Pierce designs roads and intersections.

"I get to help in projects that provide a better quality of life for people. It's a good feeling."

 What do you do as a civil engineer?

I'm a transportation engineer with a bachelor's degree in civil engineering. I do a lot of transportation studies, transportation planning, and engineering—anything to do with moving cars. Right now, my clients are about a 50-50 mix of private and public.

 What part of your job do you like best?

Transportation planning. On the planning side, you get to be involved in developments that are going to impact the community . . . being able to tap into my creative sense to help my clients get what they want.

 What do you find most rewarding about your job?

Civil engineering in civil projects. They are very rewarding because I get to see my input on a very fast time scale.

 What kinds of skills do you think a good civil engineer needs?

You need a good solid academic background. You need communication skills and writing ability. Communication is key. You should get involved in things like Toastmasters, which can help you with your presentation skills. You should get involved with your community.

 What part of your education do you think was most important?

Two years before graduation, I was given the opportunity to meet with the owner of a company who gave me a good preview of what he did. It's really important to get out there and get the professional experience as well as the academic experience before you graduate.

What advice do you have for anyone interested in civil engineering?

Have a vision. Have a goal, whatever that might be, and envision yourself in that arena. Work as hard as you can to realize that vision. Find out what you want to do, and find someone who can mentor you. Use every resource available to you in high school and college, including professors and people in the community. And in the process, have fun. It doesn't have to be dreary.

 You didn't enter college immediately after high school. Did you have to do anything differently from a younger student?

I went to school as an older student. I didn't go back to college until age 27. I knew that because I was competing with younger folks, I really had to hustle.

 internetconnect

SCI LINKS
NSTA

TOPIC: Engineer
GO TO: www.scilinks.org
KEYWORD: HK1999

Edit Element Settings Tools Utilities Workspace Window Help

Window 1

POLE "A"

620-1-1 20 LF
47-11-55 1 EA

SAND AND GROUND COVER

3' PAVED SHOULDER

GRASS MEDIAN

-2.25

-.78

-.17

1 EA

635-1

77"

132 LF

630-1

6

6

" I think my industry is going toward the 'smart' movement of vehicles and people. The future is intelligent transportation systems using automated systems."
—GRACE PIERCE

287

CHAPTER 9

Heat and Temperature

Chapter Preview

9.1 Temperature
Temperature and Energy
Relating Temperature to
Energy Transfer as Heat

9.2 Energy Transfer
Methods of Energy Transfer
Conductors and Insulators
Specific Heat

9.3 Using Heat
Heating Systems
Cooling Systems

INTEGRATING
TECHNOLOGY
and Society

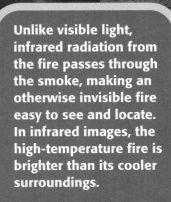

Focus ACTIVITY

Background The fire started at night. By the time firefighters arrived the next morning, the forest was filled with thick smoke. The firefighters knew the fire was still raging in the forest, but they had to see through the smoke to find the fire's exact location.

Fortunately, firefighters have instruments that detect infrared radiation. Infrared radiation is a form of light that is invisible to the eye and is given off by hot objects, such as burning wood. Infrared radiation passes through the smoke and is picked up by infrared detectors. The images formed by these instruments are then converted into pictures that we can see. From these pictures, the fire's exact location can be determined, and the firefighters can keep the fire from spreading.

Activity 1 Use a prism to separate a beam of sunlight into its component colors, and project these onto a sheet of paper. Use a thermometer to record the temperature of the air in the room, and then place the thermometer bulb in each colored band for 3 minutes. Record the final temperature of each colored band. Place the thermometer on the dark side of the red band, where infrared radiation is found, for 3 minutes. How do the final temperature readings differ? Do your results suggest why infrared radiation is associated with hot objects?

Activity 2 Obtain several cups that are about the same size but are made of different materials (glass, metal, ceramic, plastic foam). Fill one cup with hot tap water, and measure the time it takes for the outside of the cup to feel hot (at a temperature of about 35°C). Repeat this for each cup. List the materials, with the one that warms fastest listed first. Note any differences such as cup thickness, cup volume, or changes in the temperature of your hand.

Unlike visible light, infrared radiation from the fire passes through the smoke, making an otherwise invisible fire easy to see and locate. In infrared images, the high-temperature fire is brighter than its cooler surroundings.

internetconnect

SCLINKS
NSTA

TOPIC: Electromagnetic spectrum
GO TO: www.scilinks.org
KEYWORD: HK1101

Temperature

temperature
thermometer
absolute zero
heat

▶ Define *temperature* in terms of the average kinetic energy of atoms or molecules.

▶ Convert temperature readings between the Fahrenheit, Celsius, and Kelvin scales.

▶ Describe heat as a form of energy transfer.

▶ **temperature** a measure of the average kinetic energy of all the particles within an object

People use **temperature** readings, such as those shown in **Figure 9-1,** to make a wide variety of decisions every day. You check the temperature of the outdoor air to decide what to wear. The temperature of a roasting turkey is monitored to see if it is properly cooked. A nurse monitors the condition of a patient by checking the patient's body temperature. But what exactly is it that you, the cook, and the nurse are measuring? What does the temperature indicate?

Temperature and Energy

When you touch the hood of an automobile, you sense how hot or cold it is. In everyday life, we associate this sensation of hot or cold with the temperature of an object. However, this sensation serves only as a rough indicator of temperature. The Quick Activity on the next page illustrates this point.

Figure 9-1
Many decisions are made based on temperature.

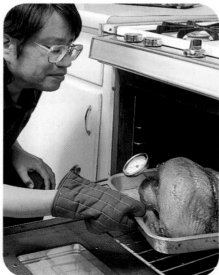
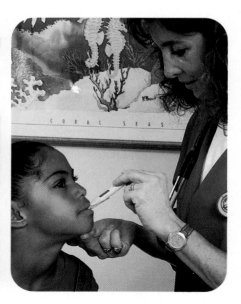

Sensing Hot and Cold

For this exercise you will need three bowls.
1. Put an equal amount of water in all three bowls. In the first bowl, put some cold tap water. Put some hot tap water in the second bowl. Then, mix equal amounts of hot and cold tap water in the third bowl.
2. Place one hand in the hot water and the other hand in the cold water. Leave them there for 15 s.

3. Place both hands in the third bowl, which contains the mixture of hot and cold water. How does the water temperature feel to each hand? Explain.

In Chapter 2, you learned that all particles in a substance are constantly moving. Like all moving objects, each particle has kinetic energy. If we average the kinetic energy of all the particles in an object, it turns out that this average kinetic energy is related to the temperature of the object. In fact, the temperature is proportional to the average kinetic energy.

In other words, as the average kinetic energy of an object increases, its temperature will increase. Compared to a cool car hood, the particles in a hot hood move faster because they have more kinetic energy. But how do we measure the temperature of an object? It is impossible to find the kinetic energy of every particle in an object and calculate its average. Actually, nature provides a very simple way to measure temperature directly.

Common thermometers rely on expansion

Icicles forming on trees, flowers wilting in the sun, and the red glow of a stove-top burner are all indicators of certain temperature ranges. You feel these temperatures as hot or cold. How you sense hot and cold depends not only on an object's temperature but also on other factors, such as the temperature of your skin.

To measure temperature accurately, we rely on a simple physical property of substances: most objects expand when their temperature increases. Ordinary thermometers are based on this principle and use liquid substances like mercury or colored alcohol that expand as their temperature increases and contract as their temperature falls. The expansion and contraction is the result of energy exchange between the thermometer and its surroundings.

For example, the thermometer shown in **Figure 9-2** can measure the temperature of air on a sunny day. As the temperature rises, the particles in the liquid inside the thermometer gain kinetic energy and move faster. With this increased motion, the particles in the liquid move farther apart causing it to expand and rise up the narrow tube.

▶ **thermometer** a device that measures temperature

Figure 9-2
A liquid thermometer uses the expansion of liquid alcohol or mercury to indicate changes in temperature.

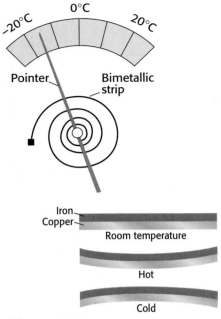

Pointer

Bimetallic strip

Iron
Copper

Room temperature

Hot

Cold

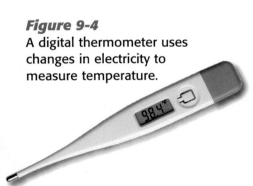

Figure 9-3
A refrigerator thermometer uses the bending of a strip made from two metals to indicate the correct temperature.

Figure 9-4
A digital thermometer uses changes in electricity to measure temperature.

internetconnect

SC LINKS
NSTA

TOPIC: Temperature scales
GO TO: www.scilinks.org
KEYWORD: HK1102

Liquid thermometers can measure only temperatures within a certain range. This is because below a certain temperature, the liquid used in the thermometer freezes. Also, above a certain temperature the liquid boils. Therefore, different types of thermometers are designed to measure extreme temperatures.

The thermometer used in a refrigerator is based on the expansion of metal, as shown in **Figure 9-3.** The thermometer contains a coil made from two different metal strips pressed together. Both strips expand and contract at different rates as the temperature changes. As the temperature falls, the coil unwinds moving the pointer to the correct temperature. A digital thermometer, shown in **Figure 9-4,** is designed to measure temperature by noting the change in current. Changes in temperature also cause electric current to change in a circuit.

Fahrenheit and Celsius are common scales used for measuring temperatures

The temperature scale that is probably most familiar to you from weather reports and cookbooks is the Fahrenheit scale. The units on the Fahrenheit scale are called degrees Fahrenheit, or °F. On the Fahrenheit scale, water freezes at 32°F and boils at 212°F.

Most countries other than the United States use the Celsius (or centigrade) scale. This scale is widely used in science. The Celsius scale gives a value of zero to the freezing point of water and a value of 100 to the boiling point of water at standard atmospheric pressure. The difference between these two points is divided into 100 equal parts, called degrees Celsius, or °C.

A degree Celsius is nearly twice as large as a degree Fahrenheit. Also, the temperature at which water freezes differs for the two scales by 32 degrees. To convert from one scale to the other, use one of the following formulas.

Celsius-Fahrenheit Conversion Equation

$$Fahrenheit\ temperature = \left(\frac{9}{5} \times Celsius\ temperature\right) + 32.0$$

$$T_F = \frac{9}{5}t + 32.0$$

Fahrenheit-Celsius Conversion Equation

$$Celsius\ temperature = \frac{5}{9}(Fahrenheit\ temperature - 32.0)$$

$$t = \frac{5}{9}(T_F - 32.0)$$

The Kelvin scale is based on absolute zero

You have probably heard of negative temperatures, such as those reported on extremely cold winter days in the northern United States and Canada. Remember that temperature is a measure of the average kinetic energy of the particles in an object. Even far below 0°C these particles are moving and therefore have some kinetic energy. But how low can the temperature fall? Physically, the lowest possible temperature is –273.13°C. This temperature is referred to as absolute zero. At absolute zero the energy of an object is minimal, that is, the energy of the object cannot be any lower.

Absolute zero is the basis for another temperature scale called the Kelvin scale. On this scale, 0 kelvin, or 0 K, is absolute zero. Since the lowest possible temperature is assigned a zero value, there are no negative temperature values on the Kelvin scale. The Kelvin scale is used in many fields of science, especially those involving low temperatures. The three temperature scales are compared in **Figure 9-5.**

In magnitude, a unit of kelvin is equal to a degree on the Celsius scale. Therefore, the temperature of any object in kelvins can be found by simply adding 273 to the object's temperature in degrees Celsius. The equation for this conversion is given below.

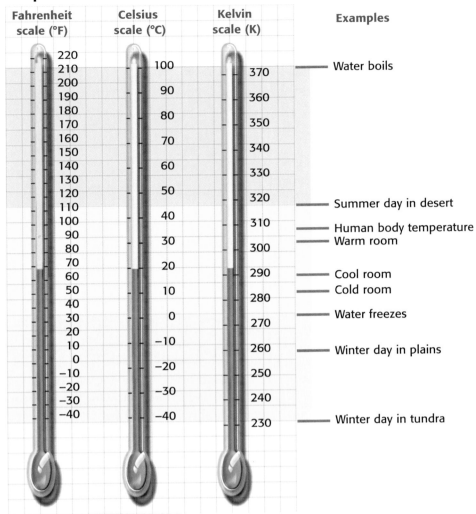

Temperature Values on Different Scales

Figure 9-5
Temperatures on the Celsius scale can be converted to both Fahrenheit and Kelvin scales. Note that all Kelvin temperatures are positive.

▶ **absolute zero** the temperature at which an object's energy is minimal

Celsius-Kelvin Conversion Equation

Kelvin temperature = Celsius temperature + 273

$$T = t + 273$$

INTEGRATING

SPACE SCIENCE
From cold deep space to hot stars, astronomers measure a wide range of temperatures of objects in the universe. All objects produce different types of electromagnetic waves depending on their temperature. By identifying the distribution of wavelengths an object radiates, astronomers can estimate the object's temperature.

Light (an electromagnetic wave) received from the sun indicates that the temperature of its surface is 6000 K. If you think that is hot, try the center of the sun, where the temperature increases to 15 000 000 K!

Disc One, Module 7: Heat
Use the Interactive Tutor to learn more about this topic.

Math Skills

Temperature Scale Conversion The highest atmospheric temperature ever recorded on Earth was 57.8°C. Express this temperature both in degrees Fahrenheit and in kelvins.

1 List the given and unknown values.
  Given: $t = 57.8°C$
  Unknown: $T_F = ?$ °F, $T = ?$ K

2 Write down the equations for temperature conversions from pages 292 and 293.
$$T_F = \frac{9}{5}t + 32.0$$
$$T = t + 273$$

3 Insert the known values into the equations, and solve.
$$T_F = \left(\frac{9}{5} \times 57.8\right) + 32.0 = 104 + 32.0 = 136°F$$
$$T = 57.8 + 273 = 331 \text{ K}$$

Practice

Temperature Scale Conversion

1. Convert the following temperatures to both degrees Fahrenheit and kelvins.
  a. the boiling point of liquid hydrogen (–252.87°C)
  b. the temperature of a winter day at the North Pole (–40.0°C)
  c. the melting point of gold (1064°C)

2. For each of the four temperatures given in the table below, make the necessary conversions to complete the table.

Example	Temp. (°C)	Temp. (°F)	Temp. (K)
Air in a typical living room	21	?	?
Metal in a running car engine	?	?	388
Liquid nitrogen	–200.	?	?
Air on a summer day in the desert	?	110.	?

3. Use **Figure 9-5** to determine which of the following is a likely temperature for ice cubes in a freezer.
  a. –20°C   **c.** 253 K
  b. –4°F   **d.** all of the above

4. Use **Figure 9-5** to determine which of the following is the nearest value for normal human body temperature.
  a. 50°C   **c.** 310 K
  b. 75°F   **d.** all of the above

Relating Temperature to Energy Transfer as Heat

When you grab a piece of ice, it feels very cold. When you step into a hot bath, the water feels very hot. Clasping your hands together usually produces neither sensation. These three cases can be explained by comparing the temperatures of the two objects making contact with each other.

The feeling associated with temperature difference results from energy transfer

Imagine that you are holding a piece of ice. The temperature of ice is lower than your hand; therefore, the molecules in the ice move very slowly compared with the molecules in your hand. As the molecules on the surface of your hand collide with those on the surface of the ice, energy is transferred to the ice. As a result, the molecules in the ice speed up and their kinetic energy increases. This causes the ice to melt.

Inquiry Lab

How do temperature and energy relate?

Materials
- ✔ glass beaker
- ✔ tongs
- ✔ 2 pieces of string, 20 cm each
- ✔ thermometer
- ✔ clock
- ✔ electric hot plate
- ✔ graduated cylinder
- ✔ 40 identical small metal washers
- ✔ 2 plastic-foam cups

Procedure

1. Tie 10 washers on one piece of string and 30 washers on another piece of string.
2. Fill the beaker two-thirds full with water, lower the washers in, and set the beaker on the hot plate.
3. Heat the water to boiling.
4. While the water heats, put exactly 50 mL of cool water in each plastic-foam cup.
5. Use a thermometer to measure and record the initial temperature of water in each cup.
6. When the water in the beaker has boiled for about 3 minutes, use tongs to remove the group of 30 washers. Gently shake any water off the washers back into the beaker, and quickly place the washers into one of the plastic-foam cups.
7. Observe the change in temperature of the cup's water. Record the highest temperature reached.

8. Repeat steps 6 and 7 by placing the 10 washers in the other plastic-foam cup.

Analysis

1. Which cup had the higher final temperature?
2. Both cups had the same starting temperature. Both sets of washers started at 100°C. Why did one cup reach a higher final temperature?

▶ **heat** the transfer of energy from the particles of one object to those of another object due to a temperature difference between the two objects

In a similar manner, a hot-water bottle transfers energy from the hot water to your skin. However, when both your hands are at the same temperature, neither hand feels warm or cold because there is no energy transfer.

The transfer of energy between the particles of two objects due to a temperature difference between the two objects is called **heat.** This transfer of energy always takes place from a substance at a higher temperature to a substance at a lower temperature.

Because temperature is an indicator of the particles' average kinetic energy, you can use it to predict which way energy will be transferred. The warmer object, such as the hot-water bottle, will transfer energy to the cooler object, such as your skin. When energy is transferred as heat from the hot water to your skin, the temperature of the water falls while the temperature of your skin rises.

When both your skin and the hot-water bottle approach the same temperature, less energy is transferred from the bottle to your skin. To continue the transfer of energy, the temperature of the hot water must be kept at a higher temperature than your skin. The greater the difference in the temperatures of the two objects, the more energy that will transfer as heat.

SECTION 9.1 REVIEW

SUMMARY

▶ Temperature is a measure of the average kinetic energy of an object's particles.

▶ A thermometer is a device that measures temperature.

▶ On the Celsius temperature scale, water freezes at 0° and boils at 100°.

▶ A kelvin is the same size as a degree Celsius. The lowest temperature possible—absolute zero—is 0 K.

▶ At absolute zero the particles of an object have no kinetic energy to transfer.

▶ Heat is the transfer of energy between objects with different temperatures.

CHECK YOUR UNDERSTANDING

1. **Define** *absolute zero* in terms of particles and their kinetic energy.
2. **Predict** which molecules will move faster on average: water molecules in a cup of hot soup or water molecules in a glass of iced lemonade.
3. **Explain** how your precautions would differ if you were preparing to enter a chamber at 100 K as opposed to one at 100°C.
4. **Predict** whether a greater amount of energy will be transferred as heat between 1 kg of water at 10°C and a freezer at −15°C or between 1 kg of water at 60°C and an oven at 65°C.
5. **Critical Thinking** Determine which of the following has a higher temperature and which contains a larger amount of total kinetic energy: a cup of boiling water or Lake Michigan.

Math Skills

6. Convert the temperature of the air in an air-conditioned room, 20.0°C, to equivalent values on the Fahrenheit and Kelvin temperature scales.
7. Convert the coldest outdoor temperature ever recorded, −128.6°F, to equivalent Celsius and Kelvin temperatures.

Energy Transfer

OBJECTIVES

▶ Investigate and demonstrate how energy is transferred by conduction, convection, and radiation.
▶ Identify and distinguish between conductors and insulators.
▶ Solve problems involving specific heat.

KEY TERMS
conduction
convection
convection current
radiation
conductor
insulator
specific heat

While water is being heated for your morning shower, your breakfast food is cooking. In the freezer, water in ice trays becomes solid after the freezer cools the water to 0°C. Outside, the morning dew evaporates soon after light from the rising sun strikes it. These are all examples of energy transfers from one object to another.

Methods of Energy Transfer

The energy transfer as heat from a hot object can occur in three ways. Roasting marshmallows around a campfire, as shown in **Figure 9-6,** provides an opportunity to experience each of these three ways.

internetconnect

SC*LINKS*
NSTA

TOPIC: Energy transfer
GO TO: www.scilinks.org
KEYWORD: HK1103

Ways of Transferring Energy

Figure 9-6

A Conduction transfers energy as heat along the wire and into the hand.

B Embers swirl upward in the convection currents that are created as warmed air above the fire rises.

C Electromagnetic waves emitted by the hot campfire transfer energy by radiation.

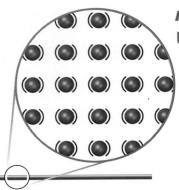

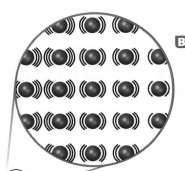

Figure 9-7

A Before conduction takes place, the average kinetic energy of the particles in the metal wire is the same throughout.

B During conduction, the rapidly moving particles in the wire transfer some of their energy to slowly moving particles nearby.

▶ **conduction** the transfer of energy as heat between particles as they collide within a substance or between two objects in contact

▶ **convection** the transfer of energy by the movement of fluids with different temperatures

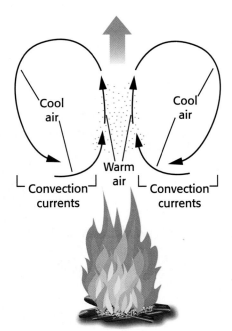

Figure 9-8
During convection, energy is carried away by a heated gas or liquid that expands and rises above cooler, denser gas or liquid.

Conduction involves objects in direct contact

Imagine you place a marshmallow on one end of a wire made from a metal coat hanger. Then you hold the other end of the wire while letting the marshmallow cook in the campfire flame. Soon you will notice that the end of the wire you are holding is getting warmer. This is an example of energy transfer by **conduction.**

Conduction is one of the methods of energy transfer. Conduction takes place when two objects that are in contact are at unequal temperatures. It also takes place between particles within an object. In the case of the wire in the campfire, the rapidly moving air molecules close to the flame collide with the atoms at the end of the wire. The energy transferred to the atoms in the wire causes them to vibrate rapidly. As shown in **Figure 9-7,** these rapidly vibrating atoms collide with slowly vibrating atoms, transferring energy as heat all along the wire. The energy is then transferred to you as the wire's atoms collide with the molecules in your skin, creating a hot sensation in your hand.

Convection results from the movement of warm fluids

While roasting your marshmallow, you may notice that tiny glowing embers from the fire rise and begin to swirl, as shown in **Figure 9-6.** They are following the movement of air away from the fire. The air close to the fire becomes hot and expands so that there is more space between the air particles. As a result, the air becomes less dense and moves upward, carrying its extra energy with it, as shown in **Figure 9-8.** The rising warm air is replaced by cooler, denser air. The cooler air then becomes hot by the fire until it also expands and rises. Eventually, the rising hot air cools, contracts, becomes denser, and sinks. This is an example of energy transfer by **convection.**

Convection involves the movement of the heated substance itself. This is possible only if the substance is a fluid—either a liquid or a gas—because particles within solids are not as free to move.

The cycle of a heated fluid that rises and then cools and falls is called a **convection current.** The glowing embers rising from the campfire are caught up in the convection currents created in the air surrounding the fire. The proper heating and cooling of a building requires the use of convection currents. Warm air expands and rises from vents near the floor. It cools and contracts near the ceiling and then sinks back to the floor. Eventually, the temperature of all the air in the room is increased by convection currents.

Radiation does not require physical contact between objects

As you stand close to a campfire, you can feel its warmth. This warmth can be felt even when you are not in the path of a convection current. The energy transfer as heat from the fire in this case is in the form of *electromagnetic waves*, which include infrared radiation, visible light, and ultraviolet rays. The transfer of energy by electromagnetic waves is called **radiation.** You will learn more about electromagnetic radiation in Chapter 10.

When you stand near a fire, your skin absorbs the energy radiated by the fire. As the molecules in your skin absorb this energy, the average kinetic energy of these molecules—and thus the temperature of your skin—increases. A hot object radiates more energy than a cool object or cool surroundings, as shown in **Figure 9-9.**

Radiation differs from conduction and convection in that it does not involve the movement of matter. Radiation is therefore the only method of energy transfer that can take place in a vacuum, such as outer space. Much of the energy we receive from the sun is transferred by radiation.

▶ **convection current** the flow of a fluid due to heated expansion followed by cooling and contraction

Quick ACTIVITY

Convection
Light a candle. Carefully observe the motion of the tiny soot particles in smoke. They move because of convection currents.

▶ **radiation** the transfer of energy by electromagnetic waves

Changes in Radiated Energy

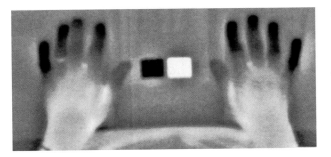

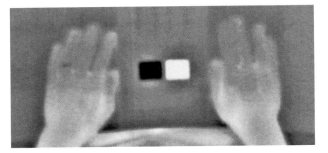

Figure 9-9

🅰 Before surgery, as seen in the infrared photo, the fingers are cooler than the rest of the hand. This results from poor blood flow in this patient's fingers.

🅱 After surgery, the blood flow has been restored, so the temperature of the fingers, and the amount of energy they radiate, increases.

Inquiry Lab

What color absorbs more radiation?

Materials
- ✔ empty soup can, painted black inside and out, label removed
- ✔ empty soup can, label removed
- ✔ 2 thermometers
- ✔ clock
- ✔ graduated cylinder
- ✔ bright lamp or sunlight

Procedure

1. Prepare a data table with three columns and at least seven rows. Label the first column "Time," the second column "Temperature of painted can (°C)," and the third column "Temperature of un-painted can (°C)."
2. Pour 50 mL of cool water into each can.
3. Place a thermometer in each can, and record the temperature of the water in each can at the start. Leave the thermometers in the cans. Aim the lamp at the cans, or place them in sunlight.
4. Record the temperature of the water in each can every 3 minutes for at least 15 minutes.

Analysis

1. Prepare a graph. Label the x-axis "Time" and the y-axis "Temperature". Plot your data for each can of water.
2. Which color absorbed more radiation?
3. Which variables in the lab were controlled (unchanged throughout the experiment)? For each of the following variables, explain your answer.
   a. starting temperature of water in cans
   b. volume of water in cans
   c. distance of cans from light
   d. size of cans
4. Use your results to explain why panels used for solar heating are often painted black.
5. Based on your results, what color would you want your car to be in the winter? in the summer? Justify your answer.

Conductors and Insulators

When you are cooking, the energy transfer as heat from the stove to the food must occur effectively. However, it is important that the handle does not get uncomfortably hot.

Energy is transferred as heat quickly in conductors

To increase the temperature of a substance using conduction, we must use materials through which energy can be quickly transferred as heat. Cooking pans are made of metal because energy is passed easily and quickly between the particles in most metals. Any material through which energy can be easily transferred as heat is called a **conductor**.

Part of what determines how well a substance conducts is whether it is a gas, liquid, or solid. Gases are extremely poor conductors because their particles are far apart, and the particle collisions necessary to transfer energy rarely occur. The particles

▶ **conductor** a material through which energy can be easily transferred as heat

in liquids are more closely packed. However, while liquids conduct better than gases, they are not very effective conductors.

Some solids, like rubber and wood, conduct energy about as well as liquids. However, metals such as copper and silver conduct energy transfer as heat very well. Some solids are better conductors than other solids. Metals, in general, are better conductors than non-metals.

Figure 9-10
The skillet conducts energy from the stove element to the food. The wooden spoon and handle insulate the hands from the energy of the skillet.

Insulators slow the transfer of energy as heat

Because energy costs money, we try to avoid wasting it. This waste is most often due to unwanted energy transfer. To reduce or stop unwanted energy transfer, we use materials that are poor conductors. A material of this type is called an insulator.

Examples of conductors and insulators are shown in **Figure 9-10.** The skillet is made of iron, a good conductor, so that energy is transferred effectively as heat to the food. Wood is an insulator, so the energy from the hot skillet won't reach your hand through the wooden spoon or the wooden handle.

▶ **insulator** a material that is a poor energy conductor

Quick ACTIVITY

Conductors and Insulators

For this activity you will need several flatware utensils. Each one should be made of a different material, such as stainless steel, aluminum, and plastic. You will also need a bowl and ice cubes.

1. Place the ice cubes in the bowl. Position the utensils in the bowl so that an equal length of each utensil lies under the ice.
2. Check the utensils' temperature by briefly touching each utensil at the same distance

from the ice every 20 s. Which utensil becomes colder first? What variables might affect your results?

Specific Heat

You have probably noticed that a metal spoon, like the one shown in **Figure 9-11,** becomes hot when it is placed in a cup of hot liquid. You have also probably noticed that a spoon made of a different material, such as plastic, does not become hot as quickly. The difference between the final temperatures of the two spoons depends on whether they are good conductors or good insulators. But what makes a substance a good or poor conductor depends in part on how much energy a substance requires to change its temperature by a certain degree.

Figure 9-11
The spoon's temperature increases rapidly because of the spoon's low specific heat.

▶ **specific heat** the amount of energy transferred as heat that will raise the temperature of 1 kg of a substance by 1 K.

Specific heat describes how much energy is required to raise an object's temperature

Not all substances behave the same when they absorb energy by heat. For example, a metal spoon left in a metal pot becomes hot seconds after the pot is placed on a hot stovetop burner. This is because a few joules of energy are enough to raise the spoon's temperature substantially. However, if an amount of water with the same mass as the spoon is placed in the same pot, that same amount of energy will produce a much smaller temperature change in the water.

For all substances, the amount of energy that must be transferred to the substance in order to raise the temperature of 1 kg of the substance by 1 K is a characteristic physical property. This property is known as **specific heat** and is denoted by c.

Some values for specific heat are given in **Table 9-1.** These values are in units of J/kg•K, meaning each is the amount of energy in J needed to raise the temperature of 1 kg of the substance by exactly 1 K.

Table 9-1 **Specific Heats at 25°C**

Substance	c (J/kg•K)	Substance	c (J/kg•K)
Water (liquid)	4186	Copper	385
Steam	1870	Gold	129
Ammonia (gas)	2060	Iron	449
Ethanol (liquid)	2440	Mercury	140
Aluminum	897	Lead	129
Carbon (graphite)	709	Silver	234

On a hot summer day, the temperature of the water in a swimming pool remains much lower than the air temperature and the temperature of the concrete around the pool. This is due to water's relatively high specific heat as well as the large mass of water in the pool. Similarly, at night, the concrete and the air cool off quickly, while the water changes temperature only slightly.

Specific heat can be used in calculations

Because specific heat is a ratio, it can be used to predict the effects of larger temperature changes for masses other than 1 kg. For example, if it takes 4186 J to raise the temperature of 1 kg of water by 1 K, twice as much energy, 8372 J, will be required to raise the temperature of 2 kg of water by 1 K. Three times that amount, 25 120 J, will be required to raise the temperature of the 2 kg of water by 3 K. This relationship is summed up in the equation below.

> **Specific Heat Equation**
> *energy = (specific heat) × (mass) × (temperature change)*
> $energy = cm\Delta t$

Specific heat can change slightly with changing pressure and volume. *However, problems and questions in this chapter will assume that volume and pressure do not change.*

Math Skills

Specific Heat How much energy must be transferred as heat to the 420 kg of water in a bathtub in order to raise the water's temperature from 25°C to 37°C?

1 **List the given and unknown values.**
    Given: $\Delta t = 37°C - 25°C = 12°C = 12$ K
        $m = 420$ kg
        $c = 4186$ J/kg•K
    Unknown: *energy* = ?

2 **Write down the specific heat equation from this page.**
    $energy = cm\Delta t$

3 **Substitute the specific heat, mass, and temperature change values, and solve.**
    $energy = \left(\dfrac{4186 \text{ J}}{\text{kg} \bullet \text{K}}\right) \times (420 \text{ kg}) \times (12 \text{ K})$
    $energy = 2.1 \times 10^4$ kJ

Practice HINT

▶ To rearrange the equation to isolate temperature change, divide both sides of the equation by mc.

$$\frac{energy}{mc} = \left(\frac{\cancel{mc}}{\cancel{mc}}\right)\Delta t$$

$$\Delta t = \frac{energy}{mc}$$

▶ Use this version of the equation for Practice Problem 4.
▶ For Practice Problems 5 and 6, you will need to isolate m and c.

Practice

Specific Heat

1. How much energy is needed to increase the temperature of 755 g of iron from 283 K to 403 K?
2. How much energy must a refrigerator absorb from 225 g of water so that the temperature of the water will drop from 35°C to 5°C?
3. A 144 kg park bench made of iron sits in the sun, and its temperature increases from 25°C to 35°C. How many kilojoules of energy does the bench absorb?
4. An aluminum baking sheet with a mass of 225 g absorbs 2.4×10^4 J from an oven. If its temperature was initially 25°C, what will its new temperature be?
5. What mass of water is required to absorb 4.7×10^5 J of energy from a car engine while the temperature increases from 298 K to 355 K?
6. A vanadium bolt gives up 1124 J of energy as its temperature drops 25 K. If the bolt's mass is 93 g, what is its specific heat?

SECTION 9.2 REVIEW

SUMMARY

▶ Conduction is the transfer of energy as heat between particles as they collide within a substance or between objects in contact.

▶ Convection currents are the movement of gases and liquids as they become heated, expand, and rise, then cool, contract, and fall.

▶ Radiation is the transfer of energy by electromagnetic waves.

▶ Conductors are materials through which energy is easily transferred as heat.

▶ Insulators are materials that conduct energy poorly.

▶ Specific heat is the energy required to heat 1 kg of a substance by 1 K.

CHECK YOUR UNDERSTANDING

1. **Describe** how energy is transferred by conduction, convection, and radiation.
2. **Rank** the following in order from the best conductor to the best insulator:
   a. iron   **c.** water
   b. air   **d.** gold
3. **Predict** whether the hottest part of a room will be near the ceiling, in the center, or near the floor, given that there is a hot-air vent near the floor. Explain your reasoning.
4. **Explain** why there are temperature differences on the moon's surface, even though there is no atmosphere present.
5. **Critical Thinking** Explain why cookies baked near the turned-up edges of a cookie sheet receive more energy than those baked near the center.

Math Skills

6. When a shiny chunk of metal with a mass of 1.32 kg absorbs 3250 J of energy, the temperature of the metal increases from 273 K to 292 K. Is this metal likely to be silver, lead, or aluminum?
7. A 0.400 kg sample of glass requires 3190 J for its temperature to increase from 273 K to 308 K. What is the specific heat for this type of glass?

Using Heat

INTEGRATING TECHNOLOGY and Society

OBJECTIVES

▶ Describe the mechanisms of different heating and cooling systems, and discuss their advantages and drawbacks.

▶ Compare different heating and cooling systems in terms of how they decrease the amount of usable energy.

▶ KEY TERMS

heating system
cooling system
refrigerant

Heating a house in the winter, cooling an office building in the summer, or preserving food throughout the year is possible because of machines that transfer energy as heat from one place to another. An example of one of these machines, an air conditioner, is shown in **Figure 9-12.** An air conditioner does work to remove energy as heat from the warm air inside a room and then transfers the energy to the warmer air outside the room. An air conditioner can do this because of two principles about energy that you have already studied.

The first principle, from Chapter 8, is that the total energy used in any process—whether that energy is transferred as a result of work, heat, or both—is conserved. This principle of conservation of energy is called the first law of thermodynamics.

The second principle, from this chapter, is that the energy transferred as heat always moves from an object at a high temperature to an object at a low temperature.

Figure 9-12

A A substance that easily evaporates and condenses is used in air conditioners to transfer energy from a room to the air outside.

B When the liquid evaporates, it absorbs energy from the surrounding air, thereby cooling it.

C Outside, the air conditioner causes the gas to condense, releasing energy.

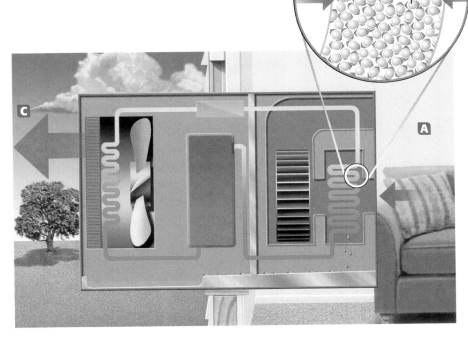

Gaseous refrigerant

Liquid refrigerant

In 1769, a Scottish engineer named James Watt patented a new design that made steam engines more efficient. During the next 50 years, the improved steam engines were used to power trains and ships. Previously, transportation had depended on the work done by horses or the wind.

Watt's new steam engines were used in machines and factories of the industrial revolution. In 1784, Watt used steam coils to heat his office. This was the first practical use of steam for heating.

Making the Connection

1. Old steam-powered riverboats are popular tourist attractions in many cities. Make a list of at least three other instances in which the energy in steam is used for practical purposes.
2. What devices in older buildings function like the steam coils Watt used for heating his office?

▶ **heating system** any device or process that transfers energy to a substance to raise the temperature of the substance

internetconnect

SCiLINKS
NSTA

TOPIC: Heating and cooling systems
GO TO: www.scilinks.org
KEYWORD: HK1104

Heating Systems

People generally feel and work their best when the temperature of the air around them is in the range of 21°C–25°C (70°F–77°F). To raise the indoor temperature on colder days, energy must be transferred into a room's air by a **heating system.** Most heating systems use a source of energy to raise the temperature of a substance such as air or water.

Work can be done to increase temperature

When you rub your hands together, they become warmer. The energy you transfer to your hands by work is transferred to the molecules of your hands, and their temperature increases. Processes that involve energy transfer by work are called mechanical processes.

Another example of a mechanical heating process is a device used in the past by certain American Indian tribes to start fires. The device consists of a bow with a loop in the bowstring that holds a pointed stick. The sharp end of the stick is placed in a small indentation in a stone. A small pile of wood shavings is then put around the place where the stick and stone make contact. A person then does work to move the bow back and forth. This energy is transferred to the stick, which turns rapidly. The friction between the stick and stone causes the temperature to rise until the shavings are set on fire.

The energy from food is transferred as heat to blood moving throughout the human body

You may not think of yourself as a heating system. But unless you are sick, your body maintains a temperature of about 37°C (98.6°F), whether you are in a place that is cool or hot. Maintaining this temperature in cool air requires your body to function like a heating system.

If you are surrounded by cold air, energy will be transferred as heat from your skin to the air, and the temperature of your skin will drop. To compensate, stored nutrients are broken down by your body to provide energy, and this energy is transferred as heat to your blood. The warm blood circulates through your body, transferring energy as heat to your skin and increasing your skin's temperature. In this way your body can maintain a constant temperature.

Heated water or air transfers energy as heat in central heating systems

Most modern homes and large buildings have a central heating system. As is the case with your body, when the building is surrounded by cold air, energy is transferred as heat from the building to the outside air. The temperature of the building begins to drop.

A central heating system has a furnace that burns coal, fuel oil, or natural gas. The energy released in the furnace is transferred as heat to water, steam, or air, as shown in **Figure 9-13.** The steam, hot water, or hot air is then moved to each room through pipes or ducts. Because the temperature of the pipe is higher than that of the air, energy is transferred as heat to the air in the room.

Solar heating systems also use warmed air or water

Cold-blooded animals, such as lizards and turtles, increase their body temperature by using external sources, such as the sun. You may have seen these animals sitting motionless on rocks on sunny days, as shown in **Figure 9-14.** During such behavior, called basking, energy is absorbed by the reptile's skin through conduction from the warmer air and rocks, and by radiation from sunlight. This absorbed energy is then transferred as heat to the reptile's blood. As the blood circulates, it transfers this energy to all parts of the reptile's body.

Solar heating systems, such as the one illustrated in **Figure 9-15,** use an approach similar to that of a basking reptile. A solar collector uses panels to gather energy radiated from the sun. This energy is used to heat water. The hot water is then moved throughout the house by the same methods other hot-water systems use.

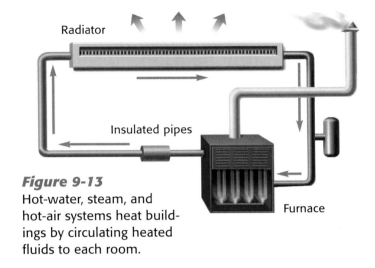

Figure 9-13
Hot-water, steam, and hot-air systems heat buildings by circulating heated fluids to each room.

Figure 9-14
Reptiles bask in the sun to raise their body temperature.

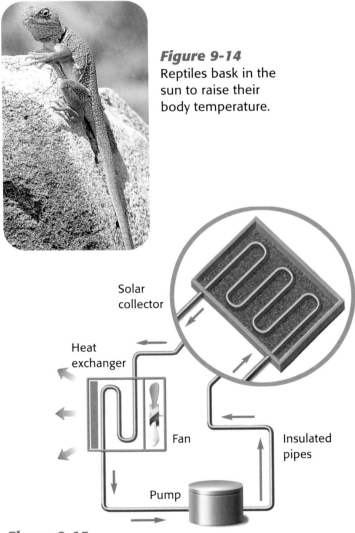

Figure 9-15
An active solar heating system moves water heated by sunlight through pipes and a heat exchanger.

Figure 9-16

(A) In a passive solar heating system, energy from sunlight is absorbed in a rooftop panel. (B) Pipes carry the hot fluid that exchanges energy as heat with the air in each room.

The warm water can also be pumped through a device called a heat exchanger, which transfers energy from the water to a mass of air by conduction and radiation. The warmed air is then blown through ducts as with other warm-air heating systems.

Both of these types of solar heating systems are called active solar heating systems. They require extra energy from another source, such as electricity, in order to move the heated water or air around.

Passive solar heating systems, as shown in **Figure 9-16,** require no extra energy to move the hot fluids through the pipe. In this type of system, energy transfer is accomplished by radiation and convection currents created in heated water or air. In warm, sunny climates, passive solar heating systems are easy to construct and maintain and are clean and inexpensive to operate.

Usable energy decreases in all energy transfers

When energy can be easily transformed and transferred to accomplish a task, such as heating a room, we say that the energy is in a usable form. After this transfer, the same amount of energy is present, according to the law of conservation of energy. Yet less of it is in a form that can be used.

The energy used to increase the temperature of the water in a hot-water tank should ideally stay in the hot water. However, it is impossible to keep some energy from being transferred as heat to parts of the hot-water tank and its surroundings. The amount of usable energy decreases even in the most efficient heating systems.

Due to conduction and radiation, some energy is lost to the tank's surroundings, such as the air and nearby walls. Cold water in the pipes that feed into the water heater also draw energy from some of the hot water in the tank. When energy from electricity is used to heat water in the hot-water heater, some of the energy is used to increase the temperature of the electrical wire, the metal cover of the water heater, and the air around the water heater. All of these portions of the total energy put into the hot-water heater can no longer be used to heat the water, and therefore are no longer in a usable form. In general, the amount of usable energy always decreases whenever energy is transferred or transformed.

Figure 9-17
Insulating materials, such as fiberglass and cellulose, are used in most buildings to reduce the transfer of energy as heat.

Table 9-2
R-Values for Some Common Building Materials

Substance	R-value
Drywall, 1.3 cm (0.50 in.)	0.45
Wood shingles, (overlapping)	0.87
Flat glass, 0.318 cm (0.125 in.)	0.89
Hardwood siding, 2.54 cm (1.00 in.)	0.91
Vertical air space, 8.9 cm (3.5 in.)	1.01
Insulating glass, 0.64 cm (0.25 in.)	1.54
Cellulose fiber, 2.54 cm (1.00 in.)	3.70
Brick, 10.2 cm (4.00 in.)	4.00
Fiberglass batting, 8.9 cm (3.5 in.)	10.90

Insulation minimizes undesirable energy transfers

During winter, some of the energy from the warm air inside a building is lost to the cold outside air. Similarly, during the summer, energy from warm air outside seeps into an air-conditioned building, raising the temperature of the cool inside air. Good insulation can reduce, but not entirely eliminate, the unwanted transfer of energy to and from the building's surroundings. As shown in **Figure 9-17,** insulation material is placed in the walls and attics of homes and other buildings to reduce the unwanted transfer of energy as heat.

A standard rating system has been developed to measure the effectiveness of insulation materials. This rating, called the *R-value,* is determined by the type of material used and the material's thickness. *R*-values for several common building and insulating materials of a given thickness are listed in **Table 9-2.** The greater the *R*-value, the greater the material's ability to decrease unwanted energy transfers.

Cooling Systems

If you quickly let the air out of a compressed-air tank like the one used by scuba divers, the air from the tank and the tank's nozzle feel slightly cooler than they did before the air was released. This is because the molecules in the air lose some of their kinetic energy as the air's pressure and volume change and the temperature of the air decreases. This process is a simple example of a **cooling system.** In all cooling systems, energy is transferred as heat from one substance to another, leaving the first substance with less energy and thus a lower temperature.

▶ **cooling system** a device that transfers energy as heat out of an object to lower its temperature

Cooling systems often use evaporation to transfer energy from their surroundings

In the case of a refrigerator, the temperature of the air and food inside is lowered. But because the first law of thermodynamics requires energy to be conserved, the energy inside the refrigerator must be transferred to the air outside the refrigerator. If you place your hand near the rear or base of a refrigerator, you will feel warm air being discharged. Much of the energy in this air was removed from inside the refrigerator.

Hidden in the back wall of a refrigerator is a set of coiled pipes through which a substance called a **refrigerant** flows, as shown in **Figure 9-18.** During each operating cycle of the refrigerator, the refrigerant evaporates into a gas and then condenses back into a liquid.

Recall from Chapter 2 and the beginning of this section that evaporation produces a cooling effect. Changes of state always involve the transfer of relatively large amounts of energy. In liquids that are good refrigerants, such as Freon®, evaporation occurs at a much lower temperature than that of the air inside the refrigerator. When the liquid refrigerant is in a set of pipes near the inside of the refrigerator, energy is transferred by heat from the air to the refrigerant. This exchange causes the air and food to cool.

▶ **refrigerant** a substance used in cooling systems that transfers large amounts of energy as it changes state

INTEGRATING

BIOLOGY

In hot regions, the ears of many mammals serve as cooling systems. Larger ears provide more area for energy to be transferred from blood to the surrounding air, helping the animals to maintain their body temperature. Rabbits and foxes that live in the desert have much longer ears than rabbits and foxes that live in temperate or arctic climates.

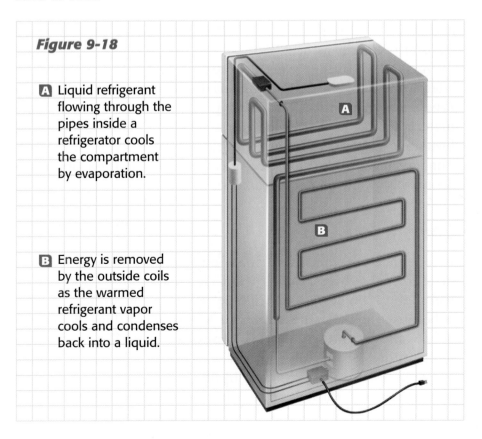

Figure 9-18

A Liquid refrigerant flowing through the pipes inside a refrigerator cools the compartment by evaporation.

B Energy is removed by the outside coils as the warmed refrigerant vapor cools and condenses back into a liquid.

Condensation transfers energy to the surroundings

The refrigerant has become a gas by absorbing energy. This gas moves to the section of coils outside the refrigerator, where electrical energy is used to power a compressor. Pressure is used to condense the refrigerant back into a liquid. Because condensation involves transferring energy from the vapor as heat, the temperature of the air outside the refrigerator increases. This explains why the outside coils stay warm.

Air-conditioning systems in homes and buildings use the same process refrigerators use. As air near the evaporation coils is cooled, a fan blows this air through ducts into the rooms and hallways. Convection currents in the room then allow the cool air to circulate as displaced warmer air flows into return ducts.

Heat pumps can transfer energy to or from rooms

Heat pumps use the evaporation and condensation of a refrigerant to provide heating in the winter and cooling in the summer. A heat pump is a refrigeration unit in which the cooling cycle can be reversed.

As shown in **Figure 9-19A,** the liquid refrigerant travels through the outdoor coils during the winter and absorbs enough energy from the outside air to evaporate. Work is done on the gas by a compressor, increasing the refrigerant's energy. Then the refrigerant moves through the coils inside the house, as shown in **Figure 9-19B.** The hot gas transfers energy as heat to the air inside the house. This process warms the air while cooling the refrigerant gas enough for it to condense back into a liquid.

In the summer, the refrigerant is pumped in the opposite direction, so that the heat pump functions like a refrigerator or an air conditioner. The liquid refrigerant absorbs energy from the air inside the house as it evaporates. The hot refrigerant gas is then moved to the coils which are outside the house. The refrigerant then condenses, transferring energy as heat to the outside air.

Figure 9-19

A Liquid refrigerant evaporates in the outdoor coils as energy is transferred from the air.

B The hot refrigerant gas moves through the coils into the indoor portion of the pump, where the refrigerant condenses back into a liquid and transfers energy as heat into the room.

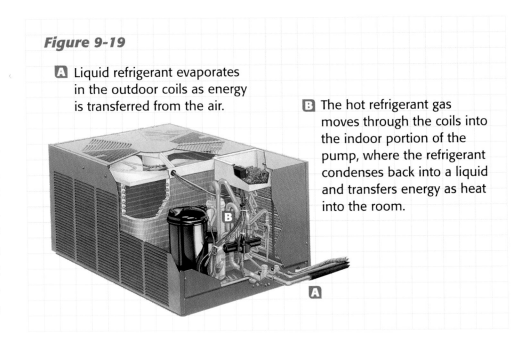

Buying Appliances Most major appliances, including those that involve the transfer of energy as heat, are required by law to have an *Energyguide* label attached to them.

The label indicates the average amount of energy used by the appliance in a year. It also gives the average cost of using the appliance based on a national average of cost per energy unit.

The *Energyguide* label provides consumers a way to compare various brands and models of appliances.

Applying Information
1. Use the *Energyguide* label shown to find how much energy the appliance uses each hour.
2. What is the daily operating cost of the appliance?

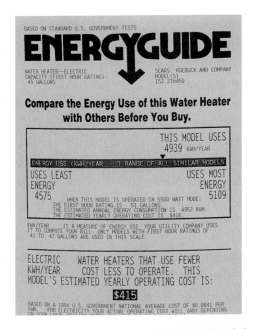

BASED ON STANDARD U.S. GOVERNMENT TESTS

ENERGYGUIDE

WATER HEATER—ELECTRIC
CAPACITY (FIRST HOUR RATING):
45 GALLONS

SEARS, ROEBUCK AND COMPANY
MODEL(S)
153.316450

Compare the Energy Use of this Water Heater with Others Before You Buy.

THIS MODEL USES
4939 KWH/YEAR

ENERGY USE (KWH/YEAR) RANGE OF ALL SIMILAR MODELS

USES LEAST
ENERGY
4575

USES MOST
ENERGY
5109

WHEN THIS MODEL IS OPERATED IN 5500 WATT MODE:
THE FIRST HOUR RATING IS 51 GALLONS.
THE ESTIMATED ANNUAL ENERGY CONSUMPTION IS 4952 KWH.
THE ESTIMATED YEARLY OPERATING COST IS $416

KWH/YEAR IS A MEASURE OF ENERGY USE. YOUR UTILITY COMPANY USES IT TO COMPUTE YOUR BILL. ONLY MODELS WITH FIRST HOUR RATINGS OF 41 TO 47 GALLONS ARE USED IN THIS SCALE.

ELECTRIC WATER HEATERS THAT USE FEWER
KWH/YEAR COST LESS TO OPERATE. THIS
MODEL'S ESTIMATED YEARLY OPERATING COST IS:
$415

BASED ON A 1994 U.S. GOVERNMENT NATIONAL AVERAGE COST OF $0.0841 PER
KWH. FOR ELECTRICITY, YOUR ACTUAL OPERATING COST WILL VARY DEPENDING
ON YOUR LOCAL UTILITY.

SECTION 9.3 REVIEW

SUMMARY

▶ Heating and cooling systems regulate temperature by transferring energy.

▶ Usable energy decreases during any process in which energy is transferred.

▶ The total amount of energy, both usable and unusable, is constant in any process.

▶ In heating systems, energy is transferred to a fluid, which then transfers its energy to the air in rooms.

▶ Heating systems use fuel-burning furnaces or sunlight for heating.

▶ Refrigerators and air conditioners use the evaporation of a refrigerant for cooling.

CHECK YOUR UNDERSTANDING

1. **Explain** how evaporation is a cooling process.
2. **List** one type of home heating system, and describe how it transfers energy to warm the air inside the rooms.
3. **Describe** how energy changes from a usable form to a less usable form in a building's heating system.
4. **Compare** the advantages and disadvantages of using a solar heating system in your geographical area.
5. **Critical Thinking** Water has a high specific heat, meaning it takes a good deal of energy to raise its temperature. For this reason, the cost of heating water is a large part of a monthly household energy bill. Describe two ways the people in your household could change their routines, without sacrificing results, in order to save money by using less hot water.
6. **Create** a spreadsheet to calculate the rate of energy transfer for each of the substances listed in **Table 9-2.** This rate can be determined using the following equation.

$$rate\ of\ energy\ transfer = \frac{(area) \times (temp.\ diff.)}{(R\text{-}value)}$$

Assume an area of 1.0 m² and a temperature difference of 20.0°C.

CHAPTER 9

Chapter Highlights

Before you begin, review the summaries of the key ideas of each section, found on pages 296, 304, and 312. The key vocabulary terms are listed on pages 290, 297, and 305.

UNDERSTANDING CONCEPTS

1. Temperature is proportional to the average kinetic energy of particles in an object. Thus an increase in temperature results in a(n)_____.
   a. increase in mass
   b. decrease in average kinetic energy
   c. increase in average kinetic energy
   d. decrease in mass

2. As measured on the Celsius scale, the temperature at which ice melts is _____.
   a. −273°C   c. 32°C
   b. 0°C   d. 100°C

3. As measured on the Fahrenheit scale, the temperature at which water boils is _____.
   a. 32°F   c. 100°F
   b. 212°F   d. 451°F

4. The temperature at which the particles of a substance have no more kinetic energy to transfer is _____.
   a. −273 K   c. 0°C
   b. 0 K   d. 273 K

5. Which kind of energy transfer can occur in empty space?
   a. convection   c. conduction
   b. contraction   d. radiation

6. Campfires transfer energy as heat to their surroundings by methods of _____.
   a. convection and conduction
   b. convection and radiation
   c. conduction and radiation
   d. convection, conduction, and radiation

7. The amount of energy required to raise the temperature of 1 kg of a substance by 1 K is determined by its _____.
   a. *R*-value
   b. usable energy
   c. specific heat
   d. convection current

8. The amount of usable energy decreases when _____.
   a. systems are used only for heating
   b. systems are used only for cooling
   c. systems are used for heating or cooling
   d. the heating or cooling system is poorly designed

9. A refrigerant in a cooling system cools the surrounding air _____.
   a. as it evaporates
   b. as it condenses
   c. both as it evaporates and as it condenses
   d. when it neither evaporates nor condenses

10. Solar heating systems are classified as _____.
    a. positive and negative
    b. active and passive
    c. AC and DC
    d. active and indirect

Using Vocabulary

11. Why is it incorrect to say that an object contains *heat*?

12. Use the concepts of average particle kinetic energy, *temperature,* and *absolute zero* to predict whether an object at 0°C or an object at 0 K will transfer more energy as heat to its surroundings.

13. How would a *thermometer* that measures temperatures using the Kelvin scale differ from one that measures temperatures using the Celsius scale?

14. Explain how water can transfer energy by *conduction* and by *convection.*

15. Explain how *convection currents* form updrafts near tall mountain ranges along deserts, as shown in the figure below.

16. Use the differences between a *conductor* and an *insulator* and the concept of *specific heat* to explain whether you would rather drink a hot beverage from a metal cup or from a china cup.

17. If you wear dark clothing on a sunny day, the clothing will become hot after a while. Use the concept of *radiation* to explain this.

18. Explain why ammonia, which has a boiling point of −33.4°C, is sometimes used as a *refrigerant* in a *cooling system*. Why would ammonia be less effective in a *heating system*?

BUILDING MATH SKILLS

19. **Temperature Scale Conversion** A piece of dry ice, solid CO_2, has a temperature of −100.°C. What is its temperature in kelvins and in degrees Fahrenheit?

20. **Temperature Scale Conversion** The temperature in deep space is thought to be around 3 K. What is 3 K in degrees Celsius? in degrees Fahrenheit?

21. **Specific Heat** How much energy is needed to raise the temperature of a silver necklace chain with a mass of 22.5 g from room temperature, 25°C, to body temperature, 37°C? (**Hint:** Refer to **Table 9-1** on p. 302)

22. **Specific Heat** How much energy would be absorbed by 550 g of copper when it is heated from 24°C to 45°C? (**Hint:** Refer to **Table 9-1** on p. 302.)

THINKING CRITICALLY

23. **Interpreting Graphics** Graph the Celsius-Fahrenheit conversion equation, plotting Celsius temperature along the *x*-axis and Fahrenheit temperature on the *y*-axis. Use an *x*-axis range from −100°C to 100°C, then use the graph to find the following values:
    a. the Fahrenheit temperature equal to 77°C
    b. the Fahrenheit temperature equal to −40°C
    c. the Celsius temperature equal to 23°F
    d. the Celsius temperature equal to −17°F

24. **Applying Knowledge** If two objects that have the same temperature come into contact with each other, what can you say about the amount of energy that will be transferred between them as heat?

25. **Applying Knowledge** If two objects that have different temperatures come into contact with each other, what can you say about their temperatures after several minutes of contact?

26. **Creative Thinking** Why does a metal doorknob feel cooler to your hand than a carpet feels to your bare feet?

27. **Creative Thinking** Why do the metal shades of desk lamps have small holes at the top ?

28. **Creative Thinking** Why does the temperature of hot chocolate decrease faster if you place a metal spoon in the liquid?

29. **Creative Thinking** If you bite into a piece of hot apple pie, the pie filling might burn your mouth while the crust, at the same temperature, will not. Explain why.

30. Applying Technology Glass can conduct some energy. Double-pane windows consist of two plates of glass separated by a small layer of insulating air. Explain why a double-pane window prevents more energy from escaping your house than a single-pane window.

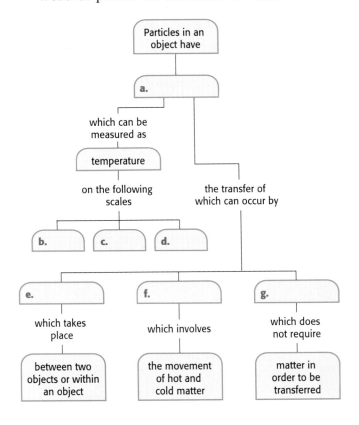

31. Understanding Systems Explain why window unit air conditioners always have the back part of the air conditioner hanging outside. Why is it that the entire air-conditioner cannot be in the room?

32. Making Decisions If the only factor considered were specific heat, which would make a better coolant for automobile engines: water or ethanol? Explain your answer.

DEVELOPING LIFE/WORK SKILLS

33. Allocating Resources In one southern state the projected yearly costs for heating a home were $463 using a heat pump, $508 using a natural-gas furnace, and $1220 using electric radiators. Contact your local utility company to determine the projected costs for the three different systems in your area. Make a table comparing the costs of the three systems.

34. Working Cooperatively Read the following statements, and discuss with a group of classmates which statement is correct. Explain your answer.
  a. Energy is lost when water is boiled.
  b. The energy used to boil water is still present, but it is no longer in a usable form unless you use work or heat to make it usable.

INTEGRATING CONCEPTS

35. Concept Mapping Copy the unfinished concept map below onto a sheet of paper. Complete the map by writing the correct word or phrase in the lettered boxes.

Particles in an object have

a.

which can be measured as

temperature

on the following scales

b. **c.** **d.**

the transfer of which can occur by

e.
which takes place
between two objects or within an object

f.
which involves
the movement of hot and cold matter

g.
which does not require
matter in order to be transferred

36. Connection to Social Studies Research the work of Benjamin Thompson, also known as Count Rumford. What was the prevailing theory of heat during Thompson's time? What observations led to Thompson's theory?

WRITING SKILL

internet**connect**

SC*LINKS*
NSTA

TOPIC: Insulators
GO TO: www.scilinks.org
KEYWORD: HK1105

Design Your Own Lab

Investigating Conduction of Heat

▶ Demonstrating Conduction in Wires

1. Obtain three wires of different thicknesses. Clip a clothespin on one end of one of the wires. Lay the wire and attached clothespin on the lab table.

2. Light the candle and place it in the holder. **SAFETY CAUTION** Tie back long hair and confine loose clothing. Never reach across an open flame. Always use the clothespin to hold the wire as you heat it and move it to avoid burning yourself. Remember that the wires will be hot for some time after they are removed from the flame.

3. Hold the lighted candle in its holder above the middle of the wire, and tilt the candle slightly so that some of the melted wax drips onto the middle of the wire.

4. Wait a couple of minutes for the wire and dripped wax to cool completely. The dripped wax will harden and form a small ball. Using the clothespin to hold the wire, place the other end of the wire in the candle's flame. When the ball of wax melts, remove the wire from the flame, and place it on the lab table. Think about what caused the wax on the wire to melt.

▶ Designing Your Experiment

5. With your lab partner(s), decide how you will use the materials available in the lab to compare the speed of conduction in three wires of different thicknesses. Form a hypothesis about whether a thick wire will conduct energy more quickly or more slowly than a thin wire.

6. In your lab report, list each step you will perform in your experiment.

7. Have your teacher approve your plan before you carry out your experiment.

Introduction

How can you determine whether the thickness of a metal wire affects its ability to conduct energy as heat?

Objectives

▶ **Develop** a plan to measure how quickly energy is transferred as heat through a metal wire.

▶ **Compare** the speed of heat conduction in metal wires of different thicknesses.

Materials

3 metal wires of different thicknesses, each about 30 cm long
clothespin
candle
lighter or matches
candle holder
metric ruler
stopwatch

Safety Needs

goggles
apron

▶ Performing Your Experiment

8. After your teacher approves your plan, you can carry out your experiment.

9. Prepare a data table in your lab report that is similar to the one shown below.

10. Record in your table how many seconds it takes for the ball of wax on each wire to melt. Perform three trials for each wire, allowing the wires to cool to room temperature between trials.

Conductivity Data

	Wire diameter (mm)	Time to melt wax (s)			
		Trial 1	Trial 2	Trial 3	Average time
Wire 1					
Wire 2					
Wire 3					

▶ Analyzing Your Results

1. Find the diameter of each wire you tested. If the diameter is listed in inches, convert it to millimeters by multiplying by 25.4. If the diameter is listed in mils, convert it to millimeters by multiplying by 0.0254. In your data table, record the diameter of each wire in millimeters.

2. Calculate the average time required to melt the ball of wax for each wire. Record your answers in your data table.

3. Plot your data in your lab report in the form of a graph like the one shown. On your graph, draw the line or smooth curve that fits the points best.

4. Reaching Conclusions Based on your graph, does a thick wire or a thin wire conduct energy more quickly?

5. When roasting a large cut of meat, some cooks insert a metal skewer into the meat to make the inside cook more quickly. If you were roasting meat, would you insert a thick skewer or a thin skewer? Why?

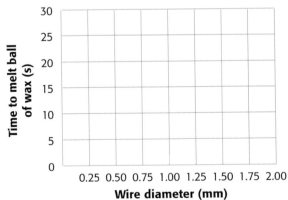

▶ Defending Your Conclusions

6. Suppose someone tells you that your conclusion is valid only for the particular metal you tested. How could you show that your conclusion is valid for other metals as well?

UNIT 4

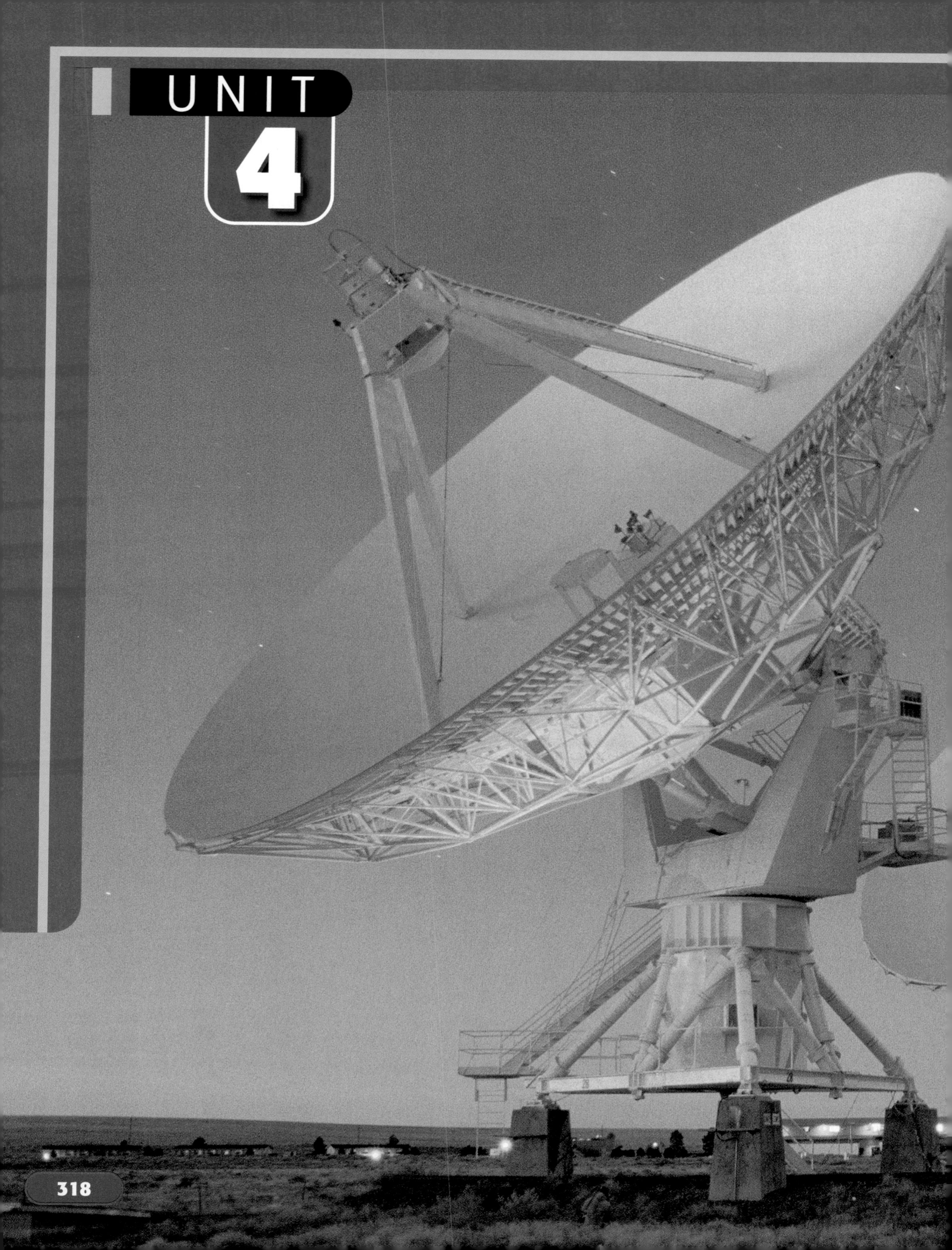

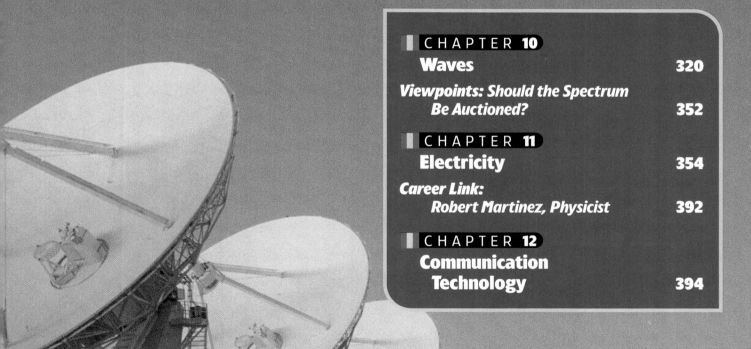

Using Energy

CHAPTER **10**
Waves 320
*Viewpoints: Should the Spectrum
Be Auctioned?* 352

CHAPTER **11**
Electricity 354
*Career Link:
Robert Martinez, Physicist* 392

CHAPTER **12**
**Communication
Technology** 394

Waves

Chapter Preview

10.1 Types of Waves
What Is a Wave?
Vibrations and Waves
Transverse and Longitudinal Waves

10.2 Characteristics of Waves
Wave Properties
Wave Speed
The Doppler Effect

10.3 Wave Interactions
Reflection, Diffraction, and Refraction
Interference
Standing Waves

Focus ACTIVITY

Background The energy in an ocean wave can lift a surfboard up into the air and carry the surfer into shore. Ocean waves get most of their energy from the wind. A wave may start as a small ripple in a calm sea, then build up as the wind pushes it along. Waves that start on the coast of northern Canada may be very large by the time they reach a beach in the Hawaiian Islands.

The winds that create ocean waves are caused by convection currents in the atmosphere, which are driven by energy from the sun. Energy travels across empty space from the sun to Earth—in the form of waves.

Waves are all around us. As you read this book, you are depending on light waves. Light bounces off the pages and into your eyes. When you talk with a friend you are depending on sound waves traveling through the air. Sometimes the waves can be gentle, such as those that rock a canoe in a pond. Other times waves can be very destructive, such as those created by earthquakes.

Activity 1 Fill a long, rectangular pan with water. Experiment with making waves in different ways. Try making waves by sticking the end of a pencil into the water, by moving a wide stick or board back and forth, and by striking the side of the pan. Place wooden blocks or other obstacles into the pan, and watch how the waves change when they encounter the obstacles.

Activity 2 Make a list of things that you do every day that depend on waves. Next to each item, write down what kind of waves you think are involved. Write a short paragraph describing some properties that you think these different kinds of waves may have in common.

A surfer takes advantage of the energy in ocean waves. Energy travels from the sun to Earth in the form of waves.

internetconnect

SC*LINKS*
NSTA

TOPIC: Waves
GO TO: www.scilinks.org
KEYWORD: HK1111

Types of Waves

▶ **KEY TERMS**

wave
medium
mechanical wave
electromagnetic wave
transverse wave
longitudinal wave

OBJECTIVES

▶ Recognize that waves transfer energy.

▶ Distinguish between mechanical waves and electromagnetic waves.

▶ Explain the relationship between particle vibration and wave motion.

▶ Distinguish between transverse waves and longitudinal waves.

When a stone is thrown into a pond, it creates ripples on the surface of the water, as shown in **Figure 10-1.** If there is a leaf floating on the water, the leaf will bob up and down and back and forth as each ripple, or wave, disturbs it. But after the waves pass, the leaf will return to its original position on the water.

What Is a Wave?

Like the leaf, individual drops of water do not travel outward with a wave. They move only slightly from their resting place as each ripple passes by. If drops of water do not move very far as a wave passes, and neither does a leaf on the surface of the water, then what moves along with the wave? Energy does. A wave is not made of matter. A **wave** is a disturbance that carries energy through matter or space.

▶ **wave** a disturbance that transmits energy through matter or space

Figure 10-1
A stone thrown into a pond creates waves.

Most waves travel through a medium

The waves in a pond are disturbances traveling through water. Sound also travels as a wave. The sound from a stereo is a pattern of changes in the air between the stereo speakers and your ear. Earthquakes create waves, called *seismic waves,* that travel through Earth.

In each of these examples, the waves involve the movement of some kind of matter. The matter through which a wave travels is called the **medium.** In the example of the pond, the water is the medium. For sound from a stereo, air is the medium. And in earthquakes, Earth itself is the medium.

Waves that require a medium are called **mechanical waves.** Almost all waves are mechanical waves, with one important exception: electromagnetic waves.

Light does not require a medium

Light can travel from the sun to Earth across the empty space between them. This is possible because light waves do not need a medium through which to travel. Instead, light waves consist of changing electric and magnetic fields in space. For that reason, light waves are also called **electromagnetic waves.**

Visible light waves are just one example of a wide range of electromagnetic waves. Radio waves, such as those that carry signals to your radio or television, are also electromagnetic waves. Other kinds of electromagnetic waves will be introduced in Section 10-2. *In this book, the terms* light *and* light wave *may refer to any electromagnetic wave, not just visible light.*

Waves transfer energy

In Chapter 8, you learned that energy can be defined as the ability to do work. We know that waves carry energy because they can do work. For example, water waves can do work on a leaf, on a boat, or on a beach. Sound waves can do work on your eardrum. Light waves can do work on your eye or on photographic film.

A wave caused by dropping a stone in a pond might carry enough energy to move a leaf up and down several centimeters. The bigger the wave is, the more energy it carries. A cruise ship moving through water in the ocean could create waves big enough to move a fishing boat up and down a few meters.

Connection to ENGINEERING

If you have ever been hit by an ocean wave at the beach, you know these waves carry a lot of energy. Could this energy be put to good use? Research is currently underway to find ways to harness the energy of ocean waves. Some small floating navigation buoys, which shine lights to help ships find their way in the dark, obtain energy solely from the waves. A few larger systems are in place that harness wave energy to provide electricity for small coastal communities.

Making the Connection

1. In a library or on the Internet, research different types of devices that harness wave energy. How much power do some of these devices provide? Is that a lot of power?
2. Design a device of your own to capture the energy from ocean waves. The device should take the motion of waves and convert it into a motion that could be used to drive a machine, such as a pump or a wheel.

▶ **medium** the matter through which a wave travels

▶ **mechanical wave** a wave that requires a medium through which to travel

▶ **electromagnetic wave** a wave caused by a disturbance in electric and magnetic fields and that does not require a medium; also called a light wave

Figure 10-2
This portrait of a tsunami was created by the Japanese artist Hokusai in 1830.

Figure 10-2 shows a woodblock print of a *tsunami,* a huge ocean wave caused by earthquakes. A tsunami may be as high as 30 m when it reaches shore, taller than a 10-story building. Such waves carry enough energy to cause a lot of damage to coastal towns and shorelines. Normal-sized ocean waves do work on the shore, too, breaking up rocks into tiny pieces to form sandy beaches.

Energy may spread out as a wave travels

If you stand next to the speakers at a rock concert, the sound waves may damage your ears. Likewise, if you look at a bright light bulb from too close, the light may damage your eyes. But if you are 100 m away, the sound of the rock band or the light from the bulb is harmless. Why?

Think about waves created when a stone falls into a pond. The waves spread out in circles that get bigger as the waves move farther from the center. Each of these circles, called a *wave front,* has the same amount of total energy. But as the circles get larger, the energy spreads out over a larger area.

When sound waves travel in air, the waves spread out in spheres, as shown in **Figure 10-3.** These spheres are similar to the circular ripples on a pond. As they travel outward, the spherical wave fronts get bigger, so the energy in the waves spreads out over a larger area. This is why large amplifiers and speakers are needed to fill a concert hall with sound, even though the same music can sound just as loud if it is played on a portable radio and listened to with a small pair of headphones.

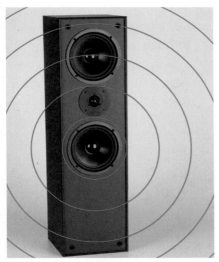

Figure 10-3
Sound waves from a stereo speaker spread out in spherical wave fronts.

Vibrations and Waves

When a singer sings a note, vocal cords in the singer's throat move back and forth. That motion makes the air in the throat vibrate, creating sound waves that eventually reach your ears. The vibration of the air in your ears causes your eardrums to vibrate. The motion of the eardrum triggers a series of electrical pulses to your brain, and your brain interprets them as sounds.

Waves are related to vibrations. Most waves are caused by a vibrating object. Electromagnetic waves may be caused by vibrating charged particles. In a mechanical wave, the particles in the medium also vibrate as the wave passes through the medium.

internetconnect

SCI*LINKS*
NSTA

TOPIC: Vibrations and waves
GO TO: www.scilinks.org
KEYWORD: HK1112

Vibrations involve transformations of energy

Figure 10-4 shows a mass hanging on a spring. If the mass is pulled down slightly and released, it will begin to move up and down around its original resting position. This vibration involves transformations of energy, much like those in a swinging pendulum.

When the mass is pulled away from its resting place, the mass-spring system gains elastic potential energy. The spring exerts a force that pulls the mass back to its original position.

As the spring moves back toward the original position, the potential energy in the system changes to kinetic energy. The mass moves beyond its original resting position to the other side.

At the top of its motion, the mass has lost all its kinetic energy. But the system now has both elastic potential energy and gravitational potential energy. The mass moves downward again, past the resting position, and back to the beginning of the cycle.

Figure 10-4
When a mass hanging on a spring is disturbed from rest, it starts to vibrate up and down around its original position.

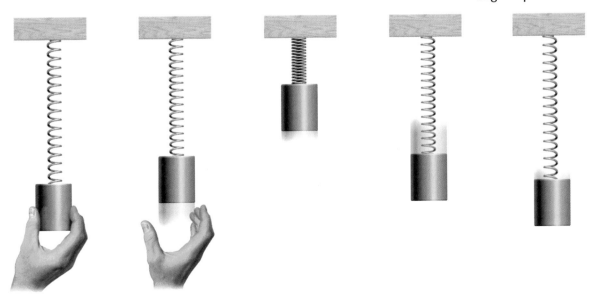

Shock Absorbers:
Why Are They Important?

Bumps in the road are certainly a nuisance, but without strategic use of dampening devices, they could also be very dangerous. To control a car going 100 km/h (60 mi/h), a driver needs all the wheels of the vehicle on the ground. Bumps in the road lift the wheels off the ground and may rob the driver of control of the car.

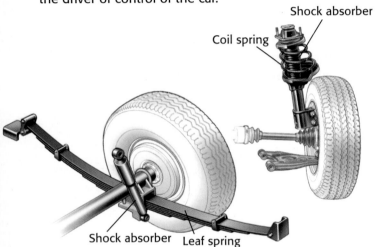

Shock absorber

Coil spring

Shock absorber   Leaf spring

Springs Absorb Energy

To solve this problem, cars are fitted with springs at each wheel. When the wheel of a car goes over a bump, the spring absorbs kinetic energy so that the energy is not transferred to the rest of the car. The energy becomes elastic potential energy in the spring, which then allows the spring to push the wheel back down onto the road.

Springs Alone Prolong Vibrations

Once a spring is set in motion, it tends to continue vibrating up and down in simple harmonic motion. This can create an uncomfortable ride, and it may also affect the driver's control of the car. One way to cut down on unwanted vibrations is to use stiff springs that compress only a few centimeters with thousands of newtons of force. However, the stiffer the spring is, the rougher the ride is and the more likely the wheels are to come off the road.

Shock Absorbers Dampen Vibrations

Modern automobiles are fitted with devices known as shock absorbers that absorb energy without prolonging vibrations. Shock absorbers are fluid-filled tubes that turn the simple harmonic motion of the springs into a damped harmonic motion. In a damped harmonic motion, each cycle of stretch and compression of the spring is much smaller than the previous cycle. Modern auto suspensions are set up so that all a spring's energy is absorbed by the shock absorbers in just one up-and-down cycle.

Shock Absorbers and Springs Come in Different Arrangements

Different types of springs and shock absorbers are combined to give a wide variety of responses. For example, many passenger cars have coil springs with shock absorbers parallel to the springs, or even inside the springs, as shown at near left. Some larger vehicles have heavy-duty leaf springs made of stacks of steel strips. Leaf springs are stiffer than coil springs, but they can bear heavier loads. In this type of suspension system, the shock absorber is perpendicular to the spring, as shown at far left.

The stiffness of the spring can affect steering response time, traction, and the general feel of the car. Because of the variety of combinations, your driving experiences can range from the luxurious "floating-on-air" ride of a limousine to the bone-rattling feel of a true sports car.

Your Choice

1. **Making Decisions** If you were going to haul heavy loads, would you look for a vehicle with coil springs or leaf springs? Why?
2. **Critical Thinking** How do shock absorbers stop an automobile from continually bouncing?

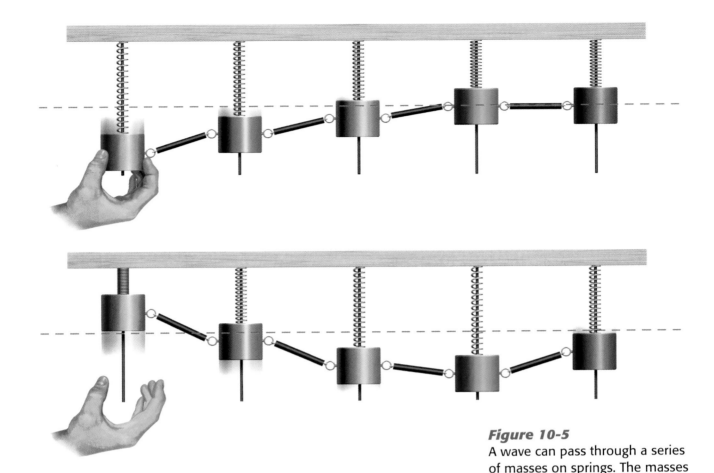

At every point in the motion of the mass, the spring is exerting a force that pushes it back to the original resting position. As a result, the mass could keep bouncing up and down forever. This type of vibration is called *simple harmonic motion.*

A wave can pass through a series of vibrating objects

Imagine a series of masses and springs tied together in a row, as shown in **Figure 10-5.** If you push down on a mass at the end of the row, that mass will begin to vibrate up and down. As the mass on the end moves, it pulls on the mass next to it, causing that mass to vibrate. The energy in the vibration of the first mass, which is a combination of kinetic energy and elastic potential energy, is transferred to the mass-spring system next to it. In this way, the disturbance that started with the first mass travels down the row. This disturbance is a wave that carries energy from one end of the row to the other.

If the first mass were not connected to the other masses, it would keep vibrating up and down on its own. However, because it transfers its energy to the second mass, it slows down and then returns to its resting position. A vibration that fades out as energy is transferred from one object to another is called *damped harmonic motion.*

How do particles move in a medium?

Materials ✔ long, flexible spring ✔ colored ribbon

Procedure

1. Have two people each grab an end of the spring and stretch it out along a smooth floor. Have another person tie a small piece of colored ribbon to a coil near the middle of the spring.
2. Swing one end of the spring from side to side. This will start a wave traveling along the spring. Observe the motion of the ribbon as the wave passes by.
3. Take a section of the spring and bunch it together as shown in the figure at right. Release the spring. This will create a different kind of wave traveling along the spring. Observe the motion of the ribbon as this wave passes by.

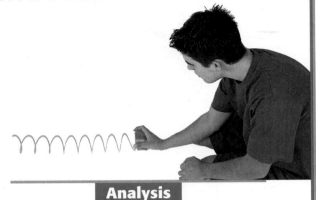

Analysis

1. How would you describe the motion of the ribbon in step 2? How would you describe its motion in step 3?
2. How can you tell that energy is passing along the spring? Where does that energy come from?

The motion of particles in a medium is like the motion of masses on springs

If you tie one end of a rope to a doorknob, pull it straight, and then rapidly move your hand up and down once, you will generate a single wave along the rope, as shown in **Figure 10-6.** A small ribbon tied to the middle of the rope can help you visualize the motion of a single particle of matter in the rope.

As the wave approaches, the ribbon moves up in the air, away from its resting position. As the wave passes farther along the rope, the ribbon drops below its resting position. Finally, after the wave passes by, the ribbon returns to its original starting point. Like the ribbon, each part of the rope moves up and down as the wave passes by.

The motion of each part of the rope is like the vibrating motion of a mass hanging on a spring. As one part of the rope moves up and down, it pulls on the part next to it, transferring energy. In this way, a wave passes along the length of the rope.

Figure 10-6
As this wave passes along a rope, the ribbon moves up and down while the wave moves to the right.

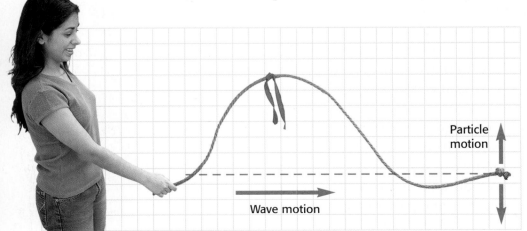

Particle motion

Wave motion

Transverse and Longitudinal Waves

Particles in a medium can vibrate either up and down or back and forth. Waves are often classified by the direction that the particles in the medium move as a wave passes by.

Transverse waves have perpendicular motion

When a crowd does "the wave" at a sporting event, people in the crowd stand up and raise their hands into the air as the wave reaches their part of the stadium. The wave travels around the stadium in a circle, but the people move straight up and down. This is similar to the wave in the rope. Each particle in the rope moves straight up and down as the wave passes by from left to right.

In these cases, the motion of the particles in the medium (in the stadium, the people in the crowd) is perpendicular to the motion of the wave as a whole. Waves in which the motion of the particles is perpendicular to the motion of the wave as a whole are called transverse waves.

Light waves are another example of transverse waves. The fluctuations in electric and magnetic fields that make up a light wave are perpendicular to the direction the light travels. For an illustration, see Section 11.4.

Longitudinal waves have parallel motion

Suppose you stretch out a long, flexible spring on a table or a smooth floor, grab one end, and move your hand back and forth, directly toward and directly away from the other end of the spring. You would see a wave travel along the spring as it bunches up in some spots and stretches in others, as shown in **Figure 10-7.**

As a wave passes along the spring, a ribbon tied to one of the coils of the spring will move back and forth, parallel to the direction that the wave travels. Waves that cause the particles in a medium to vibrate parallel to the direction of wave motion are called longitudinal waves.

Sound waves are an example of longitudinal waves that we encounter every day. Sound waves traveling in air compress and expand the air in bands. As sound waves pass by molecules in the air move backward and forward parallel to the direction that the sound travels.

▶ **transverse wave** a wave that causes the particles of the medium to vibrate perpendicularly to the direction the wave travels

▶ **longitudinal wave** a wave that causes the particles of the medium to vibrate parallel to the direction the wave travels

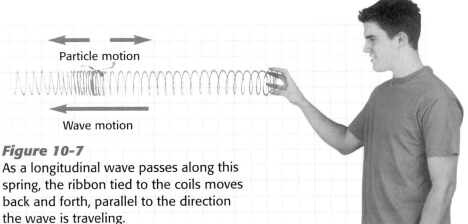

Figure 10-7
As a longitudinal wave passes along this spring, the ribbon tied to the coils moves back and forth, parallel to the direction the wave is traveling.

In a surface wave, particles move in circles

Waves on the ocean or in a swimming pool are not simply transverse waves or longitudinal waves. Water waves are an example of *surface waves*. Surface waves occur at the boundary between two different mediums, such as between water and air. The particles in a surface wave move both perpendicularly and parallel to the direction that the wave travels.

Follow the motion of the beach ball in **Figure 10-8** as a wave passes by traveling from left to right. At first, the ball is in a trough. As the crest approaches, the ball moves to the left and upward. When the ball is very near the crest, it starts to move to the right. Once the crest has passed, the ball starts to fall back downward, then to the left. The up and down motions combine with the side to side motions to produce a circular motion overall.

The beach ball helps to make the motion of the wave more visible. Particles near the surface of the water also move in a similar circular pattern.

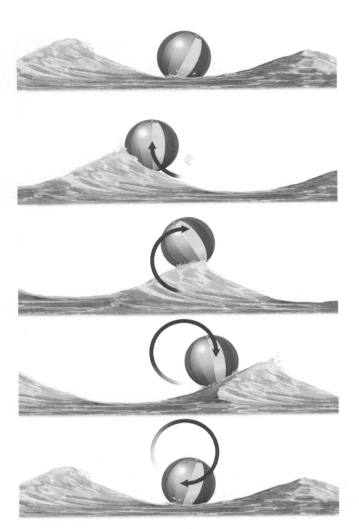

Figure 10-8
Ocean waves are surface waves at the boundary between air and water.

SECTION 10.1 REVIEW

SUMMARY

▶ A wave is a disturbance that carries energy through a medium or through space.

▶ Mechanical waves require a medium through which to travel. Light waves, also called electromagnetic waves, do not require a medium.

▶ Particles in a medium may vibrate perpendicularly to or parallel to the direction a wave is traveling.

CHECK YOUR UNDERSTANDING

1. **Identify** the medium for the following waves:
   a. ripples on a pond
   b. the sound waves from a stereo speaker
   c. seismic waves
2. **Name** the one kind of wave that does not require a medium.
3. **Describe** the motion of a mass vibrating on a spring. How does this relate to wave motion?
4. **Explain** the difference between transverse waves and longitudinal waves. Give an example of each type.
5. **Describe** the motion of a water molecule on the surface of the ocean as a wave passes by.
6. **Critical Thinking** Describe a situation that demonstrates that water waves carry energy.

Characteristics of Waves

▶ Identify the crest, trough, amplitude, and wavelength of a wave.
▶ Define the terms *frequency* and *period.*
▶ Solve problems involving wave speed, frequency, and wavelength.
▶ Describe the Doppler effect.

▶ **KEY TERMS**
crest
trough
amplitude
wavelength
period
frequency
wave speed
Doppler effect

I f you have spent any time at the beach or on a boat, you have probably observed many properties of waves. Sometimes the waves are very large; other times they are smaller. Sometimes they are close together, and sometimes they are farther apart. How can these differences be described and measured in more detail?

Wave Properties

All transverse waves have somewhat similar shapes, no matter how big they are or what medium they travel through. An ideal transverse wave has the shape of a *sine curve,* such as the curve on the graph in **Figure 10-9A.** A sine curve looks like an *S* lying on its side. Sine curves can be used to represent waves and to describe their properties.

Waves that have the shape of a sine curve, such as those on the rope in **Figure 10-9B,** are called *sine waves.* Although many waves, such as water waves, are not ideal sine waves, they can still be modeled with the graph of a sine curve.

Figure 10-9

A A sine curve can be used to demonstrate the characteristics of waves.

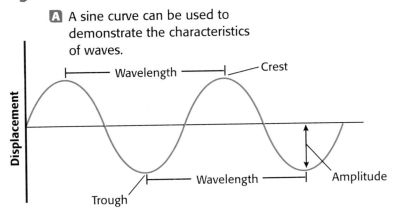

B This transverse wave on a rope is a simple sine wave.

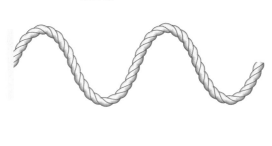

▶ **crest** the highest point of a transverse wave

▶ **trough** the lowest point of a transverse wave

▶ **amplitude** the greatest distance that particles in a medium move from their normal position when a wave passes

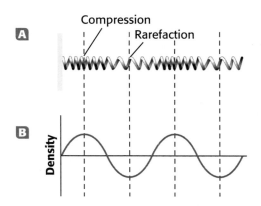

Figure 10-10
(A) A longitudinal wave has compressions and rarefactions. (B) The high and low points of this sine curve correspond to compressions and rarefactions in the spring.

▶ **wavelength** the distance between any two successive identical parts of a wave

PHYSICAL SCIENCE INTERACTIVE TUTOR

Disc Two, Module 12:
Frequency and Wavelength
Use the Interactive Tutor to learn more about these topics.

Amplitude measures the amount of particle vibration

The highest points of a transverse wave are called **crests.** The lowest parts of a transverse wave are called troughs. The greatest distance that particles are displaced from their normal resting positions because of a wave is called the **amplitude.** The amplitude is also half the vertical distance between a crest and a trough. Larger waves have bigger amplitudes and carry more energy.

But what about longitudinal waves? These waves do not have crests and troughs because they cause particles to move back and forth instead of up and down. If you make a longitudinal wave in a spring, you will see a moving pattern of areas where the coils are bunched up alternating with areas where the coils are stretched out. The crowded areas are called *compressions.* The stretched-out areas are called *rarefactions.* **Figure 10-10A** illustrates these properties of a longitudinal wave.

Figure 10-10B shows a graph of a longitudinal wave. Density or pressure of the medium is plotted on the vertical axis; the horizontal axis represents the distance along the spring. The resulting curve is a sine curve. The amplitude of a longitudinal wave is the maximum deviation from the normal density or pressure of the medium, which is shown by the high and low points on the graph.

Wavelength measures the distance between two equivalent parts of a wave

Waves crashing on the shore at a beach may be several meters apart, while ripples in a pond may be only a few centimeters apart. Crests of a light wave may be separated by only billionths of a meter.

The distance from one crest of a wave to the next crest, or from one trough to the next trough, is called the **wavelength.** In a longitudinal wave, the wavelength is the distance between two compressions or between two rarefactions. The wavelength is the measure of the distance between any two successive identical parts of a wave.

When used in equations, wavelength is represented by the Greek letter lambda, λ. Because wavelength is a distance measurement, it is expressed in the SI unit meters.

The period measures how long it takes for waves to pass by

If you swim out into the ocean until your feet can no longer touch the bottom, your body will be free to move up and down as waves come into shore. As your body rises and falls, you can count off the number of seconds between two successive waves.

The time required for one full wavelength of a wave to pass a certain point is called the **period** of the wave. The period is also the time required for one complete vibration of a particle in a medium—or of a swimmer in the ocean. In equations, the period is represented by the symbol T. Because the period is a time measurement, it is expressed in the SI unit seconds.

Frequency measures the rate of vibrations

While swimming in the ocean or floating in an inner tube, as shown in **Figure 10-11,** you could also count the number of crests that pass by in a certain time, say in 1 minute. The **frequency** of a wave is the number of full wavelengths that pass a point in a given time interval. The frequency of a wave also measures how rapidly vibrations occur in the medium, at the source of the wave, or both.

The symbol for frequency is f. The SI unit for measuring frequency is hertz (Hz), named after Heinrich Hertz, who in 1888 became the first person to experimentally demonstrate electromagnetic waves. Hertz units measure the number of vibrations per second. One vibration per second is 1 Hz, two vibrations per second is 2 Hz, and so on. You can hear sounds with frequencies as low as 20 Hz and as high as 20 000 Hz. When you hear a sound at 20 000 Hz, there are 20 000 compressions hitting your ear every second.

The frequency and period of a wave are related. If more vibrations are made in a second, each one takes a shorter amount of time. In other words, the frequency is the inverse of the period.

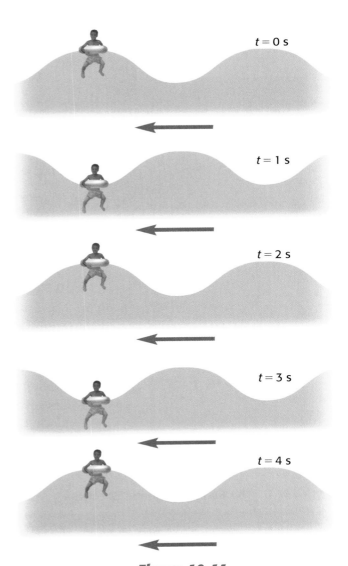

t = 0 s

t = 1 s

t = 2 s

t = 3 s

t = 4 s

Figure 10-11
A person floating in an inner tube can determine the period and frequency of the waves by counting off the number of seconds between wave crests.

Frequency-Period Equation

$$frequency = \frac{1}{period} \qquad f = \frac{1}{T}$$

In the inner tube example, a wave crest passes the inner tube every 2 s, so the period is 2 s. The frequency can be found by dividing the number of crests in a 4 s time interval by 4 s. Because 2 waves pass every 4 s, the frequency is 0.5 Hz, or half a wave per second. Note that 0.5 (1/2) is the inverse of 2.

■ **period** the time required for one full wavelength to pass a certain point

■ **frequency** the number of vibrations that occur in a 1 s time interval

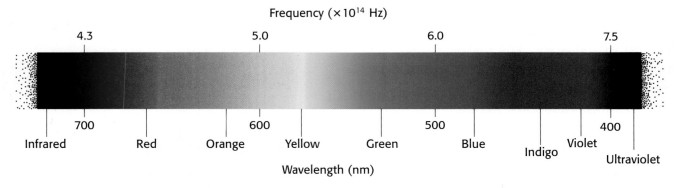

Figure 10-12
The part of the electromagnetic spectrum that we can see is called visible light.

Light comes in a wide range of frequencies and wavelengths

Our eyes can detect light with frequencies ranging from 4.3×10^{14} Hz to 7.5×10^{14} Hz. Light in this range is called *visible light*. The differences in frequency in visible light account for the different colors we see, as shown in **Figure 10-12.**

Electromagnetic waves also exist at other frequencies that we cannot see directly. The full range of light at different frequencies and wavelengths is called the *electromagnetic spectrum*. **Table 10-1** lists several different parts of the electromagnetic spectrum, along with some real-world applications of the different kinds of waves.

Table 10-1   **The Electromagnetic Spectrum**

Type of waves	Range of frequency and wavelength	Applications
Radio waves	$f < 1 \times 10^9$ Hz $\lambda > 30$ cm	AM and FM radio; television broadcasting; radar; aircraft navigation
Microwaves	1×10^9 Hz $< f < 3 \times 10^{11}$ Hz 30 cm $> \lambda > 1$ mm	Atomic and molecular research; microwave ovens
Infrared (IR) waves	3×10^{11} Hz $< f < 4.3 \times 10^{14}$ Hz 1 mm $> \lambda > 700$ nm	Infrared photography; physical therapy; heat radiation
Visible light	4.3×10^{14} Hz $< f < 7.5 \times 10^{14}$ Hz 700 nm (red) $> \lambda > 400$ nm (violet)	Visible-light photography; optical microscopes; optical telescopes
Ultraviolet (UV) light	7.5×10^{14} Hz $< f < 5 \times 10^{15}$ Hz 400 nm $> \lambda > 60$ nm	Sterilizing medical instruments; identifying fluorescent minerals
X rays	5×10^{15} Hz $< f < 3 \times 10^{21}$ Hz 60 nm $> \lambda > 1 \times 10^{-4}$ nm	Medical examination of bones, teeth, and organs; cancer treatments
Gamma rays	3×10^{18} Hz $< f < 3 \times 10^{22}$ Hz 0.1 nm $> \lambda > 1 \times 10^{-5}$ nm	Food irradiation; studies of structural flaws in thick materials

Wave Speed

Imagine watching as water waves move past a post at a dock such as the one in **Figure 10-13.** If you count the number of crests passing the post for 10 s, you can determine the frequency of the waves by dividing the number of crests you count by 10 s. If you measure the distance between crests, you can find the wavelength of the wave. But how fast are the water waves moving?

Wave speed equals frequency times wavelength

In Chapter 7, you learned that the speed of a moving object is found by dividing the distance an object travels by the time interval during which it travels that distance. Recall the speed equation from Section 7.1.

$$speed = \frac{distance}{time}$$

$$v = \frac{d}{t}$$

The **wave speed** is simply how fast a wave moves. Finding the speed of a wave is just like finding the speed of a moving object. You need to measure how far a wave travels in a certain amount of time.

For a wave, it is most convenient to use the wavelength as the distance traveled. The amount of time it takes the wave to travel a distance of one wavelength is the period. Substituting these into the speed equation gives an equation that can be used to calculate the speed of a wave.

$$speed = \frac{wavelength}{period}$$

$$v = \frac{\lambda}{T}$$

Because the period is the inverse of the frequency, dividing by the period is equivalent to multiplying by the frequency. Therefore, the speed of a wave can also be calculated by multiplying the wavelength by the frequency.

> **Wave Speed Equation**
> $$wave\ speed = frequency \times wavelength$$
> $$v = f \times \lambda$$

Suppose that waves passing by a post at a dock have a wavelength of 5 m, and two waves pass by in 10 s. In other words, 10 m of wave pass by in 10 s. Each second 1 m of the wave passes by the post. The waves in this case travel with a wave speed of 1 m/s.

Figure 10-13
By observing the frequency and wavelength of waves passing a dock, you can calculate the speed of the waves.

▶ **wave speed** the speed at which a wave passes through a medium

INTEGRATING

EARTH SCIENCE
Earthquakes create waves, called *seismic waves,* that travel through Earth. There are two main types of seismic waves, *P waves* (primary waves) and *S waves* (secondary waves).

P waves travel faster than S waves, so the P waves arrive at a given location first. P waves are longitudinal waves that tend to shake the ground from side to side.

S waves move more slowly than P waves but also carry more energy. S waves are transverse waves that shake the ground up and down, often damaging buildings and roads.

Math Skills

Wave Speed The string of a piano that produces the note middle C vibrates with a frequency of 264 Hz. If the sound waves produced by this string have a wavelength in air of 1.30 m, what is the speed of sound in air?

1 List the given and unknown values.
    Given: *frequency, f* = 264 Hz
              wavelength, λ = 1.30 m
    Unknown: *wave speed, v* = ? m/s

2 Write the equation for wave speed.
    $v = f \times \lambda$

3 Insert the known values into the equation, and solve.
    $v = 264 \text{ Hz} \times 1.30 \text{ m} = 264 \text{ s}^{-1} \times 1.30 \text{ m}$
    $v = 343 \text{ m/s}$

Practice HINT

▶ When a problem requires you to calculate wave speed, you can use the wave speed equation on the previous page.

▶ The wave speed equation can also be rearranged to isolate frequency on the left in the following way:
$$v = f \times \lambda$$
Divide both sides by λ.
$$\frac{v}{\lambda} = \frac{f \times \lambda}{\lambda}$$
$$f = \frac{v}{\lambda}$$

You will need to use this form of the equation in Practice Problem 3.

▶ In Practice Problem 4, you will need to rearrange the equation to isolate wavelength on the left.

Practice

Wave Speed

1. The average wavelength in a series of ocean waves is 15.0 m. A wave arrives on average every 10.0 s, so the frequency is 0.100 Hz. What is the average speed of the waves?

2. An FM radio station broadcasts electromagnetic waves at a frequency of 94.5 MHz (9.45×10^7 Hz). These radio waves have a wavelength of 3.17 m. What is the speed of the waves?

3. Green light has a wavelength of 5.20×10^{-7} m. The speed of light is 3.00×10^8 m/s. Calculate the frequency of green light waves with this wavelength.

4. The speed of sound in air is about 340 m/s. What is the wavelength of a sound wave with a frequency of 220 Hz (on a piano, the A below middle C)?

The speed of a wave depends on the medium

Sound waves travel through air. If they didn't, you wouldn't be able to have a conversation with a friend or hear music from a radio across the room. Because sound travels very fast, you don't notice a time delay in most normal situations. The speed of sound in air is about 340 m/s.

If you swim with your head underwater, you may hear certain sounds very clearly. Sound waves travel better—and three to four times faster—in water than in air. Dolphins, such as those in **Figure 10-14,** use sound waves to communicate with one another over long distances underwater. Sound waves travel even faster in solids than in air or in water. Sound waves have speeds 15 to 20 times faster in rock or metal than in air.

If someone strikes a long steel rail with a hammer at one end and you listen for the sound at the other end, you might hear two bangs. The first sound comes through the steel rail itself and reaches you shortly before the second sound, which travels through the air.

The speed of a wave depends on the medium. In a given medium, though, the speed of waves is constant. No matter how fast you shake your hand up and down to create waves on a rope, the waves will travel the same speed. Shaking your hand faster just increases the frequency and decreases the wavelength.

Figure 10-14
Dolphins use sound waves to communicate with one another. Sound travels three to four times faster in water than in air.

Kinetic theory explains differences in wave speed

The arrangement of particles in a medium determines how well waves travel through it. As you learned in Chapter 2, the different states of matter are due to different degrees of organization at the particle level.

In gases, the molecules are far apart and move around randomly. A molecule must travel through a lot of empty space before it bumps into another molecule. Waves don't travel as fast in gases.

In liquids, such as water, the molecules are much closer together. But they are also free to slide past one another. As a result, vibrations are transferred more quickly from one molecule to the next than they are in a gas. This situation can be compared to vibrating masses on springs that are so close together that the masses rub against each other.

In a solid, molecules are not only closer together but also tightly bound to each other. The effect is like having vibrating masses that are glued together. When one mass starts to vibrate, all the others start to vibrate almost immediately. As a result, waves travel very quickly through solids.

Light has a finite speed

When you flip a light switch, light seems to fill the room instantly. However, light does take time to travel from place to place. All electromagnetic waves in empty space travel at the same speed, the speed of light, which is 3×10^8 m/s (186 000 mi/s). The speed of light constant is often represented by the symbol c. Light travels slower when it has to pass through a medium such as air or water.

Quick ACTIVITY

Wave Speed

1. Place a rectangular pan on a level surface, and fill the pan with water to a depth of about 2 cm.
2. Cut a wooden dowel (3 cm in diameter or thicker) to a length slightly less than the width of the pan, and place the dowel in one end of the pan.
3. Move the dowel slowly back and forth, and observe the length of the wave generated.
4. Now roll the dowel back and forth faster (increased frequency). How does that affect the wavelength?
5. Do the waves always travel the same speed in the pan?

The Doppler Effect

Imagine that you are standing on a corner as an ambulance rushes by. As the ambulance passes, the sound of the siren changes from a high pitch to a lower pitch. Why? Do the sound waves produced by the siren change as the ambulance goes by? How does the motion of the ambulance affect the sound?

Pitch is determined by the frequency of sound waves

The *pitch* of a sound, how high or low it is, is determined by the frequency at which sound waves strike the eardrum in your ear. A higher-pitched sound is caused by sound waves of higher frequency. As you know from the wave speed equation, frequency and wavelength are also related to the speed of a wave.

Suppose you could see the sound waves from the ambulance siren when the ambulance is at rest. You would see the sound waves traveling out from the siren in circular wave fronts, as shown in **Figure 10-15A.** The distance between two successive wave fronts shows the wavelength of the sound waves. When the sound waves reach your ears, they have a frequency equal to the number of wave fronts that strike your eardrum each second. That frequency determines the pitch of the sound that you hear.

Figure 10-15

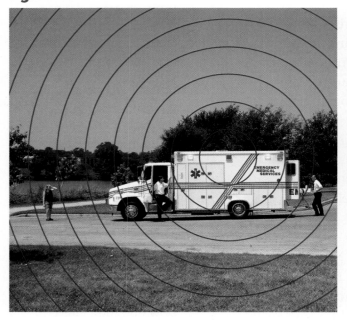

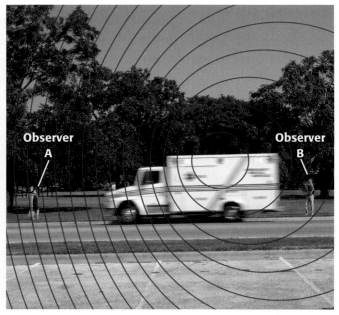

A When an ambulance is not moving, the sound waves produced by the siren spread out in circles. The frequency of the waves is the same at any location.

B When an ambulance is moving, the sound waves produced by the siren are closer together in front and farther apart behind. Observer A hears a higher-pitched sound than Observer B hears.

Frequency changes when the source of waves is moving

If the ambulance is moving toward you, the sound waves from the siren are compressed in the direction of motion, as shown in **Figure 10-15B.** Between the time that one sound wave and the next sound wave are emitted by the siren, the ambulance moves a short distance. This shortens the distance between successive wave fronts. As a result, the sound waves reach your ear at a faster rate, that is, at a higher frequency.

Because the waves now have a higher frequency, you hear a higher-pitched sound than you would if the ambulance were at rest. Similarly, if the ambulance were moving away from you, the frequency at which the waves reached your ear would be less than if the ambulance were at rest, and you would hear the sound of the siren at a lower pitch. This change in the observed frequency of a wave resulting from the motion of the source or observer is called the **Doppler effect.** The Doppler effect occurs for light and other types of waves as well.

internetconnect

SC*LINKS*
NSTA

TOPIC: Doppler effect
GO TO: www.scilinks.org
KEYWORD: HK1114

▶ **Doppler effect** an observed change in the frequency of a wave when the source or observer is moving

---

SECTION 10.2 REVIEW

SUMMARY

▶ The highest points of a transverse wave are called crests; the lowest parts are called troughs.

▶ The amplitude of a transverse wave is half the vertical distance between a crest and a trough.

▶ The wavelength is the distance between two successive identical parts of a wave.

▶ The period of a wave is the time it takes a wavelength to pass a certain point.

▶ The frequency of a wave is the number of vibrations that occur in 1 s. (1 Hz = 1 vibration/s)

▶ The speed of a wave equals the frequency times the wavelength. ($v = f \times \lambda$)

CHECK YOUR UNDERSTANDING

1. **Draw** a sine curve, and label a crest, a trough, and the amplitude.
2. **State** the SI units used for wavelength, period, frequency, and wave speed.
3. **Describe** how the frequency and period of a wave are related.
4. **Explain** why sound waves travel faster in liquids or solids than in air.
5. **Critical Thinking** What happens to the wavelength of a wave when the frequency of the wave is doubled but the wave speed stays the same?
6. **Critical Thinking** Imagine you are waiting for a train to pass at a railroad crossing. Will the train whistle have a higher pitch as the train approaches you or after it has passed you by?

Math Skills

7. A wave along a guitar string has a frequency of 440 Hz and a wavelength of 1.5 m. What is the speed of the wave?
8. The speed of sound in air is about 340 m/s. What is the wavelength of sound waves produced by a guitar string vibrating at 440 Hz?
9. The speed of light is 3×10^8 m/s. What is the frequency of microwaves with a wavelength of 1 cm?

Wave Interactions

KEY TERMS

reflection
diffraction
refraction
interference
constructive interference
destructive interference
standing wave

OBJECTIVES

▶ Describe how waves behave when they meet an obstacle, pass into another medium, or pass through another wave.
▶ Explain what happens when two waves interfere.
▶ Distinguish between constructive interference and destructive interference.
▶ Explain how standing waves are formed.

PHYSICAL SCIENCE INTERACTIVE TUTOR

***Disc Two, Module 13:* Reflection**
Use the Interactive Tutor to learn more about this topic.

reflection the bouncing back of a wave as it meets a surface or boundary

When waves are simply moving through a medium or through space, they may move in straight lines like waves on the ocean, spread out in circles like ripples on a pond, or spread out in spheres like sound waves in air. But what happens when a wave meets an object or another wave in the medium? And what happens when a wave passes into another medium?

Reflection, Diffraction, and Refraction

You probably already know what happens when light waves strike a shiny surface: they reflect off the surface. Other waves reflect, too. **Figure 10-16** shows two ways that a wave on a rope may be reflected. **Reflection** is simply the bouncing back of a wave when it meets a surface or boundary.

Figure 10-16
(A) If the end of a rope is free to slide up and down a post, a wave on the rope will reflect from the end. (B) If the end of the rope is fixed, the reflected wave is turned upside down.

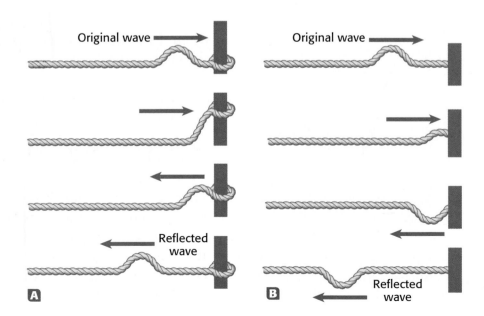

Waves reflect at a free boundary

Figure 10-16A shows the reflection of a single wave traveling on a rope. The end of the rope is free to move up and down on a post. When the wave reaches the post, the loop on the end moves up and then back down. This is just what would happen if someone were shaking that end of the rope to create a new wave. The reflected wave in this case is exactly like the original wave.

At a fixed boundary, waves reflect and turn upside down

Figure 10-16B shows a slightly different situation. In this case, the end of the rope is not free to move because it is attached to a wall. When the wave reaches the wall, the rope exerts an upward force on the wall. The wall is too heavy to move, but it exerts an equal and opposite downward force on the rope, following Newton's third law. The force exerted by the wall causes another wave to start traveling down the rope. This reflected wave is like the original wave, but it is turned upside down and travels in the opposite direction.

Diffraction is the bending of waves around an edge

If you stand outside the doorway of a classroom, you may be able to hear the sound of voices inside the room. But if the sound waves cannot travel in a straight line to your ear, how are you able to hear the voices?

When waves pass the edge of an object or pass through an opening, such as a door, they spread out as if a new wave were created there. In effect, the waves bend around an object or opening. This bending of waves as they pass an edge is called **diffraction.**

Figure 10-17A shows waves passing around a block in a tank of water. Before they reach the block, the waves travel in a straight line. After they pass the block, the waves near the edge bend and spread out into the space behind the block.

The tank in **Figure 10-17B** contains two blocks placed end to end with a small gap in between. In this case, waves bend around two edges and spread out as they pass through the opening. Sound waves passing through a door behave the same way. Because sound waves spread out into the space beyond the door, a person near the door on the outside can hear sounds from inside the room.

diffraction the bending of a wave as it passes an edge or an opening

Figure 10-17
(A) Waves bend when they pass the edge of an obstacle.
(B) When they pass through an opening, waves bend around both edges.

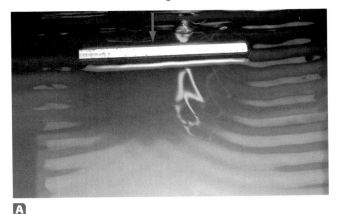

A

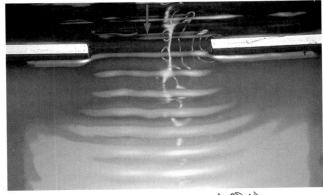

B

Waves can also bend by refraction

Figure 10-18 shows a spoon in a glass of water. Why does the spoon look like it is broken into two pieces? This strange sight results from light waves bending, but not because of diffraction. This time, the waves are bending because of **refraction.** Refraction is the bending of waves when they pass from one medium into another. All waves are refracted when they pass from one medium to another at an angle.

Light waves from the top of the spoon handle pass straight through the air from the spoon to your eyes. But the light waves from the rest of the spoon start out in the water, then pass into the glass, then into the air. Each time the waves enter a new medium, they bend slightly. By the time those waves reach your eyes, they are coming from a different angle than the waves from the top of the spoon handle. But your eyes don't know that; they just see that one set of light waves are coming from one direction, and another set of waves are coming from a different direction. As a result, the spoon appears to be broken.

Figure 10-18
Because light waves bend when they pass from one medium to another, this spoon looks like it is in two pieces.

▶ **refraction** the bending of waves as they pass from one medium to another

▶ **interference** the combination of two or more waves that exist in the same place at the same time

Interference

What would happen if you and another person tried to walk through the exact same place at the same time? You would run into each other. Material objects, such as a human body, cannot share space with other material objects. More than one wave, however, can exist in the same place at the same time.

Waves in the same place combine to produce a single wave

When several waves are in the same location, the waves combine to produce a single, new wave that is different from the original waves. This is called **interference. Figure 10-19** shows interference occurring as water waves pass through each other. Once the waves have passed through each other and moved on, they return to their original shape.

Figure 10-19
Water waves passing through each other produce interference patterns.

You can show the interference of two waves by drawing one wave on top of another on a graph, as in **Figure 10-20.** The resulting wave can be found by adding the height of the waves at each point. Crests are considered positive, and troughs are considered negative.

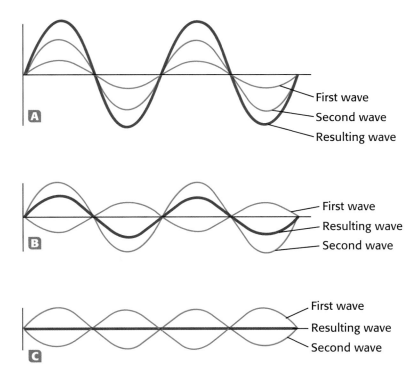

A
First wave
Second wave
Resulting wave

B
First wave
Resulting wave
Second wave

C
First wave
Resulting wave
Second wave

Figure 10-20
Constructive and Destructive Interference
(A) When two waves line up so their crests overlap, they add together to make a larger wave.
(B) When the crest of a large wave overlaps with the trough of a smaller wave, subtraction occurs.
(C) Two waves of the same size may completely cancel each other out.

Disc Two, Module 14: **Refraction**
Use the Interactive Tutor to learn more about this topic.

In constructive interference, amplitudes are added

When the crest of one wave overlaps the crest of another wave, the waves reinforce each other, as shown in **Figure 10-20A.** Think about what happens at the particle level. Suppose the crest of one wave would move a particle up 4 cm from its original position, and another wave crest would move the particle up 3 cm.

When both waves hit at the same time, the particle moves up 4 cm due to one wave and 3 cm due to the other for a total of 7 cm. The result is a wave whose amplitude is the sum of the amplitudes of the two individual waves. This is called constructive interference.

▶ **constructive interference**
any interference in which waves combine so that the resulting wave is bigger than the original waves

In destructive interference, amplitudes are subtracted

When the crest of one wave meets the trough of another wave, the resulting wave has a smaller amplitude than the larger of the two waves, as shown in **Figure 10-20B.** This is called destructive interference.

To understand how this works, imagine again a single particle. Suppose the crest of one wave would move the particle up 4 cm, and the trough of another wave would move it down 3 cm. If the waves hit the particle at the same time, the particle would move in response to both waves, and the new wave would have an amplitude of just 1 cm. When destructive interference occurs between two waves that have the same amplitude, the waves may completely cancel each other out, as shown in **Figure 10-20C.**

▶ **destructive interference**
any interference in which waves combine so that the resulting wave is smaller than the largest of the original waves

Figure 10-21
The colorful swirls on a bubble result from the constructive interference of some colors and the destructive interference of other colors.

Interference of light waves creates colorful displays

The interference of light waves often produces colorful displays. You can see a rainbow of colors when oil is spilled onto a watery surface. Soap bubbles, like the ones shown in **Figure 10-21,** have reds, blues, and yellows on their surfaces. The colors in these examples are not due to pigments or dyes. Instead, they are due to the interference of light.

When you look at a soap bubble, some light waves bounce off the outside of the bubble and travel directly to your eye. Other light waves travel into the thin shell of the bubble, bounce off the inner side of the bubble's shell, then travel back through the shell, into the air and to your eye. Those waves travel farther than the waves reflected directly off the outside of the bubble. At times the two sets of waves are out of step with each other. The two sets of waves interfere contructively at some frequencies (colors) and destructively at other frequencies (colors). The result is a swirling rainbow effect.

Interference of sound waves produces beats

The sound waves from two tuning forks of slightly different frequencies will interfere with each other as shown in **Figure 10-22A.** Because the frequencies of the tuning forks are different, the compressions arrive at your ear at different rates.

When the compressions from the two tuning forks arrive at your ear at the same time, constructive interference occurs, and the sound is louder. A short time later, the compression from one and the rarefaction from the other arrive together. When this happens, destructive interference occurs, and a softer sound is heard. After a short time, the compressions again arrive at the same time, and again a loud sound is heard. Overall, you hear a series of loud and soft sounds called *beats*.

Figure 10-22
(A) When two waves of slightly different frequencies interfere with each other, they produce beats. (B) A piano tuner can listen for beats to tell if a string is out of tune.

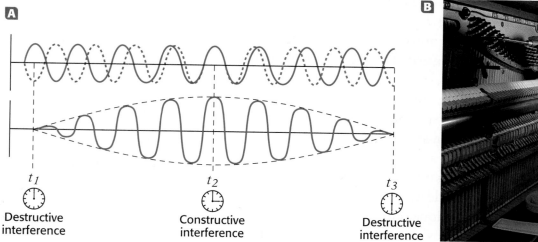

Figure 10-22B shows a piano tuner tuning a string. Piano tuners listen for beats between a tuning fork of known frequency and a string on a piano. By adjusting the tension in the string, the tuner can change the pitch (frequency) of the string's vibration. When no beats are heard, the string is vibrating with the same frequency as the tuning fork. In that case, the string is said to be in tune.

Standing Waves

Waves can also interfere in another way. Suppose you send a wave through a rope tied to a wall at the other end. The wave is reflected from the wall and travels back along the rope. If you continue to send waves down the rope, the waves that you make will interfere with those waves that reflect off the wall and travel back toward you.

Interference can cause standing waves

If the reflected waves have the same amplitude, frequency, and speed as the original waves, then standing waves are formed. Standing waves look very different from normal traveling waves. Standing waves do not move through the medium. Instead, the waves cause the medium to vibrate in a loop or in a series of loops.

Standing waves have nodes and antinodes

Each loop of a standing wave is separated from the next loop by points that have no vibration, called *nodes*. Nodes lie at the points where the crests of the original waves meet the troughs of the reflected waves, causing complete destructive interference.

One of the nodes on a fixed rope string lies at the point of reflection, where the rope cannot vibrate. Another node is near your hand. If you shake the rope up and down fast enough, you can create standing waves with several nodes along the length of the string.

Midway between the nodes lie points of maximum vibration, called *antinodes*. Antinodes form where the crests of the original waves line up with the crests of the reflected waves so that complete constructive interference occurs.

▶ **standing wave** a wave form caused by interference that appears not to move along the medium and that shows some regions of no vibration (nodes) and other regions of maximum vibration (antinodes)

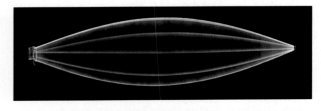

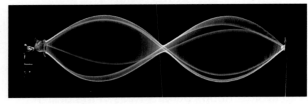

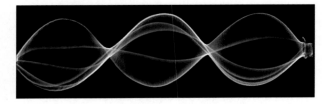

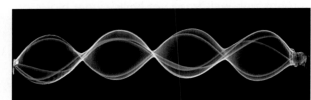

Standing waves can have only certain wavelengths

Figure 10-23 shows several different possible standing waves on a string fixed at both ends. Only a few waves with specific wavelengths can form standing waves in any given string.

The simplest standing waves occur when the wavelength of the waves is twice the length of the string. In that case, it just looks like the entire string is shaking up and down. The only nodes are on the two ends of the string.

If the string vibrates with a higher frequency, the wavelength becomes shorter. At a certain frequency, the wavelength is exactly equal to the length of the string. In the middle of the string, complete destructive interference occurs, producing a node.

In general, standing waves can exist whenever a multiple of half-wavelenths will fit exactly in the length of the string.

Figure 10-23
These photos of standing waves were captured using a strobe light that flashes different colors at different times.

SECTION 10.3 REVIEW

SUMMARY

▶ Waves bouncing off a surface is called reflection.

▶ Diffraction is the bending of waves as they pass an edge or corner.

▶ Refraction is the bending of waves as they pass from one medium to another.

▶ Interference results when two waves exist in the same place and combine to make a single wave.

▶ Interference may cause standing waves.

CHECK YOUR UNDERSTANDING

1. **Describe** what may happen when ripples on a pond encounter a large rock in the water.
2. **Explain** why you can hear two people talking even after they walk around a corner.
3. **Name** the conditions required for two waves to interfere constructively.
4. **Explain** why colors appear on the surface of a soap bubble.
5. **Draw** a standing wave, and label the nodes and antinodes.
6. **Critical Thinking** What conditions are required for two waves on a rope to interfere completely destructively?
7. **Critical Thinking** Imagine that you and a friend are trying to tune the lowest strings on two different guitars to the same pitch. Explain how you could use beats to determine if the strings are properly tuned.
8. **Critical Thinking** Determine the longest possible wavelength of a standing wave on a string that is 2 m long.

Chapter Highlights

Before you begin, review the summaries of the key ideas of each section, found on pages 330, 339, and 346. The key vocabulary terms are listed on pages 322, 331, and 340.

UNDERSTANDING CONCEPTS

1. Waves that need a medium in which to travel are called _____.
   a. longitudinal waves
   b. transverse waves
   c. mechanical waves
   d. All of the above

2. Most waves are caused by _____.
   a. velocity
   b. amplitude
   c. a vibration
   d. earthquakes

3. For which type of waves do particles in the medium vibrate perpendicularly to the direction in which the waves are traveling?
   a. transverse waves
   b. longitudinal waves
   c. P waves
   d. none of the above

4. A sound wave is an example of _____.
   a. an electromagnetic wave
   b. a transverse wave
   c. a longitudinal wave
   d. a surface wave

5. In an ocean wave, the molecules of water _____.
   a. move perpendicularly to the direction of wave travel
   b. move parallel to the direction of wave travel
   c. move in circles
   d. don't move at all

6. Half the vertical distance between the crest and trough of a wave is called the _____.
   a. frequency
   b. crest
   c. wavelength
   d. amplitude

7. The number of waves passing a given point each second is called the _____.
   a. frequency
   b. wave speed
   c. wavelength
   d. amplitude

8. The Doppler effect of a passing siren results from an apparent change in _____.
   a. loudness
   b. wave speed
   c. frequency
   d. interference

9. The combining of waves as they meet is known as _____.
   a. a crest
   b. noise
   c. interference
   d. the Doppler effect

10. Waves bend when they pass through an opening. This is called _____.
    a. interference
    b. diffraction
    c. refraction
    d. the Doppler effect

Using Vocabulary

11. How is an *electromagnetic wave* different from a *mechanical wave*?

12. You have a long metal rod and a hammer. How would you hit the metal rod to create a *longitudinal wave*? How would you hit it to create a *transverse wave*?

13. Identify each of the following as a distance measurement, a time measurement, or neither.
    a. *amplitude*
    b. *wavelength*
    c. *period*
    d. *frequency*
    e. *wave speed*

14. Imagine a train approaching a crossing where you are standing safely behind the gate. Explain the changes in sound of the horn that you may hear as the train passes. Use the following terms in your answer: *frequency, wavelength, wave speed, Doppler effect.*

15. Explain the difference between *constructive interference* and *destructive interference*.

16. Draw a picture of a *standing wave,* and label a *node* and an *antinode.*

BUILDING MATH SKILLS

17. Graphing Draw a sine curve, and label a crest, a trough, and the amplitude.

18. Interpreting Graphics The wave shown in the figure below has a frequency of 25.0 Hz. Find the following values for this wave:
   a. amplitude   **c.** speed
   b. wavelength   **d.** period

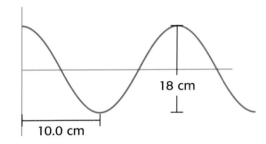

18 cm

10.0 cm

19. Wave Speed Suppose you tie one end of a rope to a doorknob and shake the other end with a frequency of 2 Hz. The waves you create have a wavelength of 3 m. What is the speed of the waves along the rope?

20. Wave Speed Ocean waves are hitting a beach at a rate of 2.0 Hz. The distance between wave crests is 12 m. Calculate the speed of the waves.

21. Wavelength All electromagnetic waves have the same speed in empty space, 3.0×10^8 m/s. Using that speed, find the wavelengths of the electromagnetic waves at the following frequencies:
   a. radio waves at 530 kHz
   b. visible light at 6.0×10^{14} Hz
   c. X rays at 3.0×10^{18} Hz

22. Frequency Microwaves range in wavelength from 1 mm to 30 cm. Calculate their range in frequency. Use 3×10^8 m/s as the speed of electromagnetic waves.

THINKING CRITICALLY

23. Understanding Systems A friend standing 2 m away strikes two tuning forks at the same time, one at a frequency of 256 Hz and the other at 240 Hz. Which sound will reach your ear first? Explain.

24. Applying Knowledge When you are watching a baseball game, you may hear the crack of the bat a short time after you see the batter hit the ball. Why does this happen? (**Hint:** Consider the relationship between the speed of sound and the speed of light.)

25. Understanding Systems You are standing on a street corner, and you hear a fire truck approaching. Does the pitch of the siren stay constant, increase, or decrease as it approaches you? Explain.

26. Applying Knowledge If you yell or clap your hands while standing at the edge of a large rock canyon, you may hear an echo a few seconds later. Explain why this happens.

27. Interpreting Graphics Draw the wave that results from interference between the two waves shown below.

a.    **b.**

28. Understanding Systems An orchestra is playing in a huge outdoor amphitheater, and thousands of listeners sit on a hillside far from the stage. To help those listeners hear the concert, the amphitheater has speakers halfway up the hill. How could you improve this system? A computer delays the signal to the speakers by a fraction of a second. Why is this computer used? What might happen if the signal were not delayed at all?

29. Applying Knowledge Describe how you interact with waves during a typical school day. Document the types of waves you encounter and how often you interact with each. Decide if one type of wave is more important in your life than the others.

30. Applying Technology With your teacher's help, use a microphone and an oscilloscope or a CBL interface to obtain an image of a sound. Determine the frequency and wavelength of the sound.

COMPUTER SKILL

31. Making Decisions A new car is advertised as having antinoise technology. The manufacturer claims that inside the car any sounds are negated. Evaluate the possibility of such a claim. What would have to be created to cause destructive interference with any sound in the car? Would it be possible to have destructive interference everywhere inside the car? Do you believe that the manufacturer is correct in its statement?

32. Working Cooperatively Work with two other classmates to research the types of architectural acoustics that would affect a restaurant. Investigate some of the acoustics problems in places where many people gather. How do odd-shaped ceilings, decorative panels, and glass windows affect echoes and noise. Prepare a model of your school cafeteria showing what changes you would make to reduce the level of noise.

33. Applying Knowledge A piano tuner listens to a tuning fork vibrating at 440 Hz to tune the string of a piano. He hears beats between the tuning fork and the piano string. Is the string in tune? Explain your answer.

34. Concept Mapping Copy the unfinished concept map below onto a sheet of paper. Complete the map by writing the correct word or phrase in the lettered boxes.

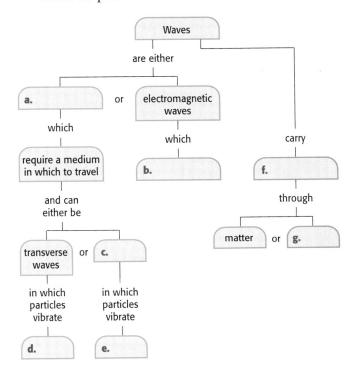

35. Connection to Earth Science What is the medium for seismic waves?

36. Connection to Architecture Buildings in areas prone to earthquakes must be able to withstand mild to severe earthquakes. Research how buildings in earthquake-prone areas, such as Los Angeles, are designed to be able to withstand earthquakes.

internet **connect**

SCI**LINKS**
NSTA

TOPIC: Seismic waves
GO TO: www.scilinks.org
KEYWORD: HK1116

Design Your Own Lab

Modeling Transverse Waves

► Making Sine Curves with a Sand Pendulum

Introduction

A model of a transverse wave may be created with a sand pendulum. What characteristics of waves can you measure using such a model?

Objectives

▶ **Create** sine curves by pulling paper under a sand pendulum.

▶ **Measure** the amplitude, wavelength, and period of transverse waves using sine curves as models.

▶ **Predict** how changes to the experiment may change the amplitude and wavelength.

▶ **Calculate** frequency and wave speed using your measurements.

Materials

paper or plastic-foam cup
nail
string and scissors
masking tape
colored sand
ring stand or other support
rolls of white paper, about 30 cm wide
meterstick
stopwatch

Safety Needs

safety glasses, gloves

1. Review the discussion in Section 10.2 on the use of sine curves to represent transverse waves.

2. On a blank sheet of paper, prepare a table like the one shown at right.

3. Use a nail to puncture a small hole in the bottom of a paper cup. Also punch two holes on opposite sides of the cup near the rim. Tie strings of equal length through the upper holes. Make a pendulum by tying the strings from the cup to a ring stand or other support. Clamp the stand down at the end of a table, as shown in the photograph at right. Cover the bottom hole with a piece of tape, then fill the cup with sand. **SAFETY CAUTION** Wear gloves while handling the nails and punching holes.

4. Unroll some of the paper, and mark off a length of 1 m using two dotted lines. Then roll the paper back up, and position the paper under the pendulum, as shown in the photograph at right.

5. Remove the tape over the hole. Start the pendulum swinging as your lab partner pulls the paper in a direction perpendicular to the cup's swing. Another lab partner should loosely hold the paper roll. Try to pull the paper in a straight line with a constant speed. The sand should trace a sine curve on the paper, as in the photograph at right.

6. As your partner pulls the paper under the pendulum, start the stopwatch when the sand trace reaches the first dotted line marking the length of 1 m. When the sand trace reaches the second dotted line, stop the watch. Record the time in your table.

7. When you are finished making a curve, stop the pendulum and cover the hole in the bottom of the cup. Be careful not to jostle the paper; if you do, your trace may be erased. You may want to tape the paper down.

Length along paper = 1 m	Time (s)	Average wavelength (m)	Average amplitude (m)
Curve 1			
Curve 2			
Curve 3			

8. For the part of the curve between the dotted lines, measure the distance from the first crest to the last crest, then divide that distance by the total number of crests. Record your answer in the table under "Average wavelength."

9. For the same part of the curve, measure the vertical distance between the first crest and the first trough, between the second crest and the second trough, and so on. Add the distances together, then divide by the number of distances you measured. Record your answer in the table under "Average amplitude."

▶ Designing Your Experiment

10. With your lab partners, decide how you will work together to make two additional sine curve traces, one with a different average wavelength than the first trace and one with a different average amplitude.

11. In your lab report, write down your plan for changing these two factors. Before you carry out your experiment, your teacher must approve your plan.

▶ Performing Your Experiment

12. After your teacher approves your plan, carry out your experiment. For each curve, measure and record the time, the average wavelength, and the average amplitude.

13. After each trace, return the sand to the cup and roll the paper back up.

▶ Analyzing Your Results

1. For each of your three curves, calculate the average speed at which the paper was pulled by dividing the length of 1 m by the time measurement. This is equivalent to the speed of the wave that the curve models or represents.

2. For each curve, use the wave speed equation to calculate average frequency.

$$average\ frequency = \frac{average\ wave\ speed}{average\ wavelength} \qquad f = \frac{v}{\lambda}$$

▶ Defending Your Conclusions

3. What factor did you change to alter the average wavelength of the curve? Did your plan work? If so, did the wavelength increase or decrease?

4. What factor did you change to alter the average amplitude? Did your plan work?

viewpoints

Should the Electromagnetic Spectrum Be Auctioned?

In the late 1990s, the Federal Communications Commission (FCC) auctioned off several portions of the electromagnetic spectrum that were not being used for broadcasting or other communications. Many private companies, especially those involved in wireless communications, bought the rights to use parts of the spectrum.

Is this a good way for the government to raise money without increasing taxes? Or should the spectrum be reserved for other uses that will benefit everyone, not just a communications company and its subscribers?

If the spectrum had not been auctioned, would that have left inventors with no way to market new technologies? What will happen if new technologies are invented that require use of the spectrum, but there's not enough of it available?

Auction the Spectrum

> FROM: Derek K., Coral Springs, FL

Private companies, like those involved in wireless communications, do benefit the public even though the companies make a profit. I think we should give the government a little credit. They must know what they are doing.

> FROM: Phillip V., Chicago, IL

By selling unused parts of the spectrum to private companies, the government can earn more money that can be used to fund different programs, without increasing the tax rate. Since no one is currently using the spectrum, why not sell it to someone who will?

Don't Auction ALL of the Spectrum

> FROM: Komal V., Chicago, IL

I think that some of the spectrum should be reserved. All of it should not be auctioned off. Some of the spectrum might be needed in an emergency.

> FROM: Chris C., Lockport, IL

Many companies who bought parts of the spectrum are on the cutting edge of technology. While they advance, they will use their part of the spectrum for newer technologies. However, the spectrum never should have been sold. It should have been leased, because there might be better uses for it in the future.

> FROM: Stacy G., Rochester, MN

I think the spectrum shouldn't be sold. It should be used in ways that will help out many people instead of helping a company become richer.

Don't Auction ANY of the Spectrum

> FROM: Maria D., Chicago, IL

The spectrum should be saved for everyone. Why does it have to be a benefit for the government? If the government collected the $3 trillion that haven't been paid in taxes, along with all the money given to foreign countries, the government could focus on things that would be more beneficial.

> Your Turn

1. **Critiquing Viewpoints** Select one of the statements on this page that you *agree* with. Identify and explain at least one weak point in the statement. What would you say to respond to someone who brought up this weak point as a reason you were wrong?

2. **Critiquing Viewpoints** Select one of the statements on this page that you *disagree* with. Identify and explain at least one strong point in the statement. What would you say to respond to someone who brought up this point as a reason they were right?

3. **Creative Thinking** If the spectrum were leased instead of sold, what should the terms be? For how long and for how much money? Develop a plan and an argument in favor of it, either as a written report, or as a poster or other form of presentation.

4. **Allocating Resources** Suppose you could decide what should be done with eight available frequencies in the electromagnetic spectrum. How would you distribute them among the following categories: emergency use, military use, National Weather Service, radio, television, wireless communication, and remote-control devices? How many frequencies would you leave open for future inventions? Write a paragraph to justify your decisions.

CHAPTER 11

Electricity

Chapter Preview

11.1 Electric Charge and Force
 Electric Charge
 Electric Force

11.2 Current
 Voltage and Current
 Electrical Resistance

11.3 Circuits
 What Are Circuits?
 Series and Parallel Circuits
 Electric Power and Electrical Energy
 Fuses and Circuit Breakers

11.4 Magnets and Electromagnetism
 Magnets
 Magnetic Fields
 Electromagnetism

Electricity arcs across the fusion chamber at Sandia National Laboratory in the large photo above. Video games and all other electrical appliances use the movement of electrons to operate.

Focus ACTIVITY

Background A race car rounds a curve and speeds to the finish line in first place. Afterward, the screen darkens and the driver's score is displayed. Video games let you pretend to drive race cars, fly airplanes, and fight warriors. They are complex pieces of electrical equipment with a detailed video display and computer chips that use electric power supplied by a power plant miles away. And in turn, that energy comes from burning fossil fuels, falling water, the wind, or nuclear fission.

At the Sandia National Laboratory, in New Mexico, powerful electrical arcs are generated in a split second when scientists fire a fusion device. Each electrical arc is similar to a bolt of lightning. A huge number of electrons move across the chamber with each arc. Although they cannot be seen, electrons move inside all electrical devices, including video games. Without electricity, we couldn't make telephone calls, use computers, watch television, or ride in high-speed trains. But electricity is not just important in technology; it is also a vital part of the natural world and every living organism.

Activity 1 Remove the bulb and battery from a flashlight. Can you use the bulb, battery, and a small piece of wire or some aluminum foil to make the light bulb light up? Try connecting the light bulb to the battery in several different ways. What makes the light bulb light up?

Activity 2 Find your electric meter at home. Observe how the horizontal gear moves and the numbers on the dials change. If you have an electric clothes dryer or air conditioner, observe the dials on the meter when one of these appliances is operating. Compare this with the rate of movement of the dials when all the electrical appliances and lights are turned off. Based on your results, what do you think the electric meter measures?

internet connect

SC**LINKS**
NSTA

TOPIC: Applications of the electric spark
GO TO: www.scilinks.org
KEYWORD: HK1131

Electric Charge and Force

KEY TERMS
electric charge
conductor
insulator
electric force
electric field

OBJECTIVES

▶ Indicate which pairs of charges will repel and which will attract.

▶ Explain what factors affect the strength of the electric force.

▶ Describe the characteristics of the electric field due to a charge.

Disc Two, Module 15:
Force Between Charges
Use the Interactive Tutor to learn more about this topic.

When you speak into a telephone, the microphone in the handset changes your sound waves into electric signals. Light shines in your room when you flip a switch. And if you step on a pin with bare feet, your nerves send messages back and forth between your brain and your muscles so that you react quickly. These messages are carried by electric pulses moving through your nerve cells.

Electric Charge

You have probably been shocked from touching a doorknob after walking across a rug on a dry day. This happens because your body picks up **electric charge** as your shoes move across the carpet. Although you may not notice these charges when they are spread throughout your body, you notice them as they pass from your finger to the metal doorknob. You experience this movement of charges as a shock.

electric charge an electrical property of matter that creates a force between objects

Figure 11-1

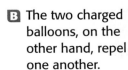

A If you rub a balloon across your hair on a dry day, the balloon and your hair become charged and are attracted to each other.

Like charges repel, and opposite charges attract

One way to observe charge is to rub a balloon back and forth across your hair. You may find that the balloon is attracted to your hair, as shown in **Figure 11-1A.** If you rub two balloons across your hair and then gently bring them near each other, as shown in **Figure 11-1B,** the balloons will push away from, or repel, each other.

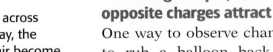

B The two charged balloons, on the other hand, repel one another.

After this experiment, the balloons and your hair have some kind of charge on them. Your hair is attracted to both balloons, yet the two balloons are repelled by each other. This means there must be two types of charges—the type on the balloons and the type on your hair.

The two balloons must have the same kind of charge because each became charged in the same way. Because the two charged balloons repel each other, we see that like charges repel. However, a rubbed balloon and your hair, which did not become charged in the same way, are attracted to one another. This is because unlike charges attract.

The two types of charges are called *positive* and *negative*. When you rub a balloon on your hair, the charge on your hair is positive and the charge on the balloon is negative. When there is an equal amount of positive and negative charges on an object, it has no net charge.

An object's electric charge depends on the imbalance of its protons and electrons

Recall from Section 3.1 that all matter, including you, is made up of atoms. Atoms in turn are made up of even smaller building blocks—electrons, protons, and neutrons. Electrons are negatively charged, protons are positively charged, and neutrons are neutral (no charge).

Objects are made up of an enormous number of neutrons, protons, and electrons. Whenever there is an imbalance in the number of protons and electrons in an atom, molecule, or other object, it has a net electric charge. The difference in the numbers of protons and electrons determines an object's electric charge. Negatively charged objects have more electrons than protons. Positively charged objects have fewer electrons than protons.

The SI unit of electric charge is the *coulomb*, C. The electron and proton have exactly the same amount of charge, 1.6×10^{-19} C. Because they are oppositely charged, a proton has a charge of $+1.6 \times 10^{-19}$ C, and an electron has a charge of -1.6×10^{-19} C. An object with a total charge of -1.0 C has 6.25×10^{18} excess electrons. Because the amount of electric charge on an object depends on the numbers of protons and electrons, the net electric charge of a charged object is always a multiple of 1.6×10^{-19} C.

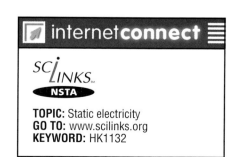

internet**connect**

SC_{LINKS}
NSTA

TOPIC: Static electricity
GO TO: www.scilinks.org
KEYWORD: HK1132

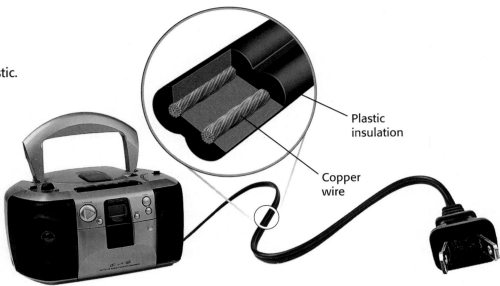

Figure 11-2
Appliance cords are made of metal wire surrounded by plastic. Electric charges move easily through the wire, but the plastic insulation prevents them from leaking into the surroundings.

Plastic insulation

Copper wire

▶ **conductor** a material that transfers charge easily

▶ **insulator** a material that does not transfer charge easily

Conductors allow charges to flow; insulators do not

Have you ever noticed that the electric cords attached to appliances, such as the stereo shown in **Figure 11-2,** are plastic? These cords are not plastic all the way through however. The center of an electric cord is made of thin copper wires twisted together. Cords are layered like this because of the electric properties of each material.

Materials like the metal in cords are called **conductors.** Conductors allow electric charges to move relatively freely. The plastic in the cord, however, does not allow electric charges to move freely. Materials that do not transfer charge easily are called **insulators.** Cardboard, glass, silk, and plastic are insulators.

Charges in the electric cord attached to an appliance can move through the conducting center but cannot escape through the surrounding insulator. This design makes the appliances more efficient and helps protect people from dangerous electric shock.

Objects can be charged by the transfer of electrons

Protons and neutrons are relatively fixed in the nucleus of the atom, but the outermost electrons can be easily transferred from one atom to another. When different materials are rubbed together, electrons can be transferred from one material to the other. The direction in which the electrons are transferred depends on the materials.

For example, when you slide across a fabric car seat, some electrons are transferred between your clothes and the car seat. Depending on the types of materials involved, the electrons can be transferred from your clothes to the seat or from the seat to your clothes. One material gains electrons and becomes negatively charged, and the other loses electrons and becomes positively charged. This is an example of *charging by friction.*

A   B

Figure 11-3
(A) When a negative rod touches a neutral doorknob, electrons move from the rod to the doorknob.
(B) The transfer of electrons to the metal doorknob gives the door- knob a net negative charge.

Objects can also be charged without friction. One way to charge a neutral object without friction is by touching it with a charged object. As shown in **Figure 11-3A,** when the negatively charged rubber rod touches a neutral object, like the doorknob, some electrons move from the rod to the doorknob. The door- knob then has a net negative charge, as shown in **Figure 11-3B.** The rubber rod still has a negative charge, but the charge is smaller. If a positively charged rod touches a neutral doorknob, electrons move into the rod from the neutral doorknob, giving the doorknob a positive charge. Objects charged in this manner are said to be charged by *contact*.

Charges move within uncharged objects

The charges in a neutral conductor can be redistributed without contacting a charged object. If you just bring a negatively charged rubber rod close to the doorknob, the movable electrons in the doorknob will be repelled. Because the doorknob is a conductor, the electrons will move away from the rod. As a result, the portion of the doorknob closest to the negatively charged rod will have an excess of positive charge. The portion farthest from the rod will have a nega- tive charge. But the doorknob will be neutral. Although the total charge on the doorknob will be zero, the opposite sides will have an *induced* charge, as shown in **Figure 11-4.**

Figure 11-4
A negatively charged rod brought near a metal doorknob induces a positive charge on the side of the doorknob closest to the rod and a negative charge on the side farthest from the rod.

Figure 11-5
The negatively charged comb induces a positive charge on the surface of the tissue paper closest to the comb, so the comb and the paper are attracted to each other.

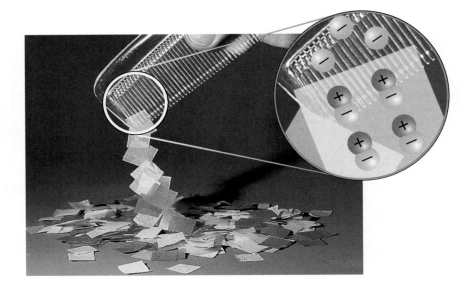

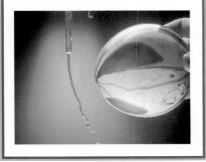

Quick ACTIVITY

Charging Objects

1. Rub two air-filled balloons vigorously on a piece of wool.
2. Hold your balloons near each other.
3. Now try to attach one balloon to the wall.
4. Turn on a faucet, and hold a balloon near the stream of tap water.
5. Explain what happens to the charges in the balloons, wool, water, and wall.

electric force the force of attraction or repulsion between objects due to charge

How can the negatively charged comb in **Figure 11-5** pick up pieces of neutral tissue paper? The electrons in tissue paper cannot move about freely because the paper is an insulator. But when a charged object is brought near an insulator, the positions of the electrons within the individual molecules of the insulator change slightly. One side of a molecule will be slightly more positive or negative than the other side. This *polarization* of the atoms or molecules of an insulator produces an induced charge on the surface of the insulator. The surface of the tissue paper nearest the comb has an induced positive charge. The surface farthest from the comb has an induced negative charge.

Electric Force

The attraction of tissue paper to a negatively charged comb and the repulsion of the two balloons are examples of **electric force.** It is also the reason clothes sometimes cling to each other when you take them out of the dryer. Such pushes and pulls between charges are all around you. For example, a table feels solid, even though its atoms contain mostly empty space. The electric force between the electrons in the table's atoms and your hand is strong enough to prevent your hand from going through the table. In fact, the electric force at the atomic and molecular level is responsible for most of the common forces we can observe, such as the force of a spring and the force of friction.

The electric force is also responsible for effects that we cannot see; it is part of what holds an atom together. The bonding of atoms to form molecules is also due to the electric force. The electric force plays a part in the interactions among molecules, such as the proteins and other building blocks of our bodies. Without the electric force, life itself would be impossible.

Electric force depends on charge and distance

The electric force between two charged objects varies depending on the amount of charge on each object and the distance between them. The electric force between two balloons is proportional to the product of the charges on the balloons.

The electric force is inversely proportional to the square of the distance between two objects. For example, if the distance between two charged balloons is doubled, the electric force between them decreases to one-fourth its original value. If the distance between two charged balloons is quadrupled, the electric force between them decreases to one-sixteenth its original value. Chapter 7 showed that the gravitational force depends on distance in the same way.

Did You Know?

Electric force and gravitational force both depend on a physical property of objects—charge and mass, respectively—and the distance between the objects. They have the same mathematical form. But gravitational force is attractive, while electric force is both attractive and repulsive. Also, the electric force between two charged particles separated by a given distance is much greater than the gravitational force between the particles.

Electric force acts through a field

As described earlier, electric force does not require that objects touch. How do charges interact over a distance? One way to model this property of charges is with the concept of an **electric field.** A charged particle produces an electric field in the space around it. Another charged particle in that field will experience an electric force. This force is due to the electric field associated with the first charged particle.

electric field the region around a charged object in which other charged objects experience an electric force

One way to show an electric field is by drawing *electric field lines.* Electric field lines point in the direction of the electric force on a positive charge. Because two positive charges repel one another, the electric field lines around a positive charge point outward, as shown in **Figure 11-6A.** In contrast, the electric field lines around a negative charge point inward, as shown in **Figure 11-6B.** Regardless of the charge, electric field lines never cross one another.

Figure 11-6

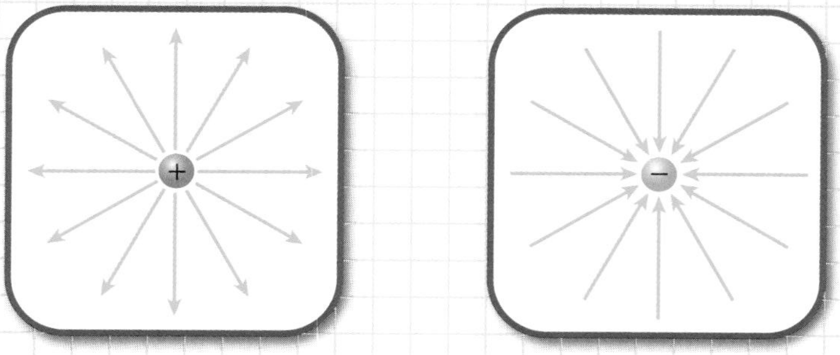

A The electric field lines show that a positive charge placed in the electric field due to a positive charge would be pushed away.

B A positive charge placed in the electric field due to a negative charge would be pulled in.

Figure 11-7

(A) The electric field lines for two positive charges show the repulsion between the charges. (B) Half the field lines starting on the positive charge end on the negative charge because the positive charge is twice as great as the negative charge.

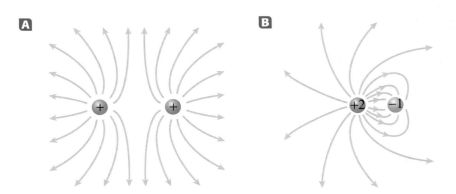

You can see from **Figure 11-7** that the electric field between two charges can be represented using these rules. The field lines in **Figure 11-7A** point away from the positive charges, showing that the positive charges repel each other. Field lines show not only the direction of an electric field but also the relative strength due to a given charge. As shown in **Figure 11-7B,** there are twice as many field lines pointing outward from the +2 charge as there are ending on the −1 charge. More lines are drawn for greater charges to indicate greater force.

SECTION 11.1 REVIEW

SUMMARY

▶ There are two types of electric charge, positive and negative.

▶ Like charges repel; unlike charges attract.

▶ The electric force between two charged objects is proportional to the product of the charges and inversely proportional to the distance between them squared.

▶ Electric force acts through electric fields.

▶ Electric fields surround charged objects. Any charged object that enters a region with an electric field experiences an electric force.

CHECK YOUR UNDERSTANDING

1. **Identify** the electric charge of each of the following atomic particles: a proton, a neutron, and an electron.
2. **Describe** the interaction between two like charges.
3. **Diagram** what will happen if a positively charged rod is brought near the following objects:
   a. a metal washer **b.** a plastic disk
4. **Categorize** the following as conductors or insulators:
   a. copper wire
   b. rubber tubing
   c. your body when your skin is wet
   d. a plastic comb
5. **Explain** how the electric force between two positive charges changes if
   a. the distance between the charges is tripled.
   b. the amount of one charge is doubled.
6. **Critical Thinking** What missing electric charge would produce the electric field shown at right?

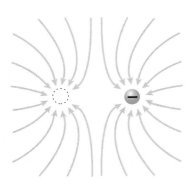

Current

▶ Describe how batteries are sources of voltage.

▶ Explain how a potential difference produces a current in a conductor.

▶ Define *resistance.*

▶ Calculate the resistance, current, or voltage, given the other two quantities.

▶ Distinguish between conductors, superconductors, semiconductors, and insulators.

▶ **KEY TERMS**
electrical potential
  energy
potential difference
cell
current
resistance

When you wake up in the morning, you reach up and turn on the light switch. The light bulb is powered by moving charges. How do charges move through a light bulb? And what causes the charges to move?

Disc One, Module 8:
Batteries and Cells
Use the Interactive Tutor to learn more about these topics.

Voltage and Current

Gravitational potential energy depends on the relative position of the ball, as shown in **Figure 11-8A.** A ball rolling downhill moves from a position of higher gravitational potential energy to one of lower gravitational potential energy. An electric charge also has potential energy—**electrical potential energy**—that depends on its position in an electric field.

Just as a ball will roll downhill, a negative charge will move away from another negative charge. This is because of the first negative charge's electric field. The electrical potential energy of the moving charge decreases, as shown in **Figure 11-8B,** because the electric field does work on the charge.

▶ **electrical potential energy** the potential energy of a charged object due to its position in an electric field

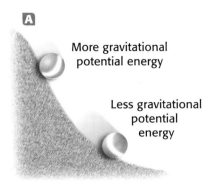

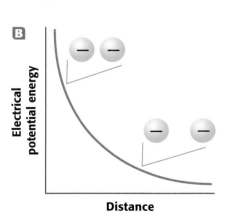

Figure 11-8
(A) The gravitational potential energy of a ball decreases as it rolls downhill. (B) The electrical potential energy between two negative charges decreases as the distance between them increases.

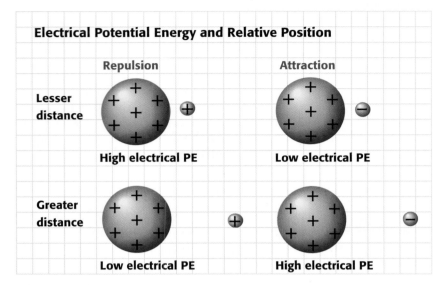

Electrical Potential Energy and Relative Position

	Repulsion	Attraction
Lesser distance	High electrical PE	Low electrical PE
Greater distance	Low electrical PE	High electrical PE

Figure 11-9
The electrical potential energy of a charge depends on its position in an electric field.

▶ **potential difference** the change in the electrical potential energy per unit charge

▶ **cell** a device that is a source of electric current because of a potential difference, or voltage, between the terminals

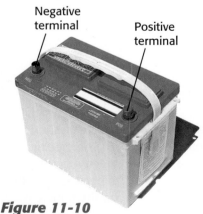

Negative terminal

Positive terminal

Figure 11-10
For a typical car battery, there is a voltage of 12 V across the negative (black) terminal and the positive (red) terminal.

You can do work on a ball to move it uphill. This will increase the ball's gravitational potential energy. In the same way, a force can push a charge in the opposite direction of the electric force. This increases the electrical potential energy associated with the charge's relative position. **Figure 11-9** shows how the electrical potential energy depends on the distance between two charged objects for both an attractive and a repulsive electric force.

Potential difference is measured in volts

When studying electricity, it is more practical to consider the **potential difference** than the electrical potential energy. Potential difference is the change in the electrical potential energy of a charged particle divided by its charge. This change occurs as a charge moves from one place to another in an electric field.

The SI unit for potential difference is the *volt*, V, which is equivalent to one joule per coulomb (1 J/C). For this reason, potential difference is often called *voltage*.

There is a voltage across the terminals of a battery

The voltage across the two *terminals* of a battery can range from about 1.5 V for a small battery to about 12 V for a car battery, as shown in **Figure 11-10.** Most common batteries are an electric **cell**—or a combination of connected electric cells—that convert chemical energy into electrical energy. One terminal is positive, and the other is negative. A summary of various types of electric cells is given in **Table 11-1.**

Electrochemical cells contain an *electrolyte*, a solution that conducts electricity, and two *electrodes*, each a different conducting material. These cells can be dry cells or wet cells. Dry cells, such as those used in flashlights, contain a paste-like electrolyte. Wet cells, such as those used in almost all car batteries, contain a liquid electrolyte. An average cell has a potential difference of 1.5 V between the positive and negative terminals.

A voltage sets charges in motion

When a flashlight is switched on, the terminals of the battery are connected through the light bulb. Electrons move through the light bulb from the negative terminal to the positive terminal.

Table 11-1 **Types of Electric Cells**

Electrical cell	Basic principle	Uses
Electrochemical	Electrons are transferred between different metals immersed in an electrolyte.	Common batteries, automobile batteries
Photoelectric and photovoltaic	Electrons are released from a metal when struck by light of sufficient energy.	Artificial satellites, calculators, streetlights
Thermoelectric	Two different metals are joined together, and the junctions are held at different temperatures, causing electrons to flow.	Thermostats for furnaces and ovens
Piezoelectric	Opposite surfaces of certain crystals become electrically charged when under pressure.	Crystal microphones and headsets, computer keypads, record stylus

When charges are accelerated by an electric field to move to a position of lower potential energy, an electric **current** is produced. Current is the rate that these charges move through a conductor. The SI unit of current is the *ampere*, A. One ampere, or *amp,* equals 1 C of charge moving past a point in 1 second.

▶ **current** the rate that electric charges move through a conductor

A battery is a *direct current* source because the charges always move from one terminal to the other in the same direction. Current can be made up of positive, negative, or a combination of both positive and negative charges. In metals, moving electrons make up the current. In gases and many chemical solutions, current is the result of both positive and negative charges in motion.

In our bodies, current is mostly positive charge movement. Nerve signals are in the form of a changing voltage across the nerve cell membrane. **Figure 11-11A** shows that a resting cell has more negative charges on the inside than on the outside. **Figure 11-11B** shows how a nerve impulse moves along the cell membrane. As one end of the cell is stimulated, channels nearby in the cell membrane open, allowing Na^+ ions to enter. Later, potassium channels open, and K^+ ions exit the cell, restoring the original voltage across the cell membrane.

Figure 11-11

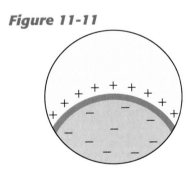

A A resting nerve cell is more negatively charged than its surroundings.

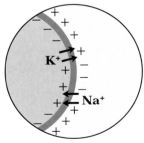

B As a nerve impulse moves along the cell membrane, the voltage across it changes.

Conventional current is defined as movement of positive charge

A negative charge moving in one direction has the same effect as a positive charge moving in the opposite direction. *Conventional current* is defined as the current made of positive charge that would have the same effect as the actual motion of charge in the material. *In this book, the direction of current will always be given as the direction of positive charge movement that is equivalent to the actual motion of charges in the material.* So the direction of current in a wire is opposite the direction that electrons move in that wire.

Which Is the Best Type of Battery?

Heavy-duty, "long-lasting alkaline," and "environmentally friendly rechargeable" are some of the labels that manufacturers put on batteries. But how do you know which type to use?

The answer depends on how you will use the battery. Some batteries are used continuously, but others are turned off and on frequently, such as those used in a stereo. Still other batteries must be able to hold a charge without being used, such as those used in smoke detectors and flashlights.

Heavy-duty Batteries Are Inexpensive

In terms of price, a heavy-duty battery typically costs the least but lasts only about 30 percent as long as an alkaline battery. This makes heavy-duty batteries impractical for most uses and an unnecessary source of landfill clutter.

Regular Alkaline Batteries Are Expensive but Long-lasting

Regular alkaline batteries are more expensive but have longer lives, lasting up to 6 hours with continuous use and up to 18 hours with intermittent use. They hold a full charge for years, making them good for use in flashlights and similar devices. They are less

of an environmental problem than they previously were because manufacturers have stopped using mercury in them. However, because they are single-use batteries, they also end up in landfills very quickly.

Rechargeable Batteries Don't Clutter Landfills

Rechargeable batteries are the most expensive to purchase initially. If recycled, however, they are the most economical in the long run and are the most environmentally sound choice. The most common rechargeable cells are either NiCads—containing nickel, Ni, and cadmium, Cd, metals—or alkaline. Either type of rechargeable battery can be recharged hundreds of times. Although rechargeable batteries last only about half as long on one charge as regular alkaline batteries, the energy to recharge them costs pennies. NiCads lose about 1 percent of their stored energy each day they are not used and should therefore never be used in smoke detectors or flashlights. However, rechargeable alkaline batteries retain a charge like regular batteries and can be used in such devices.

Your Choice

1. **Making Decisions** Which type of battery would you use in a portable stereo? Explain your reasoning.
2. **Critical Thinking** Why is it important not to use NiCads in smoke detectors?
3. **Locating Information** Use library resources or the Internet to learn more about batteries used in gasoline-powered and electric cars. Prepare a summary of the types of rechargeable car batteries available.

internet**connect**

SCI LINKS
NSTA

TOPIC: Batteries
GO TO: www.scilinks.org
KEYWORD: HK1134

Using a Lemon as a Cell

Because lemons are very acidic, their juice can act as an electrolyte. If various metals are inserted into a lemon to act as electrodes, the lemon can be used as an electrochemical cell.

SAFETY CAUTION Handle the wires only where they are insulated.

1. Using a knife, make two parallel cuts 6 cm apart along the middle of a juicy lemon. Insert a copper strip into one of the cuts and a zinc strip the same size into the other.

2. Cut two equal lengths of insulated copper wire. Use wire cutters to remove the insulation from both ends of each wire. Connect one end of each wire to one of the terminals of a galvanometer.

3. Touch the free end of one wire to the copper strip in the lemon. Touch the free end of the other wire to the zinc strip, as shown in the figure at right. Record the galvanometer reading for the zinc-copper cell.

4. Replace the strips of copper and zinc with equally sized strips of different metals. Record the galvanometer readings for each pair of electrodes. Which pair of electrodes resulted in the largest current?

5. Construct a table of your results.

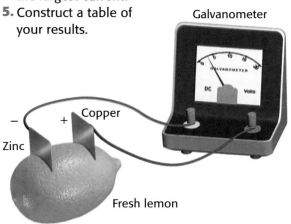

Galvanometer

Copper

Zinc

Fresh lemon

Electrical Resistance

Most electrical appliances you plug into an outlet are designed for the same voltage: 120 V. But light bulbs come in many varieties, from dim 40 W bulbs to bright 100 W bulbs. These bulbs shine differently because they have different amounts of current in them. The difference in current between these bulbs is due to their *resistance.* Resistance is caused by internal friction, which slows the movement of charges through a conducting material. Because it is difficult to measure the internal friction directly, resistance is defined by a relationship between the voltage across a conductor and the current through it.

The resistance of the *filament* of a light bulb, as shown in **Figure 11-12,** determines how bright the bulb is. The filament of a dim 40 W light bulb has a higher resistance than the filament of a bright 100 W light bulb.

▶ **resistance** the ratio of the voltage across a conductor to the current it carries

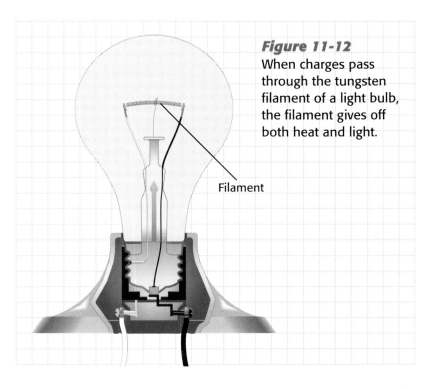

Figure 11-12
When charges pass through the tungsten filament of a light bulb, the filament gives off both heat and light.

Filament

Resistance can be calculated from current and voltage

You have probably noticed that electrical devices such as televisions or stereos become warm after they have been on for a while. As moving electrons collide with the atoms of the material, some of their kinetic energy is transferred to the atoms. This energy transfer causes the atoms to vibrate, and the material warms up. In most materials, some of the kinetic energy of electrons is lost as heat.

A conductor's resistance indicates how much the motion of charges within it is resisted because of collisions. Resistance is found by dividing the voltage across the conductor by the current.

Resistance Equation

$$resistance = \frac{voltage}{current} \qquad R = \frac{V}{I}$$

The SI unit of resistance is the *ohm*, Ω, which is equal to volts per ampere. If a voltage across a conductor of 1 V produces a current of 1 A, then the resistance of the conductor is 1 Ω.

A *resistor* is a special type of conductor used to control current. Every resistor is designed to have a specific resistance. For example, for any applied voltage, the current in a 10 Ω resistor is half the current in a 5 Ω resistor.

Did You Know?

Resistance depends on the material used as well as the material's length, cross-sectional area, and temperature. Longer pieces of a material have greater resistance. Increasing the cross-sectional area of a material decreases its resistance. Lowering the temperature of a material also decreases its resistance.

REAL WORLD APPLICATIONS

The Danger of Electric Shock If you are in contact with the ground, you can receive an electric shock by touching an uninsulated conducting, or "live," wire. An electric shock from such a wire can result in serious burns or even death.

The degree of damage to your body by an electric shock depends on several factors. Large currents are more dangerous than smaller currents. A current of 0.1 A is often fatal. But the amount of time you are exposed to the current also matters. If the current is larger than about 0.01 A, the muscles in the hand touching the wire contract, and you may be unable to let go of the wire. In this case, the charges will continue moving through your body and can cause great damage, especially if the charges pass through a vital organ, such as the heart.

Current (A)	Effect
0.001	Slight tingle
0.005	Pain
0.010	Muscle spasms
0.015	Loss of muscle control
0.070	Probably fatal (if contact is more than 1 second)

Applying Information

1. You can use the definition of *resistance* to calculate the amount of current that would be in a body, given the voltage and resistance. Using the table above as a reference, determine the effect of touching the terminals of a 24 V battery. Assume that your body is dry and has a resistance of 100 000 Ω.

2. If your skin is moist, your body's resistance is only about 1000 Ω. How would touching the terminals of a 24 V battery affect your body if your skin is moist?

Math Skills

Resistance The headlights of a typical car are powered by a 12 V battery. What is the resistance of the headlights if they draw 3.0 A of current when turned on?

1 **List the given and unknown values.**

Given: *current, I* = 3.0 A
voltage, V = 12 V

Unknown: *resistance, R* = ? Ω

2 **Write the equation for resistance.**

$$resistance = \frac{voltage}{current} \qquad R = \frac{V}{I}$$

3 **Insert the known values into the equation, and solve.**

$$R = \frac{V}{I} = \frac{12\ V}{3.0\ A}$$

$$R = 4.0\ \Omega$$

Practice

Resistance

1. Find the resistance of a portable lantern that uses a 24 V power supply and draws a current of 0.80 A.
2. The current in a resistor is 0.50 A when connected across a voltage of 120 V. What is its resistance?
3. The current in a handheld video game is 0.50 A. If the resistance of the game's circuitry is 12 Ω, what is the voltage produced by the battery?
4. A 1.5 V battery is connected to a small light bulb with a resistance of 3.5 Ω. What is the current in the bulb?

Practice HINT

▶ When a problem requires you to calculate the resistance of an object, you can use the resistance equation as shown on the previous page.

▶ The resistance equation can also be rearranged to isolate voltage on the left in the following way:

$$R = \frac{V}{I}$$

Multiply both sides by *I*.

$$IR = \frac{V\cancel{I}}{\cancel{I}}$$
$$V = IR$$

You will need this version of the equation for Practice Problem 3.

▶ For Practice Problem 4, you will need to rearrange the equation to isolate current on the left.

Conductors have low resistances

Whether or not charges will move in a material depends partly on how tightly electrons are held in the atoms of the material. A good conductor is any material in which electrons can flow easily under the influence of an electric field. Metals, like the copper found in wires, are some of the best conductors because electrons can move freely throughout them. Certain metals, conducting alloys, or carbon are used in resistors.

When you flip the switch on a flashlight, the light seems to come on immediately. But the electrons do not travel that rapidly. The electric field is directed through the conductor at almost the speed of light when a voltage source is connected to the conductor. Electrons everywhere throughout the conductor simultaneously experience a force due to the electric field and move in the opposite direction of the field lines. This is why the light comes on so quickly in a flashlight.

Some materials become superconductors below a certain temperature

Certain metals and compounds have zero resistance when their temperature falls below a certain temperature called the *critical temperature*. These types of materials are called *superconductors*. The critical temperature varies among materials, from less than −272°C (−458°F) to as high as −123°C (−189°F).

Metals such as niobium, tin, and mercury and some metallic compounds containing barium, copper, and oxygen become superconductors below their respective critical temperatures. Superconductors have been used in electrical devices such as filters, powerful magnets, and Maglev high-speed express trains.

Insulators have high resistance

Insulators have high resistance to charge movement. So insulating materials are used to prevent electric current from leaking. For example, plastic coating around the copper wire of an electric cord keeps the current from escaping into the floor or your body.

Sometimes it is important to provide a pathway for current to leave a charged object. So a conducting wire is run between the charged object and the ground, thereby *grounding* the object. Grounding is an important part of electrical safety.

How can materials be classified by resistance?

Materials
- ✔ 6 V battery
- ✔ flashlight bulb in base holder
- ✔ 2 wire leads with alligator clips
- ✔ 2 metal hooks
- ✔ block of wood

- ✔ glass stirring rod
- ✔ iron nail
- ✔ wooden dowel
- ✔ copper wire
- ✔ piece of chalk

- ✔ strip of cardboard
- ✔ plastic utensil
- ✔ aluminum nail
- ✔ brass key
- ✔ strip of cork

Procedure

1. Construct a conductivity tester, as shown in the diagram.
2. Test the conductivity of various materials by laying the objects one at a time across the hooks of the conductivity tester.

Analysis

1. What happens to the conductivity tester if a material is a good conductor?
2. Which materials were good conductors?
3. Which materials were poor conductors?
4. Explain the results in terms of resistance.

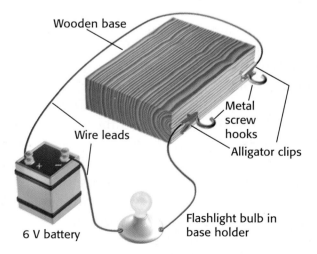

Wooden base

Metal screw hooks

Alligator clips

Wire leads

6 V battery

Flashlight bulb in base holder

Many electrical sockets are wired with three connections: two current-carrying wires and the ground wire. If there is any charge buildup, or if the live wire contacts an appliance, the ground wire conducts the charge to the Earth. The excess charge can spread over the planet safely.

Semiconductors are intermediate to conductors and insulators

Semiconductors belong to a third class of materials with electrical properties between those of insulators and conductors. In their pure state, semiconductors are insulators. The controlled addition of specific atoms of other materials as impurities dramatically increases a semiconductor's ability to conduct electric charge. Silicon and germanium are two common semiconductors. Complex electrical devices, like the computer board shown in **Figure 11-13**, are made of conductors, insulators, and semiconductors.

Figure 11-13
Most electrical devices contain conductors, insulators, and semiconductors.

SECTION 11.2 REVIEW

SUMMARY

▶ A charged object has electrical potential energy due to its position in an electric field.

▶ Potential difference, or voltage, is the difference in electrical potential energy per unit charge.

▶ A voltage causes charges to move, producing a current.

▶ Current is the rate of charge movement.

▶ Electrical resistance can be calculated by dividing voltage by current.

▶ Conductors are materials in which electrons flow easily.

▶ Superconductors have no resistance below their critical temperature.

▶ Insulators are materials with high resistance.

CHECK YOUR UNDERSTANDING

1. **Identify** which of the following could produce current:
   a. a wire connected across a battery's terminals
   b. two electrodes in a solution of positive and negative ions
   c. a salt crystal, whose ions cannot move
   d. a sugar-water mixture
2. **Predict** which way charges are likely to move between two positions of different electrical potential energy, one high and one low.
   a. from low to high
   b. from high to low
   c. back and forth between high and low
3. **State** the quantities needed to calculate an object's resistance.
4. **Explain** the function of insulation around a wire.
5. **Describe** the motion of charges through a flashlight, from one terminal of a battery to the other.
6. **Classify** the following materials as conductors or insulators: wood, paper clip, glass, air, paper, plastic, steel nail, water, aluminum can.

Math Skills

7. If the current in a certain resistor is 6.2 A and the voltage across the resistor is 110 V, what is its resistance?
8. If the voltage across a flashlight bulb is 3 V and the bulb's resistance is 6 Ω, what is the current through the bulb?

Circuits

▶ **KEY TERMS**
electric circuit
schematic diagram
series
parallel
electrical energy
fuse
circuit breaker

Disc Two, Module 16:
Electrical Circuits
Use the Interactive Tutor to learn more about this topic.

▶ **electric circuit** an electrical device connected so that it provides one or more complete paths for the movement of charges

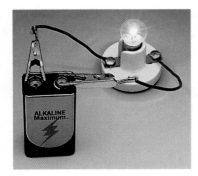

Figure 11-14
When this battery is connected to a light bulb, the voltage across the battery generates a current that lights the bulb.

OBJECTIVES

▶ Use schematic diagrams to represent circuits.
▶ Distinguish between series and parallel circuits.
▶ Calculate electric power using voltage and current.
▶ Explain how fuses and circuit breakers are used to prevent circuit overload.

Think about how you would get the bulb shown in **Figure 11-14** to light up. Would the bulb light if the bulb were not fully screwed into the socket? How about if one of the clips were removed from the battery?

What Are Circuits?

When a wire connects the terminals of the battery to the light bulb, as shown in **Figure 11-14,** charges that built up on one terminal of the battery have a path to follow to reach the opposite charges on the other terminal. Because there are charges moving uniformly, a current exists. This current causes the filament inside the light bulb to give off heat and light.

An electric circuit is a path through which charges can be conducted

Together, the bulb, battery, and wires form an **electric circuit.** In the circuit shown in **Figure 11-14,** the path from one battery terminal to the other is complete. Because of the voltage of the battery, electrons move through the wires and bulb from the negative terminal to the positive terminal. Then the battery adds energy to the charges as they move within the battery from the positive terminal back to the negative one.

In other words, there is a closed-loop path for electrons to follow. The conducting path produced when the light bulb is connected across the battery's terminals is called a *closed circuit.* Without a complete path, there is no charge flow and therefore no current. This is called an *open circuit.*

The inside of the battery is part of the closed path of current through the circuit. The voltage source, whether a battery or an outlet, is always part of the conducting path of a closed circuit.

If a device called a *switch* is added to the circuit, as shown in **Figure 11-15,** you can use the switch to open and close the circuit. You have used a switch many times. The switches on your wall at home are used to turn lights on and off. Although they look different from the switch in **Figure 11-15,** their function is the same. When you flip a switch at home, you either close or open the circuit to turn a light on or off.

The switch shown in **Figure 11-15** is called a knife switch. The metal bar is a conductor. When the bar is touching both sides of the switch, as shown in **Figure 11-15,** the circuit is closed. Electrons can move through the bar to reach the other side of the switch and light the bulb. If the metal bar on the switch is lifted, the circuit is open. Then there is no current, and the bulb does not glow.

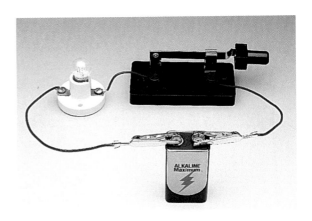

Figure 11-15
When added to the circuit, a switch can be used to open and close the circuit.

Schematic diagrams are used to represent circuits

Suppose you wanted to describe to someone the contents and connections in the photo of the light bulb and battery in **Figure 11-15.** How might you draw each element? Could you use the same representations of the elements to draw a bigger circuit, such as a string of lights?

A diagram that depicts the construction of an electrical circuit or apparatus is called a schematic diagram. **Figure 11-16** shows how the battery and light bulb can be drawn as a schematic diagram. The symbols that are used in this figure can be used to describe any other circuit with a battery and one or more bulbs. All electrical devices, from toasters to computers, can be described using schematic diagrams. Because schematic diagrams use standard symbols, they can be read by people all over the world.

internetconnect

SC*L*INKS.
NSTA

TOPIC: Electric circuits
GO TO: www.scilinks.org
KEYWORD: HK1135

▶ schematic diagram
a graphic representation of an electric circuit or apparatus, with standard symbols for the electrical devices

Figure 11-16
The connections between the light bulb and battery can be represented by symbols. This type of illustration is called a schematic diagram.

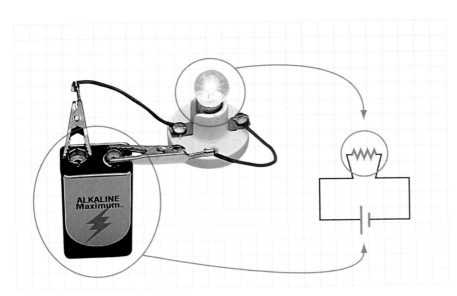

As shown in **Table 11-2,** each element used in a piece of electrical equipment is represented by a symbol that reflects the element's construction or function. For example, the schematic-diagram symbol that represents an open switch resembles the open-knife switch shown in the corresponding photograph. Any circuit can be drawn using a combination of these and other, more-complex schematic diagram symbols.

Table 11-2 **Schematic Diagram Symbols**

Component	Symbol used in this book	Explanation
Wire or conductor		Wires that connect elements are conductors.
Resistor		Resistors are shown as wires with multiple bends, indicating resistance to a straight path.
Bulb or lamp		The winding of the filament indirectly indicates that the light bulb is a resistor, something that impedes the movement of electrons or the flow of charge.
Battery or other direct current source		The difference in line height indicates a voltage between positive and negative terminals of the battery. The taller line represents the positive terminal of the battery.
Switch Open Closed	Open Closed	The small circles indicate the two places where the switch makes contact with the wires. Most switches work by breaking only one of the contacts, not both.

Series and Parallel Circuits

Section 11.2 showed that the current in a circuit depends on voltage and the resistance of the device in the circuit. What happens when there are two or more devices connected to a battery?

Series circuits have a single path for current

When appliances or other devices are connected in a series circuit, as shown in **Figure 11-17A,** they form a single pathway for charges to flow. Charges cannot build up or disappear at a point in a circuit. For this reason, the amount of charge that enters one device in a given time interval equals the amount of charge that exits that device in the same amount of time. Because there is only one path for a charge to follow when devices are connected in series, the current in each device is the same. Even though the current in each device is the same, the resistances may be different. Therefore, the voltage across each device in a series circuit can be different.

If one element along the path in a series circuit is removed, the circuit will not work. For example, if either of the light bulbs in **Figure 11-17A** were removed, the other one would not glow. The series circuit would be open. Several kinds of breaks may interrupt a series circuit. The opening of a switch, the burning out of a light bulb, a cut wire, or any other interruption can cause the whole circuit to fail.

Parallel circuits have multiple paths for current

When devices are connected in **parallel,** rather than in series, the voltage across each device is the same. The current in each device does not have to be the same. Instead, the sum of the currents in all of the devices equals the total current. A simple parallel circuit is shown in **Figure 11-17B.** The two lights are connected to the same points. The electrons leaving one end of the battery can pass through either bulb before returning to the other terminal. If one bulb has less resistance, more charge moves through that bulb because the bulb offers less opposition to the movement of charges.

Even if one of the bulbs in the circuit shown in **Figure 11-17B** were removed, charges would still move through the other loop. Thus, a break in any one path in a parallel circuit does not interrupt the flow of electric charge in the other paths.

Quick ACTIVITY

Series and Parallel Circuits

1. Connect two flashlight bulbs, a battery, wires, and a switch so that both bulbs light up.
2. Make a diagram of your circuit. Is it a series or a parallel circuit?
3. Now make the other type of circuit. Compare the brightness of the bulbs in the two types of circuits.

▶ **series** describes a circuit or portion of a circuit that provides a single conducting path

▶ **parallel** describes components in a circuit that are connected across common points, providing two or more separate conducting paths

Figure 11-17

A When bulbs are connected in series, charges must pass through both light bulbs to complete the circuit.

B When devices are connected in parallel, charges have more than one path to follow. The circuit can be complete even if one light bulb burns out.

Electric Power and Electrical Energy

electrical energy the energy associated with electrical charges, whether moving or at rest

Many of the devices you use on a daily basis, such as the toaster shown in **Figure 11-18,** require electrical energy to run. The energy for these devices may come from a battery or from a power plant miles away.

Electric power is the rate at which electrical energy is used in a circuit

When a charge moves in a circuit, it loses energy. This energy is transformed into useful work, such as the turning of a motor, and is lost as heat in a circuit. The rate at which electrical work is done is called *electric power*. Electric power is the product of total current (I) in and voltage (V) across a circuit.

> **Electric Power Equation**
> $$power = current \times voltage$$
> $$P = IV$$

Figure 11-18
Household appliances use electrical energy to do useful work. Some of that energy is lost as heat.

The SI unit for power is the watt (W), as shown in Chapter 8. A watt is equivalent to 1 A × 1 V. Light bulbs are rated in terms of watts. For example, a typical desk lamp uses a 60 W bulb.

If you combine the electric power equation above with the equation $V = IR$, the power lost, or *dissipated*, by a resistor can be calculated.

$$P = I^2R = \frac{V^2}{R}$$

Math Skills

Electric Power When a hair dryer is plugged into a 120 V outlet, it has a 9.1 A current in it. What is the hair dryer's power rating?

1 List the given and unknown values.
  Given: *voltage, V* = 120 V
    current, I = 9.1 A
  Unknown: *electric power, P* = ? W

2 Write the equation for electric power.
  power = current × voltage
  $P = IV$

3 Insert the known values into the equation, and solve.
  $P = (9.1 \text{ A})(120 \text{ V})$
  $P = 1.1 \times 10^3 \text{ W}$

Electric Power

1. An electric space heater requires 29 A of 120 V current to adequately warm a room. What is the power rating of the heater?

2. A graphing calculator uses a 6.0 V battery and draws 2.6×10^{-3} A of current. What is the power rating of the calculator?

3. A color television has a power rating of 320 W. How much current is in the television when it is connected across 120 V?

4. The operating voltage for a light bulb is 120 V. The power rating of the bulb is 75 W. Find the current in the bulb.

5. The current in the heating element of an electric iron is 5.0 A. If the iron dissipates 590 W of power, what is the voltage across it?

Electric companies measure energy consumed in kilowatt-hours

Power companies charge for energy used in the home, not power. The unit of energy that electric companies use to track consumption of energy is the kilowatt-hour (kW•h). One kilowatt-hour is the energy delivered in 1 hour at the rate of 1 kW. In SI units, 1 kW•h = 3.6×10^6 J.

Depending on where you live, the cost of energy ranges from 5 to 20 cents per kilowatt-hour. All homes and businesses have an electric meter, like the one shown in **Figure 11-19.** Electric meters are used by an electric company to determine how much electrical energy is consumed over a certain time interval.

Fuses and Circuit Breakers

When too many appliances, lights, CD players, televisions, and other devices are connected across a 120 V outlet, the overall resistance of the circuit is lowered. That means the electrical wires carry more than a safe level of current. When this happens, the circuit is said to be *overloaded*. The high currents in overloaded circuits can cause fires.

Worn insulation on wires can also be a fire hazard. If a wire's insulation wears down, two wires may touch, creating an alternative pathway for current. This is called a *short circuit*. The decreased resistance greatly increases the current in the circuit. Short circuits can be very dangerous. Grounding appliances reduces the risk of electric shock from a short circuit.

Practice HINT

▶ When a problem requires you to calculate power, you can use the power equation as shown on the previous page.

▶ The electric power equation can also be rearranged to isolate current on the left in the following way:

$$P = IV$$

Divide both sides by V.

$$\frac{P}{V} = \frac{IV}{V}$$

$$I = \frac{P}{V}$$

You will need this version of the equation for Practice Problems 3 and 4.

▶ For Practice Problem 5, you will need to rearrange the equation to isolate voltage on the left.

Figure 11-19
An electric meter, like the one shown here, records the amount of energy consumed.

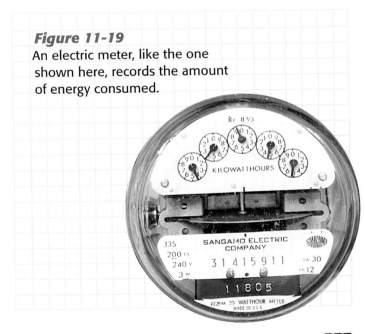

Fuses melt to prevent circuit overloads

▶ **fuse** an electrical device containing a metal strip that melts when current in the circuit becomes too great

To prevent overloading in circuits, **fuses** are connected in series along the supply path. A fuse is a ribbon of wire with a low melting point. If the current in the line becomes too large, the fuse melts and the circuit is opened.

Fuses "blow out" when the current in the circuit reaches a certain level. For example, a 20 A fuse will melt if the current in the circuit exceeds 20 A. A blown fuse is a sign that a short circuit or a circuit overload may exist somewhere in your home. It is best to find out what made a fuse blow out before replacing it.

Circuit breakers open circuits with high current

▶ **circuit breaker** a device that protects a circuit from current overloads

Many homes are equipped with **circuit breakers** instead of fuses. A circuit breaker uses a magnet or *bimetallic strip*, a strip with two different metals welded together, that responds to current overload by opening the circuit. The circuit breaker acts as a switch. As with blown fuses, it is wise to determine why the circuit breaker opened the circuit. Unlike fuses, circuit breakers can be reset by turning the switch back on.

SECTION 11.3 REVIEW

SUMMARY

▶ An electric circuit is a path along which charges can move.

▶ In a series circuit, devices are connected along a single pathway. A break anywhere along the path will stop the movement of charges.

▶ In a parallel circuit, two or more paths are connected to the voltage source. A break along one path will not stop the movement of charges in the other paths.

▶ Electric power supplied to a circuit or dissipated in a circuit is calculated as the product of the current and voltage.

CHECK YOUR UNDERSTANDING

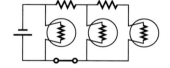

1. **Identify** the types of elements in the schematic diagram at right and the number of each type.
2. **Describe** the advantage of using a parallel arrangement of decorative lights rather than a series arrangement.
3. **Draw** a schematic diagram with four lights in parallel.
4. **Draw** a schematic diagram of a circuit with two light bulbs in which you could turn off either light and still have a complete circuit. (**Hint:** You will need to use two switches.)
5. **Contrast** how a fuse and a circuit breaker work to prevent overloading in circuits.
6. **Predict** whether a fuse will work successfully if it is connected in parallel with the device it is supposed to protect.

Math Skills

7. When a VCR is connected across a 120 V outlet, the VCR has a 9.5 A current in it. What is the power rating of the VCR?
8. A 40 W light bulb and a 75 W light bulb are in parallel across a 120 V outlet. Which bulb has the greater current?

Magnets and Electromagnetism

OBJECTIVES

▶ Recognize that like magnetic poles repel and unlike poles attract.

▶ Describe the magnetic field around a permanent magnet.

▶ Describe the orientation of Earth's magnetic field.

▶ Explain how magnetism is produced by electric currents.

▶ Summarize the conditions required for electromagnetic induction.

KEY TERMS

magnetic pole
magnetic field
solenoid
electromagnet
electromagnetic
   induction

Magnets are used in many electrical devices, but one of their most important uses has been in navigation. Magnetic stones were first used by the Chinese for navigation in the 1100s. Some animals even have small magnets in their bodies that help give them a sense of direction.

internet**connect**

SC*LINKS*
NSTA

TOPIC: Properties of magnets
GO TO: www.scilinks.org
KEYWORD: HK1142

Magnets

Magnets got their name from the region of Magnesia, which is now part of modern-day Greece. The first naturally occurring magnetic rocks, called *lodestones,* were found in this region almost 3000 years ago. A lodestone, shown in **Figure 11-20,** is composed of an iron-based material called *magnetite.*

Some materials can be made into permanent magnets

Some substances, such as lodestones, are magnetic all the time. These types of magnets are called *permanent magnets.* You can change any piece of iron, such as a nail, into a permanent magnet by stroking it several times with a permanent magnet. A slower method is to place the piece of iron near a strong magnet. Eventually the iron will become magnetic and will remain magnetic even when the original magnet is removed.

Although a magnetized piece of iron is called a "permanent" magnet, its magnetism can be weakened or even removed. Some ways to do this are to heat or hammer the piece of iron. Even then, certain materials retain their magnetism longer than others.

Figure 11-20
A naturally occurring magnetic rock, called a lodestone, will attract a variety of iron objects.

Test Your Knowledge of Magnetic Poles

1. Tape the ends of a bar magnet so that its pole markings are covered.
2. Tie a piece of string to the center of the magnet and suspend it from a support stand, as shown in the figure at right.
3. Use another bar magnet to determine which pole of the hanging magnet is the north pole and which is the south pole. What happens when you bring one pole of your magnet near each end of the hanging magnet?
4. Now try to identify the poles of the hanging magnet using the other pole of your magnet.
5. After you have decided the identity of each pole, remove the tape to check. Can you determine which are north poles and which are south poles if you cover the poles on both magnets?

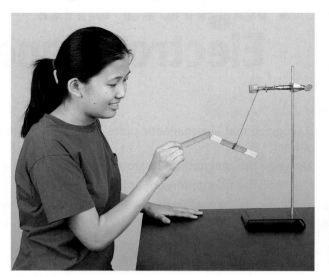

> **magnetic pole** an area of a magnet where the magnetic force appears to be the strongest

VOCABULARY *Skills Tip*

The word pole *is used in physics for two related opposites that are separated by some distance along an axis. The word* polar, *used in chemistry, has the same origin.*

> **magnetic field** a region where a magnetic force can be detected

Like poles repel, and opposite poles attract

As explained in Section 11.1, the closer two like electrical charges are brought together, the more they repel each other. The closer two opposite charges are brought together, the more they attract each other. A similar situation exists for **magnetic poles.**

Magnets have a pair of poles, a north pole and a south pole. The poles of magnets exert a force on one another. Two like poles, such as two south poles, repel each other. Two unlike poles, however, attract each other. Thus, the north pole of one magnet will attract the south pole of another magnet. Also, the north pole of one magnet repels the north pole of another magnet.

It is impossible to isolate a south magnetic pole from a north magnetic pole. If a magnet is cut into smaller pieces, each piece will still have two poles. No matter how small the pieces of a magnet are, each piece still has both a north and a south pole.

Magnetic Fields

Try moving the south pole of one magnet toward the south pole of another that is free to move. As you do this, the magnet you are not touching will move away. This is because there is a *magnetic force* between the two magnets. The magnetic force is acting at a distance. You are already familiar with other forces that act at a distance—gravitational force and electric force. The magnetic force acts through a **magnetic field.**

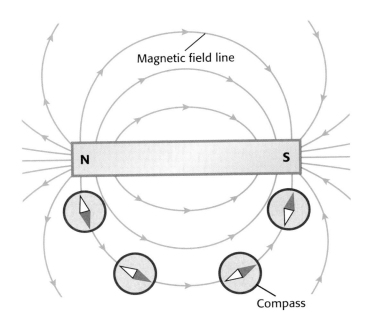

Magnetic field line

Compass

Figure 11-21

The magnetic field of a bar magnet can be traced with a compass. Note that the north pole of each compass points in the direction of the field lines from the magnet's north pole to its south pole.

Magnets are sources of magnetic fields

Magnets repel or attract each other due to the interaction of their magnetic fields. Some magnetic fields are stronger than others. Magnetic field strength depends on the material from which the magnet is made and the degree to which it has been magnetized.

Recall from Section 11.1 that electric field lines are used to represent the electric field due to a charged object. Similarly, magnetic field lines are used to represent the magnetic field of a bar magnet, as shown in **Figure 11-21.** These field lines all form closed loops. **Figure 11-21** shows only the field near the magnet. The field also exists within the magnet and farther away from the magnet. The magnetic field, however, gets weaker with distance from the magnet. Magnetic field lines that are close together indicate a strong magnetic field. Field lines that are farther apart indicate a weaker field. Knowing this, you can tell from **Figure 11-21** that a magnet's field is strongest near its poles.

Compasses can track magnetic fields

One way to analyze a magnetic field's direction is to use a compass, as shown in **Figure 11-21.** A compass is a magnet suspended on top of a pivot so that the magnet can rotate freely. The compass points in a direction that lies along, or is tangent to, the magnetic field at that point. You can make a simple compass by hanging a bar magnet from a support with a string tied to the magnet's midpoint.

Connection to
SOCIAL STUDIES

With the invention of iron and steel ships in the late 1800s, it became necessary to develop a new type of compass. The *gyrocompass*, a device containing a spinning loop, was the solution. Because of inertia, the gyrocompass always points toward Earth's geographic North Pole, regardless of which way the ship turns.

Making the Connection

1. Why does the metal hull of a ship affect the function of magnetic compasses?
2. A gyrocompass contains a device called a gyroscope. Research gyroscopes and briefly explain how they work.

Figure 11-22
Earth's magnetic field is similar to that of a bar magnet.

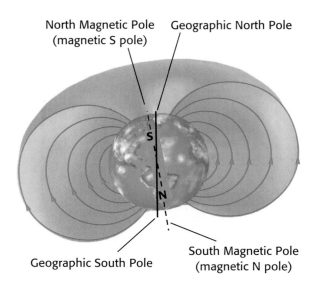

North Magnetic Pole (magnetic S pole) Geographic North Pole

S

N

Geographic South Pole South Magnetic Pole (magnetic N pole)

Earth's magnetic field is like that of a bar magnet

A compass can be used to determine direction because Earth acts like a giant bar magnet. As shown in **Figure 11-22,** Earth's magnetic field has both direction and strength. If you were to move northward along Earth's surface with a compass whose needle could point up and down, the needle of the compass would slowly tilt forward. At a point in northeastern Canada, the needle would point straight down. This point is one of Earth's magnetic poles. There is an opposite magnetic pole in Antarctica.

The source of Earth's magnetic field is not completely understood. Although Earth's core is mostly iron, the iron in the core is too hot to retain any magnetic properties. Most researchers believe that the circulation of charges in the liquid layer of the core creates the magnetic field. This motion of charges may be caused by heat rising from the central core or by Earth's rotation.

Earth's magnetic poles are not the same as its geographic poles

One of the interesting things about Earth's magnetic poles is that they are not in the same place as the geographic poles, as shown in **Figure 11-22.** Another important distinction that should be made about Earth's magnetic poles is the orientation of the magnetic field. Earth's magnetic field points from the geographic South Pole to the geographic North Pole. This orientation is similar to an upside-down bar magnet, like the one shown in **Figure 11-22.** The magnetic pole in Antarctica is actually the magnetic north pole, and the magnetic pole in northern Canada is actually a magnetic south pole.

The poles of magnets are named for the geographic pole they point toward. Thus, the end of the magnet labeled *N* is a "north-seeking" pole, and the end of the magnet labeled *S* is a "south-seeking" pole.

Electromagnetism

In the eighteenth century, people noticed that a bolt of lightning could change the direction of a compass needle. In 1820, a Danish science teacher named Hans Christian Oersted first experimented with the effects of an electric current on a compass needle. He found that a current-carrying wire produces a magnetic field. In fact, all magnetism is produced by moving electric charges.

Electric currents produce magnetic fields

The experiment shown in **Figure 11-23** uses iron filings to demonstrate that a current-carrying wire creates a magnetic field. Iron filings align with the magnetic field to make a distinct pattern around the wire.

The pattern of the filings in **Figure 11-23** suggests that the magnetic field around a current-carrying wire forms concentric circles around the wire. If you were to bring a compass close to a current-carrying wire, as Oersted did, you would find that the needle points in a direction tangent to the circles of iron filings.

The magnetic field of a coil of wire resembles that of a bar magnet

As Oersted demonstrated, the magnetic field of a current-carrying wire exerts a force on a compass needle. This force causes the needle to turn in the direction of the wire's magnetic field. However, this force is very weak. One way to increase the force is to increase the current in the wire, but large currents can be fire hazards. A safer way to create a strong magnetic field that will provide a greater force is to wrap the wire into a coil, as shown in **Figure 11-24.** This device is called a solenoid.

In a solenoid, the magnetic field of each loop of wire adds to the strength of the magnetic field of the loop next to it. The result is a strong magnetic field similar to the magnetic field produced by a bar magnet. The magnetic field of a solenoid even has a north and south pole, just like a magnet.

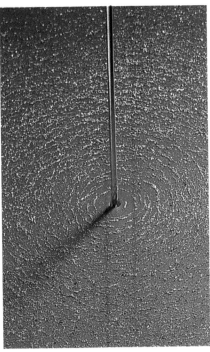

Figure 11-23
The iron filings show that the magnetic field of a current-carrying wire forms concentric circles around the wire.

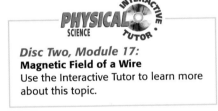

Disc Two, Module 17:
Magnetic Field of a Wire
Use the Interactive Tutor to learn more about this topic.

▶ solenoid a long, wound coil of insulated wire

Figure 11-24
The magnetic field of a coil of wire resembles the magnetic field of a bar magnet.

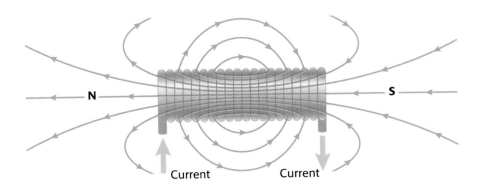

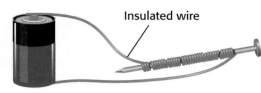
The strength of the magnetic field of a solenoid depends on the number of loops of wire and the amount of current in the wire. In particular, increasing the number of loops that make up the solenoid or increasing the current in the solenoid can create a stronger magnetic field.

The strength of a solenoid's magnetic field can also be increased by inserting a rod made of iron (or some other potentially magnetic metal) through the center of the coils. The resulting device is called an **electromagnet.** The magnetic field of the solenoid causes the rod to become a magnet as well. The magnetic field of the rod then adds to the coil's field, creating a stronger magnet than the solenoid alone.

▶ **electromagnet** a strong magnet created when an iron core is inserted into the center of a current-carrying solenoid

Electromagnetic Induction and Faraday's Law

Section 11.2 showed that there is a current in a wire connected across the terminals of a battery. Can you have current in a wire without some source of voltage? In 1831, Michael Faraday discovered that a current can be produced by pushing a magnet through a coil of wire. In other words, moving a magnet in and out of a coil of wire causes charges in the wire to move. This process is called **electromagnetic induction.** Electromagnetic induction is so fundamental that it has become one of the laws of physics—*Faraday's law.* Faraday's law states the following:

▶ **electromagnetic induction** the production of a current in a conducting circuit by a change in the strength, position, or orientation of an external magnetic field

An electric current can be produced in a circuit by a changing magnetic field.

Consider the loop of wire moving between the two magnetic poles in **Figure 11-25.** As long as the loop moves in or out in a direction that is not parallel to the magnetic field of the magnet, a current is *induced* in the circuit. Rotating the circuit or changing the strength of the magnetic field will also induce a current in the circuit.

Imagine the wire in a circuit as a tube full of charges. A charged particle moving in a magnetic field will experience a force. The force is zero when the charge moves along or opposite the direction of the magnetic field. So when the wire moves parallel to the field, no current is induced in the wire. The force is at its maximum value when the charge moves perpendicular to the magnetic field. So when the wire moves perpendicular to a magnetic field, the current in the circuit is at a maximum. As the angle between the charge's direction and the direction of the magnetic field decreases, the force on the charge decreases.

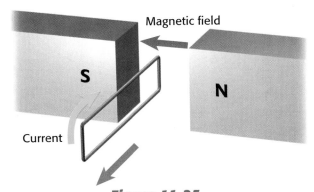

Figure 11-25
When the loop moves in or out of the magnetic field, a current is induced in the wire.

Electricity and magnetism are two aspects of a single electromagnetic force

So far you've read that a moving charge produces a magnetic field and that a changing magnetic field causes an electric charge to move. The energy that results from the interaction of electric and magnetic fields is called electromagnetic energy.

You learned in Section 10.1 that light is electromagnetic energy. Visible light travels as electromagnetic waves, or *EM* waves, as do other forms of radiation, such as radio signals, microwaves, and X rays. These waves are also called EMF (electromagnetic frequency) waves. As shown in **Figure 11-26,** EM waves are made up of oscillating electric and magnetic fields that are perpendicular to each other. This is true of any type of electromagnetic wave, regardless of the frequency.

Both the electric and magnetic fields in an EM wave are perpendicular to the direction the wave travels. So EM waves are transverse waves. As the wave moves along, the changing electric field generates the magnetic field. The changing magnetic field generates the electric field. Each field regenerates the other, allowing EM waves to travel through empty space.

Figure 11-26
An electromagnetic wave consists of electric and magnetic field waves at right angles to each other.

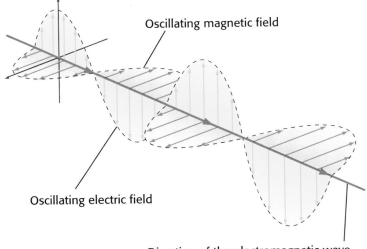

Oscillating magnetic field

Oscillating electric field

Direction of the electromagnetic wave

Figure 11-27
Transformers like this one are used to reduce the voltage across power lines so that the electrical energy supplied to homes and businesses is safer to use.

Electromagnetic Devices

Many modern devices make use of the magnetic field produced by coils of current-carrying wire. Devices as different as hair dryers and stereo speakers function because of the magnetic field produced by these current-carrying conductors.

Electric motors use a coil of wire in a magnetic field that rotates when a current is in the wire. The coil's magnetic field changes direction as it spins so that it rotates in one direction. If the coil is attached to a shaft, it can do mechanical work.

Power plants use *generators* to convert mechanical energy to electrical energy. Large turbine fans are rotated by falling water, steam, or wind. The fans are attached to a core wrapped with many loops of wire that turns within a strong magnetic field. For each half rotation, the current produced by the generator reverses direction. This *alternating current* is used in homes and industry.

Transformers, like the one shown in **Figure 11-27,** change the voltage of an alternating current source. Near power plants, the voltage is increased so less energy is lost due to the resistance of the transmission wires. Near homes and businesses, the voltage is reduced to about 120 V, for use with most appliances.

SECTION 11.4 REVIEW

SUMMARY

▶ Like magnetic poles repel each other. Unlike poles attract each other.

▶ The magnetic field of a magnet is strongest near its poles and gets weaker with distance.

▶ A magnetic field is produced around a current-carrying wire.

▶ A current is produced in a circuit by a changing magnetic field.

▶ Electromagnetic waves consist of magnetic and electric fields oscillating at right angles to each other.

CHECK YOUR UNDERSTANDING

1. **State** how many poles each piece of a magnet will have when you break it in half.
2. **Determine** whether two magnets will attract or repel when
   a. their N and S poles are near each other.
   b. their S poles are near each other.
   c. their N poles are near each other.
3. **Describe** the direction a compass needle would point if you were in Australia.
4. **Explain** why the N pole of a magnet is attracted to the geographic North Pole, yet like poles repel.
5. **Describe** the shape of the magnetic field produced by a straight current-carrying wire.
6. **Predict** whether a solenoid suspended by a string could be used as a compass.
7. **Critical Thinking** A spacecraft orbiting Earth has a coil of wire in it. An astronaut measures a small current in the coil, even though there is no battery connected to it and there are no magnets on the spacecraft. What is causing the current?

Chapter Highlights

Before you begin, review the summaries of the key ideas of each section, found on pages 362, 371, 378, and 386. The key vocabulary terms are listed on pages 356, 363, 372, and 379.

UNDERSTANDING CONCEPTS

1. Which of the following particles is electrically neutral?
   a. proton
   b. electron
   c. a hydrogen atom
   d. a hydrogen ion

2. Which of the following is not an example of charging by friction?
   a. sliding over a plastic-covered car seat
   b. scraping food from a metal bowl with a metal spoon
   c. walking across a woolen carpet
   d. brushing dry hair with a plastic comb

3. The electric force between two objects depends on all of the following except _____.
   a. the distance between the objects
   b. the electric charge of the first object
   c. how each of the two objects became electrically charged
   d. the electric charge of the second object

4. A positive charge placed in the electric field of a second positive charge will _____.
   a. experience a repulsive force
   b. accelerate away from the second positive charge
   c. have greater electrical potential energy when near the second charge than when farther away
   d. All of the above

5. The _____ is the change in the electrical potential energy of a charged particle per unit charge.
   a. circuit
   b. voltage
   c. induction
   d. power

6. An electric current does not exist in _____.
   a. a closed circuit
   b. a series circuit
   c. a parallel circuit
   d. an open circuit

7. Which of the following can help prevent a circuit from overloading?
   a. a fuse
   b. a switch
   c. a circuit breaker
   d. both (a) and (c)

8. If the poles of two magnets repel each other, _____.
   a. both poles must be south poles
   b. both poles must be north poles
   c. one pole is a south pole and the other is a north pole
   d. the poles are the same type

9. The part of a magnet where the magnetic field and forces are strongest is called a magnetic _____.
   a. field
   b. pole
   c. attraction
   d. repulsion

10. The process of producing an electrical current by moving a magnet in and out of a coil of wire is called _____.
    a. magnetic production
    b. electromagnetic induction
    c. electromagnetic radiation
    d. magnetic reduction

Using Vocabulary

11. How do charges move through an insulated wire connected across a battery? Use the terms *potential difference, current, conductor,* and *insulator.*

12. Contrast the movement of charges in a *series circuit* and in a *parallel circuit.* Use a diagram to aid in your explanation.

13. Use the terms *magnetic pole* and *magnetic field* to explain why the N pole of a compass points toward northern Canada.

14. What is made by inserting an iron core into a *solenoid?*

BUILDING MATH SKILLS

15. Resistance A potential difference of 12 V produces a current of 0.30 A in a piece of copper wire. What is the resistance of the copper wire?

16. Resistance What is the voltage across a 75 Ω resistor with 1.6 A of current?

17. Resistance A nickel wire with a resistance of 25 Ω is connected across the terminals of a 3.0 V flashlight battery. How much current is in the wire?

18. Power A portable cassette player uses 3.0 V (two 1.5 V batteries in series) and has 0.33 A of current. What is its power rating?

19. Power Find the current in a 2.4 W flashlight bulb powered by a 1.5 V battery.

20. Power A high-voltage transmission line carries 1.0×10^3 A of current. The power transmitted is 7.0×10^8 W. Find the voltage of the transmission line.

THINKING CRITICALLY

21. Understanding Systems Why is charge usually transferred by electrons?

22. Problem Solving Do you expect shocks from static electricity to be worse as the humidity increases or decreases? Explain your answer.

23. Understanding Systems The gravitational force is always attractive, while the electric force is both attractive and repulsive. What accounts for this difference?

24. Designing Systems How many ways can you connect three light bulbs in a circuit with a battery? Draw a schematic diagram of each circuit.

25. Applying Knowledge At a given voltage, which light bulb has the greater resistance, a 200 W light bulb or a 75 W light bulb?

26. Problem Solving How could you use a compass with a magnetized needle to determine if a steel nail were magnetized?

27. Interpreting Graphics Identify which of the compass-needle orientations in the figure below correctly describe the direction of the bar magnet's magnetic field.

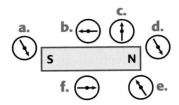

28. Understanding Systems Explain whether an electromagnet or a solenoid produces the strongest magnetic field.

29. Applying Knowledge You walk briskly into a strong magnetic field while wearing a copper bracelet. How should you hold your wrist relative to the magnetic field lines to avoid inducing a current in the bracelet?

DEVELOPING LIFE/WORK SKILLS

30. Interpreting and Communicating A metal can is placed on a wooden table. If a positively charged ball suspended by a thread is brought close to the can, the ball will swing toward the can, make contact, then move away. Explain why this happens, and predict what will happen to the ball next. Use presentation software or a drawing program to make diagrams showing the charges on the ball and on the can at each phase.

COMPUTER SKILL

31. Working Cooperatively With a small group of classmates, make a chart about electrical safety in the home and outdoors. Use what you have learned in this chapter and information from your local fire department.

32. Working Cooperatively During a field trip you find a round chunk of metal that attracts iron objects. In groups of three, design a procedure to determine whether the object is magnetic and, if so, to locate its poles. What materials would you need? How would you draw your conclusions? List all the possible results and the conclusions you could draw from each result.

33. Interpreting and Communicating Research one of the following electromagnetic devices. Write a half-page description of how electromagnetism is used in the device, using diagrams where appropriate: hair dryer, electric guitar, door bell, tape recorder, stereo speaker.

WRITING SKILL

34. Teaching Others Make a poster showing the three ways to induce a current in a circuit.

INTEGRATING CONCEPTS

35. Concept Mapping Copy the unfinished concept map below onto a sheet of paper. Complete the map by writing the correct word or phrase in the lettered boxes.

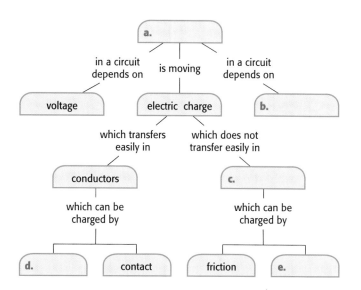

36. Connection to Social Studies The units of measurement you learned about in this chapter were named after three famous scientists—Alessandro Volta, André-Marie Ampère, and Georg Simon Ohm. Create a presentation about one of these scientists. Research the life, work, discoveries, and contributions of the scientist. The presentation can be in the form of a report, poster, short video, or computer presentation.

37. Connection to Environmental Science Research how an *electrostatic precipitator* works to remove smoke and dust particles from the polluting emissions of fuel-burning industries. Find out what industries in your community use precipitators. What are the advantages and costs of using this device? What alternatives are available? Summarize your finding in a brochure, poster, or chart.

38. Connection to Social Studies Why was the discovery of lodestones in Greece important to navigators hundreds of years later?

WRITING SKILL

39. Connection to Health Some studies indicate that magnetic fields produced by high-voltage power lines may contribute to leukemia among children. Research the history of scientific studies of the connection between leukemia and power lines. What experiments show that growing up near power lines increases the risk of leukemia? What evidence is there that there is no relation between leukemia and power lines?

internet connect

SCILINKS NSTA

TOPIC: Magnetic fields of power lines
GO TO: www.scilinks.org
KEYWORD: HK1146

Introduction

How can you show how the current that flows through an electric circuit depends on voltage and resistance?

Objectives

- ▶ **Construct** parallel and series circuits.
- ▶ **Predict** voltage and current using the resistance law.
- ▶ **Measure** voltage, current, and resistance.

Materials

dry-cell battery
battery holder
2 resistors
3 connecting wires
masking tape
multimeter

Safety Needs

safety goggles
heat-resistant gloves

Constructing Electric Circuits

▶ Preparing for Your Experiment

1. In this laboratory exercise, you will use an instrument called a multimeter to measure voltage, current, and resistance. Your teacher will demonstrate how to use the multimeter to make each type of measurement.

2. As you read the steps listed below, refer to the diagrams for help making the measurements. Write down your predictions and measurements in your lab notebook. **SAFETY CAUTION** Handle the wires only where they are insulated.

▶ Circuits with a Single Resistor

3. Measure the resistance in ohms of one of the resistors. Write the resistance on a small piece of masking tape, and tape it to the resistor. Repeat for the other resistor.

4. Use the resistance equation to predict the current in amps that will be in a circuit consisting of one of the resistors and one battery. (**Hint:** You must rearrange the equation to solve for current.)

5. Test your prediction by building the circuit. Do the same for the other resistor.

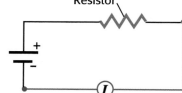

▶ Circuits with Two Resistors in Series

6. Measure the total resistance across both resistors when they are connected in series.

7. Using the total resistance you measured, predict the current that will be in a circuit consisting of one battery and both resistors in series. Test your prediction.

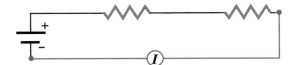

8. Using the current you measured, predict the voltage across each resistor in the circuit you just built. Test your prediction.

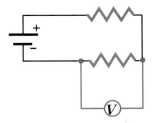

▶ Circuits with Two Resistors in Parallel

9. Measure the total resistance across both resistors when they are connected in parallel.

10. Using the total resistance you measured, predict the total current that will be in an entire circuit consisting of one battery and both resistors in parallel. Test your prediction.

11. Predict the current that will be in each resistor individually in the circuit you just built. Test your prediction.

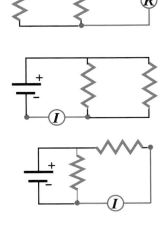

▶ Analyzing Your Results

1. If you have a circuit consisting of one battery and one resistor, what happens to the current if you double the resistance?

2. What happens to the current if you add a second, identical battery in series with the first battery?

3. What happens to the current if you add a second resistor in parallel with the first resistor?

4. **Reaching Conclusions** Suppose you have a circuit consisting of one battery plus a 10 Ω resistor and a 5 Ω resistor in series. Which resistor will have the greater voltage across it?

5. **Reaching Conclusions** Suppose you have a circuit consisting of one battery plus a 10 Ω resistor and a 5 Ω resistor in parallel. Which resistor will have more current in it?

▶ Defending Your Conclusions

6. Suppose someone tells you that you can make the battery in a circuit last longer by adding more resistors in parallel. Is that correct? Explain your reasoning.

CareerLink

Physicist

Physicists are scientists who are trying to understand the fundamental rules of the universe. Physicists pursue these questions at universities, private corporations, and government agencies. To learn more about physics as a career, read the interview with physicist Robert Martinez, who works at the University of Texas in Austin, Texas.

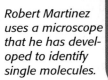

Robert Martinez uses a microscope that he has developed to identify single molecules.

 What kinds of problems are you studying?

We're working on a technique that will allow us to study single molecules. We could look at, say, molecules on the surface of a cell. What we're doing is building a kind of microscope for optical spectroscopy, which is a way to find out the colors of molecules. Studying the colors of molecules can tell us what those molecules are made of.

 How does this allow you to identify molecules?

Atoms act as little beams, and the bonds act as little springs. By exciting them with light, we can get them to vibrate and give off different colors of light. It's a little bit like listening to a musical instrument and telling from the overtones that a piano is different from a trumpet or a clarinet.

"I think of our current project a little bit like the nineteenth century explorers did. They didn't know what they would find on the other side of the ridge or the other side of the ocean, but they had to go look."

 What facets of your work do you find most interesting?

The thing that I like about what we're doing is that it's very practical, very hands-on. Also, the opportunity exists to explore whole new areas of physics and chemistry that no one has explored before. What we are doing has the promise of giving us new tools—new "eyes"—to look at important problems.

 What qualities do you think a physicist needs?

You've got to be innately curious about how the world works, and you've got to think it's understandable and you are capable of understanding it. You've got to be courageous. You've got to be good at math.

Can you remember any experiences that were particularly valuable for you?

When I was growing up, my dad was a pipe fitter for the city of Los Angeles, and I got to be his apprentice. I got a lot of practical experience that way. I think it's important to take the lawn mower engine apart, take the toaster apart—unplug it first—and see how it works.

Which part of your education was most important?

I liked graduate school a great deal. When I started in research, I had an adviser who was very hands off. What I got was the freedom to go as high as I could or to fall on my face. It was a place where I could stretch out and use things I had under my belt but didn't get to use in the classroom. Outside of school, my dad was my best teacher. He was very bright and had a lot of practical experience.

 What advice would you give someone interested in physics?

If it interests you at all, stick with it. If you have doubts, try to talk to people who know what physicists do and know about physics training. The number of people with physics training far exceed the number of people who work as physicists. A good fraction of engineering is physics, for instance.

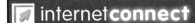

internetconnect

SCI*LINKS*
NSTA

TOPIC: Physicist
GO TO: www.scilinks.org
KEYWORD: HK1139

"I think that children are born scientists. It's just a matter of keeping your eyes open—keeping your curiosity alive."
—ROBERT MARTINEZ

CHAPTER 12

Communication Technology

Chapter Preview

12.1 Signals and Telecommunication
Signals and Codes
Telecommunication
Telecommunication Today

12.2 Telephone, Radio, and Television
Telephones
Radio and Television

12.3 Computers and the Internet
Computers
Computer Networks and the Internet

INTEGRATING
TECHNOLOGY
and Society

Focus ACTIVITY

Background When you write a letter, you assume that the recipient can read and understand what you have written. But how would you send a message to intelligent life on another planet?

NASA had to consider this question in the early 1970s when it began sending spacecraft to the outer regions of the solar system. Like bottles drifting on an ocean, these probes would eventually drift out of the solar system into deep space. With messages attached to these spacecraft, any extraterrestrial beings that discover a craft could learn where the craft came from and who made it if they could understand the message.

When the *Voyager 1* and *2* spacecraft were launched, large gold-plated copper disks were sent with them. Each disk was a large phonograph record consisting of sounds of nature, music from various nations, and greetings in all modern languages.

Activity 1 Suppose you are chosen to develop a visual message to be sent with a probe into deep space. Make a list of information you think would be most important to convey to intelligent extraterrestrial beings. What assumptions have you made about the receivers of this information?

Activity 2 On a piece of plain paper, draw the design for the space message you developed in Activity 1. Share your design with your classmates. See if they understand what you tried to communicate. Are there parts of your design that your classmates have trouble understanding? What might you do to remedy this?

Improvements in communications satellites (left) make it possible for more telephone, radio, and television signals to travel from one place to another. These advancements, in both satellites and other communication equipment, are largely the result of improvements in the speed and storage capacity of modern computers (above).

internet**connect**

SC*i*LINKS
NSTA

TOPIC: Space messages
GO TO: www.scilinks.org
KEYWORD: HK1501

Signals and Telecommunication

KEY TERMS

signal
code
telecommunication
analog signals
digital signals
optical fiber

OBJECTIVES

▶ Distinguish between signals and codes.
▶ Define and give an example of telecommunication.
▶ Compare analog signals with digital signals.
▶ Describe two advantages of optical fibers over metal wires for transmitting signals.
▶ Describe how microwave relays transmit signals using Earth-based stations and communications satellites.

You communicate with people every day. Each time you talk to a friend, wave goodbye or hello, or give someone a "thumbs up," you are sending and receiving information. Even actions such as shaking someone's hand and frowning are forms of communication.

Signals and Codes

▶ **signal** a sign that represents information, such as a command, a direction, or a warning

All of the different forms of communication just mentioned use **signals.** A signal is any sign or event that conveys information. People often use nonverbal signals along with words to communicate. Some signals, such as those shown in **Figure 12-1,** are so common that almost everyone in the United States recognizes their meaning. Signals can be sent in the form of gestures, flags, lights, shapes, colors, or even electric current.

Figure 12-1
(A) A handshake indicates friendship or good will.
(B) A green light means "go."
(C) A football referee's raised hands tell the crowd and the scorekeeper that the kick was good.

Codes are used to send signals

In a baseball game, the catcher often sends signals to the pitcher. These signals can tell the pitcher what type of pitch to throw. In order for the catcher's signals to be understood by the pitcher, the two players must work out the meaning of the signals, or code, before the game starts.

You hear and use codes every day, perhaps without even being aware of it. The language you speak is a code. Not everybody in the world understands it. An idea or message can be represented in different languages using very different symbols. The phrase "thank you" in English, for instance, is expressed as *gracias* in Spanish, شكران in Arabic, and 谢谢 in Chinese.

Some codes are routinely used by particular groups. For example, chemists around the world recognize Au, Pb, and O as symbols for the elements gold, lead, and oxygen, respectively. Also, all mathematicians recognize =, −, and + as symbols that mean *equal to, minus,* and *plus*.

In addition to signals and codes, communication requires a sender and a receiver. A sender transmits, or sends, a message to a receiver.

Signals are sent in many different forms

Signals like waving or calling out to someone can be received only if the person at the other end can see or hear the signal. As a result, these signals cannot be sent very far. To send a message over long distances, the signal needs to be converted into a form that can travel long distances easily. Both electricity and electromagnetic waves offer excellent ways to send such signals.

To send sound using electricity, the first step is to convert the sound into an electric current. This electrical signal is produced by using a microphone. The microphone matches the changes in sound waves with comparable changes in electric current. You can imagine the microphone making a copy of the sound in the form of electricity. Next, this electrical signal travels along a wire over longer distances. At the other end, the electrical signal is amplified and converted back into sound using a speaker.

In 1837, an American named Samuel Morse received a patent on a device called the electric telegraph. The telegraph uses a code made of a series of pulses of electric current to send messages. A machine at the other end marks a paper tape—a dot in response to a short pulse and a dash in response to a long pulse. Morse code, as shown below, represents letters and numbers as a series of dashes and dots.

A •—	N —•	1 •————
B —•••	O ———	2 ••———
C —•—•	P •——•	3 •••——
D —••	Q ——•—	4 ••••—
E •	R •—•	5 •••••
F ••—•	S •••	6 —••••
G ——•	T —	7 ——•••
H ••••	U ••—	8 ———••
I ••	V •••—	9 ————•
J •———	W •——	0 —————
K —•—	X —••—	
L •—••	Y —•——	
M ——	Z ——••	

Making the Connection
1. Write a simple sentence, such as, "I am here."
2. Translate it into Morse code, and send it to a partner using sounds, tapping, or a flashlight.
3. Have your partner write down the code and try to translate the message using Morse code.

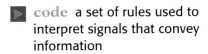 **code** a set of rules used to interpret signals that convey information

A speaker is a type of transducer, which is a device that converts a signal from one form to another. A speaker converts an incoming signal in the form of electricity into sound. After the conversion, the original sound is re-created. Two types of transducers, a speaker and a microphone, are shown in **Figure 12-2.** The microphone is a transducer that converts a sound signal into an electrical signal.

Telecommunication

Not long after the discovery of electric current, people tried to find ways of using electricity to send messages over long distances. In 1844, the first telegraph line provided a faster way to send messages between Baltimore and Washington, D.C. With this success, more telegraph lines were installed. By 1861, messages could be sent rapidly between the West Coast and the East Coast.

About 30 years after the first electric telegraph service was provided, the telephone was developed. In another 25 years, the wireless telegraph was invented. With wireless technology, a telegraph message could be sent by radio waves without the use of wires and cables. Sending and receiving signals by using electromagnetic means is referred to as **telecommunication.**

▶ **telecommunication** a communication method that uses electromagnetic means

Figure 12-2

Transducer

Current

Time

A The sound waves are converted into an electrical signal by the microphone.

Transducer

B The signal travels in the form of an electric current through a wire.

C In the speaker, the signal is amplified and converted back into sound.

Figure 12-3
This weight scale is an analog device. The spring inside the scale stretches continuously in proportion to the weight.

An analog signal varies continuously within a range

What do a thermometer, a speedometer, and a spring scale have in common? They are analog devices, which means that their readings change continuously as the quantity they are measuring—temperature, wheel rotation, or weight—changes. Readings given by each of these measuring devices are analog signals.

An example of an analog device is shown in **Figure 12-3.** As the weight on the scale increases, the needle moves in one direction. As the weight decreases, the needle moves in the opposite direction. The position of the needle on this scale can have any possible value between 0 lb and 20.0 lb (0 N and 89 N).

The audio signal from the microphone in **Figure 12-2** is an analog signal in the form of a changing electric current. Analog signals consisting of radio waves can be used to transmit picture, sound, and telephone messages.

Digital signals consist of separate bits of information

Unlike an analog signal, which can change continuously, a digital signal consists of only discrete, or fixed, values. The binary number system consists of two discrete values, 0 and 1. The combination for a lock, shown in **Figure 12-4,** is in a digital form. It is composed of discrete values, or digits, each of which can have one of six values—1, 2, 3, 4, 5, or 6.

A simple type of digital signal uses a flashing light. Sailors sometimes use a flashing *signal lamp* to send Morse code for ship-to-ship and ship-to-shore communication. Morse code, which was developed by Samuel Morse for transmitting information by telegraph, uses three "digits": a short interval between clicks, a long interval between clicks, and no click at all.

▶ **analog signal** a signal corresponding to a quantity whose values can change continuously

▶ **digital signal** a signal that can be represented as a sequence of discrete values

Figure 12-4
The code to open this lock is in a digital form, consisting of a series of whole numbers.

Figure 12-5
The English alphabet can be represented by combinations of the binary digits 1 and 0.

Alphabetic Characters and Their Binary Codes

A	01000001	**H**	01001000	**O**	01001111	**V**	01010110
B	01000010	**I**	01001001	**P**	01010000	**W**	01010111
C	01000011	**J**	01001010	**Q**	01010001	**X**	01011000
D	01000100	**K**	01001011	**R**	01010010	**Y**	01011001
E	01000101	**L**	01001100	**S**	01010011	**Z**	01011010
F	01000110	**M**	01001101	**T**	01010100		
G	01000111	**N**	01001110	**U**	01010101		

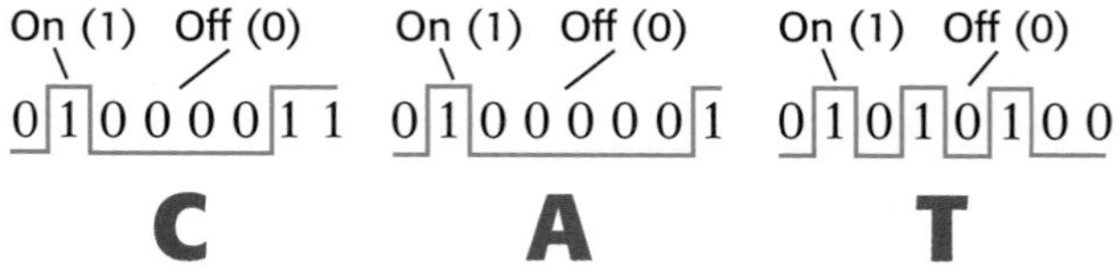
On (1) Off (0)
0 1 0 0 0 0 1 1
C
On (1) Off (0)
0 1 0 0 0 0 0 1
A
On (1) Off (0)
0 1 0 1 0 1 0 0
T

A binary digital signal consists of a series of zeros and ones

Most digital signals use *binary digital code,* which consists of two values, usually represented as 0 and 1. Each binary digit is called a *bit*. In electrical form, 0 and 1 are represented by the two states of an electric current: *off* (no current present) and *on* (current present). Information such as numbers, words, music, and pictures can be represented in binary code. **Figure 12-5** shows a binary digital code that is used to represent the English alphabet.

Most modern telecommunication systems transmit and store data in binary digital code. A compact disc (CD) player, shown in **Figure 12-6,** uses a laser beam to read the music that is digitally stored on the disc.

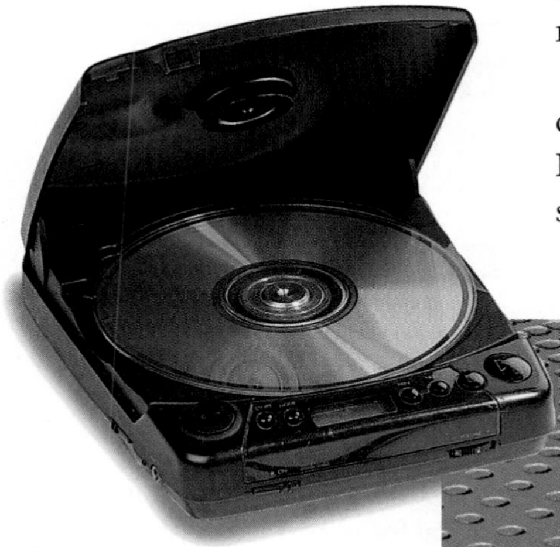

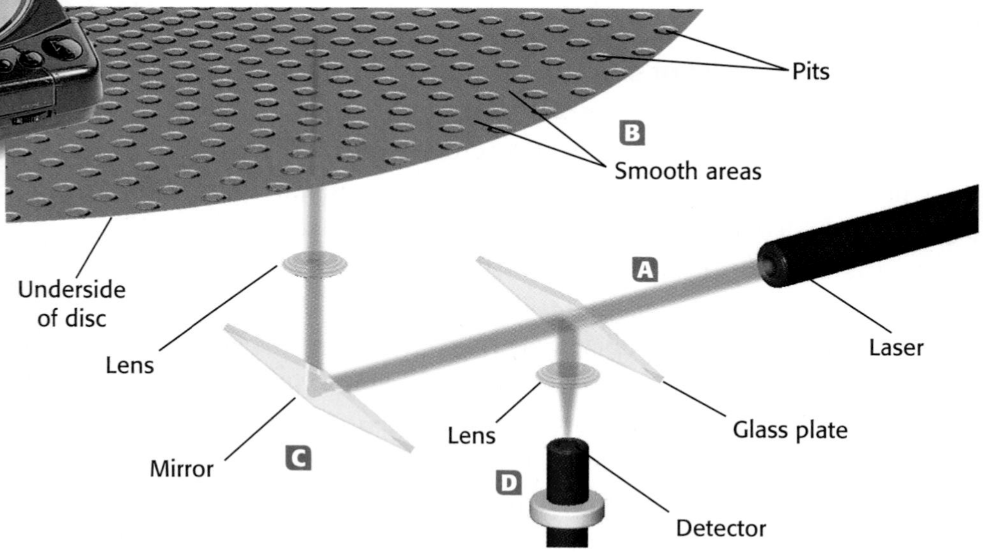
Pits
B
Smooth areas
Underside of disc
A
Laser
Lens
Lens
Glass plate
Mirror
C
D
Detector

Figure 12-6
(A) A laser beam shines on the disc. (B) The detector receives light reflected from smooth areas of the disc. (C) The reflected light is represented by a binary code. (D) The code is then reinterpreted as sound.

But how can sound be stored digitally? Sound is a wave of compressions (high air pressure) and rarefactions (low air pressure). Therefore, a sound can be described by noting the air pressure changes. The air pressure is measured in numbers and represented in binary digits.

How is the air pressure measured in numbers? This process is indirect. First, a microphone is used to convert the sound into an analog signal as a changing electric current. Then, an electronic device measures this changing current in numbers or digits at regular intervals. In fact, for CD sound recordings, the current is measured 44 100 times every second! The air pressure measurement is converted into binary digits in terms of 16 bits. For instance, 0000000010000010 is the digital representation of air pressure at a particular moment.

This conversion process is basically the same for creating digital signals from analog signals. Another device where this conversion occurs is in a digital telephone.

Digital signals can be sent quickly and accurately

Digital signals have many advantages over analog signals. Some digital "switches," consisting of electronic components, can be turned on and off up to a billion times per second. This allows a digital signal to send a lot of data in a small amount of time.

Noise and static have less effect on digital transmissions. Most digital signals include codes that constantly check the pattern of the received signal and correct any errors that may occur in the signal. By contrast, analog signals must be received, amplified, and retransmitted several times by components along the transmission route. Each time, the signal can get a little more distorted.

Telecommunication Today

Many telecommunication devices, such as telephones, transmit signals along metal wires. However, other ways are more efficient. Metal wires are being replaced with glass fibers that carry signals using pulses of light. Radio waves are also used to send signals. A call to another part of the world is likely to involve sending a signal by way of a communication satellite.

Optical fibers are more efficient than metal wires

A thin glass or plastic fiber, called an optical fiber, can be used to carry a beam of light. The light is reflected by the inside walls of the fiber, so it does not escape. Instead of carrying signals that are coded into electric currents, these fibers carry signals that are represented by pulses of light emitted by a laser.

▶ **optical fiber** a hair-thin, transparent strand of glass or plastic that transmits signals using pulses of light

Figure 12-7
A single standard metal-wire cable (A) is much thicker than an optical-fiber cable (B), yet it carries much less information than an optical fiber does.

Many telephone lines now in use in the United States consist of optical fibers. The optical-fiber system is lighter and smaller than the wire-cable system, as shown in **Figure 12-7,** making it much easier to put in place. A standard metal-wire cable, which is about 7.6 cm in diameter, can carry up to 1000 coded conversations at one time. A single optical fiber can carry 11 000 conversations at once using the present coding system.

As the use of the Internet and telephones dramatically increases, telephone companies are busy expanding fiber-optic networks. The materials used to make the optical fibers are so pure that a half-mile-thick slab made from them would transmit as much light as a clean windowpane.

Figure 12-8
A microwave relay tower picks up a signal, amplifies it, and relays it to the next tower.

Relay systems make it possible to send messages across the world

If you've traveled around the United States, you may have noticed tall steel towers with triangular or cone-shaped boxes and perhaps some dish-shaped antennas. These are microwave relay towers. They use microwave frequencies to transmit and relay signals over land.

As shown in **Figure 12-8,** a tower picks up a signal transmitted by another tower, amplifies the signal, and retransmits it toward the next tower. The next tower repeats the process, passing the signal along until it reaches its destination. Microwave transmission is often used to connect distant places with telephone signals.

Microwaves are a form of electromagnetic waves. For the microwave signals to be sent from one tower to the next, each tower must be almost visible from the top of the other. A tower built high in the Rocky Mountains would be able to relay signals for 80 to 160 km. However, a tower built in the plains can relay only a little farther than the horizon, or about 40 km.

Communications satellites receive and transmit electromagnetic waves

Microwave transmission allows you to make telephone calls across deserts or other areas without wires or fiber-optic networks. But how could you call a friend who lives across the ocean in Australia?

In the past, your call would have been carried by one of the cables that run along the ocean floor between continents. Because there are so many telephones, online computers, and fax machines today, the demand is too much for these cables. Communication satellites that orbit Earth help send these messages.

These satellites use solar power to generate electricity. This allows them to operate receivers, transmitters, and antennas. These satellites receive and send microwaves just like the towers described earlier. Because they are so high above the ground, these satellites can relay signals between telephone exchanges thousands of kilometers apart.

A satellite receives a microwave signal, called an *uplink*, from a ground station on Earth. The satellite then processes and transmits a *downlink* signal to another ground station. To keep the signals separate, the uplink signal consists of electromagnetic waves with a frequency of around 6 GHz (gigahertz, or 10^9 Hz), while the downlink signal typically has a lower frequency of about 4 GHz.

For maximum efficiency, the transmitting antenna of a communications satellite must be aimed so that it covers the largest area of land without the signal becoming too weak. This area is called a *satellite footprint*. The satellite footprint increases as the distance between the satellite and Earth's surface increases. With several satellites with large footprints, a signal from one location can be transmitted and received anywhere in the world.

Many communications satellites have geostationary orbits

If you live in an area where people receive television signals from satellites by using dish-shaped antennas, you may have noticed that the dish always points in one direction. If a satellite orbits Earth, its position would change. Why does the dish not have to be moved in order to stay pointed at the orbiting satellite?

internet connect

SCI LINKS
NSTA

TOPIC: Communications satellites
GO TO: www.scilinks.org
KEYWORD: HK1504

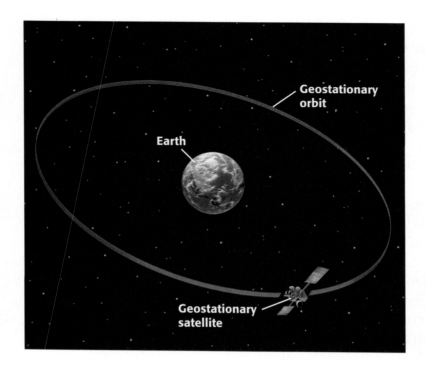

Geostationary orbit

Earth

Geostationary satellite

The answer is that these satellites orbit Earth every 24 hours, the same amount of time it takes for Earth to rotate once. Therefore the position of the satellite relative to the ground doesn't change. The orbit of this type of satellite is called a *geostationary orbit*, or a *geosynchronous orbit*. To be in a geostationary orbit, a satellite must be 35 880 km directly over Earth's equator and have a speed of 11 050 km/h, as shown in **Figure 12-9.**

Figure 12-9
A geostationary satellite appears to stay in a fixed position above the same spot on Earth. Once a dish is aimed at one of these satellites, it does not have to be moved again.

SECTION 12.1 REVIEW

SUMMARY

▶ A signal is a sign or event that conveys a message that can be sent using gestures, shapes, colors, electricity, or light.

▶ An analog signal varies continuously.

▶ A digital signal represents information in the form of discrete digits.

▶ A two-number code, called a binary digital code, represents the signal conditions of "on" or "off" by either a 1 or a 0.

▶ Telecommunication sends a signal long distances by means of electricity or light.

▶ Satellites are used to relay microwave signals around the world.

CHECK YOUR UNDERSTANDING

1. **List** five examples of telecommunication.
2. **Explain** why talking to your friend on the telephone is an example of telecommunication but talking to her face to face is not.
3. **Describe** how a sound is translated into an analog signal.
4. **Indicate** which of the following are analog signals and which are digital:
   a. music recorded on a compact disc
   b. speed displayed by the needle on a speedometer dial
   c. time displayed on a clock with three or four numerals
   d. time displayed on a clock with hands and a circular dial
   e. a motion picture on film
5. **Discuss** the advantages of optical fibers over metal wires as media for carrying signals.
6. **Explain** how communications satellites transmit messages around the world.
7. **Explain** what a geostationary orbit is and why many communications satellites are put in geostationary orbits.
8. **Critical Thinking** Explain why a taller microwave relay tower on Earth's surface has a longer transmission range than a shorter relay tower.

Telephone, Radio, and Television

OBJECTIVES

▶ Describe how a telephone converts sound waves to electric current during a phone call.

▶ Distinguish between physical transmission and atmospheric transmission for telephone, radio, and television signals.

▶ Explain how radio and television signals are broadcast using electromagnetic waves.

▶ Explain how radio and television signals are received and changed into sound and pictures.

▶ KEY TERMS

physical transmission
atmospheric transmission
modulate
carrier
cathode-ray tube
pixel

What sort of information do communication satellites relay around the world? Some information is vital business information, and some is secret government and military communication. Much of the information, however, consists of radio and television programming and telephone conversations.

Telephones

When you talk on the telephone, the sound waves of your voice are converted to an electrical signal by a transducer, a microphone in the mouthpiece of the telephone. As you hear the voice from the earpiece, a speaker, another transducer, is changing an electrical signal back into sound waves.

The electret microphone vibrates with sound waves, creating an analog signal

Most newer telephones use an *electret microphone*. In this type of microphone, an electrically charged membrane is mounted over an electret, which is a material that has a constant electric charge. The membrane vibrates up and down with the sound waves of your voice, as shown in **Figure 12-10**.

This motion causes a changing electric field so that an analog electrical signal that corresponds to your voice is produced. This signal is then transmitted as variations in an electric current between your telephone and that of the person you are talking to.

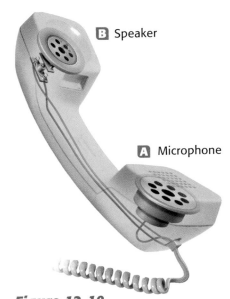

B Speaker

A Microphone

Figure 12-10
The sound waves from your voice are transformed by the microphone (A) into an analog electrical signal. A speaker (B) converts the analog electrical signal back to sound waves.

The movement of the speaker cone converts the analog signal back into sound waves

When you get a telephone call, the electrical signal enters your telephone. As you listen, the incoming electrical signal travels through a coil of wire that is fastened to a thin membrane called a *speaker cone*.

The wire coil is placed in a constant magnetic field and can move back and forth. The varying electric current of the incoming signal creates a varying magnetic field that interacts with the constant magnetic field. This causes the coil to move back and forth, which in turn causes the speaker cone to move in the same way. The movement of the speaker cone creates sound waves in the air that match the sound of your caller's voice. Speakers in radios, televisions, and stereo systems work the same way.

Telephone messages are sent through a medium in physical transmission

Telephone messages can be voice calls, faxes, or computer data. But how do the messages arrive at the right place? When you make a call, the signal is sent along wires to a local station. Telephone wires arrive at and leave the station in bundles called cables that are strung along poles or run underground. The station's switching equipment detects the number called.

If you are calling someone who lives nearby, such as a neighbor, the switching equipment sends the signal down wires that connect your phone through the station to your neighbor's phone. When the signal reaches your neighbor's phone, the phone rings. When your neighbor picks up the phone, the circuit is completed.

Sometimes telephone conversations travel a short distance by wire and then are carried by light through fiber optic cables. In this case, the varying current is fed to a laser diode, causing its laser light to brighten and dim. In this way, the electrical signal is converted into a light or optical signal. This light passes through an optical fiber to its destination, where a sensor changes light back to an electrical signal. Transmission of signals by wires or optical fibers is called **physical transmission.**

Messages traveling longer distances are sent by atmospheric transmission

Long-distance calls may be transmitted over wire or fiber-optic cables, or they may be sent through the atmosphere using microwave radiation. The transfer of information by means of electromagnetic waves through the atmosphere or space is called **atmospheric transmission.** The use of microwaves for telephone signals is one example of atmospheric transmission.

▶ **physical transmission** a transmission of a signal using wires, cables, or optical fibers

▶ **atmospheric transmission** a transmission of a signal using electromagnetic waves

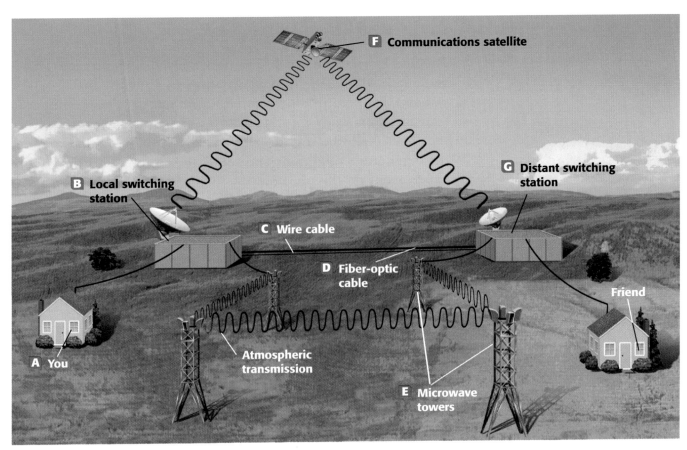

F Communications satellite

B Local switching station

G Distant switching station

C Wire cable

D Fiber-optic cable

Friend

A You

Atmospheric transmission

E Microwave towers

When you make a call, computers are used to find the most direct form of routing. Either physical or atmospheric transmission or a combination of the two may be used for long-distance calls, as shown in **Figure 12-11.** If the telephone system is very busy, computers may route your call indirectly through a combination of cables and microwave links. Your call to someone 100 mi away could actually travel for thousands of miles.

Cellular phones transmit messages in the form of electromagnetic waves

A cellular phone is just a small radio transmitter/receiver, or *transceiver.* Cellular phones communicate with one of an array of antennas mounted on towers or tall buildings. The area covered by each antenna is called a *cell.*

As the user moves from one cell to another, the phone switches to communicate with the next antenna. The user may not even notice the switching. As long as the telephone is not too far from a cellular antenna, the user can make and receive calls.

A cordless phone is also a radiowave transceiver. The phone sends signals to and receives signals from its base station, which is also a transceiver. The base station is connected to a standard phone line.

Figure 12-11
Your telephone call (A) arrives at a local switching station (B). Depending on its destination, the call is routed through a wire cable (C), fiber-optic cable (D), microwave towers (E), or communication satellites (F). The telephone signal then arrives at another switching station (G) where it travels to your friend's house, and the phone rings.

Radio and Television

The first long-distance transmission of a signal using radio waves was made across the English Channel in 1899. At the time, the signals were sent in Morse code. For the next 20 years, all radio transmissions were sent this way. It was not until 1918 that voice messages could be sent over the air using radio waves. In 1920, the first commercial radio station, KDKA, in Pittsburgh, Pennsylvania, went on the air, broadcasting sound signals by means of radio waves.

Sound waves are converted to electromagnetic waves for radio broadcast

A radio signal begins as a sound, or audio, signal that is first converted into a varying electric current from a microphone, tape deck, or CD player. This varying current is the analog of the sound waves from a voice or music source, as shown in **Figure 12-12A.**

A microphone is only capable of producing a weak signal, which has to be amplified, or increased in power, using an electronic device called an amplifier.

Now the signal is ready to be broadcast using a transmitter at the radio station. The visible part of the transmitter is an antenna, and the transmitter also contains different electric circuits including an oscillator. The oscillator produces a carrier wave, which is a signal of constant frequency and amplitude, as shown in **Figure 12-12B.** The numbers you see on your radio dial correspond to the carrier wave's frequency.

You can imagine the carrier wave as the wave on which the audio signal to be broadcasted will ride. The audio signal contains the sound information in the frequency range of the human voice, from about 100 to 3000 Hz. Also, the change in the loudness of the sound appears in the signal in terms of changing amplitude. The sound signal and the carrier signal meet in a specialized circuit in the transmitter. Here they combine and the audio signal changes, or modulates, the carrier wave. The result is a signal of constant frequency with an amplitude that is shaped by the audio signal, as shown in **Figure 12-12C.**

▶ **carrier** a continuous wave that can be modulated to send a signal

▶ **modulate** to change a wave's amplitude or frequency in order to send a signal

Figure 12-12
Amplitude Modulation
An audio signal carrying sound information modulates a carrier wave.

A

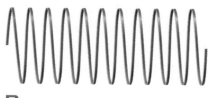 

B   C

Most broadcast carrier waves are modulated either by *amplitude modulation* (AM) or *frequency modulation* (FM). In amplitude modulation, the audio signal increases and decreases the amplitude of the carrier wave in a pattern that matches the audio signal. In frequency modulation, the audio signal affects the frequency of the carrier wave, changing it in a pattern that matches the audio signal.

Antennas transmit and receive electromagnetic waves

The modulated signal generated in the transmitter causes electric charges to move up and down along the length of the antenna. The resulting motion of the charges produces radio waves corresponding to the modulated signal.

The path that radio waves follow depends on the frequency of transmission. Higher frequency transmissions can follow only a simple straight line. This is called *line-of-sight transmission*. To receive a signal from an FM radio station, which can broadcast at frequencies between 88 and 108 MHz, your radio must be located no farther than just over the horizon from the broadcasting antenna (usually about 25 to 50 mi).

You can receive AM stations that are much farther than 50 mi away. AM frequencies between 540 and 1700 kHz can travel as *ground waves*, which can follow the curvature of the Earth for some distance, unlike line-of-sight transmissions.

Radio stations use sky waves to broadcast long distances

Another way AM radio stations can broadcast farther is by using *sky waves*. Sky waves spread out from the antenna into the sky and are reflected in the upper atmosphere, which contains charged particles. Sky waves are reflected back to Earth by these particles.

Some radio broadcasting uses sky waves to reach distant locations around the world. Certain powerful AM signals that use sky waves can be received thousands of miles away. These stations are often limited to using sky waves at night, when stations whose signals they might interfere with are off the air.

Radio receivers convert electromagnetic waves back into sound

The antenna of your radio receiver works as a transducer. When radio waves strike it, they produce very weak electric currents that match the original radio signal. But radio waves from many stations with different frequencies are striking the antenna. Fortunately, each station broadcasts with a different carrier frequency. You have to adjust the antenna circuit with a *tuner* so that the radio responds to only the frequency of the station you want to hear.

Did You Know?

In regions where broadcast signals cannot be received, such as in mountain valleys, television signals are conveyed through cables. Microwave links from satellites or microwave towers are fed by cable to local stations, and from there are either sent out by broadcast or cable.

Figure 12-13

After the detector removes the audio signal from the carrier, the signal is amplified and sent to a speaker. (Note that the amplifiers and detector shown as boxes correspond to different circuits that are part of the radio.)

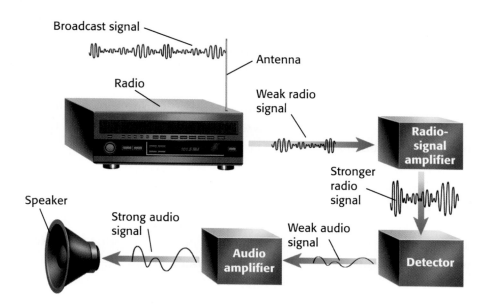

Next the modulated signal from the antenna is sent to a detector, as shown in **Figure 12-13.** The carrier wave has a very high frequency compared with the original electrical signal, so the two can be separated easily. The electrical signal then goes to an amplifier, which increases the signal's power. Finally, the amplified signal is sent to a speaker, where the sound that was originally broadcast is recreated.

Television sets convert electromagnetic waves back into images and sound

Television signals are also received by an antenna. By selecting a channel, you tune the television to the carrier frequency of the station of your choice. The carrier is passed to a detector that separates the audio and video electrical signals from the carrier. The audio electrical signals are sent to an audio amplifier and speaker, just as in a radio. The video electrical signal, which contains the color and brightness information, is used to create an image on the face of a picture tube.

The picture tube of a black-and-white television is a large cathode-ray tube, or CRT. A CRT makes a beam (ray) of electrons from a negatively charged cathode. The beam is directed toward the face of the tube that is covered with *phosphors,* which are made of a material that glows when an electron beam strikes them. Electromagnets arranged around the neck of the tube deflect the beam, causing it to move across the phosphor-coated face. The moving beam lights up the phosphors in a pattern that recreates the shot taken by the television camera. Each pass of the beam is called a *scan line.* In the United States, each complete image is made up of 525 scan lines.

cathode-ray tube a tube that uses an electron beam to create a display on a phosphorescent screen

Color picture tubes in some televisions, like the one shown in **Figure 12-14,** produce three electron beams, one for each of the primary colors of light: red, blue, and green. The phosphors on the face of the tube glow either red, blue, or green. The phosphors are arranged in groups of three dots, one of each color. Each group of three dots is a *pixel,* the smallest piece of an electronically produced picture.

To make sure the beam for red strikes only red phosphors, two different approaches can be used. In one, a screen with holes, called a *shadow mask,* lies just behind the face of the tube. The beam for each color passes through a hole in the shadow mask at an angle so that the beam strikes only the phosphor dot that glows the correct color. Another approach in some televisions use a single electron beam deflected toward the phosphor of the correct color by a charged wire grid.

▶ **pixel** the smallest element of a display image

VOCABULARY *Skills Tip*

The term pixel *is derived from the phrase* **pic***ture* **el***ement*

Figure 12-14

🅐 The video signals modulating the television carrier are detected and are then used to control the electron beams in the cathode-ray tube. The sound signal is amplified and sent to a speaker, while video signals vary the intensity of the three electron beams.

🅑 Electromagnets sweep the beams across the face of the screen. The intensity of each beam determines how bright the phosphor dots light up.

🅒 This determines the color and the brightness of each pixel.

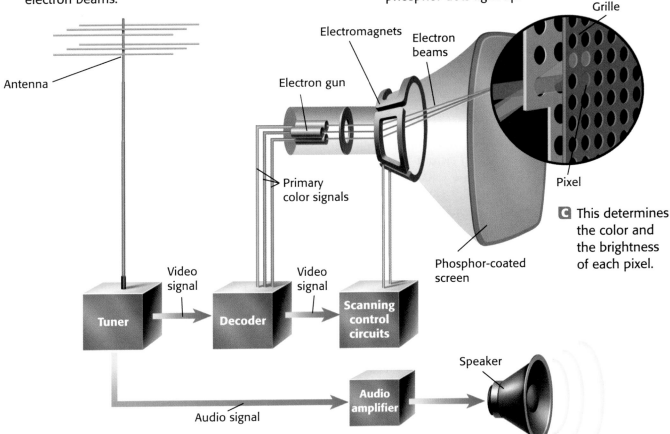

TV by the Numbers: High-Definition Digital TV

When you turn on a television in the year 2006, it may look a lot different than the one you watch now. That's because the Federal Communications Commission (FCC) has decided that all television stations in the United States must broadcast only digital, high-definition television, called HDTV for short, by 2006.

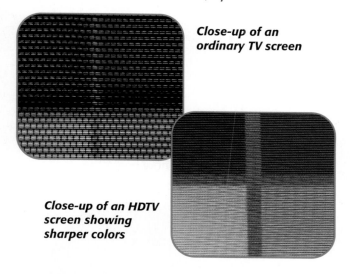

Close-up of an ordinary TV screen

Close-up of an HDTV screen showing sharper colors

Comparing HDTV with Ordinary TV

The HDTV picture looks very detailed and sharp compared with an ordinary television picture. You can even see the faces of fans at a sports event. The picture has a width-to-height ratio of 16:9, similar to many movies that you see in a theater. By 2006, you may have a TV with a large flat screen that hangs on the wall like a painting or mirror. HDTV sound is clear, digital sound, like that recorded on a CD.

However, you won't have to throw out your old television set in 2006. A converter box will let your old TV show pictures that are broadcast in HDTV. However, the picture won't look any better than if it is a regular broadcast.

History of HDTV

The development of HDTV began in the early 1980s when engineers realized that newer microprocessors would be able to both send and decode data fast enough to transmit a detailed television picture digitally. In 1988, 23 different HDTV systems were proposed to the FCC. In 1993, several companies joined the Massachusetts Institute of Technology in what was called the Grand Alliance. Its purpose was to create HDTV standards for broadcasters. In 1996, the FCC approved an entirely digital system, and by late 1998, the first commercial HDTV receivers were on sale at prices between $10 000 and $20 000.

HDTV Technology

HDTV achieves its sharp picture by using almost 1200 scan lines, compared with 525 on analog TV. The digital signal can also be continuously checked for accuracy, so the picture remains clear.

The movie industry is very interested in HDTV. It will be able to release new HDTV tapes and discs of movies already released on other video formats. Another possibility is that some movies can be released to pay-per-view HDTV at the same time they are released in theaters. The HDTV picture and sound quality should be so good that some people may prefer to stay at home to watch a new movie.

Your Choice

1. **Making Decisions** What effect do you think HDTV will have on movie theaters, especially if studios make movies available on HDTV for the same price as a theater ticket? Explain whether you think people will still want to go to theaters.
2. **Critical Thinking** When home VCRs were introduced in the mid-1970s, they cost about $2500. By 1980, the price was about $600. By 1985, the price was about $450. By the mid-1990s, you could buy a good-quality VCR for about $250. Check the current price of an HDTV, and use the VCR example to project what one will cost in 5 years.

Inquiry Lab

How do red, blue, and green TV phosphors produce other colors?

Materials
✔ three adjustable flashlights with bright halogen bulbs
✔ several pieces of red, blue, and green cellophane
✔ white paper

Procedure

1. Adjust the focus of each flashlight so that it produces a circle of light about 15 cm in diameter on a white sheet of paper. Turn off the flashlights.
2. Place a piece of red cellophane over the lens of one flashlight, green cellophane over the lens of another, and blue over the lens of the third.
3. Turn on the flashlights, and shine the three beams on white paper so the circles of light overlap slightly.
4. Adjust the distance between the flashlights and the paper until the area where all three circles overlap appears white. Add more cellophane if necessary.

Analysis

1. Describe the three colors formed where two of the beams overlap.
2. What combinations of light produced the colors yellow and cyan?

SECTION 12.2 REVIEW

SUMMARY

▶ Telephones change sound to electrical signals and electrical signals to sound.

▶ Signals can be sent by physical transmission or by atmospheric transmission.

▶ Signals modulate carrier waves by amplitude modulation (AM) and frequency modulation (FM).

CHECK YOUR UNDERSTANDING

1. **Describe** how telephones convert sound to electrical signals and electrical signals to sound.
2. **List** three ways that telephone signals can travel.
3. **Identify** which have a higher frequency—AM or FM signals.
4. **Describe** the function of phosphors in a cathode-ray tube.
5. **Explain** the function of the magnetic coils at the rear of a television picture tube.
6. **Describe** how a radio receiver converts a broadcast signal into sound waves.
7. **Critical Thinking** Why do you think there is increasing interest in using fiber-optic cables to provide homes with cable television service?

Computers and the Internet

INTEGRATING TECHNOLOGY and Society

▶ **KEY TERMS**

computer
random-access memory
read-only memory
hardware
software
operating system
Internet

OBJECTIVES

▶ Describe a computer, and list its four basic functions.
▶ Describe the binary nature of computer data and the use of logic gates.
▶ Distinguish between hardware and software, and give examples of each.
▶ Explain how the Internet works.

▶ **computer** an electronic device that can accept data and instructions, follow the instructions, and output the results

Did you heat a pastry in the microwave for breakfast? Have you ever inserted a card in a slot to pay your fare on a bus or subway? Maybe you rode to school in a car. Did you stop for a traffic light? Was the temperature in your classroom comfortable? Did a clerk scan a bar code on an item you bought at the store?

All of these situations involve computers or the use of computers to function. The computer that controls traffic lights may be large and complex, while the one in the microwave oven is likely to be small and simple.

Figure 12-15
ENIAC, the world's first practical digital computer, used 18 000 vacuum tubes, like the one shown here. The modern microprocessor has thousands of times ENIAC's computing power.

Computers

A **computer** is a machine that can receive data, perform high-speed calculations or logical operations, and output the results. Although computers operate automatically, they do only what they are programmed to do. Computers respond to commands that humans give them, even though they sometimes may appear to "think" on their own.

Computers have been changing greatly since the 1940s

The first electronic computer was the Electronic Numerical Integrator And Computer (ENIAC), shown in **Figure 12-15.** It was developed during World War II. ENIAC was as big as a house and weighed 30 tons. Its 18 000 vacuum tubes consumed 180 000 W of electric power. During the late 1940s, computers began to be used in business and industry. As they became smaller, faster, and cheaper, their use in offices and homes dramatically increased.

Today computers are so common that we hardly notice them. Try to imagine what computer developers in the 1940s would think if they could see a modern personal computer, or PC, which fits on a desk and computes thousands of times faster than the earlier cumbersome computers like ENIAC.

Computers carry out four functions

Digital computers perform four basic functions: input, storage, processing, and output. The input function can be carried out using any number of devices, as shown in **Figure 12-16.** When you use a personal computer, you can use a keyboard to input data and instructions for the computer. A mouse is another input device. You may use a mouse to draw or select text in a document.

Other input devices include a scanner, which can enter drawings or photographs, and a joystick, which sends data about the movement of the stick. A modem connected to a telephone line can be both an output and an input device.

Microphones, musical instruments, and cameras can be used as input devices. Once the data are processed, the result, or output, may be displayed on a monitor. You can also send output to a printer. Sound output goes to speakers or to a recording device.

Figure 12-16
A computer can receive data from many devices, store information on a hard drive, process data as needed, and store results or send them to an output device.

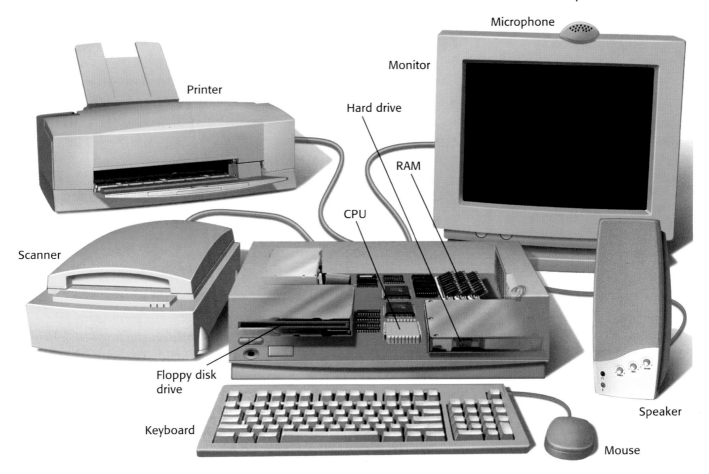

Quick ACTIVITY

How Fast Are Digital Computers?

1. With a partner, time how long it takes for each of you to solve problems involving adding, subtracting, multiplying, and dividing large numbers. Do each problem first by hand and then with the help of a hand-held calculator, which is a form of digital computer. Solve at least five problems using each method.

2. Find the average amount of time spent doing the problems by hand and with a calculator. Compare the two averages, and discuss your results.

VOCABULARY *Skills Tip*

Most disks used for computer work today are not actually floppy. The name floppy disk *originally referred to a larger-sized disk that was encased in softer plastic sleeves.*

INTEGRATING

PHYSICS

All PCs are digital computers, but analog computers also exist. An example of an analog computer in a car is the gasoline gauge, whose needle moves in response to a voltage sent from a sensor in the gas tank.

Computer input is in the form of binary code

All input devices provide data to the computer in the form of binary code. For example, a keyboard contains a small processor that detects which key is pressed and sends the computer a binary code that represents the character you typed. Devices such as temperature sensors, pressure sensors, and light sensors provide information in the form of varying voltage. This information is analog; that is, it changes continuously over the range of the quantity being measured. Such information must be passed through an analog-to-digital converter (A to D converter) before the data can be used by a computer.

Computers process binary data, including numbers, letters, and other symbols, in groups of eight *bits*. Each bit can have only one of two values, usually represented as 1 and 0. A group of eight bits is called a *byte*.

As shown in **Figure 12-5,** when you type the capital letter *W* on the keyboard, the computer receives the data byte 01010111. Similarly, the lowercase letter *e* is received as 01100101. Thus, if you type the word *We*, the computer would recognize the word as 0101011101100101, a combination of the *W* byte and the *e* byte in sequence.

Computers must have a means of storing data

Both input and output data can be stored on long-term storage devices. The most common of these devices is the *hard-disk drive*, which is sometimes simply called the hard drive. Some hard drives can store as much or more than 20 billion bytes, or 20 gigabytes (20 Gigs) of information. Hard drives are so-called to distinguish them from disk drives that use removable "floppy" disks. Floppy disks can be removed from one computer and used in another.

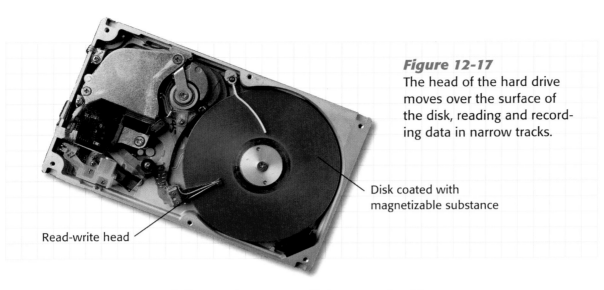

Figure 12-17
The head of the hard drive moves over the surface of the disk, reading and recording data in narrow tracks.

Disk coated with
magnetizable substance

Read-write head

Both hard drives and floppy drives use disks coated with a magnetizable substance. Disks of this type are generally referred to as *magnetic media*. A small read-write head, similar to the record-play head in a cassette tape recorder, transfers data to and from the disk, as shown in **Figure 12-17.** Each data bit consists of a very small area that is magnetized in one direction for 0 and in the opposite direction for 1. These magnetized areas are arranged in tracks around the disk.

When data are being read, the disk spins and the head detects the magnetic direction of each area that passes. When data are being recorded, or "written" on the disk, a current passes through a small coil of wire in the head. The direction of the current at any time creates a magnetic field in one direction or the other. This allows the head to record information on the disks in bits of 0's and 1's.

On a disk, the time required to access (read or write) data depends on where the information is stored on the disk and the position of the read-write head. Therefore, access time for two different pieces of data on a disk will be different.

> **random-access memory**
> a storage device that allows stored data to be read in the same access time

Random-access memory is used for short-term storage of data and instructions

For working memory, the computer needs to be able to access data quickly. This type of memory is contained on microchips as shown in **Figure 12-18** and is called random-access memory, or RAM.

Each RAM microchip is covered with millions of tiny transistors. Like a light switch, each transistor can be placed in one of two electrical states: *on* or *off*. Each transistor represents either a 0 or a 1 and can therefore store one data bit. This memory is called random-access because any of the data stored in RAM can be accessed in the same time. Unlike the data stored on the disk, accessing information in RAM doesn't depend on location.

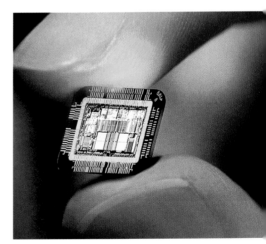

Figure 12-18
This chip is covered with tiny transistors that function as two-position switches. This feature allows the computer to operate as a binary machine.

Read-only memory is for long-term storage of operating instructions

> **read-only memory** a memory device containing data that cannot be changed

Another type of memory is called read-only memory, or ROM. The information in ROM is permanently stored when the chip is manufactured. As a result, it can be read but not changed. When you first turn on a computer, instructions that are stored in ROM set up the computer so that it is ready to receive input data from the keyboard or the hard drive.

Optical storage devices can be more permanent than magnetic disks

Information can also be stored on *compact discs* (CDs) and *digital versatile discs* (DVDs). These discs are called optical media because the information in it is read by a laser light. When they are used to store computer data, they are referred to as CD-ROMs and DVD-ROMs because the data they hold are permanently recorded on them.

Computers are guided by programs

> **hardware** the equipment that makes up a computer system

> **software** the instructions, data, and programming that make a computer system work

> **operating system** the software that controls a computer's activities

All of the physical components of a computer are called hardware. The hardware of the computer can compute and store data only if we provide it with the necessary instructions. These instructions are called computer programs, or software.

When a computer is turned on, one of the first programs executed by the computer is the operating system, or OS. The OS controls the computer hardware—memory, keyboard, disks, printer, mouse, and monitor—so they work together. It also handles the transfer of computer files to and from disks and organizes the files.

The operating system provides the environment in which other computer programs run. These other programs are called applications. Applications include word processors, drawing programs, spreadsheet programs, and programs to organize and manipulate large amounts of information, such as a store's inventory or polling data. Applications also include computer games and programs that allow you to browse the Internet.

Figure 12-19

The motherboard is the nervous system of a computer and contains the CPU, memory chips, and logic circuits.

The processing function is the primary operation of a computer

The processing function is where computing actually takes place. Computing or data processing is carried out by the *central processing unit,* or CPU. The CPU of a personal computer usually consists of one microchip, which is not much larger than a postage stamp. The CPU is one of the many chips located on the motherboard, as shown in **Figure 12-19.**

This chip, or microprocessor, consists of millions of tiny electronic parts, including resistors, capacitors, diodes, and transistors, most of which act as switches. These components form huge numbers of circuits on the surface of the chip.

Logic circuits in the CPU make decisions

The heart of the CPU is an *arithmetic/logic unit*, or ALU, which performs calculations and logic decisions. The CPU also contains temporary data storage units, called *registers*, which hold results from previous calculations and other data waiting to be processed. A control section coordinates all of the processor activities. Finally, there are conductors that connect the various parts of the CPU to one another and to the rest of the computer.

When you start a program, the program first loads into random-access memory. Next the CPU performs a "fetch" operation, which brings in the first program instruction. Then it carries out that instruction and fetches the next instruction. The CPU proceeds in this fashion, fetching new instructions and obtaining data from the keyboard, mouse, disk, or other input device. Then it processes the data and creates output that is sent to the monitor or printer.

The CPU's logic gates can be built up to evaluate data and make decisions

As with memory chips, transistors in the CPU act as switches. Here, though, the switches can operate as devices called *logic gates*. Just as a real gate can be open or shut, a logic gate can open or close a circuit depending on the condition of two inputs. One kind of logic gate, called an AND gate, closes the circuit and allows current to pass only when both inputs are in the "on" position.

You could use a device like this to alert you when it is both cold and raining so that you will know what kind of clothing to wear. You could connect moisture and temperature sensors to an AND gate and arrange to have it close a circuit and ring a bell.

The bell will ring only when the temperature falls below 40°F and it is raining. If it is raining but is not cold, the bell will not ring. Similarly, the bell will not ring if it is cold but dry outside.

Figure 12-20
This logic system evaluates three variables—temperature, moisture, and light—in order to make a decision.

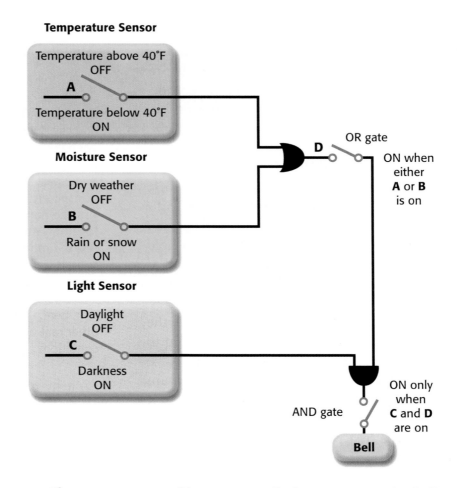

If you use a type of logic gate called an OR gate, the bell will ring when it is cold or when it is raining. If you want the bell to ring when it is cold or when it is raining, but only if it is dark outside, you could use an OR gate followed by an AND gate, as shown in **Figure 12-20.**

Computer Networks and the Internet

As the use of desktop personal computers became common in the 1980s, people looked for ways to link all of the computers within a single business, university, or government agency. The development of local area networks, or LANs, was the solution. In a LAN, all PCs are connected by cables to a central computer called a *server.* A server consists of a computer with lots of memory and several hard-disk drives for storing huge amounts of information.

This system allows workers to share data files that are stored on the server. One can also send a document to another person on the network. Soon after LANs were established, people were exchanging memos and documents over the network. This type of communication is called electronic mail, or E-mail.

The Internet is a worldwide network of computers

As the number of powerful computers increased, especially in government and universities, the U.S. Department of Defense wanted to connect them in a nationwide network. However, the department's computer experts worried about setting up a network that depended on only a few computers acting as distribution centers for information. If anything went wrong, the entire network would stop working.

Instead, a network in which every computer could communicate with every other computer was created. If part of the network were destroyed, the remainder would still be able to transmit information. This was the beginning of the Internet.

Because many companies had set up internal networks that used the same communication methods as the Defense Department's network, it was easy for them to connect to the network by telephone lines. Many other governments and corporations around the world joined to form a worldwide network that we now call the Internet, which is really a network of other networks.

If you have used the Internet, you are probably most familiar with the part known as the *World Wide Web,* or WWW, or just the Web. The Web was created in Europe in 1989 as a way for scientists to use the Internet to share data and other information.

The Web was mostly a resource for scientific information. It has since exploded into a vast number of sites created by individuals, government agencies, companies, and any other group with an interest in communicating or selling on the Internet.

▶ **Internet** a large computer network that connects many local and smaller networks

internetconnect

SCI*LINKS*
NSTA

TOPIC: Internet
GO TO: www.scilinks.org
KEYWORD: HK1506

REAL WORLD APPLICATIONS

Using a Search Engine
Search engines provide a way to find specific information in the vast amount of information that is available on the Internet. Finding information successfully depends on several things, one of which is picking appropriate keywords for your search.

Applying Information
1. Pick a science topic that interests you. Write down a few keywords that you think will occur in information about the topic.

2. Use an Internet search engine to find three Web sites that have information on the topic. Experiment with keywords until you find the kinds of sites you want.

3. Try the same keywords on other search engines. Do they all find the same sites?

4. How did the results differ? Can you detect whether an engine specializes in certain types of information?

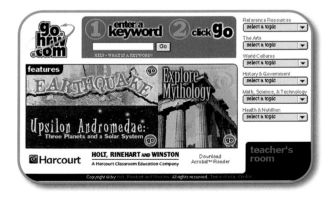

You need three things to use the Internet

To use the Internet, you need a computer with a modem to connect the computer to a telephone line. The word *modem* is short for modulator/demodulator, a device that codes the output data of your computer and uses it to modulate a carrier wave that is transmitted over telephone lines. The modem also extracts data from an incoming carrier wave and sends that data to your computer.

Next you need a software program called an Internet, or Web, browser. This program interprets signals received from the Internet and shows the results on your monitor. It also changes your input into signals that can be sent out.

Finally, you need a telephone connection to an Internet service provider, or ISP. An ISP is usually a company that connects the modem signal of your computer to the Internet for a monthly fee.

Communication across the Internet uses transmission pathways—physical and atmospheric—just like those used to relay television, radio, and telephone signals. The Internet system has advanced to the point that you can begin to communicate with a Web site anywhere on Earth in a matter of seconds.

SECTION 12.3 REVIEW

SUMMARY

- ▶ Computers are machines that carry out operations as instructed by programs.

- ▶ Computers perform four functions: input, storage, processing, and output.

- ▶ The physical components of computers are called hardware.

- ▶ Programs and instructions are called software.

- ▶ Computing activity takes place in a central processing unit, which also carries out logic functions.

- ▶ The Internet is a worldwide network of computers that can store and transmit vast amounts of data.

CHECK YOUR UNDERSTANDING

1. **List** three computer input devices and three output devices.
2. **Describe** each of the four main functions performed by a digital computer.
3. **Distinguish** between the way optical media and magnetic media function.
4. **Explain** how data are stored on and read from a magnetic hard-disk drive.
5. **Identify** which of the following components are part of a computer's hardware and which are part of its software.
   a. a CPU microchip
   b. a program to calculate when a car needs an oil change
   c. the instructions for the computer clock to be displayed
   d. RAM memory
6. **Explain** the purpose of an operating system.
7. **Indicate** how ROM and RAM differ and why RAM is necessary.
8. **Compare** an AND gate's functions with those of an OR gate.
9. **Restate** the three things, in addition to a computer, that you need to use the Internet.
10. **Creative Thinking** What is the connection between the binary operation of computers and the function of transistors?

Chapter Highlights

Before you begin, review the summaries of the key ideas of each section, found on pages 404, 413, and 422. The key vocabulary terms are listed on pages 396, 405, and 414.

UNDERSTANDING CONCEPTS

1. A _____ is necessary in order to interpret a signal.
   - **a.** CPU
   - **b.** modulation
   - **c.** operating system
   - **d.** code

2. The microphone in the mouthpiece of a telephone produces a(n) _____ signal.
   - **a.** microwave
   - **b.** analog
   - **c.** light
   - **d.** digital

3. A communications signal from a ground station to a satellite is an example of _____ transmission.
   - **a.** atmospheric
   - **b.** cellular
   - **c.** physical
   - **d.** ground-wave

4. The up-and-down movement of electrons in the wire of a transmitting antenna produces _____ waves.
   - **a.** electromagnetic
   - **b.** visible light
   - **c.** sound
   - **d.** television

5. By adjusting the _____, a radio can receive a certain station.
   - **a.** amplifier voltage
   - **b.** speaker circuit
   - **c.** tuner circuit
   - **d.** carrier frequency

6. Materials that glow when struck by an electron beam are called _____.
   - **a.** phosphors
   - **b.** pixels
   - **c.** cathode rays
   - **d.** transistors

7. A computer program that coordinates all of the computer hardware is a(n) _____.
   - **a.** read-only memory
   - **b.** application
   - **c.** operating system
   - **d.** browser

8. A modem connects a computer to a _____.
   - **a.** printer
   - **b.** transmitting antenna
   - **c.** hard-disk drive
   - **d.** telephone line

9. The most common data-storage device on a modern personal computer is the _____.
   - **a.** ROM
   - **b.** keyboard
   - **c.** hard-disk drive
   - **d.** CPU

Using Vocabulary

10. How does *telecommunication* differ from ordinary communication?

11. Describe the differences between *analog signals* and *digital signals*.

12. How does *physical transmission* differ from *atmospheric transmission*?

13. Describe two ways that a broadcasting station can *modulate* a carrier wave.

14. Which of the following diagrams correctly represents the path of a light beam through an *optical fiber*? Explain your choice. How is a binary digital signal sent through an optical fiber?

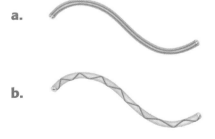

a.

b.

15. List two examples of computer *hardware* that are input devices and two that are output devices.

16. RAM stands for *random-access memory*. Why is this kind of computer memory called "random access"?

BUILDING MATH SKILLS

17. Graphing In 1965, an engineer named Moore stated that the number of transistors on integrated-circuit chips would double every 18 to 24 months. This idea became known as Moore's law. The data in the table below show the actual numbers of transistors on the CPU chips that have been introduced since 1972. Make a graph with "Years" on the x-axis and "Number of transistors" on the y-axis. Describe the shape of the graph. Does your graph support Moore's law? Does the projected value for the year 2010 seem realistic?

Year	Microprocessor	Number of transistors
1972	4004	2300
1973	8008	3500
1974	8080	6000
1978	8086	29 000
1982	80286	134 000
1986	80386	275 000
1989	80486	1.2 million
1993	Pentium	3.1 million
1996	Pentium Pro	5.5 million
1997	Pentium II	7.5 million
1999	Pentium III	9.5 million
2010	?	800 million (estimated)

THINKING CRITICALLY

18. Applying Knowledge Your basketball team and coach have a meeting in which you decide that certain hand gestures and finger positions will convey certain messages such as pass, stall, or play zone defense, etc. Use this example to explain the difference between a signal and a code.

19. Interpreting Graphics Identify the diagram that represents each of the following:
a. a carrier wave
b. an audio signal
c. an amplitude-modulated carrier

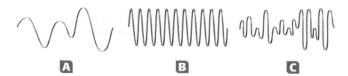

A   B   C

20. Applying Knowledge Use words or draw a diagram to explain why an FM radio signal can be received farther away as the height of the transmitting tower is increased. Also explain why you can receive more-distant television stations by using a higher television antenna.

21. Applying Knowledge Visible light from a laser can be used as a signal carrier. Describe what you would see if laser light is amplitude modulated and frequency modulated, assuming the modulation is slow enough for you to see the result. Which type of modulation do you think is more practical for visible light? Explain.

22. Problem Solving Suppose you want a light to come on automatically when someone comes to your door but only if it is dark outside. You have a proximity sensor, which is a device that closes an electric circuit when a person comes close to the door. What other sensor and what kind of logic gate do you need?

23. Applying Knowledge Suppose you are attempting to connect your computer to the World Wide Web, but it is not working. List two possible reasons why your computer is not able to connect, and explain how you could check for each one.

24. Applying Technology AM radio antennas are usually as tall as one-fourth the wavelength of the carrier. How tall is the antenna of a radio station transmitting at 650 kHz? Use the equation relating wavelength, velocity, and frequency from Chapter 10.

25. Applying Technology FM stations usually broadcast with antennas that are 1/2 the wavelength of the carrier. What is the length of an antenna for a station broadcasting at 105.5 MHz? Compare your answer with the answer in item 23, and explain why FM stations broadcast from towers much taller than the actual antenna length.

26. Applying Technology What computer-input device would work best in each of the following situations? Justify your choices.

  a. You want to use a picture from a magazine in a report for history class.

  b. You want to play a computer game in which you fly a plane.

  c. You want to compose an E-mail message and send it to a friend.

  d. You want to copy parts of several different documents on the Internet and put them all into one document.

27. Working Cooperatively Working with a group of classmates, research the achievements of the following people in the fields of communication and computer technology. Construct a classroom display that includes a picture of each person and a summary of his or her contributions.

  a. Edwin Armstrong

  b. Grace Murray Hopper

  c. An Wang

  d. Lewis Latimer

  e. Vladimir Zwyorkin

  f. John W. Mauchly

28. Concept Mapping Copy the unfinished concept map below onto a sheet of paper. Complete the map by writing the correct word or phrase in the lettered boxes.

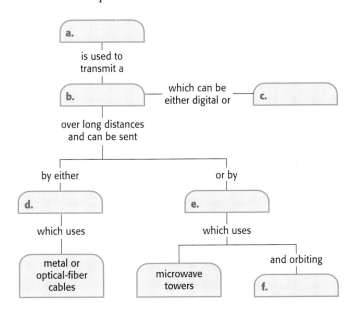

29. Connection to Social Studies Internet access has led to problems involving free speech and privacy. Should there be controls to prevent the spread of potentially dangerous or offensive information? Should others have free access to information about you? Research specific examples of these problems and find out what laws have been passed to address them. What arguments are made for and against free speech? An important fact to consider is that the Internet is not limited to one country.

internet**connect**

*SCI*LINKS
NSTA

TOPIC: Communication technology
GO TO: www.scilinks.org
KEYWORD: HK1507

Skill Builder Lab

Introduction

Can you determine the speed of sound in air?

Objectives

▶ *Observe* the reinforcement of sound in a column of air.

▶ *Determine* the speed of sound in air by calculating the wavelength of sound at a known frequency.

Materials

two tuning forks of known frequency
glass tube about 4 cm in diameter
    and 50 cm in length
tall glass cylinder
thermometer
meterstick
large rubber stopper
wood dowel or wire handle for stopper

Safety Needs

safety goggles

Determining the Speed of Sound

▶ Preparing for Your Lab

1. The speed of sound is equal to the product of frequency and wavelength. The frequency is known in this experiment, and the wavelength will be determined.
2. If you hold a vibrating tuning fork above a column of air, the note or sound produced by the fork is strongly reinforced when the air column in the glass tube is just the right length. This reinforcement is called resonance and the length is called the resonant length. The resonant length of a closed tube is about one-fourth the wavelength of the note produced by the fork.
3. On a paper, copy **Table 12-1** at right.

▶ Determining the Speed of Sound

SAFETY CAUTION Make sure the tuning fork does not touch the glass tube or cylinder, as the glass may shatter from the vibrations.

4. Set up the equipment as shown in the figure at right.
5. Record the frequency of the tuning fork as the number of vibrations per second (vps) in your **Table 12-1.**
6. Make the tuning fork vibrate by striking it with a large rubber stopper mounted on a dowel or heavy wire.
7. Hold the tube in a cylinder nearly full of water, as illustrated in the figure.
8. Hold the vibrating fork over the open end of the tube. Adjust the air column by moving the tube up and down until you find the point where the resonance causes the loudest sound. Then hold the tube in place while your partner measures the distance from the top of the glass tube to the surface of the water (which is the part of the tube sticking out of water). Record this length to the nearest millimeter as Trial 1 in **Table 12-1.**
9. Repeat steps 6–8 two more times using the same tuning fork, and record your data in **Table 12-1.**
10. Using a different tuning fork, repeat steps 4–8.

Table 12-1 Data Needed to Determine the Speed of Sound in Air

	Tuning fork 1	Tuning fork 2
Vibration rate of fork (vps)		
Length of tube above water (mm), Trial 1		
Length of tube above water (mm), Trial 2		
Length of tube above water (mm), Trial 3		

▶ Analyzing Your Results

1. On a clean sheet of paper, make a table like the one shown below.
2. Measure the inside diameter of your tube and record this measurement in your **Table 12-2.** The reflection of sound at the open end of a tube occurs at a point about 0.4 of its diameter above the end of the tube. Calculate this value and record it in **Table 12-2.** This distance is added to the length to get the resonant length. Record the resonant length in **Table 12-2.**
3. Complete the calculations shown in **Table 12-2.**
4. Measure the air temperature, and calculate the speed of sound using the information shown below. Record your answer in **Table 12-2.**

Speed of sound = 332 m/s at 0 °C + 0.6 m/s for every degree above 0°C

Table 12-2 Calculating the Speed of Sound

	Tuning fork 1	Tuning fork 2
Average measured length of air column (mm)		
Inside diameter (mm)		
Inside diameter × 0.4 (mm)		
Resonant length		
Wavelength of sound (mm), 4 × resonant length		
Wavelength of sound (m), wavelength of sound (mm) × $\frac{1}{1000}$		
Speed of sound (m/s), wavelength × vibration rate of fork		
Speed of sound (m/s), calculated from step 4		

Tuning fork

Open-ended glass tube

▶ Defending Your Conclusions

5. Should the speed of sound determined with the two tuning forks be the same?
6. How does the value for the speed of sound you calculated compare with the speed of sound you determined by measuring the air column?
7. How could you determine the frequency of a tuning fork that had an unknown value?

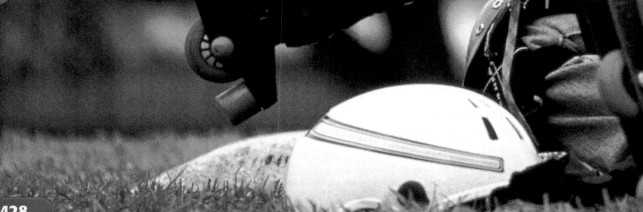

The Human Body

CHAPTER 13
Food and Diet   432
Viewpoints: Should You Buy
Genetically Engineered Food?   460

CHAPTER 14
Circulation and Respiration   462
Career Link: Vernon Henderson,
Trauma Surgeon   488

CHAPTER 15
Physical Fitness   490

CHAPTER 16
Disease Prevention and
Drug Use   518

CHAPTER 17
Reproduction and Growth   546

Food and Diet

Chapter Preview

13.1 Nutrients and Diet
  What Nutrients Are in Your Food?
  Choosing Foods for Your Health

13.2 Energy and Food
  The Role of Energy in Your Body
  Dietary Problems

13.3 Digestion
  Mechanical and Chemical Digestion
  The Start of Digestion
  Absorption of Nutrients
  Disorders of the Digestive System

Multicultural fairs like the one shown here often include opportunities to try food from other cultures.

Focus ACTIVITY

Background Every culture's food has distinctive flavors. The flavors may range from the spicy jalapeño peppers used in some Mexican dishes to the sweet-and-sour sauces of some Asian recipes. But no matter how different the food tastes, the contents of the food have some basic similarities.

These similarities exist because every human body needs nourishment. Food provides the energy and raw materials the body needs to live and grow.

Activity 1 Categorize each of the following foods as containing meat, grain product, or vegetables. What similarities are there among the ingredients from one food to another? What differences are there?

○ an Italian pastrami sandwich on rye bread with a pickle
○ a Chinese egg roll with shrimp and cabbage inside
○ a Greek gyro made of bits of roasted beef in the pocket of a doughy pita-bread
○ a Mexican taco of chicken meat with diced tomatoes and onions, rolled in a flour tortilla

Activity 2 After a meal at home, save the labels from the cans, jars, and boxes of food used to prepare it. Based on the information on the labels, estimate what percentage of the "% Daily Value" your meal provided for each of the following:

○ carbohydrates   ○ fat
○ protein   ○ vitamin A
○ vitamin C

internetconnect

SC*LINKS.
NSTA

TOPIC: Nutrients
GO TO: www.scilinks.org
KEYWORD: HJ1301

Nutrients and Diet

► **nutrient** a chemical substance required for the life and growth of an organism

OBJECTIVES

► Identify foods high in carbohydrates, fats, and proteins.
► Describe the properties and roles of different nutrients in the body.
► Use the USDA Food Guide Pyramid to select a balanced diet.

Why do we eat? When you eat a meal like the one shown in **Figure 13-1,** you are doing more than simply relieving hunger pangs. You are taking in a variety of chemical substances, called **nutrients,** that are necessary for life. You need food because your body constantly uses and needs energy.

Nutrients provide the energy for everything you do, from breathing to walking. Nutrients also contain raw materials that form structures such as bones, muscle, and hair.

What Nutrients Are in Your Food?

All foods contain at least one of the following six types of nutrients: carbohydrates, fats, proteins, water, vitamins, and minerals. As you can see in **Figure 13-1,** the first four nutrients make up virtually all of the weight of many foods. Vitamins and minerals are just as important but are needed in much smaller quantities.

Figure 13-1
The ingredients in this lunch contain different proportions of carbohydrate, fat, protein, and water.

Bread
9%
50%
38%
3%

Carbohydrate
Protein
Water
Fat

2%
22%
32%
44%
American cheese

Skim milk
5%
3%
Fat 0%
92%

Apple
13%
1%
86%
Protein 0%

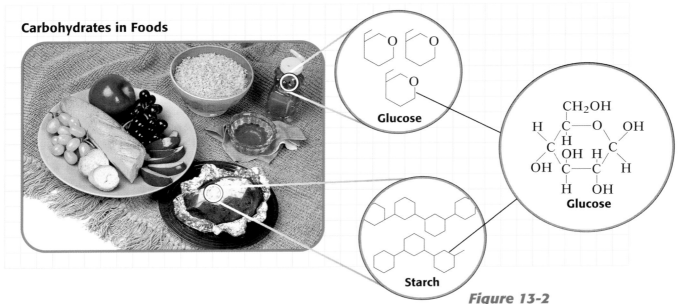

Carbohydrates in Foods

Glucose

Glucose

Starch

Figure 13-2
All of these foods are good sources of carbohydrates. Honey and fruit contain sugars. Bread, potatoes, and rice are loaded with starch. Fruits, vegetables, and grains also contain cellulose, a carbohydrate that you cannot digest.

▶ **carbohydrates** a class of nutrients containing carbon, hydrogen, and oxygen that can be used by living organisms as an energy source

Carbohydrates, such as sugar, provide quick energy

The sweet taste many people crave in desserts and fruits is due to the sugars they contain. These sugars belong to a class of compounds called **carbohydrates.**

Fruits taste sweet because they contain carbohydrates called sugars. The sugars in fruit are primarily fructose and glucose. Milk contains lactose, another sugar. Sucrose, the sugar commonly used for sweetening tea or coffee, is also used in baked goods and other foods.

Carbohydrates also include larger molecules called complex carbohydrates. These complex carbohydrates are made of many sugar molecules linked together. Carbohydrates supply most of your immediate energy needs.

When you eat carbohydrates, your body can break apart some of these molecules in a series of energy-releasing reactions called digestion. This energy is used by your body for life functions, from keeping your body warm and your heart pumping to moving your arms or legs.

Starch is a complex carbohydrate made in plants. Its structure consists of many glucose molecules linked together. Unlike the sugars from which it is made, starch does not taste sweet. Your body contains enzymes that can easily break starch down into individual sugar molecules. Once broken down into sugar molecules, foods containing starch can be digested.

Good sources of starch include bread, pasta, cereals, and potatoes. Many athletes, such as marathon runners and bicyclists, eat a lot of starchy foods prior to competing to get energy. Some foods that are high in carbohydrates are shown in **Figure 13-2.**

Did You Know ?

You cannot digest some carbohydrates such as the cellulose in plant stems and wood. Some animals, such as cows and termites, can digest cellulose. Microorganisms in their stomachs break the cellulose down into sugar molecules.

> **fats** a class of compounds containing long hydrocarbon chains that are bonded to a glycerin molecule

Fats store energy

Many people believe that **fats** are unhealthy to eat. Although a diet that is high in fats can be unhealthy, some fats are necessary for life. Fats also provide the tastes and textures that you may enjoy in salad dressings and ice cream.

Fats are very concentrated sources of energy. Your body can use them to meet your energy needs if you do not eat enough carbohydrates. When your body gets enough energy from carbohydrates, most of the fat you eat is stored under your skin and around some of your internal organs. Between meals, this stored fat is broken down to keep your body supplied with energy. Your body also uses fats to make certain cell structures.

Fats contain long chains of carbon and hydrogen atoms. There are two types of fats: saturated and unsaturated, as shown in **Figure 13-3.**

Saturated fats have the maximum possible number of hydrogen atoms in these chains and are usually solid at room temperature. Most animal fats, such as those in butter and meats, are saturated fats. A diet high in saturated fats can increase your chances of getting heart disease, as described in Chapter 14.

Unsaturated fats have fewer hydrogen atoms in their chains and are usually liquid at room temperature. Liquid fats are called *oils.* Most plant fats, including those in corn oil, canola oil, and olive oil, are mostly unsaturated fats.

No fat—whether saturated or unsaturated—can dissolve in water. For this reason, a salad dressing made of vegetable oil (a fat) and vinegar (a water solution) will separate into two layers after mixing.

Figure 13-3

A Butter consists largely of saturated fat and is solid at room temperature.

Unsaturated fat

Saturated fat

B Canola oil is over 90 percent unsaturated fat and is liquid at room temperature.

Table 13-1 **Amino Acids in the Body**

Amino acids made by the body			Essential amino acids	
Alanine	Cysteine	Histidine	Isoleucine	Phenylalanine
Arginine	Glutamate	Proline	Leucine	Threonine
Asparagine	Glutamine	Serine	Lysine	Tryptophan
Aspartate	Glycine	Tyrosine	Methionine	Valine

Proteins form the main structures of the body

Many people get **protein** from the meat, cheese, and eggs in their diet. Those who choose a vegetarian diet can get protein from grains, beans, and nuts. Your body uses some of the protein in your food to rebuild structures that wear out and to make new structures as you grow. Your muscles, skin, and blood contain a lot of protein.

Recall from Chapter 4 that proteins are polymers made by linking together many amino acid molecules. Of the 20 amino acids found in your body, your body can make only 12 of them, as shown in **Table 13-1.** The other eight amino acids are called *essential amino acids* because they must be obtained from the food you eat. Animal proteins contain large amounts of all eight essential amino acids. Most plant proteins, however, are low in one or more essential amino acids.

Water is essential for life

More than half your body's weight is due to the water it contains. Water makes your blood fluid, cools your body when you perspire, and carries the waste in your urine. Every cell in your body contains water.

Your body cannot make enough water from other compounds. Water must come from your food and drink, just like any other nutrient. To replace the water that is lost in perspiration and urine, the average adult must consume about 2.5 L (about 2.6 quarts) of water per day.

About one-third of this requirement can be met by eating solid food, which is typically 40 to 90 percent water. To get the rest of the water they require, most people should drink 7–9 glasses of water per day, as shown in **Figure 13-4.** Exercise and hot, dry weather can make your need for water much greater.

▶ **protein** a nutrient that is a polymer of amino acids, containing carbon, hydrogen, oxygen, and nitrogen

Quick ACTIVITY

Testing Foods for Fats
1. Rub samples of five foods on squares of brown paper. Label each square with the name of the food that was rubbed on it.
2. After the squares have dried, compare the food stains left. Rank the five foods you tested in order of increasing fat content, based on the stains left on the brown paper by the fatty foods.

Figure 13-4 The average person in the United States takes in about 2.3 L of water each day. This volume is less than the recommended total for healthy living.

435

Table 13-2   Vitamins Necessary for Good Health

Vitamin	Food Sources	Role
A	Carrots, leafy vegetables, butter, eggs, liver, sweet potatoes	Maintenance of healthy eyes and skin, formation of strong bones and teeth
B_1	Most vegetables, nuts, organ meats	Proper functioning of heart, nerves, and muscles
B_2	Fish, poultry, cheese, yeast, green vegetables	Tissue repair, maintenance of healthy skin
B_3	Whole grains, fish, poultry, liver, potatoes, tomatoes, legumes	Proper functioning of stomach, intestines, and nervous system
B_{12}	Meat, eggs, milk, dairy products, liver, kidneys	Formation of red blood cells
C	Citrus fruits, strawberries, potatoes	Wound healing, maintenance of healthy gums and teeth
D	Fish oils, liver, fortified milk, eggs	Formation of strong bones and teeth
E	Wheat-germ oil, leafy vegetables, milk, butter	Protection of cell components from reactive oxygen compounds
K	Leafy vegetables, liver, cauliflower (also produced by some intestinal bacteria)	Blood clotting

▶ **vitamin** an organic compound needed in trace amounts by the body

internet connect

SciLINKS
NSTA

TOPIC: Vitamins
GO TO: www.scilinks.org
KEYWORD: HJ1302

Vitamins help promote chemical reactions in the body

Vitamins are organic molecules that help the enzymes in your body function properly. As you learned in Chapter 5, enzymes are proteins that accelerate specific chemical reactions. Like enzymes, the vitamins themselves are not used up in these reactions and can be reused continually.

Because your body recycles vitamins for use again and again, you need only very small quantities of vitamins—about 0.01 to 60 mg—in your diet each day. **Table 13-2** lists the food sources and major roles of some vitamins. Of course, many people get these vitamins from vitamin supplements. This table describes some of the many important body functions that depend on vitamins.

Vitamins are water-soluble or fat-soluble

Some vitamins, such as the B vitamins and vitamin C, can dissolve in water. They are said to be *water-soluble*. Vitamins A, D, E, and K cannot dissolve in water but can dissolve in fats. These vitamins are described as *fat-soluble*.

Your body has no way to store water-soluble vitamins. If you take in more of these vitamins than you need, you simply get rid of the excess in your urine. Fat-soluble vitamins, in contrast, are stored in the fat reserves of your body. High levels of fat-soluble vitamins can build up in your body and make you very sick.

Vitamin D is the only vitamin that your body can produce. When exposed to sunlight, your skin can make vitamin D from organic molecules present in your body. But this much sunlight can be unhealthy in other ways. Prolonged exposure to sunlight is linked to skin cancer. For this reason, many people obtain vitamin D from their food or from vitamin supplements rather than from that much sunlight.

Minerals are inorganic nutrients

Your body requires a variety of minerals in amounts ranging from about 10 mg to 2 g (2000 mg) per day. Unlike carbohydrates, fats, proteins, and vitamins—which are often complex organic compounds—minerals are simple inorganic compounds.

Typically, the body needs only one element or ion from a particular compound. For this reason, rather than naming specific compounds, scientists and dieticians describe the minerals that the body needs by indicating the element that they contain.

▶ **mineral** an inorganic compound found on Earth

Inquiry Lab

How can you determine which foods contain the most vitamin C?

Materials
- ✔ lemon and other fruits
- ✔ DCPIP in a dropper bottle
- ✔ 250 mL beaker
- ✔ toothpick
- ✔ white tile plate or depression slide

Procedure

1. You will use a compound called DCPIP to test for the presence of vitamin C. DCPIP is blue but turns clear when exposed to vitamin C. Obtain a lemon, and squeeze some of its juice into a beaker.
2. Place one drop of DCPIP onto a white tile or depression slide.
3. Add a drop of lemon juice to the DCPIP, and stir the mixture with a toothpick.
4. Repeat step 3 until the mixture becomes clear. On a sheet of paper, record the number of drops of lemon juice you added.
5. Repeat steps 1–4 using other fruit juices.

Analysis

1. Compare the juices you tested and the number of drops needed for each one. Does the addition of a greater number of juice drops indicate a higher vitamin C content or a lower vitamin C content?
2. Of the juices you tested, which juice has the most vitamin C? Which juice has the least vitamin C? Did several juices have similar amounts of vitamin C?
3. What limitations could there be in using this test to compare the vitamin C content of different foods? (**Hint:** Would this test work well for a dark-colored grape juice?)

Table 13-3 Necessary Elements Supplied by Mineral Groups

Mineral	Food sources	Role
Calcium	Milk, whole-grain cereals, vegetables, meats	Formation of bones and teeth, blood clotting, muscle and nerve function
Iodine	Seafood, water, iodized salt	Production of thyroid hormone
Iron	Leafy vegetables, liver, meats, raisins, prunes	Formation of red blood cells
Phosphorus	Milk, whole-grain cereals, vegetables, meats	Formation of bones and teeth
Potassium	Vegetables, citrus fruits, bananas, apricots	Muscle and nerve function, body water balance
Sodium	Table salt, vegetables	Muscle and nerve function, body water balance

The food sources and roles of several elements of the mineral group are listed in **Table 13-3.** One of the minerals you need in fairly large amounts is calcium. Calcium is necessary for blood clotting, muscle and nerve function, and formation of bones and teeth. Your bones actually serve as a storage site for calcium. If you do not eat enough calcium, your body removes calcium from your bones until they become brittle and break easily.

Milk is a major food source of calcium. To absorb calcium from foods such as milk, however, your body also needs to have vitamin D. For this reason, federal law requires that all milk sold in the United States be fortified with vitamin D.

Choosing Foods for Your Health

balanced diet a selection of foods that provides all of the nutrients needed for healthy living

A diet that contains the right amounts of all of the nutrients for your body's needs is called a balanced diet. According to nutritionists, a balanced diet consists of about 55 percent carbohydrates, 15 percent protein, and no more than 30 percent fat. A typical diet for most people in the United States contains much more protein and fat than necessary.

Using the food pyramid to build a balanced diet

How can you be sure that the meals you eat are providing a balanced diet? One approach is to use the USDA Food Guide Pyramid, shown in **Figure 13-5.** This diagram indicates the types and amounts of foods you should eat each day to have a balanced diet.

internetconnect

SCILINKS.
NSTA

TOPIC: Food pyramid
GO TO: www.scilinks.org
KEYWORD: HJ1303

Balancing a Diet Because a marathon runner needs more food than someone who gets very little exercise, a range of servings is given in the USDA Food Guide Pyramid. This range also takes into account differences in body size and energy needs.

Applying Information

1. Monitor and record your food intake for 3 days. Classify each item you eat as a member of one of the groups in the USDA Food Guide Pyramid.

2. For each day, total the number of servings for each food group you ate. A serving size for each food group is shown in the photograph below.

3. For each day, indicate whether or not the amounts you received match the recommendations in the USDA Food Guide Pyramid.

Grains, fruits, and vegetables containing carbohydrates make up more than half of the pyramid; they should be eaten in the largest amounts. These foods are high in complex carbohydrates, including fiber, and satisfy most of your vitamin and mineral needs.

Protein-rich foods, including meat, dairy products, fish, beans, and nuts, are in the middle of the pyramid and should be eaten in smaller amounts. Foods high in sugars or fat, such as candy, butter, and ice cream, are at the top of the pyramid and should be a small part of your diet.

Figure 13-5
The USDA Food Guide Pyramid shows the amount of each type of food you should eat every day to have a balanced diet. Think about what you ate yesterday. Did you have a balanced diet?

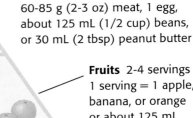

Fatty, sugary foods use sparingly

Milk, yogurt, cheese 2-3 servings 1 serving = about 250 mL (1 cup) milk or yogurt or about 45 g (1.5 oz) cheese

Meat, eggs, beans, nuts 2-3 servings 1 serving = about 60-85 g (2-3 oz) meat, 1 egg, about 125 mL (1/2 cup) beans, or 30 mL (2 tbsp) peanut butter

Vegetables 3-5 servings 1 serving = about 125 mL (1/2 cup) vegetables

Fruits 2-4 servings 1 serving = 1 apple, banana, or orange or about 125 mL (3/4 cup) fruit juice

Grains 6-11 servings 1 serving = 1 slice of bread or about 125 mL (1/2 cup) rice, pasta, or cereal

Vegetarian diets can be nutritious

Vegetarians are people that choose to eat plant products but not meat. Some vegetarians also eat animal products such as milk, eggs, and cheese. Other vegetarians do not eat any animal products at all. Because plant products contain most of the nutrients required for a balanced diet, vegetarian diets can be just as nutritious as diets that include meat.

However, vegetarians must monitor two things carefully. The first is their intake of essential amino acids. Most plant proteins are low in one or more essential amino acids. As a result, vegetarians must be sure that the foods they eat meet all of their amino acid requirements. The easiest way to do this while on a vegetarian diet is to eat a variety of plant products each day. A combination of rice and beans, as shown in **Figure 13-6,** supplies all of the essential amino acids.

The second important thing for vegetarians to consider is the vitamin content of their food. Plant products do not have much vitamin B_{12} and vitamin D. If you are a vegetarian, you can obtain both of these vitamins by adding eggs or dairy products to your diet or by taking vitamin supplements. Once a vegetarian diet has been balanced to provide all of the essential amino acids and has been supplemented with vitamins, it is just as healthy and nutritious as a meat-containing diet.

Figure 13-6
This vegetarian meal can provide plenty of protein, which contains all of the essential amino acids.

SECTION 13.1 REVIEW

SUMMARY

▶ Most of our energy needs are met by carbohydrates, such as sugars and starch, or fats.

▶ Proteins are used to rebuild structures in the body and make new structures during growth.

▶ Vitamins and minerals are needed in smaller amounts than other nutrients.

▶ The USDA Food Guide Pyramid shows the types and amounts of foods a person should eat each day in a balanced diet.

CHECK YOUR UNDERSTANDING

1. **List** two foods that are high in carbohydrate, two that are high in fat, and two that are high in protein.
2. **List** three roles of proteins in your body.
3. **Describe** the basic function of vitamins.
4. **Explain** the difference between a sugar and a complex carbohydrate.
5. **Contrast** saturated and unsaturated fats.
6. **Explain** why your bones can become weak if your diet does not contain enough calcium.
7. **Explain** why vegetarians need to be concerned about vitamin B_{12} and vitamin D in their diet. What can vegetarians do to address this concern?
8. **Critical Thinking** A student's diet for 1 day consisted of 10 servings of meat and cheese, 2 servings each of vegetables, fruits, and grains, and 5 servings of fatty, sugary foods. Was this a balanced diet? Explain why or why not.

Energy and Food

▶ Explain how the energy in food is measured.

▶ Compare the energy content of a gram of carbohydrates, fats, and proteins.

▶ Interpret food labels as a tool for choosing a balanced diet.

▶ List several factors that affect a person's metabolic rate.

▶ Discuss what happens when a person's energy consumption does not match his or her energy use.

▶ **KEY TERMS**
Calorie
metabolic rate
basal metabolic rate
obesity
undernourishment

You learned about the many roles of nutrients earlier in this chapter. They supply raw materials for making and repairing structures in your body, and they allow enzymes to work properly. But also importantly, nutrients provide energy. Without this energy, you would not be able to survive.

The Role of Energy in Your Body

If you burn food in a flame, as shown in **Figure 13-7,** energy is rapidly transferred as heat. Food contains chemical energy. Chemical reactions in the body can release this energy by rearranging the atoms and bonds within food.

Your body can also "burn" food, but it does so with several slower chemical reactions. Some of the energy in food is transferred immediately as heat. The rest is stored in your cells as chemical energy mostly within fats and carbohydrates that your body can use when it needs energy.

Even though digestion reactions are slower than the burning reaction, the results are the same. For example, the burning of carbohydrates produces carbon dioxide, CO_2, water, H_2O, and energy. These products are also formed when carbohydrates are slowly digested.

How much energy is in food?

Because the results of the reactions are the same, facts about food in a rapid burning reaction can tell you about a slower digesting reaction. Dietitians and nutrition scientists can measure a food's energy content. They burn a small sample of the food in a sealed container surrounded by water. As the food burns, the energy released warms the water.

Figure 13-7
Because food such as these peanuts contains chemical energy, it can burn. Your body harnesses slower reactions to use the peanuts as an energy source.

▶ **Calorie** a unit of energy describing the amount of energy needed to warm 1 kg of water by 1°C

Food energy measurements made this way are often given in units of **Calories.** A Calorie, abbreviated as Cal, is defined as the amount of energy needed to raise the temperature of exactly 1 kg of water by exactly 1°C. In some other countries, food energy is given in units of joules, the energy unit described in Section 8.1. One Calorie is equivalent to 4186 J.

If you measure the temperature increase of the water, you can calculate how much energy was in the food. This process is the same as the specific heat calculations described in Section 9.2. For example, if burning a food sample warms 1.0 kg of water by 25°C, then the food contained 25 Cal, according to the following calculations.

$$\text{food energy} = \text{temperature change for 1.0 kg water} \times \frac{1 \text{ Cal}}{1°C}$$

$$\text{food energy} = 25°C \times \frac{1 \text{ Cal}}{1°C} = 25 \text{ Cal}$$

Using this method, scientists have found that 1 g of carbohydrate and 1 g of protein each contain about 4 Cal, while 1 g of fat contains about 9 Cal.

Figure 13-8 shows the number of Calories in an average-sized serving for a variety of foods. If you compare **Figure 13-8** with **Figure 13-1,** you can see that the number of Calories in a particular food depends on the nutrients it contains.

Cheese is high in fat and protein, so even a small amount of cheese has a lot of Calories. In contrast, apples contain some carbohydrates but very little fat or protein. Therefore, a whole apple has fewer Calories than one slice of cheese. Most of an apple's weight is due to water, which provides no Calories at all.

internet connect

SCiLINKS
NSTA

TOPIC: Metabolism
GO TO: www.scilinks.org
KEYWORD: HJ1304

Figure 13-8
The number of Calories in a meal depends on the types and quantities of foods in the meal.

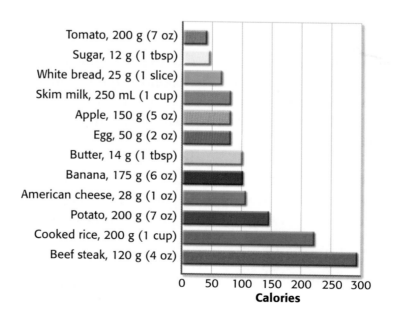

Food energy is transferred as heat and work

Your own body temperature is usually higher than the temperature of your surroundings. Maintaining this high body temperature requires energy. Colder environments require your body to expend even more energy unless you are wearing well-insulated clothes. When you put on a coat, you stay warmer because energy is not transferred away from your body as quickly.

The energy in food is used to do work. When you climb a set of stairs, for example, the muscles in your legs do work to accelerate the mass of your body against the force of gravity. Your leg-muscle cells use energy from carbohydrates and fats to do this work. Even when you sleep, you are still using energy to do internal work—to breathe, pump blood, and digest food.

Measuring your energy use for activities

Your body expends the energy in food in thousands of different chemical reactions, which are known collectively as metabolism. Therefore, scientists refer to your rate of energy use as your **metabolic rate.** Usually, metabolic rate is expressed in units of Calories per hour or Calories per day.

How can you calculate your metabolic rate? One way is to measure how quickly you consume oxygen. **Figure 13-9** shows the machine used to measure an exercising person's oxygen intake and metabolic rate.

Oxygen is crucial for your survival because the primary way your body releases energy from carbohydrates, fats, and proteins is to react these compounds with oxygen. Without oxygen, these reactions cannot continue, and your body would soon run out of the energy needed to keep it alive.

For each liter of oxygen that is consumed in these reactions, about 5 Calories of energy are released. Thus, if you consume 20 L of oxygen per hour, your metabolic rate is about 100 Calories per hour or about 2400 Calories per day.

> **metabolic rate** the amount of energy consumed by the body in a given time period

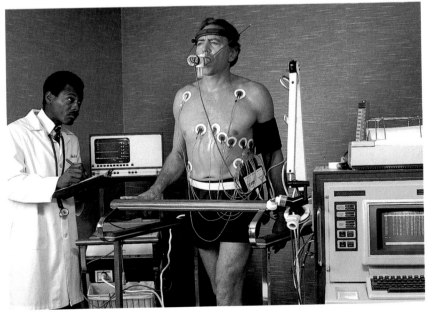

Figure 13-9
A technician is measuring the metabolic rate of this man as he exercises on a treadmill. Tubes carry the air to a gas analyzer, which calculates how much oxygen he consumes per minute.

Table 13-4 Energy Use During Different Activities

Type of activity	Energy use (Cal/h)
Sleeping	65
Awake, lying still	77
Sitting upright	100
Walking at 4.2 km/h (2.6 mi/h)	200
Swimming	500
Running at 8.5 km/h (5.3 mi/h)	570
Hard labor (lifting heavy objects, digging)	600
Walking up stairs	1100

INTEGRATING

PHYSICS

Metabolic rate is a measure of power, because it represents how much energy you use during a given time interval. How does your metabolic rate compare with other measures of power?

Because 1 Cal = 4186 J, a metabolic rate of 100 Cal/h is equal to 418 600 J/h. This in turn is equivalent to 116 J/s, or 116 W. Therefore, while you sit quietly watching a program on television, you use about as much energy per second as the TV set does.

▶ **basal metabolic rate** the rate of energy use for a living body that is not performing other activities

As **Table 13-4** shows, the more active you are, the more energy you use. Note that the values in this table are given as Calories per hour instead of Calories per day, since people do not normally perform the activities listed for a full day.

The amount of energy you use during an average day depends on how old you are as well as what you do. Because children and adolescents are growing, they use more energy than an adult of the same weight. Children between the ages of 7 and 10 need about 2400 Cal per day, while teenagers need about 2100 to 2800 Cal per day. Daily energy use for adults is about 2000 Cal for women and 2700 Cal for men.

The basal metabolic rate measures energy used for life processes

What is the lowest possible metabolic rate? There are some energy demands associated with being alive. Muscles must move to make your heart pump and your lungs expand. Energy is required for your nerves to carry messages back and forth between your brain and the rest of your body.

Your **basal metabolic rate,** or BMR, measures your body's energy use when you are lying down but awake. For the BMR to be measured accurately, all excess energy demands must be eliminated. A person's BMR is measured in a comfortably warm room, when the person has not eaten anything for at least 12 hours.

Most adults' BMRs range from about 1300 to 1800 Cal/day (55 to 75 Cal/h). A person's BMR depends on several factors, such as the person's sex, height, and weight. For example, women generally have a lower BMR than do men of the same weight.

When you do any activity, even sitting up, your metabolic rate will increase above your BMR, as shown in **Table 13-4.** The only time your metabolic rate is lower is when you are asleep.

Dietary Problems

If you take in exactly enough Calories to meet your daily energy needs, your body weight will stay the same. The parts of your brain that trigger feelings of hunger will also signal fullness to help you stop eating when your energy needs are satisfied. If this system does not work or you ignore the signals your body sends, you may be eating more or less than the amount of food needed to maintain a healthy weight.

Consuming too many calories causes obesity

Many people eat when they are not hungry or eat more than they need to feel full. Whenever you consume more energy than you use, you store the extra energy as fat and gain weight. The result is the same whether the extra energy comes from fats, carbohydrates, or proteins.

Today, there is a great controversy about how much fat is healthy. Different cultures have different ideals for a healthy and beautiful body. Throughout history, this ideal has also changed substantially within cultures. When famines were common, remaining well fed was a sign of wealth.

REAL WORLD APPLICATIONS

Sugar Substitutes Because so many people in the United States are trying to lose weight, the market for dietary aids is huge. Some products are substances that taste sweet like table sugar, sucrose, but have few or no Calories.

One such "artificial sweetener" is saccharin, a synthetic compound that tastes up to 500 times as sweet as sucrose.

Another sweetener is aspartame, which consists of two amino acids linked together. Aspartame tastes about 180 times as sweet as sucrose.

Because saccharin and aspartame taste so much sweeter than sucrose, they can be used in very small amounts. As a result, their Calorie content is insignificant.

Applying Information

1. How much saccharin would you have to add to a glass of iced tea to produce the same sweetness as 4.0 g (1 teaspoon) of sucrose?
2. How much aspartame would you have to add to a glass of iced tea to produce the same sweetness as 4.0 g (1 teaspoon) of sucrose?
3. A teaspoon of sucrose contains about 16 Cal. Using the average energy value for proteins given on page 442, determine how many Calories the equivalent quantity of aspartame contains.
4. Why do you think other substances are typically added as fillers to single-serving packets of artificial sweeteners?

> **obesity** a condition in which too much of a body's weight is stored as fat

> **undernourishment** the breakdown of the body and its organs as a result of inadequate food intake

Some people store so much extra fat and gain so much weight that they have health problems associated with **obesity**. For these people, having too much fat in their bodies increases the risk of heart disease, diabetes, and other illnesses.

Some researchers argue that obesity alone is not a major health problem, but connected with poor diet and a lack of exercise, it can be deadly. For many people, carrying some extra fat is good for them.

Most people are obese because of their body type. Others become obese because the regulatory centers in their brain do not work properly. They feel hungry even when their energy needs have been met. Some people become obese because of emotional problems that stimulate overeating to reduce stress. Still others simply get too little exercise for the amount of food they eat. Unbalanced food choices are another cause of obesity.

For all people, whether obese or not, the key to a healthy weight is to make the energy intake the same as the energy use. Those seeking to lose weight need to make their energy intake slightly less than their energy use. Usually, the solution is to eat a balanced diet and exercise regularly.

Consuming too few calories causes undernourishment

If your Calorie intake is far less than your energy use, you will lose weight. This is because your body breaks down its reserves of fat to make up the energy shortage. If weight loss continues and the body runs out of stored fat to break down, the blody starts to break down the protein that makes up muscle and brain tissue. This leads to severe muscle weakness, brain damage, and eventually death by starvation. This condition is called **undernourishment**.

Undernourishment is no longer common in the United States and other industrialized nations. However, it is a fairly common and serious problem in many developing countries, especially during droughts, famines, and wars. Frequently, undernourishment takes place immediately after large-scale natural disasters. Earthquakes, hurricanes, and floods can disrupt food supplies just as much as a drought will.

Connection to
SOCIAL STUDIES

The Potato Famine of Ireland changed Irish and American history in the mid-nineteenth century. Between 1845 and 1847, a disease called late blight destroyed virtually all of the Irish potato crop.

Because potatoes were fairly cheap and easy to grow, they were the primary food source for much of the population. During the famine, a million farmers starved to death, and almost 2 million more left Ireland for other countries, most often the United States.

SEARCHING FOR POTATOES IN A STUBBLE FIELD.

Within a decade, the population of Ireland fell from 8 million to 4 million. Many of the Irish emigrants who went to the United States settled in Boston and New York.

Making the Connection

1. Refer to **Figure 13-5.** Why are potatoes so valuable for meeting people's energy needs?
2. A large portion of Irish farmland was used for growing potatoes in the mid-1800s. How did that help make the outbreak of late blight so devastating?

Interpreting Food Labels

The U.S. Food and Drug Administration (FDA) requires that all packaged foods have a label listing the number of Calories and nutrient content in one serving of the food. These labels also list the percentage of your daily nutrient requirement for a serving. A food label is shown at right, along with an explanation.

Applying Information

1. Examine the food labels from three different breakfast cereals. Do all three labels use the same serving size? Based on your eating habits, do you think the serving size is reasonable?

2. How do the cereals compare in terms of their carbohydrate, fat, and protein content? Which cereal has the most Calories per serving?

3. If you have eaten these cereals before, which do you think tastes best? Is there any relationship between a cereal's nutrient content and taste?

1 Serving Size Serving sizes formerly were unrealistically small. New serving sizes set by the FDA are closer to the amounts that people actually eat.

2 Calories from Fat Beware of any food that gets more than one-third of its Calories from fat.

3 % Daily Value (DV) This tells you what percentage of the daily requirement for a nutrient you are getting.

4 Total Fat Keep a close eye on saturated fats, as they cause clogged arteries.

5 Cholesterol High levels of fatlike cholesterol molecules in the blood can also lead to clogged arteries. Junk foods made from vegetables, such as corn chips, may be advertised as cholesterol-free, but they are often high in other fats.

6 Sodium Sodium is abundant in table salt and many food products. Too much sodium can cause high blood pressure.

7 Total Carbohydrate Getting enough carbohydrates, especially complex ones like starches, is important. Carbohydrates are used by your cells as a source of energy.

8 Protein Although the government has not set a percent DV for proteins, it is generally agreed that protein should compose no more than about 15 percent of your total daily Calories.

9 Vitamins and Minerals A DV of about 10 percent indicates that a food is a good source of these essential nutrients.

Nutrition Facts

1 Serving Size 1 Package (258 g)
Servings Per Container 1

Amount per Serving	
2 **Calories** 270	From Fat 70
3	**% Daily Value**
4 **Total Fat** 8 g	12%
Saturated Fat 3.5 g	15%
Polyunsaturated Fat 0.5 g	
Monounsaturated Fat 1.5 g	
5 **Cholesterol** 30 mg	9%
6 **Sodium** 500 mg	20%
7 **Total Carbohydrate** 28 g	9%
Dietary Fiber 3 g	13%
Sugars 5 g	
8 **Protein** 21 g	
9 Vitamin A 8% • Vitamin C 20%	
Calcium 35% • Iron 6%	

SECTION 13.2 REVIEW

SUMMARY

▶ Your body uses the energy in food to produce heat and to do work.

▶ The energy in food is expressed in units of Calories.

▶ Labels on packaged foods list the Calories and nutrient content in one serving.

▶ Your metabolic rate is your rate of energy use.

▶ Exercise can increase your metabolic rate.

▶ If you consume more energy than you use, you will gain weight. If you consume less energy than you use, you will lose weight.

CHECK YOUR UNDERSTANDING

1. **Define** *Calorie.*

2. **Identify** the energy-containing nutrients listed on food labels. Of all of these nutrients, which one contains the most Calories per gram?

3. **Explain** why your metabolic rate is related to the rate at which you use oxygen.

4. **Use Table 13-4** to determine whether you use more energy when walking or swimming.

5. **Predict** which person is most likely to have the highest metabolic rate, and explain the reasoning for the choice you made:
   a. someone who walks a mile a day
   b. a person training for a marathon
   c. a person who does not exercise

6. **Describe** two of the health effects that undernourishment can have on the human body.

7. **Critical Thinking** Explain why a woman's basal metabolic rate increases when she is pregnant.

Digestion

KEY TERMS
digestion
salivary glands
esophagus
small intestine
pancreas
liver
large intestine
ulcer

OBJECTIVES

▶ Explain how food is mechanically and chemically digested.

▶ Identify the organs of the digestive system, and explain their functions.

▶ Describe the role of the pancreas and the liver in digestion.

▶ Explain the importance of the mucous layer that lines the digestive system.

digestion the process of breaking down food into usable molecules

The food you eat contains the nutrients and energy your body needs. But the food you eat must be broken down so it can be absorbed by your cells. Even the carbohydrates, fats, and proteins in food must be broken down into simpler molecules. This process of breaking down food is called **digestion.**

Mechanical and Chemical Digestion

Consider what happens when you eat a cheese sandwich like the one shown in **Figure 13-10.** First you bite it into pieces. Then, as you chew it, the cheese and bread in each small piece are mixed together. After you swallow it, your stomach churns the mixture even more.

Figure 13-10

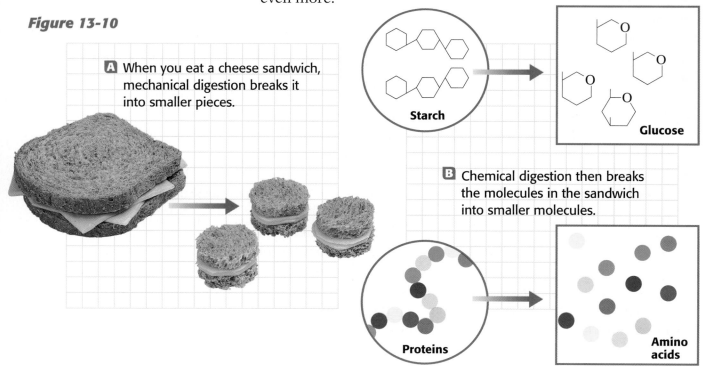

A When you eat a cheese sandwich, mechanical digestion breaks it into smaller pieces.

Starch

Glucose

B Chemical digestion then breaks the molecules in the sandwich into smaller molecules.

Proteins

Amino acids

Mechanical digestion is a physical change

The chewing, mixing, and churning of your food are processes called mechanical digestion. The molecules in the chewed-up mixture are identical to those in the original bread and cheese. These processes are all physical changes, as described in Chapter 2.

You know from Chapter 5 that one way to speed up a reaction is to break the reactants into smaller pieces, which increases the surface area available for reactions. In addition, mechanical digestion also makes the food move more easily through your digestive system.

Chemical digestion is a chemical change

While mechanical digestion is occurring, enzymes and other chemicals are being mixed with the food. By itself, this mixing is a physical change. But once mixed in, each enzyme targets a specific type of nutrient and breaks it down into smaller molecules. This process is a chemical change.

Each cell in the body is surrounded by an oily layer called the *cell membrane*. The cell membrane keeps the inside of the cell from mixing with substances around it. For nutrients to be able to pass through the cell membrane and into the cell, they must be in the form of smaller molecules.

The Start of Digestion

Digestion requires a number of organs that break food down into nutrients, transport the nutrients into the body, and eliminate wastes. Taken together, these organs are called the digestive system. **Figure 13-11** illustrates the overall structure of the human digestive system.

Digestion begins in the mouth

You already know that mechanical digestion takes place in your mouth when you chew your food. Mechanical digestion is aided by saliva, a watery substance produced by **salivary glands** beneath your tongue and at the back of your jaw. Saliva moistens the food, making it easier for your tongue to move the food around as you chew.

Saliva also contains an enzyme called amylase that helps break down starch into sugar. Both chemical and mechanical digestion occur in your mouth.

internetconnect

SC*LINKS*
NSTA

TOPIC: Digestive system
GO TO: www.scilinks.org
KEYWORD: HJ1305

▶ **salivary glands** the glands located in the bottom and top of the mouth that secrete watery saliva

Figure 13-11
The digestive system is basically a long, folded tube with an opening at each end. The salivary glands, liver, and pancreas release substances into the tube that help digestion proceed.

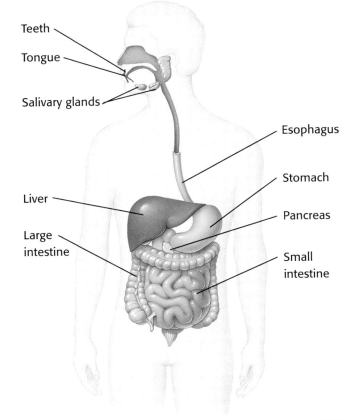

Teeth
Tongue
Salivary glands
Esophagus
Stomach
Liver
Pancreas
Large intestine
Small intestine

Demonstrating the Importance of Mechanical Digestion

1. Place 100 mL of water in each of two beakers.
2. Measure the mass of a sugar cube.
3. Add the sugar cube to one of the beakers.
4. Take another sugar cube and crush it with a metal spatula or scoop. Pour these pieces into the second beaker. You can think of these pieces as a sugar cube that has been mechanically digested.
5. Observe how much sugar remains on the bottom of each beaker.

6. Did the sugar cube or the pieces of sugar dissolve more easily? Relate your findings to what happens when you digest food.

The esophagus moves food to the stomach

Moving food from the mouth to the stomach takes a number of steps. First, your tongue pushes the food to the back of your throat. Then, as you begin to swallow, a small flap of tissue closes the opening from your throat to your lungs. This flap protects you from choking. If the flap was not there, food or liquid could enter your lungs causing you to choke.

▶ **esophagus** the muscular tube connecting the mouth and stomach

Figure 13-12
As the muscle tightens down the esophagus, the food is pushed into the stomach.

Tightened muscle

In the next step, the food enters your **esophagus,** which is connected to your stomach. Then the top of the esophagus tightens, pushing the food down. This wave of muscular contraction continues along the complete length of the esophagus. Eventually, the muscular contraction pushes the food into the stomach, as shown in **Figure 13-12.** This muscular wave is not under your conscious control. Once you begin to swallow, you cannot stop this movement of your esophagus.

Because the movement of food is driven by the muscular contractions of your esophagus, you can swallow standing on your head and eat upside down. Even astronauts in free fall as they orbit Earth are able to swallow food without the help of gravity.

Food is broken down by acid and pepsin in the stomach

If you're really hungry, your stomach may begin to feel different when you smell, taste, or even think about food. This feeling is due to specific changes in your stomach as it prepares to receive food.

Cells lining the stomach wall release two substances that help digest protein. One is hydrochloric acid, HCl, a strong acid. The other is pepsin, an enzyme that breaks food proteins into shorter chains of amino acids.

Your stomach is shaped like a muscular bag, as shown in **Figure 13-13.** Muscles in the wall of the stomach contract to thoroughly mix the pepsin and hydrochloric acid into your food.

Pepsin works best in a very acidic environment, which is provided by the hydrochloric acid. The acid also kills many of the bacteria in your food. Because of the acid, the pH of a normal stomach is between 1.0 and 3.0.

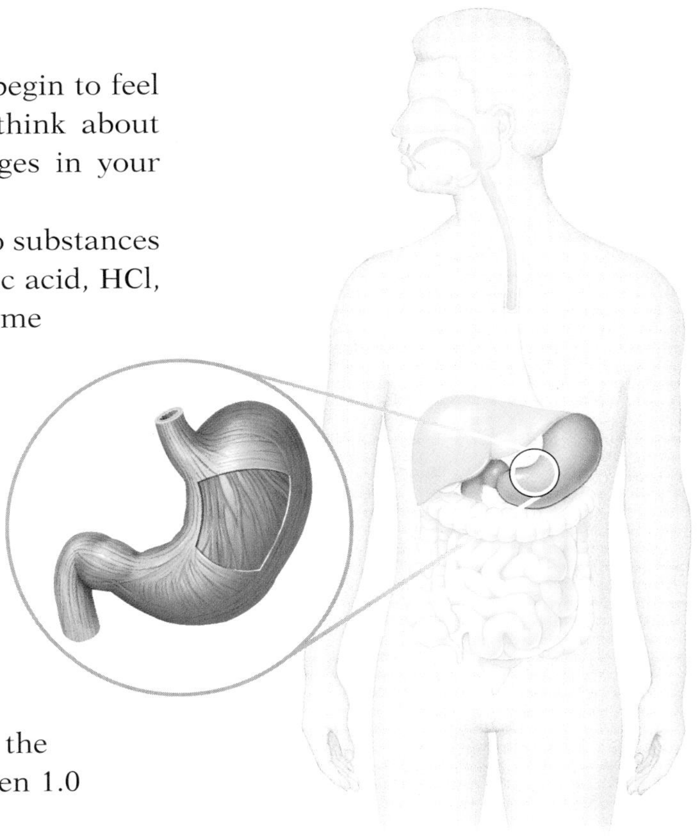

Chemical digestion is completed in the small intestine

As the stomach contracts, small amounts of the mixture of food, pepsin, and acid are pushed into the small intestine. The small intestine is a narrow but highly folded tube. It is more than 6 m (21 ft) long, the length of a small moving van. The folding is necessary for it to fit inside your abdomen. The upper portion of the small intestine completes the chemical digestion of your food.

The pancreas and liver make products needed for digestion

Near the stomach is the pancreas, which produces enzymes that break down carbohydrates, fats, and proteins. When the stomach mixture enters the small intestine, the pancreas releases these enzymes into the mixture. One of the enzymes involved is amylase, which breaks down starch into glucose, just as it did in the mouth.

However, these enzymes do not work well in the acidic mixture from the stomach. So the pancreas also adds sodium bicarbonate, $NaHCO_3$. This compound reacts with hydrochloric acid and neutralizes it. The pH of the upper part of the small intestine increases until it is between 4.8 and 8.2.

The fats in food are digested slowly. Because fats do not dissolve in water, they form large drops that float in the watery mixture. These large drops react slowly with enzymes.

Figure 13-13
The stomach is made of many layers of stomach muscles arranged in different directions. This allows the stomach to twist and turn as it digests food.

▶ **small intestine** an organ that breaks down food and absorbs nutrients

▶ **pancreas** a large gland behind the stomach that makes digestive juices

Surface Area

1. To model the difference between a large and small surface area, you will need 64 small pieces of paper.
2. Place the pieces of paper on a table or on the floor.
3. Using one hand only, pick up as many squares as you can in exactly 10 seconds.

4. Repeat Step 3 using two hands.
5. What would you expect if you had two people (four hands) picking up the squares?
6. If the squares represent nutrients and your hands represent the intestinal wall, explain the advantage of greater surface area.

► **liver** a large organ that makes bile and modifies substances in the blood

A bitter, alkaline fluid called *bile* acts on these large drops of fat and causes them to break up into smaller droplets. Enzymes digest these small fat droplets more easily. The bile comes from the **liver**, a large organ mostly located in the upper right corner of the abdomen.

Absorption of Nutrients

Digestion is not the only process that takes place in the small intestine. Once digestion is complete, the nutrients are in the form of individual molecules. These molecules must move out of the digestive system and into the body.

The villi of the small intestine increase the area for nutrient absorption

Many nutrients are absorbed in the small intestine. The nutrients gradually move from the inside of the intestine, across the intestinal wall, and into the blood stream. From there, they move to every cell in the body.

The inner surface of the intestinal wall is covered with millions of tiny, fingerlike projections, called *villi*, some of which are shown in **Figure 13-14**. Because of the villi, the area of the small intestine's inner surface is about 250 m² (2700 ft²), roughly the area of a tennis court. With such a large surface area, the small intestine can absorb most of the nutrient molecules in the food you eat.

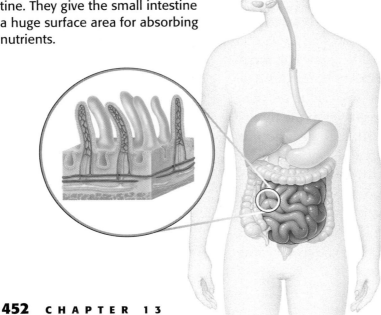

Figure 13-14
Millions of these tiny projections line the inside of the small intestine. They give the small intestine a huge surface area for absorbing nutrients.

The large intestine absorbs water from indigestible food

After most of the nutrients have been absorbed from food, what is left is mostly water and indigestible substances, such as cellulose. This material moves from the small intestine into the large intestine. The large intestine is a thicker tube about 1.5 m (5 ft) in length. It is not folded like the small intestine.

The primary function of the large intestine is to store the undigested material before it is eliminated from your body as feces. The large intestine absorbs water, which makes the feces smaller and more solid.

▶ **large intestine** an organ that stores, compacts, and eliminates indigestible material

Disorders of the Digestive System

The digestive system is very effective at breaking down large organic molecules, such as proteins, carbohydrates and fats. But those substances also make up the organs in the digestive system. Why don't the organs in this system digest themselves?

The answer has to do with the specialized cells that line the inside of the digestive system and the mucus these cells produce. This mucus serves as a protective coating. But if the mucous coating or the cells that produce it are damaged, the body's own processes can harm its organs.

▶ **ulcer** a sore that develops around a hole in the mucous lining of the digestive system

Ulcers result when bacteria break down the protective mucous lining

A hole in the mucous lining is called an ulcer. Ulcers form most often in the esophagus, stomach, and upper part of the small intestine. Ulcers can be painful because they expose cells to the very strong acid produced by the stomach.

In some cases, ulcers spread all the way through the wall of the stomach or intestine. When this occurs, partially digested food can leak into the abdomen, carrying bacteria and causing serious infection. This condition requires immediate surgery and medication.

For many years, ulcers were believed to result from the overproduction of stomach acid, which might occur when a person is under a lot of stress. Ulcers usually were treated with antacid medications. We now know that most ulcers are actually caused by bacteria that break down the mucous layer. Today, people with ulcers are generally given antibiotics to kill these bacteria.

Connection to SOCIAL STUDIES

Infants and young children produce an enzyme that breaks down lactose, the sugar found in milk. After about age four, however, many people gradually stop producing this enzyme, leading to an inability to digest lactose. This condition is called lactose intolerance.

If a person with lactose intolerance drinks milk, the undigested lactose remains in the person's digestive system, causing symptoms that range from mild pain to severe diarrhea. Lactose intolerance varies among different ethnic groups. This condition is found in more than 70 percent of African American adults but in only about 16 percent of European American adults.

Making the Connection

WRITING SKILL

1. Write a paragraph explaining why infants and young children have an enzyme that digests lactose.
2. Would you expect lactose intolerance to be more common in western Africa or in northern Europe? Explain.

Diarrhea can be caused by viruses, bacteria, or parasites infecting the large intestine

The cells lining the large intestine can also become infected by viruses, bacteria, other microorganisms, or parasitic worms. These infections interfere with the ability of the large intestine to absorb water. So large amounts of water leave the body in the feces. This condition, called diarrhea, can cause death by dehydration in as little as 2 days. Drugs can help cure the infection. People with diarrhea also need to take in a lot of fluids to prevent dehydration.

Often the intestines become infected when people drink water with disease-causing organisms in it. This kind of contamination can occur after a natural disaster, such as an earthquake, a hurricane, or a flood. Frequently such events disrupt facilities such as water treatment plants and pipelines, making clean water hard to find. In addition, people who crowd together in makeshift camps while attempting to rebuild their homes often live in unsanitary conditions, which can also increase the spread of disease.

Generally, more people die of these illnesses after a natural disaster than are killed during the actual disaster event. Worldwide, more than half of the deaths of children under the age of four are due to dehydration caused by diarrhea.

SECTION 13.3 REVIEW

SUMMARY

▶ Food is broken apart in mechanical digestion.

▶ The compounds in food are broken into simpler molecules in chemical digestion in the mouth, stomach, and small intestine.

▶ Nutrients are absorbed from food in the lower portion of the small intestine.

▶ The large intestine stores indigestible material before it is eliminated from the body.

▶ A layer of mucus protects the digestive system from digesting itself.

CHECK YOUR UNDERSTANDING

1. **List** two examples of mechanical digestion.
2. **Identify** five organs of the digestive system through which food passes.
3. **Explain** what causes most ulcers.
4. **Describe** how food is moved through the esophagus.
5. **Contrast** the roles of hydrochloric acid and sodium bicarbonate in digestion.
6. **Predict** what will happen if bile is added to a test tube containing a layer of oil floating on water and the tube is then shaken.
7. **Explain** how the inner surface of the small intestine is specialized for absorbing nutrients.
8. **Indicate** whether the following are involved in mechanical digestion, chemical digestion, both, or neither.
   - **a.** stomach
   - **b.** pancreas
   - **c.** small intestine
   - **d.** jawbone
   - **e.** large intestine
   - **f.** liver
   - **g.** mouth
   - **h.** salivary glands
9. **Creative Thinking** Frequent vomiting can accelerate tooth decay. Why do you think that is so?

Chapter Highlights

Before you begin, review the summaries of the key ideas of each section, found on pages 440, 447, and 454. The key vocabulary terms are listed on pages 432, 441, and 448.

UNDERSTANDING CONCEPTS

1. Good sources of starch include all of the following except _____.
   a. pasta   **c.** corn oil
   b. bread   **d.** potatoes
2. Vitamins are _____.
   a. inorganic nutrients
   b. required in large amounts each day
   c. made in the body
   d. needed for enzymes to work properly
3. According to the USDA Food Guide Pyramid, most of your food should consist of _____.
   a. grains   **c.** milk products
   b. meat   **d.** sugary foods
4. If vegetarians eat no animal products at all, they must take supplements to obtain enough _____.
   a. vitamin C   **c.** calcium
   b. vitamin B_{12} **d.** protein
5. The nutrients that contain the most Calories per gram are _____.
   a. fats   **c.** proteins
   b. carbohydrates   **d.** minerals
6. Your metabolic rate is lowest when you are _____.
   a. sitting upright   **c.** lying still but awake
   b. sleeping   **d.** walking
7. Consuming more energy in food than you use in exercise can lead to _____.
   a. undernourishment
   b. weight loss
   c. nervousness
   d. obesity

8. The organ that produces pepsin is labeled _____ in the diagram below.
   a. A   **c.** C
   b. B   **d.** D

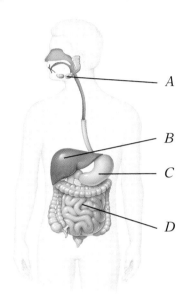

9. Bile is produced by the _____.
   a. esophagus   **c.** small intestine
   b. liver   **d.** large intestine
10. The cells that line your stomach are protected from being digested because they are covered by a layer of _____.
    a. mucus   **c.** hydrochloric acid
    b. saliva   **d.** water

Using Vocabulary

11. Distinguish between *metabolic rate* and *basal metabolic rate*. Which is usually higher?
12. Write a paragraph about the process of chemical digestion, using the following terms: *salivary gland, pepsin, bile, pancreas, liver,* and *small intestine.*
13. Someone tells you that a snack food is merely "empty calories." Explain what the person means, using the terms *Calorie, nutrient,* and *balanced diet.*

BUILDING MATH SKILLS

14. Graphing The pie chart below shows the approximate percentages of carbohydrate, protein, and fat you should have in a balanced diet. Identify which sectors *(A–C)* in the chart correspond to which nutrients.

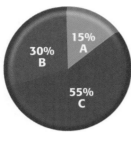

15. Food Energy If burning a sample of food raises the temperature of 1 kg of water by 32°C, how many Calories are in the sample?

16. Food Energy How much will burning a sample of food that contains 25 Cal raise the temperature of 1 kg of water?

17. Food Labels The food label for Brand X crackers lists a serving size of 32 g and a fat content of 6.0 g per serving. The food label for Brand Y crackers lists a serving size of 18 g and a fat content of 4.0 g per serving. Which brand contains more fat per gram of cracker?

THINKING CRITICALLY

18. Applying Knowledge The day before Fred left on a week-long hiking expedition, he decided to load his body with vitamins by taking a week's worth of multivitamin pills. What is dangerous about Fred's action?

19. Applying Knowledge Melissa has just declared that she is now a "fruitarian," or a person who eats nothing but fruits and fruit juices. What would you say to Melissa about whether she can have a balanced diet as a fruitarian?

20. Problem Solving A friend who is trying to lose weight gives in to the urge to eat a slice of apple pie à la mode. When you point out that the slice contains 585 Cal, he replies that he will make up for it by swimming laps in the pool. Use the information in **Table 13-4** to calculate how long he will have to swim to burn all of those Calories.

21. Problem Solving If you chew a piece of plain bread and keep it in your mouth for a while without swallowing it, the bread may begin to taste sweet. Explain why.

22. Creative Thinking The amount of glucose in your blood is controlled by the hormone insulin, which is a protein. Some people with diabetes must inject insulin into their blood several times per day. Why isn't it possible to take insulin by swallowing it, like many other medicines?

DEVELOPING LIFE/WORK SKILLS

23. Working Cooperatively Work with your classmates to obtain nutritional information from various fast-food restaurants. Many of these restaurants display this information, while others will provide it on request. Analyze the information, and prepare a list of the most nutritious and least nutritious foods in each restaurant. Post your list in class.

24. Applying Technology Make a spreadsheet on a computer that calculates an estimate of total Calories based on the number of grams of each type of nutrient present in food. (**Hint:** see page 442 of Section 13.2.) Analyze at least five different foods with your spreadsheet. How close did your estimates come to the Calorie count from the food label?

COMPUTER SKILL

25. Locating Information The enzymes papain, lactase, and alpha-galactosidase are sold for use in food preparation or to help with the digestion of certain foods. Write a short paragraph describing what each enzyme does and how it is used.

WRITING SKILL

26. Making Decisions Why is cellulose important in your diet, even though you cannot digest it or obtain energy from it?

INTEGRATING CONCEPTS

27. Concept Mapping Copy the unfinished concept map below onto a sheet of paper. Complete the map by writing the correct word or phrase in the lettered boxes.

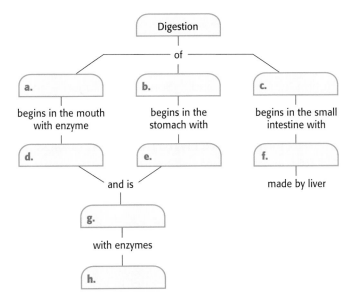

Digestion

of

a. ____
begins in the mouth with enzyme

b. ____
begins in the stomach with

c. ____
begins in the small intestine with

d. ____

e. ____

f. ____
made by liver

and is

g. ____

with enzymes

h. ____

28. Connection to Health Research what is known about the effect of pre-game meals on athletic performance. How long before a competition should an athlete eat? What types of foods should athletes eat and drink, and what types should they avoid? Are there any particular foods that can give athletes a competitive advantage?

29. Connection to Math Answer parts **a–e** in order, because each question depends on the previous question.
   a. Mayonnaise is 79 percent fat. How many grams of fat are in 28 g (2 tablespoons) of mayonnaise?
   b. All of the Calories in mayonnaise come from fat. How many Calories are in 28 g of mayonnaise? (**Hint:** the average number of Calories per gram of fat was discussed in Section 13.2 on page 442.)
   c. One Calorie equals 4186 J. How many joules are in 28 g of mayonnaise?
   d. How many joules does it take to lift a 1 kg weight to a height of 1 m?
   e. Using the energy in 28 g of mayonnaise, how many times could you lift a 1 kg weight to a height of 1 m? Assume that your body releases half the energy in the mayonnaise as heat and uses the rest of the energy to lift the weight.

30. Connection to Social Studies Salt (sodium chloride) is so widely available in developed countries today that overconsumption is a serious problem. In the past, however, the scarcity of salt in many parts of the world made this nutrient extremely valuable. Investigate the impact of salt on history and make a presentation or report. In what civilizations was salt used as currency? Are there any modern cultures that still use salt as currency? What role did salt play in Mohandas Gandhi's march to the sea in 1930?

WRITING SKILL

internetconnect

SC*LINKS*
NSTA

TOPIC: Enzymes
GO TO: www.scilinks.org
KEYWORD: HJ1306

Skill Builder Lab

Introduction

How can you identify the nutrients that are contained in food?

Objectives

▶ **Test** known and unknown samples for sugar and protein.

Materials

1 L beaker
hot plate
6 test tubes
test-tube tongs or holder
test-tube rack
grease pencil
10 mL graduated cylinder
6 glass stirring rods
disposable droppers
glucose solution
albumin solution
unknown sample
Benedict's solution
copper sulfate solution
sodium hydroxide solution
distilled water

Safety Needs

lab apron
safety goggles
disposable gloves

Testing Food for Nutrients

▶ Preparing for the Experiment

1. Fill the beaker half full with tap water. Put the beaker on a hot plate, and turn the hot plate on high.
2. While you wait for the water to boil, use the grease pencil to label six tubes with the numbers 1–6. Prepare a data table similar to the one shown at right in your lab report.
   SAFETY CAUTION Put on a lab apron, safety goggles, and gloves. If you get a chemical on your skin or clothing, wash it off at the sink while calling to your teacher. If you get a chemical in your eyes, immediately flush it out at the eyewash station while calling to your teacher.

▶ Testing for Sugar

3. Using the graduated cylinder, add 5 mL of Benedict's solution to tubes 1, 2, and 3. Benedict's solution is an indicator that forms orange or red deposits in the presence of large amounts of sugar. It forms green or yellow deposits in the presence of smaller amounts of sugar.
4. Add 10 drops of glucose solution (a sugar) to tube 1, 10 drops of the unknown sample to tube 2, and 10 drops of distilled water to tube 3. Mix the contents of each tube, using a different stirring rod for each tube.
5. When the water boils, use tongs to place tubes 1, 2, and 3 in the beaker. After 1–2 minutes, use tongs to move the tubes from the beaker to the test-tube rack. Turn off the hot plate.
6. As the tubes cool, look for deposits on the bottom of the tubes. Record your results in your data table. **SAFETY CAUTION** The hot plate remains hot even after it is turned off.

Tube	Contents	Nutrient tested	Observation	Result (+ or −)
1	glucose solution	sugar		
2	unknown	sugar		
3	distilled water	sugar		
4	albumin solution	protein		
5	unknown	protein		
6	distilled water	protein		

▶ Testing for Protein

7. Add 40 drops of sodium hydroxide solution to each of tubes 4, 5, and 6.

8. Add 40 drops of albumin solution (a protein) to tube 4, 40 drops of the unknown sample to tube 5, and 40 drops of distilled water to tube 6.

9. Add copper sulfate solution one drop at a time to tube 4. Using a clean stirring rod, mix the contents of the tube after you add each drop. Count the drops as you add them, and stop when the color of the solution in the tube changes.

10. Add the same number of drops of copper sulfate solution to tubes 5 and 6. Use a different, clean stirring rod to mix the contents of each tube.

11. Record the color of tubes 4, 5, and 6 in your data table.

▶ Analyzing Your Results

1. Based on your results, identify what nutrients were present in the unknown sample.

2. Why was it important to test each indicator solution on known nutrient solutions and on distilled water?

▶ Defending Your Conclusion

3. Suppose that the unknown sample did not produce a color change or a deposit when you added the indicator for one of the nutrients. Would that mean that the unknown sample was completely free of that nutrient? Explain.

viewpoints

Should You Buy Genetically Engineered Food?

Starting with hardier tomatoes, genetically engineered food is beginning to appear in some stores across the country.

Are there unforeseen problems associated with these foods? Are they dangerous to consume?

Some say that plant breeding, which has been used for centuries, is a form of genetic engineering. Are plant breeding and genetic engineering similar? Have the effects of plant breeding been completely safe?

BUY Genetically Engineered Food

> FROM: Carla W., Coral Springs, FL

There is always a risk involved in buying food from the grocery store—most of the time you don't know where it came from, what pesticides or other chemicals were used on it, or what invisible diseases lie inside it. No matter what kind of food you buy, there are always unforeseen problems, but they rarely occur. If the quality of genetically engineered foods is higher, you should buy them.

> FROM: Kyle H., Rochester, MN.

Have we had mutant children from tomatoes yet? No. These problems are not realistic. I will probably eat engineered food.

> FROM: Leigh Ann C., Bowling Green, KY

Ever since the time of Gregor Mendel's garden peas, genetic engineering has brought us wonders such as pickle rings as large as hamburgers and beautiful plants that fill our flower beds. Why shouldn't we use these techniques to our advantage?

> FROM: Beth W., Rochester, MN

Even though genetic engineering has been practiced for years without any problems, you never know what could go wrong. There might be a malfunction, and the consumer would be the one to learn the hard way.

> FROM: Annette A., Evergreen Park, IL

I feel that using genetically engineered food isn't wise because the seeds aren't fertile after use. Genetic engineering could allow a few people to control our food supply. Finally, how do we know these foods have the same vitamin content and taste as ordinary foods?

> FROM: Rachel G., Houston, TX

I don't understand why we need genetically engineered foods. We have lived for thousands of years without this technology.

DON'T Buy Genetically Engineered Food

> Your Turn

1. **Critiquing Viewpoints** Select one of the statements on this page that you *agree* with. Identify and explain at least one weak point in the statement. What would you say to respond to someone who brought up this weak point as a reason you were wrong?

2. **Critiquing Viewpoints** Select one of the statements on this page that you *disagree* with. Identify and explain at least one strong point in the statement. What would you say to respond to someone who brought up this point as a reason they were right?

3. **Interpreting and Communicating** Write your opinions about this issue in the form of a letter to the editor of your town's newspaper.

4. **Problem Solving** Imagine that you are a state legislator trying to draft a law that will make genetically engineered food available to those who want it, with the food carefully controlled to prevent any unforeseen problems. What precautions would you put into your law? Describe them in a paragraph.

 internet**connect**

TOPIC: Genetically engineered food
GO TO: go.hrw.com
KEYWORD: HJ1Genetic

Should genetically engineered foods be used? Why or why not? Share your views on this issue and learn about other viewpoints at the HRW Web site.

CHAPTER 14

Circulation and Respiration

Chapter Preview

14.1 Circulation and the Heart
Blood: The Living Fluid
The Heart and Blood Vessels

14.2 Breathing and the Lungs
How the Respiratory System Works

14.3 Smoking and Disease
Why Is It Hard to Quit Smoking?
Health Effects of Smoking

Focus ACTIVITY

Background Kelly has injured her knee in a basketball game. She is admitted to the hospital for minor knee surgery. Complications arise during the procedure, and Kelly loses too much blood. The surgeon operating on her needs to perform a transfusion. He requests additional blood from the hospital's blood bank, but there is a shortage of Kelly's blood type. Fortunately, Kelly donated some of her own blood days before going into surgery, and the blood bank is able to send this stored blood to the surgeon. The surgery is a success, and Kelly returns to playing basketball.

African-American surgeon Charles Drew was a pioneer in blood transfusions and plasma separation. Under his direction, the first blood banks were established by the American Red Cross during World War II. These blood banks supplied local hospitals with the blood they needed. Doctors were able to perform more blood transfusions for injured soldiers who suffered excessive blood loss. These blood banks also served as a model for the worldwide network of blood banks run by the American Red Cross. Dr. Drew's medical contributions helped save many lives and still impacts our world today.

Activity 1 Locate the local chapter of the American Red Cross in the city nearest you. Find out who can donate blood at the blood bank. Make a list of the requirements and restrictions. Also find out if the local blood bank supplies blood to all the hospitals in the area. What do you think would happen if there were not a local blood bank in your area?

Activity 2 At your local library, research the life and work of Dr. Drew. Find out what other important contributions he made in the medical field. How significant do you think these contributions were in that period of our history?

The American Red Cross interviews and screens volunteer blood donors before allowing them to donate blood.

internetconnect

SC**LINKS**
NSTA

TOPIC: Blood donations
GO TO: www.scilinks.org
KEYWORD: HJ1401

Circulation and the Heart

▶ **KEY TERMS**
circulatory system
plasma
red blood cell
hemoglobin
white blood cell
platelet
atrium
ventricle
blood pressure
artery
capillary
vein

> **OBJECTIVES**
>
> ▶ Describe the functions of plasma, red blood cells, white blood cells, and platelets.
> ▶ Describe how blood flows through the body.
> ▶ Relate the two numbers in a blood pressure reading.
> ▶ Contrast the two pathways of the circulatory system.
> ▶ Contrast arteries, capillaries, and veins.

▶ **circulatory system**
the body system that moves blood through the body

▶ **plasma** the liquid part of blood

The cells that make up your body need a constant supply of nutrients to survive and carry out their jobs. Distributing these nutrients to your cells is the job of your **circulatory system,** which consists of your blood, heart, and blood vessels. This transport system is responsible for bringing blood and vital nutrients to every cell in your body.

Blood: The Living Fluid

What makes up your blood? What path does it take through your body? Since the beginning of time, scientists have asked similar questions to guide their study of the human body.

Blood consists mostly of red and white blood cells suspended in a clear, watery solution known as **plasma.** The main components of blood are shown in **Figure 14-1.**

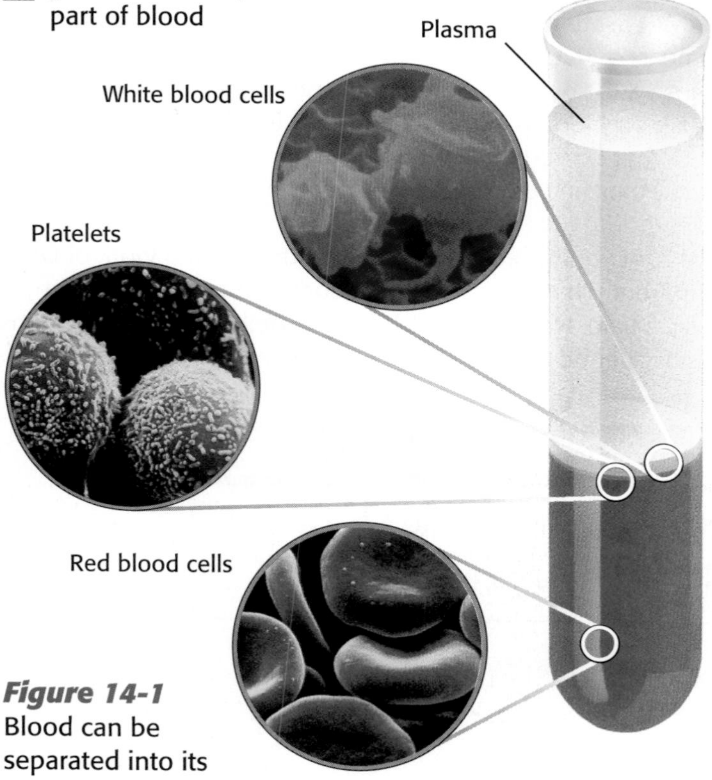

Plasma is the watery part of blood

Plasma normally makes up a little over half the volume of blood. The plasma brings nutrients and water from the digestive system to the rest of the body. It also carries a variety of hormones from the organs where they are produced to the sites where they are needed. Waste substances from cells also dissolve or float in the plasma. Eventually, this waste is taken to the lungs or the kidneys for disposal.

Plasma

White blood cells

Platelets

Red blood cells

Figure 14-1
Blood can be separated into its main components.

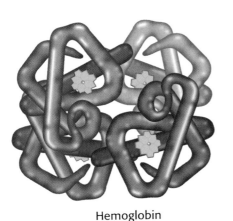

Hemoglobin

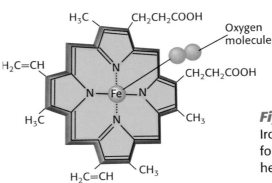

H₃C
CH₂CH₂COOH

Oxygen molecule

H₂C=CH

N

CH₂CH₂COOH

N—Fe—N

H₃C

CH₃

N

H₂C=CH
CH₃

Figure 14-2
Iron atoms are required for oxygen to bind to hemoglobin.

Red blood cells carry oxygen

The average adult has about 25 trillion (25×10^{12}) **red blood cells.** This accounts for one-fifth of all the cells in the body. The most important function of red blood cells is to carry oxygen to all cells.

▶ **red blood cell** an oxygen-transporting cell of the blood

Hemoglobin binds to oxygen

Every red blood cell contains millions of molecules of an iron-containing compound called **hemoglobin.** The structure of hemoglobin is shown in **Figure 14-2.** These molecules attract oxygen molecules and bind to them. When a hemoglobin molecule bonds to an oxygen molecule, the hemoglobin molecule turns bright red. This is why blood and red blood cells are red.

Each molecule of hemoglobin contains four iron atoms. These atoms are needed to bind oxygen and hemoglobin together. As old red blood cells are broken down and new ones are made, most of the iron is recycled, but about 10–15 mg per day is lost from the body. The iron that is lost must be replaced in your diet.

▶ **hemoglobin** a protein found in red blood cells that binds to oxygen

White blood cells fight infection

Your blood contains another type of cell, called a **white blood cell.** These cells are bigger than red blood cells, but there are fewer of them. They play an essential role in defending your body against bacteria, viruses, and other pathogens.

Different types of white blood cells have different jobs within the body. Some white blood cells produce proteins that attach to disease-causing organisms and mark them as foreign invaders. Other white blood cells recognize the marked invaders, then engulf and destroy them.

Unlike red blood cells, white blood cells can pass through the walls of intact blood vessels. Thus, they can travel to places in the body where an infection is developing. Healthy white blood cells recognize the body's own cells and leave them unharmed.

▶ **white blood cell** a blood cell that protects the body against infection

internetconnect

SCiLINKS
NSTA

TOPIC: Circulatory system
GO TO: www.scilinks.org
KEYWORD: HJ1402

The words *heart* and *blood* are used in sayings to describe far more than their scientific definitions. For example, a mother's "heart goes out" to her child because "blood is thicker than water." These phrases are used to describe emotional responses.

Making the Connection

1. Make a list of other common words, phrases, or titles of stories or poems that use *heart* or *blood*. Next to each item you list, write the meaning of each word or phrase as it is used.
2. Why do you think people have traditionally attached more symbolic significance to the blood and the heart than to other tissues and organs?

▶ **platelet** a cell fragment found in blood that functions in blood clotting

▶ **atrium** one of the two heart chambers that receive blood from the body

▶ **ventricle** one of the two heart chambers that pump blood to the rest of the body

Platelets stimulate clot formation

In addition to plasma and cells, blood also contains fragments of cells, called **platelets.** These tiny, flat structures form clots in places where blood vessels have been cut. Without platelets, even a small cut or scrape could cause you to lose most of your blood.

Clot formation begins as soon as a blood vessel is damaged. Platelets collect and stick together at the site of the cut. Next they release chemicals that trigger a clot to form. The clot plugs the hole in the damaged vessel, preventing blood from escaping. Eventually, new cells grow and the clot slowly breaks up.

The Heart and Blood Vessels

If you were a scientist, what other questions might you ask after discovering that blood is responsible for distributing nutrients to the cells, taking waste from the cells, and healing infections? You might explore how the blood moves through the body. The heart is the main organ that makes this movement happen.

The heart is a muscular pump

The heart is divided into left and right halves. Each half consists of two chambers, as shown in **Figure 14-3.** The top chamber in each half is called an **atrium,** and the bottom chamber is called a **ventricle.**

As the blood travels through the body, it flows through both the atria and ventricles. The atria receive blood from the body. Then they squeeze, pushing the blood into the ventricles. Next the ventricles squeeze, pushing the blood back to the body again. Notice in **Figure 14-3** that the ventricles are larger than the atria. This size difference is largely due to the fact that the ventricles are responsible for pumping blood back into the body, while the atria only pump blood to another part of the heart.

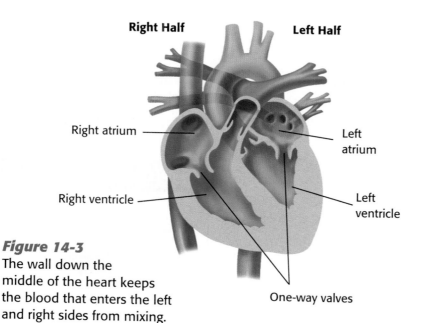

Right Half

Left Half

Right atrium

Left atrium

Right ventricle

Left ventricle

One-way valves

Figure 14-3
The wall down the middle of the heart keeps the blood that enters the left and right sides from mixing.

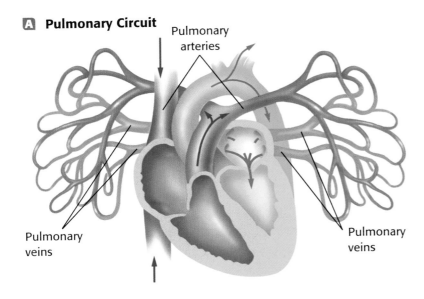

A Pulmonary Circuit

Pulmonary arteries

Pulmonary veins

Pulmonary veins

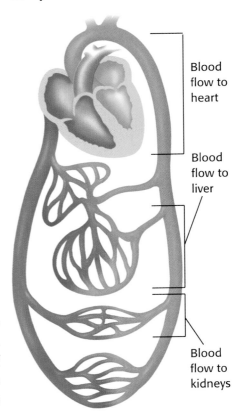

B Systemic Circuit

Blood flow to heart

Blood flow to liver

Blood flow to kidneys

Figure 14-4
(A) This pathway carries blood between the heart and the lungs.
(B) This pathway carries blood between the heart and the rest of the body.

Blood flows in one direction

Why does blood flow in only one direction? Blood flowing to the heart carries carbon dioxide away from your body's cells. Blood flowing from the heart carries oxygen to your body's cells. If blood did not flow in one direction, oxygen might be sent to the lungs instead of to the body's cells. Notice in **Figure 14-3** the one-way valve between each atrium and the ventricle below it. Another valve is located between each ventricle and the blood vessel it connects to. These valves allow blood to flow in only one direction—from the atria to the ventricles and from the ventricles to the body.

The left and right ventricles send blood along different pathways

The circulatory system is made up of two separate pathways shown in **Figure 14-4.** The first pathway starts in the right atrium. Blood moves from the right atrium to the right ventricle. The blood that fills up the right ventricle travels to the lungs. When this blood reaches the lungs, the hemoglobin in the red blood cells picks up oxygen. This oxygen-filled blood then goes to the left atrium.

The second pathway starts in the left atrium. In this loop, blood moves from the left atrium to the left ventricle. This blood carries molecules of oxygen to all parts of the body except the lungs. The blood then moves to the right atrium, and the cycle begins again.

The blood passes through each pathway once during each trip through the circulatory system. The pathway from the heart to the body is much larger than the pathway from the heart to

internetconnect

SC*L*INKS
NSTA

TOPIC: Heart
GO TO: www.scilinks.org
KEYWORD: HJ1403

the lungs. The resistance in the pathway of the body is greater than the pathway of the lungs, so the left ventricle must work harder than the right ventricle to pump blood throughout the body. This difference is seen in the thick, muscular wall of the left ventricle.

Your pulse is a measure of how fast your heart contracts

When you feel your heart beating, you are feeling the squeezing, or contracting of the chambers of your heart as they pump blood through your body.

When the atria contract, they squeeze blood into the ventricles. The contractions of the ventricles force blood into the vessels that lead to the rest of the body. While the ventricles contract, the atria fill with blood that is returning from the body. When the atria are full, the heart's contraction cycle begins again. Each cycle of the heart's contraction is a heartbeat. The heartbeat consist of two beats. The first beat occurs when the atria contract, and the second beat occurs when the ventricles contract.

Each contraction of the ventricles sends a pulse of blood out of the heart, and these pulses can be felt in blood vessels close to the surface of the skin. When you "take your pulse," you measure how fast your heart is contracting by counting the number of pulses that occur in a given period of time.

The pumping heart causes blood pressure

When a ventricle contracts, it squeezes the blood in the chamber, causing the pressure inside the chamber to increase. This elevated pressure forces blood through the vessels of the body.

Inquiry Lab

How does the structure of a heart relate to its function?

Materials
✔ mammalian heart from a grocer's meat department
✔ dissecting pan

Procedure

1. Place the mammalian heart in a dissecting pan.
2. Examine the heart closely, and compare it with **Figure 14-3** on page 466. Identify the heart's right and left sides. Locate the atria and the ventricles.
3. Locate the valves that control the flow of blood into and out of the ventricles.
4. Compare the thickness of the walls of the heart.

Analysis

1. What explains the difference in wall thickness between the atria and the left and right ventricles?

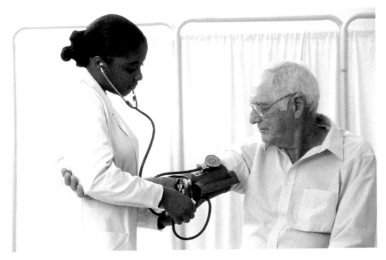

Blood pressure is an indicator of the health of the heart and blood vessels. Because it is difficult to measure pressure at the heart itself, blood pressure is typically measured in a vessel of the upper arm, as shown in **Figure 14-5.**

A blood-pressure reading is usually represented as two numbers separated by a slash, such as 120/80. The first number represents the maximum pressure in the vessel, which occurs when the left ventricle is contracting, sending blood to the body. The second number represents the minimum pressure in the vessel. The minimum pressure occurs when the left ventricle stops contracting and is filling with blood. Both numbers are given in millimeters of mercury (mm Hg), where a pressure of 1 mm Hg equals 133 newtons per meter squared (N/m^2).

Blood vessels carry blood throughout the body

When blood leaves the ventricles, it flows into large, muscular tubes called arteries. These arteries branch into smaller and smaller arteries, which carry blood to different parts of the body, as shown **Figure 14-6.** The smallest arteries branch into very narrow, thin-walled capillaries. Water, oxygen, and the many nutrients and other substances that are dissolved in the plasma are able to move through the capillary walls and into the fluid surrounding the body's cells.

▶ **blood pressure** the pressure exerted by the blood on the walls of blood vessels and heart chambers

▶ **artery** a tubelike vessel that carries blood away from the heart

▶ **capillary** a small blood vessel with two thin walls

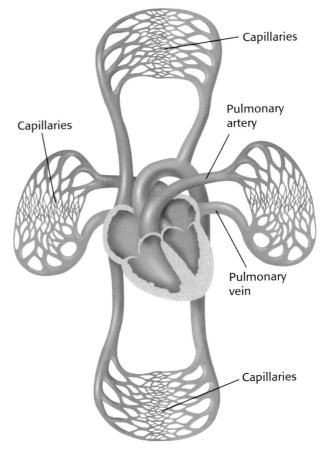

Capillaries

Capillaries

Pulmonary artery

Pulmonary vein

Capillaries

Figure 14-6
Arteries carry blood from the heart to capillaries. Blood from the capillaries is collected by veins and returned to the heart.

Quick ACTIVITY

Direction of Blood Flow

1. Find a large blood vessel that is visible on the inside of one of your forearms.
2. Using one finger, press firmly on the vessel near your elbow. Notice how the vessel swells *below* the point where your finger is compressing it.
3. As you continue to press on the vessel, slide your finger down your forearm. Notice that you can no longer see the vessel *above* the point where you finger is compressing it.
4. What do your observations in steps 2 and 3 indicate about the direction of blood flow in this vessel? What kind of vessel is it?

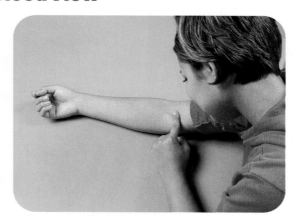

▶ **vein** a tubelike vessel that returns blood to the heart

The thin walls of the capillaries also allow waste products made by cells to enter the blood. Capillaries join together to form small **veins,** which join to form larger veins. The largest veins in the body return blood to the right and left atria. Like the heart itself, veins have valves that prevent blood from flowing backward.

SECTION 14.1 REVIEW

SUMMARY

▶ Red blood cells carry oxygen. White blood cells defend the body. Platelets help blood clot.

▶ The atria receive blood from the body. The ventricles pump blood to the body.

▶ A blood pressure reading indicates the maximum pressure as the left ventricle contracts and the minimum pressure after it relaxes.

▶ The circulatory system allows blood flow throughout the body.

▶ Arteries carry blood away from the heart. Veins return blood to the heart.

CHECK YOUR UNDERSTANDING

1. **List** two functions of blood plasma.
2. **Explain** why there is a two-beat heartbeat but only a one beat pulse?
3. **List** the heart chambers, blood vessels, and body organs in the order that blood passes through them in the pathway from the heart to the lungs. Begin with the right atrium.
4. **Explain** how oxygen is transported through the body.
5. **Describe** what the atria and ventricles do during one contraction cycle of the heart.
6. **Explain** what it means if a person has a blood pressure of 115/75.
7. **Contrast** the direction of blood flow in arteries with that in veins.
8. **Critical Thinking** If your left ventricle pumps 5 L of blood per minute, how much blood does your right ventricle pump per minute? Explain your reasoning. (**Hint:** Think about the path followed by blood as it leaves each ventricle.)

Breathing and the Lungs

OBJECTIVES

▶ Identify the main structures of the respiratory system.
▶ Explain how air is inhaled and exhaled.
▶ Describe gas exchange in the lungs and the rest of the body.
▶ Explain how the body regulates breathing.

H umans must have oxygen to survive. We use oxygen to react with the energy-containing compounds in food. These reactions produce carbon dioxide and water.

KEY TERMS
respiratory system
trachea
bronchus
alveolus
gas exchange
diaphragm
tidal volume
vital capacity
breathing rate

How the Respiratory System Works

Cells in the body must keep these reactions going or they will die. For the reactions to continue, cells need a constant supply of oxygen. Cells also need a way to get rid of carbon dioxide buildup. In the last section, you learned that blood brings oxygen to and takes carbon dioxide from cells. But how does oxygen get into the blood? How is carbon dioxide removed from the body? The structures that do this job belong to the respiratory system, as shown in **Figure 14-7.**

▶ **respiratory system**
the system that brings oxygen into the body and removes carbon dioxide

Figure 14-7

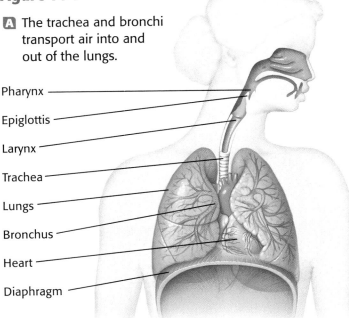

A The trachea and bronchi transport air into and out of the lungs.

Pharynx
Epiglottis
Larynx
Trachea
Lungs
Bronchus
Heart
Diaphragm

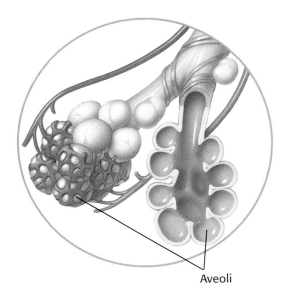

Aveoli

B In the alveoli, oxygen diffuses from the air into the blood, while carbon dioxide diffuses in the opposite direction.

trachea the tube that carries air between the throat and the chest

bronchus one of two large tubes that carry air between the trachea and the lungs

alveolus small sac in the lung where oxygen and carbon dioxide are exchanged between the air and the blood

internet**connect**

SC/LINKS
NSTA

TOPIC: Respiratory system
GO TO: www.scilinks.org
KEYWORD: HJ1404

gas exchange the exchange of oxygen and carbon dioxide between the body and the air

The respiratory system extends from the mouth to the lungs

Take another look at the respiratory system illustrated in **Figure 14-7.** It is made up of all the structures through which air passes on its way into and out of the body. In addition to the nose, mouth, and throat, the respiratory system includes the trachea, or windpipe, which extends from the back of the throat deep into the chest.

The trachea divides into two tubes called bronchi, which enter each lung. Inside the lungs, the bronchi divide into smaller passageways that end in tiny air sacs called alveoli.

As you can see in **Figure 14-7,** the thin walls of the alveoli are surrounded by capillaries. As blood circulates through these capillaries, oxygen moves from the air in the lungs into the blood. At the same time, carbon dioxide moves from the blood into the air in the lungs.

Your lungs contain about 300 million alveoli. These tiny air sacs have a combined surface area of 70 m², or about the area of a tennis court. This huge area allows large amounts of oxygen and carbon dioxide to be transferred with each breath you take.

Gas exchange is the process of exchanging oxygen and carbon dioxide

Gas exchange takes place because the concentration of oxygen and carbon dioxide in the blood is very different from the concentration of these gases in the air.

REAL WORLD APPLICATIONS

Cardiopulmonary Resuscitation A person who is not breathing and whose heart has stopped beating needs immediate help to avoid irreversible brain damage or death. The quickest way to provide such help is through cardiopulmonary resuscitation (CPR).

There are two basic parts to CPR: pressing on the victim's breastbone to compress the heart and force blood out of the ventricles, and breathing into the victim's mouth to bring oxygen into the body. CPR may stimulate the heart to resume beating and cause the victim to start breathing. If it does not, it is continued until emergency medical professionals arrive.

CPR is an effective life-saving procedure that is easy to learn. You can find CPR classes in most communities.

Applying Information
1. Why is it safe to assume that blood will flow in the right direction when the heart is compressed during CPR?
2. Why do people who perform CPR not help the victim exhale?

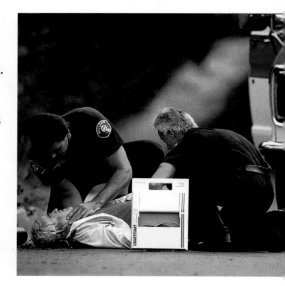

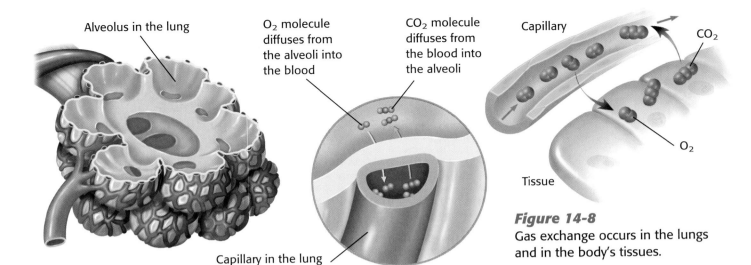

Alveolus in the lung

O_2 molecule diffuses from the alveoli into the blood

CO_2 molecule diffuses from the blood into the alveoli

Capillary in the lung

Capillary

CO_2

O_2

Tissue

Figure 14-8
Gas exchange occurs in the lungs and in the body's tissues.

Blood that enters the capillaries of the lungs has a low concentration of oxygen and a high concentration of carbon dioxide, as shown in **Figure 14-8.** In contrast, the air that you breathe is high in oxygen and low in carbon dioxide. The air that is taken in is only 0.5 μm away from the blood. The only barrier is the thin wall of the capillaries. Because both oxygen and carbon dioxide can easily pass through these thin walls, they quickly diffuse from the area where their levels are high to the area where their levels are low. That is, oxygen moves from the alveoli into the capillaries, and carbon dioxide moves from the capillaries into the alveoli.

As a result of this movement, the air you breathe out contains less oxygen and more carbon dioxide than the air you breathe in. The opposite is true for the blood. It contains more oxygen and less carbon dioxide as it leaves the lungs than it did when it entered the lungs.

Gas exchange also occurs in the body's tissues

After returning to the heart from the lungs, blood is pumped to the rest of the body. The cells of the body use oxygen and release carbon dioxide as they tap the energy stored in nutrients. So the body's cells are low in oxygen and high in carbon dioxide when oxygen-rich blood from the lungs enters nearby capillaries.

As you can see in **Figure 14-8,** gas exchange at this point occurs just as it does in the lungs. However, the direction of movement is reversed. Oxygen diffuses from the blood into the cells, and carbon dioxide diffuses from the cells into the blood. By the time the blood moves through the capillaries on its way back to the heart, it is low in oxygen and high in carbon dioxide. It returns to the heart and is pumped to the lungs, where it picks up more oxygen and releases carbon dioxide.

INTEGRATING

ENVIRONMENTAL SCIENCE

Ozone is a major air pollutant in many American cities. Most of the ozone present in the lower atmosphere of a city is produced when gasoline is burned in cars. Ozone has many harmful health effects, especially on people who are exposed to high levels for many years. It damages the alveoli of the lungs, causing shortness of breath.

It can also make people more susceptible to infections of the respiratory system, and it worsens respiratory system allergies.

On days when ozone levels are high, major cities announce an "ozone alert" and advise people to limit the time they spend outdoors.

Breathing depends on the actions of muscles around the chest

You can feel your lungs expanding and contracting as you inhale and exhale. But your lungs are not made of muscle. They cannot expand and contract on their own. This action takes place because the chest cavity around them changes size.

The chest cavity is surrounded on the sides by muscles and bones of the rib cage. Underneath the chest cavity is the **diaphragm,** a flat, sheetlike muscle.

When you breathe in, muscles between the ribs tighten. This causes the rib cage to move up and out, as shown in **Figure 14-9A.** At the same time, the diaphragm moves down. As a result, the volume of the chest cavity gets larger, and the air pressure inside the lungs decreases. Because the air pressure in the lungs is now lower than it is outside the body, air rushes into the lungs.

Breathing out is accomplished by relaxing the diaphragm and the muscles between the ribs, as shown in **Figure 14-9B.** When these structures are relaxed, they return to their original positions. The volume of the chest cavity gets smaller, which raises the air pressure inside the lungs. Because the air pressure in the lungs is now higher than it is outside the body, air is forced out of the lungs and the breathing cycle is repeated.

▶ **diaphragm** a sheet of muscle below the chest cavity that functions in breathing

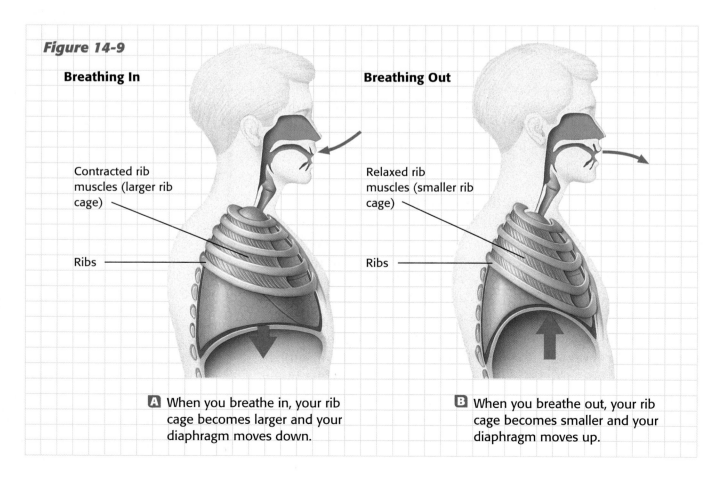

Figure 14-9

Breathing In

Contracted rib muscles (larger rib cage)

Ribs

A When you breathe in, your rib cage becomes larger and your diaphragm moves down.

Breathing Out

Relaxed rib muscles (smaller rib cage)

Ribs

B When you breathe out, your rib cage becomes smaller and your diaphragm moves up.

Inquiry Lab

How much air can your lungs hold?

Materials ✔ round balloon ✔ tape measure

Procedure

1. You will estimate your vital capacity by exhaling into a round balloon. First stretch the balloon to make it easier to inflate.
2. Take several deep breaths. After inhaling as deeply as you can, exhale as much air as possible into the balloon. Pinch the end of the balloon to prevent the air from escaping.
3. While you continue to pinch the end of the balloon, wrap the tape measure around the largest part of the balloon. Measure the balloon's circumference in centimeters.

Analysis

1. Calculate the radius of the balloon using the following formula:

$$radius = \frac{circumference}{2\pi}$$

2. Calculate the volume of the balloon (your vital capacity) using the following formula:

$$volume = \left(\frac{4}{3}\right)\pi(radius)^3$$

3. Compare your vital capacity with that of other students in the class. Is there much variation in vital capacity among students? If so, can you relate the variation to differences in weight, height, or physical fitness?

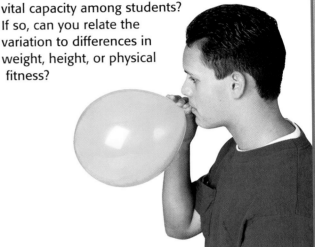

The lungs hold a maximum volume of air

When you are relaxed and breathing normally, almost the same amount of air moves into and out your lungs with each breath. This amount, called the tidal volume, averages about 500 mL in adults.

You can draw even more air into your lungs if you breathe in very deeply. You can also empty your lungs more completely by breathing out with more force than usual. The amount of air that moves into and out your lungs is known as your vital capacity. Most adults have a vital capacity of 4–5 L. Your lungs have the ability to handle a much larger volume of air than the amount that is taken in during normal breathing. This helps in moments when you need more oxygen, such as during exercise.

▶ **tidal volume** the volume of air a person breathes in and out in normal, relaxed breathing

▶ **vital capacity** the maximum volume of air a person can breathe out after breathing in fully

Automatic breathing parts; controlled breathing parts

Your brain initiates each breath you take by sending electrical signals along nerves to the diaphragm and the muscles between the ribs. These signals make the diaphragm and rib muscles contract, enlarging the chest cavity and drawing air into the lungs. The part of the brain that controls breathing allows you to breathe without thinking about it.

Measuring Breathing Rate

1. Sit quietly in your seat for about 5 minutes. Then measure how many times you breathe in 30 s. Multiply this number by 2 to calculate your breathing rate at rest.
2. Exercise vigorously by climbing stairs or performing some other strenuous activity for 5 minutes. As soon as you stop exercising, again measure

how many times you breathe in 30 s. Multiply this number by 2 to calculate your breathing rate after exercise.
3. Compare your breathing rate at rest with your rate after exercise. Did exercise produce any other change in your breathing besides your breathing rate?

This brain center is also under conscious control, however. That is why you can take a deep breath before diving into a pool, hold your breath until you return to the surface, and coordinate your breathing with your arm strokes as you swim.

What controls how often you breathe? Sensors in several arteries monitor the levels of oxygen and carbon dioxide in the blood. When the oxygen level falls too low and the level of carbon dioxide rises too high, these sensors send signals to the breathing center in the brain. The breathing center responds by increasing your **breathing rate,** which causes you to take in more oxygen.

▶ **breathing rate** the number of times per minute that a person breathes in and out

As you begin to breathe more frequently, you quickly raise the oxygen level and lower the carbon dioxide level in the blood. When these gas levels reach their normal values, the sensors stop signaling the brain, and your breathing rate returns to normal.

SECTION 14.2 REVIEW

SUMMARY

▶ The nose, mouth, throat, trachea, and bronchi are all parts of the respiratory system.

▶ Air is taken in when the diaphragm and the muscles between the ribs contract. Air is released when these muscles relax.

▶ Gas exchange occurs in the lungs and in the body's tissues.

▶ The brain controls breathing.

CHECK YOUR UNDERSTANDING

1. **List** the structures of the respiratory system that are located inside the chest cavity.
2. **List** two blood variables that are important for regulating breathing rate.
3. **Explain** what causes air to move into the lungs.
4. **Contrast** tidal volume and vital capacity.
5. **Explain** why oxygen and carbon dioxide diffuse in opposite directions in the lungs.
6. **Describe** the movement of oxygen and carbon dioxide in tissues other than the lungs.
7. **Compose** a paragraph describing two or more properties of the alveoli that help them do their job in the lungs.
8. **Critical Thinking** Explain why your breathing rate increases when you exercise vigorously.

Smoking and Disease

OBJECTIVES

- ▶ Describe two circulatory system conditions that can be caused by smoking.
- ▶ Explain how smoking affects the lungs.
- ▶ Describe two respiratory system diseases that can be caused by smoking.
- ▶ Explain how smoking affects unborn babies and infants.

▶ **KEY TERMS**

nicotine
tar
atherosclerosis
heart attack
stroke
hypertension
lung cancer
emphysema
bronchitis
asthma

Smoking has become a common activity in our society. However, medical researchers have accumulated evidence that links smoking with a variety of serious diseases of the circulatory and respiratory systems. Organizations such as the American Cancer Society publish literature like the poster shown in **Figure 14-10** to discourage smoking as a way to prevent disease.

▶ **nicotine** a toxic, addictive compound found in tobacco

Why Is It Hard to Quit Smoking ?

More than 2,000 chemicals have been found in the smoke produced when tobacco is burned in cigarettes, cigars, and pipes. One of the most dangerous of these chemicals is nicotine, an addictive drug.

Figure 14-10
The American Cancer Society uses posters like the one shown below, in their campaign against smoking.

Nicotine can affect the brain

Nicotine is absorbed through the lining of the mouth and across the alveoli into the blood. Once nicotine is in the blood, it is distributed throughout the body.

Within 10 s after smoke is inhaled, nicotine reaches the brain. There it produces the brief, mildly pleasurable sensations that smokers report feeling. As someone continues to smoke, the brain becomes less sensitive to nicotine. Eventually, a person must smoke more often to obtain the same pleasurable effects. As a result, people who smoke regularly often have trouble quitting because of nicotine's addictive properties. When a smoker stops smoking, the level of nicotine in the blood falls, and withdrawal symptoms—nervousness, jitters, and depression—can develop. Nicotine is also very toxic. In certain cigarette brands the nicotine contained in one cigarette would kill a person if all of it were to enter the bloodstream.

12 THINGS TO DO INSTEAD OF SMOKING CIGARETTES.

Health Effects of Smoking

In addition to nicotine, tobacco smoke contains a mixture of chemicals and ash particles referred to collectively as **tar.** Many of these chemicals, including carbon monoxide, hydrogen sulfide, and cyanide, are extremely poisonous. Others are known to cause genetic mutations in cells. Such mutations can lead to serious diseases, including cancer.

Smoking is linked to atherosclerosis

Smoking increases a person's risk for several problems in the circulatory system. People who smoke are two to six times more likely to develop **atherosclerosis** than nonsmokers. In atherosclerosis, fatty, cholesterol-rich deposits form in the walls of arteries. These deposits are called plaques.

The plaques become larger with time. **Figure 14-11** shows that as the plaques grow, the inside diameter of the arteries becomes smaller. This results in less blood flow to the tissues of the body, and the heart must also work harder to pump blood through the circulatory system.

Atherosclerosis can lead to heart attacks

One danger of atherosclerosis is when it occurs in the arteries that bring blood to the heart muscles. Reduced blood flow in these arteries could cause coronary heart disease, which is the leading cause of death in Americans over the age of 35.

If blood flow to the heart muscle is severely reduced, the part of the heart that does not get enough blood dies, resulting in a **heart attack.** Massive heart attacks involve a large amount of heart tissue and are often fatal. About one-fourth of all heart attacks are associated with the use of tobacco.

---

tar a complex mixture of compounds and ash particles contained in tobacco smoke

atherosclerosis a disease in which fatty deposits form in the walls of arteries

heart attack death of a portion of the heart caused by a reduced blood supply to the heart muscle

INTEGRATING

CHEMISTRY
Hemoglobin, the molecule inside red blood cells that binds to oxygen, binds to carbon monoxide about 200 times more strongly.

When a person smokes, a significant amount of carbon monoxide is present in the air that is inhaled and many of the hemoglobin molecules that pass near the lungs pick up carbon monoxide instead of oxygen. As a result, the blood delivers less oxygen to the body's cells. This is one reason why even moderate exercise often makes smokers feel breathless.

Figure 14-11
(A) Blood can flow easily through the large, open center of a normal artery. (B) Blood flow is greatly reduced in an artery of a person with atherosclerosis.

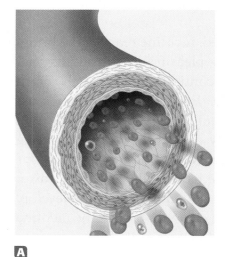

A

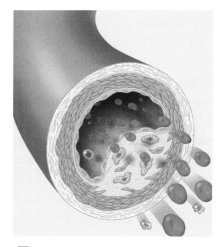

B

Atherosclerosis in the brain can cause a stroke

Another danger of atherosclerosis is the formation of blood clots. Plaques can cause blood clots that break away and travel through the circulatory system. When one of these clots gets stuck in a smaller artery, it may cut off blood flow through that vessel. This can happen in a coronary artery, causing a heart attack, or it can happen in an artery in the brain, causing a stroke.

When a stroke occurs, a part of the brain is deprived of blood and stops functioning, sometimes permanently. The symptoms can include paralysis, loss of speech, or even death. Smoking significantly increases a person's chances of having a stroke.

▶ **stroke** sudden loss of function in a part of the brain when it is deprived of its blood supply

Smoking can lead to high blood pressure

Smoking can also lead to high blood pressure, or hypertension. In a young adult, normal blood pressure is about 120/70. A person is diagnosed with hypertension when the maximum blood pressure is above 160 mm Hg or the minimum blood pressure is above 95 mm Hg.

Smoking raises blood pressure directly through the action of nicotine, which causes small arteries in the skin to tighten. Smoking also raises blood pressure indirectly by promoting atherosclerosis, which also often leads to high blood pressure.

People may not realize they have high blood pressure until they are examined by a doctor because the condition usually has no obvious symptoms. Despite its lack of symptoms, high blood pressure is a serious problem. If untreated, it can damage the heart, blood vessels, kidneys, and brain.

▶ **hypertension** a condition in which blood pressure is consistently higher than normal

Smoking harms the respiratory system's cleaning mechanisms

In a healthy lung, the air passages are covered by a thin layer of mucus that traps most foreign particles that may be taken in. Tiny hairlike structures called cilia extend from the cells that line the air passages, as shown in **Figure 14-12.** The cilia bend back and forth in unison, moving the mucus and its trapped particles out of the lungs. Any foreign material that escapes the mucus and enters the alveoli is engulfed and destroyed by white blood cells.

Tobacco smoke launches a three-pronged attack against the lungs' self-cleaning system. First, smoke irritates the lining of the air passages, causing the lungs to produce an excessive amount of mucus. Second, it paralyzes and eventually destroys the cilia. Third, it inhibits the white blood cells. As a result, smokers accumulate excess mucus in their lungs. Toxic compounds, disease-causing organisms, and cancer-causing substances stay in the lungs for a longer time and have a greater chance to produce disease.

Figure 14-12
Millions of microscopic cilia line the air passages of the lungs. Cilia sweep mucus and foreign particles out of the lungs.

Many communities have implemented bans on smoking cigarettes, cigars, and pipes in public places. Sometimes these bans apply to private businesses as well as to city, state, and federal facilities. Find out if there is a ban on cigarette smoking in your community and, if so, how the ban is specifically worded.

Making the Connection

1. Do you think your city's officials should determine whether people may smoke in public places or private businesses?
2. How do you think owners of private businesses would react to bans on smoking on their property?
3. In your opinion what kinds of businesses would have fewer customers if a ban on smoking were implemented?

▶ **lung cancer** uncontrolled growth of cells that begins in the lungs

Smoking is the major cause of lung cancer

It is now well established that smoking causes **lung cancer**. As **Figure 14-13** shows, lung cancer involves cells that grow uncontrollably, forming a large mass of abnormal tissue known as a tumor. Cancer cells can break off from the tumor in the lung and spread throughout the body, producing abnormal growths in other organs.

Scientists estimate that smoking causes 85–90 percent of all cases of lung cancer. It introduces cancer-causing agents into the lungs and disrupts the lungs' ability to cleanse themselves of these substances. In addition, smoking increases a person's risk of developing lung cancer from breathing in cancer-causing substances in polluted air.

Lung cancer develops very slowly. It usually takes about 20 years from the time a person starts smoking until that person develops lung cancer. If a smoker quits smoking, it still takes 10 years for the risk for lung cancer to drop as low as that of a person who has never smoked.

Lung cancer is rarely curable. Fewer than 10 percent of lung cancer victims live more than 5 years after they are diagnosed. Each year in the United States, about 170 000 new cases of lung cancer are reported and 150 000 people die from the disease.

Figure 14-13
(A) This lung belonged to a healthy non-smoker. (B) This lung belonged to a smoker who had developed lung cancer.

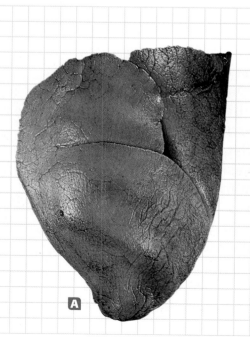

A

B

Smoking is linked to other serious respiratory diseases

Although lung cancer causes more deaths in the United States than any other type of cancer, it is not the only cancer that has been linked to smoking. Smoking also increases the risk of cancer of the bladder, pancreas, kidney, mouth, throat, larynx (voice box), and esophagus. About one-third of all cancer cases in the United States are caused by cigarette smoking.

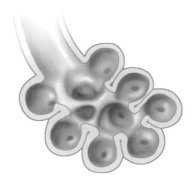 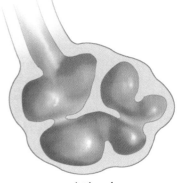

Normal Alveolus   Fused Alveolus

Figure 14-14
Emphysema occurs when the alveoli lose their elasticity and fuse together.

Smoking is also one of the major causes of emphysema. In this disease, the alveoli stop working. They lose their ability to bounce back, begin to stick together, and eventually, break apart or collapse, as shown in **Figure 14-14.** As more alveoli are lost, the surface area available for gas exchange in the lungs decreases. As a result, people with emphysema do not receive enough oxygen in their lungs.

People with severe emphysema become very short of breath when they carry out even a minimal amount of physical activity. To obtain the oxygen they need, they may have to breathe through a gas mask connected to an oxygen tank. Emphysema is often fatal. Everyone who smokes will eventually develop emphysema if they live long enough.

People who smoke often develop a long-lasting inflammation of their bronchi, as shown in **Figure 14-15.** This illness is called bronchitis. Symptoms of bronchitis include shortness of breath, soreness in the chest, and frequent coughing—commonly called "smoker's cough."

▶ **emphysema** a disease in which the lungs' alveoli break apart and collapse

▶ **bronchitis** inflammation of the bronchi

▶ **asthma** condition in which the bronchi become constricted

About 15 million Americans have asthma, a condition in which the bronchi shrink, severely reducing the flow of air into the alveoli. Bouts of asthma can result in coughing, wheezing, difficulty breathing, and even death.

Tobacco smoke is one of many things that may trigger bouts of asthma. Other factors include specific substances in food that cause allergic reactions, strenuous exercise, and emotional tension. Asthma can be controlled by medication and by avoiding tobacco smoke and other triggers.

Smoking can harm those who do not smoke

Smokers are not the only people who suffer the health effects of smoking. Anyone who breathes "secondhand smoke"—smoke from a cigarette, cigar, or pipe held by someone else—is at risk for the same diseases that affect smokers.

Normal Airways   Chronic Bronchitis

Figure 14-15
When a smoker develops bronchitis, the air passages connected to the lungs become inflamed, causing air flow to the lungs to decrease.

Quick ACTIVITY

Survey of Cigarette Smoking

1. Have your students write "Yes" or "No" on a blank sheet of paper to indicate whether they smoke cigarettes. Then ask students to write the number of cigarettes they smoke per day.
2. Ask your classmates to fold their papers in half so that their answers are not visible and to place the papers on a table at the back of the room.
3. Collect the papers, and tabulate the results. What percentage of the students in the class smoke cigarettes? How many cigarettes do those students smoke per day?

Smoking is especially dangerous among pregnant and nursing women. In pregnant women, nicotine travels across the placenta from the mother's blood to the unborn child. There is twice the risk of miscarriage among women who smoke compared with women who do not smoke. The number of premature births is also two to three times greater.

Babies of women who smoked during pregnancy weigh about 5 percent less at birth and are twice as likely to die shortly after birth than the babies of nonsmoking mothers.

An infant of a nursing mother who smokes may have as much nicotine in its blood as the mother has. Exposure to secondhand smoke also increases the risk of sudden infant death syndrome in children during their first year of life.

SECTION 14.3 REVIEW

SUMMARY

▶ Tobacco smoke contains nicotine and tar.

▶ Smoking increases a person's risk for developing diseases of the circulatory and respiratory system.

▶ Tobacco smoke reduces the ability of the lungs to clean themselves.

▶ People who breathe secondhand smoke are at risk for the same diseases as are smokers.

▶ Smoking affects the health of unborn babies.

CHECK YOUR UNDERSTANDING

1. **Identify** the addictive component of cigarette smoke.
2. **Define** *atherosclerosis*.
3. **List** three types of cancer besides lung cancer that people who smoke are more likely to develop.
4. **Describe** one way a fetus can get nicotine in its blood if the mother smokes.
5. **Explain** how smoking contributes to hypertension.
6. **Contrast** emphysema with bronchitis.
7. **Explain** how tobacco smoke hinders the lungs' ability to eliminate foreign substances.
8. **Creative Thinking** Some physicians argue that the best way to treat smokers who cannot or will not quit is to give them high-nicotine cigarettes. Write a paragraph explaining the reasoning behind this approach. Do you think this is a good idea?

WRITING SKILL

Chapter Highlights

Before you begin, review the summaries of the key ideas of each section, found on pages 470, 476, and 482. The key vocabulary terms are listed on pages 464, 471, and 477.

UNDERSTANDING CONCEPTS

1. The transport of hormones in the blood is carried out by _____.
   a. white blood cells
   c. plasma
   b. red blood cells
   d. platelets

2. Blood that enters the right atrium next flows to the _____.
   a. left atrium
   c. left ventricle
   b. right ventricle
   d. pacemaker

3. Blood flowing from the heart to the body may pass through all of the following except the _____.
   a. skin
   c. brain
   b. kidney
   d. lungs

4. Substances move from the blood to the fluid surrounding the body's cells by passing through the walls of _____.
   a. arteries
   c. veins
   b. capillaries
   d. All of the above

5. Breathing in occurs when _____.
   a. the diaphragm and the muscles between the ribs contract
   b. the diaphragm and the muscles between the ribs relax
   c. the muscles in the lungs contract
   d. the muscles in the lungs relax

6. In the respiratory system, gas exchange occurs in the _____.
   a. bronchi
   c. alveoli
   b. throat
   d. trachea

7. Smoking is estimated to cause _____ percent of all lung cancers.
   a. less than 1
   c. about 50
   b. about 10
   d. 85–90

8. A stroke occurs when _____.
   a. blood moves through the heart in the reverse direction
   b. a blood clot becomes lodged in an artery in the brain
   c. blood flow to the heart muscle is severely reduced
   d. the lungs become filled with mucus

9. The brain adjusts breathing rate in response to changes in _____.
   a. oxygen and carbon dioxide levels in the blood
   b. blood pressure
   c. the vital capacity of the lungs
   d. the number of platelets and white blood cells in the blood

10. Compared with nonsmoking mothers, smoking mothers have _____.
    a. more miscarriages
    b. more premature births
    c. babies who weigh less at birth
    d. All of the above

Using Vocabulary

11. Describe the roles of each of the following parts that make up the blood: *platelets, plasma, red blood cells,* and *white blood cells.*

    WRITING SKILL

12. Write a paragraph describing where air moves within the respiratory system on its way from the mouth to the site where gas exchange occurs. Use the following terms: *trachea, alveolus, bronchi,* and *lungs.*

13. Explain how atherosclerosis can lead to a heart attack. Use the terms *plaque* and *nicotine.*

    WRITING SKILL

14. Describe the two pathways of the circulatory system using the following terms: *heart, right atrium, left atrium, right ventricle, left ventricle, lungs,* and *body.*

BUILDING MATH SKILLS

15. Graphing The line graph below shows the relationship between the number of cigarettes smoked per day and the increased risk of dying from lung cancer.

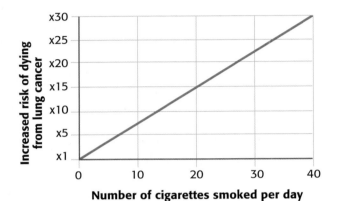

A person smokes 20 cigarettes a day. How much does the risk of dying from lung cancer increase for this person compared with the risk to a person who smokes 10 cigarettes a day? What risk is there of dying from lung cancer for the person who does not smoke at all?

THINKING CRITICALLY

16. Problem Solving Most arteries carry blood that is high in oxygen, and most veins carry blood that is low in oxygen. Considering what you have learned, name the arteries and veins that are exceptions to this generalization. Explain why they are exceptions.

17. Creative Thinking Imagine yourself as a molecule of oxygen in the air a person breathes in. Describe your journey into and through the person's body until you get to a cell in the person's left big toe. Identify each organ and structure you encounter on the journey.

WRITING SKILL

18. Applying Knowledge In which chamber of the heart would blood that had just returned from the left leg be found?

19. Applying Knowledge A person is not feeling well and decides to go see a doctor. The doctor takes a sample of blood and sends it to the lab to be examined for the number of white blood cells present. Why would this information be useful?

20. Applying Knowledge A person with anemia has too few red blood cells. A common symptom of anemia is lack of energy. Why would anemia cause this symptom? What might happen to an anemic person if too much energy is exerted during exercise?

21. Applying Knowledge The body can produce red blood cells at a faster rate if it has a greater need for oxygen transport. Given this information, predict how a person's body would respond if the person were moving from a low-altitude area to a high-altitude area, where the air contains less oxygen. How might athletes use this information to their advantage when training for major athletic events?

22. Critical Thinking The frequency of blood clots and heart attacks is much lower among the Inuit, the nomadic hunters of the North American Arctic, than it is among other North Americans and Europeans. This difference is due to fish oils in the Inuit diet that cause their platelets to be more slippery. How do you think the clotting ability of the Inuit's blood is affected by the slippery platelets?

DEVELOPING LIFE/WORK SKILLS

23. Interpreting Data A person has a blood pressure of 125/75. Explain what these two numbers mean.

24. Applying Technology Use a computer-presentation application program such as Microsoft Powerpoint to create a slide presentation that shows the different stages of the heart-beating process. Give a 3 minute presentation to the rest of the class.

25. Working Cooperatively Work with a partner and contact the local chapter of the American Cancer Society to find out if certain types of cancer are more common in your area than in other parts of the country. How many lung cancer cases have developed over the past year? Share your results with the class.

INTEGRATING CONCEPTS

26. Connection to Physics Viscosity describes how quickly or slowly a fluid flows. Consider blood being pumped by the heart. Is blood easier for the heart to pump if it is more viscous or less viscous?

27. Connection to Social Studies Newspaper, billboard, and magazine advertisements depict cigarette smoking in a very positive manner. However, these advertisements must carry warnings of the dangers to human health of smoking cigarettes. Who is the main target audience of the cigarette companies' advertisements? Do you think their advertisements are effective at selling their product? Why? Do you think the warning labels deter many people from buying the products?

internetconnect

SCI**LINKS**
NSTA

TOPIC: Smoking and health
GO TO: www.scilinks.org
KEYWORD: HJ1406

28. Concept Mapping Copy the unfinished concept map below onto a sheet of paper. Complete the map by writing the correct word or phrase in the lettered boxes.

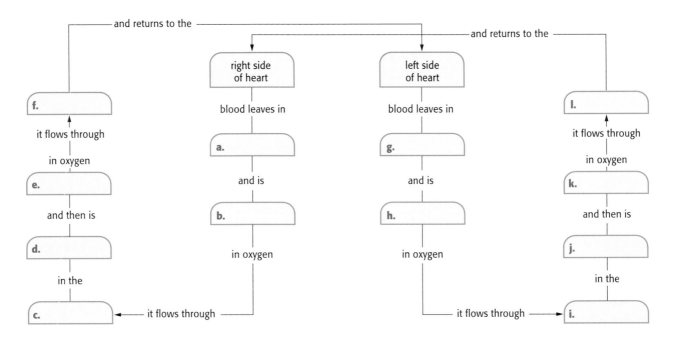

Design Your Own Lab

Introduction

Can you determine how heart rate and carbon dioxide production depend on the intensity of exercise?

Objectives

► **Measure** heart rate before and after exercise.
► **Measure** carbon dioxide production before and after exercise.

Materials

control flask
rest flask
methyl red solution in dropper bottle
NaOH, sodium hydroxide solution in dropper bottle
drinking straws
stopwatch or watch with second hand

Safety Needs

lab apron
safety goggles
disposable gloves

Studying the Effects of Exercise on Circulation and Respiration

► Preparing for Your Experiment

1. On a blank sheet of paper, prepare a table like the one shown on page 487. Leave room on the paper to add extra rows at the bottom of the table if necessary.
   SAFETY CAUTION Put on a lab apron, safety goggles, and gloves. If you get a chemical on your skin or clothing, wash it off at the sink while calling to your teacher. If you get a chemical in your eyes, immediately flush it out at the eyewash station while calling to your teacher.
2. Obtain a "Control" flask and a "Rest" flask from your teacher. Leave the plastic wrap on each flask until you are ready to perform the experiment.

► Measuring Heart Rate and Carbon Dioxide Production

3. Sit quietly for at least 2 minutes. Use two fingers to feel for your pulse on the underside of your wrist or on the side of your neck under your chin. Count the number of times your heart beats in 15 s. Record this number in your data table.
4. Remove the plastic wrap from the "Rest" flask. Exhale gently through a straw into the solution in the flask, and inhale through your nose. Continue this procedure for exactly 2 minutes.
   SAFETY CAUTION Do not inhale the solution.
5. Remove the straw, and add sodium hydroxide solution drop by drop to the flask, counting each drop. Swirl the flask as you add the drops. Sodium hydroxide neutralizes the solution, allowing methyl red's normal color to return. Stop when the solution in the flask has the same color as the solution in the "Control" flask.
6. Record the number of drops you added to the solution.

	# of heartbeats in 15 s	Heart rate (beats/min)	Drops of NaOH solution added
Rest			
Exercise 1			
Exercise 2			

▶ Designing Your Experiment

7. Form a hypothesis: How do you think exercise will affect heart rate and carbon dioxide production? A good way to exercise in the lab is to step onto and off of a step stool at a steady rate of one step every 2 seconds. How can you vary this procedure to change the intensity of exercise? Which measurements should you make?

   SAFETY CAUTION Do not attempt the exercise portion of this lab if you have a health problem or are recovering from an illness.

8. In your lab report, list each step you will perform in your experiment. Before you carry out your experiment, your teacher must approve your plan.

▶ Performing Your Experiment

9. After your teacher approves your plan, carry out your experiment. Test at least two different exercise intensities and record your results in your data table.

▶ Analyzing Your Results

1. For each measurement of the number of heartbeats in 15 s, multiply by 4 to calculate heart rate in beats per minute. Record the results in your data table.
2. Plot your data in your lab report in the form of two bar graphs.
3. How did your heart rate after exercise compare with your heart rate at rest?
4. How did the number of drops of sodium hydroxide solution you added after exercise compare with the number you added at rest?
5. **Reaching Conclusions** Based on this experiment, what can you conclude about the effect of exercise on heart rate and carbon dioxide production?
6. **Reaching Conclusions** What is the relationship between the intensity of exercise and changes in heart rate and carbon dioxide production?

▶ Defending Your Conclusions

7. Someone repeated this experiment using a different type of exercise and found no effect on either heart rate or carbon dioxide production. Assuming the person tested correctly, list three reasons that might explain the results.

Trauma Surgeon

The doctors who operate on badly injured patients who are rushed to the hospital are known as trauma surgeons. Trauma surgeons work for hospitals and perform emergency surgery on patients with severe injuries or illnesses. To find out more about trauma surgery as a career, read the interview with Dr. Vernon Henderson, who works at Morehouse School of Medicine, in Atlanta, Georgia.

"The reward in all of this is that sometimes you win, and people have you to thank for saving their lives."

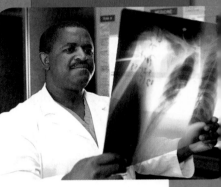

Dr. Henderson performs emergency surgery on patients in critical need of medical attention.

? What is a typical work day like for you?

I'm in the hospital 24 hours a day to take care of anyone who is injured in an accident. We operate on people who have been injured in automobile accidents, people who have been injured through interpersonal conflict, and people involved in major accidents. We do abdominal operations, operations on the chest, and vascular operations.

? What is the most satisfying aspects of your job?

One is the ability to work with patients who are in life-threatening situations. I have to think on my feet and make decisions that can save their lives. The other aspect is working the residents (doctors in training), teaching them the principles of patient care and trying to help them become good and compassionate surgeons.

? What skills does a good trauma surgeon need?

You definitely have to have the ability to think on your feet—you have to come by that skill by experience. You have to be able to work without requiring a lot of information. Trauma surgeons have to treat patients without a lot of information. To me, that requires a different mindset.

? What kind of personality should a surgeon have?

First of all, you have to have integrity—you have to stick to your principles. You have to be intelligent. You have to have a sense of self-confidence. You've got to love what you do. You have to be compassionate, because in the process of doing surgery, you end up hurting people. You have to be willing to develop your own sense of style in how you do your work.

What part of your training and education did you find most valuable?

All of it. But I think the time I spent in a cardiology (heart) lab was critical to my development as a surgeon. I learned highly technical surgical skills that really set me apart from my colleagues. It taught me to manage a surgical situation.

What advice to you have for a student who is considering a career as a trauma surgeon?

I think that you have to dedicate yourself to a life in medicine. One thing about medicine is that it's an ever-changing profession. You have to love learning. Learn to love to read. Recognize that information is your friend. The more information you have, the better off you are and your patients are.

Do you recommend that students try "shadowing," spending some time observing a surgeon at work?

I consider shadowing essential. As you go through life, embrace those people who love what they do and watch them carefully. These are the people who demonstrate the greatest skill, the greatest craftsmanship. These are the people to emulate.

internet connect

SCiLINKS
NSTA

TOPIC: Surgeon
GO TO: www.scilinks.org
KEYWORD: HK1159

"I still think that the greatest pleasure for me is to be in the operating room, applying my skills to a life-threatening situation."
—DR. VERNON HENDERSON

CHAPTER 15

Physical Fitness

Chapter Preview

15.1 Bones, Joints, and Muscles
Bones
Muscles and Force
Disorders of Bones, Joints, and Muscles

15.2 Exercise and Physical Fitness
Anaerobic Exercise
Aerobic Exercise
Using Exercise

15.3 Spaceflight and Fitness
Effects of Spaceflight on
Bones and Muscles
Other Effects of Spaceflight

INTEGRATING
TECHNOLOGY
and Society

Focus ACTIVITY

Background Can you imagine swimming 2.4 mi, biking 112 mi, or running 26.2 mi? Can you imagine doing all three on the same day? Thousands of triathletes do it every year, competing in one or more of the Ironman Triathlons held around the world. Most of the Ironman events are qualifying races for the Ironman Triathlon World Championship held every October in Kailua-Kona, Hawaii. The professional and amateur athletes who qualify for the championship race in Hawaii include men and women ages 18 to 80 with varying physical abilities. One certainty is that competitors must be physically fit in order to finish the 140.6 mi course within the cutoff time of 17 hours.

Activity 1 Athletes competing in the Ironman Triathlon World Championship have 17 hours to finish the three segments of the course. Keep a log describing the nature and duration of every physical activity, including sleeping and eating, that you perform during a continuous 17-hour period.

Activity 2 There are time restrictions on each segment of the Ironman Triathlon World Championship in addition to the 17-hour cutoff on the entire race. For example, athletes have 2 hours and 20 minutes to complete the swim course. Determine the speed in miles per hour of a swimmer who takes the maximum time available to finish the 2.4 mi course.

internet connect

SC**LINKS** NSTA

TOPIC: Physical fitness
GO TO: www.scilinks.org
KEYWORD: HJ1501

The Ironman Triathlon World Championship includes swimming, biking, and running. Physical fitness is essential for any athlete who intends to finish the race.

Bones, Joints, and Muscles

▶ **KEY TERMS**

joint
ligament
tendon
flexor
extensor
osteoporosis
arthritis

OBJECTIVES

▶ Describe the structure and function of bones.

▶ Explain the roles of joints and muscles in moving the body.

▶ Contrast skeletal, cardiac, and smooth muscle.

▶ Describe some disorders of bones, joints, and muscles.

When the goalie in **Figure 15-1** lunges to stop a shot, the muscles in her body move her skeleton in the direction of the ball. Since most of the bones in a person's skeleton are not rigidly connected to each other, they are free to move when pulled on. At the same time, the toughness of bones gives a skeleton strength, so the body is supported.

Bones

When you think of bones, you may picture the hard, dry structures that are left behind after an animal dies and its body breaks down. In a live animal, however, bones are living tissue made of cells. These cells secrete calcium phosphate, a mineral that makes bone hard.

Figure 15-1
Each movement this goalie makes is the result of muscles pulling against bones.

Bones are made of living cells

Bones contain blood vessels and nerves. The blood vessels bring nutrients to the bone cells and carry wastes away from them. Many bones have a spongy interior known as marrow, which produces blood cells.

The main functions of bones are to allow movement, to support the body, and to protect internal organs. **Figure 15-2,** on page 494, shows some of the 206 bones that make up the human skeleton.

Joints connect different bones

A joint is a place in the skeleton where two or more bones are connected. This is an important feature in the case of the skull, which protects the brain. The skull is made of several bony plates. The joints connecting them are called *fixed joints* because the bones cannot move at all. A small amount of tissue in fixed joints absorbs impact, preventing the bones of the skull from breaking.

Not all joints are fixed. If they were, you wouldn't be able to move at all. Some, like the 25 joints in your backbone, allow only a little motion. Joints that allow a little motion are called *semimovable joints*. Semimovable joints are also found in the rib cage, allowing the chest to expand during breathing.

Joints such as the ones in your elbows and feet allow more movement. For this reason, they are called *movable joints*. Because movable joints do not hold bones tightly together, another connection is required. Flexible but strong straps of tissues called ligaments hold bones together at movable joints.

Movable joints include five basic types

Movable joints include ball-and-socket, pivot, saddle, gliding, and hinge joints. An example of a ball-and-socket joint is the hip joint, which enables you to move your leg up, down, forward, and backward, as well as to rotate it in a complete circle. The shoulder joint, another example of a ball-and-socket joint, gives your arm a wide range of movement, just as the hip joint gives your leg.

Your forearm bone forms a pivot joint at your elbow, allowing you to turn your hand over by rotating your lower arm. Another example of a pivot joint is the joint formed by the top two vertebrae of your spine. This allows you to turn your head from side to side, as when shaking your head "no."

> **joint** a place where two or more bones meet

> **ligament** a strong strap of tissue that holds the bones of a joint in place

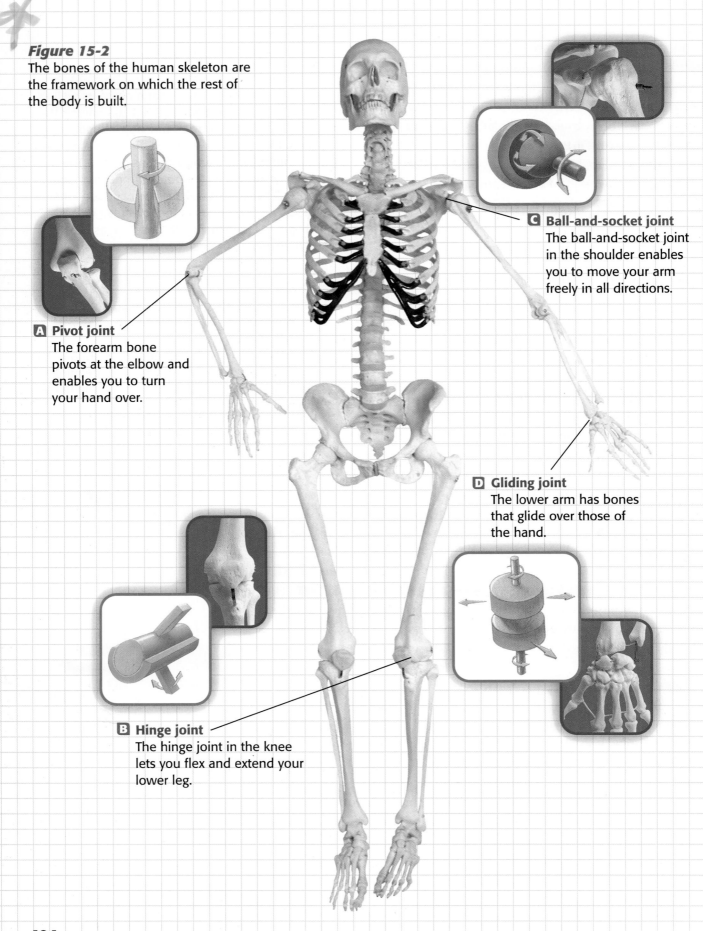

Figure 15-2
The bones of the human skeleton are the framework on which the rest of the body is built.

C **Ball-and-socket joint**
The ball-and-socket joint in the shoulder enables you to move your arm freely in all directions.

A **Pivot joint**
The forearm bone pivots at the elbow and enables you to turn your hand over.

D **Gliding joint**
The lower arm has bones that glide over those of the hand.

B **Hinge joint**
The hinge joint in the knee lets you flex and extend your lower leg.

The saddle joint, found at the base of each thumb, allows you to rotate your thumb and helps you grasp objects with your hand.

The joints between the small bones of your feet are examples of gliding joints. These allow the bones in your feet to slide over one another so you can walk. Similarly, the bones of your lower arm form gliding joints with the bones of your hand.

In the knee is a hinge joint, which allows you to move your lower leg forward and backward, much like a hinged door. **Figure 15-2** on the previous page shows examples of some of the joints in the human body.

internetconnect

SCiLINKS
NSTA

TOPIC: Joints and muscles in the body
GO TO: www.scilinks.org
KEYWORD: HJ1502

Muscles and Force

Even with joints allowing movement, bones cannot move by themselves. They move only when skeletal muscles contract and do work on them. **Figure 15-3** illustrates the major skeletal muscle systems in the human body. Force is transmitted from skeletal muscles to bones through strong cords of tissue called tendons. The amount of force a muscle can exert when it contracts—its strength—primarily depends on the muscle's cross-sectional area. Larger muscles can apply more force and lift heavier weights.

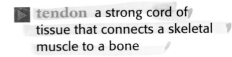

tendon a strong cord of tissue that connects a skeletal muscle to a bone

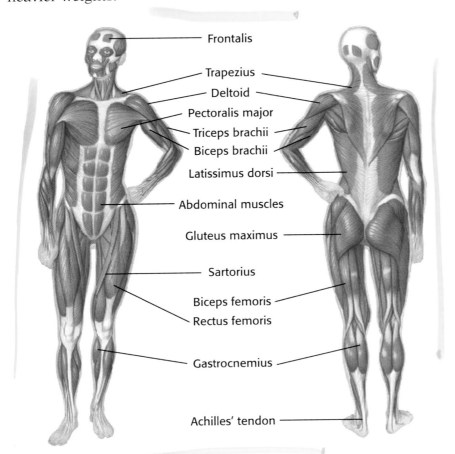

- Frontalis
- Trapezius
- Deltoid
- Pectoralis major
- Triceps brachii
- Biceps brachii
- Latissimus dorsi
- Abdominal muscles
- Gluteus maximus
- Sartorius
- Biceps femoris
- Rectus femoris
- Gastrocnemius
- Achilles' tendon

Figure 15-3
Skeletal muscles are attached to bones by cordlike tendons.

Muscles move by tightening in response to nerve signals

Skeletal muscles are responsible for moving parts of the body, like the arms, legs, face, and torso. When you move your hand to turn the pages in this book, your skeletal muscles tighten, or *contract*. This happens because you decide to do it. Your brain sends electrical signals through your nerves that cause the muscles to contract in a coordinated manner. Without a signal, these muscles remain relaxed.

The contraction of a skeletal muscle cell involves a series of chemical steps. The process begins when a nerve cell releases a specific chemical, which interacts with a protein on the surface of the muscle cell. That interaction causes calcium ions to enter the interior of the muscle cell, where they react with another protein. This in turn causes long filaments that are made of proteins called myosin and actin to slide past each other inside the cell. As they slide, they pull the ends of the muscle cell closer together, contracting the cell.

At other times your muscles move without your thinking about it. For example, as you concentrate on understanding this sentence, your chest muscles are contracting to keep you breathing. Even though you do not consciously control it, this action is also due to nerve signals sent by the brain.

Inquiry Lab

How can you estimate the strength of a muscle?

Materials ✔ metric ruler   ✔ calculator

Procedure

1. You will estimate the maximum strength of your biceps muscle. The biceps bends your arm at the elbow, bringing your hand toward your shoulder.
2. Examine **Figure 15-3** to confirm the location of the biceps, if necessary.
3. Bend the arm that you write with at the elbow. With the thumb and index finger of your other hand, determine the diameter of the biceps at its thickest part by positioning your thumb and index finger around the contracted muscle.
4. Keeping your thumb and index finger in the same position, move your hand next to a metric ruler and measure the distance in centimeters between your thumb and index finger. Use that distance as the diameter of the biceps.

Analysis

5. Convert the diameter to cross-sectional area using the following equation:
   area (in cm^2) = 3.14 × [diameter (in cm) ÷ 2]^2
6. Now estimate the maximum strength of your biceps by using the following equation:
   strength (in N) = area (in cm^2) × 35 N/cm^2
7. Is there a difference between your estimate and the amount of weight you know you can lift with that arm? (**Hint:** You can convert newtons to pounds by multiplying by 0.22.)
8. Your forearm is like a lever, with the fulcrum at the elbow. Using what you learned in Chapter 8 about simple machines, can you offer at least one reason why the biceps' force you estimated (the input force) doesn't match the force you can lift (the output force)?

Figure 15-4

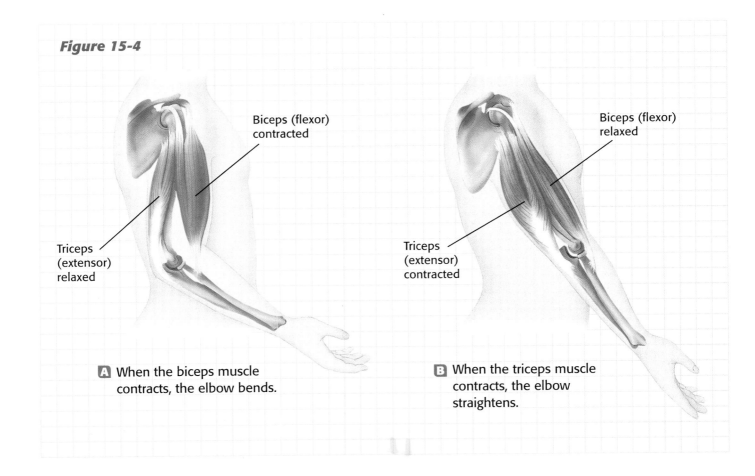

Biceps (flexor) contracted

Triceps (extensor) relaxed

A When the biceps muscle contracts, the elbow bends.

Biceps (flexor) relaxed

Triceps (extensor) contracted

B When the triceps muscle contracts, the elbow straightens.

Pairs of muscles move in opposite directions

Muscles move bones by contracting. When your biceps contracts, your elbow bends, and the upper and lower parts of your arm come together. But how are you able to straighten your arm? Another muscle, the triceps, is on the other side of your arm, as shown in **Figure 15-4.** When it contracts, your arm straightens, and the biceps relaxes.

Pairs of opposing muscles, flexors and extensors, exist around some joints in your body. During smooth movements of a limb, flexors and extensors work in a coordinated way—one contracts while the other relaxes. If both contract at the same time, the limb remains frozen in position.

▷ **flexor** a muscle that decreases the angle between two bones

▷ **extensor** a muscle that increases the angle between two bones

Two other kinds of muscles are found in internal organs

Muscles work to cause other movements within your body. Your heart contracts to push blood throughout your body. The heart is made of a specialized type of muscle known as cardiac muscle. Contraction of cardiac muscle in the walls of the heart squeezes the heart chambers, forcing blood through your arteries, veins, and capillaries.

Figure 15-5

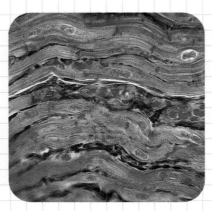

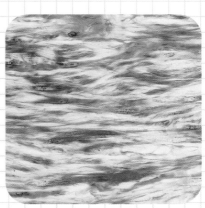

A Skeletal muscle tissue has a striped appearance when magnified 430 times under a microscope.

B Cardiac muscle tissue has interconnected fibers, shown here magnified 270 times, which allow impulses to spread rapidly.

C Seen here magnified 400 times, smooth muscle tissue is found in the digestive tract and the bladder.

INTEGRATING

ENVIRONMENTAL SCIENCE

Many Americans have been exposed to lead in their environment, mainly from the lead that used to be added to gasoline and paint. Although your body can remove most of the lead that enters it, some lead accumulates in your bones. In most cases, this is not a problem. However, if a person develops osteoporosis, lead can move from the bones into the blood. When that happens, kidney disease and high blood pressure may result.

Food moves through your digestive system because of the actions of muscles. A third type of muscle, called smooth muscle, is found in the walls of many hollow internal organs, including the stomach, intestines, and bladder. The pictures in **Figure 15-5** show the three types of muscle tissue found throughout your body.

Unlike skeletal muscle, cardiac muscle and most smooth muscles do not need to receive commands from the brain or spinal cord to contract. Instead, they have the built-in ability to contract and relax in rhythmic cycles. These cycles are reflected in the regular beating of your heart and the churning of your stomach when you digest food. Although nerve signals do not command the movements of cardiac or most smooth muscles, they can speed the movements up or slow them down.

Disorders of Bones, Joints, and Muscles

With all that your bones, joints, and muscles do every day, it is crucial that they operate well. Injuries, poor diet, and lack of exercise can have a negative impact on these systems.

A shortage of calcium in the diet leads to osteoporosis

Because calcium is one of the elements required to make bones hard, it is an essential part of everyone's diet. If too little calcium is present in the diet, it will be removed from the bones to meet other needs, as you learned in Chapter 13.

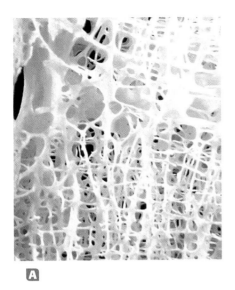
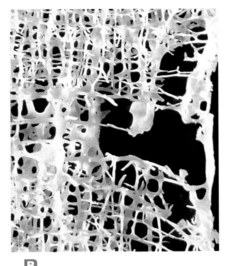

A

B

A calcium deficiency that continues over many years can lead to a condition in which bones become less dense and very fragile. When bone loss is severe, as seen in **Figure 15-6,** the condition is called osteoporosis, which means "porous bone." A person can counter the effects of osteoporosis by doing exercises that put force on bones, such as walking and running. The added force triggers the body to deposit more calcium in the bones.

> osteoporosis a disorder in which the bones become less dense and more fragile

Broken bones can heal themselves in time

If you've ever had a broken bone, or fracture, you may have spent many days wearing a cast. The cast does not actually fix the break. Like other parts of the body, bones can repair themselves. Fractures stimulate cells in the bone to produce new cells. The new cells fill in between the broken pieces of bone and re-form it, as shown in **Figure 15-7.** In the end, the healed bone is as strong as it was before the fracture. The reason for the cast is to hold the bones together so they will re-form in their original shape.

internetconnect

SCI LINKS

NSTA

TOPIC: Disorders of bones and joints
GO TO: www.scilinks.org
KEYWORD: HJ1503

A

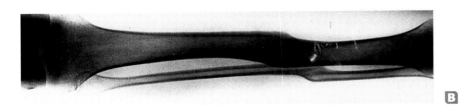

B

Figure 15-7
These X-ray photographs show a leg bone repairing itself a few days (A) and a few weeks (B) after a fracture.

Arthritis is a disease of the joints

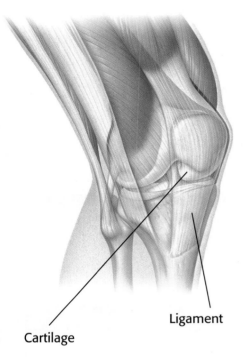

arthritis a condition in which the joints become swollen and painful

Although commonly associated with the normal aging process, the painful condition called arthritis strikes people of all ages. Normally, the ends of bones in a joint are covered with soft, smooth cartilage, as shown in **Figure 15-8.** In arthritis, this protective cushion is worn away. Without this cushioning material, the joints become stiff, swollen, and painful. Moderate exercise and pain relievers usually reduce the discomfort of arthritis.

Sprains and strains are injuries to ligaments, tendons, and muscles

Joints and muscles can also be damaged through accidents and overuse. Forcing a joint too far may injure ligaments, tendons, and muscles near the joint. The resulting injury is known as a sprain. A strain, in contrast, is an injury to a tendon or muscle that is caused by excessive physical effort, such as attempting to lift too much weight. Both sprains and strains can tear tissues. If the tear is complete, the tissue must be surgically repaired. Milder injuries are generally treated for the first 2 days by applying ice packs, wrapping and elevating the body part, and taking medicines to relieve pain and swelling. Then the injury is treated with alternating applications of heat and cold.

Figure 15-8
Pads of cartilage act as shock absorbers and protect the ends of bones where they form joints.

Ligament

Cartilage

SECTION 15.1 REVIEW

SUMMARY

▶ Bones are living tissue. They produce blood cells, allow movement, support the body, and protect internal organs.

▶ Bones move when skeletal muscles contract in response to chemical signals from the brain or the spinal cord.

▶ Dietary calcium and certain kinds of exercise can strengthen bones.

CHECK YOUR UNDERSTANDING

1. **Identify** one part of the human skeleton that protects internal organs.
2. **List** three types of joints, and give an example of each one.
3. **Define** osteoporosis.
4. **Explain** what the flexor and extensor muscles do in a limb when the limb is straightened.
5. **Distinguish** between a ligament and a tendon.
6. **Contrast** the functions of skeletal, cardiac, and smooth muscle.
7. **Distinguish** between a sprain and a strain.
8. **Critical Thinking** Two athletes of the same age—one a swimmer and one a runner—get the same amount of calcium in their diet every day. Explain why one of them might have stronger leg bones than the other.

Exercise and Physical Fitness

OBJECTIVES

▶ Define anaerobic exercise, and describe its main effects on the body.

▶ Explain how anaerobic exercise can produce muscle fatigue and an oxygen debt.

▶ Define aerobic exercise, and describe its main effects on the body.

▶ Name two ways that exercise can change body composition.

▶ Describe an exercise plan that can lead to physical fitness.

KEY TERMS

physical fitness
anaerobic exercise
muscle fatigue
oxygen debt
aerobic exercise
endurance
flexibility

▷ **physical fitness** the ability to carry out moderate physical tasks without becoming tired

Physical fitness means many things. It means having a heart, lungs, and skeletal muscles that are strong and work efficiently. But that's not all. A physically fit body is flexible and can endure prolonged physical activity. Maintaining an appropriate weight for your height and build is also important. Regular exercise is necessary for becoming and staying physically fit.

Anaerobic Exercise

Exercise, as shown in **Figure 15-9,** is any physical activity that requires your muscles to do work. Like all other kinds of work, exercise requires energy. You learned in Chapter 13 that your body can obtain energy by reacting the carbohydrates, fats, and proteins in food with oxygen.

Figure 15-9
Sprinting and lifting weights are two types of anaerobic exercise.

An oxygen-free pathway can provide energy

The oxygen-using reactions are somewhat slow. This is ideal for long-term exercise. But where can your body get energy for quick bursts of activity, like a 100 m sprint? Such exercises are powered by another set of reactions inside muscles. The reactions that release this energy do not require oxygen, so they are known as anaerobic ("without oxygen") reactions. An exercise that acquires energy from these reactions is called an anaerobic exercise.

Two examples of anaerobic exercises are shown in **Figure 15-9.** Others include swimming 50 m, doing pull-ups, shot putting, and high jumping. Notice that all of these exercises take little time. That is because anaerobic reactions cannot provide energy for more than about 30 s. Anaerobic reactions are also very inefficient. They convert only about 2 percent of the energy in food into a form that can be used to do work.

Anaerobic exercise increases skeletal muscle size and strength

Every skeletal muscle in your body consists of hundreds or thousands of long, cylindrical muscle cells. Anaerobic exercise stimulates these cells to become thicker and stronger. Because a muscle's strength is proportional to its cross-sectional area, the muscle becomes stronger through physical training. Weight lifting is a very effective way to increase muscle strength. Other anaerobic exercises can have the same effect if they force skeletal muscles to work against a load.

▶ **anaerobic exercise**
an exercise that is powered by energy-releasing reactions that do not require oxygen

REAL WORLD APPLICATIONS

Anabolic Steroids Many athletes use synthetic hormones called anabolic steroids to increase their performance. These hormones are chemically similar to the male sex hormone testosterone.

Like testosterone, they stimulate muscle fibers to thicken, promoting muscle growth and increased strength. Anabolic steroids are particularly effective in women, whose bodies normally produce very little testosterone.

These hormone supplements have very dangerous side effects. Long-term use of anabolic steroids can cause liver damage, heart disease, emotional disorders, and infertility. The side effects are particularly harmful in women, whose bodies are not adapted to high levels of male hormones.

Applying Information
1. Why do most athletic organizations ban the use of anabolic steroids?
2. In 1998, Mark McGwire smashed the single-season home run record while using androstenedione, an anabolic steroid that is legal in Major League Baseball but not in some other pro sports. Do you think McGwire's record should be erased because he used this hormone supplement? Explain why or why not.

Anaerobic exercise leads to muscle fatigue and an oxygen debt

One anaerobic reaction in muscle releases energy by converting glucose into a chemical called lactic acid. The longer a person exercises anaerobically, the more lactic acid builds up in their muscles. As lactic acid accumulates, it causes pain and muscle fatigue. These signs warn a person to stop exercising before a serious muscle injury occurs. The more often you do this type of exercise, the more lactic acid your body can handle. Then you can exercise anaerobically for longer periods of time.

When you stop exercising anaerobically, your body starts recovering. It uses oxygen to rebuild the energy stores in your muscles and to get rid of the lactic acid that has accumulated. As shown in **Figure 15-10,** this extra oxygen represents an oxygen debt—until this oxygen is taken in, your muscles can't return to their normal condition. It may take an hour or more to pay off the oxygen debt resulting from a period of hard exercise. If you begin exercising again while you still have an oxygen debt, your muscles will tire sooner.

Aerobic Exercise

As discussed earlier, slower, steadier exercise uses oxygen. This aerobic exercise is powered by energy released when food molecules are broken down during more-efficient reactions that convert about 50 percent of the energy in food into a usable form. Examples of aerobic exercises include marathon running, long-distance skating, and the exercises shown in Figure **15-11.**

▶ **muscle fatigue** the loss of muscle strength due to prolonged exercise

▶ **oxygen debt** the extra amount of oxygen needed to return muscles to their normal condition after anaerobic exercise

Figure 15-10
Oxygen debt occurs for many minutes after vigorous anaerobic exercise.

▶ **aerobic exercise** an exercise that is powered by energy-releasing reactions that require oxygen

Figure 15-11
Swimming laps and cross-country skiing are aerobic exercises.

Determining Your Target Heart Rate

1. Place your index finger and middle finger against the major artery on the underside of your wrist or on the side of your neck under your chin. Count the number of heartbeats in 15 s and multiply by 4 to calculate your resting heart rate.
2. Your target heart rate is the rate at which your heart should beat when you are exercising. It should range between 60 percent and 80 percent of your maximum heart rate. Using the table at right, calculate the lower and upper limits of your target heart rate. Then compare these values with your resting heart rate.

Age (years)	Maximum heart rate (beats/min)
13	207
14	206
15	205
16	204
17	203
18	202

Aerobic exercise strengthens the heart and increases endurance

There are many benefits to aerobic exercise, including that it strengthens and increases the size of the heart. A larger heart can pump more blood with each heartbeat, so it does not have to beat as often as a smaller heart. A male marathon runner, for example, may have a heart that pumps about 105 mL with each beat at rest and a resting heart rate of about 50 beats per minute. The corresponding values for a resting, nonathletic male are about 75 mL and 75 beats per minute.

Aerobic exercise reduces the risk of heart disease, the leading cause of death in Americans over the age of 35. Aerobic fitness also lowers a person's chances of having a stroke.

People who get plenty of aerobic exercise take in more oxygen from the air they breathe. A well-exercised body uses oxygen more efficiently. This gives aerobically fit people more **endurance.** They can walk, run, swim, or do other exercises for a long time without tiring.

▶ **endurance** the ability to continue exercising before becoming completely exhausted

Using Exercise

Exercise of all kinds keeps you healthy in other ways, too. The more you exercise, the easier exercising becomes. Your muscles get stronger, and the condition of your whole body improves.

Exercise makes the ligaments that hold your bones together more elastic. As a result, the bones at your movable joints have more range of movement. This increases your body's **flexibility.** Exercise also prevents muscles from becoming too tight. Some exercises, like those shown in **Figure 15-12,** are specifically designed to improve flexibility by stretching muscles and tendons.

▶ **flexibility** the ability of the body to move at its joints

Figure 15-12

Stretching exercises can increase flexibility, decrease the chances of injury, and contribute to overall fitness. Take time to stretch before doing any vigorous physical activity.

Shoulder stretch

With arms slightly bent, hold on to a support about shoulder height. With your hands on the support, let your chest move downward, keeping your feet under the hips and your knees slightly bent.

Achilles' tendon

Place your hands on a support and lean forward with the lead leg slightly bent and the rear leg extended. Bend the back knee slightly with the heel flat until you feel a stretch in the tendon.

Groin (a)

Put one leg in front of you and lunge forward until the knee is directly over the ankle. The other knee is bent and rests on the floor. Lean forward and hold.

Groin (b)

While sitting down with the soles of the feet together, place your hands around your feet and pull your torso forward.

Hip

Lying on your back, relax and straighten both legs. Pull one knee toward the chest. Repeat with the other knee.

Quadriceps

Stand on one leg. Now bend your other leg at the knee, hold your ankle behind you, and pull your foot upward slowly and gently until you feel a slight stretch in your thigh. Switch legs, and repeat.

Hamstring

While sitting, keep only a slight bend in the front leg, with the foot of the other leg positioned against your inner thigh. Bend forward at the hips until you feel slight pressure.

Calf

Stand slightly away from a wall, and lean forward with the lead leg bent and the rear leg extended. Move the hips forward while keeping the heel of the straight leg on the ground until you feel a stretch in the calf.

How can you measure your level of aerobic fitness?

Materials

✔ stool no more than 1 ft high   ✔ watch with second hand

Procedure

SAFETY CAUTION Do not attempt this activity if you have a health problem or are recovering from an illness.

1. You will estimate your aerobic fitness by exercising for 5 minutes and then counting your heartbeats while you rest.
2. Practice stepping on and off a stool or stair at a steady rate of one step every 2 s. Another student can count the seconds aloud to keep you in rhythm.
3. Begin the test by stepping up and down for 5 minutes.
4. Sit down and rest for 1 minute. Then count your heartbeats for 30 s. Write down your number of heartbeats on a sheet of paper.
5. Rest for 30 s. Count your heartbeats for 30 s. Write down your number of heartbeats.
6. Rest for 30 s. Count your heartbeats for 30 s. Write down your number of heartbeats.

Analysis

1. Add the heartbeats you counted in steps 4–6. Compare your total with the numbers in the table below.
2. In which fitness category did this test place you? Do you think this is a valid test of aerobic fitness? Explain why or why not.

Fitness level	Male	Female
Very fit	175 or less	190 or less
Fairly fit	about 200	about 220
Rather unfit	about 215	about 235
Very unfit	230 or more	250 or more

Exercise can change the body's makeup

Because exercise requires energy input, regular exercise can help you maintain your body weight. Just as important, it can change how much of your weight is attributable to muscle or fat.

Skeletal muscle is about 40 percent of the body weight of a physically fit man. But the weight of fat usually ranges from as little as 5 percent to as much as 18 percent. In a physically fit woman, about 32 percent of body weight is made up of skeletal muscle. The weight of fat usually ranges from 12 percent to 26 percent. Regular exercise can both increase your muscle mass and decrease your amount of body fat.

One approach used to measure physical fitness takes into account the difference between fat and skeletal muscle. Lean body mass is found by subtracting the mass due to fat from the total body mass. For example, a physically fit 75 kg man whose body fat composition is 4 percent would have 3 kg of fat on his body. Therefore, his lean body mass would be 75 kg minus 3 kg, or 72 kg. In contrast, a physically unfit man who weighs the same but has a body fat composition of 25 percent would have about 19 kg of body fat and a lean body mass of 56 kg.

Begin an exercise plan carefully and gradually

It is never too early or too late to begin an exercise plan. Exercise is important for people of all ages. You do not have to be particularly good at any form of exercise for it to keep you healthy. With the right equipment, even people with physical disabilities can become physically fit, as **Figure 15-13** shows.

To stay fit, experts recommend 20–30 minutes of vigorous exercise every day. Many people exercise too much when they begin an exercise plan and then give up when they develop sore muscles or injure themselves. It is much better to start slowly and build up to harder exercise.

One good way to develop strength and endurance without injury is to exercise different muscle groups on different days. For example, you could run one day, lift weights the next day, and run again the following day. Alternate anaerobic and aerobic training from day to day so that you benefit from both types of exercise. Remember, exercise can make your heart and muscles stronger and increase your body's efficiency in delivering oxygen to its tissues.

Figure 15-13
Achieving physical fitness through exercise is important for everyone, including people with physical disabilites.

SECTION 15.2 REVIEW

SUMMARY

▶ Anaerobic exercise is powered by chemical reactions that do not require oxygen. It increases the size and strength of skeletal muscles.

▶ Aerobic exercise is powered by chemical reactions that require oxygen. It makes the heart stronger, improves oxygen uptake and increases endurance.

▶ Physical fitness increases the body's flexibility and muscle mass and decreases the amount of fat.

CHECK YOUR UNDERSTANDING

1. **List** two examples of anaerobic exercises and two examples of aerobic exercises.
2. **Define** *oxygen debt*.
3. **Contrast** the effects of anaerobic and aerobic exercise on the body.
4. **Explain** how lactic acid causes muscle fatigue.
5. **Describe** how regular exercise increases a person's flexibility.
6. **Explain** how exercise can change a person's body composition.
7. **Describe** the features of a sensible exercise plan, including effective activities and reasonable lengths of time.
8. **Critical Thinking** James has a lean body mass of 70 kg. Aaron is the same height as James but has a lean body mass of 80 kg. With this information, can you determine which man has the lower body fat composition? Why or why not?

Spaceflight and Fitness

INTEGRATING TECHNOLOGY and Society

▶ **KEY TERMS**
atrophy
anemia

OBJECTIVES

▶ Describe the effects of spaceflight on the skeleton.
▶ Explain how spaceflight affects muscles.
▶ Explain how spaceflight interferes with coordination.
▶ Describe two changes in the circulatory system that occur during spaceflight.

You have probably seen photographs of astronauts orbiting the Earth in the space shuttle. While in orbit, they are in free fall. Although they still have mass, they feel as if they have no weight.

As you can see in **Figure 15-14,** a person can float effortlessly in space. Spaceflight also brings about some major changes in the body.

If humans are ever to visit other planets or to work in orbiting space stations, they may have to spend months or years in space. What will happen to the body of a person who remains weightless for such a long time?

Effects of Spaceflight on Bones and Muscles

Remember from Section 15.1 that one of the major functions of your skeleton is to support the weight of your body. Without bones, your body would be pulled by gravity into a shapeless blob. Muscles attached by tendons to the bones in your legs and torso help keep your skeleton upright. By contracting steadily, these muscles exert forces that counteract the downward force of gravity.

In spaceflight, however, the body no longer requires support against gravity. The body responds by altering bones and muscles.

Bones can become weaker during spaceflight

Normally, bones become stronger because of the exercise of supporting the body during walking and running. Without such exercise, the bones quickly lose calcium and become thinner, lighter, and weaker. Bone weakening is a serious problem for people who are confined to bed due to illness or injury. It is even worse in space, where the bones carry almost no weight at all.

Figure 15-14
In space, the force of gravity is very small, making astronauts essentially weightless.

When a person stands upright on Earth, the leg bones and the backbone carry most of the body's weight. Bones that do not carry much weight on Earth, such as the skull and finger bones, do not seem to be affected by spaceflight. After several months in space, bone loss gradually stops, and the skeleton is maintained in a stable but weakened state.

This weakened state is fine in space, but problems arise when space travelers return to Earth. Within minutes, they go from feeling little weight to feeling the full force of gravity. Their weak bones break more easily, just like the bones of people who have osteoporosis.

Returning astronauts can regain much of their normal bone strength by resuming weight-bearing activities. But some of their bone loss may be permanent.

internet connect

SC LINKS
NSTA

TOPIC: Atrophy
GO TO: www.scilinks.org
KEYWORD: HJ1505

In space, muscles shrink and undergo other changes

Muscles are constantly being broken down and rebuilt. Half the protein in human muscle cells is replaced every week or two. This constant change helps muscles adapt quickly to changing conditions.

When a muscle is not used very much, it is broken down more quickly than it is built up. The muscle loses protein and becomes smaller; this process is known as **atrophy.** Muscle atrophy occurs during spaceflight because the muscles no longer do any work to support the body. A decrease in muscle mass after an extended period of weightlessness seriously weakens the astronaut shown in **Figure 15-15.**

Most muscles contain two basic types of muscle cells: fast and slow. Fast cells contract quickly but tire soon. Slow cells contract slowly but are more resistant to fatigue. Leg muscles have a high proportion of slow cells, which allows these muscles to support the body for long periods without tiring.

During spaceflight, however, many of the slow cells in the leg muscles develop into fast cells. When added to muscle atrophy, this change causes many astronauts to have difficulty walking when they return to Earth after a long time in space.

▶ **atrophy** the decrease in the size of a body structure due to disease, aging, or lack of use

Figure 15-15
Muscle mass decreases noticeably during a long spaceflight because muscles do not have to work to support the body when the body is weightless.

Figure 15-16
Astronauts can help protect their bones and muscles from the effects of weightlessness by exercising during spaceflights.

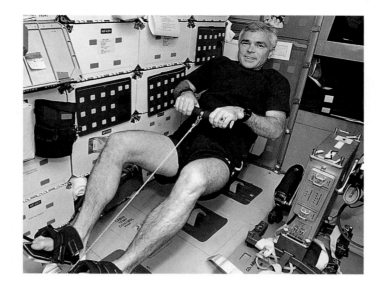

Exercising in space can prevent some bone and muscle changes

As you learned in Sections 15.1 and 15.2, weight-bearing exercises can strengthen bones and muscles on Earth. Of course, it is impossible to perform weight-bearing exercises in a weightless environment. Because there is little gravitational force in space, moving massive objects requires little muscular effort in space. Instead, astronauts use specially modified treadmills, cycles, and other exercise machines, like the one shown in **Figure 15-16.** These machines provide a resistance that muscles can work against.

Figure 15-17
Without a strong gravitational force, there is no way for the astronauts to tell which one of them is upside down.

Other Effects of Spaceflight

Because we are constantly under the force of gravity, we often do not think about it, but our bodies depend on it. Specialized organs in your inner ear sense the direction of gravity, so you know which way is up even when your eyes are closed. These organs also help you maintain your balance as you stand, walk, and run.

Without a sense of up and down, astronauts become disoriented

In space, there is no gravity sense to indicate up and down, as **Figure 15-17** shows. Without this information, the brain has trouble interpreting signals about what it sees and touches. For example, weightless astronauts may recognize a room in their spacecraft when they view it from one direction. From another direction, the same room seems unfamiliar.

Simulating Weightlessness

1. Place a stack of books on a desk, and move a wheeled swivel chair within arm's reach of the books. The desk and chair should be on a hard, smooth floor. Sit down in the chair, and lift your feet off the floor.

2. In this position, try to slide the stack of books along the desktop without touching anything but the books. First try to push the books directly away from you. Reposition the stack of books in front of you, and then try to push it to the right or to the left.

3. Using Newton's third law of motion, explain what happened in each case.

Spaceflight has an impact on physical coordination

Because arms and legs feel as if they have no weight in space, astronauts may not even know where their limbs are without looking at them! Less effort is needed to reach for and grab an object, so astronauts have a tendency to reach too far. Without the force of gravity to anchor astronauts to the floor, they have only their own inertia to keep them in place. You may have had a similar experience if you have tried to push against something while floating in water.

Astronauts quickly adjust to most disorientation and coordination problems in space. When they return to Earth, however, it may take several days for them to regain their sense of balance.

Blood is redistributed during spaceflight

Why does your face become flushed every time you do a handstand? Again, gravity is responsible. When you stand upright, the force of gravity makes blood accumulate in the veins in your legs, but when you are upside down, blood moves in the reverse direction—toward your head.

A similar thing happens when a person is in orbit. The body, which is designed to pump blood to the head against gravity's force, pumps blood just as hard. As a result, the veins in the upper part of the body contain more blood than they normally do. The extra blood in the head makes an astronaut's face appear puffy.

Spaceflight causes changes in blood volume and red-blood-cell counts

On Earth, excess blood in the head is usually a sign that the blood's volume has increased. In response, the body produces more urine, which takes water out of the blood plasma. As a result, the blood loses as much as 10 percent of its volume. In other words, an astronaut who has 5 L of blood on Earth will have only about 4.5 L during a spaceflight.

> **anemia** a condition in which the blood contains fewer red blood cells than normal

INTEGRATING

PHYSICS

One proposal for reducing the effects of spaceflight is to use a rotating wheel-shaped spacecraft. Astronauts could walk within the wheel, using the outermost wall as a floor.

The astronaut's inertia and the spacecraft's rotation could simulate the force of gravity at Earth's surface. Just as you feel pushed to one side of a car as it goes around a turn, the astronauts would feel pressed against the floor as the spacecraft turned. The strength of this "artificial gravity" would depend on the wheel's diameter and speed of rotation.

Surprisingly, tests show that the concentration of red blood cells in an astronaut's blood stays about the same as it is on Earth. This is true even though the blood's volume decreases. This means that the blood must lose red blood cells as well as water during weightlessness. This condition is called space anemia.

While anemia can be dangerous on Earth, the mild form that astronauts experience is actually an advantage in space. Muscles do less work in orbit, so they need less oxygen. That allows astronauts to get by with fewer oxygen-carrying red blood cells.

By reducing the number of red blood cells, the body keeps the blood from becoming too thick as water moves out of the plasma. Thickened blood forces the heart to work harder and raises the risk of heart attack and stroke.

These changes in the blood cause problems when astronauts return from a long spaceflight. Once an astronaut returns to Earth, the force of gravity again pulls blood into the legs. Because the blood's volume has been reduced, there may not be enough blood to supply the upper body and the brain. Astronauts may feel lightheaded, the same way you may feel when you stand up suddenly.

Returning astronauts can easily increase their blood volume by drinking fluids. However, it may take several weeks for their bone marrow to produce enough red blood cells to bring their numbers up to normal.

SECTION 15.3 REVIEW

SUMMARY

▶ During spaceflight, the skeleton loses calcium and becomes weaker. The leg bones and backbone are most affected.

▶ Spaceflight causes muscles to lose protein and become smaller. It causes many slow cells in leg muscles to develop into fast cells.

▶ During spaceflight, blood accumulates in the upper part of the body. This leads to a decrease in blood volume and a reduction in the number of red blood cells.

CHECK YOUR UNDERSTANDING

1. **Define** *atrophy*.
2. **List** two problems that may arise when astronauts return to Earth after a long time in space.
3. **Describe** the change that many leg muscle cells undergo during weightlessness.
4. **Contrast** the effects of spaceflight on finger bones and leg bones, and explain why the effects are different.
5. **Explain** why it is easy for astronauts to reach too far when they try to grab an object while in orbit.
6. **Describe** the effect of spaceflight on the blood's volume.
7. **Explain** why having fewer red blood cells can be an advantage during spaceflight.
8. **Critical Thinking** Someone suggests that astronauts should exercise with barbells in space to prevent their bones and muscles from becoming weak. Explain why that plan would not work.

Chapter Highlights

Before you begin, review the summaries of the key ideas of each section, found on pages 500, 507, and 512. The key vocabulary terms are listed on pages 492, 501, and 508.

UNDERSTANDING CONCEPTS

1. The main functions of bones include all of the following except _____.
   a. allowing movement
   b. supporting the body
   c. exerting force by contracting
   d. protecting internal organs

2. Bones are held together at movable joints by _____.
   a. muscles
   b. ligaments
   c. tendons
   d. blood vessels

3. The kind of muscle that is found in the walls of digestive organs is called _____ muscle.
   a. smooth
   b. rough
   c. cardiac
   d. skeletal

4. An injury to a joint caused by abnormal bending or twisting is known as _____.
   a. osteoporosis
   b. a fracture
   c. a strain
   d. a sprain

5. The main effect of anaerobic exercise is to increase the _____.
   a. size and strength of the heart
   b. size and strength of skeletal muscles
   c. efficiency of oxygen use by the tissues
   d. resting heart rate

6. The term *oxygen debt* refers to the oxygen that _____.
   a. is needed to get rid of lactic acid that accumulates during anaerobic exercise
   b. is lost when a person exhales
   c. is used during aerobic exercise
   d. builds up in the muscles of a person who does not exercise

7. Aerobic exercise is powered by reactions that _____.
   a. provide quick bursts of energy
   b. do not require oxygen
   c. are best suited to satisfy slow, steady energy demands
   d. are less efficient than the reactions that power anaerobic exercise

8. To achieve and maintain physical fitness, you should exercise vigorously for _____ every day.
   a. 5 minutes
   b. 20–30 minutes
   c. 1 hour
   d. 3–4 hours

9. Astronauts experience all of the following except _____ when they return to Earth after a long spaceflight.
   a. lightheadedness
   b. sense of balance
   c. difficulty walking
   d. disorientation

10. _____ is a condition in which the blood contains fewer red blood cells than it normally does.
    a. Osteoporosis
    b. Atrophy
    c. Anemia
    d. Oxygen debt

Using Vocabulary

11. Explain the connection between a movable *joint* and a *ligament*.

12. What do the *flexor* and *extensor* in your upper arm do when you move your hand toward your shoulder? What do these muscles do when you move your hand in the opposite direction?

13. Compare and contrast *anaerobic* and *aerobic* exercise in two paragraphs. Be sure to include the following terms in your discussion: *muscle fatigue, oxygen debt, endurance,* and *flexibility.*

WRITING SKILL

14. Describe the effects of muscle *atrophy* and space *anemia* on an astronaut who has returned to Earth.

BUILDING MATH SKILLS

15. Interpreting Data Muscle X has a diameter of 6 cm, and muscle Y has a diameter of 3 cm. How much stronger than muscle Y is muscle X?

16. Graphing The graph below shows the heart rates of two 15-year-old girls before, during, and after a 3-minute exercise period. Which girl is more aerobically fit? Explain your answer.

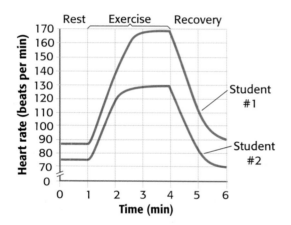

17. Interpreting Data Calculate the percentage of body fat and the lean body mass for the following individuals.
  a. male, 100 kg body weight, 18 kg of body fat
  b. female, 54 kg body weight, 7 kg of body fat
  c. male, 80 kg body weight, 7 kg of body fat

THINKING CRITICALLY

18. Creative Thinking Choose a particular joint in your body, and then imagine substituting a different kind of joint for the one that is actually there. Describe the kinds of movements that could be made by the bones connected at your imaginary joint.

19. Applying Knowledge Use a computer drawing program to design and make drawings of a device to lift heavy objects. Your device should use two fixed supports, some kind of joint, and pulleys that can work like muscles. Be certain it works on the same principles as those that apply to skeletal muscles and bones in the human body.

COMPUTER SKILL

20. Interpreting Graphics The graph below shows how the amount of oxygen taken up by an exercising person depends on heart rate before and after physical training.

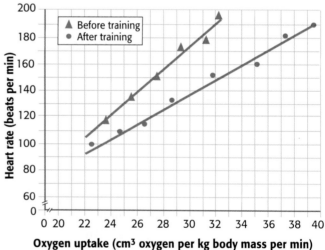

  a. What is the relationship between oxygen uptake and heart rate during exercise, as shown in the graph?
  b. What effect does physical training have on this relationship?

DEVELOPING LIFE/WORK SKILLS

21. Understanding Systems Given what you know about the problems astronauts face in low-gravity situations, predict what will happen to astronauts who spend time on the surface of a planet with a gravitational force stronger than Earth's.

22. Applying Technology Investigate the latest technology being used to replace badly damaged or diseased joints or bones. Find out how the repairs are made, the kinds of materials that are being used, and the problems that are still being encountered in this area.

23. Allocating Resources You learned in Section 15.3 that astronauts need to exercise their muscles while in space. They cannot, however, perform conventional weight-bearing activities because there is essentially no gravitational force in space. For that reason, specially modified exercise machines have been developed for use in a weightless environment. Research the types of exercise machines that have been developed for a weightless environment, and report to the rest of the class on how they work.

INTEGRATING CONCEPTS

24. Connection to Fine Arts Work with two or three other students to find pictures of the human body drawn by the artist Leonardo da Vinci, who lived from 1452 to 1519. His detailed drawings are considered to be the first accurate depictions of human anatomy. Make photocopies of the drawings or, if possible, bring books or magazines containing the pictures to class. Set up a display of a variety of da Vinci's drawings of the human body.

25. Connection to Social Studies Contrast the physical exercise that people get today with the exercise people got 100 years ago. What advancements have changed the kind and amount of exercise we get today? What effect do you think these changes are having on our overall physical fitness?

26. Concept Mapping Copy the unfinished concept map below onto a sheet of paper. Then complete it by writing the correct word or phrase in the lettered box.

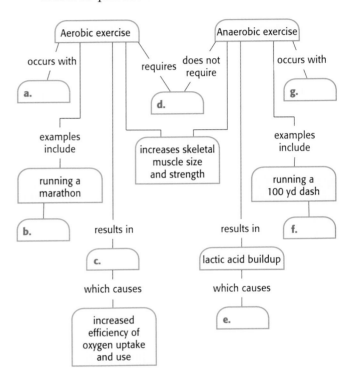

27. Integrating Biology Use library resources to find pictures of skeletons of earlier humans and other primates. Examine the pictures for similarities and differences in the skeletons. How do the skeletons of primates that walk on four legs differ from those of primates that walk on two legs? What can you infer about the mental capabilities of different primates by looking at their skulls? What differences in lifestyle can you infer for primates that have tails and those that do not?

internet**connect**

TOPIC: Skeletons of primates
GO TO: www.scilinks.org
KEYWORD: HJ1506

Skill Builder Lab

Introduction

How can you observe an example of each type of joint in your body?

Objectives

▶ *Identify* the types of skeletal joints in the body.

▶ *Compare* the movements of the major types of skeletal joints.

Materials

model of a human skull

Safety Needs

While performing this experiment, avoid physical overexertion by refraining from moving in ways that can cause injury or pain.

Comparing Skeletal Joints

▶ Preparing for Your Experiment

1. The bones of your skeleton come together at joints. In this laboratory exercise, you will explore the types of skeletal joints found in your body by observing an example of each type of joint and surveying the other joints in your body. Use a separate sheet of paper to record your observations of the skeletal joints shown below and to the right.

   SAFETY CAUTION Do not move in ways that can cause injury or pain.

▶ Observing Types of Joints

2. **Observing a Hinge Joint** Straighten one of your legs. Slowly bend the leg at the knee until your lower leg is folded behind you. Try to move the lower leg at the knee in other directions. Record your description of the movements.

3. **Observing a Ball-and-Socket Joint** Move your upper arm in as many ways as possible from the shoulder. Record your description of the movements.

4. **Observing a Pivot Joint** Place your hands on both sides of your neck to hold your neck in place. Gently move only your head in all possible directions. Try not to let your neck bend. Record your observations of the movements.

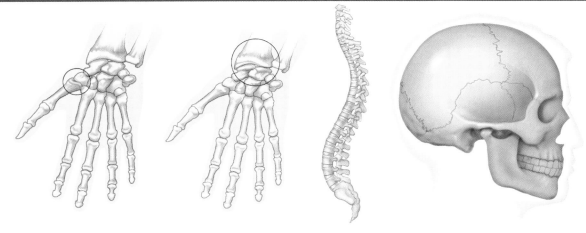

5. **Observing a Saddle Joint** Move your thumb in as many ways as possible from its base. Record your observations of the movements from the base of the thumb.

6. **Observing a Gliding Joint** Use your left hand to grip your right arm just above the wrist. Without moving your right forearm, move your right hand in all possible directions. Record your observations of the movements.

7. **Observing Semimovable Joints** Place the tips of your fingers on the lower part of your backbone. Move your torso in as many directions as possible. Record your description of the movements.

8. **Observing Fixed Joints** Examine the joints in the top of a model of a skull. Gently press on each side of the joints to see if movement is possible without damaging the skull. Record your observations.

▶ Surveying the Joints in Your Body

9. Starting with your toes, examine the movement of each of the other joints in your skeleton. Record the other locations in the body where you discover each type of joint mentioned above.

▶ Analyzing Your Results

1. Rank the types of joints according to their ability to allow movement. Start with the joint that allows the least freedom of movement.

▶ Defending Your Conclusions

2. Which types of joints are involved in walking?
3. For each type of skeletal joint, name a common, nonliving object that has a similar type of joint in its construction.

CHAPTER 16

Disease Prevention and Drug Use

Chapter Preview

16.1 Causes of Disease
   Infectious Diseases
   Noninfectious Diseases

16.2 Disease Prevention and Treatment
   Sanitation
   Environmental Health Hazards
   Your Body's Defenses
   Inherited Diseases

16.3 Drugs and Drug Abuse
   Types of Drugs
   Drug Abuse

Focus ACTIVITY

Background A New England family is delighted to receive a winter treat from a cousin in Florida—a crate of juicy grapefruit. A few days after eating the grapefruit, however, the usually energetic father becomes quiet, sleepy, and slow to answer questions. The usually cheerful mother suddenly develops headaches. The children are confused and worried. What is happening to their parents?

When the oldest daughter arrives on holiday break from pharmacy school, she sees the changes in her parents and notices the crate of grapefruit. She has just attended a lecture on drug-food interactions. She knows that a substance in grapefruit can hurt the body's ability to break down several different drugs. Her mother's symptoms are related to an excess of the drug that controls her cholesterol levels. She also realizes that her father's change could be linked to an abnormal level of his back medication.

Activity 1 Many people know that drugs can interact with other drugs. But fewer people know that there can be problems with foods as well. A group of drugs called monoamine oxidase (MAO) inhibitors were among the first drugs to be used to treat depression. Consult a pharmacist or a reference book for information about foods that should not be eaten by people who take MAO inhibitors.

Activity 2 Many people do not know that an alcohol overdose can kill them. Alcohol overdoses are particularly common among young people who are pressured by peers to drink. Using the library or the Internet, investigate how much alcohol is considered an overdose and how an alcohol overdose causes death.

Many drugs react with chemicals in certain types of foods. It is necessary to follow instructions when taking medication to avoid dangerous drug-food interactions.

internetconnect

SCILINKS
NSTA

TOPIC: Drug-food reactions
GO TO: www.scilinks.org
KEYWORD: HJ1601

Causes of Disease

KEY TERMS
pathogen
infectious disease
infection
toxin
communicable disease
AIDS
HIV

OBJECTIVES

▶ Identify five common types of pathogens.
▶ Describe three ways infectious diseases are spread.
▶ Distinguish between infectious diseases and communicable diseases.
▶ Identify two causes of noninfectious diseases.

▷ **pathogen** a virus or microorganism that causes disease

▷ **infectious disease** an illness caused by a pathogen

▷ **infection** the invasion and multiplication of pathogens in the body

Can you remember the last time you were sick? Perhaps you had a cold, an upset stomach, or an allergic reaction to something you ate. Although all these can make you feel sick, they may have very different causes.

Some diseases are caused by a genetic condition, which is passed from generation to generation. Others happen after contact with dangerous chemicals. Still others are caused by pathogens—what many people call "germs."

Infectious Diseases

An infectious disease is one that is caused by a pathogen. In an infectious disease, the pathogen invades the body and begins to reproduce. This process is called infection. You probably have heard diseases referred to as "bacterial infections" or "viral infections." These terms identify the type of pathogen that causes the disease. The most important pathogens are bacteria, protozoa, fungi, worms, and viruses.

Bacteria and protozoans are single-celled organisms that can be pathogens

Bacteria are simple, single-celled organisms. As **Figure 16-1** shows, they are so small that thousands can fit on the point of a pin. Bacteria live almost everywhere, including within and on your body. Most species of bacteria do not hurt humans, but some can cause serious diseases.

For example, the millions of bacteria that live inside your intestines normally do not harm your health. If they escape from the intestines and enter the rest of your body, however, they can cause a severe infection. That is why eating contaminated food is so dangerous.

Figure 16-1
Bacteria—shown here on the point of a pin—are the smallest living things. In large numbers, some species of bacteria can be very dangerous to health.

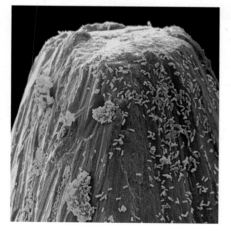

Inside your body, harmful bacteria can reproduce very rapidly. Bacteria usually cause illnesses by making poisonous substances called toxins. Cholera, botulism, and tetanus are examples of diseases that are caused by bacterial toxins.

Protozoa are the second common type of pathogen. Like bacteria, protozoa are single-celled organisms. Protozoa are larger than bacteria but still so small they can only be seen with a microscope. They act like tiny animals, moving and reacting to things around them. Protozoa are often found in bodies of water. The protozoan shown in **Figure 16-2** is a pathogen that can contaminate water supplies. However, most species of protozoa are not pathogenic.

Fungi and worms can also be pathogens

Fungi are the third type of pathogen that affects humans. You are familiar with fungi if you have eaten mushrooms or examined the mold that grows on old bread or spoiled oranges. The pathogen responsible for the skin infection known as ringworm is actually not a worm at all but a fungus. Athlete's foot and thrush, a mouth infection that occurs in infants, are also caused by pathogenic fungi.

Worms that live as parasites inside the human body make up the fourth type of pathogen. The worms usually enter the body when they are in an immature stage. They then migrate to specific tissues and mature.

Two examples of parasitic worms are hookworms and trichina worms. Hookworms hatch from eggs in the soil. They can penetrate the skin of a person who walks barefoot over the soil. This is why it is so important to wear shoes. Hookworms mature in the intestines, infecting more than 400 million people throughout the world.

Trichina worms infect many mammals, including pigs. People become infected when they eat meat—usually pork—that has not been well cooked and that still contains living worms. Meat must be cooked thoroughly to prevent such diseases.

Viruses are pathogens that are smaller than bacteria

Viruses are the fifth type of pathogen. Most viruses are too small to be seen with ordinary microscopes. In contrast to other pathogens, a virus is not a cell. Rather, it is a particle made up of protein and genetic material.

Because viruses are so simple, they can reproduce only if they infect living cells. A virus that infects a cell takes over the cell, eventually destroying it. **Figure 16-3** shows a virus that infects human cells.

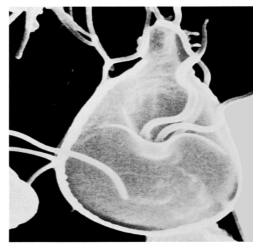

Figure 16-2
Giardia lamblia is a protozoan that lives in water. It causes giardiasis, a disease characterized by severe diarrhea and intestinal cramps.

toxin a poisonous substance

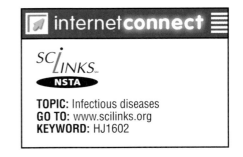

internetconnect

SCILINKS
NSTA

TOPIC: Infectious diseases
GO TO: www.scilinks.org
KEYWORD: HJ1602

Figure 16-3
Most viruses have a regular geometric structure, unlike the structure of cells.

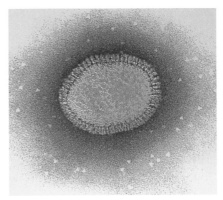

Many infectious diseases are communicable

A person with an infectious disease can often spread it to other people by spreading the pathogen that causes the disease. Such diseases are referred to as **communicable diseases.**

Some communicable diseases are passed directly when an infected person touches another person. Others can be spread by touching objects, such as doorknobs and telephone receivers, that have been used by an infected person. These diseases spread more easily where people are crowded together.

Not all infectious diseases can be spread from one person to another. Botulism and tetanus, for example, are infectious but not communicable. People get botulism by eating contaminated food, but they do not spread the disease to others. **Table 16-1** lists some common methods by which infectious diseases are transmitted.

AIDS is a communicable disease caused by a virus

Acquired immunodeficiency syndrome, or **AIDS,** is a disease in which the body loses its ability to resist pathogens and cancers. People with AIDS often get serious infections. Many AIDS patients die from bacterial pneumonia, a lung infection.

AIDS is caused by **HIV,** the human immunodeficiency virus. HIV is passed from person to person by contact with body fluids containing the virus. The most common means of transmission is through sexual contact with an infected person. The sharing of hypodermic needles among intravenous drug users also transmits HIV.

▷ **communicable disease**
an infectious disease that can be spread from person to person

▷ **AIDS (acquired immuno-deficiency syndrome)**
a viral disease that destroys the body's ability to resist other diseases by disrupting the immune system

▷ **HIV (human immuno-deficiency virus)** the virus that causes AIDS

Table 16-1   **Transmitting Infectious Diseases**

Method of disease transmission	Disease and type of pathogen
Breathing in a particle or droplet containing pathogen	Influenza, common cold, chicken pox, rubella, measles (viruses); tuberculosis, pneumonia (bacteria); histoplasmosis (fungus)
Contact with body fluids of infected person	AIDS, mononucleosis, hepatitis B (viruses)
Sexual contact	AIDS, hepatitis B, genital warts, genital herpes (viruses); syphilis, gonorrhea, pelvic inflammatory disease in females and urethritis in males (bacteria); candidiasis (fungus)
Drinking contaminated water	Cholera (bacterium); amoebiasis, giardiasis (protozoa)
Eating contaminated food	Salmonellosis, botulism (bacteria)
Skin puncture caused by contaminated object	Tetanus (bacterium)
Mammal bite	Rabies (virus)
Insect bite	Lyme disease, Rocky Mountain spotted fever (viruses)

If a blood test shows the presence of HIV, the patient is classified as HIV-positive. AIDS is said to begin when the infected person's immune system begins to fail. AIDS itself does not kill its victims. Rather, AIDS destroys their immune systems. Because people with AIDS have no ability to defend themselves against disease, even minor infections can prove deadly. AIDS victims may have multiple infections over the course of their illness. They may even get certain types of cancer.

In the past, a number of people were infected with HIV through blood transfusions. Today, however, a simple laboratory test can detect the virus in blood. All donated blood is now screened for the presence of HIV, and patients who need blood transfusions are safe from exposure to HIV.

Noninfectious diseases

All diseases that are not caused by pathogens are referred to as noninfectious diseases. Such diseases may be inherited or caused by chemicals around you. Because no pathogens are involved, noninfectious diseases are also noncommunicable.

Inherited diseases result from errors in genetic information

The list of inherited diseases is a long one. It includes many illnesses, such as muscular dystrophy, cystic fibrosis, and sickle-cell anemia. Each is caused by a defect in the genes that control a specific function in the body. Sickle cell anemia, for example, is caused by defects in the genetic instructions for making the hemoglobin found in red blood cells. The defective hemoglobin causes the cells to be misshapen, as shown in **Figure 16-4.**

TOPIC: Noninfectious diseases
GO TO: www.scilinks.org
KEYWORD: HJ1603

Figure 16-4

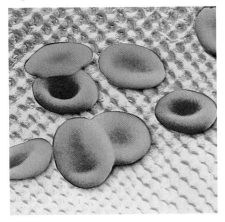

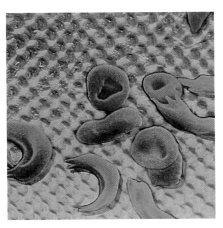

Ⓐ Normal red blood cells are smooth disks.

Ⓑ In a person with sickle-cell anemia, many of the red blood cells are crescent shaped.

Koch's Postulates Scientists use the following rules, known as Koch's postulates, to determine whether a specific pathogen causes a particular disease.

1. The pathogen must be found in diseased animals or plants but not in healthy ones.
2. The pathogen must be isolated from diseased individuals and grown in the laboratory.
3. When laboratory-grown pathogens are injected into a healthy animal or plant, they must produce the same disease.
4. When the injected animal or plant develops the disease, it must contain pathogens just like those that were injected.

Applying Information

1. Why is this method not used for human diseases?
2. A monkey has a high fever, a rash on its mouth, and an inflamed throat. Bacteria from its throat are grown in a laboratory. When the bacteria are injected into a healthy monkey, it develops a moderate fever and begins to vomit. Has the pathogen responsible for the first monkey's disease been identified?
3. What is the next step in determining the cause of the first monkey's disease?

INTEGRATING

PHYSICS
Many physicians use a technique called computed tomography (CT) to diagnose disease. In this technique, a narrow beam of X rays is directed into a patient's body from a series of different positions. An array of detectors picks up the X rays that pass through the body. A computer translates the data from the detectors into a two-dimensional image of the body, called a CT, or "cat," scan. A hundred times more detailed than conventional X-ray images, CT scans can show the exact locations and dimensions of tumors, hidden heart defects, and other abnormalities.

In Huntington's disease, the nerves responsible for muscle movements break down. The result among its victims is constant jerking movements, which usually get worse until a person dies. Children have a 50 percent chance of getting Huntington's disease if either parent is a carrier of the disease. In contrast, some other inherited diseases will not be found in any offspring unless both parents carry the defective gene for the disease.

Because genetic information is passed from parents to their children, the defect underlying an inherited disease may also be passed along. Several factors determine which children, if any, will develop a particular disease.

Some noninfectious diseases can be caused by environmental factors

Cancer can occur when a cell's genetic instructions are damaged, causing the cell to multiply uncontrollably. Often, the rapidly growing cells become large enough to be seen. The growths that result are called tumors. Although cancer occurs because of changes within a cell, these changes are often caused by exposure to substances in the environment.

Some chemicals, viruses, and even ultraviolet light in sunshine can cause damage to the cell's genetic instructions. Inhaling coal dust, for example, causes deadly black lung disease among coal miners. Exposure to chemicals at petroleum refineries and manufacturing plants raises the incidence of certain types of cancers among workers.

Many diseases are caused by a combination of heredity and environmental influences. For instance, too much sunlight can lead to skin cancer in farmers and others who work outdoors.

Table 16-2 **Noninfectious Diseases**

Disease	Causes
Cancer	Exposure to chemicals, viruses or UV light; smoking; also can be inherited
Heart disease	Too much cholesterol; smoking; also can be inherited
Lupus	Autoimmune disease in which white blood cells mistakenly attack the body's cells
Arthritis	Autoimmune disease in which white blood cells mistakenly attack the joints

However, skin cancer tends to occur most often in people who have light-colored skin, an inherited trait. In any case, it is necessary to protect your skin from too much sunlight by applying sunscreen, as shown in **Figure 16-5.** A person's risk for heart disease is also determined partly by heredity and partly by environmental factors. Those factors include specific substances in food and tobacco smoke.

Not all cancers are caused by this kind of exposure. Some of them are inherited. Other noninfectious diseases are not linked to exposure to chemicals. A few of the many noninfectious diseases and their causes are listed in **Table 16-2.**

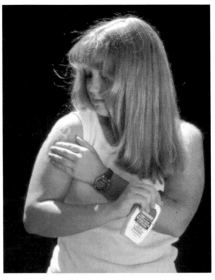

Figure 16-5
It is important to guard against skin cancer by applying sunscreen before prolonged exposure to sunlight.

SECTION 16.1 REVIEW

SUMMARY

▶ Infectious diseases are caused by pathogens, which include bacteria, protozoa, fungi, parasitic worms, and viruses. Pathogens invade the body and reproduce, producing an infection.

▶ Communicable diseases are infectious diseases that can spread from person to person.

▶ Noninfectious diseases are caused not by pathogens but by genetic defects, environmental factors, or both.

CHECK YOUR UNDERSTANDING

1. **Define** *pathogen.*
2. **List** five common types of pathogens.
3. **Identify** a disease that may result from a combination of inherited and environmental factors.
4. **Contrast** the ways hookworms and trichina worms enter the body.
5. **Distinguish** between an infectious disease and a communicable disease.
6. **Describe** three ways infectious diseases can be spread from person to person.
7. **Explain** how an HIV infection can make it more likely for a person to die from bacterial pneumonia.
8. **Critical Thinking** Some of the passengers on a ship come down with nausea and fever. What is the first step a physician should take to determine the disease and pathogen that is causing these symptoms?

Disease Prevention and Treatment

sanitation
sick building syndrome
mucous membrane
inflammatory response
histamine
immune system
vaccine
genetic counselor
gene therapy

> ► **sanitation** the practices of cleanliness and hygiene designed to help maintain health

► Identify effective ways to prevent catching or spreading an infectious disease.

► Explain why the air in some buildings can be unhealthful.

► Explain how the skin and mucous membranes protect against pathogens.

► Describe the steps in the inflammatory response.

► Explain how vaccines work.

► Identify two strategies for fighting inherited diseases.

Before the late 1800s, people did not understand that microscopic pathogens were responsible for infectious diseases. In those times, sanitation was very poor. Streets were used as sewers, and often a single water well served an entire town. This made the transmission of disease very easy. Since then, we have learned a great deal about how to stop the spread of pathogens and the diseases they cause. One key is proper sanitation.

Sanitation

Pathogens can be spread by contaminated food and water. A safe supply of food and water is essential for public health. Since the turn of the century, the United States government has regulated food and water to keep them pure, as shown in **Figure 16-6.**

Figure 16-6
Inspections performed by the U.S. Department of Agriculture help ensure the safety of our food supply.

The U.S. government works to keep food and water safe and healthy

The U.S. Department of Agriculture (USDA) inspects meat, milk, and eggs for the presence of pathogens. USDA inspectors also examine crops for the presence of parasites and pesticides. The facilities where food is produced, prepared, and preserved are inspected by government agencies. To ensure your own safety, buy only USDA-approved meat, milk, and eggs.

There are several other steps you can take to prevent disease from pathogens in food. Beware of unpasteurized milk products, which could contain pathogenic bacteria. Cook meat and eggs thoroughly to kill any organisms they may contain. Wash all fruits and vegetables before you eat them. This will eliminate many microorganisms, and it may also remove pesticides that were sprayed on the food as it was grown.

The U.S. Environmental Protection Agency also checks all municipal water systems to be sure the water they provide is safe. Users of private wells should have their water tested periodically for pathogens as well as for pesticides, mercury, and other toxins that can leach into ground water.

In times of disasters, such as earthquakes or flooding, water supplies can easily be contaminated by pathogens. In these situations, public health officials may recommend using bottled water or another source until the safety of the water supply can be ensured.

Handwashing reduces the spread of infectious diseases

One of the easiest and most effective ways to guard your health is to wash your hands frequently. Pathogens often live in large numbers on objects that many people touch, particularly in public places. These pathogens are passed from one person to another through touch.

Many pathogens are picked up on your hands and may enter your body when you touch your eyes, nose, or mouth or when you pick up food with unwashed hands. By keeping your hands away from your face and washing your hands frequently, particularly after using the restroom and before you eat, you can greatly reduce your chances of infection.

Connection to SOCIAL STUDIES

Bubonic plague is an infectious disease caused by bacteria. A severe outbreak of the plague, known as the Black Death, killed about 75 million Europeans in the middle 1300s.

People at the time understood that it was dangerous to have contact with individuals who had the disease. However, the true means of the plague's spread was not understood for many years.

We now know that the bacteria that cause bubonic plague are spread by fleas, which are carried from place to place on the bodies of rats. People get the disease when they are bitten by infected fleas.

Making the Connection

1. Using the library or the Internet, find out about the outbreak of a hantavirus in the Four Corners area of the United States in 1993. Based on your reading, explain how the virus was spread.
2. Using what you know about the spread of diseases, speculate why this small outbreak was not larger.

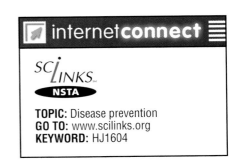

internet connect

SC_i_**LINKS**

NSTA

TOPIC: Disease prevention
GO TO: www.scilinks.org
KEYWORD: HJ1604

Figure 16-7
You can prevent food poisoning by washing utensils, containers, and cutting boards that touch raw meat or eggs.

INTEGRATING

BIOLOGY

Supermarket shelves display a variety of household products designed to kill bacteria. The list includes deodorants, disinfectant cleaners, mouthwashes, bath soaps, waterless hand sanitizers, and even kitchen cutting boards.

However, public health authorities warn that overuse of such products could further the development of bacterial strains that resist these threats. In the future, it may become more difficult to stop bacteria as a result.

Similarly, patients who stop taking antibiotic medications before finishing their prescription may inadvertently promote those bacteria that are slightly resistant.

Proper food handling can prevent food poisoning

"Food poisoning" is the common name for illnesses caused by pathogens—usually bacteria—in food. Symptoms of food poisoning range from stomach pains to death, depending on the specific pathogen and the age and overall health of the infected person.

Raw meat and eggs can contain pathogenic bacteria. Beef and pork can have parasitic worms. Although thorough cooking will kill these pathogens, you must take special care when making food. This is the best way to avoid food poisoning.

As **Figure 16-7** shows, you should use detergent and hot water to wash anything that touches raw meat or eggs before you let it touch other food. For example, you should not use a fork to pick up pieces of raw chicken and then use it again to pick up cooked chicken. Doing so could contaminate the cooked chicken with bacteria from the raw chicken.

Appropriate food storage decreases the risks of food poisoning

Another way to stop food poisoning is to keep food at a safe temperature. Pathogenic bacteria grow best at temperatures near that of the human body. They do not grow well when they are very cold. Therefore, perishable foods should be stored in a refrigerator or freezer until they are ready to be eaten or cooked.

After cooking, food should be either kept hot or immediately refrigerated. Many food-poisoning cases involve picnic food, such as potato salad, that has been left out for a few hours on a warm day. Bacteria reproduce rapidly under these conditions.

Environmental Health Hazards

Your environment includes everything around you—the air you breathe, the water you drink, and the soil you walk on. All parts of your environment, whether you are at home, in school, or even at work, can affect your health.

Buildings can contain unhealthful air

One important need for people who spend much time indoors is a supply of fresh air. When a building is poorly ventilated, the air inside the building may accumulate high levels of dangerous substances. Two of the most important of these substances are carbon monoxide and radon. They are hard to detect because both are colorless, tasteless, and odorless gases.

Carbon monoxide is made when certain fuels, such as wood, charcoal, and kerosene, are burned. Inside buildings, most carbon monoxide comes from fuel-burning heaters and furnaces that are not properly vented. Carbon monoxide is dangerous because it prevents hemoglobin from carrying oxygen efficiently through the body.

You learned in Chapter 6 that radon is a radioactive noble gas. It comes out of certain soils and can leak into buildings through cracks in the foundation or basement. Overexposure to radon can cause lung cancer.

At home, you can help keep the air you breathe safe by checking that all indoor fuel-burning appliances are in good working order and by installing a carbon monoxide detector. You can also use a simple kit to test your home for the presence of radon.

Sick building syndrome results from overexposure to chemicals indoors

The air inside buildings may also contain harmful chemicals released by vinyl flooring, synthetic carpeting, adhesives, paints, and other construction materials. If the inside air is not mixed often enough with fresh air, people who live or work in the building may develop a condition know as **sick building syndrome.** Symptoms include tiredness, headache, and eye irritation.

Sick building syndrome has become more common today because buildings are being made more airtight to increase energy efficiency. Buildings like the one shown in **Figure 16-8,** with windows that cannot be opened, must have a ventilation system that brings in plenty of fresh air.

Figure 16-8
Many modern office buildings have windows that do not open. Such buildings must have an efficient ventilation system to keep the inside air from becoming a health hazard.

▶ **sick building syndrome**
the symptoms caused by breathing air in buildings with poor ventilation

Figure 16-9
Construction workers are among those protected by OSHA rules.

Special precautions on the job can reduce health risks

Some jobs, such as firefighting, present obvious health risks. Other jobs have risks that are dangerous but much less obvious. Exterminators, chemical-plant workers, and dry cleaners, for example, use hazardous chemicals. Health care workers and sanitation workers deal with a large number of different pathogens.

The Occupational Safety and Health Administration (OSHA) monitors the safety of working conditions in the United States. OSHA makes sure that employers, such as those at the construction site shown in **Figure 16-9,** provide safety equipment and follow safety standards.

Regulations also require that information about workplace hazards be posted in the workplace for all employees to see. For any hazardous chemicals, material safety data sheets (MSDS) must be available.

Still much of the responsibility for job safety rests with the worker. How can we protect ourselves at work? Understanding the dangers of your job is critical.

Workers must follow all of their employer's safety rules and use all appropriate safety equipment, such as gloves and protective eyewear. They should also report hazardous situations and allow supervisors to assess any situation they are not sure of.

Your Body's Defenses

Pathogens and other disease-causing agents are all around you. Most of the time you stay well anyway because your body has a system of defenses against disease. These defenses work to shut out or destroy many pathogens. They can even stop some disease processes after they have begun.

Your body's exterior is the first line of defense

Skin offers an important protection against pathogens. It provides a thick, flexible, waterproof layer that most pathogens cannot get through. Cells in the skin also make chemicals that destroy pathogens. Your eyes, nasal passages, digestive tract, and urinary tract are covered by thin, moist tissues called **mucous membranes** rather than by skin. Mucous membranes secrete mucus, a thick, slippery mixture that traps pathogens.

TOPIC: The body's defense system
GO TO: www.scilinks.org
KEYWORD: HJ1605

▶ **mucous membrane** a tissue that secretes mucus; found in body cavities that open to the outside

When the skin or mucous membranes are injured, pathogens can get in more easily. Mucous membranes are injured more easily than skin because they are more delicate. Compare the inside of your mouth with the skin on your face, for example. Pathogens that penetrate injured skin or mucous membranes can infect tissues near the injury. They may get into the blood and circulate throughout the body.

VOCABULARY *Skills Tip*

The word mucous *originates from the Latin word* mucosus, *meaning "slimy."*

The inflammatory response is the second line of defense

Pathogens that get past the skin and mucous membranes may begin to reproduce inside the body. When they do, they may trigger an inflammatory response. As **Figure 16-10** shows, the area around an injury becomes red, warm, and very sore during an inflammatory response.

The inflammatory response begins when signaling molecules are released by injured tissues. Chemicals, such as histamines, are released inside the tissue and cause blood vessels to expand, so more blood enters the area of the injury. White blood cells attack pathogens that have already entered through the wound. The blood also brings fibrous components that can surround and wall off the injury site, preventing pathogens from invading the rest of the body.

The temperature of the injured area rises like a small "fever." The bacteria grow and reproduce more slowly in these warmer conditions. Chemicals that increase pain at the site encourage you to protect the injured area.

▶ **inflammatory response** a response to injury that can include redness, heat, pain, and swelling

▶ **histamine** a protein that dilates blood vessels as part of the inflammatory response

Figure 16-10

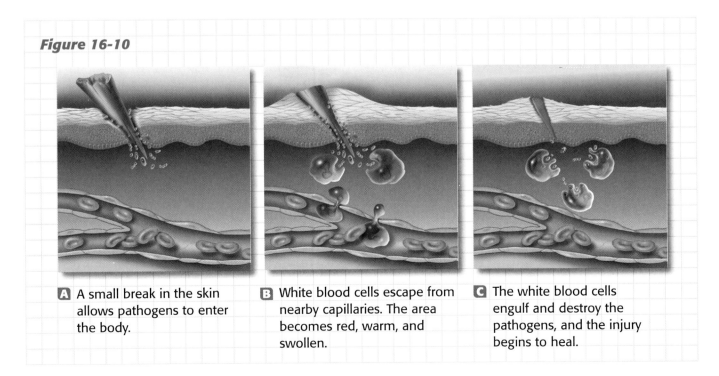

A A small break in the skin allows pathogens to enter the body.

B White blood cells escape from nearby capillaries. The area becomes red, warm, and swollen.

C The white blood cells engulf and destroy the pathogens, and the injury begins to heal.

Figure 16-11
White blood cells surround and destroy a chain of streptococcus, the bacteria that causes strep throat.

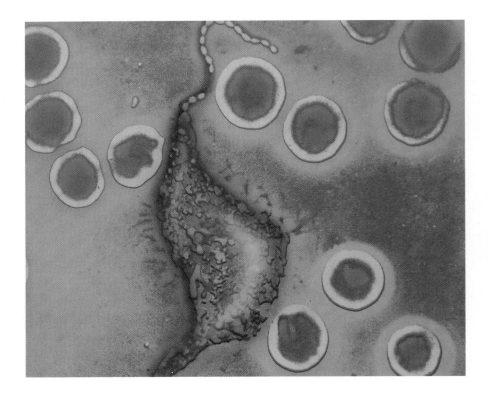

immune system the body system that attacks and destroys specific pathogens

vaccine a harmless form of a pathogen that is used to prepare the immune system for the active forms

The immune system is the third line of defense

Certain organs and blood cells work together like players on the same team to defend against specific pathogens, as shown in **Figure 16-11.** These organs and cells make up the immune system. Some cells in the immune system recognize pathogens and mark them for destruction by other cells. A third group of cells "remember" pathogens that have invaded the body, protecting you against future attacks by the same pathogen.

The ability of the immune system to remember pathogens is the basis for immunization. In an immunization, a harmless form of a pathogen, called a vaccine, is introduced into the body. The vaccine does not cause disease, but it does activate the immune system. Later, the immune system is ready if an active form of the same pathogen appears in the body. Because of the earlier activation, the immune system quickly identifies the active pathogen and destroys it.

Inherited Diseases

There are few successful treatments for most inherited diseases at this time. Researchers continue working on experiments that might be able to repair the defective genes that cause some inherited diseases. In the meantime, individuals who carry an inherited disease are given counseling so they can understand the chances of having children with the disease.

internetconnect

SCLINKS
NSTA

TOPIC: Inherited diseases
GO TO: www.scilinks.org
KEYWORD: HJ1606

Genetic counselors predict how diseases are inherited

A genetic counselor uses information from several family generations, if available, to establish a history of the disease in that family. The counselor then explains the mathematical chances of a couple's children inheriting the disease. Couples with high risk may elect to adopt children.

▷ **genetic counselor** a medical professional who advises couples on the chances of their passing an inherited disease to their children

Gene therapy repairs faulty genetic information

Scientists are attempting to develop therapies for several inherited diseases, including muscular dystrophy and cystic fibrosis. In gene therapy, a normal version of a gene from a donor individual is inserted into the genetic material of a person with an inherited disease. One problem with this therapy is that the body contains so many cells that the normal gene must get into many of them in order to have a significant effect. One promising approach is to use viruses to infect body cells without harming them. Each of these viruses can transmit genes to several cells.

▷ **gene therapy** the treatment of an inherited disease by introducing a normal gene into the body's cells

SECTION 16.2 REVIEW

SUMMARY

▶ To prevent the spread of diseases, wash your hands often, handle food safely, and store food at a safe temperature.

▶ Workers can reduce their health risks by understanding the dangers of their job and by obeying employers' safety rules.

▶ Skin and mucous membranes help prevent pathogens from entering the body.

▶ The immune system recognizes and destroys specific pathogens.

▶ A genetic counselor advises couples about the risks of transmitting inherited diseases to their children. Some inherited diseases may be treated with gene therapy.

CHECK YOUR UNDERSTANDING

1. **List** three things that workers can do to protect their health on the job.
2. **Predict** which of the following will make a better flu vaccine, and explain why.
   a. the virus that causes the flu
   b. an unrelated virus that causes skin rashes
   c. a virus that causes the flu with its cell-attacking proteins removed
3. **Identify** two ways to prevent catching or spreading an infectious disease.
4. **Describe** the function of a genetic counselor.
5. **Explain** how the air in some buildings can acquire high levels of carbon monoxide. Explain why carbon monoxide is dangerous.
6. **Compare and Contrast** skin and mucous membranes as defenses against pathogens.
7. **Creative Thinking** Applying heat to an area of skin causes blood vessels in that area to expand. Explain why applying heat might help the body heal after a minor puncture wound to the skin.
8. **Creative Thinking** Someone in your class says that genetic counselors do not really fight disease like doctors do. Explain what is wrong with this reasoning.

Drugs and Drug Abuse

OBJECTIVES

▶ List four categories of drugs used for medical purposes and three widely used social drugs.

▶ Explain how tolerance influences the effective dosage of a drug.

▶ Describe the relationship between addiction and withdrawal symptoms.

▶ Identify several short-term and long-term physiological dangers of alcohol abuse.

All **drugs** cause changes within the body. Some drugs, such as pain relievers and nasal decongestants, are designed to relieve specific disease symptoms.

Sometimes drugs are used in ways other than as medicines for sick people. Drugs are also used by some people—either legally or illegally—to change how they feel rather than to treat disease.

Types of Drugs

Drugs can be grouped according to what they do to the body. **Table 16-3** shows some of the broad categories of drugs and their medicinal uses.

The most common medicinal drugs are **analgesics,** or painkillers. You probably are familiar with aspirin and acetaminophen, which are two very common analgesics.

Not all analgesics are the same. As **Figure 16-12** shows, aspirin labels carry warnings about Reye's syndrome, a disease that can kill children and teenagers.

In most cases, Reye's syndrome occurs when a child or teenager is given aspirin or a product containing related compounds after being infected with a virus, such as chicken pox. The illness causes problems with the nervous system, beginning with vomiting and drowsiness. Eventually, seizures and death can occur.

As a result, children and teenagers should use only pain-relief products that contain acetaminophen, instead of aspirin (acetylsalicylic acid). Other products containing salicylate compounds, such as some stomach medications, should also be avoided by children and teenagers.

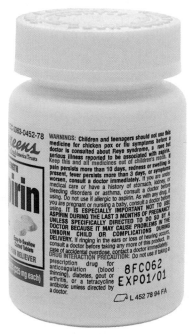

Figure 16-12
Reye's syndrome is a disorder that has been linked to taking aspirin (acetylsalicylic acid) or related compounds during a viral infection.

Table 16-3 **Categories of Medicinal Drugs**

Type of drug	Targeted conditions	Effect on body
Analgesics	Arthritis, headache, other pain	Relieve pain; some also reduce inflammation, fever
Antacids, acid reducers	Heartburn, stomach ulcers	Neutralize stomach acid; reduce acid secretion
Antibiotics	Infection by pathogens (excluding viruses)	Kill or slow growth of pathogenic microorganisms
Antihistamines	Allergy, cold, influenza	Reduce fluid in tissue; reduce swelling in nasal sinuses
Cardiovascular medications	Cardiovascular disease, high blood pressure, stroke	Reduce blood volume and fat content; inhibit clotting
Decongestants	Allergy, cold, influenza, asthma	Expand nasal sinuses and lung passages
Hormone replacements	Hypothyroidism, estrogen deficiency, diabetes mellitus	Restore normal levels of hormones
Pyschoactive drugs	Depression, anxiety, disorders of thought	Stabilize emotions and thought processes

Drugs that kill live pathogens, such as bacteria, are known as **antibiotics.** Many antibiotics come from bacteria or fungi. Penicillin, for example, is a chemical produced by the fungus *Penicillium.* Penicillin is effective in curing several bacterial diseases, including pneumonia, scarlet fever, and diphtheria.

Psychoactive drugs affect the brain, changing activity levels, thought patterns, or emotions. Although some of these drugs are abused, many have important medical uses. Antidepressants, for instance, can be enormously helpful to people with clinical depression.

antibiotic a drug that kills or slows the growth of live pathogens

psychoactive drug a drug that affects brain function

Some drugs require a prescription, while others do not

Most drugs are sold only if they are prescribed by a medical doctor for a specific condition. In the United States, the U.S. Food and Drug Administration determines which drugs require a prescription. These **prescription drugs** require regulation because they can be very dangerous if they are misused, particularly if they have side effects or interactions with other drugs.

While the FDA monitors drug safety, there is always some amount of risk with any drug. Side effects can also cause problems. For example, while some antihistamine medications can clear a stuffed-up nose, they also cause drowsiness. Consumers should always be cautious about which drugs they use and when.

prescription drug a drug that may be given only as directed by a medical doctor

Reading Drug Labels The FDA has specific requirements for labels on drugs, so that consumers are able to make informed choices. On the label shown at right, all of the ingredients are listed—the active ingredients, which make the drug work, and the inactive ingredients.

Inactive ingredients can include colors, flavors, or substances that make the mixture easier to form into pills or that keep the active ingredients well dissolved.

The label explains when to take a drug, how much of it to take, and how to store the drug. Any side effects of taking the drug are also explained, as are any cautions for people with specific conditions.

Applying Information

1. Examine the label on an empty bottle of an over-the-counter drug. Using the label shown at right as a guide, determine the type of drug the bottle used to contain and what conditions the drug was recommended for.
2. Read the warning statements on the label. Together with the rest of your class, try to determine what warning statements are common to similar types of drugs.
3. Why do almost all drugs carry warnings for pregnant women and nursing mothers?

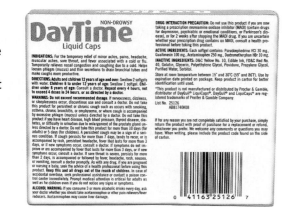

▶ **dose** the quantity of a drug to be taken at one time

Figure 16-13
A physician's prescription identifies the drug a patient needs and indicates how it should be taken.

As **Figure 16-13** shows, the doctor's prescription indicates the name of the drug, the **dose,** the number of times the drug should be taken, and the person for whom the drug is prescribed.

Drugs that may be sold legally without a prescription are known as over-the-counter drugs. They include several kinds of analgesics, antacids, antibiotics, antihistamines, decongestants, and anti-nausea drugs.

But even over-the-counter drugs can be harmful if they are misused. Always read the entire label before you use any drug. Pay particular attention to the dose, possible side effects, interactions with other drugs, and the number of times you should take the drug. Pregnant women and people with certain medical conditions should ask their physician before they take any over-the-counter drug.

All prescription drugs and over-the-counter drugs have a generic name. Most also have a brand name. Ibuprofen, for instance, is the generic name of an analgesic. Different drug companies that sell ibuprofen may give it their own brand name.

When filling many prescriptions, pharmacists can give you either a drug with a brand name or an equivalent drug with the generic name. The active ingredient in both drugs is the same, but the drug without a recognized brand name may cost less. In part, this is because generic drugs are not advertised, so some of that savings is passed on to you.

Figure 16-14
Coffee, tea, chocolate, and many soft drinks contain caffeine.

Caffeine, nicotine, and alcohol are drugs

When people talk about drugs, they often mean either medicines or illegal drugs. But the most commonly used drugs—caffeine, nicotine, and alcohol—are not taken as medicines and are not illegal. These substances are sometimes called "social drugs" because they are widely used when people get together.

Caffeine is a **stimulant** found in many foods and beverages. **Figure 16-14** shows some of the products in which caffeine is commonly found. Caffeine elevates a person's mood, reduces drowsiness, and fights muscular fatigue.

As you learned in Chapter 14, nicotine is found in tobacco products. Nicotine is a stimulant that produces in a person a brief, mildly rewarding feeling.

Alcohol refers to ethyl alcohol, or ethanol, and is found in beer, wine, and cocktails. Alcohol has been used as a **sedative** for thousands of years.

Although they are found in many places, caffeine, nicotine, and alcohol can be dangerous if misused. Some of the dangers of using these social drugs are described later in this section.

Drugs can interact with other drugs or with food

Because all drugs are chemicals, they can interact with each other or with chemicals in foods or beverages. Some of these interactions exaggerate the effects of one or both drugs. Caffeine, for example, can increase the power of some appetite suppressants, asthma drugs, and decongestants. In contrast, some drugs cancel the effects of other drugs.

Another danger is that one drug might slow the body's breakdown of a second drug. If you continue to take the second drug as advised, it could build up to toxic levels in your blood. For these reasons, it is very important that your doctor and your pharmacist know the name and dose of every drug you are taking.

▷ **stimulant** a drug that increases brain activity

▷ **sedative** a drug that decreases brain activity

INTEGRATING

BIOLOGY

The herb foxglove has been used as a medicine since the mid-thirteenth century.

By the late 1700s, foxglove was widely used to treat "dropsy," which is now referred to as congestive heart failure. In this disease, the heart's pumping is ineffective, and blood builds up in the organs, causing breathlessness and swelling.

Even today, digitalis, the chemical responsible for foxglove's effects, is given to people with some types of congestive heart failure.

Drug Abuse

🖥 internet**connect** ☰

SCI *LINKS*
NSTA

TOPIC: Drugs and drug abuse
GO TO: www.scilinks.org
KEYWORD: HJ1607

Drugs serve as powerful weapons against disease, but they can be dangerous if abused. One form of drug abuse is taking more of a drug or taking it for a longer period than is medically necessary. Using a prescription drug that was not meant for you is another form of drug abuse. Taking any drug against the law is also a form of drug abuse. **Table 16-4** lists several commonly abused drugs along with their short-term effects and dangers.

Table 16-4   **Commonly Abused Drugs**

Drug	Short-term effects	Possible dangers
Stimulants		
Amphetamines Caffeine Cocaine Nicotine	Temporary sense of excitement, decreased appetite, sleeplessness, elevated heart rate	Impaired coordination, anxiety, paranoia, brain damage, death by cardiac arrest (with cocaine and amphetamines)
Sedatives		
Alcohol Barbiturates Tranquilizers	Relaxation, relief of anxiety, sleepiness	Impaired coordination, inability to think clearly, coma, death by respiratory failure (in cases of withdrawal, death by cardiac arrest)
Narcotics (opiates)		
Codeine Heroin Meperidine Morphine	Temporary relief of pain, sense of excitement	Impaired coordination, reduced ability to see, inability to think clearly, coma, death
Hallucinogens		
Ecstasy (MDMA) LSD Marijuana, hashish Mescaline, peyote PCP (phencyclidine) Psilocybin	Feeling of removal from reality, hallucinations, elevated heart rate	Impaired coordination, reduced ability to see, confusion, agitation, paranoia, violent behavior, disordered thoughts, inability to think clearly, (for some, coma or death)
Inhalants		
Aerosol propellants Alkyl nitrates Anesthetic gases Solvents in glue and paint	Relaxation, euphoria, dizziness, hallucinations	Impaired coordination, visual distortion, severe and permanent brain damage, death by respiratory failure or massive cell damage
Anabolic steroids		
Testosterone and similar compounds	Increased muscle mass	Nausea, sleeplessness, mental depression, unwanted secondary sex characteristics, stunted growth, liver disease, cancer

Tolerance can cause people to take more of a drug

Most drugs of abuse are taken because they feel good at first. However, many such drugs also produce devastating side effects. Some, such as inhalants, kill nerve cells by the millions, resulting in permanent and irreversible brain damage.

When certain drugs are used repeatedly, the body gradually becomes less responsive to those drugs. This phenomenon is called tolerance. Because of tolerance, long-term drug abusers must take higher and higher doses of drugs to achieve the desired effects. Eventually, the user may take an overdose of the drug.

Addiction and symptoms of withdrawal make it hard to quit taking a drug

Repeated use of many drugs can also lead to addiction. A drug user who is addicted is physiologically and psychologically dependent on the drug and cannot function comfortably without it. Caffeine, nicotine, and alcohol are all capable of causing addiction, as are many illegal drugs, including cocaine and heroin.

Drug addiction is typically followed by withdrawal symptoms when an addicted person suddenly stops using the drug. A drug user in withdrawal feels a desperate need for the drug. Withdrawal symptoms can include nausea, agitation, panic, and seizures. Even daily coffee drinkers often develop a headache if they abruptly stop their caffeine consumption. Withdrawal from sedative drugs, including alcohol, can be life threatening.

Adults and teenagers suffer from alcohol abuse

Although alcohol is not illegal for adults, it is still a toxic substance. Many of the dangers of alcohol stem from its effects on the brain.

The first signs of alcohol abuse are often changes in behavior and an impairment of sound decision-making. For example, a normally quiet person may become loud and angry after drinking. If this impaired decision-making causes someone to drink more and more, that person may not realize when he or she is in danger.

Binge drinking can cause death

In some situations, referred to as *binge drinking*, people drink large amounts of alcohol in a very short time. But as drinking continues, concentration, memory, and muscle control deteriorate. Routine tasks requiring coordination become difficult and eventually impossible. At some point, the drinker loses consciousness. Drinking this much alcohol very quickly can cause death, as alcohol shuts down the brain center that controls breathing.

▷ **addiction** a physiological and psychological dependence on a drug

▷ **withdrawal symptoms** the physical and mental changes that occur when a person stops using an addictive drug

INTEGRATING

HEALTH
Alcohol is toxic to skeletal and cardiac muscle, causing deterioration of the muscle tissue. Alcohol abuse increases the risk of developing cancer of the mouth, throat, esophagus, and lungs, as well as cirrhosis, a condition in which the normal tissues of the liver are replaced by scar tissue. Alcohol abuse compromises the immune system, the reproductive system, and the central nervous system, and it causes malnutrition.

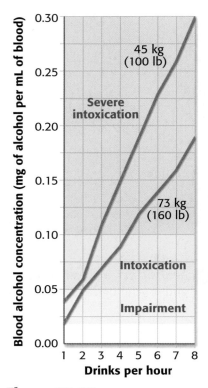

Figure 16-15
The more alcoholic beverages a person drinks in an hour, the higher the blood alcohol concentration rises. Even a single drink can produce some impairment of function.

Alcohol abuse has long-term effects

Even among people who do not go on drinking binges, alcohol abuse can become a medical problem. Alcohol causes the liver to stuff itself with too much fat and protein. Eventually, liver cells die and are replaced with scar tissue. Many long-term alcohol abusers die from liver failure. Alcohol also destroys nerve cells in the brain and throughout the body.

A pregnant woman who drinks alcohol risks having a baby with a pattern of birth defects known collectively as fetal alcohol syndrome. Children with fetal alcohol syndrome tend to be smaller than normal and to have small heads and narrow faces. Their brains are abnormally small, and they usually have intellectual and behavioral problems.

Drinking and driving can be a deadly combination

Even small amounts of alcohol can adversely affect a person's ability to drive an automobile. Alcohol is involved in many of the car accidents that occur every year, including about half of all accidents in which the driver is killed. **Figure 16-15** shows how blood alcohol concentration rises with the number of drinks consumed by people of two different weights.

What can you do about alcohol abuse? Organizations like Students Against Driving Drunk (SADD) and Mothers Against Driving Drunk (MADD) are two nationwide organizations that promote abstinence from alcohol for young people.

SECTION 16.3 REVIEW

SUMMARY

▶ A drug is any substance that alters how the body works.

▶ Some drugs require a doctor's prescription, but over-the-counter drugs do not.

▶ Drugs can interact dangerously with other drugs or with certain foods.

▶ Drug abuse may lead to tolerance, addiction, and withdrawal symptoms if use of the drug is suddenly stopped.

CHECK YOUR UNDERSTANDING

1. **Identify** three widely used social drugs.
2. **List** two short-term and two long-term dangers of alcohol use.
3. **Define** *tolerance*. Explain how tolerance can increase the risk of an overdose.
4. **Describe** the main medical uses of analgesics, antibiotics, and antihistamines.
5. **Explain** the difference between a prescription drug and an over-the-counter drug.
6. **Describe** the conditions under which a drug user may experience withdrawal symptoms.
7. **Explain** what causes fetal alcohol syndrome.
8. **Creative Thinking** Explain why physicians typically begin a physical examination by asking patients if they are taking any medications.

Chapter Highlights

Before you begin, review the summaries of the key ideas of each section, found on pages 525, 533, and 540. The key vocabulary terms are listed on pages 520, 526, and 534.

UNDERSTANDING CONCEPTS

1. A disease that can be spread from person to person is best described as _____.
   a. a communicable disease
   b. an inherited disease
   c. an environmental disease
   d. food poisoning

2. The disease AIDS is caused by a _____.
   a. bacterium   c. virus
   b. parasitic worm   d. fungus

3. An effective way to reduce the spread of communicable diseases is to _____.
   a. see a genetic counselor
   b. undergo gene therapy
   c. wash your hands
   d. share hypodermic needles

4. Mucous membranes protect against infection by _____.
   a. making chemicals that destroy pathogens
   b. trapping pathogens in a viscous, slippery mixture
   c. providing a tough layer that pathogens cannot penetrate
   d. remembering pathogens that have invaded the body

5. Which of the following events is *not* part of the inflammatory response to an injury?
   a. The injured area becomes red and sore.
   b. Blood vessels in the area expand.
   c. White blood cells attack invading pathogens.
   d. The temperature of the skin around the affected area decreases.

6. Medicinal drugs that relieve pain are known as _____.
   a. antacids   c. analgesics
   b. antibiotics   d. antihistamines

7. A commonly used social drug that acts as a sedative is _____.
   a. nicotine   c. caffeine
   b. aspirin   d. alcohol

8. A person who must take higher and higher doses of a drug to feel the drug's effects is experiencing _____.
   a. tolerance
   b. an overdose
   c. withdrawal symptoms
   d. an infection

9. A woman is most likely to have a baby with fetal alcohol syndrome if she _____.
   a. had the syndrome when she was a baby
   b. drinks alcohol while she is pregnant
   c. drinks alcohol immediately after her baby is born
   d. gives alcohol to her baby

Using Vocabulary

10. Are all *communicable diseases* also *infectious diseases*? Are all infectious diseases communicable diseases? Explain your answer.

11. Write a paragraph explaining what happens if you get a splinter. Use the following terms: *immune system, inflammatory response,* and *white blood cell.*

12. Describe the difference between *genetic counseling* and *gene therapy.*

13. Describe the properties and legal uses of each of the following types of drugs: *analgesics, antibiotics, psychoactive drugs, stimulants,* and *sedatives.*

WRITING SKILL

14. Explain how *addiction, tolerance,* and *withdrawal symptoms* are related.

BUILDING MATH SKILLS

15. Graphing The following graph shows the reproduction of pathogenic bacteria inside the body of an infected person.

   a. How many times more bacteria are present after 2 hours than are present after 1 hour?

   b. How many times more bacteria are present after 3 hours than are present after 2 hours?

   c. Predict how many bacteria will be present after 5 hours if the bacteria continue to reproduce at the same rate.

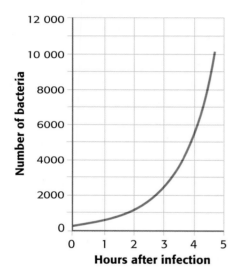

Hours after infection

16. Graphing Examine the graph shown in **Figure 16-15,** on page 540 of Section 16.3.

   a. How many drinks of alcohol would a 45 kg person have to consume in 1 hour to become intoxicated?

   b. How many drinks would the same person have to consume in 1 hour to become severely intoxicated?

   c. Is a 73 kg person who consumes five drinks of alcohol in 1 hour likely to be impaired, intoxicated, or severely intoxicated?

THINKING CRITICALLY

17. Applying Knowledge If a person has an infection that can be cured by antibiotics, is the infection likely to be caused by a virus or by some other type of pathogen? Explain your reasoning.

18. Problem Solving If someone becomes ill very soon after drinking water from a suspicious source, what kinds of pathogens might have caused the illness?

19. Creative Thinking In some cases, a pharmacist can fill a prescription either with a drug with a brand name or with a drug with a generic name. Name some differences between these two types of drugs, and explain why generic drugs are less expensive.

20. Applying Knowledge Explain how some infants can be born addicted to a drug.

DEVELOPING LIFE/WORK SKILLS

21. Applying Technology Drug tests are used to detect the presence of various commonly abused drugs in the blood or urine of an individual. Research how drug tests work, and write a paragraph explaining how drugs are detected in the common urine test.

22. Allocating Resources Offer a reason why people might buy a drug with a generic name rather than the same drug with a recognized brand name.

WRITING SKILL

internet**connect**

SCI**LINKS**
NSTA

TOPIC: Generic-brand name drugs
GO TO: www.scilinks.org
KEYWORD: HJ1608

23. Working Cooperatively Working with a group of classmates, decide which of the following statements about gene therapy is correct. Explain your answer.

a. A major problem is finding undamaged copies of certain genes.

b. A major problem is inserting normal genes into many body cells.

c. The faulty genes of only one cell must be corrected for gene therapy to work.

24. Applying Technology Using a computer drawing or presentation program, create a brief presentation portraying how the body's immune system responds to an infection by bacteria in the bloodstream.

COMPUTER SKILL

INTEGRATING CONCEPTS

25. Concept Mapping Copy the unfinished concept map below onto a sheet of paper. Then complete the map by writing the correct word or phrase in the lettered boxes.

26. Connection to Social Studies In the early 1600s, Sir Isaac Newton was forced to leave Oxford University when it closed for 2 years. Newton used this time to lay the groundwork for his important discoveries in mathematics and physics. Research Newton's life or the history of Oxford to find out why the university closed its doors.

27. Integrating Mathematics Suppose you knew the increasing doses of a drug a person had to take to compensate for tolerance over a period of time. If you also knew what dose can cause death, how could you predict when that person's effective dose would reach a level sufficient to cause death?

28. Connection to Fine Arts The Dance of Death is a medieval concept expressed in European art—poetry, drama, music, painting, and sculpture—from the mid-fourteenth century. This was a popular theme resulting from the devastation caused by the Black Death. Research the origin of this concept to determine its meaning.

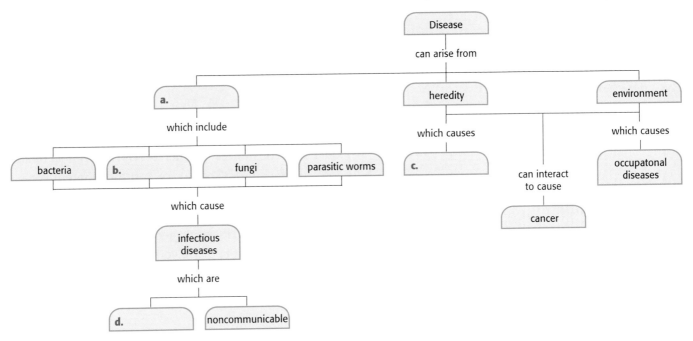

Design Your Own Lab

Introduction

Can you classify an unknown substance as a stimulant or a sedative by observing its effect on a small animal's heart?

Objectives

▶ **Observe** the effect of different chemical solutions on the heart rate of daphnia.

▶ **Classify** the solutions as stimulants or sedatives on the basis of their effects.

Materials

daphnia in pond water
medicine dropper
cotton ball
depression slide
coverslip
binocular dissecting microscope
stopwatch
paper towel
5 percent and 10 percent solutions of unknown substance 1
10 percent and 20 percent solutions of unknown substance 2

Safety Needs

protective gloves
safety goggles

Testing the Effect of Drugs on Heart Rate

▶ Measuring the Heart Rate of Daphnia

1. On a blank sheet of paper, prepare a table like the one at right.

2. Using a medicine dropper, transfer a daphnia along with a small amount of pond water from the culture jar to the center of a depression slide.

3. Add three or four fibers from a cotton ball to the slide to slow the animal's movement, and cover the slide with a coverslip. Be careful not to crush the daphnia with the coverslip or let the water on the slide dry up. **SAFETY CAUTION** Slides break easily. Use care when handling them.

4. Examine the daphnia under the low power of your microscope. You should be able to look through the animal's transparent skin to see the heart beating inside.

5. Count the daphnia's heartbeats for 10 seconds. Record the result in the first blank row of your data table, in the column labeled "Heartbeats, Trial 1." Turn off the microscope light, and wait 20 seconds.

6. Repeat step 5 two more times for trials 2 and 3. Always turn off the microscope light for 20 seconds between trials. These three trials will serve as a control for some of your tests on the unknown solutions.

▶ Designing Your Experiment

7. With your lab partners, decide how you will test the unknown substances for their effects on daphnia heart rate. In which order should you test the different concentrations of each unknown substance? Should you use the same daphnia for all tests?

8. In your lab report, list each step you will perform.

9. Your teacher must approve your plan before you carry out your experiment.

Solution	Heartbeats			Average number of heartbeats	Average heart rate (beats/min)
	Trial 1	Trial 2	Trial 3		
None					

▶ Performing Your Experiment

10. After your teacher approves your plan, carry out your experiment. To apply a test substance to the daphnia, use a medicine dropper to place a drop of the solution on the slide along one edge of the coverslip. Draw the solution into the depression by touching a piece of paper towel to the opposite edge of the coverslip.

11. Wait 1 minute for each solution to take effect. Perform three trials for each solution you test. Record your results in your data table.

    SAFETY CAUTION Do not ingest any of the solutions used in the lab.

▶ Analyzing Your Results

1. For each row of data in your table, calculate the average number of heartbeats by adding the numbers for trials 1, 2, and 3 and dividing the sum by 3. Record the result in your data table.

2. Calculate the average heart rate in beats/min by multiplying the average number of heartbeats by 6. Record the result in your data table.

3. Did unknown substance 1 increase or decrease the heart rate of daphnia? Did unknown substance 2 increase or decrease the heart rate? For each substance, which concentration produced the greatest change in heart rate?

4. What effect on heart rate would you expect a stimulant to have? What effect would you expect a sedative to have? Based on these expectations, classify unknown substances 1 and 2 as stimulants or sedatives.

▶ Defending Your Conclusions

5. Why was it important to use different daphnia for each unknown substance?

6. Is it reasonable to conclude that unknown substances 1 and 2 would have the same effects on heart rate in humans? Explain.

CHAPTER 17

Reproduction and Growth

Chapter Preview

17.1 Human Reproduction
The Male Reproductive System
The Female Reproductive System
The Female Reproductive Cycle

17.2 Pregnancy and Birth
From Fertilization to Growing Fetus
The Birth of the Baby

17.3 Growth and Development
Infancy Through Childhood
Adolescence: A Time of Change
Reproductive Health

Louise Brown, now an adult, was the first human conceived by in-vitro fertilization.

Focus ACTIVITY

Background The technology for so-called test-tube babies has been in use for several years. A "test-tube" baby is produced by a process called in-vitro fertilization, which means literally "fertilization in glass."

In this procedure, reproductive cells are taken from a man and a woman and are mixed together in a laboratory dish. If a male cell and a female cell join, this produces the first cell of a new individual. This fertilized cell is then placed in the womb of a woman. The cell divides as in any other pregnancy.

Activity 1 Research the topic of in-vitro fertilization. Write a paragraph explaining why it is used. Some people argue that in-vitro fertilization should not be used. Take a poll of 15 people, and ask them whether they think in-vitro fertilization is a good or a bad technological advancement.

Activity 2 Scientists have the ability to produce a new organism from the cells of a single existing organism. The new organism is genetically identical to the original organism—it is a clone. Are clones the same as babies produced by in-vitro fertilization? Take a poll similar to that in Activity 1, and ask people if they know the difference between the two procedures. How scientifically informed are most people?

internetconnect

SC LINKS **NSTA**
TOPIC: In-vitro fertilization
GO TO: www.scilinks.org
KEYWORD: HJ1701

Human Reproduction

▶ **KEY TERMS**

fertilization

testis

scrotum

sperm cell

penis

urethra

seminal vesicles

semen

ejaculation

bulbourethral gland

uterus

ovary

fallopian tubes

vagina

follicle

ovulation

menstruation

▷ **fertilization** the fusion of a male reproductive cell with a female reproductive cell to produce the first cell of a new individual

▷ **testis** one of a pair of organs, the testes, that produce sperm cells and the male hormone, testosterone

▷ **scrotum** the loose sac of skin that contains the testes

OBJECTIVES

▶ Describe the path that sperm cells take through the male reproductive system.

▶ Identify the organs of the female reproductive system, and describe their functions.

▶ Describe the major events of the female reproductive cycle.

When the male and female reproductive cells join during **fertilization,** the genetic information inside each reproductive cell also combines. The genetic information determines the traits the child will have and how the child's body will develop and function. Because both parents contribute genetic material, the child will have the traits of both parents.

Genetic information is encoded in a molecule called deoxyribonucleic acid (DNA), illustrated in **Figure 17-1.** DNA tells cells which proteins to make and when to make them.

The Male Reproductive System

The diagram in **Figure 17-2** at right shows the male reproductive system. The two plum-sized **testes** are contained in a loose sac called the **scrotum.** The testes produce an important hormone called *testosterone*. Testosterone is crucial for the primary sex characteristics of males, that is, the development of male reproductive organs before birth. Testosterone is also responsible for the secondary sex characteristics of adult men, which include large skeletal muscles, hair on the face, and a deep voice.

Figure 17-1
DNA exists as a coiled structure called a double helix, which is shaped somewhat like a spiral staircase. Each "stair" of the staircase is made from a sugar, a base, and a phosphate group.

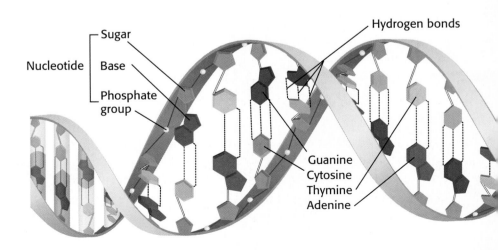

Sugar

Nucleotide

Base

Phosphate group

Hydrogen bonds

Guanine
Cytosine
Thymine
Adenine

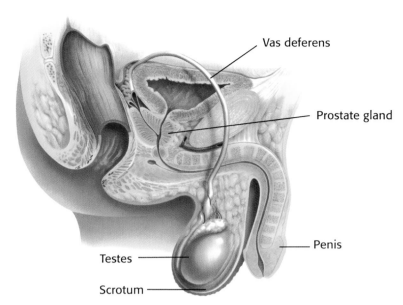

Vas deferens

Prostate gland

Penis

Testes

Scrotum

Figure 17-2
The male reproductive system produces hormones responsible for producing sperm cells and causing the sex characteristics of males.

internet**connect**

SCI*LINKS*
NSTA

TOPIC: Reproductive system
GO TO: www.scilinks.org
KEYWORD: HJ1702

Sperm cells are produced by the testes

The testes also produce the male reproductive cells, called **sperm cells. Figure 17-3** shows a single sperm cell. Sperm cells are not shaped like spheres or ovals like many other cells in the body. Their narrow, streamlined shape is specialized for movement. The narrow tail of the sperm cell lashes back and forth. This movement propels the sperm cell through the fluid environment of the female reproductive system.

The head of the cell contains genetic information—one-half of the genetic instructions needed to describe every aspect of a human being. A sexually mature male produces a continuous supply of sperm cells at a rate of between 200 million and 400 million cells every day. Sperm cell production is driven by testosterone and by hormones produced by the brain and the pituitary gland, which is located at the base of the brain.

Sperm cells move from the testes to the penis

On the outside of the body, the **penis** lies directly above the testes. The **urethra,** a hollow tube, runs down the middle of the underside of the penis. The penis serves two main functions. The urethra within the penis carries urine from the bladder to the outside of the body. The urethra can also carry the fluid that contains sperm cells.

The penis, which is specialized to deposit sperm cells, is composed of spongy tissue. Most of the time, the penis is soft. During sexual arousal, however, blood flow to the penis increases. The spongy tissue fills with blood. This makes the penis larger and firmer, producing an erection.

▶ **sperm cell** a male reproductive cell

▶ **penis** the male organ that delivers sperm cells into the female reproductive system and moves urine out of the body

▶ **urethra** the tube in the body that carries urine and, in males, semen

Figure 17-3
The head of a sperm cell contains genetic material. The active tail moves the sperm cell through the female reproductive system.

Tail

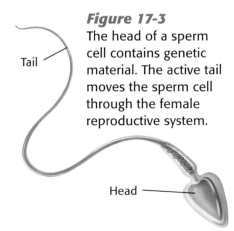

Head

Did You Know ?

Unlike other human body cells, sperm cells cannot complete their development at the normal human body temperature of 37°C. Sperm cells develop in the organs contained in the scrotum, where the temperature is about 3°C cooler than that of the rest of the body.

▶ **seminal vesicles** the glands that produce a sugar-rich fluid, which nourishes sperm cells

▶ **semen** a thick, whitish fluid containing sperm cells

▶ **ejaculation** the forceful expulsion of semen from the male reproductive system

▶ **bulbourethral gland** a gland that secretes an alkaline fluid to counteract acids in the female reproductive tract

An erection readies a male for sexual intercourse—a process by which sperm cells are deposited into the reproductive system of a female. Erections do not occur only in response to sexual stimuli. Erections may occur several times during a male's normal sleep cycle, and they even occur in infant boys.

Sperm cells take a long route from the testes, where they form, to the outside of the body. Use **Figure 17-2** to trace the path of sperm cells through the male reproductive system. Immature sperm cells move from the testes to a coiled tube on the outside of each testis. Here the sperm cells finish developing and are stored until just before they leave the body. The full process of sperm production and maturation takes about 10 weeks.

Semen contains sperm cells and other fluids

From the coiled tube, two longer tubes called the *vas deferens* move sperm cells farther from the testes. The two vas deferens come together, forming a single tube that leads to the urethra.

Near this point in the urethra, several glands, including the prostate gland, are found. The prostate gland is a donut-shaped organ that surrounds the urethra. The prostate gland and the seminal vesicles create fluids that are added to the sperm in the vas deferens and in the urethra. When these fluids mix with the sperm cells, semen is formed. Semen is mostly fluid; sperm cells add very little to the volume.

Semen is expelled from the body by ejaculation

Ejaculation is a reflex that occurs in response to a signal from the nervous system. Involuntary muscular contractions force sperm cells out of the tubes near the testes and into each of the vas deferens. The muscular vas deferens move sperm cells toward the urethra. The seminal fluids flush the sperm cells through the urethra and out of the body.

Even before ejaculation, some sperm cells can be washed out of the urethra by the watery discharge of the bulbourethral gland. So, some sperm cells can enter the female reproductive system during intercourse even if ejaculation does not occur.

The sperm cells carry the genetic material that determines the sex of the offspring. In humans, the genetic material that causes the development of a male is encoded in the DNA of the Y chromosome. Males have one X chromosome and one Y chromosome. Therefore, a sperm cell may contain either an X chromosome or a Y chromosome. Females have two X chromosomes. Because a female can donate only X chromosomes to her offspring, the sex of an offspring is determined by the male, who can donate either an X chromosome or a Y chromosome.

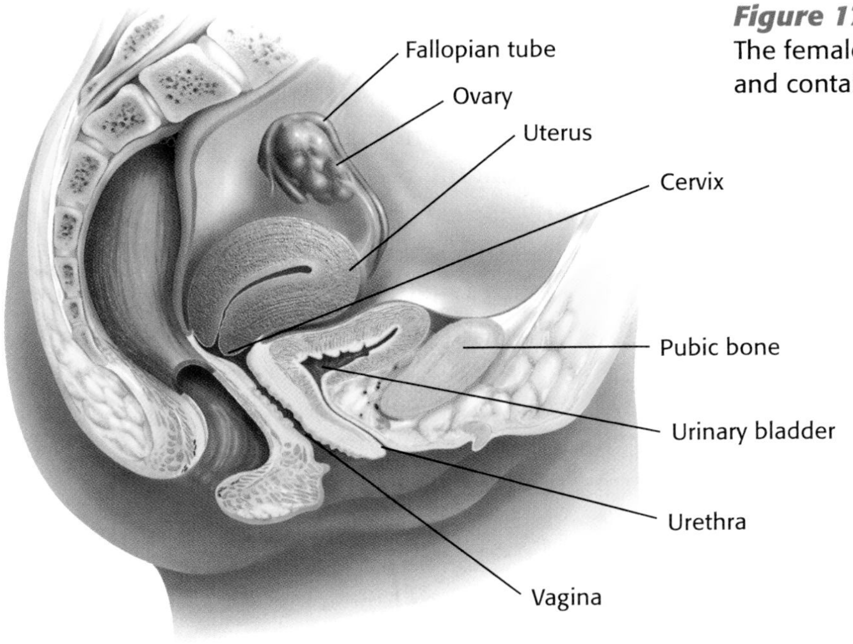

Figure 17-4
The female reproductive system produces eggs and contains a place for a developing baby.

Fallopian tube
Ovary
Uterus
Cervix
Pubic bone
Urinary bladder
Urethra
Vagina

The Female Reproductive System

The female reproductive system is shown in **Figure 17-4.** Lying deep and low in the center of the body is the uterus. It is similar in shape and size to a pear. During pregnancy, the uterus contains and nourishes the developing baby. To either side of the uterus lie the ovaries. The ovaries produce eggs, which are the female reproductive cells.

▷ **uterus** the muscular female organ that contains the developing baby

▷ **ovary** the female organ that stores and releases eggs

Eggs are released into the fallopian tubes

Each ovary contains about 400 000 immature egg cells. These egg cells are already formed and in place when a female is born. The number of egg cells does not increase over the lifetime of a female. During adolescence, the egg cells develop further so they are ready for fertilization. Although females do not produce as many reproductive cells as males do, more than enough eggs are available for the reproductive years. Eggs move from the ovaries to the uterus through the two fallopian tubes. You can see a fallopian tube and an ovary in **Figure 17-4.** Each fallopian tube opens near an ovary.

▷ **fallopian tubes** the tubular structures that move eggs from the ovaries to the uterus; the site of fertilization

The uterus connects to the vagina, a muscular tube about 7 cm long where sperm cells enter the female reproductive system. If sperm cells have been released in the vagina during the previous 72 hours, some sperm may have traveled to the fallopian tubes. Fertilization occurs in a fallopian tube when a sperm cell enters the egg. At the end of pregnancy, the baby passes through the vagina as it is born.

▷ **vagina** the passage that connects the uterus with the outside of the body

There is a worldwide effort to control population. The reason for the concern is that the world's population is growing *exponentially*, as demonstrated in the accompanying graph.

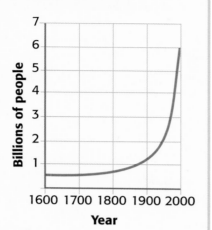

Billions of people / Year

Making the Connection

1. How many years did it take to increase the world's population from 1 billion to 2 billion?
2. How many years did it take to increase the world's population from 3 billion to 4 billion?
3. How many people do you think the world can support? Explain your answer.

▶ **follicle** a small envelope of cells surrounding an egg

▶ **ovulation** the process by which an egg moves out of the ovary

Ovulation occurs once a month

Once about every 28 days, a hormone from the pituitary gland causes an egg cell to begin to grow, as shown in **Figure 17-5.** The egg cell and its surrounding tissue, the **follicle,** continue to grow over a period of about 10 days. This tissue rises to the surface of the ovary, forming a blisterlike structure. When the blister breaks, an egg is released near the mouth of the fallopian tube. This event is called **ovulation.** After ovulation, the egg enters the fallopian tube. Then tiny hairlike structures sweep the egg through the fallopian tube to the uterus.

The Female Reproductive Cycle

In women of childbearing age, the uterus and ovaries undergo cyclical changes. This reproductive cycle is regulated by hormones, which are produced in different amounts at different times in the cycle.

The ovaries produce the primary female hormone, estrogen. Estrogen stimulates the thickening of the lining of the uterus. A rising level of estrogen causes the pituitary gland to stop producing follicle-stimulating hormone, FSH, which triggers the development of a follicle to produce an egg. Estrogen also causes the production of more lutinizing hormone, LH, which causes an egg to mature.

The hormone progesterone is also produced in the ovaries. Progesterone is the body's signal to prepare for pregnancy. It inhibits further production of FSH and LH. Other regulating hormones are produced in the pituitary gland and the brain, as they are in males.

Figure 17-5

The cross section of an ovary shows the stages an egg passes through before ovulation.

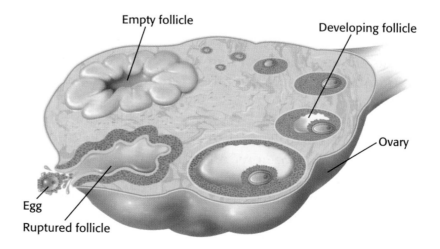

Empty follicle

Developing follicle

Ovary

Egg

Ruptured follicle

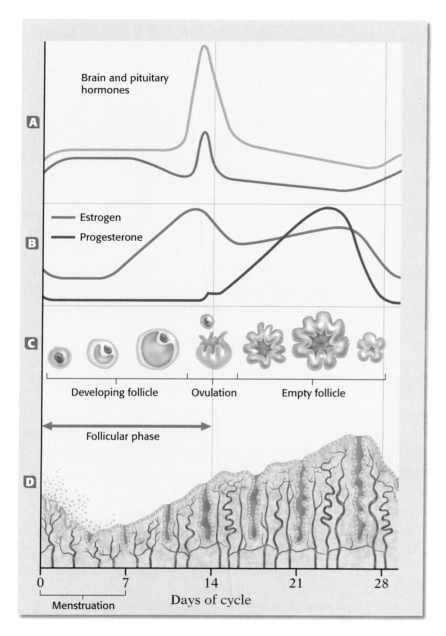

Figure 17-6
The blood levels of brain and pituitary hormones (A) govern the release of the hormones estrogen and progesterone (B). This causes changes in the ovary (C) and the inner lining of the uterus (D).

The uterus prepares for pregnancy by building a thickened lining

Figure 17-6 shows some of the ways the egg and the uterus change over the course of a single 28-day cycle. At the same time the ovary is readying the egg for ovulation, the uterus is preparing itself to receive a fertilized egg. The lining of the uterus changes in response to estrogen from the ovaries. The blood supply to the lining of the uterus increases, and the lining thickens greatly.

When ovulation occurs the egg's follicle is left in the tissues of the ovary. This follicle will also affect the uterus. The follicle left behind in the ovary produces the hormone progesterone. This hormone signals the uterine lining to make final preparations to receive a fertilized egg.

menstruation the release of uterine lining, blood, and unfertilized egg

As you probably realize, most eggs that are ovulated are not fertilized. As an unfertilized egg moves toward the uterus, the remains of the follicle in the ovary begin to break down. The follicle can no longer secrete progesterone. Without progesterone, the lining of the uterus does not receive nutrition. Most of the lining sloughs off as a mixture of blood and cells that passes through the vagina. This process is called **menstruation.** The menstrual flow is a visible sign that a pregnancy has not begun, and the female reproductive cycle is ready to begin again.

Most women menstruate until around age 50. Menstruation ceases because most of a woman's follicles have either matured and released eggs or they have degenerated. Without follicle cells the ovaries cannot secrete enough estrogen or progesterone to maintain a menstrual cycle. The pituitary gland continues to release FSH for the rest of a woman's life.

SECTION 17.1 REVIEW

SUMMARY

▶ The male reproductive system consists primarily of two testes, two vas deferens, two seminal vesicles, the bulbourethral gland, and the penis.

▶ The testes produce the male reproductive cells, sperm cells, and the male hormone, testosterone.

▶ Semen, the fluid that contains the sperm cells, exits the male body via a reflex called ejaculation.

▶ The female reproductive system consists mainly of two ovaries, two fallopian tubes, the uterus, and the vagina.

▶ The ovaries contain egg cells and produce the female hormones estrogen and progesterone.

▶ A single egg is expelled, or ovulated, by one of the ovaries every month.

CHECK YOUR UNDERSTANDING

1. **Identify** the structure in the penis that carries sperm cells during ejaculation. What is the other function of this structure?
2. **Identify** the organ where sperm cells are formed.
3. **List** three glands that contribute secretions to the makeup of semen.
4. **Discuss** two ways that sperm cells differ from eggs.
5. **Select** the item(s) below that are common to both male and female reproductive systems.
   - **a.** scrotum
   - **c.** reproductive cells
   - **b.** hormones
   - **d.** uterus
6. **Explain** the function of the fallopian tubes.
7. **Describe** what happens to the follicle after its egg has been ovulated.
8. **Compare** the actions of estrogen and progesterone in the female reproductive cycle.
9. **Explain** why menstruation stops when a pregnancy is started.
10. **Critical Thinking** Answer the following question using information that you have learned in this section. If females have two ovaries, why is it rare for a pregnancy to produce twins?
11. **Critical Thinking** Why do you think the male reproductive system has two testes, two vas deferens, and two seminal vesicles? Why do you think the female reproductive system has two ovaries and two fallopian tubes?

Pregnancy and Birth

▶ Describe the process of fertilization and implantation.

▶ Trace the development of a fertilized egg to the birth of a baby.

▶ List the events of birth.

▶ Explain how a mother's health can affect the health of her baby.

▶ **KEY TERMS**

fetus

zygote

blastocyst

embryo

amniotic fluid

placenta

▶ **fetus** a developing offspring that has most of its major structures

TOPIC: Pregnancy
GO TO: www.scilinks.org
KEYWORD: HJ1703

Early people believed that the fetus began as an extremely small version of a complete human being. Because people did not have the tools to see a fetus, they did not understand the events that start with a single sperm cell and a single egg cell. How does a complete human body form from the union of two microscopic cells, like the ones shown in **Figure 17-7**?

From Fertilization to Growing Fetus

If sperm cells are released into the female reproductive system around the time of ovulation, fertilization may occur. Timing is critical. Sperm cells can remain alive in the female reproductive system up to three days after they are ejaculated. Eggs, however, must be fertilized within about 15 hours following ovulation.

When sperm cells are ejaculated into the vagina, their tails propel them upward through the vagina, then through the uterus, and finally out through one of the fallopian tubes. Because this trip is so long, only the fastest and strongest sperm make it far enough to fertilize an egg. Of the average 200 million sperm cells that are ejaculated, only about 100 reach the area in the fallopian tube where fertilization can occur.

Fertilization is the union of an egg and a sperm cell

When fertilization occurs, one-half of the genetic information comes from the egg cell. The other half comes from the sperm cell. When the sperm cell fertilizes the egg, the new cell has a complete set of genetic information.

Figure 17-7
This scanning electron micrograph shows many sperm cells clustered around an egg cell.

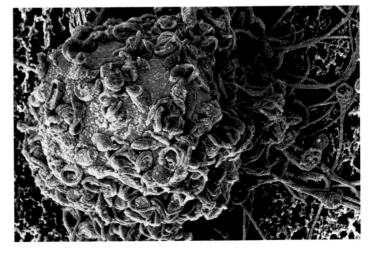

▶ **zygote** the cell resulting from fertilization of an egg cell by a sperm cell

▶ **blastocyst** the hollow ball of cells that attaches to the lining of the uterus

Figure 17-8
The zygote continually divides as it moves toward the uterus, until it becomes a ball of cells.

Fertilization has several distinct steps. First sperm cells bind to the egg while it is in the fallopian tube, close to the ovary. Chemicals produced by sperm cells weaken the egg's outer coating. At some point, a single sperm cell breaks through. The head of the sperm cell enters the egg. Immediately, the egg undergoes a change that prevents any other sperm cells from entering. The genetic material of the egg and sperm cell combine, and fertilization is complete.

All of the trillions of cells that make up a human come from this new cell, the **zygote**. Occasionally, the female ovulates two or more eggs at a single time. If more than one egg is fertilized, a multiple birth can result. The infants will not have identical genetic information and thus will be referred to as "fraternal twins" or "fraternal triplets."

The embryo develops in a fluid-filled sac

Although fertilization takes place in the fallopian tube, growth of the embryo takes place in the uterus. The zygote begins to divide as it is moved toward the uterus. First the single cell formed by the sperm and egg divides into two cells. Each of these divides, producing four cells, then eight cells, and so on. After 4–5 days, the zygote has developed into a ball of cells, like that shown in **Figure 17-8.** The growing ball of cells enters the uterus and attaches to the inner lining, where it will remain for the rest of the pregnancy.

At this time, the **blastocyst** begins secreting a hormone, human chorionic gonadotropin (HCG). This hormonal signal tells the ovary that a pregnancy has started. In response to this, the ovary continues to secrete progesterone, which maintains the uterine lining. The presence of HCG in blood or urine is the basis for pregnancy tests.

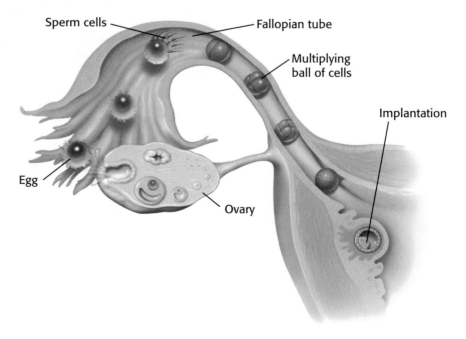

Sperm cells

Fallopian tube

Multiplying ball of cells

Implantation

Egg

Ovary

The cells of the blastocyst develop specialized structures. One of these structures is a membrane that will surround the developing embryo. The membrane produces amniotic fluid, which will cushion the developing organism. In some pregnancies, an early embryo divides in half, and each half begins to develop as a separate embryo. The resulting two infants are genetically identical and are called "identical twins" or "maternal twins."

The placenta connects the developing embryo with the mother

Following implantation, some cells of the embryo begin to form an organ called the placenta. The placenta is shown in **Figure 17-9.** It lies outside the embryo's body. It has fingerlike projections that extend into the interior layer of the uterus.

The placenta prevents direct contact between the blood of mother and the blood of the developing fetus. All nutrients and waste products pass between the mother's blood and the fetus's blood by diffusion through membranes. The umbilical cord contains the blood vessels that carry blood from the placenta to the developing fetus and then back again.

The fetus continues growing for nine months

A typical pregnancy lasts about 9 months (about 38 weeks). For the sake of discussion, this 9-month period is often divided into three 3-month segments called trimesters. During the first 8 weeks of the first trimester, the developing baby is called an embryo. It is during this time that many of the basic body systems start forming.

▶ **embryo** a growing organism that has not yet developed all of its major structures

▶ **amniotic fluid** a watery fluid in which a developing embryo or fetus is suspended

▶ **placenta** the structure attaching the embryo to the wall of the uterus

Figure 17-9
The placenta allows the nutrient and waste transport between the mother's blood and the fetus's blood.

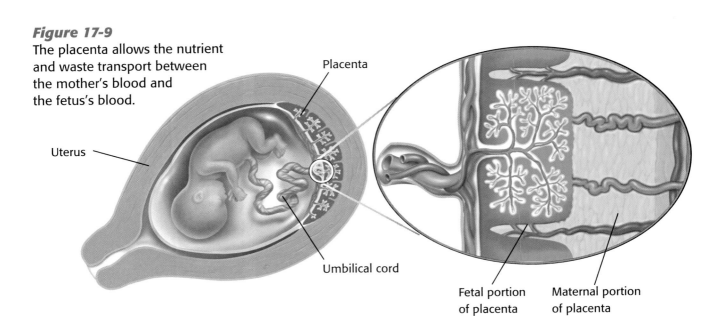

Placenta

Uterus

Umbilical cord

Fetal portion of placenta

Maternal portion of placenta

Thinking Twice

The accompanying photographs show two sets of twins. One set is identical. Identical twins are often called maternal twins. The other set of twins is not identical—they are called fraternal twins.

1. How are fraternal twins produced? Explain your answer.
2. How are identical twins produced? Explain your answer.

Within 4 weeks of fertilization, the major organs have begun to form. These include the brain, heart, eyes, ears, liver, and lungs. Also during this time, the embryo begins to develop limbs, bones, and muscles. After the initial 8-week period of pregnancy, the developing baby is referred to as a fetus. A developing fetus is shown in **Figure 17-10.**

During the second trimester, two key events occur. The fetal heart can be heard, and the fetus's movements can be felt. The fetus's arms and legs reach their final proportions, and the eyes begin to blink.

During the third trimester, all of the organ systems complete their development. The brain grows rapidly; the fetus gains weight. Late in the third trimester, the fetal lungs complete development. By third trimester's end, the fetus is about as large as can be delivered without damage to the mother or child. Neurological development and physical growth continue after birth.

Figure 17-10
The fetus steadily grows and develops throughout the 38 weeks of pregnancy.

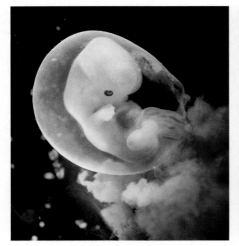

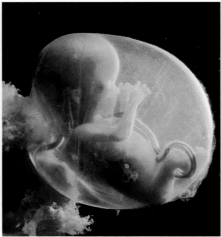

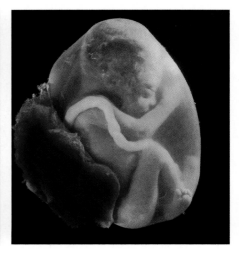

A First trimester

B Second trimester

C Third trimester

The Birth of the Baby

Babies born before 35 weeks after fertilization are considered to be born early and are called preterm or premature. If the birth occurs too early, many organ systems will not be fully developed. Premature babies require special hospital care while they complete the development that should have occurred within the uterus.

In a normal pregnancy, the fetus is ready to be born about 38 weeks after fertilization (or about 40 weeks after the last menstrual period).

The fetus is pushed out of the mother's body by very strong contractions of the uterus. These contractions are part of a process called labor. Labor can begin differently for each pregnancy. Contractions may start out as mild cramps that last for a few seconds and occur a few times an hour. As labor progresses, the contractions last longer and become stronger and more frequent.

internetconnect

SCLINKS.
NSTA

TOPIC: Birth
GO TO: www.scilinks.org
KEYWORD: HJ1704

Labor can last for 12 hours or more

In some pregnancies, the first sign of labor is the rupture of the sac that contains the fetus. About 1 L (~ 1 qt) of amniotic fluid is released through the vagina. This event is commonly called the "breaking of the water."

In most first pregnancies, the uterine contractions of labor continue for an average of 12 hours, though the time may vary. The contractions stretch the cervix, which is the mouth of the uterus, shown in **Figure 17-11.** The cervix opens from a virtually closed position to a diameter of about 10 cm. At the same time, these uterine contractions slowly move the fetus toward the cervix. The fetus passes through the cervix and then through the vagina and out of the mother's body. After birth, the fetus is referred to as an infant.

At birth, the umbilical cord still connects the infant to the placenta within the uterus. The umbilical cord is clamped shut and then cut. At this point, the mother and infant are separate. Your navel is the scar that remains after the stub of the severed umbilical cord drops off.

Following the birth of the baby, the placenta and other tissue that supported the fetus in the uterus are expelled. This event is the end of labor.

Figure 17-11
The contractions of labor move the fetus out of the uterus and through the vagina to the outside world.

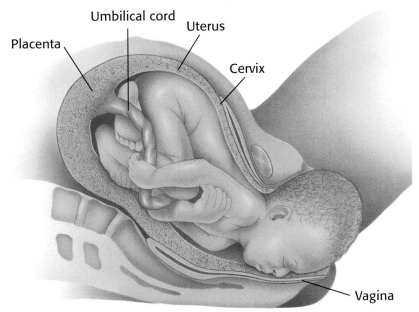

Umbilical cord

Placenta

Uterus

Cervix

Vagina

English-speaking people often call rubella *German measles*. The disease was identified and described in 1619 by Daniel Sennert, who was a German physician. Because of the red-colored rash that may be seen during the illness, he called the disease rubella from the Latin word *rubellus,* meaning "reddish."

Rubella started being called German measles around 1875, when the disease was being studied by German physicians. Rubella was not considered dangerous until 1941, when scientists discovered that a fetus infected with rubella is often born with serious birth defects, including vision defects and damage to the heart, brain, and large arteries.

A healthy baby requires a healthy mother

Mothers have a huge responsibility when carrying unborn children. "Crack babies" are eye-opening examples of what can go wrong when that responsibility is ignored. Crack babies are born damaged and addicted to cocaine because their mothers used cocaine during the pregnancy. If the mother mistreats her body, she is also mistreating the developing fetus.

The placenta is specialized for exchanging nutrients and waste products between the mother and developing baby. But dangerous substances carried in the mother's blood can pass to the fetus. Therefore, a fetus effectively "takes" any drug its mother takes, including nicotine, alcohol, and caffeine. Section 16.3 described the way children can be harmed through fetal alcohol syndrome if their mothers drink alcohol during pregnancy.

In addition, if the mother contracts a viral illness such as rubella, the virus can be transferred to the developing baby through the placenta. Rubella can have devastating effects on an embryo or fetus. Rubella in the mother can be prevented by vaccination before she becomes pregnant.

SECTION 17.2 REVIEW

SUMMARY

▶ Fertilization occurs when an egg and a sperm cell unite.

▶ A zygote forms a ball of cells, which implants in the lining of the uterus and becomes an embryo.

▶ The embryo and the mother's body cooperate to form the placenta, which provides nourishment and waste removal.

▶ Harmful substances can pass from the mother to the fetus by way of the placenta.

CHECK YOUR UNDERSTANDING

1. **Identify** the location where fertilization occurs.
   a. vagina   c. uterus
   b. cervix   d. fallopian tubes
2. **List** three important steps in fertilization.
3. **Describe** the process of implantation.
4. **List** the names used to describe a developing individual, from the earliest stage to the last.
5. **Describe** the development that occurs during the period of pregnancy.
6. **List** four important steps of labor.
7. **Explain** why a pregnant woman should avoid infectious diseases and harmful drugs.
8. **Critical Thinking** Why is the presence of HCG in the urine a good test for pregnancy?
9. **Critical Thinking** Why are events that occur early in a pregnancy more likely to cause birth defects?

WRITING SKILL

Growth and Development

OBJECTIVES

▶ List defining characteristics of childhood, adolescence, and adulthood.

▶ Describe how puberty affects the male body.

▶ Describe how puberty affects the female body.

▶ Describe practices for maintaining reproductive health.

▶ Discuss how reproductive systems are affected by aging.

KEY TERMS

empathy

altruism

puberty

sexually transmitted disease (STD)

menopause

When a baby is born, it has already developed from a single cell, the zygote, to a living thing with many parts and systems. But development continues long after birth.

Infancy Through Childhood

A baby is considered an infant for the first year of its life. The first year is a time of enormous change. A small, wailing infant becomes a child who can walk, try to talk, and demand the attention of everyone around him or her.

internetconnect

SC LINKS
NSTA

TOPIC: Growth and development
GO TO: www.scilinks.org
KEYWORD: HJ1705

Infancy requires a special diet

Throughout pregnancy, the mother's body changes to accommodate the baby. Breasts have milk-producing glands that open onto the nipple. During pregnancy, the breasts enlarge and these glands prepare to make milk. After labor and the baby's birth, the milk begins to flow. Suckling by an infant causes a reflex that stimulates milk production and release.

During the first few months of life, milk provides the baby's only food. Because the baby has no teeth and its digestive system is not fully mature, solid food cannot be digested properly. One of the first choices that a mother has to make is whether to breast-feed or bottle-feed her infant.

Infants cannot digest cow's milk easily. Therefore, bottle-fed babies, like the one shown in **Figure 17-12,** are given infant formula, which is similar in composition to breast milk. Infant formula lacks some of the components normally found in breast milk. For example, breast milk contains some antibodies from the mother, which make the infant more resistant to disease. The composition of breast milk varies according to the baby's needs as it grows, while the composition of infant formula is constant.

Figure 17-12
Infants can thrive on breast milk or bottled formula, which is similar to breast milk.

Figure 17-13
This preschool-aged child is an explorer, but he must be supervised until he can recognize danger.

Babies can be fed semi-solid food when they are several months old. Babies are said to be *weaned* when their milk diet has been replaced with a solid food diet.

Infants grow and develop very rapidly in their first year of life. At 2 months old, infants smile socially at people. A 6-month-old infant can sit up. Many infants can pull themselves to their feet at about 8 months of age. At this time, too, many infants can say simple two-syllable words, such as "mama" or "dada." A 1-year-old child may be able to walk. This child understands how to move things and can explore his or her environment.

The preschool years are times for developing reasoning and control

Childhood is the period between infancy and adolescence. Between the ages of two and five, children are able to learn important skills involving reasoning and motor control. Children learn to control urination and bowel function, and they learn to eat by themselves, drinking from a cup and using a fork or spoon.

Their language skills also improve rapidly. The clarity of speech and the size of vocabulary increase greatly. Children can make their needs understood by speaking instead of crying. Children continue to aggressively explore their environments. It is therefore very important that young children be supervised at all times. Children at this age have curiosity and advanced motor skills, but they lack the judgment and experience to recognize danger, as shown in **Figure 17-13.**

Young children often begin to learn the names of colors, the alphabet, and the counting numbers. They can sing simple songs, repeating the words correctly and mimicking tone and pitch. With instruction, some children begin to read during this period.

Children of school age continue building reasoning skills

During the time children are in elementary school, they learn to sit quietly for organized activities. Children between 5 years old and 12 years old learn a great deal from formal instruction.

Along with an improvement in reasoning and logic skills, children this age develop moral reasoning. At a younger age, children avoid wrongdoing (such as running into the street) in order to avoid punishment from parents. But during the school years, children begin to understand their parents' and society's definitions of right and wrong. They may avoid doing something because they think it is wrong or because it causes them emotional distress.

School-aged children develop empathy and become aware of the situations and motivations of the people around them. Children this age may swing back and forth between self-centered behavior and altruism. Children become aware of what others expect from them in their dress, speech, and behavior. Some children have difficulty meeting the standards of their peers, and these children often are not fully accepted into a social group.

▶ **empathy** an understanding and respect for feelings of others

▶ **altruism** the behavior that helps others but not one's self

Adolescence: A Time of Change

Adolescence is a particularly challenging period of life. It is the period of transition from childhood to adulthood. Adolescence begins at the onset of puberty, which is when the reproductive system becomes functional. The age of puberty varies greatly due to genetics, nutrition, and other environmental factors. Usually puberty begins to occur between the ages of 10 and 14, and it begins earlier in girls than in boys, as shown in **Figure 17-14.**

▶ **puberty** the time in life when secondary sex changes occur and the reproductive system becomes functional

Puberty begins the change from childhood to adulthood

Puberty usually starts with a growth spurt. In girls, the ovaries begin to secrete estrogen. In boys, the testes secrete testosterone. The hormonal signal that begins puberty in both sexes originates in the brain.

The changes that happen during puberty result from the secretion of estrogen and testosterone. These sex hormones act on many cells throughout the body. They act on brain cells, hair cells, muscle cells, and sweat gland cells. Ovaries respond to estrogen and begin preparing eggs for ovulation. Testes respond to testosterone and begin preparing to produce sperm cells. It takes three to five years to complete puberty and reach sexual maturity.

One of the most evident changes that occurs during puberty is the development of secondary sex characteristics. The secondary sex characteristics are the external differences between males and females. Males develop more body hair, including facial hair. Their skeletal muscles enlarge, and their voices become deeper. Females develop a rounder shape, wider hips, and larger breasts. Growth of pubic hair and enlargement of the external sex organs occur in both sexes.

Figure 17-14
The onset of puberty occurs at different times in different people. Girls generally begin puberty earlier than do boys.

sexually transmitted disease (STD) a disease that is transmitted by sexual contact

Figure 17-15
This false color scanning electron microscope image shows HIV particles (in red) about to penetrate human blood cells.

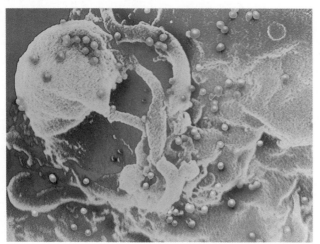

Adolescence also involves emotional and social changes

Adolescence is a challenging time, emotionally and socially, because it is a transition period. The hormonal changes may cause emotional swings that are sometimes difficult to handle. These changes stimulate the desire for greater freedom and self-expression. Conflicts may arise between the desire for independence and the need for security. Another challenge is how to control the new sexual desires that accompany puberty. Most adolescents manage well with the assistance of their parents.

Reproductive Health

You probably are aware that diseases can be spread in several different ways. For example, Lyme disease is spread by tick bites, cholera is transmitted through drinking water, and tuberculosis is transmitted in the air and in the milk of infected cows. The focus of this section, however, is the group of diseases transmitted by sexual contact. These diseases are called sexually transmitted diseases (STDs) or venereal diseases (VD).

Sexually transmitted diseases

Although STDs are often transmitted during vaginal intercourse, some can be transmitted during oral or anal sex. Acquired immune deficiency syndrome, AIDS, is an extremely serious disease because there is no cure available, and the disease is usually fatal. AIDS is caused by the human immunodeficiency virus, HIV. **Figure 17-15** shows the human immunodeficiency virus attacking healthy cells.

HIV can be transmitted from one person to another if there is a way for the virus to enter the bloodstream. AIDS is frequently transmitted by sexual contact, either heterosexual or homosexual. AIDS is also transmitted among intravenous drug users who share the needle of an infected person. Before scientists developed better screening techniques, some people contracted HIV from transfusions of blood containing the virus.

At this time, the only protection against AIDS is avoiding exposure to HIV. It is important to realize that a person who is infected with HIV can transmit the virus even if he or she has not developed AIDS. In addition, a negative blood test does not necessarily mean a person does not have the virus. Blood tests often cannot detect HIV in the early stages of infection. Therefore, sexual contact with a person who has tested negative for AIDS is still risky.

How to avoid STDs

The only sure way to avoid an STD is by abstaining from sexual relations. While the chances of spreading or catching an STD are much reduced if a person has only one sex partner who doesn't have STDs, it can be difficult to be certain that someone is not infected. Many STDs do not have highly visible symptoms. However, some people choose to have sexual relations with more than one person or with a person who cannot demonstrate that he or she is disease-free. These activities are called high-risk behaviors.

If you think that you have been infected with an STD, the information in **Table 17-1** should alert you to the importance of early treatment. Do not have sexual relations with anyone until a physician has examined you. It is important to describe your symptoms in detail to your physician, so that he or she can perform the appropriate tests.

internet**connect**

SCI*LINKS*
NSTA

TOPIC: Reproductive system disorder
GO TO: www.scilinks.org
KEYWORD: HJ1706

Table 17-1 **Sexually Transmitted Diseases**

Disease	Cause	Early symptoms	Treatment
AIDS	Human immunodeficiency virus (HIV)	Fatigue, night sweats, multiple infections	None
Candidiasis	*Candida albicans* yeast	Itching, white cheesy discharge, inflammation of tissues	Locally applied cream
Genital herpes	Herpes virus, type 2	Painful blisterlike eruptions	None
Genital warts	Papilloma virus	Soft, moist swellings	Laser or other surgery
Gonorrhea	*Neisseria gonorrhoeae* bacterium	Frequent urination, discharge of pus from the urethra	Antibiotic
Hepatitis B	Hepatitis B virus	Flulike symptoms, dark urine, yellowing of skin	Vaccine (preventative only); otherwise, no treatment
Nonspecific sexually transmitted infection	*Chlamydia tracomatis* bacterium	Uncomfortable or frequent urination, pain from the pelvis, discharge of pus from urethra or vagina	Antibiotic
Syphilis	*Trepomena pallidum* bacterium	Oozing sore (chancre), low-grade fever, rash, headache, joint pain	Antibiotic
Trichomoniasis	*Trichomonas vaginalis* protozoan	Vaginal discharge in females, bladder and urethral infections in males	Anti-protozoan agent

Figure 17-16
Older adults remain healthy longer with a good diet, good medical care, and regular exercise.

▶ **menopause** the time when a woman stops menstruating and is no longer able to conceive

Aging and reproductive health

Aging is a continuation of life as the ability to adapt to new situations begins to decrease. Aging is a natural and unavoidable process, although illness is not an inevitable part of aging. The saying "You're only as old as you feel," is truer today than it has ever been. Like the runners shown in **Figure 17-16,** people today live longer, healthier lives because of better nutrition and health care. For example, the life expectancy for a male born in 1900 was 46 years. The estimated life expectancy for a male born in 2000 is about 74 years.

In an aging male, the reproductive system produces sperm cells until death. Testosterone secretion may decrease with age, which often decreases sexual activity in males.

In contrast, the female reproductive system becomes unable to produce eggs at an average age of 51. The last menstrual period in a woman's life is called **menopause.** As the menstrual cycles stop, estrogen secretion also decreases. Sexual activity, however, is frequently not decreased.

SECTION 17.3 REVIEW

SUMMARY

▶ An infant can be breast-fed or bottle-fed.

▶ Infants grow and develop quickly.

▶ Following puberty, males have increased pubic hair, lower voices, a larger penis, and the ability to produce and ejaculate sperm cells.

▶ Following puberty, females have increased pubic hair, a more rounded body shape, larger breasts, and the ability to ovulate.

▶ An STD is a disease that is transmitted by sexual contact.

CHECK YOUR UNDERSTANDING

1. **Discuss** an advantage of breast-feeding babies.
2. **Discuss** the motor and language advancements made in the preschool years.
3. **Name** one characteristic that you can use to identify whether a child is likely to be a pre-school child, a school-aged child, or an adolescent.
4. **Identify** the hormone that is primarily responsible for the changes associated with male puberty? Which organ produces it?
5. **Define** the term *secondary sex characteristics*, and describe how one is changed by puberty in females.
6. **Define** the term *menopause,* and explain its cause.
7. **List** four STDs, and name a symptom of each.
8. **Explain** why AIDS is considered to be fatal.
9. **Critical Thinking** Is there a biological advantage for females to experience menopause?

Chapter Highlights

Before you begin, review the summaries of the key ideas of each section, found on pages 554, 560, and 566. The key vocabulary terms are listed on pages 548, 555, and 561.

UNDERSTANDING CONCEPTS

1. Male reproductive cells are formed in the _____.
   a. vas deferens
   c. penis
   b. testes
   d. prostate gland

2. The hormone responsible for the primary sex characteristics in males is _____.
   a. estrogen
   c. progesterone
   b. testosterone
   d. pituitary hormone

3. After the follicle releases an egg, the follicle begins to produce the hormone _____.
   a. estrogen
   c. progesterone
   b. testosterone
   d. pituitary hormone

4. The female organ that nourishes the developing fetus is the _____.
   a. vagina
   c. ovary
   b. fallopian tube
   d. uterus

5. In females of childbearing age, ovulation occurs about every _____.
   a. 14 days
   c. 3 months
   b. 28 days
   d. 9 months

6. After the first 8 weeks of pregnancy, an embryo is called a _____.
   a. blastocyst
   c. infant
   b. zygote
   d. fetus

7. During labor, strong muscle contractions enlarge the _____.
   a. cervix
   c. fallopian tubes
   b. uterus
   d. pelvis

8. Nutrients and drugs can pass between the mother and the fetus through the _____.
   a. zygote
   c. placenta
   b. cervix
   d. fallopian tube

9. An average pregnancy, from fertilization to birth, lasts about _____.
   a. 28 weeks
   b. 33 weeks
   c. 38 weeks
   d. 43 weeks

10. During the first 6 months of life, infants primarily live on _____.
    a. baby food
    b. milk
    c. eggs
    d. finely chopped food

Using Vocabulary

11. Describe the path sperm take, from where they are formed through their exit from the body. Use the terms *penis, testes, urethra,* and *vas deferens.*

12. Distinguish between the terms *sperm* and *semen.* Which has the larger volume?

13. Look at the diagram below and write a paragraph describing the events that occur at points A, B, and C. Use the terms *egg, follicle, immature egg cell,* and *progesterone.*

WRITING SKILL

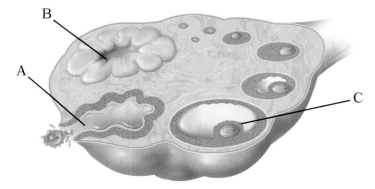

14. What ending do the words for the main three male and female sex hormones have in common?

BUILDING MATH SKILLS

15. Graphing The graph at right shows the female reproductive cycle. What hormonal event occurs just before ovulation?

16. Schedules If a woman has a menstrual cycle that lasts 28 days, and she is fertile beginning on her 13th birthday and ending on her 51st birthday, how many cycles will she have (assuming she is never pregnant)?

17. Population Using the information given in the table below, answer the following questions.

Average Daily Births in the United States	
Total	10 662
Mothers less than 20 years old	1377
Babies born with a serious birth defect	411

a. How may babies are born in a year?

b. What percentage of the total babies are born to mothers less than 20 years old?

c. The population of the United States was about 5 085 000 in 1800. At the current birth rate, how many days would it take to have 5 085 000 babies?

d. What percentage of the babies born have a serious birth defect? How many babies are born with serious birth defects in a year?

18. Cellular Division A zygote enlarges and becomes a blastocyst by cellular division. One cell becomes two; two cells become four. Identify the number of cells that arise from the third cell division to the sixth cell division. By the time the zygote reaches the uterus, it has about 100 cells. About how many cell divisions have occurred by then?

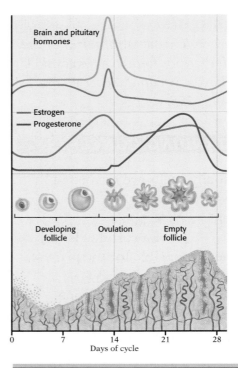

THINKING CRITICALLY

19. Creative Thinking A vasectomy is a surgery in which both of the vas deferens are cut. How would this make a male unable to have children? What would happen if one of the vas deferens were cut?

20. Problem Solving If the pituitary gland had a defect that caused it to stop secreting hormones, what effect would this have on the reproductive system of a male?

21. Applying Knowledge Does withdrawal of the penis just before ejaculation reliably prevent pregnancy? Why or why not?

22. Applying Knowledge What does it mean if a female has HCG in her blood and urine?

DEVELOPING LIFE/WORK SKILLS

23. Making Decisions Why is it important to protect the ovaries of a young girl from things that could harm egg cells, such as certain chemicals and radiation?

24. Making Decisions Why is it dangerous to have a sexual relationship with a person who recently has had sexual relations with several other partners?

25. Applying Technology Ultrasonography is a method that allows doctors to "see" the developing fetus inside the uterus. Research ultrasonography, and write a short paper on how it is used to monitor pregnancies.

26. Interpreting and Communicating Research child labor laws in the United States, and find out when these laws were first passed and the ages to which they apply. Write a paragraph on the effects of keeping children out of the work place.

INTEGRATING CONCEPTS

27. Concept Mapping Copy the unfinished concept map below onto a sheet of paper. Complete the map by writing the correct term or phrase in the lettered boxes.

28. Connection to Social Studies Research population growth in modern times. What country has the greatest birth rate (for its size)? What country has the smallest? Do countries with small birth rates attempt to control population through public policy?

29. Connection to Health Girls and women who do not have enough body fat do not have menstrual periods. Research eating disorders and write a paragraph about their effects on menstrual periods and fertility.

30. Connection to Health HIV destroys the immune system, which protects us from invading disease-causing agents. Why would very good hygiene be essential in caring for someone who has AIDS?

internet connect

SCiLINKS NSTA

TOPIC: Population growth
GO TO: www.scilinks.org
KEYWORD: HJ1707

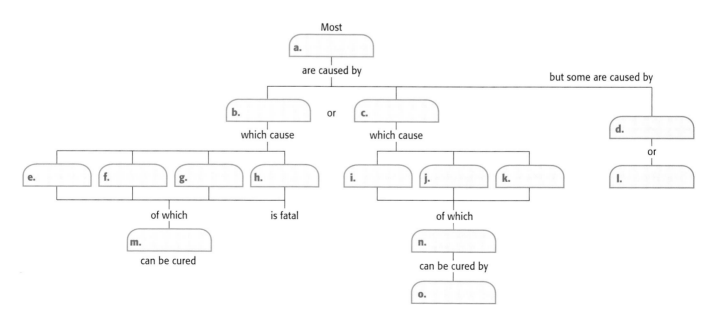

Skill Builder Lab

Introduction

How can you explain the events of the menstrual cycle in terms of changes in hormone levels?

Objectives

▶ **Graph** the concentrations of four hormones throughout the menstrual cycle.

▶ **Correlate** events during the menstrual cycle with changes in hormone levels.

Materials

colored pencils
graph paper

Investigating the Menstrual Cycle

▶ Preparing for Your Experiment

1. The human menstrual cycle lasts about 28 days. During the first half of the cycle, egg cells begin to mature in the ovaries, and the uterine lining begins to thicken.

2. At the midpoint of the cycle, an egg is released into a fallopian tube. This event is called ovulation.

3. During the second half of the cycle, the lining of the uterus continues to thicken in preparation for receiving the fertilized egg. If the egg is not fertilized, the thickened uterine lining is shed through menstruation.

4. The menstrual cycle is regulated by several hormones. Follicle-stimulating hormone (FSH) and luteinizing hormone (LH) are produced by the pituitary gland. Estrogen and progesterone are produced by the ovaries.

5. Using the data in the table below and at right, you will prepare three graphs for each day of the menstrual cycle, and draw a best-fit line through the data points.

Day in cycle	Hormone Concentrations			
	FSH (ng/mL)	LH (ng/mL)	Estrogen (pg/mL)	Progesterone (ng/mL)
1	260	80	100	0.6
2	280	110	100	0.6
3	270	115	100	0.6
4	260	110	110	0.6
5	240	105	130	0.6
6	220	100	150	0.6
7	210	95	175	0.6
8	200	90	200	0.6
9	190	85	250	0.6
10	180	80	300	0.6
11	170	100	400	0.6
12	200	160	700	0.6
13	420	400	680	1.0
14	400	380	400	1.3

▶ Graphing Hormone Levels

6. On the first graph, plot the concentrations of FSH and LH. Use a different color marker for each hormone.
7. On the second graph, plot the concentration of estrogen.
8. On the third graph, plot the concentration of progesterone.

▶ Analyzing Your Results

1. On what day does each hormone reach its maximum concentration?
2. Which hormones rise in concentration just before the midpoint of the cycle?
3. Which hormones rise in concentration gradually during the second half of the cycle?

▶ Defending Your Conclusion

4. Ovulation is triggered by high concentrations of LH. How does the rise in LH concentration during the cycle correlate with the timing of ovulation?
5. High levels of estrogen and progesterone are needed to maintain the thickened uterine lining. How do their levels correlate with the timing of menstruation?
6. Progesterone limits the release of FSH and LH by the pituitary gland. How does the rise in progesterone concentration correlate with changes in the levels of FSH and LH?

Day in cycle	Hormone Concentrations			
	FSH (ng/mL)	LH (ng/mL)	Estrogen (pg/mL)	Progesterone (ng/mL)
15	290	200	120	2.0
16	200	120	180	3.0
17	190	250	110	4.0
18	180	300	100	5.5
19	160	370	80	6.4
20	140	395	60	7.0
21	130	400	50	7.5
22	120	395	40	7.4
23	115	350	30	6.5
24	110	280	30	5.0
25	120	210	30	3.0
26	140	190	40	2.0
27	180	100	60	1.0
28	200	80	80	0.5

1 ng = 1 nanogram = 10^{-9} g
1 pg = 1 picogram = 10^{-12} g

Exploring Earth and Space

CHAPTER 18
The Universe 574

CHAPTER 19
Planet Earth 606

Career Link
    Geerat Vermeij, Paleontologist 644

CHAPTER 20
The Atmosphere 646

*Viewpoints: Should Laws Require
    Zero Emission Cars?* 676

CHAPTER 21
Using Natural Resources 678

The Universe

Chapter Preview

18.1 The Universe and Galaxies
What Is the Universe?
Galaxies
The Origin of the Universe

18.2 Stars and the Sun
What Are Stars?
The Life and Death of Stars

18.3 The Solar System
The View from Earth
The Inner Planets
The Outer Planets
Formation of the Solar System
The Moon

Focus ACTIVITY

A shooting star is really a meteor burning up in Earth's atmosphere. If a meteor survives its trip through the atmosphere, it may produce a crater when it strikes the ground.

Background Have you ever seen a shooting star? You may already know that a shooting star is not a star at all; shooting stars are meteors, tiny pieces of rock or ice that burn brightly as they enter the Earth's atmosphere. But you may not realize that more than 10 000 meteors enter the Earth's atmosphere every night.

When Earth's orbit carries the planet through a cloud of debris, observers on the ground can see a spectacular show of lights in the sky: a meteor shower.

Most meteors burn away completely in the atmosphere, forming tiny particles of dust and ash that float down to the ground. According to estimates, this matter from meteors adds an average of almost half a million kilograms of mass to Earth every day.

A few meteors survive their trip through the atmosphere and reach Earth's surface intact, producing an impact crater like Meteor Crater, in Arizona. A meteor that hits Earth is called a meteorite. Scientists study meteorites to learn more about our solar system.

Early in the history of the solar system, the moon, Earth, and all the planets were constantly bombarded with meteors. Geological activity has erased most of the impact craters on Earth. But the moon, which has less geologic activity than Earth does, is still pocked with thousands of craters.

Activity 1 Go outside on a clear evening at dusk, sit down, and look up at the sky. Spend 20 minutes counting stars as they become visible. What do you think about the first stars you see? Are they the biggest? the brightest? the closest? How many did you count in the 20 minutes? Do you see any lights in the sky that might not be stars? If so, what might they be?

Activity 2 Research the conditions on at least three other planets in the solar system. Try to find data, including surface temperature, thickness and composition of atmosphere, and the amount of water on the planet. For two of the planets, give at least two reasons why they probably could not support life as we know it.

internet**connect**

SC*i*INKS
NSTA

TOPIC: Meteors
GO TO: www.scilinks.org
KEYWORD: HK1161

The Universe and Galaxies

KEY TERMS

universe

star

galaxy

light-year

interstellar matter

cluster

red shift

big bang theory

OBJECTIVES

▶ Describe the basic structure of the universe.

▶ Introduce the light-year as a unit of distance.

▶ Describe the structure of the Milky Way galaxy, and include the location of our solar system.

▶ List the three main types of galaxies.

▶ State the main features of the big bang theory and evidence supporting the expansion of the universe.

▶ **universe** the sum of all matter and energy that exists, that ever has existed, and that ever will exist

Just imagine the following: colliding galaxies that rip stars from each other; a dead star so dense that 1 teaspoon of its matter would contain as much material as all the cars and trucks in the United States; a volcano on Mars that is nearly three times taller than Mount Everest and that has a base larger than Louisiana. All of these are part of the universe.

What Is the Universe?

By the term **universe,** scientists mean everything physical that exists in space and time. The universe consists of all matter and energy that exists, now, in the past, and in the future. There is only one universe.

Figure 18-1
The sizes of astronomical objects are so great that new measuring units, such as the light-year, are needed to describe them.

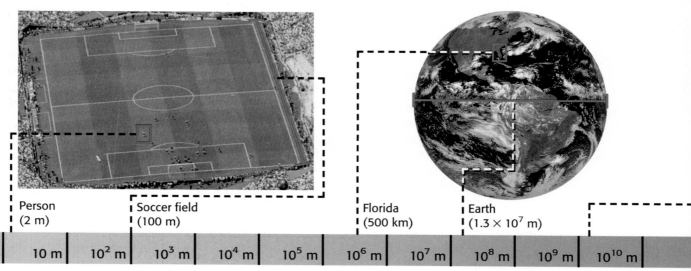

Person (2 m)	Soccer field (100 m)	Florida (500 km)	Earth (1.3×10^7 m)

1 m	10 m	10^2 m	10^3 m	10^4 m	10^5 m	10^6 m	10^7 m	10^8 m	10^9 m	10^{10} m

You are part of the universe, as is Earth and everything on it. Most of the objects beyond Earth that we can see with the unaided eye are **stars,** huge balls of hot gas that emit light. Stars are grouped together in **galaxies,** collections of millions, billions, or even trillions of stars bound together by gravity.

Astronomical distances are measured in light-years

To measure distances in the universe beyond Earth, scientists use a unit of distance called a **light-year** (ly). A light-year is the distance light travels in one year. Because light travels at a speed of 3.0×10^8 m/s in empty space, a light-year is a very large distance: 9.5×10^{15} m. This distance is so large that driving it in a car moving at highway speed would take over 10 million years.

Figure 18-1 shows objects and systems found in the universe, spanning a wide range of sizes. Beyond the solar system, the light-year is a more convenient unit of length or distance than the meter. Remember, while a *year* is a unit of time, a *light-year* is a unit of distance; it measures how far light travels in a year.

We see the universe now as it was in the past

When you go outside on a sunny day, the light that hits your skin left the sun more than 8 minutes earlier. It takes time for light to travel in space. The farther away an object is, the older the light is that we get from that object.

The three stars nearest to Earth besides the sun are 4.3 light-years away, in the star system Alpha Centauri. When you see their light from Earth, you see light that left the stars 4.3 years ago. A typical cluster of galaxies may be 10 million light-years across. How long would it take for light to travel from one side of such a cluster to the other side?

▶ **star** a huge ball of hot gas that emits light

▶ **galaxy** a collection of millions or billions of stars bound together by gravity

▶ **light-year** a unit of distance equal to the distance light travels in one year; 1 ly = 9.5×10^{15} m

Did You Know ?

Distances within the solar system are sometimes measured in *astronomical units* (AU). This is the average distance between Earth and the sun. 1 AU = 1.5×10^{11} m

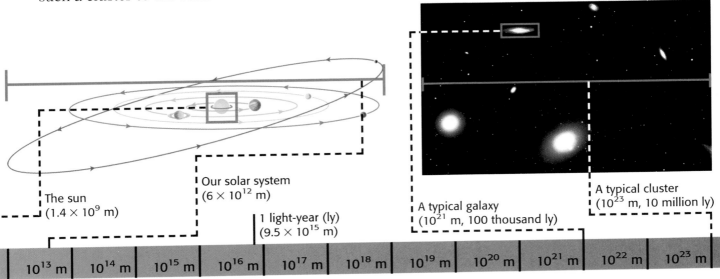

The sun
(1.4×10^9 m)

Our solar system
(6×10^{12} m)

1 light-year (ly)
(9.5×10^{15} m)

A typical galaxy
(10^{21} m, 100 thousand ly)

A typical cluster
(10^{23} m, 10 million ly)

10^{13} m | 10^{14} m | 10^{15} m | 10^{16} m | 10^{17} m | 10^{18} m | 10^{19} m | 10^{20} m | 10^{21} m | 10^{22} m | 10^{23} m

Figure 18-2
The Andromeda galaxy is 2.2 million light-years from Earth. It is one of the closest galaxies to the Milky Way galaxy, and it can be seen with the unaided eye.

interstellar matter the gas and dust located between the stars in a galaxy

Galaxies

While the nearest stars are 4.3 light-years away, the nearest full-sized galaxy to our own galaxy is more than 2 million light-years away. **Figure 18-2** shows this galaxy, the Andromeda galaxy. Many galaxies contain billions or even trillions of stars, but because they are so far away, galaxies usually look like small smudges in the sky, even through a telescope.

The deeper scientists look into the universe, the more galaxies they find. Astronomers now estimate that the universe contains 100 billion galaxies. To get a sense of how big this number is, consider this: If you counted 1000 new galaxies every night, it would take 275 000 years to count all of them.

We live in the Milky Way galaxy

If you live away from bright outdoor lights, you may be able to see a faint, narrow band of light and dark patches across the sky. **Figure 18-3** shows this band, called the Milky Way. The Milky Way consists of stars, gases, and dust in our own galaxy, the Milky Way galaxy. The Milky Way galaxy contains clouds of gas and dust between the stars, called **interstellar matter.** These clouds provide materials for new stars to form.

Almost every star you can see in the night sky is also part of the Milky Way galaxy. That is because our solar system is inside the Milky Way galaxy. Because we are inside the galaxy, we cannot see all of it at once. But scientists can use astronomical data to piece together a picture of the Milky Way galaxy like the one in **Figure 18-4** on the next page.

Figure 18-3
When we see the band of light called the Milky Way, we are looking along the plane of the Milky Way galaxy.

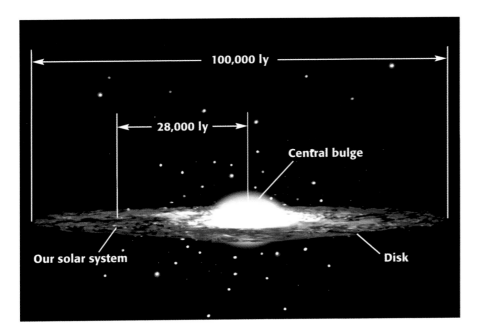

100,000 ly

28,000 ly

Central bulge

Our solar system

Disk

Figure 18-4
A picture of what the Milky Way galaxy might look like from the outside can be pieced together from astronomical data.

Our galaxy is a huge spiraling disk of stars and interstellar matter. The Milky Way galaxy has a huge bulge in its center. Earth, the sun, and the rest of the solar system are about midway between the galaxy's edge and its center.

internet**connect**

SC*i*LINKS
NSTA

TOPIC: Milky Way galaxy
GO TO: www.scilinks.org
KEYWORD: HK1162

There are three types of galaxies

Galaxies are classified into three types, based on their shape. The basic types are spiral, elliptical, and irregular.

Spiral galaxies, like the one shown in **Figure 18-5,** usually have spiral arms that contain gas and dust that provide materials for new stars to form. Young stars tend to be bluer in color than old stars, so spiral galaxies often have a bluish tint, especially in the spiral arms.

While spiral galaxies are disk-shaped, elliptical galaxies are spherical or egg-shaped. Elliptical galaxies are generally older than spiral galaxies. They contain mostly older stars, have no spiral arms, and contain relatively little gas and dust. Older stars are generally redder in color than young stars, so elliptical galaxies often have a reddish color.

Elliptical galaxies are found in a wide range of sizes and masses. Giant elliptical galaxies contain trillions of stars and can be as large as 200 000 light-years in diameter. Dwarf elliptical galaxies contain only a few million stars and are much smaller than spiral galaxies or giant ellipticals.

Irregular galaxies, as the name suggests, do not have a well-defined shape or structure. Some irregular galaxies contain relatively little gas and dust, while others are like clouds of intergalactic matter that have never given birth to stars.

Figure 18-5
Seen from above, the Milky Way galaxy might look similar to this spiral galaxy.

Figure 18-6
A cluster like the one shown here may contain thousands of galaxies held together by gravity.

▶ **cluster** a group of galaxies bound by gravity

Gravity holds galaxies together in clusters

Without gravity, the universe might just be a thin veil of gas spread out through space. With gravity, clouds of gas and dust draw together to form stars. Because of gravity, stars, gas, and dust collect into larger units, the galaxies.

Galaxies are not spread out evenly through the universe. They are grouped together in **clusters,** like the one shown in **Figure 18-6.** The members of a cluster of galaxies are bound together by gravity.

The Milky Way galaxy and the Andromeda galaxy are two of the largest members of a cluster of more than 30 galaxies called the Local Group. New members of the Local Group are being discovered as larger telescopes and better instruments are available to astronomers.

Clusters of galaxies can form even larger groups called *superclusters*. A typical supercluster contains thousands of galaxies containing trillions of stars in individual clusters. Superclusters can be as large as 100 million light-years across. They are the largest structures in the universe.

Figure 18-7

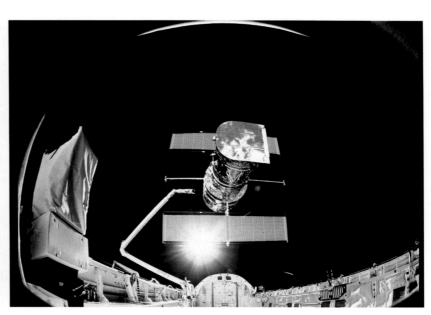

🅐 Edwin Hubble used the telescopes at Mount Wilson Observatory, in California, to explore galaxies beyond the Milky Way galaxy.

🅑 The Hubble Space Telescope, named in Hubble's honor, now probes the depths of the universe from its orbit high above the Earth's atmosphere.

The Origin of the Universe

How did the universe come to be? This is an age-old question. Scientists today study stars and galaxies for clues to the origin of the universe.

The universe is expanding

The astronomer Edwin Hubble, shown in **Figure 18-7,** spent many years studying light from distant galaxies. In 1929, he announced his conclusion that the universe is expanding.

The atoms contained in stars emit light in a characteristic pattern of spectral lines. When Hubble examined the light from stars in other galaxies, he found this pattern of lines was shifted toward the red end of the spectrum. This is called a red shift, and it can be interpreted using the Doppler effect.

When an object is moving away from us, any waves coming from that object get stretched out. The faster a light source moves away, the more that light is stretched to longer wavelengths, or shifted toward the red end of the spectrum. **Figure 18-8** illustrates a red shift in spectral lines from a galaxy. For more on spectral lines, see Section 18.2.

The red shift in light from galaxies shows that every galaxy is moving away from Earth. Hubble also found another surprising result: galaxies farther away have greater red shifts. Since the time that those older galaxies emitted the light we see now, space has stretched out, increasing the wavelength of the light. In effect, all the galaxies are moving away from each other. Or in other words, the universe is expanding.

Expansion now implies that the universe was once smaller

Imagine time running backward, like a rewinding movie. If every galaxy normally moves away from every other galaxy, then as time goes backward, the galaxies appear to move closer together. This suggests that long ago the whole universe was contained in an extremely small volume.

internet **connect**

SCI LINKS.
NSTA

TOPIC: Origin of the universe
GO TO: www.scilinks.org
KEYWORD: HK1163

▶ **red shift** a shift toward the red end of the spectrum in the observed spectral lines of stars or galaxies

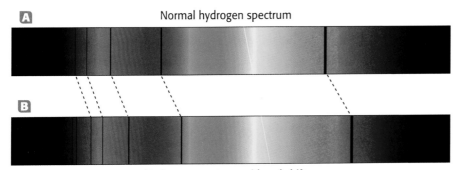

A Normal hydrogen spectrum

B

Hydrogen spectrum with red shift

Figure 18-8
(A) The spectral lines of hydrogen gas can be seen and measured in a laboratory. (B) When this pattern appears in starlight, we know the star contains hydrogen. In this case, the lines are shifted toward the red because the star is in a galaxy that is moving away from us.

Figure 18-9
The colors in this skywide map of cosmic background radiation represent slight differences in temperature above and below 2.7 K.

If time starts forward again from that point, all of the matter in the universe appears to expand rapidly outward. This would look like the result of a gigantic explosion. Scientists call this hypothetical explosion the "big bang."

Did the universe start with a big bang?

Although scientists have proposed several different theories to explain the expansion of the universe, the most complete and most widely accepted is the **big bang theory**. The big bang theory proposes that the universe began with a gigantic explosion 10 billion to 20 billion years ago. *In this book, we will assume that the universe is 15 billion years old.*

According to this theory, nothing existed before the big bang. There was no time and no space. But out of this nothingness came the vast system of space, time, matter, and energy that we now see as the universe. The explosion released all of the matter and energy that still exists in the universe today.

Cosmic background radiation supports the big bang theory

In 1965, Arno Penzias and Robert Wilson, of Bell Laboratories in New Jersey, discovered new evidence in support of the big bang theory. While making adjustments to a new radio antenna they had built, they detected a steady but very dim signal from the sky in the form of radiation at microwave wavelengths. This radiation, called the *cosmic background radiation,* had already been predicted by the big bang theory.

Imagine the changes in color as the burner on an electric stove cools off. At first the hot burner glows yellow or white. As it cools, it becomes dimmer and glows orange, then red. At all times, the burner produces light across a wide range of the electromagnetic spectrum. The color you see corresponds to the wavelength at which it radiates the most. If a burner were in outer space, it could keep cooling until the primary radiation reached very long, invisible wavelengths, such as microwaves.

Many scientists believe that the microwaves Penzias and Wilson discovered are dim remains of the energetic radiation produced during the big bang. Using computerized maps of cosmic background radiation, such as the one in **Figure 18-9,** scientists have found that the universe has an overall temperature of about 2.7 kelvins (K).

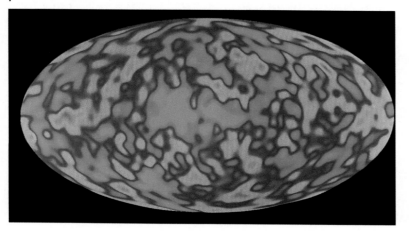

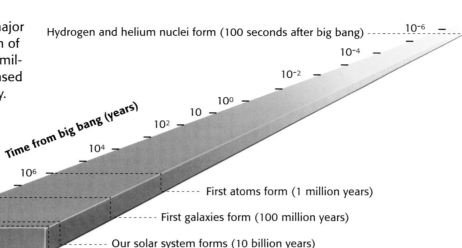

Figure 18-10
This timeline shows major events in the evolution of the universe. The first million (10^6) years are based on the big bang theory.

BIG BANG

Hydrogen and helium nuclei form (100 seconds after big bang) ------ 10^{-6}

10^{-4}

10^{-2}

Time from big bang (years)

10^0

10

10^2

10^4

10^6 ------ First atoms form (1 million years)

10^8 ------ First galaxies form (100 million years)

10^{10} ------ Our solar system forms (10 billion years)

Present (15 billion years)

From the big bang to atoms and beyond

According to the big bang theory, expansion cooled the universe enough for matter such as protons, neutrons, and electrons to form just a few seconds after the big bang. But the temperature was still too high for entire atoms to form and remain stable.

After about a million years, the universe expanded and cooled enough for regular hydrogen atoms to form. Since that time hydrogen has been the most abundant element in the universe. It serves as a fuel for stars and as a building block for stars to make other elements. Once the universe reached this point, the stage was set for the formation of stars, galaxies, and planets.

Figure 18-10 shows several key points in the evolution of the universe, following the model of the big bang theory. Note that the timeline uses a logarithmic scale, so that the last 5 billion years are squeezed into a small area at the end of the line.

The future of the universe is uncertain

The universe is still expanding, but it may not do so forever. The combined gravity of all the mass in the universe is also pulling the universe inward, in the direction opposite the expansion. The competition between these two forces leaves three possible outcomes for the universe:

1. The universe will keep expanding forever.

2. The expansion of the universe will gradually slow down, and the universe will approach a limit in size.

3. The universe will stop expanding and start to fall back in on itself.

Did You Know ?

Scientists estimate that some quasars, the most distant objects we can detect, may be as far as 15 billion light-years away. If this is true, the universe must be at least 15 billion years old in order for light from those quasars to have reached Earth.

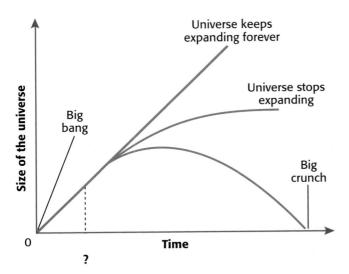

Figure 18-11
This graph shows three possible fates of the universe.

The fate of the universe depends on mass

Figure 18-11 shows three possible fates of the universe. Which one will be the outcome depends in large part on the amount of matter in the universe. If there is not enough mass in the universe, the gravitational force will be too weak to stop the expansion, so the universe will keep expanding forever. If there is just the right amount of mass, the expansion will continually slow down but never stop completely.

If there is more mass than this, gravity will eventually win out over the expansion, and the universe will start to contract. Eventually, a contracting universe might collapse back to a point in a "big crunch." This could be the end of the universe, or it could produce another big bang, starting the cycle all over again.

SECTION 18.1 REVIEW

SUMMARY

▶ The universe consists of all matter and energy that exists, that ever has existed, and that ever will exist.

▶ A light-year is the distance that light travels in one year, 9.5×10^{15} m.

▶ Galaxies consist of billions of stars held together by their own gravity. Galaxies are grouped together in clusters and superclusters.

▶ Earth and the sun are located in a spiral arm of the Milky Way galaxy. Our galaxy is about 100 000 light-years in diameter.

▶ The big bang theory describes the origin of the universe as an enormous explosion that occurred 10 to 20 billion years ago.

CHECK YOUR UNDERSTANDING

1. **Arrange** the following astronomical structures from the smallest to the largest: galaxies, planets, superclusters, stars, clusters.
2. **Determine** the distance in meters to the Alpha Centauri star system, which is 4.3 light-years from Earth. The speed of light is 3.0×10^8 m/s.
3. **Compare** the size of the Milky Way galaxy with the size of a cluster of galaxies. How many times bigger is a typical cluster?
4. **List** the three main types of galaxies.
5. **Draw** sketches of the Milky Way galaxy viewed from the side and from overhead. Label the following on each: central bulge, disk, solar system.
6. **Explain** why the Milky Way appears as a narrow band of light in the night sky.
7. **Describe** the evidence that the universe is expanding.
8. **Critical Thinking** If we observe that all the galaxies are expanding away from the Milky Way galaxy, does that mean that we are at the center of the universe? Explain. (**Hint:** Imagine an inflating balloon with dots on the surface, and picture our galaxy as one of the dots.)
9. **Creative Thinking** How would other galaxies appear to move relative to Earth if the universe were shrinking?

Stars and the Sun

OBJECTIVES

▶ Describe the basic structure and properties of stars.

▶ Explain how the composition and surface temperatures of stars are measured.

▶ Recognize that all normal stars are powered by fusion reactions that form elements.

▶ Discuss the evolution of stars.

▶ **KEY TERMS**
constellation
red giant
white dwarf
supergiant
supernova
neutron star
black hole

O n any clear night you can gaze upward and see the stars. About 6000 stars are bright enough to be seen from Earth with the unaided eye. The same stars have been observed by people on Earth for many centuries.

What Are Stars?

The ancient Greeks thought that all the stars were at an equal distance from Earth, like lights attached to a giant spherical roof. They grouped the stars together in patterns called **constellations.** The patterns often outlined characters from Greek mythology. For example, the constellation Orion, shown in **Figure 18-12,** depicts Orion the Hunter. The red star Betelgeuse represents Orion's left shoulder; the blue star Rigel represents his right foot.

▶ **constellation** a group of stars appearing in a pattern as seen from Earth

We still divide the sky into constellations, but we now know that the stars in a constellation are not necessarily grouped together in space. The patterns seen from Earth are merely products of the locations of stars along our line of sight. Although the stars appear close together in the sky, they are actually quite far apart. In Orion, Rigel is almost three times farther away from Earth than is Betelgeuse.

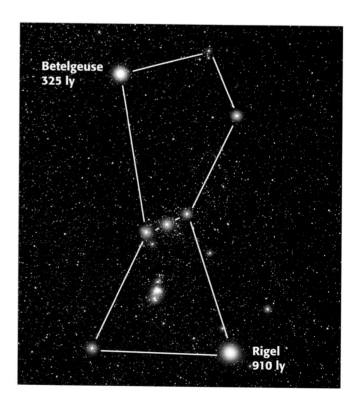

Figure 18-12
Although the stars in Orion appear close together in the sky, they are actually quite far away from each other.

Betelgeuse
325 ly

Rigel
910 ly

Figure 18-13
People on Earth are very familiar with one star in particular—the sun.

Figure 18-14
Many telescopes detect light that is beyond the visible spectrum. Data from such telescopes must be processed and displayed by a computer.

The sun is a typical star

Of all the stars, astronomers know the most about one in particular: our own sun. The sun, shown in **Figure 18-13,** is an average star, not particularly hot or cool and of average size.

Although the sun is not very big for a star, it is much bigger than Earth. The sun's diameter is about 1.4 million kilometers, or about 110 times Earth's diameter. If Earth were the size of a dime, the sun would be about 2 m in diameter and 200 m away from the dime-sized Earth.

The mass of the sun is about 2×10^{30} kg, or more than 300 000 times the mass of Earth. Although the core of the sun is extremely dense, its overall density—its total mass divided by its total volume—is about 1.4 g/cm^3, only slightly denser than water.

Why do some stars appear brighter than others?

The brightness of a star depends on the star's temperature, size, and distance from Earth. Rigel is the brightest star in the constellation Orion. Although Rigel is much farther away than Betelgeuse, it appears brighter because it is about four times hotter than Betelgeuse. Betelgeuse is not very hot for a star, but it appears brighter than the other stars in Orion because it is very large, with a diameter hundreds of times larger than the sun's.

The brightest star in the night sky is Sirius, in the constellation Canis Major. The main reason that it appears so bright is that it is relatively close to Earth, only about 9 light-years away. The sun is just an average star, but it is so close to Earth that its light dominates the entire sky during the day.

We learn about stars by studying light

Starlight is our only source for information about the nature of stars. But there is much more to starlight than meets the eye. When we look with our unaided eyes or through a telescope, we can detect only light in the visible part of the spectrum.

Stars also produce electromagnetic radiation at other wavelengths, ranging from high-energy X rays to low-energy radio waves. Astronomers today use telescopes with instruments that can detect radiation from all these different wavelengths. The data collected with such telescopes can be processed and displayed on computer screens, as shown in **Figure 18-14.**

The color of a star is related to its temperature

When light from a glowing hot object passes through a prism, it displays a continuous spectrum of light's many different colors. This spectrum changes with temperature in a definite way: hotter objects glow with light that is more intense at shorter wavelengths (toward the blue end of the spectrum), while cooler objects have greater intensity at longer wavelengths (toward the red end).

Although the light from a glowing object contains many colors, the color that we see when we look directly at any hot object, including a star, is determined by the wavelength at which the object emits the most light.

Figure 18-15 is a graph that shows the intensity, or brightness, of light at different wavelengths for three different stars. The sun appears yellow because the peak wavelength of the sun corresponds to the color yellow. This color also corresponds to a temperature of 6000 K.

Spectral lines reveal the composition of stars

How do we know what stars are made of? The spectra of most stars have dark lines where light is missing at certain wavelengths. The light at these wavelengths has been absorbed by gases in the outer layers of the stars.

Because each element produces a unique pattern of spectral lines, astronomers can match the dark lines in starlight to lines absorbed by gases of elements found on Earth and tested in the lab. **Figure 18-16** shows how the spectral lines of hydrogen and helium match lines found in the spectrum of sunlight.

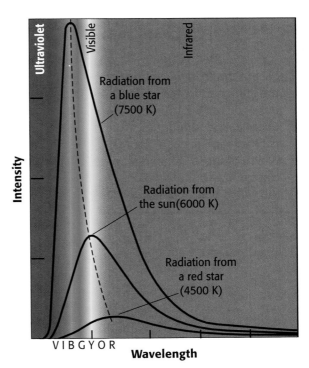

Figure 18-15
This graph shows the intensity of light at different wavelengths for the sun and two other stars.

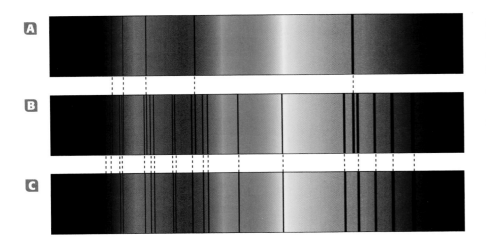

Figure 18-16
When light is passed through hydrogen gas (A) or helium gas (C), then through a prism, dark lines appear in the spectrum. Those lines match lines observed in the sun's spectrum (B).

Quick ACTIVITY

Using a Star Chart
Locate the following stars on the star chart in Appendix B: Betelgeuse, Rigel, Sirius, Capella, and Aldebaran. What constellation is each star in? Which of these stars appears closest in the sky to Polaris, the North Star?

Astronomers have analyzed more than 20 000 lines in the sun's spectrum to find the composition and chemical abundance of the sun's atmosphere. Of all the atoms in the sun, 90 percent are hydrogen, 9.9 percent are helium, and 0.1 percent are other elements. Most other stars have similar compositions.

Stars are driven by nuclear fusion reactions

Stars such as the sun are basically huge, hot balls of hydrogen and helium gas that emit light. They are held together by the enormous gravitational forces caused by their own mass. Inside the core of a star, these forces create a harsh environment. The pressure is more than a billion times the atmospheric pressure on Earth. The temperature is hotter than 15 million kelvins, and the density is over 150 times greater than that of water.

In these extreme conditions, nuclear fusion reactions combine the nuclei of hydrogen atoms into helium with a release of energy. This energy flows outward, balancing the inward pull of gravity. However, the energy released in fusion reactions inside a star does not directly produce the light we see.

Energy moves slowly through the layers of a star

Figure 18-17 shows the major parts of the sun. Other stars have similar structures, although the temperatures may be different. The energy from fusion moves through the layers of a star by a combination of radiation and convection, two of the primary ways that energy is transferred.

These processes are not very fast. In fact, it may take millions of years for the energy generated by a nuclear reaction to work its way through a star. When the energy finally reaches the surface, it is released into space as radiation, or starlight.

Once light leaves the surface of a star, it radiates across space at the speed of light in a vacuum, 3×10^8 m/s. At this speed, it takes light from the sun about 8 minutes to reach Earth. For more on radiation and convection, review Section 9.2.

Figure 18-17
Energy slowly works its way through the layers of the sun by radiation and convection.

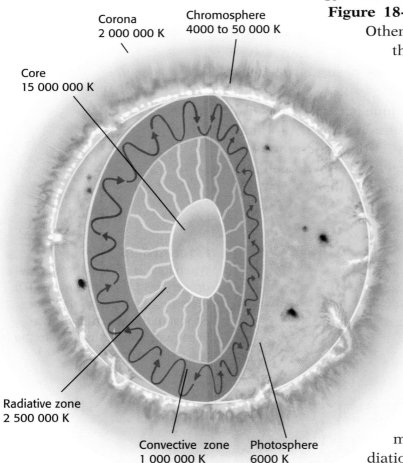

Corona
2 000 000 K

Chromosphere
4000 to 50 000 K

Core
15 000 000 K

Radiative zone
2 500 000 K

Convective zone
1 000 000 K

Photosphere
6000 K

The Life and Death of Stars

Figure 18-18 shows stars being formed in a cloud of gas and dust called a *nebula*. Like living creatures, stars are born, go through different stages of development, and eventually die. Stars appear different from one another in part because they are at different stages in their life cycles. Nearly 90 percent of all stars, including the sun, are in midlife, converting hydrogen into helium in their interiors.

Some stars, such as Rigel, are younger than the sun, while others, such as Betelgeuse, are farther along in their life cycles. Some objects in the universe are remnants of very old stars long since dead. But how do stars get started? And how do they keep on shining for billions of years?

Figure 18-18
New stars are constantly being born in clouds of gas and dust such as these columns in the Eagle nebula. This image was taken by the Hubble Space Telescope.

The sun formed from a cloud of gas and dust

About 5 billion years ago, in an arm of the Milky Way galaxy, a thin, invisible cloud of gas and dust collapsed inward, pulled by the force of its own gravity. As the cloud fell together, it began to spin, and the smaller the cloud got, the faster it spun.

About 30 million years after the cloud started to collapse, the center of the cloud reached a temperature of 15 million kelvins. Under these extreme conditions, electrons were stripped from hydrogen atoms, leaving positively charged protons.

Ordinarily, positively charged protons repel each other. But at very high temperatures, protons move very rapidly and may get as close to each other as 10^{-15} m. At such a small distance, the strong nuclear force can overpower the electrical repulsion. Through the process of nuclear fusion, the protons may combine to form helium with a release of energy.

Once nuclear fusion started in the core of the cloud, the star we call the sun was born. For more on nuclear fusion, see Chapter 6. The formation of the rest of the solar system will be covered in more detail in Section 18.3.

The sun now has a balance of inward and outward forces

The fusion reactions in the core of the sun produce an outward force that balances the inward force due to gravity. With those two forces evenly balanced, the sun has maintained an equilibrium for 5 billion years.

The sun is now in the prime of its life, fusing hydrogen into helium. Scientists estimate that the sun has enough fuel to continue nuclear fusion in its core for another 5 billion years.

internetconnect

SC*LINKS*
NSTA

TOPIC: Stars
GO TO: www.scilinks.org
KEYWORD: HK1164

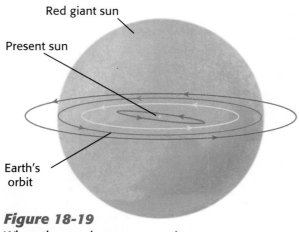

Red giant sun

Present sun

Earth's orbit

Figure 18-19
When the sun becomes a red giant, it will expand out past Earth's orbit.

▶ **red giant** a large, reddish star late in its life cycle that fuses helium into carbon or oxygen

▶ **white dwarf** a small, very dense star that remains after fusion in a red giant stops

▶ **supergiant** an extremely large star that creates elements as heavy as iron

▶ **supernova** a powerful explosion that occurs when a massive star dies

The sun will become a red giant before it dies

When fusion of hydrogen slows, the core of the sun will start to contract, and the temperature in the core will rise. The outer layers of the sun will expand out past Earth's orbit, and the sun will become a **red giant,** as shown in **Figure 18-19.** While the outer layers of the red giant sun will remain relatively cool, the core will reach temperatures high enough to spark the fusion of helium into carbon and oxygen.

After about 100 million years, the core of the red giant sun will become entirely carbon and oxygen, the core will contract further, and the outer layers will expand again. At this point, though, the temperature will not rise high enough to start the fusion of carbon or oxygen into heavier elements.

The outer layers of the sun will continue to expand out from the core, forming a *planetary nebula,* a glowing cloud or ring of gas. The remaining core of the sun will become a **white dwarf,** a dim ember about the size of Earth but extremely dense. The dwarf sun will slowly cool, producing no more energy.

Any star that ends up, after its initial stage of helium fusion, with a mass less than or equal to 1.4 times the mass of the sun will have a life cycle like the sun's and will die as a white dwarf. Most of the stars in the Milky Way Galaxy will end their lives as white dwarfs. But larger stars burn hotter and brighter, and have more dramatic deaths.

Supergiant stars explode in supernovas

Stars more than 1.4 times the mass of the sun do not become red giants. They become **supergiants.** Because of their greater mass, supergiant stars do not stop with carbon fusion. These stars produce successively heavier elements until their cores become iron.

The formation of an iron core signals the beginning of a supergiant star's violent death. This is because fusing iron atoms together to make heavier elements requires energy rather than producing energy. So when the entire core finally becomes iron, fusion stops.

When the fusion stops, there is no longer any outward pressure to balance the gravitational force. The star's core collapses and then rebounds with a shock wave that violently blows the star's outer layers away from the core. The huge, bright explosion that results is called a **supernova.** A supernova is the only natural event in the universe energetic enough to spark fusion that can create elements heavier than iron. The remains of one such explosion can still be seen in the Crab nebula, shown in **Figure 18-20.**

After a supernova, either a neutron star or a black hole forms

If the core that remains after a supernova has a mass of 1.4 to about 3 times that of the Sun, it can become a neutron star. Neutron stars are only a few kilometers in diameter—about the size of a small city—but they are very massive. The density of a neutron star is equal to that of matter in the nuclei of atoms, about 10^{17} kg/m^3. A thimbleful of the matter in a neutron star would weigh more than 100 million tons on Earth. Neutron stars can sometimes be detected as *pulsars*, rapidly rotating sources of radio waves.

If the core remaining after a supernova has a mass greater than three times that of the sun, it will collapse to form an even stranger object—a black hole. A black hole consists of matter so massive and compressed that nothing, not even light, can escape from its gravity.

Because no light comes out of a black hole, a black hole cannot be seen directly. However, black holes have a powerful gravitational influence on objects around them, so they may be detected indirectly.

Figure 18-20
The Crab nebula is the remains of a supernova seen by Chinese observers in the year 1054.

▷ **neutron star** a dead star with the density of atomic nuclei

▷ **black hole** an object so massive and dense that not even light can escape its gravity

---

SECTION 18.2 REVIEW

SUMMARY

▶ Stars are huge balls of gas that generate light through fusion in their cores.

▶ Starlight reveals the temperature and composition of stars.

▶ The sun is a typical star. It formed in a cloud of gas and dust; it will become a red giant and then die as a white dwarf.

▶ Supergiant stars die in supernovas; the cores left behind become neutron stars or black holes.

CHECK YOUR UNDERSTANDING

1. **Name** three different kinds of stars.
2. **Describe** how a star generates light.
3. **Explain** why cooler stars are red and hotter stars are blue.
4. **Describe** the formation of the sun.
5. **Describe** the final stages in the lives of the following stars:
   a. the sun
   b. a star 20 times the mass of the sun
6. **Critical Thinking** Which of the following elements are likely to be formed in the sun at some time in its life?
   a. helium   c. iron
   b. carbon   d. uranium
7. **Critical Thinking** You and a friend are looking at the stars. Your friend says, "Stars must always be shrinking because gravity is constantly pulling their particles together." Explain what is wrong with your friend's reasoning.

The Solar System

OBJECTIVES

▶ Identify the planets of the solar system and their features.
▶ Describe the formation of the solar system.
▶ Explain eclipses and the phases of the moon.

Because the Earth spins on its axis, the stars overhead appear to move in regular, circular paths across the night sky. However, a few lights in the sky deviate from these paths. The ancient Greeks named these strange lights "planets," which in their language meant "wanderers."

The View from Earth

▶ **planet** any of the nine primary bodies orbiting the sun; a similar body orbiting another star

For centuries, people have known about five of the **planets:** Mercury, Venus, Mars, Jupiter, and Saturn. Each of these can be seen from Earth with the unaided eye. **Figure 18-21A** shows an ancient model of the solar system with Earth at the center.

In 1543, the astronomer Nicolaus Copernicus argued that all of the planets—including Earth—orbit the sun. Shortly after that, the astronomer Kepler showed that the orbits of the planets are ellipses, not perfect circles. **Figure 18-21B** shows a modern representation of the solar system.

Figure 18-21

A Many old maps of the universe show the sun, the moon, and the planets orbiting Earth in perfect circles.

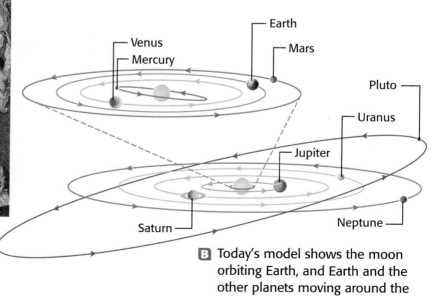

B Today's model shows the moon orbiting Earth, and Earth and the other planets moving around the sun in elliptical orbits.

Table 18-1 **Properties of the Planets**

Planet	Average surface temperature (°C)	Number of moons	Presence of rings	Atmosphere
Mercury	350	0	No	Essentially none
Venus	460	0	No	Thick: carbon dioxide, sulfuric acid
Earth	20	1	No	Nitrogen, oxygen
Mars	−23	2	No	Thin: carbon dioxide
Jupiter	−120	16	Yes	Hydrogen, helium, ammonia, methane
Saturn	−180	18	Yes	Hydrogen, helium, ammonia, methane
Uranus	−210	20	Yes	Hydrogen, helium, ammonia, methane
Neptune	−220	8	Yes	Hydrogen, helium, methane
Pluto	−230	1	No	Very thin: nitrogen and methane

Nine planets orbit the sun

After people started using telescopes to study the sky, three more planets were discovered: Uranus, Neptune, and Pluto. Pluto, which is small and very far away, was not discovered until 1930. Some facts about the planets are summarized in **Table 18-1.**

The solar system includes the sun, the nine planets, and all of the other objects orbiting the sun. These other objects include meteors, comets, and asteroids. Sometimes, one of these smaller objects strikes a planet, producing a crater.

The planets in our solar system are much smaller and much nearer than stars. As the planets move in elliptical orbits around the sun, their positions as seen against the backdrop of stars change. That is why they appear to wander through the sky.

Planets reflect sunlight

Planets do not give off their own light. They can be seen from Earth because the surfaces of the planets or clouds in their atmospheres reflect sunlight.

Besides the sun and the moon, the brightest object in the sky is Venus. It is the so-called "morning star" and "evening star" that can be seen near the sun at dawn and at dusk. Venus appears bright in the sky because it has a thick atmosphere that reflects sunlight very well.

▶ **solar system** the sun and all the objects that orbit around it

Did You Know?

Scientists now have evidence of planets orbiting other stars. However, because planets do not give off their own light, distant planets are hard to detect. So far, astronomers have only found distant planets that are larger than Jupiter. With improved telescopes, astronomers hope to someday find smaller planets that are more like Earth.

The Inner Planets

The four inner planets—Mercury, Venus, Earth, and Mars—are relatively small and have solid, rocky surfaces. Using telescopes, orbiting satellites, and surface probes, scientists can study the geologic features of these planets.

Mercury has extreme temperatures

Much of our knowledge of Mercury comes from the *Mariner 10* fly-by mission in 1974. The photographs taken from *Mariner 10,* such as the one in **Figure 18-22,** showed for the first time that Mercury is pocked with craters, much like the moon.

Mercury is so close to the sun that its surface has a temperature over 670 K (397°C), which is hot enough to melt a tin can. But on the dark side, the temperature drops to an extremely cold 103 K (–170°C). Mercury spins slowly on its axis, managing to get three spins (days) for every two orbits (years) around the sun.

Mercury would not be a likely place to find life. In addition to having very extreme temperatures, it has hardly any atmosphere at all and no water.

Figure 18-22
Mercury is pocked with craters.

Venus's thick clouds cause a greenhouse effect

On its way to Mercury, *Mariner 10* also took photos of the next planet out from the sun, Venus. The photos showed thick layers of clouds. Venus has a very thick atmosphere composed mostly of carbon dioxide. Radar maps, such as the one shown in **Figure 18-23,** indicate that Venus's surface has mountains and plains.

Although Venus is about the same size as Earth, it does not provide an environment for life. Not only is Venus hot, but its atmosphere contains high levels of sulfuric acid, which is very corrosive. In addition, the atmospheric pressure at the surface is more than 90 times the pressure on Earth. Venus's thick atmosphere prevents the release of energy by radiation, creating a greenhouse effect that keeps the surface temperature of Venus over 700 K. For more on the greenhouse effect, see Section 20.1.

Figure 18-23
Although the surface of Venus is obscured by a thick atmosphere, maps of Venus can be made by using radar. On this map, yellow and brown represent higher ground, and blue and green represent lower ground.

Earth has ideal conditions for living creatures

Earth is the third planet out from the sun. Of all the planets, Earth is by far the most likely home for life as we know it. Earth is the only planet with large amounts of liquid water on its surface. It also has an atmosphere rich with oxygen, nitrogen, and carbon dioxide, and moderate temperatures that are stable around the globe. Earth and its atmosphere will be discussed further in Chapters 19 and 20.

Figure 18-24
The Martian volcano Olympus Mons is larger than the entire state of Louisiana.

Many missions have been sent to Mars

Although humans have yet to visit Mars, we have landed several probes on the surface. *Viking 1* and *Viking 2* both arrived at Mars in 1976, and each sent a lander to the surface. In 1997, the Pathfinder mission reached Mars and deployed a rover, the *Sojourner,* which freely explored the surface using a robotic navigation system.

Earlier orbiting missions had already detected some of Mars's unique features. The Martian volcano Olympus Mons, shown in **Figure 18-24,** is the largest mountain in the solar system. Its base is larger than the entire state of Louisiana, and it is almost three times the height of Mount Everest.

Figure 18-25 shows white regions around the poles of Mars. These are polar icecaps that contain at least some water. Features on other parts of the planet suggest that water used to flow across the surface as a liquid. Mars even has an atmosphere, but it is mostly carbon dioxide and much thinner than Earth's.

The asteroid belt divides the inner and outer planets

Between Mars and Jupiter lie hundreds of smaller rocky objects ranging in diameter from 3 km to 700 km. There are probably thousands of others too small to see from Earth. These objects are called **asteroids.**

Many of the largest asteroids remain between Mars and Jupiter, but some wander away from this region. A few climb high above the plane in which the planets move. Others pass closer to the sun, sometimes even crossing Earth's orbit. The odds of a large asteroid hitting Earth directly are fortunately very small.

Figure 18-25
This picture of Mars, taken by the Hubble Space Telescope, clearly shows a polar icecap.

▷ **asteroid** a small rocky object that orbits the sun, usually in a band between the orbits of Mars and Jupiter

Figure 18-26

A Jupiter is the largest planet in the solar system.

B The Great Red Spot is a huge, hurricane-like storm in Jupiter's atmosphere.

The Outer Planets

The outer planets are Jupiter, Saturn, Uranus, Neptune, and Pluto. All of them except Pluto are much larger than the inner planets and have thick gaseous atmospheres. For this reason, they are called the *gas giants*.

Because the gas giants have no solid surface, a spaceship cannot land on one of them. However, the *Pioneer* (launched in 1972 and 1973), *Voyager* (launched in 1977), and *Galileo* (launched in 1989) spacecraft have flown to all of the outer planets except Pluto. *Galileo* even dropped a probe into the atmosphere of Jupiter in 1995.

Jupiter is the largest planet in the solar system

Jupiter, shown in **Figure 18-26A,** is the first planet beyond the asteroids. Jupiter is big enough to hold 1300 Earths. If it were only 80 times more massive than that, it would have sufficient pressure and temperature to sustain nuclear fusion, as a star does.

Images of Jupiter's atmosphere show swirling clouds of hydrogen, helium, methane, and ammonia. Complex features appear in Jupiter's atmosphere, including banded structures that appear to be jet streams and huge storms.

One of these storms, the Great Red Spot, shown in **Figure 18-26B,** is a huge hurricane about twice the diameter of Earth. The Great Red Spot has existed for hundreds of years. From year to year it changes slightly in size, shape, and color.

internetconnect

SCiLINKS
NSTA

TOPIC: Planets
GO TO: www.scilinks.org
KEYWORD: HK1165

All of the gaseous outer planets have rings and moons

The astronomer Galileo was one of the first to use telescopes to look at the planets. Among his many discoveries, he found four moons orbiting Jupiter. These were the first moons to be seen orbiting a planet other than Earth. Any object orbiting a planet, whether natural or man-made, is called a satellite. The moons Galileo discovered are now known as the Galilean satellites.

Since the time of Galileo, astronomers have discovered 12 other moons orbiting Jupiter and 18 moons orbiting Saturn, the next planet beyond Jupiter. Several of these moons were discovered by the Voyager missions that passed through the outer solar system between 1979 and 1989.

In addition to its many moons, Saturn has a spectacular system of rings, shown in **Figure 18-27.** These rings are narrow bands of tiny particles of dust, rock, and ice. Competing gravitational forces from Saturn and its many moons hold the particles in place around the planet. Jupiter, Uranus, and Neptune also have rings, but they are much thinner and harder to detect than the rings of Saturn.

Uranus and Neptune are blue giants

Beyond Saturn lie the planets Uranus and Neptune, shown in **Figure 18-28.** These two planets are similar to each other in size and color. Both are smaller than Saturn and Jupiter, but are large enough to hold very thick, gaseous atmospheres. Their upper atmospheres contain a lot of methane, which gives both planets a bluish color. Uranus has 20 known moons, and Neptune has 8. Both planets have faint rings.

Figure 18-27
Saturn, shown here in a photograph taken by *Voyager 2,* is famous for its spectacular system of rings.

Figure 18-28
(A) Methane in its atmosphere gives Uranus a uniform blue color. (B) The Great Dark Spot is a huge storm in Neptune's blue atmosphere.

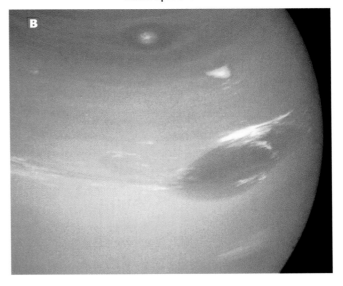

Figure 18-29
Pluto's moon, Charon, has a diameter almost half as large as Pluto. For that reason, some consider Pluto to be a double planet.

Pluto is an oddball planet

Pluto, shown in **Figure 18-29** with its moon Charon, is not like the other outer planets. It has only a thin, gaseous atmosphere, and a solid, icy surface. Pluto's orbit around the sun follows a long ellipse, and the plane of orbit is at an angle to the rest of the solar system. For these reasons, some scientists believe Pluto was captured by the gravity of the sun some time after the formation of the rest of the solar system. Pluto isn't always the farthest planet in the solar system; its orbit sometimes cuts inside the orbit of Neptune, as it was for a few years prior to 1999. The next time this will happen is in 2231.

Formation of the Solar System

According to geologic dating of rocks from Earth, the moon, and asteroids, the age of the solar system is around 4.6 billion years. The most widely accepted model of the formation of the solar system is the **nebular model.** In this model, the sun and the solar system condensed out of a nebula, a huge cloud of interstellar gas and dust.

▶ **nebular model** a model that describes the sun and the solar system forming together out of a cloud of gas and dust

The solar system may have formed from a rotating disk

According to the nebular model, the sun, like every star, formed from a cloud of gas and dust collapsing due to gravity. As this cloud collapsed, it formed into a flat, rotating disk. In the disk's center, the sun formed. Planets formed from the material farther out. This explains why all the planets lie in one plane and also why the planets orbit in the same direction that the sun rotates.

Planets formed by accretion of matter in the disk

The planets formed out of orbiting material mostly through the process of *accretion*. Accretion occurs when small particles collide and stick together to form larger masses.

Radiation from the newly born sun exerted pressure on the rest of the gas and dust in the disk. The lighter material was pushed farther away, where it combined to form the outer gas giant planets. Heavier rocky and metallic pieces that were left behind formed the solid inner planets. Even with the pressure, though, the force of gravity due to the sun was strong enough to keep most of the material in orbit.

Did You Know ?

Because our solar system contains elements heavier than iron, at least some of the dust in the original nebular cloud must have been produced in a supernova some time in the past.

The Moon

The moon is probably the most familiar object in the night sky. Like the planets, it shines because it reflects light from the sun. But the moon does not orbit the sun directly; it orbits our own planet Earth at a distance of 385 000 km.

The surface of the moon is covered with craters, mostly caused by asteroids crashing into the moon early in the history of the solar system. Larger dark patches on the moon's surface are seas of lava that flowed out of the moon's interior.

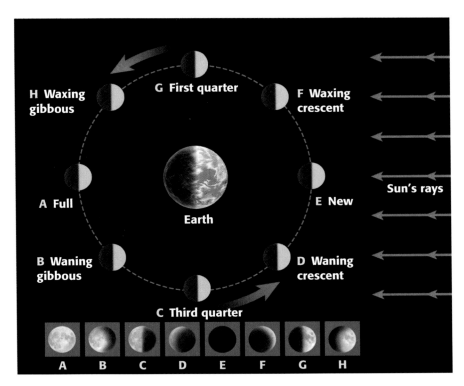

Figure 18-30
As the moon changes position relative to Earth and the sun, it goes through different phases.

The moon has phases because it orbits Earth

As the moon orbits Earth, it appears to have different shapes. These are called **phases.** The phases of the moon are determined by the relative positions of Earth, the moon, and the sun, as shown in **Figure 18-30.**

At any given time, the sun illuminates half the moon's surface, just as at any time it is daytime on one half of Earth and nighttime on the other half. When the moon is *full*, the half that is lit is facing you. The observed time from one full moon to the next is 29.5 days.

When you see a *crescent* moon, you can see only a small portion of the lit side of the moon and a lot of the dark side. Between full and crescent moons are *quarter* moons, when you can see half of the lit side of the moon, and *gibbous* moons, when you see more than half of the lit side. Times when the moon's lit side is not visible are called *new* moons.

▶ **phases** the different apparent shapes of the moon or a planet due to the relative positions of the sun, Earth, and the moon or planet

Eclipses occur when Earth, the moon, and the sun are in a line

While exploring Jamaica in 1504, Christopher Columbus impressed the native people he met by predicting an **eclipse.** He was able to do this by consulting a table of astronomical observations. Eclipses can be predicted because they happen only when Earth, the sun, and the moon are in a straight line. An eclipse occurs when one object moves into the shadow cast by another object.

▶ **eclipse** an event that occurs when one object passes into the shadow of another object

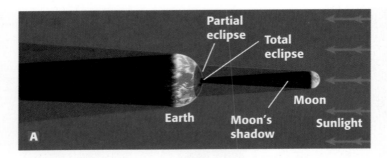

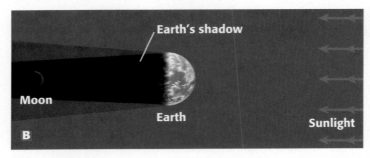

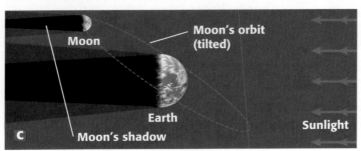

During a new moon, the moon may cast a shadow onto Earth, as shown in **Figure 18-31A.** Observers within that shadow on Earth see the sky turn dark as the moon blocks out the sun. This is called a solar eclipse.

On the other hand, when the moon is full, it may pass into the shadow of Earth, as shown in **Figure 18-31B.** Observers on Earth see the full moon become temporarily dark as it passes through Earth's shadow. This is called a lunar eclipse.

Because the moon's orbit is slightly tilted compared with Earth's orbit around the sun, the moon is usually slightly above or below the line between Earth and the sun, as shown in **Figure 18-31C.** For that reason, eclipses are relatively rare.

Figure 18-31
Eclipses occur when Earth, the sun, and the moon are in a line. (A) shows a solar eclipse, (B) shows a lunar eclipse, and in (C) there is no eclipse at all.

SECTION 18.3 REVIEW

SUMMARY

▶ The solar system consists of the sun, nine planets, and other objects orbiting the sun.

▶ The inner planets are small and rocky. The outer planets, except Pluto, are large and gaseous.

▶ The planets were formed out of the cloud from which the sun condensed.

▶ Eclipses and the phases of the moon depend on the relative positions of Earth, the moon, and the sun.

CHECK YOUR UNDERSTANDING

1. **List** the planets in order of their distance from the sun.
2. **Explain** why the surface of Venus is hotter than the surface of Mercury.
3. **Describe** some of the geologic features on Mars.
4. **Compare** the inner planets with the outer planets.
5. **Describe** the origin of the planets.
6. **Describe** the positions of the sun, the moon, and Earth during a new moon.
7. **Explain** what happens during a lunar eclipse. Why does an eclipse happen only during a full moon?
8. **Critical Thinking** If the moon is half-full as seen from Earth, what would Earth look like to a man on the moon?
9. **Creative Thinking** Some astronomers have found evidence for the formation of planets around other stars. Make a list of three characteristics these planets might need to support life.

Chapter Highlights

Before you begin, review the summaries of the key ideas of each section, found on pages 584, 591, and 600. The key vocabulary terms are listed on pages 576, 585, and 592.

UNDERSTANDING CONCEPTS

1. The basic types of galaxies are _____.
   a. spiral, elliptical, and irregular
   b. barred, elliptical, and open
   c. spiral, quasar, and pulsar
   d. open, binary, and globular

2. Which of the following is a possible age of the universe, according to the big bang theory?
   a. 4.6 million years   c. 4.6 billion years
   b. 15 million years   d. 15 billion years

3. A pattern of stars as seen from Earth is called a _____.
   a. galaxy   c. Milky Way
   b. nebula   d. constellation

4. By studying starlight, astronomers may learn which of the following things about stars?
   a. the elements that compose the star
   b. the surface temperature of the star
   c. the speed of the star relative to Earth
   d. all of the above

5. The core of a star that remains after a supernova may be any of the following except _____.
   a. a black hole   c. a red giant
   b. a neutron star   d. a pulsar

6. The shape of the orbit of Earth is _____.
   a. a circle   c. an arc
   b. an ellipse   d. a sphere

7. The only outer planet that is not a gas giant is _____.
   a. Jupiter   c. Neptune
   b. Saturn   d. Pluto

8. According to radioisotope dating of rocks from the moon, Mars, and asteroids as well as here on Earth, what is the approximate age of the solar system?
   a. 4.6 million years
   b. 15 million years
   c. 4.6 billion years
   d. 15 billion years

9. The theory that the sun and the planets formed out of the same cloud of gas and dust is called the _____.
   a. big bang theory   c. planetary theory
   b. nebular theory   d. nuclear theory

10. A lunar eclipse can occur when the moon is _____.
    a. full   c. rising
    b. new   d. setting

Using Vocabulary

11. Arrange the following from largest to smallest: *cluster, galaxy, planet, solar system, supercluster, star.*

12. What type of *galaxy* is the Milky Way galaxy?

13. Using the terms *galaxy* and *red shift,* explain the primary evidence that the universe is expanding.

14. What is the *big bang theory?*

15. Write a paragraph explaining in your own words the origin of the sun and *solar system.* Use the following terms: *planet, accretion, nebular model.*

WRITING SKILL

16. List and explain several different possible ways a star's life could end. Use the following terms: *black hole, neutron star, supernova, white dwarf.*

17. Where are most *asteroids* located?

18. Name four different *phases* of the moon.

19. What conditions are necessary for a *solar eclipse* to occur?

BUILDING MATH SKILLS

20. Interpreting Graphics The spectra shown below were taken for hydrogen, helium, and lithium in a laboratory on Earth. The spectra labeled as *Star 1* and *Star 2* were taken from starlight. What elements are found in Star 1 and Star 2?

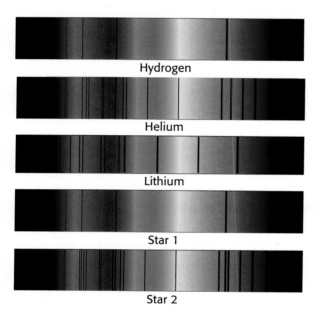

Hydrogen

Helium

Lithium

Star 1

Star 2

21. Applying Technology The free-fall acceleration, *g*, near the surface of a planet is given by the equation below.

$$g = \left(6.67 \times 10^{-11}\ \frac{m^3}{kg \cdot s^2}\right) \times \frac{(planet\ mass)}{(planet\ radius)^2}$$

Use this equation to create a spreadsheet that will calculate the free-fall acceleration near the surface of each of the planets in the table below.

Planet	Mass	Radius
Mercury	3.3×10^{23} kg	2.4×10^6 m
Venus	4.9×10^{24} kg	6.1×10^6 m
Earth	6.0×10^{24} kg	6.4×10^6 m
Mars	6.4×10^{23} kg	3.4×10^6 m

22. Applying Technology Add a column to the spreadsheet you created in item 21 that will show the weight of a 300 kg person on each of the inner planets. Use the weight equation from Chapter 7: $w = mg$. Which of the planets has gravity the most like Earth?

THINKING CRITICALLY

23. Applying Knowledge While looking through a telescope, you observe a galaxy that has mostly old, red stars, and no young, blue stars. The galaxy also does not appear to have very much gas or dust. What kind of galaxy are you probably looking at?

24. Evaluating Data If Hubble had observed that the spectral lines in light from every galaxy were shifted toward the blue end of the spectrum, what might he have concluded about the universe?

25. Understanding Systems What keeps a star from collapsing under its own weight?

26. Applying Knowledge Why will the sun never explode in a supernova?

27. Creative Thinking How can Venus be the brightest object in the sky, besides the sun and the moon, when it doesn't even produce any visible light of its own?

28. Understanding Systems You and a friend are looking at a crescent moon, and your friend comments that the phases of the moon are caused by Earth's shadow falling on the moon. How would you explain to your friend the true cause of the moon's phases?

29. Creative Thinking Name two reasons why Earth provides a better home for living creatures than would any of the other planets in the solar system.

DEVELOPING LIFE/WORK SKILLS

30. **Interpreting and Communicating** In your library or on the Internet, research the sizes of the planets and the sun and the distances between different objects in the solar system. Create a poster, booklet, computer presentation, or other presentation that can be used to teach a third-grade class about these distances.

31. **Working Cooperatively** Working with a team of at least four other students, make a list of your needs if you were planning the first human mission to Mars. Each team member should research and consider what the astronauts will need once they arrive on Mars for one of the following categories: food, shelter, clothing, air, and transportation. What ideas can your team come up with to meet these needs?

INTEGRATING CONCEPTS

32. **Connection to Fine Arts** In the years 1914 to 1916, the composer Gustav Holst created *The Planets*, a symphonic suite that portrays each of the planets according to its role in mythology. Listen to a recording of *The Planets*. Write a paragraph describing which parts of the music seem to match scientific facts about the planets and which parts do not.

WRITING SKILL

33. **Connection to Fine Arts** Holst composed *The Planets* before Pluto was discovered, so Neptune is the last planet he describes. Create your own work of art, such as a drawing, a computerized slideshow, or a brief musical theme, that portrays some of the scientific facts about the nature of Pluto.

34. **Connection to Chemistry** Based on the description in this chapter, how were hydrogen and helium first formed in the universe? What are the possible sources of elements from lithium to carbon? What are the possible sources of elements from carbon to iron? How could atoms larger than iron be formed?

35. **Concept Mapping** Copy the unfinished concept map below onto a sheet of paper. Complete the map by writing the correct word or phrase in the lettered boxes.

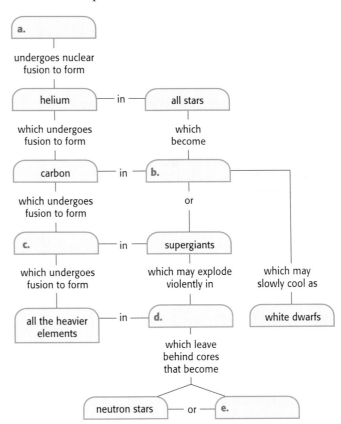

internet**connect**

SCI*LINKS*
NSTA

TOPIC: Formation of the elements
GO TO: www.scilinks.org
KEYWORD: HK1166

Skill Builder Lab

Introduction

The sun is 1.496×10^{11} m from Earth. How can you use this distance and a few simple measurements to find the size and power output of the sun?

Objectives

- ▶ **Construct** devices for observing and measuring properties of the sun.
- ▶ **Measure** the size of an image of the sun in a solar viewing device.
- ▶ **Measure** temperatures in sunlight and in light from a light bulb.
- ▶ **Calculate** the size of the sun and the power output of the sun.

Materials

shoe box and scissors
aluminum foil and pin
masking tape
index card
Celsius thermometer
very thin sheet metal (2×8 cm)
black paint or magic marker
glass jar with a hole in the lid
modeling clay
lamp with a 100 W bulb
meterstick

Safety Needs

safety goggles, gloves

Estimating the Size and Power Output of the Sun

▶ Preparing for Your Experiment

1. Construct a solar viewer in the following way.
   a. Cut a round hole in one end of the shoe box.
   b. Tape a piece of aluminum foil over the hole. Use the pin to make a tiny hole in the center of the foil.
   c. Tape the index card inside the shoebox on the end opposite the hole.
2. Construct a solar collector in the following way.
   a. Gently fit the sheet metal around the bulb of the thermometer. Bend the edges out so that they form "wings," as shown at right. Paint the wings black.
   SAFETY CAUTION Thermometers are fragile. Do not squeeze the bulb of the thermometer or let the thermometer strike any solid objects.
   b. Slide the top of the thermometer through the hole in the lid of the jar. Use modeling clay and masking tape to hold the thermometer in place.
   c. Place the lid on the jar. Adjust the thermometer so the metal wings are centered.
3. Place the lamp on one end of a table that is not in direct sunlight. Remove any shade or reflector from the lamp.

▶ Measurements with the Solar Viewer

4. Stand in direct sunlight, with your back to the sun, and position the solar viewer so that an image of the sun appears on the index card.
   SAFETY CAUTION Never look directly at the sun. Permanent eye damage or even blindness may result.
5. Carefully measure and record the diameter of the image of the sun. Also measure and record the distance from the image to the pinhole.

▶ Measurements with the Solar Collector

6. Place the solar collector in sunlight. Tilt the jar so that the sun shines directly on the metal wings. Watch the temperature reading rise until it reaches a maximum value. Record that value. Place the collector in the shade to cool.

7. Now place the solar collector about 30 cm from the lamp on the table. Tilt the jar so that the light shines directly on the metal wings. Watch the temperature reading rise until it reaches a stable value.

8. Move the collector toward the lamp in 2 cm increments. At each position, let the collector sit until the temperature reading stabilizes. When you find a point where the reading on the thermometer matches the reading you observed in step 6, measure and record the distance from the solar collector to the light bulb.

▶ Analyzing Your Results

1. The ratio of the sun's actual diameter to its distance from Earth is the same as the ratio of the diameter of the sun's image to the distance from the pinhole to the image.

$$\frac{diameter\ of\ the\ sun,\ S}{Earth - sun\ distance,\ D} = \frac{diameter\ of\ image,\ i}{pinhole - image\ distance,\ d}$$

Solving for the sun's diameter, S, gives the following equation.

$$S = \frac{D}{d} \times i.$$

Substitute your measured values, and $D = 1.5 \times 10^{11}$ m, into this equation to calculate the value of S. Remember to convert all distance measurements to units of meters.

2. The ratio of the power output of the sun to the sun's distance from Earth squared is the same as the ratio of the power output of the light bulb to the solar collector's distance from the bulb squared.

$$\frac{power\ of\ sun,\ P}{(earth - sun\ distance,\ D)^2} = \frac{power\ of\ light\ bulb,\ b}{(bulb - collector\ distance,\ d)^2}$$

Solving for the sun's power output, P, gives the following equation.

$$P = \frac{D^2}{d^2} \times b$$

Substitute your measured distance for d, the known wattage of the bulb for b, and $D = 1.5 \times 10^{11}$ m, into this equation to calculate the value of P. Remember to convert all distance measurements to units of meters. Your answer should be in watts.

▶ Defending Your Conclusions

3. How does your S compare with the accepted diameter of the sun, 1.392×10^9 m?

4. How does your P compare with the accepted power output of the sun, 3.827×10^{26} W?

CHAPTER 19

Planet Earth

Chapter Preview

19.1 Earth's Interior and Plate Tectonics
What Is Earth's Interior Like?
Plate Tectonics
Divergent Plate Boundaries
Convergent Plate Boundaries
Transform Fault Boundaries
Evidence for Plate Tectonics

19.2 Earthquakes and Volcanoes
What are Earthquakes?
Volcanoes

19.3 Minerals and Rocks
Structure and Origin of Rocks
How Old Are Rocks?

19.4 Weathering and Erosion
Physical Weathering
Chemical Weathering
Erosion

Focus ACTIVITY

Background Crater Lake, in Oregon, is the deepest lake in North America, measuring 589 m (1932 ft) at its deepest point. The lake is inside the collapsed center of a volcano called Mount Mazama.

So how did a volcano form a lake? As Mount Mazama erupted around 6800 years ago, the molten rock and volcanic ash that helped to support the cone of the volcano were ejected. The top then collapsed, creating a big hole. As the hole filled with rainwater and melted snow, Crater Lake was formed. A secondary eruption produced a small volcanic cone, which rose above the water's surface and became Wizard Island, the small island seen in the photo at left.

Activity 1 Imagine you are an early explorer who has just discovered Crater Lake. Examine the photos at left, and write two other possible explanations for how the lake may have formed. When you are finished, think of possible weaknesses in each of your explanations. Write these weaknesses down, and share your results with your class.

Activity 2 Mount Mazama exploded with a great deal of force. Go to the library and research Mount Mazama. How tall is Mount Mazama thought to have been before it erupted? How does that size compare with the size of other volcanoes in Oregon and Washington? How big was the eruption? How might the eruption have affected Earth's global climate?

Crater Lake, in Oregon, sits within the top of a collapsed volcano.

internet connect

SCI*LINKS*
NSTA

TOPIC: Volcanoes
GO TO: www.scilinks.org
KEYWORD: HK1704

Earth's Interior and Plate Tectonics

▶ **KEY TERMS**
crust
mantle
core
lithosphere
plate tectonics
asthenosphere
magma
subduction
fault

OBJECTIVES

▶ Identify Earth's different geologic layers.

▶ Describe the movement of Earth's lithosphere using the theory of plate tectonics.

▶ Identify the three types of plate boundaries and the principal structures that form at each of these boundaries.

▶ Explain how the presence of magnetic bands on the ocean floor supports the theory of plate tectonics.

You know from experience that Earth's surface is solid. You walk on it every day. You may have even dug into it and found that it is often more solid once you dig and reach rock. However, Earth is not solid all the way to the center.

What Is Earth's Interior Like?

Figure 19-1 shows Earth's major compositional layers. We live on the topmost layer of Earth—the crust. Because the crust is relatively cool, it is made up of hard, solid rock. The crust beneath the ocean is called *oceanic crust* and has an average thickness of 4–7 km (2.5–4.3 mi). *Continental crust* is less dense and thicker, with an average thickness of about 20–40 km (12–25 mi). The continental crust is deepest beneath high mountains, where it reaches depths as great as 70 km.

▶ **crust** the outermost and thinnest layer of Earth

▶ **mantle** the layer of rock between the Earth's crust and its core

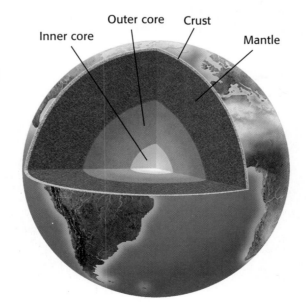

Figure 19-1
Earth is composed of an inner core, an outer core, a mantle, and a crust.

Inner core
Outer core
Crust
Mantle

Beneath the crust lies the **mantle,** a layer of rock that is denser than the crust. Almost 2900 km (1800 mi) thick, the mantle makes up about 80 percent of Earth's volume. Because humans have never drilled all the way to the mantle, we do not know for sure what it is like. However, geologic events, such as earthquakes and volcanoes, provide evidence of the mantle's consistency.

In the outer mantle, the rocks are mostly solid, as they are in the crust. The rocks in the inner portion of the mantle, however, are extremely hot and are said to be "plastic"—soft and easily deformed, like a stiff piece of gum.

The center of Earth, the _core,_ is believed to be composed mainly of iron and nickel. It has two layers. The *inner core* is solid metal, and the *outer core,* which surrounds the inner core, is liquid metal.

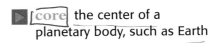

▶ [core] the center of a planetary body, such as Earth

Earth's interior gets warmer with depth

If you have ever been in a cave, you may have noticed that the temperature in the cave was cool. That's because the air and rocks beneath Earth's surface are shielded from the warming effects of the sun. However, if you were to travel far beneath the surface, such as into a deep mine, you would find that the temperature becomes uncomfortably hot. South African gold mines, for instance, reach depths of up ˜to 3 km (2 mi), and their temperatures approach 50°C (120°F). The high temperatures in these mines are caused not by the sun but by energy that comes from Earth's interior.

Geologists believe the mantle is much hotter than the crust, as shown in **Figure 19-2.** These high temperatures cause the rocks in the mantle to behave plastically. This is the reason for the inner mantle's plastic, gumlike consistency.

The core is hotter still. On Earth's surface, the metals contained in the core would boil at the temperatures shown in **Figure 19-2.** Iron boils at 3000°C (5400°F), and nickel boils at 2900°C (5300°F). But in the outer core, these metals remain liquid because the pressure due to the weight of the mantle and crust is so great that the substances in the outer core are prevented from changing to their gaseous form. Similarly, pressure in the inner core is so great that the atoms are forced together as a solid.

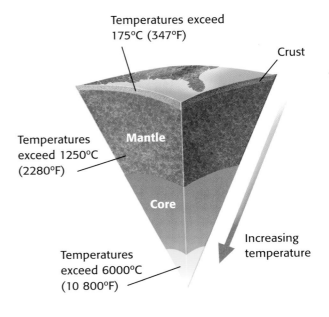

Temperatures exceed 175°C (347°F)

Crust

Mantle

Temperatures exceed 1250°C (2280°F)

Core

Increasing temperature

Temperatures exceed 6000°C (10 800°F)

Figure 19-2
Temperatures in Earth's interior increase with depth. Temperatures near the center of the core can be as hot as the surface of the sun.

Radioactive elements contribute to Earth's high internal temperature

Earth's interior contains radioactive isotopes. These radioactive isotopes (mainly those of uranium, thorium, and potassium) are quite rare. Their nuclei break up, releasing energy as they become smaller nuclei. Because Earth is so large, it contains enough atoms of these elements to produce a huge quantity of energy. This energy is one of the major factors contributing to Earth's high internal temperature.

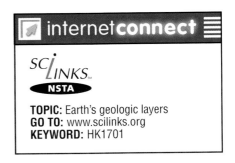

📷 internet**connect** ≣

SC*L*INKS.

⬤ NSTA ⬤

TOPIC: Earth's geologic layers
GO TO: www.scilinks.org
KEYWORD: HK1701

Plate Tectonics

In the early twentieth century, a German scientist named Alfred Wegener noticed that the eastern coast of South America and the western coast of Africa appeared to fit together like pieces of a puzzle. By studying world maps, Wegener found that several of the other continents' coastlines also seemed to fit together. Wegener pieced together parts of a map and joined all the continents together, forming a supercontinent that he called *Pangaea* (pan GEE uh). **Figure 19-3** is an illustration of what Wegener thought Pangaea might have looked like approximately 200 million years ago.

Figure 19-3
This map shows Pangaea as Alfred Wegener envisioned it.

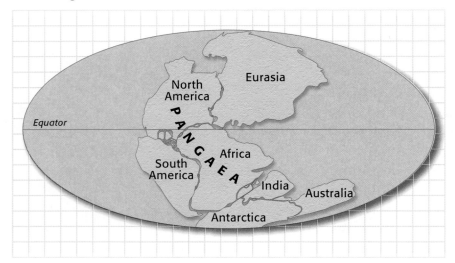

Using remains of ancient organisms, Wegener showed that 200 million years ago, the same kinds of animals lived on continents that are now oceans apart. He argued that the animals could not have evolved on separate continents. Therefore, there must have been some sort of physical connection between the continents.

The evidence was appealing, but scientists did not have an explanation of how continents could move. Wegener's theory was ignored until the mid-1960s, when structures on the ocean floor gave evidence of a mechanism for the movement of continents, or *continental drift.*

internet**connect**

SCI*LINKS*
NSTA

TOPIC: Plate tectonics
GO TO: www.scilinks.org
KEYWORD: HK1702

▶ **lithosphere** the thin outer shell of Earth, consisting of the crust and the rigid upper mantle

▶ **plate tectonics** the theory that Earth's surface is made up of large moving plates

Earth has plates that move over the tar-like mantle

Earth's stiff outer shell, called the **lithosphere,** is approximately 100 km (60 mi) thick. The lithosphere consists of the crust and the rigid, upper portion of the mantle. The lithosphere is made of about seven large pieces (and several smaller pieces) called *tectonic plates.* These plates fit together like pieces of a puzzle and move in relation to one another. The theory describing the movement of plates is called **plate tectonics.**

Figure 19-4 shows the edges of Earth's tectonic plates. The arrows indicate the direction of each plate's movement. Note that plate boundaries do not always coincide with continental boundaries. Some plates move toward each other, some move away from each other, and still others move alongside each other.

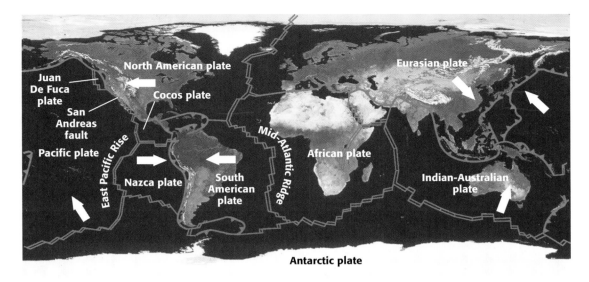

North American plate
Juan De Fuca plate
San Andreas fault
Cocos plate
Pacific plate
East Pacific Rise
Nazca plate
South American plate
Mid-Atlantic Ridge
African plate
Eurasian plate
Indian-Australian plate
Antarctic plate

▭▭ Plates move apart   ▲▲▲ Plates move together   ─── Plates slide past each other

Tectonic plates move at speeds ranging from 1 to 16 cm (0.4 to 6.3 in.) per year. Although this speed may seem slow, tectonic plates have moved a considerable distance because they have been moving for hundreds of millions of years.

Figure 19-4
Earth's lithosphere is made up of several large tectonic plates. Plate boundaries are marked in red, and arrows indicate plate movement.

It is unknown exactly why tectonic plates move

One hypothesis suggests that plate movement results from convection currents in the asthenosphere, the hot, plastic portion of the mantle. As shown in **Figure 19-5,** the plates of the lithosphere "float" on top of the asthenosphere.

▶ **asthenosphere** the zone of the mantle beneath the lithosphere that consists of slowly flowing solid rock

The soft rock in the asthenosphere might circulate by convection, similar to the way mushy oatmeal circulates as it boils. This slow movement of rock might push the plates of the lithosphere along. Some scientists believe that the plates are pieces of the lithosphere that are being moved around by convection currents. Other scientists believe that the forces generated by convection currents are not sufficient to move the plates. The origin of the forces that move the plates is not clear.

Figure 19-5
According to one theory, convection currents are the mechanism that moves tectonic plates.

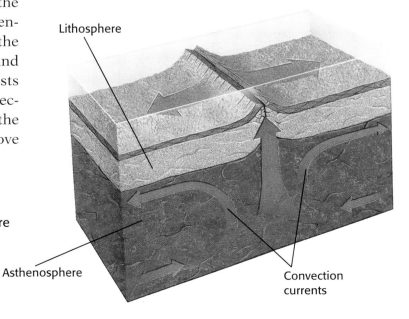

Lithosphere

Asthenosphere

Convection currents

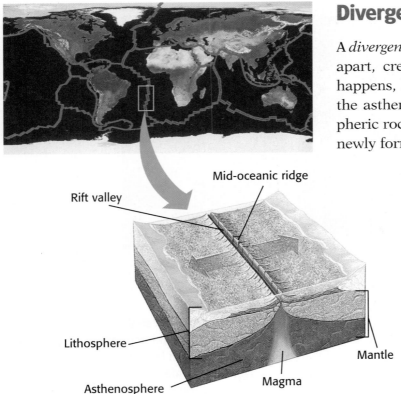

Divergent Plate Boundaries

A *divergent boundary* occurs where two plates move apart, creating a gap between them. When this happens, hot molten rock, or **magma,** rises from the asthenosphere and cools, forming new lithospheric rock. The two diverging plates then pull the newly formed lithosphere away from the gap.

Mid-oceanic ridges result from volcanic activity at a divergent boundary

Mid-oceanic ridges are mountain ranges that form at divergent boundaries in oceanic crust. **Figure 19-6** shows how a mid-oceanic ridge forms. As the plates move apart, magma rises from between the diverging plates and fills the gap. The result is new oceanic crust that forms a large central valley, called a *rift valley,* surrounded by high mountains, the mid-oceanic ridge.

Unlike most mountains on land, which are formed by the bending and folding of continental crust, mid-oceanic ridges are mountain ranges created by magma rising to Earth's surface and cooling. The most studied mid-oceanic ridge is called the Mid-Atlantic Ridge. This ridge runs roughly down the center of the Atlantic Ocean from the Arctic Ocean to an area off the southern tip of South America.

Figure 19-6
Tectonic plates move apart at divergent boundaries, forming rift valleys and mountain systems, such as this mid-oceanic ridge.

▷ **magma** molten rock within the Earth

Convergent Plate Boundaries

Knowing that lithosphere is being created at mid-oceanic ridges, you may wonder why Earth isn't expanding. The reason is that while the new lithosphere is formed at divergent boundaries, the older lithosphere is destroyed at *convergent boundaries* as oceanic plates dive beneath continental or oceanic plates.

Oceanic plates dive beneath continental plates as they collide

The Andes Mountains, in South America, are formed along a convergent boundary between an oceanic plate and the South American continental plate. At this boundary, the oceanic plate, which is denser, dives beneath the continental plate and drags the oceanic crust along with it. This process is called **subduction.** As shown in **Figure 19-7,** ocean trenches, mountains, and volcanoes are formed at *subduction zones.*

▷ **subduction** the process in which a tectonic plate dives beneath another tectonic plate and into the asthenosphere

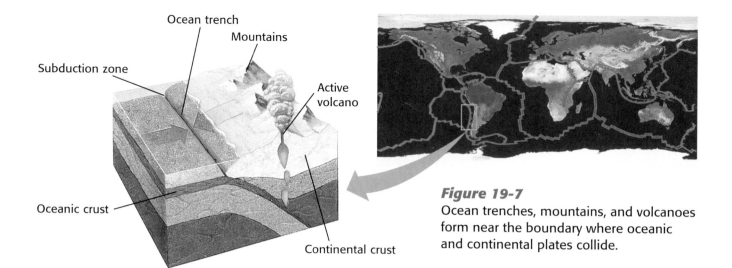

Subduction zone
Ocean trench
Mountains
Active volcano
Oceanic crust
Continental crust

Figure 19-7
Ocean trenches, mountains, and volcanoes form near the boundary where oceanic and continental plates collide.

Ocean trenches form along the boundary between two oceanic plates or between an oceanic plate and a continental plate. These trenches can be very deep. The ocean floor is deepest at the Mariana Trench, in the Pacific Ocean. Located off the coast of Asia, the trench is more than 11 km (6.8 mi) beneath the ocean surface. The Peru-Chile Trench, on the eastern side of the Pacific Ocean off the coast of South America, is associated with the formation of the Andes Mountains. This trench is more than 7 km (4.3 mi) deep.

Oceanic crust melts when it subducts

Mountains form at the boundary between oceanic crust and continental crust because of what occurs deep below Earth's surface. In the subduction zone, when the oceanic plate dives into the hotter mantle, materials in the plate reach their boiling point and begin to melt, forming magma. Because this magma is less dense than the rock above it, it rises toward the surface. This rising magma pushes the continental crust upward, forming mountains. Subtler effects of heating by the magma cause the continental crust to swell and become less dense, adding height to the continental mountains.

Volcanic mountains also form at convergent boundaries. Magma rises to the surface and cools, forming new rock. These volcanoes are formed far inland from their associated oceanic trenches. Many volcanoes in the Andes Mountains, for instance, are more than 200 km (125 mi) from the Peru-Chile Trench.

Aconcagua (ah kawng KAH gwah), the tallest mountain in the Western Hemisphere, is a volcanic mountain in the Andes. At a height of 6959 m (22 831 ft), the peak of Aconcagua is more than 13.8 km (8.6 mi) above the bottom of the Peru-Chile Trench.

INTEGRATING

PHYSICS
As mentioned earlier in this chapter, Earth's crust is cooler than the layers below. As hot magma rises, it transfers energy to the atoms in the crust and causes them to vibrate more energetically. Because of this increased vibration, the atoms press one another outward and the crust expands and swells upward.

Figure 19-8
The Himalayas are still growing today as the tectonic plate containing Asia and the plate containing India continue to collide.

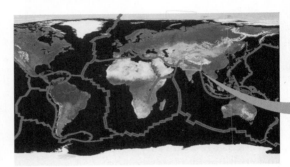

Colliding continental plates create mountains

The Himalayas, shown in **Figure 19-8,** are the tallest mountain range in the world. They formed during the collision between the tectonic plate containing India and the Eurasian plate.

The Himalayas are presently 320 km wide (about 200 mi) at their widest point. They continue to grow in both width and height as the two plates continue to collide. Mount Everest, the highest mountain in the world, is part of this range. Mount Everest's peak is 8850 m (29 034 ft) above sea level.

fault a crack in the Earth created when rocks on either side of a break move

Transform Fault Boundaries

Plate movement can cause breaks in the lithosphere as well. Once a break occurs, rocks in the lithosphere continue to move, scraping past one another. The cracks in the Earth where the rocks move past one another are called **faults.**

Faults can occur in any area where forces in the lithosphere are great enough to break rock. When rocks move horizontally past each other at faults along plate boundaries, the boundary is called a *transform fault boundary.*

Figure 19-9 shows how plates move past each other at a transform fault boundary.

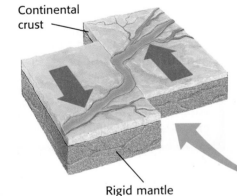

Continental crust

Rigid mantle

Figure 19-9
Plates scrape past each other at transform fault boundaries. The change in the course of the river results from plate movement.

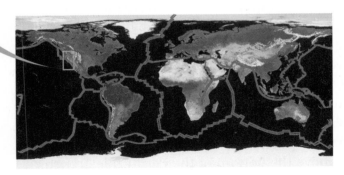

At transform fault boundaries, the great forces involved in plate movement tear at the Earth and cause earthquakes. You may have heard or read about some of the earthquakes along the San Andreas fault, which runs from Mexico through California and out to sea north of San Francisco. Transform fault boundaries occur in many places across Earth, including the ocean floor.

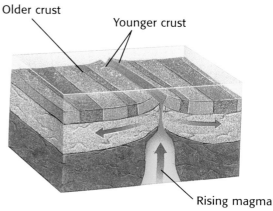

Older crust
Younger crust
Rising magma

Figure 19-10
The stripes in the crust illustrate Earth's alternating magnetic field. Light stripes represent the ocean floor when Earth's magnetic polarity was oriented the same way it is today, while the darker stripes show reversed polarity.

Evidence for Plate Tectonics

In the 1960s, evidence was discovered in the middle of the oceans that helped explain the mechanisms of plate tectonics. New technology provided images of "bands" of rock on the ocean floor with alternating magnetic polarities, like the bands illustrated in **Figure 19-10.** These bands differ from one another in the alignment of the magnetic minerals in the rocks they contain.

Inquiry Lab

Can you model tectonic plate boundaries with clay?

Materials
- ✔ ruler
- ✔ plastic knife
- ✔ paper
- ✔ lab apron
- ✔ scissors
- ✔ 2–3 lb modeling clay
- ✔ rolling pin or rod

Procedure

1. Use a ruler to draw two 10 × 20 cm rectangles on your paper, and cut them out.
2. Use a rolling pin to flatten two pieces of clay until they are each about 1 cm thick. Place a paper rectangle on each piece of clay. Using the plastic knife, trim each piece of clay along the edges to match the shape of the paper.
3. Flip the two clay rectangles so that the paper is at the bottom, and place them side by side on a flat surface, as shown at right. Slowly push the models toward each other until the edges of the clay make contact and begin to buckle and rise off the surface of the table.
4. Turn the models around so that the unbuckled edges are touching. Place one hand on each clay model. Slide one clay model toward you and the other model away from you. Apply only slight pressure toward the seam where the two pieces of clay touch.

Analysis

1. What type of plate boundary are you demonstrating with the model in step 3?
2. What type of plate boundary are you demonstrating in step 4?
3. How do the appearances of the facing edges of the models in the two processes compare? How do you think these processes might affect the appearance of Earth's surface?

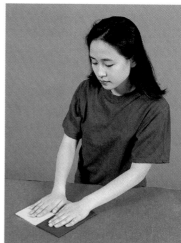

Magnetic alignment of oceanic rocks supports the plate tectonics theory

As hot, molten rock pours out onto the ocean floor, iron minerals, such as magnetite, align themselves parallel to Earth's magnetic field, just as compass needles do. After the rocks cool to about 550°C (1020°F), the alignment of these magnetic regions in the iron minerals becomes fixed. The result is a permanent record of Earth's magnetic field as it was just before the rock cooled.

So why are there differently oriented magnetic bands of rock? Earth's magnetic field has reversed direction many times during its history, with the north magnetic pole becoming the south magnetic pole and the south magnetic pole becoming the north magnetic pole. This occurs on average once every 200 000 years. This process is recorded in the rocks as bands. These magnetic bands are symmetrical on either side of the Mid-Atlantic Ridge. The rocks appear to be the youngest near the center of the ridge. The farther away from the ridge you go, the older the rocks appear. This suggests that the crust was moving away from the plate boundary.

SECTION 19.1 REVIEW

SUMMARY

▶ The layers of Earth are the crust, mantle, and core.

▶ Earth's outer layer (lithosphere) is broken into several pieces called tectonic plates. These plates ride on top of the soft mantle beneath them.

▶ Plates spread apart at divergent boundaries, collide at convergent boundaries, and slide past each other at transform fault boundaries. The entire landscape of the planet has been shaped by these processes.

▶ The alignment of iron minerals in oceanic rocks supports the theory of plate tectonics.

CHECK YOUR UNDERSTANDING

1. **Explain** why the inner core remains a solid even though it is very hot.
2. **Determine** what type of plate tectonic boundary each of the following describes:
   a. plates move alongside each other
   b. plates move toward each other
   c. plates move away from each other
3. **Describe** how the gap is filled when two tectonic plates move away from each other.
4. **Determine** whether each of the following is likely to occur at convergent or divergent boundaries:
   a. rift valley
   b. continental mountains
   c. mid-oceanic ridge
   d. ocean trench
5. **Explain** how magnetic bands provide evidence that tectonic plates are moving apart at mid-oceanic ridges.
6. **Predict** what type of plate boundary exists along the coastline near Japan's volcanic mountain ranges.
7. **Critical Thinking** The oldest continental rocks are 4 billion years old, whereas the oldest sea-floor rocks are 200 million years old. Explain the difference in these ages.

Earthquakes and Volcanoes

OBJECTIVES

▶ Identify the causes of earthquakes.
▶ Distinguish between S waves, P waves, and surface waves in earthquakes.
▶ Describe how earthquakes are measured and rated.
▶ Explain how and where volcanoes occur.
▶ Describe the different types of common volcanoes.

▶ **KEY TERMS**
focus
epicenter
P waves
S waves
surface waves
seismology
Richter scale
vent

Imagine rubbing two rough-sided rocks back and forth against each other. The movement won't be smooth. Instead, the rocks will create a vibration that is transferred to your hands. The same thing happens when rocks slide past one another at a fault. The resulting vibrations are called earthquakes.

What Are Earthquakes?

Compare the occurrence of earthquakes, shown as yellow dots in **Figure 19-11,** with the plate boundaries, marked by red lines. Each yellow dot marks the occurrence of an earthquake sometime between 1985 and 1995. You can see that earthquakes occur mostly at the boundaries of tectonic plates, where the plates shift with respect to one another.

Figure 19-11
Each yellow dot in this illustration marks the occurrence of an earthquake sometime between 1985 and 1995.

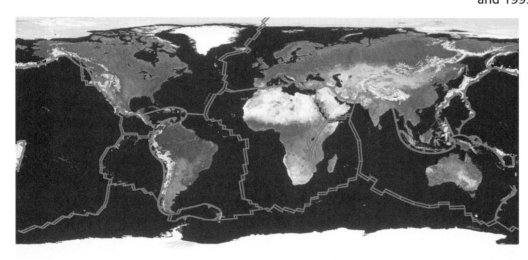

⊏⊐ Divergent boundary   ▲▲ Convergent boundary   —— Transform boundary

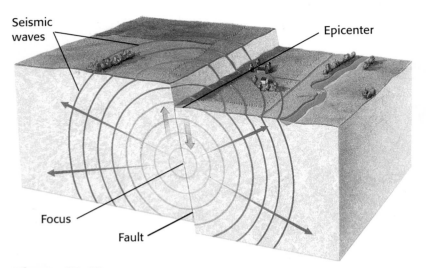

Figure 19-12
The epicenter of an earthquake is the point on the surface directly above the focus.

▶ **focus** the area along a fault at which slippage first occurs, initiating an earthquake

▶ **epicenter** the point on Earth's surface directly above the focus of an earthquake

▶ **P waves** primary waves; the longitudinal waves generated by an earthquake

Japan and California experience earthquakes often because they are situated at plate boundaries.

As plates move, the rocks along their edges experience immense pressure. Eventually, the stress becomes so great that it breaks these rocks along a fault line. As the rocks break, energy is released as *seismic waves*. As the seismic waves travel through and along the surface of Earth, they create the shaking effect that we experience during an earthquake.

The exact point inside Earth where the rocks first break, and thus where an earthquake originates, is called the **focus**. Earthquake waves travel in all directions from the focus, which is often located far below Earth's surface. The point on the surface immediately above the focus is called the **epicenter**, as shown in **Figure 19-12.** Because the epicenter is the point on Earth's surface that is closest to the focus, the damage there is usually greatest.

Energy from earthquakes is transferred through Earth by waves

The energy released by an earthquake is measured as shock waves. Earthquakes generate three types of waves. *Longitudinal waves* originate from an earthquake's focus. Longitudinal waves move faster through rock than other seismic waves. So they are the first waves to reach shock-wave recording stations. For this reason, longitudinal waves are also called *primary waves*, or **P waves.**

A longitudinal wave travels by compressing Earth's crust in front of it and stretching the crust in back of it. You can simulate longitudinal waves by compressing a portion of a spring and then releasing it, as shown in **Figure 19-13A.** Energy will travel through the coil as a longitudinal wave.

Figure 19-13

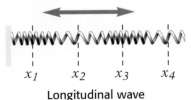

x_1 x_2 x_3 x_4

Longitudinal wave

🅐 P waves are longitudinal waves, which can be modeled by compressing and releasing a spring.

Transverse wave

🅑 S waves are transverse waves, which can be modeled by shaking a rope vertically.

The second type of wave originating from an earthquake's focus is a *transverse wave*. Transverse waves move more slowly through Earth than longitudinal waves. Thus, these slower waves are called *secondary waves,* or **S waves.** The motion of a transverse wave is similar to that of the wave created when a rope is shaken up and down, as shown in **Figure 19-13B.**

Both P waves and S waves spread out from the focus in all directions, like light from a light bulb. In contrast, the third type of wave moves only across Earth's surface. These waves, called **surface waves,** are the result of Earth's entire mass shaking like a bell that has been rung. Earth's surface bends and reshapes as it shakes. The resulting rolling motion of Earth's surface is a combination of up-and-down motion and back-and-forth motion. In this type of wave, points on Earth's surface have a circular motion, like the movement of ocean waves far from shore.

Surface waves cause more destruction than either P waves or S waves. P waves and S waves shake buildings back and forth or up and down at relatively high frequencies. But the rolling action of surface waves, with their longer wavelengths, can cause buildings to collapse.

Seismology is the science of detecting and measuring earthquakes

Seismology is the study of earthquakes. Seismologists use sensitive machines called *seismographs* to record data about earthquakes, including P waves, S waves, and surface waves. **Figure 19-14** shows a simple seismograph. Remember learning about inertia and Newton's first law from Chapter 7? Seismographs use inertia to measure ground motion during an earthquake.

Examine the seismograph in **Figure 19-14.** A stationary pendulum hangs from a support fastened to Earth as a drum of paper turns slowly beneath the pendulum, which has a pen at its tip. When the Earth does not shake, the seismograph records an almost straight line because both Earth and the pendulum are relatively still. As Earth shakes, the base of the seismograph moves with Earth, but the pendulum remains stationary because it is protected from

▶ **S waves** secondary waves; the transverse waves generated by an earthquake

▶ **surface waves** a seismic wave that travels along Earth's surface

TOPIC: Earthquakes
GO TO: www.scilinks.org
KEYWORD: HK1703

▶ **seismology** the study of earthquakes and related phenomena

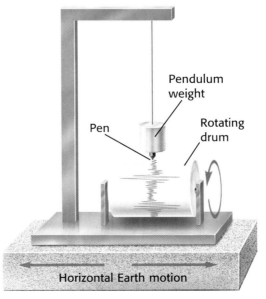

Pendulum weight

Pen

Rotating drum

Horizontal Earth motion

Figure 19-14
When the ground shakes, the pendulum on a seismograph remains relatively still while a rotating drum of paper at the seismograph's base records Earth's movement.

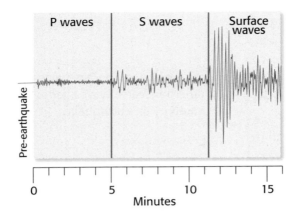

P waves | S waves | Surface waves

Pre-earthquake

0   5   10   15
Minutes

Figure 19-15
Each type of seismic wave leaves a unique zigzag pattern on a seismogram.

Earth's movement by the string. The pendulum draws zigzag lines on the paper that indicate an earthquake has occurred somewhere. Records of seismic activity are called *seismograms.*

There are more than 1000 seismograph stations across the world. At each station, three seismographs are used to measure different motions: north to south, east to west, and up and down. The north-to-south and east-to-west seismographs use a design similar to the seismograph in **Figure 19-14** but face perpendicular to each other. The up-and-down seismograph has a different design than that shown in **Figure 19-14,** but like the other seismographs, it works on the principle of inertia.

Three seismograph stations are necessary to locate the epicenter of an earthquake

As shown in **Figure 19-15,** P waves are the first to be recorded by seismographs, making a series of small, zigzag lines on the seismogram. S waves arrive later, appearing as larger, more ragged lines. Surface waves arrive last and make the largest lines. The difference in time between the arrival of P waves and the arrival of S waves enables seismologists to calculate the distance between the seismograph station and the earthquake's focus. By combining information from at least three different seismograph stations, seismologists can locate the focus and epicenter of an earthquake.

P waves →
S waves →

Epicenter

No direct P waves

Liquid outer core

Solid inner core

Mantle

105°

140°

No direct S waves

No direct P waves

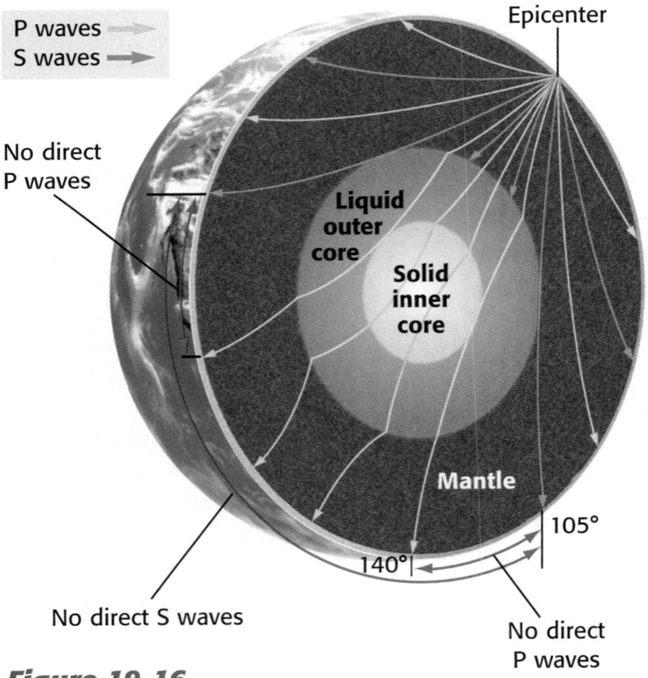

Figure 19-16
No direct S waves can be detected in locations more than 105° from the earthquake's epicenter. No direct P waves can be detected in locations between 105° and 140° from the earthquake's epicenter.

Geologists use seismographs to investigate Earth's interior

Seismologists have found that S waves do not reach seismographs on the side of Earth's core opposite the focus, as shown in **Figure 19-16.** This is evidence that part of the core is liquid because S waves, which are transverse waves, cannot travel through a liquid.

By comparing seismograms recorded during earthquakes, seismologists have noticed that the velocity of seismic waves varies depending on where they are measured. Waves change speed and direction whenever the density of the material they are traveling through changes. The differences in velocity suggest that Earth's interior consists of several layers of different densities. By comparing data, scientists have constructed the model of Earth's interior described in Section 19.1.

Table 19-1   Earthquake Magnitude, Effects, and Frequency

Magnitude	Characteristic effects of shallow earthquakes	Estimated number of earthquakes recorded each year
2.0 to 3.4	Not felt but recorded	More than 150 000
3.5 to 4.2	Felt by a few people in the affected area	30 000
4.3 to 4.8	Felt by most people in the affected area	4800
4.9 to 5.4	Felt by everyone in the affected area	1400
5.5 to 6.1	Moderate to slight damage	500
6.2 to 6.9	Widespread damage to most structures	100
7.0 to 7.3	Serious damage	15
7.4 to 7.9	Great damage	4
8.0 to 8.9	Very great damage	Occur infrequently
9.0	Would be felt in most parts of the Earth	Possible but never recorded
10.0	Would be felt all over the Earth	Possible but never recorded

The Richter scale is a measure of the magnitude of earthquakes

The Richter scale is a measure of the energy released at the focus of an earthquake. The magnitude of an earthquake is limited by the strength of the rocks of Earth's crust. The 1964 Alaskan earthquake, with a Richter magnitude of 8.4, is the largest earthquake of recent times. Each step on the Richter scale represents a 30-fold increase in the energy released. So an earthquake of magnitude 8 releases 30^4, or 810 000, times as much energy as one of magnitude 4! **Table 19-1** summarizes the effects and number of earthquakes with varying magnitudes. Notice that low magnitude earthquakes occur frequently.

The Richter scale cannot predict how severe an earthquake will be in terms of the damage it can cause. The amount of damage depends on several factors, such as the distance between populated areas and the epicenter and the type of construction used in buildings in those areas. The Armenian earthquake of 1988 and the San Francisco earthquake of 1989 both had a magnitude of 7 on the Richter scale. Yet the damage caused by each was very different. In Armenia, there was devastating property damage, and more than 25 000 people died. In contrast, 70 people died in San Francisco, and the only major damage was to an elevated freeway and some homes.

Why was there such a big difference between the effects of these two earthquakes? The depth of the focus of the earthquakes differed: the focus of the Armenian earthquake was 5 km down, but in San Francisco it was 19 km down. The deeper the focus, the less the effects will be felt at the surface.

▶ **Richter scale** scale that expresses the relative magnitude of an earthquake

Did You Know ?

The effect of an earthquake on Earth's surface is called the earthquake's intensity. The modified Mercalli scale is the most commonly used intensity scale. An earthquake is assigned a lower number if people felt the quake but it didn't cause much damage. Earthquakes that cause structural damage are assigned a higher number. The scale has been used to develop intensity maps for planners, building officials, and insurance companies.

Also, the physical properties of the rocks at the surface were different. The rocks in San Francisco are generally harder than those in Armenia. Softer rock breaks apart and changes position more easily than rigid rock, which is more likely to bend and return to its original position.

The difference in the amount of fatalities and damage between the two earthquakes was mainly due to the building construction in the two areas. California building codes require that buildings are able to withstand earthquakes of a certain magnitude. The buildings in Armenia were much less stable.

Volcanoes

As mentioned in Section 19.1, volcanoes can result from the movement of tectonic plates. A volcano is any opening in Earth's crust through which magma has reached Earth's surface. These openings are called **vents.**

Volcanoes often form hills or mountains as materials pour or explode from the vent, as shown in **Figure 19-17.** Volcanoes release molten rock, ash, and poisonous gases. All these products result from melting in the mantle or in the crust.

The type of eruption determines the volcano type

Volcanoes generally have one central vent, but they can also have several smaller vents. Magma from inside a volcano can reach Earth's surface through any of these vents. When magma reaches the surface, its physical behavior changes, and it is called *lava.*

Magma rich in iron and magnesium is very fluid and forms lava that tends to flow great distances. The eruptions are usually mild and can occur several times. The buildup of this kind of lava produces a gently sloping mountain, called a *shield volcano.* Shield volcanoes are some of the largest volcanoes. Mauna Loa, in Hawaii, is a shield volcano, as shown in **Figure 19-18A.** Mauna Loa's summit is more than 4000 m (13 000 ft) above sea level and more than 9020 m (29 500 ft) above the sea floor.

Composite volcanoes are made up of alternating layers of ash, cinders, and lava. Their magma is rich in silica and therefore is much thicker than the magma of a shield volcano. Gases are trapped in the magma, causing eruptions that alternate between flows and explosive activity that produces cinders and ash. Composite volcanoes are typically thousands of meters high, with much steeper slopes than shield volcanoes. Japan's Mount Fuji, shown in **Figure 19-18B,** is a composite volcano. Mount St. Helens, Mount Rainier, Mount Hood, and Mount Shasta, all in the northwestern United States, are also composite volcanoes.

▶ **vent** an opening through which molten rock flows onto Earth's surface

Figure 19-17
Volcanoes build up into hills or mountains as lava and ash explode from openings in the Earth called vents.

Cinder cones are the smallest and most abundant volcanoes. When large amounts of gas are trapped in magma, violent eruptions occur—vast quantities of hot ash and lava are thrown from the vent. These particles then fall to the ground around the vent, forming the cone. Cinder cones tend to be active for only a short time and then become dormant. As shown in **Figure 19-18C,** Parícutin (pah REE koo teen), in west-central Mexico, is a famous cinder cone. Parícutin first erupted in 1943. After 2 years, the top of the volcano's cone had grown to a height of 450 m (1480 ft) above the base. The eruptions finally ended in 1952.

Volcanoes form not only on land but also under the oceans. In shallow water, volcanoes can erupt violently, forming clouds of ash and steam. An underwater volcano is called a *seamount*. Seamounts look much like composite volcanoes.

Figure 19-18
The type of volcano that forms depends largely on the makeup of the magma. Differences in the fluidity of the magma determine the type of eruption that occurs.

Types of Volcanoes

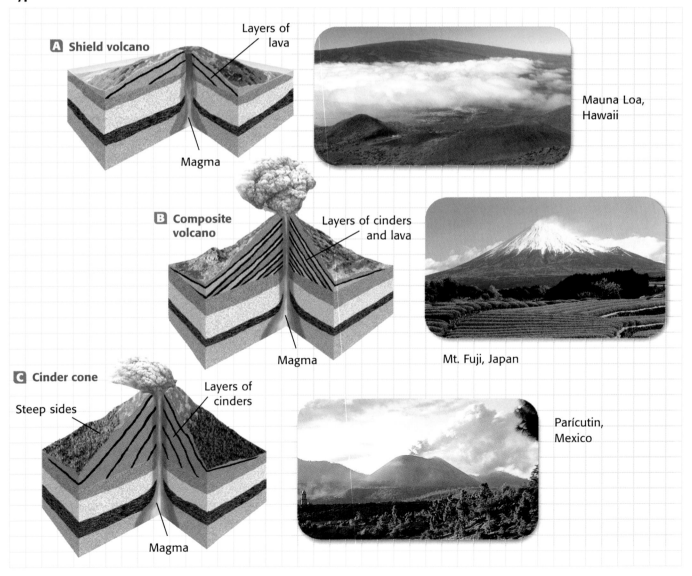

A Shield volcano

Layers of lava

Magma

Mauna Loa, Hawaii

B Composite volcano

Layers of cinders and lava

Magma

Mt. Fuji, Japan

C Cinder cone

Steep sides

Layers of cinders

Magma

Parícutin, Mexico

Figure 19-19

Seventy-five percent of the active volcanoes on Earth occur along the edges of the Pacific Ocean. Together these volcanoes form the Ring of Fire.

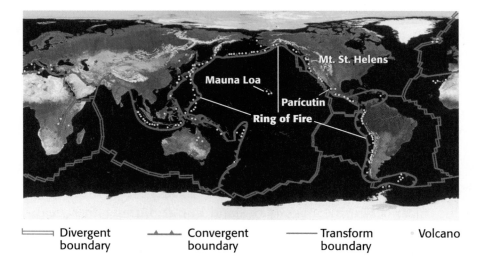

| ⊏⊐ Divergent boundary | ▲▲ Convergent boundary | — Transform boundary | · Volcano |

Volcanoes occur at convergent plate boundaries surrounding the Pacific Ocean

Like earthquakes, volcanoes are linked to plate movement. Volcanoes are common all around the edges of the Pacific Ocean, where oceanic tectonic plates collide with continental plates. In fact, 75 percent of the active volcanoes on Earth are located in these areas. As seen in **Figure 19-19,** the volcanoes around the Pacific Ocean lie in a zone known as the Ring of Fire.

As a plate sinks at a convergent boundary, part of it melts and magma rises to the surface. The volcanoes that result form the edges of the Ring of Fire. These volcanoes tend to erupt cooler, less-fluid lava and clouds of ash and gases. The sticky lava makes it difficult for the gases to escape. Gas pressure builds up, causing explosive eruptions that often lead to loss of life and damage to property.

Volcanoes occur at divergent plate boundaries

As plates move apart at divergent boundaries, magma rises to fill in the gap. This magma creates the volcanic mountains that form the ridges around a central rift valley.

The volcanic island of Iceland, in the North Atlantic Ocean, is on the Mid-Atlantic Ridge. The island is continuously expanding from its center; the eastern and western sides of the island are growing outward in opposite directions. As a result, a great deal of geologic activity, such as volcanoes and hot springs, occurs on the island.

Connection to
SOCIAL STUDIES

Mount St. Helens, in the Cascade Range in Washington, erupted explosively on May 18, 1980. Sixty people and thousands of animals were killed, and 10 million trees were blown down by the air blast created by the explosion. During the eruption, the north side of the mountain was blown away. Gas and ash were ejected upward, forming a column more than 19.2 km (11.9 mi) high. The ash was reported to have fallen as far east as central Montana.

Since the May 18 explosion, Mount St. Helens has had several minor eruptions. As a result, a small volcanic cone is now visible in the original volcano's crater.

Making the Connection

1. What might have caused the eruption of Mount St. Helens to be so explosive?
2. The force of the blast didn't push the ashes all the way to Montana. What other natural force might have transported the ashes that far?

Volcanoes occur at hot spots

Some volcanoes occur in the middle of plates. They occur because mushroom-shaped trails of hot magma, called *mantle plumes,* rise from deep inside the mantle and erupt from volcanoes at *hot spots* at the surface.

When mantle plumes form below oceanic plates, lava and ash build up on the ocean floor. If the resulting volcanoes grow large enough, they break through the water's surface and become islands. As the oceanic plate continues moving, however, the mantle plume does not move along with it. The plume continues to rise under the moving oceanic plate, and a new volcano is formed at a different point. A "trail" in the form of a chain of extinct volcanic islands is left behind.

The Hawaiian Islands, which were formed by rising mantle plumes, lie in a line that roughly corresponds to the motion of the Pacific plate. The island of Hawaii is the most recently formed volcano in the chain, and it still contains the active volcano situated over the mantle plume.

SECTION 19.2 REVIEW

SUMMARY

▶ Earthquakes occur as a result of sudden movement within Earth's lithosphere.

▶ P waves are longitudinal waves, and they travel the fastest.

▶ S waves are transverse waves, and they travel more slowly.

▶ Surface waves travel the slowest. They result from Earth's vibrating like a bell.

▶ Volcanoes are formed when magma rises and penetrates the surface of Earth.

▶ The three types of volcanoes are shield volcanoes, cinder cones, and composite volcanoes.

CHECK YOUR UNDERSTANDING

1. **Identify** which type of seismic wave is described in each of the following:
   a. cannot travel through the core
   b. cause the most damage to buildings
   c. are the first waves to reach seismograph stations
2. **Select** which of the following describes a shield volcano:
   a. formed from violent eruptions   c. formed from hot ash
   b. has gently sloping sides   d. has steep sides
3. **Identify** whether volcanoes are likely to form at the following locations:
   a. hot spot
   b. transform fault boundary
   c. divergent plate boundary
   d. convergent boundary between continental and oceanic plates
4. **Differentiate** between the focus and the epicenter of an earthquake.
5. **Explain** how a mid-oceanic ridge is formed.
6. **Explain** why Iceland is a good place to use hydrothermal power, power produced from heated water.
7. **Critical Thinking** Are quiet eruptions or explosive eruptions more likely to increase the height of a volcano? Why?

Minerals and Rocks

KEY TERMS

mineral
igneous rock
weathering
sedimentary rock
fossils
metamorphic rock

OBJECTIVES

▶ Identify the three types of rock.

▶ Explain the properties of each type of rock based on physical and chemical conditions under which the rock formed.

▶ Describe the rock cycle and how rocks change form.

▶ Explain how the relative and absolute ages of rocks are determined.

Devils Tower, in Wyoming, shown in **Figure 19-20,** rises 264 m (867 ft) above its base. According to an American Indian legend, the tower's jagged columns were formed by a giant bear scraping its claws across the rock. The tower is actually the solidified core of a volcano. Over millions of years, the surrounding softer rock was worn away by the Belle Fourche River finally exposing the core. Volcanic pipes, which are similar to volcanic cores, can be a source of diamonds. They contain solidified magma that extends from the mantle to Earth's surface.

Structure and Origins of Rocks

▶ **mineral** a natural, inorganic solid with a definite chemical composition and a characteristic internal structure

Figure 19-20
Devils Tower, in northeastern Wyoming, is the solidified core of a volcano.

All rocks are composed of **minerals.** Minerals are naturally occurring, nonliving substances found in Earth that have a composition that can be expressed by a chemical formula. Minerals also have a definite internal structure. Quartz, for example, is a mineral made of silicon dioxide, SiO_2. It is composed of crystals, as are most minerals. Coal, on the other hand, is not a mineral because it is formed from decomposed plant matter. *Granite* is not a mineral either; it is a rock composed of different minerals.

There are about 3500 known minerals in Earth's crust. However, no more than 20 of these are commonly found in rocks. Together, these 20 or so minerals make up more than 95 percent of all the rocks in Earth's crust. The nine most common of these *rock-forming minerals* are feldspar, pyroxene, mica, olivine, dolomite, quartz, amphibole, clay, and calcite.

Each combination of rock-forming minerals results in a rock with a unique set of properties. Rocks may be porous, granular, or smooth; they may be soft or hard and have different densities or colors. The appearance and characteristics of a rock reflect its mineral composition and the way it formed.

Figure 19-21

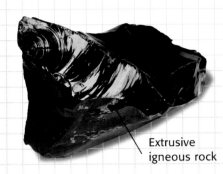

A Notice the coarse-grained texture of this sample of granite, an intrusive igneous rock.

Intrusive
igneous rock

B Obsidian, an extrusive igneous rock, cools much more quickly than granite.

Extrusive
igneous rock

Molten rock cools to form igneous rock

When molten rock cools and solidifies it forms igneous rock. Nearly all igneous rocks are made of crystals of various minerals, such as those shown in the granite in **Figure 19-21A.** As the rock cools, the minerals in the rock crystallize and grow. In general, the more quickly the rock cools, the less the crystals grow. For instance, obsidian, a smooth stone used by early American Indians to make tools, is similar to granite in composition, but it cools much more quickly. As a result, obsidian has either very small crystals or no crystals at all. **Figure 19-21B** shows a piece of obsidian.

Obsidian is categorized as an *extrusive* igneous rock because it cools on Earth's surface. *Basalt,* a fine-grained, dark-colored rock, is the most common extrusive igneous rock. Granite, on the other hand, is called an *intrusive* igneous rock because it forms from magma that cools while trapped beneath Earth's surface. Because the magma is insulated by the surrounding rocks, it takes a very long time to cool—sometimes millions of years. Because of this long cooling period, the crystals in intrusive igneous rocks are larger than those in extrusive igneous rocks. The crystals of granite, for example, are easy to see with the naked eye and are much lighter in color than those of basalt. Both rocks contain feldspar, but granite also has quartz, while basalt has pyroxene.

▷ **igneous rock** rock formed from cooled and hardened magma or lava

Connection to
SOCIAL STUDIES

Throughout history, humans have used rocks and minerals to fashion tools. During the Stone Age, the Bronze Age, and the Iron Age people used stone, bronze, and iron, respectively, to make tools and weapons. The industrial revolution began when humans learned to burn coal to run machinery. After humans learned to extract oil from Earth's crust, gasoline-powered vehicles were invented, and we entered the automobile age.

Making the Connection

1. Research minerals that have been mined for their iron content. Where are the mines that were first used to harvest these minerals?
2. Scientists have divided the Stone Age into three phases—Paleolithic, Mesolithic, and Neolithic— on the basis of toolmaking techniques. Research these phases, and distinguish between the techniques used in each.

Remains of older rocks and organisms form sedimentary rocks

weathering change in the physical form or chemical composition of rock materials exposed at Earth's surface

Even very hard rock with large crystals will break down over thousands of years. The process by which rocks are broken down is called **weathering.** Pieces of rock fall down hillsides due to gravity or get washed down by wind and rain. Rivers then carry the pieces down into deltas, lakes, or the sea. Waves beating against cliffs also knock pieces of rock away. The action of the waves and the movement of rivers and streams eventually break the pieces into pebbles, sand, and even smaller pieces. Weathering will be discussed further in Section 19-4.

As pieces of rock accumulate, they can form another type of rock—**sedimentary rock.** Think of sedimentary rocks as recycled rocks. The sediment they are made of contains fragments of older rocks and, in some cases, the remains of living organisms, called **fossils.**

sedimentary rock rock formed from compressed or cemented deposits of sediment

fossils the traces or remains of a plant or an animal found in sedimentary rock

There are two ways loose sediment can become rock. As sediment accumulates, the layers on the bottom get compressed from the weight of sediment above, forming rock. In the second way, other minerals dissolved in water seep between bits of rock and other material and "glue" them together. In **Figure 19-22A,** the pebbles and bits of rounded rock in the *conglomerate* are glued together with a brown material containing mostly quartz.

Sedimentary rocks are named according to the size of the fragments they contain. As mentioned, a rock made of pebbles is called a conglomerate. A rock made of sand is called *sandstone.* A rock made of fine mud is usually called *mudstone,* but if it is flaky and breaks easily into layers, it is called *shale. Limestone,* another kind of sedimentary rock, is made mostly of the fossils of organisms that lived in the water, as shown in **Figure 19-22B.** Sometimes the fossilized skeletons are so small or are broken up into such small fragments that they can't be seen with the naked eye. Places where limestone is found were once beneath the sea.

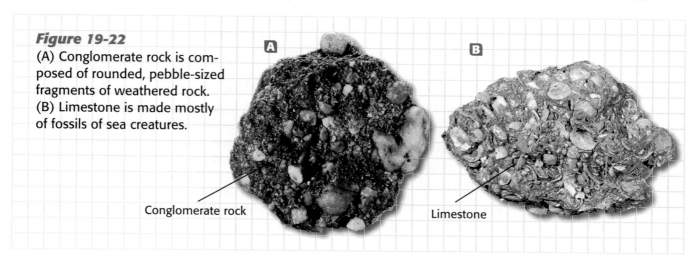

Figure 19-22
(A) Conglomerate rock is composed of rounded, pebble-sized fragments of weathered rock. (B) Limestone is made mostly of fossils of sea creatures.

A

B

Conglomerate rock

Limestone

Rocks that undergo pressure and heating without melting form metamorphic rock

Heat and pressure within Earth cause changes in the texture and mineral content of rocks. These changes produce metamorphic rocks. The word *metamorphic* comes from the Greek word *metamorphosis*, which means "to change form."

Limestone, a sedimentary rock, will turn into *marble*, a metamorphic rock, under the effects of heat and pressure. Marble is a stone used in buildings, such as the Taj Mahal, in India. **Figure 19-23** is a photo of the marble exterior of the Taj Mahal. Notice the swirling, colored bands that make marble so attractive. These bands are the result of impurities that existed in the limestone before it was transformed into marble.

Rocks may be changed, or *metamorphosed*, in two ways: by heat alone or, more commonly, by a combination of heat and pressure. In both cases, the solid rock undergoes a chemical change over millions of years, without melting. As a result, new minerals form in the rocks. The texture of the rocks is changed too, and any fossils in sedimentary rocks are transformed and destroyed.

The most common types of metamorphic rock are formed by heat and pressure deep in the crust. *Slate* forms in this way. It metamorphoses from mudstone or shale, as shown in **Figure 19-24.** Slate is a hard rock that can be split very easily along planes in the rock, creating large, flat surfaces.

Figure 19-23
The Taj Mahal, in India, is made of marble, a metamorphic rock often used in buildings.

▶ metamorphic rock rock formed from other rocks as a result of heat, pressure, or chemical processes

A Shale

Heat and pressure

B Slate

Figure 19-24
Slate (B) is a metamorphic rock that is transformed under heat and pressure from the sedimentary rocks shale (A) or mudstone.

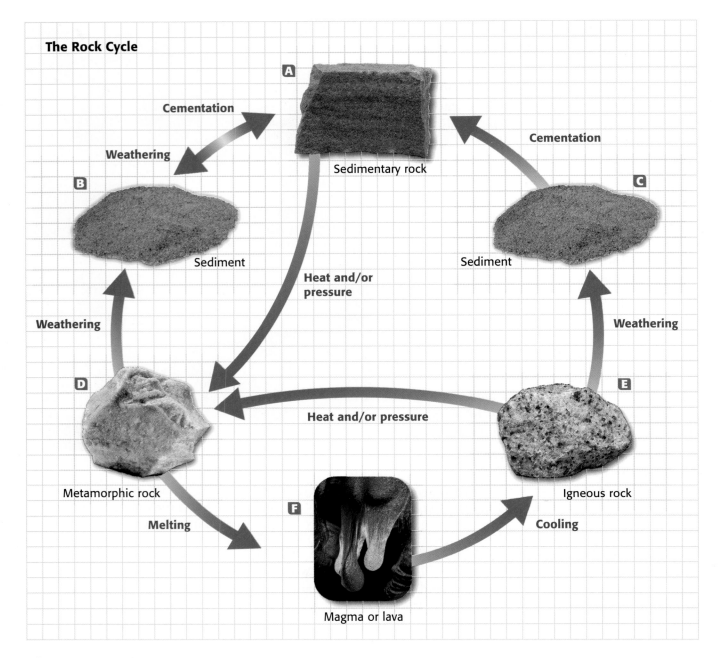

The Rock Cycle

A Sedimentary rock

Cementation

Weathering

Cementation

B Sediment

Weathering

C Sediment

Heat and/or pressure

Weathering

D Metamorphic rock

Heat and/or pressure

E Igneous rock

Melting

F Magma or lava

Cooling

Figure 19-25
The rock cycle illustrates the changes that sedimentary, igneous, and metamorphic rocks undergo.

Old rocks in the rock cycle form new rocks

So far, you have seen some examples of one type of rock becoming another. For instance, limestone exposed to heat and pressure becomes marble. Exposed rocks are weathered, forming sediments. These sediments may be cemented together to make sedimentary rock. The various types of rock are all a part of one rock system. The sequence of events in which rocks are weathered, melted, altered, and formed is described by the *rock cycle*.

Figure 19-25 illustrates the stages of the rock cycle. Regardless of which path is taken, rock formation occurs very slowly, often over tens of thousands to millions of years.

As magma (F) cools underground, it forms igneous rock (E), such as granite. If the granite is heated and put under pressure, it may become metamorphic rock (D); if it is exposed to the sea, it may be fragmented by waves and become sand (C). The sand may be transported, deposited, and cemented to become the sedimentary rock (A) sandstone. As more time passes, several other layers of sediment are deposited above the sandstone. With enough heat and pressure, the sandstone becomes a metamorphic rock (D). This metamorphic rock (D) may then be forced deep within the Earth, where it melts, forming magma (F).

How Old Are Rocks?

Rocks form and change over millions of years. It is difficult to know the exact time when a rock formed. To determine the age of rocks on a geological time scale, several techniques have been developed.

The relative age of rocks can be determined using the principle of superposition

Think about your hamper of dirty clothes at home. If you don't disturb the stack of clothes in the hamper, you can tell the relative time the clothes were placed in the hamper. In other words, you may not know how long ago you placed a particular red shirt in the hamper, but you can tell that the shirts above the red shirt were placed there more recently. In a similar manner, the *relative age* of rocks can be determined using the *principle of superposition*. The principle of superposition states the following:

Assuming no change in the position of the rock layers, the oldest will be on the bottom, and the youngest will be on top.

The principle of superposition is useful in studying the sequence of life on Earth. For instance, the cliffside in **Figure 19-26** shows several sedimentary layers stacked on top of one another. The layers on the bottom are older than the layers above them.

Although the various layers of sedimentary rock are most visible in cliffsides and canyon walls, you would also find layering if you dug down anywhere there is sedimentary rock. By applying the principle of superposition, scientists know that fossils in the upper layers are the remains of animals that lived more recently than the animals that were fossilized in lower layers.

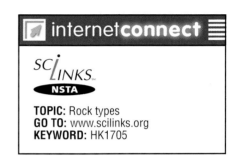

TOPIC: Rock types
GO TO: www.scilinks.org
KEYWORD: HK1705

Figure 19-26
According to the principle of superposition, the layers of sedimentary rock on top are the most recent layers if the rocks have not been disturbed.

Did You Know ?

Radioactive dating can determine a more exact, or absolute, age of rocks

The chapter on nuclear changes showed that the nuclei of some isotopes decay, emitting energy at a fairly constant rate. These isotopes are said to be radioactive. The radioactive elements that make up minerals in rocks decay over billions of years. Physicists have determined the rate at which these elements decay, and geologists can use this data to determine the age of rocks. They measure both the amount of the original radioactive material left undecayed in the rock and the amount of the product of the radioactive material's decay. The amount of time that passed since the rock formed can be calculated from this ratio.

Many different isotopes can be analyzed when rocks are dated. Some of the most reliable are isotopes of potassium, argon, rubidium, strontium, uranium, and lead.

While the principle of superposition gives only the relative age of rocks, radioactive dating gives the *absolute age* of a rock.

SECTION 19.3 REVIEW

SUMMARY

▶ Igneous rocks are formed from cooling molten rock.

▶ Sedimentary rocks form by the deposition of pieces of other rocks and the remains of living organisms.

▶ Metamorphic rocks form after exposure to heat and/or pressure for an extended time.

▶ Rocks can change type, as described by the rock cycle.

▶ The relative age of rock can be determined using the principle of superposition. Unless the layers are disturbed, the layers on the bottom are the oldest.

▶ Radioactive dating is used to determine the absolute age of rocks.

CHECK YOUR UNDERSTANDING

1. **Modify** the following false statement to make it a true statement: Fossils are found in igneous rock.

2. **Explain** how the principle of superposition is used by geologists to compare the ages of rocks.

3. **Determine** the type of rock that will form in each of the following scenarios:
   a. Lava pours onto the ocean floor and cools.
   b. Minerals cement small pieces of sand together.
   c. Mudstone is subjected to great heat and pressure over a long period of time.

4. **Explain** why a construction worker who uses a jackhammer on a rock does not produce a metamorphic rock.

5. **Identify** what type of rock might have a lot of holes in it due to the formation of gas bubbles. Explain your answer.

6. **Creative Thinking** A paleontologist who is researching extinctions notices that certain fossils are never found above a layer of sediment containing the radioactive isotope rubidium-87 or below another layer containing the same isotope. To determine when these animals became extinct, should the paleontologist use relative dating, absolute dating, or a combination of the two? Explain your answer.

Weathering and Erosion

▶ Identify the causes of rock shaping due to weathering and erosion.

▶ Explain how chemical weathering can form underground caves in limestone.

▶ Describe how acid rain affects the landscape.

▶ **KEY TERMS**

erosion

deposition

acid rain

Compared to the destructive power of an earthquake or a volcano, the force exerted by a river on Earth's surface may seem trivial. But, over time, forces such as water and wind can make vast changes in the landscape. Parunaweep Canyon, in southern Utah, shown in **Figure 19-27,** is one of the most magnificent examples of how water can shape Earth's rocky surface.

Physical Weathering

There are two types of weathering processes: physical and chemical. Physical, or mechanical, weathering breaks rocks into smaller pieces but does not alter the rocks' chemical composition. Chemical weathering breaks down rock by changing its chemical composition.

Ice can break rocks

Ice can play a part in the physical or mechanical weathering of rock. A common kind of mechanical weathering is called *frost wedging.* This occurs when water seeps into cracks or joints in rock and then freezes. When the water freezes, its volume increases by about 10 percent, pushing the rock apart. Every time the ice thaws and refreezes, it wedges farther into the rock, and the crack in the rock widens and deepens. This process eventually breaks off pieces of the rock or splits the rock apart.

Plants can also break rocks

The roots of plants can also act as wedges as the roots grow into cracks in the rocks. As the plant grows, the roots exert a constant pressure on the rock. The crack continues to deepen and widen, eventually causing a piece of the rock to break off.

Figure 19-27
Parunaweep Canyon, in Zion National Park, Utah, is a striking example of the effect of water on Earth's surface.

Figure 19-28
Red sedimentary layers in Badlands National Park contain iron that has reacted with oxygen to form hematite.

Chemical Weathering

As shown in **Figure 19-28,** many of the sedimentary layers in Badlands National Park, in South Dakota, appear red because they contain hematite. Hematite, Fe_2O_3, is one of the most common minerals on the surface of Earth. Hematite is formed as iron reacts with oxygen in an oxidation reaction. This is an example of *chemical weathering.*

You studied the process of oxidation in Section 5.2. As exemplified by the hematite, when certain elements, especially metals, react with oxygen, they become oxides and their properties change. When these elements are in minerals, oxidation can cause the mineral to decompose or form new minerals. As a result, both the chemical composition and the physical appearance of the rock change.

The results of chemical weathering are not as easy to see as those of physical weathering, but chemical weathering can have a great effect on the landscape over millions of years.

Carbon dioxide dissolved in water can cause chemical weathering

Another common type of chemical weathering occurs when carbon dioxide from the air dissolves in rainwater. The result is water that contains carbonic acid, H_2CO_3. Although carbonic acid is a weak acid, it reacts with some minerals. As the slightly acidic water seeps into the ground, it can weather rock underground.

Figure 19-29
Carbonic acid dissolved the calcite in the sedimentary rock limestone to produce this underground cavern.

For example, calcite, the major mineral in the sedimentary rock limestone, reacts with carbonic acid in water to form calcium bicarbonate. Because the calcium bicarbonate is dissolved in water, the decomposed rock is carried away in the water, leaving underground pockets filled with air or water. The cave shown in **Figure 19-29** resulted from the weathering action of carbonic acid on calcite in underground layers of limestone.

Acid rain can slowly dissolve minerals

In most areas, natural rain has a slightly acidic pH, around 5.7, because it contains carbonic acid. As humans have burned increasing amounts of fossil fuels to run car engines, power stations, and factories, the amount of acid in rain has greatly increased. For instance, because of air pollution, the pH value of rainwater in United States cities between 1940 and 1990 averaged between 4 and 5. The lowest pH measured in rainfall in the United States was in Wheeling, West Virginia, where a pH of 1.5 was recorded in 1982.

Acid rain causes damage to both living organisms and inorganic matter. In Europe, acid rain may have contributed to the death of pine trees, particularly in Germany. Acid rain can erode metal and rock, such as the statue in Brooklyn, New York, shown in **Figure 19-30.** Marble and limestone dissolve relatively rapidly even in weak acid.

▶ **acid rain** precipitation that has an unusually high concentration of sulfuric or nitric acids resulting from chemical pollution of the air

How does pollution contribute to acid rain? When fossil fuels, such as coal, oil, and gasoline, are burned, they release gases, including small amounts of sulfur dioxide from the sulfur in the fuel, and nitrogen oxides from nitrogen in the air. After these gases are released, they may react with water in the air and clouds to form nitric acid, or nitrous acid, and sulfuric acid.

In the United States, the release of chemicals that cause acid rain is declining. In 1990, the Acid Rain Control Program was added to the Clean Air Act of 1970. According to the program, power plants and factories were given 10 years to decrease the release of sulfur dioxide to about half the amount they emitted in 1980. The acidity of rain has been greatly reduced since power plants have installed *scrubbers* that remove the sulfur oxide gases.

Figure 19-30
Acid rain weathers stone structures, such as this marble statue in Brooklyn, New York.

Figure 19-31
Deltas, such as this one in New Zealand, are formed by deposition.

▶ **erosion** the process by which rock and/or the products of weathering are removed

▶ **deposition** process in which sediment is laid down

Erosion

Erosion is the removal and transportation of weathered and non-weathered materials by running water, wind, waves, ice, underground water, and gravity.

Water erosion shapes Earth's surface

Water is by far the most effective physical weathering agent. Have you ever seen a brown or murky river? Muddy rivers carry sediment in their water. As this sediment moves along with the water, it scrapes and scratches rocks and soil on the riverbanks and along the river bottom. As the water continues to scour out new places on the surface, it carries the new sediment away. This process of loosening and moving sediments is known as **erosion.**

There is a direct relationship between the velocity of the water and the size and amount of sediment it can carry. Quickly moving rivers can carry away a lot of sediment, and create extraordinary canyons.

As a river or stream becomes wider or deepens, the water flows more slowly and therefore cannot carry as much sediment. As a result, sediment is deposited on the floor of these calmer portions of the river or stream. The process of depositing sediment is called **deposition.** Rivers eventually flow into large bodies of water, such as seas and oceans, where the sediment in the water is deposited along the continental shores. As rivers widen and slow at the continental boundary, large deposits of sediment are laid down. These areas, called deltas, often have rich, fertile soils, making them excellent agricultural areas. **Figure 19-31** shows the Greenstone River delta, in New Zealand.

The oceans also have a dramatic effect on Earth's landscape. Underwater, currents carry vast amounts of sediment across the ocean floor much like rivers do on land. On seashores, the waves crash onto land, creating tall cliffs and jagged coastlines. The Cliffs of Moher, in Western Ireland, shown in **Figure 19-32,** reach heights of 204 m (669 ft) above the water. The cliffs were formed partially by the force of waves in the Atlantic Ocean eroding the rocky shale and sandstone coast.

Figure 19-32
The action of waves slowly tearing away at the rocky coast formed the Cliffs of Moher.

Figure 19-33
(A) Tustamena Glacier, in Alaska, has slowly pushed its way through these mountains.
(B) Glaciers are capable of carving out large U-shaped valleys, such as this valley in Alaska.

Glaciers erode mountains

Large masses of ice, such as the glacier shown in **Figure 19-33A,** can exert tremendous forces on rocks. The constantly moving ice mass carves the surface it rests on, often creating U-shaped valleys, such as the one shown in **Figure 19-33B.** The weight of the ice and the forward movement of the glacier cause the mass to act like a huge scouring pad. Immense boulders that are carried by the ice scrape across other rocks, grinding them to a fine powder. Glacial meltwater streams carry the fine sediment away from the glacier and deposit it along the banks and floors of streams or at the bottom of glacier-formed lakes.

Wind can also shape the landscape

Just as water or glaciers can carry rocks along, scraping other rocks as they pass, wind can also weather the Earth's surfaces. Have you ever been in a dust storm and felt your skin "burn" from the swirling dust? This happens because fast-moving wind can carry sediment, just as water can. Wind that carries sediment creates a sandblaster effect, smoothing Earth's surface and eroding the landscape.

The sandstone arches of Arches National Park, in Utah, are formed partly by wind erosion. Look at **Figure 19-34.** Can you guess how these arches might have formed? Geologists have struggled to find a good explanation for the formation of arches.

The land in and around Arches National Park is part of the Colorado Plateau, an area that was under a saltwater sea more than 300 million years ago. As this sea evaporated, it deposited a thick layer of salt that has since been covered by many layers of sedimentary rock. The salt layer deforms more easily than rock layers. As the salt layers warped and deformed over the years, they created surface depressions and bulges. Arches formed where the overlying sedimentary rocks were pushed upward by the salt.

Figure 19-34
This sandstone arch in Arches National Park, in Utah, was created as high-speed winds weathered the terrain.

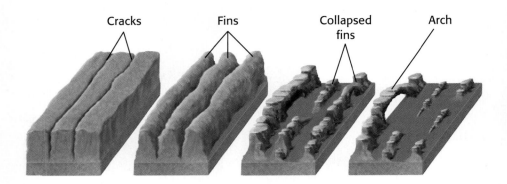

Figure 19-35
Fins are formed when sandstone is pushed upward, and cracks are slowly eroded. Wind, water, and ice erode the fins until they collapse or form arches.

Cracks   Fins   Collapsed fins   Arch

Figure 19-35 shows how one theory explains the formation of arches. As land is pushed upward in places, small surface cracks form. These cracks are eroded by water, ice, and wind until narrow free-standing rock formations, called *fins*, are formed. When these fins are exposed along their sides, the wind wears away at the cement that holds the sediment together, causing large pieces of the rock to fall away. Some fins collapse completely; others that are more sturdy and balanced form arches.

SECTION 19.4 REVIEW

SUMMARY

▶ Physical weathering breaks down rock by water erosion, ice wedging, wind abrasion, glacial abrasion, and many other physical forces.

▶ In chemical weathering, rock is altered as minerals in rock react chemically and break down.

▶ Carbonic acid acts as a chemical weathering agent and is responsible for the formation of underground limestone caves.

▶ Acid rain can weather rock and harm living organisms. It is the byproduct of fossil-fuel emissions reacting with water in the atmosphere.

CHECK YOUR UNDERSTANDING

1. **List** two agents of physical weathering that might occur in the mountains in northern Montana.
2. **Explain** how the wind may be involved in the formation of sandstone arches.
3. **Distinguish** between physical weathering, chemical weathering, and erosion in the following examples:
   a. Rock changes color as it is oxidized.
   b. Rock shatters as it freezes.
   c. Wind erodes the sides of the Egyptian pyramids in Giza.
   d. An underground cavern is formed as water drips in from the Earth's surface.
4. **Explain** why the following statement is incorrect: Acid rain is any rain that has a pH less than 7.
5. **Predict** which will experience more weathering, a rock in the Sonora Desert, in Southern Arizona, or a rock on a beach in North Carolina.
6. **Creative Thinking** On many coastlines, erosion is wearing the beach away and threatening to destroy homes. How would you prevent this destruction?

Chapter Highlights

Before you begin, review the summaries of the key ideas of each section, found on pages 616, 625, 632, and 638. The key vocabulary terms are listed on pages 608, 617, 626, and 633.

UNDERSTANDING CONCEPTS

1. The layer of tar-like mantle under the tectonic plates is called the _____.
   a. lithosphere
   b. oceanic crust
   c. asthenosphere
   d. tectonic plate boundary

2. Two tectonic plates moving away from each other form a(n) _____.
   a. transform fault boundary
   b. convergent boundary
   c. ocean trench
   d. divergent boundary

3. Vibrations in Earth caused by sudden movements of rock are called _____.
   a. epicenters   c. faults
   b. earthquakes   d. volcanoes

4. Using the difference in the time it takes for P waves and S waves to arrive at three different seismograph stations, seismologists can find an earthquake's _____.
   a. epicenter   c. fault zone
   b. surface waves   d. intensity

5. The Richter scale expresses an earthquake's _____.
   a. intensity   c. duration
   b. location   d. magnitude

6. High pressure and high temperature cause igneous rocks to become _____.
   a. sedimentary rocks
   b. limestone
   c. metamorphic rocks
   d. clay

7. The sequence of events in which rocks change from one type to another and back again is described by _____.
   a. a rock family
   b. the rock cycle
   c. metamorphism
   d. deposition

8. _____ rock is formed from magma.
   a. Igneous   c. Sedimentary
   b. Metamorphic   d. Schist

9. A common kind of mechanical weathering is called _____.
   a. oxidation   c. ice wedging
   b. carbonation   d. leaching

10. Acid rain results from pollutants reacting with water in the air to form_____.
   a. sulfuric acid   c. ice crystals
   b. carbon dioxide   d. carbonic acid

Using Vocabulary

11. Using the terms *crust, mantle,* and *core,* describe Earth's internal structure.

12. What is the name of the thin outer shell of Earth consisting of the *crust* and the rigid upper *mantle*?

13. What is the name of the field of study concerning earthquakes?

14. Use the terms *focus, epicenter, P waves, S waves,* and *surface waves* to describe what happens during an earthquake.

15. What type of rock is formed when small rock fragments are cemented together?

16. In what type of rock—*igneous, sedimentary,* or *metamorphic*—are you most likely to find a fossil?

17. What is the name of the process of breaking down rock and moving it?

18. Explain how deltas form at the continental boundary using the terms *erosion* and *deposition*.

BUILDING MATH SKILLS

19. Graphing Examine the graph in the figure below, and answer the questions that follow.

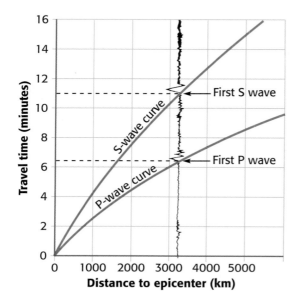

a. Approximately how far, in kilometers, was the epicenter of the earthquake from the seismograph that recorded the seismogram shown here?

b. When did the first P wave reach the seismograph?

c. When did the first S wave reach the seismograph?

d. What is the difference in travel time between the two waves?

THINKING CRITICALLY

20. Critical Thinking Why are mathematics and theory the only practical ways to determine the temperature of Earth's core?

21. Applying Knowledge Is a tall building more likely to be damaged by an earthquake if it is on a mountain of granite or in a valley of sediment? Explain.

22. Applying Knowledge You and your classmates are on a field trip to the top of a mountain. Your teacher tells you that the rocks are metamorphic. What can you tell your classmates about the geologic history of the area?

23. Problem Solving Imagine you are on a dinosaur dig and your team finds two sets of dinosaur bones entwined as if they died while engaged in battle. You know one of the dinosaurs lived 180 million to 120 million years ago and the other lived 130 million to 115 million years ago. What can you say about the age of the rock the dinosaur fossils were found in?

24. Interpreting Diagrams The figure below shows a cross-sectional diagram of a portion of a plate boundary. It shows plates, the ocean, mountains, and rivers. The mouths of the rivers reach the shore, where they deposit sediments. Using the diagram, answer the following questions:

a. What type of plate boundary is shown? How do you know?

b. What type of physical weathering processes are probably acting on the mountains?

c. What type of land-shaping processes are occurring on and near the beach?

d. What forces might have formed this coastal mountain range?

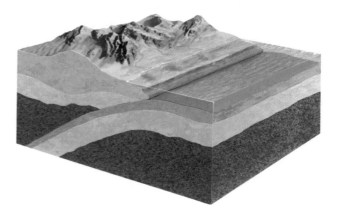

DEVELOPING LIFE/WORK SKILLS

25. Interpreting Graphics Use a map of the United States to plan a car trip to study the geology of three national parks. How many miles will you have to drive roundtrip? How many days will you stay in each park? How long will the trip take?

26. Making Decisions Pretend you are the superintendent of the Washington State Police Department. Seismologists in the area of Mount St. Helens predict that the volcano will erupt in 1 week. Write a report describing the evacuation procedures. In your report, describe the area you will evacuate and a plan for how people will be contacted.

WRITING SKILL

27. Applying Technology Sonar is the best method for identifying features under water. Sound waves are emitted from one device, and the time it takes for the wave to bounce off an object and return is calculated by another. This information is used to determine how far away a feature is. Draw a graph that could be made by a ship's sonar device as it tracks the ocean bottom from the shoreline to a deep ocean trench and farther out to sea.

28. Applying Technology Use a computer drawing program to create cutaway diagrams of a fault before, during, and after an earthquake.

COMPUTER SKILL

INTEGRATING CONCEPTS

29. Connection to Biology Charles Darwin, known for his theory of evolution by natural selection, was the first to explain how *atolls* (AT ahls) form. What are atolls? What was his explanation?

30. Concept Mapping Copy the unfinished concept map below onto a sheet of paper. Complete the map by writing the correct word or phrase in the lettered boxes.

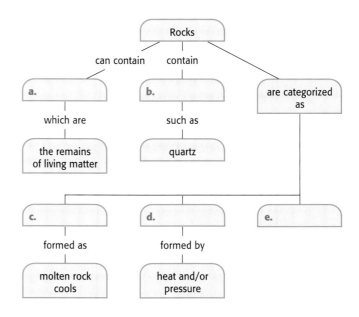

31. Connection to Social Studies The Grand Canyon is one of the most geologically informative and beautiful sites in the United States. Read about the people who have lived along the Colorado River and in the Grand Canyon. How do we know Paleo-Indians lived there? Who were the Anasazi? Who was John Wesley Powell? What role did the Mormon settlers play in the canyon's history? What is special about the region today? Write a one-page essay about the history of these people and this region.

WRITING SKILL

internetconnect

SC*LINKS*
NSTA

TOPIC: Sonar
GO TO: www.nsta.scilinks.org
KEYWORD: HK1707

Analyzing Seismic Waves

▶ Preparing for Your Experiment

1. In this lab, you will examine seismograms showing two kinds of seismic waves: primary waves (P waves) and secondary waves (S waves).
2. P waves have an average speed of 6.1 km/s. S waves have an average speed of 4.1 km/s.
   a. How long does it take P waves to travel 100 km?
   b. How long does it take S waves to travel 100 km?
   (**Hint:** You will need to use the speed equation from Section 7.1, and rearrange it to solve for time.)
3. Because S waves travel more slowly than P waves, S waves will reach a seismograph after P waves arrive. This difference in arrival times is known as the *lag time*.
4. Use the time intervals found in step 2 to calculate the lag time you would expect from a seismograph located exactly 100 km from the epicenter of an earthquake.

▶ Measuring the Lag Time from Seismographic Records

5. On a blank sheet of paper, prepare a table like the one shown below.

City	Lag time (s)	Distance from city to epicenter (km)
Austin, TX		
Portland, OR		
Bismarck, ND		

6. The illustration at the top of the next page shows the records produced by seismographs in three cities following an earthquake.
7. Using the time scale at the bottom of the illustration, measure the lag time for each city. Be sure to measure from the start of the P wave to the start of the S wave. Enter your measurements in your table.

Introduction

During an earthquake, seismic waves travel through Earth in all directions from the earthquake's epicenter. How can you find the location of the epicenter by studying seismic waves?

Objectives

▶ **Calculate** the distance from an earthquake's epicenter to surrounding seismographs.

▶ **Find** the location of the earthquake's epicenter.

Materials

drawing compass
ruler
calculator
map of the western United States

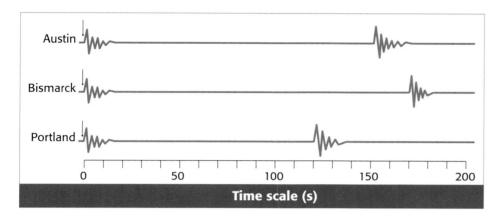

Time scale (s)

8. Using the lag time you found in step 4 and the formula below, calculate the distance from each city to the epicenter of the earthquake. Enter your results in your table.

$$\text{distance} = (\text{measured lag time} \div \text{lag time for 100 km}) \times 100 \text{ km}$$

▶ Analyzing Your Results

1. Copy the map at the bottom of this page on a blank sheet of paper. Using the scale below your map, adjust the drawing compass so that it will draw a circle whose radius equals the distance from the epicenter of the earthquake to Austin. Then put the point of the compass on Austin, and draw a circle on your map. How is the location of the epicenter related to the circle?
2. Repeat the process in item 1 using the distance from Portland to the epicenter. This time put the point of the compass on Portland, and draw the circle. Where do the two circles intersect? The epicenter is one of these two sites.
3. **Reaching Conclusions** Repeat the process once more for Bismarck, and find that city's distance from the epicenter. The epicenter is located at the site where all three circles intersect. What city is closest to that site?

▶ Defending Your Conclusions

4. Why is it necessary to use seismographs in three different locations to find the epicenter of an earthquake?
5. Would it be possible to use this method for locating an earthquake's epicenter if earthquakes produced only one kind of seismic wave? Explain your answer.
6. Someone tells you that the best way to determine the epicenter is to find a seismograph where the P and S waves occur at the same time. What is wrong with this reasoning?

Scale (km)

Career Link

Paleontologist

Paleontologists are life's historians. They study fossils and other evidence to understand how and why life has changed during Earth's history. Most paleontologists work for universities, government agencies, or private industry. To learn more about paleontology as a career, read this interview with paleontologist Geerat Vermeij, who works in the Department of Geology at the University of California, Davis.

> *"I think one needs to be able to recognize puzzles and then think about ways of solving them."*

Vermeij is a world-renowned expert on living and fossil mollusks, but he has never seen one. Born blind, he has learned to scrutinize specimens with his hands.

 Describe your work as a paleontologist.

I study the history of life and how life has changed from its beginning to today. I'm interested in long-term trends and long-term patterns. My work involves everything from field studies of how living organisms live and work to a lot of work in museum collections. I work especially on shell-bearing mollusks, but I have thought about and written about all of life.

 What questions are you particularly interested in?

How enemies have influenced the evolution of plants and animals. I study arms races (evolutionary competitions) over geological time. And I study how the physical history of Earth has affected evolution.

 What is your favorite part of your work?

That's hard to say. I enjoy doing the research and writing. I'd say it was a combination of working with specimens, reading for background, and writing (scientific) papers and popular books. I have written four books.

 What qualities make a good paleontologist?

First and foremost, hard work. The second thing is you need to know a lot. You have to have a lot of information at hand to put what you observe into context. And you need to be a good observer.

 What skills does a paleontologist need?

To me, the curiosity to learn a lot is essential. You have to have the ability to understand and do science and to communicate it.

What attracted you to a career in paleontology?

It's a love of natural history in general and shells in particular that led inexorably to my career. As long as I can remember, I have been interested in natural history. I knew pretty much what I wanted to be from the age of 10.

What education and experiences have been most useful to you?

I think it was very good for me to start early. I started school when I was just shy of my fourth birthday. I started reading the scientific literature in high school.

What advice do you have for students who are interested in paleontology?

People should work on their interests and not let them slide. They should pursue their interests outside of school. If they live near a museum, for example, getting involved in the museum's activities, getting to know the people there, and so forth is a good idea.

Why do you think paleontology is important, and did that influence your choice of career?

It gives us a window on life and the past, which like history in general, can provide lessons on what we are doing to the Earth. It gives us perspective on crises and opportunities. The main reason people should pursue interests is for their own sake. I just love the things I work on. It can be utilitarian, but that's not the rationale for my work.

TOPIC: Paleontology
GO TO: www.scilinks.org
KEYWORD: HK1900

"I hope that in 15 years' time people will be asking questions that today are inconceivable. The road ahead is not marked."
—GEERAT VERMEIJ

CHAPTER 20

The Atmosphere

Chapter Preview

20.1 Characteristics of the Atmosphere
Layers of the Atmosphere
Changes in the Earth's Atmosphere

20.2 Water and Wind
The Water Cycle
Air Pressure
Wind

20.3 Weather and Climate
Fronts and Severe Weather
Weather Maps
Climate

Focus ACTIVITY

Background Like many other weather phenomena, rainbows are caused by water in Earth's atmosphere. Rainbows are visible when the air is filled with water droplets and the viewer is positioned between the sun and the droplets. Sunlight striking the droplets passes through their front surface and is partially reflected back toward the viewer from the back of the droplet.

But why do we see the rainbow of colors? A rainbow occurs when sunlight is bent as it passes from air to water and back to air again. The degree to which the light bends depends on the frequency of the light. In this way, observers see only the frequency (the color) that is directed toward them from each droplet.

Activity 1 Look at the two rainbows in the smaller photo at left. One of these rainbows, called a secondary rainbow, results when light is reflected a second time in the raindrops. The second reflection causes the order of the colors to be reversed. Compare the order of the colors in the two rainbows with that of the rainbow in the photo of the irrigation trucks. Can you tell which rainbow is the secondary rainbow? How?

Activity 2 Rainbows are most commonly seen as arches because the ends of the rainbow disappear at the horizon. But if an observer is at an elevated vantage point, such as on an airplane or at the rim of a canyon, a complete circular rainbow can be seen.

You can create a circular rainbow in your yard. On a warm, clear day when the sun is overhead, turn on a water hose and spray water into the air above you. If the mist is fine enough, you should be able to create a rainbow encircling your body.

internet connect

SCi LINKS
NSTA

TOPIC: Visible light
GO TO: www.scilinks.org
KEYWORD: HK1801

Rainbows can be seen when the air is filled with water droplets and the observer is positioned between the sun and the droplets.

Characteristics of the Atmosphere

KEY TERMS

troposphere
temperature inversion
stratosphere
ozone
mesosphere
thermosphere
greenhouse effect

OBJECTIVES

▶ Identify the primary layers of the atmosphere.
▶ Describe how the atmosphere has evolved over time.
▶ Describe how the oxygen–carbon dioxide cycle works, and explain its importance to living organisms.
▶ Discuss the recent changes in Earth's atmosphere.

If you were to see Earth's atmosphere from space, it would look like a thin blue halo of light around the Earth. This fragile envelope provides the air we breathe, regulates global temperature, and filters out dangerous solar radiation.

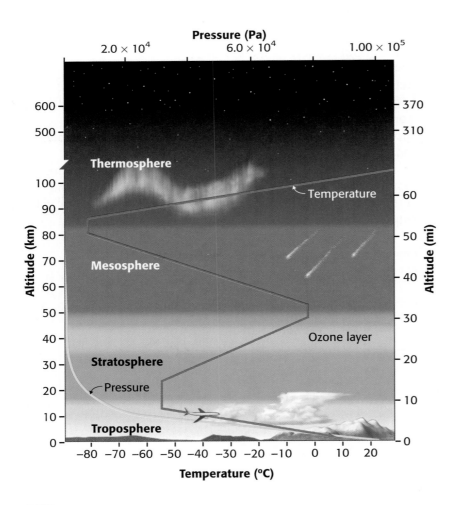

Layers of the Atmosphere

Without the atmosphere, you would have no oxygen to breathe. The atmosphere, however, does not contain oxygen alone. Earth's atmosphere consists of a variety of gases. The two main gases in the atmosphere are nitrogen (about 78 percent) and oxygen (about 21 percent). The remaining elements exist only in very small amounts and are called *trace gases*.

The atmosphere has several layers. These layers differ in temperature, density, and amount of certain gases present. **Figure 20-1** shows the order and relative sizes of Earth's atmospheric layers.

Figure 20-1
The layers of the atmosphere are marked by changes in temperature and pressure. The red line indicates temperature, and the yellow line indicates pressure in pascals.

Almost all weather occurs in the troposphere

You live in the layer closest to Earth's surface. This layer is called the troposphere. Clouds, wind, rain, and snow occur mostly in the troposphere.

The troposphere is the densest of the atmospheric layers. To understand why, consider the weight of all the other gas layers pressing down on the gases in the troposphere. The weight causes the gas molecules to squeeze together into a smaller volume. The result is a greater density than exists in higher layers of the atmosphere.

The troposphere gets cooler with increasing altitude

If you were to climb a mountain, you would notice that the air is much colder at the top of the mountain than it is at the base. The air closest to the mountain's base is warmed by the ground and oceans, which absorb solar energy during the day and heat the atmosphere by radiation and conduction. Air at higher altitudes is less dense and is not as close to those sources of heat. As you travel higher into the troposphere, the temperature decreases by about 6°C for every kilometer of altitude.

At the top of the troposphere, the temperature stops decreasing. The boundary where this occurs is called the *tropopause*. The altitude of the tropopause is different at different places on Earth. At the poles, it occurs at about 8 km (5 mi). Near the equator, it rises to nearly 18 km (11 mi).

Cold air can become trapped beneath warm air

Although the troposphere is generally warmer close to Earth's surface, cool air sometimes gets trapped beneath the warm air. This is called a temperature inversion.

When a temperature inversion occurs, the air sometimes becomes thick with pollution. This is true especially in areas surrounded by mountains, which prevent the cooler, polluted air from escaping. The Los Angeles Basin, in California, for instance, is often filled with a brown haze of pollution, as shown in **Figure 20-2.** Cool air from the Pacific Ocean blows into the basin, becomes trapped by the overriding warm air, and fills with pollutants.

> **troposphere** the atmospheric layer closest to Earth's surface where nearly all weather occurs

VOCABULARY *Skills Tip*

The names of all of Earth's atmospheric layers end in the root word sphere, *implying their spherical shape.*

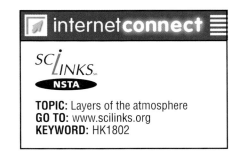

internetconnect

SCLINKS
NSTA

TOPIC: Layers of the atmosphere
GO TO: www.scilinks.org
KEYWORD: HK1802

> **temperature inversion** the atmospheric condition in which warm air traps cooler air near Earth's surface

Figure 20-2
A temperature inversion traps polluted air in the Los Angeles Basin, in California.

Figure 20-3
A heated cabin in this aircraft allows its pilot to do high-altitude atmospheric research, such as collecting air and particle samples after a volcanic eruption.

▶ **stratosphere** the layer of the atmosphere that extends upward from the troposphere to an altitude of 50 km; contains the ozone layer

▶ **ozone** the form of atmospheric oxygen that has three atoms per molecule

As long as the temperature difference remains unchanged, the trapped pollutants cannot escape. A person breathing these toxins can become ill. While these conditions exist, it is not healthy for people to exercise too much because they inhale a greater amount of pollutants as they breathe heavily.

The stratosphere gets *warmer* with increasing altitude

In 1892, unmanned balloons were built that could record temperatures in the **stratosphere,** the layer above the tropopause. Later, humans further explored this cold, oxygen-deficient layer by using balloons and airplanes with enclosed, heated cabins. The WB-57F in **Figure 20-3** is just such an aircraft. These explorers found that the temperature in the lower stratosphere remains fairly constant, staying around –55°C (–67°F) from near the tropopause to an altitude of about 25 km (about 16 mi). At 25 km, the temperature begins to increase with altitude until it reaches about 0°C (32°F).

The stratosphere extends upward to about 50 km (31 mi). In addition to getting slightly warmer instead of cooler, the stratosphere differs from the troposphere in composition, weather, and density.

Unlike the troposphere, the stratosphere has very little water vapor—the gaseous form of water. Because of this lack of water vapor, the stratosphere is relatively calm and contains few clouds and no storms.

The increase in temperature in the upper stratosphere occurs in the atmospheric layer known as the *ozone layer.* The ozone layer is warmer because it contains a form of oxygen called ozone that absorbs solar radiation. Whereas the oxygen we breathe is a molecule that consists of two oxygen atoms, ozone molecules have three oxygen atoms, as shown in **Figure 20-4.** Ozone is important because it absorbs much of the sun's ultraviolet radiation. The ozone layer shields life on Earth's surface from ultraviolet-radiation damage. Ozone will be discussed later in this section.

Figure 20-4

A Oxygen molecules have two atoms of oxygen.

B Ozone molecules have three atoms of oxygen.

The mesosphere and thermosphere exhibit extremes of temperature

Temperature begins to fall again in the mesosphere. As in the troposphere, temperatures in the mesosphere, 50–80 km (31–50 mi) above Earth's surface, decrease with increasing altitude. Near the top of this layer, temperatures fall to below –80°C (–112°F), the coldest temperature in Earth's atmosphere.

Beyond the mesosphere, temperatures begin to rise again. This layer, at an altitude of about 80–480 km (50–298 mi), is called the thermosphere. The main gases are still nitrogen and oxygen, but the molecules are very far apart. This may lead you to think that the thermosphere is very cold, but it is actually very hot. Temperatures in this layer average around 980°C (1796°F) because the small amount of molecular oxygen in the thermosphere heats up as it absorbs intense solar radiation.

The outermost portion of the thermosphere, at about 480 km, is known as the *exosphere.* In the exosphere, some gases escape from the gravitational pull of Earth and exit into space. In addition, gases in space are captured by Earth's gravity and added to Earth's atmosphere.

The ionosphere is used in radio communication

When solar energy is absorbed in the lower thermosphere and upper mesosphere, electrically charged ions are formed. The area where this occurs is sometimes called the *ionosphere.*

Electrons in the ionosphere reflect radio waves, as shown in **Figure 20-5,** allowing them to be received over long distances. Without the ionosphere, most radio signals would travel directly into space, and only locations very close to a transmitter could receive the signals.

Because these ions require solar radiation in order to form, their number in the lower layers of the ionosphere decreases at night. This means the radio waves can travel higher into the atmosphere before being reflected. As a result, the radio waves return to Earth's surface farther from their source than they do in the daytime, as shown at right.

▷ **mesosphere** the coldest layer of the atmosphere; located above the stratosphere

▷ **thermosphere** the atmospheric layer above the mesosphere

Figure 20-5
Radio waves can be received from far away because they are reflected by the ionosphere. At night, when ion density decreases in the lower atmosphere, transmissions can be received farther away.

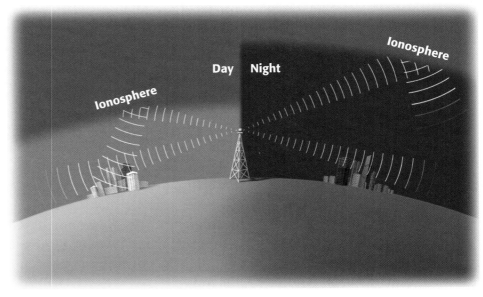

Figure 20-6
Auroras, such as this one seen above mountains in Alaska, occur in the ionosphere.

Figure 20-7

NH_3 H_2O H_2 N_2 CO CO_2 CH_4

A Early in Earth's existence, the atmosphere was filled with mostly carbon dioxide, nitrogen, and a few other trace gases.

CO_2 H_2O CO N_2 O_2 H_2 NH_3 CH_4

B Once plants evolved, they converted much of the planet's carbon dioxide into oxygen.

The ionosphere is also where colorful light displays called *auroras* can be seen encircling Earth's magnetic poles. Auroras form when energetic ions from the sun hit atoms and molecules in the ionosphere, causing photons to be emitted. The *aurora borealis*, shown in **Figure 20-6**, appears in the sky above the magnetic north pole. A similar phenomenon, the *aurora australis*, is observed in the south, above Antarctica.

Changes in the Earth's Atmosphere

When Earth began to solidify about 4.4 billion years ago, volcanic eruptions released a variety of gases. This process, called *outgassing*, created an atmosphere of gases, some of which would be poisonous to us today. As shown in **Figure 20-7A**, some of these gases included hydrogen, H_2, water vapor, H_2O, ammonia, NH_3, methane, CH_4, carbon monoxide, CO, carbon dioxide, CO_2, and nitrogen, N_2.

Photosynthetic plants contribute oxygen to the atmosphere

Amazingly, life-forms evolved that were comfortable in this early atmosphere. Bacteria and other single-celled organisms lived in the oceans. Around 2.5 billion years ago, some cells evolved a method of capturing energy from the sun and converting it to sugar that could be used as a food source. This process, called *photosynthesis*, also produced oxygen as a byproduct. Because these organisms needed only sunlight, water, and the readily available carbon dioxide for their survival, they thrived and multiplied in this environment. Gradually, the atmosphere filled with oxygen, as shown in **Figure 20-7B**. About 350 million years ago, the concentration of oxygen reached a level similar to what it is today.

Animals produce carbon dioxide necessary for photosynthesis

As *aerobic*, oxygen-breathing organisms evolved, they joined plants in a balance that led to our present atmosphere. The steps of the oxygen–carbon dioxide cycle describe this balance. These steps are summarized in **Figure 20-8.**

Figure 20-8 is a simple depiction of a series of chemical reactions. Basically, plants need carbon dioxide, CO_2, for photosynthesis and food production. Oxygen, O_2, is then released as a waste product of photosynthesis. Animals breathe oxygen during a process called *respiration* and release carbon dioxide as waste. The carbon dioxide they exhale is then used by plants and other photosynthetic organisms, and the process is repeated.

Man-made chemicals can deplete the ozone layer

Recall that the upper stratosphere contains ozone molecules in a layer called the ozone layer. Ozone is formed when the sun's dangerous ultraviolet rays strike molecules of O_2. The energy splits the molecules, and the single atoms of oxygen bond with other O_2 molecules to make O_3, ozone. These O_3 molecules in turn absorb much of the sun's damaging ultraviolet radiation.

If the ozone layer didn't exist, ultraviolet rays would cause serious damage to the DNA in the cells of living things. Thus, scientists were concerned when they found lower than expected concentrations of ozone in the stratosphere in 1985.

Low ozone concentrations are caused in part by chemicals known as chlorofluorocarbons, or CFCs. These gases were widely used in the first 80 years of the twentieth century as refrigerants and as propellants in spray cans. Even though the atmosphere is only 0.004 to 0.03% CFCs, a single molecule can react with and destroy many ozone molecules.

VOCABULARY *Skills Tip*

The word ozone *comes from the Greek word* ozein, *which means "to smell." Ozone gas has a strong odor. You may have smelled ozone after a thunderstorm when atmospheric oxygen was converted to ozone by the electrical energy of lightning.*

internet**connect**

SC*i*LINKS
NSTA

TOPIC: Ozone depletion
GO TO: www.scilinks.org
KEYWORD: HK1803

Figure 20-8

In the oxygen–carbon dioxide cycle, plants produce oxygen, which is used by animals for respiration. Animals produce carbon dioxide, which is used by plants for photosynthesis.

Persuaded by the evidence that there is a connection between CFCs and deterioration of the ozone layer, most industrialized countries stopped production of CFCs on January 1, 1996. The international bans have drastically decreased the amount of CFCs entering the stratosphere. Time is now the important factor in finding out if ozone concentrations will begin to rise again.

The greenhouse effect keeps Earth warm

Have you ever been in a greenhouse on a cold day? It is surprisingly warm inside compared with the outside. Although some greenhouses are heated by a furnace or other heating system, much of the warmth results from the sun's energy entering and becoming trapped inside the glass or plastic walls of the greenhouse.

Unlike a greenhouse, Earth's atmosphere has no walls, but certain atmospheric gases keep Earth much warmer than it would be without an atmosphere. As shown in **Figure 20-9**, energy that is released from the sun as radiation and reaches Earth's surface is absorbed. Then some of this energy is transferred back toward space as radiation. Carbon dioxide, water vapor, and other gases absorb some of this energy. Absorbing this energy makes the atmosphere warmer. The warm atmosphere in turn releases some of this energy in the form of radiation, some of which is directed back toward Earth's surface. This effect is called the **greenhouse effect.**

▶ **greenhouse effect** the process by which the atmosphere traps some of the energy from the sun in the troposphere

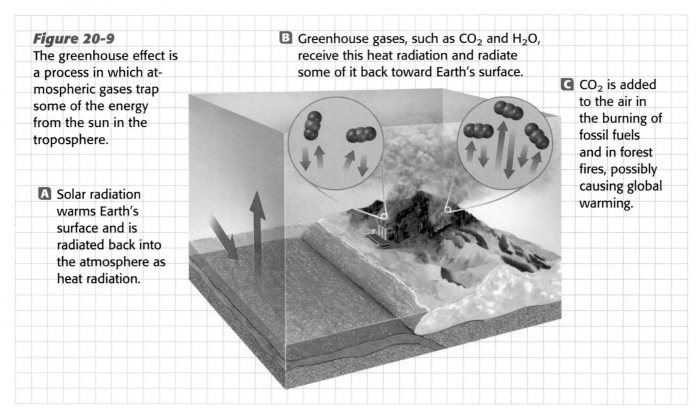

Figure 20-9
The greenhouse effect is a process in which atmospheric gases trap some of the energy from the sun in the troposphere.

Ⓐ Solar radiation warms Earth's surface and is radiated back into the atmosphere as heat radiation.

Ⓑ Greenhouse gases, such as CO_2 and H_2O, receive this heat radiation and radiate some of it back toward Earth's surface.

Ⓒ CO_2 is added to the air in the burning of fossil fuels and in forest fires, possibly causing global warming.

Increased levels of carbon dioxide may lead to global warming

Without the greenhouse effect, Earth would have a colder average temperature than it does. But too much of the greenhouse effect can cause problems. If too much heat is trapped, the global temperature will rise. This *global warming* could cause the icecaps to melt, ocean levels to rise, and droughts to occur in some areas.

Carbon dioxide occurs naturally and is necessary for plant photosynthesis. In the last 100 years, the burning of coal, oil, and gas for power plants, machinery, and cars has added excess carbon dioxide to the air. Recently, scientists have hypothesized that this increase to the amount of carbon dioxide is the reason the troposphere's average temperature has risen 0.5°C in the past 100 years. Whether carbon dioxide is responsible for global warming and what to do about it continues to be debated around the world.

SECTION 20.1 REVIEW

SUMMARY

▶ The layers of Earth's atmosphere are the troposphere, stratosphere, mesosphere, and thermosphere.

▶ The oxygen–carbon dioxide cycle produces the oxygen we breathe. Plants release oxygen. Animals breathe this oxygen and release carbon dioxide, which is used by plants.

▶ The ozone layer protects life on Earth by absorbing much of the ultraviolet radiation entering Earth's atmosphere.

▶ CFCs are linked to the deterioration of the ozone layer. For this reason, their use has been banned in most countries.

▶ The addition of CO_2 to the atmosphere by the burning of fossil fuels may cause global warming. This issue continues to be debated.

CHECK YOUR UNDERSTANDING

1. **Identify** the two atmospheric layers that contain air as warm as 25°C.
2. **Identify** which of the following gases is most abundant in Earth's atmosphere today.
   - **a.** argon
   - **b.** nitrogen
   - **c.** oxygen
   - **d.** carbon dioxide
3. **Compare** Earth's early atmosphere with its present atmosphere.
4. **Arrange** the steps of the oxygen–carbon dioxide cycle in the correct order:
   - **a.** animals breathe oxygen
   - **b.** plants produce oxygen
   - **c.** plants use carbon dioxide
   - **d.** animals exhale carbon dioxide
5. **Explain** why the following statement is incorrect:
   Global warming could cause oceans to rise, so the greenhouse effect must be eliminated completely.
6. **Predict** how much colder it is at the top of Mount Everest, which is almost 9 km above sea level, than it is at the Indian coastline. Consider only the difference in altitude. (**Hint:** The temperature in the troposphere decreases by 6°C/km.)
7. **Critical Thinking** In 1982, Larry Walters rose to an altitude of approximately 4900 m (just over 3 mi) on a lawn chair attached to 45 helium-filled weather balloons. Give two reasons why Walters's efforts were dangerous.

Water and Wind

▶ **KEY TERMS**
water cycle
transpiration
precipitation
humidity
relative humidity
dew point
barometric pressure
Coriolis effect

OBJECTIVES

▶ Describe the three phases of the water cycle.
▶ Explain how temperature and humidity are related.
▶ Identify various cloud types by their appearance and the altitudes at which they typically occur.
▶ Use the concept of pressure gradients to explain how winds are created, and explain how Earth's rotation affects their direction.

internet connect

SC*LINKS*
NSTA

TOPIC: Water cycle
GO TO: www.scilinks.org
KEYWORD: HK1804

▶ **water cycle** the continuous movement of water from the atmosphere to Earth and back

You come in contact with water throughout every day, not just when you drink it or when you shower or wash your hands. You experience water in the air because water exists as an invisible gas in the air. It also exists in air as a liquid, suspended in the atmosphere as clouds or fog, or falling as rain or snow. All of this water in the atmosphere affects the weather on Earth.

The Water Cycle

Water is continuously being moved through the troposphere in a process described by the **water cycle.** **Figure 20-10** shows the main processes that take place in the water cycle.

The major part of the water cycle occurs between the oceans and the continents. Solar energy strikes ocean water, causing water molecules to escape from the liquid and rise as gaseous water vapor. This process, as defined in Chapter 2, is known as evaporation.

Precipitation
Condensation
Transpiration
Evaporation
Ground water

Figure 20-10
Evaporation, transpiration, condensation, and precipitation make up the continuous process called the water cycle.

On the continents, some evaporation occurs as sunlight strikes water in lakes, rivers, and the soil. But much of the addition of water from land to the air occurs through transpiration. In the process of transpiration, plants lose moisture through small pores in their leaves. While this may seem insignificant, the addition of water vapor to the atmosphere through transpiration can be large. For example, 1 km² of corn typically transpires 3 400 000 L (900 000 gal) of water per day.

In the atmosphere, water vapor rises with warm air until the air is cool enough to condense the vapor into tiny droplets of liquid water. We observe these droplets as clouds. As these clouds cool and condense more vapor, they often release their moisture content in the form of precipitation. The most familiar kinds of precipitation are rain, snow, hail, and sleet. Precipitation can occur over land or water.

When precipitation falls on land, it flows across the surface until it evaporates, flows into a larger body of water, or is absorbed into the ground. *Ground water,* water that is absorbed into the ground, eventually reaches the oceans and evaporates to begin the cycle again.

Air contains varying quantities of water vapor

You have probably noticed that the air doesn't always feel the same. Sometimes it is thick and moist, while at other times it seems crisp and dry. Because the air around you contains various amounts of water vapor, you experience the effects of changing humidity, the quantity of moisture in the atmosphere.

Relative humidity is the actual quantity of water vapor present in the air compared with the maximum quantity of water vapor that can be present at that particular temperature. In weather forecasts, the relative humidity is usually given as a percentage. A relative humidity of 85 percent means that the air contains 85 percent of the water that it can contain at that temperature. A relative humidity of 100 percent means the air contains as much water vapor as is possible at that temperature. Air that has a relative humidity of 100 percent is said to be *saturated.*

Warmer temperatures evaporate more water

As illustrated in **Figure 20-11,** the temperature of the air determines the air's maximum water vapor content. At warm temperatures, molecules move very quickly and are farther apart. Thus, the water is more likely to exist as a gas. As the temperature decreases, the water molecules slow down. At these slower speeds, the attractive forces between water molecules have a greater effect, and the molecules condense into a liquid.

▶ **transpiration** the evaporation of water through pores in a plant's leaves

▶ **precipitation** any form of water that falls back to Earth's surface from clouds; includes rain, snow, sleet, and hail

▶ **humidity** the quantity of water vapor in the atmosphere

▶ **relative humidity** ratio of the quantity of water vapor in the air to the maximum quantity of water vapor that can be present at that temperature

Figure 20-11
Warm temperatures evaporate more water than cold temperatures do.

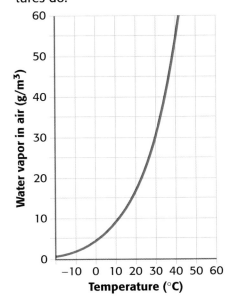

▶ **dew point** the temperature at which water vapor molecules start to form liquid water

The exact temperature at which water vapor molecules move slowly enough to form liquid water is called the **dew point.** Dew point also depends on the humidity. When the humidity is high, there are more molecules of water vapor in the air and it is easier for them to form liquid water. So the higher the humidity is, the higher the dew point is. In fact, we can measure humidity by finding the dew point.

You may have seen drops of water, or condensation, on a glass of ice water. The cold surface of the glass provides a place where the dew point is reached, and water shifts from gas to liquid.

Clouds form as warm, moist air rises

You may know from walking through fog—a low-lying cloud—that clouds are wet. Clouds are formed when warm air rises and water vapor condenses into tiny droplets of liquid as it cools. This process usually occurs in the troposphere. Clouds are made up of tiny droplets of liquid water and, at higher altitudes, small ice crystals. Depending on where clouds form, they can have many different shapes and characteristics.

Figure 20-12
Clouds are classified by their form and the altitude at which they occur.

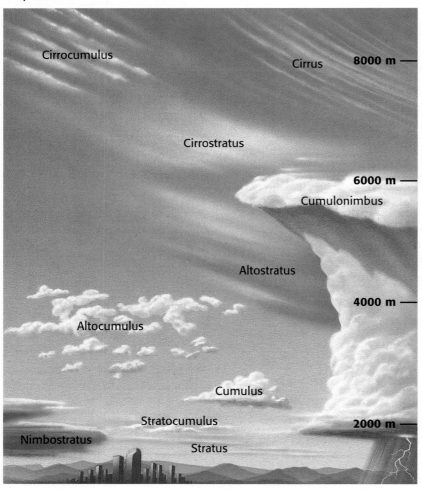

Cloud names describe their shape and altitude

Figure 20-12 shows the different kinds of clouds that can occur. Cloud names describe both their appearance and the altitude at which they occur.

There are three main types of clouds: *cirrus, stratus,* and *cumulus.* Cirrus clouds are thin and wispy, and they occur at high altitudes—between 6000 and 11 000 km (3.7–6.8 mi) above the Earth. Stratus clouds are sheetlike and layered. These clouds typically form at lower altitudes—between Earth's surface and about 6 km. Cumulus clouds are white and fluffy with somewhat flat bottoms. The flat base is the point at which rising air begins to condense. Cumulus clouds form at various altitudes—anywhere from about 500 m to about 12 km (1641 ft–7.5 mi) above the Earth.

The names of other clouds, as shown in **Figure 20-12,** are combinations of the three root words *cirrus, stratus,* and *cumulus.* These names reflect the combined characteristics of each cloud type. *Cirrostratus* clouds, for instance, are high, layered clouds that form a thin white veil over the sky. *Altostratus* and *altocumulus* clouds are simply stratus and cumulus clouds that occur at middle altitudes. When a cloud name includes the root *nimbo* or *nimbus*—as in *cumulonimbus* and *nimbostratus*—the cloud is the type that produces precipitation. Cumulonimbus clouds are the towering rain clouds that often produce thunderstorms. Nimbostratus clouds are large, featureless gray clouds that often shadow the sky and produce steady precipitation.

You may have seen a halo around the sun or moon. This halo results from the refraction of light as it passes through ice crystals in cirrostratus clouds. Sometimes the presence of a halo is the only way to tell that a very thin, transparent layer of cirrostratus clouds is present.

Air Pressure

The term **barometric pressure** is often used in weather reports in the newspaper and on television. The barometric pressure, also called *atmospheric pressure* or *air pressure,* is the pressure that results from the weight of a column of air extending from the top of the thermosphere to the point of measurement.

Air pressure is measured using a barometer

Both *barometers* shown in **Figure 20-13** are used to measure air pressure. On the left is a photo of a *mercury barometer,* and the photo on the right shows an *aneroid barometer.* Although aneroid barometers are more portable than mercury barometers, mercury barometers are more accurate.

Quick ACTIVITY

Measuring Rainfall
1. Set an empty soup can outside in the open, away from any source of runoff. At the same time each day, use a metric ruler to measure the amount of rain or other precipitation that has accumulated in the can.
2. Record your measurements. Keep a record of the precipitation in your area for a week.
3. Listen to or read local weather reports to see if your measurements are close to those given in the reports.

▶ **barometric pressure** the pressure due to the weight of the atmosphere; also called *air pressure* or *atmospheric pressure*

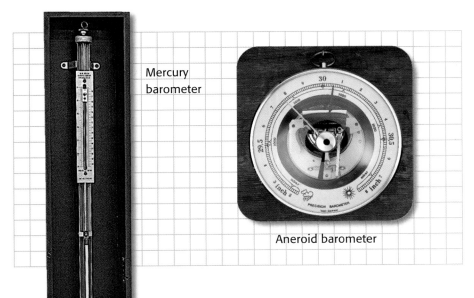

Mercury barometer

Aneroid barometer

Figure 20-13
Mercury barometers are more accurate than aneroid barometers.

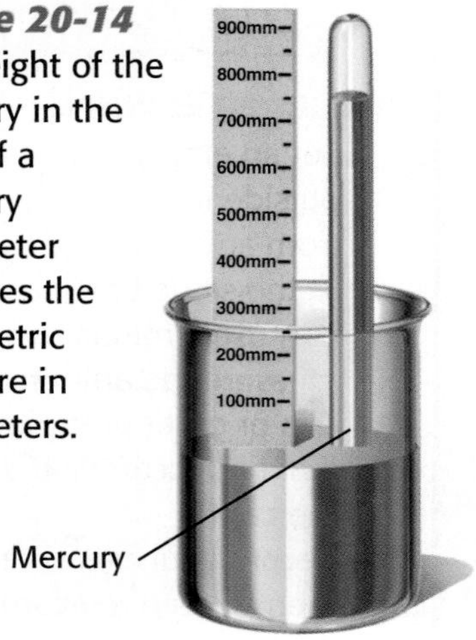

Figure 20-14
The height of the mercury in the tube of a mercury barometer indicates the barometric pressure in millimeters.

900mm—
800mm—
700mm—
600mm—
500mm—
400mm—
300mm—
200mm—
100mm—

Mercury

Figure 20-14 is an illustration of how a simple mercury barometer works. The mercury barometer contains a long tube that is open at one end and closed at the other. The tube is filled with mercury and then inverted into a small container of mercury. Once in place, some but not all of the mercury spills out of the tube and into the container. The atmosphere exerts a pressure on the mercury in the container, holding some of the mercury in the tube to some height above the mercury in the container. Any change in the height of the column of mercury means that the atmosphere's pressure has changed.

At sea level, the barometric pressure of air at 0°C is around 760 mm of mercury. This amount of pressure is defined as 1 atmosphere (1 atm) of pressure. The **SI** unit for pressure is the pascal (Pa), which is equivalent to one newton per square meter.

Aneroid barometers are more commonly used. The word *aneroid* means "without liquid." This type of barometer contains a sealed metal chamber from which part of the air has been removed. When the air pressure changes, the chamber expands or contracts, moving a needle on a dial.

Wind

Have you ever seen a movie in which an airplane window gets broken? When the window breaks, all the loose objects in the plane are pushed out the window. Although it is unlikely that an airplane window would actually break, the portrayal of objects flying out the window is correct.

Differences in pressure create winds

Commercial airplanes fly very high in the troposphere, between 10 km and 13 km above Earth. At this altitude, the air is not very dense and the atmospheric pressure is very low. The pressure inside the airplane, however, is relatively high—similar to the air pressure at Earth's surface.

If an airplane window were to break, the densely packed air in the plane's cabin would spread out into the less densely packed air outside the cabin. The airflow produced in this situation would push loose objects out the window.

Just as a difference in air pressure would create airflow from inside the airplane to the outside, differences in pressure in the atmosphere can cause wind. When air pressure varies from one place to another, a *pressure gradient* exists. The air in a pressure gradient moves from areas of high pressure to areas of low pressure. This movement of air from a high-pressure area to a low-pressure area is called wind.

INTEGRATING

HEALTH
Just as air exerts pressure on the objects around it, blood in your body exerts pressure against the walls of your arteries. To measure a person's blood pressure, a cuff is wrapped around the upper arm and a stethoscope is placed over the arteries of the forearm. Air is pumped into the cuff until the pressure exerted by the cuff stops the flow of blood.

The doctor or nurse then listens to the person's pulse as air is let out slowly until the pressure in the cuff is less than the blood pressure when the heart contracts. This pressure is called the *systolic* pressure.

More air is released until the pulsing of the heart is no longer audible. The pressure at this point, called the *diastolic* pressure, is the blood pressure when the heart relaxes.

Earth's rotation affects the direction of winds

The direction in which wind moves is influenced by Earth's rotation. The effect of Earth's rotation on the direction of wind is described by the **Coriolis effect.**

To understand how the Coriolis effect works, you must first understand that points at different latitudes on Earth move at different speeds as the Earth rotates. Consider two houses at different latitudes. A house located on the equator travels faster than a house located near one of the poles. Can you see why this must be true? Earth goes through one full rotation in 24 hours. During this time, the house at the equator must travel the distance of Earth's circumference. Closer to the poles, a circle of latitude is smaller. Therefore, the house closer to the pole moves through a shorter distance in the same amount of time. Thus, this house moves more slowly.

Now imagine a cannonball in a cannon at the equator. The cannonball is moving along with Earth as it rotates. The cannonball's speed at this time is a little greater than 1610 km/h (1000 mi/h) to the east—the speed at which all points on the equator move because of Earth's rotation. When the cannonball is fired to the north, it continues to move east at about 1610 km/hr. As the cannonball moves farther north, however, the Earth beneath the cannonball is moving more slowly. The result is a flight path like the one depicted in **Figure 20-15.** The cannonball's path appears to curve eastward relative to the Earth below.

The movement of winds is analogous to the cannonball's movement. When moving north in the Northern Hemisphere, winds curve to the right. Conversely, winds moving south from the equator curve to the left.

Now consider air moving south from the North Pole. In this case, the wind would lag behind the rotation of Earth and travel west, or to the right, relative to the ground below, because it has a slower speed than the spinning Earth. Similarly, wind moving north from the South Pole would travel west, or to the left, in respect to the ground beneath it because of its slower speed.

In summary, *winds in the Northern Hemisphere curve clockwise, and winds in the Southern Hemisphere curve counterclockwise.* The resulting circulation patterns are so regular that meteorologists have named them. **Figure 20-16** shows the directions and names of the global wind patterns.

▶ **Coriolis effect** the change in the direction of an object's path due to Earth's rotation

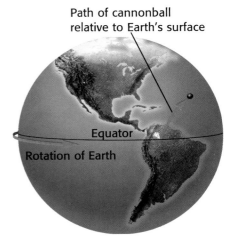

Path of cannonball relative to Earth's surface

Equator

Rotation of Earth

Figure 20-15
Because of Earth's rotation, a cannonball fired directly north from the equator will curve to the east relative to Earth's surface.

Figure 20-16
Both the Northern Hemisphere and the Southern Hemisphere have three wind belts.

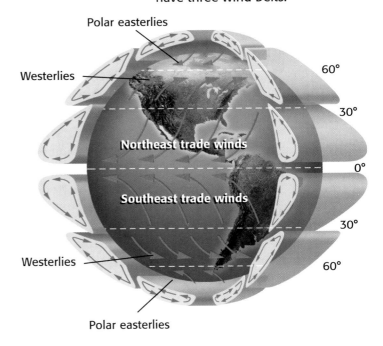

Polar easterlies

Westerlies

60°

30°

Northeast trade winds

0°

Southeast trade winds

30°

Westerlies

60°

Polar easterlies

Global wind patterns form circulation cells

Note that the wind patterns shown in **Figure 20-16** move in vertical loops. Because temperatures at the equator tend to be warmer than at other latitudes, the air there rises and creates a low-pressure belt. As this warm air rises, it moves toward the poles.

In the Northern Hemisphere, much of the northward-moving air sinks at about 30° latitude, forming a high pressure area near Earth's surface. Flowing from a high-pressure area to a low-pressure area, air flows both north and south. At about 60° latitude, air flowing along the surface from the polar high and the high pressure band at 30° converge. As these air masses converge, air rises, forming a low-pressure belt.

A similar circulation pattern, in which rising warm air is coupled with sinking cold air, occurs in the Southern Hemisphere. Thus, air in each of the hemispheres completes three loops, called *cells*.

SECTION 20.2 REVIEW

SUMMARY

▶ In the water cycle, water from oceans and lakes evaporates and rises in the atmosphere. After it cools and condenses, the water falls back to Earth as precipitation.

▶ Warm air can contain more water vapor than cold air.

▶ Clouds are classified according to their appearance and the altitude at which they occur. **Figure 20-12** summarizes the various types of clouds.

▶ Wind is caused by the air in a pressure gradient moving from a high-pressure area to a low-pressure area.

▶ Earth's rotation affects the direction of winds. This phenomenon is described by the Coriolis effect.

CHECK YOUR UNDERSTANDING

1. **Identify** which one of the following processes is not a step in the water cycle:
   a. evaporation
   b. condensation
   c. photosynthesis
   d. precipitation
2. **Determine** whether wind moving north from the equator will curve eastward or westward due to the Coriolis effect.
3. **Distinguish** between humidity and relative humidity.
4. **Select** which one of the following describes a cumulus cloud:
   a. sheetlike
   b. fluffy, white, and flat-bottomed
   c. wispy and feathery
   d. high altitude
5. **Identify** which one of the following statements describes a mercury barometer:
   a. less accurate than an aneroid barometer
   b. contains a chamber that has a lot of water inside
   c. the height of the mercury in the tube indicates the barometric pressure
   d. more commonly used than aneroid barometers
6. **Predict** which of the following would be a more humid area: the Sahara Desert on a cold night or the Texas coast on a warm day.
7. **Critical Thinking** Which has a lower pressure, the air in your lungs as you inhale or the air outside your body?

Weather and Climate

OBJECTIVES

▶ Describe the formation of cold fronts and warm fronts.
▶ Describe various severe weather situations, including thunderstorms, tornadoes, and hurricanes.
▶ Analyze weather maps.
▶ Distinguish between climate and weather.
▶ Identify factors that affect Earth's climate or that have changed it over time.

KEY TERMS

air mass
front
isobar
climate
topography

How is a weather forecast made? *Meteorologists,* people who study weather, gather data about weather conditions in different areas. By using maps, meteorologists can try to predict weather by tracking the movement of warmer or cooler air pockets called **air masses.** Interactions between air masses have predictable effects on the weather in a given location.

internetconnect

SCiLINKS
NSTA

TOPIC: Severe weather
GO TO: www.scilinks.org
KEYWORD: HK1805

Fronts and Severe Weather

You have probably heard about *cold fronts* moving down from the northwest and *warm fronts* moving in from the southeast. A **front** is the place where a cold air mass and a warm air mass meet. Clouds, rain, and sometimes snow can occur at fronts. When fronts move through an area, the result is usually precipitation and a change in wind direction and temperature.

In a warm front, a mass of warm air moves toward and over a slower mass of cold air, as shown in **Figure 20-17.** As the warm air is pushed up over the cool air, it cools and forms clouds.

▶ **air mass** a large body of air with uniform temperature and moisture content

▶ **front** the boundary between air masses of different densities

Figure 20-17
In a warm front, a warm air mass moves above a slower cold air mass.

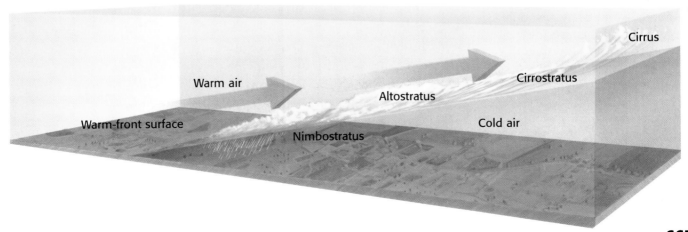

Warm air

Cirrus

Cirrostratus

Altostratus

Cold air

Warm-front surface

Nimbostratus

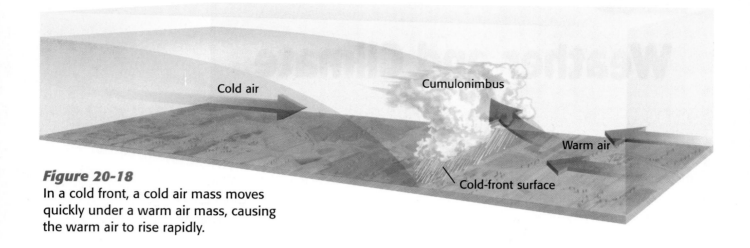

Figure 20-18
In a cold front, a cold air mass moves quickly under a warm air mass, causing the warm air to rise rapidly.

Cold air

Cumulonimbus

Warm air

Cold-front surface

Cirrus and cirrostratus clouds can be seen high in the sky as a warm front approaches. As time passes, lower-lying clouds move overhead. Often, nimbostratus clouds release steady rain or snow for one to two days.

With a cold front, the forward edge of a mass of cold air moves under a slower mass of warm air and pushes it up, as shown in **Figure 20-18.** Note that the front edge of the cold front is steeper than that of the warm front shown in **Figure 20-17.** Because of this steep edge, warm air rises quickly, forming cumulonimbus clouds. High winds, thunderstorms, and sometimes tornadoes accompany this type of front.

A *stationary front* occurs when two air masses meet but neither is displaced. Instead, the air masses move side by side along the front. The weather conditions near a stationary front are similar to those near a warm front.

Lightning is a discharge of atmospheric electrical energy

Lightning is a dangerous element of nature that occurs in the atmosphere during a thunderstorm. Thunderstorms can be very exciting to watch and listen to, but they can also be very dangerous if lightning strikes the ground somewhere near you. The electrical energy of lightning is easily conducted through water on the ground.

Lightning is a big spark. Water droplets and ice crystals in thunderclouds build up electrical charges. If the charge in a cloud is different enough from the other clouds or from Earth, sparks jump between the two to equalize the charge.

Thunder is the noise that is made when electrical charges move through the air as lightning. When lightning occurs, it superheats the air. As the air is heated, it expands faster than the speed of sound. We hear the shockwave created by this rapid expansion as thunder.

Calculating the Distance to a Thunderstorm

How can you tell if lightning is close or far away? The distance can be determined by counting the seconds between the lightning flash and the sound of thunder. This time lag occurs because light travels so fast it reaches you almost immediately, whereas sound travels more slowly and takes longer to reach you. Count the seconds between the flash of lightning and the sound of thunder, and use the following calculation:

$$\text{time (s)}/3 = \text{distance (km)}$$
$$\text{time (s)}/5 = \text{distance (mi)}$$

Applying Information

1. You see lightning in the distance and begin counting in seconds. When you reach the count of 3, you hear thunder. How far away, in kilometers, was the lightning when it struck?

2. At 3:37:45 P.M., you see lightning strike. You hear the associated thunder at 3:38:03 P.M. How many miles away did the lightning strike?

Tornadoes are funnels of high-speed wind

Figure 20-19 is a photo of a tornado. Tornadoes are high-speed, rotating winds that extend downward from thunderclouds. Tornadic winds are the most violent winds to occur on Earth. Wind speeds in the most violent tornadoes are thought to be as great as 500 km/h (about 310 mi/h).

Tornadoes occur most commonly in the United States, especially in the Midwest and in states along the Gulf of Mexico. They tend to occur during spring and early summer.

In the United States, tornadoes typically form along a front between cool, dry air from the north and warm, humid air from the Gulf of Mexico. As warm, humid air rises, more warm air rushes in to replace it. This warm air sometimes begins to rotate as it rises and can become a strong rotating thunderstorm that can spawn a tornado.

Typically a tornado begins as a tapered column of water droplets, called a *funnel cloud,* that reaches down from dark storm clouds with heavy rain and lightning. As the funnel reaches the ground, it begins sucking objects upward as air rises through its center. The rotating winds on the outer edge of a tornado can tear apart homes and trees.

Tornadoes are too fast and unpredictable to attempt to outrun, even if you are in a car. If you see a tornado approaching, move to a storm cellar or basement. The forces caused by tornadic winds can easily lift trailer homes and destroy houses. If a cellar is not available, lie flat under a table at the center of a room with few windows. If you are outside, lie in a ditch or low-lying area, and cover your head with your hands.

Figure 20-19
Tornadoes, such as this one that occurred in Pampa, Texas, in 1995, can be seen as rapidly spinning funnel clouds.

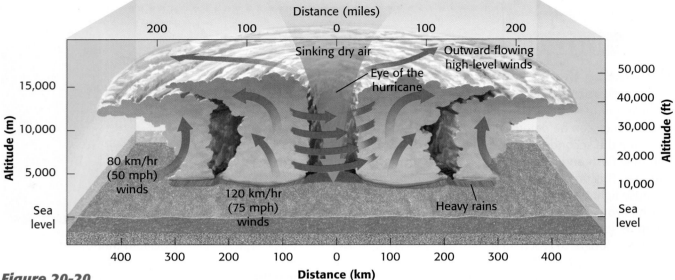

Figure 20-20
Hurricanes are nearly circular in shape and rotate around a center called the eye.

Hurricanes are large storm systems

Hurricanes are similar to thunderstorms but are much larger. Whereas these storms are called hurricanes in North America and the Caribbean, they are called *cyclones* in the Indian Ocean and *typhoons* in the western Pacific.

In the Northern Hemisphere, hurricanes occur in late summer and early fall, when the ocean temperatures are warmest. As the warm ocean water evaporates and the water vapor rises, intense low-pressure areas called *tropical depressions* form. As these tropical depressions build strength, they can become hurricanes. As shown in **Figure 20-20,** hurricanes are large circulating masses of clouds, wind, and rain with average diameters of about 600 km (373 mi).

Hurricanes are powered by the energy released as water vapor condenses to form clouds. As this condensation releases energy, the air heats and expands, and the pressure inside the clouds decreases. Warm, moist air continues to rise toward the low pressure area and condenses, releasing more energy. This rising air creates fierce winds, shown by the red arrows in **Figure 20-20,** that swirl upward around the eye of the storm. When the storm moves over land or cool water, it gradually weakens.

Although hurricanes move fairly slowly, they are extremely powerful. To be classified as a hurricane, winds in a storm must reach speeds greater than 118 km/h (73 mi/h). Winds in intense hurricanes can reach speeds greater than 250 km/h (155 mi/h).

The eye of the hurricane is very calm and free of clouds, as shown on **Figure 20-20.** This can be very dangerous because people often believe the storm has passed and leave the protective cover of their homes only to be caught in the storm again.

Weather Maps

Meteorologists use weather maps like the one shown in **Figure 20-21** when they are preparing forecasts. These maps use different symbols, such as the ones shown in Appendix B, to show weather conditions such as precipitation, wind speed, and cloud coverage. On the wind-speed symbol, wind direction is indicated by the direction from which the line comes into the circle.

Lines called **isobars** show points of equal barometric pressure. When isobars are close together, the wind is stronger. The number that appears on the isobar denotes the barometric pressure at points along the line.

Look at the wind directions in **Figure 20-21.** You might expect that winds would always blow perpendicular to isobars, from high-pressure areas to low-pressure areas. Instead, the map shows that winds near Earth's surface are directed slightly across isobars toward areas of lower pressure. This is because the direction of the wind is changed by the Coriolis effect. Because of the combined effects of force, the Coriolis effect, and friction, near-surface winds in the Northern Hemisphere generally travel across the isobars with higher pressure areas on the right.

When isobars form a closed loop, the center of the loop is called a *pressure center.* Low pressure centers (L) are areas where the air pressure is generally lower than the surrounding areas. These *lows* are usually accompanied by clouds and precipitation. High pressure centers (H), on the other hand, usually mark regions of fair weather.

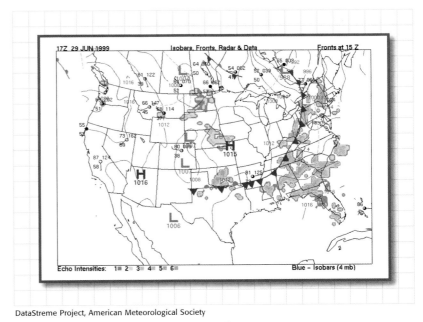

DataStreme Project, American Meteorological Society

Figure 20-21
A typical weather map shows isobars, highs and lows, fronts, wind direction and speed, temperature, and precipitation.

isobar a line drawn on a weather map connecting points of equal barometric or atmospheric pressure

Climate

Weather is something that changes day to day, moment to moment. **Climate,** on the other hand, does not change as readily. Climate is the *average* weather of a region, often measured over many years. Just as a student may receive several grades above 90 percent but still have an 85 percent average, the weather in a region may be cold and overcast on some days but still have a warm and sunny climate overall.

climate the general weather conditions over many years

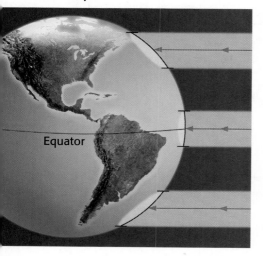

Equator

Temperatures tend to be higher close to the equator

Imagine sunlight striking Earth, as shown in **Figure 20-22.** Rays striking farther from the equator spread out over a greater area of Earth's surface and therefore are less concentrated than rays that strike Earth at the equator. At the poles, rays pass parallel to Earth's surface and do not warm the atmosphere as much. Hence, the poles are very cold.

Earth is not always oriented so that the equator is perpendicular to incoming solar radiation. However, the equator is closer to perpendicular to the incoming sunlight throughout the year than are areas closer to the poles. Because of this, countries and islands close to the equator usually have warmer climates.

Earth's tilt and rotation account for our seasons

Another major factor that affects climate is the cycling of our seasons. In summer months, the sun appears high in the sky and the days are longer and warmer. But in winter months, the sun does not appear very high, and the days are shorter and colder.

Why do we experience these differing conditions on such a regular basis? Having read in the chapter on the universe that Earth's orbit is an ellipse, you might expect that summertime corresponds with the times of year when the Earth is closest to the sun. This is not true. In fact, Earth is farthest from the sun on July 4 and closest to the sun on about January 3. Earth's seasons are actually caused by the tilt of Earth on its axis.

As shown in **Figure 20-23,** Earth's axis is tilted 23.5° from the perpendicular to the plane of the planet's orbit about the sun. Although there can be tiny changes in the amount of tilt, Earth maintains this orientation as it orbits the sun. Because of this tilted orientation, the sun seems to rise to different heights in the sky at different times of the year.

Figure 20-23
This illustration (not to scale) shows that Earth's axis is tilted 23.5° from the perpendicular to the orbital plane. The direction of tilt of Earth's axis remains the same throughout Earth's orbit.

When the North Pole is tilted toward the sun, as it is in position *A* in **Figure 20-23,** the sun rises higher in the Northern Hemisphere than when the North Pole is pointed away from the sun. When this occurs, the days in the Northern Hemisphere become longer and the temperature increases. This is summer in the Northern Hemisphere and winter in the Southern Hemisphere. The longest day of the year in the Northern Hemisphere, the *summer solstice,* occurs on approximately June 21.

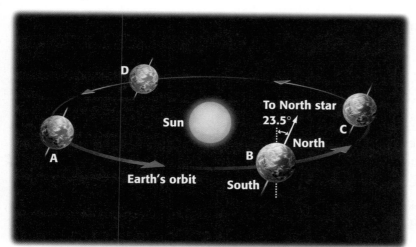

D

Sun

To North star
23.5°
C
North

B
South

A

Earth's orbit

When the South Pole is tilted toward the sun, as it is in position *C* in **Figure 20-23,** the sun rises higher in the Southern Hemisphere than when the South Pole is pointed away from the sun. In other words, it is summer in the Southern Hemisphere and winter in the Northern Hemisphere. The shortest day of the year in the Northern Hemisphere occurs on December 21. This day is called the *winter solstice.*

At positions *B* and *D,* Earth's axis is tilted neither away from nor toward the sun. When this occurs, day and night are of equal length all over the Earth. The day on which this happens is called an *equinox.* Position *D* corresponds to the *vernal* (spring) *equinox* in the Northern Hemisphere and occurs around March 21. Position *B,* on the other hand, occurs on about September 22 and is called the *autumnal* (fall) *equinox* in the Northern Hemisphere.

Earth's surface features affect climate

The rise and fall of a land surface is called topography. The hills, mountains, valleys, and wide stretches of flat surface in Earth's topography all affect the climate of a region.

Mountains can have a profound effect on the climate of an area. Tall mountains force air to rise over them. As the air rises, it cools, and clouds form. When mountains are near oceans, as shown in **Figure 20-24,** the rising air is usually so humid that the resulting clouds cannot hold all of the condensed water vapor, and precipitation results. This rain or snow is dropped over the mountains. On the other side of the mountain range, this cool, dry air warms as it descends. The deserts that form on this side of the mountain are said to lie in a rain shadow.

Broad flat surfaces, such as the Great Plains of North America, do not stop wind flow very well. Winds can come from several directions and merge on the plains. During certain seasons, this mixing of wind produces thunderstorms and even tornadoes.

INTEGRATING

PHYSICS
Large bodies of water regulate local climates because water has a high specific heat. For instance, even though Minneapolis, Minnesota, in the Midwest, and Portland, Oregon, along the Pacific Coast, are at about the same latitude, they have very different climates. The difference is caused by the Pacific Ocean. During winter months, the ocean does not get as cold as the surrounding air. As a result, Pacific winds warm the Oregon coastline. Meanwhile, Minneapolis has no large body of water to regulate its temperature.

In summertime, the Pacific Ocean does not get as warm as the surrounding air, and Pacific winds cool Portland. Minneapolis does not receive cool ocean breezes during the summertime.

▶ **topography** the surface features of Earth

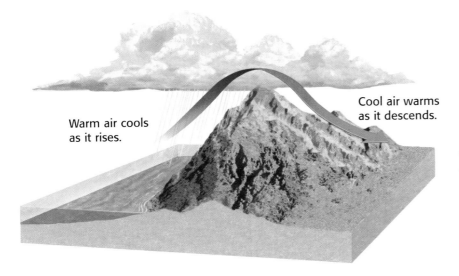

Warm air cools as it rises.

Cool air warms as it descends.

Figure 20-24
Air passing over a mountain range loses its moisture as it rises and cools. This dense, dry air warms as it descends the other side of the mountain.

Global climate changes over time

From the warm, lifeless early atmosphere to the many ice ages characterized by glaciers covering much of the continents, Earth's global climate has varied greatly over time. Many factors, such as the changes in the position of the continents and slight changes in Earth's tilt, have produced these climatic variations.

If the greenhouse effect increases because of increased carbon dioxide in the atmosphere, temperatures could rise. Volcanic eruptions can produce gases that condense in the atmosphere and reflect solar energy, causing cooling. Because of all the factors that determine global climate, Earth's climate is likely to continue to change over the millennia to come.

SECTION 20.3 REVIEW

SUMMARY

▶ A warm front forms as a warm air mass moves over a slower cold air mass. A cold front forms as a cold air mass moves under a slower warm air mass.

▶ Lightning is a discharge of atmospheric electrical energy.

▶ Tornadoes are high-speed rotating winds that form as air begins to rotate around quickly rising warm air.

▶ Hurricanes are large storm systems that are characterized by high-speed winds and very low pressures.

▶ Symbols on weather maps explain a variety of weather conditions.

▶ Climate is the average weather of a region over a length of time, usually many years.

▶ Some factors that affect climate are latitude, seasons, and topography.

CHECK YOUR UNDERSTANDING

1. **Identify** which of the following is NOT a factor of global climate change:
   a. slight changes in Earth's tilt
   b. movement of continents
   c. reversing of the magnetic poles
   d. increase or decrease of solar energy

2. **Distinguish** between thunder and lightning.

3. **Identify** which of the following probably would not have an effect on the climate of a region:
   a. the region is next to a mountain range
   b. the region is on the equator
   c. a thunderstorm just blew through the region
   d. the region is next to the Atlantic Ocean

4. **Determine** whether each of the following statements describes a warm front or a cold front:
   a. A warm air mass moves above a slower cold air mass.
   b. It is characterized by high winds and thunderstorms.
   c. A cold air mass moves quickly under a slower-moving warm air mass.
   d. It is characterized by steady rain.

5. **Determine** whether a tornado is more likely to form along a cold front or a warm front.

6. **Predict** whether wind speed will be greater when isobar lines on a weather map are closer together or farther apart.

7. **Critical Thinking** Grapes grow well in areas where the climate is generally mild. Would you recommend planting grapes on the California coast or on the plains of North Dakota? Explain your answer.

Chapter Highlights

Before you begin, review the summaries of the key ideas of each section, found on pages 655, 662, and 670. The key vocabulary terms are listed on pages 648, 656, and 663.

UNDERSTANDING CONCEPTS

1. Around Los Angeles, frequent temperature inversions are the result of cool, polluted air being trapped by _____.
   a. acid rain
   b. a layer of warmer air
   c. a thunderstorm
   d. the ocean

2. The _____ is the process in which the atmosphere traps warming solar energy near Earth's surface.
   a. summer solstice
   b. Coriolis effect
   c. greenhouse effect
   d. water cycle

3. Almost all the water vapor in the atmosphere is in the _____.
   a. exosphere
   b. ionosphere
   c. stratopause
   d. troposphere

4. The addition of _____ to the atmosphere by the burning of fossil fuels for cars, machinery, and power plants may lead to global warming.
   a. gasoline
   b. CFCs
   c. oxygen
   d. carbon dioxide

5. CFCs, chemicals that are used as refrigerants and propellants in spray cans, are partly to blame for the reduction of _____ in the stratosphere.
   a. carbon dioxide
   b. oxygen
   c. ozone
   d. clouds

6. Clouds form when water vapor in the air condenses as _____.
   a. the air is heated
   b. the air is cooled
   c. snow falls
   d. snow forms

7. When air temperature drops, the air's ability to contain water vapor is _____.
   a. slightly higher
   b. much higher
   c. about the same
   d. lower

8. Winds in the Northern Hemisphere curve to the right because of _____.
   a. isobars
   b. climate
   c. the Coriolis effect
   d. CFCs

9. Cumulonimbus and nimbostratus clouds both _____.
   a. appear white and fluffy
   b. produce precipitation
   c. occur at high altitudes
   d. look thin and wispy

10. _____ are lines on a weather map that connect points of equal pressure.
    a. Isobars
    b. Isotherms
    c. Highs
    d. Lows

11. When a moving warm air mass encounters a mountain range, it _____.
    a. stops moving
    b. slows and sinks
    c. rises and cools
    d. reverses direction

12. If you hear on the radio that a tornado is approaching, you should _____.
    a. head to high ground
    b. attempt to drive away from the tornado
    c. sit in the center of a basement
    d. hold onto a solid object, such as a tree

Using Vocabulary

13. Explain how carbon dioxide in the atmosphere relates to the *greenhouse effect*.

14. How is *ozone* formed?

15. Describe the *water cycle* using the terms *precipitation, condensation, transpiration,* and *evaporation*.

16. Using the terms *humidity* and *dew point,* explain why you might find small droplets of water on your lawn in the morning.

17. Describe the formation of a warm *front*.

BUILDING MATH SKILLS

18. **Climatography** Visual aids called climatographs are used to display information about the climate of a specific region. Using the climatograph for Moscow, Idaho, in the figure below, answer the following questions:
   a. What was the average temperature in Moscow during August?
   b. What was the total precipitation in the Moscow area for the month of January?
   c. What was the approximate total precipitation for the year?

Climatograph for Moscow, Idaho

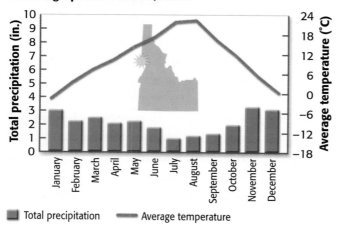

Total precipitation ——— Average temperature

THINKING CRITICALLY

19. **Critical Thinking** How would you explain why some of the mountain peaks located near the equator are covered with snow?

20. **Applying Knowledge** All use of CFCs has been banned in the United States for environmental reasons. Which one of the four layers of the atmosphere does this ban help protect? Explain your answer.

21. **Creative Thinking** Describe how your life would be changed if global temperatures were to increase by several degrees.

22. **Creative Thinking** In what ways would a knowledge of the global wind belts have helped a sixteenth-century explorer sailing between Spain and the northern part of South America?

23. **Applying Knowledge** One body of air has a relative humidity of 97 percent. Another has a relative humidity of 44 percent. If they are at the same temperature, which body of air is closer to its dew point? Explain your answer.

24. **Making Comparisons** Where would the air contain the most moisture, over Panama or over Antarctica? Explain your answer.

25. **Critical Thinking** Is it safe to be on the street in an automobile during a tornado? Explain your answer.

26. **Interpreting Graphics** Using the weather map shown in **Figure 20-25,** predict which way the winds will blow across the state of California.

27. **Acquiring and Evaluating Data** Find out the local high and low temperatures for each day of a recent 2 week period. Using a computer spreadsheet program, graph these temperatures and find the average high and low for this period.

COMPUTER SKILL

Figure 20-25

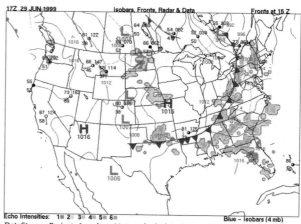

DataStreme Project, American Meteorological Society

28. Creative Thinking Predict how the strength of a Northern Hemisphere hurricane will change as it moves northward in the Atlantic Ocean, and explain why.

DEVELOPING LIFE/WORK SKILLS

29. Allocating Resources You are planning an expedition to Mount Everest, the tallest mountain in the world. Identify which four of the following items you will need the most, and explain why.
a. inflatable raft
b. insulated clothes
c. life vest
d. television
e. oxygen equipment
f. fire-starting equipment
g. raincoat

30. Applying Technology Satellites are used to observe weather and climate around the world. Research the use of weather satellites, and write a short paragraph describing how satellites help predict the weather and climate.

31. Working Cooperatively Obtain a week's worth of local or national weather maps from the paper or the Internet. In a small group, prepare a weather forecast. Interpret the daily weather, and follow any trends. Explain the high and low pressure areas and the resulting fronts, any precipitation, and average temperatures. Have a volunteer from your group present the forecast to the class.

internet connect

SCiLINKS
NSTA

TOPIC: Weather maps
GO TO: www.scilinks.org
KEYWORD: HK1806

INTEGRATING CONCEPTS

32. Concept Mapping Copy the unfinished concept map below onto a sheet of paper. Complete the map by writing the correct word or phrase in the lettered boxes.

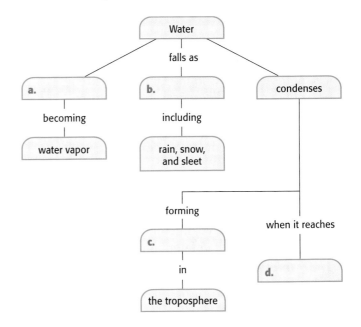

33. Connection to Chemistry Research the effects of the gas methane on the atmosphere. How is methane produced? What are some of the sources of methane in the atmosphere? What is methane's effect on global warming? Can we eliminate methane from the atmosphere?

34. Connection to Social Studies Early explorers often ventured to find resources and wealth, but they brought back more than that. They made and improved maps. They also kept journals of weather and climates of new lands. Research a famous explorer, and describe the contributions to understanding weather or climate made by the explorer. What instruments did the explorer use to make measurements?

Design Your Own Lab

Measuring Temperature Effects

▶ Preparing for Your Experiment

1. On a blank sheet of paper, prepare a table like the one shown below.

Temp. (°C)	Pull volume (mL)	Push volume (mL)	Average volume (mL)

2. Measure the air temperature in the room, and record the temperature in your data table.

3. Remove the cap from the tip of the syringe, and move the plunger. If the plunger does not move smoothly and easily, lubricate the inside wall of the syringe with a few drops of glycerin.

4. Adjust the position of the plunger until the syringe is about two-thirds full of air. Add a dab of petroleum jelly to the tip of the syringe, and replace the cap.

▶ Measuring the Volume of Air

5. Gently pull on the plunger, and then release it. When the plunger stops, read the volume of air inside the syringe. Record the volume in your data table in the column labeled "Pull volume."

6. With your finger on the cap, gently push on the plunger and then release it. When the plunger stops, read the volume of air inside the syringe. Record the volume in your data table in the column labeled "Push volume." **SAFETY CAUTION** Do not point the syringe at anyone while you push on the plunger. Wear safety goggles.

Introduction

Air rises or sinks in the Earth's atmosphere due to differences in the density of air that are caused by differences in temperature. How can you determine the effect of temperature on the density of air?

Objectives

▶ **Measure** the volume of a constant mass of air at different temperatures.

▶ **Infer** changes in density from changes in volume.

Materials

400 mL beaker
60 mL disposable syringe
glycerin
petroleum jelly
hot and cold tap water
ice
thermometer

Safety Needs

safety goggles

► Designing Your Experiment

7. With your lab partners, decide how you will use the materials available in the lab to determine the effect of temperature on air density. Test at least two temperatures below room temperature and two temperatures above room temperature. It is important that the mass of air inside the syringe does not change during your experiment. How can you ensure that the mass of air remains constant?

8. In your lab report, list each step you will perform in your experiment.

9. Before you carry out your experiment, your teacher must approve your plan.

► Performing Your Experiment

10. After your teacher approves your plan, carry out your experiment.

11. Record your results in your data table.
    SAFETY CAUTION Use care when working with hot water; it can cause severe burns.

► Analyzing Your Results

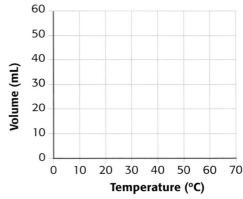

1. At each temperature you tested, calculate the average volume by adding the pull volume and push volume and dividing the sum by 2. Record the result in your data table.

2. Plot your data in your lab report in the form of a graph set up like the one at right. Draw a straight line on the graph that fits the data points best.

3. **Reaching Conclusions** How does the volume of a constant mass of air change as the temperature of the air increases? For the mass of air you used in your experiment, how much would the volume change if the temperature increased from 10°C to 60°C?

4. **Reaching Conclusions** Recall that the density of a substance equals the substance's mass divided by its volume. Do your results indicate that the density of air increases or decreases as the temperature of the air increases? Explain.

5. **Reaching Conclusions** Based on your results, would a body of air tend to rise or sink as it becomes colder than the surrounding air? Explain.

► Defending Your Conclusions

6. Suppose someone tells you that your conclusions are invalid because some of your data points lie above or below the best-fit line you drew. How could you show that your conclusions are valid?

viewpoints

Should Laws Require Zero-Emission Cars?

California law requires that by the year 2004, 10 percent of all cars sold in the state be zero-emission vehicles that produce no pollution as they are operated. Automobile companies are scrambling to develop electric cars and other technologies to meet this deadline.

Often these cars are substantially more expensive than gasoline-burning models. Is the pollution situation so desperate that this is necessary? Or is this a case of laws interfering with the car market?

> FROM: Sheneah T., Chicago, IL

As technology advances, we will be able to make better cars that won't depend on gas as much. If we were to cut down on the amount of pollution, this would make our environment better to live in. This goes back to an issue of public health. If cars emit less pollution, we would have fewer cases of respiratory disorders and a much cleaner environment.

Require These Cars Now

> FROM: Megan B., Houston, TX

A law requiring zero-emission vehicles after the year 2003 is probably the best way to prevent air pollution. The various ways companies are changing cars to be more environmentally safe just isn't cutting it. Why do we spend tens of thousands of dollars for fun but not to help save the world?

> FROM: Kathryn W., Rochester, MN

I think the government should definitely get involved in these issues. The laws can be changed later, if needed, but we can't go back in time and fix the problem.

> FROM: Margo K., Coral Springs, FL

Although zero-emission vehicles are better for the environment, there are many expenses that come along with them. I disagree with the law because of the cost of the new vehicles. Rather than making zero-emission vehicles mandatory, if the idea is spread, people will act upon it.

Don't Require These Cars Now

> FROM: Marianne C., Bowling Green, KY

Not everyone will be able to afford these expensive cars. I don't think people should be obligated to buy cars to save the planet. People should do other things instead, like planting trees or carpooling.

> FROM: Amar T., Palos Park, IL

From a car enthusiast's point of view, I feel that no state should make zero-emission cars mandatory for three main reasons: First, at this time zero-emission cars do not perform as well as cars with an internal-combustion engine. Second, zero-emission cars, like electrical cars, have small cruising ranges, and their fuel cells take up too much space. Finally, they are more expensive than gasoline-burning cars.

Your Turn

1. **Critiquing Viewpoints** Select one of the statements on this page that you *agree* with. Identify and explain at least one weak point in the statement. What would you say to respond to someone who brought up this weak point as a reason you were wrong?

2. **Critiquing Viewpoints** Select one of the statements on this page that you *disagree* with. Identify and explain at least one strong point in the statement. What would you say to respond to someone who brought up this point as a reason they were right?

3. **Interpreting and Communicating** Imagine that you work for an advertising firm that has been hired to promote a car manufacturer's new zero-emission vehicle. The new car costs more than a regular car. Create an advertisement or brochure for the car that tries to persuade people to buy the new car.

4. **Understanding Systems** Other critics of such laws point out that zero-emission cars do not end the pollution entirely. Some toxic waste is made when these cars are manufactured. Write a paragraph in which you outline a method for deciding whether the pollution emitted by a regular car is worse for the environment than the waste made in making a zero-emission vehicle.

internetconnect

go.hrw.com

TOPIC: Zero-emission vehicles
GO TO: go.hrw.com
KEYWORD: HK1Zero-emission

Should zero-emission vehicles be required? Why or why not? Share your views on this issue and find out what others think about it at the HRW Web site.

CHAPTER 21

Using Natural Resources

Chapter Preview

21.1 Organisms and Their Environment
What Is an Ecosystem?
Changes in Ecosystems
Evaluating Changes in Ecosystems

21.2 Energy and Resources
The Search for Resources
Alternative Sources of Energy
The Efficiency of Energy Conversion

21.3 Pollution and Recycling
What Causes Pollution?
Water Pollution
Pollution on Land
Reducing Pollution

INTEGRATING TECHNOLOGY and Society

Focus ACTIVITY

Background The engines are started. The drivers check their gauges one last time. The flag rises, then falls. They're off!

Is this a typical race? Not quite. These race cars are powered by solar energy. Not a drop of gasoline is needed to make them run. Teams of college students designed and built the cars to compete in an annual event called Sunrayce.

Sunrayce began in 1990, and its goal is to raise awareness of alternative energy sources, such as the sun. Each summer, students travel more than 2093 km (1300 mi) across the United States in these solar-powered cars.

Solar-powered cars must be lightweight and efficient. Although the average race speed is about 35 mi/h, the cars can reach top speeds of 65 mi/h. Each car is fueled by solar cells. These cells, which are made of thin layers of silicon, capture the sun's energy and store it in batteries.

Activity 1 Obtain a solar cell from an electronics store or your school's science lab. Using the solar cell, a low-wattage light bulb, and two pieces of insulated electrical wire, create a current in the cell and the bulb. Place the end of one wire on the metal bottom of the bulb and the end of the other wire on the side of the bulb. Place the other ends of both wires on the solar cell. In your own words, describe the movement of charges between the cell and the bulb.

Activity 2 Make a list of the energy sources you use at home. Find out from your parents which source of energy costs the most per month. Make a pie chart showing your results. Call your local power company to find out what type of resource is used to generate electrical power.

internet**connect**

SC**LINKS**
NSTA

TOPIC: Solar energy
GO TO: www.scilinks.org
KEYWORD: HK1901

Sunrayce is held each year to raise awareness of alternative energy sources. Drivers travel more than 2093 km across the United States using solar-powered cars.

Organisms and Their Environment

KEY TERMS

ecosystem
community
succession
hydroelectric power

OBJECTIVES

▶ Explain the structure of an ecosystem.

▶ Describe the effects one species can have on
an ecosystem.

▶ Discuss two ways natural forces can change ecosystems.

▶ Discuss two ways humans can change ecosystems.

internet connect

SCiLINKS
NSTA

TOPIC: Ecosystem factors
GO TO: www.scilinks.org
KEYWORD: HK1902

▶ **ecosystem** all of the living
and nonliving elements in a
particular place

Should money be spent drilling for oil in the wilderness of Alaska, or would the money be better spent promoting solar power? Should a nearby swamp be drained to provide parking for a mall in your town, or is the swamp best left alone? No matter how you feel about these issues, you need to know how they will change the world around you.

We humans, like all other living things, fill our needs by using natural resources. These resources are taken from the world around us. Every action taken, whether it is someone draining a swamp or a bird catching prey, affects all the other living things in the ecosystem, as shown in **Figure 21-1.**

To evaluate the effects of your decisions on the issues that cause change in your environment, you must first understand how the many parts of an ecosystem relate to one another.

Figure 21-1
Each living and nonliving element in this desert ecosystem directly affects the other.

What Is an Ecosystem?

Consider a squirrel in a city park. The squirrel gathers and stores food. It lives in a tree and drinks water from a sun-dappled pond. The soil, trees, sunshine, and water are natural resources found within the city park. The city park itself is an ecosystem.

Living elements in an ecosystem can include plants, animals, and people. Nonliving elements include sunlight, air, soil, water, and temperature. The different elements within a desert ecosystem are shown in **Figure 21-1.** The cactuses, sagebrush, lizards, snakes, scorpions, and birds interact with one another and with their surroundings to make a stable, balanced ecosystem.

internetconnect

SC*LINKS*
NSTA

TOPIC: Populations and communities
GO TO: www.scilinks.org
KEYWORD: HK1903

All ecosystems are not the same size

Ecosystems can be large or small. The entire planet is one big ecosystem containing all the living and nonliving things on Earth—the land and water, the organisms, and the atmosphere. A shallow forest pool no bigger than a rain puddle is also an example of an ecosystem. This ecosystem is made up of water, mud, bacteria, mosquitoes, air, and larvae all living together.

▶ **community** all of the animals and plants living in one area within an ecosystem

Living things are adapted to their ecosystem

Living things are found almost everywhere: on land, in the air, and in water. Each organism has adapted to factors in its environment, such as temperature, humidity, and the other living things around it. These factors determine where a particular organism lives. For instance, polar bears are adapted to cold, wet places, and camels are adapted to hot, dry places. Neither animal could survive in the other's environment.

Figure 21-2
Ecosystems are made up of communities that contain different populations of organisms.

Ecosystems are divided into communities

Groups of animals and plants that are adapted to similar conditions form a community. There can be several communities within an ecosystem. For example, the animals and plants of the tundra make up one community. The seals, fish, and algae of the nearby ocean make up another. Polar bears belong to *both* communities. **Figure 21-2** shows the different divisions within an ecosystem.

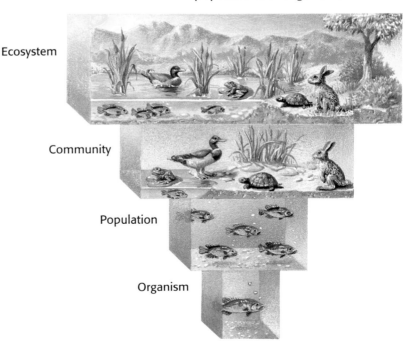

Ecosystem

Community

Population

Organism

Changes in Ecosystems

Sunlight, water, air, soil, animals, plants—the elements that make up an ecosystem are numerous. Each element is balanced with the others so that the ecosystem can be maintained over a long period of time.

Look at the aquarium shown in **Figure 21-3.** The amount of salt in the water and the temperature of the water are at the right levels. The fish, snails, and plants all have sufficient space and food. In short, there are enough resources for every living thing in the aquarium ecosystem. The ecosystem is balanced.

Figure 21-3
The living and nonliving elements of this aquarium ecosystem help to keep it balanced.

Balanced ecosystems remain stable

When an ecosystem is balanced, the population sizes of the different species do not change relative to one another. Overall, there is a natural balance between those that eat and those that are eaten. Other factors, such as disease or food shortage, prevent populations from growing too much. If the balance within an ecosystem is disturbed, change results.

The graph in **Figure 21-4** is based on a Canadian study of the snowshoe hare and its predator, the lynx. What happened to the lynx population when there where fewer snowshoe hares?

When the prey population of a particular place decreases, there is less food for the predators. As a result, some of the predators die. On the other hand, if the prey population increases, more predators may move into the area. A variety of factors, including population change, can affect the balance in an ecosystem. What happens when one factor changes?

Figure 21-4
The population of snowshoe hares directly affects the population of lynxes.

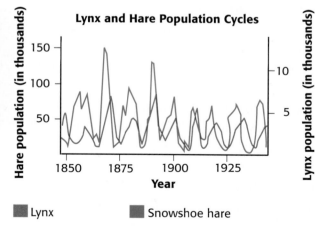

A change in one feature can affect the whole system

Throughout the 1990s, researchers have been closely watching a piece of land in Central America that was once a tropical rain forest. After the trees were logged, a species of wild pig vanished from the forest because the pigs no longer had enough food and shelter. Three species of frogs disappeared soon thereafter. Was this related to the loss of the wild pigs?

The pigs wallowed in mud, forming puddles that the frogs used for breeding. Without the pigs, there were no puddles, and the frogs had to find another place to breed. In this way, a change in one factor of an ecosystem can affect all the living and nonliving elements within the system.

The key to understanding ecosystems can be summed up in one word: *interrelatedness*. The elements that make up an ecosystem function together to keep the entire system stable. If something changes, time and natural forces often work to return the ecosystem to its undisturbed state.

Ecosystems gradually return to their original conditions

Yellowstone National Park is one of the largest tourist attractions in the United States. The park, located in northwestern Wyoming and southern Montana, covers about 2.2 million acres (3,472 square miles) of land and is know for its active geysers and hot springs.

But during the summer of 1988, large areas of the park were burned to the ground by fires, as shown in **Figure 21-5A.** The fires, which were started by lightning and careless human activity, spread quickly through the open forest during this particularly dry summer, and left nearly a third of the park blackened with ash. Firefighters and Army and Marine troops worked continuously to put the fires out but were unsuccessful. In early September, rain and snow finally put the fires out.

The following spring, the appearance of the "dead" forest began to change. Large numbers of small, green plants began to flourish and replace areas that had been covered with fallen trees. Year after year, gradual developments took place in the recovering area, as shown in **Figure 21-5B.**

Figure 21-5
(A) During the summer of 1988, Yellowstone National Park was plagued with a series of uncontrollable fires. (B) The following spring, new plant life flourished in the recovering park.

Figure 21-6
These photos of Glacier Bay, Alaska, show the change that took place over 200 years.

In time, a complex ecosystem will develop. This process, shown in **Figure 21-6,** is known as succession. The end product is a stable but complicated community where birth, death, growth, and decay take place at a steady rate. This will keep the ecosystem stable if no major disruptions occur.

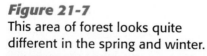 **succession** the gradual repopulating of a community by different species over a period of time

Evaluating Changes in Ecosystems

Ecosystems undergo both short-term and long-term changes. Short-term changes are usually easily reversed, but long-term changes can take many years to be reversed.

Short-term ecosystem changes
During autumn, many trees and shrubs lose their leaves. In the winter, many birds migrate to warmer places. Other animals hibernate by lowering their metabolism. These animals can sleep through the winter in snug burrows or caves. In spring, the migrating birds return, animals come out of hibernation, buds open, and seeds begin to sprout. As **Figure 21-7** shows, the same ecosystem can appear quite different during different times of the year.

Figure 21-7
This area of forest looks quite different in the spring and winter.

Long-term ecosystem changes

As you have learned, long-term changes in ecosystems can be caused by events such as volcanic eruptions. At other times, many factors act together to cause change. In these cases, it may be hard to know how much each factor adds to the change. An example is the many causes of global temperature change.

Climatic changes affect ecosystems

In your lifetime, the climate where you live probably hasn't changed much. Some years may be colder than others, but average monthly temperatures do not vary greatly from year to year. Throughout Earth's geologic history, there have been periods known as ice ages, when icy glaciers covered much of the continents. **Figure 21-8** shows the size of the glacier that covered much of North America during the last ice age. This period ended roughly 11 500 years ago.

During ice ages, temperatures are much colder than usual. These cold spells alternate with warmer, or interglacial, periods. Scientists hypothesize that ice ages are caused by a variety of factors, including the tilt of Earth's axis, continental drift, and the Earth's orbit around the sun.

The combined effect of these changes in Earth's position in space is difficult to predict. One thing we do know is that these changes cause temperature differences in ecosystems.

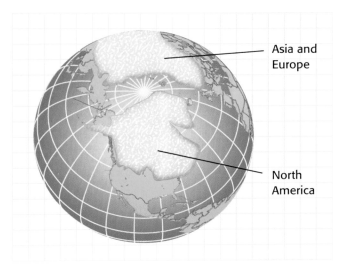

Asia and Europe

North America

Figure 21-8
Icy glaciers covered much of North America and parts of Europe and Asia during the last ice age.

Inquiry Lab

Why do seasons occur?

Materials ✔ globe   ✔ unshaded lamp

Procedure

1. Place the lamp on a table, and turn the lamp on.
2. Stand about 2 m from the table, and hold the globe at arm's length, pointing it toward the lamp.
3. Tilt the globe slightly so that the bottom half—the Southern Hemisphere—is illuminated by the lamp.
4. Keeping the axis of the Earth's rotation pointing in the same direction, walk halfway around the table.

Analysis

1. What part of the globe is lit by the lamp's light now? What season does this represent in this part of Earth?
2. Would there be any seasonal changes if the Earth's axis were not tilted? Explain your answer.
3. In addition to experiencing seasonal changes, ecosystems also experience short-term changes as day changes into night. What movement of Earth causes night and day to occur?

Figure 21-9
Clearing trees, driving cars, constructing buildings, and farming are just a few human activities that cause changes in ecosystems.

internet**connect**

SC*I*LINKS
NSTA

TOPIC: Changes in ecosystems
GO TO: www.scilinks.org
KEYWORD: HK1904

▶ **hydroelectric power**
the energy of moving water converted to electricity

Changes can be caused by human activity

Physical factors are not the only things that cause changes in ecosystems. People also alter the environment in a variety of ways, as shown in **Figure 21-9.** Activities such as driving cars, growing crops, and constructing roads and buildings change the environment.

All of those activities have some benefits, but they also cause some problems. The benefits of some human activities, such as building dams, are numerous. For instance, the El Chocon Cerros Colorados project brought much-needed flood control to the foothills of the Andes Mountains in Argentina. Formerly, the rivers that flowed down from the mountains flooded twice each year. At other times the region was too dry to grow crops. The construction of a system of dams stopped this cycle. Excess water is now stored in large reservoirs behind the dams. This water is used for irrigation. This allows farmers to grow crops year-round. In addition, the dam is used to generate **hydroelectric power** for much of the country. This energy resource will be discussed further in Section 21-2.

Such large dams, however, can cause problems. Without the floods, rivers no longer deposit rich soil, so farmers use chemical fertilizers on their crops instead. Runoff from these fertilizers can contaminate ground water and streams, making water supplies unsafe for humans and other living things.

Many of the adverse effects of dams constructed before the 1970s were not foreseen by their developers. Today scientists and engineers have a better understanding of how ecosystems work. Often, major projects such as constructing a dam must undergo an environmental analysis before construction begins. If the project is likely to destroy an entire ecosystem, it may have to be redesigned, relocated, or canceled altogether.

Changes can be caused by introduction of nonnative species

Some species move from one ecosystem to another on their own. Animals may migrate to new areas, and seeds can be carried by wind or water to different places. Even humans can influence the spread of nonnative species to other ecosystems, sometimes accidentally and sometimes on purpose.

Starlings, for instance, were purposely brought to the United States. In the 1800s, a few dozen European starlings were released in New York City. The birds rapidly multiplied, and today there are millions of them across the United States.

Both starlings and native North American bluebirds nest in holes in tree trunks and fence posts, as shown in **Figure 21-10.** As a result, the two species compete for shelter. The bluebirds nearly lost the battle. Concerned citizens launched a multistate effort to build and distribute bird boxes. These boxes, specially designed with small entrances, provided nesting places for the bluebirds and kept the larger starlings out.

There are other ways to introduce organisms to an ecosystem. For instance, small insects can be carried across borders accidentally. Often they are hidden in crates of fruit and vegetables.

In its new environment, the nonnative species may have no natural enemies to keep its numbers in check. As a result, its members can quickly multiply and take over an ecosystem. The new competing species may wipe out an existing native species and cause change in the ecosystem.

Figure 21-10
Starlings compete with bluebirds for nesting sites in the holes of tree trunks or fence posts.

SECTION 21.1 REVIEW

SUMMARY

▶ Living and nonliving elements form an ecosystem.

▶ The elements of an ecosystem work together to maintain a balance.

▶ One change can affect the entire ecosystem.

▶ A disturbed ecosystem may gradually return to its original state.

▶ Ecosystem changes can be short-term or long-term.

CHECK YOUR UNDERSTANDING

1. **List** two factors that keep populations stable.
2. **Analyze** the following statement: An ecosystem is like a fine-tuned car.
3. **Describe** how the loss of one species in a pond can affect other species.
4. **Define** *succession.*
5. **Predict** how a thunderstorm could lead to a long-term change in an ecosystem.
6. **List** two changes in the Earth's position in space that can affect climatic change in ecosystems.
7. **Critical Thinking** Describe a common human activity that can disrupt an ecosystem. Propose a solution to the problem.
8. **Critical Thinking** List several ways nonnative plants may be introduced to an environment.

Energy and Resources

How Energy Is Used Worldwide

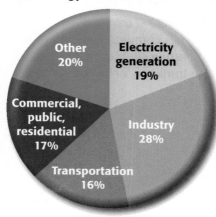

How Energy Is Used in the United States

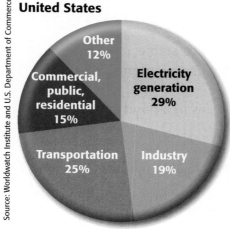

Source: Worldwatch Institute and U.S. Department of Commerce

Figure 21-11
These pie charts show how energy use in the United States compares with energy use worldwide, including the United States.

How much energy do you use in a day, a week, or a month? You probably use more than you think. Energy is needed to light streets and homes, heat water and buildings, cook food, power vehicles, and run appliances. Energy is also needed to make the products you use every day. Where does all this energy come from?

The Search for Resources

You have already learned that we rely on natural resources to meet our basic needs for food and shelter. We also depend on natural resources to provide the energy and raw materials needed at home, at work, and for growing food. **Figure 21-11** compares the patterns of energy use in the United States with the patterns of energy use worldwide.

The sun is the source of energy

Almost all of this energy comes from the sun. The sun sends out energy as radiation of various wavelengths. Living things use this energy in many different ways.

Plants change energy from the sun into chemical energy

Plants use some of the energy from sunlight to change the simple molecules of carbon dioxide and water into oxygen and more complex molecules of simple sugars. This process is called photosynthesis. It allows plants to change the sun's energy into stored chemical energy.

Some animals eat plants to obtain energy. Through a series of chemical reactions, the animals are able to convert the sugars in plants back to carbon dioxide and water. This process, which also produces energy, is known as cellular respiration. This cycle of energy transfer repeats itself continuously in nature. **Figure 21-12,** at right, shows both animals and plants undergoing cellular respiration.

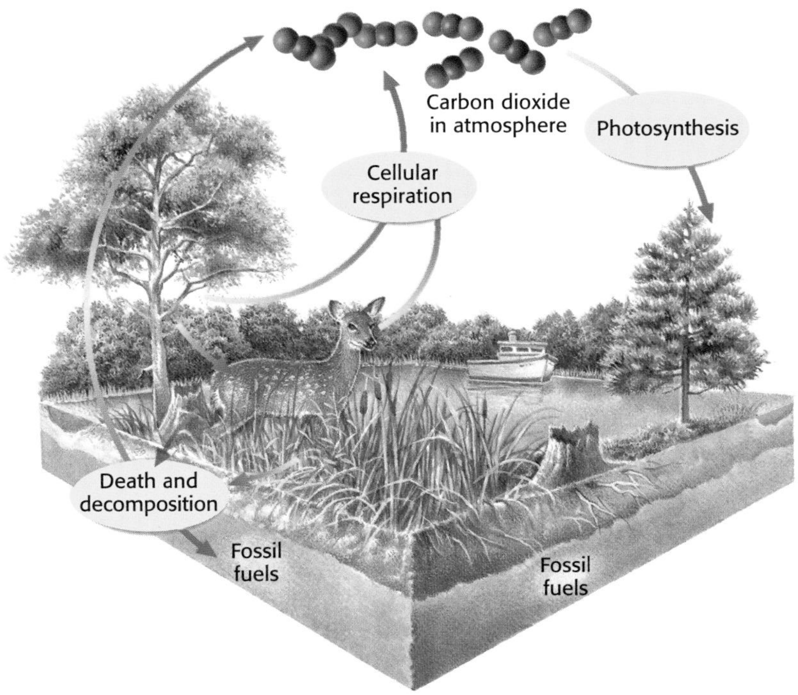

Fossil fuels form deep underground

Living things cannot decompose and release their stored energy without air. For example, microscopic plants and animals living in the ocean die and are buried under layers of sediment where they are not in contact with air. Without air, the sugars in the plants cannot combine with oxygen and change back to carbon dioxide and water. Instead, pressure and heat from the settled rock above the plants cause different chemical reactions. These reactions turn the sugars into substances that contain carbon and hydrogen, as shown in **Figure 21-13.** These substances are known as fossil fuels.

Fossil fuels can be solids, liquids, or gases

Although substances such as natural gas and coal seem very different, they have one thing in common—they are made of carbon and carbon-containing molecules.

Figure 21-12
Carbon dioxide is a product of cellular respiration.

▶ **fossil fuels** any fuels formed from the remains of ancient life

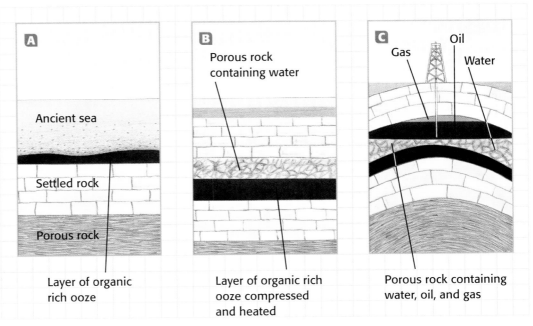

Figure 21-13
Microscopic plants and animals collect in layers of mud forming an organic rich ooze. (A) This organic rich layer is underlain and overlain by settled rock. (B) Heat and pressure "cook" the ooze, causing oil to form. (C) Geologic forces cause the rock layers to bend. The oil is forced out, migrates into porous rocks, and is trapped.

A
Ancient sea
Settled rock
Porous rock
Layer of organic rich ooze

B
Porous rock containing water
Layer of organic rich ooze compressed and heated

C
Gas   Oil
      Water
Porous rock containing water, oil, and gas

Methane

Figure 21-14
Natural gas can provide the energy needed to prepare food.

▶ **nonrenewable resources**
any resources that are used faster than they can be replaced

Figure 21-15
Although 86 percent of the world's energy is supplied by fossil fuels, oil and natural-gas reserves will soon run out.

Some fossil fuels are mixtures of liquids and gases. These fuels can leak out of porous rocks where they formed into rocks above. Porous rocks contain holes inside them and serve as reservoirs for the liquid oil and natural gas. Wells must be drilled into these porous rocks to reach the fossil fuels.

Oil is a mixture of many different substances. It comes out of the ground as a tarlike black liquid. It is useful for many things, but it must be purified and separated before it can be used. Refineries separate oil into gasoline, kerosene, diesel fuel, and other products.

Natural gas is made mostly of methane, CH_4. Methane is a colorless, odorless, poisonous gas that burns with a clean flame. It is often used for heating homes and cooking, as shown in **Figure 21-14.** In the United States, natural gas makes up 22 percent of the fossil fuels used.

Coal is a solid fossil fuel composed mainly of carbon. Unlike oil and natural gas, which formed in shallow oceans, coal formed in ancient swamps when the remains of large, fernlike plants were buried under layers of sediment.

The supply of fossil fuels is limited

When fossil fuels are burned, they form carbon dioxide and water and release energy. This energy is the energy of the sun that was trapped in plants hundreds of millions of years ago. Because fossil fuels take so long to form, they are considered **nonrenewable resources.** They are being used much faster than natural processes can replace them.

Figure 21-15A shows that the vast majority of the world's energy needs are met by the burning of fossil fuels. **Figure 21-15B** shows the estimated reserves of the world's supply of fossil fuels. If oil and natural gas use continue at current rates, the reserves may run out while you are still alive. What alternative sources of energy will provide the energy needed for everyday activities?

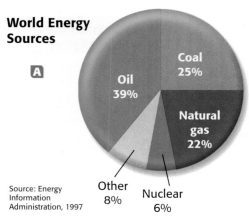

World Energy Sources

A

Coal 25%

Oil 39%

Natural gas 22%

Other 8%

Nuclear 6%

Source: Energy Information Administration, 1997

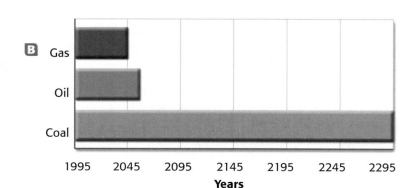

World Energy Reserves

B

Gas

Oil

Coal

1995 2045 2095 2145 2195 2245 2295

Years

Alternative Sources of Energy

Fossils fuels are not the only energy source around. We can harness energy from the sun, wind, water, and Earth. We can even obtain energy from atoms. The more these alternative sources of energy are used, the less we will rely on fossil fuels.

Another advantage of using alternative sources of energy is that many are **renewable resources.** This means they can be replaced by natural processes in a relatively short amount of time.

Solar power plants and solar cells can make electricity from sunlight

Every day, the sun makes more energy than is used to supply electricity to the United States for a year. But harnessing the sun's energy is not simple. Some parts of Earth do not get as much sunlight as other parts. Even when there is enough sunlight, tools are needed to convert the sun's energy and change it into a useful form.

In the 1990s, the first solar power plant capable of storing energy as heat was opened in the Mojave Desert, in California. This power plant, shown in **Figure 21-16,** stores the sun's heat and uses it for energy.

Another tool used to harness the sun's energy is a solar cell, shown in **Figure 21-17.** Solar cells are able to produce electricity from sunlight. But their use is limited due to high installation cost and a low output of energy.

The energy in wind can be used by windmills

Energy from the sun is a contributing factor in the production of another renewable energy resource—wind energy. Wind energy actually comes from the sun. Different places on Earth receive different amounts of sunlight, which causes variations in temperature. These temperature differences cause the movement of air, known as wind.

Wind is one of the oldest sources of renewable energy used by humans. It has been used to sail ships for thousands of years. As with other sources of energy, the use of wind energy has advantages and disadvantages. It can be unreliable. Even in exceptionally windy areas, wind doesn't blow steadily all the time. This can cause differences in the amount of power generated. However, the use of windmills is becoming increasingly popular because of their low cost.

■ internet**connect**

SC*LINKS*
NSTA

TOPIC: Alternative energy sources
GO TO: www.scilinks.org
KEYWORD: HK1906

▷ **renewable resources**
any resources that can be continually replaced

Figure 21-16
Mojave Desert, in California, is home to the first solar-power plant capable of storing heat.

Figure 21-17
Solar cells convert sunlight into electricity.

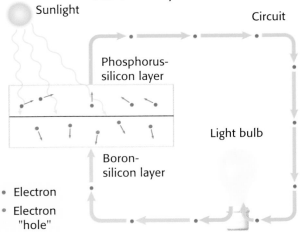

Sunlight

Circuit

Phosphorus-silicon layer

Light bulb

Boron-silicon layer

• Electron
• Electron "hole"

Figure 21-18
The spinning blades of a windmill are connected to a generator. The faster the blades spin, the more electricity that is produced.

▷ **geothermal energy** the energy drawn from heated water within Earth's crust

Windmills have been in use since about A.D. 600. Today, large windmills are set up in wind farms, like the one shown in **Figure 21-18,** to generate electrical power.

Moving water produces energy

Falling water releases a lot of energy. But even the energy produced from water depends on sunlight. For example, the water in oceans evaporates as sunlight transfers energy by heat. This water rises into the atmosphere, falls back down later as rain or snow, and flows downhill into creeks and rivers. Once the water is in the creeks and rivers, it flows back to the ocean, and the cycle begins again.

In some power plants, dams are built on fast-moving rivers to create large holding places for water. **Figure 21-19,** on page 693, illustrates how the stored water pours through turbines, making them spin. The turbines are connected to generators that produce hydroelectric power, another type of renewable resource.

Dams have already been built on most of the world's big rivers, so the potential for increasing the use of this energy source is limited.

Geothermal energy taps Earth's warmth

Another type of renewable energy resource can be found under Earth's crust. Underground reservoirs of steam or hot water produce **geothermal energy.** These holding pools usually lie near beds of molten magma, which heat the steam or water. Wells are drilled into the reservoirs, and the steam or hot water rises to the surface, where it is used to turn turbines to generate electrical power.

Connection to
SOCIAL STUDIES

To aid the nation's economic recovery following the Great Depression, President Franklin D. Roosevelt proposed a series of projects aimed at increasing employment and serving the public good. One such project was the Tennessee Valley Authority (TVA), a connected system of 40 dams spread over an area of 106 000 km². The TVA system still provides electricity to homes, farms, and factories in Tennessee, Kentucky, Virginia, North Carolina, Georgia, Alabama, and Mississippi.

Making the Connection

Go to your local library and find a map showing the area that the TVA covers. Draw your own map showing all 40 dams.

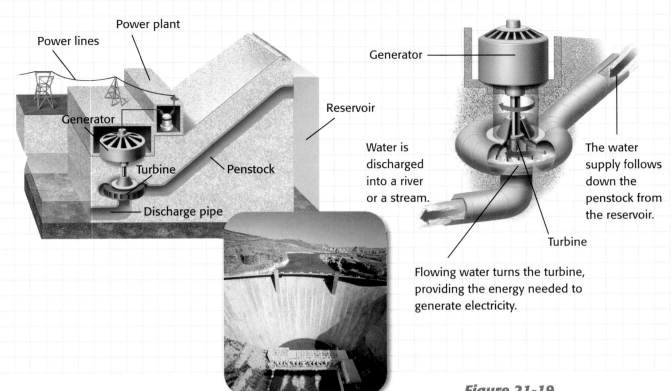

Power lines

Power plant

Generator

Turbine

Discharge pipe

Penstock

Reservoir

Generator

Water is discharged into a river or a stream.

The water supply follows down the penstock from the reservoir.

Turbine

Flowing water turns the turbine, providing the energy needed to generate electricity.

Figure 21-19
The incoming water causes the turbines in a dam to turn. The turbines run a generator that produces electricity.

Geothermal energy is a major source of electricity in volcanically active areas such as New Zealand, Iceland, and parts of California. Geothermal plants, such as the one shown in **Figure 21-20,** are common in these places. This type of energy works best when the beds of melted rock lie very close to the Earth's surface. However, not many areas have magma beds close to the surface, so widespread use of this resource is unlikely.

Atoms produce nuclear energy

In Chapter 6, you learned that atomic reactions produce a type of alternative energy resource called nuclear energy. Chain reactions involving nuclear fission produce a great deal of energy. This energy can be transferred as heat to water in a nuclear reactor. The heated water or steam can then be used to turn a turbine and generate electricity.

There are some disadvantages to harnessing nuclear energy, including the radioactive waste produced. For this reason, nuclear energy has seen limited use in the United States. It currently provides only 8 percent of our energy. Scientists working with nuclear fusion hope that it will someday be a more useful and renewable resource. But so far, more energy is needed to sustain a fusion reaction than is produced by the reaction.

Figure 21-20
This geothermal plant in New Zealand produces electricity.

The Efficiency of Energy Conversion

Regardless of which energy resource we use, some usable energy is lost each time energy is converted to another form, as you learned in Chapter 8.

Energy is wasted when input is greater than output

In a coal-fired power plant, chemical energy is released when coal burns with oxygen in the air in a combustion reaction. This energy is transferred by heat to water, which forms steam. Some energy is lost in this conversion. In order to obtain a high pressure, the steam is heated, and more energy is lost. The steam must be at a high pressure to provide the force to turn the huge steam turbines. This changes the energy into kinetic energy of the moving turbines.

The spinning turbines are connected to coils of large generators. These coils carry current and act as large electromagnets. As they spin, they generate a high voltage in the fixed coils surrounding them. The energy is now in the form of electrical potential energy. This causes a current that carries the electricity to local consumers through a cable. **Figure 21-21** shows how electricity is produced in a typical power station.

Figure 21-21
This power plant converts coal into electrical energy.

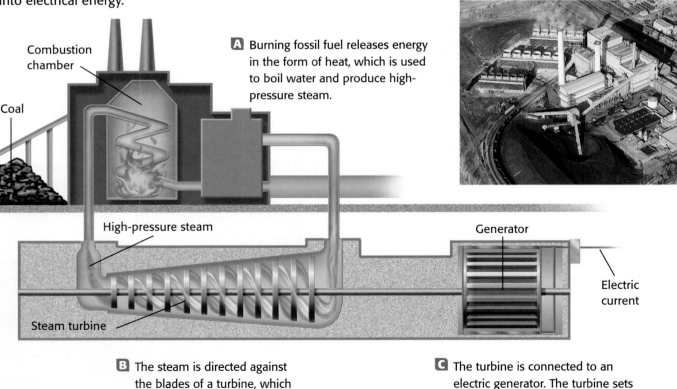

A Burning fossil fuel releases energy in the form of heat, which is used to boil water and produce high-pressure steam.

Combustion chamber

Coal

High-pressure steam

Generator

Electric current

Steam turbine

B The steam is directed against the blades of a turbine, which is set into motion.

C The turbine is connected to an electric generator. The turbine sets the generator in motion, generating electricity.

A large power station might be rated at 1000 MW. This means that it delivers 1 billion joules of energy every second. But three times the amount of fuel, equal to 3 billion joules of energy, is needed because two-thirds of the energy input is wasted. Most power stations that use fossil fuels for energy are only 30 to 40 percent efficient.

Wasted energy can be used

Wasted energy occurs in the production of all energy sources. Nuclear power stations are roughly as efficient, or inefficient, as fossil-fuel power plants. Even wind-powered plants have some inefficiency because of the energy conversions involved.

There are ways to make use of some of this wasted energy. For example, although the water from power stations is not hot enough to make electricity, it can be used to heat homes. In Germany, most towns have their own small power station. Rather than dump the warm water into a river, it is piped to people's homes to keep them heated. These are called combined heat and power schemes. They reduce wasted energy and make electricity less expensive.

SECTION 21.2 REVIEW

SUMMARY

▶ Most of the energy used in the world comes from fossil fuels, which are nonrenewable resources.

▶ Energy from the sun produces solar energy and wind energy.

▶ Hydroelectric power can be generated from large reservoirs of water.

▶ Geothermal energy is generated from underground reservoirs in volcanically active areas.

▶ The use of nuclear energy is limited.

▶ Energy is lost each time it is converted to another form.

CHECK YOUR UNDERSTANDING

1. **List** five ways that you use electricity during lunch.
2. **Describe** the cycle of energy transfer among organisms.
3. **Compare** the amount of energy used in the United States with the amount used worldwide. Write a paragraph explaining the social and economic reasons for the difference.
4. **Explain** in a paragraph the energy conversions that occur when a drop of rain falls on a mountain, rolls downhill, passes through a hydroelectric plant, and turns a turbine to generate electricity.
5. **Describe** some advantages and disadvantages of solar energy.
6. **Predict** which of the following will be more efficient in terms of capturing the most energy. Justify your answer.
   a. burning paper to boil water to make steam to turn a turbine
   b. using wind to generate electricity
7. **Critical Thinking** A classmate says that geothermal power is perfectly efficient because it never runs out. What's wrong with this reasoning?

Sun-Warmed Houses

Specially designed houses make use of the sun's heat in two different ways—passive solar heating and active solar heating.

How Does Passive Solar Heating Work?

In passive solar heating, no special devices are used. The house is simply built to take advantage of the sun's energy. For example, passive solar houses have large windows that face south, enabling them to receive a lot of sunlight throughout the day. Many have glass-enclosed fronts called sunspaces, which work to trap solar energy like glass in a greenhouse. During the winter, the energy that enters the sunspace keeps the room comfortably warm during the day. The floor is made of special tiles that absorb heat and then radiate it out into the room throughout the evening.

How Is Energy Conserved in Passive Solar Heating?

The rest of the house still has to be heated in winter, but heating costs are generally much lower than they ordinarily would be. Some of the energy that would normally escape through an outside wall is kept inside because the sunspace acts as a good insulator.

Homes that take advantage of solar heating generally have lower electric bills.

On the north side of passive solar houses, there are only small windows in order to reduce energy loss. Also, the walls are built to be good insulators. Once the house is warm, its walls and furnishings act as a large "heat store," keeping the warmth inside.

How Does Active Solar Heating Work?

In active solar heating, houses use solar heaters—active solar-energy devices—to heat water or air. In solar heaters, a flat-plate collector is placed on the roof to gather sunlight. The collector is a flat box covered with glass or plastic. The bottom of the box is often painted black because dark colors absorb radiation better than light colors do. The collector gathers and traps heat, warming the air or water inside. The heated air or water flows into an insulated storage tank. Electric pumps or fans circulate the heated air or water throughout the house. Because they can store solar energy, active solar heating systems work 24 hours a day. However, during long periods of cloudy days, backup heating systems are necessary.

Your Choice

1. **Making Decisions** A house that uses fossil fuels for energy might cost its owners $2000 in heating expenses during the winter. An energy-efficient house could reduce this cost by 50 percent, but it might cost $10 000 more to build. Do you think the energy savings are worth the added construction cost? Explain your reasoning.
2. **Critical Thinking** What problem might people who live in houses with sunspaces have in the summer? How could they solve this problem?

internet**connect**

SC*i*LINKS.
NSTA

TOPIC: Solar heated homes
GO TO: www.scilinks.org
KEYWORD: HK1900

Pollution and Recycling

OBJECTIVES

▶ Compare the economic and environmental impacts of using various energy sources.
▶ Identify several pollutants caused by fossil fuel use.
▶ Describe types of pollution in air, in water, and on land.
▶ Identify ways to reduce, reuse, and recycle.

▶ **KEY TERMS**
pollution
global warming
eutrophication
recycling

Think about the items in your classroom. You can probably identify ordinary items such as desks, lights, chalk, paper, pencils, backpacks, books, doors, and windows. Your classroom contains many products, all made from natural resources.

Making each product required energy. And the manufacture of nearly all of the products caused some kind of pollution. Whenever natural resources generate energy or become products, other things are usually made in the process. If these things are not used, they may be thrown out and cause pollution. Pollution is the contamination of the air, the water, or the soil, as shown in **Figure 21-22.**

▶ **pollution** the contamination of the air, water, or soil

What Causes Pollution?

When you think of pollution, you may think of litter, such as that cluttering the water in **Figure 21-22A.** Or you may think of smog, the clouds of dust, smoke, and chemicals shown in **Figure 21-22B.**

Pollution can be as invisible as a colorless, odorless gas or as obvious as bad-smelling trash left by the side of the road. Most forms of pollution have several common features. Understanding these features will help you make better choices.

A

B

Figure 21-22
(A) Trash polluted the water off the coast of Oahu, Hawaii.
(B) Contaminants polluted the air in Mexico City.

Table 21-1 **Air Pollutants**

Pollutant	Description	Primary Sources	Effects
Carbon monoxide	CO is an odorless, colorless, poisonous gas.	CO is produced by the incomplete burning of fossil fuels. Cars, trucks, buses, small engines, and some industrial processes are the major sources of CO.	◆ Interferes with the blood's ability to carry oxygen ◆ Slows reflexes and causes drowsiness ◆ Can cause death in high concentrations ◆ Can cause headaches and stress on the heart ◆ Can hamper the growth and development of the fetus
Nitrogen oxides (NO_x)	When combustion (burning) temperatures are greater than 538°C (1000°F), nitrogen and oxygen combine to form nitrogen oxides.	NO_x compounds come from the burning of fuels in vehicles, power plants, and industrial boilers.	◆ Can make the body vulnerable to respiratory infection, lung disease, and possibly cancer ◆ Contribute to the brownish haze often seen over congested areas and to acid rain ◆ Can cause metal corrosion and the fading and deterioration of fabrics
Sulfur dioxide (SO_2)	SO_2 is produced by chemical interactions between sulfur and oxygen.	SO_2 comes from the burning of fossil fuels. It is released from petroleum refineries, smelters, paper mills, chemical plants, and coal-burning power plants.	◆ Contributes to acid rain ◆ Can harm plant life and irritate the respiratory systems of humans and animals
Volatile organic compounds (VOCs)	VOCs are organic chemicals that vaporize readily and produce toxic fumes. Some examples are gasoline, paint thinner, and lighter fluid.	Cars are a major source of VOCs. They also come from solvents, paints, glues, and burning fuels.	◆ Contribute to the formation of smog ◆ Cause serious health problems, such as cancer ◆ May harm plants
Particulate matter (particulates or PM)	Particulates are tiny particles of liquid or solid matter. Some examples are smoke, dust, and acid droplets.	Construction, agriculture, forestry, and fires produce particulates. Industrial processes and motor vehicles that burn fossil fuels also produce particulates.	◆ Form clouds that reduce visibility and cause a variety of respiratory problems ◆ Linked to cancer ◆ Corrode metals, erode buildings and sculptures, and soil fabrics

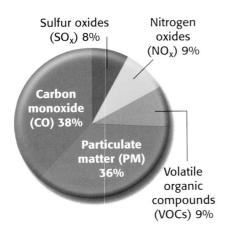

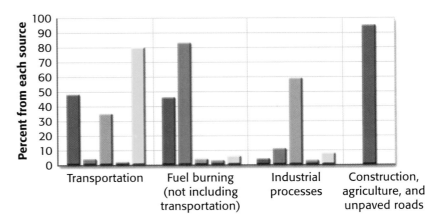

internet**connect**

SC*LINKS*

NSTA

TOPIC: Pollution
GO TO: www.scilinks.org
KEYWORD: HK1907

Figure 21-23
Carbon monoxide, produced mainly from the burning of fossil fuels, is the top air pollutant in the United States.

Some pollution has natural causes

Pollution can be caused by natural processes. For example, following an explosive volcanic eruption, dust and ash can be spread throughout the air. This can make it hard for some people to breathe. The dust and ash can also cover leaves of trees and plants, preventing them from absorbing sunlight.

Manmade pollution is more common

Most pollution is caused by human activities. As you learned in Chapter 5, many chemical reactions can be used to make new materials or to release energy. But most chemical reactions produce two or more products. If the other products are not used properly, they can add to the pollution problem.

Air pollution

Air pollution comes in many forms, from individual molecules to clumps of dust and other matter, called particulates. **Figure 21-23** shows major air pollutants and sources of air pollutants in the United States. **Table 21-1,** on page 698, describes these different forms of pollution.

Combustion of fuels produces most air pollution

As you have learned, most of the energy we use to drive cars, heat and light buildings, and power machinery comes from the burning of fossil fuels. The burning process is known as combustion.

During combustion, the fuel, which contains carbon and hydrogen, reacts with oxygen to release energy. Along with this desirable product, two other products are formed: carbon dioxide gas and water vapor. These combustion products escape into the air as invisible gases. The reaction for burning methane from natural gas is shown below.

$$CH_4 + 2O_2 \longrightarrow CO_2 + 2H_2O$$

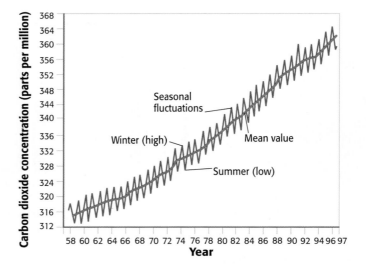

Figure 21-24
This graph shows an increase in atmospheric carbon dioxide from 1958 to 1997.

(Graph labels: Seasonal fluctuations; Winter (high); Mean value; Summer (low))

> ▶ **global warming**
> an increase in Earth's temperature due to an increase in greenhouse gases

Carbon dioxide is a greenhouse gas

Carbon dioxide is found naturally in Earth's atmosphere. It is one of the greenhouse gases, which help keep temperatures on Earth balanced. Just as the glass of a greenhouse garden traps radiation that keeps the inside warm, greenhouse gases in the atmosphere trap radiation that keeps Earth warm. Without the greenhouse effect, temperatures on Earth would be roughly 33°C lower.

Humans release about 5 billion metric tons of carbon dioxide into the air every year. **Figure 21-24** shows how the amount of atmospheric carbon dioxide has changed since 1958. Scientists hypothesize that by 2020 the amount of carbon dioxide in the atmosphere will be twice its present level. Some records indicate that the average temperature of Earth is already showing a small increase. In the past 100 years, the average temperature in the United States has increased by about 2°C. It is estimated that if the level of atmospheric carbon dioxide doubles, global temperatures will increase by about 3°C. This global warming may not sound like a lot, but it could drastically affect Earth's climate. Weather patterns could change, bringing droughts to some areas and floods to others. The level of the sea could change as more polar ice melts.

Combustion releases other pollutants

The burning of fossil fuels in vehicles, power stations, and factories releases more than carbon dioxide into the air. It also releases sulfur dioxide and nitrogen dioxide. Once these gases are released into the air, they react with other atmospheric gases and with rain to form acid rain. Chemical reactions like these can make rain, sleet, or snow acidic. Normal rain is slightly acidic, with a pH of roughly 5.6. Acid rain has a pH of between 5 and 2. In extreme cases, polluted rainfall can be as acidic as vinegar.

When acid rain falls into streams and lakes, it makes them acidic. This can harm or even kill aquatic life. Acid rain can also make soil more acidic, damaging large areas of forests. In addition, it can corrode metals and damage buildings by eroding stonework.

Air pollution can cause breathing problems

When nitrogen oxide compounds in car exhaust react with sunlight, they can produce a cloud of chemicals called photochemical smog. The result is a brown haze that can make eyes sting and cause severe headaches and breathing difficulties.

Ozone is one of the harmful chemicals in photochemical smog. High up in the atmosphere, ozone blocks harmful ultraviolet radiation. Close to Earth's surface, however, ozone is a pollutant. It can cause problems for people who suffer from asthma or other conditions affecting the throat and lungs.

Photochemical smog is most common in sunny, densely populated cities, such as Los Angeles and Tokyo. In Tokyo, many people wear masks to protect themselves from the polluted air, and companies supply fresh-air dispensers to their employees. The smog also damages plants. Decreased yields of citrus fruits, such as oranges and lemons, may be linked to photochemical smog in areas not far from Los Angeles. To combat the problem, many cities have made concerted efforts to expand public transportation systems and to encourage people to carpool. These efforts help reduce the number of vehicles on the road and thus the amount of pollutants released into the air.

Water Pollution

All living things need clean water to survive. In fact, the bodies of most organisms, including humans, are made up mostly of water. Many people believe that water is our most valuable natural resource. Unpolluted water is even more important to aquatic organisms, which spend all their life in a liquid environment.

On July 6, 1988, a load of aluminum sulfate was accidentally tipped into the water supply in Camelford, England. Before the mistake was discovered, people became ill.

Accidents are responsible for some water pollution but not all. Most water pollution can be traced to industrial waste, agricultural fertilizers, and everyday human activities. A bucket of dirty, soapy water dumped down a kitchen drain can eventually make its way into the water supply. Flushing toilets, washing cars, and pouring chemicals down drains are actions that

Quick ACTIVITY

Observing Air Pollution

1. Cut off a piece of masking tape about 8 cm long.
2. Place the sticky side of the tape against an outside wall, and press gently.
3. Remove the tape, and hold it against a sheet of white paper.
4. Did the tape pick up dust? If so, what might be the source of the dust?
5. Repeat the experiment on other walls in different places, and compare the amounts of dust observed.
6. Suggest reasons why some walls appear to have more dirt than others.

account for most of the world's water pollution.

In many countries, water is cleaned at water-purification plants before it is piped to consumers. But because many chemicals dissolve easily in water, it's difficult to remove all of the impurities from the water.

Pesticides and fertilizers often end up polluting water

Most modern farms use chemical fertilizers to increase crop yields. These fertilizers can get washed away by rain and end up in streams, rivers, lakes, or ponds. The fertilizers may contain nitrate ions, which encourage the growth of bacteria and algae.

Fed on the nitrates, the bacteria and algae grow so fast that they use up most of the oxygen in the water. The result is an algal bloom, such as the one shown in **Figure 21-25.** Fish and other aquatic wildlife suffer from the reduced oxygen and die. This process, known as eutrophication, is made worse if hot water from power stations or factories is discharged into the river or lake. The extra warmth makes the bacteria and algae multiply even faster.

Animals on land can be affected by another group of chemicals that eventually make their way into bodies of water. These chemicals, called pesticides, are used to control crop-damaging pests.

Like fertilizers, pesticides can be washed by rain into streams, rivers, lakes, or ponds. There they are ingested by fish and other aquatic animals. As larger animals eat the fish, the chemicals are passed along the food chain. In the 1970s, a pesticide called DDT was widely used to control mosquitoes and other insects. DDT caused the eggs of fish-eating pelicans and other fish-eating birds to become thin and fragile. The pelicans nearly became extinct before the use of DDT was banned in the United States.

▶ **eutrophication** an increase in the amount of nutrients, such as nitrates, in an environment

internet**connect**

SC*LINKS*
NSTA

TOPIC: Solutions to pollution problems
GO TO: www.scilinks.org
KEYWORD: HK1908

Figure 21-25
This algal bloom is the result of an abundance of nitrates in the water.

Materials
- ✔ cooking oil
- ✔ cold water
- ✔ cleaning materials
- ✔ rectangular baking pan

Procedure

1. Fill the pan halfway with cold water.
2. Pour a small amount of cooking oil into the water.
3. Try to clean up the "oil spill" using at least four different cleaning materials.

Analysis

1. Evaluate the effectiveness of each material. Which worked best? Explain why.
2. Did any of the materials "pollute" the water with particles or residue? How might you clean up this pollution?

Pollution on Land

Pollution that affects our land has many sources. In some cases, the source is obvious, as when trash is dumped illegally by a roadside. In other cases, the source is not so obvious. For example, dirt near many highways contains an unusually high amount of lead. This lead originally came from car exhaust. The lead was part of a compound added to gasoline to help car engines run more smoothly. Even though this type of gasoline was banned in the 1970s, there is still lead in the soil.

Contaminants in soil are hard to remove

A common type of land-based pollution occurs when hazardous chemicals soak into the soil. For example, in 1983, the entire town of Times Beach, Missouri, was bought by the U.S. Environmental Protection Agency. The town's soil was contaminated by a highly toxic chemical compound called dioxin.

Exposure to dioxin, a chemical used in the paper-making process, had been linked to an increased risk of cancer. The soil in the town had become contaminated because the waste oil used to keep the dust on the town's roads down contained small amounts of dioxin. After the roads were repeatedly sprayed over several years, the dioxin levels became very high. This resulted in the deaths of some livestock and other animals and it also adversely affected the health of some of the town's residents.

Dioxin, like many land-based pollutants, does not dissolve well in water. It is therefore very difficult to remove it from the soil. The EPA bought the town because it was less expensive than cleaning the entire town's soil.

Figure 21-26
Many landfills are closing because of a lack of space.

Landfill space is running out

Even when trash is taken to a landfill, like the one shown in **Figure 21-26,** and disposed of legally, it can still cause pollution. Each time an item is placed in a landfill, there is less space remaining for other materials. Throughout the United States, more and more landfills are closing because they are full. Few new landfills are opening.

   Currently, each person in the United States throws away almost a half ton of garbage every year. If the current trends continue, the United States will soon run out of landfill space.

Reducing Pollution

The are many ways to reduce or limit pollution. Government regulation is one way. In the United States there are several laws that encourage clean water supplies and discourage the pollution of air, soil, and water. Countries may also work together to combat the problem. For instance, in December 1997, international representatives met in Kyoto, Japan, to negotiate an agreement to reduce greenhouse-gas emissions.

Choosing alternatives often involves trade-offs

Even greater improvements in the pollution problem come when individuals, communities, and companies make careful choices. For example, to reduce the air pollution caused by the burning of fossil fuels, people can switch to alternative energy sources. Individuals can make a difference by conserving energy. However, even nonpolluting sources of energy, such as wind, solar, and hydroelectric power, require large amounts of land and are potentially disruptive to ecosystems.

   Small-scale sources of energy, such as disposable batteries, have an environmental impact too. These batteries contain mercury and other potentially toxic chemicals. In the United States alone, more than 2 billion disposable batteries are discarded every year. The toxic chemicals can leak into the ground, polluting water supplies and soil.

Reducing the use of energy and products can cut down on pollution

Because of the trade-offs involved, many people believe that the best solution to the problem of pollution is to reduce our overall consumption of energy and material goods. If less energy is used, less pollution is generated. Turning off lights and lowering thermostats are two simple ways to conserve energy. Carpooling is another way to conserve energy.

Recycling Codes: How Are Plastics Sorted?

More than half of the states in the United States have enacted laws that require plastic products to be labeled with numerical codes that identify the type of plastic used in them. These codes are shown in the table below. Used plastic products can be sorted by these codes and properly recycled or processed. Only codes 1 and 2 are widely accepted for recycling. Codes 3 and 6 are rarely recycled. Knowing what the numerical codes mean will give you an idea of how successfully a given plastic product can be recycled. This may affect your decision to buy or not buy particular items.

Your Choice

1. **Making Decisions** Find out what types of plastic are recycled in your area.
2. **Critical Thinking** Do you think recycling should be mandatory? Explain your views on the topic of recycling.

internetconnect

SCI LINKS
NSTA

TOPIC: Recycling plastics
GO TO: www.scilinks.org
KEYWORD: HK1910

Recycling Codes for Plastic Products

Recycling code	Type of plastic	Physical properties	Example	Uses for recycled products
1	Polyethylene terephthalate (PET)	Tough, rigid; can be a fiber or a plastic; solvent resistant; sinks in water	Soda bottles, clothing, electrical insulation, automobile parts	Backpacks, sleeping bags, carpet, new bottles, clothing
2	High density polyethylene (HDPE)	Rough surface; stiff plastic; resistant to cracking	Milk containers, bleach bottles, toys, grocery bags	Furniture, toys, trash cans, picnic tables, park benches, fences
3	Polyvinyl chloride (PVC)	Elastomer or flexible plastic; tough; poor crystallization; unstable to light or heat; sinks in H_2O	Pipe, vinyl siding, auto-mobile parts, clear bottles for cooking oil	Toys, playground equipment
4	Low density polyethylene (LDPE)	Moderately crystalline, flexible plastic; solvent resistant; floats on water	Trash bags, dry-cleaning bags, frozen-food packaging, meat packaging	Trash cans, trash bags, compost containers
5	Polypropylene (PP)	Rigid, very strong; fiber or flexible plastic; lightweight; heat- and stress-resistant	Heat-proof containers, rope, appliance parts, outdoor carpet, luggage, diapers, automobile parts	Brooms, brushes, ice scrapers, battery cable, insulation, rope
6	Polystyrene (P/S, PS)	Somewhat brittle, rigid plastic; resistant to acids and bases but not to organic solvents; sinks in water, unless it is a foam	Fast-food containers, toys, videotape reels, electrical insulation, plastic utensils, disposable drinking cups, CD jewel cases	Insulated clothing, egg cartons, thermal insulation

Figure 21-27
This recycling plant in New York City helps reduce the amount of pollution.

▶ **recycling** the process of breaking down discarded material for reuse in other products

Some people conserve water by reusing rinse water from dishes and laundry to water gardens and lawns. This way, they use less water, so less energy is required to purify it and pump it to them. In addition, the water they use does not enter the sewer system. This reduces the amount of energy used by the water-treatment plant.

Recycling is the final way to prevent pollution

After you have tried to reduce how much you use and are successfully reusing it as much as possible, there's still one more thing you can do. When something is worn out and is no longer useful, instead of throwing it away, you can try **recycling.**

Recycling allows materials to be used again to make other products rather than being thrown away. **Figure 21-27** shows a recycling plant in New York City. Such plants commonly recycle paper products such as cardboard and newspapers; metal products such as copper, aluminum, and tin; and plastics such as detergent bottles and shopping bags.

Recycling these materials can make a huge difference in the amount of waste that ends up in a landfill. Paper products alone take up 41 percent of landfill space. Yet we currently recycle less than 30 percent of our paper.

SECTION 21.3 REVIEW

SUMMARY

▶ Pollution can be caused by natural events and by human activities.

▶ Acid rain is caused when sulfur dioxide and nitrogen oxides react with moisture and other gases in the air.

▶ Government regulation and recycling can lessen the pollution of air, water, and soil.

CHECK YOUR UNDERSTANDING

1. **List** an activity related to home, work, and growing food that can lead to water pollution.
2. **Distinguish** between the greenhouse effect and global warming.
3. **Explain** how riding a bike can reduce photochemical smog.
4. **Define** *eutrophication*. Explain how it occurs.
5. **Name** an alternative energy source, and describe one benefit and one drawback.
6. **Analyze** all of the possible polluting steps in the making of a pencil. Write a paragraph describing each step.
7. **Critical Thinking** Do you think recycling should be mandatory? Explain your reasoning.

WRITING SKILL

Chapter Highlights

Before you begin, review the summaries of the key ideas of each section, found on pages 687, 695, and 706. The key vocabulary terms are listed on pages 680, 688, and 697.

UNDERSTANDING CONCEPTS

1. Hydroelectric power is a(n) _____ energy source.
   a. nonrenewable
   b. renewable
   c. small-scale
   d. atomic

2. An aquarium ecosystem is made up of _____.
   a. cactuses, sagebrush, lizards, snakes, scorpions, and birds
   b. grassland, termites, wild dogs, hyenas, and antelopes
   c. water, fish, glass, and water plants
   d. musk oxen, opposite-leaved saxifrage, wolves, and brown bears

3. When fossil fuels are burned, they form carbon dioxide and _____.
   a. water
   b. oxygen
   c. hydrocarbons
   d. carbohydrates

4. The Earth's temperature is kept slightly warmer by _____.
   a. the surface of Earth
   b. the greenhouse effect
   c. the ozone layer
   d. wind

5. In power stations, _____ of the energy input is wasted.
   a. one-third
   b. one-half
   c. two-thirds
   d. all

6. Geothermal energy is produced by _____.
   a. wind
   b. underground reservoirs of steam or hot water
   c. fast-moving water
   d. solar radiation

7. Usable energy is lost each time energy is _____.
   a. gained
   b. released
   c. converted
   d. transferred

8. Which of the following is not true of recycling?
   a. Recycling does not affect the amount of waste that ends up in a landfill.
   b. Recycling reduces litter.
   c. Recycling reduces energy usage.
   d. Recycled materials can be used to make other products.

9. What causes an algal bloom?
   a. CFCs
   b. global warming
   c. eutrophication
   d. recycling

Using Vocabulary

10. Compare *hydroelectric power* with *geothermal energy.* List advantages and disadvantages of each.

11. Driving cars releases pollutants into the atmosphere. State how these pollutants lead to *global warming* and *acid rain.*

12. A forest *ecosystem* is wiped out by disease. Using the concept of *succession,* explain how the forest might recover.

13. Most energy on Earth comes from the sun. Analyze how the burning of *fossil fuels* releases stored energy from the sun.

14. Is land a *renewable* or *nonrenewable* resource? Explain your reasoning.

BUILDING MATH SKILLS

15. **Estimating** The world population in 1999 was approximately 5.8 billion. That number is expected to double in 40 years. Assuming a steady growth rate, estimate the world population in the years 2019, 2039, 2059, and 2079. Write a paragraph explaining how population changes might affect an ecosystem.

16. Calculating Each person in the United States produces roughly 2 kg (4.4 lb) of garbage per day. How long would it take you to fill a dump truck with a 16 000 lb capacity? If each person recycled one-half of his or her trash, how much less garbage would each person produce in one year?

THINKING CRITICALLY

17. Creative Thinking Green plants use sunlight to convert carbon dioxide and water into food in the process of photosynthesis. Explain how cutting down forests might lead to increased global warming.

18. Applying Knowledge A factory is situated along the banks of a river. A large city is located farther upstream. On the outskirts of the city, farmers grow corn and wheat. **WRITING SKILL** Researchers are finding dead fish in the river. Write several paragraphs explaining the steps you would take to determine the cause.

DEVELOPING LIFE/WORK SKILLS

19. Teaching Others Using a desktop-publishing program, **COMPUTER SKILL** work in groups of three or four students to design a brochure to encourage recycling at your school. As a group, decide **WRITING SKILL** beforehand who your audience will be—do you want to reach younger students, your peers, or the school administration? List the benefits of recycling in your brochure. Explain how costs can be reduced and what products could be produced from the recycled materials.

20. Applying Technology Research recent developments and advancements in solar-power **WRITING SKILL** technology. Then write a brief report analyzing the feasibility of the technology. Share your results with the class.

21. Allocating Resources Three people live in the same neighborhood and work at the same office. One person spends $20 per week, one spends $25 per week, and one spends $30 **COMPUTER SKILL** per week for gasoline and parking. They work 51 weeks per year. If they formed a car pool, how much could each person save annually? Using a spreadsheet program, create a spreadsheet that will calculate how much each person would save in 5 years. (**Hint:** Assume that each person drives a total of 17 weeks.)

22. Interpreting and Communicating Visit a local senior center and interview elderly people who have grown up in your area. Ask them to describe the natural habitats in **WRITING SKILL** and around your area as they were 50 years ago. Compare their descriptions with your observations of how your area's environment looks now. Then write a brief paragraph describing the changes that have occurred. Share your interview with your class.

23. Improving Systems Use an atlas to find out the main sources of energy in your state. Based on the information in the atlas, identify alternative energy sources that might be used in different areas. For instance, are some places suitable for wind, hydroelectric, or solar power? Develop an alternative energy plan for your state.

24. Acquiring and Evaluating Data Call your local recycling company and find out where and how recycled materials are processed and reused. Also research how much money your city saves by using recycled materials.

25. Acquiring and Evaluating Data Using an almanac, determine which five states have the most hazardous-waste sites and which five states have the fewest sites. What factors do you think might account for the number of hazardous-waste sites located in a state?

26. Acquiring and Evaluating Data Go to your local library and research any nonnative species that have been introduced into your area. What positive and negative effects have resulted from their arrival?

27. Acquiring and Evaluating Data Research the 1986 Safe Drinking Water Act and the 1987 Clean Water Act. What incentives are in place to encourage clean water supplies?

INTEGRATING CONCEPTS

28. Connection to Health Sunscreens, which protect people from ultraviolet rays, have different sun protection factors (SPFs). For someone who burns after 10 minutes in the sun, a sunscreen with an SPF of 8 would give that person 80 minutes of protection. If the same person wanted to stay in the sun for 2.5 hours without reapplying sunscreen, what SPF should he or she use?

29. Connection to Social Studies Research a particular region of the world other than the area where you live. Find out which energy resource is used to meet the energy needs of this particular region.

30. Mapping Concepts Copy the unfinished concept map below onto a sheet of paper. Complete the map by writing the correct word or phrase in the lettered boxes.

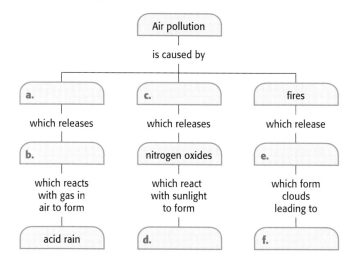

31. Connection to Social Studies One of the main causes of global warming is the burning of fossil fuels. As a group, discuss how building energy-efficient houses might help counteract this effect. Would governmental incentives help encourage people to make their homes more efficient? If so, what incentives would you suggest?

32. Connection to History Human-caused environmental pollution has occurred throughout history. Research a historical example of environmental pollution, and write a short essay about it. Also research and include information about a historic conservation effort.

WRITING SKILL

internet**connect**

SC*i*LINKS
NSTA

TOPIC: Global warming
GO TO: www.scilinks.org
KEYWORD: HK1909

Skill Builder Lab

Introduction

Can you use your familiarity with products used in or near the home to help you identify some of the products of destructive distillation?

Objectives

▸ **Observe** the process of destructive distillation.

▸ **Analyze** the amounts of products produced, and try to identify the products.

Materials

2 test tubes
one-hole stopper
two-hole stopper
bent glass tubing with fire-polished ends
20-cm long rubber tubing
gas burner
ringstand and 2 buret clamps
2 widemouthed bottles
2 glass plates, 7 × 7 cm square
gas-collecting trough
pieces of wood splints
graduated cylinder
balance

Safety Needs

safety goggles
protective gloves
laboratory apron
tongs

Changing the Form of a Fuel

▶ Preparing for Your Experiment

Destructive distillation is the process of heating a material such as wood or coal in the absence of air. The material that is driven off as a gas is called volatile matter. When cooled, some of the matter remains as a gas. Much of the matter condenses to form a mixture of liquids. These liquids can be distilled to yield a number of different products. In this investigation, you (or your teacher) will heat wood to temperatures high enough to cause the wood to break down into different components, which you will try to identify.

1. On a clean sheet of paper, make a table like the one shown below.
2. Label your glassware as shown in the illustration on page 711.
3. Determine the mass of test tube A. Record the value in your table.
4. Determine the volume of gas bottles 1 and 2. Record the values in your table.
5. Determine the volume of test tube B. Record the value in your table. Dry test tube B before setting up your equipment.

Data Table	
Mass of test tube A (g)	
Mass of test tube A with wood (g)	
Mass of wood (g)	
Mass of test tube A with solid residue (g)	
Mass of solid residue (g)	
Volume of gas bottle 1 (mL)	
Volume of gas bottle 2 (mL)	
Volume of gas produced (mL)	
Volume of test tube B (mL)	
Volume of liquid produced (mL)	

▶ Destructive Distillation of Wood

SAFETY CAUTION Wear protective gloves when inserting the glass tubing through the stoppers. Rub glycerin on the tubing and the inside of the stopper holes before pushing the tubing through the stoppers. Rotate the tubing slowly, and push gently. If you have difficulty, ask your teacher for help.

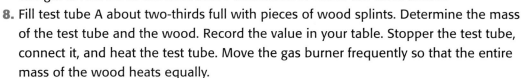

6. Set up the equipment as illustrated below.

7. The gas bottle in the pan should be completely filled with water. Insert the delivery tube into the gas bottle.

SAFETY CAUTION Protect clothing, hair, and eyes when using a gas burner. The gases formed in the destructive distillation of wood are combustible.

8. Fill test tube A about two-thirds full with pieces of wood splints. Determine the mass of the test tube and the wood. Record the value in your table. Stopper the test tube, connect it, and heat the test tube. Move the gas burner frequently so that the entire mass of the wood heats equally.

9. When all the water is driven from the gas bottle, place a glass plate over the mouth of the bottle, and remove the bottle from the pan. Set the gas bottle upright on the table, leaving it covered with the glass plate.

10. Place another water-filled bottle in the pan as before, and reinsert the gas delivery tube. Keep heating until the gas stops coming from test tube A.

▶ Analyzing Your Results

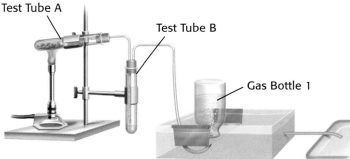

Test Tube A

Test Tube B

Gas Bottle 1

1. How much gas was produced? How much gas was produced for 1 g of wood?

2. What happens when a burning splint is thrust into the gas?

3. Describe the contents of test tube B. How much liquid was produced for 1 g of wood?

4. What does the solid material remaining in test tube A look like?

5. How much solid material was left? How much solid material is that for 1 g of wood?

6. Using insulated tongs, hold a piece of the solid material in the gas burner flame. How does it burn?

▶ Defending Your Conclusions

7. Why would you expect charcoal to give off little or no flame when it is burned?

8. Why is this type of distillation called destructive?

9. What do you think the liquids can be used for?

Reference Section

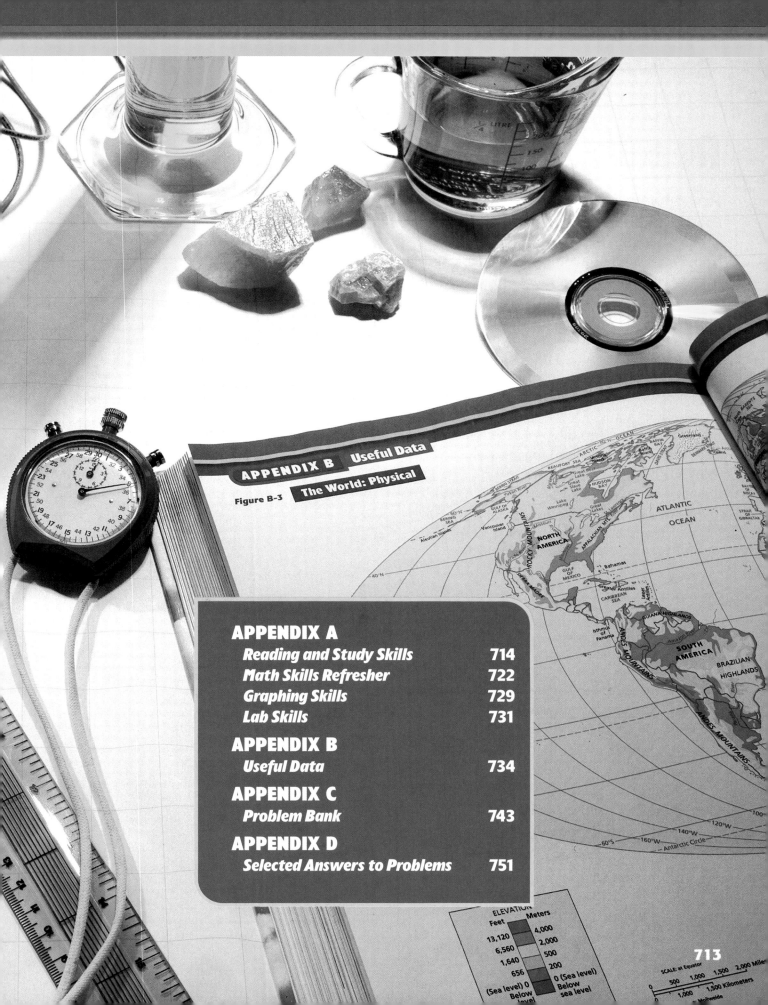

APPENDIX A
Reading and Study Skills   **714**
Math Skills Refresher   **722**
Graphing Skills   **729**
Lab Skills   **731**

APPENDIX B
Useful Data   **734**

APPENDIX C
Problem Bank   **743**

APPENDIX D
Selected Answers to Problems   **751**

ELEVATION	
Feet	Meters
13,120	4,000
6,560	2,000
1,640	500
656	200
(Sea level) 0	0 (Sea level)
Below	Below
level	sea level

SCALE: at Equator

0   500   1,000   1,500   2,000 Miles

0   500   1,000   1,500 Kilometers

Mollweide

Reading and Study Skills

Power Notes

Power notes help you organize the concepts you are studying by distinguishing main ideas from details and providing a framework of important concepts. Power notes are easier to use than outlines because their structure is simpler. You assign a power of *1* to each main idea and a *2, 3,* or *4* to each detail. You can use power notes to organize ideas while reading your text or to reorganize your class notes to study.

Start with a few boldfaced vocabulary terms. Later you can strengthen your notes by expanding these into more-detailed phrases. Use the following general format to help you structure your power notes.

Power 1 Main idea
  Power 2 Detail or support for power 1
    Power 3 Detail or support for power 2
      Power 4 Detail or support for power 3

1. Pick a Power 1 word.
We'll use the term *atom* found in Section 3.1 of your textbook.

Power 1 Atom

2. Using the text, select some Power 2 words to support your Power 1 word.
We'll use the terms *nucleus* and *electron cloud*, which are two parts of an atom.

Power 1 Atom
  Power 2 Nucleus
  Power 2 Electron Cloud

3. Select some Power 3 words to support your Power 2 words.
We'll use the terms *positive charge* and *negative charge,* two terms that describe the Power 2 words.

Power 1 Atom
  Power 2 Nucleus
    Power 3 Positive charge
  Power 2 Electron cloud
    Power 3 Negative charge

4. Continue to add powers to support and detail the main idea as necessary.
If you have a main idea that needs a lot of support, add as many powers as needed to describe the idea. You can use power notes to organize the material in an entire section or chapter of your textbook to study for classroom quizzes and tests.

Power 1 Atom
  Power 2 Nucleus
    Power 3 Positive charge
    Power 3 Protons
      Power 4 Positive charge
    Power 3 Neutrons
      Power 4 No charge
  Power 2 Electron cloud
    Power 3 Negative charge

Practice

1. Use Chapter 3 of your text and the power notes structure below to organize the following terms: *electron lost, electron gained, ionization, anion, cation, negative charge,* and *positive charge.*

Power 1 _____
  Power 2 _____
    Power 3 _____
    Power 3 _____
  Power 2 _____
    Power 3 _____
    Power 3 _____

Pattern puzzles

You can use pattern puzzles to help you remember information in the correct order. Pattern puzzles are not just a tool for memorization. They can also help you better understand a variety of scientific processes, from the steps in solving a mathematical conversion to the procedure for writing a lab report.

1. Write down the steps of a process in your own words.

We'll use the Math Skills feature on converting amount to mass from Section 3.4. On a sheet of notebook paper, write down one step per line, and do not number the steps. Also, do not copy the process straight from your text. Writing the steps in your own words helps you check your understanding of the process. You may want to divide the longer steps into two or three shorter steps.

- List the given and unknown information.

- Look at the periodic table to determine the molar mass of the substance.

- Write the correct conversion factor to convert moles to grams.

- Multiply the amount of substance by the conversion factor.

- Solve the equation and check your answer.

2. Cut the sheet of paper into strips with only one step per strip of paper.

Shuffle the strips of paper so that they are out of sequence.

- Look at the periodic table to determine the molar mass of the substance.

- Solve the equation and check your answer.

- List the given and unknown information.

- Multiply the amount of substance by the conversion factor.

- Write the correct conversion factor to convert moles to grams.

3. Place the strips in their proper sequence.

Confirm the order of the process by checking your text or your class notes.

- • List the given and unknown information.

- • Look at the periodic table to determine the molar mass of the substance.

- • Write the correct conversion factor to convert moles to grams.

- • Multiply the amount of substance by the conversion factor.

- • Solve the equation and check your answer.

Pattern puzzles can be used to help you prepare for a laboratory experiment. That way it will be easier for you to remember what you need to do when you get into the lab, especially if your teacher gives pre-lab quizzes.

You'll want to use pattern puzzles if your teacher is planning a lab practical exam to test whether you know how to operate laboratory equipment. That way you can study and prepare for such a test even though you don't have a complete set of lab equipment at home.

Pattern puzzles work very well with problem-solving. If you work a pattern puzzle for a given problem type several times first, you will find it much easier to work on the different practice problems assigned in your homework.

Pattern puzzles are especially helpful when you are studying for tests. It is a good idea to make the puzzles on a regular basis so that when test time comes you won't be rushing to make them. Bind each puzzle using paper clips, or store the puzzles in individual envelopes. Before tests, use your puzzles to practice and to review.

Pattern puzzles are also a good way to study with others. You and a classmate can take turns creating your own pattern puzzles and putting each other's puzzles in the correct sequence. Studying with a classmate in this way will help make studying fun and allow you and your classmate to help each other.

Practice

1. Write the following sentences describing the process of making pattern puzzles in the correct order.

   Place the strips in their proper sequence.

   Write down the steps of the process in your own words.

   Shuffle the strips of paper.

   Choose a multiple-step process from your text.

   Using your text, confirm the order of the process.

   Cut the paper into strips so that there is one step per strip.

KWL notes

The KWL strategy is an exciting and helpful way to learn. It is somewhat different from the other learning strategies you have seen in this appendix. This strategy stands for "what I **K**now—what I **W**ant to know—what I **L**earned." KWL differs in that it prompts you to brainstorm about the subject matter before you read the assigned pages. This strategy helps you relate your new ideas and concepts with those you have already learned. This allows you to understand and apply new knowledge more easily. The objectives at the beginning of each section in your text are ideal for using the KWL strategy. Just read and follow the instructions in the example below.

1. **Read the section objectives.**
   You may also want to scan headings, bold-face terms, and illustrations in the section. We'll use a few of the objectives from Section 2.1.

   ▶ Explain the relationship between matter, atoms, and elements.

   ▶ Distinguish between elements and compounds.

   ▶ Categorize materials as pure substances or mixtures.

2. **Divide a sheet of paper into three columns, and label the columns "What I know," "What I want to know," and "What I learned."**

3. **Brainstorm about what you know about the information in the objectives, and write these ideas in the first column.**
   It is not necessary to write complete sentences. What's most important is to get as many ideas out as possible. In this way, you will already be thinking about the topic being covered. That will help you learn new information, because it will be easier for you to link it to recently-remembered knowledge.

4. **Think about what you want to know about the information in the objectives, and write these ideas in the second column.**
   You should want to know the information you will be tested over, so include information from both the section objectives and any other objectives your teacher has given you.

5. **While reading the section, or after you have read it, use the third column to write down what you learned.**
   While reading, pay close attention to any information about the topics you wrote in the "What I want to know" column. If you do not find all of the answers you are looking for, you may need to reread the section or find a second source for the information. Be sure to ask your teacher if you still cannot find the information after reading the section a second time.

What I know	What I want to know	What I learned

What I know	What I want to know	What I learned
▶ atoms are very small particles ▶ oxygen is an element ▶ elements are listed on the periodic table	▶ Explain the relationship between matter, atoms, and elements.	▶ matter is anything that occupies space ▶ atoms are the smallest particles with properties of an element ▶ elements cannot be broken down into simpler substances with the same properties ▶ atoms and elements are matter
▶ compounds are made of elements	▶ Distinguish between elements and compounds.	▶ elements combine chemically to make compounds ▶ compounds can be broken down into elements
▶ mixtures are combinations of more than one substance ▶ pure substances have only one component	▶ Categorize materials as pure substances or mixtures.	▶ pure substances have fixed compositions and definite properties ▶ mixtures are combinations of more than one pure substance ▶ elements and compounds are pure substances ▶ grape juice is a mixture

6. It is also important to review your brainstormed ideas when you have completed reading the section.

Compare your ideas in the first column with the information you wrote down in the third column. If you find that some of your brainstormed ideas are incorrect, cross them out. It is extremely important to identify and correct any misconceptions you had before you begin studying for your test.

Your completed KWL notes can make learning science much easier. First of all, this system of note-taking makes gaps in your knowledge easier to spot. That way you can focus on looking for the content you need easier, whether you look in the textbook or ask your teacher.

If you've identified the objectives clearly, the ideas you are studying the most are the ones that will matter most.

Practice

1. Use column 3 from the table above to identify and correct any misconceptions in the following brainstorm list.
   a. Physically mixing elements will form a compound.
   b. Diamond is a compound.
   c. Sodium chloride is an element.
   d. Lemonade is a pure substance.

Two-column notes

Two-column notes can be used to learn and review definitions of vocabulary terms or details of specific concepts. The two-column-note strategy is simple: write the term, main idea, or concept in the left-hand column. Then write the definition, example, or detail on the right.

One strategy for using two-column notes is to organize main ideas and their details. The main ideas from your reading are written in the left-hand column of your paper and can be written as questions, key words, or a combination of both. Key words can include boldface terms as well as any other terms you may have trouble remembering. Questions may include those the author has asked or any questions your teacher may have asked during class. Details describing these main ideas are then written in the right-hand column of your paper.

1. Identify the main ideas.

The main ideas for each chapter are listed in the section objectives. However, you decide which ideas to include in your notes. The table below shows some of the main ideas from the objectives in Section 1.1.

2. Divide a blank sheet of paper into two columns, and write the main ideas in the left-hand column.

Do not copy ideas from the book or waste time writing in complete sentences. Summarize your ideas using quick phrases that are easy to understand and remember. Decide how many details you need for each main idea, and include that number to help you to focus on the necessary information.

3. Write the detail notes in the right-hand column.

Be sure you list as many details as you designated in the main-idea column.

The two-column method of review is perfect for preparing for quizzes or tests. Just cover the information in the right-hand column with a sheet of paper, and after reciting what you know, uncover the notes to check your answers.

Practice

1. Make your own two-column notes using the periodic table in Chapter 3. Include in the details the symbol and the atomic number of each of the following elements.

   a. neon   **c.** calcium   **e.** oxygen
   b. lead   **d.** copper   **f.** sodium

Main idea	Detail notes	
▶ Scientific theory (4 characteristic properties)	▶ tested experimentally ▶ possible explanation	▶ explains natural event ▶ used to predict
▶ Scientific law (3 characteristic properties)	▶ tested experimentally ▶ summary of an observation	▶ can be disproved
▶ Models (4 characteristic properties)	▶ represents an object or event ▶ physical	▶ computer ▶ mathematical

Concept maps

Making concept maps can help you decide what material in a chapter is important and how best to learn that material. A concept map presents key ideas, meanings, and relationships for the concepts being studied. It can be thought of as a visual road map of the chapter.

Concept maps can begin with vocabulary terms. Vocabulary terms are generally labels for concepts, and concepts are generally nouns. Concepts are linked using linking words to form propositions. A proposition is a phrase that gives meaning to the concept. For example, "matter is changed by energy" is a proposition.

1. List all the important concepts.
We'll use some of the terms in Section 2.3.

energy	chemical change
chemical property	physical change
physical property	reactivity
density	

2. Select a main concept for the map.
We will use *matter* as the main concept for this map.

3. Build the map by placing the concepts according to their importance under the main concept, *matter*.
One way of arranging the concepts is shown in **Map A.**

4. Add linking words to give meaning to the arrangement of the concepts.
When adding the links, be sure that each proposition makes sense. To distinguish concepts from links, place your concepts in circles, ovals, or rectangles. Then add cross-links with lines connecting concepts across the map. **Map B** on the next page is a finished map covering the main ideas found in the vocabulary list in Step 1.

Map A

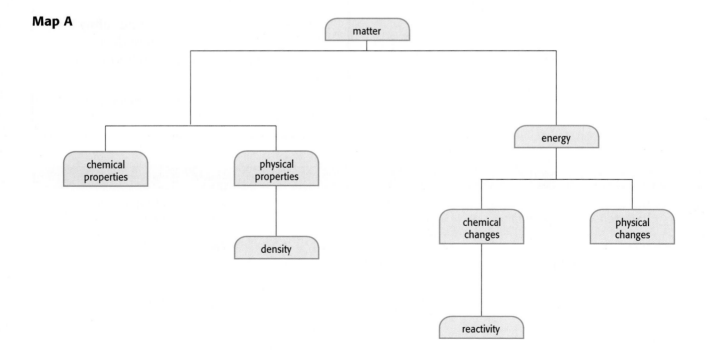

Practice mapping by making concept maps about topics you know. For example, if you know a lot about a particular sport, such as basketball, you can use that topic to make a practice map. By perfecting your skills with information that you know very well, you will begin to feel more confident about making maps from the information in a chapter.

Making maps might seem difficult at first, but the process gets you to think about the meanings and relationships among concepts. If you do not understand those relationships, you can get help early on.

In addition, many people find it easier to study by looking at a concept map, rather than flipping through a chapter full of text because concept mapping is a visual way to organize the information in a chapter. Not only does it isolate the key concepts in a chapter, it also makes the relationships and linkages among those ideas easy to see and understand.

One useful strategy is to trade concept maps with a classmate. Everybody organizes information slightly differently, and something they may have done may help you understand the content better.

Remember, although concept mapping may take a little extra time, the time you spend mapping will pay off when it is time to review for a test or final exam.

Practice

1. Classify each of the following as either a concept or linking word(s).

   a. compound
   b. is classified as
   c. forms
   d. is described by
   e. element
   f. reacts with
   g. pure substance
   h. defines

2. Write three propositions from the information in **Map B.**

Map B

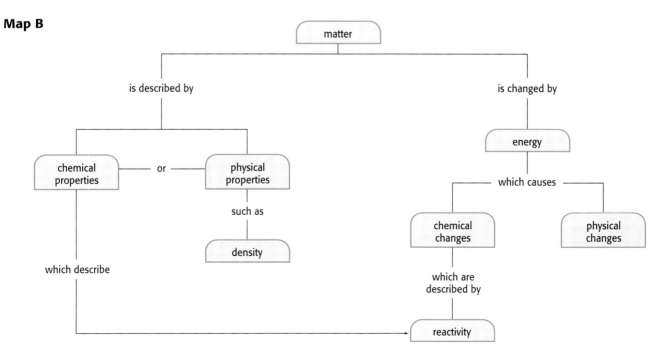

Math Skills Refresher

Fractions

Fractions represent numbers that are less than one. In other words, fractions are a way of numerically representing a part of a whole. For example, if you have a pizza with 8 slices, and you eat 2 of the slices, you have 6 out of the 8 slices, or $\frac{6}{8}$, of the pizza left. The top number in the fraction is called the numerator. The bottom number is the denominator.

There are special rules for adding, subtracting, multiplying, and dividing fractions. These rules are summarized in **Table A-1**.

Table A-1 **Basic Operations for Fractions**

Rule and example		
Multiplication	$\left(\dfrac{a}{b}\right)\left(\dfrac{c}{d}\right) = \dfrac{ac}{bd}$	$\left(\dfrac{2}{3}\right)\left(\dfrac{4}{5}\right) = \dfrac{8}{15}$
Division	$\dfrac{a}{b} \div \dfrac{c}{d} = \dfrac{\left(\dfrac{a}{b}\right)}{\left(\dfrac{c}{d}\right)} = \dfrac{ad}{bc}$	
	$\dfrac{2}{3} \div \dfrac{4}{5} = \dfrac{\left(\dfrac{2}{3}\right)}{\left(\dfrac{4}{5}\right)} = \dfrac{(2)(5)}{(3)(4)} = \dfrac{10}{12}$	
Addition and subtraction	$\dfrac{a}{b} \pm \dfrac{c}{d} = \dfrac{ad \pm bc}{bd}$	
	$\dfrac{2}{3} - \dfrac{4}{5} = \dfrac{(2)(5) - (3)(4)}{(3)(5)} = -\dfrac{2}{15}$	

Practice

1. Perform the following calculations:

   a. $\dfrac{7}{8} + \dfrac{1}{3} =$

   b. $\dfrac{7}{8} \times \dfrac{1}{3} =$

   c. $\dfrac{7}{8} \div \dfrac{1}{3} =$

   d. $\dfrac{7}{8} - \dfrac{1}{3} =$

Percentages

Percentages are no different from other fractions, except that in a percentage, the whole (or the number in the denominator) is considered to be 100. Any percentage, $x\%$, can be read as x out of 100. For example, if you have completed 50% of an assignment, you have completed $\frac{50}{100}$ or $\frac{1}{2}$ of the assignment.

Percentages can be calculated by dividing the part by the whole. When your calculator solves a division problem that is less than 1, it gives you a decimal value instead of a fraction. For example, 0.45 can be written as the fraction $\frac{45}{100}$. This is equal to 45%. An easy way to calculate percentages is to divide the part by the whole, then multiply by 100. This multiplication moves the decimal point two positions to the right, giving you the number that would be over 100 in a fraction. Try this example.

You scored 73 out of 92 problems on your last exam. What was your percentage score?

First divide the part by the whole to get a decimal value: $\frac{73}{92}$. Note that 0.7935 is equal to $\frac{79.35}{100}$
Then multiply by 100 to yield the percentage: $0.7935 \times 100 = 79.35\%$.

Practice

1. Oxygen in water has a mass of 16.00 g. The water has a total mass of 18.01 g. What percentage of the mass of water is made up of oxygen?

2. A candy bar contains 14 g of fat. The total fat contains 3.0 g of saturated fat and 11 g of unsaturated fats. What are the percentages of saturated and unsaturated fat in the candy bar?

Exponents

An exponent is a number that is superscripted to the right of another number. The best way to explain how an exponent works is with an example. In the value 5^4, 4 is the exponent on 5. The number with its exponent means that 5 is multiplied by itself 4 times.

$$5^4 = 5 \times 5 \times 5 \times 5 = 625$$

You will frequently hear exponents referred to as powers. Using this terminology, the above equation could be read as *five to the fourth power equals 625*. Keep in mind that any number raised to the zero power is equal to one. Also, any number raised to the first power is equal to itself: $5^1 = 5$.

Just as there are special rules for dealing with fractions, there are special rules for dealing with exponents. These rules are summarized in **Table A-2.**

You probably recognize the symbol for a square root, $\sqrt{}$. This means that a number times itself equals the value inside the square root. It is also possible to have roots other than the square root. For example, $\sqrt[3]{x}$ means that some number, n, times itself three times equals the number x, or $n \times n \times n = x$. We can turn our example of $5^4 = 625$ around to solve for the fourth root of 625.

$$\sqrt[4]{625} = 5$$

Taking the nth root of a number is the same as raising that number to the power of $1/n$. Therefore, $\sqrt[4]{625} = 625^{1/4}$.

A scientific calculator is a must for solving most problems involving exponents and roots. Many calculators have dedicated keys for squares and square roots. But what about different powers, such as cubes and cube roots? Most scientific calculators have a key shaped like a caret, ^. If you type in "5^4," when you hit the equals sign or the enter key, the calculator will determine that $5^4 = 625$, and display that answer.

For roots, you enter the decimal equivalent of the fractional exponent. For example, to solve the problem of the fourth root of 625, instead of entering one-fourth as the exponent, enter "625^0.25," because 0.25 is equal to one-fourth.

Practice

1. Perform the following calculations:

   a. $9^1 =$

   b. $(3^3)^5 =$

   c. $\dfrac{2^8}{2^2} =$

   d. $(14^2)(14^3) =$

   e. $11^0 =$

   f. $6^{1/6} =$

Table A-2 **Rules for dealing with exponents**

	Rule	Example
Zero power	$x^0 = 1$	$7^0 = 1$
First power	$x^1 = x$	$6^1 = 6$
Multiplication	$(x^n)(x^m) = x^{(n+m)}$	$(x^2)(x^4) = x^{(2+4)} = x^6$
Division	$\dfrac{x^n}{x^m} = x^{(n-m)}$	$\dfrac{x^8}{x^2} = x^{(8-2)} = x^6$
Exponents that are fractions	$x^{1/n} = \sqrt[n]{x}$	$4^{1/3} = \sqrt[3]{4} = 1.5874$
Exponents raised to a power	$(x^n)^m = x^{nm}$	$(5^2)^3 = 5^6 = 15\ 625$

Order of operations

Use this phrase to remember the correct order for long mathematical problems: *Please Excuse My Dear Aunt Sally.* This phrase stands for *Parentheses, Exponents, Multiplication, Division, Addition, Subtraction.* These rules can be summarized in **Table A-3.**

Table A-3 **Order of Operations**

Step	Operation
1	Simplify groups inside parentheses. Start with the innermost group and work out.
2	Simplify all exponents.
3	Perform multiplication and division in order from left to right.
4	Perform addition and subtraction in order from left to right.

Look at the following example:
$$4^3 + 2 \times [8 - (3 - 1)] = ?$$
First simplify the operations inside parentheses. Begin with the innermost parentheses:
$$(3 - 1) = 2$$
$$4^3 + 2 \times [8 - 2] = ?$$
Then move on to the next-outer parentheses:
$$[8 - 2] = 6$$
$$4^3 + 2 \times 6 = ?$$
Now, simplify all exponents:
$$4^3 = 64$$
$$64 + 2 \times 6 = ?$$
The next step is to perform multiplication:
$$2 \times 6 = 12$$
$$64 + 12 = ?$$
Finally, solve the addition problem:
$$64 + 12 = 76$$

Practice

1. $2^3 \div 2 + 4 \times (9 - 2^2) =$

2. $\dfrac{2 \times (6 - 3) + 8}{4 \times 2 - 6} =$

Geometry

Quite often, a useful way to model the objects and substances studied in science is to consider them in terms of their shapes. For example, many of the properties of a wheel can be understood by pretending that the wheel is a perfect circle.

For this reason, being able to calculate the area or the volume of certain shapes is a useful skill in science. **Table A-4** provides equations for the area and volume of several geometric shapes.

Table A-4 **Geometric Areas and Volumes**

Geometric Shape		Useful Equations
Rectangle		Area $= lw$
Circle		Area $= \pi r^2$ Circumference $= 2\pi r$
Triangle		Area $= \dfrac{1}{2}bh$
Sphere		Surface area $= 4\pi r^2$ volume $= \dfrac{4}{3}\pi r^3$
Cylinder		Volume $= \pi r^2 h$
Rectangular box		Surface area $= 2(lh + lw + hw)$ volume $= lwh$

Practice

1. What is the volume of a cylinder with a diameter of 14 cm and a height of 8 cm?

2. Calculate the surface area of a 4 cm cube.

3. Will a sphere with a volume of 76 cm^3 fit in a rectangular box that is 7 cm $\times$ 4 cm $\times$ 10 cm?

Algebraic rearrangements

Algebraic equations contain *constants* and *variables*. Constants are simply numbers, such as 2, 5, and 7. Variables are represented by letters such as *x*, *y*, *z*, *a*, *b*, and *c*. Variables are unspecified quantities and are also called the unknowns.

Often, you will need to determine the value of a variable, but all you will be given will be an equation expressed in terms of algebraic expressions instead of a simple equation expressed in numbers only.

An algebraic expression contains one or more of the four basic mathematical operations: addition, subtraction, multiplication, and division. Constants, variables, or terms made up of both constants and variables can be involved in the basic operations.

The key to figuring out the value of a variable in an algebraic equation is that the quantity described on one side of the equals sign is equal to the quantity described on the other side of the equals sign.

If you are trying to determine the value of a variable in an algebraic expression, you would like to be able to rewrite the equation as a simple one that tells you exactly what *x* (or some other variable) equals.

But how do you get from a more complicated equation to a simple one?

Again, the key lies in the fact that both sides of the equation are equal. That means if you do the same operation on either side of the equation, the results will still be equal.

Look at the following simple problem:
$$8x = 32$$
If we wish to solve for *x*, we can multiply or divide each side of the equation by the same factor. You can add, subtract, multiply, or divide anything to or from one side of an equation as long as you do the same thing to the other side of the equation. In this case, if we divide both sides by 8, we have:
$$\frac{8x}{8} = \frac{32}{8}$$
The 8s on the left side of the equation cancel each other out, and the fraction $\frac{32}{8}$ can be reduced to give the whole number, 4. Therefore, $x = 4$.

Next consider the following equation:
$$x + 2 = 8$$
Remember, we can add or subtract the same quantity from each side. If we subtract 2 from each side, we get
$$x + 2 - 2 = 8 - 2$$
$$x + 0 = 6$$
$$x = 6$$

Now consider one more equation:
$$\frac{x}{5} = 9$$
If we multiply each side by 5, the 5 originally on the left side of the equation cancels out. We are left with *x* on the left by itself and 45 on the right:
$$x = 45$$
In all cases, *whatever operation is performed on the left side of the equals sign must also be performed on the right side.*

Practice

1. Rearrange each of the following equations to give the value of the variable indicated with a letter.

   a. $8x - 32 = 128$

   b. $6 - 5(4a + 3) = 26$

   c. $-3(y - 2) + 4 = 29$

   d. $-2(3m + 5) = 14$

   e. $\left[8\dfrac{(8 + 2z)}{32} \right] + 2 = 5$

   f. $\dfrac{(6b + 3)}{3} - 9 = 2$

Scientific Notation

Many quantities that scientists deal with have very large or very small values. For example, about 3 000 000 000 000 000 000 electrons' worth of charge pass through a standard light bulb in one second, and the ink required to make the dot over an *i* in this textbook has a mass of about 0.000 000 001 kg.

Obviously, it is very cumbersome to read, write, and keep track of numbers like these. We avoid this problem by using a method dealing with powers of the number 10.

Study the positive powers of ten shown on page 22 in Chapter 1. You should be able to check those numbers on your own using what you know about exponents. The number of zeros corresponds to the exponent on 10. The number for 10^4 is 10 000; it has 4 zeros.

But how can we use the powers of 10 to simplify large numbers such as the number of electron-sized charges passing through a light bulb? This large number is equal to 3×1 000 000 000 000 000 000. The factor of 10 has 18 zeros. Therefore, it can be rewritten as 10^{18}. This means that 3 000 000 000 000 000 000 can be expressed as 3×10^{18}.

That explains how to simplify really large numbers, but what about really small numbers, like 0.000 000 001 kg? Negative exponents can be used to simplify numbers that are less than 1.

Study the negative powers of 10 on page 22 of Chapter 1. In these cases, the exponent on 10 equals the number of decimal places you must move the decimal point to the right so that there is one digit just to the left of the decimal point. Using the mass of the ink in the dot on an *i*, the decimal point has to be moved 9 decimal places to the right for the numeral 1 to be just to the left of the decimal point. The mass of the ink, 0.000 000 001 kg, can be rewritten as 1×10^{-9} kg.

Numbers that are expressed as some power of 10 multiplied by another number with only one digit to the left of the decimal point are said to be written in scientific notation. For example, 5943 000 000 is 5.943×10^9 when expressed in scientific notation. The number 0.000 0832 is 8.32×10^{-5} when expressed in scientific notation.

When a number is expressed in scientific notation, it is easy to determine the order of magnitude of the number. The order of magnitude is the power of ten that the number would be rounded to. For example, in the number 5.943×10^9, the order of magnitude is 10^{10}, because 5.943 rounds to another 10, and 10 times 10^9 is 10^{10}. For numbers less than 5, the order of magnitude is just the power of ten when the number is written in scientific notation.

The order of magnitude can be used to help quickly estimate your answers. Simply perform the operations required, but instead of using numbers, use the orders of magnitude. Your final answer should be within two orders of magnitude of your estimate.

Practice

1. Rewrite the following values using scientific notation:
   a. 12 300 000 m/s
   b. 0.000 000 000 0045 kg
   c. 0.00 006 53 m
   d. 55 432 000 000 000 s
   e. 273.15 K
   f. 0.000 627 14 kg

SI

One of the most important parts of scientific research is being able to communicate your findings to other scientists. Today, scientists need to be able to communicate with other scientists all around the world. They need a common language in which to report data. If you do an experiment in which all of your measurements are in pounds, and you want to compare your results to a French scientist whose measurements are in grams, you will need to convert all of your measurements. For this reason, *Le Système International d'Unités,* or SI system was devised in 1960.

You are probably accustomed to measuring distance in inches, feet, and miles. Most of the world, however, measures distance in centimeters (abbreviated cm), meters (abbreviated m), and kilometers (abbreviated km). The meter is the official SI unit for measuring distance.

Notice that cent*imeter* and kilo*meter* each contain the word *meter.* When dealing with SI units, you frequently use the base unit, in this case the meter, and add a prefix to indicate that the quantity you are measuring is a multiple of that unit. Most SI prefixes indicate multiples of 10. For example, the centimeter is

Table A-6 **Some SI Prefixes**

Prefix	Abbreviation	Exponential factor
Giga-	G	10^9
Mega-	M	10^6
Kilo-	k	10^3
Hecto-	h	10^2
Deka-	da	10^1
Deci-	d	10^{-1}
Centi-	c	10^{-2}
Milli-	m	10^{-3}
Micro-	μ	10^{-6}
Nano-	n	10^{-9}
Pico-	p	10^{-12}
Femto-	f	10^{-15}

1/100 of a meter. Any SI unit with the prefix *centi-* will be 1/100 of the base unit. A centigram is 1/100 of a gram.

What about the *kilo*meter? The prefix *kilo-* indicates that the unit is 1000 times the base unit. A kilometer is equal to 1000 meters. Multiples of 10 make dealing with SI values much easier than values such as feet or gallons. If you wish to convert from feet to miles, you must remember the conversion factor 1.893939×10^{-4}. If you wish to convert from kilometers to meters, you need only look at the prefix to know that you will multiply by 1000.

Table A-5 lists the SI units. **Table A-6** gives the possible prefixes and their meaning. When working with a prefix, simply take the unit abbreviation and add the prefix abbreviation to the front of the unit. For example, the abbreviation for kilometer is written km.

Table A-5 **Some SI Units**

Quantity	Unit name	Abbreviation
Length	meter	m
Mass	kilogram	kg
Time	second	s
Temperature	kelvin	K
Amount of substance	mole	mol
Electric current	ampere	A
Pressure	pascal	Pa
Volume	meters^3	m^3

Practice

1. Convert each value to the requested units.

   a. 0.035 m to decimeters

   b. 5.24 m^3 to centimeters^3

   c. 13450 g to kilograms

Significant figures

The following list can be used to review how to determine the number of significant figures in a reported value. After you have reviewed the rules, use **Table A-7** to check your understanding of the rules. Cover up the second column of the table, and try to determine how many significant figures each number has. If you get confused, refer to the rule given.

Table A-7   **Significant Figures**

Measurement	Number of significant figures	Rule
12 345	5	1
2400 cm	2	3
305 kg	3	2
2350. cm	4	4
234.005 K	6	2
12.340	5	6
0.001	1	5
0.002 450	4	5 and 6

Rules for Determining the Number of Significant Figures in a Measurement:

1. All nonzero digits are significant. **Example:** 1246 has four significant figures (shown in red).
2. Any zeros between significant digits are also significant. 1206 has four significant figures.
3. If the value does not contain a decimal point, any zeros to the right of a nonzero digit are not significant. 1200 has only two significant figures.
4. Any zeros to the right of a significant digit and to the left of a decimal point are significant. 1200. has four significant figures.
5. If a value has no significant digits to the left of a decimal point, any zeros to the right of the decimal point, and to the left of a significant digit, are not significant. **Example:** 0.0012 has only two significant figures.
6. If a measurement is reported that ends with zeros to the right of a decimal point, those zeros are significant. **Example:** 0.1200 has four significant figures.

When performing mathematical operations with measurements, you must remember to keep track of significant figures. If you are adding or subtracting two measurements, your answer can only have as many decimal positions as the value with the least number of decimal places. Study the following subtraction problem. The final answer has five significant figures. It has been rounded to two decimal places because 0.04 g only has two decimal places.

$$
\begin{array}{r}
134.050 \text{ g} \\
- \ 0.04 \text{ g} \\
\hline
134.01 \text{ g}
\end{array}
$$

When multiplying or dividing measurements, your final answer can only have as many significant figures as the value with the least number of significant figures. Examine the following multiplication problem.

$$
\begin{array}{r}
12.0 \text{ cm}^2 \\
\times \ 0.04 \text{ cm} \\
\hline
0.5 \text{ cm}^3
\end{array}
$$

The final answer has been rounded to only one significant figure because 0.04 cm has only one significant figure.

Practice

1. Determine the number of significant figures in each of the following measurements:

   a. 65.04 mL   **c.** 0.007 504 kg
   b. 564.00 m   **d.** 1210 K

2. Perform each of the following calculations, and report your answer with the correct number of significant figures and units:

   a. 0.004 dm + 0.125 08 dm
   b. 340 m ÷ 0.1257 s
   c. 40.1 kg × 0.2453 m²
   d. 1.03 g − 0.0456 g

Graphing Skills

Line graphs

In laboratory experiments, you will usually be controlling one variable and seeing how it affects another variable. Line graphs can show these relations clearly. For example, you might perform an experiment in which you measure the growth of a plant over time to determine the rate of the plant's growth. In this experiment, you are controlling the time intervals at which the plant height is measured. Therefore, time is called the *independent variable*. The height of the plant is the *dependent variable*. **Table A-8** gives some sample data for an experiment to measure the rate of plant growth.

The independent variable is plotted on the *x*-axis. This axis will be labeled *Time (days)*, and will have a range from 0 days to 35 days. Be sure to properly label each axis including the units on the values.

The dependent variable is plotted on the *y*-axis. This axis will be labeled *Plant Height (cm)* and will have a range from 0 cm to 5 cm.

Table A-8 **Experimental Data for Plant Growth versus Time**

Time (days)	Plant height (cm)
0	1.43
7	2.16
14	2.67
21	3.25
28	4.04
35	4.67

Figure A-1

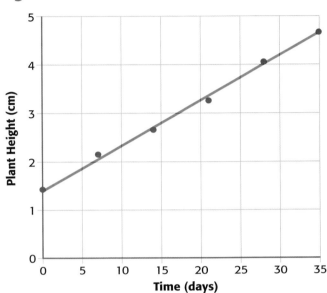

Think of your graph as a grid with lines running horizontally from the *y*-axis, and vertically from the *x*-axis. To plot a point, find the *x* (in this example time) value on the *x* axis. Follow the vertical line from the *x* axis until it intersects the horizontal line from the *y*-axis at the corresponding *y* (in this case, height) value. At the intersection of these two lines, place your point. **Figure A-1** shows what a line graph of the data in **Table A-8** might look like.

Bar graphs

Bar graphs are useful for comparing different data values. If you wanted to compare the sizes of the planets in our solar system, you might use a bar graph. **Table A-9** on the next page gives the necessary data for such a graph.

Figure A-2

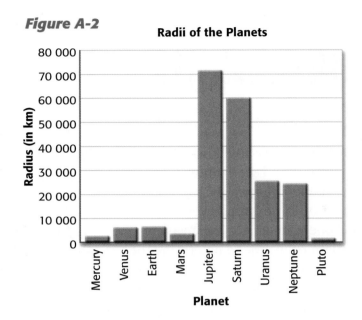

Radii of the Planets

Table A-9 Radii of the Planets in Our Solar System

Planet	Radius (km)
Mercury	2 439
Venus	6 052
Earth	6 378
Mars	3 393
Jupiter	71 398
Saturn	60 000
Uranus	25 400
Neptune	24 300
Pluto	1 500

To create a bar graph from the data in **Table A-9,** begin on the *x*-axis by labeling nine bar positions with the names of the nine planets. Label the *y*-axis *Radius (km).* Be sure the range on your *y*-axis encompasses 1500 km and 71 398 km. Then draw the bars for each planet with a bar height that matches the radius value for that planet on the *y*-axis, as shown in **Figure A-2.**

Pie charts

Pie charts are an easy way to visualize how many parts make up a whole. Frequently, pie charts are made from percentage data. For example, you could create a pie graph showing the elemental composition of Earth's crust. Data for this sample pie chart can be found in **Table A-10.**

To create a pie chart from the data in **Table A-10,** begin by drawing a circle. Then imagine dividing the circle into 100 equal sections. Shade in 46 consecutive sections, and label that region *Oxygen.* Continue in the same manner with other colors until

the entire pie chart has been filled in, and each element has a corresponding region on the chart as shown in **Figure A-3.**

Figure A-3

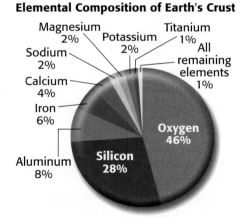

Elemental Composition of Earth's Crust

Table A-10 Elemental Composition of Earth's Crust

Element	Percentage of Earth's Crust	Element	Percentage of Earth's Crust
Oxygen	46%	Sodium	2%
Silicon	28%	Magnesium	2%
Aluminum	8%	Potassium	2%
Iron	6%	Titanium	1%
Calcium	4%	All remaining elements	1%

Lab Skills

Making Measurements in the Laboratory

Reading a balance for mass

When a balance is required for determining mass, you will probably use a centigram balance like the one shown in **Figure A-4.** The centigram balance is sensitive to 0.01 g. This means that your mass readings should all be recorded to the nearest 0.01 g.

Before using the balance, always check to see if the pointer is resting at zero. If the pointer is not at zero, check the riders. If all the riders are at zero, turn the zero adjust knob until the pointer rests at zero. The zero adjust knob is usually located at the far left end of the balance beam, as shown in **Figure A-4.** Note: The balance will not adjust to zero if the movable pan has been removed.

In many experiments, you will be asked to obtain a specified mass of a solid. When measuring the mass of a chemical, place a piece of weighing paper on the movable pan. **Never place chemicals or hot objects directly on the pan.** They can permanently damage the surface of the pan and affect the accuracy of later measurements.

Determine the mass of the paper by adjusting the riders on the various scales. Record the mass of the weighing paper to the nearest 0.01 g. Then add the mass you wish to obtain by sliding the appropriate riders on the scales. For example, if your weighing paper has a mass of 0.15 g, the balance reads 0.15 g. To measure 13g of a solid, you then need to add 13 g to this mass. Do this by sliding the 10-gram rider to 10 and the 1-gram rider to 3. The balance is no longer balanced.

Slowly add the solid onto the weighing paper until the balance is once again balanced. Do not waste time trying to obtain *exactly* 13.00 g of a solid. Instead, read the mass when the pointer swings close to zero. Remember, you must read the final mass on the balance and subtract the mass of the weighing paper (0.15 g) from this final mass to determine the solid's mass to two decimal places, as is appropriate for measurements made using a centigram balance.

Figure A-4

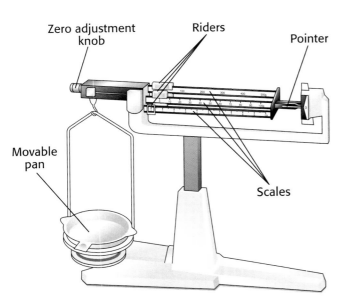

Zero adjustment knob

Riders

Pointer

Movable pan

Scales

Measuring temperature with a thermometer

A thermometer is used to measure temperature. Examine your thermometer and the temperature range for the Celsius temperature scale. You will probably be using an alcohol thermometer in your laboratory. However, you may also use a digital thermometer.

Mercury thermometers are hazardous and probably will not be available in your school laboratory, although you may still have a mercury fever thermometer at home. **If a mercury thermometer should ever break, immediately notify your teacher or parent. Your teacher or parent will clean up the spill. Do not touch the mercury.**

Alcohol thermometers, like mercury thermometers, have a column of liquid that rises in a glass cylinder depending on the temperature at the tip of the thermometer. One caution concerning alcohol thermometers is that they can burst at very high temperatures. Never let the thermometer be exposed to temperatures above its range.

When working with any thermometer, it is especially important to pay close attention to the precision of the instrument. Most alcohol thermometers are marked in intervals of 1°C. The intervals are usually so close together that it is impossible to estimate temperature values measured with such a thermometer to any more precision than a half a degree, 0.5°C. Thus, if you are using this type of thermometer, it would be impossible to actually measure a temperature like 25.15°C.

It is also very important to keep your eye at about the same level as the colored fluid in the thermometer. If you are looking at the thermometer from below, the reading you see will appear a degree or two lower than it really is. Similarly, if you look at the thermometer from above, the reading will seem to be a degree or two higher than it really is.

Reading a graduated cylinder for volume

Many different types of laboratory glassware, from beakers to flasks, contain markings indicating approximate volume in milliliters. However, these markings are merely approximate, and they were not consistently checked when the piece of glassware was made.

For truly accurate volume measurements, you should use a graduated cylinder or a buret, like the one shown in **Figure A-5.** When a graduated cylinder or a buret is made, its accuracy is checked and rechecked. You will also notice that graduated cylinders and burets are marked in smaller increments than are beakers (usually individual milliliters, although some are even more precise).

Most liquids have a concave surface that forms in a buret or a graduated cylinder. This concave surface is called a meniscus. When measuring the volume of a liquid, you must consider the meniscus, like the one shown in the buret in **Figure A-5.** Always measure the volume from the bottom of the meniscus. The markings on a graduated cylinder or a buret are designed to take into account the water that extends up along the walls slightly above the marking lines.

It may be difficult to read a volume measurement, so if you need to, hold a piece of white paper behind the graduated cylinder or buret. This should make the meniscus level easier to see.

Figure A-5

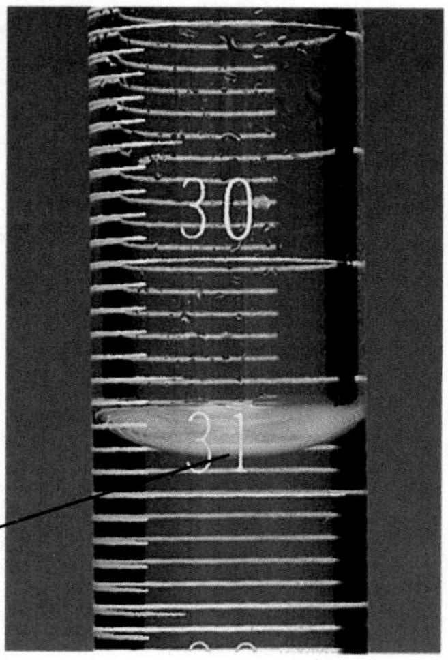

Meniscus, 30.84 mL

How to Write a Laboratory Report

In many of the laboratory investigations that you will be doing, you will be trying to support a hypothesis or answer a question by performing experiments following the scientific method. You will frequently be asked to summarize your experiments in a laboratory report. Laboratory reports should contain the following parts:

Title

This is the name of the experiment you are doing. If you are performing an experiment from this book, the title will be the same as the title of the experiment.

Hypothesis

The hypothesis is what you think will happen during the investigation. It is often written as an "If . . . then" statement. When you conduct your experiment, you will be changing one condition, or variable, and observing and measuring the effect of this change. The condition that you are changing is called the *independent* variable and should follow the "If . . ." statement. The effect that you expect to observe is called the *dependent* variable and should follow the ". . . then" statement. For example, look at the following hypothesis:

> *If salamanders are reared in acidic water, then more of the salamanders will develop abnormally.*

"If salamanders are reared in acidic water" is the independent variable—salamanders normally live in nearly neutral water and you are changing this to acidic water. "Then more of the salamanders will develop abnormally" is the dependent variable—this is the change that you expect to observe and measure.

Materials

List all of the equipment and other supplies you will need to complete the experiment. If the investigation is taken from this book, the materials are listed for you, but you will need to recopy them into your lab report. It is important that your lab report be complete enough so that someone else can repeat your experiment to test your results.

Procedure

The procedure is a step-by-step explanation of exactly what you did in the experiment. Investigations in this book will have the procedure carefully written out for you, but you must write the procedure in your lab report EXACTLY as you performed it. This will not necessarily be an exact copy of the procedure written in the book.

Data

Your data are your observations. They are often recorded in the form of tables, graphs, and drawings.

Analyses and Conclusions

This part of the report explains what you have learned. You should evaluate your hypothesis and explain any errors you might have made in the investigation. Keep in mind that not all of your hypotheses will be correct. Sometimes you will disprove your original hypothesis rather than prove it. You simply need to explain why things did not work out the way you thought they would. The labs included in this book will have questions to guide you as you analyze your data. You should use these questions as a basis for your conclusions.

Table B-1 Densities of Various Materials

Material	Density (g/cm³)	Material	Density (g/cm³)
Air, dry	1.293×10^{-3}	Iron	7.86
Aluminum	2.70	Jupiter	1.33*
Bone	1.7–2.0	Lead	11.3
Butter	0.86–0.87	Mars	3.94*
Carbon (diamond)	3.5155	Mercury (Hg)	13.5336
Carbon (graphite)	2.2670	Paper	0.7–1.15
Copper	8.96	Rock Salt	2.18
Cork	0.22–0.26	Saturn	0.70*
Earth	5.515*	Silver	10.5
Earth's moon	3.34*	Sugar	1.59
Ethanol	0.7893	Sodium	0.97
Gold	19.3	Stainless steel	8.02
Helium	1.78×10^{-4}	Steel	7.8
Ice	0.917	Water (at 25°C)	0.997 05

* Astronomical values are for mean density

Table B-2 International Morse Code

Letter	Code	Letter	Code	Number	Code	Symbol	Code
A	• —	N	— •	0	— — — — —	Period	• — • — • —
B	— • • •	O	— — —	1	• — — — —	Comma	— — • • — —
C	— • — •	P	• — — •	2	• • — — —	Interrogation	• • — — • •
D	— • •	Q	— — • —	3	• • • — —	Colon	— — — • • •
E	•	R	• — •	4	• • • • —	Semicolon	— • — • — •
F	• • — •	S	• • •	5	• • • • •	Hyphen	— • • • • —
G	— — •	T	—	6	— • • • •	Slash	— • • — •
H	• • • •	U	• • —	7	— — • • •	Quotation marks	• — • • — •
I	• •	V	• • • —	8	— — — • •		
J	• — — —	W	• — —	9	— — — — •		
K	— • —	X	— • • —				
L	• — • •	Y	— • — —				
M	— —	Z	— — • •				

Table B-3 **Specific Heats**

Material	c (J/kg·K)	Material	c (J/kg·K)
Acetic acid (CH_3COOH)	2070	Lead (Pb)	129
Air	1007	Magnetite (Fe_3O_4)	619
Aluminum (Al)	897	Methane (CH_4)	2200
Calcium (Ca)	647	Mercury (Hg)	140
Calcium carbonate ($CaCO_3$)	818	Neon (Ne)	1030
Carbon (C, graphite)	709	Nickel (Ni)	444
Carbon (C, diamond)	487	Nitrogen (N_2)	1040
Carbon dioxide (CO_2)	843	Oxygen (O_2)	918
Copper (Cu)	385	Platinum (Pt)	133
Ethanol (CH_3CH_2OH)	2440	Silver (Ag)	234
Gold (Au)	129	Sodium (Na)	1228
Helium (He)	5193	Sodium chloride (NaCl)	864
Hematite (Fe_2O_3)	650	Tin (Sn)	228
Hydrogen (H_2)	14 304	Tungsten (W)	132
Hydrogen peroxide (H_2O_2)	2620	Water (H_2O)	4186
Iron (Fe)	449	Zinc (Zn)	388

Values at 25°C and 1 atm pressure

Figure B-1 **Electromagnetic Spectrum**

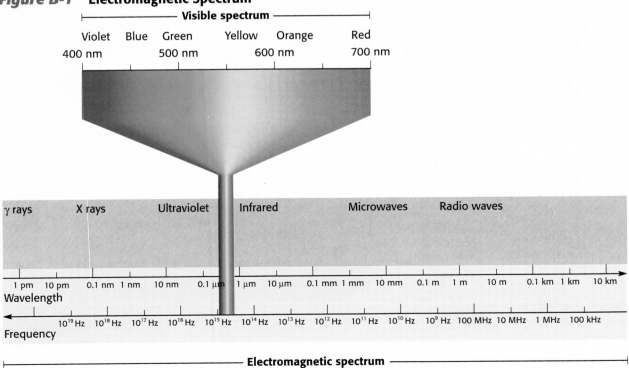

Figure B-2   **Periodic Table of the Elements**

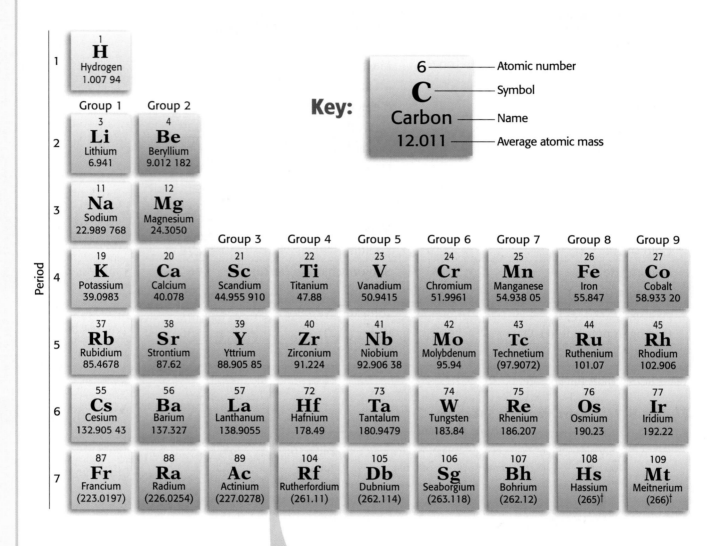

Key:

6 —— Atomic number
C —— Symbol
Carbon —— Name
12.011 —— Average atomic mass

† Estimated from currently available IUPAC data.

* The systematic names and symbols for elements greater than 109 will be used until the approval of trivial names by IUPAC.

internetconnect

TOPIC: Periodic Table
GO TO: go.hrw.com
KEYWORD: HK1Periodic

Visit the HRW Web site to see the most recent version of the periodic table.

Metals
- Alkali metals
- Alkaline-earth metals
- Transition metals
- Other metals

Nonmetals
- Hydrogen
- Semiconductors
- Halogens
- Noble gases
- Other nonmetals

Group 18

2
He
Helium
4.002 602

Group 13

5
B
Boron
10.811

Group 14

6
C
Carbon
12.011

Group 15

7
N
Nitrogen
14.006 74

Group 16

8
O
Oxygen
15.9994

Group 17

9
F
Fluorine
18.998 4032

10
Ne
Neon
20.1797

13	14	15	16	17	18
Al	**Si**	**P**	**S**	**Cl**	**Ar**
Aluminum	Silicon	Phosphorus	Sulfur	Chlorine	Argon
26.981 539	28.0855	30.9738	32.066	35.4527	39.948

Group 10 Group 11 Group 12

28	29	30	31	32	33	34	35	36
Ni	**Cu**	**Zn**	**Ga**	**Ge**	**As**	**Se**	**Br**	**Kr**
Nickel	Copper	Zinc	Gallium	Germanium	Arsenic	Selenium	Bromine	Krypton
58.6934	63.546	65.39	69.723	72.61	74.921 59	78.96	79.904	83.80

46	47	48	49	50	51	52	53	54
Pd	**Ag**	**Cd**	**In**	**Sn**	**Sb**	**Te**	**I**	**Xe**
Palladium	Silver	Cadmium	Indium	Tin	Antimony	Tellurium	Iodine	Xenon
106.42	107.8682	112.411	114.818	118.710	121.757	127.60	126.904	131.29

78	79	80	81	82	83	84	85	86
Pt	**Au**	**Hg**	**Tl**	**Pb**	**Bi**	**Po**	**At**	**Rn**
Platinum	Gold	Mercury	Thallium	Lead	Bismuth	Polonium	Astatine	Radon
195.08	196.966 54	200.59	204.3833	207.2	208.980 37	(208.9824)	(209.9871)	(222.0176)

110	111	112		114		116		118
Uun*	**Uuu***	**Uub***		**Uuq***		**Uuh***		**Uuo***
Ununnilium	Unununium	Ununbium		Ununquadium		Ununhexium		Ununoctium
(269)†	(272)†	(277)†		(285)†		(289)†		(293)†

63	64	65	66	67	68	69	70	71
Eu	**Gd**	**Tb**	**Dy**	**Ho**	**Er**	**Tm**	**Yb**	**Lu**
Europium	Gadolinium	Terbium	Dysprosium	Holmium	Erbium	Thulium	Ytterbium	Lutetium
151.966	157.25	158.925 34	162.50	164.930	167.26	168.934 21	173.04	174.967

95	96	97	98	99	100	101	102	103
Am	**Cm**	**Bk**	**Cf**	**Es**	**Fm**	**Md**	**No**	**Lr**
Americium	Curium	Berkelium	Californium	Einsteinium	Fermium	Mendelevium	Nobelium	Lawrencium
(243.0614)	(247.0703)	(247.0703)	(251.0796)	(252.083)	(257.0951)	(258.10)	(259.1009)	(262.11)

The atomic masses listed in this table reflect the precision of current measurements. (Values listed in parentheses are those of the element's most stable or most common isotope.) In calculations throughout the text, however, atomic masses have been rounded to two places to the right of the decimal.

Figure B-3 **The World: Physical**

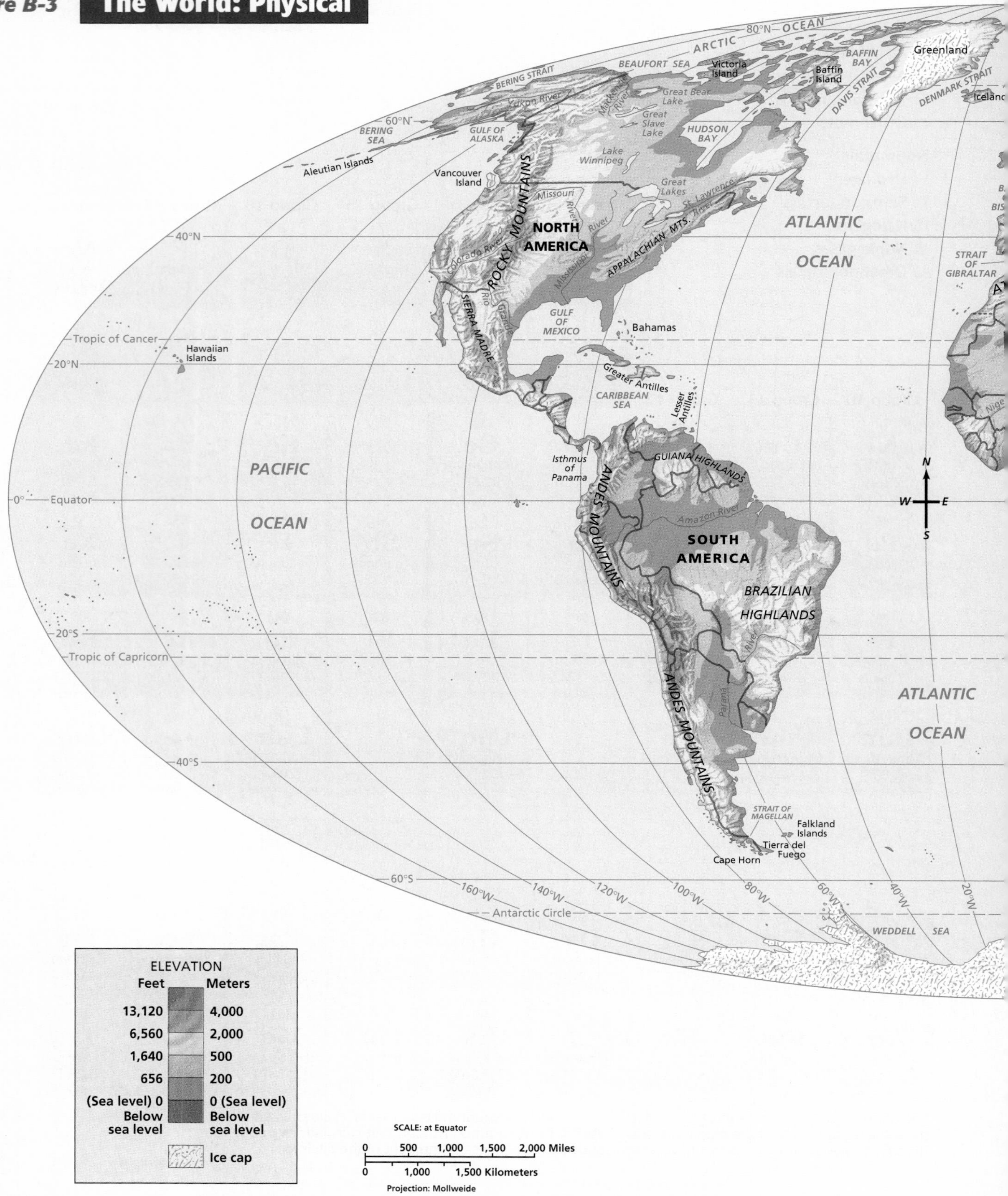

ELEVATION

Feet		Meters
13,120		4,000
6,560		2,000
1,640		500
656		200
(Sea level) 0		0 (Sea level)
Below sea level		Below sea level
	Ice cap	

SCALE: at Equator

0   500   1,000   1,500   2,000 Miles

0   1,000   1,500 Kilometers

Projection: Mollweide

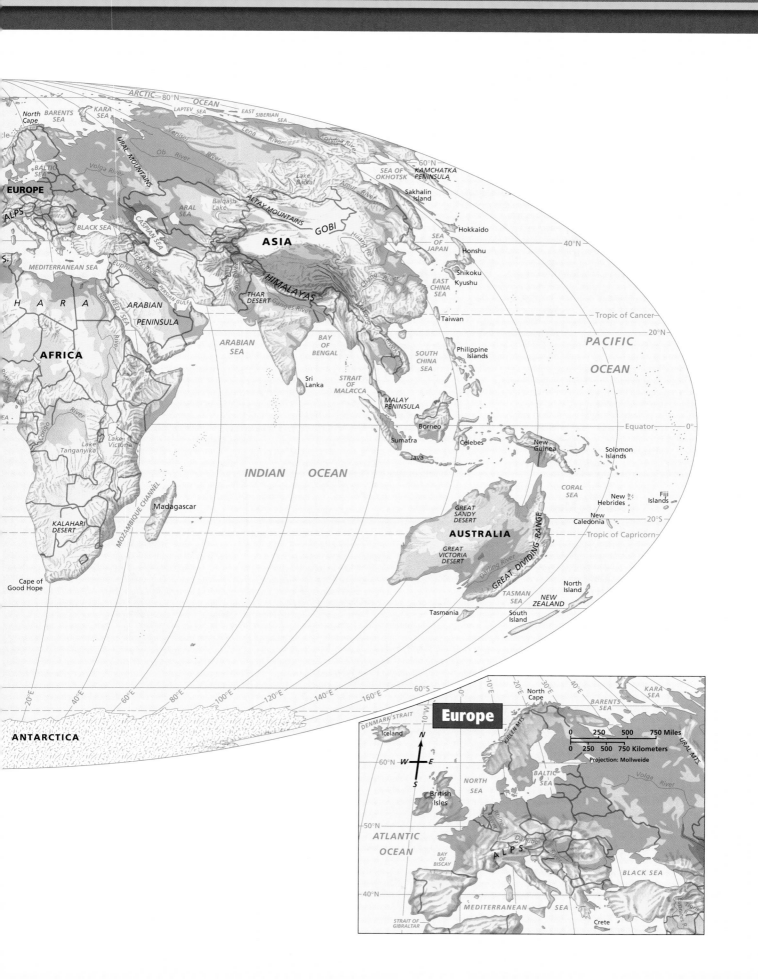

ARCTIC 80°N OCEAN
North Cape
BARENTS SEA
KARA SEA
LAPTEV SEA
EAST SIBERIAN SEA
BALTIC SEA
URAL MOUNTAINS
Ob River
Yenisey River
Lena River
Kolyma River
EUROPE
Volga River
60°N
SEA OF OKHOTSK
KAMCHATKA PENINSULA
Lake Baikal
Amur River
ALPS
Sakhalin Island
BLACK SEA
CASPIAN SEA
ARAL SEA
Balqash Lake
ALTAY MOUNTAINS
GOBI
Hokkaido
MEDITERRANEAN SEA
Tigris River
Euphrates River
PERSIAN GULF
ASIA
Huang He
40°N
SEA OF JAPAN
Honshu
Nile River
RED SEA
ARABIAN PENINSULA
THAR DESERT
HIMALAYAS
Ganges River
Chang River
Shikoku
Kyushu
SAHARA
AFRICA
ARABIAN SEA
BAY OF BENGAL
Mekong
EAST CHINA SEA
Taiwan
Tropic of Cancer
20°N
PACIFIC OCEAN
Congo River
Sri Lanka
STRAIT OF MALACCA
SOUTH CHINA SEA
Philippine Islands
Lake Tanganyika
Lake Victoria
MALAY PENINSULA
Borneo
Equator 0°
Sumatra
Celebes
New Guinea
Solomon Islands
Java
INDIAN OCEAN
Madagascar
MOZAMBIQUE CHANNEL
CORAL SEA
New Hebrides
Fiji Islands
KALAHARI DESERT
GREAT SANDY DESERT
AUSTRALIA
New Caledonia
20°S
Tropic of Capricorn
GREAT VICTORIA DESERT
Darling River
GREAT DIVIDING RANGE
North Island
Cape of Good Hope
TASMAN SEA
NEW ZEALAND
Tasmania
South Island
20°E 40°E 60°E 80°E 100°E 120°E 140°E 160°E 60°S

ANTARCTICA

Europe

DENMARK STRAIT
North Cape
KJØLEN MTS
BARENTS SEA
KARA SEA
Iceland
0 250 500 750 Miles
0 250 500 750 Kilometers
Projection: Mollweide
N
W E
S
NORTH SEA
BALTIC SEA
URAL MTS
60°N
Volga River
British Isles
ATLANTIC OCEAN
50°N
BAY OF BISCAY
Danube
Rhine
A L P S
BLACK SEA
40°N
MEDITERRANEAN SEA
STRAIT OF GIBRALTAR
Dnieper R.
Crete

Figure B-4   **Map of United States Natural Resources**

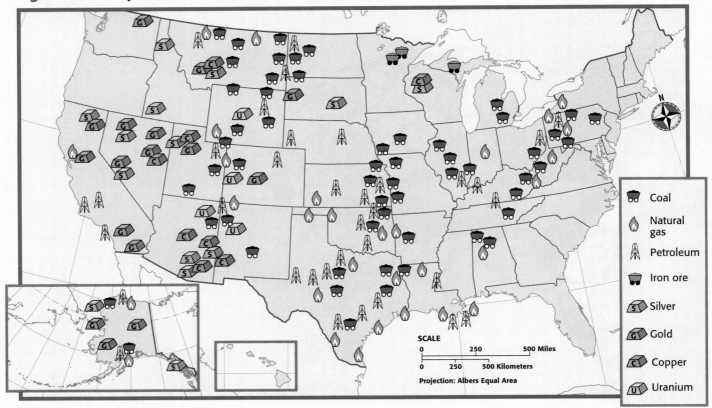

SCALE

0 — 250 — 500 Miles

0 — 250 — 500 Kilometers

Projection: Albers Equal Area

Coal

Natural gas

Petroleum

Iron ore

Silver

Gold

Copper

Uranium

Figure B-5   **Weather Map**

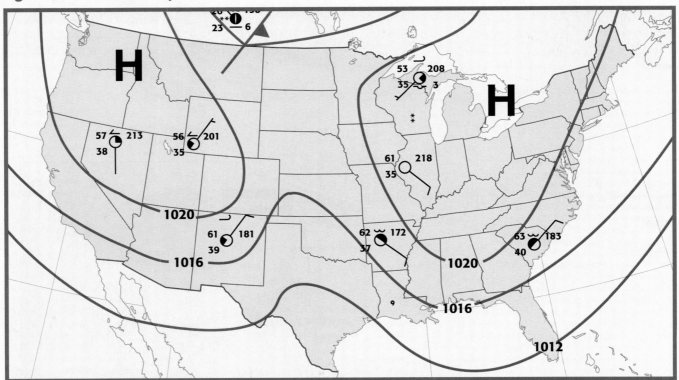

Table B-4 **International Weather Symbols**

Current Weather							
Hail	⧈	Light drizzle	,	Light rain	°	Light snow	✳
Freezing rain	∿•	Steady, light drizzle	,,	Steady, light rain	°°	Steady, light snow	✳✳
Smoke	∿	Intermittent, moderate drizzle	, ,	Intermittent, moderate rain	° °	Intermittent, moderate snow	✳✳
Tornado	)(	Steady, moderate drizzle	, , ,	Steady, moderate rain	° ° °	Steady, moderate snow	✳ ✳✳
Dust storms	⌇	Intermittent, heavy drizzle	, , ,	Intermittent, heavy rain	° ° °	Intermittent, heavy snow	✳✳✳
Fog	≡	Steady, heavy drizzle	, , , ,	Steady, heavy rain	° ° ° ° °	Steady, heavy snow	✳✳✳✳
Thunder-storm	⌐						
Lightning	⟨						
Hurricane	∮						

Sky Coverage							
No clouds	○	Two- to three-tenths covered	◔	Half covered	◑	Nine-tenths covered	◕
One-tenth Coverage	⊕	Four-tenths covered	◕	Six-tenths covered	◒	Completely overcast	●

Clouds							
Low		Stratus	—	Cumulus	⌒	Cumulonimbus calvus	⌂
		Stratocumulus	⌣	Cumulus congestus	△	Cumulonimbus with anvil	⊠
Middle		Altostratus	∠	Altocumulus	⌣	Altocumulus castellanus	M
High		Cirrus	⌡	Cirrostratus	2	Cirrocumulus	∿

Wind Speed (in km/h)					
Calm	◎	4–13	⌐	24–33	⟍
1–3	—	14–23	⌐	34–40	⟍

Figure B-6   **Sky Map for the Northern Hemisphere, Winter**

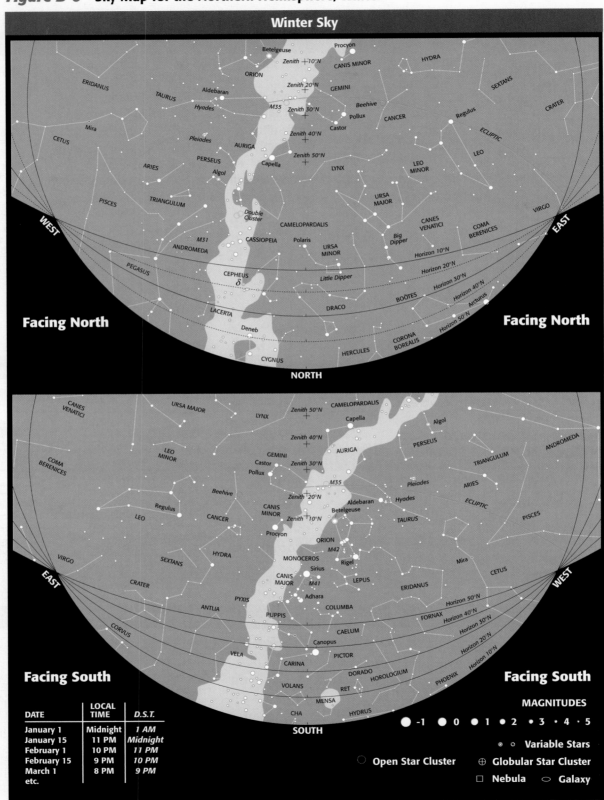

Winter Sky

Facing North · **Facing North**

Facing South · **Facing South**

DATE	LOCAL TIME	D.S.T.
January 1	Midnight	1 AM
January 15	11 PM	Midnight
February 1	10 PM	11 PM
February 15	9 PM	10 PM
March 1 etc.	8 PM	9 PM

MAGNITUDES   -1   0   1   2   3   4   5

Variable Stars
Open Star Cluster   Globular Star Cluster
Nebula   Galaxy

Conversions

1. Earth's moon has a radius of 1738 km. Write this measurement in megameters.

2. Convert each of the following values as indicated:
   a. 113 g to milligrams
   b. 700 pm to nanometers
   c. 101.1 kPa to pascals
   d. 13 MA to amperes

3. Maryland has 49 890 m of coastline. What is this length in centimeters?

4. In 1997 Andy Green, a Royal Air Force pilot, broke the land speed record in Black Rock Desert, Nevada. His car averaged 341.11 m/s. The speed of sound in Black Rock at the time that he broke the record was determined to be 0.33584 km/s. Did Andy Green break the sound barrier?

5. The mass of the planet Pluto is 15 000 000 000 000 000 000 000 kg. What is the mass of Pluto in gigagrams?

Writing Scientific Notation

6. Express each of the following values in scientific notation:
   a. 110.45 m   **c.** 132 948 kg
   b. 0.000 003 45 s   **d.** 0.034 3900 cm

7. In 1998, the population of the U.S. was about 270 000 000 people. Write the estimated population in scientific notation.

8. In 1997, 70 294 601 airplanes either took off or landed at Chicago's O'Hare airport. What is the number of arrivals and departures at O'Hare given in scientific notation?

9. The planet Saturn has a mass of 568 500 000 000 000 000 000 000 000 kg. Express the mass of Saturn in scientific notation.

10. Approximately four-and-a-half million automobiles were imported into the United States last year. Write this number in scientific notation.

Using Scientific Notation

11. Perform the following calculations involving numbers that have been written in scientific notation:
    a. $3.02 \times 10^{-3} + 4.11 \times 10^{-2}$
    b. $(6.022 \times 10^{23}) \div (1.04 \times 10^{4})$
    c. $(1.00 \times 10^{2}) \times (3.01 \times 10^{3})$
    d. $6.626 \times 10^{34} - 5.442 \times 10^{32}$

12. Mount Everest, the tallest mountain on Earth, is 8.850×10^{3} m high. The Mariana Trench is the deepest point of any ocean on Earth. It is 1.0924×10^{4} m deep. What is the vertical distance from the highest mountain on Earth to the deepest ocean trench on Earth?

13. In 1950 Americans consumed nearly 1.4048×10^{9} kg of poultry. In 1997, Americans consumed 1.2369×10^{10} kg of poultry. By what factor did America's poultry consumption increase between 1950 and 1997?

14. The following data were obtained for the number of immigrants admitted to the U.S. in major Texas cities in 1996. What is the total number of immigrants admitted in these Texas cities for that year?

City	Number of immigrants admitted
Houston	2.1387×10^{4}
Dallas	1.5915×10^{4}
El Paso	8.701×10^{3}
Ft. Worth/ Arlington	6.274×10^{3}

15. The surface area of the Pacific Ocean is 1.66×10^{14} m^2. The average depth of the Pacific Ocean is 3.9395×10^{3} m. If you could calculate the volume of the Pacific by simply multiplying the surface area by the average depth, what would the volume of the Pacific Ocean be?

Significant Figures

16. Determine the number of significant figures in each of the following values:
   a. 0.026 48 kg
   b. 47.10 g
   c. 1 625 000 J
   d. 29.02 cm

17. Solve the following addition problems, and round each answer to the correct number of significant figures:
   a. 0.00241 g + 0.0123 g
   b. 24.10 cm + 3.050 cm
   c. 0.367 L + 2.51 L + 1.6004 L

18. Solve the following multiplication or division problems, and round each answer to the correct number of significant figures:
   a. 129 g ÷ 29.20 cm^3
   b. 120 mm × 355 mm × 12.1 mm
   c. 45.4 g ÷ (0.012 cm × 0.444 cm × 0.221 cm)

19. Determine the volume of a cube with a width of 32.1 cm. Round your answer to the correct number of significant figures.

20. Solve the following subtraction problems, and round each answer to the correct number of significant figures:
   a. 1.23 cm^3 − 0.044 cm^3
   b. 89.00 kg − 0.1 kg
   c. 780 mm − 64 mm

Density

21. Sugar has a density of 1.59 g/cm^3. What mass of sugar fits into a 140 cm^3 bowl?

22. The continent of North America has an area of 2.4346×10^{13} m^2. North America has a population of 4.64×10^8 people. What is the population density of North America?

23. The average density of Earth is 5.515 g/cm^3. The average density of Earth's moon is 3.34 g/cm^3. What is the difference in mass between 10.0 cm^3 of Earth and 10.0 cm^3 of Earth's moon?

24. A rubber balloon has a mass of 0.45 g, and can hold 1.78×10^{-3} m^3 of helium. If the density of helium is 0.178 kg/m^3, what is the balloon's total mass?

25. What is the density of a 0.996 g piece of graphite with a volume of 0.44 cm^3?

Conversion Factors

26. Give the correct factor to convert between each of the following values:
   a. 4 reams of paper → 2000 sheets of paper
   b. 2.5 mol of gallium, Ga → 170 g of Ga
   c. 1.00 cm^3 of water → 0.997 g of water
   d. 1.35×10^{34} atoms of silver, Ag → 2.24×10^{10} mol of silver

27. A Calorie, as reported on nutritional labels, is equal to 4.184 kJ. A carbonated beverage contains about 150 Calories. What is the energy content in joules?

28. a. The density of gold is 19.3 g/cm^3. What is the mass of a bar of gold with dimensions of 10.0 cm × 26.0 cm × 8.0 cm?
   b. Gold is priced by the ounce. One gram is equal to 0.0353 oz. If the price of gold is $253.50 per ounce, what is the value of the bar described in part (a)?

29. How many atoms of copper are there in a piece of copper tube that contains 34.5 mol of copper, Cu? (**Hint:** There are 6.02×10^{23} atoms in one mole.)

30. In February of 1962 John Glenn orbited Earth three times in 4 hours and 55 minutes. How long did it take him to make one revolution around Earth? In June of 1983 Sally Ride became the first U.S. woman in space. Her mission lasted 146 hours, 24 minutes. If each revolution of Sally Ride's mission took the same amount of time as each revolution of John Glenn's mission, how many times did Ride orbit around Earth?

Converting Amount to Mass

31. Determine the mass in grams of each of the following:
    a. 67.9 mol of silicon, Si
    b. 1.45×10^{-4} mol of cadmium, Cd
    c. 0.045 mol of gold, Au
    d. 3.900 mol of tungsten, W

32. Fullerenes, also known as buckyballs, are a form of elemental carbon. One variety of fullerene has 60 carbon atoms in each molecule. What is the molar mass of 1 mol of this 60-carbon atom molecule? What is the mass of 5.23×10^{-2} mol of this fullerene?

33. An experiment requires 2.0 mol of cadmium, Cd, and 2.0 mol of sulfur, S. What mass of each element is required?

34. If there are 6.02×10^{27} mol of iron, Fe, in a portion of Earth's crust, what is the mass of iron present?

35. a. A certain molecule of polyester contains one-hundred thousand carbon atoms. What is the mass of carbon in 1 mol of this polyester?
    b. The same polyester molecule contains forty-thousand oxygen atoms. What is the mass of oxygen in 1 mol?

Converting Mass to Amount

36. Imagine that you find a jar full of diamonds. You measure the mass of the diamonds and find that they have a mass of 45.4 g. Determine the amount of carbon in the diamonds.

37. A tungsten, W, filament in a light bulb has a mass of 2.0 mg. Calculate the amount of tungsten in this filament.

38. One liter of sea water contains 1.05×10^{4} mg of sodium. How much sodium is in one liter of sea water?

39. Every kilogram of Earth's crust contains 282 g of silicon. How many moles of silicon are present in 2 kg of Earth's crust?

40. Chlorine rarely occurs in nature as Cl atoms. It usually occurs as gaseous Cl_2 molecules, molecules made up of two chlorine atoms joined together. What is the molar mass of gaseous Cl_2? Calculate the amount of chlorine molecules found in 4.30 g of chlorine gas.

Writing Ionic Formulas

41. Write the ionic formula for the salt made from potassium and bromine.

42. Calcium chloride is used by the canning industry to make the skin of fruit such as tomatoes more firm. What is the ionic formula for calcium chloride?

43. Write the ionic formulas formed by each of the following pairs:
    a. lithium and oxygen
    b. magnesium and oxygen
    c. sodium and chlorine
    d. magnesium and nitrogen

44. The active ingredient in most toothpastes is sodium fluoride. Write the ionic formula for this cavity-fighting compound.

45. What is the formula for the ionic compound formed from strontium and iodine?

Balancing Chemical Equations

46. Hydrogen peroxide decomposes to form water and oxygen. Balance the equation for the decomposition of hydrogen peroxide.
$$H_2O_2 \rightarrow H_2O + O_2$$

47. Iron is often produced from iron ore by treating it with carbon monoxide in a blast furnace. Balance the equation for the production of iron.
$$Fe_2O_3 + CO \rightarrow Fe + CO_2$$

48. Zinc sulfide can be used as a white pigment. Balance the following equation for synthesizing zinc sulfide.

$$Na_2S + Zn(NO_3)_2 \rightarrow ZnS + NaNO_3$$

49. Kerosene, $C_{14}H_{30}$, is often used as a heating fuel or a jet fuel. When kerosene burns in oxygen, O_2, it produces carbon dioxide, CO_2, and water, H_2O. Write the balanced chemical equation for the reaction of kerosene and oxygen.

50. When plants undergo photosynthesis, they convert carbon dioxide and water to glucose and oxygen. This process helps remove carbon dioxide from the atmosphere. Balance the following equation for the production of glucose and oxygen from carbon dioxide and water.

$$CO_2 + H_2O \rightarrow C_6H_{12}O_6 + O_2$$

Nuclear Decay

51. Potassium undergoes nuclear decay by β-emission and positron emission. Complete the following equations for the nuclear decay of potassium.

a. $^{40}_{19}K \longrightarrow\ ^{40}_{20}\underline{\quad} +\ ^{0}_{-1}e$

b. $^{40}_{19}K \longrightarrow\ ^{40}_{18}\underline{\quad} +\ ^{0}_{1}e$

52. Carbon-14 decays by β-emission. What element is formed when carbon loses a β-particle?

53. Aluminum can undergo decay by positron emission. Complete the following equation for the decay of aluminum into magnesium.

$$^{26}_{13}Al \longrightarrow\ ^{26}_{12}Mg + \underline{\quad}e$$

54. Uranium-238 decays by α-emission. What element is formed when a uranium atom loses an α-particle?

55. Complete the following equation for the decay of radon-222.

$$^{222}_{86}Rn \longrightarrow\ ^{218}_{84}\underline{\quad} +\ ^{4}_{2}He$$

Half-life

56. The half-life of thorium-232, $^{232}_{90}Th$, is 1.4×10^{10} years. How much of a 50.0 g sample of thorium-232 will remain as thorium after 4.2×10^{10} years?

57. Radium, used in radiation treatment for cancer, has a half-life of 1.60×10^3 years. If you begin with a 0.25 g sample, what mass of radium will remain after 8.00×10^3 years?

58. The half-life of iodine-131 is 8.04 days. How long will it take for the mass of iodine present to drop to 1/16?

59. What is the half-life of an element if 1/8 of a sample remains after 12 years?

60. The half-life of cobalt-60 is 10.47 minutes. What fraction of a sample will remain after 52.35 minutes?

Velocity

61. Amy Van Dyken broke the world record for a 50.0 m swim using the butterfly stroke in 1996. She swam 50.0 m in 26.55 seconds. What was her average velocity assuming that she swam the 50.0 m in a perfectly straight line?

62. If Amy Van Dyken swam her record-breaking 50 m by swimming to one end of the pool, then turning around and swimming back to her starting position, what would her average velocity be?

63. When Andy Green broke the land speed record, his vehicle was traveling across a flat portion of the desert with a forward velocity of 341.11 m/s. How long would it take him at that velocity to travel 4.500 km?

64. If a car moves along a perfectly straight road at 24 m/s, how far will the car go in 35 minutes?

65. If you travel southeast from one city to another city that is 314 km away, and the trip takes you 4.00 hours, what is your average velocity?

Momentum

66. a. A 703 kg car is traveling with a forward velocity of 20.1 m/s. What is the momentum of the car?

   b. If a 315 kg trailer is attached to the car, what is the new combined momentum?

67. You are traveling west on your bicycle at 4.2 m/s, and you and your bike have a combined mass of 75 kg. What is the momentum of you and your bicycle?

68. A runner, who has a mass of 52 kg, has a momentum of 218 kg•m/s along a trail. What is the runner's velocity?

69. A commercial airplane travels north at a speed of 234 m/s. The plane seats 253 people. If the average person on the plane has a mass of 68 kg, what is the momentum of the passengers on the plane?

70. A bowling ball has a mass of 5.44 kg. It is moving down the lane at 2.1 m/s when it strikes the pins. What is the momentum with which the ball hits the pins?

Acceleration

71. While driving at an average velocity of 15.6 m/s down the road, a driver slams on the brakes to avoid hitting a squirrel. The car stops completely in 4.2 s. What is the average acceleration of the car?

72. A sports car is advertised as being able to go from 0 to 60 mi/h straight ahead in 6.00 s. If 60 mi/h is equal to 27 m/s, what is the sports car's average acceleration?

73. If a bicycle has an average acceleration of -0.44 m/s^2, and its initial forward velocity is 8.2 m/s, how long will it take the cyclist to bring the bicycle to a complete stop?

74. An airliner has an airborne velocity of 232 m/s toward Chicago. What is the plane's average acceleration if it takes the plane 15 minutes to reach its air-borne velocity?

75. A school bus can accelerate from a complete stop at 1.3 m/s^2. How long will it take the bus to reach a speed of 12.1 m/s?

Newton's Second Law

76. A peach falls from a tree with an acceleration of 9.8 m/s^2 downward. The peach has a mass of 7.4 g. With what force does the peach strike the ground?

77. A group of people push a car from a resting position forward with a force of 1.99×10^3 N. The car and its driver have a mass of 831 kg. What is the acceleration of the car?

78. If the space shuttle accelerates upward at 35 m/s^2, what force will a 59 kg astronaut experience?

79. A soccer ball is kicked with a force of 15.2 N. The soccer ball has a mass of 2.45 kg. What is the ball's acceleration?

80. A person steps off a diving board and falls into a pool with an acceleration of 9.8 m/s^2, which causes the person to hit the water with a force of 637 N. What is the mass of the person?

Work

81. A car breaks down 2.1 m from the shoulder of the road. 1.99×10^3 N of force is used to push the car off the road. How much work has been done on the car?

82. Pulling a boat forward into a docking slip requires 157 J of work. The boat must be pulled a total distance of 5.3 m. What is the force with which the boat is pulled?

83. A box with a mass of 3.2 kg is pushed 0.667 m across a floor with an acceleration of 3.2 m/s^2. How much work is done on the box?

84. You need to pick up a book off the floor and place it on a table top that is 0.78 m above the ground. You expend 1.56 J of energy to lift the book. The book has an acceleration of 1.54 m/s^2. What is the book's mass?

85. A weight lifter raises a 227 kg weight above his head. The weight reaches a height of 2.4 m. The lifter expends 686 J of energy lifting the weight. What is the acceleration of the weight?

Power

86. A weight lifter does 686 J of work on a weight that he lifts in 3.1 seconds. What is the power with which he lifts the weight?

87. How much energy is wasted by a 60 W bulb if the bulb is left on over an 8 hour night?

88. A nuclear reactor is designed with a capacity of 1.02×10^8 kW. How much energy, in megajoules, should the reactor be able to produce in a day?

89. An electric mixer uses 350 W. If 8.75×10^3 J of work are done by the mixer, how long has the mixer run?

90. A team of three horses are hitched to a wagon. Each horse pulls with a force of 157 N. The cart travels a distance of 2.3 km in 20 minutes. Calculate the power delivered by the horses.

Mechanical Advantage

91. A roofer needs to get a stack of shingles onto a roof. Pulling the shingles up manually uses 1549 N of force. The roofer decides that it would be easier to use a system of pulleys to raise the shingles. Using the pulleys, 446 N are required to lift the shingles. What is the mechanical advantage of the system of pulleys?

92. A dam used to make hydroelectric power opens and closes its gates with a lever. The gate weighs 660 N. The lever has a mechanical advantage of 6. Calculate the input force on the lever needed to move the gate.

93. A crane uses a system of pulleys with a mechanical advantage of 27. An input force of 8650 N is used by the crane to lift a pile of steel girders. What is the weight of the girders?

94. A door that is 92 cm wide has a door knob that is 87 cm from the door hinge. What is the mechanical advantage of the door? Would the mechanical advantage be greater or less if the knob were moved 10 cm closer to the hinge?

95. A student pedals a bicycle to school. The gear on the bicycle has a radius of 8.0 cm. The student travels 1.6 km to school. During the journey, the pedals make 750 revolutions. What is the mechanical advantage of the bicycle?

Gravitational Potential Energy

96. A pear is hanging from a pear tree. The pear is 3.5 m above the ground and has a mass of 0.14 kg. What is the pear's gravitational potential energy?

97. A person in an airplane has a mass of 74 kg and has 6.6 MJ of gravitational potential energy. What is the altitude of the plane?

98. A high jumper jumps 2.04 m. If the jumper has a mass of 67 kg, what is his gravitational potential energy at the highest point in the jump?

99. A cat sits on the top of a fence that is 2.0 m high. The cat has a gravitational potential energy of 88.9 J. What is the mass of the cat?

100. A frog with a mass of 0.23 kg hops up in the air. At the highest point in the hop, the frog has a gravitational potential energy of 0.744 J. How high can it hop?

Kinetic Energy

101. A sprinter runs at a forward velocity of 10.9 m/s. If the sprinter has a mass of 72.5 kg, what is the sprinter's kinetic energy?

102. A car having a mass of 654 kg has a kinetic energy of 73.4 kJ. What is the car's speed?

103. A tennis ball with a mass of 51 g has a velocity of 9.7 m/s upward. What is the kinetic energy of the tennis ball?

104. A rock is rolling down a hill with a speed of 4.67 m/s. It has a kinetic energy of 18.9 kJ. What is the mass of the rock?

105. Calculate the kinetic energy of an airliner with a mass of 7.6×10^4 kg that is flying at a speed of 524 km/h.

Efficiency

106. If a cyclist has 26.7% efficiency, how much energy is lost if 40.5 kJ of energy are put in by the cyclist?

107. What is the efficiency of a machine if 55.3 J of work are done on the machine, but only 14.3 J of work are done by the machine?

108. A microwave oven uses 89 kJ of energy in one minute. The microwave has an output of 54 kJ per minute. What is the efficiency of the microwave?

109. A coal-burning power plant has an efficiency of 42%. If 4.99 MJ of energy are used by the power plant, how much useful energy is generated by the power plant?

110. A swimmer does 45 kJ of work while swimming. If the swimmer is wasting 42 kJ of energy while swimming, what is the efficiency for the activity?

Temperature Conversions

111. A normal body temperature is 98.6°F. What is this temperature in degrees Celsius?

112. Convert the following temperatures to the Kelvin scale.
  a. 214°F   **c.** 27°C
  b. 100.°C   **d.** 32°F

113. What are the freezing point and boiling point of water in the Celsius, Fahrenheit, and Kelvin scales?

114. What is absolute zero in the Celsius scale?

115. If it is 315 K outside, is it hot or cold?

Specific Heat

Use the values in **Table B-3** for specific heat.

116. How much energy is required to raise the temperature of 5.0 g of silver from 298 K to 334 K?

117. A burner transfers 45 J of energy to a small beaker with 5.3 g of water. If the water was initially 27°C, what is the final temperature of the water?

118. A piece of aluminum foil is left on a burner until the temperature of the foil has risen from 27°C to 98°C. The foil absorbs 344 J of energy from the burner. What is the mass of the foil?

119. If a piece of graphite and a diamond both have the same mass, and are placed on the same burner, which will become hot faster? Why?

120. The iron ore hematite is heated until its temperature has risen by 153°C. If the piece of hematite has a mass of 34 kg, how much energy was required to raise the temperature this much?

Wave Speed

121. The speed of light in a vacuum is 3.0×10^8 m/s. A red laser beam has a wavelength of 698 nm. How long, in picoseconds, will it take for one wavelength of the laser light to pass by a fixed point?

122. Two people are standing on opposite ends of a field. The field is 92 m long. One person speaks. It takes 270 ms for the person across the field to hear the sound. What is the speed of sound in the field?

123. A water wave has a speed of 1.3 m/s. A person sitting on a pier observes that it takes 1.2 s for a full wavelength to pass the edge of the pier. What is the wavelength of the water wave?

124. Jupiter is 7.78×10^8 km from the sun. How long does it take the sun's light to reach Jupiter?

125. A green laser has a wavelength of 508 nm. What is the frequency of this laser light?

Resistance

126. What is the resistance of a wire that has a current of 1.4 A in it when it is connected to a 6.0 V battery?

127. An electric space heater is plugged into a 120 V outlet. A current of 12.0 A is in the coils in the space heater. What is the resistance of the coils?

128. A graphing calculator needs 7.78×10^{-3} A to function. The resistance in the calculator is 1150 Ω. What is the voltage required to operate the calculator?

129. A steam iron has a current of 9.17 A when plugged into a 120 V outlet. What is the resistance in the steam iron?

130. An electric clothes dryer requires a potential difference of 240 V. The power cord that runs between the electrical outlet and the dryer supports a current of 30 A. What is the resistance in this power cord?

Electric Power

131. A flashlight has a potential difference of 3.0 V. The bulb has a current of 0.50 A. What is the electric power used by the flashlight?

132. What is the current in a 60 W light bulb when it is plugged into a 120 V outlet?

133. A student takes her hair dryer to Europe. In the United States, her hair dryer uses 1200 W of power when connected to a 120 V outlet. In Europe, the outlet has a potential difference of 240 V. When she uses her hair dryer in Europe, she notices that it gets very hot, and starts to smell as though it is burning. Determine the current in the hair dryer in the United States. Then calculate the resistance in the hair dryer. Calculate the current and the power in the hair dryer in Europe to explain why the hair dryer heats up when plugged into the European outlet.

134. A portable stereo requires a 12 V battery. It uses 43 W of power. Calculate the current in the stereo.

135. A microwave oven has a current of 12.3 A when operated using a 120 V power source. How much power does the microwave consume?

Selected Answers to Problems

These answers can help you determine whether or not you're on the right track as you work through the practice problems, the section reviews, and the chapter reviews.

Chapter 1
Practice, page 17
Conversions

2. $3.5 \text{ s} \times \dfrac{1000 \text{ ms}}{1 \text{ s}} = 3500 \text{ ms}$

4. $2.5 \times 10^{-3} \text{ kg}$

6. 2.8 mol

8. 3000 ng

Practice, page 23
Writing Scientific Notation

2. **a.** 4500 g
   b. 0.006 05 m
   c. 3115 000 km
   d. 0.000 000 0199 cm

Practice, page 24
Using Scientific Notation

2. **a.** $4.8 \times 10^2 \text{ L/s}$
   b. 6.9 g/cm^3
   c. $5.5 \times 10^5 \text{ cm}^2$
   d. 0.83 cm^3

Practice, page 25
Significant Figures

2. $3.02 \text{ cm} \times 6.3 \text{ cm} \times 8.225 \text{ cm} = 156.\cancel{488\ 85} \text{ cm}^3 = 160 \text{ cm}^3$

4. $3.244 \text{ m} \div 1.4 \text{ s} = 2.3\cancel{17\ 142\ 857} \text{ m/s} = 2.3 \text{ m/s}$

Section 1.3 Review, page 26
Math Skills

6. **a.** $3.16 \times 10^3 \text{ m} \times 2.91 \times 10^4 \text{ m} = 9.20 \times 10^7 \text{ m}^2$
   b. $9.66 \times 10^{-5} \text{ cm}^2$
   c. 6.70 g/cm^3

Chapter 1 Review, page 28
Building Math Skills

16. **a.** 2.6×10^{14}
    b. 6.42×10^{-7}
    c. $3.4 \times 10^8 \text{ cm}^2$
    d. $3.3 \times 10^{-3} \text{ kg/cm}^3$

Chapter 2
Practice, page 56
Density

2. $D = \dfrac{m}{V} = \dfrac{163 \text{ g}}{50.0 \text{ cm}^3} = 3.26 \text{ g/cm}^3$

4. $D = 11 \text{ g/cm}^3$
   The metal is probably lead.

6. $m = 500 \text{ g}$

8. $V = 36 \text{ cm}^3$

Chapter 2 Review, page 62
Building Math Skills

16. $D = \dfrac{m}{V} = \dfrac{67.5 \text{ g}}{15 \text{ cm}^3} = 4.5 \text{ g/cm}^3$

18. $D = 0.77 \text{ g/cm}^3$
    The substance is less dense than water (1.00 g/cm^3), so it will float.

20. $m = 1.5 \times 10^5 \text{ g}$

Chapter 3
Practice, page 98
Conversion Factors

2. $50 \text{ eggs} \times \dfrac{1 \text{ dozen}}{12 \text{ eggs}} = 4.2 \text{ dozen eggs}$
   You must buy 5 dozen eggs.
   $5 \text{ dozen} \times \dfrac{12 \text{ eggs}}{1 \text{ dozen}} = 60 \text{ eggs}$
   $60 \text{ eggs} - 50 \text{ eggs} = 10 \text{ eggs left over}$

Practice, page 99
Converting Amount to Mass

2. $1.80 \text{ mol Ca} \times \dfrac{40.08 \text{ g Ca}}{1 \text{ mol Ca}} = 72.1 \text{ g Ca}$

4. 203 g Cu

Section 3.4 Review, page 100
Math Skills

6. $0.48 \text{ mol Pt} \times \dfrac{195.08 \text{ g Pt}}{1 \text{ mol Pt}} = 94 \text{ g Pt}$

8. 0.39 mol Si

Chapter 3 Review, page 102
Building Math Skills

18. $0.54 \text{ g He} \times \dfrac{1 \text{ mol He}}{4.00 \text{ g He}} = 0.14 \text{ mol He}$

20. 407 g Al

Chapter 4
Practice, page 125
Writing Ionic Formulas

2. $BeCl_2$

4. $Co(OH)_3$

Section 4.3 Review, page 128
Math Skills

6. Cd^{2+}
   Because each CN^- has a charge of –1, the other ion must be Cd^{2+} for a neutral compound to form.

Chapter 4 Review, page 138
Building Math Skills

18. **a.** $Sr(NO_3)_2$
    b. NaCN
    c. $Cr(OH)_3$

Chapter 5
Practice, page 166
Balancing Chemical Equations
2. $Na_2S + 2AgNO_3 \longrightarrow 2NaNO_3 + Ag_2S$
4. $H_2S + 2O_2 \longrightarrow H_2SO_4$

Section 5.3 Review, page 168
2. a. $KOH + HCl \longrightarrow KCl + H_2O$
b. $Pb(NO_3)_2 + 2KI \longrightarrow 2KNO_3 + PbI_2$

Chapter 5 Review, page 178
Building Math Skills
16. $2HgO \longrightarrow 2Hg + O_2$
18. $\dfrac{1 \text{ mol } C_{12}H_{22}O_{11}}{12 \text{ mol } O_2}, \dfrac{1 \text{ mol } C_{12}H_{22}O_{11}}{12 \text{ mol } CO_2}, \dfrac{1 \text{ mol } C_{12}H_{22}O_{11}}{11 \text{ mol } H_2O},$
$\dfrac{12 \text{ mol } O_2}{12 \text{ mol } CO_2}, \dfrac{12 \text{ mol } O_2}{11 \text{ mol } H_2O}, \dfrac{12 \text{ mol } CO_2}{11 \text{ mol } H_2O}$
20. $Zn + 2HCl \longrightarrow ZnCl_2 + H_2$

Chapter 6
Practice, page 191
Nuclear Decay
2. $^{225}_{89}Ac \longrightarrow ^{221}_{87}Fr + ^{4}_{2}He$, alpha decay
4. $^{212}_{83}Bi \longrightarrow ^{208}_{81}Tl + ^{4}_{2}He$, alpha decay

Practice, page 194
Half-Life
2. $1 - \dfrac{15}{16} = \dfrac{1}{16} = \dfrac{1}{2} \times \dfrac{1}{2} \times \dfrac{1}{2} \times \dfrac{1}{2}$; four half-lives
$4 \times 3.82 \text{ days} = 15.3 \text{ days}$
4. 29.1 years

Section 6.1 Review, page 194
Math Skills
4. $^{212}_{86}Rn \longrightarrow ^{208}_{84}Po + ^{4}_{2}He$
6. $1 - \dfrac{3}{4} = \dfrac{1}{4} = \dfrac{1}{2} \times \dfrac{1}{2}$; two half-lives
$2 \times 32.2 \text{ min} = 64.4 \text{ min}$
8. 2.29×10^4 years

Chapter 6 Review, page 208
Building Math Skills
18. a. $^{212}_{83}Bi \longrightarrow ^{208}_{81}Tl + ^{4}_{2}He$
$^{208}_{81}Tl \longrightarrow ^{208}_{82}Pb + ^{0}_{-1}e$
b. $^{212}_{83}Bi \longrightarrow ^{212}_{84}Po + ^{0}_{-1}e$
$^{212}_{84}Po \longrightarrow ^{208}_{82}Pb + ^{4}_{2}He$
20. $^{149}_{62}Sm \longrightarrow ^{145}_{60}Nd + ^{4}_{2}He$
22. $15.2 \text{ days} \times \dfrac{1 \text{ half-life}}{3.82 \text{ days}} = 3.98$ half-lives
$\dfrac{1}{2} \times \dfrac{1}{2} \times \dfrac{1}{2} \times \dfrac{1}{2} = \dfrac{1}{16}$
$\dfrac{1}{16} \times 4.38 \ \mu g = 0.274 \ \mu g$

Chapter 7
Practice, page 221
Velocity
2. $v = \dfrac{d}{t} = \dfrac{38 \text{ m}}{1.7 \text{ s}} = 22$ m/s to first base
4. $t = \dfrac{d}{v} = \dfrac{2.6 \text{ km} \times \left(\dfrac{1000 \text{ m}}{1 \text{ km}}\right)}{28 \text{ m/s}} = 93$ s

Practice, page 223
Momentum
1. a. $p = mv = (75 \text{ kg})(16 \text{ m/s}) = 1200 \text{ kg} \bullet \text{m/s}$ forward
b. $p = 2.19 \times 10^3 \text{ kg} \bullet \text{m/s}$ north
c. $p = 360 \text{ kg} \bullet \text{m/s}$ eastward

Section 7.1 Review, page 224
Math Skills
8. $v = \dfrac{d}{t} = \dfrac{149 \text{ m}}{16.8 \text{ s}} = 8.87$ m/s north

Practice, page 226
Acceleration
2. $a = \dfrac{\Delta v}{t} = \dfrac{0.80 \text{ m/s} - 0.50 \text{ m/s}}{4.0 \text{ s}} = 0.075 \text{ m/s}^2$ toward shore
4. $t = 0.85$ s

Section 7.2 Review, page 233
Math Skills
8. $\Delta v = at = (4.0 \text{ m/s}^2)(3.0 \text{ s}) = 12$ m/s
The cyclist at a constant velocity of 15 m/s is faster after 3.0 s.

Practice, page 236
Newton's Second Law
2. $m = \dfrac{F}{a} = \dfrac{1.4 \text{ N}}{9.8 \text{ m/s}^2} = 0.14$ kg

Section 7.3 Review, page 240
Math Skills
6. $w = mg = (5.0 \text{ kg})(9.8 \text{ m/s}^2) = 49$ N

Chapter 7 Review, page 242
Building Math Skills
16. $v = \dfrac{d}{t} = \dfrac{72 \text{ m}}{45 \text{ s}} = 1.6$ m/s eastward
18. $p = mv = (85 \text{ kg})(2.65 \text{ m/s}) = 230 \text{ kg} \bullet \text{m/s}$ north
20. $a = \dfrac{\Delta v}{t} = \dfrac{5.5 \text{ m/s} - 14.0 \text{ m/s}}{6.0 \text{ s}} = -1.4 \text{ m/s}^2 \text{ east} = 1.4 \text{ m/s}^2$ west
22. $F = ma = (5.5 \text{ kg})(4.2 \text{ m/s}^2) = 23$ N right
24. $a = \dfrac{F}{m} = \dfrac{3.7 \text{ N}}{925 \text{ kg}} = 4.0 \times 10^{-3} \text{ m/s}^2$ away from the stop sign

Chapter 8
Practice, page 251
Work
2. $W = F \times d = (1 \text{ N})(1 \text{ m}) = 1$ J
4. $W = 30 \ (F \times d) = 30(165 \text{ N})(0.800 \text{ m}) = 3.96 \times 10^3$ J

Practice, page 253
Power

2. $P = \dfrac{W}{t} = \dfrac{9 \times 10^8 \text{ J}}{1 \text{ s}} = 9 \times 10^8 \text{ W} = 900 \text{ MW}$

4. a. $P = \dfrac{W}{t} = \dfrac{F \times d}{t} = \dfrac{(60.0 \text{ N}) \times (12.0 \text{ m})}{20.0 \text{ s}} = 36.0 \text{ W}$

 b. $P = \dfrac{W}{t} = \dfrac{F \times d}{t} = \dfrac{(300 \text{ N}) \times (1 \text{ m})}{3 \text{ s}} = 100 \text{ W}$

Practice, page 256
Mechanical Advantage

2. $mechanical\ advantage = \dfrac{output\ force}{input\ force} = \dfrac{9900 \text{ N}}{150 \text{ N}} = 66$

4. $output\ force = (mechanical\ advantage)\,(input\ force) =$
$(15 \text{ N})(5.2) = 78 \text{ N}$

Section 8.1 Review, page 256
Math Skills

6. $mechanical\ advantage = \dfrac{output\ force}{input\ force} = \dfrac{132 \text{ N}}{55.0 \text{ N}} = 2.40$

8. $P = \dfrac{W}{t} = \dfrac{1.0 \times 10^6 \text{ J}}{50.0 \text{ s}} = 2.0 \times 10^4 \text{ W}$

$2.0 \times 10^4 \text{ W} \times \dfrac{1 \text{ hp}}{746 \text{ W}} = 27 \text{ hp}$

Practice, page 265
Gravitational Potential Energy

2. $PE = mgh = (6.3 \times 10^{12} \text{ N})(220 \text{ m}) = 1.4 \times 10^{15} \text{ J}$
4. $m = 58 \text{ kg}$

Practice, page 267
Kinetic Energy

2. $v = \sqrt{\dfrac{2KE}{m}} = \sqrt{\dfrac{2(190 \text{ J})}{35 \text{ kg}}} = 3.3 \text{ m/s}$

Section 8.3 Review, page 271
Math Skills

8. $KE = \dfrac{1}{2}mv^2 = \dfrac{1}{2}(0.02 \text{ kg})(300 \text{ m/s})^2 = 900 \text{ J}$

Practice, page 279
Efficiency

2. $work\ input = \dfrac{useful\ work\ output}{efficiency} = \dfrac{1200 \text{ J}}{0.25} = 4800 \text{ J}$

Section 8.4 Review, page 280
Math Skills

8. a. $useful\ work\ output = work\ input \times efficiency =$
$(6500 \text{ J})(0.12) = 780 \text{ J}$

 b. $P = \dfrac{W}{t} = \dfrac{780 \text{ J}}{1 \text{ s}} = 780 \text{ W}$

Chapter 8 Review, page 282
Building Math Skills

16. a. $W = F \times d = (425 \text{ N})(2.0 \text{ m}) = 850 \text{ J}$

 b. $P = \dfrac{W}{t} = \dfrac{850 \text{ J}}{5.0 \text{ s}} = 170 \text{ W}$

 c. $mechanical\ advantage = \dfrac{output\ force}{input\ force} = \dfrac{1700 \text{ N}}{425 \text{ N}} = 4.0$

18. a. $PE = mgh = (2.0 \text{ kg})(9.8 \text{ m/s}^2)(12 \text{ m}) = 2.4 \times 10^2 \text{ J}$
 b. $KE\ at\ end = PE\ at\ beginning = 2.4 \times 10^2 \text{ J}$

 c. $v = \sqrt{\dfrac{2KE}{m}} = \sqrt{\dfrac{2(2.4 \times 10^2 \text{ J})}{2.0 \text{ kg}}} = 15 \text{ m/s}$

 d. The kinetic energy is changed into sound, heat, and light energy after the rock hits the beach.

Chapter 9
Practice, page 294
Temperature Scale Conversion

2. $T_F = \dfrac{9}{5}t + 32.0 = \dfrac{9}{5}(21°C) + 32.0 = 70°F$

$T = t + 273 = 21°C + 273 = 294 \text{ K}$
$t = T - 273 = 388 \text{ K} - 273 = 115°C$

$T_F = \dfrac{9}{5}t + 32.0 = \dfrac{9}{5}(115°C) + 32.0 = 239°F$

$T_F = \dfrac{9}{5}t + 32.0 = \dfrac{9}{5}(-200.°C) + 32.0 = -328°F$

$T = t + 273 = -200.0°C + 273 = 73 \text{ K}$

$t = \dfrac{5}{9}(T_F - 32.0) = \dfrac{5}{9}(110.°F - 32.0) = 43°C$

$T = t + 273 = 43°C + 273 = 316 \text{ K}$

4. c.

Section 9.1 Review, page 296
Math Skills

6. $T_F = \dfrac{9}{5}t + 32.0 = \dfrac{9}{5}(20.°C) + 32.0 = 68°F$

$T = t + 273 = 20°C + 273 = 293 \text{ K}$

Practice, page 304
Specific Heat

2. $energy = mc\Delta t = (0.225 \text{ kg})(4186 \text{ J/kg} \bullet \text{K})(35°C - 5°C) =$
$2.8 \times 10^4 \text{ J}$

4. $t = 25°C + \Delta t = 145°C$
6. $c = 480 \text{ J/kg} \bullet \text{K}$

Section 9.2 Review, page 304
Math Skills

6. $c = \dfrac{energy}{m\Delta t} = \dfrac{3250 \text{ J}}{(1.32 \text{ kg})(292 \text{ K} - 273 \text{ K})} = 130 \text{ J/kg} \bullet \text{K}$
The metal is likely to be lead.

Chapter 9 Review, page 314
Building Math Skills

20. $t = T - 273 = 3 \text{ K} - 273 = -270°C$

$T_F = \dfrac{9}{5}t + 32.0 = \dfrac{9}{5}(-270°C) + 32.0 = -454°F$

22. $energy = mc\Delta t = (0.550 \text{ kg})(385 \text{ J/kg} \bullet \text{K})(45°C - 24°C) =$
4450 J

Chapter 10
Practice, page 336
Wave Speed

2. $v = f \times \lambda = (9.45 \times 10^7 \text{ Hz})(3.17 \text{ m}) = 3.00 \times 10^8 \text{ m/s}$
4. $\lambda = 1.5 \text{ m}$

Section 10.2 Review, page 339
Math Skills

8. $\lambda = 0.77 \text{ m}$

APPENDIX D Selected Answers

Chapter 10 Review, page 348
Building Math Skills

18. **a.** 9 cm

b. 20 cm

c. $v = f \times \lambda = (25.0 \text{ Hz})(20 \text{ cm})\left(\dfrac{1 \text{ m}}{100 \text{ cm}}\right) = 5 \text{ m/s}$

d. $T = \dfrac{1}{f} = \dfrac{1}{25.0 \text{ Hz}} = 0.04 \text{ s}$

20. $v = 24 \text{ m/s}$

22. f range $= 1 \times 10^9$ Hz to 3×10^{11} Hz

Chapter 11
Practice, page 369
Resistance

2. $R = \dfrac{V}{I} = \dfrac{120 \text{ V}}{0.50 \text{ A}} = 240 \text{ }\Omega$

4. $I = 0.43$ A

Section 11.2 Review, page 371
Math Skills

8. $I = 0.5$ A

Practice, page 377
Electric Power

2. $P = IV = (2.6 \times 10^{-3} \text{ A})(6.0 \text{ V}) = 1.6 \times 10^{-2}$ W

4. $I = 0.62$ A

Section 11.3 Review, page 378
Math Skills

8. $I = 0.3$ A for the 40 watt bulb
$I = 0.62$ A for the 75 watt bulb

Chapter 11 Review, page 388
Building Math Skills

14. $R = \dfrac{V}{I} = \dfrac{12 \text{ V}}{0.30 \text{ A}} = 4.0 \times 10^1 \text{ }\Omega$

16. $I = 0.12$ A

18. $I = \dfrac{P}{V} = \dfrac{2.4 \text{ W}}{1.5 \text{ V}} = 1.6$ A

Chapters 12–21
none

Appendix C Problem Bank, pages 743–750
Conversions

2. **a.** $113 \text{ g} \times \dfrac{1000 \text{ mg}}{1 \text{ g}} = 113\,000$ mg

b. $700 \text{ pm} \times \dfrac{10^{-12} \text{ m}}{1 \text{ pm}} \times \dfrac{1 \text{ nm}}{10^{-9} \text{ m}} = 0.7$ nm

c. $101.1 \text{ kPa} \times \dfrac{1000 \text{ Pa}}{1 \text{ kPa}} = 101\,100$ Pa

d. $13 \text{ MA} \times \dfrac{10^6 \text{ A}}{1 \text{ MA}} = 13\,000\,000$ A

4. 341.11 m/s>335.84 m/s
Yes, he did break the sound barrier.

Writing Scientific Notation

6. **a.** 1.1045×10^2 m

b. 3.45×10^{-6} s

c. $1.329\,48 \times 10^5$ kg

d. $3.439\,00 \times 10^{-2}$ cm

8. $7.029\,4601 \times 10^7$ airplanes

10. 4.5×10^6 automobiles

Using Scientific Notation

12. $(8.850 \times 10^3 \text{ m}) + (1.0924 \times 10^4 \text{ m}) =$
$(0.8850 \times 10^4 \text{ m}) + (1.0924 \times 10^4 \text{ m}) = 1.9774 \times 10^4$ m

14. 5.2277×10^4 immigrants

Significant Figures

16. **a.** 4

b. 4

c. 4

d. 4

18. **a.** $\dfrac{129 \text{ g}}{29.20 \text{ cm}^3} = 4.417\,808\,219 \text{ g/cm}^3 = 4.42 \text{ g/cm}^3$

b. $120 \text{ mm} \times 355 \text{ mm} \times 12.1 \text{ mm} =$
$5.1546 \times 10^5 \text{ mm}^3 = 5.2 \times 10^5 \text{ mm}^3$

c. $\dfrac{45.4 \text{ g}}{0.012 \text{ cm} \times 0.444 \text{ cm} \times 0.221 \text{ cm}} =$
$3.855\,665\,62 \times 10^4 \text{ g/cm}^3 = 3.9 \times 10^4 \text{ g/cm}^3$

20. **a.** $1.23 \text{ cm}^3 - 0.044 \text{ cm}^3 = 1.19 \text{ cm}^3$

b. $89.00 \text{ kg} - 0.1 \text{ kg} = 88.9$ kg

c. $780 \text{ mm} - 64 \text{ mm} = 716$ mm

Density

22. $density = \dfrac{people}{area} = \dfrac{4.64 \times 10^8 \text{ people}}{2.4346 \times 10^{13} \text{ m}^2} = 1.91 \times 10^{-5} \text{ people/m}^2$

24. $m = 0.45 \text{ g} + (1.78 \times 10^{-3} \text{ m}^3)(0.178 \text{ kg/m}^3) =$
7.7×10^{-4} kg *or* 0.77 g

Conversion Factors

26. **a.** $\dfrac{2000 \text{ sheets}}{4 \text{ reams}}$

b. $\dfrac{170 \text{ g Ga}}{2.5 \text{ mol Ga}}$

c. $\dfrac{0.997 \text{ g H}_2\text{O}}{1.00 \text{ cm}^3 \text{ H}_2\text{O}}$

d. $\dfrac{2.24 \times 10^{10} \text{ mol Ag}}{1.35 \times 10^{34} \text{ atoms Ag}}$

28. **a.** $19.3 \text{ g/cm}^3 \times (10.0 \text{ cm} \times 26.0 \text{ cm} \times 8.0 \text{ cm}) = 4.0 \times 10^4$ g

b. $(4.0 \times 10^4 \text{ g}) \times \dfrac{0.0353 \text{ oz}}{1 \text{ g}} \times \dfrac{\$253.50}{1 \text{ oz}} = \$3.6 \times 10^5$

30. 98.3 min/rev for John Glenn

$\dfrac{\left(146 \text{ h} \times \dfrac{60 \text{ min}}{1 \text{ h}}\right) + 24 \text{ min}}{98.3 \text{ min/rev}} = 89.4$ rev for Sally Ride

Converting Amount to Mass

32. $60 \times \dfrac{12.01 \text{ g C}}{1 \text{ mol C}} = 720.6 \text{ g/mol C}_{60}$

$5.23 \times 10^{-2} \text{ mol C}_{60} \times \dfrac{720.6 \text{ g C}_{60}}{1 \text{ mol C}_{60}} = 37.7 \text{ g C}_{60}$

34. 3.36×10^{29} g Fe

Converting Mass to Amount

36. $45.4 \text{ g C} \times \dfrac{1 \text{ mol C}}{12.01 \text{ g C}} = 3.78 \text{ mol C}$

38. 0.457 mol Na

40. 70.90 g/mol Cl_2
6.06×10^{-2} mol Cl_2

Writing Ionic Formulas

42. $CaCl_2$

44. NaF

Balancing Chemical Equations

46. $2H_2O_2 \longrightarrow 2H_2O + O_2$

48. $Na_2S + Zn(NO_3)_2 \longrightarrow ZnS + 2NaNO_3$

50. $6CO_2 + 6H_2O \longrightarrow C_6H_{12}O_6 + 6O_2$

Nuclear Decay

52. $^{14}_{6}C \longrightarrow ^{14}_{7}N + ^{0}_{-1}e$; nitrogen

54. $^{238}_{92}U \longrightarrow ^{234}_{90}Th + ^{4}_{2}He$; thorium

Half-life

56. $\dfrac{4.2 \times 10^{10} \text{ y}}{1.4 \times 10^{10} \text{ y}} = 3$ half-lives

$50.0 \text{ g} \times \dfrac{1}{2} \times \dfrac{1}{2} \times \dfrac{1}{2} = 6.25 \text{ g Th}$

58. 32.2 days

60. 1/32

Velocity

62. $v = 0$ m/s (velocity is change in position over time, but at the end there was no change in position)

64. $d = vt = 35 \text{ min} \times \dfrac{60 \text{ s}}{1 \text{ min}} \times \dfrac{24 \text{ m}}{1 \text{ s}} = 5.0 \times 10^4 \text{ m}$

Momentum

66. **a.** $p = mv = (703 \text{ kg})(20.1 \text{ m/s}) = 1.41 \times 10^4 \text{ kg} \bullet \text{m/s forward}$
b. $p = mv = (703 \text{ kg} + 315 \text{ kg})(20.1 \text{ m/s}) = 2.05 \times 10^4 \text{ kg} \bullet \text{m/s}$ forward

68. $v = 4.2$ m/s along the trail

70. $p = 11 \text{ kg} \bullet \text{m/s}$ down the lane

Acceleration

72. $a = \dfrac{\Delta v}{t} = \dfrac{27 \text{ m/s} - 0 \text{ m/s}}{6.00 \text{ s}} = 4.5 \text{ m/s}^2$

74. $a = 0.258 \text{ m/s}^2$ toward Chicago

Newton's Second Law

76. $F = ma = (7.4 \times 10^{-3} \text{ kg})(9.8 \text{ m/s}^2) = 7.3 \times 10^{-2} \text{ N}$

78. $F = 2.1 \times 10^3 \text{ N}$

80. $m = 65 \text{ kg}$

Work

82. $F = \dfrac{W}{d} = \dfrac{157 \text{ J}}{5.3 \text{ m}} = 3.0 \times 10^1 \text{ N}$

84. $m = 1.3 \text{ kg}$

Power

86. $P = \dfrac{W}{t} = \dfrac{686 \text{ J}}{3.1 \text{ s}} = 2.2 \times 10^2 \text{ W}$

88. $W = 8.81 \times 10^9 \text{ MJ}$

90. $P = 9.0 \times 10^2 \text{ W}$

Mechanical Advantage

92. $input \ force = \dfrac{output \ force}{mechanical \ advantage} = \dfrac{660 \text{ N}}{6} = 110 \text{ N}$

94. *mechanical advantage* = 0.95
If the knob were moved closer to the hinge, the mechanical advantage would be less.

Gravitational Potential Energy

96. $PE = mgh = (0.14 \text{ kg})(9.81 \text{ m/s}^2)(3.5 \text{ m}) = 4.8 \text{ J}$

98. $PE = 1.3 \times 10^3 \text{ J}$

100. $h = 0.33 \text{ m}$

Kinetic Energy

102. $v = \sqrt{\dfrac{2KE}{m}} = \sqrt{\dfrac{2(7.34 \times 10^4 \text{ J})}{654 \text{ kg}}} = 15.0 \text{ m/s}$

104. $m = 1.73 \times 10^3 \text{ kg}$

Efficiency

106. $energy \ lost = energy \ input \times \left(\dfrac{100 - efficiency}{100}\right) =$

$40.5 \text{ kJ} \times \left(\dfrac{100 - 26.7}{100}\right) = 29.7 \text{ kJ}$

108. *efficiency* = 61%

110. *efficiency* = 6.7%

Temperature Conversions

112. **a.** $T = t + 273 = \dfrac{5}{9}(T_F - 32.0) + 273 =$

$\dfrac{5}{9}(214°F - 32.0) + 273 = 374 \text{ K}$

b. $T = t + 273 = 100.°C + 273 = 373 \text{ K}$

c. $T = t + 273 = 27°C + 273 = 3.00 \times 10^2 \text{ K}$

d. $T = t + 273 = \dfrac{5}{9}(T_F - 32.0) + 273 =$

$\dfrac{5}{9}(32°F - 32.0) + 273 = 273 \text{ K}$

114. $t = T - 273 = 0 \text{ K} - 273 = -273°C$

Specific Heat

116. $energy = mc\Delta t =$
$(5.0 \text{ g Ag})(1 \text{ kg}/1000 \text{ g})(235 \text{ J/kg} \bullet \text{K})(334 \text{ K} - 298 \text{ K}) = 42 \text{ J}$

118. $m = 5.4 \times 10^{-3} \text{ kg}$

120. $energy = 3.4 \times 10^6 \text{ J}$

Wave Speed

122. $v = \dfrac{92 \text{ m}}{2.7 \times 10^{-1} \text{ s}} = 3.4 \times 10^2 \text{ m/s}$

124. $t = 2.6 \times 10^3 \text{ s}$

Resistance

126. $R = \dfrac{V}{I} = \dfrac{6.0 \text{ V}}{1.4 \text{ A}} = 4.3 \ \Omega$

128. $V = 8.95 \text{ V}$

130. $R = 8 \ \Omega$

Electric Power

132. $I = \dfrac{P}{V} = \dfrac{60 \text{ W}}{120 \text{ V}} = 0.5 \text{ A}$

134. $I = 3.6 \text{ A}$

Glossary

Key to Phonetic Spellings

Sound symbol	Key word(s)	Phonetic spelling	Sound symbol	Key word(s)	Phonetic spelling
a	map	MAP	uhr	paper fern	PAY puhr FUHRN
ay	face day	FAYS DAY	yoo	yule globule	YOOL GLAHB yool
ah	father cot	FAH thuhr KAHT	yu	cure	KYUR
aw	caught law	KAWT LAW	y	yes	YES
ee	eat ski	EET SKEE	g	get	GET
e	wet rare	WET RER	j	jig	JIG
oy	boy foil	BOY FOYL	k	card kite	KARD KIET
ow	out now	OWT NOW	s	cell kiss	SEL KIS
oo	shoot suit	SHOOT SOOT	ch	chin	CHIN
u	book put	BUK PUT	sh	shell	SHEL
uh	sun cut	SUHN KUHT	th	thin	THIN
i	lip	LIP	zh	azure	AZH uhr
ie	tide sigh	TIED SIE	ng	bring	BRING
oh	over coat overcoat	OH vuhr KOHT OH vuhr KOHT	nj	change	CHAYNJ
			z	is	IZ

CAPS = primary stress; SMALL CAPS = secondary stress; lowercase = unstressed

absolute zero (AB suh LOOT ZIR oh) the temperature at which an object's energy is minimal (293)

acceleration (ak SEL uhr AY shuhn) the change in velocity divided by the time interval in which the change occurred (225)

accuracy (AK yur uh see) the extent to which a measurement approaches the true value (25)

acid rain (AS id RAYN) any precipitation that has an unusually high concentration of sulfuric or nitric acids resulting from chemical pollution of the air (635)

addiction (uh DIK shuhn) physiological and psychological dependence on a drug (539)

aerobic exercise (er OH bik EK ser siez) an exercise that is powered by energy-releasing reactions that require oxygen (503)

AIDS (acquired immunodeficiency syndrome) a viral disease that destroys the body's ability to resist other diseases by disrupting the immune system (522)

air mass (ER MAS) a large body of air with uniform temperature and moisture content (663)

alkali metals (AL kuh LIE MET uhls) the highly reactive metallic elements located in Group 1 of the periodic table (87)

alkaline-earth metals (AL kuh LIN UHRTH MET uhls) the reactive metallic elements located in Group 2 of the periodic table (88)

alpha particle (AL fuh PAHRT i kuhl) a positively charged particle, emitted by some radioactive nuclei, that consists of two protons and two neutrons (187)

altruism (al TROO iz uhm) the behavior that helps others but not one's self (563)

alveolus (al VEE uh luhs) a small sac in the lung where oxygen and carbon dioxide are exchanged between the air and the blood (472)

amino acid (uh MEE noh AS id) any one of 20 different naturally occurring organic molecules that combine to form proteins (134)

amniotic fluid (AM nee uh tik FLOO id) a watery fluid in which a developing embryo or fetus is suspended (557)

amplitude (AM pluh TOOD) the greatest distance that particles in a medium move from their normal position when a wave passes by (332)

anaerobic exercise (an uhr OH bik EK ser siez) an exercise that is powered by energy-releasing reactions that do not require oxygen (502)

analgesic (an uhl JEE zik) a drug that relieves pain (534)

analog signal (AN uh LAWG SIG nuhl) a signal corresponding to a quantity whose values can change continuously (399)

anemia (uh NEE mee uh) a condition in which the blood contains fewer red blood cells than normal (512)

anion (AN IE ahn) an ion with a negative charge (81)

antibiotic (an tie bie AHT ik) a drug that kills or slows the growth of live pathogens (535)

artery (AHRT uhr ee) a tubelike vessel that carries blood away from the heart (469)

arthritis (ahr THRIET is) a condition in which the joints become swollen and painful (500)

asteroid (AS tuhr OYD) a small rocky object that orbits the sun, usually in a band between the orbits of Mars and Jupiter (595)

asthenosphere (as THEN uh SFIR) the zone of the mantle beneath the lithosphere that consists of slowly flowing solid rock (611)

asthma (AZ muh) a condition in which the bronchi become constricted (481)

atherosclerosis (ath uhr oh skluh ROH sis) a disease in which fatty deposits form in the walls of arteries (478)

atmospheric transmission (AT muhs FIR ik trans MISH uhn) the transmission of a signal using electromagnetic waves (406)

atom (AT uhm) the smallest particle that has the properties of an element (39)

atomic mass unit (amu) (uh TAHM ik MAS YOON it) a quantity equal to one-twelfth the mass of a carbon-12 atom (84)

atomic number (uh TAHM ik NUHM buhr) the number of protons in the nucleus of an atom (82)

atrium (AY tree uhm) one of the two heart chambers that receive blood from the body (466)

atrophy (AH truh fee) the decrease in the size of a body structure due to disease, aging, or lack of use (509)

average atomic mass (AV uhr ij uh TAHM ik MAS) the weighted average of the masses of all naturally occurring isotopes of an element (84)

Avogadro's constant (AH voh GAH drohz KAHN stuhnt) the number of particles in 1 mol; equals 6.022×10^{23}/mol (96)

B

background radiation (BAK grownd RAY dee AY shuhn) the nuclear radiation that arises naturally from cosmic rays and from radioactive isotopes in the soil and air (201)

balanced diet (BAL uhnsd DIE uht) a selection of foods that provides all of the nutrients needed for healthy living (438)

balanced forces (BAL uhnst FOHR sez) the forces acting on an object that combine to produce a net force that is equal to zero (229)

barometric pressure (BAR uh ME trik PRESH uhr) the pressure due to the weight of the atmosphere; also called *air pressure* or *atmospheric pressure* (659)

basal metabolic rate (BAY suhl met uh BAHL ik RAYT) the rate of energy use for a living body that is not performing other activities (444)

beta particle (BAYT uh PAHRT i kuhl) an electron emitted during the radioactive decay of a neutron in an unstable nucleus (187)

big bang theory (BIG BANG THEE uh ree) a scientific theory that states that the universe began 10 billion to 20 billion years ago in an enormous explosion (582)

biochemical compound (BIE oh KEM i kuhl KAHM pownd) any organic compound that has an important role in living things (134)

black hole (BLAK HOHL) an object so massive and dense that not even light can escape its gravity (591)

blastocyst (BLAS toh sist) the hollow ball of cells that attaches to the lining of the uterus (556)

blood pressure (BLUHD PRESH uhr) the pressure exerted by the blood on the walls of blood vessels and heart chambers (469)

boiling point (BOYL ing POYNT) the temperature at which a liquid becomes a gas below the surface (54)

bond angle (BAHND AYN guhl) the angle formed by two bonds to the same atom (110)

bond length (BAHND LENGKTH) the average distance between the nuclei of two bonded atoms (110)

Glossary

breathing rate (BREETH ing RAYT) the number of times per minute that a person breathes in and out (476)

bronchitis (BRAHN kiet is) inflammation of the bronchi (481)

bronchus (BRAHN kuhs) one of the two large tubes that carry air between the trachea and the lungs (472)

bulbourethral gland (buhl boh yoo REETH rahl GLAND) a gland that secretes an alkaline fluid to counteract acids in the female reproductive tract (550)

buoyancy (BOY uhn see) the force with which a more dense fluid pushes a less dense substance upward (57)

C

Calorie (KAL uh ree) a unit of energy describing the amount of energy needed to warm 1 kg of water by 1°C (442)

capillary (KAP uh layr ee) a small blood vessel with two thin walls (469)

carbohydrate (CAHR boh HIE drayt) any organic compound that is made of carbon, hydrogen, and oxygen and that provides nutrients to the cells of living things (134)

carrier (CAR ee uhr) a continuous wave that can be modulated to send a signal (408)

catalyst (CAT uh list) a substance that changes the rate of chemical reactions without being consumed (171)

cathode-ray tube (CATH OHD RAY TOOB) a tube that uses an electron beam to create a display on a phosphorescent screen (410)

cation (CAT IE ahn) an ion with a positive charge (81)

cell (SEL) a device that is a source of electric current because of a potential difference, or voltage, between the terminals (364)

chemical bond (KEM i kuhl BAHND) the attractive force that holds atoms or ions together (109)

chemical change (KEM i kuhl CHAYNJ) a change that occurs when a substance changes composition by forming one or more new substances (58)

chemical energy (KEM i kuhl EN uhr jee) the energy stored within atoms and molecules that can be released when a substance reacts (151)

chemical equation (KEM i kuhl ee KWAY zhuhn) an equation that uses chemical formulas and symbols to show the reactants and products in a chemical reaction (161)

chemical formula (KEM i kuhl FOHR myoo luh) the chemical symbols and numbers indicating the atoms contained in the basic unit of a substance (41)

chemical property (KEM i kuhl PRAHP uhr tee) the way a substance reacts with others to form new substances with different properties (53)

chemical structure (KEM i kuhl STRUHK chuhr) the arrangement of bonded atoms or ions within a substance (110)

chemistry (KEM is tree) the study of matter and how it changes (38)

circuit breaker (SUHR kit BRAYK uhr) a device that protects a circuit from current overloads (378)

circulatory system (SUHR kyoo lah toh ree SIS tuhm) the body system that moves blood through the body (464)

climate (KLIE muht) the general weather conditions over many years (667)

cluster (KLUHS tuhr) a group of galaxies bound by gravity (580)

code (KOHD) a set of rules used to interpret signals that convey information (397)

combustion reaction (kuhm BUHST shuhn ree AK shuhn) a reaction in which a compound and oxygen burn (155)

communicable disease (ku MYOO ni kuh buhl di ZEEZ) an infectious disease that can be spread from person to person (522)

community (kuh MYOO nuh tee) all of the animals and plants living in one area in an ecosystem (681)

compound (KAHM pownd) a substance made of atoms of more than one element bound together (39)

compound machine (KAHM pownd muh SHEEN) a machine made of more than one simple machine (262)

computer (kum PYOOT uhr) an electronic device that can accept data and instructions, follow the instructions, and output the results (414)

condensation (KAHN duhn SAY shuhn) the change of a substance from a gas to a liquid (49)

conduction (kuhn DUK shuhn) the transfer of energy as heat between particles as they collide within a substance or between two objects in contact (298)

conductor (kuhn DUK tuhr) a material through which energy can be easily transferred as heat (300); a material that transfers charge easily (358)

constellation (KAHN stuh LAY shuhn) a group of stars appearing in a pattern as seen from Earth (585)

constructive interference (kuhn STRUHK tiv IN tuhr FIR uhns) any interference in which waves combine so that the resulting wave is bigger than the original waves (343)

convection (kuhn VEK shuhn) the transfer of energy by the movement of fluids with different temperatures (298)

convection current (kuhn VEK shuhn KUHR uhnt) the flow of a fluid due to heated expansion followed by cooling and contraction (299)

conversion factor (kuhn VUHR zhuhn FAK tuhr) a ratio equal to one that expresses the same quantity in two different ways (97)

cooling system (KOOL ing SIS tuhm) a device that transfers energy as heat out of an object to lower its temperature (309)

core (KOHR) the center of a planetary body, such as

Earth (609)

Coriolis effect (KOHR ee OH lis e FEKT) the change in the direction of an object's path due to Earth's rotation (661)

covalent bond (KOH VAY luhnt BAHND) a bond formed when atoms share one or more pairs of electrons (119)

crest (KREST) the highest point of a transverse wave (332)

critical mass (KRIT i kuhl MAS) the minimum mass of a fissionable isotope in which a nuclear chain reaction can occur (199)

critical thinking (KRIT i kuhl THINGK ing) the application of logic and reason to observations and conclusions (12)

crust (KRUHST) the outermost and thinnest layer of Earth (608)

current (KUHR uhnt) the rate that electric charges move through a conductor (365)

D

decomposition reaction (DEE kahm puh ZISH uhn ree AK shuhn) a reaction in which one compound breaks into at least two products (155)

density (DEN suh tee) the mass per unit volume of a substance (55)

deposition (DE puh ZISH uhn) the process in which sediment is laid down (636)

destructive interference (di STRUK tiv IN tuhr FIR uhns) any interference in which waves combine so that the resulting wave is smaller than the largest of the original waves (343)

dew point (DOO POYNT) the temperature at which water vapor molecules start to form liquid water (658)

diaphragm (DIE uh fram) a sheet of muscle below the chest cavity that functions in breathing (474)

diffraction (di FRAK shuhn) the bending of a wave as it passes an edge or an opening (341)

digestion (di JES chun) the process of breaking down food into usable molecules (448)

digital signal (DIJ i tuhl SIG nuhl) a signal that can be represented as a sequence of discrete values (399)

Doppler effect (DAHP luhr e FEKT) an observed change in the frequency of a wave when the source or observer is moving (339)

dose (DOHS) the quantity of a drug to be taken at one time (536)

double-displacement reaction (DUHB uhl dis PLAYS muhnt ree AK shuhn) a reaction in which a gas, a solid precipitate, or a molecular compound is formed from the apparent exchange of ions between two compounds (158)

drug (DRUHG) a substance that changes how the body works (534)

E

eclipse (i KLIPS) an event that occurs when one object passes into the shadow of another object (599)

ecosystem (EK oh SIS tuhm) all of the living and non-living elements in a particular place (680)

efficiency (e FISH uhn see) a quantity, usually expressed as a percentage, that measures the ratio of useful work output to work input (278)

ejaculation (ee jak yoo LAY shuhn) the forceful expulsion of semen from the male reproductive system (550)

electric charge (ee LEK trik chahrj) an electrical property of matter that creates a force between objects (356)

electric circuit (ee LEK trik SUHR kit) an electrical device connected so that it provides one or more complete paths for the movement of charges (372)

electric field (ee LEK trik FEELD) the region around a charged object in which other charged objects experience an electric force (361)

electric force (ee LEK trik FOHRS) the force of attraction or repulsion between objects due to charge (360)

electrical energy (ee LEK tri kuhl EN uhr jee) the energy associated with electrical charges, whether moving or at rest (376)

electrical potential energy (ee LEK tri kuhl poh TEN shuhl EN uhr jee) the potential energy of a charged object due to its position in an electric field (363)

electrolysis (EE lek TRAHL i sis) the decomposition of a compound by an electric current (155)

electromagnet (ee LEK troh MAG nit) a strong magnet created when an iron core is inserted into the center of a current-carrying solenoid (384)

electromagnetic induction (ee LEK troh mag NET ik in DUHK shuhn) the production of a current in a circuit by a change in the strength, position, or orientation of an external magnetic field (384)

electromagnetic wave (ee LEK troh mag NET ik WAYV) a wave that is caused by a disturbance in electric and magnetic fields and that does not require a medium; also called a light wave (323)

electron (ee LEK trahn) a tiny negatively charged subatomic particle moving around outside the nucleus of an atom (72)

element (EL uh muhnt) a substance that cannot be broken down into simpler substances (39)

embryo (EM bree oh) a growing organism that has not yet developed all of its major structures (557)

empathy (EM puh thee) an understanding and respect for feelings of others (563)

emphysema (em fuh SEE muh) a disease in which the lungs' alveoli break apart and collapse (481)

empirical formula (em PIR i kuhl FOHR myoo luh) the simplest chemical formula of a compound that tells the smallest whole-number ratio of atoms in the compound (126)

endothermic reaction (EN doh THUHR mik ree AK shuhn) a reaction in which energy is transferred to the reactants from the surroundings usually as heat (151)

endurance (en DOOR uhns) the ability to continue exercising before becoming completely exhausted (504)

energy (EN uhr jee) the ability to change or move matter (48)

energy level (EN uhr jee LEV uhl) any of the possible energies an electron may have in an atom (73)

enzyme (EN ziem) a protein that speeds up a specific biochemical reaction (171)

epicenter (EP i SEN tuhr) the point on Earth's surface directly above the focus of an earthquake (618)

equilibrium (EE kwi LIB ree uhm) the state in which a chemical reaction and its reverse occur at the same time and at the same rate (174)

erosion (ee ROH zhuhn) the process by which rock and/or the products of weathering are removed (636)

esophagus (i SAHF uh guhs) the muscular tube connecting the mouth and stomach (450)

eutrophication (yoo TRAHF i KAY shuhn) an increase in the amount of nutrients, such as nitrates, in an environment (702)

evaporation (ee VAP uh RAY shuhn) the change of a substance from a liquid to a gas (49)

exothermic reaction (EK soh THUHR mik ree AK shuhn) a reaction that transfers energy from the reactants to the surroundings usually as heat (151)

extensor (ek STEN suhr) a muscle that increases the angle between two bones (497)

F

fallopian tubes (fuh LOH pee uhn TOOBZ) the tubular structures that move eggs from the ovaries to the uterus; the site of fertilization (551)

fats (FATS) a class of compounds containing long hydrocarbon chains that are bonded to a glycerin molecule (434)

fault (FAWLT) a crack in Earth created when rocks on either side of a break move (614)

fertilization (FUHRT il iez ay shuhn) the fusion of a male reproductive cell with a female reproductive cell to produce the first cell of a new individual (548)

fetus (FEET uhs) a developing offspring that has most of its major structures (555)

fission (FISH uhn) the process by which a nucleus splits into two or more smaller fragments, releasing neutrons and energy (197)

flexibility (FLEK suh bil uh tee) the ability of the body to move at its joints (504)

flexor (FLEKS uhr) a muscle that decreases the angle between two bones (497)

focus (FOH kuhs) the area along a fault at which slippage first occurs, initiating an earthquake (618)

follicle (FAHL i kuhl) a small envelope of cells surrounding an egg (552)

force (FOHRS) the cause of an acceleration, or change in an object's velocity (228)

fossil fuels (FAHS uhl FYOO uhlz) any fuels formed from the remains of ancient plant and animal life (689)

fossils (FAHS uhlz) the traces or remains of a plant or an animal found in sedimentary rock (628)

free fall (FREE FAWL) the motion of a body when only the force of gravity is acting on it (237)

frequency (FREE kwuhn see) the number of vibrations that occur in a 1 s time interval (333)

friction (FRIK shuhn) the force between two objects in contact that opposes the motion of either object (231)

front (FRUHNT) the boundary between air masses of different densities (663)

fuse (FYOOZ) an electrical device containing a metal strip that melts when current in the circuit becomes too great (378)

fusion (FYOO zhuhn) the process in which light nuclei combine at extremely high temperatures, forming heavier nuclei and releasing energy (200)

G

galaxy (GAL uhk see) a collection of millions or billions of stars bound together by gravity (577)

gamma ray (GAM uh RAY) the high-energy electromagnetic radiation emitted by a nucleus during radioactive decay (188)

gas exchange (GAS eks CHAYNJ) the exchange of oxygen and carbon dioxide between the body and the air (472)

gene therapy (JEEN THER uh pee) treatment of an inherited disease by introducing a normal gene into the body's cells (533)

genetic counselor (juh NET ik KOWN suh luhr) a medical professional who advises couples on the chances of their passing an inherited disease to their children (533)

geothermal energy (JEE oh THUHR muhl EN uhr jee) the energy drawn from heated water within Earth's crust (692)

global warming (GLOH buhl WAHRM ing) an increase in Earth's temperature due to an increase in greenhouse gases (700)

gravity (GRAV i tee) the force of attraction between two particles of matter due to their mass (232)

greenhouse effect (GREEN HOWS e FEKT) the process by which the atmosphere traps some of the energy from the sun in the troposphere (654)

group (GROOP) a vertical column of elements in the periodic table; also called a family (80)

half-life (HAF LIEF) the time required for half a sample of radioactive nuclei to decay (191)

halogens (HAL oh juhnz) the highly reactive elements located in Group 17 of the periodic table (92)

hardware (HAHRD WER) the equipment that makes up a computer system (418)

heart attack (HART uh TAK) death of a portion of the heart caused by a reduced blood supply to the heart muscle (478)

heat (HEET) the transfer of energy from the particles of one object to those of another object due to a temperature difference (296)

heating system (HEET ing SIS tuhm) a device that transfers energy as heat to a substance to raise the temperature of the substance (306)

hemoglobin (HEE moh gloh bin) a protein found in red blood cells that binds to oxygen (465)

histamine (HIS tuh meen) a protein that dilates blood vessels as part of the inflammatory response (531)

HIV (human immunodeficiency virus) the virus that causes AIDS (522)

humidity (hyoo MID uh tee) the quantity of water vapor in the atmosphere (657)

hydroelectric power (HIE DROH ee LEK trik POW uhr) the energy of moving water converted to electricity (686)

hypertension (HIE puhr ten shuhn) a condition in which blood pressure is consistently higher than normal (479)

igneous rock (IG nee uhs RAHK) any rock formed from cooled and hardened magma or lava (627)

immiscible (im MIS uh buhl) describes two or more liquids that do not mix into each other (42)

immune system (im MYOON SIS tuhm) the body system that attacks and destroys specific pathogens (532)

inertia (in UHR shuh) the tendency of an object to remain at rest or in motion with a constant velocity (235)

infection (in FEK shuhn) the invasion and multiplication of pathogens in the body (520)

infectious disease (in FEK shuhs di ZEEZ) an illness caused by a pathogen (520)

inflammatory response (in FLAM uh tohr ee ri SPAHNS) a response to injury that can include redness, heat, pain, and swelling (531)

insulator (IN suh LAYT uhr) a material that is a poor energy conductor (301); a material that does not transfer charge easily (358)

interference (IN tuhr FIR uhns) the combination of two or more waves that exist in the same place at the same time (342)

Internet (IN tuhr NET) a large computer network that connects many local and smaller networks (421)

interstellar matter (IN tuhr STEL uhr MA tuhr) the gas and dust between the stars in a galaxy (578)

ion (IE ahn) an atom or group of atoms that has lost or gained one or more electrons and therefore has a net electric charge (81)

ionic bond (ie AHN ik BAHND) a bond formed by the attraction between oppositely charged ions (116)

ionization (IE uhn i ZAY shuhn) the process of adding electrons to or removing electrons from an atom or group of atoms (81)

isobar (IE soh BAHR) a line drawn on a weather map connecting points of equal barometric or atmospheric pressure (667)

isotopes (IE suh TOHPS) any atoms having the same number of protons but different numbers of neutrons (83)

joint (JOYNT) a place where two or more bones meet (493)

![K]

kinetic energy (ki NET ik EN uhr jee) the energy of a moving object due to its motion (266)

![L]

large intestine (LAHRJ in TES tuhn) an organ that stores, compacts, and eliminates indigestible material (453)

length (LENGTH) the straight-line distance between any two points (18)

ligament (LIG uh ment) a strong strap of tissue that holds the bones of a joint in place (493)

light-year (LIET YIR) a unit of distance equal to the distance light travels in one year; $1 \text{ ly} = 9.5 \times 10^{15}$ m (577)

lithosphere (LITH oh SFIR) the thin outer shell of Earth, consisting of the crust and the rigid upper mantle (610)

liver (LIV uhr) a large organ that makes bile and modifies substances in the blood (452)

Glossary

longitudinal wave (LAHN juh TOOD uhn uhl WAYV) a wave that causes the particles of the medium to vibrate parallel to the direction the wave travels (329)

lung cancer (LUHNG KAN suhr) uncontrolled growth of cells that begins in the lungs (480)

M

magma (MAG muh) the molten rock within Earth (612)

magnetic field (mag NET ik FEELD) a region where a magnetic force can be detected (380)

magnetic pole (mag NET ik POHL) an area of a magnet where the magnetic force appears to be the strongest (380)

mantle (MAN tuhl) the layer of rock between Earth's crust and its core (608)

mass (MAS) a measure of the quantity of matter in an object (18)

mass number (MAS NUHM buhr) the total number of protons and neutrons in the nucleus of an atom (82)

matter (MAT uhr) anything that has mass and occupies space (38)

mechanical advantage (muh KAN i kuhl ad VANT ij) a quantity that measures how much a machine multiplies force or distance (255)

mechanical energy (muh KAN i kuhl EN uhr jee) the sum of the kinetic and potential energy of large-scale objects in a system (268)

mechanical wave (muh KAN i kuhl WAYV) a wave that requires a medium through which to travel (323)

medium (MEE dee uhm) the matter through which a wave travels (323)

melting point (MELT ing POYNT) the temperature at which a solid becomes a liquid (54)

menopause (MEN uh pahz) the time when a woman stops menstruating and is no longer able to conceive (566)

menstruation (men STRAY shuhn) the release of uterine lining, blood, and unfertilized egg (554)

mesosphere (MES oh SFIR) the coldest layer of the atmosphere; located above the stratosphere (651)

metabolic rate (met uh BAHL ik RAYT) the amount of energy consumed by the body in a given time period (443)

metallic bond (muh TAL ik BAHND) a bond formed by the attraction between positively charged metal ions and the electrons around them (118)

metals (MET uhls) the elements that are good conductors of heat and electricity (87)

metamorphic rock (MET uh MOHR fik RAHK) any rock formed from other rocks as a result of heat, pressure, or chemical processes (629)

mineral (MIN uhr uhl) a natural, inorganic solid with a definite chemical composition and a characteristic internal structure (626)

miscible (MIS uh buhl) describes two or more liquids that are able to dissolve into each other in various proportions (42)

mixture (MIKS chuhr) a combination of more than one pure substance (41)

modulate (MAHJ uh LAYT) the process of changing a wave's amplitude or frequency in order to send a signal (408)

molar mass (MOH luhr MAS) the mass in grams of 1 mol of a substance (96)

mole (MOHL) the SI base unit that describes the amount of a substance (96)

mole ratio (MOHL RAY shee OH) the smallest relative number of moles of the substances involved in a reaction (168)

molecular formula (moh LEK yoo luhr FOHR myoo luh) a chemical formula that reports the actual numbers of atoms in one molecule of a compound (128)

molecule (MAHL i KYOOL) the smallest unit of a substance that exhibits all of the properties characteristic of that substance (40)

momentum (moh MEN tuhm) a quantity defined as the product of an object's mass and velocity (222)

mucous membrane (MYOO kuhs MEM brayn) a tissue that secretes mucus; found in body cavities that open to the outside (530)

muscle fatigue (MUHS uhl fuh TEEG) the loss of muscle strength due to prolonged exercise (503)

N

nebular model (NEB yuh luhr MAHD uhl) a model that describes the sun and the solar system forming together out of a cloud of gas and dust (598)

neutron (NOO trahn) a neutral subatomic particle in the nucleus of an atom (72)

neutron emission (NOO trahn ee MISH uhn) the release of a high-energy neutron by some neutron-rich nuclei during radioactive decay (188)

neutron star (NOO trahn STAHR) a dead star with the density of atomic nuclei (591)

nicotine (NIK uh teen) a toxic, addictive compound found in tobacco (477)

noble gases (NOH buhl GAS iz) the unreactive gaseous elements located in Group 18 of the periodic table (93)

nonmetals (NAHN MET uhlz) the elements that are usually poor conductors of heat and electricity (87)

nonrenewable resources (NAHN ri NOO uh buhl REE sohrs uz) any resources that are used faster than they can be replaced (690)

nuclear chain reaction (NOO klee uhr CHAYN ree AK shuhn) a series of fission processes in which the neutrons emitted by a dividing nucleus cause the division of other nuclei (198)

nuclear radiation (NOO klee uhr RAY dee AY shuhn) the charged particles or energy emitted by an unstable nucleus (186)

nucleus (NOO klee uhs) the center of an atom; made up of protons and neutrons (72)

nutrient (NOO tree uhnt) a chemical substance required for the life and growth of an organism (432)

O

obesity (oh BEES i tee) a condition in which too much of the body's weight is stored as fat (446)

operating system (AHP uhr AYT ing SIS tuhm) the software that controls a computer's activities (418)

optical fiber (AHP ti kuhl FIE buhr) a hair-thin, transparent strand of glass or plastic that transmits signals using pulses of light (401)

orbital (OHR bit uhl) a region in an atom where there is a high probability of finding electrons (75)

organic compound (ohr GAN ik KAHM pownd) any covalently bonded compound that contains carbon (129)

osteoporosis (AHS tee oh puh ROH sis) a disorder in which the bones become less dense and more fragile (499)

ovary (OH vuh ree) the female organ that stores and releases eggs (551)

ovulation (ahv yoo LAY shuhn) the process by which an egg moves out of the ovary (552)

oxygen debt (AHKS i jen DET) the extra amount of oxygen needed to return muscles to their normal condition after anaerobic exercise (503)

ozone (OH ZOHN) the form of atmospheric oxygen that has three atoms per molecule (650)

P

P waves (PEE WAYVZ) primary waves; the longitudinal waves generated by an earthquake (618)

pancreas (PAN kree uhs) a large gland behind the stomach that makes digestive juices (451)

parallel (PAR uh LEL) describes components in a circuit that are connected across common points, providing two or more separate conducting paths (375)

pathogen (PATH uh juhn) a virus or microorganism that causes disease (520)

penis (PEE nis) the male organ that delivers sperm cells to the female reproductive system and moves urine out of the body (549)

period (PIR ee uhd) a horizontal row of elements in the periodic table (80); the time required for one full wavelength to pass a certain point (333)

periodic law (PIR ee AHD ik LAW) the properties of elements tend to repeat in a regular pattern when elements are arranged in order of increasing atomic number (77)

phases (FAYZ iz) the different apparent shapes of the moon or a planet due to the relative positions of the sun, Earth, and the moon or planet (599)

physical change (FIZ i kuhl CHAYNJ) a change that occurs in the physical form or properties of a substance that occurs without a change in composition (59)

physical fitness (FIZ i kuhl FIT nis) the ability to carry out moderate physical tasks without becoming tired (501)

physical property (FIZ i kuhl PRAHP uhr tee) a characteristic of a substance that can be observed or measured without changing the composition of the substance (54)

physical transmission (FIZ i kuhl trans MISH uhn) the transmission of a signal using wires, cables, or optical fibers (406)

pixel (PIKS uhl) the smallest element of a display image (411)

placenta (pluh SEN tuh) the structure attaching the embryo to the wall of the uterus (557)

planet (PLAN it) any of the nine primary bodies orbiting the sun; a similar body orbiting another star (592)

plasma (PLAZ muh) the liquid part of blood (464)

plate tectonics (PLAYT tek TAHN iks) the theory that Earth's surface is made up of large moving plates (610)

platelet (PLAYT lit) a cell fragment found in blood that functions in blood clotting (466)

pollution (puh LOO shuhn) the contamination of the air, water, or soil (697)

polyatomic ion (PAHL ee uh TAHM ik IE ahn) an ion made of two or more atoms that are covalently bonded and that act like a single ion (120)

polymer (PAHL i MUHR) a large organic molecule made of many smaller bonded units (133)

potential difference (poh TEN shuhl DIF uhr uhns) the change in the electrical potential energy per unit charge (364)

potential energy (poh TEN shuhl EN uhr jee) the stored energy resulting from the relative positions of objects in a system (264)

power (POW uhr) a quantity that measures the rate at which work is done (252)

precipitation (pree SIP uh TAY shuhn) any form of water that falls back to Earth's surface from clouds; includes rain, snow, sleet, and hail (657)

precision (pree SIZH uhn) the degree of exactness of a measurement (24)

prescription drug (pree SKRIP shuhn DRUHG) a drug that may be given only as directed by a medical doctor (535)

pressure (PRESH uhr) the force exerted per unit area of a surface (47)

product (PRAHD uhkt) a substance that is the result of a chemical change (149)

protein (PROH teen) a biological polymer made of bonded amino acids (134)

Glossary

proton (PROH tahn) a positively charged subatomic particle in the nucleus of an atom (72)

psychoactive drug (SI koh ak tiv DRUHG) a drug that affects brain function (535)

puberty (PYOO buhr tee) the time in life when secondary sex changes occur and the reproductive system becomes functional (563)

pure substance (PYUR SUB stuhns) any matter that has a fixed composition and definite properties (41)

R

radiation (RAY dee AY shuhn) the transfer of energy by electromagnetic waves (299)

radicals (RAD ik uhls) the fragments of molecules that have at least one electron available for bonding (159)

radioactive tracer (RAY dee oh AK tiv TRAYS uhr) a radioactive material added to a substance so that the substance's location can later be detected (204)

radioactivity (RAY dee oh ak TIV uh tee) a process by which an unstable nucleus emits one or more particles or energy (186)

random-access memory (RAN duhm AK SES MEM uh ree) a storage device that allows any stored data to be read in the same access time (417)

reactant (REE AK tuhnt) a substance that undergoes a chemical change (149)

reactivity (REE ak TIV i tee) the ability of a substance to combine chemically with another substance (54)

read-only memory (REED OHN lee MEM uh ree) a memory device containing data that cannot be changed (418)

recycling (ree SIE kuhl ing) the process of breaking down discarded material for re-use in other products (706)

red blood cell (RED BLUHD SEL) an oxygen-transporting cell of the blood (465)

red giant (RED JIE uhnt) a large, reddish star late in its life cycle that fuses helium into carbon or oxygen (590)

red shift (RED SHIFT) a shift toward the red end of the spectrum in the observed spectral lines of stars or galaxies (581)

reduction/oxidation (redox) reaction (ri DUK shuhn AHKS i DAY shuhn (REE DAHKS) ree AK shuhn) a reaction that occurs when electrons are transferred from one reactant to another (159)

reflection (ri FLEK shuhn) the bouncing back of a wave as it meets a surface or boundary (340)

refraction (ri FRAK shuhn) the bending of waves as they pass from one medium to another (342)

refrigerant (ri FRIJ uhr uhnt) a substance used in cooling systems that transfers large amounts of energy as it changes state (310)

relative humidity (REL uh tiv hyoo MID uh tee) the ratio of the quantity of water vapor in the air to the maximum quantity of water vapor that can be present at that temperature (657)

renewable resources (ri NOO uh buhl REE sohrs uhz) any resources that can be continually replaced (691)

resistance (ri ZIS tuhns) the ratio of the voltage across a conductor to the current it carries (367)

respiratory system (RES puhr uh tohr ee SIS tuhm) the body system that brings oxygen into the body and removes carbon dioxide (471)

Richter scale (RIK tuhr SKAYL) a scale that expresses the relative magnitude of an earthquake (621)

S

S waves (ES WAYVZ) secondary waves; the transverse waves generated by an earthquake (619)

salivary glands (SAL uh ver ee GLANDZ) the glands located in the bottom and top of the mouth that secrete watery saliva (449)

sanitation (san uh TAY shuhn) the practices of cleanliness and hygiene designed to help maintain health (526)

schematic diagram (skee MAT ik DIE uh GRAM) a graphic representation of an electric circuit or apparatus, with standard symbols for the electrical devices (373)

science (SIE uhns) a system of knowledge based on facts or principles (6)

scientific law (SIE uhn TIF ik LAW) a summary of an observed natural event (8)

scientific method (SIE uhn TIF ik METH uhd) a series of logical steps to follow in order to solve problems (13)

scientific notation (SIE uhn TIF ik noh TAY shuhn) a value written as a simple number multiplied by a power of 10 (22)

scientific theory (SIE uhn TIF ik THEE uh ree) a tested, possible explanation of a natural event (8)

scrotum (SKROHT uhm) the loose sac of skin that contains the testes (548)

sedative (SED uh tiv) a drug that decreases brain activity (537)

sedimentary rock (SED uh MEN tuh ree RAHK) any rock formed from compressed or cemented deposits of sediment (628)

seismology (siez MAHL uh gee) the study of earthquakes and related phenomena (619)

semen (SEE muhn) a thick, whitish fluid containing sperm cells (550)

seminal vesicles (SEM uh nul VES i kuhls) the glands that produce a sugar-rich fluid, which nourishes sperm cells (550)

semiconductors (SEM i kuhn DUHK tuhrz) the elements that are intermediate conductors of heat and electricity (87)

series (SIR eez) describes a circuit or portion of a circuit that provides a single conducting path (375)

sexually transmitted disease (STD) (SEK shoo uhl lee trans MIT tuhd di ZEEZ) a disease that is transmitted by sexual contact (564)

sick building syndrome (SIK BIL ding SIN drohm) a collection of symptoms caused by breathing air in buildings with poor ventilation (529)

signal (SIG nuhl) a sign that represents information, such as a command, a direction, or a warning (396)

significant figures (sig NIF uh kuhnt FIG yurz) the digits in a measurement that are known with certainty (24)

simple machine (SIM puhl muh SHEEN) any one of the six basic types of machines of which all other machines are composed (257)

single-displacement reaction (SING guhl dis PLAYS muhnt ree AK shuhn) a reaction in which atoms of one element take the place of atoms of another element in a compound (157)

small intestine (SMAHL in TES tuhn) an organ that breaks down food and absorbs nutrients (451)

software (SAWFT WER) the instructions, data, and programming that enables a computer system to work (418)

solar system (SOH luhr SIS tuhm) the sun and all the objects that orbit around it (593)

solenoid (SOH luh noyd) a long, wound coil of insulated wire (383)

specific heat (spuh SIF ik HEET) the amount of energy transferred as heat that will raise the temperature of 1 kg of a substance by 1 K (302)

speed (SPEED) the distance traveled divided by the time interval during which the motion occurred (218)

sperm cell (SPERM SEL) a male reproductive cell (549)

standing wave (STAN ding WAYV) a wave form caused by interference that appears not to move along the medium and that shows some regions of no vibration (nodes) and other regions of maximum vibration (antinodes) (345)

star (STAHR) a huge ball of hot gas that emits light (577)

stimulant (STIM yoo lant) a drug that increases brain activity (537)

stratosphere (STRAT uh SFIR) the layer of the atmosphere that extends upward from the troposphere to an altitude of 50 km; contains the ozone layer (650)

stroke (STROHK) sudden loss of function in a part of the brain when it is deprived of its blood supply (479)

strong nuclear force (STRAWNG NOO klee uhr FOHRS) the force that binds protons and neutrons together in a nucleus (196)

subduction (suhb DUHK shuhn) the process in which a tectonic plate dives beneath another tectonic plate and into the asthenosphere (612)

sublimation (SUHB luh MAY shuhn) the change of a substance from a solid to a gas (50)

substrate (SUHB STRAYT) the specific substance affected by an enzyme (172)

succession (suhk SESH uhn) the gradual repopulating of a community by different species over a period of time (684)

supergiant (SOO puhr JI uhnt) an extremely large star that creates elements as heavy as iron (590)

supernova (SOO puhr NOH vuh) a powerful explosion that occurs when a massive star dies (590)

surface waves (SUHR fis WAYVZ) the seismic waves that travel along Earth's surface (619)

synthesis reaction (SIN thuh sis ree AK shuhn) a reaction of at least two substances that forms a new, more complex compound (154)

tar (TAR) a complex mixture of compounds and ash particles contained in tobacco smoke (478)

technology (tek NAHL uh gee) the application of science to meet human needs (7)

telecommunication (TEL i kuh MYOO ni KAY shuhn) a communication method using electromagnetic means (398)

temperature (TEM puhr uh chuhr) measure of the average kinetic energy of all particles in an object (290)

temperature inversion (TEM puhr uh chuhr in VUHR zhuhn) the atmospheric condition in which warm air traps cooler air near Earth's surface (649)

tendon (TEN duhn) a strong cord of tissue that connects a skeletal muscle to a bone (495)

terminal velocity (TUHR muh nuhl vuh LAHS uh tee) the maximum velocity reached by a falling object, occurring when resistance of the medium is equal to the force due to gravity (238)

testis (TES tis) one of a pair of organs, the testes, that produce sperm cells and the male hormone testosterone (548)

thermometer (thuhr MAHM uht uhr) a device that measures temperature (291)

thermosphere (THURM oh SFIR) the atmospheric layer above the mesosphere (651)

tidal volume (TIED uhl VAHL yoom) the volume of air a person breathes in and out in normal, relaxed breathing (475)

toxin (TAHKS in) a poisonous substance (521)

trachea (TRAY kee uh) the tube that carries air between the throat and the chest (472)

topography (tuh PAHG ruh fee) the surface features of Earth (669)

transition metals (tran ZISH uhn MET uhls) the metallic elements located in Groups 3–12 of the periodic table (89)

transpiration (TRAN spuh RAY shuhn) the evaporation of water through pores in a plant's leaves (657)

transverse wave (TRANS VUHRS WAYV) a wave that causes the particles of the medium to vibrate perpendicularly to the direction the wave travels (329)

troposphere (TRO poh SFIR) the atmospheric layer closest to Earth's surface where nearly all weather occurs (649)

trough (TRAWF) the lowest point of a transverse wave (332)

U

ulcer (UL suhr) a sore that develops around a hole in the mucous lining of the digestive system (453)

urethra (yoo REE thruh) the tube in the body that carries urine and, in males, semen (549)

unbalanced forces (UHN BAL uhnst FOHR sez) the forces acting on an object that combine to produce a net nonzero force (229)

undernourishment (uhn der NUR ish ment) the breakdown of the body and its organs as a result of inadequate food intake (446)

universe (YOON uh VUHRS) the sum of all matter and energy that exists, that ever has existed, and that ever will exist (576)

uterus (YOOT uhr uhs) the muscular female organ that contains the developing baby (551)

V

vaccine (vak SEEN) a harmless form of a pathogen that is used to prepare the immune system for the active forms (532)

vagina (vuh JIE nuh) the passage that connects the uterus with the outside of the body (551)

valence electron (VAY luhns ee LEK trahn) an electron in the outermost energy level of an atom (76)

variable (VER ee uh buhl) anything that can change in an experiment (13)

vein (VAYN) a tubelike vessel that returns blood to the heart (470)

velocity (vuh LAHS uh tee) a quantity describing both speed and direction (220)

vent (VENT) an opening through which molten rock flows onto Earth's surface (622)

ventricle (VEN tri kuhl) one of the two heart chambers that pump blood to the rest of the body (466)

viscosity (vis KAHS uh tee) the resistance of a fluid to flow (48)

vital capacity (VIET uhl kuh PAS i tee) the maximum volume of air a person can breath out after breathing in fully (475)

vitamin (VIET uh min) an organic compound needed in trace amounts by the body (436)

volume (VAHL yoom) a measure of space, such as the capacity of a container (18)

W

water cycle (WAH tuhr SIE kuhl) the continuous movement of water from the atmosphere to Earth and back (656)

wave (WAYV) a disturbance that transmits energy through matter or space (322)

wave speed (WAYV SPEED) the speed at which a wave passes through a medium (335)

wavelength (WAYV LENGTH) the distance between any two successive identical parts of a wave (332)

weathering (WETH uhr ing) the change in the physical form or chemical composition of rock materials exposed at Earth's surface (628)

weight (WAYT) the force with which gravity pulls on a quantity of matter (18)

white blood cell (WIET BLUHD SEL) a blood cell that protects the body against infection (465)

white dwarf (HWIET DWOHRF) a small, very dense star that remains after fusion in a red giant stops (590)

withdrawal symptoms (with DRAH uhl SIMP tuhms) a set of physical and mental changes that occur when a person stops using an addictive drug (539)

work (WUHRK) a quantity that measures the effects of a force acting over a distance (250)

Z

zygote (ZIE goht) the cell resulting from fertilization of an egg cell by a sperm cell (556)

Index

Boldfaced page references denote illustrations.

A

Absolute zero, 293
Acceleration, 225–228, 231, **231**, 233, 237–238, 602
Accretion, 598
Accuracy, 25
Acetaminophen, 534
Acetate ions, 122
Acetic acid, 127
Acetylsalicylic acid, 129, 534
Acidity. *See* pH
Acid rain, 635, 700–701
Aconcagua, Mount, 613
Acoustics, 345
Acquired immunodeficiency syndrome (AIDS), **522,** 522–523, 564, **565**
Addiction, 539
Adenine, 136, **136**
Adolescence, 563–564
Aerobic exercise, 503–504, 507
Aging, 566
AIDS (acquired immunodeficiency syndrome), **522,** 522–523, 564, **565**
Air bags, 230
Air conditioning, 305, **305,** 311
Air density, 55, 674
Air pollution, **649,** 649–650, 653–654, **698, 698**–701
Air resistance, 232, **232,** 238
Alcohol, 132, 537, **537, 538,** 539–540, **540**
Alkali metals, 87, **87,** 158
Alkaline-earth metals, 88, **88**
Alkanes, 130–131
Alpha particles, 187, 189
Alternating current (AC), 386
Altocumulus clouds, **658,** 659
Altostratus clouds, **658,** 659, **663**
Altruism, 563
Aluminum, **21, 70,** 90, 123, 302
Aluminum chloride, 157
Aluminum sulfate, 178
Alveolus, **471,** 472–473, **473,** 481, **481**
American Cancer Society, **477**
American Red Cross, 463
Amino acids, 134–135, 435, **435,** 440
Ammonia, **120,** 168, 175, **175,** 302
Ammonium nitrate, 121
Ammonium sulfate, 121, **175**
Amniotic fluid, 557, 559
Amperes, 365
Amplification, 408
Amplitude, **331,** 332, 343, **343**
Amplitude modulation (AM), 409
Amylase, 171, 449, 451
Anabolic steroids, 502, **538**
Anaerobic exercise, 501–503, 507
Analgesics, 534, **535**
Analog signals, 399, 405–406
Andromeda galaxy, **578,** 580
Anemia, 512, 523, **523**
Anions, 81, 91, 121, 122, 124

Anodes, 5
Antacids, **535**
Antennas, 409
Antibiotics, 528, 535, **535**
Antibodies, 74, 561
Antifreeze, 57, 62
Antihistamines, **535**
Antimony, 93, **93**
Antinodes, 345
Archaeology, 193
Architecture, 91, 345, 419
Argon, 53, **93**
Arms, in levers, 258, **258**
Arsenic, 93, **93**
Arteries, 467, **467,** 469, **469**
Art forgeries, 185
Arthritis, 500, **525**
Aspartame, 129, **129,** 445
Aspirin, 129, 534
Astatine, **92**
Asteroids, 595
Asthenosphere, 611–612
Asthma, 481
Astronomical units (AU), 577
Atherosclerosis, **478,** 478–479
Atmosphere, 646–670
  air pressure, 659–660
  changes in, 652–655
  layers of, 648–652
  of planets, 593–595
  transmission, 406
  wind patterns, **660,** 660–662
Atomic mass, 84, **85**
Atomic mass units (amu), 84, 97
Atomic number, 82, **84**
Atomic structure, 70–76
Atoms
  definition, 39
  kinetic energy, 268, **268**
  mass, 84, **85**
  models of, 73–76
  overview, 70–72
Atrium, **466,** 466–468, 470
Atrophy, muscular, 509
Auroras, 652, **652**
Autoimmune diseases, **522,** 522–523, **525**
Avogadro's constant, 96

B

Background radiation, 201, **201**
Bacteria, **520,** 520–521, 527, 556
Baking soda, 121, 451
Ball-and-socket joints, 493, **494**
Barometers, **659,** 659–660, **660**
Basal metabolic rate (BMR), 444
Basalt, 627
Batteries
  chemical potential energy in, 276
  in circuits, 372, 375
  in symbols, **374**

types of, 366
  voltage, **364,** 364–365
Beats, 344
Beryl, 126, **126**
Beta particles, 187–189
Betelgeuse, **585,** 585–586, 589
Biceps, **495, 497**
Big bang theory, 582–584, **583**
Bile, 452
Binary digital code, **400,** 400–401, 416
Binge drinking, 539
Biochemistry, 7
Biodegradation, 704
Biology
  anaerobes, 704
  branches of, 6, **6**
  disease bacteria, 5
  nervous systems, 406
  work, 251
Bioluminescence, 153, **153**
Birth defects, 560
Birth process, **559,** 559–560. *See also* Pregnancy; Reproduction
Bismuth, 208
Black Death, 527
Black holes, 591
Blastocysts, 556–557
Block and tackle, 259
Blood
  blood pressure, 468–470, **469,** 479, 660
  clots, 466, 479, 484
  composition of, **464,** 464–466, **465**
  flow direction, 467, **467, 469,** 470
  gas exchange, 472–473, **473**
  immune system, 465, 530–532, **532**
  during spaceflight, 511–512
  transfusions, 463, 564
Blood vessels, 467, **467,** 469, **469**
Body fat, 506
Bohr, Niels, 73
Boiling, energy for, 49–50, 54, 111, 113–114
Bonds. *See* Chemical bonds
Bone loss, 498–499, **499,** 508–509
Bones, 492–495, **494,** 498–500, **499,** 508–510
Boron, 93, **93**
Bose, S.N., 46
Bose-Einstein condensate, 46
Botulism, 522
Bread, **432**
Breast milk, 561
Breathing
  gas exchange, 472–473, **473**
  rate, 476
  respiratory system, **471,** 471–476, **473, 474**
  tidal volume, 475
  vital capacity, 475
Bromine, 92, **92**
Bronchi (bronchus), **471,** 472
Bronchitis, 481, **481**

Brown, Louise, 547
Bubbles, **344**
Bubonic plague, 527
Buckminsterfullerene, 91
Bulbourethral gland, 550
Buoyancy, 57
Burning, 51, 155–156, 160, 164
Butter, **434**

C

CAD (computer-aided design), 419
Caffeine, 537, **538**
Calcite, **634,** 635. *See also* Limestone
Calcium, 88, 103, 123, **438,** 496, 498
Calcium carbonate, 88, **88,** 174, **628,**
  628–629
Calcium fluoride, **117**
Calcium phosphate, 492
Caloric theory, 9
Calories, 269, 296, **442,** 442–444, 447
Cancer, **480,** 480–481, 524–525, **525**
Candidiasis, **565**
Canola oil, **434**
Capillaries, **469,** 469–470, 472
Capsaicin, 61
Carbohydrates, 134, **432,** 433, **433,** 447
Carbon. *See also* Organic compounds
  bonding, 130–132, **132**
  carbon dating, 193, 209
  half-life of, 208
  nuclear decay, **190,** 192
  properties, 91
  specific heat, 302
Carbon dioxide
  atmospheric, 652–653, **653,** 655
  chemical weathering by, 634–635
  dry ice, **50**
  greenhouse effect, 700, **700**
  from plants, 689
  production, 149, **150**
  in soft drinks, **173,** 173–174
Carbon monoxide, 155–156, **156,** 529,
  698, **699**
Carrier waves, 408, **408,** 410
Cars
  air bags in, 230
  air resistance, 232, **232**
  crash-test dummies, 217
  solar, **678–679,** 679
  suburbs and, 220
Cartilage, 500, **500**
Catalase, 172
Catalysts, 171, 176
Cathode-ray tubes (CRT), **4,** 4–5, 410
Cathodes, 5
Cations, 81, 123, 124
CAT scans, 524
CDs (compact discs), **400,** 400–401, 418
Cell membranes, 449
Cellular phones, 407
Cellular respiration, 689, **689**

Cellulase, 171
Cellulose, 433
Celsius scale, 292–294, **293**
Cement, 174, **174**
CFCs (chlorofluorocarbons), 653–654
Chain reactions, **198,** 198–199
Charge. *See* Electrical charge
Charon, 598, **598**
Chemical bonds, 109–110, 115–120, **117,**
  132
Chemical changes, 58–59
Chemical energy, 151–152, **152,** 269
Chemical equations, 161–166
Chemical formulas
  compounds, 109
  definition, 41
  empirical, 126–127
  formula units, 117
  molecular, 128
  parentheses in, 121
  structural, 131
  subscripts in, 41
Chemical properties, 53–54, 113–114, 133
Chemical reactions. *See also* Chemical
    equations
  electrons and, 159–160
  equations, 161–166
  overview, 148–153
  potential energy in, 269
  rates of change, 169–176
  signs, **148**
  types, 154–160
Chemical structure, **110,** 110–112
Chemistry, 38, 556
Chlamydia tracomatis, **565**
Chlorine
  gas, 92
  isotopes, **84, 85**
  molecular structure, **40**
  properties, 92, **92**
  reactions of, 108, **108**
Chlorophyll, 91
Cholesterol, 447
Cilia, 479
Cinder cones, 623, **623**
Cinnamaldehyde, **45**
Circuit breakers, 377–378
Circuits. *See* Electrical circuits
Circulatory system, 464, **466,** 466–470,
  467
Cirrostratus clouds, **658,** 659, **663,** 664
Cirrus clouds, 658, **658, 663,** 664
Claw hammers, **258**
Clay, 110
Climate, 667–670, 685, **685.** *See also*
    Weather
Climatographs, 672
Closed systems, 277
Clot formation, 466, 479, 484
Clouds, 658–659, 665, **665**
Clusters, 580
Coal, 690, 694, **694**
Codes, **397,** 397–398
Coffee, 539

Cold fronts, 664, **664**
Columbus, Christopher, 599
Comb jellies, **153**
Combustion reactions, 51, 155–156, 160,
  164
Communicable diseases, 522–523. *See also*
    Diseases
Communities, 681, **681**
Compact discs (CDs), **400,** 400–401, 418
Compasses, 381–382
Composite volcanoes, 622, **623**
Compound machines, 262
Compounds
  biochemical, 134–136
  covalent, 112, 119–120, 126–128
  definition, 39
  ionic, 112, 117, 123–125
  law of definite proportions, 167–168
  names of, 123–128
  organic, 129–132, **133**
  overview, 39–40, 108–110
Compressions, 332
Computed tomography (CT), 524
Computer models, 10–11
Computers, 416–422, **415**
Concentration, 170, 175
Condensation, 49, 311, **311, 656**
Conduction. *See* Electrical conductivity,
    heat
Conductors, 300–301, 358, **358,** 368–369,
  374
Conglomerates, 628
Congreve, Sir William, 163
Conservation of energy, 51, 276–277
Conservation of mass, 51, 162, 166
Conservation of momentum, 224
Constellations, 585, **585**
Constructive interference, 343, **343**
Continental crust, 608, **613**
Continental drift, 610
Contractions, 496–497, **497,** 559
Convection, **297, 298,** 298–299, 304, 308,
  611, **611**
Conventional current, 365
Conversion factors, 97–100, **99**
Cooling systems, 305, 309–311
Copernicus, 592
Copper, 57, 90, **118**
Copper(II) chloride, 157
Coral, 88, **88**
Core of the Earth, 609, **609**
Coriolis effect, 661, **661**
Corrosion, 151
Cosmic background radiation, 582, **582**
Coulombs, 357
Covalent bonds, 119, 130
Covalent compounds, 112, 119–120,
  126–128
CPR (cardiopulmonary resuscitation), 472
CPUs (central processing units), 418–419
Crab nebula, 590, **591**
Cranium, 493
Crash tests, **10**
Crater Lake (Oregon), **606–607**

Crests, **331,** 332, **343**
Critical mass, 199
Critical temperature, 370
Critical thinking, 12–13
Crust of the Earth, 608, **608**
Crystals, 111, **112**
Cumulus clouds, 658, **658**
Curie, Marie, 188, **188**
Curie, Pierre, 188
Current, electrical, 365, 368, 383, **383**
Cyclohexane, **131**
Cyclones, 666, **666**
Cytosine, 136, **136**

D

Dalton, John, 71, 73
Data presentation, 20–26
Data storage, 416–417
DDT, 702
Dead spots, 345
Decomposition reactions, 155
Decongestants, **535**
Democritus, 70
Density, 55–56, 674
Deposition, 636
Destructive interference, 343, **343**
Deuterium, 83, **83**
Dew point, 658
Diaphragms, 474, **474**
Diarrhea, 454
Diet. *See* Food
Diffraction, 341, **341**
Digestion. *See also* Food
    absorption of nutrients, 452–453
    digestive system, **449,** 449–452
    disorders of, 453–454
    mechanical and chemical, **448,**
        448–449
    muscle tissue in, **498**
Digitalis, 537
Digital signals, 399–401
Dihydrogen sulfide, 113
2,3-dimethylbutane, **131**
Dinitrogen tetroxide, **126**
Dioxins, 703
Direct current (DC), 365
Diseases
    communicable, 522–523
    defenses against, 530–532, **532**
    environmental health hazards, 529–530
    heart, 478, **525,** 537
    infectious, 520–523, **522**
    inherited, 532–533
    noninfectious, 523–525
    sanitation and, 526–528
    sexually transmitted, 564
Dissolution, 60, **60**
Distillation, 43
DNA, **7,** 134–136, **136,** 203, **203, 548**
DNA polymerases, 136, 171
Doppler effect, **338,** 338–339, 581
Doses, 536

Double-displacement reactions, 158, 160
Double helix, 135, **136**
Downlinks, 403
Drew, Charles, 463
Drugs
    abuse, **538,** 538–540
    design of, 74
    drug-food interactions, 519, 537
    prescription, 535–537
    psychoactive, 535, **535**
    tolerance, 539
    types of, 534–537
Dry cleaning, 43
Dry ice, **50.** *See also* Carbon dioxide
DVDs (digital versatile discs), 418
Dwarf elliptical galaxies, 579

E

Eagle nebula, **589**
Earth, 606–638. *See also* Plate tectonics
    composition, **39, 83,** 90
    diameter and mass, 586, 602
    gravitational constant, 237
    interior, **608,** 608–609, 620
    magnetic field, 382, **382**
    photograph from space, **576**
    radioactive isotopes, 192
    seasons, 668–669
    surface temperatures, 668
Earthquakes
    focus, 618, **618,** 621
    intensity, 621
    magnitude, **621,** 621–622
    plate boundaries and, **617,** 617–618,
        618
    P (primary) waves, 335, 618, 620
    seismographs, **619,** 619–620, **620**
    specific events, 621
    S (secondary) waves, 335, 619–620
Earth science, 44, 92, 156, 193, 303, 335,
    382
Eclipses, 599–600, **600**
Ecosystems
    balanced, 682
    changes in, 682–687
    definition, 680
    human activities and, 686
    nonnative species, 687
    overview, 681, **681**
Efficiency of machines, 278–280
Eggs, human, 551–556, **552, 553, 555, 556**
Einstein, Albert, 46, 197
Ejaculation, 550
Elasticity, 133
Elastic potential energy, 264
Electret microphones, 405
Electrical charge, 123, 125, 356–360, **360**
Electrical circuits
    fuses and breakers, 377–378
    overview, 372–374
    series and parallel, 375, **375**
    shorts, 377

Electrical conductivity
    chemical bonding, 117, 119
    copper and, 57, **118**
    semiconductors, 93–94
Electric current, 365, 368, 383, **383**
Electricity, 354–386. *See also* Electrical
        charge; Electrical circuits; Electrical
        conductivity; Electric current
    electrical resistance, 367–371
    electric fields, 361, **361**
    electric force, 360–362, 388
    electric power and energy, 270, 276,
        376–377
    fuses and circuit breakers, 377–378
    from nuclear power, 204
    production of, 694, **694**
    sound from, 397–398, **398**
Electric meters, **377**
Electric motors, 386
Electrochemical cells, 364–365
Electrodes, 364
Electrolysis, **59,** 155
Electrolytes, 364
Electromagnetic waves (EMF waves). *See
        also* Light; Waves
    definition, 323
    electrical and magnetic components,
        385, **385**
    energy transfer through, 271, 299
    radio transmissions, 409–410
    spectrum 334, **334.** *See also* Light.
    television transmissions, 410–411
Electromagnetism. *See also* Electromag-
        netic waves
    electromagnetic devices, 384, 386
    electromagnetic induction, 384–385,
        385
    overview, **383,** 383–386, **385**
Electronegativity, 116
Electrons
    beta particles, 187–189
    charge and mass, 72
    clouds, **115,** 115–116, 119–120
    in covalent bonds, 119, **119**
    definition, 72
    electrical charge, 357–358
    energy levels, 73, **73,** 75
    in ionic bonds, 116
    location of, 73–74
    orbitals, 75, **75**
    valence, 76, **76**
Elements
    creation of, 206
    families, 86–94
    overview, 39–40
    radioactive, 609
Elliptical galaxies, 579
Embryo, 557
Emeralds, **126**
Empathy, 563
Emphysema, 481, **481**
Empirical formulas, 126–127, **127**
Endergonic reactions, 153
Endothermic reactions, 151–152, **152**

Endurance, 504
Energy
  to break bonds, 149
  for change of state, 48–49, **49**
  chemical, 151–152, **152**, 269
  coal, 690, 694, **694**
  conservation of, 51–52, 272–280
  definition, 48, 263
  efficiency, 278–280, **694,** 694–695
  electrical, 270, 276, 376–377
  electrical potential, **363,** 363–364, **364**
  food, 269, 296, 306, 441–444, **442, 443, 444**
  geothermal, 692–693, **693**
  gravitational potential, 264–265, 271, 274, 276, 363, **363**
  heat, 295–296
  in human body, 443–444
  hydroelectric, 692, **693**
  kinetic, **266,** 266–268, **268, 273,** 273–274, 291
  light, 271
  mass-energy equation, 197
  mechanical, 268, 275, 280
  nuclear, 197–198, 270, 693
  potential, 264–265, 269, **273,** 273–274
  reduction in use, 704–706
  solar, 688–689, 691, **691**
  sources, **690**
  in stars, 588–589
  transfer, 297–304, 308
  transformations, 272–275
  usage, 688, **688**
  waves, 323–327
  wind, 691–692, **692**
  work and, 263
Energyguide labels, 312, **312**
Energy levels, 73
Engineering, 323
ENIAC (Electronic Numerical Integrator and Computer), 414, **414**
Environmental hazards, 529–530
Environmental Protection Agency (EPA), 527
Environmental science, 473, 498, 562
Enzymes, 74, 153, 171–172, **172,** 451
Epicenters of earthquakes, 618, **618,** 620, **620**
Equations
  acceleration, 225–226
  chemical, 161–163, 165–166
  efficiency, 278–279
  electric power, 376
  frequency-period, 333
  gravitational potential energy, 264–265
  kinetic energy, 266–267
  mass-energy, 197
  mechanical advantage, 255–256
  momentum, 223
  Newton's second law, 235–236
  power, 252
  resistance, 368–369
  specific heat, 303–304
  speed, 220–221
  temperature conversion, 292–294
  universal gravitation, 9
  wave speed, 335–336
  work, 250–251
Equilibrium systems, 174–176
Equinoxes, 668–669
Erections, 549–550
Erosion, **636,** 636–638, **637, 638**
Esophagus, 450, **450**
Estrogen, 552–553, **553,** 563
Ethane, 130, **130,** 138
Ethanol, 132, **132,** 302
Ethene, 133, 138
Ethylene glycol, 57, 62
Ethyne, 138
Eutrophication, 702, **702**
Evaporation, **48,** 48–49, **49,** 310, **656**
Everest, Mount, 614
Exercise
  aerobic, 503–504, 507
  anaerobic, 501–503, 507
  benefits of, 504–507
  nutritional requirements, 439
  during spaceflights, 510
  stretching exercises, **505**
Exergonic reactions, 153
Exosphere, 651
Exothermic reactions, 151–152, **152,** 158
Experiments, 14
Exponential growth, 552
Exponents, 23
Extensors, 497, **497**
Extrusive igneous rock, 627, **627**

F

Fahrenheit scale, 292–294, **293**
Fallopian tubes, 551, **551, 556**
Faraday, Michael, 384
Fats, **432,** 434, **434,** 445, 447
Faults, 614, **614**
FDA (Food and Drug Administration), 447, 535–536
Female reproductive cycle, **552,** 552–554, **553**
Female reproductive system, **551,** 551–552, **552**
Fermi, Enrico, 197
Fertilization, 547–548, **555,** 555–556
Fetus, 555, **557,** 557–558, **558**
Fibula, 493
Fine arts, 110, 159, 185
Fire extinguishers, 164
Fire retardants, **175**
Fireworks, 163, **163**
Fish oils, 484
Fission, 197–199, **198,** 205, 270
Flammability, 54
Fleming, Alexander, 5
Flexors, 497, **497**
Floppy disks, 416
Fluids, 48. *See also* Gases; Liquids
Fluorine, **81,** 81–82, 92, **92**
FM (frequency modulation), 409
Foams, 44, 160
Focus, earthquake, 618, **618,** 621
Follicles, **552,** 552–554, **553**
Follicle-stimulating hormone (FSH), 552
Food. *See also* Digestion
  drug-food interactions, 519, 537
  energy in, 269, 296, 306, 441–444, **442, 443, 444**
  food pyramid, 438–439, **439**
  inspection, 527
  labels, 447
  nutrients in, **432,** 432–438, **433, 434, 436**
  obesity, 445–446
  poisoning, 528
  storage, 528
  undernourishment, 446
  vegetarian diets, 440
Food and Drug Administration (FDA), 447, 535–536
Forces
  acceleration, 225–228
  balanced and unbalanced, 229, **229, 231,** 235
  definition, 228
  electric, 360–362, 388
  frictional, 231–232
  gravitational, 232–233, 237–238, 361
  machines and, 254, **258,** 260, **260**
  magnetic, 380–382, **381, 382**
  net, 228–229, 235
  Newton's Laws of Motion, 234–240
  nuclear, 195–196
Formaldehyde, 127–128
Formulas. *See* Chemical formulas
Formula units, 117
Fossil fuels, 635, **689,** 689–690
Fossils, 628, **628,** 631
Fractures, bone, 499, **499**
Franklin, Benjamin, 357
Franklin, Rosalind, 29
Free fall, 237–238, 602
Free radicals, 159–160
Freezing, **49**
Freon, 310
Frequency, 333, **333,** 335, 338–339, 410
Friction, 231–232, 358–359
Frisch, Otto, 195
Fronts, weather, **663,** 663–666, **664**
Frost wedging, 633
Fruits, **432,** 433, **433, 442**
FSH (follicle-stimulating hormone), 552
Fuels
  coal, 690, **694**
  fossil, **689,** 689–690
  gasoline, 42, 52, 55, 59
  rocket, 147, **240**
Fuji, Mount (Japan), 623, **623**
Fulcrum, 258, **258**
Fuller, R. Buckminster, 91
Fullerenes, 91
Fungi, 521

Funnel clouds, 665, **665**
Fuses, 377–378
Fusion, 200, 206, 270, **270,** 588–590

G

Galaxies, 577, **577, 578, 579,** 580, **580,** 584
Galileo, 597
Gamma radiation, 188, 190
Gamma rays, 188, 334
Gases
    dissolved in liquids, 44
    gas exchange, 472–473, **473**
    kinetic theory of matter, 46, **46**
    noble, 93, **93**
    pressure, 47, **47,** 170
    trace atmospheric, 648
Gasoline, 42, 52, 55, 59
Gemstones, **126**
Generators, 386
Gene therapy, 533
Genetic counselors, 533
Genetic mutations, 203
Genital herpes, **565**
Geodesic domes, 91, **91**
Geostationary orbits, 403–404
Geosynchronous orbits, 404
Geothermal energy, 692–693, **693**
Germanium, 94
German measles, 560
Giardia lamblia, **521**
Gibbous moons, 599
Glaciers, 221, 637, **637,** 685, **685.**
Glass-blowing, 37–38, **38**
Global warming, 655, 670, 700. *See also*
    Climate; Weather
Glucose, 91, 127, 134, **433, 448**
Glycogen, 134
Gold, **21,** 89, **89,** 90
Gonorrhea, **565**
Granite, 626–627, **627**
Grape juice, 41
Graphite, 197, 302
Graphs, 21–22, **21–22,** 219, **219,** 227–228
Graves's disease, 204
Gravitational force, 232–233, 361
Gravitational potential energy, 264–265,
    271, 274, 276
Gravity, 232–233, 237–238, 512, 580, 602
Great Pyramid, 261
Great Red Spot, 596, **596**
Greenhouse effect, 654, **654,** 700, 704
Grounding, 370
Ground waves, 409
Guanine, 136, **136**
Gyrocompasses, 381

H

Haber process, 168, **175,** 175–176
Hahn, Otto, 195, 197–198
Half-life, **191,** 191–193

Hallucinogens, **538**
Halogens, 92, **92**
Hardware, computer, 418
Harmonic motion, 327
Hawaiian Islands, 625
HCG (human chorionic gonadotropin),
    556
HDTV (high-definition television), 412
Heart, **466,** 466–470, **467,** 497, **498,**
    504
Heart attacks, 478
Heart disease, **525,** 537
Heat
    caloric theory, 9
    definition, 296
    from electricity generation, 695
    kinetic theory, 9
    semiconductors and, 93
    solar, **307,** 307–308, 696
    specific, 302–304
    temperature and, 295–296
    using, 305–312
Heat exchangers, 308
Heating systems, 305–309
Heat pumps, 311, **311**
Helicases, 136
Helium
    alpha particles, 189
    amount in universe, 51
    atomic structure, **72**
    ballooning, **55**
    density, 55
    properties, 93, **93**
    rate of motion, 46
Hemoglobin, 202, 465, **465,** 478, 523
Hepatitis B, **565**
Heterogeneous mixtures, 42
Hexane, **131**
Hexokinase, **172**
High-definition television (HDTV), 412
Himalayan Mountains, 614, **614**
Histamines, 531
HIV (human immunodeficiency virus),
    522–523, 564, **564, 565**
Holst, Gustav, 603
Homogeneous mixtures, 42, 44
Hookworms, 521
Hormones, 502, 552–553, **553,** 563–564
Horsepower, 252
Hot spots, 625
Hubble, Edwin, 580–581
Hubble Space Telescope, **580**
Human body. *See also* Reproduction
    bones, 492–495, **494**
    circulatory system, 464, **466,** 466–470,
        467, 469
    composition, **39**
    digestive system, **449,** 449–452
    exercise and, 506
    immune system, 465, 530–532, **532**
    nerves, 365, **365**
    respiratory system, **471,** 471–476, **473,**
        474
    simple machines in, **258**

Human immunodeficiency virus (HIV),
    522–523, 564, **564, 565**
Humidity, 657
Huntington's disease, 524
Hurricanes, 666, **666**
Hydrocarbons, 130
Hydrochloric acid, 451
Hydroelectric power, 686, 692, **693**
Hydrogen
    amount in universe, 51
    bonds, **115,** 115–116
    isotopes of, 83, **83**
    molecular structure, **40**
    nuclear decay, 192
    nuclear fusion, 200, 206
    radicals, 159
    rate of collisions, 171
    reactions, **109**
    spectral lines, **581**
Hydrogen carbonate, 121
Hydrogen peroxide, 166, 172
Hydrogen sulfide, 166
Hydroxide ions, **121**
Hypertension, 479
Hypothesis testing, 13, **13**

I

Ice, 55, **57,** 221, 633
Igneous rocks, 627, **627, 630**
Immiscibility, 42, **42**
Immune system, 465, 530–532, **532**
Inclined planes, **260,** 260–261, **261**
Indigo, 41, **41**
Inertia, 235, 237
Infants, 559, 561–562
Infection, 520
Inflammatory responses, 531
Infrared (IR) light, 334
Inhalants, **538**
Inhibitors, 171
Insulators, 301, 309, 358, **358,** 370–371
Insulin, 135, **135**
Interference, **342,** 342–346, **343**
International System of Units, 15–19, **16**
Internet, 420–422
Internet service providers (ISPs), 422
Interstellar matter, 578
Intoxication, **540.** *See also* Alcohol
Intrusive igneous rock, 627, **627**
Inuit people, 484
In-vitro fertilization, 547
Iodine, 92, **92,** 192, 208, **438**
Ionic bonds, 116–117, **117**
Ionic compounds, 112, 117, 123–125
Ionization, 81, 187
Ionosphere, **651,** 651–652
Ions, 81–82, 88, 112, 120–122
Iron
    abundance and cost, 90
    in blood, 465, **465**
    compounds, 124
    density, 55

dietary, **438**
melting point, **21**
molar mass, 99
scanning tunneling micrograph, **39**
Ironman Triathlon World Championship, 491–492
Iron oxide, 124, 634
Isobars, 667, **667**
Isooctane, 91, **149, 150**
Isopropanol, 132
Isotopes, 83, 609. *See also* Radioactivity

J

Joints, 493, **494, 497**
Joules, 251, 263
Jupiter, 593, **596,** 596–597

K

Kelvin scale, 293–294
Kepler, Johannes, 592
Kilowatt-hours, 377
Kinetic energy, **266,** 266–268, **268, 273,** 273–274, 291
Kinetic theory, 9, 45–48, 52, 170, 337
Koch's postulates, 524
Krypton, **93**

L

Labor, **559**
Lactose intolerance, 453
Landfills, 704, **704**
Language arts, 15, 466, 493, 560
LANs (local area networks), 420
Large intestine, 453–454
Lasers, 400, **400,** 418
Lava, 622
Law of action and reaction, 239. *See also* Newton's laws of motion
Law of conservation of energy, 51, 276–277
Law of conservation of mass, 51, 162, 166, 224
Law of definite proportions, 167–168
Laws, scientific, 8
Lead, **21,** 55, 185, 498
LeChâtelier's principle, 175–176
Leonardo da Vinci, 7, **7,** 515
Leukemia, 204
Levers, **257–258,** 257–260
Life expectancy, 566
Ligaments, 493, **500**
Light
    energy, 271
    intensity, 587, **587**
    interference, 344, **344**
    speed, 337
    visible, 334, **334**
Light bulbs, 367, **367,** 375

Lightning, 357, 664
Light-year, 577, 584
Limestone, 88, **88,** 156, 174, **628,** 628–629
Line-of-sight transmission, 409
Lipase, 171
Liquids, 46, **46**
Lithium, 80, **81,** 158, 206
Lithosphere, 610, **611,** 612
Liver, 452
Local Group, 580
Locks, 399, **399**
Lodestones, 379, **379**
Logic gates, 419–420, **420**
Loschmidt, Joseph, 96
Luciferase, 153
Lunar eclipses, 599–600, **600**
Lung cancer, 480, **480,** 529
Lungs, 467, **471,** 472–473, **473,** 475, 479, **479**
Lupus, **525**
Lutenizing hormone (LH), 552
Lyme disease, 564
Lye (sodium hydroxide), 121, 202

M

Machines
    compound, 262
    efficiency, 278–280
    perpetual motion, 279–280
    simple, **257–258,** 257–262
    work and force, 254, **254**
MADD (Mothers Against Driving Drunk), 540
Magma, **612,** 612–613, 627
Magnesium, 53, 88, **163**
Magnesium fluoride, 111
Magnetism. *See also* Electromagnetism
    magnetic fields, 380–385, **381, 382, 383, 385**
    magnetic media, 417
    magnetic poles, 380, 382, **382**
    magnets, 379–380, **381,** 384
    overview, 615, **615**
Magnetite, 379
Male reproductive system, 548–550, **549**
Mantle, **608,** 608–609, **609**
Mantle plumes, 625
MAO (monoamine oxidase), 519
Marble, 629
Mars, 238, 593, 595, **595,** 602
Mass
    atomic, 84, **85**
    during changes of state and, 50
    conservation of, 51, 162, 166, 224
    critical, 199
    definition, 18
    density and, 55–56
    gravity and, 232–233
    molar, 96, **96,** 98–100, **99**
    nucleus, 198
    universe fate and, 584

Mass-energy equation, 197
Mass number, 82, **84**
Matter, 36–60, 106–136
    definition, 38
    kinetic theory of, 45–52
    overview, 38–41
    properties of, 53–60
Mauna Loa, 623, **623**
Mazama, Mount, 607
Mechanical advantage, 255–256, 259. *See also* Machines
Mechanical energy, 268, 275, 280
Mechanical waves, 323
Medicine, nuclear, 203. *See also* Diseases; Health
Medium, 323, 336–337
Meitner, Lise, 195
Melting, **21,** 48, 54, 111, 113–114, 117, 138
Menopause, 566
Menstruation, **553,** 554
Mercalli scale, modified, 621
Mercurial barometers, 660, **660**
Mercury metal, 89, **89**
Mercury (planet), 593–594, **594,** 602
Meringue, 44
Mesosphere, 651
Metabolic rate, **443,** 443–444
Metallic bonds, 118
Metalloids (semiconductors), 87, **93,** 93–94, 371, **371**
Metals
    abundance and cost, 90
    alkali, 87
    alkaline-earth, 88, **88**
    chemical bonding, 118
    definition, 87
    transition, 89, **89,** 124
Metamorphic rocks, 629, **629, 630**
Meteorology, 11. *See also* Weather
Methane, 130, **130,** 156, **156, 161,** 699
Methanol, 132, **132**
3-methylpentane, **131**
Microchips, 417, **417, 418,** 419
Microphones, 398, 405
Microscopes, 14, 564
Microwaves, 334, 402–403, 406–407, **407,** 409
Mid-oceanic ridges, 612, **612,** 616, 624
Milk and milk products, 57, **432,** 433, 438, 442, 561
Milky Way galaxy, **578,** 578–580, **579,** 584
Minerals, 437–438, 447, 626
Miscarriages, 482
Miscibility 42, **42**
Mixtures, 41–42, 44
Models, 9–11, 73–76, 110–111
Modems, 422
Modulation, 408, **408**
Molar mass, 96, **96, 98,** 98–100, **99**
Molecular formulas, 128
Molecules, **40,** 112–114, **114,** 171, 268, **268**
Mole ratios, 166–168

Moles, 96–100, 166–168, **167**
Momentum, 222–224
Monoamine oxidase (MAO), 519
Monomers, 133, 136
Moon, **599,** 599–600, **600**
Moons, 597
Moore's law, 424
Morse, Samuel, 397
Morse code, **397,** 399
Motion, 218–224
MSDS (material safety data sheets), 530
Mucous membranes, 530–531
Muscles
    contractions, 496–497, **497**
    exercise and, 502
    fatigue, 503
    force and, 495–498
    proportion, 5–6
    spaceflight and, 509
    strength, 496
    tissues, **498**

N

Naismith's rule, 222
Narcotics, **538**
Natural gas, 690. *See also* Methane
Nebulas, **589,** 590, **591,** 598
Neisseria gonorrhoeae, **565**
Neon, **40, 76,** 80, 93, **93**
Neptune, 238, 593, 597, **597**
Nerves, 365, **365,** 406
Neutron emission, 188
Neutrons
    charge and mass, 72
    definition, 72
    fast, 188
    isotopes, 83–84
    mass number, 82
    in nuclear decay reactions, 189–190,
        190, 196, 198
Neutron stars, 591
Newton, Sir Isaac, 234, 543
Newton's Laws of Motion, 234–240, **235,
    239**
Newtons (units), 236
Nicotine, 477, 479, 482, 537, **538**
Nimbostratus clouds, **658,** 659, 664
Nitrogen, **48,** 55, 80
Nitrogen oxides, 698
Nitroglycerin, **169**
Noble gases, 93, **93**
Nodes, 345
Nomenclature
    covalent compounds, 126
    ionic compounds, 123–125
    organic compounds, 132
    polyatomic anions, 121–122
Nonmetals, 87, 91–94
Nonpolar covalent bonds, 119, **119**
Nonrenewable resources, 690, **690**
Nuclear bombs, 116, 199–200
Nuclear chain reactions, **198,** 198–199

Nuclear energy, 270, 693
Nuclear fission, 197–199, **198,** 205, 270
Nuclear forces, 195–196
Nuclear fusion, 200, 206, 270, **270,** 588–590
Nuclear power, 204–206
Nuclear radiation. *See also* Radioactivity
    background, 201, **201**
    beneficial uses, 203–204
    dangers, 201–203
    decay rates, **191,** 191–193
    decay reactions, 189–191, 194
    definition, 186
    health effects, 202–204, **203**
    overview, 186–188
    types of, 187–188
Nuclear reactors, 197
Nuclear wastes, **205,** 205–206
Nuclear weapons testing, 116
Nucleus, 72, 82
Nuclides, 195–196
Nutrition. *See* Food
Nylon, 39

O

Obesity, 445–446
Obsidian, 627, **627**
Occupational Safety and Health Adminis-
    tration (OSHA), 530
Oceanic crust, 608, 613, **613**
Oceans, 636, 669
Odors, 45
Oersted, Hans Christian, 383
Ohms, 368
Oil, 155, 690
Oils, dietary, 434, **434**
Olympus Mons, **595**
Open systems, 277
Operating systems, 418
Optical fibers, 401–402, **402, 407**
Optical media, 418
Orbitals, 75, **75,** 80
Orbits, geostationary, 403–404
Organic compounds, 129–133, **133**
Orion, **585**
OSHA (Occupational Safety and Health
    Administration), 530
Osteoporosis, 498–499, **499**
Outgassing, 652
Ovaries, 551, **551, 552, 556,** 563
Ovulation, 552–553, **553**
Oxygen
    atmospheric, 652
    in combustion, 155–156, **156**
    discovery of, 178
    exercise and, 502–503
    human requirement for, 443, 465
    molecular structure, **40**
    rate of motion, 46, 171
    reactions, **109**
    respiratory system, **471** (*See also*
        Breathing)
Ozone, 473, 650, **650,** 653–654

P

P (primary) waves, **618,** 618–620, **620**
Pancreas, 451
Pangaea, 610, **610**
Parallel circuits, 375, **375**
Parícutin (Mexico), 623, **623**
Particle accelerators, 15
Particles, 45–48, 187–189, 291, 328
Particulate matter (PM), 698
Patella, 493
Pathogens, 520, 526
Pauling, Linus, 116
Pendulum, energy in, 277
Penicillin, 5, 535
Penis, **549,** 549–550
Penzias, Arno, 582
Pepsin, 451
Periodic law, 77
Periodic table, 77–85, **78–79**
    halogens, 92
    illustration of, **78–79**
    metals, **87,** 87–90
    noble gases, 93, **93**
    nonmetals, **91,** 91–94
    organization of, 77–80
    semiconductors, **93,** 93–94
Periods, 80, 332–333
Perpetual motion machines, 279–280
pH, 451, 556, 635
Phases, 599, **599**
Phosphors, 410
Phosphorus, **40, 438**
Photoelectrical cells, 365
Photography, 150, **150**
Photosynthesis
    atmosphere and, 652–653
    chemical reactions, 152, **152,** 155, **155**
    energy transfer, **152,** 269, 688
    fossil fuels and, **689**
Physical changes, 59
Physical fitness, 501, 507. *See also* Exercise
Physical properties, 54
Physical transmission, 406
Physics, 444, 613, 669
Piano tuners, 344–345
Piezoelectric cells, 365
Pitch, 338
Pixels, 411
Placenta, 557, **557, 559,** 560
Planets, 592–593
Plants, 633, 652
Plasma, blood, 464, **464**
Plasma, phase of matter, 46
Plastic recycling, 705
Platelets, blood, 466
Plate tectonics
    earthquakes and, **617,** 617–618, **618**
    evidence for, 615–616
    origin of word, 616
    overview, **610,** 610–611, **611,** 616
    plate boundaries, **14,** 612–614, **613,
        614, 617,** 624, **624**
    transform faults, **614,** 614–615

Pluto, 593, 598, **598**
Plutonium, 192
Polar covalent bonds, 120, **120**
Poles, magnetic, 380, 382, **382**
Pollution
    acid rain, 635, 700–701
    air, **649,** 649–650, 653–654, 697–701
    definition, 697
    land, 703–704
    reduction of, 704–706
    water, 701–703
Polyatomic ions, 120–122
Polyethylene, 133, **133,** 154, **154**
Polymerases, 136
Polymerization reactions, 154
Polymers, **133,** 133–135
Polystyrene, **160**
Population growth, 552, 569, 707
Potassium, 158, **158,** 192, **438**
Potato Famine of Ireland, 446
Potential difference, 364, 386
Potential energy
    chemical, 269, 276
    elastic, 264
    electrical, **363,** 363–364, **364**
    gravitational, 230–231, 264–265, 271, 274, 363, **363**
    from kinetic energy, 273, **273**
Power
    electrical, 376–377
    hydroelectric, 686, 692, **693**
    nuclear, 204–206
    units of, 252–253, 256
Power plants, **694,** 694–695
Precipitation, in water cycle, **656,** 657
Precision, 24
Prefixes, **16,** 126
Pregnancy. *See also* Reproduction
    birth, **559,** 559–560
    drinking alcohol during, 540
    drug abuse during, 560
    process of, **555,** 555–558, **556, 557, 558**
    smoking during, 482
Prescription drugs, 535–537
Pressure
    air, 659–660
    atmospheric, **648,** 667
    blood, 468–470, **469,** 479, 660
    definition, 47
    effect on equilibrium, 175–176
    gas, 47, **47,** 170
    gradients, 660
    reaction rates and, 170
    wind and, 660
Priestly, Joseph, 178
Products, 149, **150,** 165
Progesterone, **553,** 553–554
Propane, 130, **130,** 166
Prostate gland, **549,** 550
Protease, 171
Proteins, 134–135, **432,** 435, **435,** 447, 451. *See also* Enzymes

Protium, 83, **83**
Protons, 72, 82, 196, 357
Protozoa, 521, **521**
Psychoactive drugs, 535, **535**
Puberty, 563
Pulleys, 259, **259,** 278
Pulmonary circuit, **467**
Pulse, 468
Pumice, 44
Pure substances, 41, 54
Pyramids, 261

Q

Qualitative/quantitative statements, 8
Quartz, 111, **111,** 626
Quasars, 583

R

Radiation, 186, **297,** 299–300. *See also* Nuclear radiation
Radicals, 159–160
Radioactivity. *See also* Nuclear radiation
    dating, 632
    definition, 186, **186**
    in Earth's interior, 609
    tracers, 204
    uses of, 90, 203
Radio telescopes, 15
Radio transmissions, **408,** 408–410
Radio waves, 334, 651, **651**
Radium, **188,** 188–189, 192–193
Radon
    health effects, 186, 202, 529
    nuclear decay, 189, 192, 208
Rainbows, **646–647,** 647
Random-access memory (RAM), 417
Rarefactions, 332
Reactants, 149, **150,** 165
Reaction rates, 169–172, 174
Reactivity, 54
Read-only memory (ROM), 418
Recycling, 705–706
Red blood cells, **464,** 465, 512, **523**
Red giants, 590, **590**
Redox reactions, 159–160, 634
Red shifts, 581, **581**
Reflections, **340,** 340–342
Refraction, 342, **342**
Refrigerants, **310,** 310–311, 653–654
Relative humidity, 657
Relativity, 197
Relay systems, **402,** 402–403, **407**
Rems, 204
Renewable resources, 691
Reproduction
    birth, **559,** 559–560
    breast milk, 561–562
    female reproductive cycle, **552,** 552–554, **553**

    female reproductive system, **551,** 551–552, 566
    male reproductive system, 548–550, **549,** 566
    pregnancy, **555,** 555–560, **556, 557, 558, 559**
    sexually transmitted diseases, 564
Repulsion, 356–357, 362
Resistance, electrical, 367–371
Resistors, 368, 374, 376
Respiration, 269, 653, **653.** *See also* Breathing
Reversibility, **173,** 173–174
Reye's syndrome, 534, **534**
Richter scale, 621, **621**
Rift valleys, 612, **612**
Rigel, 585, **585**
Ring of Fire, 624, **624**
Rockets, 240, **240**
Rocks
    age of, 631–632
    cycle, **630,** 630–631
    igneous, 627, **627,** 630
    magnetic bands in, 616
    metamorphic, 629, **629, 630**
    sedimentary, 628, **628,** 630
    structure and origin, 626–631
    weathering, 628, **630,** 633–638, **634, 635, 636, 638**
Roentgen, Wilhelm, 5–6
Roller coasters, **272,** 272–273, **273,** 275
Roosevelt, Franklin D., 692
Rubella, 560
Rust, **54,** 124
Rutherford, Ernest, 76, 187, 189
R-values, 309

S

S (secondary) waves **618,** 618-620, **620**
Saccharin, 445
SADD (Students Against Driving Drunk), 540
Safety
    electric shock, 368
    grounding, 370–371
    occupational, 530
St. Helens, Mount (Washington), 624
Salivary glands, 449, **449**
Sandstone, 628
Sanitation, 526–528
Satellites, 403–404, **404**
Saturation, 657
Saturn, 593, 597, **597**
Scan lines, 410
Scanning electron microscopes (SEM), 564
Schematic diagrams, **373,** 373–374
Science, 4–7, **6,** 11
Scientific data presentation, 20–26
Scientific laws, 8
Scientific method, 13, **13**
Scientific notation, 22–24

Scientific theories, 8–11
Screws, 261, **261**
Scrotum, 548, **549,** 550
Seamounts, 623
Search engines, 421
Secondary sex characteristics, 563
Sedatives, 537, **538**
Sedimentary rocks, 628, **628,** 630
Seismic waves, 323, 335, **618,** 618–620, **620,** 642–643
Seismograms, 620, **620**
Seismographs, 619, **619**
Seismology, 619–620. *See also* Earthquakes
Semen, 550, 554
Semiconductors, 87, **93,** 93–94, 371, **371**
Seminal vesicles, 550
SEM (scanning electron microscopes), 564
Series circuits, 375, **375**
Servers, 420
Sexually transmitted diseases (STDs), 522–523, 564–565, **565**
Shadow masks, 411
Shale, 628, **628**
Shepard, Alan B., 147
Shield volcanoes, 622, **623**
SI (International System of Units), 15–18, **16**
Sick building syndrome, 529
Sickle cell anemia, 523, **523**
SIDS (sudden infant death syndrome), 482
Signals
analog, 399, **405,** 405–406
codes, 397–398, **398**
digital, 399–401
microwave, 406–407
overview, 396, **396**
Significant figures, 24–26
Silicon, 94, **94**
Silicon dioxide, 111
Silver, **21,** 90
Silver bromide, **150**
Simple machines, **257–258,** 257–262. *See also* Machines
Sine curves, 331, **331**
Single-displacement reactions, 157–158
Sirius, 586, 589
Skin, 530–531
Skin cancer, 524–525, **525**
Sky diving, 238
Sky waves, 409
Slopes of lines, 219
Small intestine, 451–452, **452**
Smog, 701. *See also* Air, pollution
Smoke alarms, 203, **203**
Smoking
addictive nature of, 477
bans on, 480
carbon monoxide and, 478
health effects, **478,** 478–482, **480, 481**
secondhand, 481–482

Social studies
bubonic plague, 527
cars and suburbs, 220
fireworks, 163
Benjamin Franklin, 306
gyrocompasses, 381
lactose intolerance, 453
mineral use, 627
Morse code, 397
Linus Pauling, 306
population growth, 552, 569, 707
potato famine, 446
pyramids, 261
Mount St. Helens, 624
smoking, 480
steam engines, 306
Tennessee Valley Authority, 692
Sodium
dietary, **438,** 447
properties of, 87, **87**
reactions of, 108, **108,** 158
states of matter, **46**
Sodium carbonate, 121
Sodium chloride, **47,** 111–112, **112,** 116–117
Sodium hydrogen carbonate, 121, 451
Sodium hydroxide, 121
Soft drinks, 173, **173**
Software, 418
Solar cars, **678–679,** 679
Solar energy, 403, 691
Solar heating, **307,** 307–308, 696
Solar system, **577, 592,** 592–593, 598
Solenoids, 383–384
Solids, **46,** 46–47, **47**
Solstices, 668–669
Solvents, dry-cleaning, 43
Sonar, 641
Sorbitol, 129, **129**
Sound
from electricity, 397–401, **398,** 405–406
radio transmissions, 408–410
telephones, **405,** 405–407
waves, **10**
Spaceflight
artificial gravity, 512
physiological effects, 508–512
planetary probes, 205, 594–595
Space science
electromagnetic waves, 294
element formation, 206
forces, 238–239
organic molecules, 121
Speakers, 397–398, **398**
Specific heat, 302–304
Spectral lines, **581, 587,** 587–588
Spectrophotometers, 15
Speed, 218–221, **219,** 224, 335–337. *See also* Velocity
Sperm cells, **549,** 549–550, **555,** 555–556, **556**
Spiral galaxies, 579, **579**
Sprains, 500
Spring motions, 325, **325, 327,** 327–328

Starch, 134, 433, **433**
Stars, 577, 585–591, **589, 590**
Stationary fronts, 664
Statue of Liberty, 159, **159**
STDs (sexually transmitted diseases), 522–523, 564–565, **565**
Steam engines, 306
Steel, 53, 55
Stimulants, 537, **538**
Stomach, 451, **451**
Strains, 500
Strassman, Fritz, 195, 197–198
Stratosphere, 650
Stratus clouds, 658, **658**
Strokes, 479
Strong nuclear force, 196, **196**
Structural formulas, 110
Subduction zones, **612,** 612–613
Sublimation, 50, **50**
Subscripts, 41
Substances, pure 41
Substrates, 172
Succession, 684
Sucrose. *See* Sugar
Sudden infant death syndrome (SIDS), 482
Sugar
calories in, 445
chemical formula, 41, 178
chemical structure, 112, **433**
dissolution, **60**
properties, 113
Sugar substitutes, 445
Sulfur, 40
Sulfur dioxide, 698
Sun, **83,** 586–590
Sunlight, cancer from, 524–525, **525**
Sunscreen, 525, 709
Superclusters, 580
Superconductors, 370
Supergiants, 590
Supernovas, 590, 598
Superposition, principle of, 631–632
Surface area, 170
Surface waves, 619–620, **620**
Sweating, 48, **48,** 310. *See also* Evaporation
Switches, 373–374, 401
Synthesis reactions, 154–155
Syphilis, **565**
Systemic circuit, **467**
Systems, open and closed, 277

T

Tars, 478
Technology, 7, **7,** 276
Telecommunication, 398–401
Telegraphs, 397, **397**
Telephones, 402, **405,** 405–407
Telescopes, 15, **15, 580,** 586
Television, 409–413, **411**
Tellurium, 93, **93,** 208

Temperature
    absolute zero, 293
    air density and, 674
    in the atmosphere, **648,** 649–651
    during changes of state, **49**
    critical, 370
    definition, 290
    of Earth's interior, 609, **609**
    effect on equilibrium, 175–176
    energy and, 290–294
    heat and, 295–296
    humidity and, 657–658
    kinetic energy and, 268, **268,** 291
    light and, 294
    of planets, 593–594
    reaction rates and, 170, **170**
    scale conversions, 292–294, **293**
    specific heat, 302–304
    sperm cells and, 550
    of stars, 587, **587**
    of the universe, 582
    work and, 306
Temperature inversions, 649, **649**
TEM (transmission electron micro-
    scopes), 564
Tendons, 495, **495**
Terminal velocity, 238
Testes, 548, **549,** 554, 563
Testosterone, 502, **538,** 548, 563
Tetrachloroethylene, 43
Theories, scientific, 8–11
Thermoelectric cells, 365
Thermometers, 61, **291,** 291–292
Thermosphere, 651
Thunderstorms, 664–665
Thymine, 136, **136**
Thyroid gland, 204
Tidal volume, 475
Tidal waves, 324, **324**
Tin, 90
Titanium, 62
TNT (trinitrotoluene), 197
Tobacco. *See* Smoking
Tolerance, 539
Topography, 669, **669**
Tornadoes, 665, **665**
Toxins, 521
Trachea, **471,** 472
Transceivers, 407
Transducers, 398
Transformers, 386
Transform faults, 614–615
Transition metals, 89, **89,** 124
Transmission, 406
Transmission electron microscopes
    (TEM), 564
Transpiration, **656,** 657
Trepomena pallidum, **565**
Triceps, **495, 497**
Trichina worms, 521
Trichomoniasis, **565**
Tritium, 83, **83**
Tropical depressions, 666
Tropopause, 649

Troposphere, 649
Troughs, **331,** 332, **343**
Tsunamis, 324, **324**
Tuberculosis, 564
Tumors, 524. *See also* Cancer
TVA (Tennessee Valley Authority), 692
Twins, 556–557, **558**
Typhoons, 666, **666**

U

Ulcers, 453
Ultraviolet (UV) light, 334
Umbilical cord, 557
Undernourishment, 446
United States Department of Agriculture
    (USDA), 527
Units of measurement
    for acceleration, 225, 233
    base units, **16**
    conversions, 16–17
    derived, 16
    for electricity, 357, 364–365, 368,
        376–377
    for energy, 263, 269
    for force, 236
    International System of Units,
        15–18
    for momentum, 223
    for nuclear radiation, 204
    for power, 252
    prefixes, **16,** 16–17, 126
    for specific heat, 302
    for speed, 219
    for temperature, 292–294
    for weight, 237
    for work, 251
Universal gravitation equation, 9
Universe
    future of, 583–584, **584**
    galaxies, 577, **577, 578, 579,** 580, **580,**
        584
    origin and age, 581–584, **583**
    overview, 576–577
    solar system, **577, 592,** 592–600
    stars, 585–591
Uplinks, 403
Uranium
    chain reactions, **198,** 198–199
    isotopes, 84
    nuclear decay, 192, **197**
    in nuclear power plants, 205
Uranus, 593, 597, **597**
Urethra, 549
Uterus, 551, **551,** 553–554

V

Vaccines, 532, **532**
Vagina, 551, **551**
Valence electrons, 76, **76,** 80–81, **81,** 119
Vanillin, **45**

Van Meegeren, Han, 185
Variables, 13
Vas deferens, **549,** 550
VD (venereal diseases), 522–523, 564–565,
    565
Veins, **467, 469,** 470
Velocity, 220–222, 227, 238, 266–267. *See
    also* Speed
Ventricles, **466,** 466–468
Vents, in the Earth, 622, **622**
Venus, 238, 593–594, **594,** 602
Vibrations, 325–328
Villard, Paul, 188
Villi, 452
Vinegar, 127
Viruses, 521, **521**
Viscosity, 48
Vital capacity, 475
Vitamins, **436,** 436–437, 440, 447
Volatile organic compounds (VOCs), 698
Volcanoes
    cores, **626**
    pipes, 626
    plate tectonics and, **624,** 624–625
    rock, 44
    subduction and, 613, **613**
    types, 622–623
Voltage (potential difference), 364, 386
Volts, 364
Volume, 18, 55–56

W

Warm fronts, 663, **663**
Washington, George, 58
Water
    in the atmosphere, 657
    changes of state, 49, **49,** 55
    density, 55
    in food, **432**
    heating, 307–308
    human requirement for, 435
    ice, 55, **57,** 221, 633
    molecular structure, **40, 48, 71**
    pathogens in, 454
    pollution, 701–703
    properties, 113
    specific heat, 302–303
    water cycle, **656,** 656–659
Watt, James, 306, 376
Watts, 252, 376
Wavelengths, **331,** 332, 335, 346, **346**
Waves, 320–346, 323, 334, **334.** *See also*
    Electromagnetic waves
    amplitude, **331,** 332, 343, **343**
    definition, 322
    diffraction, 341, **341**
    energy in, 271
    fronts, 324
    ground, 409
    interference, **342,** 342–345, **343**
    longitudinal, 329, **329,** 332, **332, 618,**
        618–619

mechanical, 323
microwaves, 334, 402–403, 406–407,
    407, 409
motion of, 328, **328**
ocean, 323–324, **324,** 330, **330**
overview, 322–324
properties, 331–334
radio, 651, **651**
reflections, **340,** 340–341
refraction, 342, **342**
seismic, 323, 335, **618,** 618–620, **620,**
    642–643
sky, 409
sound, **10,** 324, 329, 337–339, **344,**
    344–345, 641
speed of, 335–337
standing, 345–346
surface, 330, **330,** 619
tidal, 324, **324**
transverse, 329, 331, **331, 618,**
    618–619
vibrations, **325,** 325–328, **327**
Wave speed equation, 335
Weather
    electrical storms, 664–665
    fronts, **663,** 663–666
    hurricanes, 666, **666**
    maps, 667, **667**
    tornadoes, 665, **665**
    in the troposphere, 649
Weathering, 628, **630,** 633–638, **634–638**
Wedges, 261, **261**
Wegener, Alfred, 610
Weight, 18, 237–238. *See also* Mass
Weightlessness, 237, **237,** 508–509
Wheel and axle, 260, **260**
Wheelbarrows, **258**
White blood cells, **464,** 465, **531**
White dwarf, 590
Wilson, Robert, 582
Wind energy, 691–692, **692**
Winds, 637–638, 660–662, **661,** 665
Withdrawal symptoms, 539
Work, 250–251, 254–256, 278–280, 306
World Wide Web, 421
Worms, parasitic, 521, 528

Xenon, **93**
X rays, 6, 334

Zinc, 90
Zygotes, 556, **556**

Art Credits

Front matter: Page vi-viii, Kristy Sprott; ix, Uhl Studios, Inc.; xii, Christy Krames; xiv, Ortelius Design; xv, Uhl Studios, Inc.; xvi, Christy Krames. Chapter 1: Page 6, Leslie Kell; 10, Kristy Sprott; 13, Leslie Kell; 18, Uhl Studios, Inc.; 21, Leslie Kell; 28, Leslie Kell. Chapter 2: Page 40, Kristy Sprott; 42, Kristy Sprott; 47, Stephen Durke; 48, Kristy Sprott; 49, Leslie Kell; 51, Uhl Studios, Inc.; 60, Kristy Sprott; 61, Uhl Studios, Inc.; 63, Leslie Kell. Chapter 3: Page 71, Kristy Sprott; 72, Kristy Sprott; 73, Uhl Studios, Inc.; 75, J/B Woolsey Associates; 76, Kristy Sprott; 78-83, Kristy Sprott; 85-89, Kristy Sprott; 91-93, Kristy Sprott; 96, Kristy Sprott; 99, Leslie Kell. Chapter 4: Page 109, Kristy Sprott; 111 (t), Kristy Sprott; 111 (b), J/B Woolsey Associates; 112, Kristy Sprott; 114, Kristy Sprott; 116, Kristy Sprott; 117-121, Kristy Sprott; 127, Leslie Kell; 129-131, Kristy Sprott; 132 (tl, tr), J/B Woolsey Associates; 132 (bl), Kristy Sprott; 133, Kristy Sprott; 135, Kristy Sprott; 136, Morgan-Cain & Associates; 137, J/B Woolsey Associates. Chapter 5: Page 149-150, Kristy Sprott; 151, Uhl Studios, Inc.; 152, Kristy Sprott; 154-158, Kristy Sprott; 161, Kristy Sprott; 163, Kristy Sprott; 167, Kristy Sprott; 169, Kristy Sprott; 173, Kristy Sprott; 179, Kristy Sprott. Chapter 6: Page 186-187, Kristy Sprott; 190-191, Kristy Sprott; 196-198, Kristy Sprott; 203, Kristy Sprott; 205, Uhl Studios, Inc. Chapter 7: Page 231, Uhl Studios, Inc.; 233, Uhl Studios, Inc.; 239-240, Uhl Studios, Inc.; 242, Uhl Studios, Inc. Chapter 8: Page 258-260, Stephen Durke; 268, Stephen Durke; 277, Uhl Studios, Inc. Chapter 9: Page 293, Uhl Studios, Inc.; 295, Uhl Studios, Inc.; 298, Stephen Durke; 305, Uhl Studios, Inc.; 307-308, Uhl Studios, Inc.; 310, Uhl Studios, Inc.; 314, Uhl Studios, Inc. Chapter 10: Page 325, Uhl Studios, Inc.; 326, Kent Leech; 327, Uhl Studios, Inc.; 330, Uhl Studios, Inc.; 331-332, Mark Schroeder; 333, Uhl Studios, Inc.; 340, Mark Schroeder; 343, Uhl Studios, Inc. Chapter 11: Page 358, Uhl Studios Inc.; 359, Uhl Studios Inc./Kristy Sprott; 360, Uhl Studios Inc./Kristy Sprott; 363-364, Kristy Sprott; 367, Stephen Durke; 370, Stephen Durke; 381, Boston Graphics; 382, Stephen Durke; 383, Boston Graphics; 384, Boston Graphics; 385 (tr), Stephen Durke; 385 (br), Kristy Sprott. Chapter 12: Page 400, Stephen Durke; 402, Uhl Studios, Inc.; 404, Uhl Studios, Inc.; 405, Uhl Studios, Inc.; 407, Uhl Studios, Inc.; 410, Uhl Studios, Inc.; 411, Uhl Studios, Inc.; 415, Uhl Studios, Inc.; 420, Leslie Kell; 423-424, Uhl Studios, Inc.; 427, Uhl Studios, Inc. Chapter 13: Page 439, Yves Larvor; 442, Leslie Kell; 449, John Karapelou; 450 (bl), Christy Krames; 450 (br), John Karapelou; 451 (bl), Christy Krames; 451 (br), John Karapelou; 452, John Karapelou; 455, John Karapelou. Chapter 14: Page 466, Kip Carter; 467, Christy Krames; 469, Christy Krames; 471, John Karapelou; 473, Christy Krames; 474, John Karapelou; 478, John Karapelou; 481, Christy Krames. Chapter 15: Page 495, John Karapelou; 497, Keith Kasnot; 500, John Karapelou; 515-517, Christy Krames. Chapter 16: Page 531, Christy Krames; 540, Leslie Kell. Chapter 17: Page 548, Morgan-Cain & Associates; 549 (tl), Keith Kasnot; 549 (br), Morgan-Cain & Associates; 551, Keith Kasnot; 552, Christy Krames; 553, Morgan-Cain & Associates; 556-557, Christy Krames; 559, Alexander & Turner; 567, Christy Krames; 568, Morgan-Cain & Associates. Chapter 18: Page 577, Uhl Studios, Inc.; 579, Uhl Studios, Inc.; 583, Uhl Studios, Inc.; 588, Tony Randazzo; 590, Uhl Studios, Inc.; 592, Uhl Studios, Inc.; 599, Uhl Studios, Inc.; 600, Uhl Studios, Inc. Chapter 19: Page 608, Ortelius Design; 610, Ortelius Design; 611(br), Uhl Studios, Inc.; 612 (t), Uhl Studios, Inc.; 613 (tl), Uhl Studios, Inc.; 614 (bl), Uhl Studios, Inc.; 615, Uhl Studios, Inc.; 618 (tl), Uhl Studios, Inc.; 618 (b), Mark Schroeder; 619-620, Uhl Studios, Inc.; 623, Uhl Studios, Inc.; 638, Uhl Studios, Inc.; 640, Uhl Studios, Inc.; 643, Doug Walston. Chapter 20: Page 648,
Stephen Durke; 650, Kristy Sprott; 651-652, Uhl Studios, Inc.; 654, Uhl Studios, Inc.; 656, Uhl Studios, Inc.; 658, Uhl Studios, Inc.; 660, Stephen Durke; 661, Uhl Studios, Inc.; 663-664, Craig Attebery; 666, Uhl Studios, Inc.; 668-669, Uhl Studios, Inc.; 672, Leslie Kell. Chapter 21: Pages 680-681, Robert Hynes; 685, Ortelius Design; 688, Leslie Kell; 689, Robert Hynes; 690 (tl), Uhl Studios, Inc.; 690, (b)Leslie Kell; 691, Stephen Durke; 693-694, Uhl Studios, Inc.; 699, Leslie Kell; 705, Kristy Sprott; 711, Uhl Studios, Inc. Back matter: Page 730, Leslie Kell; 731, Thomas Gagliano; 736-737, Kristy Sprott; 738-740, MapQuest.com, Inc.

Photo Credits

List of Abbreviations

AA=Animals Animals; ES=Earth Scenes; FPG=FPG International; PA=Peter Arnold; PR=Photo Researchers Inc.; SS=Science Source; TSI=Tony Stone Images; TSM=The Stock Market; VU=Visuals Unlimited.

Integrating Icon Images: Biology, Health, Images Copyright 2001 Photodisc, Inc; Earth, ESA/K. Horgan/TSI; Space, Corbis Images; Physics, Richard Megna/Fundamental

Images by Sam Dudgeon/HRW Photo: vi(cl), x(tl), 1(br), 19(balance), 32 ,40(l,c), 42(bl), 45(b), 60, 95(t), 95(bl,br), 96(b), 97(all), 98(all), 108(br), 113(cr), 117,118(all), 132(t), 133, 162(tl), 173(all), 235(t), 253, 258(b), 277, 290(c), 291(b,t), 292, 300, 301(all), 315, 364(bl), 372, 373(all), 375(all), 392, 393(bl), 394-395(inset), 432, 450, 463, 470, 487, 505(tr, br, bcl, tcl), 517, 518-519, 526(br), 534, 536(all), 562(bl), 571(cr), 615, 629(bl), 630(tc), 712-713.

Unless otherwise noted all other photographs by Peter Van Steen/HRW Photo.

Page iii, David Malin/Anglo-Australian Observatory; v, VU/Glen M. Oliver; vi(bl), Michael Keller/TSM; viii(tl), Sergio Purtell/ Foca/HRW; xiii(tr), Rick Stewart/Allsport; xiii(bl), NIBSC/Science Photo Library/PR; xiii(bc), VU/E. White xiv(cl), Celestial Image Picture Co./Science Photo Library/PR; xv(cr), VU/Richard Thom; xv(bl), Mark Richards/Photo Edit; xv(bc), Myrleen Ferguson/Photo Edit; xv(br), Peter Dean/Grant Heilman Photography; xix(br), Nicholas Pinturas/TSI; xix(tr), Matthew Stockman/Allsport; xx(cl), Bob Peterson 1988/FPG International; xx(tl), Andy Christiansen/ HRW; 2-3, Roger Ressmeyer/Corbis; 2-3(inset), Corbis-Bettmann; 4(l), Hulton Getty/Liaison Agency; 4(r), Phil Degginger/Color-Pic, Inc.; 6, AIP Emilio Segrè Visual Archives; 7(br), Corbis/ Bettmann; 7(bl), Sheila Terry/Science Photo Library/ PR; 7,(bc), SuperStock; 7(t), Leonard Lessin/PA, Inc.; 10(t), Kristian Hilsen/ TSI; 10(c,b), BMW of North America, Inc.; 11, Chris Johns/TSI; 14(b), Science Photo Library/PR; 15(l), Roger Ressmeyer/Corbis; 15(r), Celestial Image Co./Science Photo Library/PR; 19(nickle), EyeWire, Inc.; 19(CD), Image Copyright ©2001, Photodisc, Inc.; 34-35, Alfred Pasieka/PR; 36, Theresa Batty/Dale Chihuly Studio; 37(inset), Russell Johnson/Dale Chihuly Studio; 38, James L. Amos/PA, Inc.; 39(t), IBM Corporation/Research Division/Almaden Research Center; 39(bl), Tom Van Sant/The Geosphere Project/TSM; 39(br), Image Copyright ©2001, Photodisc, Inc.; 40(r), Ken Eward/SS/PR; 42(br), Sergio Purtell/Foca/HRW; 45(t), Bruce Byers/ FPG; 46(all), Sergio Purtell/Foca/HRW; 47, Andrew Syred/Tony Stone/Allstock; 48, John Langford/HRW; 49(l), Steve Joester/FPG; 49(c), Michael Keller/TSM; 49(r), E. R. Degginger/Color-Pic, Inc.; 50(b), Uniphoto Picture Agency; 50(t), Charles D. Winters; 53, Robert

The Periodic Table of the Elements

Key:

6	Atomic number
C	Symbol
Carbon	Name
12.011	Average atomic mass

Period

Period 1

1
H
Hydrogen
1.007 94

Group 1

Period 2

3
Li
Lithium
6.941

Group 2

4
Be
Beryllium
9.012 182

Period 3

11
Na
Sodium
22.989 768

12
Mg
Magnesium
24.3050

Group 3 | **Group 4** | **Group 5** | **Group 6** | **Group 7** | **Group 8** | **Group 9**

Period 4

19	20	21	22	23	24	25	26	27
K	**Ca**	**Sc**	**Ti**	**V**	**Cr**	**Mn**	**Fe**	**Co**
Potassium	Calcium	Scandium	Titanium	Vanadium	Chromium	Manganese	Iron	Cobalt
39.0983	40.078	44.955 910	47.88	50.9415	51.9961	54.938 05	55.847	58.933 20

Period 5

37	38	39	40	41	42	43	44	45
Rb	**Sr**	**Y**	**Zr**	**Nb**	**Mo**	**Tc**	**Ru**	**Rh**
Rubidium	Strontium	Yttrium	Zirconium	Niobium	Molybdenum	Technetium	Ruthenium	Rhodium
85.4678	87.62	88.905 85	91.224	92.906 38	95.94	(97.9072)	101.07	102.906

Period 6

55	56	57	72	73	74	75	76	77
Cs	**Ba**	**La**	**Hf**	**Ta**	**W**	**Re**	**Os**	**Ir**
Cesium	Barium	Lanthanum	Hafnium	Tantalum	Tungsten	Rhenium	Osmium	Iridium
132.905 43	137.327	138.9055	178.49	180.9479	183.84	186.207	190.23	192.22

Period 7

87	88	89	104	105	106	107	108	109
Fr	**Ra**	**Ac**	**Rf**	**Db**	**Sg**	**Bh**	**Hs**	**Mt**
Francium	Radium	Actinium	Rutherfordium	Dubnium	Seaborgium	Bohrium	Hassium	Meitnerium
(223.0197)	(226.0254)	(227.0278)	(261.11)	(262.114)	(263.118)	(262.12)	(265)†	(266)†

Estimated from currently available IUPAC data.

* The systematic names and symbols for elements greater than 109 will be used until the approval of trivial names by IUPAC.

58	59	60	61	62
Ce	**Pr**	**Nd**	**Pm**	**Sm**
Cerium	Praseodymium	Neodymium	Promethium	Samarium
140.115	140.908	144.24	(144.9127)	150.36

90	91	92	93	94
Th	**Pa**	**U**	**Np**	**Pu**
Thorium	Protactinium	Uranium	Neptunium	Plutonium
232.0381	231.035 88	238.0289	(237.0482)	244.0642

internet connect

go.hrw.com
Visit the HRW Web site to see the most recent version of the periodic table.